Biological Psychology

Biological Psychology

Kelly G. Lambert

New York   Oxford

OXFORD UNIVERSITY PRESS

Oxford University Press is a department of the University of Oxford. It furthers the University's objective of excellence in research, scholarship, and education by publishing worldwide. Oxford is a registered trade mark of Oxford University Press in the UK and certain other countries.

Published in the United States of America by Oxford University Press 198 Madison Avenue, New York, NY 10016, United States of America.

© 2018 by Oxford University Press

Library of Congress Cataloging-in-Publication Data
Names: Lambert, Kelly.
Title: Biological psychology / Kelly G. Lambert.
Description: New York : Oxford University Press, [2018] | Includes
    bibliographical references.
Identifiers: LCCN 2016046060 (print) | LCCN 2016047113 (ebook) | ISBN
    9780199766109 (hardcover) | ISBN 9780190654498 (loosleaf) | ISBN
    9780190650322 (ebook)
Subjects: LCSH: Psychobiology—Textbooks.
Classification: LCC QP360 .L357 2018 (print) | LCC QP360 (ebook) | DDC
    612.8—dc23
LC record available at https://lccn.loc.gov/2016046060

9 8 7 6 5 4 3 2 1
Printed by LSC Communications, United States of America

Brief Contents

Contents

Preface

As I write this preface, I am attending the International Behavioral Neuroscience Society meeting in Budapest, Hungary. After an engaging dinner discussing recent neuroscience findings with both long-time and new colleagues, I am reminded of how fortunate I am to be a professor and researcher in the fascinating field of behavioral neuroscience. As I have spent the past several years writing *Biological Psychology*, I have become a student of Biopsychology once again—and have encountered exciting and fascinating neurobiology information every step along the way. Writing this book has been an incredible learning journey, one that has reintroduced my brain to, well, my brain.

What about you? Have you met your brain? My hope is that your brain has performed so well throughout your life that you haven't had to give it a second thought. Some of you, however, have no doubt been introduced to your brain as a result of challenges such as depression, addiction, concussions, or neurological disease. Regardless of the nature of your introduction thus far, I look forward to beginning this brain journey with you—introducing you to the most exciting and relevant past, present, and future brain stories.

If you have ever wondered why you have to study harder than your best friend to earn an A, are more fearful of insects than your sister, or why you tend to feel sadder than others in your peer group, you have embarked on your own biopsychological investigations. In my own research endeavors, I am so captivated by the many unanswered questions in biopsychology that my undergraduate students and I are never at a loss for research projects. In our small laboratory, we have been busy trying to answer real-life questions such as:

- How does a mother rat know how to take care of her offspring (appx 12-14!) without the benefit of parenting classes?
- What makes wild raccoons so curious, bold, and mischievous, allowing them to adapt to new environments all over the world?
- How does a natural environment affect us differently than an artificial environment?
- What effect does the stress we all encounter in life have on our brain, behavior, and overall health?
- How can we build resilience against the toxicity of that stress?
- In addition to drugs, what are the most effective ways to treat psychiatric illnesses?

If you speak with another biopsychologist, he or she will likely be interested in a completely different set of research questions—all just as relevant for enhancing our understanding of how to maintain healthy brains—*Better living through Biopsychology!*

As a professor at Randolph-Macon College for 27 years and, more recently, at the University of Richmond, I never tire of sharing information about the brain with my students. It is my sincerest wish that you, too, will share in the excitement as we begin this fascinating journey. So, buckle up your brain and get ready for a very exciting ride!

KELLY LAMBERT
DECEMBER 1, 2016

About *Biological Psychology*

Although behavioral neuroscience has many aspects, the theme of *context* is especially relevant and is central to the approach of *Biological Psychology*. Your surroundings influence whether or not you view certain situations as rewarding or stressful, threatening or challenging, engaging or overwhelming. For example, consider a skydiver anticipating her first jump. Appropriate training would likely reduce the skydiver's physiological stress response, as would meeting others who have skydived many times before without getting hurt. Regardless of past experience, however, the stress response might be further enhanced by external and internal environmental variables—the sudden outbreak of a thunderstorm might cause more stress; whereas, an efficient cardiovascular system would likely reduce stress.

A closely related theme to the discussion of context throughout *Biological Psychology* is *neuroplasticity*. The brain's ability to change in response to altered environmental pressures is nothing short of amazing. As an undergraduate student in a physiological psychology course, I was mesmerized by the classic enriched environment studies conducted by Rosenzweig, Krech, Bennet, and Diamond at Berkeley in the 1960s. I became fascinated with the idea that the brain was not carved in stone but could adapt, if necessary, to altered environmental demands. I recently interviewed Dr. Marian Diamond, and she conveyed that the first time she presented the data about changing neural tissue in the enriched rats, an audience member stood up and shouted "Young lady, the brain does not change!" Biological psychology has certainly come a long way over the past half-century—today neuroplasticity has emerged as one of the most relevant topics in the discipline.

Biological Psychology captures both the classic and current developments in the field of biological psychology/behavioral neuroscience. Whether or not you continue in the discipline, I hope that this text, facilitated by the expertise of your dedicated instructors, will prepare you to be informed consumers of behavioral neuroscience information, resulting in a positive effect on your own neural and mental health.

Organization

Rather than the more commonly seen 15 chapters in this type of text, *Biological Psychology* has 13 chapters and an epilogue and is divided into four parts: *I. The Brain in Context; II. The Nervous System: Essential Components; III. The Nervous System: Essential Functions;* and *IV. Neurobiology in Action.*

Although the content of *Biological Psychology* retains the classic work and categories that characterize the discipline, its presentation/format also represents the changing field. Over the past several decades, the psychology curriculum has changed. For example, whereas most biological psychology texts include two chapters on sensation and perception, *Biological Psychology* includes only one. Incorporating the sensory information into a single chapter (Chapter 6) allows me to superimpose overarching themes about the functions of each sensory system in interpreting crucial environmental variables. Of course, more specific information about each sensory system is often covered in the traditional Sensation and Perception course.

In addition, aside from the more traditional learning and memory chapter(s), several texts also include other chapters on cognitive-related topics: language and communication; lateralization; and neurocognition, for example—all topics covered in various cognitive courses in contemporary psychology departments. Instead of covering these topics separately and extensively, *Biological Psychology* includes a single chapter emphasizing learning, memory, and decision making (Chapter 12). However, topics such as language and lateralization are covered in other chapters. Specifically, language is presented in a novel way in the movement chapter (Chapter 7—because language is itself a specialized movement), and lateralization is included in the chapter on structure and functions of the nervous system (Chapter 2). The delegation of these topics to other relevant chapters permits more extensive coverage of decision making, representing the most recent exciting findings in the literature and providing innovative ways to think about topics such as language.

Finally, the reproduction chapter is also unique. Because the role of affiliative social relationships has been increasingly investigated in the past several decades, positive social interactions are emphasized in the "Affiliative and Reproductive Strategies" chapter (Chapter 11)—addressing topics such as the neurobiological mechanisms accompanying parenting and interactions with offspring, maintaining trust in social interactions, and social responses characterizing disorders such as autism spectrum disorder. Antagonistic social interactions (i.e. aggression) appear in the "Emotional Expression and Regulation" chapter (Chapter 10).

Distinguishing Features

In addition to the topical coverage, *Biological Psychology* includes several distinguishing features. Throughout the text, a **"storytelling" approach** presents novel and relevant information to capture your attention. I will consider *Biological Psychology* to be a success if the research and/or case studies prompt you to continue the process of storytelling yourselves by relating various topics to your friends, family, and other instructors.

Clinical applications appear woven throughout the narrative of each chapter. For example, in addition to the disorders discussed in the mental illness chapter, I discuss autism spectrum disorder in the development/evolving brains chapter (Chapter 5); obesity is featured in the motivation chapter (Chapter 8); posttraumatic stress disorder is incorporated in the emotion chapter (Chapter 10); Parkinson's disease and several movement disorders are discussed in the movement chapter (Chapter 7); and addiction is prominently featured in the neurochemistry chapter (Chapter 4). I have drawn on my experience writing a Clinical Neuroscience text as well as my current laboratory research to present relevant and instructive examples.

Each chapter opens with a **"Brain Scene Investigation"**: a case study or behavioral mystery intended to interest you and provide potential biopsychological explanations in the accompanying "Behind the Scenes" sections.

A **"Context Matters" feature** within each chapter presents an experiment/research study that demonstrates the importance of different contextual variables (mentioned previously) on specific dependent variables. The detailed presentation of the experiment will enable you to appreciate the intricate methodological details, statistical analyses, and conclusions that accompany each research investigation. I hope that these mini-summaries of original research, accompanied with engaging, explanatory artwork, will provide a virtual laboratory experience and ignite a sense of discovery in you along with a curiosity about reasonable next steps for these studies.

While several texts include a chapter devoted solely to methodology in the discipline, I find it more relevant to discuss the methods/techniques in the context of the pertinent chapter content. Consequently, in addition to a summary of classic and current research approaches presented in the introductory chapter, a **"Laboratory Exploration" feature** illustrating a relevant research technique concludes each chapter. Through this feature and the main chapter narrative, you will encounter both classic and novel laboratory techniques in the context of relevant chapters.

Finally, *Biological Psychology* also features **contextual and relevant art** depicting more realistic features of animal and human models than appear in other texts. Presenting the art in a more natural, realistic style facilitates the processing of information more than sterile, cartoon-like images.

Ancillaries

For Students
Companion Website

Available at no additional cost, the Companion Website provides students with the following review resources:

- **Chapter Outlines:** Detailed outlines give an overview of each chapter. Chapter Summaries: Full summaries of each chapter provide a thorough review of the important facts and concepts covered.
- **Flashcards:** Interactive flashcard activities are an effective way for students to learn and review all of the important terminology.
- **Practice Quizzes:** Each chapter includes a practice quiz, which students can use as a self-review exercise, to check their understanding.
- **Animations:** A set of detailed animations helps students understand some of the book's more complex topics and processes by presenting them in a clear, easy-to-follow narrative.

For Instructors

An extensive and thoughtful supplements program offers instructors everything they need to prepare their course and lectures, and assess student progress.

Ancillary Resource Center (ARC)
Available exclusively to adopters, the Ancillary Resource Center (ARC) includes all of the instructor resources that accompany Biological Psychology 1/e

Instructor's Manual: For each chapter of the textbook, the Instructor's Manual includes the following:

- Chapter Outlines
- Key Concepts
- Journal Articles and Press Releases
- Video Links

Textbook Figures and Tables: All of the textbook's illustrations and tables are provided in a variety of formats, including high and low resolution, with and without balloon captions, and unlabeled (all balloon captions, labels, and leaders removed).

PowerPoint Resources:

- **Figures and Tables:** This presentation includes all of the figures and tables (all formats) from the chapter, with titles.
- **Lecture:** A complete lecture outline, ready for use in class. Includes coverage of all important facts and concepts presented in the chapter along with selected figures and tables.

Animations: All of the animations from Dashboard are available in the ARC for download, making it easy to include them in lecture presentation and online course materials. (Also available in Dashboard.)

Videos: A collection of videos selected to accompany each chapter helps bring some of the key concepts from the textbook to life. Ideal for use as lecture starters or paired with assignments.

Test Bank: A complete test bank provides instructors with a wide range of test items for each chapter, including multiple-choice, fill-in-the-blank, short-answer, true/false, and essay questions. Questions are noted for whether they are factual or conceptual, and for level of difficulty.

Computerized Test Bank: The Test Bank is also provided in Blackboard Diploma format (software included). Diploma makes it easy to create quizzes and exams using any combination of publisher-provided questions and an instructor's own questions and to export those assessments for print or online delivery in a wide range of learning management system formats.

Dashboard
For more information, go to www.oup.com/us/dashboard

Oxford's Dashboard learning management system features a streamlined interface that connects instructors and students with the functions they perform most often, simplifying the learning experience to save instructors time and put students' progress first. Dashboard's prebuilt assessments were created specifically to accompany *Biological Psychology* 1/e and are automatically graded so that instructors can see student progress instantly. Dashboard includes the following resources:

- Quizzes: For each chapter of the textbook, there is a quiz to test student comprehension of important facts and concepts introduced in the chapter.
- Animations: A set of detailed animations helps students understand some of the book's more complex topics and processes by presenting them in a clear, easy-to-follow narrative.

LMS Course Cartridges
For those instructors who wish to use their campus learning management system, a course cartridge containing all of the Dashboard resources is available for a variety of e-learning environments. (For more information, please contact your local Oxford representative.)

Acknowledgments

I am extremely grateful to my husband, Gary Lambert, and our daughters, Lara and Skylar, for understanding the inordinate amount of time this project required over the past six years. Their collective support for this book project allowed me to push through to completion. I also appreciate their tolerance for the never-ending Biopsychology stories I told them as I gathered new information for this text.

OUP's Editorial Director, Patrick Lynch, saw value in a brain text with nontraditional stories and an emphasis on context; I appreciate his enthusiastic support from the very beginning of this process. Senior Editor Jane Potter has listened to every idea and concern I have thrown her way from her first day's association with this project; I value both her wisdom and friendship during this time. Developmental Editor Anne Kemper scrutinized each chapter with her keen editing eye. Her positive influence is seen throughout the entire text. Finally, Senior Developmental Editor Lisa Sussman has guided the final editing process with an impressive editorial surgical precision. The collective wisdom of these three dedicated women greatly improved the quality of this book as they trimmed all the rough edges and polished the final draft.

Throughout this process, I have certainly learned that writing a book takes a village. Beyond the wonderful OUP staff, including Editorial Assistant Larissa Albright and Senior Production Editor Keith Faivre, the team at Dragonfly Media created a beautiful art program. In addition, a considerable number of faculty reviewers took time out of their busy schedules to carefully consider the content of each chapter of *Biological Psychology*. Their collective expertise elevates this book to a level that could not have been achieved without them. I can't thank these neuroscience and biopsychology colleagues enough for their generosity and expertise:

Khaleel Abdulrazak, University of California, Riverside; Dawn Albertson, Minnesota State University, Mankato; Robin Arkerson, University of Massachusetts, Dartmouth; Bryan C. Auday, Gordon College; Michael Babcock, Montana State University; N. Jay Bean, Vassar College; Taunjah P. Bell, Jackson State University; Jeanette M. Bennett, University of North Carolina, Charlotte; Michael J. Beran, Georgia State University; Joan Brugman, Belmont Abbey College; Susanne Brummelte, Wayne State University; John E. Bryant, Bowie State University; Jessica Cail, Pepperdine University; Martha Leah Chaiken, Johnson State College and Hofstra University; Evangelia Chrysikou, University of Kansas; Jennifer Coleman, Western New Mexico University; Derek Daniels, University at Buffalo, The State University of New York; Scott L. Decker, University of South Carolina; Darragh Devine, University of Florida; Ira Driscoll, University of Wisconsin, Milwaukee; Thom Dunn, University of Northern Colorado; Jeff Dyche, James Madison University; William Essman, University of Indianapolis; Stephanie Fowler, University of Missouri; Nicholas Grahame, Indiana University-Purdue University, Indianapolis ; Ruth Grahn, Connecticut College; Jeffrey W. Grimm, Western Washington University; Joshua M. Gulley, University of Illinois, Urbana-Champaign; Rebecca Gullan, Gwynedd Mercy University; F. Scott Hall, University of Maryland, College Park; Nancy Hamilton, University of Kansas; Sayamwong "Jom" Hammack, University of Vermont; Donna Hardy, California State University, Northridge; Christopher Hayashi, Southwestern College; Chelcie Heaney, University of Nevada, Las Vegas; Michael R. Hoane, Southern Illinois University-Carbondale; Trevor Hyde, Cardinal Stritch University; Michael Hylin, Southern Illinois University; Michael Jarvinen, Emmanuel College; Chris Jones-Cage, College of the Desert; N. Bradley Keele, Baylor University; John E. Kelsey, Bates College; Norman E. Kinney, Southeast Missouri State University; Meg Kirkpatrick, Wheaton College; Lori Knackstedt, University of Florida; Robert E. Krout, Southern Methodist University; Shannon Kundey, Hood College; Daniel W. Leger, University of Nebraska, Lincoln; Vincent P. Markowski, State University of New York at Geneseo; Amanda Kentner, Massachusetts College of Pharmacy & Health Sciences University; Tara Anne McCloskey, City University of New York, Hunter & John Jay Colleges; Daniel McConnell, University of Central Florida; Kai McCormack, Spelman College; Sandra L. McFadden, Western Illinois University; Bill Meil, Indiana University of Pennsylvania; Holly C. Miller, Universitè de Lille, Nord de France; Maura Mitrushina, California State University, Northridge; Lorenz S. Neuwirth, State University of New York, Old Westbury; Jeane He Norden, Vanderbilt University; Jason L. Parker, Old Dominion University; Terry F. Pettijohn, Ohio State University; Brady J. Phelps, South Dakota State University; Jay W. Pope, Fresno Pacific University; Joseph H. Porter, Virginia Commonwealth University; Andrea Rashtian, California State University Northridge; Neelam Rattan, San Jose State University; Paul J. Reber, Northwestern University; Joshua Rodefer, Florida State University; Michael Anch, Saint Louis University; Mark S. Schmidt, Columbus State University; Gwendolyn Scott-Jones, Delaware State University; Leslie C. Skeen, University of Delaware; Robert Sorge, University of Alabama at Birmingham; James L. Spencer, West Virginia State University; Patricia Stifter, DePaul University; Elizabeth Jeffress Thorsteinson, Georgia State University; Saurabh Kokane, University of Texas at Arlington; Jennifer Valad, Queens College, City University of New York; Thomas E. Van Cantfort, Fayetteville State University; Meg Waraczynski, University of Wisconsin, Whitewater; Beth Wee, Tulane University; Robin Wellington, St. John's University; Kathleen West, University of North Carolina, Charlotte; Shannon N. Whitten, University of Central Florida; Guangying Wu, George Washington University; Paul Young, Houghton College; Janna Taft Young, James Madison University; Susan Zup, University of Massachusetts, Boston.

Biological Psychology

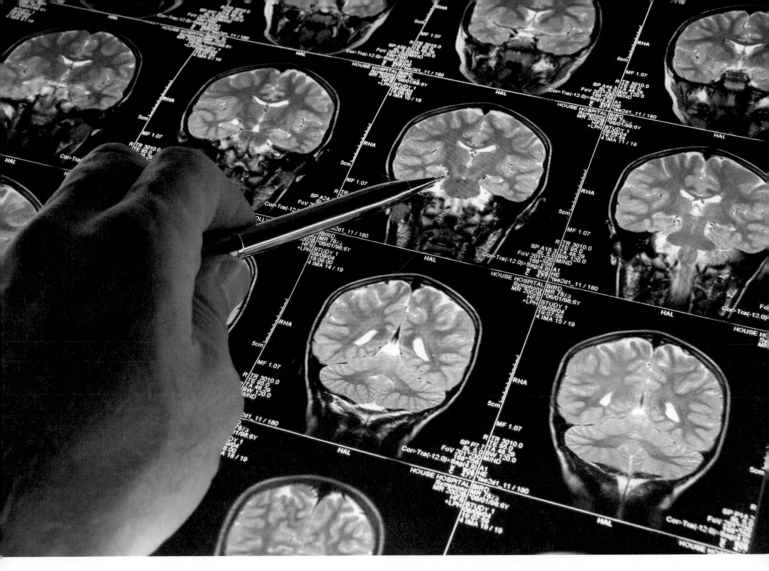

Introduction to Biological Psychology

Your brain knows a lot about you, but what do you know about your brain? Could you identify the brain areas that allow you to read and process the written words on this page? Are you familiar with how the billions of neurons in your brain communicate with one another? Do you know how to maintain a healthy brain? Biological psychology introduces your brain to . . . well, your brain, and all of the mental and behavioral functions that it controls.

Biological psychology, also known as **biopsychology**, merges relevant information from the fields of biology, neuroscience, and psychology to reveal how the brain produces behavior. Biological psychologists are committed to recognizing the influence of both the brain and the environment on behavior. This commitment requires both a broad and a deep understanding of the brain and behavior. Because of the emphasis on behavior, the discipline of biological psychology is often called *behavioral neuroscience*.

As you will discover throughout this text, specializations exist within the field of biological psychology. For example, cognitive neuroscientists examine the influence of brain activity in cognitive functions such as memory; psychophysiologists investigate the role of basic physiological functions such as heart rate in various psychological functions; neuropsychologists focus on the role of specific brain areas in psychological dysfunction; and psychopharmacologists investigate the influence of psychoactive drugs on brain and behavior. My students and I emphasize a more traditional physiological psychological approach. We attempt to identify brain areas and neurochemicals involved in specific behaviors such as learning and stress responses. We often employ a comparative psychological approach using different animal species to investigate our research questions. Although exceptions exist, cognitive neuroscientists, psychophysiologists, and neuropsychologists work most often with human subjects, whereas nonhuman animals are often used with psychopharmacological, physiological, and comparative research approaches.

Regardless of the title of the course you are taking, biological psychology is, in my opinion, the most fascinating topic on earth—the Cirque du Soleil of academic disciplines! Similar to each new act in the riveting Cirque du Soleil shows, each chapter in this book presents a cast of intriguing researchers and pioneering thinkers along with the most captivating research findings that inform our thoughts about behaviors as diverse as dancing, laughing, falling in love, eating, and learning new information. On this journey, you will learn how your own brain enables you to make informed decisions that will keep it healthy for the rest of your life.

Throughout this book, you will encounter the important theme of **context**, the specific setting in which an event occurs. In biological psychology, the term *context* refers to the circumstances surrounding an event and the unique interactions that exist among behavior, the brain, and one's external and internal environment. If you are pushed out of a plane at 3,500 feet above the ground, the context of that event will affect your brain's response. For example, your brain will act a certain way if it knows this is the final assignment in a skydiving course, but it will respond differently if it knows an adversary pushed you out—without a parachute! Despite the brain's complexity, scientists have identified many of its fundamental responses and the brain regions that are most involved in these responses. Later in this chapter, you will learn about some early pioneers in brain research and their groundbreaking observations about the brain's functions.

Our current knowledge of the brain's functions depends on emerging technology and methods that are available to investigate the brain's components and activity. This chapter provides an overview of the classic methodological approaches used to investigate brain functions. Subsequent chapters will expand on these techniques and describe additional techniques. As technology changes at a rapid pace, we gain greater opportunities to learn more about the cornerstones of biological psychology. Thus, students learning biological psychology today will know more about their brains than do all of their student predecessors! ▇

Establishing Relevant Biopsychological Context

As you begin reading this chapter, many factors will influence the impact of these words on your thoughts and memories. Are you in a good mood? Do you feel a little under the weather? Are you sitting in a quiet room? Are you anticipating an enjoyable outing with friends after completing this reading assignment? Are you taking any medication that may influence your ability to concentrate on the material? Did you recently drink a cup of coffee? Are you hungry? Is the room temperature comfortable? The types of variables that can potentially influence your comprehension of this chapter's content are endless.

As previously mentioned, the circumstances surrounding the process of reading this chapter can be thought of as context. It probably comes as no surprise that it will be more difficult to concentrate on new material if you are distracted by a few friends chatting, or if you skipped lunch and you are starving, or if your allergy medication is making you a little drowsy. Even if you are an excellent student who consistently earns high marks, you are not immune to varying contextual influences. No one exists in a vacuum; on the contrary, the context of our world is multifaceted and ever changing.

As you progress through this textbook and learn about how the brain influences behavioral responses, we will also consider how these established brain–behavior interactions change in different situations. Before learning more about the various dimensions of biopsychological context, we will consider the journey of Charles Darwin, a pioneer in biological science who identified the importance of variations in external contexts on the formation and survival of species.

Darwin's Observations and the Importance of Variations in Environmental Contexts

As Charles Darwin stepped onto the ship H.M.S. *Beagle* in late December 1831, few of his acquaintances expected him to make a breakthrough discovery that would change the face of biological science. Disappointed that Charles was not pursuing a medical career, his father had told him, "You care for nothing but shooting, dogs, and rat-catching, and you will be a disgrace to yourself and all your family" (Boulter, 2010, p. 8). To make matters worse, the captain of the *Beagle*, Robert Fitzroy, had read that certain facial characteristics revealed information about mental abilities (a nonscientific but popular theory at that time) and suspected that Darwin did not have the appropriately shaped nose to be a seafarer. But, against these doubts, Darwin joined the five-year journey to explore potential trading routes and the changing geography of South America. Darwin also collected specimens to inform other naturalists (individuals studying the natural world) about geological and geographical distributions of plants and animals in these regions (Boulter, 2010).

After Darwin returned from his long tour on the *Beagle*, he started organizing and categorizing his many specimens from his journey and reviewing the meticulous notes in his travel diary. Some of his observations were intriguing. The finches' beaks, for example, were variable in their physical characteristics, such as size and shape. As seen in Figure 1.1, short beaks (such as those of large ground finches) seemed to be useful for readily cracking seeds, whereas long beaks (such as those of woodpecker finches) seemed to be useful for fishing insects out of tree bark. On reflection, it appeared to Darwin that these physical characteristics were **adaptations**, biological modifications that enhanced survival in varying challenging environments. The finches with beaks that were best adapted to successfully retrieve food were the finches most likely to survive long enough to reproduce, passing to their offspring the likelihood of having a similarly adaptive beak. In contrast, the finches with beaks that were less well adapted to retrieve food were more likely to die without reproducing, so that the genes contributing to their poorly adapted beaks would eventually disappear. Could it be that changing geological characteristics such as a sandy beach or a winding brook were associated with changes in species that increased their likelihood of survival in different environments? As the physical structure of environments changed, animals had to adapt to new ways of finding mates and food sources to maintain their individual survival and the continued existence of their species. Inflexibility in changing environments led to death.

These thoughts led to Darwin's famed **theory of natural selection**, which emphasized that species that are uniquely adapted to their environments, the physical *context* of their habitats, tend to have higher survival rates than species that are not. The survivors produce more offspring than do those species that are less well adapted, thereby increasing the proportion of organisms in each succeeding generation with adaptive traits.

For example, during his visit to the Galápagos Islands, Darwin acknowledged that the black iguanas sunning on the black lava rocks (depicted in Figure 1.2) were well suited for their environment. Darwin was less than impressed with the beauty of the black iguanas. In fact, he described them as the "imps of darkness," claiming that they were ugly and clumsy. However, Darwin found remarkable evidence for behavioral adaptations in the black iguanas. He reported tossing one in the water and observing that it kept coming right back to him so that he could, once again, pick it up by the tail and toss it in the water. Given that their only predators were located in the water, it was actually adaptive for the iguanas to quickly escape from the water after being thrown in to decrease their probability of being eaten. Moreover, after diving into the cold water on warm days, sunning on the black rocks allowed these cold-blooded iguanas to warm their bodies. After the sun set on chilly nights, the iguanas' behavior of sleeping in huddles continued to keep their bodies warm (Keynes, 2001).

After Darwin returned from his journey, his own environment in London influenced his responses. At his country garden home, Down House, he cultivated many gardens and breeding colonies of various animals to test and develop his ideas. Subsequently, he published the groundbreaking book entitled *On the Origin of Species* in 1859. Similar to the iguanas, Darwin also seemed to be well adapted to his surroundings at Down House because he apparently benefitted from living in the midst of gardens and animals. In fact, he wrote that the path pictured in Figure 1.3 was his *thinking path*, where he mentally processed the reams of information informing him about the survival of species in changing environments.

Darwin's emphasis on context in the development of species' successful reproductive and survival strategies inspired other scientists to examine this important variable. In the mid-20th century, the Harvard University naturalist

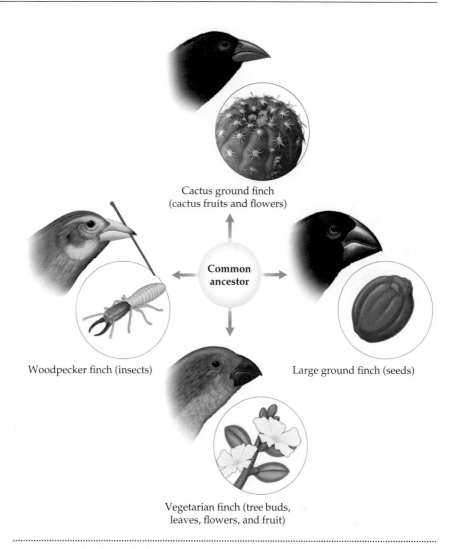

FIGURE 1.1 Adaptive evolution. The finches of the Galápagos Islands evolved from a common ancestor to have differently sized and shaped beaks based on their primary food source.

Ernst Mayr distinguished between two different contextual variables that influence animal behavior. Darwin's observations about specialized environments and specific adaptations, such as the varying beak shapes of the finches and the sunning behavior of the marine iguanas on the rocks in the Galápagos Islands, suggested that evolutionary forces shaped responses associated with the survival of species. Mayr referred to these long-term evolutionary causes of physical and behavioral characteristics as **ultimate causes**. He referred to more short-term causes of behavior, such as hormonal secretions or an unexpected loud noise, as **proximal causes** (Kulathinal, 2010; Lalano, Sterelny, Odling-Smee, Hoppitt, & Uller, 2011).

The Nobel prize–winning scientist Nikolaas Tinbergen reinforced the importance of understanding short- and long-term influences on animal behavior when he more specifically described relevant questions that should be answered as researchers attempted to understand various behaviors. These questions required an understanding of the mechanisms, development, function, and evolution of behavioral

FIGURE 1.2 **Evolutionary adaptations.** Marine iguanas evolved to blend in with their environment. This camouflage provides protection against predation while the iguanas sun themselves on black rocks to maintain warm body temperatures.

FIGURE 1.3 **Cognition and context.** Darwin altered his environmental context in beneficial ways when he walked along this "thinking path" on his property each day.

responses. Using Tinbergen's framework, the proximal (mechanisms and development) questions are sometimes referred to as the "how" questions and the ultimate (function and evolution) questions are referred to as the "why" questions (Bateson & Laland, 2013).

Throughout this text, we will examine many behaviors by attempting to understand the causes, development, function, and evolutionary history of the targeted responses. For example, your motivation to spend time with your friends this evening could be understood by identifying its proximal causes: the developmental pattern of such social responses

from childhood through adulthood, as well as the brain areas and neurochemicals (chemicals in the brain involved in various functions) associated with social behavior. Your desire to see your friends could also be studied based on its ultimate causes: the function and survival benefits of social behavior and the evolutionary history of social behavior in primates.

Although Darwin focused on the physical specializations that facilitated adaptation and survival of animals, other evolutionary strategies exist. Animals that do not depend on a particular habitat or food source have more flexibility in their options of where to live, and they can survive in different environments. Mammals such as humans, bears, raccoons, foxes, and rats have varied diets and are considered more *generalists* than *specialists* in their food preferences.

Raccoons, for example, are known for their ability to adapt to eating novel foods from almost any new food source, an inclination that keeps them breaking into trash cans in urban environments (Zeveloff, 2002; Figure 1.4). Such opportunistic mammals may lead riskier lives as they venture out to unknown territories, but they are more likely to survive than other animals when a familiar environment changes or when expected resources are suddenly depleted. As they are forced out of one type of habitat, they readily adapt to another.

Perhaps the most extreme example of adapting to eat new foods from different sources occurred centuries ago, in opportunistic rats that served as castaways on ships traveling from Europe to what would later become the United States. Surviving on human food during the trip, the rats departed from the ships when they landed and, along with their fellow human travelers, established colonies in the new territory. Although both the humans and the rats survived their journey to a new environment in this example, such a move is not always met with success and more plentiful resources. The rats' behavioral strategy of following humans to take advantage of human food sources (rats and humans prefer similar

FIGURE 1.4 **Opportunistic raccoons.** Raccoons often use opportunistic strategies to solve novel problems such as breaking into garbage cans for human leftovers.

types of foods) prompted the rats to explore new habitats such as buildings and ships, a strategy that eventually led to the establishment of these opportunistic animals in the new habitats. Regardless of an animal's awareness of the process, survival depends on a strategic and realistic cost/benefit analysis, in this case between safe but restricted resources and riskier but more plentiful resources (Lambert, 2011).

Explorations of Environmental Context in the Laboratory and Beyond

Of all the lectures I heard as an undergraduate, the most exciting was the one in which my professor described the classic **enriched environment** studies. In these studies, experimenters housed some rats in social groups in cages along with stimulating objects for the rats to interact with (known as either an enriched or a complex environment) and compared them with "control" rats that were housed individually or in groups in standard laboratory cages with food and water but no stimulating objects. Compared with the control rats, the enriched-environment rats showed increased physical activity and social interactions (Bennett, Diamond, Krech, & Rosenzweig, 1964).

In the 1960s, a research team at the University of California at Berkeley systematically evaluated the impact of a complex environment on rat development. The complex enriched environments consisted of social groups of three rats per cage; further, objects were placed in each cage and replaced after several days to ensure that the environment was dynamic, as it would be in the wild. These "enriched" rats were compared with animals housed individually in cages, as well as with groups of rats housed in cages with no enriching objects. After a month, the rats' brains were removed and examined. The rats that had experienced the enriched environment (that is, the group-housed rats that were presented with new objects) had thicker areas of the brain (e.g., the most recently evolved *cortex* known to be involved in "higher" cognitive functions) and more connections among the cells of the nervous system. Although it was thought at the time that brains were fixed from birth, the brains of these animals appeared to change in response to the external environment (Diamond, 1988; Diamond, Krech, & Rosenzweig, 1964). This enrichment research provided evidence that the

context of these rats' home cages, consisting of complex social and environmental stimuli, influenced the brain's structure after birth.

Since the initial enriched environment studies, researchers have continued to explore the impact of complex environments on the brains of various species. As seen in Figure 1.5, evidence indicates that enriched environments also facilitate recovery of function following brain trauma. In this study, rats experienced brain trauma from temporary interruption of blood flow to the brain (similar to a **stroke**) and received transplanted healthy neural tissue from fetal rat brains as a treatment. Rats that were housed in an enriched environment regained more lost function (e.g., balance and agility) than their counterparts that were housed in the standard, boring cages (Dobrossy & Dunnett, 2001).

Recently, my students and I explored the impact of the source of the stimuli placed in the enriched environments on rats' neural and behavioral responses. For example, in enriched environments, do natural stimuli such as dirt, sticks, and rocks influence the brain differently than do artificial stimuli such as plastic toys and ladders? Using varying levels of the **independent variable** that is manipulated in a controlled laboratory study—in this case, natural-enriched, artificial-enriched, and standard environments—allowed us to more thoroughly examine the effects of the type of environment on the **dependent variables**—the specific behaviors and hormone levels that are measured in research investigations.

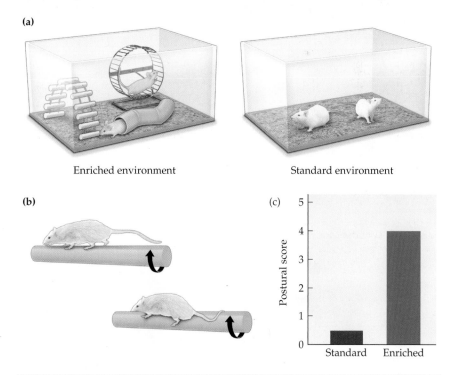

FIGURE 1.5 Enriched environments and brain recovery. (a) Following experimental brain damage, rats were either housed in an enriched or standard environment. The rats were then subjected to (b) motor testing in which they were challenged to walk and balance on a rod. The rats housed in the enriched environment (top) performed better than those housed in the standard environment (bottom). (c) These results suggest that an enriched environment facilitates recovery from brain damage.

Initial investigations suggest that although the rats' learning abilities seem to be comparable in the artificial-enriched environments and the natural-enriched environments, the rats exposed to natural-enriched environments secrete hormones, or neurochemicals, and exhibit bold behaviors that are more consistent with emotional resilience, the ability to bounce back from challenging situations. When the rats exposed to natural-enriched environments were placed in a small swim tank, they had higher levels of a hormone called dehydroepiandrosterone (DHEA), known to be involved with resilience, than did the rats in artificially enriched environments (the ones with toys) and those in standard laboratory cages. The DHEA likely buffered against the spike in the stress hormone corticosterone that all the rats experienced in this challenging situation (more information about hormones and stress will be presented in Chapter 10). Further, the distribution of brain cells differed across the groups in this study. When compared with the rats housed in standard cages, the naturally enriched environment rats had more cells in parts of the brain associated with memory and processing emotional information. Although the artificially enriched environment group's average number of cells was higher than that of the standard-housed group, the difference was not statistically significant

(Kaufman et al., 2012; Lambert, Nelson, Jovanovic, & Cerda, 2015; see Figure 1.6). These findings provide evidence that an animal's **environmental context** (internal or external conditions) can indeed have a powerful impact on many aspects of the animal's brain and behavioral systems.

Human research has produced some similar findings suggesting that exposure to natural environments contributes to resilience and the reduction of stress. For example, one study showed that in an urban public housing complex, women residents who had a window overlooking grass and trees engaged in less violent and aggressive behavior than did women residents who had a window overlooking barren concrete scenes. The study's authors theorized that exposure to natural contexts diminishes mental fatigue or inability to focus one's attention on a critical issue (Kuo & Sullivan, 2001). In another study in the same housing complex, young girls (aged 7–12 years) with more natural views outside their windows were found to have more self-control in the form of inhibited impulsivity, enhanced concentration, and an increased ability to delay gratification (Taylor, Kuo, & Sullivan, 2002). Perhaps the designer of Manhattan's Central Park, Frederick Law Olmsted, was on to something in 1865 when he stated that "It is a scientific fact that the occasional contemplation of natural scenes of an impressive character.... is favorable to the health and vigor of men" (as cited in Hartig, 2007, p. 165).

The Context Conundrum

If the environmental context is important for the development and maintenance of healthy and successful species, what happens to the brain as the environment changes from that of our ancestors? As you see in Figure 1.7, our environmental habitats have changed drastically over the past few centuries. Manhattan has been transformed from a lush, green, natural habitat with plentiful wildlife to a city that is, except for a few cherished parks, characterized more by architectural than natural wonders. Compared with our hunter-gatherer ancestors, our survival is much less dependent on physical exertion—the activities of tracking, spearing, and preparing our dinners have been replaced by pressing a series of buttons or lightly touching screens to either heat up our food or have it delivered to our door (Pontzer et al., 2012).

Although we consider that our contemporary environment represents "advances" in our culture, have those advances been good for the

(a)

(b)

(c)

(d)

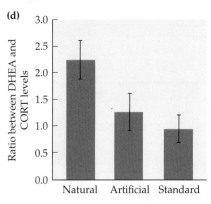

FIGURE 1.6 **Rat behavior in different environments.** Rats were housed in one of three conditions: (a) a natural-enriched environment with stimuli found in nature, and a standard bare cage (not pictured), (b) an artificial-enriched environment with manufactured stimuli. (c) All the rats underwent a brief forced swim task. (d) When stress-related hormones were subsequently tested, the rats in the natural-enriched group had DHEA/corticosterone ratios indicating greater resilience than the rats found in the artificial-enriched groups.

(a)

(b)

FIGURE 1.7 **Environmental transformations.** In a relatively short period of time, human habitats have changed drastically, often transitioning from natural to artificial environments. (a) Manhattan in 1609 and (b) Manhattan today.

development of our brains? The ease with which we can access calorie-laden food, for example, differs markedly from the experience of our hunter-gatherer ancestors and has likely contributed to a worldwide epidemic in obesity (Pontzer et al., 2012). Considering that our brains direct our behavioral responses, drastic changes in daily behavior directed toward food collection and preparation also alter the brain's processing (as we will discuss in Chapter 8).

As humans have transitioned from living in challenging wild environments to living in the drastically different environments that characterize most contemporary cities, have our brains, thoughts, emotions, and behavior also been transformed? Currently, half the world's population lives in cities, and by 2050, nearly 70% of all humans are predicted to live in urban areas (Dye, 2008). Overall, compared with inhabitants of rural areas, city dwellers (particularly in the developed world) are wealthier and have improved health care, sanitation, and nutrition. However, urban living is also associated with an increased risk for chronic illnesses and heightened levels of stress stemming from restricted resources or dangerous living conditions (Lambert et al., 2015; Lederbogen et al., 2011).

In addition to increasing our vulnerability to chronic illnesses, our contemporary lifestyles may be changing the physical structure of our brains. Research suggests that domestication produced by selectively breeding animals in captivity decreases the size of brains. Pet rabbits, for example, which have been paired by breeders to promote desirable traits such as floppy ears as opposed to being allowed

to breed naturally in the wild, have brains that are about 20% smaller than those of their counterparts in the wild (Hemmer, 1990). These observations lead us to contemplate whether our contemporary environments have resulted in the domestication of the human species. Although the concept of human domestication is complex and differs from the captive breeding of animals, finding mates via social media and computer dating services differs from the mate selection strategies used by our ancestors. Accordingly, it is interesting to consider whether humans have produced an environment that has led to a more "tame" human species that is less competent in the wilderness than our earlier ancestors (Brune, 2007). Even if we are less likely to survive on a deserted island, does this have meaningful consequences for our species? Should we be concerned?

According to the University of Wisconsin paleoanthropologist John Hawks, analyses of skulls from 5,000 years ago suggest that the size of the human brain has decreased by approximately 10%. Considering that our brains consume disproportionately large amounts of energy compared with other body organs, it is not clear whether this physical downsizing corresponds with a downsizing of our intelligence. The current, more streamlined brain model may be more coordinated and efficient, representing an improved model, or it may be less complex and sophisticated, representing a compromised model. Indeed, recent research suggests that students at the University College London who reported more media multitasking (including concurrent use of print, television, computer, and cell phone applications) had a smaller brain area known as the anterior cingulate cortex, known for its involvement in cognitive and emotional information processing (Loh & Kanai, 2014). Although these findings do not prove that media multitasking shrinks our brains, the results are informative about our evolving multimedia lifestyles and provide a potential explanation for previous research findings suggesting that such activities are associated with compromised cognitive abilities and unhealthy emotional responses (Becker, Alzahabi, & Hopwood, 2013; Ophir, Nass, & Wagner, 2009;). For the purposes of this discussion, the key point is that the human brain is still evolving and changing in response to environmental demands (Choi, 2009; McAuliffe, 2011).

Regardless of the brain changes that accompany domestication, does the removal of animals from their natural habitats compromise their ability to return to that habitat and survive, as suggested in the case of humans? Manuel Berdoy, a scientist at Oxford University, sought to answer this question. He took rats that had lived in laboratories for 200 generations and released them in a barnyard that was fenced in from some, but not all, predators. Could they find food? Water? Shelter? Other rats? Could they reproduce and successfully raise their offspring? Would they recognize a predator and retreat to safety? This experiment was an adventure for both the scientists and the rats. Overall, the rats exhibited adaptive responses that were characteristic of wild animals the minute they were released. For example, they figured out how to drink from a large pool of rainwater instead of from a water bottle, and they cautiously tasted berries and raw eggs that had replaced the lab chow that had once been readily available. When they detected a barn cat, they retreated for almost a day until there was no sign of danger. Further, they became increasingly nocturnal, which made them less visible to predators. All in all, these laboratory rats passed the challenge with flying colors.

The only difference that distinguished these rats from their wild counterparts was their diminished fear of novelty. In contrast to wild rats, which cautiously approach any new item in a familiar environment, the rats that had been raised in laboratories were more curious and quicker to explore novel items. This lingering effect of domestication resulted in an increased probability of being lured into shiny metal traps with enticing food treats (Berdoy, 2002). Thus, although curiosity is often viewed as beneficial, in the wild it often leads to an animal's demise. Overall, this study reminds us that although rats have been living in laboratories for generations, for the most part, their brains and capacity for responses are similar to those of their wild ancestors. Similarly, aspects of the human brain may still be geared for our ancestral surroundings.

The Importance of Context in Biopsychological Research

Although context is a general term, the concept can be broken down into environmental and experiential dimensions, which influence various biopsychological factors

such as activation of specific brain areas, processing speed in the brain's billions of cells, and neurochemical levels. As described throughout the subsequent chapters, such biopsychological factors potentially have a significant impact on behavioral responses and mental functions. Examples of each dimension appear in Figure 1.8.

Environmental Context. Environmental context can take the form of external or internal conditions. Both can influence behavior as well as mental functions. A thorough analysis of neurobiological variables should always consider these relevant contexts.

EXTERNAL CONDITIONS. In the early 1980s, Bruce Alexander and his colleagues at Simon Fraser University in British Columbia investigated the effects of external environment on drug addiction in rats. At that time, plenty of research had already demonstrated that rats housed in standard laboratory cages would press a bar to obtain drugs such as morphine or cocaine, suggesting that animals may be predisposed to consume these mind-altering substances. The rats often chose the drugs over life necessities such as food and water. Alexander wondered whether the stark differences between the sparse environment of the laboratory cages and the rich natural habitat of rats in the wild had any impact on rats' consumption of these drugs. In other words, did the boring laboratory environments drive the rats toward addiction?

To investigate this question, Alexander and his colleagues built a habitat that was 200 times larger than the

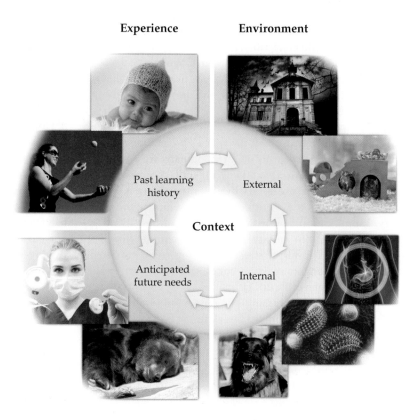

FIGURE 1.8 **The brain in context.** Varied contexts in the form of experience and environment influence neural functions and behavioral responses. Past experiences and anticipated events influence responses as well as stimuli from both external and internal origins.

standard rat cage. Colorful murals of nature scenes were painted on the walls, and objects were placed in the habitat to interact with and climb over. Instead of being housed in isolation, as was the case in typical drug addiction research, large groups of rats were placed in the habitat to provide rich social stimulation. The researchers referred to this new rodent community, a modified version of the enriched environments described earlier in the chapter, as "Rat Park" (Figure 1.9).

When given a choice between morphine and water, the residents of Rat Park chose water. Even when the rats had a previously established preference for morphine, their preference shifted to water when they were moved and housed in Rat Park. These researchers suggested that one reason animals consume psychoactive drugs is to stimulate their brains. Accordingly, when rats were housed in an environment with lots of competing, engaging distractions (alternative forms of brain stimulation), the allure of the drugs diminished (Alexander, Beyerstein, Hadaway, & Coambs, 1981; Lambert, 2011).

Although Alexander was excited by the results and their implications, he had difficulty getting them accepted for publication in the highest-profile science journals. If you have taken a research methods course, you likely understand why these results may have been received with caution. Because the researchers manipulated multiple variables to

FIGURE 1.9 Rat addiction intervention. Rats living in the enriched "Rat Park" habitat displayed enhanced protection against addiction when offered free access to substances such as morphine.

create the enriched environment, they had difficulty identifying which variables contributed most to the results. That is, which variables were most critical in suppressing the rats' motivation to consume psychoactive drugs? Was it the social interactions? Increased physical exercise? The interactive stimuli in the habitat? Regardless of the differing effects of these factors, this series of studies demonstrates the significant influence of external environment on biopsychological variables, in this case, addiction.

Focusing on the impact of a more specific external environmental variable, could something in the environment explain a phenomenon as mystical and complex as feeling that you are in a haunted house? In Edgar Allen Poe's 1839 short story "The Fall of the House of Usher," Poe wrote, "What was it—I paused to think—what was it that so unnerved me in the contemplation of the House of Usher?" According to environmental scientists, Poe was likely unnerved by carbon monoxide poisoning from the coal gas used during that time period for indoor lighting (Donnay, 1999). Dr. William Wilmer, an ophthalmologist at Johns Hopkins University, published an account in 1921 about one of his patients whose family moved into an old home in 1912 that was in dire need of repairs. After settling into the house, they started having strange experiences—sensing that someone was with them when no one was actually in the room, hearing sounds that did not seem to be real, feeling lethargic, looking pale, and noticing that the plants were dying. It appeared to them that their house was haunted. The simpler explanation, however, was revealed when a relative identified that the furnace was emitting toxic levels of carbon monoxide. Although a poisonous gas is much less dramatic than a haunted house, this is yet another example of the powerful influence of the environment on biopsychological variables (Wilmer, 1921).

INTERNAL CONDITIONS. Your digestive system hosts many different types of microorganisms that are associated with both healthful and unhealthful effects, such as normal digestion of our food or an upset stomach. For example, in the lower part of the digestive system, known as the colon, 5,600 species or strains of microorganisms have been identified (Dethlefsen, Huse, Sogin, & Relman, 2008). Bacteria known as probiotics are generally thought to have a positive impact on internal functions such as digestion, explaining why these microorganisms are sold as supplements at health food stores. But what about behavior and neural processes? When researchers in Ireland fed mice probiotics, they found that the mice exhibited less anxiety and lower levels of stress hormones than mice that did not receive the probiotic diet (Bravo et al., 2011).

Viruses also invade our bodies and influence our behavior. Rabies, a fatal viral disease, is characterized by a behavioral change of increased aggression. A rabid animal typically attacks and bites another animal at the height of the rabies infection—passing on the virus—and then dies. Examinations of the brains of animals and humans infected with rabies indicate that the virus travels to the areas of the brain known to be involved in aggression. This is a case of a virus spreading by exploiting the complex mammalian brain's functioning, forcing us to rethink who is controlling whom in the biosphere of life (Schnell, McGettigan, Wirblich, & Papaneri, 2010).

Experiential Context The **experiential context** refers to the context provided by past or future experiences. As with the environmental context, the experiential context influences behavior and mental functions.

PAST EVENTS. Even if you have an identical twin, your experiences differentiate your brain and behavior from your twin's brain and behavior in multiple ways. Adding to the impact of your external and internal environmental conditions, your past emotional, cognitive, and social experiences also sculpt your neurobiology. In one study, brain scans of preschool-age children provided evidence that the degree of maternal support directed toward a child may influence the brain by increasing the size of the hippocampus, which is involved in both emotions and memory. This study evaluated the degree of maternal support in children diagnosed with depression and in healthy children by examining the correlation between the two variables, or the degree to which maternal support and measures of depression varied in a similar or different fashion. The results revealed that higher levels of maternal support were predictive of larger hippocampal volumes in the children, especially in nondepressed children. By providing evidence that the supportive interactions between a child and his or her caregiver are important for the healthy development of the child's hippocampus, this study illustrated the importance of past events on biopsychological responses (Luby et al., 2012).

Even hobbies that require us to fine-tune our movements shape our brains. In one study, subjects were instructed to juggle for three months, performing a classic three-ball routine for 60 seconds. Compared with their brain scans taken prior to the juggling training, subjects' brain scans taken after the three months of training provided evidence that the juggling training expanded the brain's gray matter, where the cell bodies of the nerve cells are located. In fact, the better the subjects' juggling skills, the greater the expansion. However, these structural changes in the brain did not last forever. Three months after the juggling practice stopped, most of the subjects could no longer juggle. A brain scan at this point indicated that the volume of gray matter had started to diminish, although it was still increased compared with the prejuggling scan—supporting the adage "use it or lose it" (Draganski et al., 2004).

In a follow-up study, the research team wondered whether studying abstract information would produce similar effects in the brain's gray matter. In this study, German medical students' brains were scanned before the students began their intense three-month study period for their preliminary medical examination taken two years into their medical education. As you may imagine, substantial medical information is studied, memorized, and processed during this time. The subjects' brains were scanned again shortly after the exam. Once again, compared with the earlier scans before this intense study session began, the brain's gray matter increased (Draganski et al., 2006).

FUTURE AND ANTICIPATED EVENTS. Our bodies and brains also monitor the likelihood of future events, and these anticipated events affect current biopsychological processes such as stress hormone levels and the degree of brain activation in certain areas. For example, when the outdoor temperature drops below a certain threshold, certain behavioral and physiological modifications occur in animals that hibernate during the coldest winter months. Going into hibernation with little stored energy would be fatal, so an increase in eating, along with a decrease in the animals' metabolic rate, typically accompanies the preparation for hibernation. For some bears that can survive up to 100 days without eating or drinking, survival takes considerable biological preparation. During the preceding summer months, bears increase their food intake and, consequently, gain up to 30 pounds per week. During early fall, they prepare the hibernation den for the long winter's slumber (Reardon, 2011).

Evidence indicates that anticipation of impending events influences biopsychological processes in humans. For example, knowledge of certain impending events affects pain perception, an ability that is important for survival. Many patients are anxious when they are about to undergo a dental or other type of medical procedure. Research indicates that when patients are provided with both procedural and sensory information in preparation for the procedure (e.g., when they are told that they will feel a specific way after a certain step of the procedure), they report feeling less pain during the procedure than do patients who go into the procedure blind to expectations (Suls & Wan, 1989). Further research has suggested that when patients are uncertain about the outcome of a medical procedure, the hippocampus is activated to process escape and threat situations aligned with the worst possible outcome. When subjects were exposed to uncomfortable thermal stimulation (i.e., heat) while having their brains scanned, less activity in the hippocampus was observed if the level of thermal pain was predictable than if the subjects were uncertain about the degree of pain that they would experience at various times. Thus, uncertainty about the presentation of painful procedures appears to exacerbate the perceived pain. When relevant and accurate preparatory information is provided, however, brain scans indicate that certain areas of the hippocampus are disengaged (Ploghaus et al., 2001).

Thus, anticipated events modify behavior in many ways, further supporting the important influence of experiential context on biopsychological functions. Such research can provide valuable information about the most effective ways for medical professionals to interact with patients, perhaps leading to less use of pain medications.

Return to Figure 1.8 and reconsider the examples described in this section. It should be evident that the brain is directly influenced by its experiential and environmental context. With this knowledge, we become more accountable for the context in which we place our brains. Now that you know that factors such as physical activity, studying, friends, and past experiences influence brain health, you understand why we all should thoughtfully evaluate the activities that characterize our daily lives. Throughout this book, you will learn valuable information about being an informed user of your brain, maximizing its output and your chances of well-being and success.

Our understanding of the impact of various environmental and experiential contexts is a result of the diligent and insightful work of passionate brain explorers who wanted to understand the inner workings of the brain. In the next section, you will be introduced to some of these fascinating pioneers and their journeys to reveal the brain's many mechanical and functional mysteries.

Pioneers in Brain Research

Once researchers began focusing on the brain as the organ responsible for mental and behavioral functions, the next question was how closely specific brain functions were mapped onto specific brain areas. For example, when you decide that you want to grab a snack out of the pantry, does your entire brain, or only specific areas of your brain, play a role in that decision? This question addresses the issue known as **localization of brain function**.

One of the first pioneers to formally investigate this question was an Austrian physician named Franz Joseph Gall. Gall began pondering the origins of various mental functions long before he attended medical school. He reminisced that when he was in elementary school, he had noted that some of the boys in his class had excellent memories. Similar to many of us, Gall felt that he did not possess this enviable trait. On further examination, the schoolboy thought that the supermemorizers had bulging eyes and a high forehead, perhaps evidence of a larger brain that was literally pushing beyond the boundaries of the skull. At that time, similar to the notions that influenced Fitzroy's conclusion that Darwin did not have the right shape nose to be a seafarer, a trend existed associating facial characteristics with personality traits (e.g., sinister individuals having beady little eyes). In this respect, Gall's interest in the characteristics of the head and face were aligned with the intellectual trends of the time period.

As Gall finished medical school, he began revisiting those childhood observations, this time incorporating the size of certain areas of the brain into his ideas. Specifically, he hypothesized that certain brain structures were associated with specific functions or, as they were called in that time, **mental faculties**. To put this emerging theory to the test, he had to get creative. In a later section of this chapter, you will learn about some excellent methodological tools that biological psychologists use, but in the 18th century, Gall had access to none of them. An astute student of the brain, Gall had conducted many postmortem dissections of human brains, even being the first to formally describe a few of the brain's areas. He theorized that any higher-functioning areas of the cortex would be represented by a bulge in the cortex. Further, he thought that the associated cortical bulge could be assessed by merely feeling the skull with one's hands.

With his new theory in hand (literally!), Gall set out to measure and assess the skulls of many people and question them about specific abilities so he could correlate the size of the bumps with their personal mental faculties. After this data collection phase, he settled on 27 mental faculties such as wisdom, poetic talent, and satire that he proposed were specifically localized on the brain's cortical surface. If you are following this story closely, you may have slipped your hand over your skull to search for these proposed bumps. Any luck? Unless your skull is different from that of most humans, it probably feels surprisingly smooth, without enough variation for one of Gall's neuropsychological exams. As you know, logic does not always prevail in human pursuits, so let's set aside our skepticism and continue with this story.

Forced out of Austria because his new brain theory equated the human soul with the material brain, Gall started touring and lecturing throughout Europe. He made the acquaintance of Johann Spurzheim, who would become his assistant. Spurzheim modified Gall's list of mental faculties by removing some of the negative ones, such as destructive and secretive tendencies, so that the theory presented humans in a more positive light. It is not clear whether this decision was based on a closer examination of the perceived evidence (which would make Spurzheim a pioneer in the current movement known as positive psychology) or whether it was merely a marketing strategy to attract more interest in Gall's theory. Spurzheim also popularized the term **phrenology** (after *phren* for mind and *logos* for discourse) to represent Gall's theory of brain localization. To the public, phrenology was known as the mapping of mental characteristics to bumps on the skull. As seen in Figure 1.10, phrenology busts, or representative labeled skulls, were made to assist phrenologists in their brain assessments.

The lack of **empirical evidence** (observable support for a scientific claim) supporting the premise of phrenology eventually caught up with Gall. By 1840, phrenology was no longer viewed as scientific and was associated more with parlor humor. A French scientist, Marie-Jean-Pierre Flourens, attacked Gall's theory with the most valuable

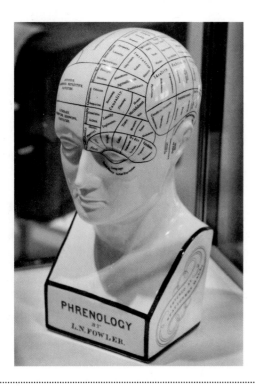

FIGURE 1.10 **Phrenology bust.** Gall's theory about localization of function on the brain's surface was popularized by Spurzheim as "phrenology" and marketed with phrenology busts.

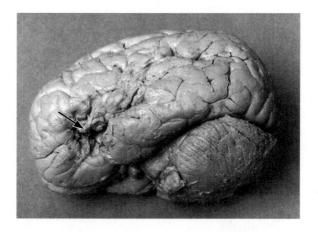

FIGURE 1.11 **Broca's area.** An autopsy of Tan's brain revealed a lesion in the frontal cortical area that was later referred to as Broca's area.

weapon—empirical evidence. Taking Gall's ideas into the experimental laboratory, he surgically removed one of the proposed "bumps" that was associated with amorous relations (romance) in a female cat. If Gall's theory were correct, this cat would show no interest in romantic relations with a male suitor. Flourens's picture of this experimental cat being followed by her litter of kittens was all the evidence he needed to squash Gall's reputation as a pioneer in brain research. Consequently, Flourens concluded that the moral and intellectual faculties proposed by Gall, such as circumspection and satire, could not be specifically localized to the brain's cortex. But, was Flourens correct?

A few decades later, the notion that higher faculties could be localized to the brain's cortex continued in the minds of a few researchers. Two French physicians, Jean-Baptiste Bouillaud and his son-in-law, Simon Aubertin, believed that language was localized in the cortex. Paul Broca, a future pioneer in brain research, listened intently to Bouillaud and Aubertin lecture on their case studies describing patients with simultaneous damage to a specific brain area and language deficits. Bouillaud and Aubertin had not been able to locate an individual with a visible frontal lobe injury to provide evidence in support of their theory of the localization of language. However, Broca successfully located a 51-year-old patient who, after suffering from epilepsy, had been unable to speak for 20 years. On his death, the brain of this patient (known as Tan) was examined and, as shown in Figure 1.11, found to have had damage in the same brain

area that Bouillaud and Aubertin had predicted. Whereas Gall's ideas about cortical localization were ultimately ridiculed, Broca's study of actual brain damage provided evidence of the localization of language function, an idea that was enthusiastically received by the scientific community (Finger, 1994, 2000).

This intriguing story of pioneers in brain research serves as a reminder of the importance of empirical evidence in biopsychological research. Scientists must strive to maintain integrity by providing appropriate and sufficient evidence to assess **hypotheses** (testable scientific predictions) and theoretical models that are being investigated. Although Gall lost his methodological way, his early observations, scientific curiosity, and passion for his work influenced the work of others who provided further clarification on the localization of brain function. The answers to the localization question continue to evolve—answers that are complex, multifaceted, and always changing.

As you progress through each chapter of this book, you will learn about defined areas of the brain involved with specific brain functions. You will also be introduced to countless **brain circuits**, also known as "neural networks," representing multiple brain areas linked in critical ways so that they are concurrently involved in certain functions. Thus, the most current evidence suggests that both specific areas and integrated networks in the brain are involved with specific brain functions.

Another pioneer discussed previously in this chapter was Charles Darwin. Although his work was not specifically related to understanding the functions of brain tissue, he laid the groundwork for an exciting new methodological approach that would redefine the way scientists explored various biological functions. It is difficult for us living in contemporary society to imagine a time when genetics was not part of the scientific dialogue; however, before and during Darwin's time, the genetics story was yet to be told. The new details about genetics and the transmission of biological traits described in the next section revolutionized biological science, including neuroscience.

The Genetics Story: From Gemmules to Genomes

As Darwin studied the transmission of traits from one generation to another, he sought to understand exactly how these traits were passed down. He reported being fascinated by animal breeders, especially pigeon fanciers, who were well aware of the hazards of inbreeding (the mating of closely related individuals). If unrelated birds were bred, their offspring were more variable—expressing differences in physical and behavioral characteristics such as size, feather color, and behavioral tendencies—whereas inbreeding reduced this variability. Thus, Darwin's time spent with fanciers and breeders emphasized the importance of variability in the transmission of traits from parents to offspring. Such variability would produce a species that had the capacity for diverse responses should the environment change in either subtle or dramatic ways.

Recall the varying beak shapes of the finches that Darwin described. If the environment were to change, birds with slightly different beak shapes might be more likely to obtain different sources of food and thus survive the changes. For example, imagine that insects in the bark of a tree become unavailable to finches with beaks that are adapted to dig through the bark. The members of this finch species most likely to survive will be those whose beaks differ enough from the norm to allow them to obtain food from other sources as well. Variability, in this case, is an important aspect of survival.

Although Darwin examined plants, insects, and cells under the microscope, he could only speculate about the mechanisms of **heredity** (the biological transmission of physical and mental characteristics from parents to offspring) of the characteristics he was monitoring in his plants and animals. He once thought that heredity was transmitted through the blood. However, blood transfusions in rabbits, conducted by his cousin, Sir Francis Galton, failed to alter any of their physical characteristics (Bulmer, 1999). Although Darwin's endless search for the hypothetical unit of inheritance transmitted through sexual reproduction never produced any

tangible evidence, he referred to this proposed unit as the *gemmule* (Boulter, 2010).

The Components of Heredity

Unbeknownst to Darwin, an Austrian monk, Gregor Mendel, was also seeking the unit of inheritance. Mendel focused his studies on plants, primarily the pea plant. Mendel's theory about how certain traits were expressed and suppressed in subsequent generations ultimately identified peas with varying observable, physical characteristics such as shape and color; these characteristics are known as **phenotypes**. After seven years of breeding different varieties of the pea plant with one another and recording the phenotype of the second and subsequent generations of plants, Mendel started to understand the rules of heritable transmission. He assigned letters representing specific **alleles** or varying versions of biological factors, now known as **genes**, containing the inherited information for a particular species for varying forms of physical characteristics. Animals and plants receive one allele of the gene from each parent. For example, the rock pocket mouse (*Chaetodipus intermedius*) has two different coat colors, a light sandy color and a dark color. As seen in Figure 1.12, in the southwestern United States where sections of pale rocks adjoin areas of black lava beds, the coat color is important for providing camouflage against predators such as owls with a keen sense of vision. Biologists have determined that this dramatic change in coat color is determined by a single gene, consisting of a dark-fur-colored allele and a sand-fur-colored allele (Majerus & Mundy,

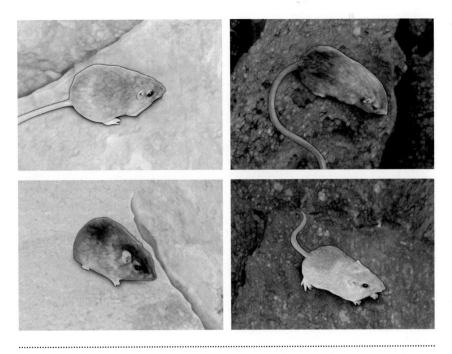

FIGURE 1.12 Evolved camouflage. Different color variations have evolved in the rock pocket mouse. Specific coat colors have survival value in specific environmental contexts. Coat colors that blend in with the environment lead to protection from predators (above), while coat colors that contrast with the environment make the mouse more vulnerable to predation (below).

2003). Initially, the allele associated with the dark coat was a product of a **mutation**, a random but permanent alteration that suddenly occurs in the DNA sequence of a gene. In this case, the mutation had survival consequences for mice living in the territories covered with dark lava rock. You are probably not surprised to learn that the mice with the dark fur are most often found in the lava habitat and the light-colored mice are found on the sandy rocks.

Mendel suggested that when animals or plants with varying characteristics were bred, these characteristics were not blended; on the contrary, the genes responsible for some varieties of the traits always won out. For example, as shown in Figure 1.13, when pea plants with yellow seeds were bred with those with green seeds, all of the offspring in the first generation had yellow seeds. When some of these offspring were bred, some members of the second generation had green seeds. The yellow-seeded plants of the first generation thus must

have carried the green-seeded allele, which was not expressed. The yellow-seeded allele was **dominant**, whereas the green-seeded allele was **recessive**. When a dominant gene is paired with a recessive gene, the characteristics of the dominant gene are expressed. In the case of the pocket mice, the dark-colored coat has been found to be dominant over the light-colored coat (Nachman, Hoekstra, & D'Agostino, 2003). Mendel's assignment of alleles that appeared to be responsible for the expression of a particular phenotype is known as the plant or animal's **genotype**. As seen in Figure 1.13, the peas with the same alleles (e.g., both dominant or recessive) are considered **homozygous**, whereas the peas with different alleles (one dominant, one recessive) are known as **heterozygous**.

Mendel presented a summary of his research on inheritance to a local scientific society in 1865, just six years after Darwin's publication of *On the Origin of Species*. Unfortunately, Mendel's work was not recognized as being revolutionary until nearly four decades later, when a zoologist from Cambridge University, William Bateson, read a summary of the work in preparation for a talk he would deliver to the Royal Horticultural Society. Mendel's previously unnoticed paper inspired Bateson to change the emphasis of his talk. He recounted Mendel's pivotal findings and told the audience,

> *An exact determination of the laws of heredity will probably work more change in man's outlook on the world, and in his power over nature, than any other advance in natural knowledge that can be foreseen. There is no doubt whatever that these laws can be determined. (Henig, 2000, p. 3)*

After Bateson had Mendel's paper translated from German into English, he coined the term **genetics** to refer to the branch of biology that would pursue the study of heritable transmission and variability of inherited phenotypes (Henig, 2000).

The work of the German anatomist Walther Flemming in the mid-19th century would eventually be viewed as revealing the cellular mechanisms of heredity, further supporting the preliminary observations of Darwin and Mendel. Using the best microscopy (microscope techniques) of his time, Flemming described an interesting fibrous network in the cell's **nucleus**, the command center of the cell that contains

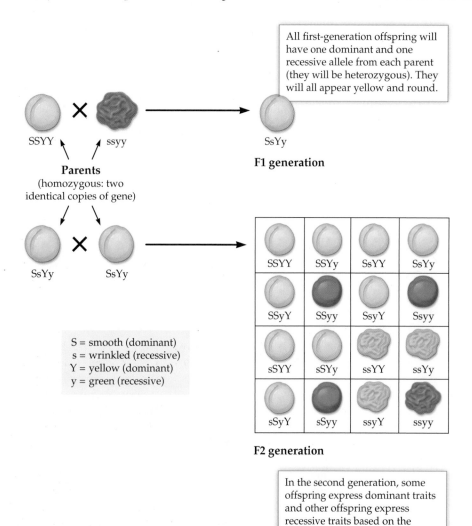

All first-generation offspring will have one dominant and one recessive allele from each parent (they will be heterozygous). They will all appear yellow and round.

SSYY × ssyy

Parents
(homozygous: two identical copies of gene)

SsYy × SsYy

SsYy

F1 generation

S = smooth (dominant)
s = wrinkled (recessive)
Y = yellow (dominant)
y = green (recessive)

SSYY	SSYy	SsYY	SsYy
SSyY	SSyy	SsyY	Ssyy
sSYY	sSYy	ssYY	ssYy
sSyY	sSyy	ssyY	ssyy

F2 generation

In the second generation, some offspring express dominant traits and other offspring express recessive traits based on the various possible alleles they could have inherited.

FIGURE 1.13 Inheritance. Mendel's pioneering genetic work with peas emphasized the inheritance of traits based on alleles received from each parent. As seen in the F2 generation, different genotypes are expressed as different phenotypes.

the genetic code (specific information about the transmission of specific characteristics) for the cell's functions. When he attempted to identify certain parts of the cell by staining the cells with basic dyes, he noted that this fibrous network stained darker than the other components of the cell, prompting him to refer to it as *chromatin*, or stained material. Flemming noted movement of this chromatin, later known as **chromosomes** (colored bodies), during cell division.

This information led to the subsequent discovery of **sex chromosomes**, which were shaped differently from the other chromosomes, and their role in the transmission of heritable traits during sexual reproduction (O'Conner, 2008). The sex chromosomes consist of both X and Y chromosomes, and the combination inherited from the parents determines the sex of the offspring—XX for a female and XY for a male. Further, certain traits can be linked to these sex chromosomes (they are influenced by the genes on those chromosomes). For example, Fragile X syndrome is linked to the X chromosome and is associated with intellectual delays, repetitive behavior, and increased social anxiety. Understanding more about the effects of this genetic condition on brain functioning may lead to effective treatment strategies for types of intellectual disabilities (Maurin, Zongaro, & Bardoni, 2014).

A half century later, several pioneering scientists at Cambridge University and King's College in London made further progress toward understanding the unit of inheritance. When James Watson received his Ph.D. in zoology at Indiana University in 1950, he was interested in learning more about the structure of **deoxyribonucleic acid (DNA)**, which made up the chromosomes, and how it replicated itself. (The Swiss chemist Friedrich Miescher had first identified DNA in the late 1860s.) At Cambridge University, Watson began a collaboration with Francis Crick, who shared his interest in DNA. At the nearby King's College, the two young scientists shared notes with Maurice Wilkins, who was taking X-ray photographs of DNA. Based on the information at hand, Watson and Crick built a physical model of DNA. However, this model was deemed inaccurate and was criticized by their colleagues.

Another critical scientist in the DNA story was a young woman named Rosalind Franklin at King's College, who applied her skills in X-ray techniques to the project of determining the structure of DNA. After working for two years, she produced an image that provided the earliest evidence of DNA's double-helix shape. According to historical accounts, Maurice Wilkins showed this image to Watson and Crick without Franklin's knowledge. The enlightening photo gave Watson and Crick the information they needed to construct a second model, this time with the **nucleotide bases** (the chemical building blocks of DNA) appearing in consistent pairs, either adenine–thymine or cytosine–guanine, to form the inner rungs of the double-helix shape (see Figure 1.14).

As can be seen in Figure 1.15, the DNA structure could be divided into two strands that are effectively mirror images of one another, enabling it to reproduce biological messages

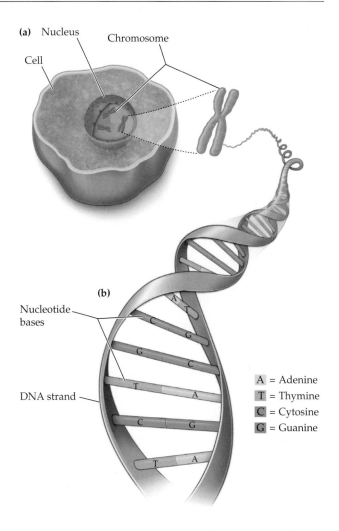

FIGURE 1.14 Chromosomes. (a) Every animal cell contains a nucleus with chromosomes. (b) Chromosomes are made of strands of DNA, which are characterized by specific sequences of nucleotide bases: adenine, thymine, cytosine, and guanine.

that governed the cell's protein production. This happens with the help of **ribonucleic acid (RNA)**, which is similar to DNA but single stranded and with the base uracil instead of thymine. First, the DNA strands separate, and a strand of **messenger RNA (mRNA)** assembles opposite one of the DNA strands such that its nucleotide bases are in the order that DNA prescribes. Then, the mRNA leaves the nucleus and meets a ribosome, which assembles **amino acids** into proteins based on the order of the nucleotide bases in the mRNA (see Figure 1.15).

The discovery of this process solved the mystery of the unit of inheritance theorized by Darwin and tested by Mendel. In 1962, Watson, Crick, and Wilkins received the Nobel Prize for their pioneering work on DNA. Four years prior to the Nobel Ceremony, Rosalind Franklin, just 37 years old, died from ovarian cancer (possibly related to her work with X-rays) and was not recognized at that time for her contributions to this discovery (Maddox, 2002).

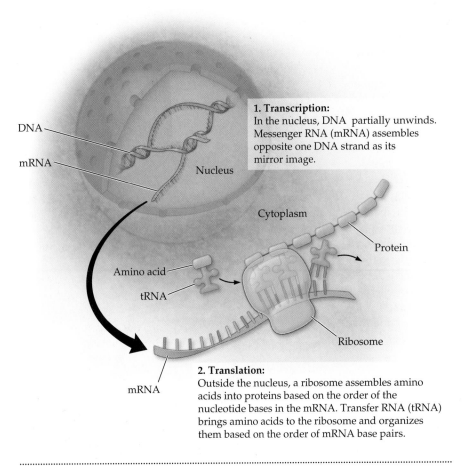

In the nucleus, DNA partially unwinds. Messenger RNA (mRNA) assembles opposite one DNA strand as its mirror image.

2. **Translation:**
Outside the nucleus, a ribosome assembles amino acids into proteins based on the order of the nucleotide bases in the mRNA. Transfer RNA (tRNA) brings amino acids to the ribosome and organizes them based on the order of mRNA base pairs.

FIGURE 1.15 Transmission of genetic information. Genetic traits are communicated through transcription, in which DNA is divided and "read" by messenger RNA, and translation, in which ribosomes assemble amino acids into proteins.

In the late 20th century, a race to decode the complete set of genes (the **genome**) in humans began. The National Institutes of Health, led by Francis Collins, competed with a private laboratory, Celera Genomics, established by a former National Institutes of Health geneticist, Craig Venter. Much excitement and hope surrounded this project. People anticipated that scientists would begin to understand the genetic causes of various diseases, opening new avenues for treatment of those diseases. For example, if we learned that a certain medical condition was associated with a deficit in a specific protein from a malfunctioning genetic sequence, new therapies could potentially restore levels of that particular protein. During this time, the methodology used to read the nucleotide bases making up the genes got much faster as it became fully automated, allowing both teams to complete the project faster than anticipated.

In the end, nearly 3 billion base pairs were decoded to illuminate the formula for being human—an ambitious accomplishment! This undertaking was known as the **Human Genome Project**. In June 2000, President Bill Clinton announced that the two labs shared credit for sequencing the human genome, that is, for determining the sequence of nucleotide bases in human DNA. This accomplishment was considered a milestone for humanity that would soon bring cures for numerous diseases (Public Broadcasting Service, 2001). As described below, however, the sequencing of the human genome has been slow to provide those much-awaited cures for various brain-related diseases.

The next step was to determine what the sequenced human genome meant. The decoded genome revealed several surprises. Although scientists had previously estimated that humans had approximately 100,000 genes, the actual number turned out to be closer to between 20,000 and 30,000 (Lander, 2011; Lander et al., 2001; Venter et al., 2001). This was only twice the number of genes found in fruit flies, indicating that the basic building blocks of living species were similar. Another unexpected finding was the percentage of DNA that actually consisted of genes; at 1.5%, it was much lower than expected (Lander, 2011; Lander et al., 2001; Venter et al., 2001). This means that the function of about 98% of DNA, which is not associated with defining genes for protein production, sometimes referred to as *junk DNA*, is unknown. The sequence variability across humans was also much less than expected. As diverse as humans appear on the surface, the genome tells a different story. Only 0.1 to 0.5% of the entire genome varies across individuals. Perhaps this is because humans in existence today, regardless of their home continent, descended from a small population of our human ancestors in Africa approximately 100,000 years ago. For an older species such as the chimpanzee, however, much more genetic variation has been observed (Bowden et al., 2012).

From Genes to Behavior

A relevant finding for the field of biological psychology is that 84% of all the human genes are expressed in the brain. Thus, a majority of human genetic machinery is utilized in the brain (Hawrylycz et al., 2012). Trying to determine how this genetic material is translated into behavior, thoughts, and emotions is a challenge.

Even if a gene is known to contribute to a phenotype such as a disease, the mechanisms of how the gene contributes to such a disorder must be determined before genetically driven medical interventions can be developed. For example,

Tay–Sachs disease is a fatal condition that is associated with a particular gene. If two mutated copies of the recessive Tay–Sachs gene are inherited, a vital **enzyme** in the brain, hexosaminidase A (Hex-A), will not be produced. (An enzyme is a protein that facilitates a chemical reaction but is not changed by it.) Because Hex-A is an important enzyme for breaking down fatty substances (lipids) in the brain, lipid levels build up in individuals with Tay–Sachs disease, destroying brain tissue. After about six months of apparently normal development, babies with this condition start to miss important developmental milestones such as sitting and crawling. The disease is cruel and relentless, typically ending in death at two to three years of age when basic biological functions such as swallowing and breathing are no longer possible (National Institutes of Health, 2012). Unlike Tay–Sachs disease, most diseases are likely to involve the interactions of many genes.

Identifying the genes related to diseases such as Tay–Sachs disease offers hope via several strategies. First, through genetic counseling, parents can be alerted to the probabilities of having a child who will develop Tay–Sachs disease. Second, researchers may be able to develop treatments to counteract the detrimental effects of Hex-A deficiency.

A cure for Tay–Sachs disease, however, still eludes scientists, who continue to investigate potential treatments and cures.

The example of Tay–Sachs disease reminds us that the gene is only the starting point for the ultimate expression of a behavior or disease phenotype. Scientists currently searching for relevant genes related to language, for example, realize that identification of such genes would be only the *first* step in a series of research investigations to understand how genes may influence language. As seen in Figure 1.16, DNA making up a particular gene dictates the productions of proteins that influence cells and, further, cellular networks in the brain, to ultimately influence the ability to speak and comprehend language. With so many steps from the DNA molecule to ultimate behavioral expression, there are many potential points to intervene in the process. For example, genetic therapies may be introduced early in fetal development to alter the genetic sequence, drugs may be given to correct protein or neurochemical imbalances at specific time points, or behavioral training may be used to modify brain responses altered by a mutated gene.

Although the sequencing of the human genome is a celebrated accomplishment, it is only part of the biological code,

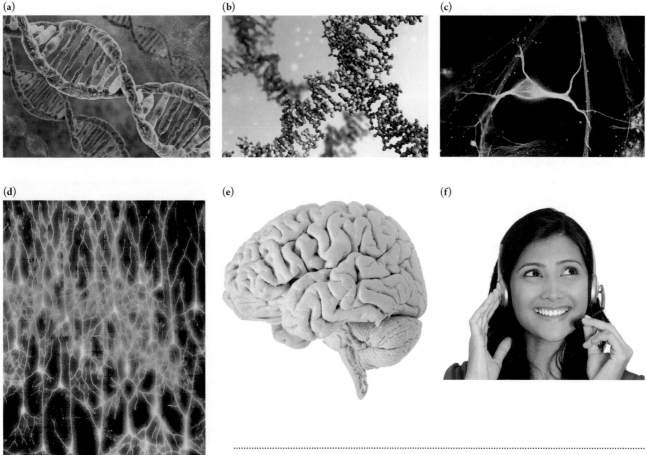

(a) (b) (c)

(d) (e) (f)

FIGURE 1.16 From genes to behavior. In a progressively more complex manner, behavioral abilities emerge from genes (a) transcribed to proteins (b), formed into neurons (c) that are part of neural circuits (d) in targeted brain areas (e), to ultimately produce a multifaceted behavioral and cognitive response such as language (f).

or map of life. If you were given a map that only had coordinates and legends indicating distances on it, you would not find it helpful. Only when the cities, roads, lakes, rivers, and mountain ranges are filled in does the map become useful. Similarly, it is important to incorporate lifestyle data (e.g., health status, food preferences, personality style) with the genome data to understand genetic influences on an individual's phenotype. In 2005, Harvard University's George Church launched the Personal Genome Project. This project aims to collect both genetic sequencing and lifestyle data for 100,000 individuals to investigate how genes interact with the environment to form human traits.

As you will learn in Chapter 5, variations in life experiences and the environment can alter the expression of proteins dictated by the genetic template—a process known as **epigenetics**. By understanding how **gene–environment interactions** alter the production of genetically prescribed proteins, scientists can attempt to create more sophisticated treatments for illness that will account for the context of an individual's lifestyle. It will be interesting to see how the ambitious Personal Genome Project influences our views of genetic influences.

With rapidly changing technology (Mardis, 2011), it is not unrealistic to sequence the genome of many individuals. From the time the first human's genome was sequenced, the price has dropped from hundreds of millions of dollars to less than $10,000 per genome and continues to drop quickly. Although it took more than a decade to produce the first human genome sequence, a lab can now produce one in a day. Thus, the enhanced speed and lower costs will open the door to collect a wealth of data to generate new theories about genetic influences on behavior and mental processes. Whereas the challenge just a few decades ago was how to sequence the human genome, today the challenge is how to manage the deluge of genetic information emerging from laboratories across the world (Cohen, 2010; Pollack, 2011). With a human genome containing more than 3 billion nucleotide bases, storage of these data is becoming increasingly challenging (Lathe, Williams, Mangan, & Karolchik, 2008).

The field of biological psychology will benefit from projects such as the Personal Genome Project because the collection of information from large populations will enable specialists working in the subdiscipline of behavioral genetics to learn more about how genetic variation contributes to behavioral variation. Researchers have long known that the genetic blueprint does not provide all the answers, as illustrated when one identical twin develops schizophrenia but the other does not. An individual's environment and lifestyle, or the context of an individual's life, may ultimately affect whether an individual with a specific genotype develops a genetic disorder. In fact, in the future, behavioral genomics, the investigation of how an individual's genome interacts with one's life context, may replace the field of behavioral genetics (Dick & Rose, 2002). Researchers hope that such an approach will yield both genetic and lifestyle remedies for disease and maladaptive behavior. Genetic

research, however, is just one methodological approach to understanding the brain's impact on behavior. As you will read in the next section and throughout the text, biological psychologists have many research methods in their toolbox.

The Tools of Biological Psychology: Classic and Contemporary Methods

Look closely at the human brain in Figure 1.17. Admittedly, first impressions are somewhat lackluster because the brain looks more like a heaping mound of mush than the most advanced biological organ in the known universe. However, as you will learn throughout this book, there is much more to this amazing brain than meets the eye. Before we get into all the fascinating details, however, let's consider *how* we have learned so much about the brain, an approximately 3.3-pound (1,500-gram) mass of gelatinous tissue in the average adult (Herculano-Houzel, 2009). How have researchers investigated the human brain's functions and mechanisms? We will discuss some of the more historically relevant research methods here and learn about others, especially more contemporary methods, throughout this book. (See the Appendix for a complete list of techniques covered by this text.)

Human Research Methods

Investigators study the human brain by conducting case studies, tracking the brain's electrical activity, and using various imaging techniques.

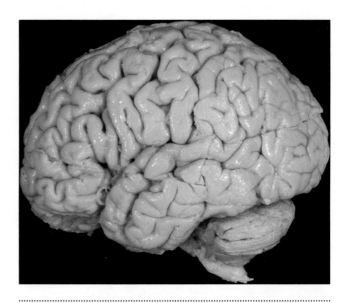

FIGURE 1.17 The human brain. Although the brain looks like a heaping mound of mush, it is the most advanced biological organ in the known universe.

Case Studies Long before scientists could systematically investigate brains in the laboratory, they were collecting evidence from **case studies**, investigations of individuals who had suffered injury or disease that had an impact on behavior or mental functions. Tan, the previously described patient who had a brain injury and language impairment, is a 19th-century example of a case study that pointed to the localization of specific language functions to Broca's area. This paved the way for an understanding of localization of different functions in the human brain. At that time, however, the brain could be examined only after the death of the patient.

Despite all the advanced techniques utilized in hospitals and research settings today, case studies still provide a springboard for learning about brain conditions that are not easily studied through experimentation in the laboratory. For example, have you ever wondered how the brain would respond to having a 3.5-inch nail lodged in it? Of course, this would never be part of an experimental protocol, but when Dante Autullo's nail gun shot a nail close to his head, he felt fortunate to have only a small flesh wound. Little did he know that the nail had actually lodged in his brain! Autullo finished working and initially felt fine, but by the next day he went to the hospital with a headache and nausea. The doctors were amazed that he was still functioning with such a brain intrusion, as seen in Figure 1.18. The nail was removed 36 hours following the incident, with Autullo expected to make a full recovery.

The outcomes of such accidents provide valuable information about the brain's resilience and vulnerabilities. However, case studies are far from experimental studies that control for other variables such as diet, age, and gender.

Experimental Studies Controlled experimental studies typically attempt to isolate the effect of one specific variable, the independent variable (e.g., damage to a specific brain area), on one or more measures (e.g., brain function), the dependent variable(s). For example, an experimental study investigating the effects of brain damage using animal models such as rats would include an experimental group and a control group. The experimental group of animals would have damage to the same brain area. The control group would have no brain damage, but would be the same age and sex as the experimental group. The control group would also be treated the same way as the experimental group to isolate the effects of the brain damage and avoid **confounding variables**, variables other than the independent variable of interest that may affect the dependent variable(s).

Electroencephalography One of the first techniques that allowed investigators to measure the human brain's activity was **electroencephalography (EEG)**, which detects the electrical activity of large populations of the brain's cells. Electrodes, which are positioned at regularly spaced intervals on the scalp, pick up the electrical activity across the brain. This activity is then amplified and recorded on a computer. This technique is often used to document the extreme activation

(a)

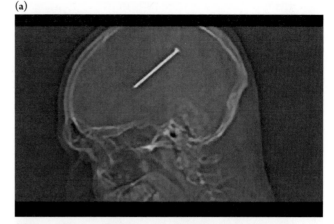

(b)

FIGURE 1.18 **Brain invasion case study.** (a) An X-ray showing a nail embedded in Dante Autullo's brain. (b) Dante, following the successful removal of the nail.

of cellular populations that accompanies an epileptic seizure. Additionally, as seen in Figure 1.19, experimenters use EEG to assess healthy subjects' brain activity accompanying their performance on various tasks in the laboratory, such as cognitive or perceptual tasks. For example, an experimenter may use EEG to record the electrical activity of subjects' brains as they perform a memory task or listen to music. Chapter 9 will describe the use of EEG in sleep studies.

Rather than collecting the brain's spontaneous activity, investigators using EEG may record the brain's response to a specific task or stimulus. The small voltages that result are called **event-related potentials (ERPs)**. Tracking the location of ERPs in the brain has provided valuable information about functions of different brain areas (Sur & Sinha, 2009). For example, one study examined three populations of subjects: subjects with the sleep disorder narcolepsy (characterized by sudden, uncontrollable bouts of falling asleep during waking life, discussed in Chapter 9), subjects with the motor disorder Parkinson's disease (characterized by an inability to initiate smooth movement, discussed in Chapter 7), and healthy control subjects. In this study, narcolepsy and Parkinson's disease were of interest because of

FIGURE 1.19 EEG. Electroencephalography is a noninvasive method of assessing activity of large populations of neurons through electrodes placed on the skull's surface.

(a)

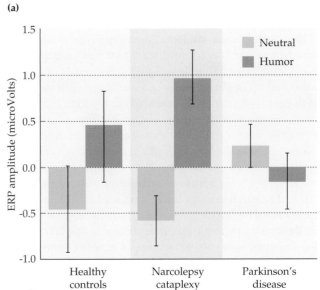

(b)

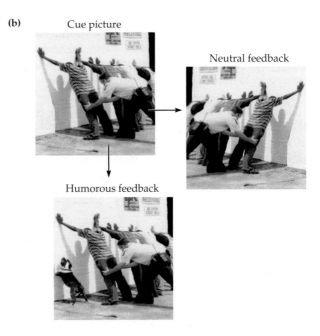

FIGURE 1.20 Contextual cues and brain responses. (a) Researchers categorized subjects into three groups: healthy controls, narcolepsy, or Parkinson's Disease. All subjects were shown the cue picture followed by either a humorous or neutral version of the cue picture. (b) Evoked response potentials were higher in the frontal cortical region in the healthy control and narcolepsy subject groups, in response to the humor cue, than observed in the Parkinson subject group.

dysfunctional reward and humor processing that had been observed in each disorder. As their brain wave activity was recorded, subjects viewed neutral images followed by the same image that was either flipped to make it slightly visually different or had an added humorous touch (as seen in Figure 1.20a). This design allowed the researchers to investigate the timing and intensity of neural responses to humor. As seen in Figure 1.20b, the ERP records indicated that subjects with narcolepsy had larger ERP responses (possibly leading to abrupt transitions in consciousness between the waking and sleep states), whereas subjects with Parkinson's disease did not exhibit the higher ERP amplitudes, possibly because of altered levels of neurochemicals involved in both movement and attention (Mensen, Poryazova, Schwartz, & Khatami, 2014).

Whereas the EEG research methods discussed thus far monitor the activity of large populations of neurons, some researchers are interested in the activity of a single neuron to answer more specific questions about the brain's contributions to various responses. In Chapters 6 and 12, you will read about a recording technique called **single-unit recording** (or single-cell recording), which records the activity of individual neurons. As seen in Figure 1.21, microelectrodes are positioned in proximity to the neuron so that its activity can be recorded. This technique has been used in experimental studies with animals such as monkeys, cats, and rats to determine specific neuronal responses associated with particular tasks.

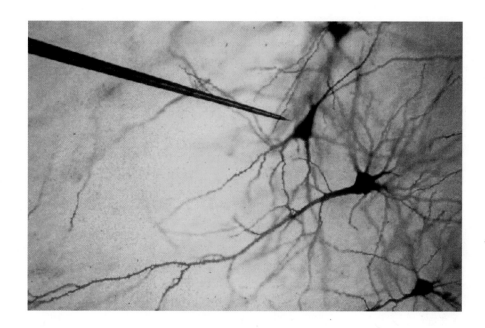

FIGURE 1.21 Single-unit recording. Using the single-unit recording method, the activity of an individual neuron is monitored by a small, precise micropipette.

More recently, a related methodology known as magnetoencephalography (MEG) has been utilized to assess brain function by detecting the magnetic fields generated by neural networks. An advantage of this technique over EEG is that MEG provides a more accurate image of real-time functions of the brain because of its more sensitive temporal resolution, which has fewer time delays than EEG monitoring. Both EEG and MEG methodologies will likely provide new insights into effectively treating disorders such as Parkinson's disease and Alzheimer's disease (Stam, 2010).

Neuroimaging Various imaging techniques allow researchers to examine brain tissue in a living human without surgery. **Computed tomography (CT)** scans use X-rays and computer technology to provide horizontal images of the brain. An X-ray beam moves in a circle around the head, allowing for different views of the brain. The X-ray information is transmitted to a computer, which interprets it and displays it in a two-dimensional form on a monitor. **Positron emission tomography (PET)** scans convey real-time images of functioning in areas of the brain involved in various tasks. For the PET scan, a substance such as radioactive-labeled **glucose**, a simple sugar, is injected into the bloodstream of the subject and then crosses over into the brain's territory. Because glucose is considered a fuel for the brain, consumed by active areas, this labeled glucose allows observers to track the activity of specific brain areas. Subsequently, the PET scan displays images of activity in those brain areas that are actively metabolizing, or using, glucose.

As Figure 1.22a shows, a PET scan can determine functional differences between subjects who have consumed low and moderate doses of alcohol and those who have received a **placebo**, or inactive substance. In this case, the placebo produces none of the effects observed with alcohol consumption. The darker colors denote less activity, providing evidence that alcohol significantly slowed down neural functioning in the alcohol-consuming subjects (Volkow et al., 2006).

Higher-resolution images are provided by structural **magnetic resonance imaging (MRI)**, which shows brain structure. Patients or subjects lie in a large cylindrical tube so that the brain can be exposed to a powerful magnetic field. As shown in Figure 1.22b, an MRI scan can be used to detect structural brain differences between a healthy subject and a subject diagnosed with alcoholism. Both subjects were men who were about 60 years old. Even before you read the chapter in this book emphasizing neuroanatomy, you can see structural differences between these two brains; specifically, there is less tissue in the alcoholic brain (Rosenbloom, Sullivan, & Pfefferbaum, 2003).

An additional imaging technique that can reveal important clues about the constitution of the brain is **diffusion tensor imaging (DTI)**. This technique uses the movement of water in the brain to detect characteristics of the fibers that make up the *white matter*, or the communication pathways, in the brain. DTI scans are also depicted in Figure 1.22b. DTI has provided an important tool to allow researchers to visualize the massive network of fibers supporting the brain's communication network. This information is important in helping researchers understand the critical role of white-matter communications in the brain in various brain diseases such as Alzheimer's disease (Oishi, Mielke, Lyketsos, & Mori, 2011).

Functional magnetic resonance imaging (fMRI), shown in Figure 1.22c, measures brain activity by detecting changes in blood flow and oxygenation. Subjects lie in the same type of magnetic scanner used to record structural MRI (and a structural MRI is often done simultaneously). Like the PET scan, the fMRI provides a measure of brain activity; however, there is no need to inject a radioactive substance with fMRI (making the fMRI scan safer and less expensive than the PET scan). The fMRI technique is

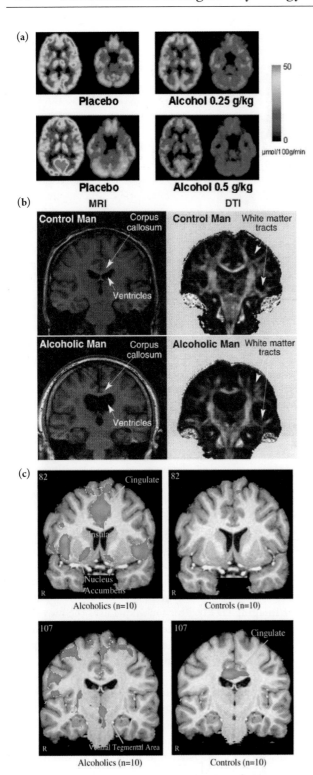

frequently used in research studies to investigate which brain areas are involved in various cognitive functions.

The increased popularity of the fMRI technology has led to the emergence of the field of **cognitive neuroscience**, the exploration of brain functions that accompany various cognitive functions such as perception, memory, and language. However, a disadvantage of the fMRI technique is that it requires the subjects to remain very still in the scanner, which restricts the types of tasks that experimenters can ask the subjects to perform. Figure 1.23 shows a person entering an fMRI imaging scanner. One clear advantage of both PET and fMRI (as well as CT and MRI) scans is the fact that they are noninvasive, requiring no brain surgery (as is needed for electrode implantation in single-unit recording).

These valuable neuroimaging techniques have further informed scientists' views of the localization of function questions discussed earlier in this chapter. Although specific tasks can indeed be associated with specific brain areas using neuroimaging techniques, few brain areas are activated in a neural vacuum. That is, neuroimaging studies have revealed that even simple tasks often activate widespread areas of the brain, causing scientists to reconsider how localized brain functions are (Dolan, 2008).

Although the images provided by neuroimaging have contributed valuable information about the brain's functions, they leave out substantial important information that is occurring at a more microscopic, or cellular, level of analysis. As discussed in the next section, researchers use a diverse array of animal research methods to explore questions that cannot be fully addressed with the human imaging research studies.

Animal Research Methods

In addition to focusing on the human brain, researchers have investigated specific biopsychological questions using appropriate nonhuman **animal models**. Various animal

FIGURE 1.22 Neuroimaging and alcohol consumption.
(a) Positron emission tomography scans depict metabolic rates in healthy (nonalcoholic) subjects during baseline and following alcohol consumption. (b) Structural information is provided by magnetic resonance imaging (MRI) and diffusion tensor imaging (DTI) scans in alcoholic and healthy control subjects. (c) Physiological activation is viewed against a high-resolution brain image in functional MRI (fMRI) scans conducted on alcoholic and control subjects. The MRI, DTI, and fMRI brain images all reveal different response levels between alcoholic and control subjects.

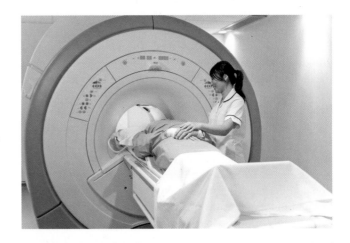

FIGURE 1.23 Functional magnetic resonance imaging (fMRI) scanner. A subject enters the fMRI scanner for brain imaging.

models, which use a specific species to investigate a specific function or disease, have been developed based on appropriate biological similarities with humans, such as the ability to develop the same disease or carry out a behavior that a researcher wants to study. These models allow researchers systematically to investigate a neurobiological system or symptoms of psychiatric illnesses with animals in a controlled laboratory setting. A key element in selecting an appropriate species for an animal model, however, is determining whether the animal exhibits the behavior or symptom the researcher is interested in targeting. Of course, no animal model will perfectly mirror the human condition or experience, so researchers must use animal models with caution.

Because they are easy to house in the laboratory, rats and mice are the most popular mammalian models used in biopsychological research. These rodents generally have all the same areas and chemicals in their brains as humans (although proportions differ), so the rodent brain is viewed as an appropriate, but scaled-down model of the human brain (Lambert, 2011; Narayanan, Cavanagh, Frank, & Laubach, 2013). As seen in Figure 1.24, the mouse is considerably smaller than the rat and, because of its small size and lower costs, is more commonly used than the rat for most models of brain-based diseases such as Alzheimer's disease and Parkinson's disease. Further, because there exist more genetically modified strains of mice than of any other mammal (as we will see later in the chapter), researchers interested in genetic variables contributing to various behaviors often use these genetically engineered mouse species. However, rats have more complex and sophisticated behavioral responses than mice do. Consequently, rats are often used for models of more complex cognitive responses such as complex decision making or solving challenging cognitive tasks (Baker, 2011).

Lesion Methods and Brain-Stimulation Techniques To understand the role of specific brain areas on behavioral functions, researchers can create a lesion by damaging, destroying, or removing animals' brain tissue to determine the effect of losing specific brain areas on a particular

behavior. If a certain brain area is suspected to play a role in aggression, for example, the specific brain area can be carefully removed so the effect on aggression can be investigated. If the animals with a brain lesion behave differently than similar control animals exposed to **sham lesion** (preparing the animal for surgery without actually damaging the tissue), then the targeted brain area is thought to be associated with aggression.

To create lesions, experimenters often use **stereotaxic surgery**, frequently carried out with a precise surgical instrument known as a **stereotaxic apparatus**, to accurately target the specific area (see Figure 1.25). A guidebook known as a brain atlas or **stereotaxic atlas** is used to determine the precise location of the brain area of interest based on the location of a specific landmark, such as **bregma**, the connection point between the coronal and sagittal sutures

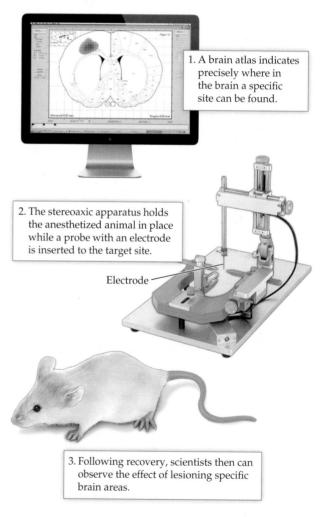

1. A brain atlas indicates precisely where in the brain a specific site can be found.

2. The stereoaxic apparatus holds the anesthetized animal in place while a probe with an electrode is inserted to the target site.

Electrode

3. Following recovery, scientists then can observe the effect of lesioning specific brain areas.

FIGURE 1.25 Stereotaxic surgery. (a) A brain guide known as a stereotaxic atlas is used to determine the exact location of a brain area of interest. (b) An electrode is positioned in the targeted brain area with a stereotaxic apparatus. (c) After surgery, the animal's recovery is monitored closely so that the effects of subsequent stimulation through the electrode can be determined.

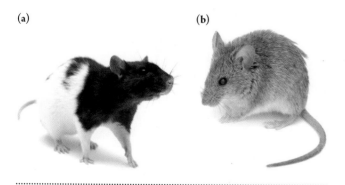

(a)   (b)

FIGURE 1.24 Animal models. Rats (a) and mice (b) are the most commonly used model animals in biomedical research, including biopsychological investigations.

(seams) in the skull. The typical method of damaging the tissue is via an electrical current; in this case it is said that the animal experienced an *electrolytic lesion*.

This electrolytic lesion technique has several potential complications. Often, it damages not only the area of interest but also fibers that connect relevant brain areas and other nearby areas. Additionally, individual differences exist in all mammals, meaning that even with the use of specific guides, the researcher may miss the area of interest in a particular animal. Such techniques have been refined in many ways throughout the years, but it is impossible to damage a brain area without influencing other brain areas; thus, researchers must be careful when interpreting results in such a study. This concern extends to other methods of inducing lesions or brain damage, such as through the use of chemicals, discussed in subsequent chapters.

Still, when the electrolytic lesion technique is used in combination with other brain manipulation techniques, such as **brain stimulation techniques**, an informed picture of the role of various areas emerges. Brain stimulation requires the same preparatory surgery as a brain lesion, except that a permanent electrode is implanted so that the brain area can be stimulated, as opposed to damaged or destroyed, in an attempt to determine the effects of increased activation of a specific brain area on behavioral functions. In Chapter 8, you will learn about a certain brain area involved in hunger motivation (i.e., the lateral hypothalamus) that results in increased eating when stimulated and decreased eating when lesioned (Anand & Brobeck, 1951). You will also learn that the functions of these brain areas are much more complicated than originally perceived based on these early investigation techniques.

Genetic Engineering We have discussed various techniques that researchers use to activate or inhibit various brain areas to learn more about the localization of brain functions. Many techniques allow researchers to modify specific genes, either diminishing or enhancing their activity, to investigate their role in specific behaviors or illnesses.

One popular genetic approach is to make a specific targeted gene inoperative to determine the impact on the animal's functions. An animal with such an inoperative gene is known as a **gene knockout** model. Such genetic engineering has produced specialized animal models that have been used in biopsychological research. Additionally, as previously mentioned, strains (genetic variations) of mice have been identified as optimal models for various behavioral or mental disorders. One example is alcoholism. Although all of the aspects of human alcoholism will not be captured in a single animal model, different strains have been developed to study various aspects of alcoholism, such as alcohol preference, withdrawal, and metabolism of alcohol. Once the researchers feel that the genetically prepared animal model adequately represents the variable of interest (e.g., alcohol preference), then it is considered

an appropriate model for further investigation. As shown in Figure 1.26, a two-bottle test can be used to assess alcohol preference in mice. The experimenter simply measures how much liquid is consumed from each bottle (in this case, one contains an alcoholic solution and the other a nonalcoholic solution). Higher consumption rates are associated with stronger preferences (Sillaber et al., 2002).

Behavioral Tests Behavioral tests assess various behavioral phenotypes in animals. Many traditional behavioral tests that have been developed to assess behaviors such as learning, memory, stress, anxiety, sexual motivation, and other important behaviors will be discussed extensively throughout the text. Newer to the listing of behavioral tests are those that have been developed to learn more about disorders of social functions, such as autism spectrum disorder, in which effective social interactions are disrupted. For example, the social preference test has been developed to determine whether animals are more likely to spend time with another animal (indicating higher social preference) or alone. As depicted in Figure 1.27, this test consists of a three-chamber arena that allows the mouse to choose among the following response options: approach another mouse in an enclosure, approach just the enclosure itself, or remain in the middle chamber. This task has been used to assess social anxiety and social preferences. It has been considered an animal model that may be informative

FIGURE 1.26 **Two-bottle preference test.** Preferences for substances such as alcohol can be assessed in the two-bottle preference test with one bottle containing alcohol and the other containing water.

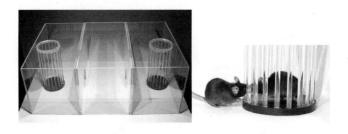

FIGURE 1.27 **Social preference test.** In the social preference test, mice can freely choose to spend time either in proximity to a container holding another mouse or in an empty container.

for understanding some of the symptoms of autism spectrum disorder because decreased social motivation is a symptom of this disorder (Silverman, Yang, Lord, & Crawley, 2010). The social preference test represents only one of hundreds of behavioral tasks used in biopsychological research.

Field Research Even the best animal models used in laboratories have limitations because of the artificial surroundings in most laboratory settings. The importance of the natural environment discussed previously in this chapter also applies to laboratory research. The sterile and controlled environments that scientists prefer for their studies may alter behavior in important ways. For example, the results of the enriched-environment studies suggest that animals kept in traditional laboratory cages may have compromised brains resulting from their impoverished environments. Further, merely picking up the animals to transport them from their home cages to testing cages or during cage cleaning may be stressful for animals and interfere with their performance on a subsequent behavioral task (Castelhano-Carlos & Baumans, 2009). Being picked up by human hands was not part of these animals' evolutionary history (Baker, 2011).

Scientists can avoid potential confounding variables or other limitations of a restricted laboratory environment by conducting **field research**, in which the animals are observed in natural habitats. Such research offers valuable insights about how physiological and behavioral phenotypes have adapted to specific environmental challenges. The snub-nosed monkeys, for example, have adapted to the harsh winter conditions of China's Qinling Mountains. As seen in Figure 1.28, they have an interesting phenotype that they were named for, that is, their snub noses. They also have excessive fur compared with other primates and spend considerable time huddling with family members. Although it is easy to see how fur and huddling can keep the animals warm, the functional significance of the shapes of their noses is more of a mystery. It has been suggested that a flat nose makes it less probable that the snub-nose monkey will be injured by frostbite (Ruoso, 2011).

Observing animals in their natural environmental and social groups provides a rich source of information but also has its limitations. Researchers often have little knowledge about the past life histories of the animals or other extenuating circumstances that could influence the animals' responses. For example, such circumstances might include a loud thunderstorm that took place just before the experimenter arrived. Further, there is much less control of other variables, such as the diet of the animals and social contact, which are easily controlled in the laboratory. Hence, both laboratory and field research have costs and benefits.

Regardless of whether a scientist is conducting laboratory or field research on humans or nonhuman animal models, a wider array of research methods is available today than ever before. Only a small sampling has been discussed in this chapter to give you a mental framework of some of the approaches and technologies used in biopsychological research.

FIGURE 1.28 Adaptive huddling. Researchers conducting field research observe spontaneous behaviors displayed by animals in their natural habitats, such as the huddling of snub-nosed monkeys in freezing temperatures.

(the Appendix lists all of the methods covered in this text and their locations.) Further, you have been introduced to the historical journeys of pioneering brain scientists to gain an appreciation of just how far the discipline has come over the past century. Subsequent chapters will introduce you to many additional research technologies and approaches.

Evaluation of Research Outcomes

Because there is no perfect brain assessment technique, animal model, or behavioral task, it is often important to combine as many research strategies as possible to determine the most accurate conclusions. Ideally, a convergence of evidence, or consideration of multiple types of data, is used to determine the validity of a research model or approach that a researcher develops as an effective research strategy, such as the use of rats to explore maternal behavior.

For example, if a particular brain area is considered important in maternal behavior, a lesion study in the rat may be a good place to start. If destruction of this brain area leads to decreased maternal attentiveness, then the targeted brain area is likely involved in maternal behavior. To provide more evidence of a particular brain area's involvement, a researcher may electrically stimulate the targeted brain area by inserting an electrode in that area (electrical brain stimulation). If maternal behavior is enhanced, this is additional evidence of the function of this brain area. Recording from this brain area while the animal is interacting with her pups provides even further evidence. Finally, finding neuroanatomical differences such as a smaller volume of this structure in animals that neglect their offspring (compared with those who care for their offspring) would provide additional valuable information suggesting that the targeted brain area is involved in maternal behavior. Hence, a convergence of lesion, activation, real-time recording, and imaging data provides more convincing evidence in biopsychological research than a single research strategy.

As researchers evaluate the various tests used in research, it is critical to confirm the **validity** of all tasks used in research programs. Validity is generally viewed as the degree with which a chosen test actually measures what the researcher is interested in measuring—in the real world as well as in a laboratory setting (Baker, 2011). For example, a biological psychology exam should be a valid assessment of your mastery of the knowledge in this course. If your first biological psychology exam included questions about the weather patterns that had been observed during the past week, you would question the validity of the exam as an accurate assessment of your knowledge of the material covered in class.

Conclusion

This chapter has introduced you to some fundamental information to prepare you for your journey through the subsequent chapters of this book. By discussing the concept of context and its importance for the exploration of brain functions, it has prepared you to learn about the many ways in which an environment influences behavior. Both internal and external contextual variables must be considered in the investigation of neural influences on behavior. Otherwise, only a single snapshot of a concept is obtained. To develop a full understanding of the brain and its influence on behavior, we need a three-dimensional animation that can be viewed from multiple perspectives. A respect for context will help researchers develop a more complete picture, regardless of its format, of the field of biological psychology.

This introductory chapter highlighted the topic of genetics, which provides the foundation for all aspects of biological psychology. The history of how researchers went from a discussion of gemmules to the human genome reinforces the monumental nature of this accomplishment. Considering that a high proportion of human genes are expressed in the brain, a solid understanding of genetics is critical for understanding brain functions.

The formal pursuit of brain research has a relatively short history because the sophisticated tools necessary for brain investigations have not been available long. We have come a long way since the time of phrenology. Multiple neuroimaging options and other sophisticated techniques allow us to understand more about how the brain influences behavior. The use of both humans and nonhuman models has produced a recent explosion of knowledge in this area.

Now that you have an appreciation for the critical role of context in biopsychological investigations, coupled with your recently acquired knowledge of noteworthy pioneers in brain research, classic methodological techniques, and insights about the current status of genetics research, you are prepared to embark on this journey in biological psychology. You will navigate through chapters describing the essential elements and functions of the nervous system before encountering chapters describing the fascinating ways brains adjust to changing environments and physiological demands: neurobiology in action. Some adjustments are adaptive, such as learning, whereas others are maladaptive, such as mental disorders.

Your knowledge of the nervous system will build as you progress through this book, enabling you to be a critically thinking, informed reader as you approach each new topic. To further enhance your understanding of biological psychology, each chapter also contains the following features.

A *"Brain Scene Investigation"* opens each chapter with a biopsychological mystery and then presents relevant research findings about the underlying biological psychology. This feature aims to foster intrigue and interest in a relevant biopsychological phenomenon to increase your motivation to learn more about how the brain contributes to this functional area.

The *"Context Matters"* feature of each chapter follows a research study that has emphasized some aspect of environmental or experiential context from beginning to end—allowing you to trace the important steps of the brain researchers in each study.

The *"Laboratory Exploration"* feature introduces additional important laboratory techniques that have been used to conduct research related to neuroscience topics discussed in each specific chapter. These techniques will range from cutting-edge to classic—both of which are vital for conducting meaningful research revealing the many secrets of the nervous system.

Let the journey begin!

KEY TERMS

biological psychology (p. 3)
biopsychology (p. 3)
context (p. 3)

**Establishing Relevant
Biopsychological Context**

adaptations (p. 4)
theory of natural selection (p. 4)

ultimate causes (p. 5)
proximal causes (p. 5)
enriched environment (p. 7)
stroke (p. 7)
independent variable (p. 7)
dependent variable (p. 7)
environmental context (p. 8)
experiential context (p. 12)

Pioneers in Brain Research

localization of brain
   function (p. 13)
mental faculties (p. 13)
phrenology (p. 13)
empirical evidence (p. 13)
hypotheses (p. 14)
brain circuits (p. 14)

The Genetics Story: From Gemmules to Genomes

heredity (p. 15)
phenotypes (p. 15)
alleles (p. 15)
genes (p. 15)
mutation (p. 16)
dominant (p. 16)
recessive (p. 16)
genotype (p. 16)
homozygous (p. 16)
heterozygous (p. 16)
genetics (p. 16)
nucleus (p. 16)
chromosomes (p. 17)
sex chromosomes (p. 17)
deoxyribonucleic acid (DNA) (p. 17)
nucleotide bases (p. 17)
ribonucleic acid (RNA) (p. 17)

messenger RNA (mRNA) (p. 17)
amino acids (p. 17)
genome (p. 18)
Human Genome Project (p. 18)
enzyme (p. 19)
epigenetics (p. 20)
gene–environment interactions (p. 20)

The Tools of Biological Psychology: Classic and Contemporary Methods

case studies (p. 21)
confounding variables (p. 21)
electroencephalography (EEG) (p. 21)
event-related potentials (ERPs) (p. 21)
single-unit recording (p. 22)
computed tomography (CT) (p. 23)
positron emission tomography (PET) (p. 23)

glucose (p. 23)
placebo (p. 23)
magnetic resonance imaging (MRI) (p. 23)
diffusion tensor imaging (DTI) (p. 23)
functional MRI (fMRI) (p. 23)
cognitive neuroscience (p. 24)
animal models (p. 24)
sham lesion (p. 25)
stereotaxic surgery (p. 25)
stereotaxic apparatus (p. 25)
stereotaxic atlas (p. 25)
bregma (p. 25)
brain stimulation techniques (p. 26)
gene knockout (p. 26)
field research (p. 27)
validity (p. 28)

REVIEW QUESTIONS

1. What is Charles Darwin's theory of natural selection? What was Darwin's basis for this theory?

2. What is an enriched environment? What have studies of enriched environments in rats suggested about the role of context in the brain's influence on behavioral responses? Explain.

3. What was Franz Joseph Gall's theory with respect to the localization of brain function? What evidence did Marie-Jean-Pierre Flourens provide against Gall's theory?

4. What did the study of Paul Broca's patient, known as Tan, contribute to the scientific knowledge regarding the localization of brain function?

5. Describe Watson and Crick's model of DNA. What significant events contributed to the discovery of the structure of DNA?

6. What is the Human Genome Project, and what is its significance?

7. What is the difference between the techniques of PET and fMRI? What advantages and disadvantages does each of these techniques have?

CRITICAL-THINKING QUESTIONS

1. What do you foresee as the major environmental demands of the near future, to which the human brain will need to evolve and adapt? Explain.

2. Would you be willing to volunteer to contribute your own data to the Personal Genome Project? Why or why not? What do you see as the potential benefits and risks of contributing your own data? Explain.

3. Imagine that a research team has developed a new behavioral test that they claim can be used to diagnose autism spectrum disorder (which is generally characterized by social interaction difficulties, communication difficulties, and repetitive behaviors) in 18-month-olds. How would you assess the validity of this new test? Explain.

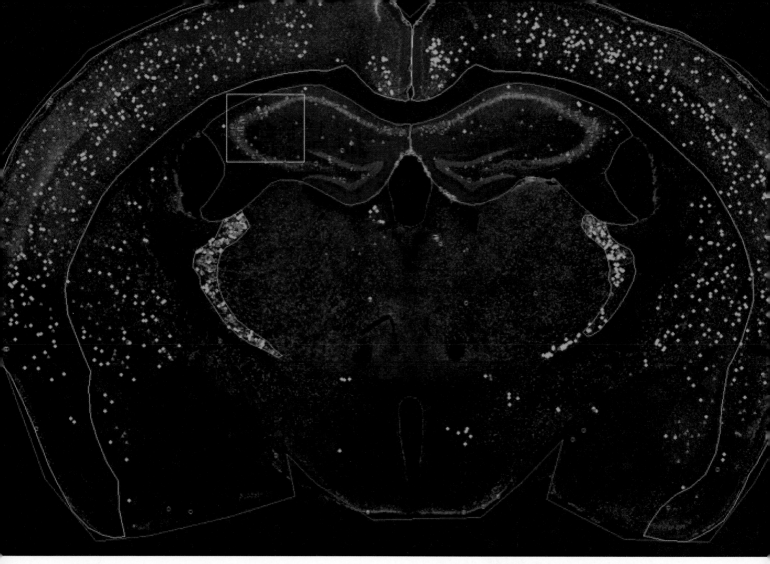

The Nervous System: Structure and Function

David Blaine's Breath-Defying Act

David Blaine, a self-declared endurance artist, has pushed his physiological limits to unprecedented extremes. He was buried alive for a week and frozen in a block of ice for three days. As a child, he was captivated by stories of Houdini holding his breath for more than three minutes and started practicing the feat himself. According to his accounts, he matched Houdini's breath-holding record by the age of 11.

As it turns out, Houdini's record was not that impressive. As Blaine investigated the extreme limits of the human capacity for breath holding, he learned that humans could rival other aquatic mammals with their underwater capabilities. For example, after training, free divers regularly hold their breath longer than 3 minutes as they dive to depths exceeding 600 feet. Some have exceeded 9 minutes after taking deep breaths of ordinary air. After breathing pure oxygen, the duration of breath holding in humans can exceed 16 minutes. Blaine decided to test how long he could go without breathing.

After consulting with physicians, Blaine initially lost 50 pounds. He then began a training regimen to maximize the efficiency of his body's use of oxygen. He learned to slow his heart rate to about 38 beats per minute, which declined further to 12 beats per minute as he was holding his breath.

In contrast to the free divers who are obviously expending energy, Blaine chose to remain still and hold his breath underwater for as long as possible (a discipline known as static apnea) to maximize his efficient use of oxygen. Each morning he practiced holding his breath for 44 of a total of 52 minutes, taking breaks, of course. After planning to perform the pure oxygen, static apnea breath-holding stunt on Oprah Winfrey's television show, he began sleeping in a hypoxic altitude tent, a structure that provides a low-oxygen environment similar to that found in high altitudes, in an

FIGURE 2A **Self-control.** Through extensive training, David Blaine learned to hold his breath for an extended period of time, exerting extraordinary control over his nervous system's reflexive functions.

attempt to increase his red blood cell count. Because red blood cells transport oxygen throughout the body, the body generates more of them to compensate for chronically low oxygen levels (Wehrlin, Zuest, Hallon, & Marti, 2006). Obviously, Blaine was serious about achieving this goal.

Did this breath-holding training regimen pay off? Blaine later reported that the breath-holding duration test got off to a scary start. To his dismay, the elaborate stage set, crew, and audience were distracting and thereby impaired his ability to control his heart rate, which was visible to everyone on a large monitor. After being submerged in the tank and securing his feet so that he would not float to the top, his typical, extremely low starting heart rate was suddenly 120 beats per minute . . . and never changed throughout his entire breath-defying attempt. Much to Blaine's chagrin, the background setting for this endurance test was a critical factor that he should not have ignored.

Blaine knew that his high heart rate was wasting precious oxygen. After 8 minutes, he was certain he would fail to break the breath-holding record in humans of 16 minutes. At 10 minutes, he felt blood shunting from his fingers and toes to his core vital organs; at 11 minutes, he felt throbbing in his legs; at 12 minutes, his arm felt numb, causing him to think that he was having a heart attack. The next few minutes brought on chest pains and, not surprisingly, an overwhelming urge to breathe! Blaine could tell from the heart monitors that his heart had an insufficient supply of blood, wildly bouncing from low to high heart rates. At 16 minutes, Blaine removed his feet from their restraints so he could be removed from the tank easily if he passed out. Then Blaine heard the cheers from the audience confirming that he had indeed exceeded the world record for breath holding. Like a true endurance artist, Blaine pushed the limits, finally emerging from the tank after 17 minutes and 4 seconds. In a lecture given later, Blaine reported that he felt his best when he was able to push through the pain to display superhuman abilities (Blaine, 2009; Tierney, 2008).

Behind the Scenes

How did David Blaine demonstrate such control over his physiology? Which parts of Baine's brain allowed him to exert control over essential functions? As opposed to behaviors such as walking or reaching that are known as *somatic functions* under voluntary control, the moment-by-moment, life-sustaining functions of our internal organs that are known as *autonomic functions* are typically considered involuntary.

The view that autonomic functions are beyond individual control was challenged in the 1960s by the physiological psychologist Neal Miller. He conducted a series of studies that provided evidence that rats could control their heart rates and dogs could control their salivation in anticipation of a water reward (N. E. Miller, 1969, 1978). These findings remain controversial because of difficulty replicating the original studies (Dworkin & Miller, 1986), yet scientists continue to be intrigued by them. Various **biofeedback techniques** are regularly used in laboratories, demonstrating that, with the appropriate feedback, humans can alter functions such as heart rate and blood flow. If such techniques could be identified as consistently effective in altering these autonomic functions, especially outside of a controlled laboratory, it might lead individuals to opt for biofeedback instead of pharmacological treatment.

Neuroscientists have more recently identified a few brain areas that may facilitate the shift from involuntary to voluntary control of autonomic functions. A prime suspect is the **insular cortex** (also known as the **insula**), a brain area located in the most recently evolved **cerebral cortex** (the brain's outer layer). The insular cortex provides representations of the "state of the body" to other relevant brain areas by integrating input both from within the body and from the external environment (Craig, 2010a, 2010b). In the past, scientists described the insular cortex as being involved solely in more basic automatic functions. However, recent data indicate that these descriptions were premature (Churchland, 2011). The insular cortex's function in facilitating *interoception*, the ability to monitor the body's internal processes (Craig, 2010a, 2010b), makes it a likely candidate for Blaine's extraordinary ability to monitor and control his physiological processes.

Although no convincing evidence exists that David Blaine has an overactive insular cortex, research suggests that patients with higher levels of activity in this area could suppress ongoing chronic pain (deCharms et al., 2005). Another study reported that subjects able to accurately judge the timing of their own heartbeats exhibited increased activity in the area of the insular cortex, measured by the neuroimaging technique fMRI (discussed in Chapter 1; Critchley, Wiens, Rotshtein, Ohman, & Dolan, 2004).

Considering the complexity of the nervous system, multiple brain areas are likely involved in the biofeedback techniques that Blaine used to monitor physiological processes such as heart rate. Yet, research provides compelling evidence that our awareness of internal contexts is influenced by the insular cortex. ▪

The Building Blocks of the Nervous System

The nervous system that allowed David Blaine to exert control over his internal organs is an extensive network of neural connections that can be investigated on many levels. This chapter begins with the fundamental unit of the nervous system, the **neuron**, and its complex connections that ultimately form specialized brain areas and functional neural systems, as depicted in Figure 2.1.

Neurons

A text describing the nervous system's building blocks would have looked different a mere 150 years ago. Until that time, scientists believed that the nervous system consisted of a continuous network of connected nerves. The 19th-century neuroscientist Camillo Golgi (1843–1926) advocated this view, known at the time as the *nerve net theory* (see Figure 2.2). However, with no way to clearly view the brain's tissue, these thoughts were mere speculation. Golgi's work in the laboratory finally paid off when he discovered that he could impregnate nerve cells with a silver stain that would allow him to view the unique structure of the nervous system tissue.

Santiago Ramón y Cajal (1852–1934), working in Spain, was fascinated by Golgi's new **histological technique**, or method to study the microscopic structure of tissues, allowing him to view neurons. An artist, Cajal spent hours perched over his microscope viewing nerve cells in various brain areas and drawing them. Even today, Cajal's depictions of neurons are considered accurate.

With more detailed images of the cellular constituents of the nervous system, Cajal came to realize that the nervous system was not continuous, as suggested by Golgi. Instead,

FIGURE 2.2 Camillo Golgi. In the late 19th century, Golgi invented the first technique that enabled scientists to see the structure of neurons.

his examination of these cells convinced him that each cell, or neuron, was a distinct unit that was physically separate from the others. Accordingly, Cajal abandoned the nerve net theory and endorsed the *neuron doctrine*, the notion that neurons are discrete units, not part of a continuous network. Although more recent research has revealed many complexities about how individual neurons interact with and form networks, or ensembles, with other neurons, the neuron doctrine remains a central tenet of modern neuroscience (Bullock et al., 2005).

The important contributions of Golgi and Cajal were acknowledged in 1906 when they shared the Nobel Prize in Physiology or Medicine. At this ceremony, Cajal declared how Golgi's histological breakthrough had confirmed the accuracy of the neuron doctrine; that is, the nervous system was composed of individual cells known as neurons. Interestingly, Golgi had difficulty letting go of his initial ideas of neurons being a single continuous structure. Although his work provided evidence against the nerve net theory, in contrast to Cajal, Golgi declared his allegiance to the nerve net theory. Thus, Golgi's thoughts were considered uninformed, even as he accepted the Nobel Prize. This is a lesson for all of us to reassess data often to reevaluate theories in the most informed ways (Mazzarello, 2010).

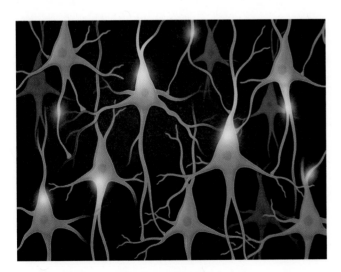

FIGURE 2.1 Neuronal connections. Individual neurons form connections with other neurons to build critical neuronal structures and circuits for optimal functioning.

Once techniques for viewing the structure of the neuron emerged, scientists examined the neuron's characteristics in more detail. Although neurons can take several forms, Figure 2.3 depicts the typical neuronal structure.

A prominent cell body, or **soma**, ranging in size from 5 to 100 micrometers in diameter, encloses a collection of microstructures found in all cells throughout the body. Figure 2.4 shows the neuron's microorganelles (internal components of the cell body) (Siegel et al., 1999).

Unique characteristics of neurons are the projections extending from the soma: **dendrites** and **axons**. Dendrites, named after the Greek word for "tree" because of their similarity to a tree's branches, typically extend from multiple points on the soma. A close examination confirms the complexity and extent of dendrites; they continue to branch, again and again, establishing networks with many neurons. Although the soma is prominently represented in most images of neurons, it accounts for only a small percentage (perhaps 4–10%) of the total surface area of the neuron. The dendrites account for the bulk of a neuron's surface area.

In **multipolar neurons**, the most common shape of neuron in the nervous system, multiple dendrites extend from the soma. Additional surface area is also provided by small protrusions known as **dendritic spines** located throughout the dendritic processes, or branches. A single neuron may have as many as thousands of dendritic spines, greatly increasing its surface area (Fiala & Harris, 1999).

Why all the interest in increased surface area of neurons? Dendrites receive information from other neurons mostly via their connections with the dendritic spines. Therefore, the greater the surface area, the greater the opportunities for receiving information from other parts of the nervous system. By analogy, when purchasing a network plan for your latest cell phone, a critical selling point is the range of the network. Accordingly, for some neurons, it is critical to have far-reaching connections to build effective and efficient neural networks.

Once the information is received through the dendrites, it is processed through the soma and along another specialized neuronal extension known as the axon. Once this neural message clears the entrance gate of the axon, known as the **axon hillock**, it is propagated away from the soma toward a target such as another neuron. Returning to our cell phone analogy, an expansive network is valuable only in the presence of a strong, reliable, fast signal. To ensure the delivery of a consistently strong signal at a rapid rate, many vertebrate axons have a special insulating covering known as the **myelin sheath**. If you look closely at Figure 2.3, you will see tiny gaps, or **nodes of Ranvier**, between these myelin segments. The myelin sheath facilitates the speed of the neural impulse as it is propagated down the axon (see Chapter 3 for additional details). Although there are exceptions, when the nerve impulse does not need to travel very far, a myelin sheath typically is not present on the axon (Olave,

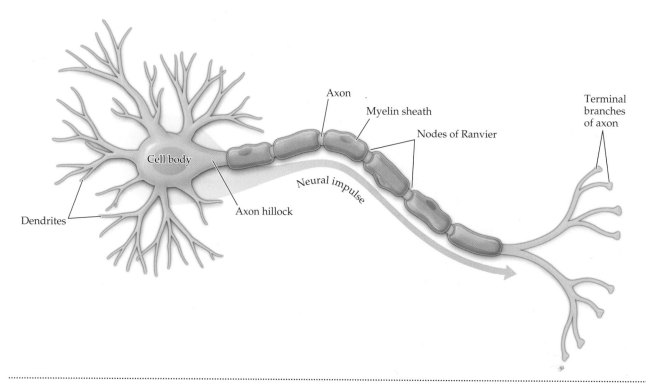

FIGURE 2.3 The structure of a typical neuron. The neural impulse travels from the dendrites of the cell body down the axon. From the terminal branches of the axon the impulse is passed on to neighboring neurons. The myelin sheath covering the axon helps speed the progress of the neural impulse.

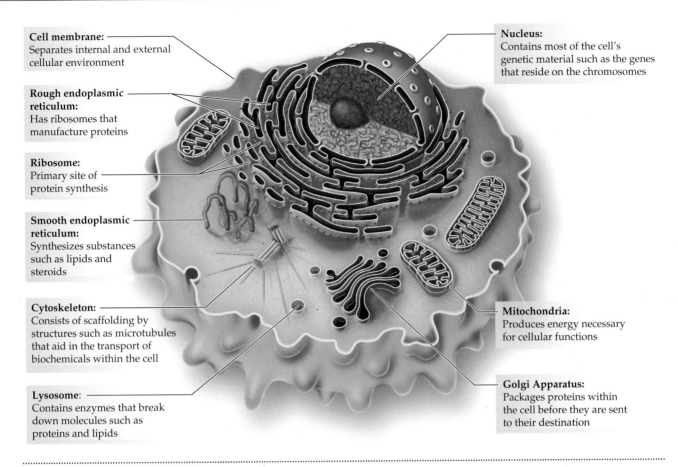

Cell membrane:
Separates internal and external cellular environment

Rough endoplasmic reticulum:
Has ribosomes that manufacture proteins

Ribosome:
Primary site of protein synthesis

Smooth endoplasmic reticulum:
Synthesizes substances such as lipids and steroids

Cytoskeleton:
Consists of scaffolding by structures such as microtubules that aid in the transport of biochemicals within the cell

Lysosome:
Contains enzymes that break down molecules such as proteins and lipids

Nucleus:
Contains most of the cell's genetic material such as the genes that reside on the chromosomes

Mitochondria:
Produces energy necessary for cellular functions

Golgi Apparatus:
Packages proteins within the cell before they are sent to their destination

FIGURE 2.4 **Internal components of the cell body.** The neuron's cell body includes many internal structures (*microorganelles*) that enable it to function.

Puri, Kerr, & Maxwell, 2002). For example, small neurons in the spinal cord that transmit information about pain are unmyelinated (Neuman, Braz, Skinner, Llewellyn-Smith, & Basbaum, 2008).

On the arrival of the nerve impulse at the end of the axon, a transfer of messages usually occurs between the **terminal ending** of the neuron and some component of a second neuron, such as a dendritic spine. In other cases, neurons transfer messages to nonneuronal tissue, such as muscles and glands throughout the body. Chapter 3 discusses the specific nature of the nerve impulse, as well as the characteristics of the "message" that is exchanged between neurons.

Although most neurons are multipolar neurons with multiple dendrites protruding from the cell body, neurons can be found in other shapes as well. In addition to a multipolar neuron, Figure 2.5 depicts a **bipolar neuron** with two processes extending from the soma (a dendrite and an axon) and a **unipolar neuron** with one process extending from the cell body that divides into an axonal and dendritic segment. The bipolar and unipolar neurons are generally found in sensory areas of the brain. Like a diverse array of flowers in a botanical garden, different types of neurons make up the neuronal networks that support our behavioral, physiological, and cognitive functions.

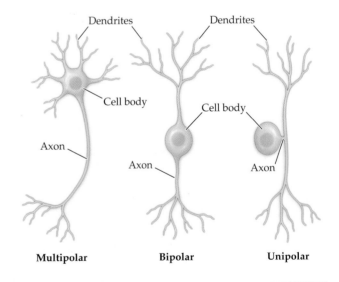

FIGURE 2.5 **Neuron morphology.** The number of processes extending from the cell body determine whether the neuron is unipolar, bipolar, or multipolar.

Glial Cells

As it turns out, neurons are only part of the story when it comes to the nervous system. Although neurons have received the bulk of attention, there is another class of cells known as glial cells (also called **glia** or neuroglia, literally *nerve glue*). Generally, glial cells are thought to support neurons. More recent research suggests, however, that these long-ignored cells may process information in similar ways as neurons. Increasing evidence suggests that the glial cells are just as critical to the ongoing functions of the nervous system as the neurons (Fields, 2004; Hamilton & Attwell, 2010).

What do the various types of glial cells do? **Astrocytes**, the most abundant type of glial cell, are shaped like stars. They fill in the spaces between neurons (see Figure 2.6) and transport essential nutrients from the brain's blood vessels to the neurons. Astrocytes also maintain a constant chemical environment. When cells die, astrocytes help eliminate the potentially dangerous remnants of the dead cells. Astrocytes also play a key role in the regulation of cerebral blood flow (Attwell et al., 2010) and communication between neurons (Hamilton & Attwell, 2010; Nedergaard, 1994). A close working relationship between the astrocytes and the brain's arterial system is essential because just a few minutes of an interrupted oxygenated blood supply can result in permanent brain damage.

Furthermore, astrocytes are involved in the brain's primary security system, the **blood–brain barrier**, which restricts the entry of substances into the brain. The blood–brain barrier acts as a filter and protects the brain from potentially harmful substances. As seen in Figure 2.7, the presence of astrocytes provides an additional security buffer to keep unwelcome substances in the bloodstream and away from the vulnerable brain tissue. Generally, the blood–brain barrier does such a good job of establishing a defense

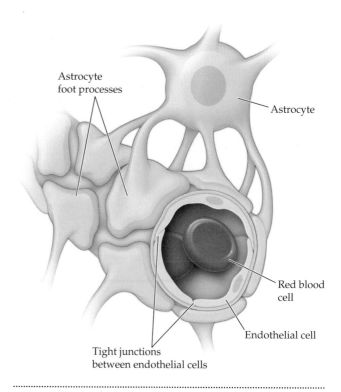

FIGURE 2.7 **Blood–brain barrier.** Astrocytes and endothelial cells with tight junctions are positioned on blood vessels in the nervous system to prevent the blood and any accompanying substances from reaching the cells of the nervous system.

between the body's circulatory system and the internal environment of the brain that the body's traditional security cells (immune cells, discussed later in the chapter) are also prevented from entering this high-security brain terrain. Ironically, the astrocytes that help to protect the brain can also pose a threat: they can give rise to astrocytomas, a relatively common form of brain tumor.

Microglia are smaller glial cells that are sometimes considered the brain's first-responder cells. Just as it is important to protect the body from invaders, it is important to protect the brain. Microglia act as a cellular cleanup crew as they search for dead cells and cellular debris throughout the brain (Davalos et al., 2005). The microglia monitor the microenvironment of the nervous system and are alerted to various threats. Sometimes, however, this process can go awry. Not too different from a spy thriller, there have been cases in which microglia have become double agents by emitting neurotoxins to the brain's *resident* cells, as opposed to *intruding* cells. Therefore, microglial activity may be a factor in neurodegenerative diseases (Kim & de Vellis, 2005; Li, Lu, Tay, Moochhala, & He, 2007). For example, microglia have been investigated as the source of destruction of a brain area that regulates a neurochemical involved in movement, leading to compromised movement (Qian & Flood, 2008).

Oligodendrocytes (also known as *oligodendroglia*) make up the myelin sheath that encapsulates axons of myelinated neurons that are located within the brain and spinal cord.

FIGURE 2.6 **Neuronal cell bodies and astrocytes.** In this photomicrograph, neuronal cell bodies are shown in red and astrocytes in green.

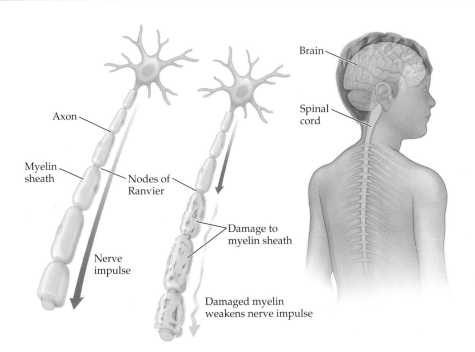

Oligodendrocytes have multiple projections, each serving as one segment of the neuron's myelin sheath. Neurons located outside of the brain and spinal cord also have a myelin sheath. On these neurons, however, the segments of myelin sheath are the product of another type of glial cell, **Schwann cells**. In this case, the pancake-shape cells wrap their entire cell body around the axon. The critical functions of the glial cells forming the myelin sheath are easily seen in patients suffering from **multiple sclerosis**, a neurodegenerative disease associated with impaired movement. These patients have exposed axons because of the mysterious death of the cells making up the myelin sheaths. As seen in Figure 2.8, the damaged myelin compromises the conduction of the nerve impulse, like an exposed portion of an electrical cord that grounds out, leading to both sensory and motor impairments. Researchers are currently exploring oligodendrocyte and Schwann cell transplants as a therapy for multiple sclerosis and other neurodegenerative diseases (Kocsis & Waxman, 2007).

Whereas neuroscientists have traditionally assumed that glial cells greatly outnumber neurons—by a factor of 10 glial cells per neuron or, stated another way, that glial cells make up 85% of the brain's cells (Fields, 2009)—other reports tell a different story (Hilgetag & Barbas, 2009). Several published reports of cell counting using a novel method called *isotropic fractionation* have investigated the number of neurons and nonneural cells (mostly glia) in the brains of about 20 different species. The isotropic fractionation technique, discussed further in Chapter 5, involves transforming the cells into a uniform fluid, with all cells distributed equally throughout so that the cell nuclei can be counted (Herculano-Houzel & Lent, 2005). This research suggests that the number of glial cells varies drastically by brain structure. For example, although glial cells are numerous in the thalamus (17 glial cells per neuron), they are few in number in the cerebellum (1 glial cell for every 25 neurons). However, this new technique suggests that the total number of glial cells in the brain is approximately equal to the total number of neurons in the brain.

Brain analyses with isotropic fractionation have revealed another surprising finding. Whereas researchers once thought that the cerebral cortex contained the majority of the brain's neurons, Brazilian researchers report that, in humans, the actual percentage of the brain's neurons that the cerebral cortex contains is closer to 19%. So where do the majority of neurons reside in the brain? The **cerebellum**, a structure primarily responsible for motor coordination (as described later in the chapter), contains up to 80% of all the brain's neurons (Herculano-Houzel, 2009, 2010; Herculano-Houzel, Collins, Wong, & Kaas, 2007; Herculano-Houzel, Collins, Wong, Kaas, & Lent, 2008). According to these recent reports, the need to make well-coordinated physical movements in our environments requires a relatively large neural investment. From an evolutionary perspective, this investment appears to have paid off.

Divisions of Labor in the Nervous System

Nervous systems exist in many forms across the animal kingdom. In vertebrates (including mammals), however, nervous systems have a consistent form, with subdivisions that efficiently manage the many physiological functions necessary to sustain life. This division of labor ensures that we continue to breathe, digest our food, and produce immune cells although we have no awareness of these activities.

Evolutionary Considerations

Nervous systems are not new to the evolutionary scene. If you look at a worm (as in Figure 2.9), a nervous system is certainly apparent. However, it differs from the vertebrate nervous system. A tiny brain, consisting of two clusters of neurons—called **ganglia** (*ganglion is the singular form*)—resides in the head region of the worm, but the brain does not seem to be necessary for the worm to move its body. The nerve cord with interspersed ganglia provides independent functioning in the absence of the brain. The earthworm version of neural government is closer to autonomous neural "city-states" because it has no clear leadership from the worm's "head of state," its rudimentary brain.

The nervous system of vertebrates (including mammals) differs from that of the worm in that a clear "leader" has emerged, the brain. The brain evolved into a complex structure that assumed critical responsibility for the organism's survival. The new leadership role of the brain required a considerable amount of neural infrastructure. This infrastructure supports the sophisticated interplay between the brain and the rest of the body, including internal organs and muscles. Life-sustaining functions needed to be consistently maintained while allowing the animal to constantly survey its environment, move around, and obtain resources.

This more recent neural organization strategy redistributed neural energy, enabling vertebrates to interact with the environment in far more sophisticated ways than invertebrates such as the worm. But this sophisticated, complex brain came with a cost—should something happen to the brain that prevented it from functioning, the animal would not survive. Consequently, the brain had to be protected at all costs. We have learned about one of the brain's security systems, the blood–brain barrier. Additional security systems will be introduced later in the chapter. The next section discusses the various functions performed by the two major divisions of the vertebrate nervous system.

The Central Nervous System and Peripheral Nervous System

The nervous system has two divisions. The **central nervous system (CNS)** consists of the brain and spinal cord. The **peripheral nervous system (PNS)** is the part of the nervous system that lies outside of the brain and spinal cord.

Key components of the neural infrastructure include the long axons protruding from the billions of neurons in the brain and spinal cord. As Figure 2.10 indicates, axons with similar destinations are bundled together like a cable. They connect to various organs and muscles throughout the body. The cabled axons within the brain and spinal cord, the CNS, are called **tracts**, whereas the cabled axons extending beyond the CNS are called **nerves** or *peripheral nerves* because they travel to various sites in the PNS. Thus, tracts are found in the CNS and the nerves are in the PNS.

The function of these nerves and tracts is simple—communication. The ability to successfully adapt to the changing context of our lives requires considerable transmission of information, both incoming and outgoing. In the nervous system, **afferent nerves** (sensory nerves) transmit information from the environment or other body areas

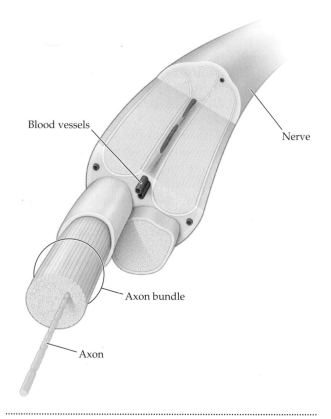

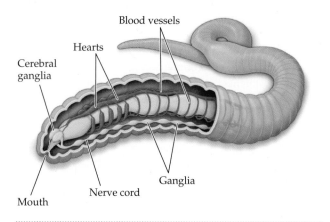

FIGURE 2.9 Worm nervous system. Through evolution, the nervous system has transitioned from the distributed ganglia of the earthworm toward a more central operating system in vertebrates, with the neural tissue concentrated in the brain and spinal cord.

FIGURE 2.10 Nerves. Nerves consist of bundles of axons traveling to various destinations in the central and peripheral nervous systems.

toward the CNS. For example, if a mosquito lands on your arm, **sensory neurons** detect its arrival and afferent nerves send information to the CNS so that you can shake off the mosquito before its impending bite. If your afferent nerves are too slow to prevent the bite, you will eventually get the message from your itchy skin.

As information about the mosquito makes its way to the CNS, it is directed to the appropriate **motor neurons** involved in initiating movement via appropriate **interneurons** (neurons that transmit impulses between other neurons) so that the **efferent nerves** (motor nerves) assigned to the arm can be activated to evade the mosquito. If it is too late to prevent the bite, the efferent nerves assigned to the hands are activated to scratch the irritated skin. When responding to such immediate threats, speed is critical. Information must be quickly transmitted to your brain and from your brain to your arm muscles, so that you can shake away the mosquito (see Figure 2.11). The myelin sheath drives this speed. Without it, we would be covered in bites. In Chapter 7, we will look more closely at the way the nervous system reacts to immediate threats, like moving one's hand away from a pot on a hot stove.

The cells in the brain and spinal cord use two categories of nerves to communicate with the body. The 12 **cranial nerves** exit various areas of the brain and extend to target destinations in the head, face, and shoulder region. As seen in Figure 2.12, these nerves may be considered to have primarily motor, sensory, or mixed (motor and sensory) functions. Note that cranial nerve X, the *vagus nerve*, extends to the body's internal organs.

A larger population of nerves exits the spinal cord to final destinations throughout the body. As seen in Figure 2.13, these 31 left–right pairs of **spinal nerves** in humans shuttle information to and from all areas of the body. The spinal nerves are divided into the following: 8 cervical spinal nerve pairs (C1–C8), 12 thoracic spinal nerve pairs (T1–T12), 5 lumbar spinal nerve pairs (L1–L5), 5 sacral spinal nerve pairs (S1–S5), and 1 coccygeal spinal nerve pair. Each spinal nerve travels to a distinct area of skin, or **dermatome**. Doctors of patients with shingles (*Herpes zoster* infection)

can detect the origin of the virus by determining the specific area, or dermatome, affected (Haanpaa, Laippala, & Nurmikko, 1999). As you can see in Figure 2.14, the pattern of skin irritation on the patient's back is similar to the area of a dermatome supplied by a specific thoracic nerve.

With the vertebrate central neural control model, in which the brain exerts neural control over the body, damage to the spinal cord—and its accompanying nerves—is unforgiving. No working spinal nerves means no sensation and no movement. One reminder of this system's fragility came when Christopher Reeve, the actor famous for playing Superman in a series of movies, suffered a tragic horse-riding accident in the mid-1990s, severing his spinal cord at the C1 level. This level of injury leaves the brain with insufficient information and neural communication to direct the body's movements, resulting in paralysis. Although research looks promising, a cure for spinal cord injuries remains elusive. Vertebrate CNS neurons do not easily regenerate, although peripheral nerves, composed of axons and Schwann cells, regenerate readily.

As seen in Figure 2.15, damage to PNS neurons provokes immune cells to clean up debris. This activity ultimately results in regrowth. In contrast, CNS neurons do not regenerate because of their lack of immune-system cells, the presence of inhibitory proteins, and the migration of astrocytes to the threatened site, which can leave scar tissue on the damaged axon (Strittmatter, 2010; Toy & Namgung, 2013). All of Christopher Reeve's nervous system tissue was still in place after his accident—a simple slit in the spinal cord blocked this essential CNS/PNS connection. Neuroscientists have been working diligently on this nervous system puzzle—can they discover how to make CNS neurons regenerate from studying the regenerating peripheral nerves? Time will tell.

Further Divisions of the PNS

The PNS is divided into the **somatic nervous system** that generally controls voluntary movement (discussed in further

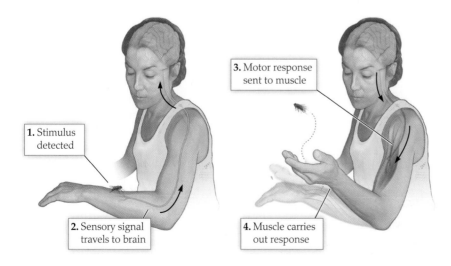

1. Stimulus detected

2. Sensory signal travels to brain

3. Motor response sent to muscle

4. Muscle carries out response

FIGURE 2.11 Responding to threat. Sensory neurons send signals warning of threats, such as a mosquito. The information travels via sensory nerves to the brain. The brain responds by signaling the appropriate motor nerves to tell the arm muscle to shake away the mosquito.

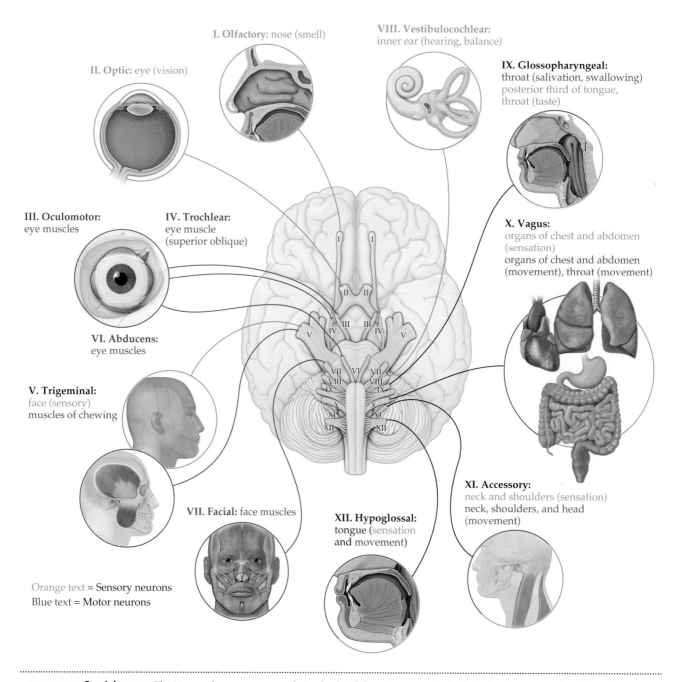

FIGURE 2.12 Cranial nerves. The 12 cranial nerves are primarily involved with functions associated with the head, neck, and shoulders. The vagus nerve, however, extends beyond this area.

detail in Chapter 7) and the **autonomic nervous system** that controls involuntary functions (e.g., heart rate, digestion). We saw in the chapter opening that David Blaine demonstrated voluntary control over his supposedly involuntary physiological processes. But most of us do not think about the number of times our hearts beat per minute, the dilation of our pupils when we walk outside on a sunny day, or the intensity of our gastric secretions following the consumption of a large meal. It all just seems to take care of itself. You may want to pause for a moment as your neurons are processing just how amazing this neural engineering plan really is.

The autonomic nervous system is further divided into the **sympathetic nervous system** and **parasympathetic nervous system**. This division is based on the fact that, at times, animals face challenging situations. Challenges can take the form of something perceived as a positive experience (e.g., running the winning lap of a race) or a negative experience (e.g., running to escape an attacker). Good or bad, these challenges still require a substantial redistribution of energy throughout the body. In these cases, our responses demand special attention so that we can identify important stimuli in our environment and respond accordingly.

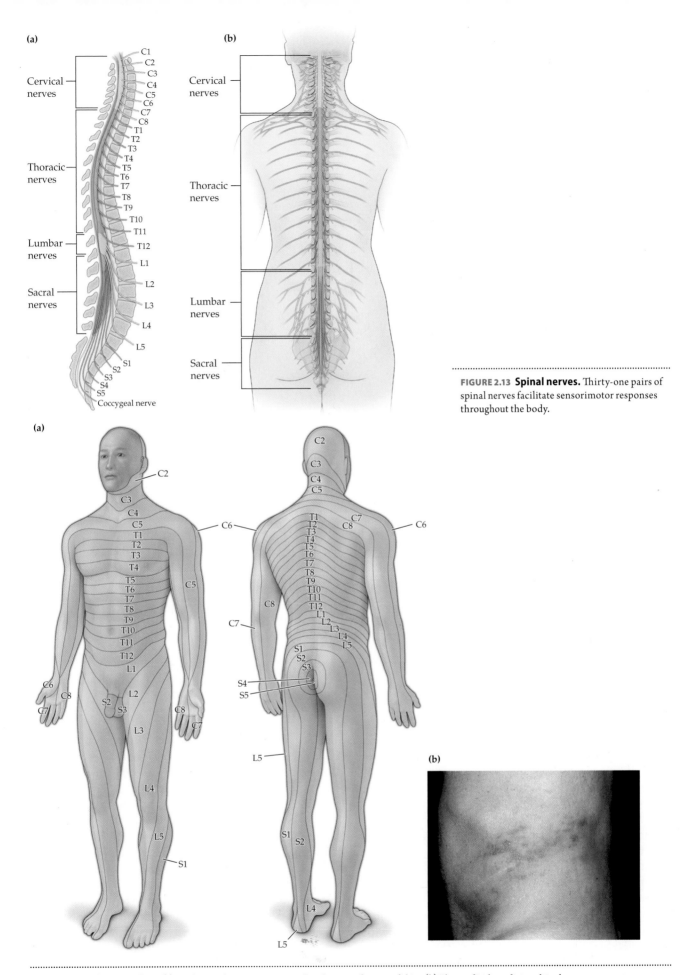

(a)

Cervical nerves
C1
C2
C3
C4
C5
C6
C7
C8
T1
T2
T3
T4
T5
T6
T7
T8
T9
T10
T11
T12

Thoracic nerves

Lumbar nerves
L1
L2
L3
L4
L5

Sacral nerves
S1
S2
S3
S4
S5
Coccygeal nerve

(b)

Cervical nerves

Thoracic nerves

Lumbar nerves

Sacral nerves

FIGURE 2.13 Spinal nerves. Thirty-one pairs of spinal nerves facilitate sensorimotor responses throughout the body.

(a)

(b)

FIGURE 2.14. Dermatomes. (a) Each spinal nerve is associated with a specific area of skin. (b) The medical condition shingles produces a painful rash in a specific and distinct area of the skin corresponding to a given dermatome.

41

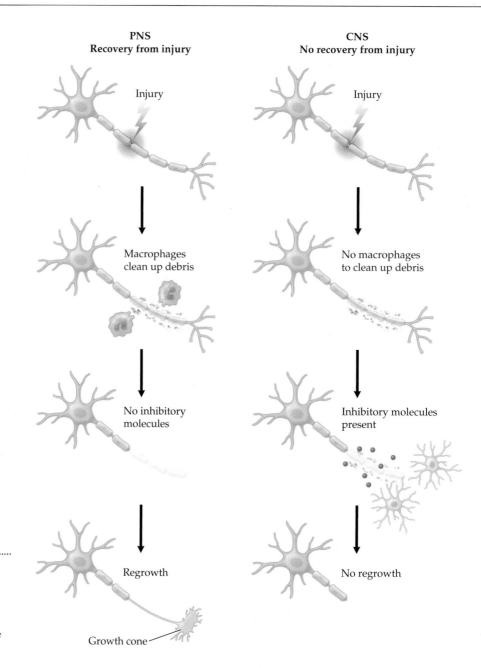

PNS
Recovery from injury

CNS
No recovery from injury

Injury

Injury

Macrophages
clean up debris

No macrophages
to clean up debris

No inhibitory
molecules

Inhibitory molecules
present

Regrowth

No regrowth

Growth cone

FIGURE 2.15 **Axonal regeneration.**
Regrowth of damaged axons occurs in
the peripheral nervous system (PNS)
but not in the central nervous system
(CNS); research is focused on identifying aspects of PNS recovery that may be
applied to CNS recovery.

Although the somatic nervous system facilitates the decision to run or jump in response to a challenge or an impending threat, the body needs additional help executing
the brain's motor demands. If the decision is made to run
from a potential attacker, the body must increase its heart
rate to pump more blood to the muscles, increase hormonal
secretions to maintain heightened arousal, and, in the spirit
of efficiency, scale back other ongoing operations (e.g.,
growth processes) that are not critical for the survival task
at hand. The American physiologist Walter Cannon coined
the term **fight-or-flight response** to refer to the function of
the sympathetic nervous system in preparing the body for
strenuous physical responses to life's threats and challenges
(Cannon, 1915; Jacobs 2001; see Figure 2.16).

Once the behavior has been successfully executed and
the threat is no longer present, the parasympathetic nervous
system reestablishes normal baseline functions. Energy is a
valued commodity in all animals, and the autonomic nervous system works diligently to ensure that energy is ex-
pended on an as-needed basis. As seen in Figure 2.16, the
parasympathetic nervous system regulates baseline functions necessary for survival. For example, it slows the heart
rate, stimulates gastric secretions necessary to digest breakfast, and directs energy toward long-term physiological
investments such as growth, reproductive functions, and
immune functions. In contrast to the fight-or-flight characterization of the sympathetic nervous system, the parasympathetic nervous system can be characterized as the

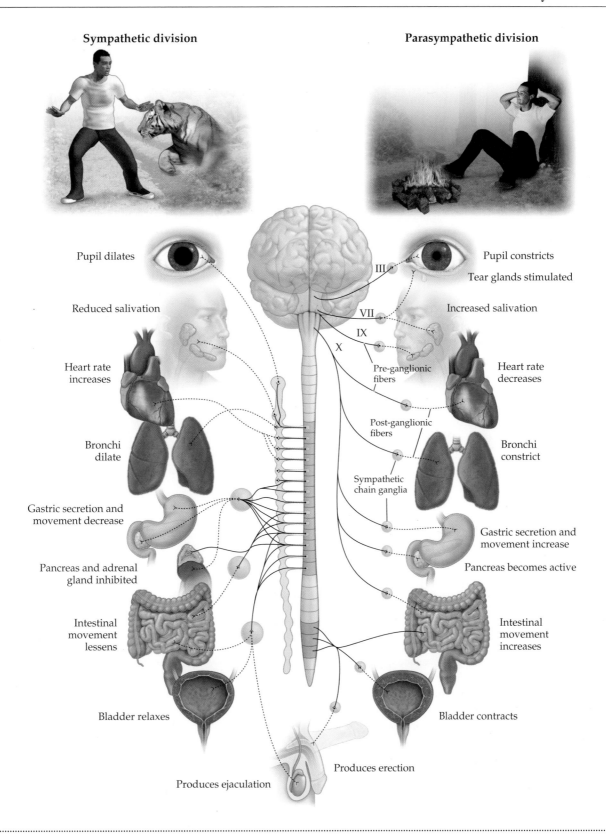

Sympathetic division

Parasympathetic division

Pupil dilates

Reduced salivation

Heart rate increases

Bronchi dilate

Gastric secretion and movement decrease

Pancreas and adrenal gland inhibited

Intestinal movement lessens

Bladder relaxes

Produces ejaculation

III

VII

IX

X

Pre-ganglionic fibers

Post-ganglionic fibers

Sympathetic chain ganglia

Pupil constricts

Tear glands stimulated

Increased salivation

Heart rate decreases

Bronchi constrict

Gastric secretion and movement increase

Pancreas becomes active

Intestinal movement increases

Bladder contracts

Produces erection

FIGURE 2.16 Autonomic nervous system. The autonomic nervous system consists of the sympathetic nervous system ("fight or flight") and the parasympathetic nervous system ("rest and digest").

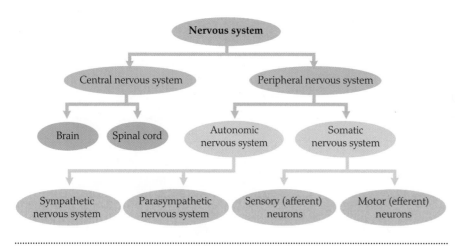

FIGURE 2.17 **Organization of the nervous system.** The peripheral nervous system has more extensive categories than the central nervous system.

"rest-and-digest" system. The priorities switch to high alert, however, when the sympathetic nervous system is activated.

The efficiency of these systems is critical for the short- and long-term survival of animals. Considering that the brain is the ultimate energy hog, consuming about 20% of the body's fuel, it must micromanage energy expenditure in proportion to specific physiological demands. Thus, the various divisions of labor in the nervous system enable the brain to operate reliably and efficiently. Of course, the design of the vertebrate nervous system is not perfect. However, through evolution's constant tweaking, the vertebrate nervous system has allowed more sophisticated interactions with the environment than the invertebrate worm's nervous system described at the beginning of this section.

Figure 2.16 also shows differences in the anatomy of the sympathetic and parasympathetic nervous systems. Specifically, the sympathetic nerves extend from the thoracic and lumbar areas of the spinal cord, and the parasympathetic nerves extend from the cranial and sacral areas. The sympathetic nerves also make contact with other nerves in the sympathetic chain ganglia, small clusters of neurons just outside of the spinal cord, so that the sympathetic nerves have short preganglionic fibers and long postganglionic fibers that extend to the final organ destination. The parasympathetic nerves, by contrast, have long preganglionic fibers and short postganglionic fibers that extend to the final organ destination.

Now that you have been introduced to all the major organizational divisions of the nervous system, the overall organization is depicted in Figure 2.17. Together, the components of the CNS and PNS enable you to function from day to day in an adaptive manner.

CONTEXT MATTERS

Friends, Marathons, and New Neurons

Stranahan, A. M., Khalil, D., & Gould, E. (2006). Social isolation delays the positive effects of running on adult neurogenesis. Nature Neuroscience, 9, 526–533.

Neuroscientists originally assumed that the number of neurons in a given brain was fixed. However, today we know that the adult mammalian brain can create new neurons in certain brain areas, a process called **neurogenesis**. Results from several studies established that the context of an animal's life, referring to both internal and external conditions, could both enhance and diminish rates of cellular proliferation. For example, evidence indicates that in rodents, running increases neurogenesis (van Praag, Christie, Sejnowski, & Gage, 1999) and stress exposure suppresses neurogenesis (Gage & van Praag, 2002; Gould, Cameron, Daniels, Woolley, & McEwen, 1992).

Elizabeth Gould and her colleagues at Princeton University examined the influence of a rat's social living conditions on neurogenesis. If a rat was exposed to running wheels for 12 days, its neurogenesis rates should increase. But would it make a difference if the rat was housed with two other rats (socially housed) or housed individually (socially isolated)? Would the social context alter the expected neurogenesis?

In this study's research design, four groups of rats were used: (1) a socially housed running group, (2) a socially housed nonrunning (control) group, (3) an individually housed running group, and (4) an individually housed nonrunning (control) group. (See Context Matters Figure 2.1.) Beginning on the second day of a 12-day running regimen, the rats received daily injections of bromodeoxyuridine, a marker of new dividing cells. The rats spent 12 days running or spending time in their cage. Then, the researchers assessed the rats' brains for the existence of new cells.

The researchers found that in the running groups, the socially housed rats had significantly more new cells (including neurons) than the individually housed (socially isolated) running group did. These findings supported the past research that running enhanced neurogenesis. The results, however, got more interesting when the brains of the individually housed (socially isolated) groups were examined. In these groups, the socially isolated runners showed less neurogenesis than the

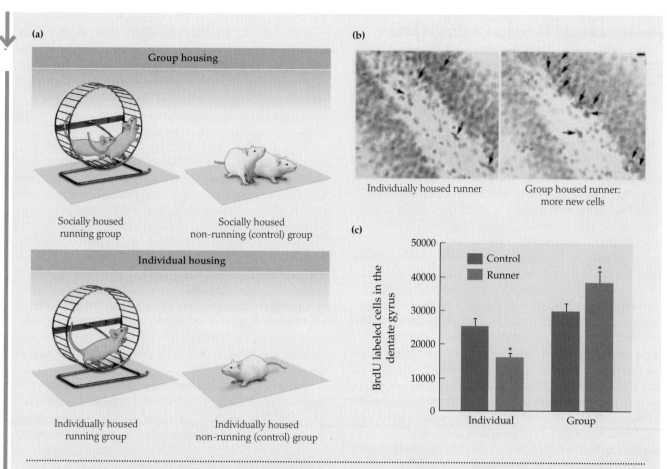

(a) Group housing

Socially housed
running group

Socially housed
non-running (control) group

Individual housing

Individually housed
running group

Individually housed
non-running (control) group

(b) Individually housed runner

Group housed runner:
more new cells

(c)

CONTEXT MATTERS FIGURE 2.1. Lifestyle and neuron production. (a) Rats were initially assigned to either a social or an isolated group and then assigned to a running or control group. (b) Following bromodeoxyuridine injections that marked new neurons, the brains of the rats were examined for the presence of newly divided cells, or neurogenesis. (c) The results indicated that the social runners experienced the highest rates of neurogenesis.

socially isolated nonrunners. Thus, it appeared that even if an animal is exposed to tried-and-true methods to enhance neurogenesis, certain contextual conditions (e.g., social contact) must be met for enhanced neurogenesis to occur.

The next step in this study was to rule out other possible reasons for this result (i.e., confounding variables). A close examination of videos sampling running behavior throughout the study revealed no differences in the levels of running between the socially housed and socially isolated groups. The researchers then sought to identify the benefits of a social environment. Social contact may have reduced the rats' stress levels and accompanying levels of toxic stress **hormones** (chemicals that travel throughout the body with various effects). Running increases energy demands and is considered a stressor of sorts, although it is typically considered healthful. But do certain conditions determine whether the demands of running are stressful or healthful?

To address this question, the Princeton researchers repeated the experiment, but this time rats in all groups were placed in a restraint tube, a Plexiglas tube that confines movement. Most rats find this situation aversive. The researchers were interested in the rats' baseline stress hormone levels prior to entering the tube, their hormone levels during the stressful experience, and, finally, their hormone levels on recovery two hours later. In the

control (nonrunning) rats, regardless of the housing condition, stress hormones were elevated during the stress phase and returned to baseline levels two hours later. Although it is critical to have sufficient levels of stress hormones in a challenging situation, once the threat is gone, the lingering effects of these hormones can lead to wear and tear of physiological systems.

What about the stress hormones in the two running groups? The social context mattered here. Specifically, no increase in the level of stress hormone was observed in the socially housed runners. The stress hormone response of the socially isolated runners, however, was similar to that of the control (nonrunning) groups. The researchers found evidence that the level of stress hormones was key when they removed the source of stress hormones (that is, the adrenal gland that sits on top of the kidney) in the socially isolated running rats. Sure enough, similar to the socially housed running rats, when the source of stress hormones was removed, the socially isolated (individually housed) running rats responded to running with increased neurogenesis rates.

These findings provide evidence that harmful elevations in stress hormones are mitigated if the stressful experience occurs in the context of affiliative contact (that is, friends). In the absence of stress hormones, more energy is devoted to building up the brain's neuronal count, or neurogenesis rates.

The Brain's Geography

The most influential component of the CNS is the brain because of its control over all of our voluntary movements. Although you may not have realized it, your brain has been the central executive organ that has facilitated all of your decisions since you awakened this morning. You have met its fundamental units, neurons and glia, as well as various communication structures: cranial nerves and spinal nerves. In this section, we will discuss the various specialized communities of neurons throughout the brain and describe their basic functions. Just as people use maps to help navigate unfamiliar territory, neuroscientists use specific directional terminology to describe the anatomical positions of various brain structures. The use of these terms in four-legged and two-legged animals is depicted in Figure 2.18. Key terms include **rostral** or **anterior** (toward the front or mouth), **caudal** or **posterior** (toward the tail), **dorsal** (toward the top or back), **ventral** (toward the bottom or chest), **medial** (toward the center), and **lateral** (toward the side). In addition, **proximal** means closer to the CNS, and **distal** means farther from the CNS.

If you are reading this book, you are likely a college student who has studied some psychology or biology previously, depending on your major. If you are at a traditional academic institution, you began with the basics—the introductory courses—and then moved to the courses for majors that teach you the tools and fundamentals of your discipline, still basic but becoming more specialized. By your senior year, you will be taking more advanced courses that prepare you for successful careers or graduate school. Generally speaking, the progression of courses in the traditional college curriculum resembles the evolution of the brain's anatomical structures and the progression of their functional specialization.

We will begin with the brain's fundamental structures making up the hindbrain and then move to the lower-level specialization courses as we discuss the midbrain before arriving at the advanced senior courses: the forebrain. Of course, the advanced courses are most effective if they integrate relevant information from other courses taken throughout a student's college experience. This hierarchical integration is also essential for effective brain functions. This brief tour through the structures of the brain introduces the most basic functions associated with specific brain areas. You will learn more about these brain sites as we discuss topics in more detail in subsequent chapters.

The Hindbrain (Myelencephalon and Metencephalon)

Introductory courses cover fundamental information, preparing students to succeed in the upper-level courses. The same organizational purpose exists for the brain. As neural information from the body travels through the spinal nerves

and up the spinal cord, it enters the most ventral (lower) area of the brain, the **medulla oblongata (myelencephalon)**. The medulla oblongata, together with the pons and midbrain (described in this section), form the **brainstem**. Just as all students must take required fundamental courses, regardless of their major and future career specializations, all vertebrate species have a hindbrain—fish, lizards, frogs, rats, and pigs all have brainstems.

The medulla oblongata regulates fundamental life-supporting systems such as respiration, blood pressure, arousal, and muscle tone. These basic functions are essential for survival. Lizards may not need to demonstrate sophisticated problem-solving skills, but, like humans, they must breathe, move around, sleep, and digest their food.

Just above the myelencephalon sits the **metencephalon**. One structure in this area is a bulge on the ventral side of the brain known as the **pons** (the Latin term for *bridge*). This area is rich in nerve-fiber pathways that transfer information to more dorsal (upper) areas and from one side of the brain to the other. In a sense, the pons is the brainstem hub for information transfer. Just across the medulla is the cerebellum (briefly introduced earlier in this chapter), another part of the metencephalon.

Returning to the curriculum analogy, the cerebellum is more of a specialized course than the other hindbrain areas. The cerebellum, literally "little brain," is a large neural structure that dangles off the dorsal section of the brainstem. As mentioned in this chapter's section on glia, it contains approximately 80% of all the brain's neurons and regulates motor coordination and balance (Herculano-Houzel, 2009). To accomplish these feats, the cerebellum must accurately process information about the environment through sensory input as well as from within the body. This brain area is one of the first to be affected when alcohol is consumed. The tests that a police officer requests of individuals suspected of being intoxicated (e.g., walking a straight line, touching one's nose while one's eyes are closed) are cerebellum dependent. In subsequent chapters you will learn that the cerebellum has also been implicated in nonmotor functions such as attention, learning, and executive control (Strick, Dum, & Fiez, 2009).

In a stained section of rat brain tissue, the cerebellum stands out. The darker tissue depicted in Figure 2.19 shows that the tissue of the cerebellum, compared with that of other brain areas, is more densely populated with neurons. The great neuronal investment in the cerebellum suggests that this structure is critical for an animal's survival. A common histological method for staining neuron cell bodies is the *cresyl violet stain*, which, as Figure 2.19 illustrates, stains the neuronal cell bodies a vibrant violet color.

The **reticular formation** is a cluster of neurons, called **nuclei** (singular *nucleus*), and fibers that are located throughout the central area of the brainstem. (*Nucleus* refers to a group of neurons in the CNS as well as to the central, DNA-containing component of every animal cell.) So . . . what percent of the brain's neurons are in the cerebellum? If you are paying attention, you will recall that the answer to

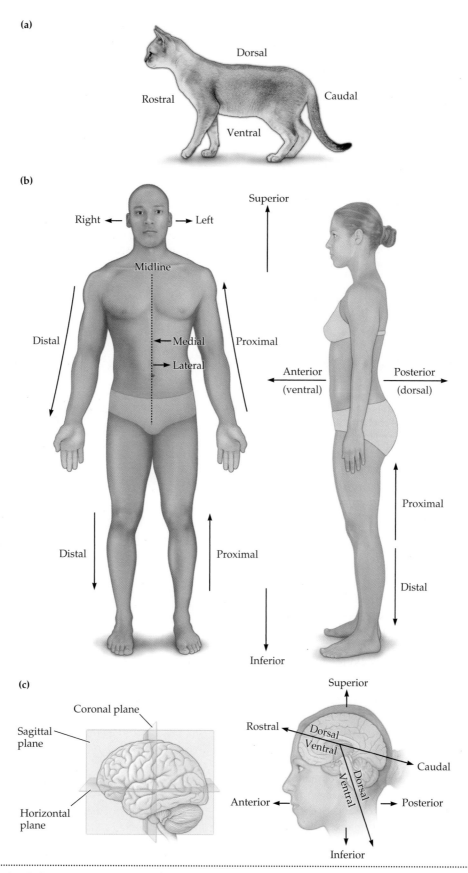

FIGURE 2.18. Directional planes. Systematic positions throughout the body are used as landmarks to communicate specific and relative areas within the nervous system in both (a) four-legged animals and (b) humans. (c) Within the brain, coronal, horizontal, and sagittal sections are used when examining neural tissue.

(a)

(b)

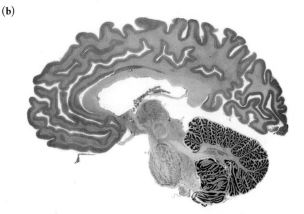

FIGURE 2.19 **Neuron density in cerebellum.** The cerebellum contains the majority of the brain's neurons in both (a) rats and (b) humans.

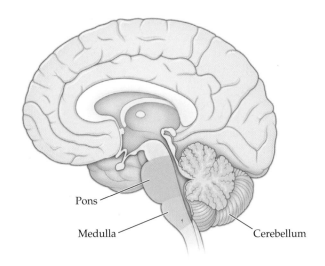

FIGURE 2.20 **The hindbrain.** Basic functions such as glandular secretions, breathing, arousal, and muscle tone are controlled by the components of the hindbrain.

(a)

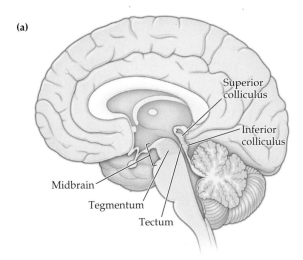

(b)

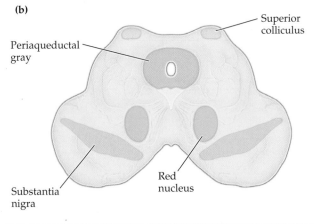

FIGURE 2.21 **The midbrain.** (a) The rather small midbrain area. (b) Several midbrain nuclei involved in sensory and motor responses.

the preceding question is 80%. If you answered the question correctly, then it is safe to say that your reticular formation is activated as you are reading this text. The reticular formation maintains sufficient levels of arousal necessary for animals to direct their attention toward relevant targets in the environment. It is also involved in sleep/wake cycles.

Thus, the hindbrain (Figure 2.20) covers the basic component of the nervous system's curricular design. As you are probably already realizing, even the most basic brain function is far from simple. As we move up to the midbrain and forebrain, the brain's ability to interact with the environment becomes increasingly complex, presenting new options to add to the mammalian behavioral repertoires.

The Midbrain (Mesencephalon)

The midbrain is small compared with the hindbrain and forebrain. Generally, this brain area contains nuclei where fine-tuned sensory and motor messages interact, enhancing the responsiveness of animals to complex environments. As animals can detect more specific information about relevant external stimuli, they can respond in more effective ways as they navigate through their environment. For example, being able to visually evaluate the speed of an animal such as a rabbit as it runs across a field enables a predator to respond accordingly with running speed to successfully capture the prey.

The midbrain (see Figure 2.21) is divided into two regions, the **tectum**, or "roof," and the **tegmentum**, or "floor."

The tectum contains two sets of nuclei related to sensory processing, namely the **superior colliculi** (important for processing visual information) and the **inferior colliculi** (important for processing and localizing auditory information).

The tegmentum contains several nuclei including the most dorsal region of the reticular formation described above, the **periaqueductal gray** central region, involved in the sensation of pain, and the **substantia nigra**, or "black substance," known for its production of a neurochemical important for integrated (smoother) physical movement. A pinkish area known as the **red nucleus** is prominent in this area and seems to have evolved as limbs (such as arms) emerged on the larger evolutionary scene as they play a role in limb movement (Gruber & Gould, 2010). With the abilities offered by the midbrain area, behavioral options become more specialized in preparation for the brain's upper-level major course areas discussed in the next section.

The Forebrain (Diencephalon and Telencephalon)

At the top of the brainstem, we reach a proverbial fork in the road. As we moved from the hindbrain to the midbrain, we began to see more structures in duplicate, on the right and left side of the midbrain (e.g., superior colliculi, substantia nigra). This trend continues as most of the structures described from this point forward appear in both the right and the left sides of the brain. As you might guess, communication between these two sides of the brain, or **cerebral hemispheres**, is critical. The **corpus callosum**, a thick band of myelinated axons, connects the dorsal sections of the hemispheres, whereas the **anterior commissure** provides more ventral communication. The contrasts between the **white matter** (myelinated axons) and **gray matter** (neuronal cell bodies) are depicted in Figure 2.22. We will discuss

more about communication between the two cerebral hemispheres at the end of this section.

Diencephalon As seen in Figure 2.23, a primary component of the *diencephalon* is the **thalamus**, composed of two large egg-shape structures, one in each cerebral hemisphere. It is difficult to imagine all of the sensory information entering the brain at one time. Regardless of where you are, there are typically several sounds, sights, smells, tastes, and tactile stimuli bombarding the sensory neurons and arriving in the CNS at any given moment. The thalamus filters and directs the information to the appropriate higher area in the cerebral cortex. The thalamus comprises several nuclei (i.e., distinct groups of similarly functioning neuronal cell bodies) specialized for identifying specific types of sensory stimuli and directing them to the appropriate cortical location. All sensory stimuli are initially processed through this sensory hub except olfaction (smell), an evolutionarily old sensory system that is quickly directed to relevant brain areas as it enters the brain to facilitate survival.

Under the thalamus is the **hypothalamus**, a favorite destination for many behavioral neuroscientists because of its prominent role in motivational systems. Interested in sexual behavior? Aggression? Parenting? Hunger? Thirst? Stress? These are just a sample of the behaviors regulated by the hypothalamus.

Dangling from the hypothalamus is the **pituitary gland**, a component of the body's hormonal system, called the *endocrine system*. On receiving the appropriate information from the hypothalamus, the pituitary gland triggers the release of various hormones, which travel to destinations throughout the body. This pea-size brain structure is small compared with other brain areas, but its job is critical. A disruption in endocrine functions may result in symptoms such as

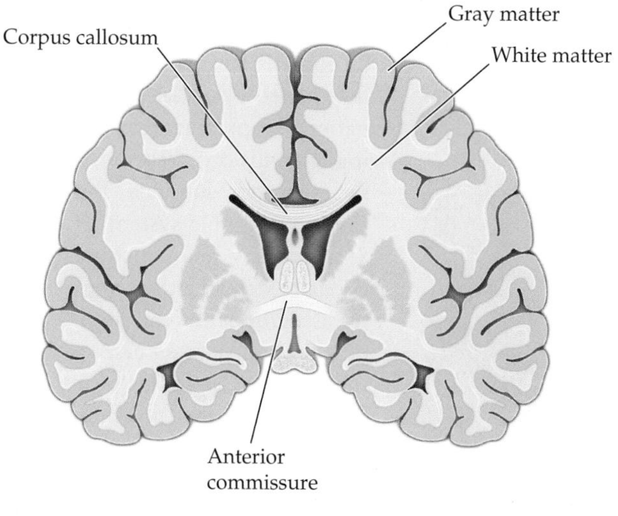

Corpus callosum

Gray matter

White matter

Anterior commissure

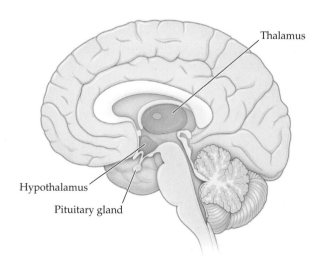

Thalamus

Hypothalamus

Pituitary gland

FIGURE 2.22 Connecting the hemispheres. The corpus callosum and anterior commissure provide vital connections between the two hemispheres of the brain.

FIGURE 2.23 Diencephalon. The diencephalon consists of the thalamus, hypothalamus, and pituitary gland.

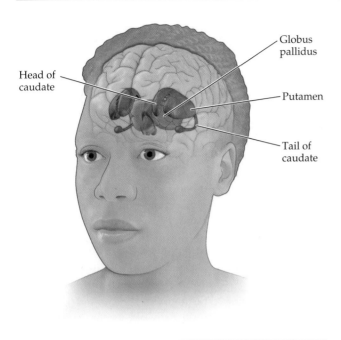

Head of caudate

Globus pallidus

Putamen

Tail of caudate

FIGURE 2.24 Basal ganglia. The cluster of structures surrounding the thalamus known as the basal ganglia is primarily involved in motor functions.

fertility problems, excessive weight gain, anxiety disorders, and stunted or extreme growth, to name just a few. You will learn more specific information about hormones and their functions in Chapter 11.

Telencephalon: Subcortical Systems (Basal Ganglia and Limbic System) Finally, we have made it through the brain's foundational requirements and the introductory courses in our major . . . and now is the time for specialized and sophisticated integration. As we move away from the diencephalon, we encounter two essential subcortical systems that modulate the complex information processing in the *telencephalon*. The interconnections of these two systems are multifaceted and will be discussed more extensively in subsequent chapters. In the meantime, the primary functions and most influential components are briefly described here.

The first subcortical system of the telencephalon is a collection of nuclei known as the **basal ganglia**. As seen in Figure 2.24, three components of the basal ganglia include the **caudate** (both head and tail), **globus pallidus**, and **putamen**. These structures are critical for the regulation of movement and, as you may guess, coordinate with the cerebellum. If you are able to carry out movements with minimal thought and planning; if you have not noticed any abnormalities in your movement sequences; if you rarely think about the limitations of your body's movement, then it is safe to say that your basal ganglia are probably working well. More information about the functions and integrations of all brain areas involved in movement appears in Chapter 7.

The degenerative neuromuscular disease **Parkinson's disease** results from suboptimal activation of the various components of the basal ganglia—the caudate, globus pallidus, and putamen. When these structures fail to receive appropriate neurochemical fuel in the form of the neurotransmitter dopamine, problems with movement emerge. Symptoms include difficulty initiating movements, slowness carrying out certain movements, excessive muscle tone (rigidity), and excessive involuntary movements such as tremors. The most highly functioning basal ganglia are hard at work to keep their functions from ever crossing your mind.

The **limbic system** is the second subcortical system of the telencephalon. Like the basal ganglia, the limbic system consists of a collection of structures that surround the thalamus. Functionally, these structures are involved in emotional regulation and include the fornix, septum, **amygdala**, cingulum, and **hippocampus**, as seen in Figure 2.25. The limbic system received its official name from the neuroanatomist Paul MacLean. Epileptic seizures are normally accompanied by convulsions. However, MacLean discovered a population of epileptic patients who, rather than experiencing convulsions, reported intense feelings and emotions. Borrowing the term "limbic system" from the 19th-century neuroanatomist Paul Broca to describe the circular form of structures in the mid-section of the brain, MacLean extended the term to the cluster of interconnected structures positioned in a circle around the thalamus.

MacLean used a *neuroethological approach*; that is, he considered the role of these structures in several species with various environmental landscapes and behavioral repertoires. This scientific approach

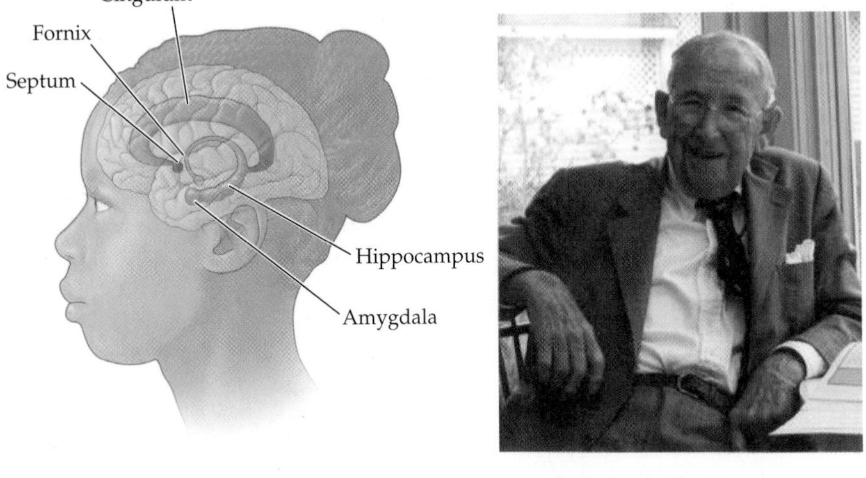

(a)

Cingulum

Fornix

Septum

Hippocampus

Amygdala

(b)

FIGURE 2.25 Limbic system. (a). The key structures contributing to the limbic system form a circular structure around the thalamus in a similar manner to the basal ganglia. (b) Paul MacLean initially referred to these structures with a common function in emotional processing as the "limbic system."

led him to believe that the limbic system evolved to facilitate play behavior, parental behavior, and the cry of infants on separation from their mothers, all behaviors that seemed to be new to mammals as they evolved from reptiles. Have you ever seen lizards frolicking in play? Turtles cuddling with their young in a nest? Quite the contrary, it is every baby turtle for itself. No parental energy is directed toward the offspring past the point of burying the eggs (MacLean, 1990). More highly evolved components of the telencephalon, including the cerebral cortex, are discussed below; these subcortical systems paved the way for more sophisticated responses.

Today, we still consider this cluster of interconnected brain areas known as the limbic system to be associated with emotional expression because it directly influences neurophysiological and behavioral mechanisms (Tien, Felsberg, Krishnan, & Heinz, 1994). Limbic structures are likely responsible for many emotional (affective) disorders, such as anxiety disorders. Two limbic structures, the hippocampus and amygdala, have received the most research attention in the context of emotional expression. The hippocampus, involved in learning and memory, is activated by the brain's stress hormones so that appropriate memories can be formed relating to

Layer I. Molecular layer
Axons and dendrites.

Layer II. External granular layer
Stellate cells and small pyramidal cells.

Layer III. Pyramidal cell layer
Pyramidal cells.

Layer IV. Inner granular layer
Densely grouped stellate cells.
Sensory information.

Layer V. Inner pyramidal cell layer
Large pyramidal cells. Motor action.

Layer VI. Fusiform layer
Fusiform cells.

White matter. Axons.

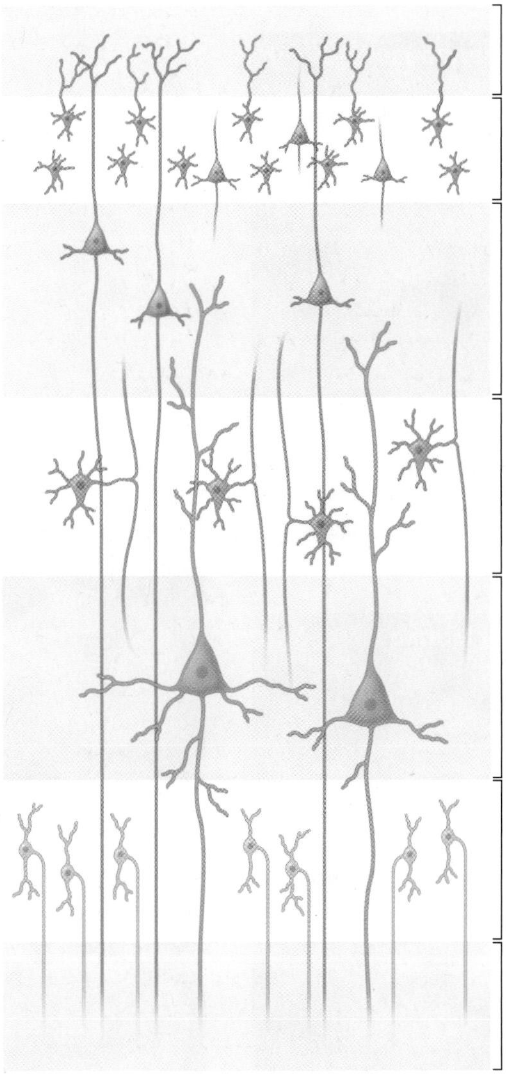

FIGURE 2.26 **Neocortex.** The neocortex is composed of six distinct layers characterized by unique cellular populations.

these experiences. Research suggests that depression is associated with eventual decreased functioning of the hippocampus (Sapolsky, 2001). Further, lesions of the amygdala have been shown to prevent rodents from being trained to fear certain stimuli. Research with humans indicates that a damaged amygdala compromises a person's ability to interpret fearful faces in other individuals (Adolphs, Tranel, Damasio, & Damasio, 1995). Thus, the amygdala is closely associated with fear.

Telencephalon: The Cerebral Cortex The cerebral cortex surrounds the basal ganglia and the limbic system. The human brain's cerebral cortex is 1–4 millimeters thick, is divided into six distinct cellular layers (see Figure 2.26), and has a total surface area of about 1.5 square meters (the size of a small desk). Because it contains dense collections of neuronal cell bodies and blood vessels, it is also called the "gray matter" (Fischl & Dale, 2000). How does so much brain tissue fit inside the skull? This feat occurs via an ingenious packing

strategy that results in many bulges, known as **gyri** (singular, *gyrus*), and grooves, known as **sulci** (singular, *sulcus*). As you may guess, animals with less cortical tissue than humans have fewer gyri and sulci than humans do (see Figure 2.27).

With so much brain area packed into the cortex, an organizational plan is definitely in order. As Figure 2.28 illustrates, four broad lobes distinguish large areas of the cerebral cortex: the **frontal lobe** (involved in movement and in higher executive functions such as reasoning and decision making), the **parietal lobe** (involved in interpreting sensory information), the **occipital lobe** (involved in visual processing), and the **temporal lobe** (involved in hearing, language, visual processing, and emotional processing). Additional landmarks include the central fissure that separates the **primary motor cortex** in the frontal lobe from the **primary somatosensory cortex** in the parietal lobe (Nolte, 2002).

The complex functioning of the human frontal cortex is often viewed as a critical factor distinguishing the human brain from the brains of other mammals. Our college

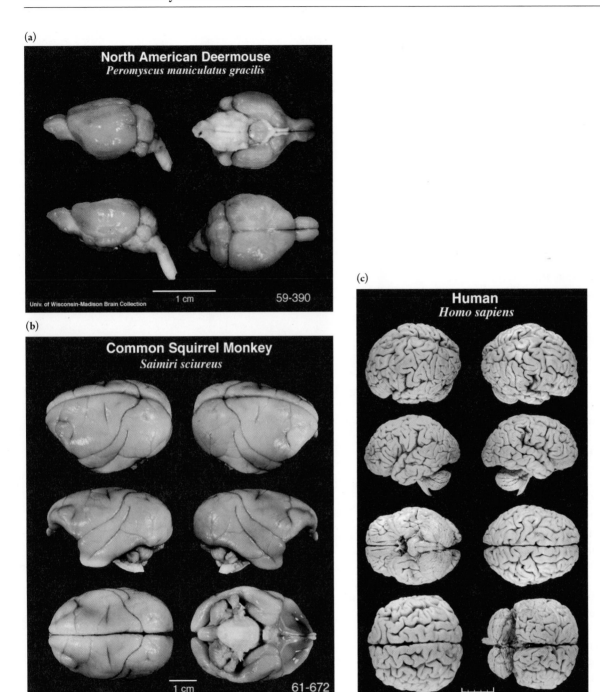

(a)

North American Deermouse
Peromyscus maniculatus gracilis

1 cm

Univ. of Wisconsin-Madison Brain Collection

59-390

(b)

Common Squirrel Monkey
Saimiri sciureus

1 cm

Univ. of Wisconsin-Madison Brain Collection

61-672

(c)

Human
Homo sapiens

5 cm

Univ. of Wisconsin-Madison Brain Collection

69-314

FIGURE 2.27 Cortical size across mammals. Compared with other mammals, such as (a) mice and (b) monkeys, (c) humans have a disproportionately large cerebral cortex.

curriculum analogy may help explain the functions of this brain structure. Consider the first week of classes, when you sit down at your desk with all your syllabi in hand looking at your master calendar. You have multiple assignments and exams in each course, not to mention extracurricular activities, family events, work, or volunteer obligations. To be a successful student, you must integrate all the information to produce an overall schedule for the semester. Your highly functioning frontal cortex allows you to organize and plan your schedule so that you can successfully achieve your goals for the semester. To accomplish this task, your brain will integrate the functions of different areas (from the myelencephalon to the telencephalon) that will enable you to utilize memories, emotions, and various decision-making strategies.

The classic case of Phineas Gage reveals the importance of an intact frontal cortex and its interconnections with the subcortical areas. When Gage was working as a railroad foreman in 1848, he suffered a life-changing accident. An explosion sent

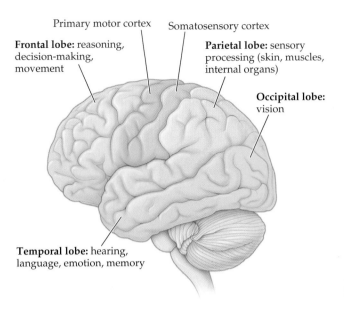

FIGURE 2.28 **Cerebral cortex.** The expansive cerebral cortex includes four lobes with varying functions.

a tamping iron (43 inches in length, 1.25 inches in width, and 13.25 pounds in weight) through Gage's left cheek, his brain, and his skull. It is not clear that Gage even lost consciousness following this incident; however, he did lose his left eye.

In a recent investigation of Gage's skull, researchers estimated the potential volume of white matter that was damaged in the explosion. To do so, they compared Gage's brain with the brains of contemporary right-handed men of a similar age. Based on their model (see Figure 2.29), the investigators estimated that Gage lost about 11% of his white matter, drastically reducing his brain's ability to communicate. Specifically, connections between the frontal lobes and both the limbic and the basal ganglia would have been lost with the lesion he suffered (van Horn et al., 2012). It was reported that Gage changed from a competent employee to a man who was "fitful, capricious, impatient of advice, obstinate, and lacking in deference to his fellows" (MacMillan, 2002, p. 13; Twomey, 2010). However, recent evidence suggests that this change was not permanent and Gage was able to support himself with various jobs throughout his life. The engaging context of his varied employment experiences such as working on the family farm and learning to be a stagecoach driver may have facilitated neuroplasticity mechanisms and his subsequent neurorehabilitation (Macmillan & Lena, 2010). Gage's case became famous because his brain damage and subsequent behavioral changes were the first to be documented in detail, allowing scientists to learn about which brain areas controlled which behaviors.

Now that you have been introduced to the fundamental divisions and structures of the brain, it is important to consider an important overarching theme for the two brain hemispheres: from a functional perspective, the left and right hemispheres are not created equal.

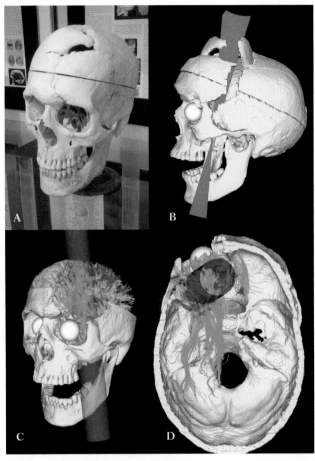

FIGURE 2.29 **Phineas Gage's brain.** Neuroimaging of Phineas Gage's skull revealed the specific path of the tamping iron that blasted through his left hemisphere.

Taking Sides: Brain Lateralization

On first glance, the two hemispheres of the brain look identical. However, just as you cannot judge a book by its cover, you cannot judge a brain's functions by its structure alone. Research has slowly revealed that, although the hemispheres are more similar than different from a neuroanatomical perspective, they harbor different functions. This difference in function between the two hemispheres is called brain **lateralization**. A significant finding pointing toward the existence of brain lateralization occurred a half-century ago with the neuroscientists Michael Gazzaniga and Roger Sperry's groundbreaking discovery of lateralized functions in patients who were diagnosed with epilepsy. The patients had had their corpus callosum surgically severed to diminish the intensity of their epileptic seizures. This process is known as split-brain surgery. Because the corpus callosum acts as a major pathway for information transfer between the hemispheres, medical opinion at the time held that inactivating the corpus callosum would prevent seizures from traveling from one hemisphere to the other, thereby reducing seizure intensity.

How did splitting people's brains affect their thoughts, movements, emotions, and personalities? This was fascinating, unexplored terrain for neuroscience. One patient, Vicki, reported some annoying effects during the first months following her surgery. For example, grocery shopping became extremely frustrating. When she saw an item on the shelf that she wanted to purchase, she found it difficult to actually retrieve the item. "I'd reach with my right for the thing I wanted, but the left would come in and they'd kind of fight. . . . almost like repelling magnets" (Wolman, 2012, p. 260). This interhemisphere conflict subsided over the next year, and once again, her two hands worked as partners to accomplish tasks such as tying her shoelaces and slicing vegetables.

In the 1960s, Gazzaniga and Sperry embarked on a research program to evaluate these **split-brain patients**. They compared these patients with healthy, age-matched subjects. As Figure 2.30 illustrates, in these studies, subjects were asked to carry out a particular task in response to a stimulus presented briefly to either the left or the right visual field (Gazzaniga, Bogen, & Sperry, 1962). (The *visual field* is the visual information that we process at a given time.) If the split-brain patients were asked to verbally indicate what they saw, the patients complied if the stimulus was presented to the right visual field. When the visual stimulus was flashed to the left visual field and processed by the right hemisphere, patients could not respond verbally. However, they could point to the correct stimulus or answer with their left hand (see Figure 2.30).

Because the brain has *contralateral control* over the body (i.e., one side of the brain controls the opposite side of the

body), the results confirmed that patients could respond verbally only if the left hemisphere was activated by the right visual field. As you will learn in Chapter 6, visual information crosses over from one side of the visual field (e.g., left) to the other hemisphere (e.g., right).

Gazzaniga and Sperry's Nobel Prize–winning research suggested that the two cerebral hemispheres were specialized for specific functions. Namely, the left hemisphere was specialized for language and the right hemisphere for visual–spatial processing (e.g., pointing to an object) and facial recognition (Gazzaniga, Ivry, & Mangun, 1998; Gazzaniga & Sperry, 1967). As a result, when information prompting a verbal response was delivered to the right hemisphere, the brain could not respond with language. However, when the prompt was received by the left hemisphere, it could respond verbally. More recently, brain imaging has confirmed more activity in the left hemisphere than in the right hemisphere when a subject is processing language (Wolman, 2012).

Initial research suggested that the volume of certain brain structures such as the **planum temporale**, an area of the temporal cortex that is thought to be involved in language, was consistently larger in the left hemisphere than in the right hemisphere (Foundas, Leonard, Gilmore, Fennell, & Heilman, 1994). However, as imaging techniques have become more sophisticated and less invasive (allowing many more subjects to be evaluated), researchers are observing fewer distinct anatomical differences between the left and right hemispheres than originally proposed (Greve et al., 2013). Additional information about how the brain generates language will be discussed in Chapter 7.

Why are certain brain functions lateralized? Neuroscientists do not have the answer. However, several theories have

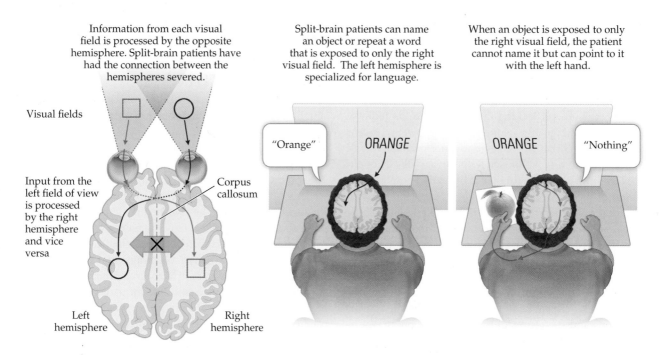

FIGURE 2.30 **Split-brain studies.** Close examination of split-brain patients revealed unique functions of each hemisphere.

been proposed. Perhaps, the old adage of "too many cooks in the kitchen" applies to some brain functions. For example, researchers have suggested that stuttering may be a result of having both hemispheres actively participating in language production (Fox et al., 2000). Or maybe it is just more economical to assign certain tasks to a specific hemisphere so that more can be accomplished with minimal brain activation (Halpern, Gunturkun, Hopkins, & Rogers, 2005).

Although the original split-brain patients are getting too advanced in age to continue participating in research, one of the final studies with these patients suggested that both hemispheres are necessary to make ethical judgments. In this study, both healthy and split-brain subjects were asked to make a moral judgment about a hypothetical case in which a person accidentally killed her boss with rat poison (thinking it was sugar) versus one in which she tried but failed to kill her boss with rat poison. In the split-brain subjects without a corpus callosum, the left hemisphere that processed language appeared to be unable to differentiate the two scenarios from an ethical perspective. To the split-brain subjects, both scenarios involved administering rat poison, so they were similar scenarios. Of course, most people would consider the employee's *intent to harm* the boss a factor distinguishing the scenarios. This finding suggests that the right hemisphere, also known to be involved in emotional processing, is instrumental in making complex decisions such as moral judgments (M. B. Miller et al., 2010). Thus, having two hemispheres on board may not be necessary for some simple tasks such as pointing but appears beneficial when making complex decisions—weighing evidence from many different perspectives to arrive at the most effective solutions.

CNS Security Systems

Although evidence now suggests that neurons continue to be produced throughout our lives, there is no assurance that new neurons will take over the lost functions of damaged brain tissue. In fact, considering the staggering number of debilitating brain injuries that occur worldwide each year, our brains are obviously vulnerable. To offer protection, the brain has developed an elaborate security system.

Cerebrospinal Fluid and the Ventricular System

In addition to the gray and white matter, the CNS contains a configuration of chambers known as **ventricles** that are filled with **cerebrospinal fluid (CSF)**. This clear fluid provides the appropriate chemical environment for the brain's cells. CSF is produced by the **choroid plexus**, a dense collection of small blood vessels located in the ventricles. Thus, as shown in Figure 2.31, the ventricular system includes the central canal, the four ventricles, and the CSF flowing through it. The CSF is in high production because 0.35 milliliters are produced per minute, 500 milliliters per day, so that the total volume in humans is renewed three times per day. It is eventually absorbed into the brain's blood supply. The CSF provides buoyancy and physical space that acts as a buffer when the brain is jolted as a result of sudden movement, a consistent environment for the brain's cells, and a drainage system for waste products.

Covering the outside of the brain and the spinal cord's fragile tissue are the **meninges**, a three-layer structure, similar to a tri-layer shower cap, stretched across the tissue. The outer layer, the **dura mater**, lies just beneath the skull and, along with the skull and vertebral column, provides another layer of protection for the CNS. The *arachnoid mater* (middle layer) has an underlying space with blood vessels running through it (similar to a spider's web, for which it was named). The **pia mater** is the layer immediately covering the brain's surface. As shown in Figure 2.32, the meninges extend to the spinal cord where they, along with the vertebrae, protect the vulnerable spinal cord.

Internal and External Surveillance Systems

Organisms clearly face many threats, and the delicate nervous system has evolved various means of protection. The meninges, skull, and spinal column offer physical defense

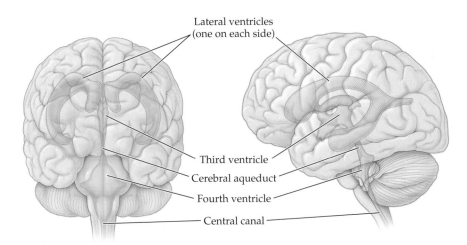

Lateral ventricles (one on each side)

Third ventricle

Cerebral aqueduct

Fourth ventricle

Central canal

FIGURE 2.31 Ventricles. Cerebrospinal fluid flows through the brain's four ventricles.

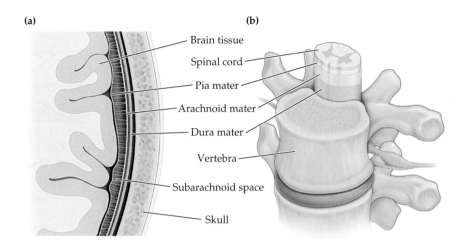

(a)   (b)

Brain tissue
Spinal cord
Pia mater
Arachnoid mater
Dura mater
Vertebra
Subarachnoid space
Skull

FIGURE 2.32 The nervous system's protective gear. (a) The brain is protected by the meninges and cerebrospinal fluid filling the space between the meninges and skull. (b) The vertebrae provide further protection for the spinal cord.

against harm, as we have seen. The sympathetic branch of the PNS produces the **stress response**, which helps guide both behavior and physiological responses to danger. The **immune system** continuously surveys the body and brain for evidence of invasions of pathogens (disease-causing agents) that can wreak havoc on the body's physiological systems.

The Stress Response As you sit quietly reading this text, your body is in a resting state. You are probably influenced more by your parasympathetic nervous system than by your sympathetic nervous system. Should you detect smoke coming in from under the door of your room, however, drastic changes would occur in your brain and body to enable you to escape the threat. Decisions about the safest escape path would need to be made, visual vigilance would be required to assess the distribution of the smoke, and an energized heart rate and muscles would be needed to enable you to escape the emergency quickly.

Once the brain perceives a stressor in the environment, the sympathetic nervous system activates the release of adrenaline (also known as epinephrine) from the adrenal medulla, located in the central portion of the adrenal gland. In addition, neural messages travel from various brain areas such as the prefrontal cortex and the amygdala to the hypothalamus, which in turn sends a chemical known as **corticotropin-releasing hormone** to the pituitary gland, prompting the release of **adrenocorticotropic hormone**. Adrenocorticotropic hormone travels through the blood to the adrenal gland, where it triggers the release of stress hormones known as **glucocorticoids** from the adrenal cortex. As a whole, this **hypothalamic–pituitary–adrenal axis** modulates cardiovascular responses, brain activity, and other physiological systems (see Figure 2.33). These stress-induced responses facilitate escape—in the form of fight or flight—from the threatening situation (Fink, 2009; Joels & Baram, 2009).

Once the threat is gone, the stress response must end so that physiological responses can return to their baseline levels (as you learned in the "Context Matters" feature with the running rats). This resting state has typically been called a homeostatic state (*homeo* referring to similar and *static* to condition), suggesting that physiological systems have ideal constant values that are maintained under healthy, nonthreatening conditions. The term **homeostasis** refers to the body's tendency to preserve this constant internal environment. Recent findings indicate, however, that few physiological systems are maintained at a constant state; indeed, our physiological responses vary depending on the situation (Sterling, 2004). Your cardiovascular system changes in response to sitting, walking, climbing steps, and running. Such change in response to varying demands is known as **allostasis**.

The stress response orchestrates energy distribution throughout the brain and body to facilitate survival of the impending threat. Because stress is often associated with excessive energy expenditure, cuts must be made to balance the physiological budget (Reese, Bhatnagar, & Young, 2009). Thus, energy typically directed toward more long-term investments, such as growth, reproduction, and immune functions, is redirected toward the immediate threat (Sapolsky, 2010). If stress continues for too long, the system becomes more difficult to manage and wears down, a process known as *allostatic overload*. When this occurs, the individual is at increased risk for various diseases.

According to the stress researcher Bruce McEwen, allostatic overload can be avoided if the intensity of the stress response is relative to the intensity of the actual stressor and if the stress response stops once the stress ends. Maintaining one's health so that the resources necessary to respond to stressful situations are available also decreases the likelihood of allostatic overload. Finally, it is beneficial to avoid environments that frequently or constantly activate stress responses. For people living in poverty with little control over their lives, it is virtually impossible to avoid allostatic overload (McEwen, 2009). Thus, although the stress response is essential to facilitate our escape from life-threatening situations, it must be kept in check to avoid harmful effects. The immune system, discussed next, is similar to the stress response system in that the very system built to protect you from dangerous substances can harm you if it gets out of control.

The Immune System To keep out potential invaders, the body has several barriers, including approximately 2 square meters of skin and an extensive network of mucosal-lined tracts in

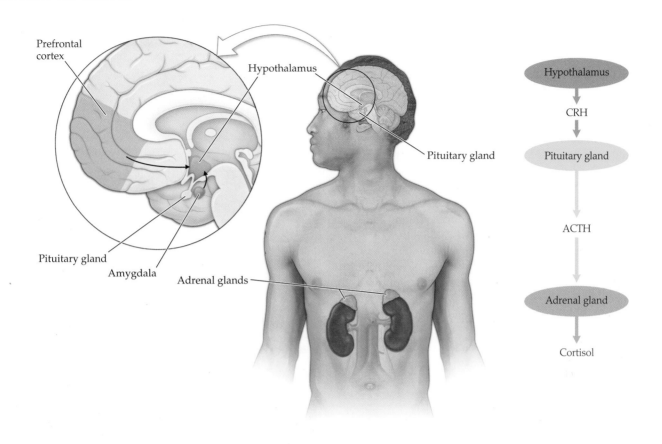

FIGURE 2.33 **The hypothalamic–pituitary–adrenal axis.** The hypothalamus, pituitary gland, and adrenal cortex regulate the stress response that is critical for survival.

the digestive system. If these boundaries are penetrated, the **innate immune system** dispatches cells such as **phagocytes** and **macrophages**, which indiscriminately engulf and digest pathogens via a process called **phagocytosis**. Microglia and astrocytes, which you learned about earlier in this chapter, are also important components of the innate immune system.

In addition to the innate immune system, a second component of the immune system allows the immune cells to adapt to unfamiliar threats—viruses, bacteria, and other dangerous substances. This **acquired immune system**, or **adaptive immune system**, was identified following an unorthodox experiment conducted by an 18th-century English country doctor. Dr. Edward Jenner observed that milkmaids who had been exposed to cowpox virus never seemed to be infected with the disfiguring and deadly smallpox virus. Thinking that the cowpox virus protected against the development of smallpox, he tested his theory by injecting a little boy first with cowpox virus and then with smallpox pus (see Figure 2.34). As Jenner suspected, the boy did not contract smallpox. We now see that the boy was vaccinated against smallpox (via the cowpox exposure) and subsequently developed immunity. In fact, *vacca* is Latin for cow, the origin of the term *vaccination*. Of course, strict ethical guidelines for medical research would prohibit such an experiment today.

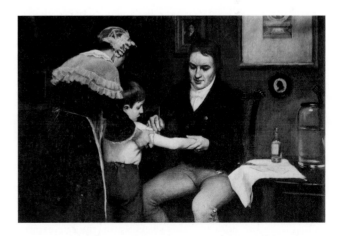

FIGURE 2.34 **First vaccination.** Acting on an idea that exposure to small amounts of a pathogen enabled the body to build resilience against the immunological threat, the European physician Edward Jenner exposed a young boy to fluid from a cowpox sore to provide protection against smallpox.

We now know that the immune system contains cells that have amazing memories for any past introductions to pathogens (viruses, bacteria, and so forth) so that, should a previously encountered pathogen ever enter the body again, the immune system is ready. **T cells** form in the bone marrow and then mature in the thymus (hence, the "T"), an immune organ below the neck region. These cells have specialized detection abilities and immediately migrate to the infected areas to kill the pathogens.

Another component of the adaptive immune system is a group of cells known as **B cells** because they originate in bone marrow. On recognizing a pathogen, B cells secrete a type of ammunition known as **antibodies** into the bloodstream. These specialized chemical missiles travel to the infected area to tag infected cells for T cells to destroy. Any substances leading to the production of antibodies are sometimes referred to as **antigens** (*anti* after antibody and *gen* after generator; Strebhardt & Ullrich, 2008). Thus, T cells and B cells work together to establish adaptive immunity by maintaining a memory of the pathogens following the first exposure (see Figure 2.35 for examples of different types of cells in the immune system).

As Jenner demonstrated, exposing an individual to a small amount of a pathogen gives the immune system a "heads up." Should the person encounter a more dangerous amount of the pathogen at a later date, the immune system will be ready for the attack.

Today, we know that the immune system is complex, with many different types of specialized cells that protect against invaders. Until the latter part of the 20th century, the disciplines of immunology and neuroscience were kept separate from one another. The dichotomy, however, between immune and nervous systems was viewed differently following the work of the behavioral neuroscientist Robert Ader and his immunologist colleague, Nicholas Cohen.

In the 1970s, Ader and Cohen conducted research with rats on conditioned taste aversion (the avoidance of substances that were paired with negative outcomes). Through drinking water that contained sugar to make the water more appealing, they administered a drug that would suppress the rats' immune systems (Ader & Cohen, 1975). In this straightforward study, Ader and Cohen demonstrated that the rats avoided the sweet water because of its association with the symptoms of sickness the drug produced.

The most interesting research finding came next, when the researchers used eyedroppers to administer the sweet water (to be certain that the rats actually consumed the substance to which they had developed an aversion). During this phase of the research, the drug was not added to the water; only sugar was added to the water to sweeten its taste. When forced to consume this sweet water, the rats experienced symptoms of sickness similar to those they had demonstrated during the experimental phase of the study, as if they were still consuming the drug. What was going on?

Based on his behavioral training, Ader realized that the rats had made an association between the sweet water and the drug during the experiment. For this association to occur, there had to be some cross-talk between the nervous system that detected the sweet taste of the water and the immune system that led to the sickness responses. Ader

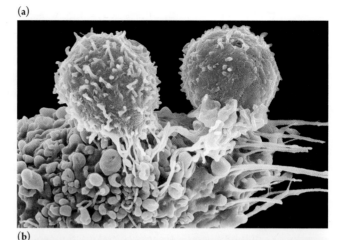

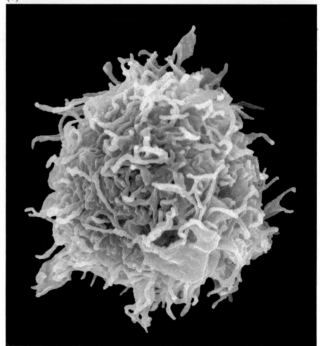

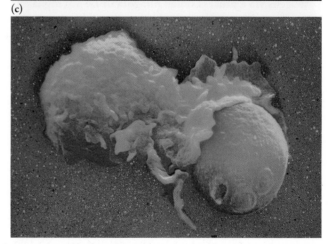

FIGURE 2.35 Immune cells. (a) T cells (shown attacking a cancer cell) and (b) B cells contribute to adaptive immunity, whereas (c) phagocytes (one shown engulfing a yeast cell) contribute to innate immunity.

and Cohen continued to work on this neuroimmune mystery, finding increasing evidence that the nervous system and immune function are closely integrated. Ader and his colleagues introduced the term **psychoneuroimmunology** to formally establish the connections among psychology, neuroscience, and the immune system (Ader, Cohen, & Felten, 1995).

In addition to establishing that the brain influences immune function throughout the body, researchers have recently focused on the brain's ability to protect itself against pathogens. Although the blood–brain barrier provides significant protection for the brain, backup surveillance is necessary to monitor the brain for signs of trauma or infection. As described earlier in the chapter, microglial cells, the most prevalent immune cells in the brain, take action when a brain injury is detected (Ousman & Kubes, 2012).

Representative immune cells from the body also migrate into the brain to aid in surveillance. For example, T cells can be found in the brain's CSF. However, even with substantial immune activity in the brain, the response is not as strong as that observed in the PNS. Because of its large size and enhanced exposure to the outside world and all of its threats, the body's peripheral components such as skin could be considered more of a battleground for pathogen exposure and injury than the more protected brain. The relatively weaker CNS immune response, compared with the PNS immune response, may explain why damaged CNS nerves do not regenerate nearly as readily as damaged PNS nerves regenerate. Apparently, the fast-acting immune cells in the PNS, including phagocytes (review Figure 2.35), do a better job at cleaning the damaged area and preparing the nerve for growth than CNS immune cells do (Popovich & Longbrake, 2008).

LABORATORY EXPLORATION

The Brain in Technicolor

Considering the vast number of cells in the nervous system, it is mind-boggling to comprehend how they all ultimately connect to form functioning neural networks. Clusters of neurons in the cerebellum, for example, form connections with populations of cell bodies in the prefrontal cortex. In humans, nearly 90 billion neurons must establish connections to various destinations across the brain. How they do so remains a mystery.

In the past, these networks have been difficult to observe visually. The histological technique introduced by the 19th-century researcher Camillo Golgi (described earlier in this chapter) provided valuable images of neurons, but the number of stained cells was sparse. Staining a few neurons helped scientists view the characteristics of a single neuron, but did not allow them to view complete neural networks. Even if more cells were stained, if they were the same color, the single cells would appear as a blur. Consequently, progress was slow toward producing a histological technique that provided more information about the connections of neurons. Recent technological advancements, however, have moved this field forward by taking advantage of fluorescent proteins found in jellyfish and coral.

When scientists insert these fluorescent protein genes into mouse genes, the mouse genes produce the fluorescent proteins. Working at Harvard University, microbiologist Jeff Lichtman has refined his technique to produce "fluorescing mice." These mice produce three proteins that can be randomly produced to tag each neuron with a distinctive color from about 100 different potential colors. This technique enables scientists to visualize different neurons in crowded brain regions. When the brains of these genetically engineered, or

transgenic, mice, known as Brainbow mice, are processed and viewed with high-resolution specialized microscopes, each neuron can easily be seen even in the midst of all its neighboring neurons (see Laboratory Exploration Figure 2.1).

Although these vivid images are impressive, researchers working with this technology currently face the challenge of having too much data. As you might imagine, staining the cell bodies, dendrites, and axons for all the neurons in the brain produces an inordinate amount of data. According to Lichtman, even if he had several dozen electron microscopes scanning brain tissue around the clock, it would take months or years to reconstruct all the connections in just a single mouse brain (Lehrer, 2009).

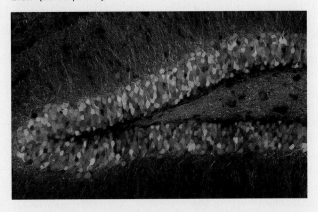

LABORATORY EXPLORATION FIGURE 2.1. Brainbow technology.
In contrast to the sparsely stained neurons using the Golgi staining technique, the Brainbow staining technique allows scientists to examine dense clusters of neurons in the brain.

Although the prospect of tracing all the neural connections in the human brain seems daunting, the National Institute of Mental Health has invested $40 million in this project, hoping it will reveal clues about various brain functions and mental illnesses. The *Human Connectome Project* will result in revealing structural and functional maps of the brain's neural wiring. Thus, there is cautious optimism that this project will reveal important information about the brain, with potential clinical applications such as cures for neurological diseases (Lichtman & Smith, 2008; Lichtman, Livet & Sines, 2008).

Conclusion

With so many cells and connections in the nervous system, organization is critically important. Consequently, brain organization was the theme of this chapter, which moved from the smallest functioning units of the brain in the form of neurons and glia to the most integrative neural networks, such as the autonomic nervous system, which process information from multiple neural sites.

In the CNS, clusters of similarly functioning neurons contribute to larger brain structures that become increasingly complex in more recently evolved brain areas. Whereas more similarities are observed across vertebrate brainstems, differing amounts of complexity are observed across vertebrate species in the higher cortical areas.

CNS tissue located along the spinal cord communicates with the body via a vast array of peripheral nerves that carry information back and forth from the environment to the CNS and from the CNS to the muscles. Peripheral nerves allow us to respond to an arousing situation and then quickly reestablish a more comfortable baseline. Working together, the delicately balanced CNS and PNS enable us to grab a cup of coffee in the morning, digest our lunch, text our friends about dinner plans, and strategize about effective study strategies for the upcoming week.

A few security systems help keep the nervous system healthy and effective. Physical protection comes in the form of the skull, vertebrae, meninges, and cerebrospinal fluid. Further protection from both external and internal threats is provided by the stress response and immune functions. If any of the physiological systems get out of balance, an individual becomes vulnerable to accidents, diseases, and illnesses. Thus, the exquisite choreography of the nervous system, with all of its complexity, contributes to our day-to-day survival with what seems like minimal effort. The effort, however, is anything but minimal. The brain is an energy hog, consuming a significant chunk of the body's energy.

KEY TERMS

biofeedback techniques (p. 32)
insular cortex (p. 32)
insula (p. 32)
cerebral cortex (p. 32)

The Building Blocks of the Nervous System

neuron (p. 33)
histological technique (p. 33)
soma (p. 34)
dendrites (p. 34)
axons (p. 34)
multipolar neurons (p. 34)
dendritic spines (p. 34)
axon hillock (p. 34)
myelin sheath (p. 34)
nodes of Ranvier (p. 34)
terminal ending (p. 35)
bipolar neuron (p. 35)
unipolar neuron (p. 35)
glia (p. 36)
astrocytes (p. 36)

blood–brain barrier (p. 36)
microglia (p. 36)
oligodendrocytes (p. 36)
Schwann cells (p. 37)
multiple sclerosis (p. 37)
cerebellum (p. 37)

Divisions of Labor in the Nervous System

ganglia (p. 38)
central nervous system (CNS) (p. 38)
peripheral nervous system (PNS) (p. 38)
tracts (p. 38)
nerves (p. 38)
afferent nerves (p. 38)
sensory neurons (p. 39)
motor neurons (p. 39)
interneurons (p. 39)
efferent nerves (p. 39)
cranial nerves (p. 39)
spinal nerves (p. 39)
dermatome (p. 39)

somatic nervous system (p. 39)
autonomic nervous system (p. 40)
sympathetic nervous system (p. 40)
parasympathetic nervous system (p. 40)
fight-or-flight response (p. 42)
neurogenesis (p. 44)
hormones (p. 45)

The Brain's Geography

rostral (p. 46)
anterior (p. 46)
caudal (p. 46)
posterior (p. 46)
dorsal (p. 46)
ventral (p. 46)
medial (p. 46)
lateral (p. 46)
proximal (p. 46)
distal (p. 46)
medulla oblongata (myelencephalon) (p. 46)
brainstem (p. 46)

REVIEW QUESTIONS

1. Explain the difference between the nerve net theory and the neuron doctrine. Which is a central tenet of modern neuroscience?

2. What is the most abundant type of glial cell in the nervous system? What are the functions of this type of glial cell?

3. How do sensory (afferent) nerves differ in function from motor (efferent) nerves?

4. Compare and contrast the functions of the sympathetic nervous system and the parasympathetic nervous system.

5. Name the four lobes of the human brain, and describe the functions of each lobe.

6. In what ways do scientists theorize that brain lateralization is adaptive?

7. What are the roles of the CSF and the ventricular system in protecting the brain against injury and infection?

CRITICAL-THINKING QUESTIONS

1. Based on your knowledge from this chapter, what do you think might be the most promising avenues for research to cure spinal cord injuries? What would the major challenges be in this research? Explain your answer.

2. In addition to the potential benefits of brain lateralization described in this chapter, what other potential benefits do you think that brain lateralization might confer to humans? Explain your answer.

3. Propose two important questions about the interactions between the nervous system and the immune system that would be important for future researchers to address. What methods should researchers use to address these questions? How would answers to these questions advance scientific knowledge?

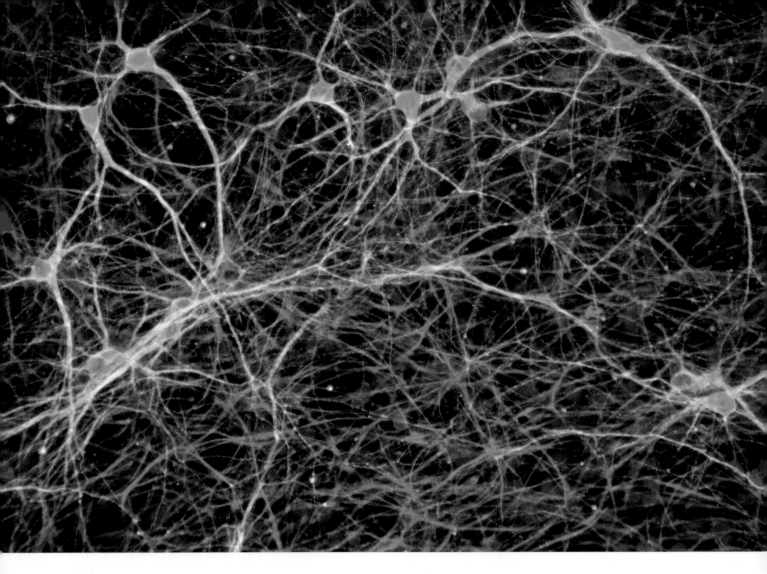

Cells and Circuits

Intuition, Hunches, and Self-Awareness: Potential Role of von Economo Neurons?

We have all been in situations in which we decided to do something and then had trouble explaining our decision to someone else. A business owner may feel confident about her hiring decision for the job of sales representative, although all of the candidates had similar credentials and experience. After meeting with the candidates, the owner may have a clear favorite and yet be unable to articulate her rationale to her regional managers. She may tell them instead that she had a "gut feeling" that the person would be the best for the job.

Although we all make some decisions based on "hunches," seemingly without conscious reasoning, the process of making such decisions is challenging to study systematically in the laboratory. However, one experimental task known as the Iowa Gambling Task has enabled researchers to explore these hunches from an experimental perspective (Bechara, Damasio, Tranel, & Damasio, 1997).

One version of the Iowa Gambling Task involved four decks of cards (A, B, C, and D). Each subject began with $2,000 (in pretend money). Subjects were told that they would receive an immediate reward (either $100 or $50) when they selected a card from each deck. However, in an unpredictable manner, some card selections were accompanied by a financial penalty. Although the subjects were

not informed of the odds of winning or losing money in this task, two decks (A and B) were more likely to yield the higher payoff ($100) but were also more likely to result in a high financial penalty. By contrast, the remaining two decks (C and D) had a lower payoff ($50) but were more likely to result in a lower financial penalty, yielding more money overall over the course of the experiment.

How did healthy subjects respond? During the experiment, a measure known as the **skin conductance response (SCR)** indicated a heightened emotional response characterized by increased electrodermal activity in the palms of the subjects (e.g., sweaty palms). The researchers reported that after healthy subjects had selected a few of the cards that were associated with the higher financial penalty, they began to exhibit an SCR prior to selecting another card from that deck. Subsequently, they started avoiding the decks with the higher financial penalty (decks A and B). But when asked to describe their response strategy early in the task (after selecting about 20 cards), they typically reported having no clue what was going on—although their bodies were exhibiting a heightened emotional response to the "risky" decks. After selecting about 50 cards, the subjects conveyed that they had a hunch that certain decks were riskier than others. After selecting about 80 cards, subjects had started to conceptualize the payoffs and penalties associated with all of the decks and the advantages of selecting from decks C and D.

However, when patients who had experienced frontal lobe damage completed this task, different results emerged. These subjects never showed anticipatory SCRs or adopted a strategy of bypassing the risky A and B decks for the higher-payoff C and D decks. It appeared that the neural circuits enabling messages from the emotional areas of the brain to reach brain areas involved in decision making were disrupted (Bechara et al., 1997; Turnbull, Bowan, Shanker, & Davies, 2014).

Behind the Scenes

The findings from the Iowa Gambling Task suggest that in certain situations, the brain is taking in information and making decisions at a pace faster than our conscious awareness can process. This suggests that our hunches that we generally think of as vague and unsubstantiated may be just the opposite—a result of efficient neural processing occurring at a pace that is difficult for us to keep up with. A *gut feeling* appears to be an emotional or body perception (indicated by physiological reactions like SCRs) that is being monitored by the brain's decision-making areas via the establishment of formidable neural networks.

One particular type of neuron in the brain's neural networks, the **von Economo neuron,** may be crucial in our ability to make quick intuitive judgments about seemingly random events. Named after the researcher who formally identified the cells in 1925, these bipolar neurons are larger than typical neurons and have two similarly sized dendrites extending from the cell body (Allman et al., 2010; von Economo & Koskinas, 1925; see Figure 3A). Complex information is more likely to be coded in neural networks than in individual neurons. Von Economo neurons and their connections within neural networks seem to play a key role in an individual's ability to make quick, intuitive assessments of complex situations.

The von Economo neurons, sometimes called spindle cells, are located in the *anterior cingulate cortical area* and the *frontoinsular cortical area* of the brain. They are about five times denser in the right hemisphere than in the left hemisphere. In contrast to most other neurons in humans, von Economo neurons appear late in fetal brain development—in the 35th week of pregnancy (Allman et al., 2011; Allman, Watson, Tetreault, & Hakeem, 2005).

fMRI studies yield clues as to which brain regions are involved in intuition. As described in Chapter 1, the fMRI research technique assesses the functions of different brain regions by determining which brain regions are "activated" as human research participants perform a specified (typically cognitive) task. As a participant performs a task, the fMRI technique detects associated changes in the blood flow to different regions of his or her brain. One fMRI study revealed that two brain areas activated during fast-paced decisions based on hunches and "intuitive thinking" are the anterior cingulate and frontoinsular cortical areas, in which von Economo neurons are located (Critchley, Mathias, & Dolan, 2001).

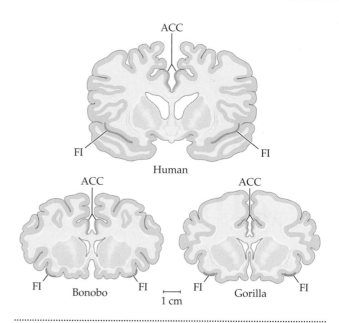

FIGURE 3A von Economo neurons. The von Economo neurons may enable us to make quick, intuitive judgments about seemingly random events. They are located in the anterior cingulate cortical area and the frontoinsular cortical area of the brain.

Thus, evidence suggests that during complex intuitive responses, the von Economo neurons in the anterior cingulate and frontoinsular cortical areas are likely engaged. Initial reports that von Economo neurons were found only in the highly evolved brains of humans and great apes solidified our understanding of von Economo neurons as involved in advanced, complex social interactions and interpretations (Allman et al., 2010). However, scientists have recently discovered von Economo neurons in other primate species such as the macaque monkey, as well as in nonprimate mammalian species that may have advanced social interactions—specifically, elephants and dolphins (Butti, Sherwood, Hakeem, Allman, & Hof, 2009; Evrard, Forro, & Logothetis, 2012; Hakeem et al., 2009).

Although many questions persist about the von Economo neurons, researchers are identifying neurobiological mechanisms that provide the basis of our intuitions and hunches, which have been difficult to capture in laboratory investigations. More research is needed before we can make more definitive claims about von Economo neurons. This research question is so intriguing that it inspired my lab to search for von Economo neurons in another mammal with impressive cognitive strategies, the raccoon. Did we find them? Those findings appear in the epilogue of this book. ▶

What mechanisms underlie the functioning of the neurons that make up the brain's tissue? In this chapter, after learning how a single neuron operates, you will learn about the mechanisms of communication among neurons. In addition, you will see how neurons collaborate with other brain cells to form **neural circuits** that produce behavioral and physiological responses. The importance of appropriately functioning neural circuits becomes clear, as you will see, when threats such as epileptic seizures disrupt these neural circuits. We will explore how the brain's cells and circuits work seamlessly to produce the behavioral functions that are necessary for surviving and living meaningful lives. Such functions range from grasping a ripe fruit from a tree branch to sympathizing with a friend who is having a bad day.

Neurons: Structure and Function

As discussed in Chapter 2, the landmark research of Santiago Ramón y Cajal and Camillo Golgi led to the eventual identification of neurons as the individual cellular units of the nervous system. This was only the beginning of the journey toward understanding the complex lives of neurons. Cajal never missed an opportunity to view neurons, even setting up a microscope on his kitchen table and revisiting his neurons after dinner each evening (Rapport, 2005) (see Figure 3.1). When he was invited to give a lecture to the English Royal Society in 1894, his host, the British physiologist Charles Sherrington, was eager to discuss the neuronal doctrine with him. True to his character, Cajal set up a makeshift laboratory in Sherrington's guest room. Even with Cajal's devotion to his microscope, however, Sherrington found time to discuss the characteristics of the neuron with his colleague. Sherrington was especially interested in the controversial topic of a "gap" between neurons that Cajal had mentioned in his lecture. Cajal did not have microscopes with a sufficiently high magnification to actually see such a gap, but his endless observations of neuronal networks prompted him to suggest the notion of a gap separating the neurons.

Sherrington introduced a more formal term for the proposed gap between neurons when he compiled material to be included in Michael Foster's 1897 edition of *Textbook of Physiology.* **Synapse,** meaning "to clasp," is the term still used today to describe the minuscule gap between neurons (Rapport, 2005). However, more questions continued to emerge: How did one neuron communicate with another, especially given the fact that neurons do not actually touch one another? What "language" did a neuron use to speak to a neighboring cell? What activated a neuron—and, conversely, what inhibited it? Throughout the 20th century, improved microscopes and more advanced recording technologies revealed important answers.

The Neuron's Microstructure

As we saw in Chapter 2, the neuron has all of the standard components that are found in other cell types located throughout the body, devoted to managing the general workings of the cell. However, axons and dendrites, specialized extensions projecting from the cell body, are structures unique to the neuron. Early-20th-century scientists struggled to identify the specific characteristics and functions of axons and dendrites.

An examination of the axon reveals an interesting neuroarchitecture. The cell **membrane** is composed of a

(a)

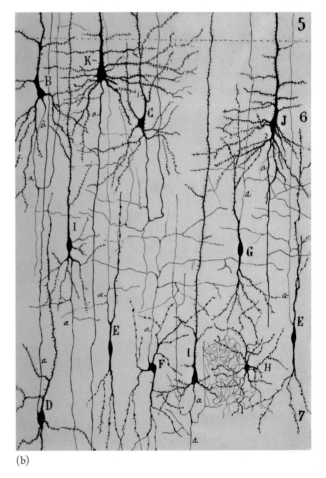

(b)

FIGURE 3.1 Santiago Ramón y Cajal. (a) Cajal adapted Golgi's neuronal stain to examine brain tissue. (b) Cajal drew accurate depictions of various forms of neurons in the brains of different species.

double layer of phospholipids that isolates the cell's inner components from the extracellular fluid. This membrane contains a phosphate head region that is hydrophilic (attracted to water) and a tail that is hydrophobic (oriented away from water and toward the inside of the layer). The cell membrane is also porous, containing various channels that either remain open or can be triggered to open. **Ion channels,** made from proteins, are pores in the neuronal cell membrane. In many cases, ion channels are specific to certain **ions,** or charged molecules. Channels characterized by ion selectivity, for example, may be *selectively permeable* to potassium (i.e., allow potassium to pass through the membrane more freely than other molecules). Most ion channels are **gated ion channels,** meaning that they open and close based on the environmental conditions around the membrane.

As seen in Figure 3.2, an unequal distribution of sodium and potassium ions is present in the interior and exterior of the cell. The distribution of ions is strategically managed to contribute to the optimal functioning of the membrane. In addition to the selectively permeable ion channels, the membrane contains **ion pumps** that play an essential role in the distribution of ions inside and outside the neuron. Throughout this chapter, we will discuss the importance of the distribution of ions across the cellular membrane.

Although dendrites share some properties with axons, such as cell membranes and ion channels, they also possess many other unique, essential features. As we learned in Chapter 2, dendritic spines are tiny protrusions that extend

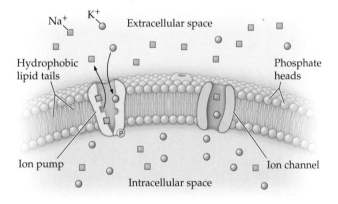

FIGURE 3.2 Ion movement through cell membrane. The semipermeable cell membrane composed of a double layer of phospholipids and strategically placed sodium–potassium pumps contributes to the unequal distribution of sodium ions (Na^+) and potassium ions (K^+) inside and outside the cell.

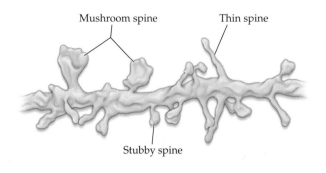

FIGURE 3.3 Diversity of dendritic spines. Dendritic spines come in varied forms, most often categorized as stubby, thin, or mushroom in shape.

from the dendrite. The synapse typically comprises the space between one axon terminal and a dendritic spine. The dendritic spines, providing opportunities for synaptic connections with other neurons, vary in size and shape. Some are fine filopodialike extensions (thin spines), others are short (stubby spines), and still others have a large, bulbous head (mushroom spines); see Figure 3.3.

Moreover, dendritic spines can change their shapes over time. When rats are placed in an enriched environment, the dendritic spines appear to be flexible, or plastic, in response to changes in the rats' environment (Holtmaat & Svoboda, 2009). For example, my colleagues and I have found that dendritic spines become increasingly dense in the hippocampal area of pregnant rats (Kinsley et al., 2006). These changing connections, created by modified dendritic spines, contribute to the establishment of neural circuits in the brain. As we will discuss in Chapter 12, these circuits are composed of axons and their terminal endings, dendrites and their spines, and the synapses they form. The circuits constantly change as the brain learns to adapt to new challenges as necessary for survival.

The sensory neurons, motor neurons, and interneurons that were introduced in Chapter 2 are the building blocks for the brain's neural circuits. As information travels to and from the CNS via these specialized neurons, our experiences facilitate processing speed by influencing neural plasticity and modifying the synapses between neurons. This occurs via the promotion of cellular changes such as modifications to the shape of dendritic spines. The study described in this chapter's "Context Matters" provides evidence that a pregnant rat's social context influences the context of her uterus where the fetal rats are developing, resulting in alterations in measures such as dendritic length and spine density in her offspring. Thus, the building of neural networks based on the brain's external and internal environment starts early in an animal's life.

CONTEXT MATTERS

Social Distress and Neuronal Connections

Featured study: Mychasiuk, R., Gibb, R., & Kolb, B. (2011). Prenatal bystander stress induces neuroanatomical changes in the prefrontal cortex and hippocampus of developing rat offspring. Brain Research, 1412, 55–62. doi:10.1016/j.brainres.2011.07.023

The rapid period of neuronal growth during fetal development provides a unique opportunity for researchers to explore variables that disrupt neural functions. Accordingly, researchers have investigated the internal contexts (i.e., intrauterine environments) created by exposing pregnant rats to various prenatal stressors. Most often, researchers expose pregnant rats to **restraint stress,** in which the rats are confined in small tubes for a few hours (C. M. McCormick, Smythe, Sharma, & Meaney, 1995). Richelle Mychasiuk, Robin Gibb, and Bryan Kolb at the University of Lethbridge wondered whether prenatal neural development would be disrupted if the pregnant rat were exposed to indirect, as opposed to direct, stress. For example, what would happen if the pregnant rat were exposed to "bystander stress" (i.e., merely housed with a rat that was experiencing a direct form of stress, rather than experiencing it herself)?

These researchers designed a study in which five pregnant rats were exposed to bystander stress (experimental group) during gestational days 12–16 and five pregnant rats were exposed to no stress (control group). The gestational period for rats is 21 days, much shorter than that of many other mammals. Each pregnant rat was housed in a cage with a nonpregnant rat.

The nonpregnant rat cage-mates were stressed by being placed on a small elevated platform and exposed to a bright light for 30 minutes twice a day (Context Matters Figure 3.1). The nonpregnant cage-mates of the control pregnant rats were simply removed from the cage for the same 30-minute period twice a day. When the females in the experimental group (who had been exposed to bystander stress) delivered their pups, they were housed individually with their pups.

The rat pups from the experimental (bystander stress) and control groups were allowed to develop until 21 days after their birth, at which time they are typically weaned from their

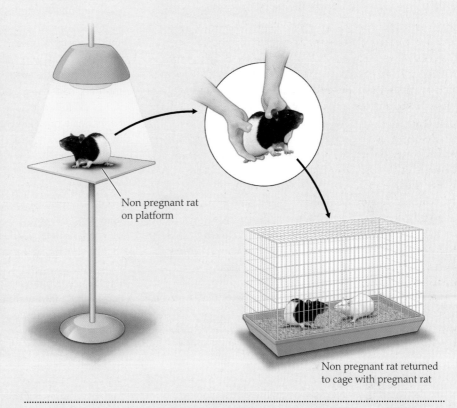

Non pregnant rat on platform

Non pregnant rat returned to cage with pregnant rat

CONTEXT MATTERS FIGURE 3.1　Causing rats stress. In this study, a rat was stressed by being placed on a small elevated platform under a bright light for two 30-minute sessions daily before being placed back in the home cage with a pregnant cage-mate.

mothers. They were then sacrificed so that their brains could be prepared for histological processing using the Golgi and cresyl violet stains. Recall from Chapter 2 that the Golgi stain marks the entire neuron (Context Matters Figure 3.2); alternatively, the cresyl violet stain only marks the cell bodies.

The brains were then sliced or sectioned in the medial prefrontal cortex, the orbitofrontal cortex, and the dorsal area of the hippocampus. These brain areas have previously been shown in rats to be affected by stress (McKittrick et al., 2000; Radley & Sawchenko, 2011) and are also known in rats, humans, and monkeys to be involved in emotional and learning processes, including decision making (Abela & Chudasama, 2013; Alexander & Brown, 2011). After each brain area was examined under the microscope, several neuronal measures, such as dendritic length and spine density, were recorded for the experimental (bystander stress) and control groups.

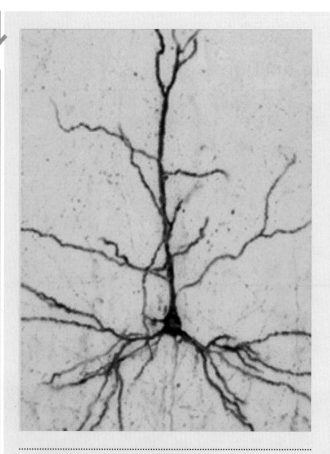

CONTEXT MATTERS FIGURE 3.2 **Golgi stain.** The Golgi stain is absorbed by the entire neuron. This technique provided the first accurate images of neurons.

Did the bystander stress create an environmental context that affected the maternal rats and their developing pups? The results showed that bystander stress was unrelated to the duration of the pregnancy or the number of pups delivered. Bystander stress was, however, associated with differences in the pups' developing neurons—emphasizing just how sensitive these neurons are to their prenatal conditions. Among the many fascinating effects observed were decreased dendritic length and increased spine density in the orbitofrontal cortex of both male and female pups in the experimental (bystander stress) group, compared with the same measures in pups in the control group. Increased spine density increases potential synaptic sites with other neurons and may serve as a compensation for the decreased dendritic length. In the hippocampus, female pups whose mothers had experienced bystander stress during pregnancy exhibited increased spine density and a lower neuron count. Male pups whose pregnant mother had experienced bystander stress also exhibited increased spine density but did not exhibit a lower neuron count (Context Matters Figure 3.3).

These findings provide evidence that bystander stress—being in the mere presence of another animal that had experienced stress—did indeed alter the neuronal architecture in developing rats. Overall, females seemed to be more affected than the males, and many of the changes were different for male and female pups. The results suggest that both the external social context (stressed cage-mate) and the internal context (the intrauterine environment that influences male and female development) interact to alter the cellular characteristics of the developing pups. It would be interesting for future research to assess whether such differences in neuronal architecture are related to differences in the behavior of the pups. That is, would the behavior of pups in the experimental (bystander stress) group differ from that of the pups in the control group? If so, how?

CONTEXT MATTERS FIGURE 3.3
Bystander stress. The bystander stress experienced by the pups' mothers during pregnancy increased dendritic spines in the orbital prefrontal cortex, medial prefrontal cortex, and hippocampus in all groups, potentially increasing sites for synapses and altering the stress neural circuits.

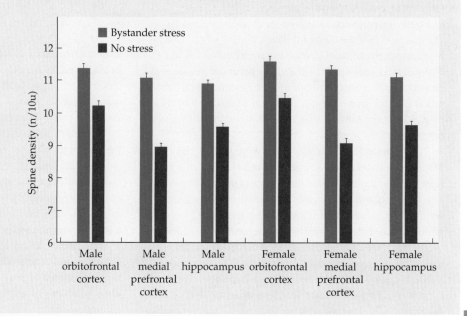

The Neuron's Resting Membrane Potential

When a neuron is at rest, its **membrane potential** (the difference in charge between the inside and outside of a cell) is regulated by the distributions of sodium (Na^+) and potassium (K^+) ions previously described. Specifically, a neuron's resting membrane maintains a gradient whereby positively charged Na^+ ions are much higher in concentration in the **extracellular space** (outside of the neuron) than in the **intracellular space** (inside of the neuron), and K^+ ions are higher in concentration in the cell's intracellular space than in the cell's extracellular space (refer back to Figure 3.2).

Negatively charged chloride ions (Cl^-) and positively charged calcium ions (Ca^{2+}) are found in the extracellular space (and play a more limited role in regulating a neuron's membrane potential when it is at rest; D. A. McCormick, 1999). The unequal distribution of ions contributes to a negative polarity of the resting membrane—typically about −50 to −80 millivolts (a millivolt is a standard unit of energy equal to 1/1,000 of a volt) as measured by cellular recordings—known as the **resting membrane potential.**

The neuron's resting membrane potential is maintained by several mechanisms. The resting membrane's selective permeability to potassium, for example, allows K^+ ions to flow through the membrane at a moderate rate through K^+ ion channels, but restricts the flow of Na^+ ions through the membrane to a very low rate (since the Na^+ ion channels are closed when the membrane is at rest). The varying distribution of ions inside and outside of the axon determines the **concentration gradient.**

To balance the unequal distribution of ions inside and outside of the axon, ions diffuse from an area of greater ionic density to an area of sparser ionic density. By analogy, consider that if a perfume bottle is opened in one corner of the room, the perfume particles will diffuse across the room as they move from areas of greater perfume particle density to areas of sparser perfume particle density. In nature, an

electrical gradient, in which oppositely charged particles attract, is also at work. As a result, at some point, the K^+ ions in our discussion of the resting membrane potential are drawn back into the negatively charged intracellular space of the neuron. Table 3.1 sums the effects of the concentration and electrical gradients on the different types of ion.

Na^+ ion channels are closed to the flow of Na^+ ions when a neuron is at rest. Another mechanism known as the **sodium–potassium pump** (a type of ion pump) plays an important role in maintaining the unequal distribution of Na^+ ions and K^+ ions across the membrane (see Figure 3.4). Sodium–potassium pumps are specialized membrane protein channels that transport three Na^+ ions out of the cell for every two K^+ ions they transport into the cell. This provides a net exit of positive Na^+ ions to the extracellular space.

The sodium–potassium pump is an active transport system that is fueled by the high-energy molecule adenosine triphosphate, in contrast to the passive transport system of ion flow that occurs through open ion channels in the membrane. Given the membrane's lack of selective permeability for Na^+ ions in its resting state, the sodium–potassium pumps help keep Na^+ ions in the neuron's extracellular space when they do not easily cross the membrane on their own. This function, however, comes at a great cost because approximately 40% of the neuron's metabolic resources are used to operate these pumping sites (Erecinska & Dagani, 1990).

Why would neurons not be electrically neutral at rest? A neuron's negative resting membrane potential prepares it to fire strongly and rapidly in response to a stimulus. Why does the brain divert so many resources to maintaining the resting membrane potential during the time when the neuron may be viewed as running at idle speed? The answer is that responding to environmental challenges is critical for survival, and so neurons must be ready to respond quickly to a stimulus. In a sense, maintaining the resting membrane potential ensures that a neuron is relaxed, yet poised to respond to the next critical message in the nervous system.

TABLE 3.1.

Resting Membrane Potential

RESTING MEMBRANE	SODIUM IONS (NA⁺)	POTASSIUM IONS (K⁺)	CALCIUM IONS (CA²⁺)	CHLORIDE IONS (CL⁻)
Concentration gradient	Draws into cell (more concentrated outside)	Pushes out of cell (more concentrated inside)	Draws into cell (more concentrated outside)	Draws into cell (more concentrated outside)
Electrical gradient	Draws into negatively charged cell interior	Draws into negatively charged cell interior	Draws into negatively charged cell interior	Pushes out of negatively charged cell interior
Effect	Flows into cell when its ion channels open		Ion channels usually closed	

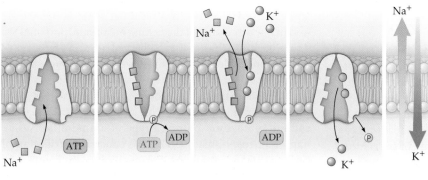

1. Three sodium ions bind to pump

2. Phosphate breaks off ATP and binds to pump, causing pump to open and release the sodium ions outside the cell

3. As sodium ions exit, pump binds two potassium ions

4. Channel releases phosphate and shuts to the outside, re-opening to the inside of the cell and releasing potassium ions there

FIGURE 3.4 **Sodium-potassium pump.** Sodium-potassium pumps located on the cell membrane help maintain the unequal distribution of sodium and potassium in the intracellular and extracellular spaces during the resting membrane potential.

The Action Potential

Given the nervous system's massive complexity, it is difficult to single out the most critical element for effective neural functioning. However, the nerve impulse, known as the **action potential,** is a prime candidate for this distinction. The action potential is triggered in response to relevant and meaningful information, whether it originates from the environment (e.g., a bright light or shrill sound) or from another neuron (as part of a neural network).

Suppose an interneuron, stimulated by an individual's visual perception of an intruder entering a building, is activated and sends a message to another neuron in a relevant emotional response neural circuit. This message will cause the neuron that receives the message to alter its membrane potential. If the message from the interneuron is weak—perhaps the threat of the intruder has diminished—it is likely that the neuron will not respond.

As shown in Figure 3.5, a mild stimulation from a microelectrode may alter a neuron's membrane potential by making its inside less negative (**depolarization**) or more negative (**hyperpolarization**). However, after these modest changes in membrane potential, the neuron quickly drifts back to its original resting membrane potential. Yet, if the stimulation is sufficiently strong, the neuron will respond with a larger depolarization or hyperpolarization. The neuron has a **threshold** (typically around −55 millivolts), a membrane potential that must be reached to trigger an action potential. Thus, if a neuron is resting at −70 millivolts and incoming neural messages change the membrane potential so that it is at −55 millivolts, this message would meet the criterion for response and would, almost instantaneously, trigger an action potential.

Once the action potential is set in motion, the depolarization continues with the inside of the cell reaching a potential of close to +40 millivolts. This rapid depolarization is achieved as a result of the opening of ion channels in the cell membrane that allows Na$^+$ ions to enter the cell. With the concentration gradients and electrical gradients luring sodium to the inside, the Na$^+$ ions rush into the cell when

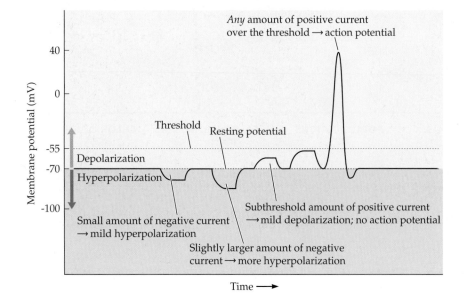

FIGURE 3.5 **Depolarization and hyperpolarization.** When a neuron is stimulated, the membrane potential must depolarize to a specific threshold level before an action potential is activated.

the ion channels open. These ion channels have a high density and are industrious. Given that a single ion channel can transport up to 100 million ions per second when it is open (as reviewed in Gadsby, 2009), it is important for these ion channels to open and close at precisely the right time. Local anesthetic drugs such as Xylocaine and Novocain work by manipulating the movement of Na^+ ions within a patient's nervous system. These drugs block the sodium channels, thereby blocking the influx of sodium as well as the message telling the patient that he or she is experiencing pain (Ragsdale, McPhee, Scheuer, & Catterall, 1994).

The sodium ion channels are **voltage-gated ion channels,** meaning that they open and close in response to changes in the membrane potential. A joke among neuroscientists is that the neuronal membrane was the first "gated community." Even before these voltage-gated channels were visualized, Alan Hodgkin and Andrew Huxley, physiologists at Cambridge University (Figure 3.6), proposed their existence. Their informed predictions about the ionic flow associated with varying membrane potentials, proposed after extensive work with giant squid nerve fibers, was recognized in 1963 when they were awarded the Nobel Prize (Shepherd, 1991).

Although the cell membrane also contains voltage-gated K^+ ion channels, these respond more slowly to depolarization than the voltage-gated Na^+ ion channels. Therefore, the voltage-gated K^+ ion channels open after the Na^+ ion channels. During the action potential sequence, once the depolarization threshold is reached, the Na^+ ion channels open to allow a massive influx of Na^+ ions into the cell. This event is typically allowed to occur for only about a single millisecond, after which a **refractory period** occurs.

The refractory period sets a maximum limit on a neuron's firing frequency. Throughout the refractory period, the membrane's permeability to Na^+ ions is low. The first part of

the refractory period is described as being *absolute*, during which no amount of stimulation can trigger an action potential. The second part of the refractory period is described as being *relative*, during which a greater change in membrane potential than usual is required to trigger an action potential.

With the degree of depolarization now meeting the criterion level for the voltage-gated K^+ channels to open, the focus shifts to K^+ ions. Since the inside of the cell is now positively charged because of the massive immigration of Na^+ ions, the electrical and concentration gradients drive the freely moving K^+ ions out of the cell. This exit of K^+ ions forces the cell membrane back to its resting membrane potential level. In addition, this prompts the closing of the K^+ ion channels, but not before overshooting the initial −70-millivolt potential as the final K^+ ion channels close. This is the mechanism behind the process of hyperpolarization. As seen in Figure 3.7, the changes in membrane potential are regulated by the specific movement of Na^+ and K^+ ions.

Once the action potential has been triggered, it must travel down the axon to the axon terminal. This neural propagation is similar to one of those elaborate domino displays in which the dominos are set up perfectly, so that when a single domino falls, it triggers a chain reaction down the line. In this chain reaction, because the preceding domino has already been knocked down, the falling force can move in only one direction (forward). Similarly, the spreading

(a)

(b)

....

FIGURE 3.6 Nobel Prize–winning neuroscientists. (a) Alan Hodgkin and (b) Andrew Huxley were awarded the Nobel Prize in 1963 for their pioneering work identifying the contribution of voltage-gated channels in the neurons of the giant squid.

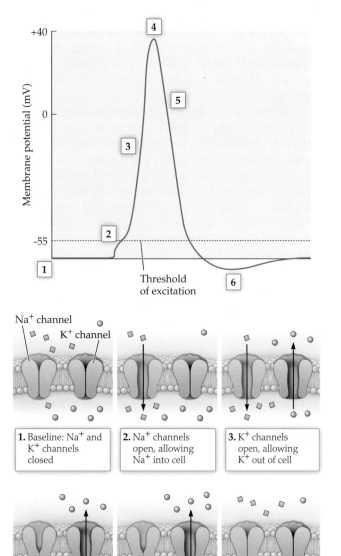

1. Baseline: Na⁺ and K⁺ channels closed

2. Na⁺ channels open, allowing Na⁺ into cell

3. K⁺ channels open, allowing K⁺ out of cell

4. Refractory period: Na⁺ channels close, preventing Na⁺ from entering cell

5. K⁺ channels remain open; K⁺ outflow continues

6. K+ channels close; system resets

FIGURE 3.7 Ion movement in action potentials. Each stage of the action potential is accompanied by differential movement of sodium and potassium ions through the appropriate ion channels.

wave of depolarization alters the membrane potential in the next area of the axon's membrane. Because the preceding area is in a refractory period, the depolarization will not generate or propagate itself backward.

Axon diameter is positively correlated with the speed of the action potential, or *conduction velocity*. The much-studied giant squid axon is the prototypical example of an axon with a very fast conduction velocity (Adrian, 1975; Rosenthal & Bezanilla, 2002). Axons regulating the more essential life functions have evolved rather large axon diameters for fast

conduction velocity (Assaf, Blumenfeld-Katzir, Yovel, & Basser, 2008; Hursh, 1939; Waxman, Kocsis, & Stys, 1995).

The nervous system has another fundamental property that enhances conduction velocity in myelinated axons. (Note that in completely *unmyelinated* axons, cable conduction occurs. That is, the action potential at one location of the membrane stimulates the next location to produce a new action potential, a process that continues down the entire axon membrane.) In myelinated axons, the myelin sheath (described in Chapter 2) increases the speed of the action potential by forcing the impulse to jump from one node of Ranvier to another node of Ranvier, that is, from one short unmyelinated section of axon to another. This jumping movement is known as **saltatory conduction** (after *saltere*, Latin for "to jump"). Saltatory conduction greatly enhances the speed of neural processing by allowing the action potential to jump ahead to the next node of Ranvier, just as tossing a ball to every fifth person down a long line of people is faster than passing it from one person to the next person.

Saltatory conduction is possible because of the insulation provided by two types of glial cells, which build myelin sheaths that wrap around and insulate axons: oligodendrocytes and Schwann cells. Oligodendrocytes extend their processes to wrap around axon segments in the CNS (Figure 3.8a), whereas Schwann cells wrap around axons in the PNS (Figure 3.8b). The nodes of Ranvier, critical for saltatory conduction, are formed between the units of myelin that these glial cells provide. Voltage-gated Na⁺ channels cluster in these nodes of Ranvier to promote saltatory conduction.

The need for mechanisms to increase the speed of neural conduction is especially great in the case of longer vertebrate neurons. For example, the axons of the human sciatic nerve, which extend from the base of the spine to the big toe, require this saltatory conduction to allow your toes to

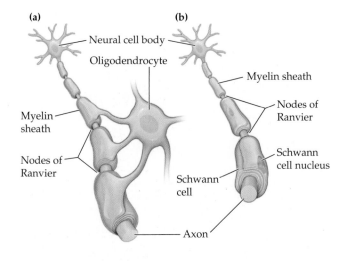

FIGURE 3.8 Components of the myelin sheath. Specialized glial cells form the myelin sheath. (a) Oligodendroglia processes create segments of the central nervous system myelin sheath. (b) Schwann cells wrap around the neural processes to form individual segments of the peripheral nervous system myelin sheath.

respond to stimuli (e.g., stubbing) in a timely manner. These axons of the sciatic nerve are the longest axons in humans; they extend up to a meter in length. Neural impulses making the long journey up and down the neck of a giraffe also require fast neural speed.

In some neurons, the action potential is initiated in the axon hillock, whereas in other neurons, the action potential originates in the axon initial segment, which is about 30 micrometers down from the axon hillock (Colbert & Johnston, 1996). A neuron's **spike-initiation zone** is the area in that neuron in which the action potential is initiated. Revisiting the domino example, you may have noted that, once the movement of dominos is initiated, the dominos fall at a consistent speed (rather than some dominos falling immediately and others wobbling back and forth before finally hitting the flat surface). This principle of consistent speed also holds for the action potential. Regardless of the strength of the initiating stimulus, the intensity of the action potential is set and that intensity remains constant as the action potential moves down the axon. Furthermore, as long as the membrane potential reaches the threshold value, an action potential occurs. However, if the membrane potential does not reach the threshold value, no action potential is triggered. This principle is known as the **all-or-none law.**

The Cambridge University neurophysiologist Edgar Adrian (Figure 3.9) discovered evidence for the all-or-none law. The Nobel Prize for Physiology in 1932 was awarded jointly to Adrian and Charles Sherrington (mentioned earlier in this chapter) in recognition of their respective discoveries regarding the functions of neurons (Finger, 2000).

In addition to facilitating saltatory conduction, the myelin sheath provides insulation for the axons. However, this evolutionary advancement comes with a cost. If myelin is missing or degenerated in a given individual's nervous system (or in part of it), the action potential is halted because of a lack of sodium channels in the spaces previously occupied by the myelin. As we saw in Chapter 2, this is the case in multiple sclerosis, a neurodegenerative disease that impairs the ability of the brain and spinal cord neurons to communicate effectively with one another. To treat conditions such as multiple sclerosis, researchers have been exploring factors that initiate the growth of new myelin to encapsulate the existing healthy neurons. The reproductive hormone **progesterone,** for example, is showing promise as a means of facilitating the remyelination of axons affected by demyelinating diseases such as multiple sclerosis (Hussain et al., 2011).

Synaptic Transmission

Thus far in this chapter, we have discussed a great deal of basic information about neurons: the subunits of the membrane, the functions of ion channels, the importance of depolarizing membrane potentials, and the strategies utilized to increase the speed of neural processing. Even so, we have not yet described how neurons actually communicate with one another.

For the billions of neurons in our brains to build the circuits required to direct our behavior in various situations, as well as maintain the many physiological functions necessary for survival, an efficient mode of neuron-to-neuron communication is necessary. In this section, we will examine the underlying mechanisms of **synaptic transmission,** the process by which a neuron communicates with another neuron or neurons across a synapse.

Once Cajal, Sherrington, and others established that there was indeed a synapse between neurons, scientists were eager to determine just how one neuron communicated with another neuron. With so much excitement about electricity, many physiologists hypothesized that some type of electrical spark jumped from one neuron to the next. The focus shifted, however, when the physiologist Henry Dale, who was working with a chemical known as **acetylcholine** (extracted from a type of fungi), noted similarities between the chemical's effects and the functions of the autonomic nervous system. These parallels prompted Dale to consider the possibility that natural chemical substances such as acetylcholine might be transported across the synapse.

Dale's ideas remained speculations until 1921, when physiologist Otto Loewi reported that a dream inspired the perfect experiment to test the hypothesis that acetylcholine was indeed a natural substance secreted by neurons. Loewi wrote,

The night before Easter Sunday of that year I awoke, turned on the light and jotted down a few notes on a tiny slip of thin paper. Then I fell asleep again. It occurred to me at six o'clock in the morning that during the night I had written down something most important, but I was unable to decipher the scrawl. The next night, at three o'clock, the idea

FIGURE 3.9 Edgar Adrian. Adrian, working as a neurophysiologist at Cambridge University, won a Nobel Prize in 1932 for his introduction of the all-or-none law of neurotransmission.

returned. It was the design of an experiment to determine whether or not the hypothesis of chemical transmission that I had uttered seventeen years ago was correct. I got up immediately, went to the laboratory, and performed a simple experiment on a frog heart according to the nocturnal design. (Loewi, 1960, p. 17)

What was the nature of Loewi's brilliant experiment? Loewi prepared the hearts of two frogs so that they were isolated: one with nerves intact, the other without. After stimulating the vagus nerve of the first heart that was immersed in a special physiological solution (which slowed the heart rate), he carefully transferred that solution to the second heart. The transferred liquid solution slowed the heart rate, just as the stimulation of the vagus nerve had done. In contrast, when he stimulated an alternate nerve of the first heart that was immersed in a special physiological solution (which accelerated the heart rate) and then transferred that solution to the second heart, the rate of the second heart was accelerated. Loewi referred to the physiological solution that slowed the heart rate in the first experiment as *Vagusstoff* (German for "vagus stuff"), a substance later identified as acetylcholine (see Figure 3.10). Although this was a simple, elegant demonstration, several years elapsed until the findings were consistently replicated and accepted by Loewi's colleagues.

The contributions of both Henry Dale and Otto Loewi were recognized in 1936 when they were jointly awarded the Nobel Prize in Physiology or Medicine (Valenstein, 2005). Although neurochemical transmission is now known to be the most prevalent mode of neuronal communication, electrical synapses do indeed exist. In addition to being commonplace in both invertebrate and cold-blooded vertebrate species (Pereda et al., 2013), electrical synapses have been observed to exist temporarily while chemical synapses are being formed in mammalian nervous systems (Marin-Burgin, Eisenhart, Baca, Kristan, & French, 2005). Later in this chapter, we will examine their role in adults.

With the knowledge that neurons used chemical messengers to communicate among themselves, the next wave of neuroscience pioneers worked hard to learn more about the necessary conditions for the neurochemical exchange. They also sought to identify the various types of neurochemicals, or **neurotransmitters** (see Chapter 4), exchanged between neurons. As seen in Figure 3.11, the axon of one neuron has extended to the dendrites and cell body of a second neuron. The axon terminal, also referred to as the **presynaptic terminal,** is occupied with small spheres surrounded by membranes, known as **synaptic vesicles.** These neurochemical-containing vesicles cluster around active zones on the **presynaptic membrane.** Looking across the **synaptic cleft,** typically approximating 20 nanometers between the two neuron membranes, the **postsynaptic membrane** contains receptors for the specific neurotransmitter released by the synaptic vesicles in the presynaptic membrane.

The critical event in synaptic transmission is the release of an appropriate and specific type of neurotransmitter between neurons. Once an action potential arrives at the terminal ending of the presynaptic neuron, the change in membrane potential in this area triggers another set of voltage-gated ion channels to open. In this case, the ions are calcium, and they produce a subsequent influx of Ca^{2+} ions into the terminal. As seen in Figure 3.11, the elevation of Ca^{2+} ions provides another trigger, this time driving the synaptic vesicles to merge with the presynaptic membrane and release their components, the neurotransmitters, into the synaptic cleft. The release of neurotransmitters from the vesicles is known as **exocytosis.**

Neural communication does not occur, however, unless the postsynaptic neuron contains receptors that can bind to the released neurotransmitter. Receptors can have multiple binding sites, and the ability of various drugs to bind to receptor sites has important clinical implications (as you will learn in Chapter 4).

If a neurotransmitter binds to a receptor, the membrane potential changes in the postsynaptic membrane, altering the flow of ions in and out of the postsynaptic membrane. If the neurotransmitter–receptor binding makes the membrane potential depolarized (with an influx of sodium ions into the membrane), it produces an **excitatory postsynaptic potential (EPSP).** Conversely, if the neurotransmitter-receptor binding makes the membrane channels more permeable to negative ions such as Cl^-, which makes the membrane potential hyperpolarized, it produces an

(a)

1. Stimulation of vagus nerve slows heart rate.

2. Solution from first heart causes second heart to slow.

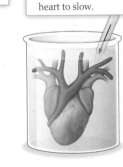

Donor   Recipient

(b)

FIGURE 3.10 **Critical neurochemical experiment.** (a) Otto Loewi's simple experiment of manipulating hearts emphasized the importance of chemical neural transmission in controlling various functions throughout the body. (b) Henry Dale (left) and Otto Loewi (right) outside the Grand Hotel before the Nobel Prize ceremonies in 1936.

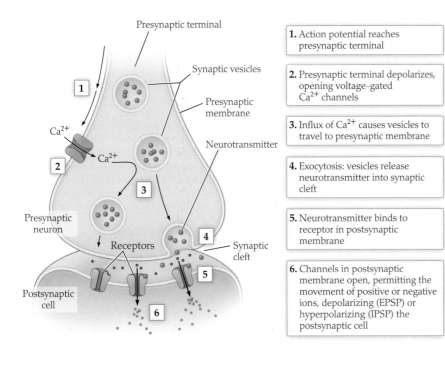

Presynaptic terminal

Synaptic vesicles

Presynaptic membrane

Neurotransmitter

Ca²⁺

Ca²⁺

Presynaptic neuron

Receptors

Synaptic cleft

Postsynaptic cell

1. Action potential reaches presynaptic terminal

2. Presynaptic terminal depolarizes, opening voltage-gated Ca²⁺ channels

3. Influx of Ca²⁺ causes vesicles to travel to presynaptic membrane

4. Exocytosis: vesicles release neurotransmitter into synaptic cleft

5. Neurotransmitter binds to receptor in postsynaptic membrane

6. Channels in postsynaptic membrane open, permitting the movement of positive or negative ions, depolarizing (EPSP) or hyperpolarizing (IPSP) the postsynaptic cell

FIGURE 3.11 Anatomy of a synapse. Many presynaptic steps are required to mobilize a neurochemical to the presynaptic membrane, across the synapse, and onto the postsynaptic receptor, where a postsynaptic effect occurs.

inhibitory postsynaptic potential (IPSP). Different neurotransmitter substances invoke EPSPs and IPSPs; we will explore the many neurotransmitters and their specific functions further in Chapter 4. In this chapter, we introduce the basic premises of neurochemical transmission.

Postsynaptic receptors that alter the membrane potential immediately on binding to neurotransmitters are called **ionotropic receptors.** The binding of a neurotransmitter to an ionotropic receptor almost immediately opens a specific type of ion channel, thereby enabling a specific type of ion to enter the postsynaptic cell (e.g., when the neurotransmitter glutamate binds to certain ionotropic receptors, it opens sodium channels). Chemicals that bind to other chemicals are known as ligands, and the channels involved in this process are therefore known as **ligand-gated** (or neurotransmitter-gated) **channels.**

In contrast to ionotropic receptors, which respond within a few milliseconds of neurotransmitter release from the presynaptic membrane, **metabotropic receptors** are generally slower to respond to neurotransmitter release. However, variability is found among the response times of metabotropic receptors (Craig & McBain, 2014). Metabotropic receptors are slower to respond to neurotransmitter release because they work via intracellular molecules called **second messengers** to cause changes in the postsynaptic neuron. When a ligand binds to a metabotropic receptor, the receptor activates a protein called a **G-protein,** which is coupled with the energy-storing molecule guanosine triphosphate. Once activated, the G-protein activates second messengers within the postsynaptic neuron. Second messengers have several roles, including the opening of ion channels in the postsynaptic membrane. See Figure 3.12 for more information about ionotropic and metabotropic receptors.

It is important at this stage of the synaptic transmission discussion to note that the neurotransmitter exchange occurring across a single synapse does not alter the membrane potential by the approximately 15 millivolts necessary to reach the action potential threshold. As seen in Figure 3.13, it is possible for a single neuron synapsing onto the postsynaptic membrane to be stimulated quickly in succession before the first transmitter release decays. This process, known as **temporal summation,** enables the subthreshold changes to build on themselves, or summate, to action potential threshold. The action potential threshold can also be reached by **spatial summation,** in which multiple synaptic inputs originating from different locations have a cumulative effect on depolarizing the neuron to the action potential threshold. The mechanisms of temporal and

(a) Ligand-gated ion channels   **(b) G protein-coupled receptors**

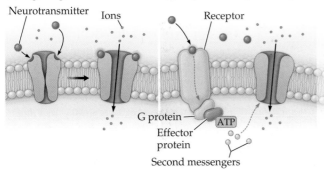

Neurotransmitter   Ions

Receptor

G protein

ATP

Effector protein

Second messengers

When the neurotransmitter binds to the receptor, the G protein binds to the effector protein, producing second messenger molecules that activate enzymes to open the channel.

FIGURE 3.12 Ionotropic and metabotropic receptors. (a) Neurotransmitters binding to ionotropic receptors directly open the ion channels. (b) Neurotransmitters binding to metabotropic receptors activate a series of events that indirectly open the ion channels.

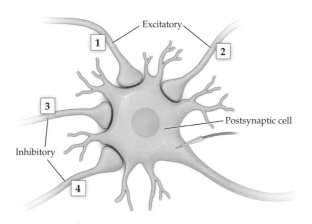

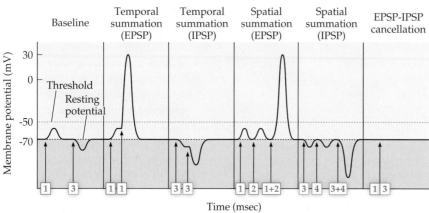

FIGURE 3.13 **Temporal and spatial summation.** Two mechanisms enable the resting membrane potential to depolarize toward the threshold for action potential (EPSP): *Spatial summation* requires multiple presynaptic neurons each altering the membrane potential. *Temporal summation* involves rapid firing of presynaptic neurons that build on graded potentials to depolarize toward the action potential threshold. Both spatial and temporal summation can also hyperpolarize the membrane (IPSP), moving the resting membrane potential away from the action potential threshold.

spatial summation also apply to inhibitory neural input that hyperpolarizes the membrane instead of depolarizing it.

Although the all-or-none law reflects the fixed nature of action potential firing, neurons have ways of modulating this system that affect the amount of neurotransmitter release. In nature, many neurons form networks such that multiple EPSPs and IPSPs are directed toward single neurons, and the net effects become complex.

As Figure 3.14 illustrates, different types of synaptic arrangements are found in the CNS, including **axodendritic,** **axosomatic,** and **axoaxonic.** It has been shown that axoaxonic synapses, in which axon B is synapsing onto axon A, can alter the amount of neurotransmitter released across the synaptic cleft to the dendrite of the postsynaptic membrane of Neuron C. Neurons accomplish this via various mechanisms such as hyperpolarizing an axon terminal or altering calcium influx in an activated axon terminal. If the interactions result in increased excitation and neurotransmitter release, the effect is known as **presynaptic facilitation.** If the interactions result in decreased neurotransmitter release, the effect is known as **presynaptic inhibition.**

We have now outlined the basics of the complex process of neural transmission at chemical synapses. The series of steps that neurons go through as they transmit impulses is similar to a dance you jump into after the music begins playing—you coordinate your movements with the music and the actions

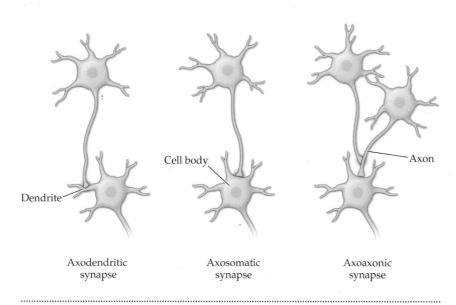

FIGURE 3.14 **Synaptic arrangements.** The synapse is the tiny gap between the presynaptic and postsynaptic neurons. Synapses are characterized as axodendritic, axosomatic, or axoaxonic depending on the area of the postsynaptic neuron contacted by the presynaptic neuron.

of everyone else on the dance floor. Review Figure 3.11 for a summary of the steps of synaptic transmission.

Neurons and Glial Cells: Collaborations

As we have discussed, glial cells are critical support cells for neurons because they form the important myelin sheaths that facilitate the propagation of action potentials down the axon. In addition to the crucial roles that oligodendrocytes and Schwann cells play in neural transmission, the astrocytes play an essential supporting role. Astrocytes extend their fine membranous processes to ensheath both the synapses and the fine blood vessels. Research suggests that these astrocytes monitor and control levels of ions such as K^+ ions in the extracellular space; they also possess receptors for many neurotransmitters (Barres, 2008).

Pfrieger and Barres (1997) investigated the specific role of astrocytes at the synapse, focusing on neurons in the eye's retina. When these neurons were cultured, or grown in the laboratory, without astrocytes, they had low levels of synaptic activity although the neurons possessed the requisite axons, dendrites, and membrane excitability. When cultured with astrocytes, however, their synaptic activity increased by 100-fold. This dramatic effect was specific to the presence of astrocytes. When the neurons were cultured with another type of glial cells, oligodendrocytes, the researchers observed no changes in synaptic activity.

How do astrocytes enhance synaptic excitability? Karen Christopherson and her colleagues at Stanford University (2005) identified a protein called *thrombospondin* that is released by astrocytes. This protein facilitates **synaptogenesis** (the creation of synapses), most notably during fetal brain development and following injury. Thrombospondin-deprived brains from genetically engineered mice have significantly fewer synapses than normal, typically developing mice; further, blocking thrombospondin release leads to impaired synaptogenesis (Barres, 2008). Astrocytes also secrete cholesterol, which serves as a powerful facilitator of presynaptic function (Mauch et al., 2001) and is thought to release other **neurotrophic factors,** or nerve growth factors.

This research indicates that glial cells play an essential role in facilitating and modulating synaptic transmission. In addition to providing the building blocks for the myelin sheath, glial cells (specifically, astrocytes) are essential for both the sculpting and the maintenance of effective neural connections. Thus, glial cells maintain existing neural functions while contributing to the synaptic plasticity that accompanies necessary neural modifications (Barres, 2008).

Turning our focus to the Schwann cells that form the myelin in the PNS, we see that another fascinating line of research is exploring how these cells facilitate the regeneration of PNS-damaged axons following an accident or the onset of a neurodegenerative disease. As we saw in Chapter 2, this regeneration does not naturally occur in the CNS. Findings revealed by the PNS investigations may provide important clues about how to develop interventions to regenerate CNS myelin (Weinstein, 1999). A successful intervention that regenerates CNS myelin would provide relief for many patients suffering from traumatic brain injury and other CNS diseases.

In addition to the various critical roles of glial cells in synaptic transmission, the role of glial cells in the blood–brain barrier is another critical area of research investigation. As we learned in Chapter 2, the **blood–brain barrier** consists of tight junctions between endothelial cells (cells lining body cavities and blood vessels), creating a filter between the brain and its incoming blood supply. This barrier prevents certain dangerous substances from entering the brain's blood supply. Interestingly, the brain area known as the **area postrema,** located in the medulla, has a weak blood–brain barrier. This is likely related to its function because it is known as the vomiting center. Thus, the area postrema is an additional security system in the brain that prompts the expulsion of ingested food should a threat be detected, and the relaxed blood–brain barrier enables the area postrema to detect such threats before they penetrate the body's other defenses. Astrocytes have been hypothesized to play a role in maintaining the blood–brain barrier by adding an additional layer of cellular defense to the barrier, especially following brain injury (Bush et al., 1999).

A recent line of research suggests that oligodendrocytes may play a role in *major depressive disorder* (also called *major depression*), a debilitating mental illness (discussed in Chapter 13). Postmortem examination of the temporal lobes of brains from patients with major depressive disorder has revealed that such patients have decreased gene expression devoted to oligodendrocyte function compared with nondepressed individuals (Aston, Jiang, & Sokolov, 2005). As described earlier in this chapter, oligodendrocytes build myelin sheathes in the CNS. Myelin loss is one of the most dramatic abnormalities observed in the brains of individuals with major depression. Therefore, some researchers have suggested that optimal neuronal functions rely on a delicate balance between axons and myelin. According to this view, when the balance is disrupted, various neuropsychiatric disorders such as major depression emerge (Edgar & Sibille, 2012).

As you will learn in Chapter 13, a popular and established theory of depression is that depression is caused primarily by low levels of a specific neurotransmitter, serotonin, in the brain. Although this theory is controversial (Castren, 2005; Kirsch, 2010), it is interesting to note that oligodendrocytes secrete an enzyme (dopa decarboxylase) that is critical for serotonin synthesis. It is plausible that a reduction in the number of oligodendrocytes and the accompanying reduction in serotonin synthesis in the temporal lobes, perhaps even exacerbated by prolonged stress, contributes to the onset of depression (Cahoy et al., 2008).

Lessons from Epilepsy: Neural Transmission in Review

Evidence of seizures and epilepsy has been found in the artifacts and records from the earliest human civilizations, long before any knowledge of brain functions existed. Trephined skulls (skulls with holes drilled in them), dating back more than 10,000 years to the Neolithic period, suggest that early humans may have tried to release energy from the head or to penetrate the head in search of the cause of a malady. In the Middle Ages, possessing this mysterious energy was associated with being possessed, or *seized*, by demons. This gave rise to the related term *seizures* (Penfield & Erikson, 1941).

Toward the end of the 19th century, the English neurologist John Hughlings Jackson formally defined the symptoms of epilepsy, writing that the seizures accompanying epilepsy are characterized by abnormal neural discharge, a symptom more accurately described as an atypical synchronized excitation of a population of neurons (Penfield & Erikson, 1941). In general, the seizures are thought to be caused by clusters of neurons becoming hyperexcitable and easily enticed to discharge abnormally (Scharfman, 2007). Epileptic seizures, sometimes involving muscular contractions, persist from seconds to minutes. Seizures that originate in a localized area of the brain are referred to as partial seizures, whereas those originating from larger areas dispersed across both hemispheres are known as generalized seizures (Figure 3.15). It is only when seizures are recurrent and seemingly spontaneous that a diagnosis of epilepsy is made. The term *epileptogenesis* refers to the transformation of a normal brain into a brain that supports seizures (Scharfman, 2007). Following a brain injury, posttraumatic seizures are a primary complication that leads to further cognitive and behavioral impairment and a more discouraging prognosis for recovery (Tucker, 2005).

Considering the basic process of neural transmission that we have described in this chapter, it should not be difficult to imagine the many opportunities for neuronal missteps leading to seizures. Regardless of the contributing factors, if neurons begin to fire out of context with the demands of the internal and external environments, the brain loses its ability to respond adaptively to the real-time challenges a person may be experiencing in any given situation, such as driving a car or walking a dog along a winding sidewalk. Further, the neuronal hyperexcitability leading to seizures can modify and even damage brain tissue.

Potential Mechanisms of Changes in Neural Excitability

As described earlier, the neuronal membrane potential is set so that a neuron is not firing constantly, but can fire readily if its membrane potential is changed by a modest

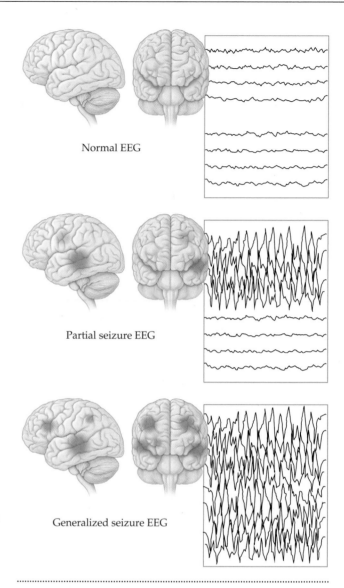

Normal EEG

Partial seizure EEG

Generalized seizure EEG

FIGURE 3.15   **Brain activity during seizures.** In partial and generalized seizures, desynchronized brain waves are prevalent in either specific or global brain areas.

degree. But what if the ionic balance maintaining this critical membrane potential is perturbed in some way? Or if the glial cells that interact with the neurons altered the resting membrane potential in a manner that made neurons more likely to fire action potentials? Or if the principal excitatory or inhibitory neurotransmitters and their accompanying receptors became altered in some way? These are just some of the neural situations that could lead to a change in the excitability of certain neuronal populations (Dzhala et al., 2005).

Potential Mechanisms of Synchronization

Although most of the synapses in the nervous system are of the chemical nature, some are electrical synapses. As seen in Figure 3.16, electrical synapses are characterized by the alignment of two neurons so that specific channels known

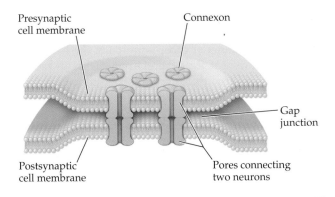

Presynaptic cell membrane

Connexon

Gap junction

Postsynaptic cell membrane

Pores connecting two neurons

FIGURE 3.16 Gap junctions. Electrical currents are exchanged through gap junctions, resulting in alterations in membrane potential.

as **connexons** align perfectly to form a **gap junction** where electrical currents can be exchanged between the two cells. Whereas chemical synapses operate directionally from the presynaptic neuron to the postsynaptic neuron, electrical synapses are bidirectional (Pereda, 2014).

Cortical neurons are richly interconnected, forming the previously described gap junctions, spaces of about 2–4 nanometers that exchange electrical currents (Lo & Reese, 1993). These gap junctions or other synaptic communication systems may alter the membrane potential of cortical neurons in various ways to ultimately produce cellular excitation, triggering a seizure.

Furthermore, in individuals who are susceptible to seizures, environmental stimuli such as video games with rapidly changing patterns of lights can affect large populations of neurons in the brain in such a way as to induce a seizure. Accordingly, terms such as *electronic screen game-induced seizure* and *video-game epilepsy* have been generated to describe such conditions. The brain's sensitivity to photo patterns displayed on liquid crystal display screens can be monitored with EEG to track the generation of photo-induced electrical alterations that may lead to these video-induced seizures (Funatsuka, Fujita, Shirakawa, Oguni, & Osawa, 2001).

A final factor thought to facilitate the generation of seizures is the excessive growth of axon extensions, or collaterals, which may increase the neural network excitability, especially in the area of the hippocampus (Scharfman, 2007). In this case, neurons may become too "networked" so that excessive synchronized activity occurs when the neurons are stimulated in certain ways. The proposed mechanisms of seizures introduced in this section serve as a reminder that factors disrupting the precision of neural communications can lead to chaotic neural responses.

Research with Animal Models

Seizures can be induced in rodent models by delivering electrical stimulation to the brain to trigger action potentials or by administering convulsant drugs such as pilocarpine or kainic acid that result in involuntary contractions of muscles. The animal models suggest that the seizure sets a chain of events into motion that leads to altered gene expression in the brain and subsequent modifications of excitatory neural networks (e.g., strengthening of the networks). These modifications may be caused by an increased activation of brain growth factors such as brain-derived neurotrophic factor (Scharfman, 2007).

Treatment of Epilepsy

Continued investigations of epilepsy over the past century and a half have revealed several clues about the disease. However, a cure still eludes the contemporary field of neurology. A number of different methods have been developed to treat epilepsy in humans. One treatment is the administration of drugs that increase levels of γ-aminobutyric acid in the synapse, an effect that ultimately suppresses neuronal excitation and enhances neuronal inhibition in the brains of patients. Another treatment strategy that is considered for patients who do not respond to medications, as discussed in Chapter 2, is severing the patient's corpus callosum to prevent the seizure from spreading from one side of the brain to the other. In the most severe cases of epilepsy, the treatment is to surgically remove the affected brain area or sometimes even an entire hemisphere (hemispherectomy).

Mirror Neurons, Specialized Neural Circuits, and Investigations into Autism Spectrum Disorder

As you have learned, researchers have identified the fundamental components of neural transmission. The application of this knowledge to complex behaviors such as social interactions is a subject of great interest in the field of biopsychology. I start with a personal example illustrating that our brains are predisposed to attend to the responses of others. My daughter is a gymnast, which means that on several weekends during the year I find myself sitting in large gymnasiums watching her compete in four "events" against many other young women. The most nerve-racking part of these gymnastic meets is the balance beam. I never cease to be amazed at the poise and balance the gymnasts exhibit as they leap and flip along this 10-centimeter-wide beam (Figure 3.17). Even with their extensive training, missteps occur that require quick repositioning attempts to prevent the dreaded fall (and half-point deduction).

FIGURE 3.17 **Maternal mirror neurons?** When my daughter performs on the balance beam as shown here, my body moves reflexively in response to her wobbles as if my compensatory movements will correct her movements and prevent a fall.

As I watch my daughter, I am fascinated by my own seemingly reflexive movement. If she sways too far to the left, my body jerks to the right as if I am helping her reestablish her balance on the beam. If she lands in an unbalanced position and is fighting with both hands to balance herself to achieve a solid standing position, I throw my hands up—in that poised position with the flared gymnast hands as if my movement is going to help her stand up and finish the move—with confidence and style.

Logically speaking, this is a ridiculous behavior. I am sitting at least 20 meters from my daughter; nothing I do is going to help her stay on that beam. And, just in case you are wondering, the other moms do this as well. I have not extended this informal observation to dads, but I imagine they also exhibit similar responses. In my experience with moms, however, at any given competition one can reliably expect to see them jerking around like marionette puppets to try to "help" their daughters complete their routines.

This behavior underscores how predisposed our brains are to anticipate the movements of others. In some cases, such as with children or other loved ones, the barrier between self-movement and other-movement begins to blur. It appears that social-motor activity-anticipation networks exist to allow us to save a falling child, enjoy a football game, or even dance the waltz with a partner.

The chapter opening described the role of von Economo neurons and their role in fast-paced neural processing. These neurons have also been implicated in social interactions (Insel & Young, 2001). Although controversial, another type of specialized neurons called **mirror neurons** have received considerable attention for their contributions to neural networks implicated in social interactions.

A team of Italian neuroscientists first discovered these specialized mirror neurons in the early 1990s. While recording from a single neuron in the premotor cortex of a macaque monkey, the Italian researchers noted that certain neurons were active both when the monkey was engaged in an activity like grabbing something to eat and when the monkey *observed* another animal grab some food (Di Pellegrino, Fadiga, Fogassi, Gallese, & Rizzolatti, 1992). It was as if these neurons mirrored the actions of others, a response that likely facilitated effective social interactions (see Figure 3.18). Other research suggested that these neurons played a role in empathy (Gazzola, Aziz-Zadeh, & Keysers, 2006), speech perception (D'Ausilio et al., 2009), language comprehension (Aziz-Zadeh, Wilson, Rizzolatti, & Iacoboni, 2006), imitation (Iacoboni, 2005), and behaviors typically impaired in individuals with **autism spectrum disorder (ASD),** a disorder characterized by disruptions in social interactions and communication, as well as the presence of repetitive behaviors (Dapretto et al., 2006).

Figure 3.19 shows proposed mirror neuron areas in the human brain, including an area in the inferior frontal cortex containing the *posterior inferior frontal gyrus* and the *ventral premotor cortex.* A second, more posterior area is found in the rostral area of the *inferior parietal lobule* and in the *posterior superior temporal sulcus,* an area that provides the primary visual input to the proposed mirror neurons. Based on these initial findings, it has been proposed that these areas form the core circuit for imitation (Iacoboni, 2009a,b; Iacoboni & Dapretto, 2006).

Stephen Suomi and his colleagues at the National Institutes of Health have conducted research suggesting that if you look at just the right time in development, you can track social-focused neural networks in young rhesus macaque monkeys. They observed frequent visual contact between macaque mothers and their infants during the first two months of the infants' lives. Initially, as the infants aged, the tendency for mutual gazes increased, but after about three weeks of age, the response diminished. As seen in Figure 3.20, a mother macaque stares at her 10-day-old infant and then smacks her lips together, an important social behavior that likely draws the infant's attention toward the mother (Ferrari, Paukner, Ionica, & Suomi, 2009).

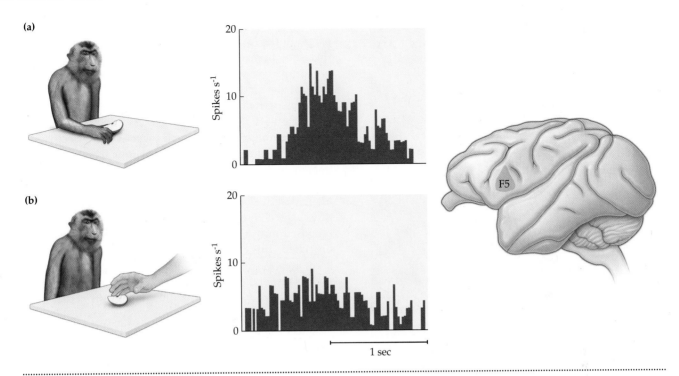

FIGURE 3.18 **Mirroring neuronal activity.** Similar neuronal activation is seen in the inferior frontal cortex in two situations. (a) The monkey grabs the food itself. (b) The monkey watches an experimenter grasp the food.

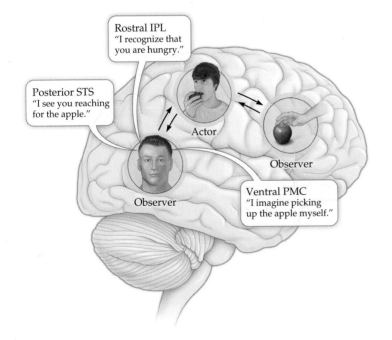

FIGURE 3.19 **The frontoparietal mirror neuron system.** Specific components of the proposed mirror neuron system contribute to the perception of the actor's movements and intentions in the observer's brain.

In a previous study, Suomi and his research group had observed other evidence of imitative responses in young rhesus macaque monkeys. The ability to imitate adult facial expressions and movements was once thought to be unique to humans and apes. However, in this study, three-day-old infant macaques imitated human facial and hand gestures, including opening and closing the mouth, sticking out the tongue, smacking the lips together, and opening and closing the hand. These imitative responses were confined to a narrow window of time; the responses almost completely disappeared by seven days of age.

Suomi and his colleagues suggested that this early imitation may work to tune infant macaques' attention and behaviors toward the grown animals that show affiliative and nurturing responses, animals that would likely provide critical care for the infants throughout their infancy

FIGURE 3.20 Maternal facial expressions. This maternal rhesus macaque interacts with her offspring via facial expressions and vocal communications.

(Ferrari et al., 2006). Figure 3.21 shows a three-day-old rhesus macaque imitating mouth opening and tongue protrusion. The next step for this team was to develop an EEG cap to measure the activity in proposed mirror neuron areas during these imitative responses (Paukner, Ferrari, & Suomi, 2011; Suomi, 2011).

Even with increasing evidence supporting the existence of mirror neurons in nonhuman primates, the notion that humans possess similar mirror neurons is controversial. Human neuroimaging studies have not obtained findings similar to those of the single-cell recording studies conducted in the monkeys (Dinstein, Thomas, Behrmann, & Heeger, 2008; Gallese, Gernsbacher, Hayes, Hickock, & Iacoboni, 2011; Turella, Pierno, Tubaldi, & Castiello, 2008). A challenge for researchers in this field is that it is sometimes difficult to compare humans and monkeys in their behaviors of observing and imitating the actions of others. Monkeys fail to demonstrate the same imitative behaviors exhibited by humans that are often linked to complex responses such as social learning and cultural transmission of responses (Rizzolatti & Craighero, 2004). The complexity

of interpreting similar responses in different contexts is apparent in the fMRI study results shown in Figure 3.22. In this study, humans showed more brain activation in the proposed mirror neuron areas when they observed an action associated with the intention of drinking compared with an action associated with the intention of cleaning.

Regardless of the challenges in assessing this proposed mirror neuron system, research suggests that selective impairment of the proposed mirror neuron areas specifically impairs imitative behavior. For example, when researchers used repetitive **transcranial magnetic stimulation** (a technique described in "Laboratory Exploration" at the end of this chapter) to cause temporary disruption of activity in a proposed mirror neuron area, imitative behavior was also disrupted. This effect was not observed when an unrelated brain area was disrupted, nor were nonimitative behaviors such as responding to spatial cues affected when the mirror neuron circuit was disrupted. Thus, the results in this study suggested that the mirror neuron circuit was involved in imitative behavior (Heiser, Iacoboni, Maeda, Marcus, & Mazziotta, 2003). Further, a study of human patients with epilepsy whose treatment involved single-cell recording in various brain areas provided evidence that mirror neurons were present in the predicted brain areas (Mukamel, Ekstrom, Kaplan, Iacoboni, & Fried, 2010). Thus, a growing body of evidence suggests that the brain areas designated as mirror neuron sites in the earlier nonhuman primate studies play a role in human imitative behavior.

It is interesting to speculate about how mirror neurons might develop in humans. How early in infant development might such neurons become functional? One study compared the goal-directed eye movements of 6-month-old and 1-year old infants to those of adults to determine the development of functional imitative responses. When adults and 1-year-old infants viewed a video of toys being moved by a hand, their eye movements shifted to the location goal of the toy placement before the toy physically arrived in that location. When the toys were moved automatically (without help from a human) in a video, these goal-oriented eye movements were not observed. In contrast, 6-month-olds did not shift their gaze in this manner in either scenario. Behavioral competencies such as imitation and use of gestures that are necessary to engage in goal-directed eye movements do not develop until 9 to 12 months of age. Therefore, the researchers were not surprised by the younger (6-month-old) infants' inability to demonstrate goal-directed eye movements (Falck-Ytter, Gredeback, & von Hofsten, 2006). Another study demonstrated that 9-month-old infants show similar EEG patterns when they grasp an object as when they merely observe someone grasp an object (Southgate, Johnson, Osborne, & Csibra, 2009).

The *associative sequence learning model* indicates how mirror neurons and their circuits may be formed during infant development. When infants see their parents' faces and imitate their parents' expressions simultaneously, the infants' sensory and motor neurons are activated

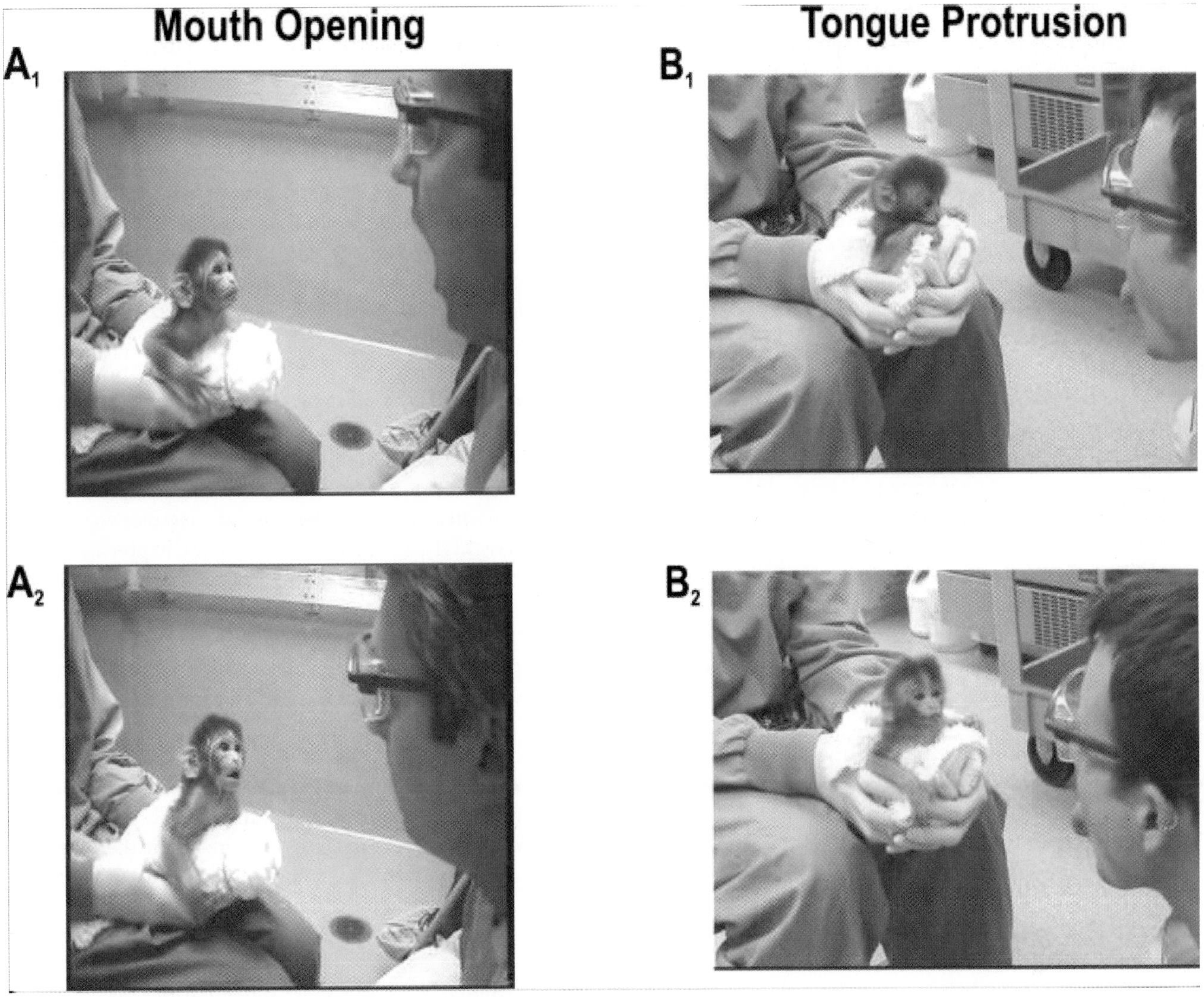

Mouth Opening

A₁

A₂

Tongue Protrusion

B₁

B₂

FIGURE 3.21 **Monkey see, monkey do.** This young monkey imitates the facial expressions of the human experimenter, including (a) open mouth and (b) tongue protrusion.

FIGURE 3.22 **Role of intentions in mirror neuron system.** The mirror neuron system is sensitive to varying intentions accompanying similar motor actions. The glass full of orange juice is associated with the intention of drinking, whereas the empty glass is associated with cleaning.

simultaneously. According to this model, after repeated episodes of the same sensory and motor events occurring simultaneously, stronger connections form between the sensory and motor neurons so that neurons in the proposed mirror neuron circuit are activated by neuronal input from multiple sensory and motor areas. These repeated experiences and corresponding strengthening of synaptic communication among these neurons fine-tunes social imitative responses. Just as having experience with thunderstorms leads to your anticipation of a clap of thunder following a lightning bolt, the neuronal circuits associated with imitative and goal-directed behavior prompt you to predict a friend's familiar responses. Consequently, once these circuits are formed, researchers propose that infants understand more about the predictions of movements in certain sensory contexts (such as meal time) and begin to engage in behaviors such as reaching for a delicious treat that another person is attempting to grasp (Heyes, 2010).

But what if these associations among sensory stimuli, the intended actions of other people, motor events, and the activation of appropriate motor/mirror neurons are delayed or impaired in some way? You probably will not be surprised to learn that researchers have explored the possibility that mirror neuron networks may be involved in the emergence of symptoms associated with ASD. Signs of ASD appear fairly early in a child's development. Because of the early observations of imitation deficits in children diagnosed with autism, mirror neurons have been considered a viable candidate for causing the deficits that children with ASD display in social interactions (Oberman & Ramachandran, 2007; Perkins, Stokes, McGillivray, & Bittar, 2010; Williams, Whiten, Suddendorf, & Perrett, 2001). However, the role of mirror neurons in ASD is far from clear. Researchers have observed reduced activity, increased activity, or no abnormalities in the proposed mirror neuron circuits in individuals with autism (Oberman et al., 2013).

In one study, children with autism and typically developing children were studied with fMRI on a facial expression task that required them to either observe or imitate various facial expressions. Results showed that compared with typically developing children, children with autism exhibited less activity in the proposed frontal mirror neuron system area in the inferior frontal cortex. The results revealed an inverse relationship between ASD symptom severity (as measured by traditional assessments for ASD) and the brain activity in the proposed frontal mirror neuron system area. The greater the severity of the ASD symptoms, the lower the activity in the proposed frontal mirror neuron area (Dapretto et al., 2006).

Using an experimental apparatus that tracks eye movements, other researchers have reported that children with ASD do not visually follow other people to the same extent as typically developing children do. In fact, the gaze durations of children with ASD do not appear to distinguish between objects and people in these studies (Klin, Jones, Schultz, Volkmar, & Cohen, 2002). The characteristic pattern of avoiding eye contact with parents and caregivers places these children at a disadvantage for strengthening the proposed mirror neuron networks. Accordingly, researchers are currently exploring treatment strategies such as synchronized dance therapy, in which children are taught to anticipate the moves of their dance partners, for stimulating and restoring the proposed mirror neuron functions in individuals with ASD (Iacoboni, 2009b; Ramachandran & Seckel, 2011). The most successful treatment strategy for ASD, applied behavior analysis, involves structured social interactions that provide incentives for appropriate social and behavioral responses (Foxx, 2008). More information about the effectiveness of behavioral therapies for various types of mental illness will be covered in Chapter 13.

The studies described in this section suggest that the development, connections, and firing patterns of neurons, as well as their associated neural circuits, are necessary for the development of social interactions that are critical for many aspects of survival—from securing appropriate nurturing responses to forming social bonds with others.

Recognizing the role of neural circuits in the most complex social interactions reminds us of the importance of having a thorough understanding of the brain and its neurons. As researchers discover more about the proposed mirror neuron circuit in humans, as well as other social neural networks, they will be better able to develop interventions for treating disorders characterized by impaired social interactions such as ASD, social anxiety disorder, and schizophrenia. Further, important similarities may exist between the characteristics and functions of the von Economo neurons discussed earlier in the chapter and mirror neurons, given that both types of neurons have been implicated in the anticipation of others' actions (Evrard et al., 2012). Future research may yield results that differentiate the roles of such neurons and their associated circuits in social interactions.

LABORATORY EXPLORATION

Altering Brain Functioning with Transcranial Magnetic Stimulation

Transcranial magnetic stimulation (TMS) is known as a *perturbation technique* because it disrupts, or perturbs, neural processing via the placement of a magnet over the cortex and the subsequent administration of brief electrical currents in a specific region of the cerebral cortex. When this magnet is used on a patient, the current passes along a stimulating coil positioned over the scalp. It induces an increase in the strength of the magnetic field and, subsequently, a rise in electrical current in the affected brain tissue. The disrupted electrical current in neurons located in proximity to the magnet takes the affected brain area momentarily offline. As seen in epilepsy, these neuronal disruptions render the neurons temporarily unable to respond to real-time neuronal messages (Barker, Jalinous, & Freeston, 1985).

The noninvasive TMS method involves disrupting a particular brain area and assessing the consequences of having that brain area temporarily malfunctioning. Consequently, researchers have referred to the use of TMS as a form of *virtual lesion*. Unlike the traditional lesioning techniques used with animal models or human brain trauma and brain surgery patients (discussed in Chapter 1), this noninvasive technique can be used in experimental settings with humans. TMS complements the use of fMRI and PET scans that measure the activity of certain brain areas while subjects are engaged in various tasks. By using TMS to disrupt activity in a brain area, researchers can see the behavioral consequences when the subject is asked to complete a task (Pascual-Leone, Bartres-Faz, & Keenan, 1999).

One way that TMS can be used as a "perturbing technique" is to ask the subject to engage in a particular task, such as auditory discriminations in which subjects must distinguish between two sounds, and then to disrupt neural processing in a cortical area known to play a role in that particular function. In this case, the auditory cortex would be such a cortical candidate.

As can be seen in Laboratory Exploration Figure 3.1, a figure 8–shape coil is used. This shape minimizes the intensity and undesirable spread of current associated with TMS. Even with this accommodation, TMS is not as specific as fMRI or PET when it comes to spatial resolution or pinpointing exact functional areas in the brain. However, this technique allows researchers to disrupt neural functions in areas that have been identified with imaging techniques (Chouinard & Paus, 2010). The TMS perturbation technique provides yet another reminder of the importance of the neurons' ability to fire in response to moment-by-moment demands. Any disruption, such as that introduced by the presence of a strong magnetic field or seizures, renders affected areas of the brain temporarily dysfunctional. As you will read in Chapter 13, a repetitive

version of this technique is used as a therapy for treatment-resistant major depression.

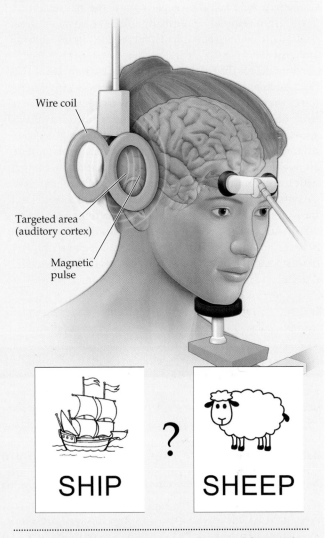

LABORATORY EXPLORATION FIGURE 3.1 Transcranial magnetic stimulation. This noninvasive technique activates or "perturbs" targeted brain areas and is used both in brain research studies and in treatment protocols for psychiatric illness.

Conclusion

This chapter has introduced you to neurons and the circuits they build to influence behavior, thoughts, and emotions. The action potential can be viewed as the neuron's basic—or neural—operating system. Neurons experience strategic shifts in ionic densities across the axonal membrane that ultimately result in neural communication.

We know that neurotransmitter molecules interact with specific receptors on the postsynaptic neuron, resulting in either activation or inhibition of neurons and, ultimately, behavioral responses. Glial cells support neural functions by providing the cellular basis for the myelin sheath, contributing to the blood–brain barrier, and facilitating synaptic interactions. Although not apparent to the casual observer, the architecture and continuous functions of the neurons and glial cells, as well as their associated neural circuits, define behavioral responses such as eating, running, studying for an exam, and talking to your roommate.

Malfunctioning of the intricate neural transmission process sometimes results in neural chaos, as is the case in epilepsy. Instead of responding to constant changes in the environment, large populations of neurons become synchronized, resulting in seizures that render an epileptic patient momentarily helpless until the neurons once again begin responding normally. We have learned a great deal about neural functions from patients suffering from epilepsy.

Support for the role of neural networks in specific functions such as regulating social interactions is also emerging in the field of neuroscience. In this chapter, you learned that von Economo neurons and mirror neurons may play a specialized role in social functions, facilitating anticipated responses and imitative behaviors that may contribute to emotions such as sympathy and empathy. The discovery that neurons communicate via neurochemicals revolutionized neuroscience research, yielding extensive information about the types of neurochemicals and their functions.

In addition to serving as a foundation for material on neurons and neurotransmitters in the subsequent chapters of this book, the knowledge gained in this chapter provides a basis for understanding the challenges and promise of research on disorders such as epilepsy and ASD. It also enables us to consider important future directions for research with both humans and nonhuman animals to identify the neural mechanisms that underlie behavior.

The next chapter will build on this information to focus on how neurochemical communication systems modulate the brain's existing neural circuits to enable us to perform the behaviors necessary for survival. These behaviors include regulatory behaviors such as sleeping and eating, as well as social behaviors such as caring for offspring. The brain's natural levels of neurotransmitters can be manipulated by drugs for medicinal and recreational reasons. As you will learn in the next chapter, the manipulation of these neurochemicals via taking drugs can sometimes lead to neural disaster in the form of drug addiction. Thus, our ability to intervene with the brain's neurochemical functions leads to both promise, as researchers develop treatments for mental illness, and peril, as drug use sometimes leads to chronic addiction and other neural challenges.

KEY TERMS

skin conductance response (SCR) (p. 63)
von Economo neuron (p. 64)
neural circuits (p. 64)

Neurons: Structure and Function

synapse (p. 65)
membrane (p. 65)
ion channels (p. 66)
ions (p. 66)
gated ion channels (p. 66)
ion pumps (p. 66)
restraint stress (p. 67)
membrane potential (p. 69)
extracellular space (p. 69)
intracellular space (p. 69)
resting membrane potential (p. 69)
concentration gradient (p. 69)
electrical gradient (p. 69)
sodium–potassium pump (p. 69)
action potential (p. 70)
depolarization (p. 70)
hyperpolarization (p. 70)
threshold (p. 70)
voltage-gated ion channel (p. 71)
refractory period (p. 71)

saltatory conduction (p. 72)
spike-initiation zone (p. 73)
all-or-none law (p. 73)
progesterone (p. 73)
synaptic transmission (p. 73)
acetylcholine (p. 73)
neurotransmitters (p. 74)
presynaptic terminal (p. 74)
synaptic vesicles (p. 74)
presynaptic membrane (p. 74)
synaptic cleft (p. 74)
postsynaptic membrane (p. 74)
exocytosis (p. 74)
excitatory postsynaptic potential (EPSP) (p. 74)
inhibitory postsynaptic potential (IPSP) (p. 75)
ionotropic receptors (p. 75)
ligand-gated channels (p. 75)
metabotropic receptors (p. 75)
second messengers (p. 75)
G-protein (p. 75)
temporal summation (p. 75)
spatial summation (p. 75)
axodendritic (p. 76)
axosomatic (p. 76)

axoaxonic (p. 76)
presynaptic facilitation (p. 76)
presynaptic inhibition (p. 76)

Neurons and Glial Cells: Collaborations

synaptogenesis (p. 77)
neurotrophic factors (p. 77)
blood–brain barrier (p. 77)
area postrema (p. 77)

Lessons from Epilepsy: Neural Transmission in Review

connexons (p. 79)
gap junction (p. 79)

Mirror Neurons, Specialized Neural Circuits, and Investigations into Autism Spectrum Disorder

mirror neurons (p. 80)
autism spectrum disorder (ASD) (p. 80)
transcranial magnetic stimulation (p. 82)

REVIEW QUESTIONS

1. Compare and contrast the characteristics and functions of axons and dendrites.

2. Describe the various mechanisms that maintain the neuron's resting membrane potential.

3. How does ionic movement lead to the initiation of an action potential and the eventual restoration of the resting membrane potential?

4. Describe the influence of various types of glial cells on the transmission of action potentials along the axon.

5. What are neural circuits? How is an individual's experience thought to modify neural circuits?

6. List several potential ways in which neural transmission can malfunction, causing epileptic seizures.

7. How were mirror neurons discovered in animals? How have the proposed mirror neuron circuits in humans been investigated to determine their influence on imitative responses?

CRITICAL-THINKING QUESTIONS

1. Suppose an individual's nervous system loses its ability to maintain a negative resting membrane potential. How might this affect the person's behavior?

2. Provide examples of how environmental and experiential changes alter the anatomical features of neurons. Are these changes consistently beneficial for adaptive brain functions? Explain.

3. Disrupted activity of proposed mirror neurons was associated with autism in this chapter. What effects might enhanced activity of mirror neurons have on the behavior of individuals who do not have autism?

Neurochemistry, Neuropsychopharmacology, and Drug Addiction

Methamphetamine "Tweaks" the Brain

After more than a decade of drug abuse, including a run with methamphetamine, the 20-year-old college dropout Nic Sheff (shown with his father in Figure 4A) wrote in his journal,

> *How the hell did I get here? It doesn't seem that long ago that I was on the water-polo team. I was an editor of the school newspaper, acting in the spring play, obsessing about which girls I liked, talking Marx and Dostoevsky with my classmates. The kids in my class will be starting their junior years of college. This isn't so much sad as baffling. It all seemed so positive and harmless, until it wasn't. (Sheff, 2005)*

Nic's father, David Sheff, chronicles the story of his son's addiction in his harrowing memoir, *A Beautiful Boy*. Nic's involvement with drugs began early in his life—his father found marijuana in his backpack when he was just 12 years old. David became increasingly devastated as he witnessed his son's transition from a bright, energetic boy to a drug addict. Each time Nic remained sober for an extended period, David had hope that his

son had finally turned a corner, only to be disappointed by yet another relapse.

After cleaning up his act, Nic was accepted into Manchester College, far away from his San Francisco home and all of the drug-related cues that had kept leading him into relapse. Elated to pick up his son after his first full year of college, David's excitement turned to panic when he looked at Nic and saw the telltale signs that Nic was definitely using drugs again—pale skin, unkempt hair, a vibrating body, gyrating jaw, and darting eyes. Nic's old habits were evident that painful summer because he would disappear for weeks without contacting his parents. Consequently, David was certain that Nic was somewhere on the street abusing methamphetamine. He feared he would never see his son again.

Somehow, Nic found enough sobriety in the next couple of years to write his own memoir, *Tweak: Growing Up on Methamphetamine*. "Tweaking," a word that usually refers to minor alterations, is anything but a minor alteration in the context of drug use. In this most dangerous stage of methamphetamine abuse, the user has reached the end of a binge—several days of continuous use without sleeping, accompanied by an emotional tsunami of irritability and paranoia—and can no longer get satisfaction from the drug. During a tweak, methamphetamine users have been known to engage in dangerous behavior, threatening and hurting friends or loved ones and committing crimes (Sheff, 2008).

Behind the Scenes

What changes in Nic's brain accompanied his transition from a highly functioning child to a methamphetamine addict? Animal research has established that amphetamine and **methamphetamine** alter neurons that secrete the neurotransmitter dopamine into the striatum. Dopamine is a neurochemical involved in reward and motor systems and is one of the most investigated neurochemicals in addiction research. Addiction, in Nic's case, involved an uncontrollable desire to consume methamphetamine. Addiction, as you will learn throughout this chapter, is the compulsive dependence on a behavior or substance—a complex response that involves many neurochemicals.

Specifically, research suggests that chronic methamphetamine use leads to a type of toxicity characterized by decreased numbers of dopamine-sensitive (dopaminergic) synaptic endings, as well as lower dopamine levels in the brain (Berman, O'Neill, Fears, Bartzokis, & London, 2008). In one study, rats that received high-dose methamphetamine injections showed a 35% reduction in dopaminergic synaptic endings relative to control rats that received saline injections (Pubill et al., 2003). This study provided evidence that methamphetamine restructures the dopaminergic neural circuits that keep the brain's movement, emotions, and thoughts running smoothly.

Using MRI, researchers have found evidence that the human brain is similarly affected by the use of methamphetamine. In one study, autopsied brains of methamphetamine users showed up to 97% lower dopamine levels in an area of the striatum known as the caudate nucleus relative to the autopsied brains of control subjects (Moszcynska et al., 2004). In a PET study that imaged human subjects' living brains, Nora Volkow and her colleagues at the National Institute on Drug Abuse (NIDA) reported reduced availability of a specific subtype of dopamine receptor in chronic methamphetamine users compared with non-drug-abusing control subjects (Volkow et al., 2001).

In these types of studies of drug abusers, researchers use a control (non-drug-abusing) group of subjects as the comparison group (since it is typically not possible to conduct a controlled study in which individuals participate once before they are drug abusers and again after they are drug abusers). Brain differences observed between the drug-abusing group and the non-drug-abusing control group are generally interpreted as evidence of the changes that drug abuse causes in the brain.

FIGURE 4A David and Nic Sheff. David Sheff chronicles the story of his son Nic's addiction in his harrowing memoir, *A Beautiful Boy.*

Other researchers have observed less gray matter in limbic structures such as the cingulate cortex, as well as white matter hypertrophy, or enlargement, and smaller hippocampal volumes in methamphetamine addicts compared with non-drug-abusing control subjects. Chronic methamphetamine abuse is associated with a pattern of abnormal brain structure that is comparable in effect size to deficits observed in schizophrenia (see Chapter 13) and early dementia (see Chapter 5) (Thompson et al., 2004).

What behavioral patterns are associated with these findings of abnormal brain structure? Research on humans has identified positive relationships between striatal dopamine receptor availability and impulsiveness (Lee et al., 2009). Even when they stop taking the drug, methamphetamine users demonstrate impaired response inhibition and decision making (Paulus et al., 2002; Salo et al., 2002). Early in the abstinence period, users experience a range of troubling symptoms including fatigue, decreased pleasure, agitation, vivid dreams, irritability, anxiety, and poor concentration. Most of these patients also experience cravings for the drug (C. McGregor et al., 2005). These **withdrawal symptoms** (those troubling symptoms that emerge once the drug use ceases) make it especially difficult for users like Nic to continue to abstain from drug use.

The dopamine neurotransmitter that is affected by methamphetamine is one of more than 100 identified neurotransmitters that the brain uses. Other psychostimulant drugs affect the dopamine neurotransmitter as well. This chapter will describe several key neurotransmitters and the ways in which **psychoactive drugs** can disrupt their normal functioning.

Neurotransmitters: A Brief Introduction

As introduced in Chapter 3, neurons communicate with one another by secreting neurotransmitters that activate specific receptors on neighboring neurons. Specific neurotransmitters can be divided into four major categories based on chemical structure and function, as shown in Table 4.1.

As we learned in Chapter 3, it is generally beneficial for neurons to return to their baseline functions quickly after being activated by specific neurotransmitters. Just how does a neurotransmitter terminate its activation of the postsynaptic receptors? Two processes are **enzymatic deactivation** (the neurotransmitter is broken down by enzymes) and **reuptake** (the neurotransmitter is transported back to the presynaptic neuron and repackaged for reuse). Specific neurotransmitters are discussed in the next section. Additionally, several neurotransmitters will be discussed in relevant contexts throughout this text.

Contributing to the complexity of the neurochemical systems, a single neurotransmitter can have several different types of receptors. As more specific information about the function of neurotransmitters is discussed throughout the text, relevant information about specific receptors will be introduced.

Monoamine Neurotransmitters

The **monoamines,** containing a single ("mono") amine group (a specific class of organic compounds), include **catecholamines,** a group composed of **dopamine** (mentioned earlier in this chapter), **norepinephrine,** and **epinephrine**. The other class of monoamines is the **indolamines,** represented by the neurotransmitter **serotonin.** Figure 4.1 shows the synthesis pathways for dopamine, norepinephrine, epinephrine, and serotonin.

As seen in Figure 4.2, the monoamine neurotransmitter systems are widely distributed throughout the brain.

TABLE 4.1.

Neurotransmitter Categories

NEUROTRANS-MITTER CATEGORY	REPRESENTATIVE EXAMPLES
Monoamines	*Catecholamines* (dopamine, norepinephrine, and epinephrine) and *indolamines* (serotonin)
Amino acids	Glutamate, γ-aminobutyric acid, and glycine
Peptides	Endorphins, oxytocin, and vasopressin
Other	Acetylcholine, lipid-derived transmitters such as anandamide, adenosine, and certain gases such as nitric oxide and carbon monoxide

Dopamine, produced in the substantia nigra and **ventral tegmental area,** is involved in movement, reward systems, and increased vigilance. The pathway from the substantia nigra to the **striatum** (caudate and putamen) is known as the **nigrostriatal pathway,** and the pathway from the ventral tegmental area to the brain reward area (including the nucleus accumbens) is called the **mesolimbic pathway** (Koob, 2009). Dopamine pathways and their relevance for addiction will be discussed more extensively later in this chapter. Norepinephrine is produced in the **locus coeruleus,** a brainstem area involved in arousal, and in sympathetic nerves. It is involved in increased vigilance, focused attention, and enhanced energy. Epinephrine is structurally similar to norepinephrine but is released from the adrenal gland, which sits atop the kidney. In times of acute stress, epinephrine plays a similar role to

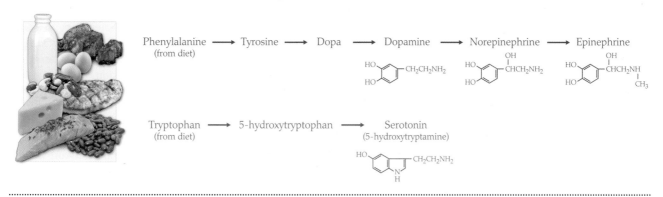

FIGURE 4.1 Neurotransmitter metabolic pathways. Proteins consumed in our diet undergo specific chemical transformations and ultimately become neurotransmitters.

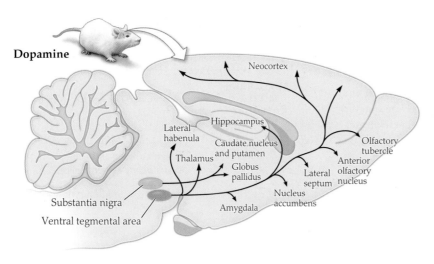

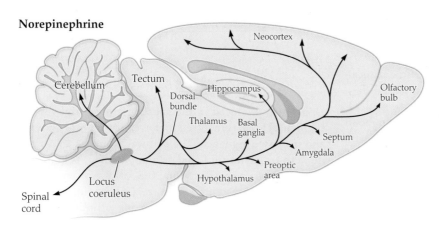

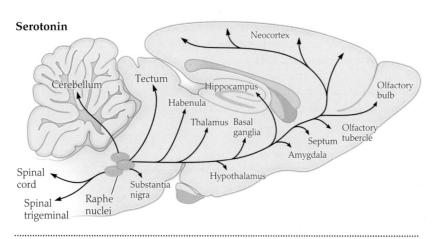

FIGURE 4.2 Neurotransmitter brain pathways. After being produced in specific nuclei, each neurotransmitter has specific pathways leading to relevant areas throughout the brain. (We will look at acetylcholine pathways later in the chapter.)

Amino Acid Neurotransmitters

The **amino acid neurotransmitters** are among the most abundant of the neurotransmitters in the CNS. One of these neurotransmitters, **glutamate,** is considered the workhorse transmitter for excitatory signaling pathways in the brain. Although glutamate has many functions, it is perhaps best known for its involvement in brain plasticity mechanisms such as the creation of synapses (synaptogenesis) as neural networks are formed. Once the foundation for these networks is established, glutamate plays a role in strengthening the existing synapses, a process facilitating both learning and memory (which we explore further in Chapter 12). Two types of receptors that glutamate molecules activate are the **NMDA receptor** (because of its affinity for *N*-methyl-D-aspartate) and the **AMPA receptor** (because of its affinity for alpha (α)-amino-3-hydroxy-5-methyl-4-isoxazole propionic acid).

Figure 4.3 depicts a transgenic (genetically engineered) mouse with enhanced NMDA receptor function in the hippocampus being assessed in an object recognition test that requires the mouse to recognize objects that it has previously encountered. Transgenic mice with enhanced NMDA receptor function exhibit enhanced learning in an object recognition task in which they spend more time exploring novel, rather than familiar, objects. They remember events longer and solve complex mazes better than normal mice (Tsien, 2000). These smart mice were referred to as "Doogie mice" after the 1990s television series, *Doogie Howser, M.D.,* which featured a genius teenager as a physician. Chapter 12 ("Learning, Memory, and Decision Making") will cover more details on the role of glutamate in learning.

Gamma (γ)-aminobutyric acid (GABA), derived from glutamate, is the principal inhibitory neurotransmitter in the brain.

norepinephrine in the sympathetic nervous system. The final monoamine neurotransmitter, serotonin, is produced in the **raphe nuclei,** where it is synthesized from the dietary amino acid tryptophan. Serotonin affects mood regulation, sleep/wake cycles, temperature regulation, sexual activity, and aggression.

GABA inhibition leads to seizures (as discussed in the previous chapter) and death. The GABA system is subject to activation by various ingested substances. In the case of alcohol (in part a GABA **agonist,** or drug that mimics or enhances the effects of specific neurotransmitters), this activation results in inhibition of the brain's cognitive and behavioral systems (as will be

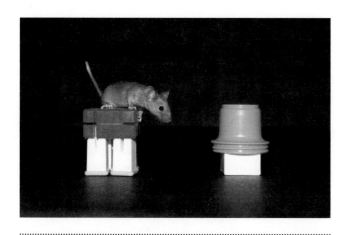

FIGURE 4.3 Mouse intelligence? This transgenic mouse is exposed to both a familiar and an unfamiliar object. If the mouse spends more time exploring the new object than the familiar object, the mouse is viewed as having an established memory of the familiar object.

discussed further later in this chapter). Another GABA agonist is muscimol, a psychoactive chemical compound present in certain kinds of mushrooms. In this case, GABA system activation results in intoxication and hallucinatory effects, similar to the effects of **hallucinogenic drugs** such as lysergic acid diethylamide (LSD), psilocybin mushrooms, and peyote, which will be discussed later in the chapter. Different from agonists, neurochemicals that are **antagonists** block or decrease the effects of specific neurotransmitters. For example, a GABA antagonist may counteract the agonist effects of alcohol on GABA receptors (Paul, 2006).

In addition to GABA, **glycine** is a prevalent major inhibitory neurotransmitter in the brainstem and spinal cord. It plays an important role in the control of many sensory and motor pathways. Strychnine is a strong antagonist that blocks ionotropic glycine receptors. By blocking inhibition, strychnine can cause convulsions, muscle cramping, and respiratory problems.

Peptide Neurotransmitters

Peptides are composed of approximately 3–40 amino acids. As discussed later in this chapter, endorphins are one type of **peptide neurotransmitter** and are involved in both pain and reward processes. Two additional examples of peptide neurotransmitters are oxytocin and vasopressin, both involved in the

regulation of specific fluids and social relationships. Oxytocin and vasopressin will be discussed extensively in Chapter 11.

Other Neurotransmitters

Acetylcholine (ACh) is synthesized from *acetyl coenzyme A* (from metabolism) and *choline* (from metabolism or diet). Figure 4.4 shows the synthesis pathway for ACh. Note that the precursors for ACh come partly from the human diet. We will learn more about the impact of nutrients on brain functions in Chapter 8. Otto Loewi confirmed ACh as a neurotransmitter in his frog-preparation experiment, as discussed in Chapter 3. ACh is produced by clusters of neurons in the basal ganglia and brainstem areas. Figure 4.5 shows the distribution of ACh throughout the brain.

ACh is involved in motor functions and parasympathetic functions outside of the CNS, and it is involved in memory and cognitive functions inside the CNS. The two main classes of ACh receptors are *nicotinic ACh receptors* and *muscarinic ACh receptors*. The deadly poison curare is a nondepolarizing muscle relaxant that blocks nicotinic receptors at the neuromuscular junction (synapse between a neuron and muscle), thereby blocking neuromuscular transmission.

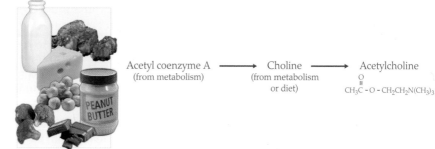

Acetyl coenzyme A ⟶ Choline ⟶ Acetylcholine
(from metabolism)   (from metabolism or diet)

$$CH_3C-O-CH_2CH_2N(CH_3)_3$$

FIGURE 4.4 Acetylcholine pathway. Dietary choline is transformed into the neurotransmitter acetylcholine.

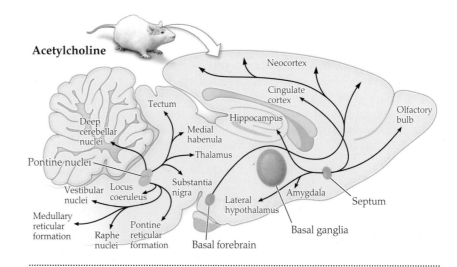

FIGURE 4.5 Acetylcholine brain pathway. Cholinergic pathways extend from nuclei located in the forebrain and brainstem.

The deadly poison botulin blocks the release of ACh at the neuromuscular junction, thereby interfering with nerve impulses. In the CNS, the drug pilocarpine, used to treat dry mouth, serves as an agonist for muscarinic receptors, whereas the drug scopolamine, often taken to treat motion sickness, antagonizes muscarinic receptors.

Recent research has highlighted the existence of lipid-derived transmitter substances, the most notable examples being the neuroactive lipids known as **endocannabinoids:** substances produced by the body itself that mimic the physiological effects of the cannabis (marijuana) plant. Endocannabinoids are not stored in vesicles; rather, they are released as needed by the plasma membrane in the postsynaptic synaptic neuron (Basavarajappa, 2007; Kreitzer, 2005). **Anandamide,** the first of these substances to be identified, has been shown to be involved in hippocampal plasticity in close association with the glutamatergic neurotransmitter system (Nyilas et al., 2008).

A few gases such as **nitric oxide** and carbon monoxide have also been found to alter synaptic function. Gaseous transmitters can readily pass through the cell membrane. Therefore, like endocannabinoids, they are not stored in synaptic vesicles as the other transmitters are (Dawson & Snyder, 1994; Kuriyama & Ohkuma, 1995; Johnson & Johnson, 2000; Xue et al., 2000). Nitric oxide and endocannabinoids are *retrograde neurotransmitters*, meaning that they are released by postsynaptic neurons to the axons of presynaptic neurons, where they affect relevant receptors. Although more research is necessary to determine the mechanisms and functions of gaseous neurotransmitters, nitric oxide has been shown to modulate several different transmitter systems (Artinian, Tornieri, Zhong, Baro, & Rehder, 2010). Nitric oxide has been associated with the brain's control of the cardiovascular system and may lead to new therapeutic approaches for cardiovascular disease (Ufnal & Sikora, 2011). It has also been implicated in learning (Bon & Garthwaite, 2003).

Table 4.1 summarizes the major categories of neurotransmitters that we have discussed and well-known examples of neurotransmitters within each category. Although these neurotransmitters have been conveniently categorized in this section, interactions among neurotransmitters lead to an unfathomable range of potential functions and effects. Because the vast complexity of the brain's neurochemicals is difficult to capture in the limited space of this chapter, the discussion of neurotransmitters (including the introduction of new neurotransmitters) continues throughout the rest of this book.

Overview of Neuropsychopharmacology

A goal of the field of **neuropsychopharmacology** is to identify specific drugs that interact with the nervous system to alter behavior that has been disrupted by disease, injury, or environmental factors. Such targeted drugs serve as medicinal aids to treat various mental illnesses ranging from attention-deficit/hyperactivity disorder (ADHD) to addiction. Essentially, regardless of whether a **psychoactive drug** has been researched and developed by pharmaceutical companies or generated from plant substances for recreational use, it acts as either an antagonist or an agonist for targeted neurochemical systems. Drugs can serve as agonists or antagonists at any one of several stages of neurotransmission, and drugs may affect multiple neurotransmitters in different ways. Some drugs work directly at the receptor sites, whereas others change the amount of neurotransmitter that is released.

As described earlier, antagonist drugs block or decrease the effects of specific neurotransmitters. They block the receptor sites, increase the speed of neurotransmitter removal from the synapse, or decrease the production of neurotransmitters. For example, antagonists known as beta (β)-blockers decrease the effects of epinephrine, typically experienced during the stress response. This calms a person's cardiovascular responses during a music recital or other stressful event.

Agonists mimic or enhance the effects of specific neurotransmitters. They mimic neurotransmitters at the receptor site, stop the removal of neurotransmitters from the synapse, or increase the production of neurotransmitters. Alcohol, as previously mentioned, inhibits activation of the nervous system through agonistic effects as it activates the GABA neurotransmitter system in the amygdala (Roberto, Madamba, Moore, Tallent, & Siggins, 2003).

Figure 4.6 depicts how antagonists and agonists that interact with the receptor influence the receptor site. Agonists fit the receptor site and result in a pharmacological response.

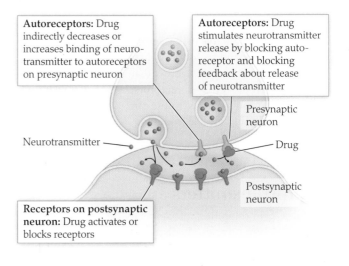

FIGURE 4.6 **Drug influences on synaptic transmission.**
Psychoactive drugs affect neural transmission by enhancing (agonists) or blocking (antagonists) the actions of natural transmitters in the synapse.

Antagonists only partially fit the receptor site, so they do not result in a pharmacological response. However, antagonists block the receptor site and prevent other molecules, including the normal neurotransmitter and agonists, from interacting with the receptor site. This blocks or decreases the effects of a specific neurotransmitter.

Major Goals of Neuropsycho-pharmacological Research

Neuropsychopharmacological research has a number of important goals. The typical objective of pharmaceutical research is to develop a drug that has an **affinity** (or a tendency for close binding) for the targeted neurotransmitter's natural receptors in the brain. Regardless of the strategy, the most important goal is to develop drugs that have a high **efficacy,** or ability to produce desired effects for a targeted condition. For example, currently, although most antidepressant drugs have a high affinity rate for blocking serotonin reuptake in the synapse, their efficacy is frustratingly low.

One way to assess a drug's efficacy is through a controlled study involving a placebo (as described in Chapter 1, a placebo is an inactive substance administered as a control in drug studies). In a typical clinical research study, patients with a given condition (e.g., depression) are divided into two groups, given pills, and told that the pills may improve their condition. One group of patients receives the actual medication under study, but the other group receives a chemically inactive placebo as a control. Such studies are **blind studies,** meaning that patients do not know to which group they have been assigned. Some are **double-blind studies,** in which neither the patients nor the researchers know the group assignments. Placebos may cause the patients to believe that the treatment will improve their conditions, and this may lead to their subjective perception that their condition has improved or to an actual improvement in their condition (the **placebo effect**). The efficacy of the actual drug is compared with that of the placebo. Sometimes the efficacy of antidepressant drugs is no different from that of a placebo (see Chapter 13).

It is extremely important to assess the **therapeutic effects** of a drug (i.e., the targeted and beneficial consequences, such as a reduction in a patient's depression symptoms). Sometimes, however, the therapeutic effects of a drug are outweighed by undesirable side effects such as gastrointestinal problems and sexual dysfunction. A drug's **potency,** or its ability to induce a given effect relative to other drugs, is also important.

As research institutions and pharmaceutical companies develop a given drug, they must understand the drug's **pharmacokinetics,** or the process by which the drug is absorbed, distributed, metabolized, and eliminated by the body. The concept of pharmacokinetics focuses on what the body does to the drug. By contrast, the concept of **pharmacodynamics** focuses on what the drug does to the body: the effects of the drug and the mechanisms of how the drug works.

For a drug to be considered a safe and effective treatment option for a specific disorder, the following questions must be investigated and, eventually, definitively answered:

- *Route of administration.* What is the route of administration, and what is the lowest amount of drug necessary to produce optimal responses in the patient? The speed of the drug's absorption into the patient's bloodstream depends on the route of drug administration (e.g., inhalation, injection, or oral administration in pill form). For each route of administration, **dose–response curves** should be established to determine the lowest amount of drug necessary to produce optimal responses. Most drugs have different dose–response curves for different outcome measures. As shown in Figure 4.7, this is the case for the analgesic (pain-relieving) effect of morphine and for the depressive effect of morphine on respiration.

- *Absorption and distribution.* Which areas of the brain and body does the drug affect? How quickly do these effects occur? Most drugs are distributed throughout the body, which often leads to undesired side effects.

- *Binding.* In addition to the active target sites for which the drug was developed, where else does it bind or find itself stored as a temporarily inactive substance?

- *Inactivation.* What metabolic processes eventually render the drug inactive? Most drugs are metabolized by the liver via the actions of specific enzymes. Other neural actions such as the employment of deactivating enzymes may also render the drug or its downstream effects inactive in the brain.

- *Excretion.* How are the final metabolites (substances produced by metabolism) of the drug eliminated from the body?

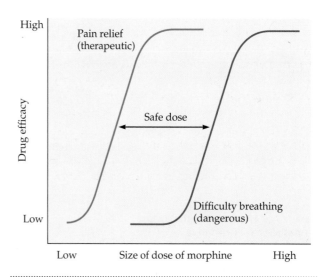

FIGURE 4.7 Dose–response curve of morphine. Research is necessary to determine the specific range of morphine doses that target symptoms without putting the patient in danger.

Figure 4.8 summarizes these pharmacokinetic and pharmacodynamic factors that influence the impact of drugs as they travel through the body. Researchers must explore each factor carefully when developing new drugs.

Development of New Drugs for Specific Symptoms: A Thought Experiment

If you were a researcher with the assignment of developing a drug to enhance cognitive functions by increasing the effects of the excitatory neurotransmitter glutamate, how would you approach this challenge? Think back to the discussion of synaptic transmission in Chapter 3, as well as the information about neurotransmitters in this chapter. Any ideas? As you mentally revisit the steps of synaptic transmission, the ideas from Figure 4.9 and Table 4.2 may emerge.

Of course, if you wanted to *reduce* the effects of glutamate by developing a drug that serves as an antagonist—as you may be instructed to do if the pharmaceutical company is looking for pharmacological treatments to minimize seizures—your strategies would be just the opposite of those in Table 4.2.

Actual pharmacological research focusing on cognitive enhancement has targeted one of the glutamate receptors—the AMPA receptor. Drugs such as ampakines interact strongly with the AMPA receptor. Interestingly, these drugs exert an indirect effect on AMPA receptors by modulating neurotransmitter release when the neuron is activated by glutamate, ultimately increasing glutamate release (Holst et al., 1998; Ingole, Rajput, & Sharma, 2008). Chapter 12 will provide more information on the important role of glutamate transmission in learning.

Throughout history, the identification of chemicals that alter psychological functioning has not always required scientists and advanced laboratory equipment. The discovery that some of the same chemicals are present in both plants and brains provided the first gateway to neuropsychopharmacology. As discussed in the next section, the development of drugs that alter psychological functioning began many centuries ago in cultures across the world. Although the emphasis in the next section is on common psychoactive drugs that have been associated with drug addiction, the use of psychoactive drugs for therapeutic purposes such as the treatment of schizophrenia and depression will be described in Chapter 13.

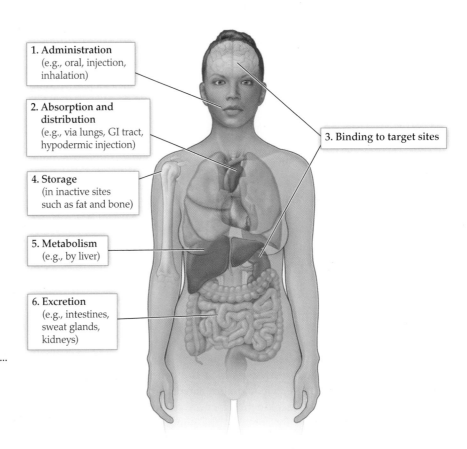

1. Administration
(e.g., oral, injection, inhalation)

2. Absorption and distribution
(e.g., via lungs, GI tract, hypodermic injection)

3. Binding to target sites

4. Storage
(in inactive sites such as fat and bone)

5. Metabolism
(e.g., by liver)

6. Excretion
(e.g., intestines, sweat glands, kidneys)

FIGURE 4.8 Pharmacokinetics. To have a physiological effect, drugs have specific metabolic pathways accompanying their entry into the body, impact on targeted systems, and subsequent breakdown and release. The metabolic actions occur at various sites throughout the body.

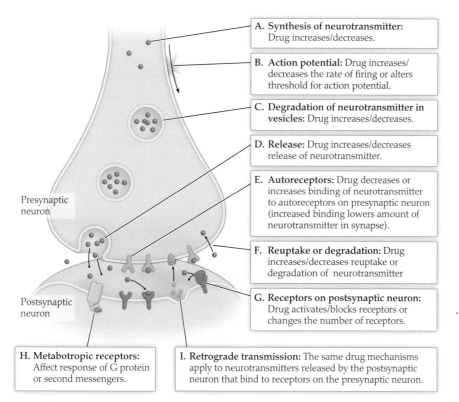

A. **Synthesis of neurotransmitter:** Drug increases/decreases.

B. **Action potential:** Drug increases/decreases the rate of firing or alters threshold for action potential.

C. **Degradation of neurotransmitter in vesicles:** Drug increases/decreases.

D. **Release:** Drug increases/decreases release of neurotransmitter.

E. **Autoreceptors:** Drug decreases or increases binding of neurotransmitter to autoreceptors on presynaptic neuron (increased binding lowers amount of neurotransmitter in synapse).

F. **Reuptake or degradation:** Drug increases/decreases reuptake or degradation of neurotransmitter

G. **Receptors on postsynaptic neuron:** Drug activates/blocks receptors or changes the number of receptors.

H. **Metabotropic receptors:** Affect response of G protein or second messengers.

I. **Retrograde transmission:** The same drug mechanisms apply to neurotransmitters released by the postsynaptic neuron that bind to receptors on the presynaptic neuron.

Presynaptic neuron

Postsynaptic neuron

FIGURE 4.9 Drugs and synaptic operations. Psychoactive drugs interfere with a diverse array of functions necessary for the manufacturing, transport, and reception of neurotransmitters.

TABLE 4.2.

Strategies to Increase the Effects of Glutamate

PRESYNAPTIC POSSIBILITIES

~ Increase the level of precursors to glutamate production, so that more glutamate can be produced

~ Alter the glutamatergic neurons so that they fire action potentials more readily, or change membrane threshold in a more pronounced way so that more glutamate is released

~ Enhance or speed up the transport of glutamate down the axon on its way to the terminal ending

~ Keep the calcium channels open in the synaptic ending so that an influx of calcium can propel the synaptic vesicles toward the presynaptic membrane, facilitating the release of glutamate

~Ensure that no substances (such as reserpine) cause the synaptic vesicles to leak glutamate after glutamate is stored in the vesicles

~Activate presynaptic autoreceptors in such a way as to inhibit glutamate release

~ Block or delay the reuptake of glutamate into the presynaptic terminal following its release

~Reduce the number or delay the action of enzymes in the synapse that rapidly inactivate glutamate

POSTSYNAPTIC POSSIBILITIES

~Inhibit enzymes on the postsynaptic surface that render glutamate inactive (i.e., inhibit deactivating enzymes)

~Increase the number of postsynaptic glutamate receptors [Hint: Remember that more than one type of postsynaptic glutamate receptor exists (e.g., NMDA, AMPA receptors)]

~Develop a drug that serves as an agonist to glutamate and activates the postsynaptic glutamate receptors

~Modulate aspects of metabotropic receptors (e.g., activation of the G-protein) to slow down the response to receptor activation

Psychoactive Drugs: Precursors to Drug Addiction

Which common psychoactive drugs have been associated with drug addiction? In his book *Forces of Habit: Drugs and the Making of the Modern World*, the historian David Courtwright (2001) provides an engaging account of humans' fascination with neurochemicals throughout history. Courtwright differentiates between the most consumed drugs, including alcohol, caffeine, and nicotine, and drugs such as opium, cannabis, and coca that are popular in various cultures but consumed at lower rates. These substances have altered the consciousness of billions of people worldwide (Courtwright, 2001).

In this section, we will learn about the most consumed psychoactive drugs as they are typically categorized by neuropsychopharmacologists (see Table 4.3). Focusing on substances with the greatest historical influence and highest contemporary consumption rates, this section will discuss several drugs in the stimulant category and will focus on a single representative drug in the other categories. Although far from exhaustive, these examples present the basic pharmacology of various types of psychoactive drugs.

As shown in Figures 4.10 and 4.11, the illicit use of prescribed **stimulants,** drugs that facilitate arousal; **depressants,** drugs that suppress arousal; and **analgesics** (pain relievers) continues in high school seniors. Further, the data from a University of Michigan study of high school seniors (Figure 4.10) indicate that 7 of the 14 most frequently abused drugs were prescribed or over-the-counter medications. These trends suggest that the *regulation* of drug use via medical prescriptions is more of a perception than a reality.

CNS Stimulants

In general, stimulants facilitate CNS arousal systems. The most common drugs in this category include caffeine, nicotine, cocaine, amphetamine, and 3,4-methylenedioxymethamphetamine (MDMA).

Caffeine The stimulant **caffeine,** which is found naturally in the leaves, seeds, and fruit of several plants, wins the prize for being the earth's most widely used psychoactive

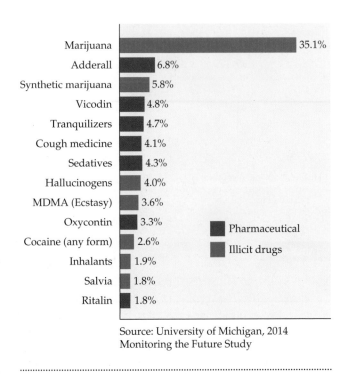

Source: University of Michigan, 2014 Monitoring the Future Study

FIGURE 4.10   Drug use trends. In general, there is little difference between use rates of prescription and recreational drugs in high school seniors.

TABLE 4.3.	
Categorization of Psychoactive Drugs	
TYPE OF DRUG	**FUNCTION(S) AND EXAMPLES**
CNS stimulants	General activation and arousal (amphetamine, cocaine, caffeine, nicotine)
CNS depressants	General suppression and relaxation (alcohol, barbiturates, benzodiazepines)
Analgesics	Pain relief and altered psychological experience (opium, morphine; codeine; heroin)
Hallucinogens	Altered perceptual experience (mescaline, LSD, psilocybin)
Drugs with diverse CNS effects	Marijuana (used for some medicinal uses such as the treatment of pain, nausea and glaucoma; psychoactive symptoms include relaxation and mild hallucinations)
Psychotherapeutics	Therapy target for various mental illnesses (Prozac, thorazine)

Number of prescriptions for stimulants*
dispensed by US retail pharmacies, years 1991–2009
*excludes modafinil and atomoxetine products

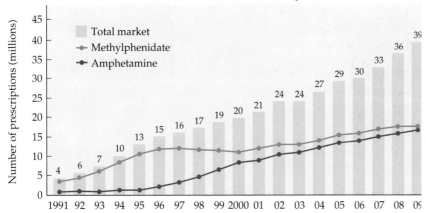

Number of prescriptions for hydrocodone and oxycodone products
dispensed by US retail pharmacies, years 1991–2009

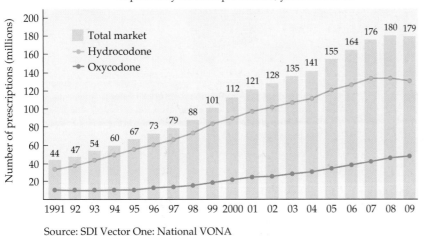

Source: SDI Vector One: National VONA

FIGURE 4.11 **Prescription drug use.** These graphs depict the rising rates of stimulant and pain medication use.

produces increased energy, efficiency, creativity, self-confidence, alertness, and ability to focus on one's work (Griffiths & Mumford, 1995).

What does caffeine do to the brain that keeps its users coming back, time after time, for just one more cup? Research in rats suggests that caffeine produces psychoactive effects by blocking receptors of **adenosine** (an inhibitory neurotransmitter), especially two specific receptors known as adenosine A_1 and A_{2A} receptors. These receptors are located throughout the entire brain, but the highest levels are in the hippocampus, cerebral cortex, and cerebellar cortex (see Figure 4.12; Fastbom, Pazos, & Palacios, 1987; Fredholm & Dunwiddie, 1988). As you learned in Chapter 2, the hippocampus and cerebral cortex (especially the prefrontal areas of the cerebral cortex) are involved in learning, memory, and the formation of complex cognitive associations. Further, the cerebrum contains a dense population of the brain's neurons and is involved in conscious awareness and various forms of cognition. Caffeine has also been implicated in increased attention and focus, given that adenosine receptors are concentrated in dopamine-rich areas of the brain such as the prefrontal cortex (Fredholm & Dunwiddie, 1988).

Exactly how does caffeine alter brain functions? Because of the pervasiveness of adenosine receptors throughout the brain, the answer to this question is complex. However, a few overarching mechanisms have been proposed. Interestingly, adenosine works in some brain areas by inhibiting the release of excitatory neurotransmitters. By blocking adenosine, caffeine consumption may result in an overall increase in excitatory neurotransmitter release (Fredholm & Dunwiddie, 1988). This suggests that adenosine works to match the rate of energy supply with energy consumption and, if called for, decrease the firing rate of neurons (Phillis & Edstrom, 1976). Perhaps this is why adenosine is thought to play a role in sleepiness, an effect that is sometimes thwarted by that late-night cup of caffeinated coffee (see Figure 4.13; Landolt, Dijk, Gaus, & Borbely, 1995). (See Chapter 9 for more information about adenosine and sleepiness.)

Nicotine In 1492, sailors in Christopher Columbus's expedition brought back knowledge of the Taino Indian custom of rolling the dried leaves of a special plant into cigars, lighting

drug. Although tea has been consumed in Asian cultures for thousands of years, the effects of caffeine did not become known in the West until more recently. According to legend, in the 9th century, Ethiopian herdsmen noted that certain berries and leaves their goats were chewing seemed to make the goats "perkier" (Pendergrast, 1999). Consequently, the herdsmen started chewing the berries themselves. By the 15th century, a drink prepared by infusing these berries (i.e., coffee beans) with boiling water had become popular throughout the Middle East. The practice spread to Europe, and coffee became a global commodity. Eventually, coffee houses became fashionable (Courtwright, 2001). In the meantime, tea and chocolate had become popular beverages in Europe.

Today, coffee remains the preferred method of caffeine consumption. In the United States, approximately 150 million coffee consumers drink a daily average of 3.2 cups per day. Self-report data indicate that a low dose of caffeine

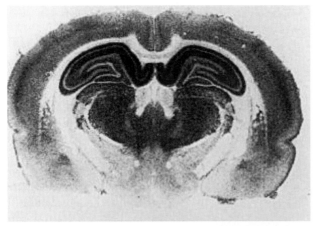

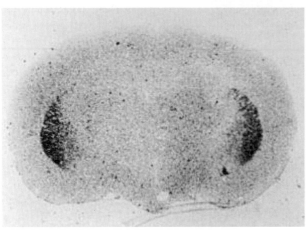

FIGURE 4.12 **Adenosine receptors.** The dark patches on these brain images indicate the presence of dense populations of adenosine receptors in the hippocampus. The top image depicts adenosine A_1 receptors and the bottom image shows adenosine A_{2A} receptors.

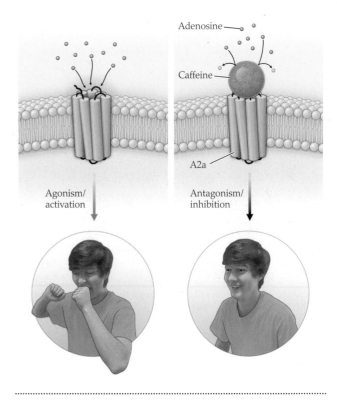

FIGURE 4.13 **Adenosine receptors and sleep.** Adenosine agonists activate receptors and lead to sleep, whereas adenosine antagonists, such as caffeine, suppress the activation of the receptor, keeping the person awake.

them afire, and inhaling the smoke. The plant, which the Europeans called *tabaco*, was used by many native cultures in the Americas and was believed to have medicinal properties. This was the beginning of a worldwide industry that has continued to the present day (Courtwright, 2001).

Currently, approximately 21% of individuals 12 and older in the United States (56 million people) smoke cigarettes (National Survey on Drug and Health, 2014). In their book *Prescription for a Healthy Nation*, the physicians Tom Farley and Deborah Cohen (2005) pointed out that smoking cigarettes accelerates death in many users, killing 440,000 Americans each year—equivalent to three 747 aircrafts filled to maximum capacity crashing every day. The death rate associated with cigarette smoking represents 20 times that caused by HIV, even higher if we include the 50,000 Americans dying each year from secondary smoke. Poignantly, Farley and Cohen state that "if we cured all other forms of cancer, vanquished the AIDS epidemic, prevented all murders, suicides, and car/plane crashes, and wiped out all deaths from alcohol we still would not have saved as many

lives as we could by merely cutting smoking rates in half" (Farley & Cohen, 2005, p. 133).

Nicotine is the active ingredient in tobacco and is found in the leaves of the family of plants known as *solanaceae*. Nicotine gained popularity when 16th-century French diplomat Jean Nicot delivered tobacco leaves imported from America to the wife of King Henry II as a potential treatment for her migraines (Figure 4.14). She was impressed by nicotine's therapeutic effects and Nicot became forever entrenched in tobacco history—with the active ingredient, nicotine, bearing his name and the pervasive delivery system receiving a French name, the cigarette (Sciolino, 2008).

Delivered via the cigarette, nicotine enters the smoker's lungs on tiny particles of tar (a mixture of hydrocarbons, some known to have the potential to cause cancer). Once the cigarette smoke is inhaled, the vaporized nicotine passes through the lungs. If the tobacco is snorted (e.g., as snuff) or chewed, nicotine is absorbed to a lesser extent by the membranes of the mouth and nose. Each of the 10 typical puffs a cigarette smoker takes per cigarette delivers a rush of nicotine to the brain (Kozlowski, Whetzel, Stellman, & O'Connor, 2008).

After entering the brain, nicotine activates the *nicotinic cholinergic receptors*, which are normally activated by acetylcholine. Nicotinic cholinergic receptors, chemical destinations for nicotine molecules, exist in many brain areas,

FIGURE 4.14 Jean Nicot. Nicotine gained popularity in the 16th century after Jean Nicot, a French diplomat, presented the tobacco plant to the wife of King Henry II, as shown in this illustration. Nicot became forever entrenched in tobacco history—with the active ingredient, nicotine, bearing his name.

including the cerebral cortex, striatum, hippocampus, thalamus, substantia nigra, ventral tegmental area, locus coeruleus, and raphe nuclei (Jones, Sudweeks, & Yakes, 1999; Rahman, Lopez-Hernandez, Corrigall, & Papke, 2008). The nicotine inhaled from three cigarettes will occupy a majority of the brain's nicotinic cholinergic receptors.

Nicotine receptors are also found in the PNS in the autonomic nervous system. When activated by nicotine, the adrenal gland releases epinephrine and norepinephrine. This PNS activation also leads to increased heart rate and elevated blood pressure, both of which may increase a smoker's risk for cardiovascular disease. Furthermore, nicotine has a stimulating effect on the metabolic rate of humans.

Regarding CNS effects, when nicotine binds to nicotinic cholinergic receptors, sodium channels open to allow the influx of sodium and subsequent depolarization of the neuronal membrane. Because most of the nicotinic receptors are presynaptic, nicotine alters the release of acetylcholine and alters other neurotransmitter systems in which nicotinic receptors are situated on the presynaptic terminal (Exley & Cragg, 2008). Hence, occupation of nicotinic receptors can have far-reaching effects beyond those observed in the cholinergic system.

To determine the psychological effects of nicotine, researchers must separate it from the standard delivery system (the cigarette) and simply inject it into subjects or administer it via nicotine patches or nicotine gum. Generally, smokers associate nicotine use with feelings of calm and relaxation. This calming effect, however, may simply be a result of the individual's history of smoking. Nonsmokers who receive the same dose of nicotine via injection, patch, or gum report feelings of heightened tension and arousal (Parrott & Kaye, 1999).

Researchers have found evidence that nicotine addiction may be centered in the insula, a cortical area involved in processing information from both internal and external sources (interoception and the insula were discussed in Chapter 2). In one study, chronic smokers who had experienced traumatic brain injury with specific damage to the insula were able to quit smoking more easily than smokers who had not sustained damage to this brain area (Naqvi, Rudrauf, Damasio, & Bechara, 2007). Perhaps compromised processing in the insula diminishes awareness of the uncomfortable withdrawal effects occurring during smoking cessation.

Nicotine may have other psychological effects. Evidence suggests that nicotine may activate brain areas involved in cognition (Amitai & Markou, 2009). Abstinent smokers who subsequently consume nicotine exhibit enhanced cognitive performance, especially in the realm of sustained arousal and attention (Sherwood, 1993).

Finally, nicotine delivery is reinforcing. The existence of high-affinity nicotinic receptors in the ventral tegmental area leads to increased firing of dopaminergic neurons and, subsequently, the release of dopamine from the **nucleus accumbens** (a brain area known for its role in reward and motivational responses). In one rodent study, when this dopaminergic area was lesioned with the toxic chemical 6-hydroxydopamine, rats were less likely to self-administer nicotine (Corrigall, Franklin, Coen, & Clarke, 1992).

Cocaine As with the other drugs discussed in this section, humans have long known of the effects of the coca plant and its active ingredient, **cocaine,** a stimulant that combats the effects of hunger and fatigue. Archaeological evidence of humans chewing coca leaves dates back as early as 3000 bce. A lively coca trade flourished in the Spanish colonies of the Americas in the 16th century. In 1862, a packaging strategy opened the trade of coca across the world. Soon products, including beverages and throat lozenges, were marketed with cocaine as an active ingredient. Cocaine was an ingredient in the best-selling soft drink *Coca-Cola* before government regulations required its removal. As cocaine became more readily available, use of the drug peaked in the United States around the turn of the 20th century, accompanied by cases of cocaine poisoning and addiction (Courtwright, 2001). The main route of administration changed as well, as people began sniffing and injecting the drug.

The psychological effects of cocaine include euphoria, a sense of increased energy, heightened mental alertness, and feelings of competence and power. In the form of cocaine hydrochloride, the drug can be easily mixed in solution and taken orally, intranasally, or via injection. A later transformation mixing cocaine hydrochloride with baking soda, known as **crack,** created a more efficient form to smoke.

Regardless of the route of administration, once it enters the CNS, cocaine blocks the reuptake of three monoamine neurotransmitters: dopamine, norepinephrine, and serotonin. Specifically, cocaine binds to the proteins that act as **transporters** for neurotransmitter reuptake back into the presynaptic membrane. The result of this transporter block is that the neurotransmitters remain in the synaptic cleft longer (see Figure 4.15). Research suggests that cocaine binds more strongly to dopamine and serotonin transporters than to norepinephrine transporters (Ritz, Lamb, Goldberg, & Kuhar, 1988; Peng et al., 2010). As you will see in the next section on the neurobiological bases of drug addiction, the majority of psychoactive drugs with addictive potential work by modifying the dopamine system.

Amphetamine and MDMA In addition to the stimulants already discussed, several variations of natural and synthetic CNS stimulants exist, including methamphetamine (discussed at the beginning of this chapter). Before leaving this section, we will discuss two additional stimulant compounds, amphetamine and MDMA.

Arriving on the pharmacological scene later than the previously described CNS stimulants, **amphetamine** was developed in the 1930s and marketed for its antiasthmatic effects. It soon became known to boost alertness and produce a sense of well-being, which led to its use for a range of conditions from fatigue and depression to narcolepsy. Amphetamine was initially sold in the form of inhalers, but findings indicated they were being abused, so the drug was subsequently produced in tablet form and restricted to prescription use. By the 1960s, however, amphetamines ("uppers") were once again being taken in a more casual manner, especially by students wishing to stay awake for all-night study sessions. Although it remains a problem in young adults, recent statistics suggest that amphetamine use in college students has leveled off and slightly declined since 2006 (Johnston, O'Malley, Bachmen, & Schulenberg, 2009).

Similar to methamphetamine, amphetamine is an indirect catecholamine agonist that not only blocks catecholamine reuptake but also enhances its release from the presynaptic neurons. Because of the increased release of the catecholamine dopamine, amphetamine results in psychological effects that are similar to those produced by cocaine, including a sense of well-being, confidence, heightened alertness, and diminished fatigue. Although the rewarding effects of amphetamine have led to abuse, amphetamine is a treatment approved by the U.S. Food and Drug Administration for ADHD (discussed in Chapters 5 and 12) and narcolepsy (Berman, Kuczenski, McCracken, & London, 2009).

Before leaving the psychostimulant story, it is worth noting that the "designer" drug **MDMA,** commonly known as ecstasy, is a form of amphetamine. Developed in 1914, ecstasy did not receive much attention until the 1970s, when psychotherapists began using it as a supplement to their talk therapy treatments. Although it became a controlled substance in 1985, the popularity of ecstasy for promoting feelings of well-being led to recreational use by adolescents and young adults, especially at rave dances (Foderaro, 1988). In addition to the common effects of cocaine, MDMA produces enhanced sensory perception and a desire for social interaction (Atkins, Burks, Swann, & Dafny, 2009).

At the level of the synapse, MDMA is considered a messy drug because of the extent to which it affects more than one neurotransmitter system (Parrott, 2002). Specifically, laboratory research suggests that MDMA is a monoamine agonist because it leads to the release of stored serotonin and dopamine (Capela et al., 2009). MDMA has been found to have numerous adverse side effects and long-term effects. These include sleep disruptions, depression, anxiety, cognitive deficits, involuntary teeth clenching, temperature dysregulation, cardiovascular effects, and potential kidney injury and liver disease (Burgess, O'Donohoe, & Gill, 2000; Campbell & Rosner, 2008; Green, King, Shortall, & Fone, 2012).

CNS Depressants: Alcohol

Following caffeine, alcohol is the most used psychoactive drug in the United States (World Health Organization, 2012). Alcohol is the most *abused* drug. Because alcohol is legal in most countries, many people do not consider it a

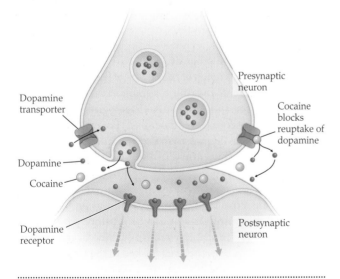

Dopamine transporter

Presynaptic neuron

Cocaine blocks reuptake of dopamine

Dopamine

Cocaine

Dopamine receptor

Postsynaptic neuron

FIGURE 4.15 Cocaine's activation of the brain. Cocaine blocks the reuptake sites for dopamine, leading to the prolonged presence of dopamine in the synapse, where it activates postsynaptic receptors.

drug—this despite the unintended negative consequences of alcohol use, ranging from automobile accidents caused by drunk drivers to long-term effects such as liver disease and memory impairment. As seen in Figure 4.16, worldwide alcohol consumption rates are high, with an average per capita consumption rate of 6.2 liters of pure alcohol per year (World Health Organization, 2014).

The Egyptians are thought to have prepared the first beer around 3700 BCE. In the late 15th century, books were printed in Europe describing the alcohol distilling process, and the Dutch became leaders in alcohol production. In colonial America, alcoholic beverages were considered part of a normal diet, and taverns emerged as the meeting point for conducting business. It was not until the 1830s that the temperance movement began to educate the public about the dangers of alcohol consumption. In 1919, temperance crusaders scored a decisive victory with the passage of the 18th Amendment to the U.S. Constitution, prohibiting the manufacturing and distribution of alcohol. However, prohibition turned out to be ineffective in reducing actual alcohol consumption. Consequently, the amendment was repealed in 1933 (Courtwright, 2001; Goode, 1993).

The effects of low doses of alcohol include an improved mood, drowsiness, and increased self-confidence, as well as impaired judgment and muscle coordination. As the doses of alcohol increase, further cognitive and reflexive impairment occur. The highest physiological doses of alcohol can lead to acute alcohol poisoning. This is a life-threatening condition that occurs when an individual has consumed a toxic amount of alcohol, usually over a short time period. The alcohol causes the individual's CNS to slow down, leading to extreme confusion and disorientation, as well as slow and irregular breathing patterns. As breathing and heart rate become slower and slower, the patient can become comatose and die.

Alcohol's positive mood effects continue to make it popular. Worldwide, approximately half of all men and one-third of all women report consuming alcohol in the past year (World Health Organization, 2011). In the United States, approximately 20% of adults self-report binge drinking (defined as consuming four drinks in a row for women and five drinks in a row for men) during the previous year (Schoenborn & Adams, 2010). Approximately 40% of college students are categorized as heavy drinkers (defined as having at least one binge episode during the past two-week period; Ross & DeJong, 2008). Unfortunately, reports suggest that these rates are continuing to increase, especially among male students (Courtney & Polich, 2009). Students have reported negative consequences of binge drinking, including hangovers, unplanned and unprotected sex, and incidents of violence, as well as missed classes (Wechsler, Moeykens, Davenport, Castillo, & Hansen, 1995). Overall, if you are a male, young adult, in a high-income category, or attend college, you are at risk for both binge and heavy drinking (Paul, Grubaugh, Frueh, Ellis, & Egede, 2011).

Research has identified several effects of alcohol on brain functioning. Once alcohol crosses the blood–brain barrier, it influences several ionotropic and metabotropic receptors. In general, alcohol consumption has a profound impact on the transmission of glutamate, the principal excitatory neurotransmitter in the nervous system. Alcohol inhibits glutamate transmission by interacting with the NMDA receptors in several brain areas including the hippocampus, an area involved in learning and memory. This effect may contribute to the cognitive deficits associated with long-term, excessive alcohol consumption. To compensate for the continuous effects of consuming alcohol, the NMDA glutamate receptors adapt by increasing their numbers in both the cerebral cortex and the hippocampus (Willis & Winder, 2013). In another attempt to counteract alcohol's effects, glutamate release increases in the striatum. This apparent compensatory effect is likely related to the hyperexcitability and irritability that are typically observed in individuals who are undergoing alcohol withdrawal (see Fadda & Rossetti, 1998, for review.)

Alcohol also impacts the major inhibitory neurotransmitter GABA by binding to the GABA$_A$ receptor and enhancing the effects of GABA. Other types of sedative drugs such as **benzodiazepines** and barbiturates function similarly, but bind to different receptors. Similar to the glutamate system, the GABA system adapts to chronic use of alcohol (Heilig, Goldman, Berrettini, & O'Brien, 2011; Wallner, Hanchar, & Olsen, 2006). Such GABA effects explain the initial sedative-like effects including drowsiness and a sense of relaxation and why, after

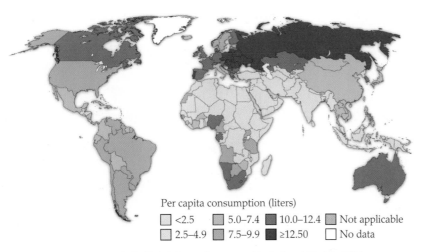

Per capita consumption (liters)

☐ <2.5   ☐ 5.0–7.4   ■ 10.0–12.4   ☐ Not applicable
☐ 2.5–4.9   ■ 7.5–9.9   ■ ≥12.50   ☐ No data

Source: WHO Global Status Report on Alcohol and Health, 2014

FIGURE 4.16 Worldwide alcohol consumption. Extreme variations in alcohol consumption exist across the world, with the highest rates in Russia.

a stressful day at work, many people self-medicate with their alcoholic beverage of choice.

Another neurotransmitter system altered by alcohol is the previously mentioned dopaminergic system. During alcohol withdrawal, the brains of animals with a history of alcohol use exhibit reduced firing rates of the mesolimbic neurons, decreasing the dopamine release in the nucleus accumbens (Diana, Pistis, Carboni, Gessa, & Rosetti, 1993). Decreased activity in the brain's reward center during withdrawal can lead to **anhedonia** (i.e., lack of reward perception, experienced by the individual as the inability to experience pleasure).

Analgesics: Opium

Opium (Greek for "poppy juice"), derived from the liquid extracts of certain poppy plants (see Figure 4.17), was likely used as early as 4000 bce, considering that the Sumerians drew an ideograph for the poppy plant that was identified as the "joy plant" (Jaffe, 1975). In the 18th century, smoking opium became a widespread practice in East Asia. The practice spread to America, while in Europe the practice of ingesting opium in the form of an alcohol-based tincture became popular.

FIGURE 4.17 Natural sources of opioids. The opium poppy and its sap drippings contain natural narcotics such as morphine and codeine.

One factor leading to the increased use of **morphine,** the principal psychoactive substance in opium, was the invention of the hypodermic needle in 1855 by the British physician Alexander Wood. Physicians used this efficient delivery system to inject morphine to relieve pain and other symptoms (Courtwright, 2001).

Opium continued to be consumed in liquid form as a medicinal aid throughout the 19th century. It was advertised, for example, in the 1897 *Sears, Roebuck and Co. Catalog* in various forms to treat cough and diarrhea. Products such as "Mrs. Winslow's Soothing Syrup" were marketed to help relieve pain in teething infants (see Figure 4.18). Today, variations of opium and morphine still have medicinal value. However, they are controlled substances under U.S. law, and their use is strictly regulated through prescriptions.

In addition to the principal active ingredient, morphine, other ingredients such as the cough suppressant and analgesic codeine have been chemically isolated from opium. **Heroin,** developed in the 19th century, was manufactured from morphine by adding two acetyl groups to the morphine molecule. Taken orally, morphine and heroin have similar effects, but when injected, heroin is much more potent (because it passes into the brain more easily and is converted to morphine). When high doses of **opioids** are administered either intravenously or inhaled, they rapidly penetrate into the brain and give users a subsequent feeling of euphoria.

What are the biological mechanisms of opioids? In the 1970s neuroscientists Solomon Snyder and Candice Pert identified **opioid receptors** throughout the brain (see Figure 4.19; Pert & Snyder, 1973). These scientists later demonstrated that the affinity of opioids for the opioid receptors was strongly correlated with the psychological and physiological effects of the drug (Snyder, 1977). In the midst of this research, several types of opioid receptors were identified, including the mu (μ), delta (δ), and kappa (κ) receptors (Snyder & Pasternak, 2003).

The *μ receptors* have a high affinity for opioids and are widely distributed throughout the brain and spinal cord.

FIGURE 4.18 Medicinal morphine. Prior to government regulations, morphine appeared in various 19th-century consumer products, such as this tonic for restless infants.

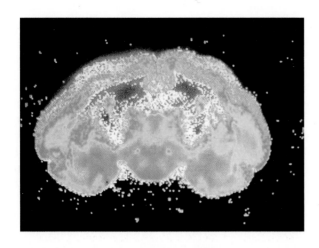

FIGURE 4.19 **Distribution of opiate receptors.** Areas of the highest density of opiate receptors (shown in red) are located in the nucleus accumbens and surrounding areas associated with reward functions.

High-density areas of μ receptors, related to the analgesic effects of opioids, include the thalamus, periaqueductal gray, raphe nuclei, certain areas of the spinal cord, and areas associated with reward including the nucleus accumbens. The brainstem areas regulate the cough control and antinausea effects of opioids (Mansour & Watson, 1993).

The δ receptors are localized more in the forebrain structures including the striatum, olfactory areas, substantia nigra, and nucleus accumbens. These receptors likely mediate the olfactory, motor, cognitive, and rewarding effects of the opioid drugs.

The κ receptors are located in the striatum, amygdala, hypothalamus, and pituitary and are most closely involved with dysphoria (a state of unease or dissatisfaction with life) and hallucinations, pain perception, temperature control, and certain neuroendocrine functions such as the stress response.

After the discovery of these receptors, researchers were puzzled as to why so many receptors existed for the byproducts of this poppy plant. Did the brain contain a natural substance to which the receptors had evolved to respond? In the 1970s researchers identified a peptide that activated the opioid receptors (Terenius & Wahlstrom, 1974; Hughes, 1975). This peptide was referred to as **enkephalin;** literally "in the brain." Several such opioid peptides were identified, including **endorphins.** These peptides were **endogenous** (i.e., produced within the organism itself) variations of morphine. Endorphins interact with the dopamine system by diminishing GABA's inhibitory effects leading to increased secretion of dopamine (Koneru, Satyanarayana, & Rizwan, 2009).

The United States was reminded of the addictive properties of opioids when the drug Oxycontin (oxycodone), introduced in 1996, rapidly became the country's best-selling narcotic pain reliever. Although Oxycontin was marketed with claims that it had less abuse potential than other drugs,

the drug became commonly abused, destroying many lives. Recently, a drastic increase in heroin abuse has been attributed to high rates of prescription painkillers. Approximately four of five individuals with a heroin addiction report that their addiction resulted from an initial addiction to prescription painkillers. The shift from prescribed opioids occurred because heroin was cheaper and more easily purchased (Kolodny et al., 2015). Another prescription opioid drug, methadone, is used to treat opioid drug addiction. Often used as a component of opioid maintenance treatment programs, this drug is prescribed to reduce withdrawal from illegal opioids since it engages opioid receptors in a similar manner as the abused drugs. However, when methadone is consumed, the euphoric response is diminished. Although the effectiveness varies, the goal of methadone maintenance treatment is to reduce opioid relapses (Walcher et al., 2016).

Hallucinogens: LSD

LSD is a semisynthetic product of a natural substance, lysergic acid, extracted from a rye fungus known as *Claviceps purpurea* (Passie, Halpern, Stichtenoth, Emrich, & Hintzen, 2008). The psychological effects of LSD were discovered when the substance was synthesized by Albert Hofmann, a chemist working for the Sandoz pharmaceutical company (Figure 4.20). Although his goal was to create a compound that would serve as a respiratory and circulatory stimulant, Hofmann had a clue that the substance produced other effects after he accidentally absorbed a small amount while working with it in the laboratory. He later described this first LSD "trip":

> Last Friday, April 16, 1943, I was forced to interrupt my work in the laboratory in the middle of the afternoon and proceed home, being affected by a remarkable restlessness, combined with a slight dizziness. At home I lay down and sank into a not unpleasant intoxicated-like condition, characterized by an extremely stimulated imagination. In a dreamlike state, with eyes closed (I found the daylight to be unpleasantly glaring), I perceived an uninterrupted stream of fantastic pictures, extraordinary shapes with intense, kaleidoscope play of colors. After some two hours this condition faded away. (Hofmann, 1979, p. 58)

Being a thorough scientist, Hofmann consumed a small amount of the drug the next week and confirmed that it was the LSD that was responsible for his rather bizarre experience. With the help of his laboratory assistant, he managed to ride his bicycle home. This time his hallucinations took on more of a threatening theme (a "bad trip"), but he reported having a profound sense of well-being the next morning (Hofmann, 1979).

In the late 1940s and early 1950s, LSD was marketed to the medical community as a tool to induce temporary psychosis in healthy individuals and enhance the effectiveness

FIGURE 4.20 Albert Hofmann. The chemist Alfred Hofmann first synthesized lysergic acid diethylamide (LSD) and was also the first to experience and describe its hallucinogenic effects.

of psychotherapy in individuals suffering from mental illnesses such as schizophrenia. In the later 1960s the drug became popular for recreational and spiritual uses, leading to its placement on a list of government-regulated drugs in 1966. After this time, enthusiasm for LSD as a therapeutic tool diminished. Consequently, little legal research has been conducted with human subjects since the 1970s (Passie et al., 2008). A wide array of psychological effects (as described by Hofmann), including altered emotions, enhanced introspection, and a sense of being in a dreamlike state, have been ascribed to LSD. Most noteworthy are the unusual perceptual changes such as hallucinations, illusions, alterations in perception of time and space, and **synesthesia** (a blurring of the boundaries among senses, e.g., seeing music, which is discussed in Chapter 6) (Passie et al., 2008).

Laboratory research with animals has revealed clues about the neurobiological mechanisms of LSD. Generally, the drug acts as a partial agonist of serotonin 2_A (5-HT$_{2A}$) receptors (Nichols, 2004). However, LSD is a complex drug, with other neurotransmitters such as glutamate either directly or indirectly affected (Hanks & Gonzalez-Maeso,

2012). The Purdue neurochemist David Nichols has suggested that 5-HT$_{2A}$ receptors in the brainstem raphe nucleus contribute to the sleep and dreamlike effects of the drug, whereas these receptors in the locus coeruleus enhance attention to novel stimuli. These serotonin receptors are also found in the thalamus, the brain structure that filters sensory information to the cortical areas, and the nearby reticular nucleus, a gateway to the thalamus. Thus, the typical filtering and dispersal of neural information becomes disrupted under the influence of LSD. Additionally, LSD has been proposed to indirectly inhibit GABA neurons in the pyramidal cells of the cortex. This, along with other cellular effects of the drug, is thought to enhance activation and suppress normal filtering that typically accompanies neural activity in the decision-making and executive areas of the cortex (Nichols, 2004).

After more than 40 years, recent research with LSD and other hallucinogens has prompted a renewed interest in their potential clinical uses for psychiatric disorders. In general, neuroimaging data suggest that *psychedelic* drugs (known for altering thought and perceptual experiences) influence brain areas implicated in affective disorders (Vollenweider & Kometer, 2010). Providing further evidence of the involvement of 5-HT$_{2A}$ receptors in psychiatric illness, one study found more of these receptors in the prefrontal cortex and hippocampus, but not in the nucleus accumbens, of teenage suicide victims than of mentally healthy control subjects (Pandey et al., 2002; see Figure 4.21). In Chapter 13, you will learn about the use of ketamine, a hallucinogenic anesthetic, for the treatment of depression. More research, however, is required to determine whether LSD and other hallucinogens hold any value in the treatment of mental health and mental illness.

A Drug with Diverse CNS Effects: Cannabis

Cannabis, or marijuana, was grown in China more than 6,000 years ago. India had the first cannabis-oriented culture resulting from the drug's use, peaking during the 16th to 19th centuries, to treat diseases such as malaria. By the 1920s, the *ganja* preparation, consisting of the dried flowering tops of plants rich in δ-9-tetrahydrocannabinol, or **THC,** was popular in Caribbean nations. However, it was not until the 1930s that cannabis entered the United States via Mexican laborers as well as South American and Caribbean sailors. In the 1960s, marijuana use became common among middle- and upper-class Americans. By 1979, 55 million Americans had tried the drug, with two-thirds of the users in the 18–25 age range. From there, marijuana use became a worldwide phenomenon (Courtwright, 2001).

Today, marijuana remains the most heavily used illegal drug in the United States, but the illicit nature of marijuana is rapidly changing. As of 2016, 24 states and the District of Columbia had either legalized medical marijuana or decriminalized possession of the drug (although it remains illegal

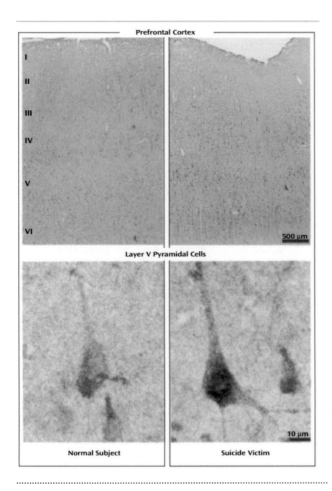

Prefrontal Cortex

I

II

III

IV

V

VI

500 μm

Layer V Pyramidal Cells

10 μm

Normal Subject   Suicide Victim

FIGURE 4.21 Serotonin receptors and suicide. In one study, teenage suicide victims showed a higher density of 5-HT$_{2A}$ receptors in the prefrontal cortex compared with healthy control subjects.

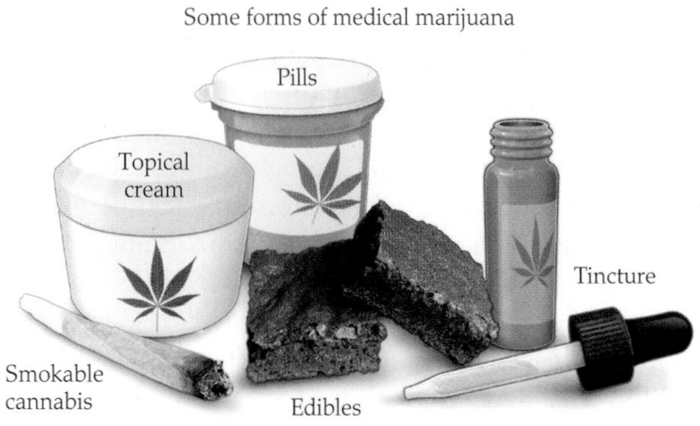

Some forms of medical marijuana

Pills

Topical cream

Tincture

Smokable cannabis

Edibles

FIGURE 4.22 Medical marijuana. Several states have legalized the medical use of marijuana in different forms.

under federal law). Such legalizations have primarily applied to medicinal uses (Figure 4.22), including the treatment of nausea in cancer patients undergoing chemotherapy and the treatment of appetite loss in AIDS patients (Boyette & Wilson, 2015; *New York Times*, 2012).

The issue of legalizing marijuana and the potential long-term effects of such legalization remain hotly contested. Research studies have identified both positive and negative effects of marijuana, depending on the variables being assessed. Since marijuana is sometimes prescribed for chronic pain, states that have legalized the use of medical marijuana have lower mortality rates for overdose of opioids (also used to treat pain) than do states that have not legalized medical marijuana (Bachhuber, Saloner, Cunningham, & Barry, 2014). Regarding the long-term effects of recreational use, a survey conducted in Australia and New Zealand indicates that individuals who used marijuana daily prior to the age of 17 were less likely to complete high school and were more likely to use other illicit drugs and attempt suicide than their nonuser counterparts (Silins et al., 2014).

Research suggests that the use of cannabis leads to several diverse psychological effects including altered sensations, increased appetite, euphoria, disinhibition, and

relaxation. Negative effects include impaired memory and motor performance, as well as other cognitive impairments. In agreement with the previously described study (Silins et al., 2014), a longitudinal study (following subjects over many years) indicated that individuals who started using marijuana as adolescents exhibited more cognitive decline in adulthood than nonusers, with a positive correlation between persistence of use and extent of cognitive decline (Meier et al., 2012). Diminished academic performance and lack of motivation are also correlated with chronic marijuana use. Several health risks, such as respiratory problems, are associated with smoking marijuana (Anderson, Rizzo, Block, Pearlson, & O'Leary, 2010; Jo, Chen, Chua, Talmage, & Role, 2005; Moore, Augustson, Moser, & Budney, 2004).

The Israeli scientists Raphael Mechoulam and Yehiel Gaoni identified THC, the primary active ingredient in marijuana, in 1964 and proceeded to conduct further research on its effects (Mechoulam, 1970). The receptors activated by THC, known as **cannabinoid receptors**, were identified in the 1980s by Lawrence Melvin and Allyn Howlett, scientists at St. Louis University, and Ross Johnson, a neurochemist at Pfizer (Devane, Dysarz, Johnson, Melvin, & Howlett, 1988). The cannabinoid receptors are concentrated in the basal ganglia, substantia nigra, cerebellum, hippocampus, and cerebral cortex (Herkenham et al., 1991).

Cannabis users experience alterations in coordination, memory, and locomotor activity, which are key functions of the brain areas in which the cannabinoid receptors are concentrated. Studies have revealed that by acting on presynaptic receptors, cannabinoids can inhibit several neurotransmitters including dopamine, norepinephrine, acetylcholine, glutamate, and GABA (Iverson, 2003). Researchers are extensively studying the different types of cannabinoid receptors as drug targets for obesity management and analgesia (Grant, Atkinson, Gouaux, & Wilsey, 2012; Vickers & Kennett, 2005).

Once these cannabinoid receptors were identified, Mechoulam's lab identified an endogenous substance that mimicked the cannabinoids—30 long years after first identifying THC! As mentioned earlier in this chapter, this substance was named anandamide, the Sanskrit word for "bringer of inner bliss and tranquility" (Felder & Glass, 1998). Activation of the cannabinoid receptors, whether through drug use or through endogenous production of anandamide, modulates dopaminergic functions in a manner similar to that of the opioids. Cannabinoid receptor activation affects GABAergic neurons so that they no longer inhibit dopaminergic neurons. Dopaminergic neurons are not affected directly, since they lack cannabinoid receptors. However, with decreased inhibition from GABAergic neurons, the dopaminergic neurons ultimately increase their release of dopamine (Pierce & Kumaresan, 2006).

Now that you are familiar with the specific effects of various neurotransmitter systems throughout the brain and how certain psychoactive drugs influence these neurotransmitter systems, you are prepared to learn more about how a person's casual or medicinal use of these substances can reach a tipping point for the emergence of addiction. Once the brain adjusts to the continued presence of a particular psychoactive drug, new waves of neural effects occur as the brain attempts to compensate for the unnatural flow of neurotransmitters. In some cases, the brain's ability to compensate for and manage these changing tides of neurochemicals collapses, leading to devastating results for drug users. In the next section, we will discuss characteristics of the addicted brain and current methods of treating drug addiction.

Drug Addiction

Drug addiction is a complex phenomenon that typically begins because a drug generates a pleasurable experience and decreases pain, stress, and anxiety, but is often maintained because of an uncomfortable response when the drug is no longer consumed (Cardinal & Everitt, 2004). Thus, drug addiction spirals into an abnormal motivated behavior.

Before psychoactive drugs were manufactured in the laboratory, they existed only in nature in the form of plants. Exemplifying the conservation of neurotransmitters, chemicals in plants such as marijuana, tobacco, opium poppies, and psilocybin mushrooms contain molecules that can cross the blood–brain barrier and activate specific receptors in the brain. This results in psychological experiences ranging from pleasure to hallucinations.

Most drugs of abuse hijack the brain's mesolimbic pathway, or mesolimbic dopaminergic pathway. This pathway consists of cell bodies located in the ventral tegmental area projecting to the nucleus accumbens. This system also projects to the frontal cortex and amygdala (see Figure 4.23). The entire pathway projecting from the ventral tegmental area to the frontal cortex is known as the mesocorticolimbic dopamine pathway (Koob, 2009). The mesolimbic dopaminergic pathway is known as the common neural pathway for addiction because activation of key areas in the circuit has

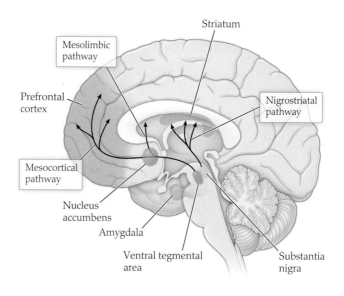

FIGURE 4.23 Dopamine pathways of the brain. The mesocorticolimbic pathway that is involved in addiction projects from the ventral tegmental area to the frontal cortex. It differs from the nigrostriatal pathway, which is associated with movement and extends from the substantia nigra to the striatum.

the ability to motivate and sustain drug use (Gardner, 2011; Stewart, 2000). For example, injections of amphetamine into the nucleus accumbens increase firing in dopaminergic cells and cause rats previously exposed to heroin to search for heroin (Stewart & Vezina, 1988). Regardless of the type of drug, these addictive substances eventually alter the mesolimbic dopaminergic pathway, a system designed to motivate animals to engage in life-sustaining endeavors such as eating, drinking, and maintaining social relationships. Thus, generally, drugs of abuse utilize the neurobiological pathways typically involved in motivating animals to engage in behaviors necessary for species preservation (Koob & Volkow, 2010).

As is the case for most complex responses, however, drug addiction ultimately involves many neurotransmitters in addition to dopamine such as serotonin, norepinephrine, glutamate, and GABA (Tomkins & Sellers, 2001). Chapter 8 will thoroughly describe the biological systems of reward and pleasure.

The power of addiction to guide human behavior is often striking. Consider the case of a man who finds out that his drug of choice led to a vascular inflammatory condition that had caused him to have his leg amputated at the age of 22. Most people would expect him to quit using the drug after learning this, especially after he hears that further use would result in additional amputations. However, the pull of the drug with the anticipation of its immediate effects is stronger than the long-term fear of losing a limb.

In this case, the young man, Brandon Carmichael, suffers from the rare vascular condition known as **Buerger's disease** (see Figure 4.24), a condition characterized by

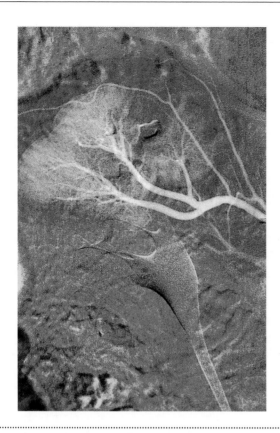

FIGURE 4.24 **Buerger's disease.** Buerger's disease is characterized by smoking-induced inflammation blockblood flow to the arms and legs. Shown here, inflamed arteries disrupt blood flow to this patient's kidney.

inflammation and blockage of blood vessels in the hands and feet that is triggered by smoking cigarettes. Ultimately, Brandon's knowledge that he had this disease and the devastating consequences of continuing to smoke did not curtail his addiction because he needed to have his other leg amputated as well (Arkkila, 2006). As mentioned earlier in this chapter, although it is legal, cigarette smoking represents the most prevalent preventable cause of premature death in the United States and the developed world (Peto, Lopez, Boreham, Thun, & Health, 1992; Volpp et al., 2009).

Drug addiction is generally viewed as an uncontrollable desire to consume a drug. Many factors, such as the strength of the initial high, determine the intensity of addiction. Drug addiction is a complex, ongoing process that continues to change the brain as the user continues to consume the drug. As the brain changes in response to continued use of the drug, **drug dependence,** the need for the drug to maintain physiological functions, develops. **Tolerance,** for example, occurs when an individual's reaction to a drug decreases with repeated exposure to that drug, such that increasingly larger doses of the drug are required to achieve the same desired effect. Evidence suggests that drugs restructure the brain's neurochemical systems by altering physiological mechanisms such as decreasing receptor sensitivity or increasing the efficiency of metabolic processes that break down the drugs. With continued use and increased tolerance, the user

requires more and more of the given drug to achieve a high, and it becomes increasingly difficult to break away from the drug's firm grasp.

Two distinct types of tolerance include *pharmacodynamic tolerance* and *behavioral tolerance.* Pharmacodynamic tolerance results from exposure to high drug doses and is not considered directly impacted by the environment. Behavioral tolerance is sensitive to behavioral and environmental manipulations; it involves learning and memory. If an individual consumes a drug repeatedly in the same environmental setting, he or she will develop behavioral tolerance to it. However, if he or she takes the same amount of the drug in an unfamiliar setting, the drug will have its original effect (Doweiko, 2009; Vogel-Sprott, 1997). As discussed in "Context Matters," **sensitization,** an *increase* in drug efficiency on repeated use, occurs in other cases (Stewart & Badiani, 1993).

Stages of the Addiction Cycle

The clinical characteristics of the **drug addiction cycle** include a compulsion to seek and consume a drug, an inability to control the intake of a drug, and the onset of a negative emotional state when access to the drug is prevented (Koob & Le Moal, 1997). Drug addiction is also characterized by the tendency for chronic **relapse,** the recurrence of drug use following a period of abstinence.

Survey research from 2013 indicates that nearly 25 million Americans (12 years and older), representing approximately 9.5% of the population, had either used an illegal drug or abused a psychotherapeutic medication such as a pain medication during the past month (Substance Abuse and Mental Health Services Administration, 2014). This rate had increased from 8.3% in 2002, with the rise attributed to increased use of marijuana, which is the most frequently used illicit drug (National Institute on Drug Abuse, 2011). Statistics indicate that alcohol is used by 52% of individuals over the age of 12, with 23% reporting a binge episode (five or more drinks on one day during the past month) and 6% identifying as heavy drinkers (five binge episodes in the past month). In addition, nicotine use is reported by 25.5% of Americans aged 12 or older (Substance Abuse and Mental Health Services Administration, 2014). Hence, the use of drugs for nonmedicinal purposes is common in the United States and, as you have seen in this chapter, across the world.

Neuroscientists are currently investigating the potential biological processes that are involved in an individual's transition from occasional, controlled drug use to a pattern of drug abuse that is characterized by the drug addiction cycle described below. According to recent research, the behavioral effects of drug use include aspects of impulse-control disorders and compulsive disorders (Everitt et al., 2008). For example, the University of Cambridge behavioral neuroscientists Barry Everitt and Trevor Robbins have suggested that, as individuals transition from the voluntary consumption of a given drug to the habitual use of that drug, neural control shifts from the prefrontal cortex (involved in executive decision making) to brain areas involved in movement such as the striatum (Everitt & Robbins, 2005). This neural shift provides an explanation for the diminishing cognitive control and informed decision-making abilities often observed in drug-using individuals as the drug addiction cycle emerges. The close proximity of the nucleus accumbens to the striatum and the importance of dopamine in both areas likely facilitate this shift from *controlled drug use* to *drug addiction*.

The transition to drug dependence may also be accompanied by neuroplastic changes that prompt drug use during vulnerable developmental stages—such as the adolescent years (Figure 4.25; Koob, Kandel, & Volkow, 2008). Impulsivity, or risky behavior, is known to be high during adolescence and may play a role in increased vulnerability to drug use (Blakemore & Robbins, 2012). Specifically, addiction rates have been correlated with high impulsivity in humans. Research with animal models of addiction has further indicated that impulsive rats respond at higher rates (or work harder) to self-administer cocaine than nonimpulsive control rats. Additionally, highly impulsive rats had lower dopamine function in the nucleus accumbens area than nonimpulsive control rats (Everitt et al., 2008).

According to Salk Institute neuroscientist George Koob and the NIH scientist Nora Volkow (2010), the drug addiction cycle consists of the three stages discussed below.

Binge/Intoxication Stage When a drug creates a positive psychological state, it has, either directly or indirectly, influenced the brain reward pathway described above (the mesolimbic dopaminergic pathway). Direct influences include immediate alterations of the dopamine system, as seen in cocaine's ability to block the reuptake of dopamine into the presynaptic synapse. Indirect influences include the ability of opioids, such as heroin, to enhance GABA functions in

the ventral tegmental area that ultimately enhances dopaminergic functions (Pierce & Kumaresan, 2006). Mice that have been genetically altered so that they lack the D1 receptor, a specific type of dopamine receptor prevalent in the prefrontal cortex component of the mesolimbic dopaminergic pathway (Takahashi, Yamada, & Suhara, 2012), do not self-administer cocaine as mice with unaltered dopaminergic receptors do (Caine et al., 2007). This provides evidence that dopamine is important in the initial rewarding experience of drug use.

The central amygdala also plays a role in the acute reinforcing effects of drugs of abuse. When dopamine (D1) antagonists are injected into the central amygdala of rats, cocaine self-administration is blocked (Caine, Heinrichs, Coffin, & Koob, 1995; A. McGregor & Roberts, 1993). Further, lesions of the central amygdala also block self-administration of alcohol in rats (Hyytia & Koob, 1995; Heyser, Roberts, Schulteis, & Koob, 1999).

Finally, the **ventral pallidum,** a site for considerable output from the nucleus accumbens, appears to be a crucial component of the reward circuit. When this area is lesioned, rats do not work for cocaine or heroin injections (Hubner & Koob, 1990; Robledo & Koob, 1993). Although the exact mechanisms for each drug of abuse vary to some degree, research points to the role of dopaminergic activity in the nucleus accumbens, ventral pallidum, and central amygdala for the generation of the early rewarding experiences associated with abused drugs. Ultimately, the nervous system comes to classify an abused drug as being just as biologically relevant as other natural rewards (see Figure 4.26a; Koob & Volkow, 2010).

Brain imaging studies with humans provide an opportunity to determine which areas of the brain are activated when an individual consumes a drug and reports a pleasurable effect. Nora Volkow's neuroimaging studies have indicated that subjects report a pleasurable experience when drugs

FIGURE 4.25   Teens and addiction. Because of the continuing neural adaptations occurring in the adolescent brain, this stage of development represents the highest vulnerability to risk-taking behavior that can lead to addiction.

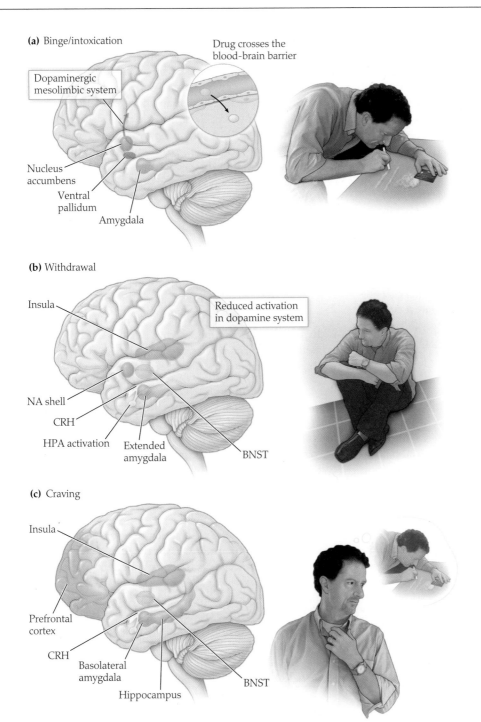

(a) Binge/intoxication

Dopaminergic mesolimbic system

Drug crosses the blood-brain barrier

Nucleus accumbens

Ventral pallidum

Amygdala

(b) Withdrawal

Insula

Reduced activation in dopamine system

NA shell

CRH

HPA activation

Extended amygdala

BNST

(c) Craving

Insula

Prefrontal cortex

CRH

Basolateral amygdala

Hippocampus

BNST

FIGURE 4.26 **The brain's role in addiction.** (a) During the initial stage of addiction, the nucleus accumbens and associated areas are activated to reinforce the positive effects of the drug. (b) When the drug is no longer present, the brain areas involved in processing negative emotions, such as the amygdala, are disproportionately activated, as well as the stress hormone system (corticotropin-releasing hormone). (c) Following detoxification, drug-associated environmental cues activate brain areas involved in memory and distress, such as the hippocampus and amygdala.

such as the psychostimulant **methylphenidate** (Ritalin) quickly and significantly increase dopaminergic activity in the areas of the ventral pallidum and nucleus accumbens. However, slow and stable increases in dopaminergic activity, brought about by typical medicinal doses of dopaminergic drugs, fail to trigger such a pleasurable experience (Volkow & Swanson, 2003). Thus, when children take methylphenidate as a treatment for ADHD, they do not experience a "high" because their controlled and sustained doses do not mimic natural dopaminergic firing in striatal cells.

Withdrawal/Negative Affect Stage Following the initial introduction and subsequent binge on a drug, agonizing symptoms of withdrawal arise when the drug is no longer available to an individual. For example, when people stop taking psychostimulants such as amphetamine, withdrawal symptoms include depressed mood, fatigue, and psychomotor slowness. When rats are removed from a drug, they have shown a reduced willingness to work for natural rewards such as food (Barr & Phillips, 1999). Chronic activation of the mesolimbic dopaminergic system and its related brain structures compromises its responsivity. This effect is magnified during withdrawal, when the drug is no longer available to provide the boost to the dopaminergic system to which the system had become accustomed. More dramatic physiological effects are observed in heroin withdrawal.

Researchers have found a neuroanatomical system known as the *extended amygdala* to be activated during the negative emotional states accompanying withdrawal. As seen in Figure 4.26b, the extended amygdala includes the central amygdala, bed nucleus of the stria terminalis, and a portion of the nucleus accumbens shell region. The extended amygdala receives inputs from various regions of the limbic system and has traditionally been viewed as being important in fear and pain processing (Le Doux, 2000; Neugebauer, Li, Bird, & Han, 2004). Hence, the message the brain is receiving during drug withdrawal resembles those related to real threats. The diminished availability of a specific drug, at one point a substance not necessary for survival, now seems like a matter of life or death.

The negative emotional effects accompanying withdrawal are also observed in animal models of drug withdrawal. In one study, rats in withdrawal from amphetamine exhibited reduced motivation to work for another positive stimulus, a sweet solution. However, when they were given a partial dopamine agonist, the rats were, once again, as motivated to work for the sweet solution as were the nonwithdrawal (control) rats (Orsini, Koob, & Pulvirenti, 2001). The inability to experience pleasure is a symptom of depression (as we will discuss in Chapter 13). This study's findings of diminished motivation to experience non-drug-related rewards suggest that symptoms of depression may characterize this withdrawal stage. Additionally, withdrawal is characterized by a heightened stress response. Animals in withdrawal exhibit an activated hypothalamic–pituitary–adrenal axis (with elevated adrenocorticotropic hormone and corticosterone; Koob, 2008), as well as increased anxiety (Koob & Volkow, 2010).

Because of the uncomfortable nature of withdrawal, few neuroimaging studies have been conducted with human patients who are experiencing this phase of the addiction cycle. However, researchers have observed diminished activity in the mesolimbic dopaminergic pathway once patients' withdrawal symptoms have subsided (Koob & Volkow, 2010). Such effects could lead to anhedonia (defined earlier in this chapter as a lack of reward perception), preventing the individual undergoing withdrawal from experiencing pleasure or enjoyment (Martinez et al., 2004, 2005).

Preoccupation/Anticipation (Craving) Stage The craving stage is a definitive aspect of addiction, often leading to relapse and restarting the downward spiral of addiction. For example, research suggests that the depressive and psychotic symptoms of methamphetamine withdrawal dissipate after about a week, with craving decreasing in the second week, both continuing to decline for about five weeks (Zorick et al., 2010). However, data suggest that individuals who have

abused cocaine may have cravings for *months* or even *years* after having stopped using it (Nestler, 2005). As described earlier in this chapter, other drugs such as nicotine produce similar persistent cravings that lead to relapse (Killen & Fortmann, 1997). Thus, when any drug of abuse produces long-term alterations in the brain, the user is susceptible to cravings and, unfortunately, relapse long after the person ceases use of the drug (National Institute on Drug Abuse, 2012). Understanding the persistent effects of these drugs makes it easier to understand why, when faced with so many negative consequences, a person will continue to consume a drug of abuse such as methamphetamine.

Generally, individuals who have abstained from drug use for some time tend to relapse in response to one or more of the following experiences:

- Exposure to the drug once again (considered a **priming effect** in which an individual is reminded of an earlier memory of effects of the drug);
- Exposure to environmental cues that are strongly associated with drug use (i.e., **conditioned cues**); or
- Exposure to acute (i.e., short-term) stress.

As in the case of Nic Sheff and his father, described at the beginning of this chapter, you can imagine how frustrating it must be to see a loved one or patient/client go for years without touching a drug, only to relapse and begin the painful process all over again. Relapse activates the multiple neural systems that make it so difficult to control the urge to consume drugs again . . . and again. The susceptibility to relapse for individuals addicted to drugs provides strong evidence that drugs alter the brain in long-term ways.

Animal studies suggest that relapse resulting from drug-related cues (a priming effect) is localized to the medial prefrontal cortex, nucleus accumbens, and ventral pallidum. By contrast, research in rats provides evidence that relapse resulting from conditioned cues involves the basolateral amygdala that communicates with the prefrontal cortex, brain areas implicated in learning (Koob & Volkow, 2010). Finally, research with rats has shown that relapse is associated with compromised hippocampal functioning (Caine, Humby, Robbins, & Everitt, 2001; see Figure 4.26c).

Jane Stewart's laboratory at Concordia University has conducted extensive research on the triggers for relapse, especially on the impact of acute stress exposure (Stewart, 2000). Her laboratory's model requires the rat to self-administer the drug of interest by pressing one lever of two lever choices. Subsequently, the levers are left in the cage, but the drug is no longer made available to the rats. During this time of *extinction training* (a form of conditioning that removes the reward that is associated with a specific behavior), the animals eventually stop pressing the lever associated with the drug. This model allows the Stewart laboratory to investigate the ability of various stimuli and experiences to reignite the rat's motivation to press the lever for drugs. After a period of abstinence, what sends the rats back to the "bar"?

If the experimenter gives the rat an injection of the drug previously delivered by the lever setup and places the rat in the former drug-taking environment, the rat starts pressing the lever for drugs again. This supports the existence of a priming effect of a drug during abstinence. The higher the dose of the drug, the longer the rat persists in its attempts to obtain the drug. Thus, the administration of the drug served as a strong reminder of the drug's effects, resulting in a renewed interest in drug seeking and drug consumption.

This research suggests that the presence of the drug in the body and brain prompts an individual to focus on drug-related cues and then engage in drug-seeking and consumption behaviors. Because of the strong associations formed between two stimuli in classical conditioning (discussed in Chapter 12), certain environmental cues become associated with the effects of drug use when a drug is repeatedly consumed. These conditioned cues direct the individual's attention toward the drug, just as the drug itself does (Jaffe, Cascell, Kumor, & Sherer, 1989).

In a series of studies, Stewart and her colleagues systematically investigated the influence of various factors on facilitating the role of acute stress in relapse. This research has pointed to the important role of a particular neurochemical in a specific brain area. Specifically, corticotropin-releasing hormone (CRH), a neurochemical released by the hypothalamus, travels to the pituitary to trigger the release of another stress hormone, adrenocorticotropic hormone (see Chapter 10). In this research, CRH and a brain area involved in anxiety, the bed nucleus of the stria terminalis (BNST), have been implicated in relapse. The BNST was investigated because of the location of CRH receptors in this area. The role of stress in relapse was evident in one experiment, for example, in which rats were trained to self-administer cocaine and then given five drug-free days. When the rats were returned to their drug administration chambers and given brief intermittent foot shock as an acute stressor, they resumed their cocaine seeking by pressing the levers.

Further, bypassing the environmental stress (shock), if CRH was infused into the BNST but not the amygdala, the animals reinstated their cocaine-seeking responses (Erb & Stewart, 1999).

Additional research suggests that the CRH system may be modulated by the neurotransmitter norepinephrine. Specifically, a norepinephrine receptor agonist, *clonidine*, blocks the stress-induced relapse in cases of both cocaine and heroin abuse (Erb et al., 2000; Shaham, Highfield, Delfs, Leung, & Stewart, 2000). Clonidine enhances norepinephrine function. This research provides evidence that, in addition to drug presentation, acute stress also has a priming effect on animals exhibiting extinction.

Are animals more likely to revisit other previously extinguished responses, unrelated to drug use, under stressful conditions? According to the research conducted on rats, the answer is no. If lever pressing is associated with a sugar drink, for example, and then the response is extinguished, the rat is not more likely to go back to the levers when presented with an acute stressor. The psychoactive drugs seem to impact this CRH system in a unique manner, making the animal more vulnerable to stressful events or at least more likely to attempt to "self-medicate" during subsequent stressful events (Stewart, 2000).

This research reinforces the important role of the environment and personal experiences in triggering relapses in drug addiction. Being in environments rich in cues associated with past drug use places a person at great risk for relapse. Consequently, clinicians acknowledge the importance of drug-related cues in relapse and recommend that former drug users who are trying to abstain from drug use not spend time with friends who use the drug nor spend time in environments in which they previously used the drug. Stress reduction strategies (e.g., effective coping strategies, pharmacological aids) may also build resilience against relapse (Anton, 1999; National Institute on Drug Abuse, 2012).

CONTEXT MATTERS

Treating Cocaine Addiction with Environmental Enrichment

Featured study: Solinas, M., Chauvet, C., Thiriet, N., El Rawas, R., & Jaber, M. (2008). Reversal of cocaine addiction by environmental enrichment. Proceedings of the National Academy of Sciences of the USA, 105, *17145–17150.*

Marcello Solinas and his colleagues at the University of Poitiers in France investigated the effect of environmental enrichment on the likelihood of cocaine addiction (Solinas, Chauvet, Thiriet, El Rawas, & Jaber, 2008). As discussed previously in this text, environmental enrichment consists of several different contextual elements including novelty, cognitive complexity, physical exercise, and social contact that may have

therapeutic value. As seen in Context Matters Figure 4.1, after receiving a series of cocaine injections, group-housed mice were randomly assigned to either a standard or an enriched environment. In the standard environment, the rats had food and water. In the enriched environment, they had food and water, as well as a running wheel, plastic house, and new toys that were changed every few days. After 1, 7, or 30 days

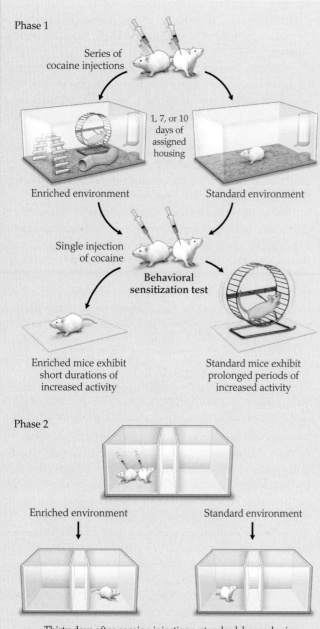

Phase 1

Series of cocaine injections

1, 7, or 10 days of assigned housing

Enriched environment

Standard environment

Single injection of cocaine

Behavioral sensitization test

Enriched mice exhibit short durations of increased activity

Standard mice exhibit prolonged periods of increased activity

Phase 2

Enriched environment

Standard environment

Thirty days after cocaine injections, standard-housed mice preferred the compartment where the injections took place, but mice housed in enriched environments did not.

Phase 3

Enriched environment

Standard environment

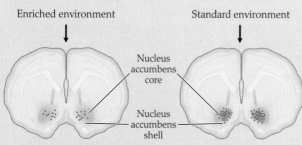

Nucleus accumbens core

Nucleus accumbens shell

When all the mice were reexposed to cocaine, the enriched-environment mice showed less nucleus accumbens activation than did standard-environment mice.

following the final cocaine injection, the mice's response, or sensitization, to a subsequent cocaine injection was assessed by observing the animals' motor activity.

Behavioral sensitization is characterized by increased responsiveness to the repeated exposure to a stimulus such as a specific drug. In this case, behavioral sensitization persisted longer for the standard-housed mice after they received a final injection of cocaine. In fact, the standard-housed mice showed up to twice as much motor activity in response to the cocaine injection as a separate group that had no prior experience with cocaine. Mice housed in enriched environments showed reduced sensitization when compared with the standard-housed mice; in fact, they were indistinguishable from the mice with no prior experience with cocaine.

In a second phase of the study, the researchers exposed mice to a **conditioned place-preference test** to assess their motivation to consume the drug. Mice were exposed to cocaine and then housed in standard or enriched environments for 1, 7, or 30 days. To assess conditioned place preference, the cocaine injections were administered in a dual-compartment box. This apparatus had a central area for mice to be placed before two doors were lifted to allow them to explore either of the two compartments. Different combinations of objects were placed on the walls in each compartment to make the two areas appear as two distinct spaces. The mice received cocaine injections when they were in one specific compartment.

As expected, if mice were placed in the standard environment following this training, they spent more time in the compartment associated with drug delivery after 1, 7, and 30 days. However, if mice were placed in the enriched environment for 30 days following this training, they did *not* prefer the compartment associated with drug delivery. But what if something about the enriched environment simply led to increased memory loss . . . so that the mice just failed

....

CONTEXT MATTERS FIGURE 4.1 Behavioral sensitization. After exposing mice to either a standard or an enriched environment, their memory of cocaine administration was assessed after 1, 7, or 30 days by being placed in a place preference box. After 30 days of exposure to an enriched environment, cocaine sensitization, or a preference for the side of the box where the drug was administered, was no longer present. Thus, the enriched environment functioned as a treatment for cocaine sensitization.

to remember the positive effects associated with the compartment in which they received cocaine injections? To test this possibility, the experimenters conducted a similar experiment with injections of the aversive drug lithium. In this case, mice in both the standard and the enriched environments showed evidence of a memory for the aversive drug (translated as *not* spending time in the chamber associated with the injections of the aversive drug).

After examining the animals' brains, researchers found that, in a mouse with no history of cocaine exposure, a single injection resulted in cellular activation in the orbitofrontal cortex, regardless of housing history. Of the mice that had received the series of cocaine injections as described above, the animals in the enriched environment exhibited less activation than standard-housed mice in the infralimbic cortex (part of the prefrontal cortex), the nucleus accumbens, the ventral tegmental area, and the basolateral amygdala. Perhaps enhanced processing in these motivational and emotional areas contributes to a heightened vulnerability for sensitization and eventual relapse (Solinas et al., 2008).

These findings provide a springboard for neuroscientists trying to develop addiction treatment strategies for humans. The evidence that the enriched environment reduced activation of the brain's reward system in the cocaine-using mice, likely via modifications in the mesolimbic dopaminergic system, suggests that windows of opportunity exist to reclaim this system once it has been hijacked by a drug.

In line with the results of the Rat Park studies discussed in Chapter 1, the results of the Solinas et al. (2008) cocaine study suggest that the use of positive and stimulating environmental conditions can diminish craving and help addicts stay clean (Carroll & Onken, 2005). Indeed, these findings may help explain why addicted human drug users held in prison cells for extended periods (a human version of an impoverished or standard environment) without access to drugs often relapse soon after being released from prison. The potential effectiveness of positive and stimulating environmental contexts may explain why participation in social meetings such as Alcoholics Anonymous and Narcotics Anonymous is associated with lower relapse rates (Krentzman et al., 2011).

Addiction Therapies

Considering that drug addiction has been a prevalent worldwide problem for centuries, with an estimated financial cost in the United States alone exceeding $600 billion annually, one might think that great strides would have been made toward the discovery of cures for this condition (Robison & Nestler, 2012). Although a variety of therapeutic approaches have been used over the years, a cure for drug addiction still eludes scientists. Nevertheless, many modern-day therapies do show promise.

Although removing a drug from a person's physiological system—detoxification—is an important first step in addiction recovery, the complex factors contributing to addiction suggest that this single step is far from a cure. Certain pharmacological approaches, in combination with behavioral and psychosocial therapies, have proved effective as addiction therapies. This is particularly the case for opioid, nicotine, and alcohol addiction.

Much hope surrounds the promise that targeted genetic therapies for addiction will prove to be more effective than other approaches (Robison & Nestler, 2012). However, because the neuroanatomy underlying addiction is intimately involved in natural emotional processing, the thought of manipulating genetic expression related to the emotional reward neural network should be approached with great caution. Behavioral therapies such as contingency management interventions may facilitate treatment for most addictions. In this type of therapy, a patient may receive vouchers or prizes for drug-free urine, with the incentives getting stronger with longer periods of abstinence (Budney, Moore, Rocha, & Higgins, 2006). Finally, technological advances have facilitated the introduction of treatment strategies such as the electronic cigarette. This device includes an electronic inhaler that vaporizes a liquid containing nicotine to simulate the act of smoking. Research has yet to confirm the safety and clinical efficacy of this strategy (Bullen et al., 2013). See Table 4.4 for brief descriptions of existing and experimental therapeutic approaches for drug addiction.

How effective are these treatments? That is a complex question with few simple answers. Because drug addiction is considered a chronic disease, addiction therapies emphasize disease management and reduced relapse rates rather than cure rates. Accordingly, for most patients, treatment consists of a combination of several therapy approaches and continued monitoring over a long period of time. As shown in Table 4.5, the relapse rates for drug addiction are similar to those for other diseases that are influenced by both physiological and behavioral components. In general, combinations of treatment therapies are more effective than treatment with a single type of therapy. For example, behavioral therapies combined with pharmacological therapies produce more successful outcomes than either treatment delivered alone. The good news is that most people who go into and remain in treatment are able to stop using drugs. The diminished drug use achieved in therapy also leads to decreased criminal offenses and improvement in other areas of life such as career and family satisfaction (National Institute of Drug Abuse, 2012; O'Brien & McLellan, 1996).

TABLE 4.4.

Therapies for Drug Addiction

THERAPEUTIC APPROACH	DESCRIPTION
Detoxification	Patient is not allowed to consume drug; typically, hospitalization is recommended to prevent patient's access to drugs and to avoid medical complications of withdrawal effects
Pharmacological therapies	Drugs are prescribed to counteract withdrawal effects of abused drugs; examples include buprenorphine and methadone for heroin/opioid addiction
Vaccinations	Antibodies are presented that are designed to render the drug and any psychological effects of the drug inactive (described in "Laboratory Exploration"); experimental therapy
Genetic therapies	Specific drugs are delivered to alter genetic functions involved in neural systems related to addiction, such as dopamine receptor density and sensitivity throughout the mesolimbic dopaminergic pathway; experimental therapy
Contingency management therapies	This approach may offer rewards or incentives for drug abstinence or punishment for drug usage
Cognitive behavioral therapy	This psychotherapeutic approach examines the relationships among thoughts, feelings, and behavior; helps patients to identify and change negative patterns of thinking, thereby leading to positive feelings and behavioral changes
Psychosocial therapies	Social groups such as Alcoholics Anonymous provide continuous support and accountability as individuals meet in groups frequently (daily in some situations)

Source: Adapted from Lambert and Kinsley, 2010.

TABLE 4.5.

Relapse Rates in Chronic Diseases with Physiological and Behavioral Components

DISEASE	RELAPSE RATES (%)
Diabetes	30–50
Drug addiction	40–60
Hypertension	50–70
Asthma	50–70

Source: National Institute of Drug Abuse, 2012.

LABORATORY EXPLORATION

A Nicotine Vaccine?

With so many people dying from diseases related to nicotine addiction and cigarette smoking, pharmaceutical companies are motivated to develop drugs to help smokers kick the habit. Approaches such as nicotine gum and patches have been approved for general use, but they have not been effective in helping people quit smoking. Up to 70% of all smokers try to quit each year, but only about 5% succeed (Volpp et al., 2009).

One line of research focuses on developing a vaccine for nicotine addiction. Kim Janda's laboratory at the Scripps Research Institute has been working on developing vaccines for various abused drugs since the 1980s. Because of the large potential market, pharmaceutical companies seem most interested in a nicotine vaccination, but a vaccine approved by the U.S. Food and Drug Administration has yet to materialize.

As seen in Laboratory Exploration Figure 4.1, the idea behind drug vaccinations is that a given drug molecule is injected into the bloodstream so that antibodies are formed and attach to any subsequent molecules of that specific drug (in this case, nicotine) that are presented to the body. Because the nicotine molecule is so small, Janda and his colleagues developed a hapten (a small molecule that modifies the nicotine molecule so that it will elicit an immune response) that would latch onto the nicotine molecule and make it larger so it would be noticed by the immune system (Moreno et al., 2010). If the presence of nicotine eventually prompts self-generated antibodies to latch on to the nicotine–hapten molecule, then the overall complex becomes too large to cross the blood–brain barrier. If nicotine is restricted from entering the brain, then the nicotine user fails to experience the reinforcing psychological effects that would otherwise sustain an addiction. In a sense, the reward faucet is cut off in these individuals. At least, that is the way this treatment is supposed to work.

Although Janda's findings with animal models have been difficult to transfer to the human clinical population because of more variable levels of nicotine antibodies in the blood serum of humans compared with rats, some predict that his career-long efforts directed toward this single cause will one day succeed (Lockner et al., 2015; Roiko et al., 2008). It is interesting to consider how a vaccination strategy to treat addiction, expanded to other drugs, could change attitudes toward addiction (Long, 2011; Quenqua, 2011). Will nicotine vaccinations, as well as cocaine and heroin vaccinations, become a standard part of our children's vaccinations someday? If so, will motivated users simply look for new drug variations to cross the blood–brain barrier? For the approximately 25% of the U.S. population currently using nicotine and 6 million smokers worldwide who will die of

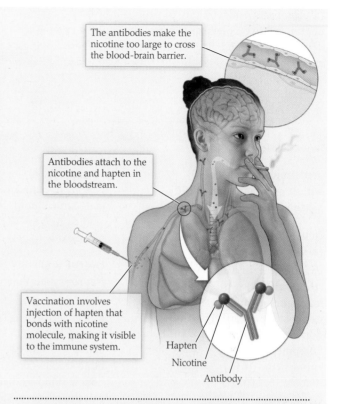

The antibodies make the nicotine too large to cross the blood-brain barrier.

Antibodies attach to the nicotine and hapten in the bloodstream.

Vaccination involves injection of hapten that bonds with nicotine molecule, making it visible to the immune system.

Hapten
Nicotine
Antibody

LABORATORY EXPLORATION FIGURE 4.1 Nicotine vaccine. The concept of the nicotine vaccine involves the binding of the nicotine with the antibody so that the new complex is too large to cross the blood–brain barrier.

smoking-related effects each year (Substance Abuse and Mental Health Services Administration, 2014; World Health Organization, 2011), the short-term possibility of finding help in fighting nicotine addiction outweighs these unknown long-term consequences.

Conclusion

This chapter discussed the fundamentals of neurochemistry, neuropsychopharmacology, and drug addiction. Knowledge of the brain's neurotransmitters and their associated functions is critical for understanding how drugs can produce both adaptive and maladaptive effects. Specific types of neurotransmitters help to regulate functions such as movement, sleep regulation, learning, reward, and pain management. Building on the scientific knowledge of these neurotransmitters, neuropsychopharmacological research aims to develop drugs that modify existing neural circuits to treat symptoms related to mental illness or impaired psychological functions. A detailed understanding of synaptic transmission is critical to the development of drugs to treat psychological disorders.

Aside from the medicinal goals of neuropsychopharmacology, certain natural and synthesized chemicals have been used throughout human history to alter psychological functions. Psychoactive drugs modify psychological functions by altering the brain's natural neurochemical systems. Further, these chemicals' potential for abuse relates to their tendency to interact with the brain's natural reward system, known as the mesolimbic dopaminergic pathway.

Because the brain is constantly adapting to changing internal and external contexts, it adapts to the chronic consumption of psychoactive drugs. For example, drug tolerance demonstrates the brain and body's increased efficiency, in response to larger and larger doses of drugs, in metabolizing drugs to clear them from the system. When the individual stops consuming a drug, withdrawal effects provide additional evidence of physiological adaptations to the abused drug.

The brain's adaptations to drug use lead to long-term neural and psychological effects that result in craving the drug when it is not being readily consumed. These cravings, even after long-term abstinence, often lead to high relapse rates. Although a cure for drug addiction remains elusive to scientists, many treatment strategies continue to be developed and assessed in the search for a strategy that will offer relief to individuals affected by drug addiction.

KEY TERMS

methamphetamine (p. 90)
withdrawal symptoms (p. 90)
psychoactive drugs (p. 90)

Neurotransmitters: A Brief Introduction

enzymatic deactivation (p. 91)
reuptake (p. 91)
monoamines (p. 91)
catecholamines (p. 91)
dopamine (p. 91)
norepinephrine (p. 91)
epinephrine (p. 91)
indolamines (p. 91)
serotonin (p. 91)
ventral tegmental area (p. 91)
striatum (p. 91)
nigrostriatal pathway (p. 91)
mesolimbic pathway (p. 91)
locus coeruleus (p. 91)
raphe nuclei (p. 92)
amino acid neurotransmitters (p. 92)
glutamate (p. 92)
NDMA receptor (p. 92)
AMPA receptor (p. 92)
gamma (γ)-aminobutyric acid (GABA) (p. 92)
agonist (p. 92)
hallucinogenic drugs (p. 93)
antagonists (p. 93)
glycine (p. 93)

peptides (p. 93)
peptide neurotransmitter (p. 93)
endocannabinoids (p. 94)
anandamide (p. 94)
nitric oxide (p. 94)

Overview of Neuropsychopharmacology

neuropsychopharmacology (p. 94)
psychoactive drug (p. 94)
affinity (p. 95)
efficacy (p. 95)
blind studies (p. 95)
double-blind studies (p. 95)
placebo effect (p. 95)
therapeutic effects (p. 95)
potency (p. 95)
pharmacokinetics (p. 95)
pharmacodynamics (p. 95)
dose–response curves (p. 95)

Psychoactive Drugs: Precursors to Drug Addiction

stimulants (p. 98)
depressants (p. 98)
analgesics (p. 88)
caffeine (p. 98)
adenosine (p. 99)
nicotine (p. 100)
nucleus accumbens (p. 101)
cocaine (p. 101)

crack (p. 102)
transporters (p. 102)
amphetamine (p. 102)
MDMA (p. 102)
benzodiazepines (p. 103)
anhedonia (p. 104)
opium (p. 104)
morphine (p. 104)
heroin (p. 104)
opioids (p. 104)
opioid receptors (p. 104)
enkephalin (p. 105)
endorphins (p. 105)
endogenous (p. 105)
synesthesia (p. 106)
cannabis (p. 106)
THC (p. 106)
cannabinoid receptors (p. 107)

Drug Addiction

Buerger's disease (p. 108)
drug dependence (p. 109)
tolerance (p. 109)
sensitization (p. 109)
drug addiction cycle (p. 109)
relapse (p. 109)
ventral pallidum (p. 110)
methylphenidate (p. 111)
priming effect (p. 112)
conditioned cues (p. 112)
conditioned place-preference test (p. 114)

REVIEW QUESTIONS

1. Name and describe the four major categories of neurotransmitters described in this chapter, giving examples of neurotransmitters in each category.

2. List the specific functions of the neurotransmitters covered in this chapter.

3. What is neuropsychopharmacology, and what do neuropsychopharmacologists do?

4. What pharmacokinetic aspects of a drug are evaluated when the drug is being developed for medicinal uses?

5. Name the five major categories of psychoactive drugs and give an example of a psychoactive drug in each category.

6. Describe the three-stage drug addiction cycle and the brain areas associated with each stage. What is the common neural pathway used by most psychoactive drugs that are abused?

7. What treatment strategies are currently used for drug addiction? How does the effectiveness of these strategies compare with that of treatment strategies for other illnesses such as hypertension and diabetes?

CRITICAL-THINKING QUESTIONS

1. Of the various factors and concerns that psychopharmacologists must be aware of in their research, which do you believe is the most important? Explain your answer.

2. From a neurochemical standpoint, is any one stage of the addiction cycle more powerful than the others? How might researchers use this knowledge to develop more effective strategies for preventing or treating addiction?

3. Why have cultures around the world historically tended to permit the recreational use of caffeine, alcohol, and tobacco, while generally outlawing the recreational use of opium, cocaine, and cannabis? In what ways, if any, do you think laws regarding psychoactive drugs should be changed? Explain your position.

Evolving Brains: Neural Development, Neuroplasticity, and Recovery of Function

Traumatic Brain Injury and an Unlikely Neurochemical Intervention

The car crash that sent Marc Baskett by helicopter to Grady Memorial Hospital in Atlanta, Georgia, left no trace in his memory. The hospital staff listed him in critical condition as a result of blunt force trauma to his brain. The news was not encouraging when his parents hurried to his side. Marc was just 19 years old, but his future was now in jeopardy. Even if he survived, his functioning would likely be severely compromised (Tricoles, 2007).

But the frightening news came with a sliver of hope. Grady Memorial Hospital was participating in a clinical trial evaluating the effectiveness of a hormonal intervention for

FIGURE 5A Marc Baskett. Baskett after recovering from a traumatic brain injury.

traumatic brain injury (TBI) patients. After hearing that they could volunteer their son as a participant in the clinical trial, Marc's parents agreed, although at the time they did not know whether Marc would be assigned to the experimental (drug) group or the control (placebo) group. As Marc's medical team fully evaluated his condition, they predicted that he would likely be hospitalized for up to one year.

To everyone's surprise, Marc was released after only seven weeks. Other than injuries to his legs and feet that compromised his movement, he showed little evidence of his ordeal (see Figure 5A). He was able to live on his own and return to work. Was Marc's impressive recovery a result of the intervention in the clinical trial? Perhaps it was, because Marc learned he had received the actual hormonal intervention.

Behind the Scenes

What was the neurochemical intervention being assessed in the clinical trial? Surprisingly, it was not a newly synthesized drug: it was the hormone progesterone. The trial investigated the clinical effectiveness of progesterone versus a placebo in TBI patients.

But why progesterone? Most people know of progesterone as a sex hormone present at much higher levels in women than in men. Historically, far from being considered a promising neurochemical for TBI patients, it was mostly known for its role in maintaining and nurturing a developing fetus. But, as a student in the 1960s, Emory neuroscientist Don Stein noted that his female rats seemed to recover faster from brain damage than male rats of the same age. His curiosity led him to consider the effects of progesterone. Progesterone is present in both males and females and can cross the blood–brain barrier to enter the CNS. Also, some progesterone is actually produced in the brain. Even so, few scientists were impressed with Stein's research. Consequently, it was difficult for Stein to secure funding to investigate this hormone when there was more of a push for the discovery of exotic synthetic drugs that could be patented and manufactured by pharmaceutical companies (Weir, 2013).

Despite funding challenges, scientists have conducted informative research on the effects of progesterone on neural functions. Today, we know that progesterone has many functions that are relevant to neural growth. Indeed, in many ways, recovery from TBI requires similar neural processes to those that exist during the fetal neural growth that progesterone maintains. Decades of research on progesterone indicate that, among other functions, progesterone reduces swelling

in the brain, promotes the expression of neural growth factors, protects neurons that surround the site of damaged neural tissue from eventual death, and enhances myelination of neuronal axons (Stein, 2011). Eventually, support grew for the investigation of progesterone as a possible effective intervention in clinical trials for TBI patients. Given the absence of a widely effective treatment for TBI, it would be exciting to determine that progesterone has **clinical efficacy** or effectiveness for TBI.

Based on laboratory work in animals, it seemed possible that Marc's recovery was the result of progesterone treatment. Ultimately, however, evaluations of large-scale, controlled clinical trials provide the most informative answers. Early clinical trials yielded promising results. For example, in one early clinical trial, adult patients diagnosed with moderate to severe TBI who received progesterone intravenously for three days following their injury had mortality rates of 13.6% compared with 30.4% mortality rates in control patients who received a placebo (Wright et al., 2007).

As encouraging as these data were, later, large-scale clinical trials failed to replicate the beneficial effects of progesterone over placebo for TBI (Stein, 2015). Because the results of phase III clinical trials (assessing the safety and effectiveness of the drug in large human populations) conflicted with a large number of preclinical studies, researchers are investigating possible reasons for the discrepancy. Don Stein has contemplated the discrepancies between the approximately 300 preclinical studies that showed beneficial effects of progesterone in TBI and the failed clinical trials (Stein, 2015). Focusing on drugs for all disorders, up to 62% of phase III trials fail, an observation that has researchers scratching their heads (Amiri-Kordestani & Fojo, 2012).

Thus, the greater recovery of function in female versus male rats that Stein noted a half century ago may or may not ultimately contribute to a therapy that benefits human lives. The phase III clinical trials in humans suggest that progesterone is an ineffective treatment for TBI. This story highlights the significant challenges that scientists face in translating success at the laboratory bench to success at the bedside of patients. Scientists must reevaluate their research strategy with regard to TBI and consider whether they will need to develop new research paradigms to improve bench-to-bedside success. In the process of learning from their failures, scientists will learn more about how the brain recovers from TBI.

In this chapter, we begin by considering how the brain develops. This will provide a foundation for understanding how recovery of brain function may occur after injury.

Building Brains

Imagine being given the task of building a brain. That's right—an organ that will detect all relevant environmental information, monitor all internal physiological systems, and, looking both to the past and future, determine the most adaptive responses at every moment of an animal's life. Even developing a brain for a relatively simple vertebrate, such as a lizard, would be daunting. If you accomplished this challenging task, however, and were asked to build a brain for another species, you would likely borrow a few tried-and-true tricks from your first build-a-brain assignment. After all the work of designing a functioning brain that would keep the lizard alive long enough to reproduce, it definitely would not be efficient for you to reinvent the neural wheel for a new animal.

Throughout time, the brains of thousands of different vertebrate species have been built, each working efficiently and effectively. And each time a new species arrived on the evolutionary scene, nature did not start from scratch to give it a brain. Rather, comparative analysis of these brains suggests that the evolution and development of different species' brains has been a **conservative process**. That is, many more similarities (evidence that principles have been *conserved*) than differences exist among the brains of various species.

Recurring Evolutionary Themes

The conservative nature of brain and body evolution was reinforced by the drawings of the German zoologist Ernst Haeckel, an early proponent of Darwinism in the 19th century. In fact, Haeckel's drawings, depicting the similarity of vertebrate embryos, were considered supporting evidence of common descent strategies observed in nature. As seen in Figure 5.1, these famous artistic renderings conveyed an extreme similarity in various developing vertebrates such as salamanders, chicks, and humans—they looked almost identical in the earlier stages of development.

Although these images persist in textbooks today, scientists have raised criticisms about the accuracy of Haeckel's drawings. Photographs of actual embryos suggest that Haeckel may have either miscopied or taken artistic liberties when generating these images. For example, different-size embryos appear as the same size and in the same position. Because he frequently gave lectures to mainstream audiences, his drawings and accompanying comments had an impact on the social, religious, and political climate of the day. In advocating for Darwin's provocative ideas about natural selection, Haeckel wondered what the nobles would "think of the thoroughbred blood that circulates in their privileged veins, when they learn that all human embryos, those of nobles as well as commoners, during the first two months of development, are scarcely distinguishable from the tailed embryos of the dog and other mammals" (Hopwood, 2006, p. 270).

Although Haeckel's drawings may have strayed from the truth, his point about the conservative nature of vertebrate evolution is important to acknowledge. Looking more specifically at the structure of the nervous system, the similarities across vertebrates are even more striking than Haeckel depicted in his embryo illustrations. For example, the structure of cortical neurons is similar in birds and humans. Conservation is also evident in the larger landscape of neural circuits, consisting of functioning units of neuronal connections. Note the similarity in the hippocampal structures of the kitten and the human in Figure 5.2.

Focusing on the evolution of the mammalian cortex, a neuroscientist at the University of California at Davis, Leah Krubitzer, and her colleagues have mapped the specific cortical areas of many mammals and noted how the size of various cortical areas changes depending on the extent of use of various sensory and motor systems. Figure 5.3 shows three mammals with similarly sized cortical areas. Yet, the sizes of the auditory, visual, and somatosensory areas differ across the three mammals' brains. The visual cortical area is largest in the opossum, the auditory cortex is largest in the vole, and the somatosensory cortex is largest in the mouse. Thus, the presence of similar types of cortical areas in these species emphasizes the importance of similar genetic factors in the development of the cortex. However, interspecies differences also emphasize the importance of the animals'

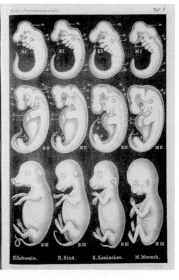

FIGURE 5.1 Similarities in developing vertebrate organisms. The development of embryos from various vertebrate species, shown in these drawings by Ernst Haeckel, go through similar transformations prior to more specialized development occurring later in the gestational period.

(a)

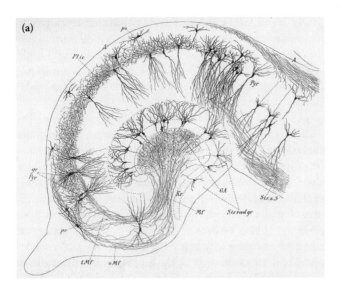

(b)

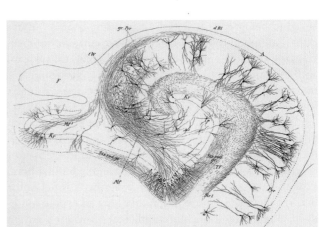

FIGURE 5.2 **Conservation of hippocampus.** In both (a) kittens and (b) humans, the hippocampal structures are similar, confirming conservation in mammalian nervous systems.

lifestyle in the development of these fundamental areas (Larsen & Krubitzer, 2008). We will return to this issue later in the chapter and learn about the evolution of cortical sensory mapping in Chapter 6.

Commonalities in brain development across species provide further support for conducting behavioral neuroscience research with animal models. The similarities in the cells of the nervous system and common developmental pathways validate the use of various animal models to learn more about developing nervous systems of humans. Although various species share many common neural development strategies early in development, at some point their paths diverge, leading to unique neural profiles for specific vertebrate and mammalian species. The varying sizes of the cortical areas depicted in Figure 5.3 provide clear evidence of these divergent neural paths characterizing mammals with different habitats and lifestyles.

We have learned about the similarities in neural structures across vertebrates. This conservation through evolution validates the use of animal models for studying human brain development. In addition to neural structures, certain *behaviors* have been conserved through mammalian evolution. We will next turn to a discussion of one such behavior.

The Importance of Play Behavior in Developing Brains

Although not typically a subject of serious study among scientists, playfulness is among the most prominent behaviors observed in young mammals across species—that is, a conserved mammalian response. Speaking to its evolutionary significance, the late National Institute of Mental Health researcher Paul D. MacLean suggested that, along with maternal behavior and vocal communication, play was one of the defining behaviors of mammals (MacLean, 1990). Because of the seemingly instinctive tendencies for mammals to engage in this complex behavior, play is categorized in the more specific discipline of **neuroethology**. Neuroethology is the study of the neural basis of animals' natural behavior. It includes the study of the

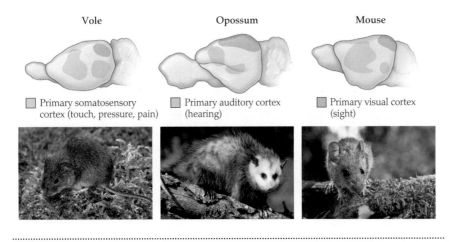

Vole   Opossum   Mouse

☐ Primary somatosensory cortex (touch, pressure, pain)

☐ Primary auditory cortex (hearing)

☐ Primary visual cortex (sight)

FIGURE 5.3 **Cortical variations.** The functional areas of the cortex change in accordance with the sensory and motor needs for the specific species' survival.

neural basis of natural responses, such as sexual behavior and aggressive responses that animals acquire and use without training. The presence of play is a recurring theme in the lives of young mammals.

When placed in a nonthreatening environment, laboratory rat pups engage in distinctive patterns of play including object-play, movement-play, and play fighting, or rough-and-tumble play. Researchers observing play typically assess three behaviors: *chasing*, *dorsal contacts* (in which one animal climbs on another's back), and *pins*, in which one animal flips another onto its back and pounces on top of its belly. (Figure 5.4 depicts how the pin has been conserved in two mammalian species, rats and humans.) In addition to their physical antics, during play rats emit complex chirps at around 50 kilohertz, vocalizations that are also emitted during other socially rewarding situations such as sexual encounters (Panksepp, 2010).

Although the exact function of play remains unknown, researchers have suggested that it helps animals learn about their physical and social environments (Panksepp, 2010). However, engaging in play comes at a cost. In both free-living and captive animals, play consumes as much as 20% of an animal's daily activities and up to 10% of its daily energy expenditure (energy used during physical activity) that could be directed toward growth in young animals (Pellegrini, Horvat, & Huberty, 1998). Rolling around and vocalizing not only forces young animals to expend energy, but also makes them more easily noticeable to predators and exposes them to the risk of injury. For example, juvenile fur seals suffer their highest mortality rates while playing because playing in the water often makes them vulnerable to predation (Harcourt, 1991; Pellis & Pellis, 2009). Yet the drive to play appears to be strong. When deprived of play and then

given the opportunity to engage in it with another animal, rats compensate by spending more time in play (Panksepp & Beatty, 1980). This trend continues until the rat reaches the end of its juvenile stage (about 40 days of age), diminishing as the rat reaches puberty. Although greatly diminished in adult rats, playful behaviors continue to exist at lower levels (Panksepp, 2010).

Which brain areas are involved in play? In hamsters and rats, the complete removal of the neocortex has no effect on play responses (M. R. Murphy, MacLean, & Hamilton, 1981; Pellis, Pellis, & Whishaw, 1992). These findings suggest that the core driver of play responses is located in the subcortical areas of the brain. In support of this claim, research suggests that the mesolimbic dopamine system is important for the reward aspects of play. Additionally, evidence indicates that certain areas of the thalamus, such as the parafascicular area, regulate somatosensory input necessary for choreographing specific play responses along with the striatum's influence on intentional movement patterns. Finally, evidence indicates that the periaqueductal gray area, known for its role in switching between different behavioral patterns, regulates the play response (Gordon, Kollack-Walker, Akil, & Panksepp, 2002; Siviy & Panksepp, 2011).

Several neurochemicals appear to be active in play. In addition to dopamine involved with the mesolimbic system, *endogenous opioids* have been observed to be released from several relevant brain areas during play (Normansell & Panksepp, 1990; Vanderschuren, Niesink, Spruijt, & Van Ree, 1995a, 1995b). Serotonin also influences play in rats, although the effect depends on the established relationship between the two rat playmates. If one rat is more dominant, evidence indicates that a decrease in serotonin levels increases the number of pins in the wrestling bout (Knutson &

(a)

(b)

FIGURE 5.4 Rough-and-tumble play. Mammalian play responses are similar across species, including behaviors such as running, chasing, and pinning—shown here in (a) rats and (b) children.

Panksepp, 1997). Furthermore, play is associated with increases in the levels of growth factors in the brain (Burgdorf, Kroes, Beinfeld, Panksepp, & Moskal, 2010). Thus, play seems to provide an enriching and stimulating climate for the developing brain. However, research suggests that psychostimulants such as amphetamine and methylphenidate (Ritalin) significantly reduce, rather than enhance, play duration (Beatty, Dodge, Dodge, White, & Panksepp, 1982), perhaps because of an increase in norepinephrine (Siviy & Panksepp, 2011).

The effect of amphetamine on play responses has led the Washington State University neuroscientist Jaak Panksepp to consider a possible relationship between the opportunities for children to engage in play and the prevalence of ADHD, which has increased in recent years (see Figure 5.5; Akinbami, Liu, Pastor, & Reuben, 2011). Specifically, just as rats deprived of the opportunity to play exhibit an increased desire for play, play-deprived children may also experience such play urges, a response that adults may interpret as a form of impulse-control disorder (Panksepp, 2007). The observation that psychostimulants such as Ritalin prescribed to children with ADHD appear to diminish the play response further supports a potential connection between play and ADHD. Although ADHD is a complex illness, Panksepp suggests that some cases may be influenced by a child's social and physical environment, with decreased opportunities to engage in physical play leading to increased susceptibility to ADHD symptoms (Panksepp, 2007; Siviy & Panksepp, 2011).

Further, the movement patterns of children exhibiting ADHD symptoms may provide additional insight into neurobiological variables associated with the disorder. One study, for example, investigated gross motor development in boys with and without ADHD and found that those with ADHD were less effective in their skilled movement patterns than their peers without ADHD (Harvey et al., 2009). If physical activity is important for development, then it is important to monitor activity levels in children and adolescents. When a representative sample of U.S. mothers was asked to compare the duration of active outdoor play of their children with their own experiences with play, 85% of the mothers reported that their children play less than they did when they were children. Whereas 70% of the mothers reported engaging in active play every day when they were children, this was the case in only 30% of their children (Clements, 2004). These findings suggest that the quantity and quality of play behavior are changing rapidly.

Recently, researchers have focused on the effect of limited outdoor play on the visual abilities of young children in China. Playing outdoors provides a richer visual landscape, with distant horizons, than playing in smaller spaces indoors. Therefore, some researchers have hypothesized that limited outdoor play is contributing to the rising rates of myopia, or nearsightedness. In one study, a 40-minute outdoor play period was added to the daily curriculum of some schools for three years. Myopia decreased by 10% in children who experienced the extra outdoor play versus children who did not (He et al., 2015). Research suggests that play behavior is important to the developing mammalian brain; therefore, these changes in play behavior should be monitored closely.

We have learned about the critical importance of play behavior, a conserved mammalian response, in developing brains. Further, we have learned about the brain areas and neurochemicals implicated in play behavior. Given that the play response has been conserved across species and is costly because of energy expenditure and vulnerability to injuries or predation, it likely plays an important role in development. Play is generally unique to mammals, but not to humans. Is there any aspect of the human brain that distinguishes it from other brains? We will address this question next.

Is the Human Brain Unique?

Revisiting the build-a-brain assignment considered earlier in the chapter, how would you design a brain that would equip an animal with the cognitive abilities of a human? What exactly is special about the human brain? The answer to that question is debatable, but as far as we can tell, humans are the only species studying the nervous systems of other animals. Compared with other mammals, humans have superior cognitive abilities. In the words of the neuroscientist Osvaldo Cairo, "The human brain is undoubtedly the most impressive, complex, and intricate organ that has evolved over time" (Cairo, 2011).

Regarding the distinctive properties of the human brain, the neuroscientist Michael Gazzaniga has pointed out in his book, *Human: The Science behind What Makes Us Unique*, that one distinctive feature of the human brain is its large size. After diverging from the chimpanzee brain, the human

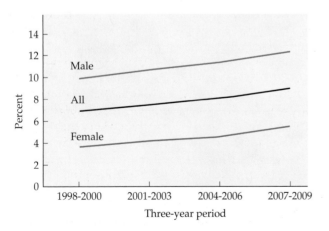

Source: CDC/NCHS, Health Data Interactive and National Health Interview Survey

FIGURE 5.5   ADHD prevalence. Although they are higher in males than in females, rates of attention-deficit hyperactivity disorder continue to rise in both groups.

brain seemed to take off in size—becoming more than three times larger than the 400-gram chimp brain (Gazzaniga, 2008). Acknowledging that the human brain is not the largest mammalian brain, however, weakens the idea that *absolute* brain size is a distinguishing factor in defining human intelligence and abilities.

What about *relative* brain size—that is, brain mass in proportion to body mass? Killer and sperm whales share the distinction of having the largest mammalian brain mass (Ridgway & Hanson, 2014). If we take brain size into consideration in the form of a simple brain-to-body-mass ratio, humans still do not have the largest brain (Cairo, 2011). Even so, it is informative to consider the proportion of cerebral cortex mass to total brain mass in certain categories of mammals.

Although past studies have revealed that a distinguishing characteristic of the primate brain is the proportion of cerebral cortex to total brain mass, even this ranking fails to distinguish several types of mammals (as reviewed in Hofman, 2014). Compared with other mammalian brains, the proportion of cerebral cortex mass to total brain mass in the human brain is impressive but not particularly distinctive (Herculano-Houzel, 2010, 2011a, 2011b). Perhaps, however, we have approached our brain data collection from too broad of a species spectrum. Focusing more narrowly, how does the human brain compare with other primate brains?

When the brain data are evaluated for various *primate* species, is the large size of the human brain (approximately 1.5 kilograms) for the human body size an outlier? To answer this question, Brazilian neuroscientist Suzana Herculano-Houzel worked with Roberto Lent and other colleagues to assess how many neurons the human brain contains. At the time that these researchers embarked on this question, the often-quoted statistic of 100 billion neurons in the human brain was not actually linked to a publication that was based on observation or experiment; on the contrary, its origin is unknown (Lent, Azevedo, Andrade-Moraes, & Pinto, 2011). However, based on the more recent cell-counting technique of isotropic fractionation (described in Chapter 2), Herculano-Houzel and her colleagues estimated that the human brain contains closer to 86 billion neurons with 12–15 billion in the telencephalon, 70 billion in the cerebellum, and fewer than 1 billion in the brainstem (Herculano-Houzel, 2009).

Could the human brain be unique by having the greatest *number of neurons* among the brains of all mammalian species? Answers to this question may help scientists resolve the mysteries surrounding brain size and cognitive abilities.

A key question about brain size is whether it is a reliable measure of neuronal count (as well as glial count). The African elephant brain weighs up to six times more than the human brain. But does that mean that the elephant brain has six times more neurons than the human brain? Clearly, humans possess far more sophisticated cognitive abilities than elephants do.

Traditionally, it was thought that the **Encephalization Quotient** (EQ; an index determined by comparing the actual brain mass of an animal with the expected brain mass for an animal of that particular body mass based on measurements of representative mammals) would differentiate the most complex brains. The calculation of expected brain mass was based on the observation that across species, the relationship of brain mass to body mass generally varies according to a mathematical rule. The EQ is a measure of the deviation from the expected brain mass. Compared with gorillas and chimpanzees, humans have a larger brain size for the average human body size, suggesting that humans have a higher EQ than gorillas and chimps.

But considering that researchers did not know exactly what was the most important factor correlated with brain weight (e.g., number and/or size of neurons, number and/or size of glia, and so forth), the EQ was too general a measure to provide specific information about the factors that distinguished the human brain from that of other mammalian species. It was not necessarily the case that all 50-gram brains contained the same number of neurons because *density* of neurons and nonneuronal cells could vary from species to species. For example, if an animal had a large brain with sparsely populated neurons, that brain might be less complex and efficient than a smaller brain with more densely populated neurons. Researchers therefore needed to determine actual *neuron densities* before declaring that the largest brains are the superior brains.

When scientists eventually determined the neuronal and glial cell counts for various species including rodents, insectivores, and primates using the isotropic fractionation technique, answers started to emerge. The cerebral cortex contains only 13–28% of the brain's neurons. Surprisingly, the number of neurons in the cerebral cortex is not correlated with the total number of neurons in the brain (Herculano-Houzel, 2012). Instead, a more accurate indicator of the total number of neurons in the brain is the number of neurons in one part of the brain: the cerebellum.

Although the cerebellum occupies only up to 15% of the total brain area, it contains more neurons than the cerebral cortex. Specifically, across species, approximately 3.6 neurons are found in the cerebellum for every neuron located in the cerebral cortex (Herculano-Houzel, 2010, 2011b). In humans, the cerebellum occupies up to 15% of the total brain area, whereas the cerebral cortex occupies approximately 80% of the total brain area (Herculano-Houzel, 2009).

Once scientists had determined neuronal densities in primate brains, the human brain neuronal count was within 10% of the expected numbers for a primate with the body size of an average human. According to the neuronal counts across the brains of various primate species, it is the great apes (orangutans, chimpanzees, gorillas) who are the outliers, with a smaller brain size than expected given their large bodies (Herculano-Houzel, Collins, Wong, & Kaas, 2007). Across the broader range of primate brains, humans have the largest brain (both in absolute terms and relative to body size), which, unsurprisingly, has the most neurons. When it comes to brains of many species, size can be misleading.

However, among primates specifically, a larger brain reliably indicates more neurons.

As seen in Figure 5.6, in mammalian species, the number of neurons does not reliably increase with brain mass (Herculano-Houzel, 2009). Further, if the rodent brain were enlarged to the size of the human brain, it would have only 12 billion neurons, fewer neurons than exist in the human cerebral cortex alone and approximately seven times less than the number of neurons in the human brain as a whole. If a rat brain were enlarged to have the same number of neurons as the human brain, the rat brain would weigh a whopping 35 kilograms, four times greater than the brain mass of the blue whale. Based on mathematical scaling rules emerging from these cell-counting data, one would expect a primate brain weighing 1.5 kilograms (the size of a human brain) to have 93 billion neurons and 112 billion glial cells, producing a ratio of neurons to glial cells that is closer to 1:1 (as indicated in Chapter 2). Further, based on the scaling rules, the human-size primate cerebral cortex should

contain 25 billion neurons with a cerebellum containing 61 billion neurons. If you review the projected brain sizes in Table 5.1, you will see how accurately these scaling rules predict the parameters of the human brain. Using these rules, the human brain is far from "off the charts." Rather, it is very much on track for expected parameters of a primate brain.

More recent research indicates that although humans do not have the largest cerebral cortex, the human cerebral cortex contains the most neurons of any known mammal. This characteristic may be related to the advanced cognitive abilities of humans. As human ancestors extended their range into new environments with challenging weather patterns and physical terrains, the increase in the number of neurons in the cerebral cortex may have been related to more sophisticated cognitive abilities that enhanced the likelihood of survival and reproduction (Lent et al., 2011).

Where does this innovative research leave us? Is the human brain unique? Yes and no. The human brain follows the same evolutionary scaling rules observed for other primate species, so in that sense, we do not possess a unique brain when it comes to overall brain size. The realization that, when it comes to sophisticated cognitive abilities, size does not matter is similar to the ever-changing views in the world of supercomputers. We are no longer impressed with the largest computers. In fact, we value most greatly the computers with the most efficient processing speed, flexibility, and storage ability that fit into the smallest computer shells. Perhaps big brains, like supersized computers, are less than impressive in nature as well. Big brains certainly require a lot of energy to maintain. Among primates, the human brain packs the highest number of neurons. And it is highly probable that humans have more neurons than any species on earth (Herculano-Houzel, 2011a).

Recent findings indicate that the elephant's cortical area is roughly twice the size of the human cerebral cortex although it contains only 3 billion neurons (20% of the human cortical neuron count). Yet, the cerebellum cell count of the elephant reveals three times more neurons than the cerebellum cell count of the human reveals. It is not clear why the elephant cerebellum is so rich in neurons, but the addition of an entirely new appendage, the trunk, may require substantial neuronal real estate in the cerebellum (Herculano-Houzel et al., 2014). These emerging data about the number of neurons that are packed into brains of different sizes reveal important factors in building effective and efficient brains during the course of development.

What other factors are important in building such brains? As you will see next, another critical factor is the influence of people's lifestyles on gene activity that extends across several generations. Lifestyle factors such as stress and impoverishment can have effects on gene activity that have long-lasting impacts on brain development.

TABLE 5.1.

Projected Values for Generic Rodent and Primate Brains Compared with Actual Values in the Human Brain

The researchers began with a hypothetical generic rodent brain and a hypothetical generic human-size primate brain of 1500 grams each.

	GENERIC RODENT BRAIN	GENERIC PRIMATE BRAIN	ACTUAL HUMAN BRAIN
Brain mass	1500 grams	1500 grams	1508 grams
Total neurons	12 billion	93 billion	86 billion
Total non-neurons (e.g., glial cells)	46 billion	112 billion	85 billion
Cerebral cortex mass	1154 grams	1412 grams	1233 grams
Neurons in cerebral cortex	2 billion	25 billion	16 billion
Cerebellum mass	133 g	121 g	154 g
Neurons in cerebellum	10 billion	61 billion	69 billion

Adapted from Herculano-Houzel, S. (2009). The human brain in numbers: A linearly scaled-up primate brain. *Frontiers in Human Neuroscience*, doi: 10:3389/neuro.09.031.2009

Data from Azevedo et al. (2009).

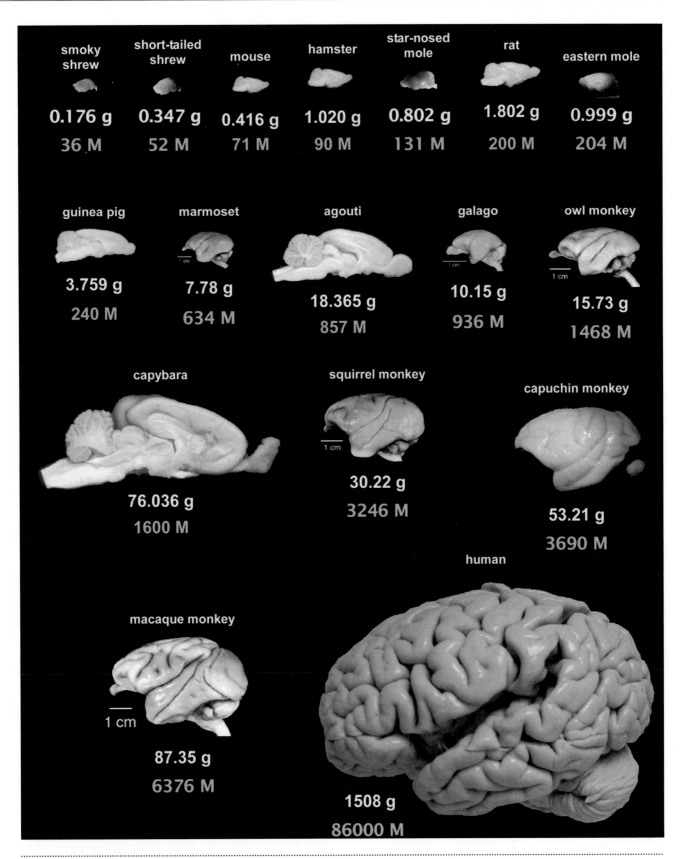

FIGURE 5.6 Diversity of mammalian brains. The brains of different mammals share similar structural templates but vary greatly in size and number of neurons.

Epigenetics: How Lifestyles Influence Inheritance

Sweden's northernmost county, Norrbotten, is home to only six people per square mile. During the 19th century, this territory was so remote that in years of poor harvests, the inhabitants risked starving to death. The stress associated with crop failures was exacerbated by their unpredictability. Historical records indicate that starvation occurred during the years 1800, 1812, 1821, 1836, and 1856, whereas in 1801, 1822, 1828, 1844, and 1863 crops were so plentiful that residents were able to gorge themselves (Cloud, 2010).

Fast-forwarding to the 1980s, the scientist Lars Bygren, now at the Karolinska Institute, wondered about the long-term effects of poor harvests in the survivors of Norbotten's starvation years. Additionally, Bygren wondered whether these famines influenced subsequent generations. Earlier research had indicated that poor fetal nutrition increased the risk of cardiovascular disease later in life, suggesting that variables present early in development may program later physiological effects (Barker, 1995). To answer his questions about potential longer-term generational effects of food scarcity, Bygren sampled individuals born in Norrbotten in 1905 and used archival evidence to discern the amount of food available during their parents' and grandparents' childhoods (Bygren, Kaati, & Edvinsson, 2001).

Bygren's line of thinking conflicted with the traditional ideas of offspring being born with a clean DNA slate—representative of the unchangeable DNA of their parents, not affected by any life events occurring throughout the parents' lives. Further, it supposedly took painstakingly long periods of time, spreading over hundreds and thousands of generations, for changes to occur in the genetic blueprint. However, interesting **transgenerational** findings (i.e., genetic trends influenced by life events of a single generation that can extend beyond an individual's lifetime across several generations) suggested that there was more to the genetic inheritance story originally espoused by Darwin. (For a review on potential mechanisms of transgenerational effects, see Bohacek & Mansuy, 2015.)

What did Bygren find in those historical agricultural records? Boys who abruptly switched from a normal or deprived diet to a gluttonous diet had sons and grandsons who lived much shorter lives. Individuals with paternal grandfathers who had experienced the two extremes of feast and famine lived, on average, 32 years less than a cohort of individuals whose grandparents lived at the same time but were not exposed to such extreme feeding conditions (Bygren et al., 2001). Thus, going from a year of starvation to a year of abundant food, in many cases just a single winter of overeating, appeared to initiate a series of biological events that left a genetic imprint on eggs and sperm, producing long-term effects for the child's descendants. These transgenerational effects appeared to result in reduced longevity and increased risk for diabetes and cardiovascular disease (Bygren et al., 2001; Cloud, 2010; Kaati, Bygren, & Edvinsson, 2002).

Important clues about this fascinating family inheritance story can be found in the rodent research that the neuroscientist Michael Meaney and his colleagues at McGill University have conducted. They report that the number of times a mother rat licks her offspring can profoundly affect the development of the offspring's stress response (see Figure 5.7). The offspring of high-licking mothers have a reduced level of stress hormone (corticosterone response) compared with the offspring of low-licking mothers. The offspring of the more attentive (high-licking) mothers also exhibit evidence of more glucocorticoid receptor activity in the hippocampus and, accordingly, a more sensitive stress hormone system, resulting in a more efficient and healthier stress-response system. With increased sensitivity to existing levels of glucocorticoids, the stress response system is able to respond quickly to the changing levels of stress hormones, resulting in a more effective feedback system.

These effects also extend to behavior. Adult offspring of high-licking mother rats exhibit diminished startle responses, more exploration in a novel environment, and shorter latencies overcoming fear in a novel environment to approach a desirable food source (Meaney, 2001). Further, rats born to low-licking mothers but subsequently placed with high-licking rats serving as foster parents ("foster mothers") also exhibited the benefits of a more sensitive stress response. These rats also continued the cycle by acting more like their foster mothers than their biological mothers when they became parents. That is, although a rat was born to a low-licking mother, it engaged in high-licking maternal behavior after being raised by a high-licking foster mother. This line of research suggests that the environmental influence of the degree of maternal attentiveness seemed to override the genetic transmission of factors related to the degree of maternal attentiveness that the rat provided to its own pups (Champagne & Curley, 2009). This behavioral transmission of maternal traits is known as *nongenomic transmission*. These initial results provided convincing evidence that a mother's response to her offspring could *program* both neuroendocrine (hormonal) and behavioral responses to stress. These findings provided additional evidence that lifestyle experiences alter genetic programming, even when they occur after birth. As seen in Figure 5.7c, offspring born to high-licking maternal rats exhibit less anxiety in the elevated plus-maze compared with offspring from low-licking offspring (Masis-Calvo, Sequeira-Cordero, Mora-Gallegos, & Fornaguera-Trias, 2013).

More relevant to the issue of famine in Norrbotten residents, Meaney's team tracked behavioral patterns in the offspring of the low-licking mothers that were fostered by high-licking mother rats. The offspring of the low-licking mothers were less fearful, as their foster mothers were. When allowed to mature and become mothers, their maternal behavior looked more like that of their foster high-licking grandmothers than that of their biological grandmothers (Meaney, 2001). Thus, these rodent studies provided a

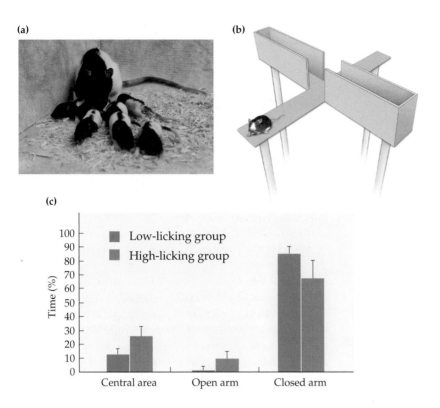

Source: Masís-Calvo, M., Sequeira-Cordero, A., Mora-Gallegos, A., & Fornaguera-Trías, J. (2013). Behavioral and neurochemical characterization of maternal care effects on juvenile Sprague-Dawleyrats. *Physiology & Behavior, 118, 212 -21*

FIGURE 5.7 Maternal care and offspring anxiety. (a) Slight variations in the amount of maternal contact with the pups can have long-lasting neuronal and behavioral effects. (b) One study of the influence of maternal care on the anxiety of the offspring used an elevated plus-maze. Rats that spent more time in the open arm were considered less anxious, and those that spent more time in the closed arm were considered more anxious. (c) Rats who had been more frequently licked by their mother showed less anxiety in the maze.

laboratory model of the transgenerational transmission of physiological and behavioral traits.

This rodent maternal attention model has allowed researchers to explore the phenomenon of epigenetics, modified gene activity that is transmitted to subsequent generations, as opposed to the more permanently ingrained genetic code. Similar to on–off switches, important environmental events such as extreme diets or stressful experiences leave an imprint that is passed on to subsequent generations along with the DNA code. In contrast to the transmission process described by Darwin, the maternal research suggested that the genetic blueprint may be modified, at least transiently, by key environmental events. Although the potential impact of postnatal nurturing on an animal's genetic code has been extensively investigated in the field of behavioral neuroscience, these findings are not without controversy. Microbiologists have expressed reservations about the subtlety of the physiological changes and whether such changes alone are extensive enough to alter actual phenotypes such as maternal strategies (Buchen, 2010).

In 2004, Meaney's team reported evidence that increased maternal attention during the first week of a rat's life modified the genetic material at a specific hippocampal glucocorticoid receptor gene promoter (the region of DNA that signals to start transcription of the gene) by altering a process known as **DNA methylation**. This refers to a mechanism in which genes can be modified by the addition of a methyl chemical compound to the cytosine nucleotide base in DNA (DNA structure is reviewed in Chapter 1). The presence of a methyl group at a gene promoter usually prevents the expression of the gene in question. Methyl groups can be added and removed at various points in an animal's development. In addition, these researchers reported that the altered genetic material known as the *epigenome* could be altered by environmental conditions such as the cross-fostering investigated by Meaney and his colleagues.

Furthermore, the epigenome was associated with re-modeling mechanisms such as histone acetylation, the addition of a functional chemical compound known as an acetyl group to the **histones**. As seen in Figure 5.8, the histones are proteins located in cellular nuclei. They act as spools around which DNA coils (Buchen, 2010; Curley, Jensen, Mashoodh, & Champagne, 2010; Weaver et al., 2004). The addition of an acetyl group to a histone changes the shape of nearby DNA, making those genes more likely to be expressed. (The removal of an acetyl group from a histone makes genes in nearby DNA less likely to be expressed.) Thus, DNA methylation and histone acetylation are two mechanisms that modify the expression of an animal's genetic blueprint.

The epigenetic process may be a way to override the painstakingly slow process of changing the DNA code, a

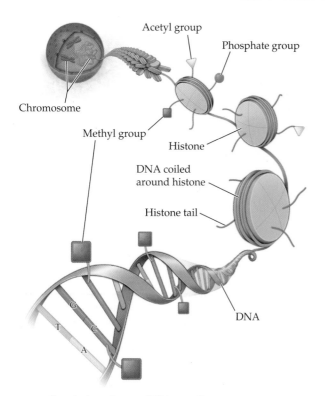

Chromosome

Acetyl group

Phosphate group

Methyl group

Histone

DNA coiled
around histone

Histone tail

DNA

Chemical markers on DNA can affect gene expression.
Histone modification occurs throughout an organism's
life. Removal of methyl groups occurs at fertilization,
during fetal development, and immediately after birth.

FIGURE 5.8 The elements of epigenetics. Although the genetic
blueprint was once thought to be permanent, the blueprint can be
altered by specific chemical markers throughout an individual's life.

necessary response for survival in constantly changing environments. But the fundamental integrity of the DNA code is protected against premature changes. Although epigenetic changes can be inherited across many generations, if the environmental pressures are altered, these genetic modifications will fade over time, reverting to the original expression pattern. Thus, although evolutionary biologists have focused on the role of natural selection in the creation of permanent changes in the genome, epigenetic mechanisms enable the permanent code to be transiently tweaked to enhance survival in changing environments. Because the field of epigenetics is in its infancy, scientists are still struggling to reconcile the notion of real-time rapid evolutionary changes and the more conservative long-term evolutionary changes described by Darwin. Consequently, many questions remain as scientists are reconsidering our genetic foundation.

As we have seen, the epigenetic mechanisms are valuable for modifying an animal's established genetic material. However, the brain itself also needs the capacity to change through both qualitative and quantitative modifications of various types of cells that reside in the nervous system. In the next section, we discuss the process of neural development. We describe the mechanisms underlying **neuroplasticity** (the brain's ability to restructure itself) during the process of neural development.

Neural Development

Once the brain begins to form during prenatal development, a series of events occurs so that the brain, at birth, is mature enough to help sustain survival. As neurons are born, they are positioned within functioning neural networks, allowing animals and humans to breathe, eat, walk, and navigate life's many challenges.

A Brain Is Born: Neuroplasticity in Action

On conception, the fertilized human egg starts dividing at a rapid pace. In just three short weeks, a swelling appears that will ultimately develop into the human brain. The earliest stages of this process are shown in Figure 5.9 as tissue forms folds around a tube that will ultimately result in the central canal surrounded by the spinal cord and, in the more dorsal direction, ventricles surrounded by brain tissue (Nicholls, Martin, Wallace, & Fuchs, 2001). Additionally, distinctive brain categories such as the forebrain and hindbrain begin to appear by four weeks, accompanied by more specific brain areas such as the hippocampus and cerebellum at six weeks. By two months, the swellings are reminiscent of a human brain (Nicholls et al., 2001; figure after Nolte, 1988). As seen in Figure 5.9, at around 100 days of prenatal development, the gross structure of the developing brain closely resembles the adult brain, except for the smaller size and smooth cortex. By the time the fetus is full-term, the surface area of the cerebral cortex contains an impressive number of cortical gyri and sulci.

Because the brain is rapidly growing during prenatal development, it is important for the neurons to arrive at their appropriate destinations. As you might imagine, this task requires specific micromanaging to avoid brain development mistakes that could eventually lead to functional mishaps. These fundamental processes are directed by the genes regulating brain development. At the earliest stages of development, new cells are considered **pluripotent**, meaning that they are able to become many different types of cells, ranging from brain cells to the cells that produce fingernails. Learning how to guide the differentiation of various pluripotent cells, also called **stem cells**, into specific tissue is an ongoing challenge in medical research. **Progenitor cells** are another category of rapidly dividing cells. Although progenitor cells retain their ability to eventually produce a specific type of cell, they do not have the ability of stem cells to produce pluripotent (unspecialized) cells (Abrous, Koehl, & Le Moal, 2005). Thus, the progenitor cells are more specialized than stem cells. For example, neural progenitor cells can develop

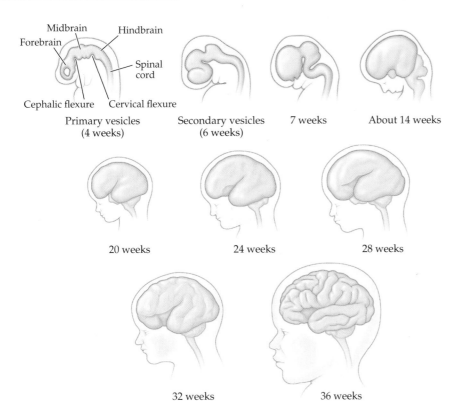

Midbrain **Hindbrain**
Forebrain
Spinal cord
Cephalic flexure **Cervical flexure**
Primary vesicles (4 weeks) Secondary vesicles (6 weeks) 7 weeks About 14 weeks

20 weeks 24 weeks 28 weeks

32 weeks 36 weeks

....

FIGURE 5.9 Brain development. The development of the human brain occurs at a rapid pace. Early in the process, the overall brain structure is similar to that of other mammals, with the more specific differentiation characteristic of the human brain occurring toward the end of gestational development.

into various types of neural cells, but they cannot differentiate into other types of cells such as muscle or cardiac cells.

Figure 5.10 shows key stages in the process of transitioning a burgeoning undifferentiated cell into a specific type of neuron that will eventually be incorporated into a neural network. Determining the role of new neurons in the sustained functions of mature brains has become a popular topic of investigation in many behavioral neuroscience labs.

Following neurogenesis (as described in Chapter 2), the cells must migrate to a specific geographical area of the developing brain where similar types of neurons will aggregate, or cluster together. Following this **aggregation** phase of development, the cells continue to differentiate, forming neural *communities* consisting of similar types of neurons. Functional circuits are formed as **synaptogenesis** (the formation of new synapses among neurons) occurs. Inevitably, some neurons will be deemed unnecessary during circuit formation and will degenerate via a form of programmed cell death known as **apoptosis**. Often synapse rearrangement will take place as neurons are pruned throughout the brain. This pruning process removes unnecessary cells so that neuronal processes once attached to now-degenerated cells must find new cells with which to form synapses.

Although the brain does not have a navigational system like the one that so many of us rely on to get us to our driving destinations, it does have a few navigational tricks up its neural sleeve. Certain glial cells known as **radial cells** provide a pathway reminiscent of *The Wizard of Oz*'s yellow-brick road that developing neurons follow to their destinations. These radial cells may turn into astrocytes (Chapter 2), another type of glial cell, after guiding the young neurons. Alternatively, they may continue to exist as radial cells, guiding young neurons and, impressively, generating young undifferentiated cells (Kriegstein & Alvarez-Buylla, 2009) (see Figure 5.11). Radial cells play an extremely important role in the developing cortex, considering that none of the cortical neurons in mammals is actually born in the cortex. The cortical neurons are generated in **proliferative** (cell-producing) **areas** such as the ventricular and subventricular zones (located near the lateral ventricles) and must migrate to their final cortical destinations (Rakic, 2009).

As neurons reach their destinations, they must branch out and form new synapses with other like-minded neurons. One of neuroscience's most remarkable stories reveals the discovery of a neurochemical known as **nerve growth factor** (**NGF**) and its role in neural development. Because the Mussolini government prohibited Jews from practicing medicine in World War II Italy, Rita Levi-Montalcini (Figure 5.12) set up her own makeshift laboratory in her bedroom. Working in these less-than-ideal conditions in Italy and later in laboratories in the United States, she and her colleagues discovered the NGF protein, which facilitates the growth of axons and dendrites and enhances the probability of neuronal survival (Abbott, 2009; S. Cohen, Levi-Montalcini, & Hamburg, 1954; Levi-Montalcini & Hamburger, 1951).

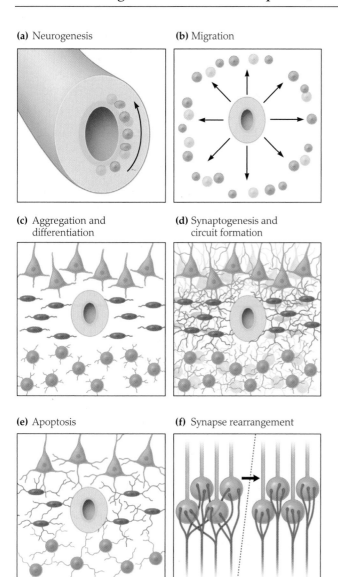

(a) Neurogenesis

(b) Migration

(c) Aggregation and differentiation

(d) Synaptogenesis and circuit formation

(e) Apoptosis

(f) Synapse rearrangement

FIGURE 5.10 Stages of neuronal development. Following neurogenesis, immature neurons go through several processes that ultimately lead them from the neural tube (depicted in yellow) to their final destination with appropriate neuronal connections.

The discovery of NGF marked the beginning of the identification of additional neurochemicals that alter the programmed genetic development of neurons. **Brain-derived neurotrophic factor (BDNF)** promotes the maturation of neurons and synapse formation throughout the brain (Bao, Chen, Qiao, & Thompson, 2011). BDNF has also been implicated in complex behaviors such as learning and in disorders such as depression. BDNF-knockout mouse models, in which mice are genetically engineered to lack BDNF, indicate that the absence of forebrain BDNF early in development is associated with hyperactivity, whereas later in development, the lack of BDNF is associated with disruption of learning processes (Monteggia et al., 2004).

Another way that neurons migrate is via specific membrane proteins located on the cell's surface that react differentially to other cell surfaces. These membrane proteins serve as **cell adhesion molecules (CAMs)** that are attracted to certain proteins located on specific types of cells (McClain & Edelman, 1982). Considering that the brain has in excess of a trillion connections that are most likely maintained by CAMs, there is much enthusiasm about the utilization of CAMs to develop therapeutic targets for disorders in which the brain's connections have gone awry (Uhl & Drgonova, 2014).

The proteins and other substances that influence various neuroplasticity functions are known collectively as *neurotrophic factors*. Considering the rate at which neuronal connections must be generated among the billions of neurons in the newborn's brain, neurotrophic factors are essential for the development of a healthy brain. Although the necessary neural cell bodies and emerging processes are present in the newborn's brain, the abundance of established neuronal connections is created through the early childhood years. In the human brain, the growth of dendritic processes (known as dendritic arborization) becomes more complex as the child experiences the world around her (as seen in Figure 5.13). In the mouse cortex, new synapses are formed when spines emerge from axons and migrate toward another strategically placed axon or another terminal ending (Holtmaat & Svoboda, 2009). Whereas cortical maturation occurs quickly

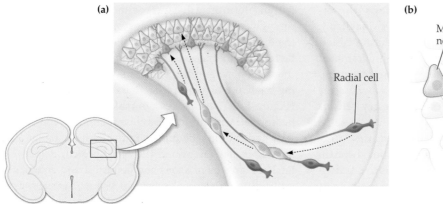

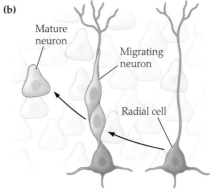

FIGURE 5.11 Neuronal pathways. Radial cells serve as guidance paths for immature neurons, marking the way to their final destinations.

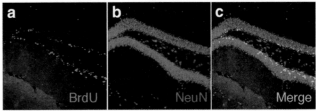

FIGURE 5.14 Detecting new neurons. To determine whether new cells were neurons and not glial cells, (a) mice were injected with BrdU, and the reactive cells were illuminated. (b) All of the neurons were stained. (c) When the new green cells merged with all of the new neurons, the yellow cells were known to be new neurons.

FIGURE 5.12 Rita Levi-Montalcini. Working in Italy, Levi-Montalcini and her colleagues discovered nerve growth factor.

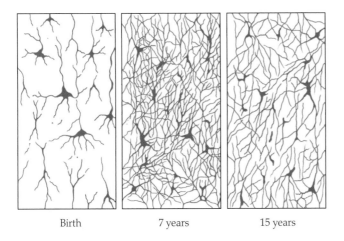

Birth	7 years	15 years

FIGURE 5.13 Age-related neuronal complexity. Following birth, the immature neurons develop synaptic connections that enable a child to engage in complex behavior. In adolescence, synaptic pruning occurs resulting in decreased density of neuronal processes to maximize neural efficiency.

in many mammalian species, it continues through early adulthood in humans, as neural circuits are formed and subsequently pruned following birth (Tau & Peterson, 2010). Life experiences provide the context for determining the most effective networks for optimal functioning.

Another mode of plasticity that has been observed in mature neurons is the restructuring of the neuron's existing **cytoskeleton**, the cellular infrastructure made up of the fibers contained within the cell's cytoplasm. This occurs in response to various neural adaptations that accompany learning in different contexts. The protein *nestin*, which contributes to the formation of the thin strands of proteins known as microfilaments that make up the cell's infrastructure, is typically expressed in developing neurons. It has also been observed in a specific type of nestin-expressing cell. One class of nestin cells includes mature cells that are found in the

adult brain in areas such as the basal forebrain, hippocampus, and striatum (Hendrickson, Rao, Demerdash, & Kalil, 2011). Just as it is sometimes more economical to renovate a home as opposed to building a new one, at times it is likely more economical to reconstruct existing neurons rather than create new neurons that must be integrated into mature neural networks. The previously mentioned modifications in dendritic arborization patterns and spines are additional examples of these efficient neural renovations. As new behaviors are acquired, additional growth in the neuron's cell body can support new dendritic growth and connections.

We have now learned about the remarkable process of neural development. Neuroplasticity is a critical component of neural development, and neurogenesis plays a key role in neuroplasticity. But how is neurogenesis itself thought to occur?

Fundamentals of Neurogenesis

Now that we know that neurons continue to be produced throughout the mammalian life span, behavioral neuroscientists face the challenge of determining the function of these new neurons. Neurogenesis has been established in the hippocampus of the adult human brain (Eriksson et al., 1998). Because scientists can systematically investigate rodent brains in ways they cannot investigate human brains, the rodent model has become a popular means of exploring neurogenesis.

Protocols that scientists use to provide evidence of neurogenesis rely on exposing the animals to bromodeoxyuridine (BrdU), a marker of cell division in the CNS. BrdU is a marker of neurogenesis in behavioral neuroscience research (Gould, 2007; Gratzner, 1982). Generally, BrdU is injected into the rat's abdominal area, although it can also be administered via the rat's drinking water or injected directly into the brain's ventricles (Wojtowicz & Kee, 2006). After a designated period of time, the researchers assess the number of dividing brain cells that are marked with BrdU.

Research has revealed two discrete areas of the mature mouse brain in which neurogenesis occurs: the **subgranular zone** of the dentate gyrus in the hippocampus and the **subventricular zone** of the lateral ventricle (see Figure 5.14). The cells produced in the subgranular zone eventually mature and migrate to the existing neurocircuitry of the dentate gyrus, where they likely play a role in learning and memory. The cells generated in the subventricular zone give rise to cells that migrate to the olfactory bulb and differentiate into interneurons that have olfactory function (Ma et al., 2010).

It is important to understand that not all dividing, or proliferating, cells in the CNS will become mature neurons that are integrated into functional neuronal circuits. Many will die, and some will mature into glial cells or endothelial cells migrating close to the brain's vascular system. This finding suggests that the production of new cells in the nervous system may play a role in the development or expansion of the brain's blood supply (Abrous et al., 2005). Accordingly, researchers must label the developing cells with markers that provide more definitive evidence that the new cells are indeed committed neurons to assure that they are investigating neurogenesis as opposed to the production of glial cells, known as *gliogenesis*.

Timing is a critical component of neurogenesis investigations. It will likely take up to a week for the cells to begin showing evidence of maturation and several weeks before the cells are classified as mature neurons. Focusing on the dentate gyrus cells, research suggests that it may take as long as four to eight weeks for a cell to become synaptically integrated into the hippocampal neural circuitry and up to four months for the cells to reach their final mature form with soma, dendrite length, and branching similar to other mature neurons (Carlen et al., 2002; Song, Stevens, & Gage, 2002). Thus, if a researcher wants to assess the effects of some manipulation, such as a training program or special diet, on the production and maturation of neurons, it is best to wait a few weeks for the cells to become mature. Other markers such as glial fibrillary acid protein can be used to determine whether the cells mature into glial cells (Abrous et al., 2005).

In this section, you have learned how and where neurogenesis occurs. Further, you have learned how new neurons are integrated into neural circuits. Of course, the brain continues to develop throughout our lives. Once the neural circuits are established throughout childhood, the next developmental milestone is adolescence, the preparation phase for the adult brain. As any person who has survived this developmental phase can confirm, the transition from childhood to adulthood via adolescence is rarely seamless. You will learn about various neural adaptations accompanying this turbulent developmental phase in the next section.

The Human Adolescent Brain

The slow maturation of the human brain, especially the executive functioning areas, results in a protracted period of immature responses such as impulsivity and risky decision making throughout the developmental stage of adolescence. Information in this section may provide some long-awaited answers to puzzling questions about your own behavior

during adolescence. As white matter, composed of myelinated axons, continues to develop throughout adolescence and early adulthood, more adult-like executive functioning and impulse controls begin to appear more consistently. Until that time, however, the adolescent brain can find itself in precarious situations that too often result in deadly circumstances (Asato, Terwilliger, Woo, & Luna, 2010). For example, compared with the adult brain, the adolescent brain is less likely to compute the long-term consequences of engaging in risky behaviors such as texting while driving (Dobbs, 2011). In this section, we will discuss some of the neural adaptations that accompany the transition to the more sophisticated cognitive and emotional functions that appear more consistently in adulthood.

To investigate the influence of development and maturity on voluntary planned behaviors, Beatriz Luna and her colleagues at the University of Pittsburgh have explored these responses in children, adolescents, and adults. One of the tasks these researchers used required sustained focus on a goal. That is, it required an ability to plan and carry out the appropriate response and, finally, the ability to inhibit irrelevant responses that interfere with the completion of the task—also known as **response inhibition**. For example, researchers tested children, adolescents, and adults in an fMRI scanner. They instructed subjects to stare at a light. When a stimulus suddenly appeared to one side of the light, subjects were to look in the opposite direction (for example, to the left if the stimulus were to the right). Looking at the stimulus was considered an error (Luna & Sweeney, 2001). Because we naturally orient toward new visual stimuli, success on this task requires cognitive control to override the impulse to focus on the stimulus. Such control can be thought of as **top-down processing** that requires executive cognitive function. As Figure 5.15 depicts, the subject

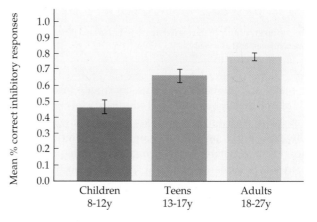

Source: Luna, B., Padmanabhan, A., Ohearn, K. (2010). What has fMRI told us about the development of cognitive control through adolescence? *Brain and Cognition, 72,* 101-113.

FIGURE 5.15 Gaining inhibitory control. Throughout human development, the ability to inhibit inappropriate responses increases with age.

groups demonstrated a graded improvement on this task from childhood to adulthood, with children improving from 50% of trials containing errors to only about 15% in adulthood. At about the time of late adolescence, the number of trials in which subjects correctly inhibited errors matched that of the adults. Thus, improvement on this response inhibition task, as well as executive function, improved through adolescence (Luna, Garver, Urban, Lazar, & Sweeney, 2004; Luna, Padmanabhan, & O'Hearn, 2010).

fMRI scans of the subjects conducting this visual task provided evidence that the anterior cingulate cortex (ACC) and right dorsolateral prefrontal cortex (DLPFC) were necessary to control eye movement in this task (Luna et al., 2010). Past research suggests that, during adolescence, activation of the DLPFC is increased compared with activation of the DLPFC in adult brains. Thus, even when teens match adult performance, they do so by exerting more brain effort in this area (Luna & Sweeney, 2001).

The DLPFC is associated with perceptual integration and motor planning. The prefrontal cortex (PFC) in general also seems to enhance perceptual integration with other brain areas such as the thalamus, striatum, and cerebellum during adolescence. These strengthened circuits may enhance inhibitory control in this task. The dorsal ACC, in contrast, seems to play a role initially in disengaging from a default mode of functioning present in the dorsal ACC when a person is not focusing on a specific task (Velanova, Wheeler, & Luna, 2008). Additionally, this area integrates past error information as an individual monitors performance and plans future responses (Polli et al., 2005).

Interestingly, whereas children, adolescents, and adults showed decreased activation of the rostral ACC during trials performed correctly compared with trials when they were not focused on the task, in the incorrect trials only adults showed a differential response characterized by an increase in the dorsal ACC. This suggests that adults are employing the ACC in all trials, resulting in more consistent and effective monitoring of responses (see Figure 5.16; Luna et al., 2010; Velanova et al., 2008). Overall, this research provides evidence for a role of the ACC and the DLPFC in the improvements in response inhibition and executive function through adolescence.

In another study, researchers assessed the correlation of the actual size or thickness of various cortical areas with intelligence. To do so, they imaged the brains of more than 300 children via fMRI and MRI scans at various ages throughout their childhood, adolescence, and early adulthood. Researchers were interested in the natural trajectory of cortical development and how it varies with intellectual ability. More important to intelligence than the actual size of the cortical area was the *dynamic* nature or plasticity of the cortical area, especially in the frontal cortex area. For example, the children who tested in the superior (highest) intelligence category started with thinner cortical widths than the average and high-intelligence groups but exhibited more change in these areas up until about 11 years of age, at which

point overall cortical thinning began again. In contrast, the lower-intelligence groups reached their peak in cortical width a few years earlier. Once again, the flexibility of brain tissue appears to be critical for optimal development. The results of this study suggest that a prolonged period of growth is also essential for optimal intellectual performance (Shaw et al., 2006).

Adolescents are more likely than adults to engage in risky behaviors, and one reason for this tendency is a less-developed ability to weigh short-term and long-term consequences, as implied previously. Researchers have hypothesized that in the adolescent brain, the ventral striatum, involved in processing of rewards, appears to be hyperactive, whereas the amygdala, involved in harm avoidance, and the PFC, involved in regulatory control, are less activated relative to the adult brain when processing long-term consequences of specific responses. In adolescents, this is thought to result in enhanced attention directed toward immediate rewards and less attention directed toward long-term payoffs or consequences (Grier, Terwilliger, Teslovich, Velanova, & Luna, 2010).

Although risk-taking is observed more often in adolescents than in adults, research contradicts the stereotypes that teens are irrational individuals who are unaware of potential harm that may result from different behaviors. On the contrary, the logical reasoning ability of adolescents is similar to that of adults (Steinberg, 2007), and there is a lack of convincing evidence that risk taking is related to an immature PFC (Romer, 2010).

Far from any deficit, the normal trajectory of brain development involves the maturation of the reward circuits in the frontal and striatal (frontostriatal) brain areas, an effect accompanied by a rise in dopamine activity involved in anticipation and reward responses (Chambers, Taylor, & Potenza, 2003). The incongruent maturation of the PFC and limbic areas such as the nucleus accumbens involved in reward contribute to a developmental phase of disproportionately high risk-taking behavior during adolescence that levels off during adulthood (Casey, Jones, & Hare, 2008; see Figure 5.17).

Research with animal models has suggested that this rise in dopamine activity may play a role in prompting juvenile animals to leave the family for novel territories and potential mates (Spear, 2007). In humans, these novel responses are often risky (e.g., driving, sex), especially considering that adolescents have considerably less experience than adults. For example, the number of car crashes significantly decreases after about 1,000 miles of driving experience (McCartt, Shabanova, & Leaf, 2003). This finding suggests that lack of experience may be more influential for the perception of increased risky decision making, impulsivity, and sensation seeking than immature brain circuits. Accordingly, interventions enhancing experience with dangerous adult behaviors such as extended driving training courses may play a significant role in reducing the occurrence of decisions or cognitive errors leading to harmful

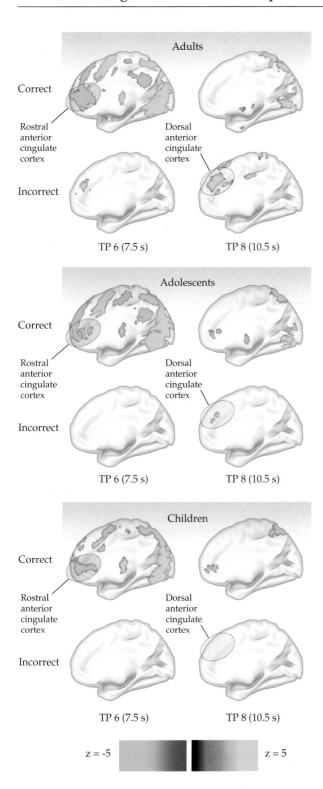

Source: Velanova, K., Wheeler, M.E., & Luna, B. (2008). Maturational changes in anterior cingulate and frontoparietal recruitment support the development of error processing and inhibitory control. *Cerebral Cortex, 18,* 2505-2522.

outcomes during adolescence (Romer, 2010). More information about the influence of various cortical areas in decision making and the determination of optimal response outcomes will be discussed in Chapter 12.

Another insightful research finding is that adolescence is the time when individuals are most susceptible to the emergence of mental health disorders. Depression, eating disorders, anxiety disorders, schizophrenia, and substance abuse are most likely to become apparent during adolescence (Kessler et al., 2005). Scientists have suggested that these illnesses may be related to some type of anomaly or exaggeration of the typical maturation of the adolescent brain. Of course, context is important. Other influences, ranging from psychosocial to various biological and environmental conditions, also influence brain development during this time. Scientists have suggested that an understanding that "moving parts get broken" helps to clarify why the adolescent brain is especially vulnerable to the onset of psychopathology. In other words, adolescence is a time of tremendous change in the brain, during which brain development may go awry. This may predispose adolescents to mental health disorders (Paus, Keshavan, & Giedd, 2008).

As you have learned, the human brain continues its development throughout childhood and adolescence into early adulthood. This extended developmental period is a hallmark of more complex brains and, although it leaves young people vulnerable for longer, it allows for more neural fine-tuning to respond to dynamic environmental demands throughout adulthood. This section has provided some insights into the neural basis of the behavioral changes of adolescence. However, adolescence is not the only vulnerable developmental phase for the brain. As we age, the brain encounters multiple neural challenges that may compromise cognitive and behavioral functions. These age-related challenges are discussed in the next section.

The Aging Brain

Once the brain emerges from adolescence, does neuroplasticity come to a screeching halt? In the earlier part of the 20th century, Santiago Ramón y Cajal, who penned the beautiful drawings of neurons presented earlier in the chapter (refer back to Figure 5.2), asserted that once the brain

FIGURE 5.16 Anterior cingulate and inhibitory control. When asked to perform a visual task during a fMRI scan, it was observed that adults, adolescents, and children all decreased activity in the rostral anterior cingulate cortex when responding correctly. Only the adults exhibited increased activation in the dorsal anterior cingulate when responding incorrectly. In this figure, blue colors indicate decreased activity, and yellow/red colors indicate increased activity.

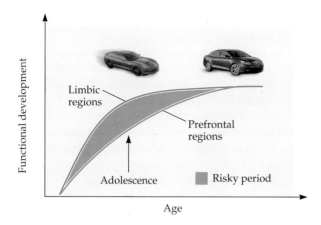

Source: Casey, B. J., Jones, R. M., & Hare, T. A. (2008). The adolescent brain. *Annals of the New York Academy of Sciences, 1124*, 111 -126.

FIGURE 5.17 Brain maturation and risk-taking in adolescence. The limbic regions of the brain mature at a faster rate than the prefrontal cortical areas during adolescence. Consequently, without the prefrontal regions to regulate the emotional and reward functions of the limbic areas, high levels of risk-taking are observed during this time.

completed its development, it was fixed and immutable in adulthood. This conclusion is not surprising considering that Cajal spent his time drawing two-dimensional static neurons from fixed tissue. Even so, there are hints that he began to see evidence of mutability rather than immutability in the adult nervous system, especially following damage, a process he referred to as *restorative plasticity* (Stahnisch & Nitsch, 2002). Hints of neuroplasticity were also observed by the biopsychology pioneer Karl Lashley, who observed plasticity in the brain of an adult rhesus monkey (Lashley, 1923). However, these ideas were not embraced initially, likely because of limited techniques to investigate these proposed plastic processes. As advanced neuroscience techniques became more readily available, however, it was only a

matter of time before scientists realized that the brain continues to change across the life span.

When the University of Illinois neuroscientist William Greenough and his colleagues investigated the effects of enriched environments (discussed in Chapter 1) on old, listless rats that had been sitting in cages their entire lives, he found that their brains were just as malleable as those of their younger rodent counterparts assessed in his original studies (Green, Greenough, & Schlumpf, 1983; Greenough, McDonald, Parnisari, & Camel, 1986). But what about the primate brain? How much restructuring was possible throughout adulthood? The neuroscientist Michael Merzenich, working originally with the Johns Hopkins neuroscientist Vernon Mountcastle, began identifying areas of the cortex that received specific sensory information, areas known as sensory receptive fields. For example, Merzenich would record from a particular area of a monkey's sensory cortex and then tap the monkey's fingers to determine the specific nature and location of the sensory input that would stimulate the neurons in the specific section of the sensory cortex. He continued this meticulous process until he had determined the sensory map of the entire hand onto the appropriate section of the sensory cortex (Kaas, 1991; Merzenich & Kaas, 1982).

In a key study, Merzenich and his colleagues amputated the third finger on an adult owl monkey's hand and waited up to 8 months to see whether the monkey's brain had reorganized itself to accommodate the loss of the finger. Would the brain sensory map on the somatosensory cortex remain the same after there was no longer any input coming to the sensory cortex from that finger? As previously mentioned, up until this time it was generally accepted that the brain could not rewire itself so late in the developmental game. Merzenich was not surprised, however, when he found the brain map to be completely restructured so that the adjoining fingers to the amputated fingers now included larger areas on the somatosensory cortex to provide more sensitivity to accommodate for

FIGURE 5.18 Cortical reorganization. Just two months after losing a digit, the owl monkey's cortical area representing each digit reorganizes to compensate for the lost incoming sensory information from the lost digit, maximizing responsiveness of the remaining digits.

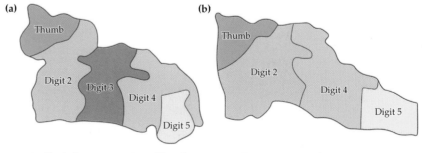

(a) Typical representation of hand

(b) Representation after amputation

the loss of the third finger (see Figure 5.18) (Merzenich et al., 1984).

After establishing that the adult primate brain was indeed plastic, the next question focused on how day-to-day experience altered the brain's mapping. To answer this question, monkeys received specific and controlled training in which certain fingers were stimulated. Accordingly, the cortical maps associated with these trained fingers became larger (Figure 5.19). These results provided strong evidence that training could alter the responsive maps of the brain (W. M. Jenkins, Merzenich, Ochs, Allard, & Guic-Robles, 1990).

Humans have also shown evidence of use-dependent cortical reorganization. In one study, after receiving extensive training with simultaneous stimulation of the thumb and "pinky" finger, it was more difficult for human subjects to differentiate stimulation of the two fingers. The representations of these fingers suggested that the dedicated cortical areas for each finger had become overlapped following training (Braun, Schweizer, Elbert, Birbaumer, & Taub, 2000). Additionally, MRI study results have provided evidence that musical training results in brain reorganization that is not observed in control subjects who are not training as musicians. Specifically, enlarged cortical representation of the fingers in the right hemisphere has been reported in string players (e.g., violin, cello) who, during their extensive musical training, become more sensitive to sensation generated from their individual fingers on their left hand as they play their instruments (Elbert, Pantev, Wienbruch, Rockstroh, & Taub, 1995).

During the aging process, however, many sensory abilities change. For example, our vision and hearing become less acute, meaning that the accompanying sensory signals entering our brains become a bit muddled as we age. If less clear sensory information is delivered to the brain areas designated to promptly process it, the neurons may become less responsive to the appropriate incoming sensory information. This process could lead to a functional downward spiral in which less sensory information is processed by the brain, accompanied by a downsizing of the area of the brain devoted to processing the sensory stimuli because

of decreased use dependence (Mahncke, Bronstone, & Merzenich, 2006).

In addition to sensory abilities, research suggests that cognitive abilities in general begin to decline with age, perhaps as early as age 30 (Bishop, Lu, & Yankner, 2010; Park & Gutchess, 2003; Park et al., 1996). Although the cognitive decline is not noticeable initially, it slowly builds as we age. Further, most adults will experience a reduction in processing speed as they age (Salthouse, 1996). In experimental populations consisting of a continuum of young to old adults, postmortem studies reveal reduced brain weight, shrinkage of neurons, reduced synaptic density, and loss of dendritic spines with age (Raz & Rodrigue, 2006).

Researchers have investigated the potential role of age-related changes in the genome as an influential factor in the functional decline of various body organs, including the brain, during aging. One candidate for such genetic decline is telomere function. **Telomeres** are critical for keeping our genes intact during chromosome replication, a protective function that becomes increasingly important as we age. Structurally, telomeres are repetitive DNA sequences located at the end of chromosomes that, over time, get worn down and lose their ability to function. Remember when that plastic cap comes off the laces on your worn tennis shoes? The ends of the laces become unraveled, making part of the lace unusable for tying knots. Similarly, as the telomeres shorten, their productivity declines, resulting in increased cell death and age-related cognitive decline (Jaskelioff et al., 2011).

The risk of **Alzheimer's disease (AD)**, which is characterized by severe memory loss and eventual loss of essential functions such as swallowing, increases dramatically with age. Age-related cognitive deficits are even more pronounced in individuals suffering from AD relative to their healthy, aging peers (Morrison & Hof, 1997). The brains of individuals with AD, as confirmed on autopsy, are characterized by the buildup of **amyloid plaque protein**, deposits of the protein known as β-amyloid found in spaces between neurons. Additionally, neurofibrillary tangles are found in brains diagnosed with AD. These tangles consist of knotted threads of **tau (τ) protein**, important in supporting the

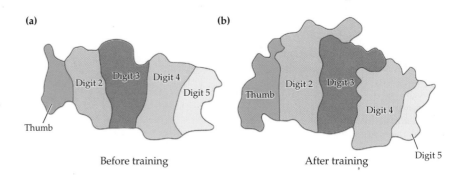

FIGURE 5.19 Training-induced neuroplasticity. Training in digits 2, 3, and 4 produces larger cortical areas for these digits in comparison with the digits that were not trained.

microtubules that form the infrastructure of the neuron. Finally, severely enlarged ventricles and a shrinking of the hippocampus have been observed in the brains of Alzheimer's patients (see Figure 5.20). Up to 20% of adults 65 years and older have a mild version of the disease, and about 15% of these individuals develop severe AD each year. It is disturbing to learn that half of those living to age 85 will develop AD (Alzheimer's Association, 2011). Although advances in medicine are leading to longer lives for our bodies, our brains do not seem able to endure these long lives without loss of function.

Michael Merzenich and his colleagues have described the changes associated with cognitive decline as **negative plastic changes**, changes that, even in healthy elderly populations, occur as the signal-to-noise ratio (important for distinguishing meaningful stimuli from background information) discerned by the brain's neurons becomes less and less distinct (Mahncke et al., 2006). Accordingly, since aging-related brain changes have been observed to be reversible in aged rats exposed to enriched environments, scientists have asked whether it is possible to reverse, or at least slow, aging-related cognitive decline in older humans (Winocur, 1998; Mahncke et al., 2006). To answer this question, researchers have developed software for individuals to engage in extensive cognitive training to build neural reserves and slow the aging process. Research provides evidence that these brain plasticity–based training programs aimed at enhancing sensory functions, processing speed, and memory have significantly improved people's performance in these areas. However, the effectiveness of these programs outside of the laboratory requires further research (Ball et al., 2002; Mahncke et al., 2006; Willis et al., 2006).

Far from Cajal's original notions about the lack of plasticity in the healthy developed nervous system, research now illuminates the many ways in which brains change as we age. Indeed, Cajal would likely be surprised, if he were alive today, to learn that thousands of new neurons are generated every day in the adult mammalian brain (Cameron & McKay, 2001). The sustained plasticity of the brain throughout our lives makes sense because our behaviors would be constrained if we could not continue to modify them in response to changing environments. In general, the adult brain has two challenges—preserving essential components of established neural circuits and allowing the circuits to adapt to changing environmental challenges (Abrous et al., 2005). In connection with this discussion of age-related changes in the brain, "Context Matters" focuses on a study that investigates the basis for the decrease in neurogenesis and the cognitive decline associated with aging.

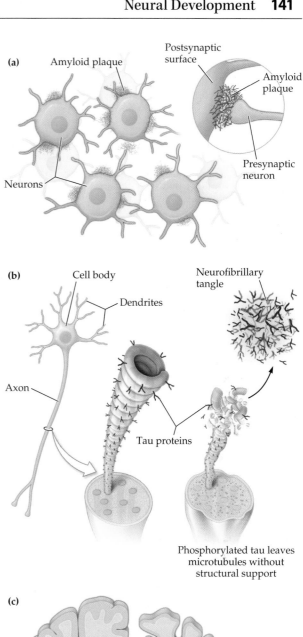

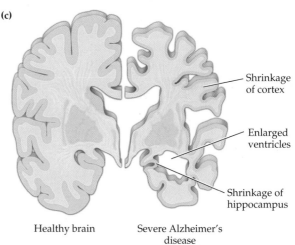

FIGURE 5.20 **The Alzheimer's brain.** (a) Alzheimer's disease is characterized by amyloid plaques interrupting neuronal functioning, especially in the hippocampal area. (b) Normally, τ works to stabilize microtubules, but in Alzheimer's disease τ destabilizes microtubules, leading to neurofibrillary tangles and diminished neuronal processing and communication. (c) Patients with Alzheimer's also show enlarged ventricles and significant shrinkage of the cortical and hippocampal areas.

Aging: Is It in Our Blood?

Featured study: Villeda, S. A., Luo, J., Mosher, K. I., Zou, B., Britschgi, M., Bieri, G., ... Wyss-Coray, T. (2011). The ageing systemic milieu negatively regulates neurogenesis and cognitive function. Nature, 477, 90–94.

Is it possible that some component of an individual's internal context interacts with the nervous system to regulate the aging process? In this study, Saul Villeda and his Stanford University colleagues investigated the influence of blood components on age-related neurogenesis and cognitive decline. After noting that specific areas in the brain where neurogenesis takes place are clustered around blood vessels, these scientists wondered whether some factor in the blood interacted with the nervous system and regulated these aging-related reductions in neurogenesis. To answer their questions, Villeda and colleagues used young mice (3–4 months old) and old mice (18–20 months old) as their subjects.

To enable the young and old mice to share blood, they employed a technique known as **parabiosis**, in which portions of the animals are surgically bound so that the blood supply is shared between the two animals. Using this technique, the animals could either be the same age or, more important for this study, they could vary in age. In an additional procedure, blood from young mice was merely injected into older mice and vice versa.

As seen in Context Matters Figure 5.1, when young mice received old mouse blood, their levels of young neurons declined, indicated by the decrease in the doublecortin antibody that marks newly developing neurons in the dentate gyrus of the hippocampus. Although the generation of new neurons was practically nil in the old mice, the infusion of young mouse blood appeared to produce a modest increase (based on representative

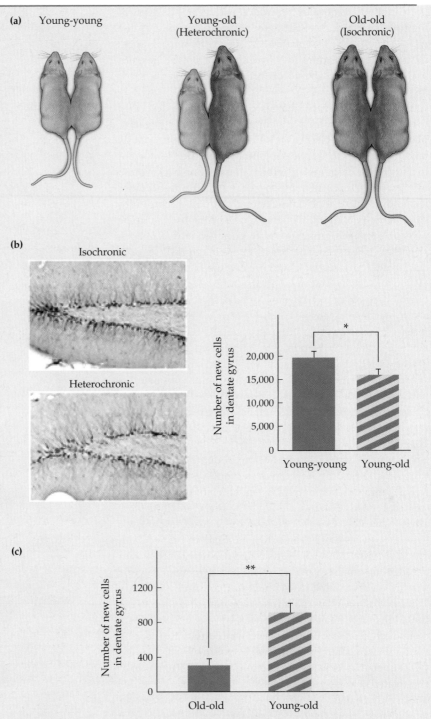

(a) Young-young   Young-old (Heterochronic)   Old-old (Isochronic)

(b) Isochronic

Heterochronic

(c)

CONTEXT MATTERS FIGURE 5.1 **Aging and neurogenesis.** When the blood of old mice was transfused into younger mice in a heterochronic preparation (a), neurogenesis declined to a level closer to that of the old mice (i.e., fewer stained developing cells) (b); alternatively, when the blood from young mice was transfused into old mice, neurogenesis rates increased to a level closer to that of young mice (c).

images of the brain). To quantify this change, the number of new cells stained with the BrdU antibody was examined. As indicated by the graphs, exposure to old blood decreased the rates of neurogenesis in young mice. In old mice exposed to young blood, the rate of proliferating cells increased (by 200%) in the dentate gyrus.

To determine whether these neural alterations resulted in behavioral and cognitive changes, researchers gave another group of mice intravenous injections of either young or old blood and then tested them on two tasks. In the contextual fear conditioning task, animals learned to associate a specific environmental context with an aversive stimulus such as mild electric shock. Evidence of strong memories of this association are determined by the strength of the freezing response (a common response to threat) when the animals are placed back into the environment in which they were previously shocked. Researchers also assessed the mice's spatial memory with the radial arm water maze. In this task, mice must remember which of the eight arms of a maze contains a platform allowing them to escape from the water. Fewer errors in

an attempt to locate the safe platform indicate stronger spatial memories. The results suggested that the infusion of the old blood resulted in impaired contextual fear conditioning and spatial learning and memory.

In an attempt to identify the element in the blood that was influencing neurogenesis, the researchers conducted a statistical analysis to identify the signaling proteins in the blood that were most closely associated with improved performance in the old animals receiving the young blood. In this process, they eventually identified eotaxin, a specific immune molecule involved in allergic responses such as asthma. When eotaxin was injected into young mice, the young mice took on the older characteristics by exhibiting declines in their performance on cognitive tasks and reduced rates of neurogenesis.

This study provides evidence that eotaxin plays a role in the reduction in neurogenesis and the cognitive decline associated with aging. It suggests that the internal context of our blood components interacts with the nervous system to regulate the process of aging.

Recovering from Brain Injury

Up until this point in the chapter, we have largely focused on the importance of the brain's ability to change during neural development. However, through the course of a brain's life, change is not always good. As previously mentioned, as brains age, their functions begin to slow down. In our contemporary, fast-paced society, brains are also vulnerable to many types of injuries. The brain's safeguards against potential injuries (e.g., skulls, meninges, and cerebrospinal fluid) may have been effective for our ancestors who could rely only on their feet to transport their bodies. However, with the introduction of planes, trains, and automobiles (as well as bullets and a host of other fast-moving objects) into our evolutionary landscape, traumatic brain damage became a significant threat to healthy brains.

Approximately 5 million individuals in the United States are currently living with **traumatic brain injury (TBI)** and its physical, emotional, and financial aftermath (B. A. Cohen et al., 2007). Further, about 1.7 million TBIs occur each year in the United States (Faul, Xu, Wald, & Coronado, 2010; Rozenbeek, Maas, & Menon, 2013). Aside from firearms and humans' various rapid modes of transportation, health circumstances such as strokes, seizures, and other debilitating diseases also leave an unfavorable mark on the brain's terrain. Thanks to the continual neuroplasticity of mammalian brains, however, hope exists for either partial or full recovery from brain injury in many cases.

Damage Control in Injured Brains

What happens when the brain is injured, and how does the brain recover from injury? Once the brain is damaged by an external or internal destructive force, the body initiates a series of events not only to contain the damage, but also to increase the likelihood of resuscitating the damaged tissue. For example, as seen in Figure 5.21, when a person suffers an automobile accident causing the brain to slam against the inside of the skull, damage occurs as axons twist and tear, a process known as **axon shearing**. Such an injury from an accident often leads to a **subdural hematoma** (a localized blood clot). The disruption of blood flow, known as **ischemia**, following an event such as an accident or a stroke is a key factor predicting the extent of damage following the brain injury.

Cerebral blood flow is critical for the delivery of glucose and oxygen to the cells. Without these precious resources, the cell enters a phase of **ionic flux**, characterized by altered concentrations of ions such as decreased levels of magnesium and potassium and increased levels of calcium. In this precarious state, if the cell fails to locate the resources necessary for homeostatic functioning, it will die (Giza & Hovda, 2001). Further, the release of excitatory amino acids such as glutamate, a frequent effect of brain trauma, also often leads to cell death (L. W. Jenkins et al., 1988).

When a brain injury occurs, it is important to determine the extent of damage. Often this is accomplished with a standard neurological assessment known as the *Glasgow Coma Scale*, which determines the patient's ability to speak, move, engage in conversation, and perform other basic cognitive functions. Glasgow Coma Scale scores at various time

(a)

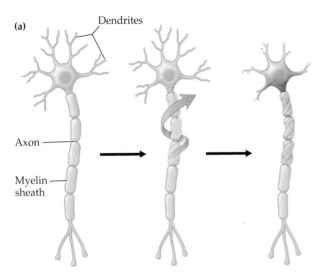

Axon rips, leading to cell death

(b)

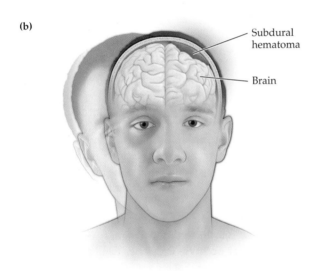

FIGURE 5.21 **Traumatic brain injury.** During forceful blows to the head, the impact of the brain against the skull can result in ripped axons and blood clots, both of which disrupt the flow of glucose, oxygen, and relevant neurochemicals.

points serve as important predictors of the possible degree of recovery of function (Kraus & Chu, 2005).

Recovering from injury is perhaps the biggest challenge ever encountered by the brain. One important type of emergency rescue cell in these situations is the astrocyte, a type of glial cell (see Chapter 2). Unlike neurons, astrocytes are not vulnerable to the toxic effect of glutamate release that typically follows brain damage. Consequently, not unlike workers who are brought in to clean up hazardous waste sites, astrocytes are recruited to vacuum up excessive glutamate to prevent additional neuronal loss. In the process, they scavenge for the presence of **oxygen free radicals** that can also harm vulnerable neurons. These multitasking astrocytes also modify levels of extracellular potassium and hydrogen ions

to provide a buffer against swelling, or edema. Thus, the response of the glial cells to brain injury is an important step toward recovery (Buffo et al., 2008; Chen & Swanson, 2003).

Neurologists, neuropsychologists, and other rehabilitation specialists use several approaches, including pharmacological therapy and behavioral therapy, to further promote recovery. Drugs such as amphetamine are sometimes used to activate certain areas. Behavioral therapies such as **constraint-induced movement therapy**, which restricts the use of the functional limb to encourage the use of the impaired limb, force new neural circuits to be formed that regulate the performance of the impaired limb (see Figure 5.22).

In one study, children diagnosed with cerebral palsy who consequently had paralysis on one side of their body were assigned to either a constraint-induced movement therapy intervention group or a control group. The children in the treatment group wore a sling on their functioning limb for six hours per day for up to 12 days and, during this time, were encouraged to participate in active play and other functional tasks (e.g., eating with their impaired limb). Even after this short time, the children developed improved dexterity of their impaired limb and better movement efficiency, effects that persisted at the six-month follow-up assessment (Charles, Wolf, Schneider, & Gordon, 2007). A similar study with children with cerebral palsy found that the effects extended outside of the laboratory to increased use of the affected limb in the child's home (Taub, Ramey, DeLuca, & Echols, 2004).

Animal studies also emphasize the importance of training in recovery of function following damage to the nervous system. In one study in which rats experienced an experimentally induced spinal cord injury, half the animals were trained in a reaching task. That task required the animal to use the impaired limb to retrieve a food treat for six weeks. Compared with injured animals that were not provided with training, the trained animals had higher levels of cortical BDNF. Further, a similar group of injured animals that received training exhibited improved functional movement in the reaching task, relative to the injured animals that were not provided with

FIGURE 5.22 **Constraint-induced therapy.** To enhance rehabilitation of the injured arm, the functioning arm is constrained to encourage the movement and use of the injured limb to regain neural functioning through repeated use.

training (Girgis et al., 2007). Such experiments are important in determining just how effective the brain is in remapping its circuits following intensive behavioral therapy.

Thus, recovery from brain damage is possible, but it requires a considerable amount of effort and training. As discussed previously in this chapter, younger brains that are still exhibiting optimal levels of neuroplastic functions have an advantage over older, less plastic brains. As you have learned in this section, the recovery process begins with the actions of glial cells and neurons and continues with the efforts of therapists working with the patient in hopes of establishing new neural circuits to recover or compensate for the lost function. In the next section, you will learn about how vulnerable the brain is to injury in certain types of collision sports, as well as why it is so important to minimize trauma to the brain.

A Case to Consider: Repetitive Head Injuries in Athletes

In many organized sports, athletes do not have to step into a fast vehicle to experience a head injury. Not only do trained athletes run at impressive speeds—but also, in some athletic matches such as both European and American versions of football, it is commonplace to use one's head as a weapon or tool to propel the ball toward the desired goal. In other sports such as boxing, the use of the head is less subtle. In boxing, the goal is to punch opponents' heads in hopes of disorienting opponents and forcing them off their feet. Obviously, evolutionary mechanisms directed toward protecting the brain sometimes run counter to the goals of our society's quest to win a game.

The havoc that athletic games may wreak on the brain started to become evident in the 1920s, when head injuries from boxing appeared to result in progressive neurological deterioration. This condition, known informally as *punch-drunk syndrome*, was originally referred to as *dementia pugilistica* but was more recently referred to as **chronic traumatic encephalopathy (CTE)** when the neuropathologist Bennet Omalu and his colleagues published a case-study report of the brain of Mike Webster, a retired football player for the Pittsburgh Steelers (Figure 5.23). (The story was dramatized in the 2015 movie *Concussion*, starring Will Smith.)

CTE is associated with memory loss, behavioral/personality changes, and speech and movement (gait) abnormalities. The brains of CTE patients exhibit atrophy in the cerebral hemispheres in general, with specific loss in the temporal lobe, thalamus, hypothalamus, and brainstem. As occurs in other conditions such as schizophrenia, the ventricles are enlarged as well. When the brain tissue of CTE patients is more closely examined under the microscope, similar to the tissue of an Alzheimer's brain, neurofibrillary tangles of τ, amyloid plaques, and a host of other neural abnormalities are observed. CTE differs from AD, however, in that it is a slowly progressing condition (likely more slowly developing than AD) with a clear environmental cause (McKee et al., 2009).

FIGURE 5.23 Dr. Bennet Omalu. Dr. Omalu was the first doctor to discover chronic traumatic encephalopathy in football players. He is shown here with Will Smith (left), who played him in the 2015 movie *Concussion*.

In 2012, some 2,000 former professional football players brought new attention to CTE by filing a lawsuit against the National Football League for ignoring knowledge about the risk to players of brain injuries (Simon, 2012). One year later, the National Football League reached a $765 million settlement with a larger group of 4,500 former players in an attempt to end existing and future lawsuits over debilitating, football-related brain injuries (Thompson & Red, 2013). As with boxers (and participants in other contact sports, including rugby, wrestling, lacrosse, hockey, soccer, and skiing), football players frequently suffer **concussions**, brain injuries with symptoms ranging from loss of consciousness to a sustained headache to memory loss.

It is estimated that 1.6 to 3.8 million sports-related TBIs including concussions occur each year in the United States (Langlois, Rutland-Brown, & Wald, 2006; Thurman, Branche, & Sniezek, 1998). From 1997 through 2007, emergency room visits from children 8–13 years of age doubled. The rate tripled among 14- to 19-year-olds, with 70% occurring in males. In these children and adolescents, most injuries are from football and cycling (Sahler & Greenwald, 2012). Although most patients with concussions recover within a few days or weeks, others will embark on a long-lasting, progressive condition. For example, it was estimated that about 17% of boxers experiencing repetitive concussions would develop punch-drunk syndrome (CTE) (Roberts, Allsop, & Bruton, 1990). In collision sports such as football and boxing, players may encounter thousands of hits that do not cause a concussion during a single season. However, as you may guess, the cumulative damage from these hits can trigger CTE. Further, since players know that they will be pulled from playing the game if a concussion is confirmed, many players may feel pressure to report their symptoms inaccurately so that they can continue competing.

In 2009, Ann McKee and her colleagues at Boston University School of Medicine published a report confirming CTE in five football players. They found that the trajectory of the illness seems accelerated in football players compared with boxers and wrestlers. The average life span of football players with CTE was 44 years, whereas the average life span of boxers was closer to 60 years (McKee et al., 2009). As seen in Figure 5.24, areas of dense τ protein deposits have been observed in football players.

The confirmation that the University of Pennsylvania's former captain of the football team, 21-year-old Owen Thomas, exhibited evidence of CTE although he had never been diagnosed with a concussion throughout his football career raises concerns about predicting who is at risk for CTE. Additionally, this case suggests that CTE may lead to debilitating symptoms much earlier than originally thought. Thomas was a successful defensive end on the celebrated Penn team, an all-Ivy player who, in 2009, started all of Penn's games (see Figure 5.25). After calling his mother and mentioning that he was struggling in a few classes, this accomplished student appeared to have committed suicide by hanging himself. His mother reported that, although her son had been playing football since he was 9 years old, he had never been officially diagnosed with a concussion. She insightfully stated in a newspaper interview, "The evidence coming in from Owen . . . is that this [injury] is not just a question of a person getting big hits and then ignoring them. This is a person getting many little hits, starting from a young age. Football linebackers might get 1,000 little hits. Now we're thinking these are like teaspoons. A thousand teaspoons of water could be the same as a big jug. It's possible" (ESPN, 2010). Owen Thomas was the youngest football player to be diagnosed with CTE (ESPN, 2010).

Of course, the results of a single case study cannot be generalized to a wider population. More research on the probability of these conditions developing in athletes playing collision sports is necessary before we can draw definite conclusions. However, research suggests that attempts to minimize trauma to the brain are necessary to avoid some form of brain degeneration. Consequently, sports equipment companies have directed attention toward developing more effective sports helmets.

The former Harvard football player Vin Ferrara, after receiving an M.D. and an M.B.A., launched a company that manufactures a helmet thought to reduce impact to the brain in the event of collisions. As seen in Figure 5.26, this new helmet design borrows from the idea of installing airbags in automobiles to minimize the impact to the driver and passengers in accidents. The helmet contains patches of air cells that act as shock absorbers when the player's head crashes into another player or the ground (Lambert, 2010).

Continued research is necessary to track reductions in concussions,

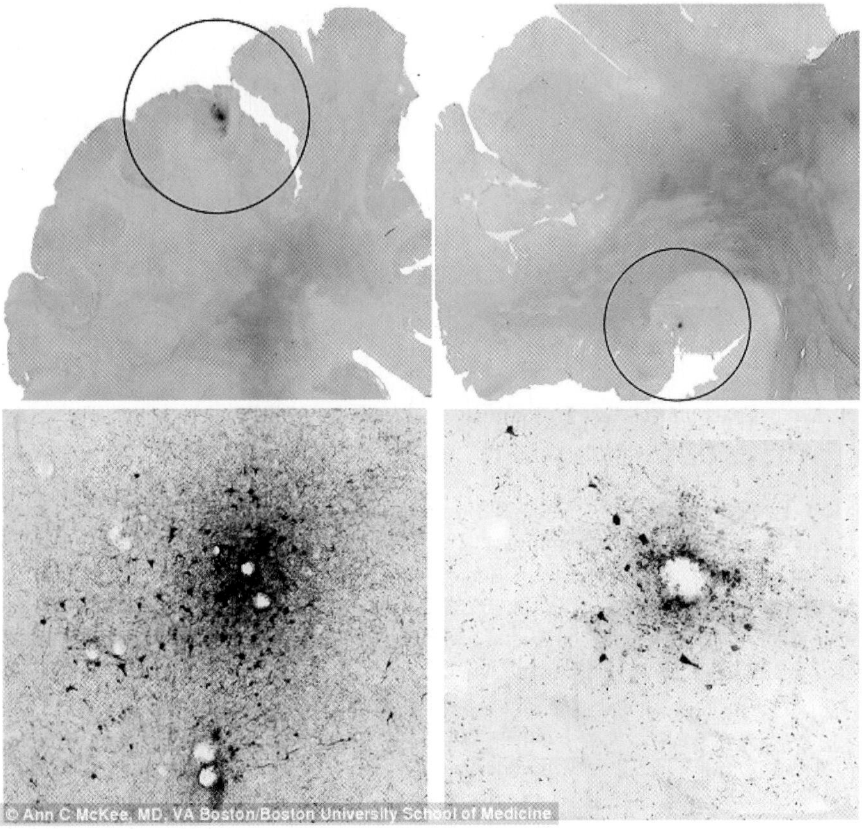

© Ann C McKee, MD, VA Boston/Boston University School of Medicine

FIGURE 5.24 Chronic traumatic encephalopathy. When the brains of football players who exhibited unexplained psychiatric illness were closely examined, evidence of τ deposits in neuronal processes were observed throughout the temporal lobe, thalamus, hypothalamus, and brainstem. The top row indicates τ deposits (circles). Under the microscope, the deposits reveal neurofibrillary tangles (dark spots shown in the bottom row).

FIGURE 5.25 **Youngest case of CTE.** The University of Pennsylvania football player, Owen Thomas (in middle), was the youngest football player to be diagnosed with CTE.

FIGURE 5.26 **CTE-preventive helmets?** In response to fears about football players developing CTE, more technologically advanced helmets are being designed. Research is necessary to determine whether such helmets will provide protection against forceful hits and CTE.

brain injuries, and confirmations of CTE in football players using different styles of helmets. Having a safer helmet could also send a signal to players to use their heads even more forcefully. Time—and data—will provide informed answers to these questions.

As researchers continue to learn how the brain recovers from injuries such as repetitive concussions, we are reminded just how vulnerable the brain is to external threats. As we wait for the latest technologies and protocols to prompt the most effective neuronal and functional recoveries, perhaps we could all practice "safe neural functions" by wearing helmets while biking, skating, skiing, and playing contact sports—as well as avoiding blows to the head altogether, to the extent this is possible.

Unfortunately, although we have seen in this chapter that our brains are constantly evolving, the human brain will likely never generate adequate preventive and safety mechanisms to compensate for humans' desire to propel themselves at speeds our ancestors never imagined. The survival of neurons in these cases is literally *a battle of the brains*. We end this chapter with "Laboratory Exploration," which examines how animal models are informing our understanding of how specific missteps in neural development may lead to neurodevelopmental disorders.

LABORATORY EXPLORATION

Behavioral Profiling and Genetic Engineering: In Search of Animal Models for Autism Spectrum Disorder

ASD is a socially debilitating condition with an extraordinarily high rate of heritability. The prominent role of genetics in ASD has prompted scientists to search for genetic candidates for the disorder, a process that often involves the development of genetically engineered mice. For example, if a genetic mutation is identified through human studies as a possible candidate for ASD, researchers can develop an analogous mutation in the mouse genome. Mouse knockout models, in which genetically modified stem cells are strategically injected into pregnant females, can be used to generate a desired mutant strain of mice.

Once the genetically engineered strain of mouse has been generated, the next step is **behavioral phenotyping**, a form of behavioral profiling to determine whether the new mouse strain is a "match" for the human disorder of interest. A challenge with ASD is that no definitive biological cause has been identified, so researchers have emphasized behavior (Silverman, Yang, Lord, & Crawley, 2010). According to the

Fifth Edition of the *Diagnostic and Statistical Manual of Mental Disorders* (DSM-5), ASD is characterized by (1) "persistent deficits in social communication and social interaction across multiple contexts" and (2) "restricted, repetitive patterns of behavior, interests, or activities" (American Psychiatric Association, 2013). With these behavioral targets in mind, several strains of mice have been engineered, each meeting the criteria described in the DSM-5 with varying success.

One mouse model that shows promise as a model of ASD is the black and tan brachyuric (BTBR) mouse strain (Clee, Nadler, & Attie, 2005). Compared with a more standard mouse strain, the BTBR strain of mice exhibits compromised social interactions such as diminished reciprocal social interactions, delayed approaches to mouse peers, decreased evidence of social communication, and repetitive self-grooming (Scattoni, Gandhy, Ricceri, & Crawley, 2008). In a study conducted by Jacqueline Crawley and her colleagues at the National Institute of Mental Health, the BTBR and control mice were placed, one at a time, in an apparatus with three chambers. One chamber had a mouse placed in a small enclosure, another had the enclosure object with no mouse, and the third compartment was empty (Laboratory Exploration Figure 5.1). The question was simple: where would each mouse prefer to spend time, with another mouse, with an object, or in an empty chamber? The control mice spent more time with the mouse, whereas the BTBR mice spent more time with the object. Each control mouse sniffed the mouse in the apparatus, whereas each BTBR mouse showed no preference, sniffing the object as much as it did the other mouse (Silverman et al., 2010).

With the identification of a potential animal model, scientists begin trying to identify biological correlates of the targeted symptoms of ASD. When neuroscientists examined the mice brains, they found a surprise. These mice lack a corpus callosum, an effect not characteristic of human ASD patients—although smaller volumes of the corpus callosum have been observed in ASD patients compared with healthy controls (Vidal et al., 2006). Other neurological differences between the BTBR and standard mice include a smaller hippocampus and greater number of unmyelinated axons in

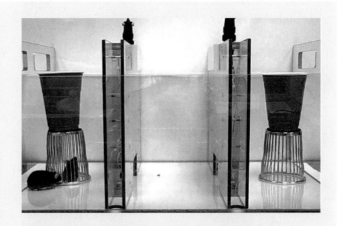

LABORATORY EXPLORATION FIGURE 5.1 Social preference chamber. In research assessing animal models of autism-like behavior, mice are placed in the middle chamber to determine whether they prefer to spend time with either the novel object or the novel object with the mouse (social preference).

the BTBR strain (Stephenson et al., 2011). Do these neuroanatomical differences invalidate this seemingly valid model of autism? Although the results are preliminary, compromised hippocampal neurons and decreased myelination have been observed in human cases (Raymond, Bauman, & Kemper, 1996; Zikopoulis & Barbas, 2010).

Although this animal model is far from perfect, it has helped scientists to explore the symptoms of ASD in new ways. After learning throughout this chapter about the dramatic changes that the brain experiences during development, we can see how certain missteps may occur along the developmental path. Early-stage research on ASD suggests that these neural missteps can have far-reaching effects. Once scientists learn more about the cause or causes of ASD in humans, they may be able to create an even better animal model of ASD for laboratory studies. Scientists will continue to learn as much as possible about the developing brain to identify specific mechanisms of functional impairments associated with the broad spectrum of neurodevelopmental disorders.

Conclusion

An overarching theme of this chapter is *change*. Our brains have changed through evolutionary adaptations, arriving at a human brain that contains more neurons than any other primate brain and more neurons in the cortex than any other mammal. Throughout the phases of development, newborn brains change from structures with limited neural processes to brains with mature neural networks that continue to develop through adolescence. The adult brain continues to generate new neurons and build new networks to accommodate changing environmental demands. Advanced age brings minimal neuronal loss and mild cognitive decline, with accelerated decline associated with neurodegenerative disorders such as AD.

Change can have a negative impact when the brain is injured, but evidence indicates that some damage can be reversed, especially with extensive behavioral training. Other medical interventions may slow down the negative effects of TBI. Finally, harmful effects on the brain can be minimized through prevention tactics such as wearing helmets and engaging in less risky behavior.

KEY TERMS

clinical efficacy (p. 122)

Building Brains

conservative process (p. 123)
neuroethology (p. 124)
Encephalization Quotient (EQ)
   (p. 127)
transgenerational (p. 130)
DNA methylation (p. 131)
histones (p. 131)
neuroplasticity (p. 132)

Neural Development

pluripotent (p. 132)
stem cells (p. 132)
progenitor cells (p. 132)
aggregation (p. 133)

synaptogenesis (p. 133)
apoptosis (p. 133)
radial cells (p. 133)
proliferative areas (p. 133)
nerve-growth factor (NGF) (p. 133)
brain-derived neurotrophic factor
   (BDNF) (p. 134)
cell-adhesion molecules (CAMs)
   (p. 134)
cytoskeleton (p. 135)
subgranular zone (p. 135)
subventricular zone (p. 135)
response inhibition (p. 136)
top-down processing (p. 136)
telomeres (p. 140)
Alzheimer's disease (AD) (p. 140)
amyloid plaque protein (p. 140)

tau (τ) protein (p. 140)
negative plastic changes (p. 141)
parabiosis (p. 142)
traumatic brain injury (TBI) (p. 143)

Recovering from Brain Injury

axon shearing (p. 143)
subdural hematoma (p. 143)
ischemia (p. 143)
ionic flux (p. 143)
oxygen free radicals (p. 144)
constraint-induced movement therapy
   (p. 144)
chronic traumatic encephalopathy
   (CTE) (p. 145)
concussions (p. 145)
behavioral phenotyping (p. 147)

REVIEW QUESTIONS

1. Describe the conservative process of brain evolution, giving examples. How do today's scientists assess the similarities and differences between the human brain and those of other species?

2. Define epigenetics and give an example of research in which scientists observed epigenome marking.

3. Describe the formation of the human nervous system during prenatal development, including the gestational ages at which certain stages of development occur. Identify the respective roles of stem cells, progenitor cells, NGF, BDNF, and nestin.

4. Describe some key developmental differences between the human adolescent brain and the adult brain. How do these differences manifest in behaviors?

5. Name some developmental changes that are typical of the older adult brain. How do the brains of AD patients differ from those of healthy adults?

6. Describe what happens inside the brain when a TBI is sustained. How does the body respond to attempts to contain the damage and heal from such injuries? What therapies are used to help TBI patients recover?

7. Define CTE and describe how it may be prevented.

CRITICAL-THINKING QUESTIONS

1. Consider the cross-generational changes described in the section on epigenetics. What implications does this information have for the lifestyle choices of people who intend to have children?

2. Given that adolescence has been found to be a vulnerable time for the onset of psychopathology, can you imagine neuroscientists finding a way to "immunize" the preadolescent brain against mental illnesses? What knowledge would be necessary to approach this problem? What potential challenges do you foresee?

3. Imagine that humans will someday evolve to have brains that are more resilient to TBI than those we have today. What changes might need to occur in the human brain for it to confer this resilience?

Sensation, Perception, and Adaptation

Seeing Without Vision

In a recent interview with a journalist, 44-year-old Daniel Kish appeared to be an ordinary man. When the journalist arrived at Daniel's home, Daniel teased him about his poor parking job. During the interview, Daniel described his interests, which included camping alone in the wilderness, climbing trees, and riding his mountain bike on dirt trails and through city traffic (see Figure 6A). Engaging in these activities and also traveling, cooking, swimming, and dancing, Daniel exhibited more independence than most people. He mentioned living for several weeks at a time in a tiny cabin two miles from the nearest road.

While describing the ordinary details of his life, Daniel suddenly did something extremely startling. With the same casual motion one might use to clean one's eyeglasses, Daniel removed his eyeballs—his prosthetic, or artificial, eyeballs, that is. Daniel explained that the prosthetic eyes get a bit gummy throughout the day, so he has to remove them occasionally and wipe them with a cloth before replacing them in his eye sockets.

Daniel was born with a retinoblastoma, an aggressive form of cancer that attacked his eyes' retinas. His real eyes were removed when he was 13 months old to protect him

FIGURE 6A **Daniel Kish.** Despite being blind, Daniel Kish manages to "see" his surroundings when biking.

151

from the cancer. How could Daniel have just "seen" the journalist's bad parking job when he was standing a full 10 feet away from the street? And how could he navigate through traffic on a bicycle or hike in the wilderness on his own?

Behind the Scenes

From a young age, Daniel trained himself to produce a clicking sound with his tongue and sharpened his auditory skills to the point where he could hear the ever-so-slight echoes of the tongue clicks, enabling him to interpret their location. Daniel's "flash sonar" technique resembles sound localization techniques utilized by bats and dolphins. For example, when the journalist arrived at his home, Daniel opened the door and generated the clicking sounds. The echoes from the clicks presented an image of two pine trees on his lawn, the curb at the edge of his yard, and the rental car, parked about a foot and a half from the curb. Although he accomplishes it in a unique way, Daniel could "see" the landscape in front of his house (Finkel, 2011).

How does the brain see without eyes? Research suggests that blind individuals interpret their surroundings by relying on nonvisual sensory information to compensate for the lack of incoming visual stimulation. It is most often their auditory capacities that are enhanced, most likely from the established neural network integrating both auditory and tactile sensory domains (Cattaneo et al., 2008). Further, recent fMRI studies indicate that, compared with sighted individuals, blind individuals have more neural connections between the primary auditory and visual cortical areas (Klinge, Eippert, Roder, & Buchel, 2010; Kupers, Pietrini, Ricciardi, & Ptito, 2011). Such compensatory mechanisms may enable blind individuals, with sufficient training, to use different strategies to achieve perceptual outcomes similar to those of sighted individuals.

In addition, researchers have observed similarities between blind and sighted individuals' responses to environmental events. In Chapter 3, you learned about proposed cortical neurons known as mirror neurons. Although this view is controversial, these neurons are thought to respond similarly when a subject watches the action of another individual and when the subject carries out the same action herself. Evidence suggests that similar mirror neuron networks exist in both sighted and congenitally blind subjects.

Sighted and congenitally blind subjects showed similar patterns of fMRI brain activation when they were exposed to auditory presentations of hand-executed action (such as the sound of scissors) and when they pantomimed that action via manipulation of a virtual tool such as a hammer. Thus, imagining a person using scissors and, in this case, virtually using scissors, was associated with similar activation patterns in both sighted and blind subjects. These findings suggest that visual experience is not necessary for the presence of a functional mirror neuron network. Blind individuals may "see" the actions of others using neural networks similar to those used by sighted individuals (Ricciardi et al., 2009).

As this chapter will demonstrate, multiple sensory systems in humans and other animals are characterized by flexibility and plasticity. The sensory receptors and corresponding receptive cortical areas *adapt* to the many changing modes of presentation encountered in the environment throughout an organism's life. As in the case of Daniel Kish, the brain of a blind individual is far from a disabled brain—it is more aptly described as a brain with altered means of sensory processing (Kupers et al., 2011).

Most of us are unaware of the moment-by-moment work of our sensory systems as they continually interpret our surroundings. We effortlessly take in visual scenes, listen to our favorite music, savor the taste of an afternoon snack, feel comforted by the soft texture of our sweatshirt keeping us warm on a snowy day, and enjoy the aroma of our favorite meal cooking in the oven—perhaps all at the same time. Making sense of these perceptual experiences by analyzing sensory stimulus characteristics such as relevant light waves, chemical structures, sound waves, and tactile pressures would be impossible for the most advanced robots, but it is a constant process—the default mode—in our brains.

Humans are especially well equipped for the sense of vision, with approximately 30% of the cortex devoted to decoding light into images and complex scenes (Kupers et al., 2011). It is humbling to consider, however, that some other animals have greater visual capacities than humans do, and many species surpass us in the strength of all of the other traditional senses as well. In addition to describing the encoding, decoding, and subsequent interpretation of various modes of sensory information, this chapter will highlight examples of sensory superstars. Exhibiting *uber* sensory abilities that extend far beyond the norm for other animals, these creatures are not fictional comic book characters, but rather animals from nature's book of evolutionary adaptations.

Because of the importance of vision in primates, much of this chapter is devoted to the visual sensory system. Taste, hearing, touch, and smell are covered as well. However, even more important than each individual sensory system function is the brain's amazing ability to integrate multiple sensory systems and respond appropriately.

Fundamentals of Sensation and Perception

All sensory systems share common characteristics and basic operating principles. In fact, the discovery of these fundamental properties of **sensation** and **perception** played a pivotal role in the birth and advancement of the discipline of psychology. For us to exhibit effective and adaptive behavior, we must detect information about our environmental context (sensation) and interpret that information (perception).

Fechner's Dream

In 1850, Gustav Theodor Fechner (Figure 6.1), who had studied mathematics and biology at the University of Leipzig, had a "flash of insight" as he lay in bed one morning that provided the foundation for the emerging science of psychology (Hunt, 1993, p. 123). This insight prompted Fechner to appreciate that intersections between the mind

FIGURE 6.1 Gustav Fechner. Fechner's insights about sensory perception provided the framework for experimental psychology.

and the physical world could be investigated by measuring a person's perception in response to a changing material stimulus. Fechner's new approach to this complex problem focused on the specific physical qualities of the sensory stimulus and one's perception of that stimulus, an area now known as **psychophysics**.

When an experimenter gradually and systematically increased the intensity of a light from an extremely dim luminance, a subject would eventually report a change in intensity. The minimum amount that a stimulus must change for the subject to detect a difference, regardless of whether the stimulus was light, sound, pressure, or heat, was labeled a **difference threshold**, or **just noticeable difference (JND)**. Further research showed that the JND was a constant proportion of the initial stimulus. This is known as **Weber's law**. For example, for a subject to detect a JND in the loudness of low-intensity sounds, one sound must be about 10% louder than the other sound. In contrast to the difference threshold, the **absolute threshold** is the lowest intensity of a stimulus that a person can detect 50% of the time.

Why was Fechner's insight so significant? Fechner's JND permitted the measurement of subjective mental experiences. Scientists could systematically alter light intensities, sounds, temperature, chemicals, and tactile pressures in standard laboratories to investigate mental experiences objectively. Fechner's most important influence was probably his physiology professor, Ernst Heinrich Weber, known for contributing Weber's law. Weber taught Fechner about his work on tactile thresholds across the body (Murray, 1983).

Although neither Weber nor Fechner was especially interested in how the nervous system processed sensory information, the empirical tradition inspired by Fechner's dream still serves as the basis for much research in behavioral neuroscience and neuropsychology.

Tuning in to Environmental Cues

It likely comes as no surprise that a brain built to respond to relevant cues in one's environment would prove advantageous for survival. Using high-resolution x-ray technology, scientists recently examined the fossilized skull of a mouse-size mammal known as the Morganucodon (Figure 6.2) that lived about 205 million years ago, during the late Triassic period. Evaluation of the Morganucodon's brain provided valuable knowledge about the factors that drove brain enlargement and the accompanying rise and success of mammals. The Morganucodon's brain was about 50% bigger, relative to body size, than the brains of the Triassic reptiles. The images of its skull suggested that the Morganucodon's enlarged olfactory bulbs and olfactory cortex (brain areas that help to enable the sense of smell) were critical features that differentiated the premammalian brain from that of its reptilian ancestors (Rowe, Macrini, & Luo, 2011).

The increase in brain size relative to body size was also observed in the skull of a Hadrocodium, a small mammal that lived about 10 million years after the Morganucodon.

FIGURE 6.2 Morganucodon evolutionary transition. These reptile-like animals had larger brains than other reptiles, a trait more characteristic of early mammals. This upgrade in brain size is thought to be a result of their enhanced processing of olfactory information.

The Hadrocodium's brain was 50% larger than that of the Morganucodon, similar in size to the brains of representative modern mammals. Once again, the enlargement of the animal's brain seemed to be related to increased brain tissue supporting enhanced olfactory capacities. Based on this limited fossil evidence, it appears that sensory systems, specifically smell, played a significant role in the evolution of the mammalian brain. Indeed, considering that the complex neocortex is unique to mammals, its presence was likely necessary to decode and interpret the massive amounts of sensory information streaming in from an animal's unique environment.

As animals (including mammals) began to live in various habitats, a vast array of sensory adaptations evolved. Honey bees can see ultraviolet light that humans cannot detect; male dogs can smell the social hormones excreted by a female dog two blocks away; and dolphins rely on reflected sounds to locate food in their sometimes murky underwater environment. For each sensory ability, animals possess specialized **sensory receptors** (e.g., specialized receptors in the eye's retina and olfactory cells in the nasal cavity), as we will see.

Although the individual skills exhibited by different animals are impressive, no single species of animal possesses the ability to *fully* interpret the surrounding world. To prevent mass confusion and sensory overload, sensory specializations have evolved in various species to provide information about the *most* relevant stimuli in the animals' surroundings. As evident throughout the chapter, the environmental context comprising the territory of each species has powerfully influenced the animal's most prevalent sensory abilities. For example, a rat, which navigates the world in the dark of night, has little use for clear, detailed color vision.

Even with limited sensory abilities, overload will occur without **sensory adaptation**. When you get dressed in the morning and slip your feet into your shoes, the pressure of the shoes on your feet translates into an awareness that you are now wearing shoes. After a while, however, it is not meaningful to have a constant reminder that you are wearing shoes. Your sensory receptors adapt so that you are no longer consciously aware of the shoes' pressure on your feet. The situation may be different, however, if the shoes are hurting your feet. Pain, addressed in Chapter 10, is an exception to the rule when it comes to sensory adaptation, because pain relays an important biological message relevant to one's health.

Beau Lotto, a neuroscientist at University College in London, has studied variations in sensory abilities—especially color vision, a valuable sensory acquisition in the animal kingdom—and has emphasized that the contexts of our lives construct our personalized perceptual realities. According to Lotto,

> *no one is an outside observer of nature.... We are not defined by our central properties, by the bits that make us up. We're defined by our environment and our interaction with that environment—by our ecology. And that ecology is necessarily relative, historical and empirical.... Last, and perhaps most important, I am more and more struck by the reality that context is everything. In all disciplines, in all ethics, in all wisdom, and in all understanding, context rules. And to remove or extract pieces out of context is to dismiss truth, reality, and our personal and fundamental engagement with what is "real" in the world. (Lotto, 2009)*

Context is critical for successful neural adaptation and functioning. However, perhaps in no other neural domain is context more important than for sensory processing.

The Big Sensory Picture: Taste and Multisensory Integration

Although sensory systems have traditionally been investigated one sense at a time, our real-world sensory experiences are influenced by the simultaneous integration of multiple sensory systems (Ghazanfar & Schroeder, 2006), a function known as **multisensory integration**. As an example, multiple sensory systems converge to produce the sense of smell. When the biologist Esther Sternberg visited the Monell Chemical Center in Philadelphia, she participated in an experiment in which she placed her face in a chamber containing a single aroma as she looked at a beautiful mountainous scene. She described the aroma as pleasant and fresh. In the next phase of the study, Sternberg again placed her face in a chamber containing a single aroma. However, this time, she did so as she looked at a picture of a city scene with smoke stacks expelling billows of dark smoke. In this situation, Sternberg described the aroma as toxic, pungent, and unpleasant. Surprisingly to her, the aroma was identical in both situations. The visual scene in each case contributed to the final interpretation and perception of the odor. Sternberg's olfactory perception was influenced by **cross-modal stimuli** (stimuli from two senses) (Sternberg, Cohen, & Cohen, 2010).

Smell, Taste, and Flavor: An Example of Multisensory Processing. When 22-year-old Molly Birnbaum was jogging across a street one afternoon, she was hit by a car. A Brown University graduate and aspiring chef, Birnbaum suffered a fractured skull, a broken pelvis, and other musculoskeletal injuries (Birnbaum, 2011). Her broken bones healed, but an invisible injury had a huge impact on her life journey and career aspirations. After returning from the hospital, Molly noticed that she couldn't smell . . . *anything*. This lost sensation also affected her taste, a highly valued sense for someone who planned to earn a living cooking.

The perception of **flavor** that we experience when we bite into a slice of pizza is based on the convergence of cues from several senses, including vision, smell, taste, and touch (Spence, Levitan, Shankar, & Zampini, 2010). In Molly's case, taking smell out of the flavor formula diminished her discriminating palate when tasting various foods. However, she could still detect the basic tastes of food because her tongue's taste buds were unharmed. Molly's loss of flavor perception after her accident was a result of impairments in multisensory integration.

Taste buds are small structures of soft tissue located on the tongue, soft palate, and areas of the throat; they contain taste receptors that are specialized for detecting salty, sweet, sour, bitter, and the rich, meaty taste known as umami (Chaudhari & Roper, 2010; Frank & Hettinger, 2005; see Figure 6.3). Molly's taste buds were able to transfer this

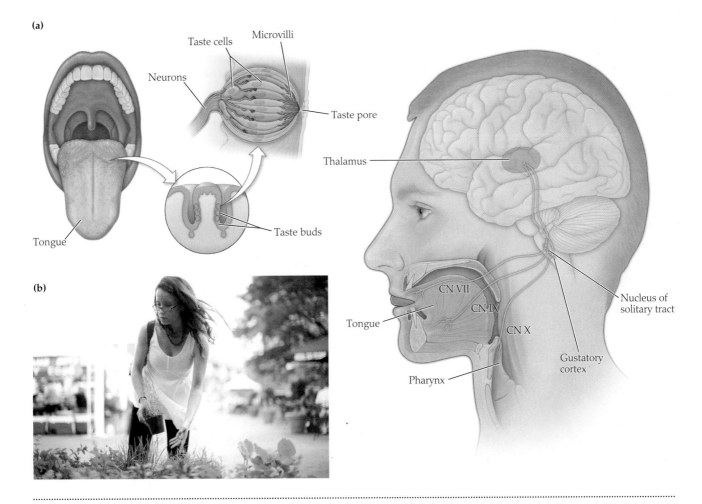

FIGURE 6.3 Taste sensation. (a) In taste, chemicals activate the taste buds, and neural messages travel via specific cranial nerves to various areas of the brain as the chemicals are interpreted as taste variations. (b) When aspiring chef Molly Birnbaum lost her sense of smell in an accident, she also lost much of her multisensory-influenced ability to taste.

information to her brain via facial and glossopharyngeal cranial nerves (see Chapter 2), where this taste information travels through the nucleus of the solitary tract and thalamus before finally reaching the cortical insula area (Schoenfeld et al., 2004). One effect of Molly's brain injury was that she did not experience the final product of this multisensory integration, that is, flavor. Unfortunately, this impairment left Molly unable to pursue her career interest in the culinary arts. As chronicled in her book *Season to Taste*, Molly eventually regained her sense of smell and flavor years later, likely because of the regenerative ability of olfactory neurons (Birnbaum, 2011).

The Functions and Neural Basis of Multisensory Integration. As seen in Figure 6.4 (Stein & Sanford, 2008),

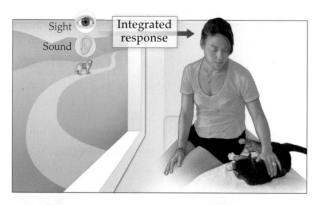

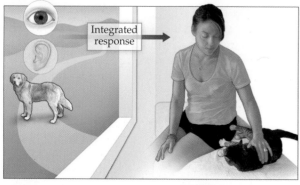

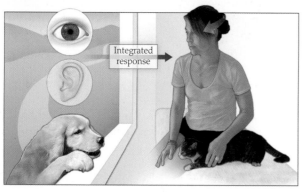

FIGURE 6.4 Multisensory integration. As the dog gets closer to the woman and her cat, the additive neural component is less exaggerated because the sensory stimuli are more distinctive and recognizable.

multisensory integration facilitates the timely detection of relevant stimuli in our environment. When a dog begins to approach a woman and cat sitting by a window, the woman and cat receive only mild auditory and visual cues to warn of its approach. However, because these incoming stimuli are highly relevant, the integrated response is exaggerated in what is known as a **superadditive neural response** (an integrated response much stronger than any of its components). This enhanced response prompts the woman to orient toward the meaningful canine stimulus to protect her feline companion. As the dog approaches the window, the unisensory audio and visual cues become stronger, and the level of exaggeration of the integrated neural response becomes proportionately smaller—a mere **additive response**. When the dog reaches the window, the sight and sound of it become even stronger, and the integrated response becomes even less exaggerated—a **subadditive neural response**. Indeed, one could hardly fail to notice the salivating dog leaning in the window (Stein & Sanford, 2008).

Finally, some individual cells respond to multiple senses. In this case, each **multisensory neuron** contains several receptive fields for different sensory modalities. Whereas traditional sensory neurons have **receptive fields** that receive information from a specific sensory area, such as visual neurons that are activated in accordance with certain areas of the visual field being activated, multisensory neurons have more diverse receptive fields. Such neurons are located throughout the brain but are especially abundant in the midbrain's superior colliculus. As observed in cats, a single cell in this area may respond to both visual and auditory information. Based on information received from the cortical areas, this midbrain structure controls gaze shifts as the animal orients toward relevant visual information. Thus, multisensory neurons such as the ones located in the superior colliculus interpret information from multiple sources to arrive at the most informed interpretation of a particular external event. If the incoming sensory information is incomplete (e.g., a predator hiding behind a tree), the addition of relevant sounds would help resolve the uncertainty about the identity and potential threat of the animal.

In fact, our sensory systems are so intertwined that it is disturbing if their synchronization is disrupted. If you have ever tried to watch a movie where the audio is slightly off from the lip movement, you have experienced flawed sensory integration—in this case because of the audiovisual equipment, not your brain. Another vivid example of the importance of the sensory systems being synchronized is demonstrated by the **McGurk effect**. Typically, watching a speaker's face helps us to perceive speech because we integrate auditory cues (the sounds of speech) with visual cues (lip movements). However, if slightly mismatched auditory and visual cues are paired (e.g., the sound for "bows" with the lip movements for "goes"), people report hearing something more consistent with their visual input (like "doze" or "those"). This perceptual experience occurs as the brain's cross-modal systems attempt to correct the disparity (Stein & Stanford, 2008). This is just one example of how the brain's multisensory neurons make adjustments in our perceived worlds to diminish anxiety-producing discrepancies—serving as a reminder that our virtual perceptual experience does not always match the external reality.

Proposed multisensory regions of the monkey cortex are shown in Figure 6.5. Because of its role in audiovisual and facial integrative sensory processing, the superior temporal sulcus likely plays a role in the McGurk effect because it is activated during vocalization and audiovisual discrepancies. As depicted in the image, a significant proportion of the cortex is devoted to multisensory processing. When animals find themselves in uncertain environments, integrating inputs from several sensory systems increases perceptual sensitivity and the probability of a more accurate assessment of relevant environmental components (Ohshiro, Angelaki, & DeAngelis, 2011).

Now that we have outlined the "big picture" of multisensory integration and its role in sensation and perception, we will examine specific sensory systems individually. We will begin with vision.

Ventral intraparietal area:
Vision, hearing, touch, balance

Parietal reach region (medial intraparietal area) (PRR(MIP)):
Vision, hearing, taste

Ventrolateral prefrontal cortex (VLPFC):
Vision and hearing correspondence, speech

Lateral intraparietal area (LIP): Vision and hearing

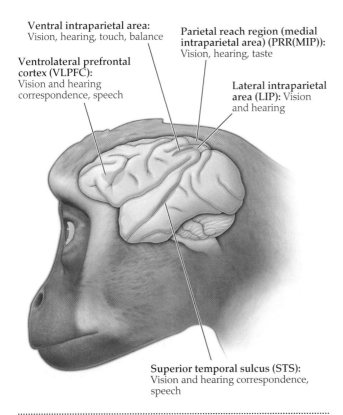

Superior temporal sulcus (STS):
Vision and hearing correspondence, speech

FIGURE 6.5 Multisensory cortical areas. Several regions of the cortex respond to multiple modes of sensory information, an important aspect of the interpretation of complex sensory stimuli.

Vision

Once visual information is processed in the eyes, it still has quite a journey to make through the brain. As visual information travels, it gathers more relevant information to produce a meaningful image. Seemingly simple visual information is imperative for our day-to-day interactions with our environments: ducking to avoid a Frisbee coming a little too close to your head as you walk through the park, noticing a baby's first smile, or seeing a fleeting image of a snake as you hike through the forest. As we will see, interpreting these various images requires the actions of unique neural pathways and centers in your brain.

Light's Journey to the Cortex

Once the appropriate visual stimulus is detected by the specialized cells in the eye, this information is transformed into neural energy that begins a journey to the back of the brain. As the visual information makes key stops along the way to the cortex, information is gathered at each stop to determine exactly what your eyes are detecting. Thus, in a sense, the eyes translate the world around us to a neural language that can be easily understood by the brain.

Stimulus and Receptor. The first **photoreceptors**, specialized neurons that are sensitive to light, are thought to have evolved about 600 million years ago in single-cell organisms such as algae and bacteria. However, the first structure that resembles the eyes we recognize was the eye of the lamprey, an eel-like organism that evolved around 530 million years ago. Sea squirts and hagfish had a rudimentary form of an eye, referred to as an eye patch, prior to the lamprey's cameralike eye, complete with many of the components of the human eye (Lamb, Collin, & Pugh, 2007).

Light is the type of physical energy that photoreceptors in the eye respond to effectively; thus, light is the **adequate stimulus** for photoreceptors. (As we will see later in the chapter, disrupted air waves represent the adequate stimulus for auditory receptors.) Applying pressure to the eyelid will also evoke bursts of apparent light (close your eyes and gently tap your eyelid to demonstrate this effect), but the applied tactile pressure provides minimal information compared with light.

Humans can detect light only within a narrow band of the **electromagnetic spectrum**, or all possible wavelengths of electromagnetic radiation (see Figure 6.6). Humans can detect wavelengths ranging from approximately 400 to 750 nanometers, with purple and blue represented by the shorter waves, green by medium-length waves, and red by the longer waves. (A meter contains a billion nanometers.) Shorter, ultraviolet rays can be detected by bees and longer, infrared rays can be detected by snakes.

The color qualities perceived by humans, however, are influenced by three dimensions of the light stimulus: **hue**, **brightness**, and **saturation**. The wavelength of the light

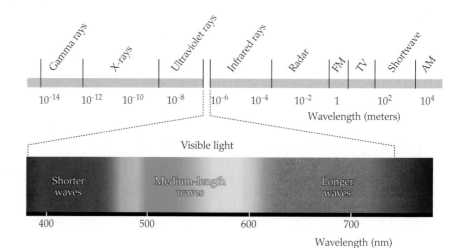

FIGURE 6.6 Visual perception and the electromagnetic spectrum. The small segment of the electromagnetic spectrum that is visible to humans reinforces the notion that sensory abilities are specifically adapted and fine-tuned to enhance survival.

stimulus determines the perceived hue, or color; the intensity of the light stimulus determines the perceived brightness; and the purity of the light stimulus, represented by the precision of the wavelength bandwidth of the visual output, determines the perceived color saturation. When you select a paint color card at your local home improvement store that contains eight variations of blue, each color represents a different color saturation. In this case, saturation is weakened by the varied wavelengths—perhaps spanning several hundred nanometers—created using so many different shades of blue.

As seen in Figure 6.7, the human eye, containing photoreceptors, is held in the optic socket by the **extraocular muscles** and **optic nerve**. Light enters the eye through the **pupil**, which accommodates darkness by dilating to let more light in and accommodates brightness by constricting to minimize the amount of incoming light. The **iris** controls the size of the pupil. The pupil and iris are covered by a transparent surface known as the **cornea**. Along with the **lens** that is located behind the pupil, the cornea focuses the image so that it is projected to the specialized photoreceptors

contained in the **retina** at the back of the eye. The internal cavity of the eye is filled with a jellylike substance, consisting mostly of water with specific amounts of salt, sugar, and proteins, known as the **vitreous humor**. The vitreous humor is more viscous than the watery **aqueous humor**, which occupies the space between the cornea and lens. The vitreous humor and aqueous humor maintain a healthy internal environment for the eye (Kaufman, Alm, & Adler, 2003).

A critical step in decoding light occurs when the image is projected onto the retina in the back of the eye. The visual photoreceptors, **rods** and **cones**, are located in this layer of specialized neurons along with other important types of cells. As illustrated in Figure 6.7, rods and cones line the most peripheral layer of the retina. The rods and cones form synapses with **bipolar cells**, and the bipolar cells subsequently form synapses with **ganglion cells**. The bundle of axons emerging from the ganglion cells makes up the optic nerve that exits the back of the eyeball. At this exit point there are no photoreceptors, making this small section of the retina a **blind spot** (see Figure 6.8). An individual will not

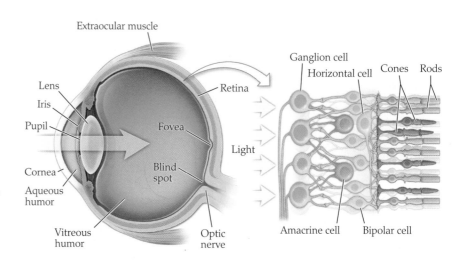

FIGURE 6.7 The human eye. The organ for vision, the eye, interprets visual stimuli so that the neural information can be processed through the cells of the retina.

FIGURE 6.8 **The visual blind spot.** Although human visual acuity is impressive, there are imperceptible gaps in our ability to visually detect the entire surrounding environment. View this image at arm's length. Cover your left eye and stare at the red pepper (left) with your right eye. Move the image toward you until the yellow pepper disappears.

see any image that falls on this blind spot unless the information is coming from the other eye. However, even when only one eye is functional, we are not consciously aware of the visual deficit. This is because higher cortical areas fill in the visual gaps left by the blind spot—a clue that our personal visual reality does not always accurately reflect the environment. Although the brain's ability to fill in the blind spot is usually adaptive, if critical stimuli occupy that blind spot—such as an approaching car in your rearview mirror—the results could be deadly.

Two other types of specialized cells, the **horizontal cells** and **amacrine cells**, process information in a lateral direction in the retina. Essentially, these cells facilitate the integration of the vast amount of information processed in the retina. As different types of visual information, including

information about color contrast and perceived brightness, are carried simultaneously to the brain, a uniformed image is constructed from the various pieces of the visual perception puzzle (Nassi & Callaway, 2009; Wassle, 2004).

In general, the rods are more densely packed around the periphery of the retina, whereas the cones are clustered in the center. The most densely populated area of cones is in the **fovea**, the part of the retina where our vision is sharpest. The human retina contains approximately 100 million rods, compared with 5 million cones. In dimly lit environments such as the outside environment at night, the rods are activated because they are more sensitive to light than the cones. Under well-lit conditions, the cones contribute to visual interpretation by providing information about color (as described later in this section) and other relevant visual details.

The conversion of physical energy to neural energy (**transduction**) requires the presence of **photopigments** in the photoreceptors. Photopigments are molecules consisting of an **opsin** (a specific type of protein) and **retinal** (made up of fatty substances such as lipids). In the rods, the photopigment is **rhodopsin**. A few unique features characterize light transduction in the rods. In contrast to most neurons, which are activated when they are depolarized to reach the absolute threshold for an action potential (see Chapter 3), rods are *hyperpolarized* by light. Thus, the rods are in a depolarized state in the dark, with a membrane potential of approximately -40 millivolts. The flow of sodium ions contributes to the depolarized state of rods maintained under dark conditions. The open or closed position of sodium ion channels is regulated by levels of cyclic guanosine monophosphate (cGMP). Levels of cGMP are lower in the presence of light. This leads to closed channels and to the corresponding hyperpolarization and reduced levels of transmitter release.

As shown in Figure 6.9, when a photon of light is absorbed by the photopigment rhodopsin in the rods, a change

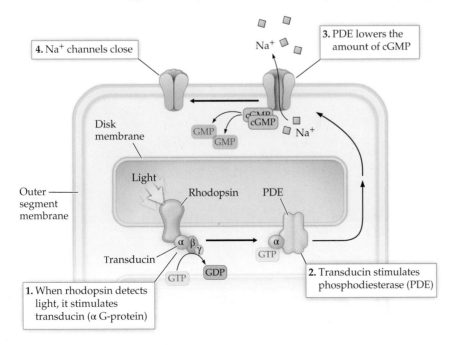

FIGURE 6.9 **Visual transduction.** Light triggers a series of chemical events that transform the light stimulus into neural messages that are ultimately interpreted as visual stimuli.

occurs in the shape of the photopigment component retinal. This activates the transformation of one form of a G-protein known as transducin to another form that activates a cGMP **phosphodiesterase**, an enzyme that reduces cGMP concentrations that maintain the open channels. The ultimate result is the closure of the sodium channels and hyperpolarization of the receptor. Although we usually think of hyperpolarization as an inhibition, it is important to remember that the key to the success of photoreceptors is the *detection* of the presence of light, regardless of whether that detection results in a depolarization or hyperpolarization. This hyperpolarization ultimately results in the activation of the ganglion cells that carry information to the brain (Berson, 2007; Montell, 1999).

The Central Nervous System Visual Pathway. As shown in Figure 6.10, in the human visual system, the visual image is both inverted and left–right reversed as it is received by the retina, and information from the right and left visual fields is processed separately for each eye. Input from the left visual field (that is, the left half of the visual field for each eye) strikes the right side of each retina and is sent to the right visual cortex. Input from the right visual field strikes the left side of each retina and is sent to the left visual cortex.

How does this occur? The visual information carried by the ganglion cells exits the back of the eyeball through the blind spot in the form of the optic nerve (cranial nerve II) and crosses over in a midline structure known as the **optic chiasm**. After exiting the optic chiasm, the visual information travels in the form of the **optic tract** to the **lateral geniculate nucleus (LGN)** of the thalamus. At that point, the visual information travels in the form of optic radiations to the **primary visual cortex (V1)** (also known as the **striate cortex** because of a noted stripe in the tissue). A disproportionately large area of the cortex receives visual input from the richly detailed foveal region of the retina (Purves & Lotto, 2003).

As illustrated in Figure 6.11, the LGN contains three types of cellular layers. The **magnocellular layers** are the ventral layers and are characterized by larger cells ("magno" means *great*). They provide information about the position of a visual stimulus (i.e., "where"), whereas the **parvocellular layers** ("parvo" means *small*) are located on the dorsal surface of the LGN and provide identifying details about a visual stimulus (i.e., "what"). An additional **koniocellular layer** is interspersed throughout the LGN, falling below each parvocellular and magnocellular layer; this layer has been associated with color perception (P. R. Martin, White, Goodchild, Wilder, & Sefton, 1997). These differentiated sections of the LGN allow for the efficient delivery of relevant visual information to V1 and to the visual cortex located outside of the V1, known as the **extrastriate cortex** (Nassi & Callaway, 2009).

Visual Details. The final perception of a visual scene requires multiple types of specialized cells and receptive

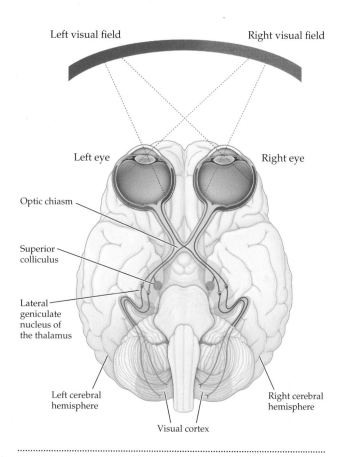

FIGURE 6.10 Lateralization of visual neural pathways. As visual information travels from the eye to the visual cortex, portions of the visual neural pathways cross over at the optic chiasm and are directed to the opposite hemisphere.

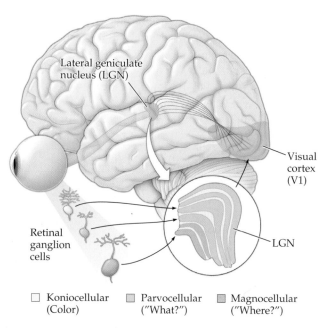

FIGURE 6.11 The lateral geniculate nucleus (LGN) pathways. Visual information travels from the retinal ganglion cells through striated regions of the LGN on the way to the visual cortex.

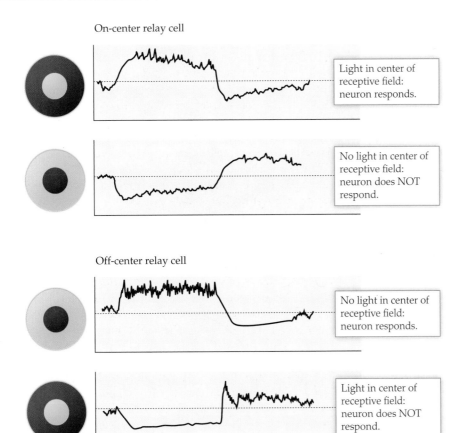

On-center relay cell

> Light in center of receptive field: neuron responds.

> No light in center of receptive field: neuron does NOT respond.

Off-center relay cell

> No light in center of receptive field: neuron responds.

> Light in center of receptive field: neuron does NOT respond.

FIGURE 6.12 On- and off-center lateral geniculate nucleus (LGN) cells. The receptive field shifts from the cell's center area to the surrounding area in specific cells of the LGN.

cortical areas. Information about specific visual elements is added at every step along the visual pathway.

The retina and LGN contain cells with a **concentric receptive field**. Bipolar and ganglion cells in the retina, for example, respond to detailed visual information in very specific areas of their representative visual fields. Retinal cells designated as **on-center cells** become stimulated when a light is focused on the center of the cell; **off-center cells** become inhibited when a light is focused on the center of the cell. Similar types of cells are located in the LGN (see Figure 6.12 for on-center and off-center cells in the LGN; Wang, Vaingankar, Sanchez, Sommer, & Hirsch, 2011). These concentric receptive fields add a layer of detail to the big picture the brain is constructing, much in the same way that a painter adds shadows and bits of light to make a portrait appear more realistic.

Information about edges and contrasts is perceived through a process known as **lateral inhibition**, in which a cell's neighboring neurons inhibit the activation of that particular cell (Hartline, 1949). When bipolar cells are excited, a corresponding horizontal cell in the retina is activated. This ultimately inhibits adjacent bipolar cells in a graded manner laterally across the bipolar cellular field, fading as it travels from its origin. As the horizontal cell's inhibitory effect expands across neighboring bipolar cells that were not as excited as the original bipolar cell was, the effect is that they are more strongly inhibited than the original activated bipolar cell.

Lateral inhibition emphasizes perceived contrast, a visual feature known as **contrast enhancement** that provides valuable information about our environment— perhaps keeping us from stepping off a cliff or tripping over a dip in the sidewalk. The lateral inhibition of interconnected retinal cells creates the perception of lighter and darker bands called *Mach bands*, shown on the edge of each panel in Figure 6.13 (Platanov & Goosens, 2013). Although each panel in Figure 6.13 is actually the same color from edge to edge, the edges of the panels appear to be lighter or darker.

FIGURE 6.13 Lateral inhibition. Differential inhibition of the retinal bipolar cells results in contrast enhancement perceived as Mach bands.

This effect comes from lateral inhibition in your retinal cells to emphasize the contrast between panels.

Different visual features are also processed by the previously described parvocellular and magnocellular layers of the LGN. The parvocellular neurons receive input from parvocellular ganglion cells, which have small receptive fields that enable them to process information about visual details, including color. By contrast, the magnocellular neurons receive input from magnocellular ganglion cells, which have larger receptive fields that respond to movement and more general visual patterns such as the course of a tree-lined street. Thus, the parvocellular system contributes information to higher cortical areas about *what* a visual stimulus is, whereas the magnocellular system contributes information about *where* a visual stimulus is. As you walk into the kitchen, your parvocellular system identifies the visual stimulus on the counter as your favorite coffee cup as the magnocellular system locates the coffee maker. The koniocellular system is involved in more diverse functions ranging from color detection to contextual processing, depending on the location of the cells (Hendry & Reid, 2000).

Not all of the visual information travels to the LGN from the optic chiasm. Some optic tract axons project to the midbrain's **superior colliculus**. In addition to its role in multisensory integration, research with various species suggests that the superior colliculus is also involved in eye movements and visual orientation (MacKinnon, Gross, & Bender, 1976). Cells in the superior colliculus appear to integrate both repeated and novel information in our ever-changing visual world (Boehnke et al., 2011). You can imagine that this system is paramount to the survival of military troops surveying potentially hostile territories. When scanning the visual environment, the soldier's visual system must instantaneously detect potential threats that are inconsistent with the predicted visual scene. The superior colliculus, more primitive than the cortical areas discussed later in the chapter, likely plays a role in this visual vigilance necessary for survival.

Visual information leaves the LGN via fibers called optic radiations that travel to V1. Pioneering research conducted by the Nobel Laureates David Hubel and Torsten Wiesel revealed specialized types of V1 neurons. After implanting microelectrodes in V1 of cats and exposing them to various visual scenes and stimuli, Hubel and Wiesel (1962) discovered several types of V1 cortical cells that responded to very specific features of the visual stimulus. Different from the receptive fields of LGN cells, the receptive fields of V1 **simple cells** respond to bar-shape stimuli located in specific areas in specific orientations (e.g., vertical, horizontal). **Complex cells** also respond to the bar-shape stimuli but are less selective about the location of the bar in the visual field. **Hypercomplex cells** respond to bars of a particular length by detecting endpoints as well as aspects of position and orientation (see Figure 6.14). The preferences of these cells dictate the organization of V1 as cells that respond to lines of a particular orientation are grouped in specific **orientation columns** (DeValois, Albrecht, & Thorell, 1982).

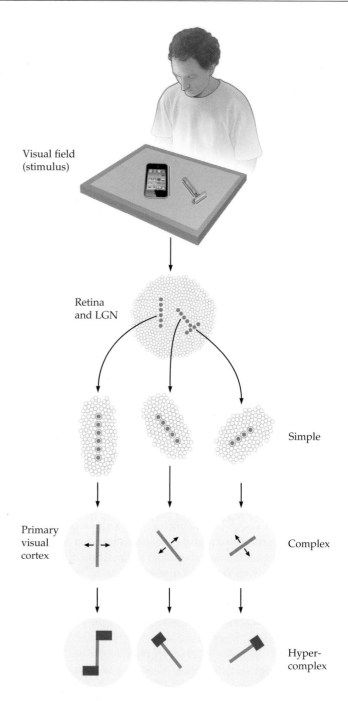

FIGURE 6.14 Specific feature-detecting cells in the visual cortex. In the V1 cortical area, designated cells respond to varying types of stimuli, ranging from simple orientations to hypercomplex characteristics of a visual stimulus. These cells are grouped into organizational columns in the cortex.

In addition to V1, other areas of the visual cortex have been associated with specific visual functions, based on both single-cell recordings (see Chapter 1) in monkeys and, more recently, fMRI data in humans. For example, cells in **Area V2** respond to outlines or defining shapes, including illusory contours that do not actually exist (see Figure 6.15). **Area V3** cells are involved in form analysis and motion,

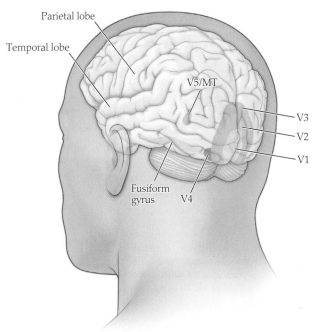

FIGURE 6.15 **Visual illusory contours.** V2 cortical cells generate perceived visual contours in the absence of an actual visual outline.

FIGURE 6.16 **Visual cortical areas.** Several cortical visual areas converge to produce perceived visual images.

facilitating, for example, your interpretation of a fast-moving visual stimulus as a car speeding through a stop sign (Felleman & Van Essen, 1987; Grosof, Shapley, & Hawken, 1993). **Area V4** cells facilitate the ability to identify objects, as well as color perception (Roe et al., 2012). **Area V5**, also known as the medial temporal area, contributes to the perception of motion (Zeki, 2004). Damage to this area would make the pedestrian crossing the street appear as a series of still-frame pictures as opposed to a seamless motion. See Figure 6.16 for various specialized areas of the visual cortex in humans and other primates.

Additional areas of the cortex have been associated with the perception of individual faces. Humans' ability to recognize and analyze faces allows us to maintain effective social interactions. Damage to the fusiform gyrus in the **fusiform face area** leads to **prosopagnosia**, or the inability to recognize faces (Saygin et al., 2011). Although these individuals perceive a face, they cannot recognize a particular person, sometimes not even their own face in the mirror (Gainotti, 2013). Further research has identified the roles of two additional cortical areas in face perception, the occipital face area located in the occipital lobe and the superior temporal sulcus facial recognition area located in the temporal lobe. Damage to these cortical areas reduces the quality of visual information about parts of the face, eliminating the person's ability to recognize individual faces. Figure 6.17 shows the result of disruption of the occipital face area (Downing, 2007).

For visual images to be recognized and interpreted as quickly as possible, their specific details, such as facial components, are processed in the context of broader categorical information such as a person's surroundings.

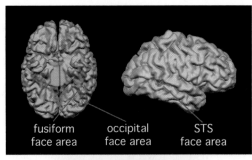

FIGURE 6.17 **Disrupting facial recognition.** When areas of the brain that are critical for perception of faces are interrupted or damaged, it becomes difficult or impossible to recognize a person by seeing his or her face.

As shown in Figure 6.18, a ventral stream and a dorsal stream extend from V1. Expanding on similar functions described for the parvocellular and magnocellular layers of the LGN, the **ventral stream** provides information about the

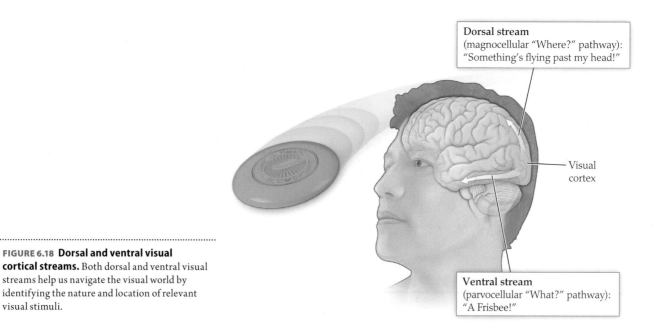

FIGURE 6.18 Dorsal and ventral visual cortical streams. Both dorsal and ventral visual streams help us navigate the visual world by identifying the nature and location of relevant visual stimuli.

identification of various objects, and the **dorsal stream** contributes information about the location of particular objects. Thus, the ventral stream addresses the "what" and the dorsal stream the "where" of a visual stimulus.

As you walk through the park and the dorsal stream identifies a nondescript stimulus hurtling toward your head, the ventral stream keeps working to identify the object. When the ventral stream communicates that it is a Frisbee thrown by a young child, you try to catch the Frisbee to return it to the child. Your response would be different, however, if the ventral stream communicates that the object is a knife thrown by a suspicious adult. The existence of multiple sources that contribute to the verification of the nature and location of visual stimuli reinforces the importance of this process for our survival—it is indeed occurring at multiple levels of our visual systems. Further, a large portion of the primate cortex is devoted to processing visual information. Evidence indicates that 55% and 30% of the cortex participates in visual functions in the macaque and human, respectively (Tootell, Tsao, & Vanduffel, 2003).

Processing Contextual Cues

In the real world, we are rarely interested in visual details such as edges, borders, and illusory contrast. Rather, the brain uses these details to inform us about relevant components of the visual scenes that we are constantly processing. As we scan a crowd of soldiers returning home from a dangerous mission, we want to identify our loved one—a person—not specific, seemingly irrelevant visual details. In short, we are interested in the big picture, the relevant visual scene that represents the convergence of incoming information from many neural sites.

As the Harvard cognitive neuroscientist Moshe Bar has indicated, we see the world in scenes, not specific details like

lines and edges. If you evoke a mental image of a cat, you rarely envision the cat against a blank background; instead, the visual image has a context filled with rich surroundings. You may picture the cat sitting in a window or chasing a mouse down the sidewalk. Information about the different aspects of the entire visual scene also plays a role in identifying visual stimuli. Firing of ganglion cells is considered a form of **bottom-up visual processing** (processing specific visual information in increasing levels of complexity). The cortical processing of information from the context of a visual scene to determine that the object in a person's hand is a plate instead of a Frisbee is an example of **top-down visual processing** (processing more integrated visual information based on context and expectations). As important as the specialized receptor cells are to visual perception, our past experiences also dictate our interpretation of a particular visual stimulus. Consider the visual stimulus presented in Figure 6.19.

Identification of the center element of this stimulus depends on whether you read it in the context of the row of numbers or column of letters. The image activates bipolar and ganglion cells (bottom-up processing), yet cortical input based on the context dictates the final identification as the number 13 or the letter B (top-down processing).

The more complex visual scenes in Figure 6.20 indicate how information about the larger visual setting is needed to identify the dark object as a hair dryer or a drill. Without the brain's ability to make accurate context-based predictions about the identity of objects, our safety would be severely compromised. Imagine having to take a few minutes to discern whether the object a person is pointing at you is a gun or a cell phone . . . such a delay in recognition time could mean the difference between life and death. However, as described in frequent news reports, this predisposition to make probability-based decisions can also lead to false

A 12 13 14 C

FIGURE 6.19 **Visual context.** An ambiguous visual cue is further defined by the context in which it appears.

identifications because a police officer in a specific visual scene may interpret a cell phone as a gun. Further, cultural stereotypes influence the final interpretation of such ambiguous scenes (Correll, Park, Judd, & Wittenbrink, 2002). In such cases, it is critical to be informed of our visual biases. Thus, our past experiences have led us to develop **context frames**, or prepackaged visual perceptual templates that we are likely to encounter. For example, our context frames suggest that it is very likely for a person to be holding a dog, but not for a dog to be holding a person.

Which areas of the brain contribute to the interpretation of visual context? Moshe Bar has proposed several cortical areas that interpret contextual information to facilitate accurate object recognition (Bar, 2004; Bar & Aminoff, 2003). To increase interpretative speed, objects are not represented in rich detail in the relevant cortical areas responding to contextual cues. For example, objects may be grouped into certain categories based on physical appearance in the visual

cortex, whereas the **parahippocampal cortex (PHC)** is sensitive to contextual relations based on the presence of other objects. I feel the value of these two perceptual systems operating simultaneously when I first encounter a student outside of the context of the classroom. In the classroom, my visual system had always easily recognized the student. However, in this case the PHC cannot give my visual cortex the added contextual clues necessary to identify the student. It is not until I consider the person in various contexts—grocery store, gym, class, and so forth—that I recognize the student from my biopsychology class.

In an fMRI study (see Figure 6.21), Bar's team exposed subjects to two types of visual stimuli—one type characterized by a strong visual context (such as a bowling pin or a construction hat) and one type characterized by a weak visual context (such as a camera or scissors). Most of us would automatically associate a bowling pin with a bowling alley and a construction helmet with a construction zone. In contrast, a camera and scissors are used in many different contexts, so we are less likely to associate them with one specific context. When Bar's subjects were exposed to the strong visual context objects as opposed to the weak visual context objects, they showed increased activation in the PHC as well as activation of an additional cortical area implicated in context perception, the **retrosplenial cortex**. Additionally, the **superior orbital sulcus** was activated in tasks that required higher-order integration to continuously update the interpretation of the visual stimulus (Bar, 2004; Bar & Aminoff, 2003). Thus, supporting the value of top-down processing, specific brain areas are associated with the interpretation of context. Other specific brain areas are associated with processing more specific detailed information to give us further information about what we see.

Color Vision

Although technicolor movies have only been around for about a century, our visual systems have been producing technicolor images since the emergence of our primate ancestors. Although we often take the vivid colors making up the context of our lives for granted, the perceptions of these colors are a result of complex brain functions.

The Neural Basis of Color Vision. As described earlier in the chapter, specialized neurons in the retina, known as cones, enable us to detect color. Cones allow us to distinguish differences in certain wavelengths of the electromagnetic spectrum. Around 1800, the British physicist Thomas Young proposed that there were three different receptors maximally sensitive to the perception of blue, green, and red. He theorized that the many colors making up our visual color

FIGURE 6.20 **Context frames.** The parahippocampal cortex and associated cortical areas help the brain determine the identification of ambiguous stimuli based on the surrounding environmental context.

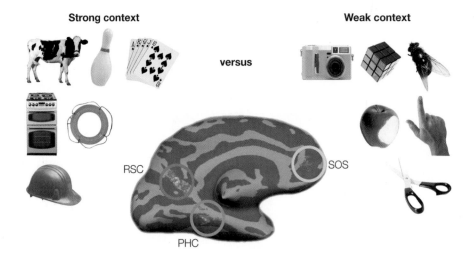

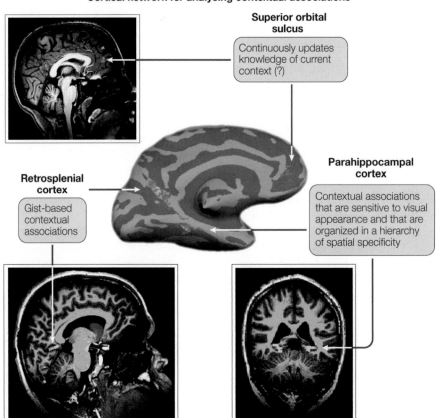

FIGURE 6.21 Visual context. Certain brain areas show more activity when we look at items that are strongly associated with a specific context: RSC, retrosplenial cortex; SOS, superior orbital sulcus; PHC, parahippocampal cortex.

repertoires—including all those colors in your 64 Crayola pack in preschool—result from various relative activations of the three types of receptors. Young showed that differentially mixing medium, short, and long wavelengths of light produced all of the colors that we can see. When all three colored lights were superimposed, the viewer reported perceiving the color white—entirely different from the color that results from mixing different paint colors.

Fifty years later, the German physiologist Hermann von Helmholtz wrote about the role of the cones in color perception, although not always in agreement with Young's observations (Hurvich & Jameson, 1949). Since both Young and Helmholtz wrote about this theory, it became known as the **Young–Helmholtz trichromatic theory of color vision**. According to this theory, specialized receptor cells respond specifically to medium, short, and long wavelengths of light, ultimately informing our perception of all recognized colors.

Later in the 19th century, the physiologist Ewald Hering proposed a different theory to explain the basis for color vision. Hering theorized that the visual system was designed to detect opposed pairs of colors, specifically, green versus red, blue versus yellow, and black versus white (Solomon & Lennie, 2007). This theory, known as the **opponent-process theory of color vision**, is supported by afterimage visual demonstrations such as the one in Figure 6.22. After staring at the image for about a minute, look at a blank, white piece of paper for a few seconds. An afterimage, a lingering but altered visual perception in the absence of the actual stimulus, will appear with the traditional red, white, and blue colors of the American flag. According to Hering, the opponent colors are perceived because of fatigue resulting from overstimulating the receptors for the opposing colors in the actual image.

In actuality, both the trichromatic theory and the opponent-process theory are correct to some extent. The sensitivity zones of the three types of cones are less specific than predicted by Helmholtz. Their *peak* sensitivity responds to 420 (blue–violet spectrum), 560 (yellow–green spectrum), and 630 nanometers (orange–red spectrum). (Each type of cone contains a different type of photopigment that makes it sensitive to a different set of wavelengths.) But, as seen in Figure 6.23, each type of cone will respond to a range of wavelengths of light. In general, on the one hand, cones are considered maximally sensitive to short, medium, and long wavelengths of light, providing supporting evidence for the trichromatic theory in the retina. Opponent cells that respond to two different colors, on the other hand, have been identified in the LGN and visual cortex (Buzas et al., 2013; Shapley & Hawkins, 2011). Thus, contemporary evidence continues to support the 19th-century theories of color perception.

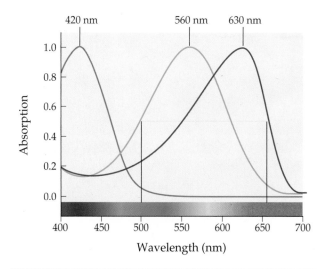

FIGURE 6.23 **Peak sensitivity of cone cells.** The three types of cones respond maximally to different wavelengths in the visual spectrum.

Color is also processed at the cortical level. As previously mentioned, Area V4 in the visual cortex contains color-sensitive cells. Specifically, these cells may play a role in **color constancy** (the ability to continue to perceive that an object is a specific color even under varying perceptual conditions). For example, after recognizing the flower on your desk as red in the light, you will continue to perceive it as red when the lights are dimmed. Area V4 is not activated when humans focus on black-and-white stimuli (Zeki et al., 1991).

Adaptive Functions of Color Vision. For many animals, the colors perceived from the electromagnetic spectrum provide important information for survival. As you look at the image in Figure 6.24a, do any visual stimuli trigger your sympathetic "fight-or-flight" circuits? Now look at the color version of this image (Figure 6.24b). Do you feel the adrenaline? With the added information of color, the contextual network described earlier in this chapter activates a context frame including a predator that deserves immediate attention.

These images suggest that the ability to perceive color may have survival advantages. The variation of cone densities and distributions across animals suggests that specific cone/rod ratios have been selected for various habitats and lifestyles. Although both rats and squirrels are dichromats possessing two types of cones, as opposed to the three that characterize trichromats such as humans, the diurnal (active in daylight) squirrel's retina contains about 86% cones, whereas the nocturnal rat retina contains only about 1% cones (Jacobs, 2009). The squirrel needs the detail and color information from the cones to jump from tree limb to tree limb during the day, abilities that are useless to a rat navigating its territory at night.

Primates are the only types of mammals that have three kinds of cones. Indeed, it has been hypothesized that

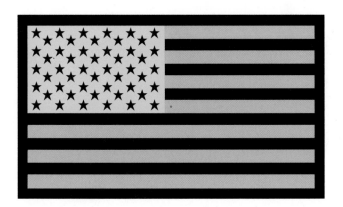

FIGURE 6.22 **Visual afterimages.** This flag is used to demonstrate visual afterimages in support of the opponent-process theory of color vision. Stare at the red dot in the center of this image for about a minute and then look at a blank, white piece of paper for a few seconds. An afterimage will appear with the traditional red, white, and blue colors of the American flag.

FIGURE 6.24 **The illumination of color.** The ability to detect color in the environment provides more information about an animal's surroundings and a heightened ability to detect threats and resources.

primates were originally nocturnal, with dichromatic color vision (R. D. Martin, 1979). For various reasons, many primate species became diurnal, requiring more accurate visual assessments of their environment to detect important stimuli. An exception is the owl monkey that appears to have switched from being diurnal to nocturnal (R. D. Martin, 1990). Although these primates have large eyes that are characteristic of nocturnal mammals, they lack a tapetum

lucidum, a layer of tissue behind the retina that reflects light back through the retina. This structure is typically observed in animals that evolved to be nocturnal, as it creates a form of internal night goggles to help the animals see their way through the darkness. Even without a tapetum lucidum, the large size of the owl monkey's eyes allows more light to enter the eyes to enhance visibility during darkness. As some primates emerged from the darkness and depended on eating fruits, trichromatic color vision may have enabled them to be more efficient harvesters of ripened fruit (Regan et al., 2001). Computational models have provided evidence that the medium and long wavelength–sensitive pigments give primates an advantage for foraging for fruits that are embedded in the foliage (Regan et al., 2001).

Does color vision have additional potential functions? Look at the image in Figure 6.25 and write down the colors you see. There are many brightly colored hand parts in the image. Did you get them all: yellow, green, blue, red, pink, orange, turquoise, purple? If so, your trichromatic color vision and supporting cones are working well. But are those all the colors? What about the child's skin color? After all, there is more surface covered with that color than any other color in the picture.

Mark Changizi (2009), a theoretical neuroscientist, has proposed the **skin theory of color vision**: the colors emphasized in our visual repertoires allow us to see changes in skin color that provide information about a peer's health or emotional status. To see physiological changes in another person's skin color, we must perceive the skin, regardless of race, as a noncolor or a colorless palette. The observation that skin color is perceived as more of a background color is reinforced by the fact that many individuals find it difficult to find an accurate color description of even their own skin. In fact, the nondescript color "base" is often used to describe

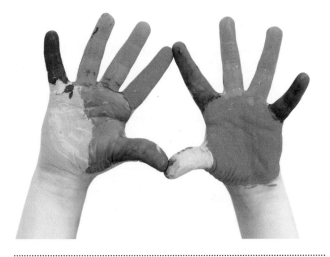

FIGURE 6.25 **The skin backdrop.** If asked to identify colors in this image, many people would ignore the skin color while identifying all the vivid colors. Yet, the somewhat neutral color variations of skin allow physiological markers related to factors such as oxygenation to be visible.

facial makeup that is supposed to match a person's skin color, avoiding the process of having to describe the actual color.

What physiological clues can the skin reveal? Consider the baseline skin color of a Caucasian person's wrist. If a tourniquet is placed on the person's wrist, trapping blood in the palm, the palm appears reddish. On the contrary, if blood is forced out of the hand, it appears yellowish. The oxygen levels of blood also influence the perceived color of the palm because rich, oxygenated blood will appear bluish or purple, whereas the deoxygenated veins will give the skin a greenish appearance. Red, blue, yellow, green—do those colors sound familiar? Those are the colors that the rods and opponent cells discussed in the previous section respond to and may play an adaptive role in social communications, facilitating the interpretation of emotional or health status.

Supporting the importance of color perception of skin, neuroscientists in Scotland have provided evidence that, regardless of race, we judge the health of individuals by the color of their faces. These scientists presented subjects with an unaltered photo of a Caucasian woman. Subjects who were asked to adjust her image to make her appear healthier responded by making her face appear redder, consistent with increased oxygenated blood flow (Figure 6.26). Various ethnicities assessed in the study increased the redness of faces to make them appear healthier; for example, African subjects increased the redness in black faces more than they did in other groups (Stephen, Coetzee, Smith, & Perrett, 2009). Facial redness in the form of blushing provides clues about an individual's emotions. Thus, in different contexts, reading facial colors may indeed have communicative value. This information would be meaningless without the photoreceptors to detect changes in this particular wavelength.

In further support of the skin theory of color vision, nonhuman primates with trichromatic color vision have no fur on their faces, leaving the color of their skin visible. Primates that have retained dichromatic color vision have also retained full facial hair. The skin color changes may have also influenced the use of colors to verbally describe emotional states such as *yellow cowardice* or *red-hot passion* or being described as *green (or sick) with envy*.

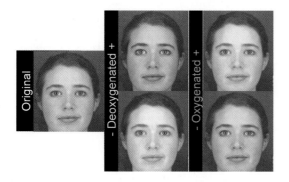

FIGURE 6.26 Color perception of skin. A study found that participants associated greater health with redder skin (which corresponds to more oxygenated blood).

Whatever its function, primates have excellent color vision. Research suggests that human trichromats can reliably discriminate between colors differing in wavelength by a distance as small as 0.25 nanometers (Mollon, Estevez, & Cavonius, 1990). In fact, humans can discern approximately 2.3 million surface colors (Pointer & Attridge, 1998). Some individuals, however, lack either the long or the middle wavelength–sensitive visual photopigments. They have a common genetic disorder known as **red–green colorblindness**, making them human dichromats. To these individuals, the world looks very different than it does to other people. Although colorblind individuals can see all the objects in their environment in varying shades of colors, they are not be able to view subtleties in the environment that can be adaptive (such as discerning whether a piece of meat is too raw to eat).

In a fascinating study, squirrel monkeys that had been colorblind since birth were treated with a virus carrying a gene to alter the responsiveness of the cones. When the virus was injected behind the eye, the virus delivered the gene to the retinal cells. After being altered by the gene, the cones started producing a protein sensitive to red light, and when the monkeys were tested for the ability to perceive red, they passed—and you can see this one coming—with flying colors! The visual world of the colorblind monkey is simulated in Figure 6.27a, and the visual world of the trichromatic monkey is depicted in Figure 6.27b (Mancuso et al., 2009). Because of safety concerns, this technique has not been attempted in humans, but gene therapy may someday lead to a safe treatment for colorblindness.

Uber-vision: Hawks

There's a reason why a person with exceptional **visual acuity** (clearness of vision) is sometimes described as "hawk-eyed." Like other diurnal birds of prey, hawks have excellent visual acuity. One contributing factor to their enhanced visual abilities is their large eyes. If human eyes matched the proportional size of the hawk's eyes to its facial area, they would be the size of tennis balls, much like the eyes of prototypic "space aliens" in science fiction films (Preston, 2000). Furthermore, a hawk's eyes are positioned at the front of its face, a position contributing to **binocular vision** (vision dependent on two eyes) and superior depth perception (Figure 6.28).

Another important reason for hawks' enhanced visual acuity is that it has two foveae, cone-dense areas of great visual acuity, in each eye. Humans, by comparison, have only one fovea in each eye. Hawks and other birds of prey also have up to five times more photoreceptors per square millimeter than humans (Sinclair, 1985). These sophisticated visual systems are extremely adaptive for hunting. A hawk can fly through the woodland, chasing a rodent, while avoiding branches and other objects. In a similar situation, humans would see the fast-paced scenes as a blur, not being able to zero in on the prey. As the hawks soar through the

(a)

(b)

FIGURE 6.27 A colorful, bountiful feast. Gene therapy can transform (a) colorblind squirrel monkeys into (b) color-perceiving monkeys, enhancing their ability to discriminate among stimuli in their environment.

FIGURE 6.28 Hawk-eyed. Like fictional renderings of space aliens, hawks have very large eyes in proportion to their head size.

sky, they keep their eyes on the target by keeping their heads very steady and using compensatory motor reflexes to maintain a consistent position (Sinclair, 1985). In addition, hawks are sensitive to objects moving more slowly than humans can perceive, which allows hawks to follow the changing positions of the constellations across the sky to orient themselves during migration (Jones, Pierce, & Ward, 2007).

Hearing

In addition to vision, animals rely on auditory processing for communication and other functions relevant for survival. Audition, or hearing, is the perception of sound produced by variations in sound waves. Even if an animal cannot see an important object in the environment, through auditory perception the animal can detect the vibrations of objects as they change positions.

Stimulus and Receptor

Human ears respond to sound vibrations ranging from about 30 to 20,000 cycles per second (or Hertz). The frequency of sound waves is perceived as **pitch**, and the intensity of sound waves measured as intensity is perceived as **loudness**.

As depicted in Figure 6.29, once the air vibrations are funneled through the pinna (outside) of the ear, sound

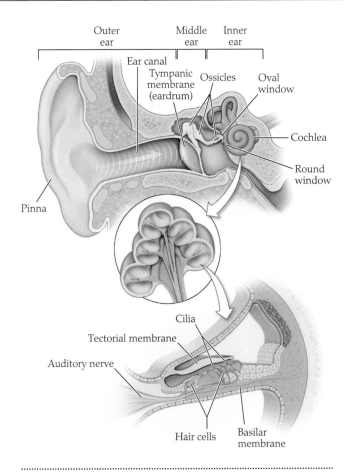

Outer ear · Middle ear · Inner ear

Ear canal
Tympanic membrane (eardrum)
Ossicles
Oval window
Cochlea
Round window
Pinna
Cilia
Tectorial membrane
Auditory nerve
Hair cells
Basilar membrane

FIGURE 6.29 Anatomy of ear. Sound waves are funneled by the pinna and subsequently travel through the ear canal to the middle and inner ear areas.

waves are channeled through the ear canal to the **tympanic membrane**, also known as the eardrum, where vibrations continue. Three small bones, known collectively as the **ossicles**, then transmit the air vibrations. Specifically, the malleus (hammer) transmits vibrations to the incus (anvil) and stapes (stirrup), which are located behind the tympanic membrane. These tiny bones are located in the middle ear, an important passageway to the fluid-filled **cochlea** (Greek for "land snail"). The receptive area is found on the **basilar membrane** containing **hair cells**. This area contacts the **tectorial membrane** positioned above these cells. The pitch of the sound waves projected onto the **oval window** activates various sections of the basilar membrane. The cochlea is more responsive to the vibrations because of the presence of the **round window**, allowing fluids to move back and forth in the structure.

More specifically, the hair cells located on the basilar membrane contain tiny hair growths known as **cilia**. The hair cells form synapses with the **auditory nerve** stretching into the cochlea. When the basilar membrane moves in response to sound waves, the hair cells are slightly displaced, creating a shearing force when the cilia move against the tectorial membrane above them. Thus, the movement of the

cilia is a critical component of the auditory transduction process as sound wave characteristics are translated into neural energy. As shown in Figure 6.29, the **organ of Corti** contains the area of the cochlea that contains the receptive cells (hair cells) for audition.

In many deaf individuals with impaired cochlear function, a small electronic device known as a **cochlear implant** can restore some aspects of sound perception. As shown in Figure 6.30, this device consists of a microphone, speech processor, receiver, and transmitter that relay auditory information to the auditory nerve. Hence, the cochlear implant bypasses damaged portions of the ear and stimulates the auditory nerve. Cochlear implants differ significantly from conventional hearing aids, which amplify sound so that individuals with hearing loss can better perceive the incoming sounds. The auditory message transmitted through a cochlear implant is an unnatural representation of sounds in the environment, such that the person with the implant must go through a period of learning to perceive and interpret the implant's signals effectively (National Institutes of Health, 2012).

The Central Nervous System Auditory Pathway

The auditory nerve is a component of the eighth cranial nerve (Chapter 2), which controls both hearing and balance. As depicted in Figure 6.31, after leaving the cochlea, auditory signals travel through the auditory nerve and synapse in the cochlear nuclei in the brainstem. These in turn send projections to the **superior olivary nucleus** and the **trapezoid body**, both located in close proximity to the cochlear nuclei. From the cochlear nucleus and superior olivary nucleus, projections are sent to the **inferior colliculus** in the midbrain. In the inferior colliculus, auditory pathways continue to the

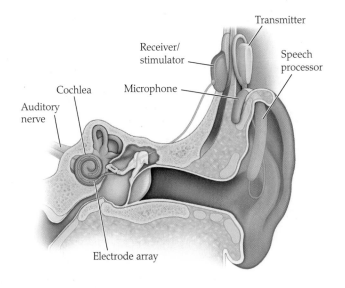

Transmitter
Receiver/ stimulator
Speech processor
Cochlea
Microphone
Auditory nerve
Electrode array

FIGURE 6.30 Cochlear implant. Cochlear implants are devices that amplify and transmit auditory information to the auditory nerves.

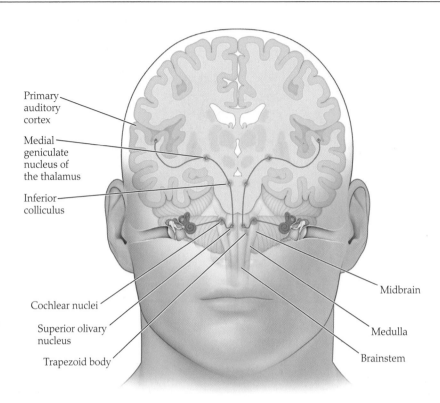

Primary auditory cortex

Medial geniculate nucleus of the thalamus

Inferior colliculus

Cochlear nuclei

Superior olivary nucleus

Trapezoid body

Midbrain

Medulla

Brainstem

FIGURE 6.31 Central nervous system auditory pathway. After leaving the inner ear, auditory information travels through nuclei in the medulla, midbrain, and thalamus on its journey to the auditory cortex.

medial geniculate nucleus in the thalamus before projecting to the **primary auditory cortex** (area A1) and related areas (see Appler & Goodrich (2011) for review).

Beyond the primary auditory cortex, projections toward the temporal lobe help us identify certain sounds (e.g., a bird chirping in a tree). By contrast, information directed toward the parietal lobe plays a role in spatial localization and guides our movements in certain directions. The **posterior parietal cortex** is activated when subjects are asked to localize certain sounds; for this reason, auditory information passing through this cortical area is referred to as the "where" stream of auditory processing (Rauschecker & Tian, 2000).

An extreme version of this process appeared in the case of Dan Kish in this chapter's opening. Recall that Kish used spatial auditory information (flash sonar) to envision his environment so well that he could tell the position of the parked car of the journalist who came to interview him. A further example of this variation of **cross-modality**, or integration between senses, is seen in individuals who have been deaf since birth. Research suggests that these individuals experience enhanced visual sensitivity, as well as reorganization of the sensory areas of the cortex. The auditory cortex, important for the processing of auditory information, has been found to be activated in deaf individuals when *viewing* sign language. Additionally, larger visual field areas have been observed in deaf individuals than in hearing subjects (Codina et al., 2011). These observations provide evidence of adaptation and plasticity in the brain's processing of sensory information.

Uber-audition: Echolocation in Bats

As you might imagine, it is quite a sensory challenge for bats to hunt moving insects in the dark of night. Not being in close proximity to their prey rules out the use of tactile or olfactory sensation, and hunting at night renders vision far less useful than it is during the day. Such a challenge requires the fascinating auditory adaptation known as **echolocation**. Bats generate sounds and analyze the echoes of those sounds to detect the presence of small insects up to 10 meters away. Once a bat detects an insect, the bat's brain must process this information in ways that enable the bat to alter its aerial movements to travel to the precise location of the insect prey.

Although the ability of blind people to use flash sonar to identify the presence of objects in their environment is impressive and adaptive, it is modest compared with the amazing ability of bats. These animals use their self-generated echoes to track the distance, velocity, and size of multiple elements within a complex environment and fine-tune their aerial movements to capture the moving prey. To accomplish this feat, bats hunting for insects emit a sonar signal characterized by a long duration and narrow bandwidth to detect prey. Once in pursuit of insects, the bat emits more rapid, shorter-duration sonar signals that alter the **frequency modulation (FM)**, or frequency of the sound wave, so that it can be carried to the receiver (similar to FM radio waves), or bat, in this case, which can then detect the position of the insect. This practice optimizes the bat's ability to hone in on its prey. To determine the position and distance of the insect

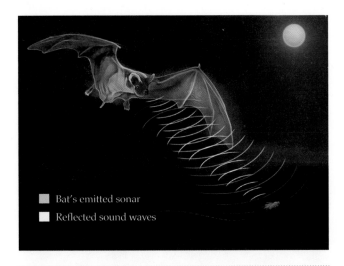

from the bat, bats use specialized delay-tuned neurons to process the time delay between their emitted sonar signal and the perception of the returning signal. More specifically, these delay-tuned neurons respond to the delay between the FM component of the signal sent by the bat and a higher-FM component of the returning auditory signal. Consequently, these specialized neurons are called **FM-FM neurons**.

One species of echolocating bats that has received research attention is the mustached bat (Figure 6.32). The specialized delay-tuned FM-FM neurons have been found in the inferior colliculus, medial geniculate nucleus, and auditory cortex of echolocating bats, brain regions that are also involved in human auditory processing. Projections from the auditory midbrain area to the pontine nuclei in the upper brainstem have also been identified as playing a critical role in the adaptive behavioral modifications that occur during echolocation, allowing the bat to capture the small moving prey (Wenstrup & Portfors, 2011).

Bats are not the only animals to use echolocation. Whales and dolphins also use it to locate food sources in the water. This technology was replicated by scientists who developed sonar used by the military to detect the location of underwater objects such as submarines.

Touch

Our skin is our body's largest organ, and our sense of touch enables us to monitor what comes into contact with it. Our complex skin-related sensory systems convey messages to the brain about pressure, temperature, and pain. The **somatosensory system** relays information about the body's interaction, through touch, position, and movement, with the external world.

Helen Keller's Unique Sensory Portal

As a young child, I often traveled with my family through the small town of Talladega, Alabama, to visit my grandparents. I was always intrigued by the big buildings of the Alabama Institute for the Deaf and Blind, which included a school named after one of the state's most accomplished citizens, Helen Keller. In elementary school, I had learned that Keller was both deaf and blind but was able largely to compensate for these challenges. I could not imagine how a person could live without these critical senses. Without the use of either visual or auditory sensory systems, Helen Keller needed another sensory portal to understand her immediate surroundings.

Born in 1880, Keller lost her sight and hearing as a result of a mysterious bout of fever (likely either scarlet fever or meningitis) when she was 19 months old. In her autobiography, she described her discovery of the most important sensory portal following her illness: the sensation of touch. While she was still a toddler, she realized that she could learn about objects in her environment by touching them with her hands. When she was 6 years old, her teacher, Anne Sullivan, taught her to associate letters signed on her hand with various objects. As Anne poured water on one of Helen's hands, Anne signed the letters W-A-T-E-R slowly, then quickly, on Helen's other hand. At this point, Helen made the connection between the letters and the substance, realizing how touch could provide very specific information about her world. She started learning new words with this manual alphabet technique as fast as her teacher could reveal them to her. She went on to learn to read Braille in five different languages, as well as to study other academic subjects. In 1904, she graduated from Radcliffe College. For the rest of her life, Keller was an activist for social justice.

As we have learned throughout this chapter, the brain flexibly adapts to the most relevant sensory information. Once touch gained its relevance, Keller later wrote that she felt a "misty consciousness" (Whitman, 1968) for the first time, a sentiment that conveys a sense of enhanced awareness of her surroundings. Prior to this experience, her life was bereft of such consciousness, truly a frustrating, if not nearly devastating, circumstance for most humans. Demonstrating just how sensitive her hands were to touch, she learned to interpret spoken language by touching a person's face and throat to detect specific movements of the throat, mouth, and face (see Figure 6.33) (Keller, 1914).

Touch Receptors and the Somatosensory Pathway

Helen Keller's ability to detect movement on her hand depended on the somatosensory axons traveling from the skin on her palm to the central nervous system by way of the dorsal root ganglia in the spinal nerves. In Keller's case, information about fine touch traveled through the dorsal columns in the spinal cord's white matter at the cervical level to the lower medulla. **Meissner's corpuscles** represent a type

FIGURE 6.33 Communication through touch. Being both deaf and blind, Helen Keller learned to read lips with her fingers, as she did here when meeting with President Eisenhower.

of **mechanoreceptor**, a receptor in the skin that responds to touch or pressure. Meissner's corpuscles are sensitive to light touch and are concentrated in sensitive skin areas, such as fingers and lips. Other important types of mechanoreceptors exist in the skin as well. For example, **Pacinian corpuscles** respond to deep pressure, and **free nerve endings** respond to tissue damage and temperature changes, which we experience as pain (Cauna & Ross, 1960). Figure 6.34 illustrates

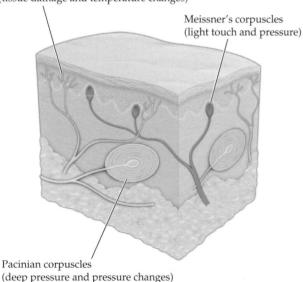

Free nerve endings
(tissue damage and temperature changes)

Meissner's corpuscles
(light touch and pressure)

Pacinian corpuscles
(deep pressure and pressure changes)

FIGURE 6.34 Touch and pressure receptors. Specialized receptors in the skin transmit information about touch and pressure to the central nervous system.

these touch receptors. (More information about pain sensory processing and perception is presented in Chapter 10.)

As discussed in Chapter 2, tactile information arriving from other areas of the body has specific dermatomes, or body territories, each innervated by a specific spinal nerve. Subsequently, the tactile information travels via the **dorsal column–medial lemniscus pathway** to the relay nucleus of the thalamus specialized for **somatosensation**, known as the **ventral posterior nucleus of the thalamus**. From the thalamus, the axons' next destination is the **primary somatosensory cortex**, followed by the secondary somatosensory cortex. Figure 6.35a illustrates the somatosensory pathway.

Whereas the axons carrying information about tactile discrimination from the mechanoreceptors in the skin travel along the dorsal column–medial lemniscus pathway, axons mediating pain and temperature sensation in the skin travel along the **spinothalamic (anterolateral) pathway** (see Figure 6.35b) (Kubota, Nagano, Baba, & Sato, 2004; Wasner, Lee, Engel, & McLachlan, 2008).

Uber-touch: Raccoons

In Chapter 1 you learned about raccoons being classified as opportunistic mammals that exhibit high rates of exploration in their surroundings. One physical characteristic that helps the raccoon explore new environments is an extremely sensitive sense of touch. As depicted in Figure 6.36, raccoons have five fingers on their hands, or forefeet, as well as five toes on their hind feet. The skin on their digits (fingers and toes) is soft. Unlike the digits of other carnivores, raccoon digits do not have webbing between them. The top region of the raccoons' digits is

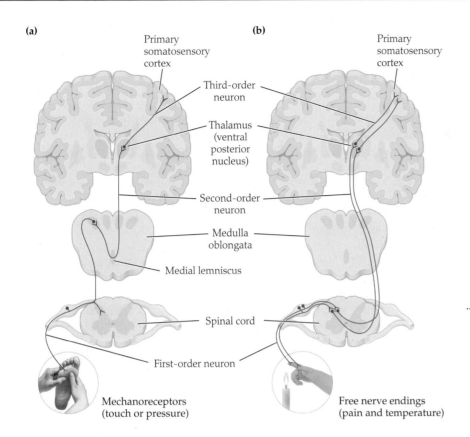

(a)

(b)

Primary somatosensory cortex

Third-order neuron

Thalamus (ventral posterior nucleus)

Second-order neuron

Medulla oblongata

Medial lemniscus

Spinal cord

First-order neuron

Mechanoreceptors (touch or pressure)

Primary somatosensory cortex

Free nerve endings (pain and temperature)

FIGURE 6.35 Central nervous system tactile and pain pathways. (a) The dorsal column–medial lemniscal pathway carries tactile information through the spinal cord and medulla to the somatosensory cortex. (b) The spinothalamic tract that transmits information about tactile pain and temperature follows a similar path.

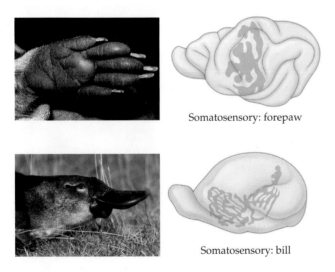

Somatosensory: forepaw

Somatosensory: bill

FIGURE 6.36 Mammalian cortical specialization. The raccoon and platypus have evolved specialized cortical areas to accommodate their impressive use of the forepaw and bill, respectively.

covered with short hairs; however, the palms and soles are hairless.

As indicated in Figure 6.36, a large proportion of the raccoon's cortex is devoted to the sensory functions of the forepaw. In comparison, Figure 6.36 also depicts the platypus, another mammal with an extraordinarily sensitive body

part (in this case, the bill). Platypuses use their bills to explore their surroundings as they search for food or other resources. The sensitivity of both the platypus bill and the raccoon forepaw suggests that the amount of cortical territory devoted to a sensory or motor function is related to the importance of that particular function to the animal's survival. For both the raccoon forepaw and the platypus bill, much more area is devoted to the sensory function than to the motor function. Although raccoons have more motor capability in their forepaws than other carnivores do, their most prominent strength is their ability to discriminate between objects based on tactile cues. This supersensitivity does not extend to their hind paws because their forepaw skin has approximately four times more sensory receptors than their hind paw skin.

As impressive as the raccoon forepaw is, however, the human hand is likely more sensitive since the raccoon lacks the sensitive Meissner's corpuscles discussed previously (Zeveloff, 2002). Yet, whereas humans rely mostly on vision to navigate the world, raccoons use touch as their primary sensory portal. For example, when presented with a garbage bag, in contrast to other animals that may rip the bag open to smell, taste, and view the contents, raccoons stick their forepaws through a small hole to determine whether there is anything worth exploring and eating. Their sensory systems provide sufficient information about the bag's contents for their brains to make the decision to dive in.

The Healing Touch and Recovery from Brain Injury

Featured study: Gibb, R. L., Gonzalez, C. L. R., Wegenast, W., & Kolb, B. E. (2010). Tactile stimulation promotes motor recovery following cortical injury in adult rats. Behavioral Brain Research, 214, 102–107.

A report indicating that massages in premature human babies were associated with increased alertness, ability to move spontaneously and independently, and body weight brought attention to the possible medical benefits of massage therapy (Field et al., 1986). Subsequent rodent models have provided further evidence that tactile stimulation facilitates recovery following brain injury as a newborn (Chou et al., 2001). Robin Gibb and colleagues at the University of Lethbridge explored this connection further. Specifically, they set out to determine the effect of providing the contextual element of tactile stimulation on the recovery of adult male rats that had experienced lesions of the bilateral medial frontal cortex.

The researchers assigned 18 rats to one of three groups:

1. An experimental group that received frontal brain lesions and tactile therapy,

2. A control group that received frontal brain lesions with *no* tactile therapy, and

3. A sham surgery control group that was prepped for surgery and experienced everything the surgery groups experienced but received no brain damage and no tactile therapy.

One week prior to the surgery, the rats in the tactile therapy group were placed in the experimenter's lap and stroked with a baby hairbrush for 15 minutes three times per day (Context Matters Figure 6.1). At the end of each tactile session, rats were given a food treat. A food treat was given to non-tactile-trained animals as well.

Following surgery and a three-week recovery period, rats were trained in a reaching task. Specifically, rats were trained to reach through two bars, grasp one or more chicken feed pellets, and retract the pellets for consumption (more detail appears in Chapter 7, "Movement," "Laboratory Exploration"). At the completion of the behavioral training and assessment, the researchers processed the rats' brains using the Golgi stain technique (discussed in Chapter 2). The investigators cut the tissue into 200-micrometer-thick sections (one micrometer equals one millionth of a meter) throughout the cortical area so that they could trace and evaluate five complete neurons in each hemisphere of each rat.

The results indicated that the frontal injured-tactile experimental group's rates of successful reaching were closer to those of the noninjured sham control group than to those of the injured control group that received no tactile treatment. These findings suggest that the tactile treatment facilitated functional recovery from the brain injury. Tactile stimulation appeared to increase the branching, or arborization, of the dendrites in the pyramidal cells adjacent to the lesioned area, an effect associated with enhanced neural connections.

A direction for future research may be to identify the specific mechanisms of how tactile therapy appears to promote recovery from brain injury. For example, tactile stimulation has been hypothesized to increase production of a growth factor in the skin and brain known as fibroblast growth factor 2. Future research is necessary to learn more about the specific mechanisms mediating the contextual effect of providing heightened tactile stimulation, so that any relevant findings can eventually be directed toward improving human health.

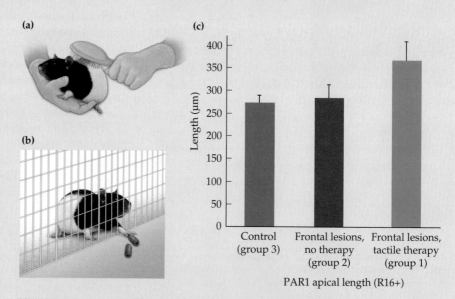

CONTEXT MATTERS FIGURE 6.1 **Study components.** (a) Rats were stroked with a hairbrush for 15 minutes in three daily sessions for a week prior to receiving frontal lesions. (b) Rats in all the groups were trained to reach through the bars of a cage to retrieve food pellets. (c) The animals that received surgery and tactile stimulation exhibited better recovery, defined as successful retrievals of food, than those that received surgery without the tactile stimulation. Additionally, the frontal lesion/tactile therapy group had longer extensions of the cortical apical dendrites.

Smell

The sense of smell, or olfaction, is an important feature of our everyday lives. We depend on this sensory system to help us identify desirable foods and to direct us away from foul-smelling stimuli that may be associated with dangerous pathogens. As previously mentioned, olfaction may have been the most important sense for the earliest mammals, driving the expansion of the mammalian brain. In this section, you will learn more about how certain chemicals activate your neurons and, ultimately, influence behavior.

Stimulus and Receptor

In mice and humans, the approximately 1,000 genes that code for receptors of **odorant molecules** (molecules that we can smell) constitute the largest gene family in the vertebrate genome. However, only 300–400 of the odorant receptor genes are functional in humans. Two neuroscientists, Linda Buck and Richard Axel, won the Nobel Prize in 2004 for their 1990s work at Columbia University identifying the molecular structure of the odorant receptors (Laurant, 2005). The rodent brain devotes a larger proportion of the cortex to olfaction than the human brain does, suggesting that rodents rely on this sense more than humans do. Thus, a human who lost the ability to smell would likely experience minimal challenges related to survival, whereas a rat that lost the ability to smell would likely experience significant challenges (see the section on uber-olfaction).

The environment produces a diverse array of odorant molecules. Humans can detect up to 10,000 different odors, which is even more impressive considering that natural odors often consist of up to hundreds of different chemical molecules. As odorants are inhaled, they reach the nasal cavity, where the chemicals interact with the olfactory sensory neurons in the **olfactory epithelium** (also known as the mucous membrane), located at the top of the nasal cavity.

When the odorant molecules reach the olfactory sensory cells in the olfactory epithelium, they bind to receptors on the cilia of the sensory bipolar neurons. The cilia are the site of the olfactory transduction process. As shown in Figure 6.37, the odorant interacts with the receptor cells in the epithelium, resulting in the depolarization of the olfactory neurons (i.e., olfactory transduction) (Menini, Lagostena, & Boccaccio, 2004).

Olfactory Neural Destinations and Emotional Connections

The olfactory sensory neurons synapse in the **olfactory bulbs** that lie at the ventral surface of the brain just above the olfactory epithelium. The olfactory bulbs contain clusters of axonal and dendritic processes known as olfactory **glomeruli** (after the Latin *glomus*, meaning "ball"). Humans have approximately 10,000 of these glomeruli. From the olfactory bulbs, the olfactory axons travel deeper into the brain into the areas of the amygdala, the **piriform cortex**, and the **entorhinal cortex**. These evolutionarily ancient structures serve as portals to other structures of the limbic system.

Multiple studies and demonstrations have provided evidence for close associations between olfaction and emotions. The calm feeling you get when you smell your mother's homemade chocolate-chip cookies or some other comforting, familiar smell is one bit of evidence for these close associations. Figure 6.38 indicates just how integrated smell is into the brain's emotional circuits. In Figure 6.38, a single neuron originating in the posterior piriform cortex is depicted with all of its far-reaching axonal branches extending to the amygdala as well as to the entorhinal, perirhinal, and insular cortical areas (Johnson, Illig, Behan, & Haberly, 2000). As previously described, smell interacts with taste to produce perceptions of varying flavors—more evidence of the integrative and far-reaching effects of the olfactory system.

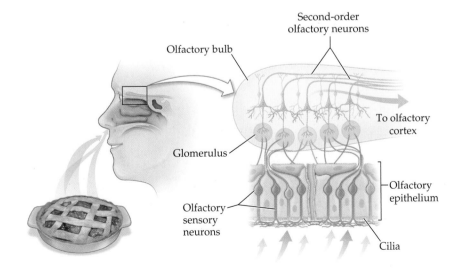

Olfactory bulb

Second-order olfactory neurons

To olfactory cortex

Glomerulus

Olfactory epithelium

Olfactory sensory neurons

Cilia

....

FIGURE 6.37 Olfactory central nervous system. After volatile chemicals are received by nasal receptors, neural messages progress to the olfactory bulb on their path to the olfactory cortex.

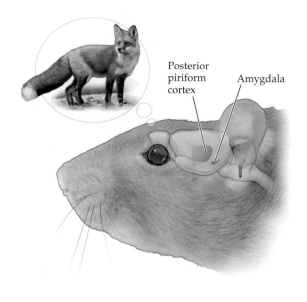

Posterior piriform cortex

Amygdala

FIGURE 6.38 Extensive reach of olfactory-sensitive piriform neurons. When this rat sniffs a predator odor, the odorant molecules activate expansive cells in the piriform cortex that alert the animal's cortical areas to respond appropriately to the threat.

A recent study at the Monell Chemical Senses Center in Philadelphia provided an example of just how well integrated the olfactory information is with the limbic system. Researchers reported that children (ages 5–8) of women who used alcohol to counter negative emotional states ("escape drinkers") found the smell of beer and other alcoholic beverages more aversive than did the age-matched children of mothers who did not use alcohol in such a way (control group). In fact, the children of nonsmoking escape drinkers rated the smell of cigarettes as more desirable than that of alcohol, an effect not found in the control group. Thus, the study provided evidence that children's association of the smell of alcohol with their mothers' distraught emotions influenced their individual preferences for other odors encountered in their day-to-day lives (Mennella & Forestell, 2008).Whereas some of our olfactory preferences and aversions are biologically predisposed (e.g., aversion to odors such as ammonia), others, such as a preference for a best friend's favorite perfume, are learned based on our individual olfactory life stories.

Pheromones

At certain times of the year, female dogs seem to attract a larger audience of male canine suitors than at other times. It is as if the male dogs all receive the same memo when females are receptive to mating with males, which happens in the phase of the reproductive (estrous) cycle known as estrus (as discussed in Chapter 11). The "memo" the male neighborhood dogs receive is a chemical that the female dog releases during estrus. Such chemicals, released from one animal and detected by another, are known as **pheromones**.

For example, specific pheromones are released into the animals' environments to change the social behavior of members of their own species. The effects of pheromones are diverse, ranging from eliciting aggression in **conspecific** males (males of the same species) to triggering sexual receptivity in females.

Pheromones are detected by an **accessory olfactory system** that consists of the **vomeronasal organ (VNO)** located in the nasal cavity and its neuronal projections to the accessory olfactory bulbs, which then project to the hypothalamus and amygdala. This system appears as a supplement to the main olfactory system (see Figure 6.39) (Keller, Baum, Brock, Brennan, & Bakker, 2009). The VNO is the structure that the dog uses in the previously described example. Do humans have such a well-developed accessory olfactory system? Evidence suggests that the VNO develops in the human fetus, but regresses after that time. Thus, it appears that humans have only remnants of this structure. Even so, humans have been shown to be able to detect the presence of certain steroid hormones, so some social communication of hormones may take place (Trotier, 2011).

A classic laboratory demonstration of pheromonal processing is the case of pregnancy block observed in mice. This effect, known as the **Bruce effect**, is associated with a disruption of pregnancy when a female mouse is exposed to the scent of an unfamiliar male's urine. If a female mouse's VNO is lesioned, however, the presence of unfamiliar urine fails to disrupt her pregnancy (Halpern & Martinez-Marcos, 2003).

Whereas volatile molecules traveling through the air have been shown to activate cells in the main olfactory bulb,

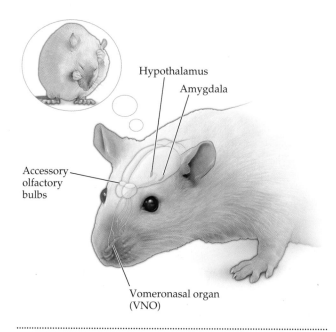

Hypothalamus

Amygdala

Accessory olfactory bulbs

Vomeronasal organ (VNO)

FIGURE 6.39 The vomeronasal organ. Pheromones are detected by the vomeronasal organ and neural processes subsequently progress to the accessory olfactory bulbs, and from there to the hypothalamus and amygdala.

FIGURE 6.40 **Flehman response.** This horse rolls its upper lip to detect the presence of pheromones, revealing important information about the hormonal status of other horses in proximity.

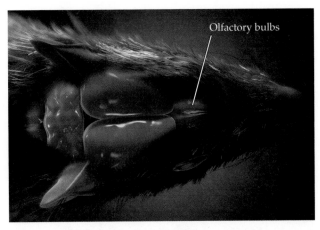

FIGURE 6.41 **Rodent olfactory bulb.** The importance of olfaction in the life of a rat is obvious when the large size of the olfactory bulbs is observed.

the VNO typically requires actual physical contact with the urine (Tirindelli, Dibattista, Pifferi, & Menini, 2009). This is the likely function of the mammalian *Flehman response* observed in species such as cats and horses. Flehman (German for "curls upper lip") responses involve a male's physical contact with social chemicals such as the female's urine. After sampling the female's urine and then rolling the lip back so that the VNO can assess the chemicals, the male can determine the reproductive status of the female, as observed in Figure 6.40 (Stahlbaum & Houpt, 1989). Referring back to the example of the neighborhood dogs, once the male identifies the presence of a female in heat (perhaps through the main olfactory system or some combination of the main and accessory olfactory systems), the male will sample the female's urine and vaginal secretions on making contact with her (Tirindelli et al., 2009).

Uber-olfaction: Rats

Although olfaction is important in primates, its relevance pales in comparison to that in rodents. As indicated by the proportionately large size of the rat olfactory bulbs to the rest of the brain (Figure 6.41), the sense of smell is very important in almost every aspect of a rodent's life (Slotnick, Schellinck, & Brown, 2005). In fact, rats can identify the location of odorants, without even moving their heads, at a rate that is three orders of magnitude faster than in humans. Compared with the human genome, a larger proportion of the rat genome is devoted to olfaction. The VNO is much more prominent in rats than in humans (Burn, 2008).

In a striking example of the sensitivity of the rat olfactory system, the giant African pouch rat has been trained to detect the presence of trinitrotoluene (TNT) in land mines in Mozambique, Africa (Figure 6.42). The philanthropist Bart Weetjens has led an international campaign to use the

FIGURE 6.42 **HeroRats.** Because of their sensitive olfactory abilities, giant African pouched rats are trained to detect TNT in landmines in Mozambique.

sensitive olfactory systems of the rats. Operant conditioning is used to train the rats (known as HeroRats) to respond to the presence of the TNT odor by making a scratching movement with their forepaws. Although it takes six months to one year and costs up to $8,000 to train a single rat, it is still more efficient to train the rats than to train dogs to detect the presence of TNT in land mines. The rats are so small that they will not trip the mines, and they are cheaper to transport than dogs. The program has been successful: Between 2008 and 2009, 30 accredited HeroRats canvassed more than a million square meters of mine-infested Mozambican land. The rats identified approximately 400 mines that could have harmed children or others who might have encountered the mines (McLaughlin, 2010).

African pouch rats are being trained to detect the presence of tuberculosis in human saliva by motioning when they smell *Mycobacterium tuberculosis*, the bacterium that causes tuberculosis. Impressively, the rats are more efficient at this task than human laboratory assistants using visual screening techniques enhanced with chemical tests and microscopes. Compared with the human rate of visually assessing 20 saliva samples in a day, the rats can easily detect up to 1,000 samples per day with their noses (Lambert, 2011). The TNT- and tuberculosis-sniffing rats provide additional examples of how a human sensory system, olfaction in this case, pales in comparison to that system in other animals.

Final Thoughts on Sensory Integration and Adaptation

Although you have reviewed several distinct senses—including vision, audition (hearing), touch, and olfaction (smell), as well as taste—it is important to remember that multisensory integration represents the most relevant perceptual experiences of animals, including humans. In fact, the more traditional practice of separating the senses to investigate them may limit our ability to thoroughly understand the interconnections between brain and behavior (Ghazanfar & Schroeder, 2006). Thus, in this section, we revisit the idea of multisensory integration. In a study focusing on the responses of individual neurons in one multisensory cortical area, researchers found that 23% of the same neurons responded to both the sight of a person ripping paper and the sound of ripping paper (Barraclough et al., 2005). Hence, multisensory processing may be a more accurate representation of the typical sensory experience than the often-studied unisensory (or single-mode sensory experience) processing in the mammalian cortex.

Recently, I was struck by how relevant multisensory and **cortical association areas** are to the adaptive responses of mammals when I viewed a phylogenetic tree depicting the proportion and placement of various sensory cortical areas throughout the evolution of mammals. (A phylogenetic tree is a type of diagram that represents the relationships among diverse biological species.) Leah Krubitzer, a neuroscientist at the University of California at Davis (featured in this chapter's "Laboratory Exploration"), has gathered evidence about these cortical areas in various mammals through fossils and real-time single-cell recordings conducted in her laboratory to generate the phylogenetic tree depicted in Figure 6.43.

At the base of the tree, the common ancestor's cortex appeared to be dominated by the specific sensory cortical areas (i.e., unisensory cortical areas). However, as mammalian brains morphed in the various horizontal and vertical branches of the tree, the primary sensory areas became smaller in many species. As the unisensory areas diminished in size, association areas, including multisensory areas, became more prevalent. Approximately 75% of the primate cortex comprises cortical association areas, providing more opportunities for integrative analysis of environmental surroundings than were available to the common mammalian ancestor, which likely resembled a rodent with a long snout. With more integration potential, more advanced cognition became possible because the decisions to engage in certain responses could be influenced by multiple factors. Further, additional complex and integrative cortical areas could more accurately make decisions between competing responses and perhaps even anticipate and plan future responses. These are interesting ideas to ponder with our extensive cortical association areas.

Finally, further evidence of sensory integration appears in **synesthesia** (Greek for *unified senses*), a rare condition in which stimulation of one sense triggers additional, seemingly unrelated perceptual experiences. For example, when a person with synesthesia hears a voice, he or she may simultaneously taste a certain flavor. For another such individual, touching sandpaper may result in not only tactile stimulation but also the perception of a color. Different synesthetes (people with synesthesia) report many different perceptual experiences in response to different stimuli. Because human brains are so rich in integrative sensory cortices, it is easy to predict that, in some cases, the cross-talk between the areas crosses a perceptual border that results in synesthesia.

Affecting about 1% of the population, synesthesia generally does not appear to interfere with daily functions—it just provides a unique perspective (Eagleman, 2010). As long as the brain still identifies the most salient sensations in our environments, a little sensory decoration does not seem to impede perceptual function and adaptation. In fact, cross-modal processing may lay the groundwork for one of humanity's most unique cognitive abilities—creativity. Musical artists such as Billy Joel and Sting have associated their synesthesia with their creative success (Seaburg, 2012).

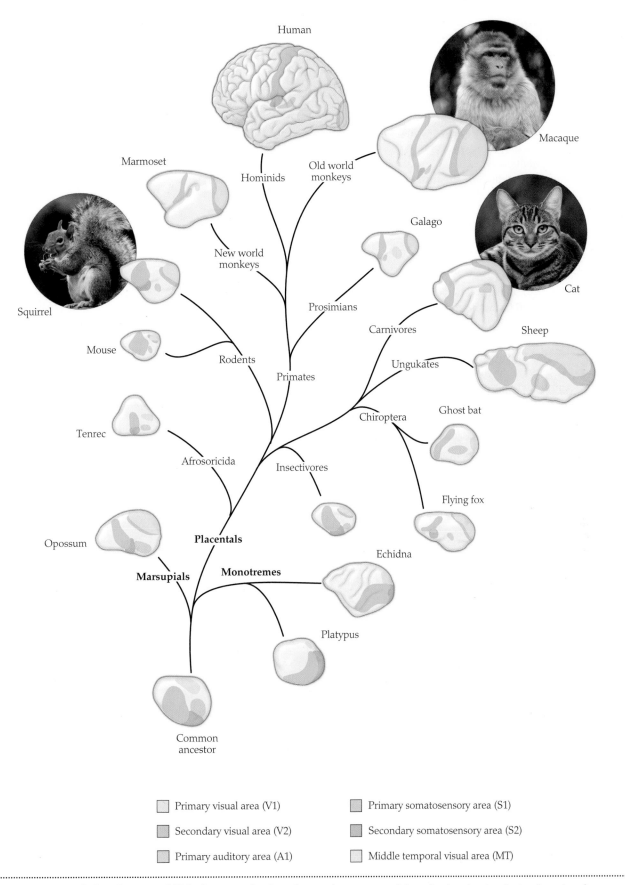

LABORATORY EXPLORATION

Somatosensory Cortical Maps in the Rat

Throughout this chapter, you have learned that certain areas of the cortex respond to specific types of sensory stimulation or, in some cases, multiple types of sensory stimulation. You may have wondered exactly how scientists know that a certain area of the cortex responds to a specific type of sensory stimulation. Our knowledge about specialized sensory cortical areas is, in part, a result of extensive meticulous work in which scientists have used electrophysiological recordings to systematically map the location of primary and secondary sensory areas in the cortex.

Here, we will focus on the technique that Leah Krubitzer's lab at the University of California at Davis uses to determine rats' somatotopic maps (maps of correspondences between specific areas of the body and specific areas in the brain's somatosensory system) (modified from Seelke, Dooley, & Krubitzer, 2012; personal communication, May 3, 2012).

A single-unit recording electrode (connected to an amplifier) is placed in cortical layer 4 of a rat's brain; additionally, a corresponding set of speakers is utilized for listening to the neural activity, and a computer allows the experimenter to see the neural signal. At that time, the experimenter stimulates the rat's body by lightly running a paintbrush over its skin—all the while listening for neural activity. When stimulation of a specific region of the skin triggers neural activity, the boundaries of the neuron's receptive field are determined and then marked on the rat's body (Laboratory Exploration Figure 6.1). This process continues until the entire primary somatosensory cortex (in this particular study) has been mapped. In the rat, this process requires dozens of electrode placements. In larger animals, however, the process can require hundreds of electrode placements.

When the electrophysiological process is complete, the experimenters remove the brain for histological processing. In this case, the cortex is separated from the subcortical areas so that a functional and anatomical organization of the primary sensory areas of the cortex can be constructed. The somatotopic organization provides important clues about an animal's sensory world, revealing the type of stimulation that is most important for its survival. In the case of the rat, the area responding to the rat's whiskers is the most prevalent. Rats use information from their whiskers to provide information about their environment during the darkness. As previously noted, rats also depend on smell, and, as you will notice on the final somatosensory map, the area for the nose is larger than the area for the entire trunk of the body (which is much larger than the nose!). The mouth area is also very important for the rat.

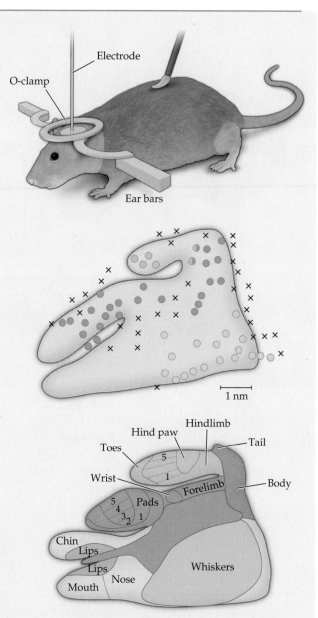

LABORATORY EXPLORATION FIGURE 6.1 **Defining the brain's specific sensory areas.** (Top) Electrophysiological recording is used to determine which areas of the cortex respond to specific sensory stimuli. Body part colors are represented in areas of the primary somatosensory cortex, with similarly colored dots representing electrode placements. (Bottom) The final somatotopic map indicates the sensory stimuli that are most important for the rat (e.g., note the expansive area for the whiskers).

Conclusion

This chapter introduced you to the many ways the brain decodes the events of the external world to allow us to survive day to day. Regardless of the mode of transportation (light, airwaves, chemicals, and so forth), sensation produces a relevant picture of our surroundings so that we can take advantage of potential resources and avoid threats to our survival. The visual sensory system received the most thorough coverage because primates depend more on sight than on their other senses. Specific aspects of light are decoded through the eye and retina before traveling through the brain to the primary visual cortex. Interpretation of the visual stimulus continues as the information is processed through the relevant cortical areas. You learned that the same stimulus can be interpreted in different ways depending on current context and past experiences.

The chapter also discussed the roles of the ears, skin, tongue, and nose, respectively, in hearing, touch, taste, and smell. Ultimately, transduction of the appropriate environmental stimuli in the sensory-specific receptor cells takes place. These messages then project to the cortex, where they are processed by unisensory and multisensory areas. Individuals frequently compensate for sensory impairments by honing their other senses. For example, blind individuals may develop a more sensitive auditory system, such as the use of flash sonar to "see" the world with echoing sounds.

Although several animals surpass human sensory capacities, humans possess impressive sensitivity in most sensory systems. Primates have evolved a cortex containing primarily association areas that integrate sensory information. This "sensory merge" enables complex responses that enhance survival. The extensive association areas allow for the effortless integration of multiple modes of information, an ability that likely leads to varying perceptual and cognitive experiences such as synesthesia and creativity.

KEY TERMS

Fundamentals of Sensation and Perception

sensation (p. 153)
perception (p. 153)
psychophysics (p. 153)
difference threshold (p. 153)
just noticeable difference (JND) (p. 153)
Weber's law (p. 153)
absolute threshold (p. 153)
sensory receptors (p. 154)
sensory adaptation (p. 154)
multisensory integration (p. 154)
cross-modal stimuli (p. 155)
flavor (p. 155)
taste buds (p. 155)
superadditive neural response (p. 156)
additive response (p. 156)
subadditive neural response (p. 156)
multisensory neuron (p. 156)
receptive fields (p. 156)
McGurk effect (p. 156)

Vision

photoreceptors (p. 157)
adequate stimulus (p. 157)
electromagnetic spectrum (p. 157)
hue (p. 157)
brightness (p. 157)
saturation (p. 157)

extraocular muscles (p. 158)
optic nerve (p. 158)
pupil (p. 158)
iris (p. 158)
cornea (p. 158)
lens (p. 158)
retina (p. 158)
vitreous humor (p. 158)
aqueous humor (p. 158)
rods (p. 158)
cones (p. 158)
bipolar cells (p. 158)
ganglion cells (p. 158)
blind spot (p. 158)
horizontal cells (p. 159)
amacrine cells (p. 159)
fovea (p. 159)
transduction (p. 159)
photopigments (p. 159)
opsin (p. 159)
retinal (p. 159)
rhodopsin (p. 159)
phosphodiesterase (p. 160)
optic chiasm (p. 160)
optic tract (p. 160)
lateral geniculate nucleus (LGN) (p. 160)
primary visual cortex (V1) (p. 160)
striate cortex (p. 160)
magnocellular layers (p. 160)

parvocellular layers (p. 160)
koniocellular layer (p. 160)
extrastriate cortex (p. 160)
concentric receptive field (p. 161)
on-center cells (p. 161)
off-center cells (p. 161)
lateral inhibition (p. 161)
contrast enhancement (p. 161)
superior colliculus (p. 162)
simple cells (p. 162)
complex cells (p. 162)
hypercomplex cells (p. 162)
orientation columns (p. 162)
Area V2 (p. 162)
Area V3 (p. 162)
Area V4 (p. 163)
Area V5 (p. 163)
fusiform face area (p. 163)
prosopagnosia (p. 163)
ventral stream (p. 163)
dorsal stream (p. 164)
bottom-up visual processing (p. 164)
top-down visual processing (p. 164)
context frames (p. 165)
parahippocampal cortex (PHC) (p. 165)
retrosplenial cortex (p. 165)
superior orbital sulcus (p. 165)
Young–Helmholtz trichromatic theory of color vision (p. 166)

opponent-process theory of color
  vision (p. 167)
color constancy (p. 167)
skin theory of color vision (p. 168)
red–green colorblindness (p. 169)
visual acuity (p. 169)
binocular vision (p. 169)

Hearing

pitch (p. 170)
loudness (p. 170)
tympanic membrane (p. 171)
ossicles (p. 171)
cochlea (p. 171)
basilar membrane (p. 171)
hair cells (p. 171)
tectorial membrane (p. 171)
oval window (p. 171)
round window (p. 171)
cilia (p. 171)
auditory nerve (p. 171)
organ of Corti (p. 171)
cochlear implant (p. 171)

superior olivary nucleus (p. 171)
trapezoid body (p. 171)
inferior colliculus (p. 171)
medial geniculate nucleus (p. 172)
primary auditory cortex (p. 172)
posterior parietal cortex (p. 172)
cross-modality (p. 172)
echolocation (p. 172)
frequency modulation (FM) (p. 172)
FM-FM neurons (p. 173)

Touch

somatosensory system (p. 173)
Meissner's corpuscles (p. 173)
mechanoreceptor (p. 174)
Pacinian corpuscles (p. 174)
free nerve endings (p. 174)
dorsal column–medial lemniscus
  pathway (p. 174)
somatosensation (p. 174)
ventral posterior nucleus of the
  thalamus (p. 174)

primary somatosensory cortex
  (p. 174)
spinothalamic (anterolateral)
  pathway (p. 174)

Smell

odorant molecules (p. 177)
olfactory epithelium (p. 177)
olfactory bulbs (p. 177)
glomeruli (p. 177)
piriform cortex (p. 177)
entorhinal cortex (p. 177)
pheromones (p. 178)
conspecific (p. 178)
accessory olfactory system (p. 178)
vomeronasal organ (VNO) (p. 178)
Bruce effect (p. 178)

Final Thoughts on Sensory Integration and Adaptation

cortical association areas (p. 180)
synesthesia (p. 180)

REVIEW QUESTIONS

1. Define multisensory integration and explain how it works in humans, giving at least two different examples.

2. Explain the difference between taste and flavor. What are the principal body parts and brain areas involved in each of these sensory capabilities?

3. Describe how light waves are processed and perceived as visual images, naming the major anatomical components in the eye and the brain that facilitate this process.

4. Describe how sound waves are processed and perceived as sounds, naming the major anatomical components in the ear and the brain that facilitate this process.

5. Explain how tactile impulses travel from the skin to the nervous system. Are there differences in the pathways for touch, pressure, temperature, and pain? What are the principal brain areas that interpret tactile sensations?

6. What are the key anatomical and neural structures that enable us to smell? How does olfactory transduction take place? What role does the limbic system play in the perception of odors?

7. What does the phylogenetic tree depicting the proportion and placement of sensory cortical areas tell us about the evolution of sensation and perception in mammals?

CRITICAL-THINKING QUESTIONS

1. If you had to go through life without one of the major sensory abilities (i.e., vision, hearing, touch, or smell), which one would you give up? Explain your answer, citing anatomical and physiological details provided in this chapter.

2. Considering the close associations between olfaction and emotions, do you think the popular practice of aromatherapy has scientific validity in promoting health and well-being? Why or why not? How might you design an experiment to evaluate this claim?

3. Imagine that scientists can develop a clinical application that endows humans with "uber" sensory abilities—the ability to see like a hawk, hear like a bat, feel like a raccoon, or smell like a rat. What neurological and technological challenges would have to be met to develop such an application? What are the ethical implications?

Movement

The Frozen Addicts

In the summer of 1982, six individuals found themselves in emergency rooms in the San Jose, California, area with odd symptoms. Although these patients were young adults, they were "frozen" as if they had advanced Parkinson's disease, a degenerative disorder that limits movement and typically affects older individuals. In these mysterious cases, the movement restriction resulted in complete paralysis. When the neurologist Bill Langston met his first patient, George Carillo, he saw a young man propped up in bed with his arms in an awkward position as if he had suddenly frozen while making a gesture. When Langston held George's arms out in front of him and let go, they stayed in that position.

Doctors had no clues about the cause of George's condition and no way to obtain a medical history. A week later, someone gave George a pencil and paper to see whether he could move his fingers. George finally wrote his name and, after a half hour, a few more sentences:

> I'm not sure what is happening to me. I only know I can't function normally. I can't move right. I know what I want to do. It just won't come out right. (Langston & Palfreman, 1995, p. 19)

George then wrote that his girlfriend was also experiencing the same symptoms. When asked whether they had taken any medication, he wrote, "heroin." Over the next several days, four additional heroin users exhibited the same paralysis symptoms. Although heroin is associated with many health risks, becoming frozen was not one of them. This prompted a press conference warning the public to go to the hospital immediately if they developed paralysis symptoms following heroin use.

Behind the Scenes

When the police searched George's apartment, they found what appeared to be heroin. As Langston and his colleagues waited for the lab results on the identity of the substance, they decided to give the frozen patients the drug **L-DOPA (L-3, 4-dihydroxyphenylalanine)**. The drug is used to treat Parkinson's disease by increasing levels of dopamine in patients experiencing deficits in this essential neurotransmitter. Within only a few hours, the frozen patients regained their movement—and emotionally conveyed what it was like to be trapped in their motionless bodies.

The lab results revealed that the samples were a "designer" analogue of the narcotic pain medicine Demerol (meperidine). The toxic substance in the "heroin" was 1-methyl-4-phenyl-1,2,3,6-tetrahydropyridine (MPTP). Although MPTP had less severe effects in rats than in humans, it became evident in subsequent research with monkeys that MPTP attacked the cells of the substantia nigra (a brain area that produces dopamine), producing a form of Parkinson's disease. Ironically, the MPTP tragedy prompted research in primates that led to the production of a clinically relevant model for Parkinson's disease (Chiueh et al., 1984; Porras, Li, & Bezard, 2012).

But was L-DOPA a cure-all for the San Jose frozen patients? Unfortunately, L-DOPA worked for only about a year before patients became sensitized to it, exhibiting increased involuntary movements as well as hallucinations. At this point, the work of the Swedish neuroscientist Anders Björklund, who had experimented with the transplantation of rodent fetal cells in the substantia nigra as a treatment for Parkinson's disease, came to the attention of the investigators.

Typically, researchers focus on rat and nonhuman primate models before moving to clinical studies of human patients. In this case, research provided evidence that the transplantation of developing dopaminergic neurons from a fetus into an adult host brain of the same species increases the chances of the cells surviving and maturing into dopamine-producing cells in the adult host brain (Björklund et al., 2003). Because the San Jose patients were still young, researchers believed they might be candidates for Björklund's fetal transplant surgery. If the treatment succeeded in these patients, it was possible that their brains would be responsive enough to the new dopamine-producing brain tissue that they would be cured of drug-induced Parkinson's disease.

George Carillo was the first patient to travel to Sweden for this experimental surgery. Every two weeks, Langston evaluated George. Subtle improvements became apparent approximately a year following the surgery. Several months later, George was walking with a natural arm swing, and more natural facial expressions began to return (see Figure 7A). With such encouraging results, two more patients underwent the surgery with comparable improvements. Langston reported that George enjoyed relief from Parkinson's

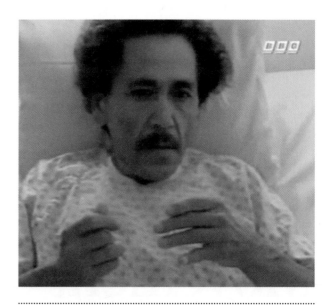

FIGURE 7A George Carillo. After consuming an altered "designer" form of heroin that was toxic to the substantia nigra, Carillo exhibited a statuelike pose.

symptoms until his death in 2011 (personal communication, July 11, 2012).

Although the fetal transplant surgery appeared to successfully treat the symptoms of these patients, subsequent clinical trials demonstrated individual differences in the patients' recovery rates (Barker, Barrett, Mason, & Bjorklund, 2013). Moreover, ethical questions about the use of fetal tissue led to political controversy. For these reasons, researchers have also considered the use of existing lines of human stem cells and fetal cells of animals such as pigs for this type of surgery (Bjorklund et al., 2003). We will return to the subject of Parkinson's disease treatment later in the chapter. ▶

After hearing that you are taking a "brain" course, suppose your roommate asks you what the brain's function is. What is your answer? If you are like many people, you will state that the brain's purpose is to allow us to carry out some type of cognitive function: to think, communicate, assess, perceive, evaluate, reflect, sympathize, and experience the moment.

According to Daniel Wolpert, a neuroscientist at Cambridge University, the brain exists to produce movements. He suggests that movement is the only way to affect the world around us. Even talking and breathing require muscular contractions. Consider the sea squirt (Figure 7.1). This animal is born with a nervous system and swims around as a juvenile searching for a rock to become its permanent home. Once it finds a home, however, and it no longer needs to move, the sea squirt digests its own nervous system (Wolpert, 2009).

Although contemporary robotics is sophisticated, human cognitive functions (e.g., those used in playing chess)

FIGURE 7.1 Brainless sea squirt. Once the sea squirt locates a home and no longer needs to move, it digests its own nervous system.

are much easier for robots to replicate than are motor functions. Among the most sophisticated dexterous tasks that robots have achieved include the simple tasks of unscrewing a cap from a bottle and pouring the bottle's contents into a cup (Figure 7.2a). Compare this type of task with the children's cup-stacking competition pictured in Figure 7.2b, in which contestants stack plastic cups into pyramid configurations in a matter of seconds. The remarkable sensory, motor, and cognitive integration executed at such a fast pace in these children confirms that robotics has a long way to go before it approaches the complexity of the human brain.

The mechanisms built into the human brain, spinal cord, and muscles enable us to perform impressive feats. Considering that we have approximately 600 muscles that control more than 200 joints, the fact that many of us move throughout our lives with little effort is indeed impressive. Although simple in nature, the ability to consistently exhibit predictable movements in the context of changing conditions is highly valued

(a)

(b)

FIGURE 7.2 Complex movements. (a) The most advanced robot can pour a liquid into a glass. (b) In contrast, even children can perform far more intricate movements, like quickly stacking cups.

in our society. Consider golf, for example. If an individual can hit a ball into a hole with consistency, minimalizing the effects of wind, crowd noises, and varying golf course conditions, our society rewards that person with millions of dollars. Other professional sports, including team sports such as basketball in which athletes *collectively* use their motor systems to move a ball into a net, indicate just how much humans value movement (D. W. Franklin & Wolpert, 2011).

Movement Basics

Although some may argue that the brain has purposes beyond generating movement, movement does begin in the brain. This section explores how the brain, spinal cord, and muscles enable us to move.

The Brain and Spinal Cord

The brain and the spinal cord coordinate the many neural components that activate movement. These key areas appear throughout the CNS, from the most dorsal cortical area to relevant gray matter areas in the most caudal section of the spinal cord.

The Motor Cortex. During the 19th century, when scientists sought to localize function in the brain, the work of the German physiologists Gustav Fritsch and Eduard Hitzig supported a certain degree of specificity in the brain. When Fritsch and Hitzig stimulated small areas of the cortex of conscious dogs, they found that certain areas, when stimulated, produced specific movements in the dogs. These areas were generally located in the front of the dogs' brains. The British neurologist and physiologist Sir David Ferrier found specific motor areas of the brain in monkeys. In the mid-20th century, the neurosurgeon Wilder Penfield stimulated the cortex of his human patients undergoing brain surgery (who remained conscious during the surgery) and mapped out the motor and sensory cortical areas.

Penfield's work culminated in the now famous **motor homunculus** (literally, "little man") depicting the proportion of motor cortex areas devoted to certain body parts (Figure 7.3). Known for his work mapping the brain, Penfield contributed to the knowledge of how specific cortical areas were involved with specific movements (Murray, 1983). However, as this chapter will explain, Penfield's research literally only scratched the (cortical) surface because many subcortical areas (as well as additional cortical areas) also play critical roles in movement.

Generally, activation of specific areas of the motor cortex accompanies voluntary control of corresponding muscle groups in your body. Thus, a specific area of the motor cortex is activated before you execute a movement such as moving your hand. Note the order of body parts represented on the

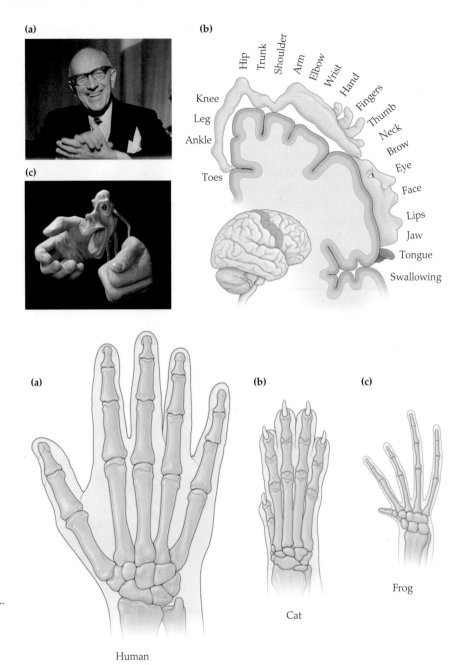

FIGURE 7.3 **Motor cortex.** (a) Dr. Wilder Penfield's work as a neurosurgeon identified the cortical strip known as the motor cortex involved in movement. (b) Specific areas of the motor cortex control specific body areas, with the space devoted to each area representing the degree of motor control for each area. (c) The motor homunculus illustrates the amount of control the motor cortex has over each body area.

FIGURE 7.4 **A common hand.** The hands of (a) a human, (b) a cat, and (c) a frog all share the same anatomical plan, with five fingers attached to bones at the wrist.

motor cortex. Feet are toward the top, and the mouth is on the ventral section of the motor cortex. Additionally, the size of the cortical area devoted to a certain body area relates to the body area's function, rather than its size. For example, the areas representing the hands and mouth require a greater area of motor cortex than the larger surface areas representing the legs and back.

The area of the motor cortex devoted to hand movement suggests that the hand is one of the brain's most valued instruments for interacting with the world. In an article in *National Geographic* magazine, science writer Carl Zimmer stated that "the hand is where the mind meets the world" (2012, May, p. 98). As seen in Figure 7.4, although a similar template has been conserved in nature for hands and forepaws, the human hand is far more complex. The thumb, for

example, is controlled by nine muscles. The human wrist consists of a cluster of bones and ligaments amid an intricate collection of blood vessels and nerves. Such neural and muscular control leads to a wide variety of uses for human hands, ranging from building a miniature dollhouse to throwing a curveball (Zimmer, 2012).

Corticospinal Tracts. As neurons in specific areas of the motor cortex are activated, their axons travel to the spinal cord via **corticospinal tracts**. In the mid-19th century, these tracts were identified (see Figure 7.5), although their functional relationships remained unclear until several decades later.

Today, we know that this motor system includes two separate tracts: the **lateral corticospinal tract** and the

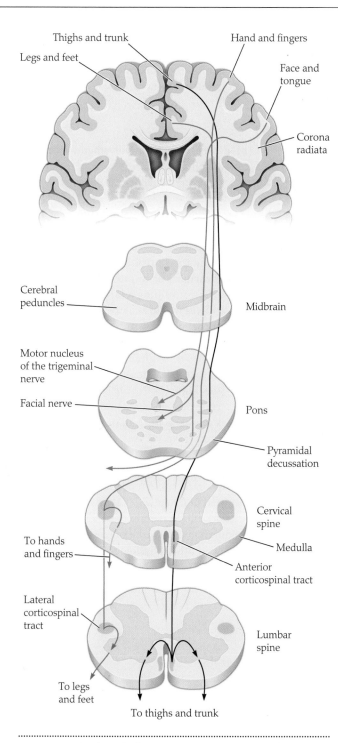

FIGURE 7.5 Corticospinal tracts. The corticospinal tracts extend from the motor cortex to the spinal cord on their way to activating muscles involved in the desired movement.

anterior corticospinal tract (sometimes called the ventral corticospinal tract). Most of the cells in the corticospinal tracts originate in layer V of the primary cortex, where **Betz cells**, a form of pyramidal cells, are located. Traveling through the **corona radiata** (a projection of nerve fibers that connect the cerebral cortex to the brainstem and spinal cord) to the

brain's lateral ventricle, the fibers continue to descend to the midbrain, pons, and anterior medulla, forming the **medullary pyramids**. In the caudal section of the medulla, a majority of the fibers (approximately 80%) in the pyramidal area cross over to the other (contralateral) side of the body, whereas the remaining fibers stay on the same (ipsilateral) side. The contralateral fibers from the lateral corticospinal tract play an integral role in moving the distal limbs and digits. The ipsilateral fibers form the anterior corticospinal tract and control the muscles of the core or midline of the body. Thus, the corticospinal tract essentially consists of bundles of axons extending from the cell bodies in the motor cortex, sometimes referred to as **upper motor neurons**. Essential motor neurons also exist in the gray matter of the spinal cord (see Figure 7.6), specifically arising from the ventral horn. These are the **lower motor neurons** (Ai Masri, 2011).

The corticospinal tracts are essential for voluntary movement. As a child learns to play the piano, Betz cells in the arm and finger areas of the primary motor cortex are activated. The Betz cells send their axons downward through the brain, crossing over at the medulla to form part of the lateral corticospinal tract, which will ultimately activate the appropriate finger muscles to press the keys. The anterior corticospinal tract will control the muscles maintaining the child's posture as he leans forward at certain times during the performance to be closer to the keys. The **decussation**, or crossing over, of the corticospinal tracts in the medulla explains why individuals who suffer a stroke or experience trauma in one side of the brain experience paralysis on the opposite side of the body.

The Spinal Cord. Another essential player in movement, the spinal cord is the transit system for motor neural signals. As discussed in Chapter 2, the spinal cord, encased in protective

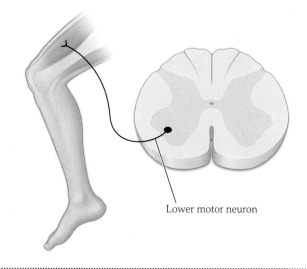

FIGURE 7.6 Lower motor neurons. Motor neurons located in the anterior horn of the spinal cord activate the movement of specific muscles.

vertebrae and meninges, is divided into several sections that direct neural traffic to specific body areas (dermatomes) via the 31 spinal nerves. When part of a city's transit system shuts down for a maintenance issue, accident, or safety threat, access to that part of the city is blocked. This diminishes the city's functions until service is restored. Similarly, when neural transmission in the spinal cord is disrupted, access to the body's muscles is also disrupted, resulting in either diminished capacity or a shutdown of movement.

Extending from the gray matter in the spinal cord are the dorsal and ventral roots making up each spinal nerve (Figure 7.7). As you process sensory information, such as feeling a sharp edge on the surface of a glass, that sensory message is relayed to the spinal cord via the dorsal root of the spinal nerve, which, in this case, is carrying information from the fingers. Once that information arrives in the gray matter of the spinal cord, interneurons connect the information to the appropriate **α motor neurons** in the ventral horn of the gray matter. The axons of these α motor neurons exit the spinal cord via the ventral roots as they travel to the appropriate finger muscles, allowing you to quickly remove the finger from the sharp surface. Thus, the dorsal roots carry sensory, or *afferent*, information, and the ventral roots carry motor, or *efferent*, information.

Have you ever touched a hot stove and jumped back so quickly that you really did not know what had happened? This suggests that your behavior was under the control of **reflexes** outside of the domain of your brain's sophisticated cortex. Eventually, your eyes communicate to the occipital cortex that your finger touched the stove. Given this information and the real-time perception of pain in the finger, cortical neural networks eventually inform you of exactly what happened. The delay is justified when you consider the consequences of having to wait until the appropriate brain circuits informed the appropriate muscle circuits. Your hand would be severely injured! This example illustrates how, for basic adaptive responses, very fast neural networks are

engaged. The benefit, obviously, is speed. The cost is that you have little control over these responses once they are triggered. Figure 7.8 illustrates the fundamental **reflex arc** that occurs when a person touches something hot.

Muscles

Regardless of the degree of brain involvement, all movement requires muscle contraction. This section focuses on muscles and how they are controlled by the nervous system.

Muscle Types. Generally, there are three types of muscles. Both the **cardiac muscle** located in the heart and the **smooth muscles** located in organs such as the stomach are considered under involuntary control. You do not have to remember to initiate a heartbeat or to move your food along your digestive tract after consuming a large meal. Can you imagine how short our lives would be if we were responsible for these life-sustaining details?

Unlike the cardiac muscle and smooth muscles, the **skeletal (striatal) muscles** throughout the body depend on your own volition to be activated, making these the body's voluntary muscles (see Figure 7.9). Of course, there are exceptions to most rules in behavioral neuroscience. For example, the muscles allowing us to maintain our posture while engaging in various tasks are skeletal, but often under involuntary control.

Research in the field of **biofeedback** suggests that with training, humans can control more movement than we typically do. As you learned in Chapter 2, David Blaine learned to control his breathing and heart rate to be able to hold his breath for extreme durations. Research suggests that patients can be trained to control other physiological responses that

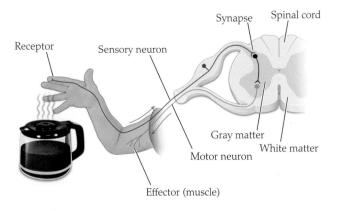

FIGURE 7.8 Reflex arc. When the person's hand touches the hot coffeepot, afferent pain messages are sent to the dorsal root of the spinal nerve and enter the gray matter of the spinal cord. Once the information is aligned with the appropriate efferent neuron, the arm muscle is stimulated, such that the hand is quickly removed from the hot surface before further damage is done. Because these neural processes happen below the level of the brain, the reflex response occurs before the person is fully aware of the situation.

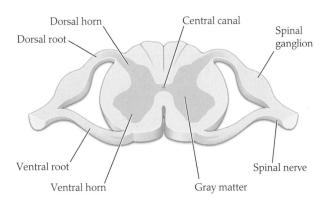

FIGURE 7.7 Spinal cord anatomy. The components of the spinal cord and extending nerves can be viewed in a cross-section of the spinal cord.

FIGURE 7.9 **Muscle types.** During gardening, the cardiac and smooth muscles are under involuntary control as they regulate heart rate and facilitate the digestion of breakfast, respectively, whereas the skeletal muscles in the arm are voluntarily moved in different directions as plants are pruned and new seeds are planted.

are typically viewed as involuntary, such as blood pressure and the relaxation of their internal anal sphincter (Engel, 2003). As research progresses in this field, it will be interesting to determine how the boundaries between involuntary and voluntary movement can be modified with intensive training.

Regardless of whether a movement is voluntary or involuntary, motor responses require an efferent (motor) nerve to contract a muscle. Skeletal muscle tissue consists of two types of fibers, **extrafusal fibers** (muscle cells that contract to shorten a muscle) and **intrafusal fibers** (muscle cells that detect changes in muscle length). The **motor unit** consists of the α motor neuron in the ventral horn of the gray matter of the spinal cord, its axon, and the extrafusal muscle fibers it innervates (Figure 7.10a). Motor units with fewer innervated muscle fibers are characteristic of muscles over which you have more control (such as your fingers), whereas motor units with greater numbers of innervated muscle fibers by a single axon are typical of muscles over which you have little fine control (such as your back muscles).

Generally, the information that you learned in Chapter 3 about neuron–neuron synapses applies to the neuron–muscle synapses, or junctions. However, we will need a few new terms. The **neuromuscular junction** is the synapse formed when the axon terminal of a motor neuron positions itself in a section of the extrafusal muscle fiber known as the **motor end plate**, an area that is highly excitable and appropriate for the initiation of action potentials (see Figure 7.10b). In each neuromuscular junction, acetylcholine is the neurotransmitter released. Recall from Chapter 4 that toxins that block acetylcholine result in paralysis and often death.

Sensory Feedback in Muscles. For muscles to function in a coordinated and effective fashion, the nervous system requires constant feedback about their status. As shown in Figure 7.11, the biceps flex the arm and the triceps extend the arm. These muscles are known as **antagonistic muscles** because they produce actions that are opposite of one another. If the nervous system detects excessive contraction, it may compensate by activating the antagonist muscle.

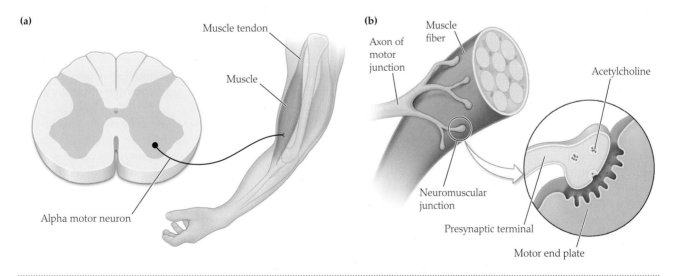

FIGURE 7.10 **Motor unit anatomy and neuromuscular junction.** (a) Axons of α motor neurons in the spinal cord extend to the muscle fiber. (b) Neurotransmitter molecules are released from the synaptic vesicles, travel across the synaptic cleft, and activate specific receptors on the postsynaptic membrane (motor end plate).

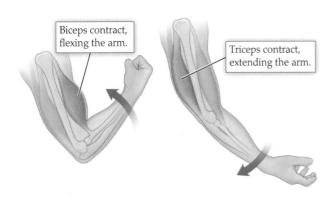

FIGURE 7.11 Antagonistic arm muscles. Biceps and triceps enable the arm to move toward and away from the body.

The tendons that connect the bone to the muscle are also monitored so that the muscle does not contract so much that the tendon is ripped from the bone. The stretching of muscles must also be monitored so that damage is not produced from extending the muscle too much.

Sensory receptors (in this case, muscle sensory receptors) are strategically located in the muscles and tendons to monitor the muscle's activity. The ability to sense the position, orientation, and movement of one's own body is known as **proprioception** and is necessary to maintain a working muscular system. Using the field sobriety test, police officers often assess a driver's proprioception by asking the driver to take the *walk-and-turn test*. In this test, the driver takes nine steps heel-to-toe along a straight line. Then, the driver turns on one foot and returns in the exact same manner in the opposite direction. To perform well on this test, one must use multiple parts of the brain, including parts that help one to maintain balance. Because alcohol impairs motor coordination, an individual who is intoxicated finds this task quite challenging and shows deficits such as failing to touch heel-to-toe and losing balance.

To provide sensory feedback to the muscles, the **muscle spindle** has receptor endings extending from **γ motor neurons** in the spinal cord that wrap around the intrafusal muscle fibers. If the muscle is stretched, this intrafusal muscle sensory organ is also stretched and communicates this status via the afferent spinal root to the nervous system. When the nervous system receives the message, the movement can be corrected by the stimulation of an antagonist muscle or the inhibition of the stretch to relieve the muscle before it rips into two pieces (see Figure 7.12).

If the muscle contracts excessively, another sensory organ, the **Golgi tendon organ**, sends a message back to the nervous system to initiate appropriate compensatory action. This prevents the muscle from contracting so far as to rip itself from the bone. As Figure 7.12 shows, the Golgi tendon organs are located in the tendons. The muscle spindles detect excessive stretch in the muscle, and the Golgi tendon organs detect excessive contraction.

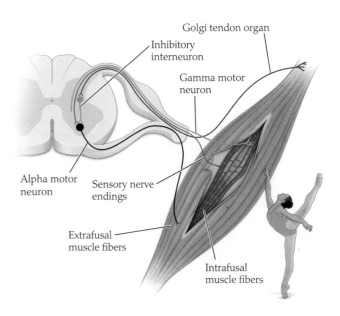

FIGURE 7.12 Muscle spindles and tendon organs. Elaborate sensory systems monitor and guide movement to protect against muscles tearing and ripping. The muscle spindle organ detects and inhibits muscle extension via gamma motor neurons, sensory nerve endings, and intrafusal muscle fibers, as shown in this image. The Golgi tendon organ detects and inhibits excessive muscle contraction.

These counterbalancing actions of the nervous system are evident in a fundamental neurological test to determine the efficiency of the **monosynaptic spinal reflex**, determined by the familiar medical assessment known as the knee-jerk test. In this test, the doctor asks the patient to let his leg hang free. When the doctor taps the patient's patellar tendon with a small rubber hammer, the healthy nervous system will detect an extra stretch of the quadriceps as the manipulated tendon hit by the hammer extends the muscle ever so slightly. Accordingly, the muscle spindle sends information via the afferent root of the appropriate spinal nerve, leading to activation of the efferent α nerve fibers to contract the muscle. In this case, the contraction of the quadriceps muscle, accompanied by the lower leg lifting up with a swift kick, is just what the doctor ordered to determine the health of the patient's nerve fibers.

Our discussion of movement thus far has focused on very simple movements—reflexes and basic movements that do not require much thought. Even the more complex movement of walking is considered by some a chain of reflexes, requiring little thought. Indeed, locomotion became more complex as water-based vertebrates morphed into land-based animals. Researchers have proposed that networks of neurons that spontaneously generate patterns of activity such as walking are under the control of **central pattern generators** (Goulding, 2009). This explains how humans can walk and talk to someone, walk and read text messages, or even walk and chew gum at the same time. Land-based locomotion, however, requires more sensory feedback, as well as proprioception, than was necessary for our swimming-based ancestors. Sensory feedback helps to guide and shape these default motor patterns when necessary, such as when you are walking on a winding path or need to increase your speed to catch up with a friend.

Complex Movement

As I write this chapter, I am typing on my keyboard, flipping through folders containing my constantly expanding collection of articles on movement, and running back and forth to our departmental kitchen for coffee breaks. These movements are not that impressive—we engage in similar types of activity all day, every day—but they require more brain territory than the primary motor cortex, the corticospinal tracts, and the spinal cord.

Our complete behavioral repertoires consist of much more complex movements than reflexes and movement patterns such as walking. Humans use their muscles to build machines, create art, and cook fabulous meals—motor responses that require more brain areas than reflexive movements require. Further, athletes must be able to alter rehearsed movements instantaneously to react to constantly changing positions of both team players and opponents. It takes a considerable amount of brain to initiate, coordinate, and guide these complex movements. In this section, we will discuss the brain areas that perform these impressive motor feats.

Cortical Areas

Other than the primary motor cortex, a cluster of cortical areas known as the **supplementary motor complex** helps to guide the execution of complex behavior. Specifically, this complex consists primarily of the **supplementary motor area (SMA)** and the **presupplementary motor area (pre-SMA)**. Generally, this cortical complex plays a key role in self-initiated (voluntary) movements as opposed to responses triggered by external events (Nachev, Kennard, & Husain, 2008).

Both the SMA and the pre-SMA are located in the dorsomedial frontal cortex in humans (Figure 7.13). The **premotor cortex** is located ventral to the supplementary motor complex, positioned directly in front of the primary motor cortex.

To learn more about the specific function of cortical motor areas, researchers have used sophisticated recording, stimulation (e.g., transcranial magnetic stimulation), and imaging techniques over the past several decades (Chouinard & Paus, 2010; Nachev, Kennard, & Husain, 2008). For example, an early study using PET indicated that the SMA is activated when a person simply imagines himself performing a complex motor task, such as the complex finger movement sequences executed by musicians playing keyboard or string instruments (Roland, Larsen, Lassen, & Skinhoj, 1980). When the task involves more executive control, such as deciding to suppress a response (response inhibition) or switch tasks, perhaps while conducting a difficult

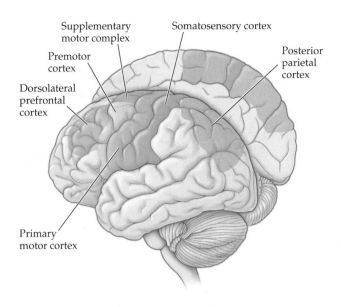

FIGURE 7.13 Cortical areas involved in movement. Several cortical areas contribute to the initiation and successful execution of movement necessary for the completion of complex tasks.

neurosurgery with constantly changing conditions, the pre-SMA is activated (Chouinard & Paus, 2010). For skills that are less dependent on self-initiation and more dependent on external guidance of movement, such as using a template to trace an image, the premotor cortical areas are more activated (Halsband, Matsuzaka, & Tanji, 1994).

How are these cortical areas involved when a person is learning fast, complex skills such as juggling? fMRI and PET studies suggest that, early on, while you are still dropping as many balls as you are catching, the DLPFC, primary motor cortex, and pre-SMA are involved. As you become more proficient at the task, however, activity in these areas decreases (Dayan & Cohen, 2011). Single-cell recording in monkeys has revealed similar results. For example, researchers found evidence that the pre-SMA was involved in monitoring performance of the monkeys early in task acquisition but was less important once the task had been sufficiently learned (Shima & Tanji, 2006). Following the initial learning, increased activity was observed in the premotor cortex and SMA. As the brain's mechanisms that enable neuroplasticity led to learning of the task, activation of these areas diminished. Similarly, in humans, once a person has learned to juggle, less cortical area appears to be necessary to initiate and monitor the newly learned task (see Figure 7.14; Dayan & Cohen, 2011). Of course, juggling is a visual task as well. In the early stages of learning to juggle, juggling is more dependent on a person's visual perception than it is after the person masters the skill. Seasoned jugglers typically focus on the audience while juggling, since they no longer need to watch the balls.

As you learn to juggle and after you master the skill, the cortical areas regulating the planning and sequencing of

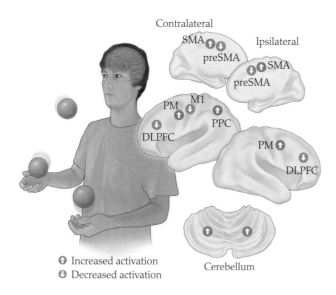

Contralateral

SMA
preSMA
Ipsilateral
SMA
preSMA
PM M1
DLPFC
PPC
PM
DLPFC

⬆ Increased activation
⬇ Decreased activation

Cerebellum

FIGURE 7.14 **Skilled motor learning.** Several brain areas are recruited when a person begins to learn a task involving skilled movements.

events require help from subcortical areas. Coordination, muscle tone, balance, and precise timing of the responses are regulated by the basal ganglia and cerebellum, discussed in the next two sections.

The Basal Ganglia

The basal ganglia are a collection of interconnected nuclei that surround the thalamus and regulate movement (Chapter 2). As shown in Figure 7.15, among the primary components of the basal ganglia are the **caudate nucleus**, **putamen**, and **globus pallidus**. The nearby **substantia**

nigra communicates with these structures but is not universally considered part of the basal ganglia. The caudate and putamen are often collectively referred to as the **striatum**. Generally, the basal ganglia communicate regularly with the cerebral cortex to contribute to the efficient execution of appropriate movements. In the previous juggling example, however, the basal ganglia facilitate the acquisition of the movement sequencing and control the height and direction of the juggler's ball throwing.

In the past, the basal ganglia have been viewed simply as a "go-through" system, creating a motor loop in which these structures modulate the information from the cortical areas discussed above and then send it back to the cortex for final movement execution. More recently, however, researchers have recognized that, beyond the motor loop, the basal ganglia process information from several surrounding brain areas. In addition, the components of the basal ganglia monitor internal feedback from within the basal ganglia. It is now clear that the functions associated with the basal ganglia extend well beyond movement regulation. Focusing on cortical areas serving as projection destinations for the basal ganglia, research suggests that the basal ganglia are also involved in learning and habit formation, attention, rewarded behaviors, and emotional responses (Obeso et al., 2008). Thus, the basal ganglia provide strong evidence that movement is a core component of a majority of responses in our behavioral repertoire.

We have learned much about the function of the basal ganglia by observing the movements and brain functions characteristic of Parkinson's disease. This disease, which we will examine later in the chapter, disrupts the basal ganglia (Obeso et al., 2008). In healthy individuals, output from the globus pallidus typically inhibits unwanted movements. However, when there is too much output of the basal ganglia,

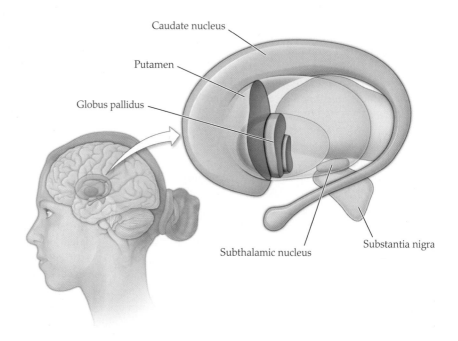

Caudate nucleus

Putamen

Globus pallidus

Subthalamic nucleus

Substantia nigra

FIGURE 7.15 **Basal ganglia.** A collection of brain structures contributes to the basal ganglia and communicates with the cortex to facilitate the successful execution of movements.

then the projections to the cortex become too inhibited. This typically leads to problems initiating movement. Additionally, the basal ganglia structures become hyperresponsive to peripheral input. This makes it more difficult to filter through the most salient input to select among competing motor programs, such as putting your empty glass in the sink rather than the refrigerator (Leblois, Boraud, Meissner, Bergman, & Hansel, 2006; Rubchinsky, Kopell, & Sigvardt, 2003).

The Olympics present wonderful displays of movement in a variety of sports. One event that requires extreme motor memory is platform diving (see Figure 7.16). In this sport, the diver stands on a stationary platform of various regulated heights and, after jumping, performs a series of precisely timed acrobatic movements before entering the water in the perfect vertical position. With little sensory feedback available (other than air and time!) to guide the movements in the acrobatic sequence of responses that unfold between leaving the platform and entering the water, the athlete relies on the basal ganglia to execute the solidified motor memories that have been consolidated throughout years of practice. Once these movement memories (informally referred to as "muscle memory") are formed, they become similar to reflexes in that they are resistant to interference and can be retrieved after long periods of time without training. The popular adage emphasizing how one never forgets how to ride a bicycle is a testament to just how well the basal ganglia, in concert with other brain areas, forms long-lasting motor memories. (More about the creation and persistence of several types of memories will be discussed in Chapter 12.)

Why is it important for certain activities that we perform repeatedly to become "automatic?" Once these memories are formed, the individual can perform a secondary task; thus, the basal ganglia enable us to multitask (Doyon et al., 2009). Although many of our motor skills, such as driving, require some sensory feedback, most people can carry on a conversation while driving. However, regardless of one's degree of driving skill, sensory feedback is critical to provide information about cars stopping in front of the driver or sharp bends in the road. Consequently, tasks that minimize or distract a driver from this feedback, such as cell phone use or—even worse—texting, will increase the chances of the driver making a fatal error. Statistics indicate that 28% of all car crashes are caused by either talking or texting on cell phones (Halsey, 2010).

Do you have any habits? As we learn to perform certain tasks in certain ways, habits are thought to emerge to continue to automate the selection and activation of specific movements and free up brain processing for more important tasks. Although these habits are efficient in many ways, our brains relinquish valuable real-time processing of the environment if they rely on too many habitual responses, even those that have served us well in the past. Habits can become such strong responses that a person engages in them repeatedly without conscious awareness. Adjusting one's hair may be important to keep it from obstructing one's view, but can be distracting if done repeatedly during a job interview. According to Ann Graybiel, a neuroscientist at the Massachusetts Institute of Technology who has extensively studied the role of the basal ganglia in habit formation, "Whether good, bad, or neutral, habits can have great power over our behavior" (Graybiel, 2008, p. 360). Thus, although habits become automatic, it is important to monitor our habitual responses to ensure that they are being used effectively and not repeated excessively.

Research indicates that both the striatum and the frontal cortex play a role in habit formation (Graybiel, 2008). The brain's preparedness to form habits may contribute to dysfunctional behavior such as addiction and obsessive–compulsive disorder. This predisposition may also extend to other responses such as cultural/religious rituals and

FIGURE 7.16 Movements requiring motor memory. Platform divers must develop extreme motor memory to successfully perform the timed acrobatic movements necessary to obtain high scores in competition.

superstitious behaviors. The famous baseball player Wade Boggs ate chicken before each game and drew a specific symbol in the dirt before each at-bat. Many athletes are notorious for exhibiting ritualistic responses, such as eating certain foods on the day of the game, touching their gloves and hat in a certain order prior to batting (in the case of baseball players), or even growing facial hair (Figure 7.17). If these responses facilitate a desired outcome and do not interrupt other responses, they are likely more adaptive than disruptive. Indeed, superstitious behavior across the animal kingdom is often an adaptive response enhancing animals' attention toward cause and effect, or contingencies, in their surrounding environment (Foster & Kokko, 2009).

Although the basal ganglia allow us to operate in a default mode at times, we must pay close attention to our changing environment to survive. The next section discusses the role of the cerebellum in the acquisition and maintenance of movement patterns.

The Cerebellum

In our tour of brain areas involved in movement, we have traveled from multiple areas of the cerebral cortex to the expansive area of structures known as the basal ganglia, as well as to the spinal cord and the nerves extending throughout the entire body to the muscles. The cerebellum, the large structure located at the base of the skull that makes up approximately 10% of the brain's total volume, is the last stop on our tour of major brain areas involved in movement. As described in Chapter 2, the cerebellum contains about four times more neurons than the more recently evolved cerebral cortex (Herculano-Houzel, 2010). As you now appreciate, the massive amount of brain territory devoted to moving the body suggests that movement is indeed a top priority of our nervous systems.

The cerebellum is divided into several functional sections including the vermis, cerebellar hemispheres, and **flocculonodular lobe**. The oldest part of the cerebellum is likely the flocculonodular lobe; it is thought to support fundamental motor functions such as the maintenance of balance and posture. Muscle tone is thought to be regulated by the **vermis** and the **lateral cerebellar hemispheres**, which contain the deep nuclei such as the **dentate nucleus** that communicates in a structured, maplike fashion with the various motor and nonmotor areas of the cerebral cortex. The **cerebellar peduncles** serve as a neural communication transit system to other brain areas such as the cerebral cortex, providing opportunities for the cerebellum to play a role in cognitive functions as well (see Figure 7.18; Hoppenbrouwers, Schutter, Fitzgerald, Chen, & Daskalakis, 2008).

The cerebellum plays an essential role in movement coordination, balance, and muscle tone (Ghez, 1991). Although the cerebellum cannot initiate movement on its own, it receives feedback related to the programming and execution of movement sequences and uses this internal and external feedback to monitor and modify movements as they occur. The extensive connections between the cerebellum and basal ganglia allow for continual adjustment of movement patterns (Hoshi, Tremblay, Feger, Carras, & Strick, 2005).

Although the cerebellum has been associated primarily with motor control over the past century, evidence has also pointed toward the cerebellum's involvement in nonmotor functions (Tedesco et al., 2011). For example, clinical observations of patients with cerebellar lesions have identified nonmotor symptoms such as diminished pleasure, anxiety, repetition of certain responses, and aggression

FIGURE 7.17 **Ritualistic response.** Kendrys Morales of the Kansas City Royals exhibits a common ritual known as the "playoff beard." If his team keeps winning during the playoffs, he cannot shave. In 2015, the Royals won the World Series.

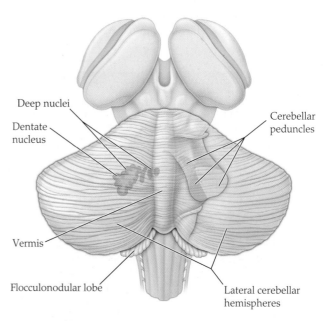

FIGURE 7.18 **Cerebellum anatomy.** Similar to the cerebral hemispheres, the cerebellum has two hemispheres, a convoluted cortex and deep nuclei.

(Schmahmann, Weilburg, & Sherman, 2007). These cognitive and emotional characteristics are observed in psychiatric disorders such as depression, autism, and obsessive–compulsive disorder, implicating the cerebellum in various mental disorders (Hoppenbrouwers et al., 2008).

Further, building evidence confirming the emergence of cognitive deficits following cerebellar damage led Dr. Jeremy Schmahmann of Harvard Medical School and his colleagues to describe a new clinical disorder called the **cerebellar cognitive affective syndrome**. In one study, the charts of approximately 150 patients with various forms of cerebellar damage were analyzed to identify patterns of cognitive impairment. Among the most prevalent

effects were impairments in executive function, language, sequencing events, and visuospatial abilities (Tedesco et al., 2011). The extensive connections between the cerebellum and both sensorimotor and association areas of the cerebral cortex might explain the cerebellum's involvement in both movement and cognitive functions (Stoodley, Valera, & Schmahmann, 2012).

Research has produced several unexpected revelations about the function of the cerebellum. As seen in this chapter's "Context Matters," the cerebellum also plays a role in interpreting unexpected tactile stimulation, a unique somatosensory stimulation that results in the tickle sensation.

CONTEXT MATTERS

How the Brain Gets Tickled

Featured Study: Blakemore, S. J., Wolpert, D. M., & Frith, C. D. (1998). Central cancellation of self-produced tickle sensation. Nature Neuroscience, 1, 635–640.

Have you ever noticed that you cannot tickle yourself? You may flail wildly and laugh uncontrollably when another person gently strokes the bottom of your feet (Context Matters Figure 7.1), but when you generate the same strokes on your foot, there is no response at all.

Scientists were interested in how the brain responds when a person experiences a self-generated versus an other-generated tickle stimulus. To investigate this question, they used an experimental setup with a tactile stimulus device (see Context Matters Figure 7.2) and an fMRI scanner. Methodological limitations of the fMRI technique required the experimenters to develop a task involving minimum movement. Six young-adult subjects each underwent a series of fMRI scans during four experimental conditions. The independent variables were the presence of self-generated movement and the presence of tactile stimulation.

The experimental conditions were as follows:

CONTEXT MATTERS FIGURE 7.1 **Tickle response.** Tactile stimulation from another person results in the unique tickle response.

- Condition A: self-generated movements producing tactile stimulation (subjects moved the rod to produce tactile stimulation on their left palm);

- Condition B: self-generated movements without tactile stimulation (subjects moved the rod but did not experience any tactile stimulation);

- Condition C: externally produced tactile stimulation (the experimenter moved the tactile stimulus to produce tactile stimulation on subjects' left palm); and

- Condition D: no movement and no tactile stimulation (rest).

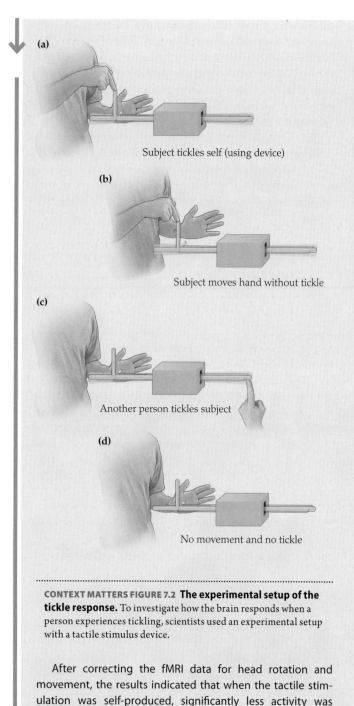

(a) Subject tickles self (using device)

(b) Subject moves hand without tickle

(c) Another person tickles subject

(d) No movement and no tickle

CONTEXT MATTERS FIGURE 7.2 **The experimental setup of the tickle response.** To investigate how the brain responds when a person experiences tickling, scientists used an experimental setup with a tactile stimulus device.

After correcting the fMRI data for head rotation and movement, the results indicated that when the tactile stimulation was self-produced, significantly less activity was observed in the somatosensory cortex, the anterior lobe of the cerebellum, and the anterior cingulate area of the frontal cortex than when the tactile stimulation was externally produced (Context Matters Figure 7.3). These findings supported previous evidence that the cerebellum plays a role in generating precise predictions of the sensory consequences resulting from various movement commands (Blakemore et al., 1998). For example, when you decide to stroke the bottom of your foot, your cerebellum predicts the resulting tactile sensation, resulting in less activation in the somatosensory cortex and anterior cingulate. A surprise tactile stimulus, however, cannot be canceled out by the anterior cerebellum, and the unintended event is marked with the rather curious responses that accompany tickling. The specific context of the person on the receiving end of a tickle stimulus has a dramatic impact on the brain and behavioral responses. That is, knowing that stimulation is self-directed results in less tickle sensation, whereas knowing that the tactile stimulation was not self-produced results in a more exaggerated tickle sensation.

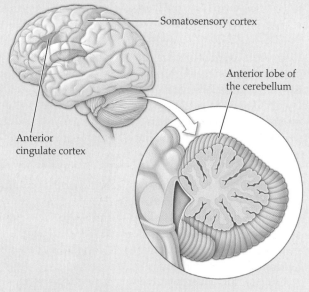

Somatosensory cortex

Anterior lobe of the cerebellum

Anterior cingulate cortex

CONTEXT MATTERS FIGURE 7.3 **Brain areas involved in the tickle response.** The results of the study indicated that when the tactile stimulation was self-produced, significantly less activity was observed in the somatosensory cortex, the anterior lobe of the cerebellum, and the anterior cingulate area of the frontal cortex than when the tactile stimulation was externally produced.

Adaptive Moves

If you have observed the movement trend known as *parkour*, you know the extreme agility and flexibility of the human movement system. Individuals trained in parkour navigate their urban environments by scaling walls, leaping great distances between building roofs, and hanging from lampposts (Figure 7.19; Wilkinson, 2007). Although I am certain these superhuman feats often land the followers of parkour in the emergency room, these movements seem more like those displayed by our distant ancestors than the movements of our contemporary daily lives. If humans can learn these movements, perhaps aspects of them helped our ancestors navigate the environment to escape from predators or other threats.

FIGURE 7.19 **Parkour form of complex movement.** Parkour showcases the flexibility of human movement.

Outside of the protected confines of a laboratory experiment, movement demands become exponentially more complex. Daniel Wolpert and his colleagues have emphasized the importance of **optimal actions** that minimize costs and maximize benefits. For example, in a hockey game, the goaltender must be in tune with his own movements as well as the uncertainty of the movements of opposing players attempting to shoot the puck into the net. Thus, in addition to monitoring his own 600 muscles and 200 joints to position himself in front of the net and impending puck, the goaltender must predict the movement of the opposing player in control of the puck, which is based on other players in pursuit of the approaching player. Sensory feedback in hockey games is muted to some extent by the noise of the crowd, the protective helmets worn, the fast pace of the players, and the unpredictable conditions of the ice. Considering the amount of uncertainty in such movement scenarios, it is amazing that humans perform as optimally as they do.

Bayesian decision theory presents a possible explanation of how a nervous system selects optimal actions for movement in an uncertain world. It involves applying probabilistic reasoning to make inferences based on uncertain circumstances (e.g., how fast will the hockey player approach the net, exactly when will he hit the puck, which direction will the puck go within the net?). Both past experiences and current likelihoods are factored into the Bayesian statistics to arrive at an optimal response choice (D. W. Franklin & Wolpert, 2011). Hence, according to this theory, your brain has been solving probability problems long before you consciously learned about them in your math class. We will revisit this decision-making process in Chapter 12.

Of course, even with our sophisticated calculations, movement errors often occur. Such mistakes happen especially when there are too many variables to accurately process (e.g., excessive crowd noise, changing conditions of the ice, unpredictability of opponent's ability) or a false belief

about a physical circumstance. If someone asks you to pick up a brick on a desk, you apply your past experience of the weight of a brick as you plan the movement required to retrieve the brick. If the brick, however, is actually a piece of Styrofoam painted like a brick, your arm will lift wildly in the air because the object is much lighter than anticipated. In this case, your experience with heavier bricks interfered with the motor system's assessment of the task, rendering the typically vigilant cerebellum unable to respond quickly enough to correct the misjudgment.

Aside from solving impressive real-life probability problems, the purpose of optimizing actions is to optimize survival including behaviors associated with reproduction, health, and regulation of movement during stressful or threatening times. Accordingly, this section of the chapter discusses three optimal actions, including the adaptive functions of having just the right dance moves, the factors enabling athletes to avoid choking under pressure, and the diffuse benefits of repetitive movement comprising exercise.

All the Right Moves

In the avian (bird) world, the male blue manakin spends up to 90% of its waking hours in a dancing duel with another male blue manakin (Figure 7.20). The blue manakin with the best moves wins the sexual attention of the female. Using multiple motor circuits in the brain, the moves must be synchronized, so timing and prediction are critical to winning the female's attention.

The skills required to capture the attention of the female blue manakin take years to perfect. When the male birds are about two years old, they begin practicing their dance moves, but it is not until about age eight that they become official apprentices to a senior expert dancer—dancing in duos for the female blue manakins. And only when the senior

FIGURE 7.20 **The blue manakin.** Precisely timed movements are required for the male manakin's dancing rituals, which are used to attract females.

dancer dies does the apprentice become a leader and obtain access to the females. Perfected dance moves are adaptive in the sense that they are associated with reproductive success. Although manakins have vividly colored feathers, observers have reported that their true colors are not revealed until they start dancing (Goymer, 2009).

What about humans? Does being an awkward dancer render human males childless as well? Obviously, compared with manakins, humans do not devote the same amount of time to perfecting their dancing skills. Yet, the U.K. anthropologist Nick Neave and his colleagues recently investigated the precise movements in human males to determine the types of moves that females found most attractive. To answer their research question, they brought males who were not professional dancers into the lab and, as awkward as it seems, instructed them to dance.

Before presenting their dance moves to the females, the researchers used 3-D motion capture technology to create computer-generated "avatars" to ensure that all dancers were equal in attractiveness; thus, only their dance moves would be evaluated by the female observers (see Figure 7.21). The dancers were subsequently divided into good dancers and bad dancers based on female evaluations, and the researchers used mathematical analysis techniques to identify key features of the movements that the females classified as most attractive. What were the most attractive moves? The speed and movement of the right knee was determined to be attractive as well as the variation in neck and back movements (Neave et al., 2010).

Other researchers have explored the question of why dance moves are a valid assessment of the value of a male mate in various species. After Charles Darwin suggested that both male ornaments (feathers, horns) and displays (courtship dances) evolved as a result of sexual selection by females, sexual selection has remained a dominant topic among animal behaviorists. Today, it is known that motor performance is widely used across the animal kingdom as a selection method for male mates. Motor performance, as displayed in courtship dances, reveals important information about the fitness of the male and suitability as a mate.

First, impressive dancing displays convey vigor, an animal's ability to energetically perform complex motor or challenging acts in a repeated fashion. More accurate evaluations are derived from having an opportunity to compare multiple males, as is the case with the blue manakin. Whereas physical vigor can be faked in online dating profiles, it cannot be faked in these marathon motor displays. Physical vigor may also provide clues about the male's entire functional genome consisting of immune function, movement efficiencies, anatomy, and motivation (to name just a few functions). In addition to vigor, motor skill is a valuable marker of overall organism health and performance potential. Thus, having just the right dance moves confers adaptive advantages. Adaptive dance moves are examples of optimal actions that are associated with health and reproductive success.

Athletic Performance

Certain individuals obviously acquire a high level of athletic skill through extensive practice. It may seem like many athletes are "naturals." Indeed, certain inborn predispositions may facilitate expert motor achievement. Even so, practice is key to athletic performance. According to one estimate, individuals who become skilled professional athletes previously practiced for approximately 10,000 hours over the course of a decade (Ericsson, Krample, & Tesch-Romer, 1993). Thus, both trial and error (learning from one's mistakes) and reinforcement learning (being rewarded for making certain responses) characteristic of practice sessions are important aspects of becoming a skilled professional athlete. In such cases, a coach is helpful in guiding the trial-and-error responses, minimizing the breadth of potential relevant responses while reinforcing the movements that represent improvements toward the desired motor outcomes.

Recently, researchers have tried to identify how the brain changes as athletes transform from novice to expert. Not surprisingly, several of the previously discussed brain areas involved in movement have been suggested to play a role in impressive athletic performances. One such area is the cerebellum. Patients with cerebellar damage exhibit an impaired sense of timing of movements that is so critical for sports performance. In addition, research with nonhuman primates suggests that neurons in the primary motor cortex orchestrate movements toward a consistent goal or intended outcome of movement (S. H. Scott, 2003). That is, the primary motor cortex keeps our eyes on the final prize—landing on the balance beam or hitting the ball. Rats, for example, that

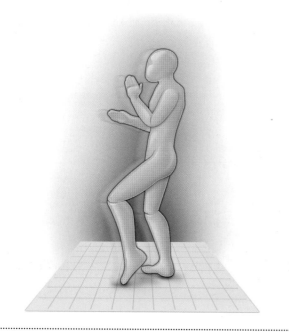

FIGURE 7.21 Attractive dance moves. Computer-generated avatars were used to identify the dance moves that female subjects found consistent with sexual attractiveness.

have been trained in a motor task performance exhibit more synaptic complexity in the primary motor cortex, as well as a modified cortical map representation accompanying more precise performance in motor skills (Kleim et al., 2002).

Another critical component of expert performance is an increased **automaticity** of the movement, requiring less cortical input—as discussed in the juggling and diving examples earlier in this chapter. Professional athletes exhibit automaticity with expert-level skills. In one study, both expert and novice female golfers were shown a picture of a golf course and then instructed to prepare to make a shot to an observed pin that was 100 yards away. Being in an fMRI scanner as opposed to on an actual golf course, the women were told to flex their right fingers when they were ready for the shot. Expert golfers exhibited increased activation in the parietal cortex, lateral premotor cortex, and occipital lobes compared with the novice golfers, who exhibited more activity in the limbic areas and basal ganglia (see Figure 7.22 for different responses in expert and novice golfers; Milton, Solodkin, Hlustik, & Small, 2007).

Thus, although the types of learning tasks previously mentioned in this chapter were laboratory tasks, similar themes have emerged from research focusing on well-practiced athletes. Namely, research provides evidence that as we improve athletic skills, less of the brain is required to perform these skills. Finally, the mirror neuron system discussed in Chapter 5 may contribute to learning from watching others or to success in interactive sports requiring individuals to predict and, sometimes, work in tandem with another player's movements (Yarrow, Brown, & Krakauer, 2009).

After acquiring expert skills, some athletes "choke" under pressure. That is, they perform below their actual ability level in a high-stakes context, such as the final game of the World Series or the last heat in the Olympic swim trials. Why, after so much practice, does their motor performance diminish at such critical times? When the University of

Chicago psychologist and kinesiologist Sian Beilock was watching the 2008 Beijing Olympics, she saw the American gymnast Alicia Sacramone pulled aside by an official (because of a lengthy delay) as she approached the balance beam. Beilock knew, based on her research on sports performance, that the imposed waiting period could lead to disaster at this critical moment in the gymnast's career. Unfortunately, Beilock's fears became a reality. Sacramone fell after doing a front flip to mount the beam (Figure 7.23). However, like a true professional, she regained composure and her confidence and completed a beautiful routine. Even so, in an unforgiving sport such as gymnastics, a single mistake typically leads to a loss. In this case, the U.S. team lost the all-around title they were chasing.

Beilock's research suggests that athletes who have achieved the high-level automaticity discussed previously but who then step back to think about the individual moves introduce error into the highly trained movement machine. It is true that multiple factors, such as distraction from the task, can contribute to choking under pressure. However, the pressure causing an athlete to monitor his movements directs the brain's attention to working memory and attentional mechanisms that detract from and interfere with the well-practiced movements. When Beilock asked golfers to

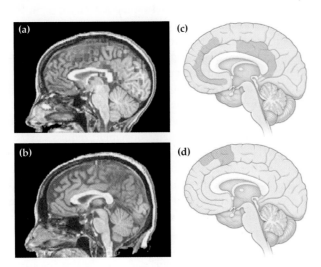

FIGURE 7.22 **Brain activation in golfers.** Novice (a and c) and expert (b and d) golfers exhibit different patterns of brain activity when preparing to make a shot.

FIGURE 7.23 **Choking in motor performance.** Following extensive training, when the U.S. gymnast Alicia Sacramone had to wait before her beam routine at the 2008 Beijing Olympics, her motor memory was likely disrupted, resulting in a phenomenon known as "choking."

think about the movement of their elbows prior to taking a shot, their performance declined. Recruiting the prefrontal cortex to intrude on the perfectionist actions of the motor cortex and basal ganglia when asked to "think" about their movement appeared to disrupt the golfers' intended outcome of the movement.

The rationale behind "icing" a kicker by calling a time out at a critical play in a football game, such as a potentially game-winning field goal, derives from observations that giving the kicker time to think about his automated kicking response will interfere with the accuracy of the kick. Thus, although thinking about our responses is typically recommended, in certain sports situations thinking too much can lead to performance disaster (Beilock, 2010; DeCaro, Thomas, Albert, & Beilock, 2011). It seems that the high-level automaticity discussed above normally helps professional athletes to take optimal actions—and to thereby avoid choking under pressure.

Exercise

Unlike the finely tuned movements observed in athletic performances, exercise focuses on movement repetition, intensity, and duration. When it comes to exercise, endurance is more important than precision and style. We have already discussed the brain's role in the execution of the precise movements that are necessary for athletic performance. In this section, we will discuss how the movement involved in exercise benefits the brain.

Research with children, young adults, and the elderly suggests that exercise enhances intelligence scores and learning and also helps to stave off cognitive decline in older age (van Praag, 2009). MRI scans indicate that elderly subjects participating in exercise programs had larger prefrontal and temporal lobe gray matter volumes than their sedentary counterparts (see Figure 7.24; Colcombe et al., 2003). Considering that humans gradually lose brain tissue from their mid-thirties onward, with accompanying cognitive declines, these findings suggest that exercise is a viable strategy to prevent cognitive decline for our society's aging populations. More research, however, is needed to specify the "dosage" of exercise for various ages and how the activity interacts with diet and pharmacological interventions such as hormone replacement therapies (Kramer, Colcombe, McAuley, Scalf, & Erickson, 2005).

Research with rodents suggests that exercise affects the brain in several ways. Increased oxygen and nutrient delivery resulting from regular physical exercise increases neurogenesis (Duman, 2005; van Praag, Kempermann, & Gage, 1999). Additionally, BDNF, a neural growth factor, is increased in exercising animals; in turn, BDNF is associated with increased cellular survival in the brain (Russo-Neustadt, Ha, Ramirez, & Kesslak, 2001). Evidence also suggests that exercise in rodents enhances production of new blood vessels, or **angiogenesis**, especially in the cerebellum (Isaacs, Anderson, Alcantara, Black, & Greenough, 1992) and motor cortex (Swain et al., 2003). For example, rats that were allowed to exercise exhibited 19% more blood flow in the motor cortex than control animals (Swain et al., 2003). In humans, the increased rates of neurogenesis and angiogenesis associated with participation in exercise programs have been linked to optimal cognitive, emotional, and behavioral functions (Portugal et al., 2013).

Thus, movement and brain activity are closely intertwined. Movement requires extensive activation of the brain to plan and execute the desired responses. Additionally, activation of the body's muscles changes the resource distribution to the brain, altering the infrastructure of the nervous system to more readily accommodate the dynamic conditions associated with persistent movement. Exercise is an optimal action that is associated with health improvement. Fortunately, it appears that exercise generates benefits for the brain that extend beyond the specific movements in the exercise routine.

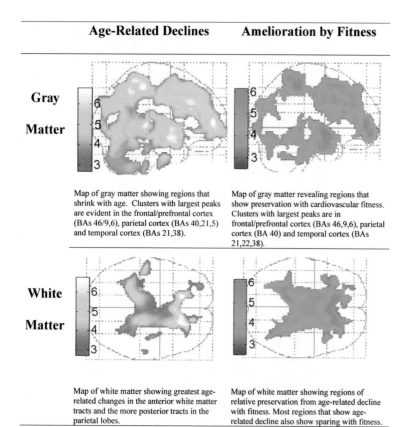

Age-Related Declines	Amelioration by Fitness

Gray Matter

Map of gray matter showing regions that shrink with age. Clusters with largest peaks are evident in the frontal/prefrontal cortex (BAs 46/9,6), parietal cortex (BAs 40,21,5) and temporal cortex (BAs 21,38).

Map of gray matter revealing regions that show preservation with cardiovascular fitness. Clusters with largest peaks are in frontal/prefrontal cortex (BAs 46,9,6), parietal cortex (BA 40) and temporal cortex (BAs 21,22,38).

White Matter

Map of white matter showing greatest age-related changes in the anterior white matter tracts and the more posterior tracts in the parietal lobes.

Map of white matter showing regions of relative preservation from age-related decline with fitness. Most regions that show age-related decline also show sparing with fitness.

FIGURE 7.24 Exercise and the aging brain. The hot colors (left) depict more shrinkage and cool colors (right) less shrinkage in brain areas. There was more aging-related loss in nonexercising aging subjects and less loss in exercising aging subjects.

Movement Disorders

Considering the complexity of the neural systems involved in movement, it is not hard to imagine plenty of opportunities for certain functional components to fail, resulting in movement disorders. Movement disorders are generally considered to result from any disease or injury that disrupts a person's movement. Neuromuscular diseases may result from the degeneration of motor neurons, as is the case with **amyotrophic lateral sclerosis**, or the degeneration of the myelin sheath, as is the case with **multiple sclerosis**. Key brain areas such as the substantia nigra or striatum may become compromised (as seen in Parkinson's disease and Huntington's disease, respectively), or key neurochemicals may be altered in such a way to affect movement (as seen in seizures). Damage to the motor systems may also occur as a result of trauma, an effect that is especially debilitating when the spinal cord, the nervous system's pathway to the muscles, is injured. In this section of the chapter, we will discuss two very different movement disorders: Parkinson's disease and movement impairment resulting from spinal cord injury. Although many conditions diminish motor capacity, these two examples demonstrate how such damage can have very different causes.

Parkinson's Disease

Parkinson's disease is one of the most common movement disorders, characterized by a diminished capacity for voluntary movement (**akinesia**), muscle tremors, and rigidity of movement. As the disease progresses, cognitive decline and loss of autonomic functions accompany the movement symptoms. Parkinson's typically affects older adults; most cases are first diagnosed when patients are in their fifties.

Although its causes remain a mystery, Parkinson's is associated with a progressive degeneration of neurons in the substantia nigra, accompanied by decreased levels of dopamine (see Figure 7.25). Further pathology has been observed in the brainstem and both subcortical and cortical brain areas. Brain areas affected by Parkinson's contain abnormal protein deposits that are known as **Lewy bodies** when they are present in the cell body and **Lewy neurites** when they are present in the neuronal processes. Although the function of these protein deposits is unknown, research suggests that they contribute to the death of the substantia nigra neurons. Recall from this chapter's opener that one treatment option for Parkinson's disease under exploration is the transplantation of substantia nigra cells into the brains of Parkinson's patients. Because Lewy bodies have been observed to form in tissue that has been transplanted into a patient's substantia nigra, it is likely that some aspect of the patient's extracellular environment may transfer the disease to the patient's healthy neurons following the transplant surgery (Brundin, Li, Holton, Lindvall & Revesz, 2008).

In addition to the substantia nigra, areas of the striatum have been implicated in Parkinson's symptoms. As previously discussed, studies have provided evidence that various sections of the striatum, consisting of the caudate and putamen, regulate both habit- and goal-directed learning. Thus, patients with Parkinson's may exhibit lower rates of automatic behaviors such as arm swinging during walking than they exhibited prior to the onset of the disease. Considering that at the time a patient is diagnosed with Parkinson's the putamen contains only about 60% of normal levels of dopamine in a healthy brain, we can easily see how various movements are inhibited. Interestingly, if a salient external stimulus is available to guide a patient's behavior, a notable improvement in movement is typically observed (Redgrave et al., 2010). For example, if a Parkinson's patient is struggling to walk across the street, a car horn indicating imminent danger may activate the appropriate brain circuits to jumpstart the behavior and enable the patient to cross quickly to avoid danger.

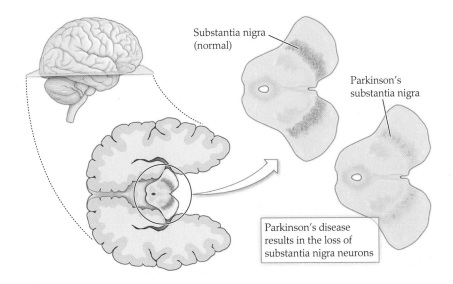

Substantia nigra (normal)

Parkinson's substantia nigra

Parkinson's disease results in the loss of substantia nigra neurons

FIGURE 7.25 Parkinson's disease.
The substantia nigra is compromised in Parkinson's disease.

Although no cure for Parkinson's has been found, many treatment options exist. Drugs that increase dopamine levels in the brain, such as L-DOPA, offer temporary relief of symptoms. However, the benefits of these drugs on movement subside after a certain period of time, and in some cases even more severe symptoms emerge, such as complete inability to move (freezing) or drug toxicity. Surgery is another treatment option for Parkinson's. In this chapter's opener, you learned about the surgical neural transplantation of dopaminergic cells in Parkinson's patients. Because of this procedure's high variability in success rates in patients, along with ethical considerations associated with the use of fetal tissue, research is focusing on alternatives such as using an existing, continuing line of human stem cells for the transplantation (Barker et al., 2013; Bjorklund et al., 2003).

Over the past six decades, close to 100,000 patients with Parkinson's and other motor diseases have undergone more traditional surgery to lesion various areas of the basal ganglia. These lesions appear to decrease the "noise," or disruptive neural messages, in the motor system, helping to decrease excessive tremors and unwanted movements and ultimately making movement more efficient for Parkinson's patients. Research suggests that the lesion-induced damage blocks distorted motor, or efferent, messages that interfere with goal-directed behavior. Although it is paradoxical that a treatment strategy of damaging a brain area enhances function, these surgeries have provided relief to many patients (Redgrave et al., 2010).

Another type of surgery, **deep brain stimulation**, has successfully reduced Parkinson's symptoms (Figure 7.26). Tens of thousands of patients have benefited from the placement of electrodes into various areas of the brain such as the subthalamic nucleus (Wojtecki, Colosimo, & Fuentes, 2012). The batteries for the electrodes, which need to be replaced about every three years, are implanted in the patient's chest. The writer Steven Gulie recounted his personal experience with deep brain stimulation; in this case, he referred to his neurosurgeon as "Henderson" and his surgical team as "Team Hubris":

    I'm lying in an operating room at the Stanford University hospital, head shaved, waiting for my brain surgery to begin.... I'll be kept awake for the entire procedure. Unfortunately, this also means I'm conscious when Henderson produces what looks like a hand drill and uses it to burr two dime-sized holes into the top of my skull. It doesn't hurt, but it's loud. Team Hubris is installing a deep brain stimulator, essentially a neurological pacemaker, in my head. This involves threading two sets of stiff wires in through my scalp, through my cerebrum—most of my brain—and into my subthalamic nucleus, a target the size of a lima bean, located near the brain stem. Each wire is a little thinner than a small, unfolded paper clip, with four electrodes at one end. The electrodes will eventually deliver small shocks to my STN. How did I get into this mess? Well, I have Parkinson's disease. If the surgery works, these wires will continually stimulate my brain in an attempt to relieve my symptoms. (Gulie, 2007, paras. 1–4)

Following surgery, Gulie had to undergo extensive fine-tuning of the levels of current transmitted through the implants before finally arriving at a symptom-free state. Remarkably, he went from being incapacitated with Parkinson's symptoms to exhibiting no evidence of Parkinson's. It is not clear, however, how long these effects will last. The degeneration of substantia nigra cells continues, so this treatment strategy is far from a cure. But this surgery seems to give patients another chance for movement for a period of at least four years in their lives. Although the success rate is far from perfect, research generally suggests that for the patients who meet the criteria for surgery, deep brain stimulation is more effective than more traditional medical management (Deuschl et al., 2006). At a cost of up to $100,000 for surgery and variable insurance coverage, however, not every patient has the opportunity to receive this surgical treatment (Okun & Zeilman, 2014).

Far from the invasiveness of drugs and surgery, dance therapy has capitalized on the findings that Parkinson's patients can overcome diminished voluntary movement with salient guiding cues. Research suggests that with an instructor, music, and a dance partner to lead the way, dance classes effectively address impaired balance and walking. Specifically, in one study, Parkinson's patients who participated in

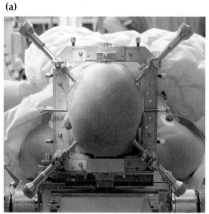
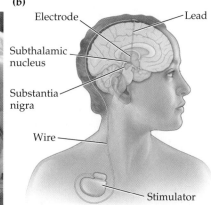

FIGURE 7.26 Deep brain stimulation for Parkinson's disease. (a) The patient remains awake during the surgery. (b) In this procedure, doctors implant electrodes into the targeted brain areas and secure the associated battery-powered stimulator in the upper chest area.

Electrode

Lead

Subthalamic nucleus

Substantia nigra

Wire

Stimulator

a six-week dance therapy program showed improvements in movement initiation relative to Parkinson's patients who participated in an exercise group for the same period of time (Westbrook & McKibben, 1989). This type of therapy may also benefit Parkinson's patients who have had surgical therapies or are continuing with pharmacological therapies (Earhart, 2009).

Spinal Cord Injury

Worldwide, about 2.5 million individuals live with spinal cord injuries. These injuries typically result from automobile and sports accidents. They occur more frequently in males than in females and predominantly in the age range of 16 to 30 years. Although the vertebrae provide substantial support to and protection of the fragile spinal cord, high-speed impacts can easily crush the vertebrae and leave the spinal cord vulnerable to damage.

Although the intricate network of brain areas necessary for movement remains functional, the damaged area of the spinal cord reduces its communication with the muscles—affecting the point of damage and all muscles served by the spinal cord below that point. For reasons scientists still do not understand, the chances for regeneration of transected axons are very different between the CNS and PNS. Specifically, peripheral nerve axons can regenerate under appropriate conditions, whereas transected axons in the CNS are rarely able to regenerate. Thus, CNS damage, such as damage to the spinal cord, has a much poorer prognosis than injury to the peripheral nerves (Ferguson & Son, 2011; R. J. M. Franklin & Blakemore, 1990).

In addition to the primary effects of the trauma itself, secondary effects arise that can cause further damage to the affected area. For example, swelling can cause the damage to spread around the initial area of impact. Consequently, drugs are given to contain this effect. Excessive release of excitatory neurotransmitters such as glutamate can lead to cell death (National Institute of Neurological Disorders and Stroke, 2013).

Whereas the decline in movement ability is gradual in many disorders, an individual who suffers spinal cord injuries undergoes an abrupt transformation from being a fully functioning person to one with very limited ability. One of my daughters' friends, Cole Sydnor, severed his spinal cord at the age of 16 while diving in a local river (Figure 7.27). Cole wrote an essay for his English class about the moment he went from the life of a celebrated athlete to the physical constraints of **quadriplegia**, losing control of his arms, legs, and torso:

Impact. An impact too familiar. An impact identical to the violent collision of two football players slamming head-to-head at full speed. I remember it too vividly, an audible thud, a flash of white, and an aching headache, the same impact which drove me to quit football. Yet, part of this impact was unfamiliar—The Crunch. The sound reminded me of chomping down on a chip.

I couldn't decide where the crunch came from, since most of my body was now numb and tingly, a sensation I had never experienced before. My mind raced as I tried to figure out what the ominous crunch meant. The haunting realization I was underwater brought me back to my now dire situation. Aware of the next set of rapids only twenty yards downstream, I knew I had to swim to the other side with haste. I began kicking and stroking as hard as possible. What happened then made the crunch seem irrelevant. My limbs wouldn't budge.

Unnaturally, I opened my eyes in the murky water. What I saw was the most horrifying sight I had ever beheld. Two arms, now foreign to me, jostled about the rushing water like a rag doll's. A deep red slowly began staining the white water around me, a dismal sight for someone so comfortable in water all his life.

My lungs were clawing for fresh air. Luckily, my instincts held, and I did not inhale the bloody water clouded about me. So close to the surface, all it would take would be lifting my head to satiate my screaming lungs. However, like the other limbs, my head would not cooperate. Looking upward was like solely using my neck to lift the ten foot rock we had just been jumping from. My "happy place" had never been so far gone as I floated face down, soaking up not the sun.

Cole's spinal cord was damaged at the C5 level, meaning that he has little motor control of muscles below his shoulders. He can, however, lift his arms and maneuver his hands to type and engage in other manual tasks. With so many patients suffering from similar injuries, scientists hope that research—the research we are discussing in this chapter (and also in the Epilogue)—will lead to life-changing benefits for Cole and enable his perfectly functioning brain to once again manage the spinal cord's control over his body's movements.

Although spinal cord injuries can be managed much more effectively today than in the past, obviously, as in Cole's case, a cure still eludes both practitioners and researchers. Even so, enthusiasm surrounds the use of cellular transplantations to provide multiple benefits, including a bridge for missing tissue and/or to replace dead cells, a replacement of myelin on affected neurons, or the provision of an appropriate cellular environment for axon regeneration (Thuret, Moon, & Gage, 2006). For example, following transplantation of fetal spinal cord using rodent models, scientists have observed small numbers of regenerated axons. However, the regenerated axons do not extend beyond the border of the transplant tissue. Also encouraging is the fact that modest functional recovery has been observed in rat and cat models of spinal cord injury (Bregman, McAtee, Dai, & Kuhn, 1997; Bregman et al., 1993; Jakeman & Reier, 1991; Reier, Stokes, Thompson, & Anderson, 1992).

Because they allow researchers to avoid the ethical controversy of using fetal cell transplants, autologous (self-generated) transplants are currently being explored in many

FIGURE 7.27 Drastic changes in movement ability. (a) Cole Sydnor (in blue) playing lacrosse. (b) During his junior year at Atlee High School in Virginia, following a diving accident, Cole suffered a spinal cord injury that left him with quadriplegia. Here, he assists his coach from the sidelines.

laboratories. The goal is to find a proliferative cell (a cell that is capable of dividing) from the patient that can be modified so that it is viable in the spinal cord. Thus, if such cells are harvested from a patient, the strategy is to expose the developing cells to the proper chemical environment to guide their development into the desired type of neuron prior to the transplantation surgery. Many factors—cell type, growth factors, cellular threats in the transplant area—influence the probability that a cell will both live and sprout functional processes involving intended targets (Ferguson & Son, 2011).

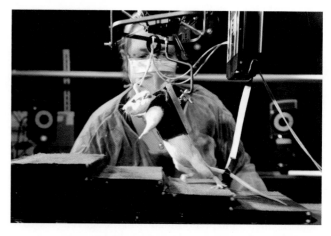

FIGURE 7.28 Neurorehabilitation in rats. Following spinal injury, a multifaceted rehabilitation approach consisting of electrical stimulation, neurochemical treatments, and training in a robotic harness has yielded promising results.

In another exciting research program, rats with spinal cord injury regained the ability to walk toward a treat following nine weeks of neurorehabilitative therapy. The therapy in this study consisted of placing the rats in a specialized robotic harness and delivering intense electrical stimulation and neurochemical treatments (i.e., monoamine agonists meant to activate dopamine, serotonin, and noradrenaline receptors) intended to activate the neurons. The neurorehabilitative therapy required the rats to make a decision to reach the treat. Compared with the rats that had merely been trained on a treadmill, the rats that had undergone neurorehabilitative therapy were more likely to walk voluntarily (van den Brand et al., 2012) (see Figure 7.28).

Gregoire Courtine, the lead scientist for this research, referred to this approach as "new ontogeny" because it is intended to replicate the original growth phase for the spinal nerve connections that the nervous system encountered during development. In an interview about the results, Courtine said, "This is the World Cup of neurorehabilitation. Our rats have become athletes when just weeks before they were completely paralyzed. I am talking about 100% recuperation of voluntary movement." Of course, moving from rats to humans is a challenge; accordingly, clinical trials are being planned in Switzerland to assess whether these results generalize to humans (*Science Daily*, 2012).

Thus, scientists are currently investigating many therapeutic approaches to restore valuable motor function in the millions of **paraplegic** (paralyzed in the lower half of the body) and quadriplegic patients across the world. Scientists have proposed that a combination of therapies, perhaps cellular transplant, rehabilitative, and neurochemical/pharmacological (e.g., growth factors) strategies, will be necessary to maximize recovery of lost function (Thuret, Moon, & Gage, 2006).

In addition to the mystery associated with rebuilding damaged motor circuits to enable patients to regain control of their bodies, another movement mystery has been brewing in the neuroscience community for the past decade. When a gene related to language was identified, researchers were eager to follow its functions to learn more about the evolution and neurobiology of language, considered a uniquely human ability. To the researchers' surprise, this gene has been most closely linked to brain areas related to movement (Vargha-Khadem, Gadian, Copp, & Mishkin, 2005). These fascinating findings, along with other relevant research, have prompted some researchers to reenvision language as an extension of movement. We will take this perspective as we focus on understanding specific aspects of language in the next section.

Language as an Extension of Movement

Here's an assignment for you. Next time you have a very exciting story to tell your friend, sit on your hands while you convey the details of the story. That's right, try to tell the story with no gestures whatsoever. It even sounds difficult, doesn't it? Have you ever thought about why we so readily move our hands when we speak?

Language is a broad, complex topic that is covered in depth in cognition-focused courses such as cognitive psychology, neuropsychology, and cognitive neuroscience. This textbook's coverage of the topic of language will focus on evolutionary perspectives involving the role of movement in the acquisition of language. As previously mentioned, based on the emergence of exciting research, this textbook explores language as an extension of movement (Vicario, 2013). After all, in addition to hand gestures, speech articulation requires the fast and precise coordinated movement of more than 100 muscles (Ackermann & Riecker, 2004).

Evolution of Language

Michael Arbib, neuroscientist and computer scientist, has proposed that language began with manual movements, or **protosigns**, that eventually provided the neural groundwork for the first signs of vocal-based language, or **protolanguage**. This evolutionary trajectory toward language acquisition did not exist in a genetic vacuum, as cultural innovations occurring in the context of human evolution facilitated the emergence of complex spoken languages (Arbib, 2005). These cultural effects are apparent when one considers the vast number of languages across the world—close to 7,000 (Rymer, 2012)!

Communication via hand gestures has been observed in two of our closest living relatives, chimpanzees and bonobos. Because gestures are rarely observed outside of a communicative context, they are thought to be a reliable measure of natural communication. When gestures were recorded in

FIGURE 7.29 Primate communication and gestures. (a) This chimp's hand is extended in a begging gesture. (b) Humans exhibit the same gesture when soliciting desired items from others.

these primate species, it was apparent that certain gestures observed in these apes had been conserved in human species. For example, the open-arm gesture, known as a begging gesture, is observed in chimps and humans (see Figure 7.29; Pollick & de Wall, 2007).

Although apes, humans, and monkeys look and behave differently, they possess some similarities in manual dexterity and have similar brain infrastructure. Even so, only humans normally acquire functional language. However, the region of the monkey brain specialized for visual and motor control of hand movements includes an area called F5, which is an area proposed to contain mirror neurons. As discussed in Chapter 3, these specialized neurons are active not only when the animal grasps an object or gestures, but also when the animal observes *another* animal grasping or gesturing. The **homologous** area in the human brain is Broca's area, an area traditionally touted as the speech area of the brain (see Chapter 2). Similar to F5 in the monkey brain, Broca's area in the human brain is also active when humans either execute or observe grasping responses. This may explain why, even when we talk on the phone and we know the person we are speaking with cannot see us, we continue to gesture throughout our conversations (see Figure 7.30).

FIGURE 7.30 **Hand gestures and conversation.** A brain area involved in language, Broca's area, is activated during both gesturing and language expression, perhaps explaining why it is difficult to speak on the phone without gesturing.

Adding further evidence to this interesting yet controversial idea is the observation that Broca's area is active when both spoken and sign languages are in use (Horwitz et al., 2003).

The **mirror system hypothesis of language** suggests that the primate mirror system involved in grasping responses eventually evolved into critical components that prepared the human brain for language (Arbib, 2005). This does not mean, however, that primates are the only animals with some aspect of mirror systems (other social mammals such as elephants have already been shown to possess mirror neurons). With this knowledge about language acquisition, the notion of *grasping a concept* takes on a new level of meaning.

Another theory, the **motor theory of speech perception**, suggests that speech is perceived as an extension of gestures generated by individuals articulating communicative sounds. In support of this idea, in studies in which the motor cortex was disrupted with TMS, subjects could no longer perceive specific language sounds in the speech stimuli presented in the study (Meister, Wilson, Deblieck, Wu, & Iacoboni, 2007). Because the true value of language is to be able to have

a conversation with another person, it is important for individuals to coordinate their verbal and manual gestures with others. Although monologues exist, dialogues appear to be the most functional use of conversation. And when it comes to coordinating conversations, humans are adept. One study reported that 45% of turn transitions (when the conversation switches from one person to another) in 1,500 phone conversations occurred within the narrow window of 250 milliseconds. This expert degree of timing coordination in language has been proposed to rely on the motor system (S. K. Scott, McGettigan, & Eisner, 2009).

Recent research focusing on large clusters of families with language disabilities such as **dyslexia** (a disorder characterized by difficulty reading) point to another factor that has influenced the evolution of language abilities. Genetic analyses have revealed a mutation of a specific gene, the FOXP2 gene, which may have played a role in adapting the cortical and basal ganglia systems (covered earlier in this chapter) for language production and comprehension (Enard, 2011; Kang & Drayna, 2011). In addition to being implicated in speech comprehension and production, this gene has also been linked to the coordination of gestures (Vicario, 2013). As more families with additional language deficits are investigated, additional genetic markers will most likely be identified, leading to revised theories of speech production.

Language and Sounds of Nature

The neurotheorist Mark Changizi (2011) has proposed a creative theory of language production. Changizi has proposed that three basic types of sounds capture physical interactions in nature. These sounds are hits, slides, and rings (see Figure 7.31). Explosive sounds that are similar to a tennis ball hitting the court represent hits. Consonant sounds such as b, p, d, t, g, and k are characteristic of hit sounds. Slides are more extensive sounds, such as running a finger across a page. Consonant sounds such as s, z, th, and sh represent slides in nature. Tapping your coffee mug with a spoon represents a ringing sound in nature. According to Changizi, vowel and certain consonant sounds, collectively called sonorants, such as r, y, w, m, n, and l, sound like these rings in nature.

FIGURE 7.31 **The sounds of movement.** The neurotheorist Mark Changizi has proposed that human language captures the sounds of nature since the brain is predisposed to differentiate these sounds.

Hits

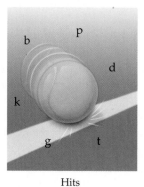

Slides

Rings

Changizi proposes that the brain's language system "harnessed" the sounds of nature because the brain was predisposed to hearing these sounds. In fact, music that is associated with movement also seems to be readily received by the brain. Remember "I'm a little teacup" and its associated movements? Or the chicken dance? Or the hokey pokey? Once again, the brain appears to be especially receptive to language incorporated with movement. That may be why some of these songs get stuck in our minds—making them a form of auditory parasites known as *earworms*.

Language Localized in the Brain

Regardless of how language arose in humans, brain injury case studies and neuroimaging research have identified several key brain areas involved in language production and comprehension. In Chapter 2 you learned that language is typically localized in the left hemisphere. As shown in Figure 7.32, Broca's area, known for its involvement in language production, is located anterior to **Wernicke's area**, known for its involvement in speech perception. Recently, Wernicke's area was found to be positioned a bit more anterior than originally proposed (DeWitt & Rauschecker, 2012). Connecting these two areas is the bundle of fibers known as the **arcuate fasciculus**. The **angular gyrus** in the parietal lobe is involved in visual and auditory processing of words. Additionally, the visual cortex is involved in reading, whereas the auditory cortex is necessary for hearing spoken words. As previously discussed, the primary motor cortex is involved in the movement of the mouth and is associated with both language production and gesture production. Damage to these areas leads to specific language disorders—**aphasias**—which affect people's ability

to communicate. Although these brain areas are generally thought to be critically involved in language, recent imaging studies have revealed that language is influenced by a more diffuse array of brain areas located throughout a broader range of cortical areas. Hence, the key language-related brain areas and the specific boundaries of these areas continue to be updated through informative neuroimaging studies (Gernsbacher & Kaschak, 2003).

With language typically localized in the left hemisphere, it is interesting to consider what would happen if, for some unfortunate reason, the left hemisphere was no longer functional or, even worse, was removed. The literature is riddled with cases of individuals who experienced brain trauma or disease in the left hemisphere and subsequently suffered from severe language impairments. For example, after the former Arizona Congresswoman Gabrielle Giffords (Figure 7.33) was shot in the head in 2011, leaving her left hemisphere damaged, she lost her ability to speak. Although she has made progress through intense rehabilitation therapy, her current language ability is far from her ability prior to her injury. Today, her language is largely characterized by single words and gestures. In an interview in which she was asked about her recovery, she responded "Stronger, better, tougher," rather than in complete sentences (Bash, 2013).

Other cases reveal an impressive degree of plasticity in language recovery following massive brain damage. In some cases of intractable epilepsy or related diseases, individuals have had a hemispherectomy in which most or all of one hemisphere is disconnected or removed from the rest of the brain (see Figure 7.34). When this occurs to the left hemisphere, it would be easy to conclude that there would be no chance for a child's brain to reorganize so the right

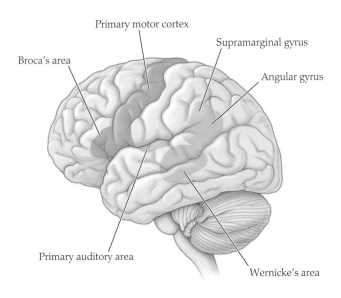

FIGURE 7.32 Language areas in the brain. Areas of the brain associated with language are distributed across the cortex.

FIGURE 7.33 Language recovery following traumatic brain injury. The congresswoman Gabrielle Giffords (center) had extensive damage to her left hemisphere after being shot in the head; following extensive rehabilitation therapy, her oral communication consists of simple words and gestures.

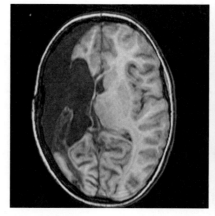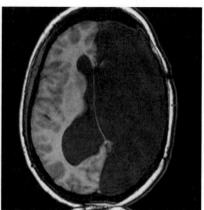

FIGURE 7.34 Language following hemispherectomy. If the left hemisphere is removed during childhood via a hemispherectomy, language can be retrained. Such plasticity is not seen in adults with comparable damage.

hemisphere could gain control over language. However, amazingly, that is often not the case. One study followed 13 individuals who underwent this surgery from the ages of 4 months to 13 years. The authors reported that all participants (those having either the left or the right hemisphere removed) exhibited highly intelligible speech, making few phonological and articulation errors (Liegeois et al., 2010).

These remarkable cases suggest that the right hemisphere has the innate potential to support various aspects of

language processing (Boatman et al., 1999). However, the transfer of language to the right hemisphere is more likely to occur before the age of six. Consequently, although individual differences exist, older children, adolescents, and adults do not experience the same language recovery rates following left hemispherectomy because of slower rates of neural growth and subsequent formation of neural networks following the early childhood years (Choi, 2007; Loddenkemper et al., 2004; see Chapter 5).

LABORATORY EXPLORATION

Using Reaching Tasks to Assess Models of Brain Injury and Recovery

As researchers develop animal models of various human neurological diseases and conditions, they need appropriate assessment tools to determine the extent of impairment following surgically induced damage. This way, they can determine any changes in motor function that occur following a particular treatment or intervention. Damage to the motor cortex and other associated areas such as the caudate nucleus results in deficits in skilled movements such as reaching for food. Consequently, reaching tasks serve as valuable assessment tools to test models of injuries and diseases of the motor system, ranging from stroke-induced damage to Parkinson's disease (Whishaw, 2005).

Ian Whishaw and his colleagues at the University of Lethbridge have developed two reaching tasks to systematically test rat models of injuries and diseases of the motor system. For example, to investigate recovery from stroke, a blockage of the middle cerebral artery is used to produce damage in the rodents (Schaar, Brenneman, & Savitz, 2010). As shown

in Laboratory Exploration Box Figure 7.1, in the *single pellet reaching task*, rats are placed in an apparatus that requires them to use only one paw to reach for a piece of food. The location of the food can be manipulated so that the rat needs to use a limb that has diminished function (because of injury or illness). The experimenters closely observe the rat's paw to evaluate successful grasping and the efficiency with which the rat uses its paw to carry food to its mouth. By contrast, in the much simpler *tray reaching task*, the rat reaches through bars for chicken feed in a tray.

The single pellet reaching task requires more motor skill than the tray reaching task. This variation of skill necessary to successfully perform these tasks provides the researchers with a more informed view of the animal's motor ability and recovery. Video recordings of sessions allow researchers to assess many variables in the single pellet reaching task such as the latency, or time delay, for the rat to initiate the reach; the number of attempts before the rat successfully retrieves

the food pellet; the quality of the rat's grasp for the food; and the rat's efficiency in carrying the pellet to its mouth for consumption (Gharbawie, Gonzalez, Williams, Kleim, & Whishaw, 2005; Whishaw, 2005).

Rats and humans show similarity in their grasping movements. As rats and humans are presented with food, the extension, grasp, and retrieval components of their responses as they grasp the food and then direct it to their mouths suggest that these basic movements have been conserved through mammalian evolution. Further, these species' similarities in this movement enhance the likelihood that the findings from the rodent studies will translate to human movement disease and recovery, increasing the chances of identifying key therapeutic approaches that will generalize from preclinical animal models such as the tasks described above to human disease (Klein, Sacrey, Whishaw, & Dunnett, 2012). For example, certain critical periods of training following an injury may be identified in animal models that could be beneficial for human recovery. Further, exposure to certain types of enriched environments known to enhance neuroplasticity may enhance the effectiveness of the motor training.

LABORATORY EXPLORATION FIGURE 7.1 Rodent motor task. Motor rehabilitation is investigated in rats trained on a reaching task. Rodent studies are valuable considering the similarities in grasping responses between humans and rodents.

Conclusion

Although the most basic motor responses represent complex neurobiological responses, in most cases, movement is seamless and is not something that we consciously monitor. However, in the case of athletes who must enhance performance or in the unfortunate cases of patients with movement disorders, movement arrives at the forefront of our awareness. Researchers hope that learning more about the fundamental cells and circuits of the motor system will lead to effective therapies and, even better, cures for the many movement disorders that plague our society.

Further, in one of the most impressive displays of voluntary fine-tuned movements, humans have evolved the ability to communicate with spoken language. This ability facilitates the communication of successes and failures of past movements with others, thereby minimizing the necessity of reinventing the wheel with each new learned motor task and maximizing the potential to move to new levels of motor sophistication.

Chapter 12 will explore further how the brain influences specific motor responses when voluntary action, coupled with varying degrees of uncertainty, is part of the equation. Thus, the ability to respond with movement is most adaptive when it is associated with the ability to determine *whether* and *when* to respond in specific situations—a determination based on a diverse array of neurobiological variables.

KEY TERMS

L-DOPA (L-3, 4-dihydroxyphenylalanine) (p. 187)

Movement Basics

motor homunculus (p. 189)
corticospinal tracts (p. 190)

lateral corticospinal tract (p. 190)
anterior corticospinal tract (p. 191)
Betz cells (p. 191)
corona radiata (p. 191)
medullary pyramids (p. 191)
upper motor neurons (p. 191)

lower motor neurons (p. 191)
decussation (p. 191)
α motor neurons (p. 192)
reflexes (p. 192)
reflex arc (p. 192)
cardiac muscle (p. 192)

smooth muscles (p. 192)
skeletal (striatal) muscles (p. 192)
biofeedback (p. 192)
extrafusal fibers (p. 193)
intrafusal fibers (p. 193)
motor unit (p. 193)
neuromuscular junction (p. 193)
motor end plate (p. 193)
antagonistic muscles (p. 193)
proprioception (p. 194)
muscle spindle (p. 194)
γ motor neurons (p. 194)
Golgi tendon organ (p. 194)
monosynaptic spinal reflex (p. 194)
central pattern generators (p. 194)

Complex Movement

supplementary motor complex
    (p. 195)
supplementary motor area (SMA)
    (p. 195)
presupplementary motor area
    (pre-SMA) (p. 195)

premotor cortex (p. 195)
caudate nucleus (p. 196)
putamen (p. 196)
globus pallidus (p. 196)
substantia nigra (p. 196)
striatum (p. 196)
flocculonodular lobe (p. 198)
vermis (p. 198)
lateral cerebellar hemispheres (p. 198)
dentate nucleus (p. 198)
cerebellar peduncles (p. 198)
cerebellar cognitive affective
    syndrome (p. 199)

Adaptive Moves

optimal actions (p. 201)
Bayesian decision theory (p. 201)
automaticity (p. 203)
angiogenesis (p. 204)

Movement Disorders

amyotrophic lateral sclerosis (p. 205)
multiple sclerosis (p. 205)

Parkinson's disease (p. 205)
akinesia (p. 205)
Lewy bodies (p. 205)
Lewy neurites (p. 205)
deep brain stimulation (p. 206)
quadriplegia (p. 207)
paraplegic (p. 208)

Language as an Extension of Movement

protosigns (p. 209)
protolanguage (p. 209)
homologous (p. 209)
mirror system hypothesis of language
    (p. 210)
motor theory of speech perception
    (p. 210)
dyslexia (p. 210)
Wernicke's area (p. 211)
arcuate fasciculus (p. 211)
angular gyrus (p. 211)
aphasias (p. 211)

REVIEW QUESTIONS

1. Describe the role of the nervous system in voluntary and involuntary movement, citing the key parts of the brain and spinal cord described in the chapter. Why does the motor homunculus give only a partial picture of how humans are able to move?

2. Name the major types of muscle, and explain the role of each type in voluntary and/or involuntary movement.

3. How are the supplementary motor complex, basal ganglia, and cerebellum involved in enabling the performance of complex movement?

4. Explain the evolutionary advantages of dancing and achieving athletic prowess. Why do athletes sometimes choke in competition? What does research suggest about the effects of exercise on the human brain?

5. Describe the symptoms of Parkinson's disease, and identify the principal parts of the nervous system that have been implicated in this disorder. What are some of the therapeutic approaches that have been evaluated for Parkinson's disease, and why are they effective?

6. Describe how a person is affected by a spinal cord injury, citing the components of the nervous system named in the chapter. What are some experimental methods of repairing spinal cord injuries, and how do they work?

7. Name several key brain areas associated with the complex motor activity of speech, and describe at least two evolutionary theories of how speech developed.

CRITICAL-THINKING QUESTIONS

1. Suppose you were assigned to design a robot capable of the full range of human movements. What information and equipment would you need to approach this task? Discuss the ethical implications of such a robot.

2. Imagine that you are an athlete, musician, or other performer preparing for a high-stakes competition or audition. What will you do to make the most of your practice time? How will you reduce the likelihood of choking under pressure? How would you apply these same principles to coaching someone else for competition?

3. Do you anticipate that in the near future doctors will be able to repair spinal cord injuries by means of surgery or other therapies? What challenges would researchers need to meet for such treatments to be successful?

Maintenance and Motivation

Runaway Motivation

As a graduate student, I ran across a motivational mystery involving some odd rat behavior: a series of articles by William Pare at the Maryland Veterans Hospital on the topic of activity-stress (Pare, 1975, 1976, 1977). I've been conducting research on this topic and considering the underlying motivational factors ever since.

The **activity-stress** research condition involved housing rats in cages, restricting their feeding to one hour per day, and giving them unlimited access to activity wheels (Figure 8A). The rats could eat as much as they wanted for that one hour. For the remainder of the time, they could either rest in their cage or run in the wheel. That wasn't so bad . . . was it? Pare's initial studies indicated that the health consequences for these animals were severe. Rats are notorious for their tendency to run 1 to 15 miles per day when housed in cages with activity wheels (Mather, 1981), but in this case, food was restricted. Didn't it make sense to conserve energy when resources were limited? Apparently not.

When I conducted my own version of this experiment as a graduate student, I observed rats run up to seven miles per day. Although rats are typically active at night, the rats in this experiment became increasingly active during the light hours. Additionally, when food was eventually placed in their cages, instead of jumping on top of the food bowl as expected, the rats typically hopped in their activity wheels and ran before finally orienting toward the food bowls. If an experimenter did not intervene, these animals would literally run themselves to death, exhibiting stomach ulcers (stress ulcers), hypertrophied or swollen adrenal glands, and shriveled thymus glands that are involved in immune functions. Similarities to anorexia nervosa became obvious—restricted eating, increased activity, and significant weight loss.

The altered feeding schedule had stressed the rats exposed to this condition. Many research studies have explored these

FIGURE 8A **Rat in running wheel.** When their food is restricted, laboratory rats increase their running behavior.

217

stress effects in an attempt to determine which variables (e.g., temperature, type of diet, duration of food exposure) made the animals more susceptible to the ulcers and other maladaptive health effects (reviewed in Lambert, 1993). More relevant to this chapter, however, is the question of what specific biological mechanisms fuel such bizarre, seemingly self-destructive behavior. What factors would motivate an animal to do this? And, if identified, would such factors provide clues to maladaptive compulsive behavior observed in humans?

Behind the Scenes

A plausible explanation is that running somehow becomes more reinforcing than eating. In one study, when dopamine was blocked by an antagonist (at a dose that did not interfere with movement), the rats' excessive amounts of running subsided (Lambert & Porter, 1992). As you learned in Chapter 4, dopamine fuels a reward circuit in the brain that involves the nucleus accumbens. In another study, rats kept in cooler ambient temperatures exhibited greater amounts of running than did rats kept in warmer-temperature climates (Lambert & Hanrahan, 1990). Apparently, the more uncomfortable the laboratory conditions became, the more likely it was that these activity-stress rats would run.

Was this a case of extreme maladaptation? Probably not. In a more natural context, this would likely be a life-saving response. If food in the wild became scarce, movement to another area would likely lead the animal to locate more plentiful food. A caged rat has the same biological urge to run, but in this case, the behavior leads to its demise rather than to its rescue from starvation. Additionally, the enhanced response is consistent with a classic learning effect known as the *reinforcement-omission effect*, in which responses strengthen when an animal is not rewarded, perhaps because of frustration (Amsel & Roussel, 1952; Stout, Boughner, & Papini, 2003). For example, if a rat expects a reward after running down an alley and does not receive the reward, the next time, it runs faster!

As this chapter indicates, the brain's reward system is the product of a complex circuit of brain areas and neurochemicals. Altered environmental conditions and availability of resources can recalibrate these responses. As seen in the activity-stress paradigm, these recalibrations—run even more to receive food—may be highly detrimental.

Although it is a stretch to move from rats to humans, the activity-stress paradigm provides clues about the impact of increased activity and decreased food consumption on the brain and body. Research with patients who have anorexia nervosa suggests that, like the rats, these individuals are also searching for something to make them feel less anxious and more secure. Further, dopamine has been implicated in the excessive activity and dieting that are characteristic of this disorder (Kontis & Theochari, 2012). In this chapter, we will examine influential factors in both eating disorders and many behaviors we engage in every day. ■

The Brain's Reward Circuitry

Imagine that all obligations have been removed from your schedule for a day: You have no need to worry about going to class, studying for exams, doing laundry, or going to work. With no responsibilities, how would you spend your day? The basic drives are a given; you will eat, drink, maybe even catch up on sleep. The brain gives the body strict orders to follow through with these pleasurable responses, regardless of one's schedule. But what else would you be motivated to do? Would you opt to spend time with friends, watch television, go on a hike, read the book that has been on your nightstand for months, or cook a meal?

The U.S. Department of Labor, Bureau of Labor Statistics (2013), has collected data on how full-time college students in the United States, with all of their obligations, spend their time each weekday (Figure 8.1). Sleeping tops the list at 8.7 hours, followed by leisure and sports at 4.1 hours. Obligations in the form of working and related activities (2.4 hours) and educational activities such as attending class and studying (3.3 hours) are not far behind. Students spend approximately 1 hour eating and drinking, close to

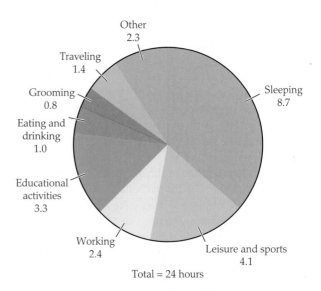

Source: Bureau of Labor Statistics, American Time Use Survey

FIGURE 8.1 Student daily time budget. An important first step in determining the degree of motivation animals and humans have for various activities is to complete accurate time budgets. This pie chart depicts the allocation of time for full-time students. How closely does this match your time budget?

an hour grooming, and an hour and a half traveling (taking public transportation, commuting, walking to class). That leaves about 2 hours for other miscellaneous activities. Of course, just because we spend a lot of time engaging in an activity such as working does not mean that we enjoy that activity or find it especially pleasurable—at least not the same way as we enjoy a piece of chocolate cake.

When the London researchers Mathew White and Paul Dolan (2009) asked subjects from a German university to report their "feelings" associated with various activities, they determined that activities such as eating, resting, and watching television were characterized as pleasurable but not very rewarding, whereas work was characterized as rewarding but not very pleasurable. Activities such as self-care or grooming were considered neither very pleasurable nor rewarding, whereas prayer and meditation were considered both pleasurable and rewarding. In this study, *pleasurable* referred to immediate positive emotions; *rewarding* represented more complex responses that may involve more long-term learning and anticipation in addition to positive emotions.

This chapter discusses the brain mechanisms involved in the subjective feelings of pleasure and reward, also known as *subjective well-being*, and how these responses drive various behavioral responses. Although subjective well-being research is conducted with human participants, aspects of various motivational systems can also be studied with appropriate animal models. A mother rat may not be able to tell you how much she enjoys being with her pups, but an experimenter can observe various behaviors such as the amount of time she spends with her pups or how hard she works to gain access to her pups. (In this chapter, we define *work* as physical or mental effort undertaken to obtain desired resources.) We will also explore mechanisms involved with motivating animals to engage in essential behaviors such as grooming that do not appear to be as pleasurable or rewarding as other responses. The convergence of results from human research and research with animal models provides the most informed views on the brain's role in motivating us to engage in various behaviors.

More than a half century ago, the researchers James Olds and Peter Milner implanted electrodes in the brains of rats and observed something unexpected. The rats received electrical stimulation in specific brain areas if they stayed in a particular location. The rats seemed to *really* like this brain stimulation. These findings were unexpected because the scientists were targeting a brain area known as the reticular formation involved in sleep/wake cycles and arousal functions. What they were seeing exceeded mere arousal. Olds and Milner seemed to have stumbled on brain areas involved in pleasure and reward. Indeed, further tests revealed that the stimulation of specific brain areas was rewarding enough to keep the rats working for the continued stimulation of these brain areas (Olds & Milner, 1954).

When the rats were allowed to voluntarily press a lever to receive mild jolts of electrical stimulation (as depicted in Figure 8.2) targeted at limbic structures such as the **septal nuclei** and nucleus accumbens, they would press the lever up to 2,000 times per hour! This motivational response seemed more intense than mere curiosity. Further research implicated the neurotransmitter dopamine in this mesolimbic dopaminergic pathway (discussed in Chapter 4). Wise and Schwartz (1981) administered the dopamine receptor blocker pimozide (at a dose that did not interfere with motor functions) and found evidence that it diminished the rats' motivation to respond for a food reward. At that time, it appeared that the brain's reward pathway had been identified.

Stimulation of the brain's hot spots for reward also had a dramatic impact on humans. In the 1950s, the psychiatrist Robert Heath implanted electrodes in the septal nuclei (a limbic structure involved in brain reward) in a few human patients (Heath, 1972). The patients receiving this electrical brain stimulation pressed the button to stimulate their brains extremely frequently, similar to what the rats did in Olds and Milner's research. Several human patients with this electrode placement reported pleasurable responses that they described as orgasmic, providing evidence that a reward pathway also existed in humans.

Elements of the Reward Circuits

Kent Berridge and Morten Kringlebach have conducted extensive research on how the mesolimbic dopamine reward circuit facilitates adaptive behavior. As shown in Figure 8.3, they believe that some basic aspects of motivation may be similar between humans and rodents. Bitter stimuli, for example, promote a similar facial expression that is consistent with avoidance behaviors. The more research that is done

(a)

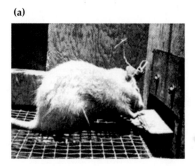

(b)

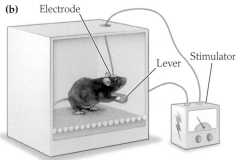

Stimulation occurs when rat presses lever

FIGURE 8.2 Motivation fueled by brain stimulation. (a) Rats press a bar to receive electrical stimulation to the mesolimbic dopaminergic pathway. (b) If rats increase bar press responses to obtain stimulation to a specific brain area, this indicates that the stimulation is rewarding.

in this area, however, the more complex the brain's reward system appears to be. For example, mesolimbic dopaminergic neurons are activated by *aversive*, or negative, stimuli as well as rewarding stimuli (Ferrari, van Erp, Tornatzky, & Miczek, 2003; Scott, Heitzeg, Koeppe, Stohler, & Zubieta, 2007). Additionally, at least two lines of evidence suggest that mesolimbic dopamine is not the sole neurochemical involved in the brain's reward circuit:

1.   Mesolimbic dopaminergic neurons are more reliably activated by predictive, attentional, and motivational factors as opposed to the more pleasurable aspects of stimuli (Carelli, 2004; Salamone, Correa, Farrar, & Mingote, 2007).
2.   When behaviors indicating that an animal finds a stimulus pleasurable are monitored (i.e., protruding tongue when drinking desired sweet water, as shown in Figure 8.3), manipulations of mesolimbic dopamine fail to modulate the degree of liking for the stimulus (Berridge, 2007; Leyton, 2009).

Berridge and Kringlebach have suggested that dopamine may play a role in shifting our arousal and motivation toward pleasurable aspects of a stimulus. For example, dopamine may play a role in focusing our attention toward the cheesecake on the dessert tray and imagining just how wonderful it will taste (Berridge & Kringelbach, 2008). However, if you never liked cheesecake, an extra dose of dopamine will not make you suddenly enjoy its taste. In fact, after two decades of investigating dopamine's role in responses that are related to pleasure, the researchers reported that dopamine fluctuations were never observed to change the intensity of the

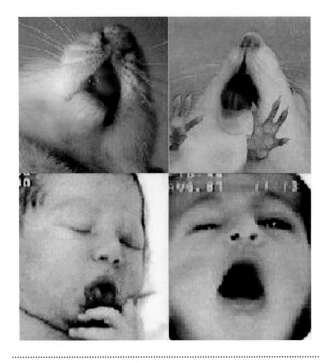

FIGURE 8.3 Conserved facial responses to taste. Similarities observed between rodents and humans suggest that facial responses to sweet and bitter tastes have been conserved across mammalian species.

pleasurable impact of food, even when the intensity of the drive to obtain it had been profoundly changed (Berridge, Ho, Richard, & DiFeliceantonio, 2010).

After reconsidering the role of dopamine from strictly enhancing reward to directing responses toward rewarding contexts, these researchers have also proposed different brain circuits associated with the brain's reward pathways. The notion of the brain's reward system being associated solely with the mesolimbic dopaminergic pathway does not appear to tell the whole story. Although the terms are somewhat subjective, evidence is emerging for three related systems defining pleasure responses—*liking*, *wanting*, and *learning*. The networks for each system are distinct, yet overlapping.

As shown in Figure 8.4, according to Berridge and Kringlebach, these terms can be defined as follows:

*   **Liking**: When you take that first bite of ice cream and savor its taste, you are experiencing liking. Liking is a sensory-stimulating emotional experience, closely associated with pleasure. Relevant brain areas for this proposed system include the orbitofrontal cortex, anterior cingulate cortex, insula, nucleus accumbens shell, ventral pallidum, periaqueductal gray, and amygdala, with opioids as the system's key neurochemicals.
*   **Wanting**: When children jump up and down in anticipation of birthday presents, they are experiencing wanting. Wanting is closely related to motivation and drive; it is an emotional experience that builds as the children think about the possible gifts and imagine themselves playing with them. You may feel this way as you anticipate an exciting trip and imagine the fun you will have. Relevant brain areas include the orbitofrontal cortex, anterior cingulate cortex, insula, nucleus accumbens, ventral tegmental area, and hypothalamus. The key neurochemical in this "wanting" system is dopamine.
*   **Learning**: As children grow older and build associations between events or responses that lead to pleasurable outcomes, their behavioral and cognitive reward repertoires expand. We learn to associate smells, tastes, thoughts, images, verbal phrases, certain faces, and holidays with rewarding outcomes. Learned associations can also be negative, but this chapter focuses on positive emotional experiences that lead animals to seek life-sustaining resources (i.e., searching a field for food if you are a rat or driving to your grandmother's house for apple pie if you are a human). Relevant brain areas include the orbitofrontal cortex, medial prefrontal cortex, anterior cingulate cortex, insula, amygdala, and hippocampus. Key neurochemicals in this "learning" system include dopamine, serotonin, and acetylcholine.

Dividing the brain's reward system into these more specific components helps to explain some of the paradoxes we see in the real world. The mesolimbic dopaminergic pathway and areas associated with *wanting* likely drive the drug-seeking behavior of addicts described in Chapter 4, explaining why the addicts are driven to obtain drugs that do not

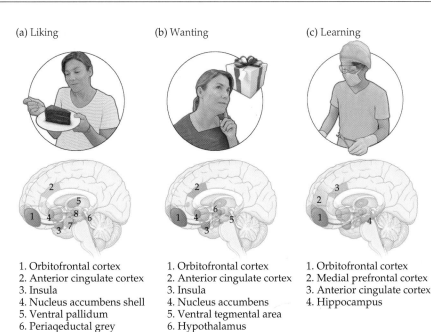

(a) Liking

1. Orbitofrontal cortex
2. Anterior cingulate cortex
3. Insula
4. Nucleus accumbens shell
5. Ventral pallidum
6. Periaqeductal grey
7. Amygdala
8. Hypothalamus

(b) Wanting

1. Orbitofrontal cortex
2. Anterior cingulate cortex
3. Insula
4. Nucleus accumbens
5. Ventral tegmental area
6. Hypothalamus

(c) Learning

1. Orbitofrontal cortex
2. Medial prefrontal cortex
3. Anterior cingulate cortex
4. Hippocampus

FIGURE 8.4 Motivational systems of the brain. Various brain areas and neurochemicals guide us to desired outcomes based on how much we enjoy the activity (liking), wish to engage in the activity (wanting), or have come to associate specific stimuli with subsequent desired activities (learning).

necessarily make them happy or lead to extended pleasurable experiences. In fact, recent research has demonstrated that rats can exhibit a desire or wanting for something they never really liked. In one such study, following a period of salt deprivation, the rats preferred a very salty taste that they previously disliked (Tindell, Smith, Berridge, & Aldridge, 2009). This compartmentalization also helps explain why activating the brain areas involved in wanting and learning while you plan a summer vacation may seem to be more rewarding than the trip itself; the anticipation dissipates, replaced by the reality of a less-than-perfect vacation. In addition, although our founding fathers did not take a biopsychology course or conduct research on the brain's reward system, their suggestion in the Declaration of Independence that one of our inalienable human rights is "the pursuit of happiness"—as opposed to just outright happiness—is quite insightful. They seem to have recognized that the anticipation of a pleasurable event is more important than the pleasurable experience itself. The pursuit of happiness is likely to utilize the *wanting* and *learning* pleasure circuits in addition to those associated with the more pleasurable emotional state of *liking* that is all too often more fleeting than we might wish.

Environmental Tuning of the Reward Circuits

With his colleague Sheila Reynolds, Kent Berridge has also explored the impact of the environment on the nucleus accumbens, a central player in the brain's reward circuitry. It turns out that the shell of the nucleus accumbens is a bit

like a piano keyboard in that activation of certain areas of the shell results in very specific desirable, or *appetitive*, behaviors. To identify the specific notes of this emotional keyboard, researchers have administered microinjections of a drug that blocks the neurotransmitter glutamate. Depending on the area of the accumbens shell affected, researchers observe different outcomes. In more rostral regions of the medial shell, glutamate enhances appetitive responses such as eating. In the caudal shell, glutamate generates negative avoidance and defensive responses (aggression or escape). Injections in intermediate locations in the shell produce mixtures of appetitive and negative (*aversive*) responses. In short, you need the equivalent of a musical score to keep track of the functional outputs of the specific areas of the accumbens shell.

Reynolds and Berridge (2008) wondered whether they could adjust the "tuning" of the nucleus accumbens by exposing rats to one of three environments: a more natural environment that was dark, familiar, and quiet; a standard laboratory environment with artificial light; or a stressful environment bombarded with extrabright light and loud sounds like punk-rock music. As the researchers predicted, the rats preferred their familiar homelike environment to the standard and overstimulating environments.

When the researchers investigated the standard laboratory environment animals for potential changes in the areas of the accumbens shell that were sensitive to certain emotional responses, they found no reassignment or reorganization of rewarding areas. This finding was expected since the standard environment served as a control group. However, that was not the case for the natural and stressful environments. In the homelike, familiar environment, the appetitive zone expanded to fill approximately 90% of the entire accumbens shell. The more aversive zone shrank to about one-third of its original territory. Thus, being housed in the preferred dark, quiet environment seemed to restructure the nucleus accumbens shell so that the zone responding to pleasure increased in size. This finding is profound; rats housed in this preferred environment experienced changes in a brain area involved with the processing of pleasurable responses that seemed to maximize their potential of experiencing more pleasure.

What about the stressful environment? In this group, the defensive, aversive zone expanded to fill more than 80% of the medial shell; this area was about twice the size of the aversive zone observed in the animals exposed to the standard laboratory environment. The appetitive sites still existed but were much smaller than that in the other groups

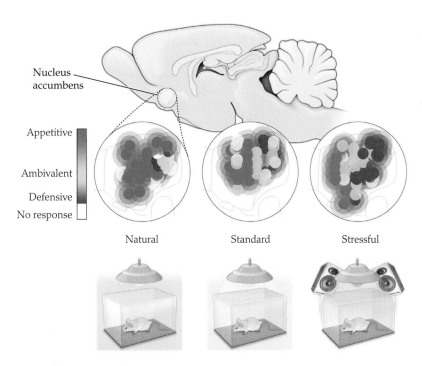

Nucleus accumbens

Appetitive

Ambivalent

Defensive

No response

Natural   Standard   Stressful

FIGURE 8.5 Tuning the nucleus accumbens. In this study, the rat's habitat influenced the proportion of the nucleus accumbens shell assigned to positive and negative emotional responses.

that happiness is more complex than we ever imagined. The ancient Greek philosopher Aristotle declared that happiness consisted of two fundamental aspects: **hedonia** (pleasure) and **eudaimonia** (a life well lived; Waterman, 1993). In this view, pleasure can be viewed as a more immediate response or an *outcome*, whereas eudaimonia refers to the adoption of a lifestyle or a *process* that facilitates positive emotional responses throughout one's lifetime (Deci & Ryan, 2008; Huta, & Ryan, 2010). Although philosophers continue to deliberate on the criteria for a life well lived, neuroscientists are making progress identifying various aspects of pleasure. It can be difficult, however, to understand reward and pleasure in the abstract, so in the next section we will explore a pleasurable response that motivates us each day: eating.

and pushed to the very frontal region of the accumbens shell. This dramatic rezoning is shown in Figure 8.5.

These results provide insights into how stressful contexts may lead to stress-related disorders such as posttraumatic stress disorder (PTSD), as well as to depression. PTSD patients report heightened responsiveness to stimuli after living in a war zone or experiencing other emotional trauma. Sounds, such as popping noises, that used to be emotionally neutral become associated with intense aversion and defensiveness. Depressed patients often report difficulty experiencing pleasure or being motivated to engage in previously enjoyed activities. This emotional shift could coincide with the rezoning of the accumbens shell. The researchers' seeming ability to increase the size of the appetitive zone of the rats' nucleus accumbens by changing their living conditions suggests that environmental conditions and perhaps cognitive-behavioral therapies can also produce more positive accumbens responses (e.g., happiness, pleasure, anticipation) in humans by physically altering the nucleus accumbens shell. As emphasized throughout this text, context, here in the form of a stressful home cage, influences the brain's emotional responses in significant ways. Hence, an animal's physical and social environment should always be evaluated when examining neurobiological effects. Further, these findings reinforce the importance of considering the environmental context of humans when exploring mechanisms of mental illness and other maladaptive functions.

Thus, research on pleasure and happiness has identified several brain areas and neurochemicals, suggesting

Hunger Regulation

If there is any task that the brain has mastered, it is motivating us to eat. Eating is essential for survival. If caloric intake stops, in time the body will enter a state of starvation, and physiological functions will begin to fail. One of the first organs to feel the effects of food deprivation is the brain, which is the energy hog of the body, consuming up to 20% of the fuel we expend (Wrangham, 2009).

Too much food can be as harmful as too little, however, especially over the long term. In today's developed societies, where food is plentiful, the motivation to eat has led to adverse consequences for many. The World Health Organization has stated that the obesity epidemic is a significant contributor to the global burden of disease, with worldwide rates of obesity doubling since 1980 (World Health Organization, 2014). Whereas **obesity** refers to having an excessive amount of fat, overweight refers to possessing excessive weight because of muscle, fluids, fat, or bone composition. Using the body mass index (BMI) as a factor, normal-weight BMIs range from 18 to 24, with overweight BMIs ranging from 25 to 29 and BMIs categorized as obese in the range of 30 and above (U.S. Department of Health and Human Services, National Institutes of Health, National Institute of Diabetes and Digestive and Kidney Diseases, 2012). One survey found that from 2009 to 2010, 32% of children and adolescents in a representative sample of the U.S. population were either overweight or obese (Ogden, Carroll, Kit, & Flegal, 2012).

In past generations, when most people were more physically active throughout the day, caloric intake closely matched caloric expenditure. Even considering that our society consumes more food than needed to carry out basic physiological functions, the ability of humans and other mammals to monitor eating behavior is impressive. The typical human adult male consumes a whopping 900,000 calories a year. Straying from this amount by consuming a mere extra 11 calories a day (approximately 4,000 calories a year) will result in a weight gain of about one pound per year. Consequently, the margin of error for maintaining one's adult weight is less than 0.5% (Seeley & Woods, 2003). Those calibrated energy consumption/expenditure circuits that were so finely tuned in our ancestors seem to have become confused in our contemporary society with excess food availability, particularly of high-fat and high-sugar products. In this section, we will discuss the evolution of the strict regulation of caloric consumption and energy expenditure that characterized our human ancestors, as well as potential factors leading to compromised functioning of the hunger regulation system.

The Evolution of Efficient Eating Strategies and Brain Enlargement

Many anthropologists look to the environment for perhaps the single most important human discovery, which simultaneously catapulted the brain's growth to exceed the brain size of early human ancestors and greatly reduced the amount of time required to provide a daily portion of calories. Can you guess the identity of this environmental factor? If you are thinking "fire," then you are on the right track. In the 19th century, Charles Darwin declared that the ability to make fire was "probably the greatest [discovery], excepting language, ever made by men" because it made difficult-to-eat roots digestible and diminished the poisons in various herbs (Darwin, 1874; p. 54). This proposal was more recently advocated by Harvard biological anthropologist Richard Wrangham in his book *Catching Fire: How Cooking Made Us Human.* Let's consider the evidence for the claim that the advent of cooked food sparked the growth of the human brain.

In 2006, nine volunteers with high blood pressure participated in a study called the Evo Diet Experiment to explore the diet our primate ancestors consumed, that is, a diet of raw food (such as the fruits and vegetables in Figure 8.6) (Fullerton-Smith, 2007). For 12 days, the participants lived in a tent in England's Paignton Zoo and ate only raw fruits and vegetables, about 2,300 calories worth, an ideal level for human adults. Their diet consisted of peppers, melons, cucumbers, tomatoes, carrots, broccoli, grapes, dates, bananas, peaches, and various nuts. Further, during the second week, portions of cooked oily fish were also included to mimic a hunter–gatherer diet. To consume the number of calories needed to maintain ideal adult weights, each participant had to eat about 10 pounds of food a day. As you might imagine, eating this much food takes a lot of time, leaving less time for

FIGURE 8.6 Raw food diet. To maintain a healthy body weight on a raw-food diet, humans must consume excessive amounts.

other activities. And, although their caloric intake was not what we would consider "dieting," in just 12 days, participants lost an average of 9.7 pounds—nearly a pound a day.

As this experiment suggests, modern humans on a raw-food diet have difficulty maintaining a healthy body weight, even while consuming 10 pounds of food a day. So, where does all this food go? About half of the proteins in the raw food exit the small intestine undigested. In contrast, if those foods were cooked, their proteins would be more digestible through the process of **denaturing**, or weakening the protein's internal bonds. Denaturation can also be increased by exposing food to acidity (e.g., pickling), salt, or drying. With this in mind, the traditional recipe for adding lemon to dried salted cod (bacalhau) makes evolutionary sense.

The physical anthropologist Loring Brace has proposed that our human ancestors began manipulating fire and heating food about 200,000 years ago; others have suggested that this process originated later (Brace, 1995). Brace further speculates that the teeth and stomachs of these early humans started adapting to eating less raw food and increased amounts of soft food. Now that humans required smaller storage capacities for their food, there was no need to carry around large stomachs. Interestingly, whereas there are strict sizing regulations for most of the body's organs (e.g., a large body requires a large heart), a considerable amount of variation exists for the intestinal system across species. This may explain why stomachs are smaller in humans than in nonhuman primates (see Figure 8.7).

Likely prompted by cooked food, humans now have small teeth and guts for an animal of our size. With fewer resources going to the stomach, more resources could be directed to the brain. As suggested in the raw-food experiment, cooked-food diets allow us to eat more calories much faster and in smaller quantities than raw-food diets. Contemporary primate species show considerable variability in intestinal sizes. Primates with smaller intestinal sizes relative to their body sizes generally have higher-quality

(a)

(b)

FIGURE 8.7 **Diet and stomach size.** (a) Orangutans, who eat only raw foods, require a large stomach for storage. (b) Eating cooked foods enables humans to have smaller stomachs, since they obtain necessary levels of nutrients from smaller volumes of food.

diets, meaning that they do not have to spend the bulk of their day foraging for food and chewing raw foods (Aiello & Wheeler, 1995). The primates with more complex food-searching strategies have larger brains than simple leaf foragers. As shown in Figure 8.8, although the spider monkey and howler monkey have similar body sizes, the fruit-eating spider monkey has a smaller stomach and larger brain than the leaf-eating howler monkey. Consider the potential role of a behavior such as cooking on the unrivaled number of neurons in the human brain as described in Chapter 5.

In addition to channeling more glucose to the brain from more calorically rich foods, cooking led to several lifestyle changes in humans. Controlling fires provided protection that may have prompted early humans to leave the safety of the trees and join one another around a fire to sleep. Sleeping in groups, as well as cooking around and maintaining a campfire, may have facilitated social cooperation. A transportable heat source also allowed humans to explore and survive in colder environments. Finally, a preference for soft food allows human mothers to wean their young early, providing shorter intervals between births.

Although anthropological assumptions are largely speculative, we now have considerable corroborating evidence that using fire for cooking food helped mold modern humans. The cognitive powers required to direct food production and preparation, in collaboration with the physical changes in the stomachs that occurred in modern humans, may have been the perfect recipe for an enlarged brain with enhanced cognitive potential (Wrangham, 2009). Such evolutionary modifications in humans confirm the far-reaching influence of hunger motivation on our species. Transitioning from global evolutionary factors to neurobiological mechanisms of hunger motivation, as will be discussed in the next section, provides further clues about this critical behavior.

(a) (c)

Howler monkey
(leaf-eating generalists)

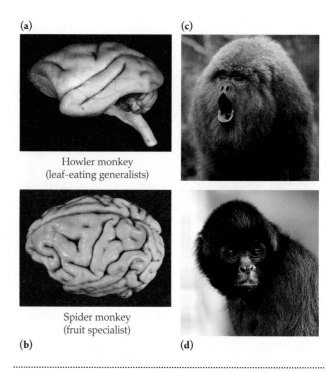

Spider monkey
(fruit specialist)

(b) (d)

FIGURE 8.8 **Diet and brain size.** The type of diet consumed by an animal is associated with its brain size. Howler monkeys eat leaves and have a smaller brain, proportionally, than do spider monkeys, which consume a more calorie-dense diet of fruit. Additionally, the spider monkey also has a more complex cortex with additional gyri and sulci.

The Neurobiology of Hunger Regulation

We have just considered some broad anthropological and evolutionary perspectives on eating. However, behavioral neuroscientists also investigate smaller-scale neural mechanisms within our brains and bodies to understand hunger and eating. Evolutionarily speaking, the maintenance of a healthy body weight under constantly changing environmental conditions was and remains a formidable challenge. This challenge was met by the evolution of a multifaceted system consisting of specific neural circuits and neurochemical activation patterns. Because eating is critical for survival, multiple physiological systems affecting hunger regulation ensure that food will continue to be consumed if one system malfunctions. Although the hunger regulation system usually keeps mammals eating, malfunctions do arise—these malfunctions, in the form of anorexia nervosa, bulimia nervosa, and obesity, will be discussed in the next few sections.

Interest in the neural mechanisms of hunger regulation coincided with the observation that food intake and body weight could be dramatically altered by lesioning specific nuclei of the hypothalamus in rats. Research in the 1960s provided evidence that bilateral lesions of the **ventromedial hypothalamus (VMH)** led to overeating (**hyperphagia**) and obesity in laboratory rats (Grossman, 1967, 1973). Additionally, research provided evidence that bilateral lesions of the **lateral hypothalamus (LH)** resulted in reduced eating and decreased body weight in laboratory rats (Anand & Brobeck, 1951). This research led to the view that the brain contained a hunger and satiety center, like a switch to turn hunger on and off. However, scientists subsequently learned that central nervous system control of hunger is more complicated.

Later research identified the VMH's role in **insulin** secretion, suggesting that the VMH plays a more indirect role in body weight than if it were a satiety center (Woods, Schwartz, Baskin, & Seeley, 2000). For example, even VMH-lesioned rats that were kept from overeating secreted increased insulin, which increases fat storage (Rohner-Jeanrenaud & Jeanrenaud, 1980). Concerning the LH, early lesion studies in rats damaged fibers known collectively as the **dopaminergic nigrostriatal bundle**, involved in motor and sensory systems. Damage to these fibers appeared to produce a general motivational deficit, more widespread than just a deficit in hunger motivation. Subsequent research leaving this bundle intact provided evidence that certain cells in the LH play a role in initiating food intake, independent of the dopaminergic nigrostriatal bundle (Clark, Clark, Bartle, & Winn, 1991; Winn, Tarbuck, & Dunnett, 1984). In fact, a population of neurons in the monkey LH was shown to respond to the taste and sight of food, but not to the taste or sight of a nonfood substance (Rolls, 1981a, 1981b, 1986; Rolls, Sanghera, & Roper-Hall, 1979). The LH cells were only temporarily quieted when the monkey was full of one type of food substance; they became activated when a new, appealing food was presented. The sensitivity of the LH neurons to food diminished, however, when monkeys were fed the new food to satiety. This phenomenon, known as **sensory-specific satiety** (Rolls, 1981a), explains why you cannot eat another bite of your main dinner entrée but seem to have plenty of room for dessert! It was becoming clear that these early hunger and satiety "switches" were part of larger neural circuits, an observation that further research strongly supported.

Neurochemicals and Appetite Control. More recent scientific literature suggests the difficulty of disentangling the roles of certain brain areas and various neuropeptides, neurotransmitters, and hormones in hunger regulation. One of the earliest neurochemicals to become associated with food intake and energy regulation was insulin, a hormone that facilitates the storage of energy in body fat and liver tissue. When patients with diabetes begin insulin treatment, for example, higher levels of insulin in the blood lead to increased glucose absorption and body weight gain. It was a mystery in the beginning, however, how a hormone that facilitated the storage of food (and removal of food metabolites from circulation) could lead to decreased hunger.

This mystery was solved as researchers learned that insulin enhanced satiety by crossing the blood–brain barrier and activating receptors in an area of the hypothalamus known as the **arcuate nucleus** (Woods et al., 2000). Diets high in fat and sugar have been shown to decrease insulin's effectiveness at lowering blood glucose levels, a condition known as **insulin resistance**. The unfortunate result of insulin resistance is increased food consumption and fat storage (Davidoff et al, 2004; Erlanson-Albertsson, 2005; Kim et al, 2004).

In the 1990s, a hormone called **leptin** was found to play a key role in hunger regulation when mice that expressed a recessive gene that made them leptin deficient became obese (**ob/ob mice**). As seen in Figure 8.9, in one human case study, a young boy with low levels of leptin was overweight, but lost weight following leptin treatment (Farooqi et al., 2002). Similar results were found in rodents (Figure 8.10 depicts a normal mouse and an ob/ob mouse). The leptin hormone, produced in fatty tissue, is a critical hunger regulatory signal conveying metabolic information from the body to the hypothalamus. Researchers further discovered that leptin receptors reside in the arcuate nucleus of the hypothalamus along with insulin receptors. The medical community hoped that this line of research would lead to an effective medical approach to treat obesity. However, most obese people do not have a leptin deficiency as originally thought (Farr, Gavrieli, & Mantzoros, 2015; Friedman & Halaas, 1998; Horvath & Diano, 2004). Alternatively, leptin replacement therapy in patients with metabolic disturbances and accompanying weight loss (e.g., anorexia) has been associated with weight gain (Blüher & Mantzoros, 2009). Further, in addition to its role in energy expenditure, leptin is currently being investigated for its therapeutic role in neuroendocrine and reproductive dysfunction (Chou and Mantzoros, 2014).

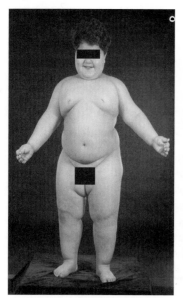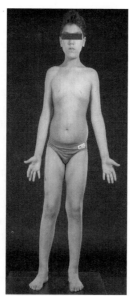

3yr old weighing 42kg   7yr old weighing 32kg

FIGURE 8.9 **Leptin-deficiency.** After being treated for his leptin deficiency, this boy lost weight, approaching a more typical weight for his age.

FIGURE 8.10 **Leptin-deficient mice.** Mice expressing a recessive gene associated with leptin deficiency have more body fat than mice that do not express the recessive gene.

Ghrelin, a chemical secreted by endocrine cells in the stomach, is another hunger signal secreted outside of the CNS that is subsequently detected in the brain to regulate hunger and food consumption. Ghrelin levels increase during fasting and decrease following a meal; thus, ghrelin is known as a meal initiator. As ghrelin migrates from the peripheral bloodstream to the brain, it activates receptors in the arcuate nucleus of the hypothalamus. Long-term ghrelin treatment results in increased body weight and fat accumulation.

A cleverly designed study in rats demonstrated the influence of the central administration of a drug similar to ghrelin, growth hormone–releasing protein-6. As shown in Figure 8.11, rats that were given access to as much food as they wanted exhibited decreased activation in the arcuate nucleus surrounding the third ventricle following an intravenous injection of growth hormone–releasing protein-6. In contrast, activation was increased in animals that had fasted. Activation in this study was determined by the detection of a protein (in this case the **Fos** protein) that indicates recent activity in a particular brain area (more about this technique appears in Chapter 12's "Laboratory

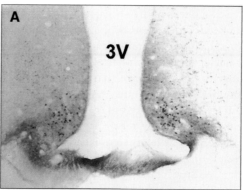

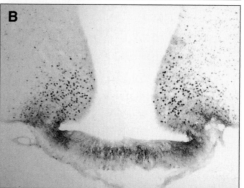

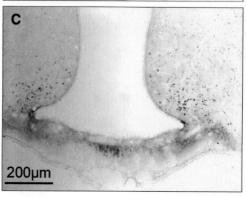

FIGURE 8.11 **Hunger and the arcuate nucleus.** As indicated by the presence of darkly stained Fos-positive cells, there is less activation in the arcuate nucleus of (a) rats that are fed to satiety and administered saline than in that of (b) rats that are food deprived with a saline infusion. (c) However, if the hungry animals receive an insulin infusion, less Fos activity is observed.

Exploration"). Animals that had fasted but had also received injections of insulin to the lateral ventricles showed decreased activation, although insulin levels remained low outside the brain. These results emphasized the dominant role of CNS levels of these satiety signals over PNS levels (Hewson, Tung, Connell, Tookman, & Dickson, 2002).

Another neurochemical that has received considerable attention for its role in hunger regulation is **neuropeptide Y (NPY)**, a neuropeptide neurotransmitter similar to those described in Chapter 4. In the 1980s, researchers showed that NPY caused increased food intake (Clark et al., 1984). Administration of NPY to the cerebral ventricles in rats produced a robust eating response that had not been seen in previous research exploring the effects of modulators in the feeding response. In addition, NPY is released from the hypothalamus when energy demands increase, as in the case of exercise or lactation (Erlanson-Albertsson, 2005). Research has shown that leptin and insulin inhibit NPY expression and activity (Erikson et al., 1996; Schwartz et al., 1991). Further, ghrelin activates NPY neurons (Wren et al., 2002). Hypothalamic neurons also produce **agouti-related peptide (AgRP)**, a neurochemical that works in conjunction with NPY neurons to maintain energy regulation by increasing appetite and decreasing energy expenditure when necessary (Hahn, Breininger, Baskin, & Schwartz, 1988; Horvath & Diano, 2004) (see Figure 8.12). Recent research has indicated that the **paraventricular nucleus** of the hypothalamus, an area of the hypothalamus long thought to be

involved with the inhibition of appetite, contains a subset of neurons that enhance hunger by stimulating the AgRP neurons in the arcuate nucleus (Krashes et al., 2014). Such findings confirm the complex, interactive nature of the CNS circuits mediating hunger regulation (Trivedi, 2014).

The hunger and satiety signals mentioned thus far represent just a few on the long list of chemical signals that have been identified as **orexigenic** (appetite stimulating) or **anorexigenic** (appetite suppressing). We can view the vast distribution of these substances throughout the body as multiple backup and detection systems to protect against malfunctions in hunger regulation. With so many substances involved, it is unlikely that the vital hunger and satiety signals will be ignored. However, diets that differ drastically from that of our ancestors may interfere with this finely tuned energy-regulating system and associated neurochemicals. Consuming a highly appetizing diet rich in fat, sugar, and salt likely results in the breakdown of several safeguards, contributing to the high rates of obesity in today's society (Erlanson-Albertsson, 2005).

The impact of so many neurochemical factors (e.g., neuropeptides and hormones) has stirred much enthusiasm in the pharmaceutical industry. Might it be possible to create an anti-ghrelin pill or NPY blocker to suppress hunger? Although you may see advertisements for various products that claim to enable people to lose weight effortlessly, thus far, an effective pharmacological treatment has not been found. In a review on this topic, Gerard Smith and Nori Geary (2002) declared that "the current status of this work on central neuropeptides can be described as a few small islands of scientific understanding surrounded by a vast area of uncertain phenomena" (p. 1667). This summary remains true today. Realistically, the fine-tuning of these peptides may be dwarfed by the more influential roles played by the environment—with its abundance of high-fat and high-sugar foodstuffs. Changes in our environment over the past century—leading to decreased physical activity and the overproduction of highly desired food—have likely contributed to the apparent breakdown of the energy maintenance system that evolved in our ancestors.

Why Can't We Eat Just One? In this section, we will revisit the brain's reward circuit. We will consider how the same system that was designed to keep us eating when resources were hard to come by contributes to our inability to say no to our favorite junk food.

Given the importance of the mesolimbic dopamine reward circuit in guiding our behavior, it is no surprise that it plays a role in eating as well. The activation of "liking" reward circuits ensures that humans consume sweet, fatty, and salty foods. The pleasurable response is powerful enough to activate wanting circuits as well so that we remain attentive when these types of foods are in our midst or even in our thoughts (Berridge et al., 2010). These observations confirm the marketing genius of the creators of fast-food restaurants serving high-fat, salty food and sugary soft drinks.

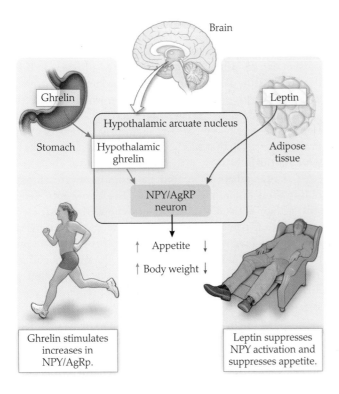

FIGURE 8.12 Contributions of leptin and ghrelin to hunger responses. Leptin and ghrelin interact with the arcuate nucleus to affect hunger and energy regulation.

In 1963, the advertising firm Young and Rubicam launched a wildly successful campaign for Lay's potato chips with the slogan, "Bet you can't eat just one." This was an advertising campaign, not a serious scientific claim. However, these advertising executives may have been onto something by suggesting that these high-fat and salty chips were *addictive*. Although potato chips are tempting, sweets are even harder for many people to refuse. Some people report that they feel as compelled to eat sweet foods as an alcoholic is to drink. Intrigued by the notion of sugar addiction, Princeton University neuroscientist Bart Hoebel and his colleagues explored similarities between addiction to highly desired foods and addiction to drugs of abuse (discussed in Chapter 4).

The rat model that Hoebel and his colleagues developed involved a daily feeding schedule of 12 hours without food followed by 12 hours of access to sugar solution and rat chow. The rats drink more on this intermittent schedule, providing a model of binging similar to human behavior. Rats in a comparative control group had sugar access for a half hour per day, along with unrestricted access to chow. After a month of this sweet-solution diet, the 12-hour-exposure rats exhibited various behaviors characteristic of responses to drug abuse, including binging and "withdrawal" symptoms characterized by signs of increased anxiety and depression. Implicating the dopaminergic system that is involved in drug addiction, dopamine in the nucleus accumbens increased in rats with intermittent access to the sugar solution, leading to modified sensitivity of dopamine receptors (Avena, Rada, & Hoebel, 2008). As shown in Figure 8.13, rats with 12 hours of daily exposure to a sugar solution increased their lever pressing for sugar by 123% following an abstinence period of 14 days. This increase was much higher than that shown by the half-hour exposure group.

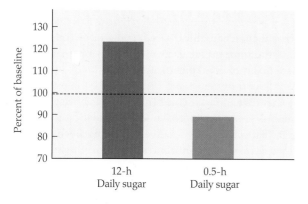

Source: Avena, N. M., Rada, P., Hoebel, B. G. (2008). Evidence of sugar addiction: Behavioral and neurochemical effects of intermittent, excessive sugar intake. *Neuroscience and Biobehavioral Reviews, 32,* 20-39.

FIGURE 8.13 Sugar withdrawal. Rats that had experienced greater access to sugar consumed much more sugar after a period of sugar deprivation than did control rats.

Further investigations produced even stronger evidence of parallels between drug and sugar addiction. These researchers observed a **cross-sensitization** between sugar consumption and amphetamine. Rats that were maintained on the intermittent-sugar diet and given daily amphetamine injections exhibited typical drug-induced hyperactivity after tasting 10% sugar solution one week later. Additionally, rats that had developed this "sweet tooth" demonstrated hyperactivity in response to a low dose of amphetamine that had no effect on animals not exposed to drugs or sugar. This effect remained even after eight days of sugar abstinence (Avena & Hoebel, 2003). Such cross-sensitization occurs with other drugs of abuse. These results prompted researchers to suggest that sugar addiction may serve as a "gateway drug" for other drugs of abuse, just as nicotine may serve as a gateway to illegal drugs such as cocaine (Avena et al., 2008; Lai, Lai, Page, & McCoy, 2000).

Perhaps the most compelling evidence of sugar addiction occurs when such rats have no access to sugar or other food for 24 hours. In another study using the same intermittent-exposure protocol, the rats showed dramatic somatic signs of withdrawal such as teeth chattering, head shaking, and forepaw tremor (Colantuoni et al., 2002). Other studies have shown that decreased body temperature and heightened aggression also accompany spontaneous withdrawal following the removal of sugar (Galic & Persinger, 2002; Wideman, Nadzam, & Murphy, 2005). It appears that sugar addiction and drug addiction cause similar behavioral and brain changes.

The Scripps Research Institute neuroscientists Paul Johnson and Paul Kenney (2010) decided to go right to the source of brain reward to learn more about how compulsive eating influenced the experience of reward. They implanted stimulating electrodes in the lateral hypothalamus of rats. After 14 days of training in which the rats responded vigorously to receiving electrical brain stimulation, the researchers recorded the minimal intensity of the brain stimulation that was necessary to motivate the rats to work for the reward.

The researchers compared these brain-reward thresholds in three different groups of rats. The "chow-only" (control) group received only laboratory chow. The "restricted-access" group had free access for 1 hour a day to a "cafeteria" diet, with many energy-dense foods (in this study, sausage, bacon, pound cake, cheesecake, frosting, and chocolate). The "extended-access" group received the same cafeteria diet, but for 18 to 23 hours per day. All groups had unrestricted access to rodent chow.

Although weight increased in the restricted-access group, only the extended-access group exhibited statistically significant weight gain. The extended-access group also exhibited higher thresholds for rewarding brain stimulation, similar to rats with extended access to heroin or cocaine self-administration. That is, when the extended-access group was assessed in the brain stimulation task, it required more intense levels of electrical brain stimulation before the animals would work to receive the stimulation. The stimulation itself appeared to have become less intrinsically motivating. Thus, extended access to highly appealing, high-fat food appeared to induce addiction-like deficits in brain reward functions.

In this study, the intensity of the brain stimulation had to be elevated for the rats to experience reward. In their natural habitat, this finding would likely translate into the rats having to eat more to experience expected levels of reward. This speculation was confirmed when these researchers monitored food consumption among the three groups. The chow-only and restricted-access groups did not show any differences in food consumption. However, the extended-access group consumed twice the number of calories of the other groups. Further analyses revealed that rats in the restricted-access group consumed only 33% of their calories from chow. This result suggests that even limited exposure to a high-fat diet results in binge-like eating when the high-fat food is available. These rats consumed 66% of their diet during this one-hour buffet. Even more disturbing was the eating pattern of rats in the extended-access group, which consumed only 5% of their total calories from chow, eating the cafeteria diet almost exclusively.

Following 40 days of the cafeteria diet, all groups were given standard rodent chow. The researchers continued to monitor brain reward thresholds and noted that these deficits persisted for two weeks, longer than had been observed for rats in other studies undergoing abstinence from self-administered cocaine (Markou & Koob, 1991). Thus, the urge for a double cheeseburger, especially if it has become a regular part of your diet, should not be underestimated! See Figure 8.14 for weight gain and brain reward thresholds for each group.

A second phase of this study assessed the density of dopamine receptors using a new cohort of animals placed on the same diet. The expression of dopamine DA2 receptors was lower in the striatum of the extended-access groups than in the other groups. The investigators suggested that the easy access humans have to cafeteria-style diets is an important contributor to the obesity epidemic threatening Western societies today. In a depressing downward spiral, this study provides evidence that humans' overconsumption of high-fat foods leads to higher thresholds for satiety and pleasure, resulting in further overeating and weight gain. The sensitive feedback system consisting of peripheral and central distributions of satiety and hunger peptides discussed previously can no longer modulate the system. Just as flooding a gallery containing beautifully detailed art with white light diminishes our retinal cells' ability to detect the color and form represented on each canvas, flooding our physiological systems with more food than Nature ever intended has masked our safeguards for maintaining healthy weight levels and energy balances. Behavioral neuroscientists interested in the causes of obesity must consider our contemporary environments and lifestyles.

(a)

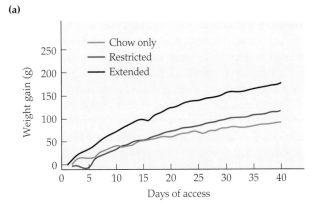

(b)

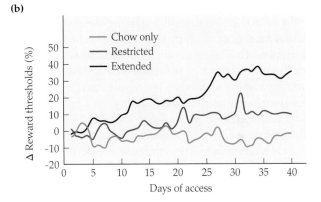

Source: Johnson, P.M., & Kenney, P.J. (2010). Dopamine D2 receptors in addiction-like reward dysfunction and compulsive eating in obese rats. *Nature Neuroscience, 13*, 635-641.

FIGURE 8.14 The powerful effects of "all you can eat." Having extended access to calorie-rich, highly desired foods altered weight gain and brain threshold levels for rewarding stimuli in rats.

Environmental Influences on Eating

Other than perhaps heat production, overeating has few benefits. Knowing that continued access to high-fat diets leads not only to obesity but also to symptoms of depression and addiction is even more disconcerting. Yale psychologist Kelly Brownell has conducted research that provides evidence for the toxic effects of excessive food exposure on humans, especially on children who are establishing lifelong eating habits. In addition to the effects of low physical activity and increased food consumption, he has also explored the effects of food advertisements on hunger regulation and food consumption. On average, children view about 15 food commercials per day, with 98% of these commercials promoting diets high in fat, sugar, and sodium (Powell, Szczypka, Chaloupka, & Braunschweig, 2007). Additionally, these ads promote the artificial association between unhealthy eating patterns and positive outcomes (e.g., snacking at nonmeal times, having fun when eating certain unhealthy foods).

Although earlier research had confirmed that these advertising campaigns successfully motivate children to consume the advertised products (Story & French, 2004), Brownell and his colleagues conducted a study to explore the consistency with which food and beverage advertisements would prompt both children and adults to exhibit corresponding eating responses (Harris, Bargh, & Brownell, 2009). When you see a commercial with warm chocolate-chip cookies, do you find yourself sprinting to the kitchen for a glass of milk and a cookie? In these studies, the food advertisements were embedded within a television program. In the children's portion of the experiment, the children watched a cartoon with food advertisements while having the opportunity to snack on goldfish crackers. Children watching the cartoon with the food advertisements ate 45% more goldfish crackers than those watching the cartoon without the food advertisements. This increased food consumption, coupled with the obvious fact that television viewing restricts physical activity, leads to a lifestyle strategy that will quickly add pounds to these young children's bodies.

Would this effect generalize to more mature individuals, in this case university students between the ages of 18 and 24? In this phase of the study, the subjects viewed the television program with the embedded food ads. This time, one group watched snack ads, one group viewed ads for nutritious foods, and one group viewed nonfood ads. In this phase of the study, no snack food was available. The subjects were asked to stay in the lab following the program to test consumer products, rating their taste and perceived nutritional value. Although the results were not as dramatic in the adults as in the children, the subjects viewing the snack food ads consumed more of both healthful and unhealthful foods than did the subjects in the other groups. In addition, viewing the food ads was associated with enhanced consumption of unadvertised foods, regardless of hunger status. But the subjects viewing the snack ads consumed healthful foods, even when those foods were competing with cookies and trail mix. In fact, the subjects viewing the snack ads consumed more vegetables than other food substances, suggesting that, even after bombardment with unhealthful food ads, the human predisposition for healthful vegetables persisted. Thus, although we should all take heed of these results, we should also appreciate that there is still hope of returning to some semblance of our ancestral diets.

Another aspect of our environment that greatly affects our food consumption rates may surprise you—it involves the company we keep while we are eating. Do you eat more when you are alone or with a group of friends? Most people eat more when with others, an effect called the **social facilitation of eating**. Let's consider research that has investigated this phenomenon.

John de Castro has conducted informative research in the real world of eating behavior. He argued that the laboratory presents too many artificial obstacles to accurately investigate human feeding patterns (for example, food costs are a significant factor rarely considered in laboratory experiments). Therefore, he gave his subjects eating diaries and requested that they write down the type of food, amount consumed, their feelings/emotional responses, and the number of people present each time they ate for seven days (de Castro, 2000).

The results in several such studies have been surprising. Meals eaten in the presence of others are on average 44% larger than those consumed alone. These social meals include more carbohydrates, fat, protein, and alcohol. And as the number of people increases, the larger the meals become (as Figure 8.15 illustrates). Subjects consumed 58% more with three people, 69% with four people, 70% with five people, and 96% more with a group larger than seven people. It is amazing how little we sometimes know about our own behavior.

The definitive explanation for social facilitation of eating is still unknown, but several possibilities have emerged. We remain around food longer when we are in the company of others; we may pay less attention to how much we are eating when we are otherwise engaged with our friends' conversations; and the presence of others may trigger some unconscious competition, prompting us to keep reaching for the tortilla chips more often than we would when eating alone. Regardless of the reason, it is important for us to be aware of this trend in eating.

Clinical Implications of Eating Strategies: Eating Disorders, Diet, and Hunger Regulation

The hunger regulation system usually motivates humans to eat. However, individuals suffering from **anorexia nervosa** are an unfortunate reminder that no physiological system

(a)

(b)

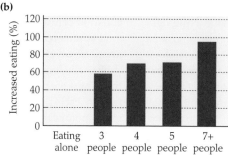

FIGURE 8.15 **Social influence on food consumption.** (a) Eating with friends may be enjoyable, (b) but it leads us to consume more calories.

is perfect. According to the fifth edition of the *Diagnostic and Statistical Manual of Mental Disorders*, the diagnostic criteria for anorexia nervosa include being at a significantly low body weight for one's developmental stage, having an exaggerated fear of gaining weight, having an unrealistic perception of weight, and demonstrating persistent behavior that interferes with weight gain. Although it is not officially a diagnostic criterion, excessive exercise often accompanies this disorder. Anorexia is rare, affecting about 0.3% of the U.S. population, but it has the highest mortality rate of any psychiatric disorder (Hoek, 2006; Kaye, Fudge, & Paulus, 2009).

Walter Kaye, a neuroscientist at the University of California at San Diego, and his colleagues have conducted extensive research on the causes of anorexia nervosa. They describe it as a disorder of complex causes rather than a single imbalance of a neurochemical. Research suggests that multiple factors, ranging from sociocultural to genetic, interact to contribute to increased vulnerability for the development of this disorder. A general pattern of symptoms follows: Anorexia nervosa typically starts in the teen years when an individual goes on a strict diet and successfully loses weight. Then the weight loss progresses to an "out-of-control spiral" (Kaye et al., 2009; p. 582). Several predisposed temperaments and traits have been associated with this disorder, for example, negative emotionality, perfectionism, and obsessive–compulsive tendencies. Additionally, genetic factors are believed to account for about 50–80% of the variance (i.e., how spread out a certain variable is across a population) in both anorexia nervosa and a related disorder, **bulimia nervosa** (Kaye et al., 2009' Walters & Kendler, 1995).

Bulimia nervosa and anorexia nervosa are both disorders in which eating regulation is altered in dangerous ways. However, bulimia is characterized by the behaviors of binging (excessive overeating) and purging (removing food from one's system via strategies such as self-induced vomiting or use of laxatives). If continued, such behaviors lead to symptoms such as damaged tissue in the mouth and throat resulting from an excess of digestive enzymes. Whereas brain scans of anorexia patients in one study revealed less gray matter area in the cerebellum and a few cortical areas such as the primary motor cortex compared with healthy controls, brain scans of bulimia patients revealed reduced volume of the caudate putamen compared with healthy controls (Amianto et al., 2013). Since the subjects in this neuroimaging study were patients who had engaged in these behaviors for some time, however, it is difficult to know whether these different effects were a cause or a consequence of the disorder.

In another study, when patients with bulimia were compared with healthy controls on a spatial task in which subjects were instructed to respond to the direction of arrows while suppressing irrelevant information about the positioning of the visual stimuli, the bulimia patients exhibited less activation in the **frontostriatal** brain area. This brain area is implicated in the self-regulation necessary to perform such a task. The frontostriatal brain area connects the frontal cortex to the striatum. The researchers hypothesized that bulimia involves a compromise of the brain areas involved in regulatory control, leading to binging when the individual encounters eating opportunities (Marsh et al., 2011).

Although neurobiological research has been conducted on both patients with bulimia nervosa and patients with anorexia nervosa, more informative research has been conducted on anorexia patients. From the biopsychological research conducted on this disorder, three interesting observations stand out:

- *Anorexia patients often exercise compulsively and report experiencing* **anhedonia** *(the inability to experience pleasure in previously rewarding or enjoyable activities).* Given the complicated role of dopamine in reward and motivation systems, it should be no surprise that dopamine has been suggested as playing a causal role in anorexia. Dysfunctional mesolimbic dopamine functions may be associated with altered reward and emotional experiences, shifts in decision making and executive control, excessive repetitive movements, and decreased hunger (Kontis & Theochari, 2012). Supportive evidence for this hypothesis includes the finding of lower levels of dopamine metabolites in the CSF of anorexia patients both ill and in recovery, suggesting that this may be a chronic condition as opposed to a result of the starvation during anorexia (Frank et al., 2005; Kaye, Frank, & McConaha, 1999). Recall the compulsively running rats described at the beginning of this chapter: A dopamine blocker reduced the excessive running and weight loss in these rats. Accordingly, modifications of the dopamine system may normalize the behavior of anorexia patients.

- *Another neurochemical suspect in the emergence of anorexia symptoms is serotonin.* As discussed in Chapter 4, serotonin is a pervasive neurotransmitter that is present in several brain areas thought to be involved in the relevant responses of patients with anorexia, such as modifications in impulse control, satiety, and mood. When serotonin metabolites are measured in the CSF of ill anorexia patients, low levels of 5-hydroxyindoleacetic acid (5-HT) are observed. These low levels of serotonin metabolites are thought to indicate low extracellular levels of serotonin. In patients who have recovered from anorexia, however, elevated serotonin metabolites are observed in the CSF. Imaging studies have provided further evidence of specific serotonin receptor involvement in the brains of ill patients and patients who have recovered from anorexia. Results have consistently shown that anorexia patients have different patterns of specific serotonin receptors (i.e., 5-HT_{1A} and 5-HT_{2A}) than healthy individuals do (as shown in Figure 8.16) (Audenaert et al., 2003; Bailer et al., 2005; Kaye, Wierenga, Bailer, Simmons, & Bischoff-Grethe, 2013). In such cases, dieting may calm anxieties in the short term, but lead to dangerous health consequences in the long term. Thus, the propensity for extreme dieting practices may serve a self-medicating function by recalibrating serotonin and other related neurochemical systems that initially led to the dysfunctional psychological symptoms discussed previously. Of course, extreme food deprivation and significant weight loss become a bigger problem than neurochemical alterations as the restricted eating continues. As more information about underlying neurochemical alterations in anorexia emerges, more specific treatments can be developed.

• *The anterior insular cortex responds to taste and the physical properties of foods as well as their rewarding properties.* Consequently, this brain area may play a role in the development of anorexia. The insula may be a key component of a more integrative neural circuit consisting of the amygdala, anterior cingulate cortex, orbitofrontal

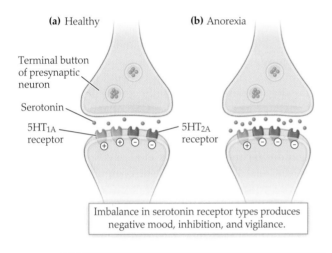

(a) Healthy   **(b)** Anorexia

Terminal button of presynaptic neuron

Serotonin

$5HT_{1A}$ receptor $5HT_{2A}$ receptor

Imbalance in serotonin receptor types produces negative mood, inhibition, and vigilance.

FIGURE 8.16 Serotonergic receptors and anorexia. Research suggests that the proportion of 5-hydroxyindoleacetic acid 1A and 2A receptors in (a) healthy patients is distorted in (b) patients diagnosed with anorexia.

cortex, dorsolateral prefrontal cortex, and parietal cortex. Additionally, activation of the tongue's taste receptors (also known as chemoreceptors) subsequently stimulates the brainstem areas (medulla and **nucleus tractus solitari**) before activating the thalamus taste center. The activation of this circuit in a patient with anorexia may lead to an enhanced top-down modulation (or higher cortical control of lower brain circuits) of food intake, an ability that, if experienced to a lesser degree, would serve overweight individuals well. The enhanced ability to regulate the basic function of hunger in the case of anorexia, however, leads to an avoidance of food in the patient, accompanied by chronic weight loss and sickness. We have discussed the importance of the insula previously in this text (see Chapter 2). Its potential involvement in anorexia further supports its pivotal role in integrating information about the internal and external variables associated with our bodies and brains (see Figure 8.17). For example, patients with anorexia may have a distorted insula response that does not appropriately prompt increased eating to maintain body weight at a healthy level.

Thus, these three neurobiological systems (dopamine, serotonin, and insular neural network) appear to play important roles in the onset of anorexia nervosa. The facts that this disorder is more typically observed in females and that the usual time of onset is puberty, when menstruation begins, may also be important pieces of the puzzle (Kaye et al., 2009). Learning about the factors involved in anorexia allows scientists to better understand the functions of hunger and satiety systems in healthy individuals.

Although some eating strategies can be toxic for one's health, others can be therapeutic. Informed food choices can result in various benefits to the brain, such as enhanced cognition. For example, **omega (ω)-3** has received substantial press for its role in supporting cognitive functions by activating genes involved in neuroplasticity (McCann & Ames, 2005; Wu, Ying, & Gomez-Pinella,

FIGURE 8.17 Insula involvement with anorexia. The insula plays a role in determining whether food is perceived as positive or negative.

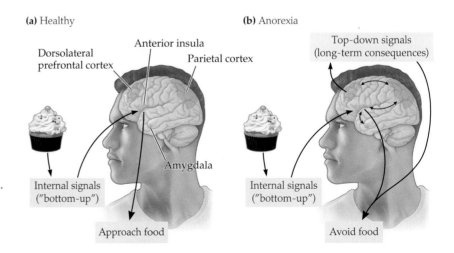

(a) Healthy

Dorsolateral prefrontal cortex

Anterior insula

Parietal cortex

Amygdala

Internal signals ("bottom-up")

Approach food

(b) Anorexia

Top-down signals (long-term consequences)

Internal signals ("bottom-up")

Avoid food

2007). **Docosahexaenoic acid (DHA)** is the ω-3 fatty acid that most commonly appears in the cell membranes of neurons. Humans derive this DHA from dietary sources, such as fish, rather than generating it ourselves. Researchers have proposed that DHA contributed to modern humans' large brains in proportion to body size. If DHA is critical for the maintenance of healthy brains, then there may be cause for concern regarding recent trends in Western diets of replacing the more healthful ω-3 fatty acids with more saturated fatty acids, trans-fatty acids, and linoleic acid. As shown in Figure 8.18, depression rates have been inversely correlated with DHA consumption, suggesting a potential relationship between DHA consumption and depression (Hibbeln, 1998).

The foods we consume can influence several brain processes by altering neurotransmitter pathways, synaptic transmission, and the extracellular chemical environment. Table 8.1 summarizes a select group of nutrients and their proposed effects on cognition and emotion (Gomez-Pinilla, 2008). Because of the preliminary nature of these findings, additional research is necessary to confirm these proposed effects.

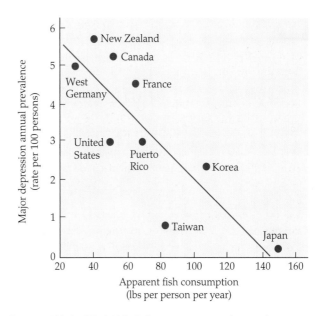

Source: Hibbeln, J.R. (1998). Fish consumption and major depression. *Lancet, 35,* 12-13.

FIGURE 8.18 Diet and depression. Cultures that consume higher amounts of fish report lower rates of depression.

TABLE 8.1.

Effects of nutrients on cognition and emotion

NUTRIENT	EFFECTS ON COGNITION AND EMOTION	FOOD SOURCES
ω-3 fatty acids (for example, docosahexaenoic acid)	Amelioration of cognitive decline in the elderly; basis for treatment in patients with mood disorders; improvement of cognition in traumatic brain injury in rodents; amelioration of cognitive decay in mouse model of Alzheimer's disease	Fish (salmon), flax seeds, krill, chia, kiwi fruit, butternuts, walnuts
Curcumin	Amelioration of cognitive decay in mouse model of Alzheimer's disease; amelioration of cognitive decay in traumatic brain injury in rodents	Turmeric (curry spice)
Flavonoids	Cognitive enhancement in combination with exercise in rodents; improvement of cognitive function in the elderly	Cocoa, green tea, Ginkgo tree, citrus fruits, wine (higher in red wine), dark chocolate
Saturated fat	Promotion of cognitive decline in adult rodents; aggravation of cognitive impairment after brain trauma in rodents; exacerbation of cognitive decline in aging humans[3]	Butter, ghee, suet, lard, coconut oil, cottonseed oil, palm kernel oil, dairy products (cream, cheese), meat
B vitamins	Supplementation with vitamin B_6, vitamin B_{12}, or folate has positive effects on memory performance in women of various ages; vitamin B_{12} improves cognitive impairment in rats fed a choline-deficient diet	Various natural sources. Vitamin B_{12} is not available from plant products
Vitamin D	Important for preserving cognition in the elderly	Fish liver, fatty fish, mushrooms, fortified products, milk, soy milk, cereal grains
Vitamin E	Amelioration of cognitive impairment after brain trauma in rodents; reduces cognitive decay in the elderly	Asparagus, avocado, nuts, peanuts, olives, red palm oil, seeds, spinach, vegetable oils, wheat germ

(continued)

Effects of nutrients on cognition and emotion (*continued*)

NUTRIENT	EFFECTS ON COGNITION AND EMOTION	FOOD SOURCES
Choline	Reduction of seizure-induced memory impairment in rodents; a review of the literature reveals evidence for a causal relationship between dietary choline and cognition in humans and rats	Egg yolks, soy beef, chicken, veal, turkey liver, lettuce
Combination of vitamins (C, E, carotene)	Antioxidant vitamin intake delays cognitive decline in the elderly	Vitamin C: citrus fruits, several plants and vegetables, calf and beef liver. Vitamin E: see above
Calcium, zinc, selenium	High serum calcium is associated with faster cognitive decline in the elderly; reduction of zinc in diet helps to reduce cognitive decay in the elderly; lifelong low selenium level associated with lower cognitive function in humans	Calcium: milk, coral. Zinc: oysters, a small amount in beans, nuts, almonds, whole grains, sunflower seeds. Selenium: nuts, cereals, meat, fish, eggs
Copper	Cognitive decline in patients with Alzheimer's disease correlates with low plasma concentrations of copper	Oysters, beef/lamb liver, Brazil nuts, blackstrap molasses, cocoa, black pepper
Iron	Iron treatment normalizes cognitive function in young women	Red meat, fish, poultry, lentils, beans

Source: Gomez-Pinilla, F. (2008). Brain foods: The effects of nutrients on brain function. *Nature Reviews Neuroscience, 9,* 568–578.

CONTEXT MATTERS

Neurodevelopment and Weight Regulation: Influence of Mother's Diet During Pregnancy

Featured study: Chang, G. Q., Gaysinskaya, V., Karatayev, O., & Leibowitz, S. F. (2008). Maternal high-fat diet and fetal programming: Increased proliferation of hypothalamic peptide-producing neurons that increase risk for overeating and obesity. The Journal of Neuroscience, 28, 12107–12119.

Typically, when we consider the impact of the environment on our brains, we focus on the immediate context. However, as discussed in Chapter 5, contextual effects, especially dietary effects, on the brain are far-reaching. The Rockefeller University neuroscientist Sarah Leibowitz and her colleagues conducted a study providing evidence that the type of diet consumed by a mother rat during pregnancy had long-lasting effects on the areas of her offspring's brains associated with hunger regulation. This dietary fetal programming led to a significant modification of eating patterns and overall body weight of the offspring. Thus, this study demonstrates the role of epigenetics in the development of hunger regulatory circuits.

How did the Leibowitz team find evidence that the type of diet consumed by the pregnant rat played a role in her offspring's future dietary preferences? Pregnant rats were divided into two groups: a group receiving a high-fat diet (defined as 50% fat) beginning on day six of the pregnancy and a group receiving a balanced control diet (25% fat) for the entire pregnancy. During the pregnancy, food consumption was measured three times per week, and the pregnant rats were weighed once each week. The high-fat diet did not result in higher calorie intake or body weight in the pregnant rats; further, lactation seemed to be unaffected. The litters were also comparable between the two groups, similar in number and body size of pups. The actual amount of food consumed did not differ between the two diet groups. The only difference between the two groups was the percentage of fat in the mother's prenatal diet.

On the birth of the pups, three groups were created:

1. High-fat pups raised by high-fat diet mothers;
2. High-fat pups cross-fostered and raised by balanced-diet mothers, and
3. Balanced-diet pups raised by balanced-diet mothers.

Cross-fostering refers to the pups being raised by a non-biological "foster" mother. This strategy allows researchers to investigate the impact of being raised by a healthier mother following birth even if the biological mother consumed an unhealthful prenatal diet. The researchers analyzed the brains of representative pup cohorts of different ages.

Another phase of the study focused on behavioral and physiological assessments of pups under the same conditions.

(a)

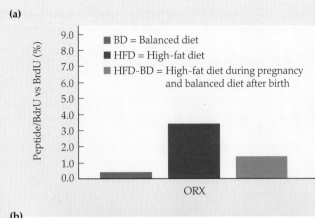

- BD = Balanced diet
- HFD = High-fat diet
- HFD-BD = High-fat diet during pregnancy and balanced diet after birth

(b)

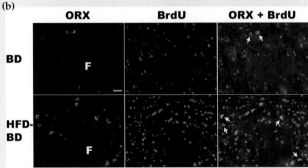

CONTEXT MATTERS FIGURE 8.1 Maternal diet influences offspring neurons. (a) The pups of rats placed on a high-fat diet during pregnancy developed more orexin-producing neurons than did offspring from mothers kept on a balanced diet during pregnancy, even if these offspring consumed a balanced diet after birth. (b) As indicated by the arrows, more orexin cells were double stained for bromodeoxyuridine in the brain tissue of offspring from the mothers with the high-fat diet than from offspring of mothers with the balanced diet.

They remained on a balanced diet following weaning until postnatal day 50. At that time and for the next 20 days, the young rats were given access to both the high-fat and balanced diets. Would their mothers' prenatal diet influence their eating preferences?

Pups that were born to a mother fed a high-fat diet exhibited increased caloric intake and body weight. Even if pups born to mothers fed a high-fat diet were raised by mothers fed a balanced diet, they exhibited overeating and weight gain by 70 days of age. Increased leptin and insulin levels were observed in both males and females fed a high-fat prenatal diet.

Another experiment in this study indicated increased activity of peptides such as orexin (involved in triggering hunger) in the lateral hypothalamus of pups with the high-fat prenatal diet compared with the pups of mothers placed on the balanced diet at 15 days of age. Similar changes were observed in the high-fat prenatal-diet pups raised by mothers on a balanced diet, suggesting that a high-fat diet, even if it is restricted to pregnancy, leads to long-term changes in the offspring following birth.

To explore the mechanisms mediating these long-term brain changes, researchers looked at the production of new neurons (neurogenesis) in the fetal pups of both high-fat and balanced-diet moms. The pups of the high-fat mothers exhibited an increased density of new neurons even when neurogenesis was assessed just 5 days following the beginning of the diet. The same effect was observed later at days 8 or 15 after birth. These results strongly suggested that just a few days of an in utero high-fat diet exposure resulted in an increased production of neurons. The investigators found that these new neurons expressed orexigenic peptides (see Context Matters Figure 8.1). Although neuroscientists typically praise the production of new neurons, in this case, more neurons that stimulate the brain to search for food may not be desired, especially when living in an environment with plentiful food sources.

This study provides evidence that a high-fat diet can set events in motion that have long-term effects on the neurobiological components of hunger regulation and energy storage. As shown in Context Matters Figure 8.2, the mother rat's high-fat diet is associated with increased lipids in the fetus that are detected around the third ventricle of the developing fetus' brain. Altered levels of fat increase the production of neurons that eventually migrate to the LH and paraventricular nucleus and regulate the production of orexigenic peptides such as orexin. These early neurobiological foundations set the stage for the young rat's increased food intake, early-onset puberty, and increased body weight.

CONTEXT MATTERS FIGURE 8.2 Maternal diet influences offspring brain and behavior. The consumption of a high-fat diet during pregnancy has long-lasting effects on eating behaviors and associated neural production in offspring.

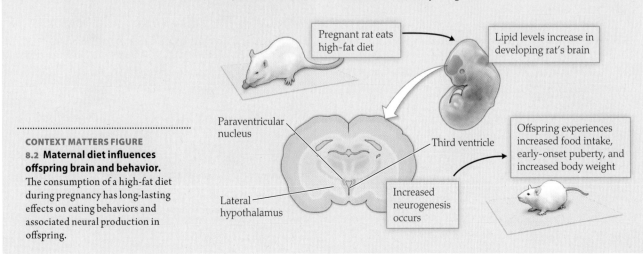

Pregnant rat eats high-fat diet

Lipid levels increase in developing rat's brain

Paraventricular nucleus

Third ventricle

Lateral hypothalamus

Increased neurogenesis occurs

Offspring experiences increased food intake, early-onset puberty, and increased body weight

In this section, we discussed various contexts associated with eating patterns. The variables, ranging from aspects of the environment to fluctuations in neuropeptides, are all important to the complete picture of hunger regulation. Along with hunger regulation, our bodies and brains closely regulate necessary fluid intake to maintain healthy physiological systems. We next turn to this essential function.

Thirst Regulation

Just as we need nutrients from food resources to keep our bodies functioning, we also need fluids to maintain our physiological health. Your urge to drink water after working out is a result of your body's ability to regulate and monitor its internal fluids that are critical for survival. Although you may accept a drink simply because someone has offered it to you, several neurobiological and physiological mechanisms are also at work to make sure that you drink fluids before you reach dangerous levels of dehydration.

Water resides both inside and outside of our cells in the body. Additionally, water is an important component of our blood. As shown in Figure 8.19, an **isotonic solution** is characterized by equal concentrations of solutes (dissolved substances) inside of cells (in the **intracellular** space) and outside of cells (in the **extracellular** space). After you eat too many salty snacks, however, the fluid outside of your cells may become a **hypertonic solution**, with a higher concentration of solutes (in this case, salt) outside of the cells than inside of the cells. Several conditions, including blood loss (with its associated water and salt solute loss), can lead to **hypotonic solution** in the extracellular space, meaning a lower concentration of solutes outside the cells than exists inside the cells. This situation can lead to dangerous situations, such as the movement of excessive water into the cells to establish solute equilibrium but resulting in excessive swelling of the cells. Thus, when hypertonic or hypotonic conditions arise, water moves outside or inside of the cells to reestablish isotonic fluid conditions. Accordingly, we need multiple sensors to detect the first signals of altered fluid

and solute levels, regardless of the origin. The systems for detecting fluid loss both inside and outside of the cells are described below (McKinley & Johnson, 2004).

Osmoregulatory Thirst

Early research investigating brain areas involved in thirst regulation pointed to the role of the hypothalamus. Initially, when small amounts of hypertonic solution of sodium salts were injected into the hypothalamus of goats with homeostatic, isotonic fluid conditions (see Figure 8.20), the goats started to drink (Andersson 1953). Further, when the hypothalamus was either electrically or chemically stimulated, the goats began to drink, even if they had recently consumed water and showed no evidence of thirst. Lesions to this brain area seemed to eliminate the goats' urge to drink, and they became severely dehydrated (Andersson, 1978; Andersson & Eriksson, 1971).

Additional research pointed to the existence of **osmoreceptors**, cells that are sensitive to cellular dehydration, in the anterior wall of the third ventricle of the brain. When this area was lesioned in goats and rats, they developed **adipsia**, an apparent absence of thirst (Andersson, 1978). More specifically, very sensitive osmoreceptors have been

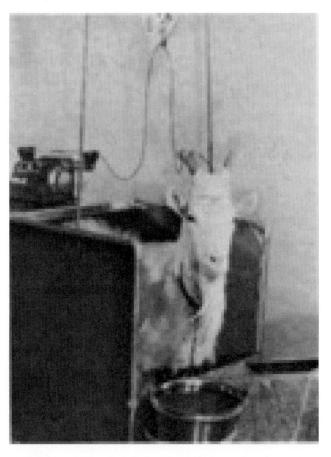

FIGURE 8.20 Hypertonic solutions and thirst. When a hypertonic solution was infused into the hypothalamic area of goats, they started drinking water from the bucket.

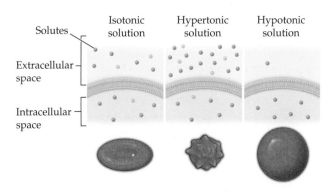

FIGURE 8.19 Solute density and cellular fluids. The density of solutes inside or outside of the cell influences the movement of liquids.

identified in two areas of the anterior third ventricle known as the **organum vasculosum of the lamina terminalis (OVLT)** and the **subfornical organ (SFO)**. These circumventricular organs (located around the ventricle) lack a blood–brain barrier. Being located in the ventricle with no blood–brain barrier places these organs in an ideal location to sample and respond to changes in solutes and fluid levels in the brain (McKinley & Johnson, 2004).

As indicated in Figure 8.21, a PET study in humans showed that both anterior and posterior areas of the cingulate cortex are activated when hypertonic saline solution is infused into the brain. When the human subjects were hydrated, activity in the cingulate cortex diminished (Denton et al., 1999). Another PET study examining thirst in human subjects infused with a hypertonic saline solution to produce thirst indicated that increased activation occurs in the insula, as well as the cingulate cortex (Farrell et al., 2006). As you recall from Chapter 2, the insula is associated with

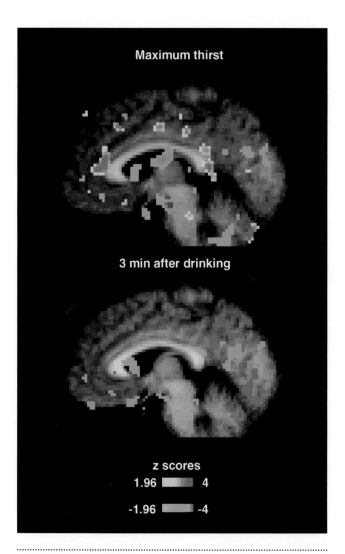

FIGURE 8.21 Thirst-induced brain activity. When human subjects were thirsty, more activity along the cingulate cortex was observed than after the subjects relieved their thirst by drinking water.

the interoceptive system that monitors internal homeostatic functions, so it should be no surprise that it is involved in monitoring thirst (Craig, 2003).

Thus, as we experience normal physiological functions such as urinating and sweating that are associated with the loss of fluids, the movement of intracellular fluids to extracellular spaces triggers a series of actions that promote fluid consumption and other compensatory mechanisms to replace the lost fluids. **Osmosis** is the net movement of fluid (e.g., water) through a semipermeable membrane into a region of higher solute concentration. To maintain the appropriate levels of fluids in our bodies, the many components of osmoregulatory thirst work together to monitor changes and to restore both fluids and solutes to appropriate levels.

Hypovolemic Thirst

Fluids can be depleted from the extracellular space or blood supply following many conditions, such as loss of blood (hemorrhage). On the detection of low blood volume, or **hypovolemia**, the endocrine and autonomic systems respond to correct the fluid depletion. Specific pressure receptors known as **baroreceptors** are located in the blood vessels. Baroreceptors located in the heart initially detect low blood volume. When the cardiac baroreceptors activate the autonomic nervous system, fluid-deprived rats develop urges to drink and consume salt to correct the drop in blood pressure (Stocker, Stricker, & Sved, 2001).

In the brain, the neuropeptide **vasopressin** is released from the posterior pituitary gland in response to hypovolemia. In addition to constricting the blood vessels as a mechanism to increase blood pressure, vasopressin triggers a response in the kidneys to reduce fluid release to the bladder. Thus, vasopressin is also known as the **antidiuretic hormone** since the term *diuresis* refers to the production of urine.

When hypovolemia is detected by the kidneys, the hormone **renin** is released into the circulatory system. Renin interacts with the protein angiotensinogen to produce angiotensin I and then **angiotensin II**. Angiotensin II increases blood pressure. It constricts blood vessels, triggers the release of the hormones **aldosterone** (which stimulates reabsorption of sodium and water and is released by the adrenal cortex) and vasopressin, and stimulates drinking (likely induced by activating the OVLT and SFO). This works to restore appropriate fluid and solute levels. When the peptide angiotensin II is infused into the brains of several animal species (dogs, sheep, rats, and goats), they appear to be suddenly thirsty and begin drinking, although they are not water deprived. This effect likely results from angiotensin II's actions on the OVLT and SFO (McKinley & Johnson, 2004).

In the final two sections of this chapter, we will examine two very different types of motivated responses that appeared on the time budget analysis for college students presented earlier in the chapter—work and grooming. Examining our consistent motivation to engage in these behaviors is critical for a complete understanding of how we maintain healthy bodies and secure appropriate resources for survival throughout our lives.

Motivating the Brain to Work

Recall from the surveys described earlier in this chapter that we spend a lot of time working. On average, individuals in the United States work outside of the home close to eight hours per day. On the days they report doing housework, they report spending a little over two hours per day on those tasks (U.S. Department of Labor, Bureau of Labor Statistics, 2013). Other animals also demonstrate sustained work habits that result in long-term, rather than immediate, payoffs. According to the neuroscientist John Salamone, motivated behavior is characterized by persistence, vigor, and elevated levels of work output (Salamone & Correa, 2002). To better understand the basis of motivated responses, behavioral neuroscientists have recently begun studying the specific neurobiological factors that prompt an animal to work. Before addressing these biological systems, we will review a few examples of animals, including humans, known for their tendencies to work.

Male bowerbirds spend weeks building their towering nests to catch the attention of females. Once these impressive structures are built, the nests are then "decorated" with valuable and colorful items such as flowers or pieces of plastic. Working as aviary interior designers, the birds usually decorate with a theme—large piles of one type of object, such as rocks or leaves or flowers, or multiple objects with a single color. Once the females arrive, the males dance and sing to further impress the females, with the ultimate payoff being the opportunity to mate (Morell, 2010).

As shown in Figure 8.22, the beaver provides a valuable mammalian model for sustained work. Enos Mills, a naturalist and "father" of the Rocky Mountain National Park, was fascinated with the sustained work and engineering feats of the beavers, which built dams to provide themselves with a safe habitat and a reservoir of resources. The beavers built their homes of sticks and mud and positioned them with the entrance below water level. Mills observed the final foundation to generally be about 8 feet across and 5–10 feet in height, but the size of beaver dams can be much larger. Each autumn, the beavers plastered the outside with mud. This behavior seems to be learned as young beavers work alongside the adults, who also cut trees and build the dams (Mills, 1909).

Humans are known for their work ethic as well. I consider myself extremely fortunate to have a career that I enjoy—teaching courses that I find fascinating, conducting interesting research projects, and even writing textbooks. Even so, if I am going to classify my motivation for work along the wanting–liking–learning scale discussed earlier in the chapter, I must admit that I rarely get to work and savor the moment in the same way that I savor the first bite of a favorite pasta dish. And, considering that I rarely find myself craving or binging on my tasks during work hours, it is safe to say that my brain places work closer to the wanting category than the liking category. The learning category also plays an increasingly prevalent role as the brain learns more about relationships between work and payoffs for various degrees of effort directed toward different jobs and tasks. Although aspects of liking are no doubt involved in one's motivation to work, wanting and learning appear to be more closely aligned with this motivation. Thus, for humans, our desire to work is more of an acquired motivation as we learn how to interact with our environment to produce resources necessary for survival and life satisfaction.

(a)

(b)

FIGURE 8.22 Species-specific work patterns. Persistent effort directed toward a goal, or work, is seen in (a) the beavers' construction of dams and (b) the carpentry projects of humans. Both of these work efforts result in desired habitats for these species.

Neurobiology of Sustained Work

Recent research has identified several neurochemicals and brain areas that are involved in sustaining the work exhibited by animals such as the bowerbirds, beavers, and humans. Building on the research presented earlier in the chapter regarding the role of dopamine in reward processes, researchers have studied how alterations in dopamine influence rats' willingness to exert effort to obtain a reward. When rats are given a choice of two levers, one that produces common laboratory chow every time it is pressed (low-effort option) and one that produces highly desirable food every fifth time it is pressed (high-effort option), the rats will obtain most of their food from the high-effort option that delivers the preferred food. Healthy rats, in this case, indicate that the highly appealing food is worth the extra effort. However, if the rats are treated with dopamine antagonists or receive accumbens dopamine depletions, the highly desired food is no longer worth the extra effort, and the rats shift their responses to the standard chow with the low-effort option (Salamone et al., 1991). Other studies have reported similar findings suggesting that impaired dopaminergic activity impacts the animals' willingness to work, leading them to recalculate the amount of effort they are willing to exert for a reward.

The upper boundary of the amount of work an animal will do to receive a desired outcome is called **ratio strain**. For example, whereas the previously mentioned study trained rats to press a lever 5 times to receive a reward, as the ratio is increased to 10 presses for a reward, the animal may be less motivated to work for the reward. (Ratio strains are also closely monitored in casinos because the casino directors are all too aware of the fact that humans will only work for so long without rewards.) This research with rats indicates that disruptions of the mesolimbic–dopamine system alter the ratio strain and the amount of work an animal will engage in to receive a reward (see Figure 8.23; Salamone & Correa, 2007).

Do you ever wonder why you get an extra boost in your work energy after a cup of coffee? Caffeine, the active stimulant in your afternoon cup of java, is a nonselective adenosine antagonist (as discussed in Chapter 4). Because adenosine receptors are most dense in the nucleus accumbens and striatum, drinking coffee directly influences the brain areas that are involved in effort-related functions. If adenosine is injected into the rat nucleus accumbens, the effects resemble the effects described in studies in which dopamine has been depleted—the rats shift their responses to the reward associated with the least amount of work (Salamone, Correa, Nunes, Randall, & Pardo, 2012). Thus, coffee antagonizes the work-suppressing effects of the brain's natural levels of adenosine, perhaps enabling humans to work for a longer duration.

In a different type of task, the **medial frontal cortex** (comparable to the human medial prefrontal cortex; Preuss, 1995) was found to contribute to a rat's decision to exert effort to obtain a high-value reward. In this two-choice maze, the rat could enter an arm that was baited with standard chow and/or another arm with a high-value food reward. For us, this setup is similar to having a choice between instant oatmeal or our favorite blueberry pancakes for breakfast. The high-value arm of the maze had a barrier requiring the rat to climb over it and work harder to obtain the preferred food. Healthy rats climb the barriers for the desired reward. However, when the medial frontal cortex was lesioned, the same rats shifted their responses to obtain the standard chow (Walton, Bannerman, & Rushworth, 2002). Similar lesion studies have implicated the anterior cingulate cortex, basolateral amygdala, ventral pallidum, and nucleus accumbens core in effort-related decisions (Hauber & Sommer, 2009).

Finally, a neuroimaging study in humans suggests that the caudate nucleus, a component of the striatum, is also involved in effort-based decisions (Zink et al., 2004). In this study, researchers at Emory University placed subjects in fMRI scanners to monitor the activity in the striatum, an area involved in movement that has close connections with the nucleus accumbens, as well as the activity in the right nucleus accumbens. In this task, a video showed various visual stimuli that the subjects were asked to track. In one group, the subjects were told that if they saw money drop in a money bag, they would receive a monetary reward (passive group). In the other group, the subjects were told that if they pressed the correct buttons to direct the money to the money bag (active group), they would receive the money. Subjects' self-reports and skin conductance responses indicated that money was more salient (i.e., meaningful, rewarding) in the active group in which subjects had to work for the reward. In the fMRI scans of these trials, the caudate and nucleus accumbens were more active, yet no differences in activation were observed in other areas such as the putamen (also part of the striatum). These results provide evidence that the brain responds differently to rewards that are actively earned rather than passively presented.

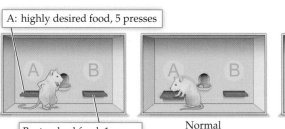

A: highly desired food, 5 presses

B: standard food, 1 press

Normal

Low dopamine

FIGURE 8.23 Dopamine and work productivity. Rats are more likely to exert more effort for highly desirable food when their dopaminergic system is intact and functioning normally.

It appears that the nucleus accumbens, medial prefrontal cortex, and striatum, perhaps fueled by dopamine, underlie the sustained work exhibited by various animals, including humans (see Figure 8.24). Could it be that dog breeders who have developed lines of "working dogs" unknowingly also selected for altered sensitivity of these brain circuits, motivating the animals to work harder for salient rewards? To my knowledge, that research project has not yet been undertaken. However, researchers have investigated the ways these effort-related responses can be changed in animal models, an area especially relevant to mental disorders such as depression.

Plasticity of Effort-Related Responses

In the 1960s, a series of classic research studies demonstrated that effort-related responses could be altered by manipulating the consequences of an animal's actions. In this now famous research, Martin Seligman and Steven Maier exposed dogs to an electrified grid and provided opportunities for one group to escape the shock. The second group could not escape from this shock, regardless of their actions. In subsequent tests in which all dogs were given an opportunity to escape the shock, the dogs from the group that had not previously been able to escape the shock no longer attempted to escape. The researchers referred to this acquired shift in motivation as **learned helplessness**. Although the learned helplessness task was originally designed to investigate the effects of stressor controllability, the learned helplessness paradigm is currently considered a valuable model for human depression. Individuals learn that their behavior is not associated with successful outcomes, so they cease responding. Indeed, depression is characterized by an overall deficiency in motivation and behavioral activation (Salamone et al., 2007).

In addition to the behavioral similarities between learned helplessness and depression, interesting resemblances in underlying neurochemical mechanisms have been identified. For example, activation of serotonergic neurons in the dorsal raphe nucleus of the brainstem has confirmed a prevalent role of serotonin in learned helplessness. In rats, lesions of the dorsal raphe nucleus block the emergence of learned helplessness symptoms (Maier et al., 1993). Corticotropin-releasing hormone, involved in the stress response and depression (see Chapter 13), is also necessary for the learned helplessness symptoms (Maier & Watkins, 2005).

Students in my laboratory recently wondered whether it would be possible to demonstrate **learned persistence**, the opposite of learned helplessness, in which animals would continue attempting to improve their situation (e.g., escape attempts) regardless of the effectiveness of their latest attempt. To explore this notion, students habituated rats to (i.e., made them used to receiving) sweet cereal rewards. Rats would consistently work to retrieve these rewards. The animals were subsequently placed on a mild food restriction diet. Each day, for 10 minutes, they were introduced to an apparatus with four mounds of bedding. During these work sessions, the rats, known as the contingent group, learned that they could dig up sweet cereal rewards in each mound. A second group, known as the noncontingent group, received the cereal regardless of their effort. Instead of disrupting connections between behavior and consequences, as in learned helplessness, this study design strengthened connections between an animal's efforts and their outcome.

As depicted in Figure 8.25, after five weeks, the rats were presented with an unsolvable task to test their persistence. This test consisted of a small plastic ball with the cereal strategically placed inside so that it could be seen, smelled, and touched, but not removed. The contingent group worked longer to try to retrieve the cereal. Thus, experience with work that consistently produced desired rewards led to increased persistence when the problem became more difficult and unfamiliar (Lambert et al., 2007).

Grooming: The Silent but Essential Motivator

We have discussed various aspects of motivation and reward in the chapter thus far. Most behaviors in this category are considered pleasurable (food), meaningful (careers), or somewhere in between (surfing the Internet; White & Dolan, 2009). We have not covered even a small sampling of these behaviors: responses such as sex, parenting, play, and learning are discussed in other chapters. In this final section of the chapter, we will discuss **grooming**, a motivational response that humans report as less rewarding than most of their other daily behaviors. However, humans and other animals spend a significant amount of time engaged in grooming—some more than virtually any other behavior (Figure 8.26). As described in the time budget analysis presented at the beginning of this chapter, humans spend

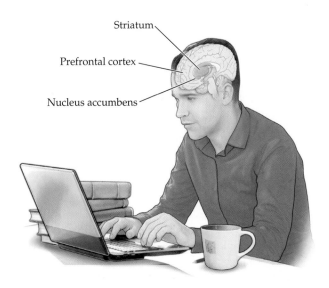

Striatum
Prefrontal cortex
Nucleus accumbens

FIGURE 8.24 The working brain. Several brain areas have been implicated in directing and sustaining work efforts.

(a)

(b)

....

FIGURE 8.25 Learned persistence. (a) When rats are trained to dig for sweet cereal in mounds of bedding for several weeks, (b) they exhibit more persistence in a problem-solving task that challenges them to remove the cereal from a toy ball.

(a)

(b)

(c)

....

FIGURE 8.26 Mammalian grooming patterns. Grooming responses are critical for maintaining healthy skin. They include specific motor patterns in various mammals, as seen in the (a) lion, (b) rat, and (c) human.

almost as much time grooming (e.g., bathing, styling hair) as they do eating and drinking, so it is important to understand this behavior. Grooming is a prevalent response with a strong survival value, yet it is carried out in such habitual ritualistic patterns that it can often be completed without cognitive awareness.

Components of the Rodent Grooming Response

Self-grooming in mammals serves many functions, including maintaining the skin and fur by removing parasites, transmitting important odors to potential mates or aggressors, facilitating wound healing, and maintaining thermoregulation. Self-grooming may also occur during anxiety-provoking situations, functioning as a mechanism to reduce anxiety (Kalueff, Aldrige, LaPorte, Murphy, & Touhimaa, 2007; Kalueff & Touhimaa, 2005). If you have ever caught yourself stroking your hair or picking at a scab incessantly while anxiously waiting for your final exam score, you have engaged in antianxiety grooming.

Most terrestrial mammals spend between 20 and 40% of their time during waking hours self-grooming (Spruijt, van Hooff, & Gispen, 1992). Rats, not often associated with cleanliness, spend up to 50% of their waking time engaged

in grooming (Aldridge, 2005). Even with the prevalence of this behavior in the lives of animals, it was not until the elegance and complexity of this response was described that scientists began to devote more attention to this topic.

In the early 1970s, John Fentress hired the aspiring science illustrator Frances Stilwell to do some clerical tasks and work with mice in his laboratory. Fentress was an ethologist, a scientist who studies animal behavior as it occurs in the natural environment. As Stilwell watched the mice with her artist's eye, she saw what she described as a *syntax*, even a grammar, in the rodents' movements as they groomed. "I loved watching the mice do their thing, especially in slow motion. It was like witnessing a ballet. I liked working with the DBAs (the little gray mice) the most, as they seemed to thrive on grooming. The overhand strokes particularly were executed with robustness, verve, sensuousness, and pride" (Stilwell & Fentress, 2010, pp. 6–7). Together, Stilwell and Fentress (Fentress & Stilwell, 1973) published their work on grooming patterns in the premier journal *Nature* in an article titled "Grammar of a movement sequence in inbred mice."

Scientists have conducted much research on the sequence of rodent grooming since that time. The stereotyped grooming response consists of approximately 25 movements—all in a brief five seconds. These grooming bouts consist of four phases that are described in Figure 8.27. In addition to this fixed-chain grooming sequence, rodents also engage in more variable nonchain sequences that do not always follow the grooming script. They may stop before the sequence is completed or begin a sequence in the middle of the expected grooming chain. The fixed grooming response sequences reinforce the importance of this behavior with disruptions leading to dysfunction, as discussed in the next section.

Neural Circuits and Clinical Applications

Although rats have not been shown to bar press to earn grooming privileges as they do for cocaine privileges, the nervous system ensures that grooming behavior will be carried out each day. Specific neural mechanisms critical for maintaining high rates of grooming behavior are incorporated in neural circuits composed of the basal ganglia and brainstem, brain areas that are important for the execution of an animal's most basic movement (Cromwell & Berridge, 1996). Research has shown that lesions of the striatum are associated with a decrease in the number of completed grooming sequences by about 50% in rats. Interestingly, small lesions of the dorsolateral quadrant of the striatum disrupted the grooming sequences as much as larger striatal

lesions (Cromwell & Berridge, 1996). This research provides evidence that the striatum and other areas of the basal ganglia are important for the implementation of motor sequences, making them central to the more basic, almost automatic, routines or habits of our lives.

Similar deficits in grooming and other basic motor responses are observed in patients with neurodegenerative movement diseases resulting from striatal damage such as Parkinson's disease (Berridge & Fentress, 1987). Damage to some aspect of the striatum or other components of the basal ganglia circuitry may result in various complications, ranging from a lack of motivation to groom to a diminished ability to effortlessly execute the movements once the response has been triggered. Although the human grooming response may not be as *stereotyped*, or biologically programmed, as the rodent grooming response, we spend substantial time grooming (as described earlier in the chapter). We are aware of the amount of time we spend bathing our bodies, washing and drying our hair, and applying various hygiene products.

However, other more habitual grooming routines are often carried out with little awareness (e.g., picking wounds or sunburned skin, twirling hair). Accordingly, researchers have used their knowledge of an animal's healthy levels of motivation to groom as they have developed animal models to investigate psychological disorders in addition to the previously mentioned neurodegenerative disorders. For example, because decreased attention to personal hygiene is often observed in patients diagnosed with depression, grooming behavior has been used as a key dependent measure to assess the effects of therapies for depression (Smolinsky, Bergner, LaPorte, & Kalueff, 2009). In one study, grooming behavior was indirectly determined in mice exposed to chronic unpredictable stress by assessing the quality of their fur on eight different areas of their body. When the fur was viewed as greasy, fluffy, thin, or protruding, then it was recorded as dirty. When antidepressants were given to the mice, the state of their fur coat improved (Mutlu et al., 2012). (More about animal models of depression appears in Chapter 13.)

Although a notable drive to engage in these behaviors is often absent, the role of dopamine is as prevalent in these responses as it is in the other motivated responses discussed in this chapter. Chemical lesions via a drug that destroys the dopaminergic neuronal tracts in the striatum are just as damaging to the sequenced grooming responses as were lesions to the actual tissue of the striatum (Berridge, 1989). Dopamine agonists also facilitate grooming sequences. When rats receive such agonists, they spend up to twice the amount of time grooming as control animals do (Berridge & Aldridge, 2000).

As scientists have discovered more about the neurobiology of grooming responses, this behavior

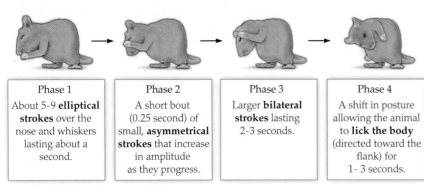

Phase 1	Phase 2	Phase 3	Phase 4
About 5-9 **elliptical strokes** over the nose and whiskers lasting about a second.	A short bout (0.25 second) of small, **asymmetrical strokes** that increase in amplitude as they progress.	Larger **bilateral strokes** lasting 2-3 seconds.	A shift in posture allowing the animal to **lick the body** (directed toward the flank) for 1- 3 seconds.

FIGURE 8.27 Rodent grooming. Very specific behavioral patterns characterize each phase of the rodent grooming response.

has become a useful model system for the investigation of the neuronal mechanisms and organization of behavioral sequences. Because grooming is composed of both consistent and variable responses, it is a rich model to investigate multiple aspects of both motivation and mental health. By understanding an animal's motivation to engage in a particular response, as well as the behavior that corresponds with the response, researchers can assess these behaviors to detect impairments in neural and psychological functioning.

Barbering: Extreme Grooming for Extreme Circumstances

Biopsychologists typically search for adaptive explanations for various behaviors. Common adaptive functions include enhanced reproductive fitness, health, or acquisition of resources. However, one behavior seen in some strains of captive laboratory mice has had scientists scratching their heads for some time now. **Barbering** is the plucking of whiskers and fur of cagemates, typically in a similar pattern for each barber. A mouse may just remove the whiskers or pluck the fur around the eyes, the entire face, or a certain area on the cagemate's back. Some mice are creative with their signature barbering patterns. In reference to the biblical story, this response is sometimes referred to as the **Dalila effect** (Sarna, Dyck, & Whishaw, 2000). After learning that Samson's power came from his long locks of hair, Dalila decided to weaken him by cutting his treasured hair. A barbering bout between two mice is like a strange dance. Surprisingly, even the recipient seems to cooperate by approaching the barber at times. Once contact is made, the barbering mouse holds the recipient and systematically begins to pluck hair or whiskers. Figure 8.28 shows mice that are engaged in barbering (Dufour & Garner, 2010).

Considering that barbering has never been observed in wild animals, that it has no obvious benefit to the plucker, and that it is costly to the recipient, there seems to be no real adaptive value to this behavior. Being on the receiving end of a barbering interaction results in reduced sensitivity input from the missing whiskers and less efficient thermoregulation (Dufour & Garner, 2010). Why engage in this puzzling behavior? Some researchers have characterized barbering as pathological, a result of living in an artificial, restrictive, boring laboratory environment. Even if this behavior is not adaptive for wild animals, researchers have continued to search for triggers or reasons for barbering in the laboratory animals.

Three potential explanations for this behavior have been explored: (1) *Establishing dominance.* Although barbering may seem to be a way to obtain dominance, most of the research suggests that barbering does not cause dominance. However, dominant animals are less tolerant of being barbered (Garner, Dufour, Gregg, Weisker, & Mench, 2004). (2) *Coping with stress.* At this time, little corroborating evidence supports the idea that barbering decreases anxiety in animals housed under impoverished laboratory conditions. However, this remains a plausible theory (van den Broek, Omtzigt, & Beynen, 1993).

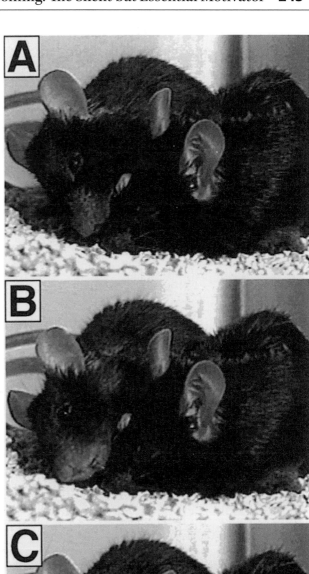

FIGURE 8.28 Barbering mice. For unknown reasons, mice exhibit barbering behavior consisting of plucking whiskers and pulling out patches of fur.

(3) *Compensatory activation response.* Animals are housed in restricted, artificial laboratory cages. A compensatory activation of the natural behavioral sequences that comprise grooming responses may be triggered to enhance general arousal in an otherwise boring environment. If another animal is in the

(a)

(b)

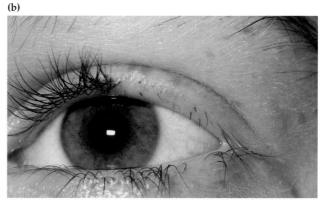

FIGURE 8.29 **Grooming extremes.** Barbering patterns in (a) mice resemble the bald patches resulting from hair picking in (b) humans diagnosed with a condition known as trichotillomania.

cage, barbering is typically directed toward the cagemate. However, self-barbering has also been observed (Dufour & Garner, 2010). This self-barbering may also be related to other self-injurious behaviors such as head banging and self-directed injuries (e.g., biting) that are observed in about 10% of captive primates that are housed individually (Dorey, Rosales-Ruiz, Smith, & Lovelace, 2009). Regardless, when both external and internal environments are altered from natural patterns, disruptions of fundamental motivational systems can occur.

Could this abnormal grooming response extend to humans? **Trichotillomania**, a disorder characterized by compulsive hair plucking, is one of the earliest documented psychiatric disorders (Christenson & Mansueto, 1999; see Figure 8.29 for a comparison of plucking patterns in a mouse and a human). This condition occurs in about 3% of women and 1.5% of men and has been associated with stress and social loss (e.g., loss of a loved one or the end of a romantic relationship). In contrast to barbering in mice, it is predominately self-directed (Dufour & Garner, 2010). Other disorders that involve repetitive behaviors, such as **obsessive–compulsive disorder**, have been associated with trichotillomania. However, compulsions in patients with obsessive–compulsive disorder relieve anxiety associated with certain stress triggers (i.e., washing hands to calm one's fear of germs). Regardless of

the specific mechanisms and functions, enhanced knowledge about this often neglected sector of behavior may provide valuable information about various neurobiological aspects of mental illness and mental health.

In this chapter, we have covered the gamut of motivational responses. Some responses are savored. Other responses are less pleasurable, but more meaningful. Yet others, such as grooming, are unremarkable. Regardless of their pleasure status, predisposed neural circuits keep us engaging in these responses day after day. Predisposed grooming responses provide valuable natural models to assess both an individual's motivation to perform a behavior and the brain's ability to execute important behaviors with minimal conscious awareness, freeing up the neural responses for more complex functions. Barbering is a unique behavioral reminder that when animals are placed in environments that differ from their natural habitats, predisposed habitual responses such as hair plucking easily emerge from the subcortical areas of the brain such as the basal ganglia—systems that are predisposed for activation. Thus, to maintain healthy motivational patterns, an animal requires a specific level of arousal. When that level is not experienced, compensatory mechanisms appear to be activated in the nervous system to make up for the deficit—sometimes leading to pathological responses.

LABORATORY EXPLORATION

Microdialysis and Motivation Research

In this chapter, we have discussed the role of neurochemicals such as dopamine in the regulation of certain behaviors, revealing time-sensitive information about neurochemical involvement. For example, earlier in this chapter, you learned that dopaminergic activity plays an important role in the

anticipation of a pleasurable experience. That is, a rat experiences activation in the brain's reward pathway as it merely prepares to receive a reward by pressing a bar for cocaine or food. Tracking the activity of key neurotransmitters known to be involved in anticipation and pleasure has been critical for understanding the neurobiology of motivation, the central theme of this chapter.

How do scientists know exactly when the brain is using a neurotransmitter? A technique known as **microdialysis** can provide this information. Since the late 1970s, microdialysis has often been used to sample neurotransmitter or drug concentrations from brain tissue. In these studies, microdialysis enables scientists to monitor time-dependent alterations in the brain's chemistry, such as the release and uptake of neurotransmitters or drug delivery to a certain brain area (Kehr, 1999).

In general, microdialysis uses the principle of separation (*dialysis* is Greek for separate) using a membrane known as a microdialysis probe that is designed to be permeable to water and small solutes, such as neurotransmitter molecules. When this probe is subsequently inserted into the brain tissue (as shown in Laboratory Exploration Figure 8.1), a liquid is perfused, or transported, across the semipermeable probe membrane, at which time the solutes on the interior and exterior of the probe diffuse to achieve equilibrium (equal distribution inside and outside). This movement of solutes allows the experimenters to determine the levels of targeted neurotransmitters or drugs in the tissue (Shippenberg & Thompson, 2001).

A key advantage of microdialysis is that it is used in a freely moving animal, allowing researchers to explore the role of specific neurochemicals in various behavioral tasks, such as the motivation tasks described in this chapter. For example, a recent study indicated that rats trained to press a bar in an operant chamber for alcohol delivery experienced a spike in dopamine in the nucleus accumbens when they were being transported from their home cage to the

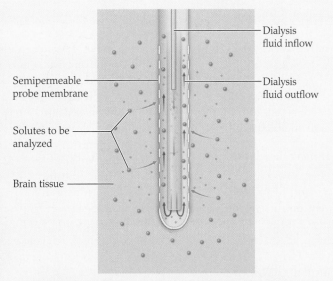

Dialysis fluid inflow

Semipermeable probe membrane

Dialysis fluid outflow

Solutes to be analyzed

Brain tissue

LABORATORY EXPLORATION FIGURE 8.1 Microdialysis and motivation. This technique allows researchers to track the flow of specific neurochemicals in specific areas as an animal is engaged in a task.

testing chamber (Howard, Schier, Wetzel, & Gonzales, 2009). One possible explanation for this finding is that the rats' dopaminergic system became activated as the variables in their environment changed to those that predicted the upcoming alcohol session. This is an example of how microdialysis has been used to demonstrate the relationship between enhanced dopamine and the anticipatory phase of consumption.

Conclusion

In this chapter we have discussed how the brain keeps us engaging in behaviors that are important for survival. The brain's reward pathway directs us toward important survival behaviors by influencing motivational categories such as liking, wanting, and learning. The specific behavior of eating, corresponding to the complex interactions of various brain areas, neural circuits, and neurochemicals, confirms the multifaceted nature of many motivational responses. When the reward is less immediate than the taste of a desired food substance, the brain's motivational systems are engaged in different ways. This is also the case for sustained work exhibited by various animals such as bowerbirds, beavers, and humans. Other behaviors such as grooming provide an example of frequent responses exhibited by animals, although the responses do not seem to be associated with immediate salient rewards.

In addition to neurobiological mechanisms, the context, or environment, plays an influential role in all motivational responses. Social and physical environments influence hunger, thirst, work, and hygiene responses such as grooming. In fact, as environments become less natural and more stressful, disruptions of these basic motivational systems may cause individuals to transition from adaptive responses to maladaptive responses, characteristic of mental illness. Of course, animals and humans are motivated to engage in more diverse behaviors than were covered in this chapter. Accordingly, you will read about additional motivated behaviors such as sex, parenting, and sleep in subsequent chapters.

KEY TERMS

activity-stress (p. 217)

The Brain's Reward Circuitry

septal nuclei (p. 219)
hedonia (p. 222)
eudaimonia (p. 222)

Hunger Regulation

obesity (p. 222)
denaturing (p. 223)
ventromedial hypothalamus (VMH)
   (p. 225)
hyperphagia (p. 225)
lateral hypothalamus (LH) (p. 225)
insulin (p. 225)
dopaminergic nigrostriatal bundle
   (p. 225)
sensory-specific satiety (p. 225)
arcuate nucleus (p. 225)
insulin resistance (p. 225)
leptin (p. 225)
ob/ob mice (p. 225)
Ghrelin (p. 226)
Fos (p. 226)
neuropeptide Y (NPY) (p. 227)

agouti-related peptide (AgRP) (p. 227)
paraventricular nucleus (p. 227)
orexigenic (p. 227)
anorexigenic (p. 227)
cross-sensitization (p. 228)
social facilitation of eating (p. 230)
anorexia nervosa (p. 231)
bulimia nervosa (p. 231)
frontostriatal (p. 231)
anhedonia (p. 231)
nucleus tractus solitari (p. 232)
omega (ω)-3 (p. 232)
docosahexaenoic acid (DHA) (p. 233)
Cross-fostering (p. 234)

Thirst Regulation

isotonic solution (p. 236)
intracellular (p. 236)
extracellular (p. 236)
hypertonic solution (p. 236)
hypotonic solution (p. 236)
osmoreceptors (p. 236)
adipsia (p. 236)
organum vasculosum of the lamina
   terminalis (OVLT) (p. 237)

subfornical organ (SFO) (p. 237)
osmosis (p. 237)
hypovolemia (p. 237)
baroreceptors (p. 237)
vasopressin (p. 237)
antidiuretic hormone (p. 237)
renin (p. 237)
angiotensin II (p. 237)
aldosterone (p. 237)

Motivating the Brain to Work

ratio strain (p. 239)
medial frontal cortex (p. 239)
learned helplessness (p. 240)
learned persistence (p. 240)

Grooming: The Silent but Essential Motivator

grooming (p. 240)
Barbering (p. 243)
Dalila effect (p. 243)
Trichotillomania (p. 244)
obsessive–compulsive disorder
   (p. 244)
microdialysis (p. 245)

REVIEW QUESTIONS

1. Which three pleasure responses have researchers identified, and how do they differ from one another? Name the principal brain areas and neurotransmitters involved in these three pleasure responses.

2. What does the research that shows evidence of the re-zoning of the nucleus accumbens in rats, in response to different environments, suggest? What might the implications of this work be for the treatment of PTSD and clinical depression in humans?

3. Which regions of the brain are thought to be involved in hunger regulation? What are their functions in hunger regulation thought to be?

4. Which brain systems are thought to be involved in the onset of anorexia nervosa? Describe the evidence for the involvement of these brain systems in anorexia. How does anorexia nervosa differ from bulimia nervosa?

5. Why is it important for the brain to monitor fluid and solute concentrations in the body? How does the brain regulate internal and external fluid levels?

6. What is the difference between learned helplessness and learned persistence? What do learned helplessness and learned persistence demonstrate about motivation?

7. Which brain regions are thought to be involved in effort-based decisions?

8. What is trichotillomania, and how might it relate to barbering in mice?

CRITICAL-THINKING QUESTIONS

1. Which do you think has more influence on how much people eat: (a) television advertisements for high-fat foods or (b) the social facilitation of eating? Do you think this depends on the age of the individuals who are eating? Explain.

2. Why do you think that scientists have failed thus far in their efforts to develop an effective drug to regulate hunger? Explain.

3. What do you see as the limitations of using animal models to study motivation and reward? Explain.

Sleep, Wakefulness, and Conscious Awareness

The Sleep-Murder Legal Defense

After falling asleep on the couch, 23-year-old Kenneth Parks got up in the early morning hours, put on his shoes and jacket, and drove his car for 20 minutes, through traffic lights and down a winding road, to his in-laws' home. He grabbed the tire iron from his car and a knife from the kitchen and proceeded to strangle his father-in-law to the point of unconsciousness. He then stabbed his mother-in-law to death. He did not harm his in-laws' teenage daughters, who reported that Parks was grunting like a wild animal. Parks later drove himself to a police station, where he reported that he thought he had killed his mother-in-law because he had memories of her being in pain. The deep cuts and blood on his fingers provided evidence to support his story.

Although this appeared to be an open-and-shut case leading to a guilty verdict, after considering the testimony of sleep experts, the jury acquitted Mr. Parks of the murder of his mother-in-law and the attempted murder of his father-in-law (Figure 9A). They found that he could not be held responsible for his actions that dreadful night.

FIGURE 9A Kenneth Parks. Shown here leaving a courthouse.

249

Behind the Scenes

What led to the acquittal of Kenneth Parks? The jury determined that he was sleepwalking and sleep-attacking, with no conscious control over his actions. Surprising conclusion, isn't it? Sleep violence has been self-reported in about 2% of the population, but such sleep responses rarely become murderous (Siclari et al., 2010; Siclari, Tononi, & Bassetti, 2012). When the sleeping brain turns to violence, the behavior is considered an example of an **automatism**, an involuntary complex response that occurs outside of conscious awareness, not unlike the behavior of zombies appearing on movie and television screens (Moorcroft, 2003).

Sleep is considered an altered state of consciousness characterized by diminished awareness. Researchers investigate the biological basis of sleep primarily through **electroencephalograms (EEGs)**, which reveal shifts in brain wave activity, several of which occur at various points throughout sleep. The different stages of sleep can be easily determined in sleep laboratories by measuring patients' EEGs with electrodes. However, the jury had no EEG recordings to determine whether Parks was indeed asleep the night he murdered his mother-in-law. Such cases recruit the expertise of forensic psychiatrists who work within the legal system to determine criminal intent and psychological competency of defendants.

The sleep clinician Carlos Schenck, who worked as a consultant on this case, agrees with the jury's decision. Schenck based his conclusion on the following factors: (1) Parks had both a personal and a family history of **parasomnias** (i.e., talking, walking, and eating during sleep, as reported by his family members); (2) he had been sleep deprived prior to the incident and had experienced significant physical stress playing rugby; (3) he had recently experienced significant emotional stress because of a gambling debt; (4) he had cut the tendons in his fingers yet reported experiencing no pain; and (5) he had organized a picnic at his in-laws' home the next day, which suggested that driving to his in-laws was likely an event that he had mentally rehearsed the day of his mother-in-law's death (Schenck, 2011).

Indeed, considering that past research has shown that men are more likely than women to behave violently when they have sleep disorders, Parks appeared to be a textbook case for sleep violence. This gender difference may exist because men are more susceptible than women are to excessive life stressors, disturbed sleep, and drug abuse (although no drug abuse was reported in this case) (Siclari et al., 2012).

No absolute truths exist in this case, just a convergence of evidence. Yet, this case raises many intriguing questions about the brain activity that underlies conscious awareness and about just what our brains and minds do after midnight. ■

Until the mid-20th century, scientists interested in behavior did not spend much time investigating sleep, a response that appeared, on the surface, to be associated with absolutely *no* behavior. The notion that sleep is a passive response, however, changed in the 1950s when a graduate student, Eugene Aserinsky, started recording eye movements and brain waves from his eight-year-old son in a run-down lab at the University of Chicago. Aserinsky was desperate to find some interesting data—any data—that would lead to the completion of his Ph.D. degree (Rock, 2004).

Why focus on sleep? Aserinsky's advisor, Nathaniel Kleitman, just happened to be the first scientist in the world to devote his career to the study of sleep. Apparently, in those early days of sleep research, subjects were hard to come by; consequently, Kleitman was a guinea pig in several of his own studies. He lived in a dark underground chamber for a month to determine whether internal sleep–wake rhythms persisted without external cues such as sunlight (they did) (Figure 9.1). He was also curious about the maximum amount of time that humans can endure sleep deprivation. After staying awake for 180 consecutive hours, he determined that such extreme sleep deprivation was an effective form of torture (Rock, 2004).

For his Ph.D. dissertation, Aserinsky decided to explore eye movements that he had previously observed while watching others sleep. Was there a rhythm or a pattern to these movements throughout an entire night's sleep?

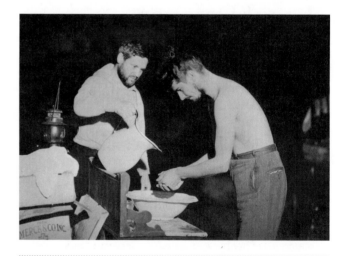

FIGURE 9.1 **Nathaniel Kleitman in Mammoth Cave.** The sleep research pioneer Nathaniel Kleitman (left) monitored rest and activity cycles with his student Bruce Richardson (right) in a dark cave environment, with no external markers of time, to investigate the presence of internal clocks regulating activity and rest cycles.

Aserinsky's curiosity and persistence in recording eye movements and brain activity during sleep yielded revolutionary findings. Ironically, when subjects' eyes moved back and forth during sleep, their brain wave activity looked like that when they were awake. Were Aserinsky's subjects waking up? He checked to make sure they were still sleeping and indeed they were, although their brain waves suggested otherwise. Referring to this stage of sleep as **rapid eye movement (REM) sleep**, Aserinsky also found that, on being awakened during this stage of sleep, many subjects reported dreaming (Aserinsky & Kleitman, 1953).

Suddenly, what scientists had considered a passive brain state appeared to be just the opposite, a brain state of varied movements and brain wave patterns, a time when vivid stories were being projected to the mind's eyes. William Dement, a medical student assigned by Kleitman to Aserinsky's studies, continued to pursue his interest in studying sleep and dreaming (Dement & Kleitman, 1957). Dement later became the director of the world's first sleep clinic at Stanford University. Dement charted subjects' brain wave activity throughout the entire night of sleep, identifying several stages and patterns of the brain's activity during this seemingly quiet time (Brown, 2003; Rock, 2004).

The Rhythms of Sleep and Wakefulness

If you recorded your daily activities for a month, you would probably note patterns after several days. Generally, you likely tend to sleep, get hungry, and be most active at consistent times of the 24-hour day. Indeed, our physiological and behavioral responses have optimal schedules that are biologically driven and important for our health. In this section, you will learn more about the biological relevance of these rhythms for all animals.

Circadian Rhythms

At the time that Kleitman decided to stay in an underground compartment to determine whether he would maintain sleep–wake cycles similar to those he experienced with normal light and dark conditions, no formal discipline studied questions about rhythms of wakefulness and sleepiness. Unbeknown to Kleitman, however, this project focusing on rest and activity cycles was the unassuming launch of an important new discipline focusing on **circadian rhythms**: responses, such as the timing of our sleep and wake cycles, with distinct daily rhythms. By removing the presence of light, a powerful **zeitgeber** (German for "time-giver"), he was able to demonstrate that daily rest and activity cycles are regulated by internal mechanisms when the environmental triggers such as light are removed. Such internal rhythms are known as **free-running rhythms**, as demonstrated by the maintenance of rest and running rhythms in rats housed in total darkness (Honma, von Goetz, & Aschoff, 1983). Humans who are blind also exhibit these free-running rhythms (Sacks, Brandes, Kendall, & Lewy, 2000), although there are plenty of other zeitgebers in our contemporary society (e.g., alarm clocks, city sounds, and the voices of family members) to regulate or synchronize their rest and activity cycles.

Explorations of the neurobiology of circadian rhythms point to the key role of a nucleus of the hypothalamus known as the **suprachiasmatic nucleus (SCN)**, which receives stimulation from light via tracts extending from the retina (i.e., the **retinohypothalamic tracts**). Working at the University of Virginia, Michael Menaker bred a mutant strain of hamster that had a shorter than normal circadian rhythm (about 21 hours) and restored the atypical rhythm to a normal duration after transplanting cells from the SCN of wild-type hamsters (Ralph, Foster, Davis, & Menaker, 1990). These SCN neural messages are related solely to the detection of light in the environment, not to the interpretation of visual stimuli. The detection of the sun rising in the morning and setting in the evening has had a significant impact on the evolution of sleep–wake cycles.

When the SCN is disrupted, physiological systems are desynchronized (Spiga, Walker, Terry, & Lightman, 2014). For example, when the SCN is lesioned in laboratory rats, the peak in the hormone corticosterone that occurs just prior to the dark phase disappears. However, the rats still experienced the pulsing bursts of corticosterone that typically recur throughout the 24-hour cycle (Waite et al., 2012). This finding provides evidence that the **ultradian rhythms** (rhythms with a period shorter than 24 hours) of this system do not appear to be under the control of the SCN. Although the exact source of ultradian rhythms remains unknown, some evidence suggests that cells in the hypothalamus (outside of the SCN) respond in this short pulsing fashion (Mershon, Sehlhorst, Rebar, & Liu, 1992). Because rats are nocturnal, the circadian rhythm of stress hormone release differs from that in humans (who are active during the day). For humans, the stress hormone cortisol (which is similar to corticosterone in animals) peaks around 6:00 am as we are rising and preparing for a day of activity. Thus, for both rats and humans, the peak in stress hormone occurs prior to the active period. If this pattern is disrupted, stress-related illnesses (e.g., depression) become more prevalent (Spiga et al., 2014).

Although light is the strongest external zeitgeber that entrains circadian rhythms, the hormone **melatonin**, secreted by the pineal gland, acts as an internal zeitgeber. The pathway of light from the retina to the pineal gland is shown in Figure 9.2. Specifically, melatonin appears to be a chemical trigger signaling increased blood flow in distal areas of the body, promoting heat loss and the onset of sleep. Melatonin, rather than light, likely entrains circadian rhythms in blind individuals (Sacks et al., 2000). When melatonin secretion increases, wakefulness is less likely to appear during scheduled sleep phases of the day. Thus, melatonin is considered a sleep facilitator and has been investigated as a potential treatment for insomnia. Indeed, some research has indicated that melatonin can be used to induce **phase shifts**, or realignment, in circadian clocks for those suffering from **jet lag** or for shift workers who are experiencing sleep problems (Cajochen, Krauchi, & Wirz-Justice, 2003).

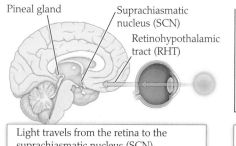

Pineal gland
Suprachiasmatic nucleus (SCN)
Retinohypothalamic tract (RHT)

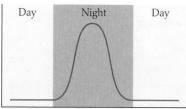

Day   Night   Day

Light travels from the retina to the suprachiasmatic nucleus (SCN), regulating daily patterns of sleep, activity, appetite, temperature, and other cycles

Darkness causes the pineal gland to produce melatonin, which facilitates sleep. Melatonin secretion peaks around 3-4 am

FIGURE 9.2 **Neural circuits involved in circadian rhythms and peak melatonin response.** Melatonin appears to be a chemical trigger signaling increased blood flow in distal areas of the body, promoting heat loss and the onset of sleep.

If you have ever flown to another time zone, you have triggered such a phase shift. Flying from the eastern to western United States, or vice versa, for example, your biological rhythms shift by as much as three hours. If this desynchronization of rhythms produces negative side effects such as difficulty going to sleep, early wakening, changes in appetite, changes in gastrointestinal functions, and daytime tiredness, an individual is considered to suffer from jet lag (Rajaratnam & Arendt, 2001).

In addition to the previously discussed SCN lesions, a desynchronization of biological rhythms also takes place with **shift work** that requires employees to work at night. As seen in Figure 9.2, melatonin levels rise at night, peaking between about 3:00 and 4:00 am. Alertness and reaction time

suffer when melatonin levels are highest, making accidents more likely for these night workers. Over time, these workers can adapt so that their peak melatonin secretion occurs during the day when they are sleeping. However, because many shift workers work some days and some nights in irregular schedules, their biological clocks have trouble making such frequent adjustments. Consequently, most long-term shift workers suffer negative health effects like obesity, diabetes, and, as mentioned, increased risk of accidents. Some individuals report successfully realigning their biological rhythms by taking melatonin supplements, using light therapy (exposure to intense light during certain times of day), or some combination of the two (Arendt, 2010).

Even without the circadian challenges of shift work or jet lag, we often have difficulty both maintaining wakefulness and shifting from sleep to wakefulness. One behavioral response that may help us navigate these shifts in arousal is yawning. A yawn is generally characterized by the gaping of the mouth, accompanied by a long inhalation and brief exhalation. Further, people often stretch while yawning, a response that is most likely to be observed before sleep and following waking (Provine, Hamernik, & Curchack, 1987). Even reading about yawning may prompt the yawning response. And, because yawns are socially contagious, if you yawn in the presence of others, you are likely to see others joining in.

Although the function of yawning is uncertain, some researchers propose that it may help regulate brain temperature because the inhalation of cool air into the lungs lowers the cerebral blood temperature. When rats are sleep deprived, their brain temperature increases. This observation suggests that rising brain temperatures may prompt a few yawns, a response associated with feelings of sleepiness (Everson, Smith, & Sokoloff, 1994; Gallup & Gallup, 2007). Additionally, increased blood flow accompanying yawning and stretching may activate some neural circuits that have low levels of activity. The brain-cooling theory of yawning is far from conclusive. However, given that yawning has been conserved across species throughout evolution, it likely has some important physiological function, such as helping an animal maintain wakefulness during times of drowsiness, as well as a social function (Gallup, 2011; Leone, Ferrari, & Palagi, 2014) (see Figure 9.3).

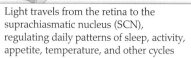

(a)

(c)

(b)

(d)

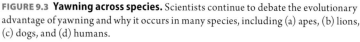

FIGURE 9.3 **Yawning across species.** Scientists continue to debate the evolutionary advantage of yawning and why it occurs in many species, including (a) apes, (b) lions, (c) dogs, and (d) humans.

Looking beyond the broad rhythms of sleep and wakefulness, specific rhythms exist within the sleep period itself. In the next section, these sleep phases are discussed in detail.

Stages of Sleep

From a behavioral perspective, **sleep** can be defined as a reversible state characterized by minimal movement, a relaxed posture, and diminished attention directed to the environment. In addition to these overt behavioral signs of sleep, other signs can be observed using a physiological recording technique known as **polysomnography**, which creates a record called a **polysomnograph**. This technique involves the recording of three physiological measures: an EEG assessing brain wave activity; an **electrooculogram** (EOG) assessing eye movements; and an **electromyogram** (EMG) assessing muscle tension, typically in the muscles located under the chin (see Figure 9.4).

The EEG sleep record displays the characteristic features of the awake state, drowsy state, and each sleep stage. EEG waves are typically characterized by their shape and frequency, measured in Hertz (cycles per second). The most active waves are the **beta (β) waves** (13–30 Hertz), which are fast, irregular, low-intensity waves; they typically occur in brains that are awake and active. **Alpha (α) waves** are more regular or consistent in their shape and a little slower (8–12 Hertz); they are predominant in awake, but drowsy brains. **Theta (θ) waves** are low-intensity sleep waves that are slower (3–7 Hertz), whereas **delta (δ) waves** are even lower-frequency sleep waves (0.5–3 Hertz). Two additional characteristics seen in sleep EEGs are **k-complexes**, which are large waves with a slow rise to the peak followed by a faster decline, and **sleep spindles**, moderately fast and intense oscillations (12–14 Hertz) that last up to 1.5 seconds.

After decades of research, the various stages of sleep have been clearly mapped. In addition to the REM sleep that Aserinsky witnessed, our nights include **non-REM sleep** composed of three distinct stages. For example, on entering a sleep lab, a typical young adult (let's call him Josh) prepares to sleep through the night. Once settled in bed with the lights turned off, Josh's EOG reflects decreased activity as he enters non-REM sleep (a flat line), and his EEG starts to transition from β waves to the slower α waves as the EMG shows relaxing muscles. Following this transitional phase, after a few minutes, signs of **Stage 1 sleep** begin to emerge. The lab technician notes slow eye movements on the EOG, as well as EEG waves transitioning from α waves to slower θ waves. During this early sleep stage, if awakened, Josh may report that he was not quite asleep but was in a relaxed state, feeling like he was floating as conscious awareness was fleeting. In some cases, he may even report simple, transitory dreams.

After about 10 minutes, a k-complex, a sleep spindle, or both emerge as signs of **Stage 2 sleep** in Josh's polysomnograph record. If the technician tried to wake Josh, it would take longer than in Stage 1, and Josh would appear groggier.

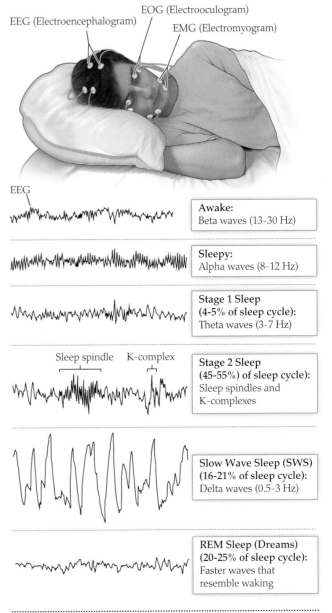

FIGURE 9.4 Stages of sleep. Over the course of a night, sleeping individuals cycle through several distinct stages: Stages 1 and 2, slow wave sleep, and REM sleep, during which dreams occur. A polysomnograph records the different brain wave patterns that characterize these stages.

Josh's EOG reflects no eye movements during this stage. If Josh remains asleep, after about 20 minutes, slow δ waves start to dominate his EEG, indicating the transition from Stage 2 to **slow wave sleep (SWS)**, which is dominated by low-frequency δ waves. Waking Josh during this stage would take some effort. He would be extremely groggy—and probably quite annoyed. The δ waves start to disappear after another 30 minutes, at which time evidence of Stage 2 reemerges.

After about 80 minutes, the technician notes a flat EMG reflecting diminished muscle tone. The EEG waves become faster, looking like β waves but sometimes referred to as sawtooth waves. The EOG amplitude increases, reflecting bursts of rapid eye movements. It would be easier to awaken Josh during this stage than during SWS, but probably more difficult than in Stage 2. This is known as REM sleep.

This cycle repeats throughout the night, with the interval between REM periods approaching about 100 minutes for adults. As the night progresses, the length of the REM periods increases (up to 30 minutes per REM period), and the amount of SWS decreases (see Figure 9.5). Toward morning, non-REM sleep is characterized mostly by Stage 2 sleep, accompanied by multiple brief arousals (brief episodes of wakefulness) and evidence of Stage 1 appearing once again, perhaps coming full circle to prepare the body to enter the stage of alert wakefulness (Moorcroft, 2003; Peter-Derex, Magnin, & Bastuji, 2015).

Extreme Sleep: Hibernation

As mammals moved into the harsh conditions of terrains located in higher latitudes, they evolved the ability to engage in a form of a prolonged sleep known as **hibernation**. Hibernation is a seasonal rhythm enhancing survival by allowing an animal to withdraw from harsh environmental conditions (such as a cold climate with limited food). During hibernation, observed in mammals ranging from bats to bears, an internal timer alerts the animals to the imminent onset of winter and stimulates them to prepare accordingly (e.g., to find a safe nest or den). The body's functions come close to shutting down during this time, allowing the animal to persist on very low caloric resources, an adaptive response to low food availability. An animal's body temperature is maintained as low as -3°C; additionally, its brain's cortical EEG activity is minimal, representing suppressed neuronal activity (Siegel, 2009; see Figure 9.6).

Researchers are interested in learning more about the mechanisms contributing to hibernation. Clues about emergence from long durations of reduced conscious awareness may inform researchers about arousal mechanisms necessary to shift the brain back into real-time responsiveness—even from a prolonged state of unconsciousness, as we will discuss later in the chapter. In addition, understanding the mechanisms that contribute to hibernation may have relevant applications for stalling or halting the progression

FIGURE 9.6 Hibernation. Many animals, such as the (a) chipmunk, enter an extended state of unconsciousness (b) in response to harsh winter weather.

of diseases. For example, bats housed in the laboratory die within about six days when infected with the rabies virus; however, rabies-infected bats can survive the long winter when they hibernate. In this case, the virus hibernates as the animals do, but returns to an active state as the animals' body temperature increases (George et al., 2011).

The Neurobiology of Sleep

The EEGs obtained in the early days of sleep research provided highly valuable information on the brain waves that characterized the different stages of sleep. However, the EEGs did not identify specific areas of the brain that were involved in sleep each night. Targeted animal studies and, more recently, human studies using high-resolution imaging techniques have revealed specific brain areas associated with various stages of sleep.

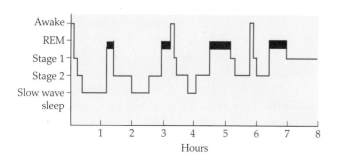

FIGURE 9.5 A full night's rest. Slow wave sleep decreases and REM sleep increases as the night progresses.

Early Neuroanatomical Explorations

In the 1930s, some 20 years before Aserinsky and Kleitman reported the landmark findings that the brain was indeed active during its seemingly passive slumber, the Belgian physiologist Frederick Bremer studied what the brain does when an animal sleeps. As discussed by Moorcroft (2003), Bremer worked with cats, a popular animal model for sleep since they spend up to two-thirds of their day sleeping. His first thought was that sleep occurred when no incoming stimuli (such as lights, sounds, or smells) activated the brain. According to this theory, sleep was a passive response to diminished brain activation.

To test this idea, Bremer made a cut at the top of a cat's spinal cord, separating it from the brain. He thought that this action would cut off all incoming stimulation to the brain, leaving it in a permanent state of sleep. Although the cats were paralyzed, Bremer found evidence that they were awake at times. This observation threatened his theory that sleep was a passive response to diminished incoming sensory stimuli.

Bremer realized that some stimuli were entering the brain via the cranial nerves. Accordingly, he made a higher cut (transection) in the brain, around the midbrain area. With just the visual and olfactory nerves intact, the cats did sleep longer, waking in the presence of strong odors or lights. Bremer thought he had confirmed his theory that sleep was the passive response to limited sensory stimulation and, alternatively, that wakefulness occurred in response to sensory stimulation arousing the brain (Moorcroft, 2003).

In the late 1940s, the research of Giuseppe Moruzzi and Horace Magoun (scientists working in France and the United States, respectively) provided evidence that wakefulness, even in the absence of sensory stimulation, came from activation of the **ascending reticular activating system (ARAS)**, a neural network that sends projections from the brainstem and hypothalamus throughout the forebrain (see Figure 9.7). In fact, when the ARAS was lesioned in cats but the sensory pathways were left intact, a permanent sleep state resulted that was interrupted only by very strong stimuli (Batini, Beaumanoir, & Tyc-Dumont, 2011; Moruzzi & Magoun, 1949).

A decade later, when the French researcher Cesira Batini and his colleagues made a transection through the pons of cats, they found that the cats showed no signs of sleeping (Batini, Moruzzi, Palestini, Rossi, & Zanchetti, 1958). This intriguing finding suggested that a brainstem area below the mid-pontine cut played an important role in sleep production. Today, we know that the **raphe nuclei**, a cluster of serotonin-secreting neurons in the brainstem, play a role in sleep regulation. The raphe nuclei and the ARAS are both components of the larger reticular formation (introduced in Chapter 2), a neural system involved in sleep–wake cycles that runs up the midline area of the brainstem. Following these early observations, it became apparent that sleep, like wakefulness, resulted from active neuronal processes, a finding confirmed by Aserinsky's report of active brain waves

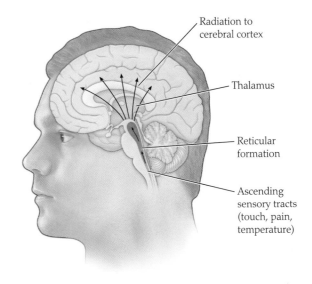

Radiation to cerebral cortex

Thalamus

Reticular formation

Ascending sensory tracts (touch, pain, temperature)

FIGURE 9.7 **The ascending reticular activating system (ARAS).** The ARAS conveys sensory information to other parts of the brain and is essential for maintaining wakefulness.

during REM sleep. These early studies identified the important role of the brainstem in sleep production. Subsequent research, described below, has further elucidated the neural basis of sleep production (Moorcroft, 2003).

Integrated Neuroanatomical and Neurochemical Circuits

Since the initial sleep studies conducted more than a half century ago, abundant research has confirmed the existence of specific neuroanatomical and neurochemical sleep circuits. To understand how sleep occurs, however, researchers first had to understand the brain areas involved in wakefulness. We now know that the acetylcholine-secreting neurons making up the cholinergic systems in the brainstem and **basal forebrain area** comprise the ARAS.

As seen in Figure 9.8, two relevant cholinergic pons/midbrain areas are the **pedunculopontine tegmental nuclei** and **laterodorsal tegmental nuclei**. Essentially, this system contributes to producing and sustaining wakefulness by maintaining the fast desynchronized β waves during the waking hours and facilitating the transmission of neural messages to the thalamus and basal forebrain. Some of these projections ultimately travel to the cortex (Holmstrand & Sesack, 2011; Saper, Chou, & Scammell, 2001). Additionally, both noradrenaline inputs from the **locus coeruleus** in the pons as well as serotonin from the raphe nuclei located in the brainstem activate thalamocortical neurons (neurons projecting from the thalamus to the cortex; Jones & Muhlethadler, 1999). Although serotonin was initially thought to promote sleep universally, evidence also suggests that spontaneous activity of serotonergic dorsal raphe neurons is highest during waking hours with maximal activity

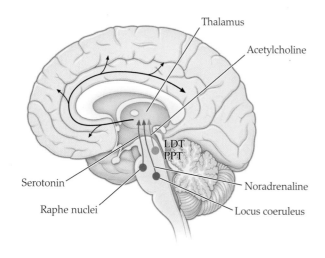

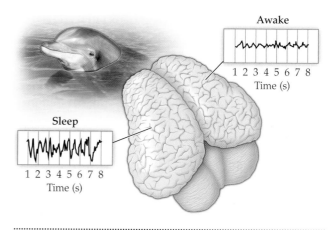

FIGURE 9.9 **Dolphin sleep.** EEG records of dolphins reveal that only one hemisphere sleeps at a time.

FIGURE 9.8 **The neurochemistry of wakefulness.** Acetycholine from the pedunculopontine tegmental nuclei (PPT) and laterodorsal tegmental nuclei (LDT) contributes to the maintenance of wakefulness.

observed during activities such as grooming in cats (B. L. Jacobs & Fornal, 1991). More recent research suggests that the raphe nuclei are more accurately described as a heterogeneous group of serotonergic neurons, some contributing to sleep and some contributing to wakefulness (Sakai, 2011).

Slow Wave Sleep. During SWS, when the brain is no longer responding to environmental sensory cues, neurons in the neocortex and thalamus fire in synchrony because of the decreased activation from the activating brainstem areas—producing the δ waves characteristic of this stage of sleep (Steriade & Contreras, 1995). The slow waves during non-REM sleep have been found to occur in localized areas of the brain at any given time, rather than throughout the entire brain. For example, at certain times of the night, especially in later stages of sleep, some brain areas are active, whereas others are silent. A similar pattern has been observed with the presence of sleep spindles.

This uneven distribution of sleep spindles and slow brain waves seems to protect against prolonged durations of slow, synchronized brain waves throughout the brain, an effect that could result in dangerously low levels of brain activity. Thus, the local pockets of slow brain waves may be a way of maintaining more activity in the brain's cells throughout the night than would be the case if the entire brain were in an inactive neuronal state (Nir et al., 2011).

What does the brain wave activity of animals that are not completely inactive during sleep look like? Dolphins and other marine mammals that do not have the luxury of being completely inactive during sleep exhibit slow waves in only one hemisphere at a time while they are sleeping (see Figure 9.9). Unlike terrestrial mammals, these animals never show evidence of both hemispheres sleeping at the same time. If the entire brain were asleep, it would be

difficult for an animal to swim, avoid obstacles, and occasionally surface to take a breath. Thus, the unequal distribution of synchronized brain wave activity observed during SWS in terrestrial mammals is even more pronounced in marine mammals (Mukhametov, Supin, & Polyakova, 1977; Purves et al., 2001; Siegel, 2011).

Whereas most neurons decrease their activation levels during SWS, the neurons in one brain area, the **ventrolateral preoptic area (VLPO)**, increase their activity during this time (Sherin, Shiromani, McCarley, & Saper, 1996). Neurons in this area that are characterized as GABAergic and galaninergic neurons (because they produce GABA and **galanin** as their output, respectively) project to the **tuberomammillary nucleus (TMN)**, an area involved in sleep–wake cycles and circadian rhythms that also contains histamine neurons that are active during immune functions such as allergic responses. Both the VLPO and the TMN nuclei are located in the hypothalamus. Research provides evidence that the inhibitory GABAergic and galaninergic neurons activated by the VLPO work to diminish wakefulness (see Figure 9.10). Galanin is an inhibitory neurotransmitter that is widely expressed throughout the brain. In addition to being involved in sleep–wake cycles, it plays a role in eating, learning, mood regulation, and protection of neurons from damage (J. M. Monti, 2010). Now you understand why your allergy medicine sometimes makes you drowsy: An antihistamine accomplishes the same function as GABA and galanin by simply blocking the histamine receptors on the TMN neurons, leading to their decreased firing rates and an individual's accompanying reduced ability to stay awake (Saper et al., 2001; Toth & Jhaveri, 2003).

Another neurochemical that plays an important role in sleep and wakefulness is adenosine. Interestingly, adenosine decreases neural activation and facilitates the onset of sleep (Bjorness, Kelly, Gao, Poffenberger, & Greene, 2009). Thus, building levels of adenosine may trigger sleep onset. Since adenosine is a byproduct of **adenosine triphosphate** metabolism, which is important for the production and

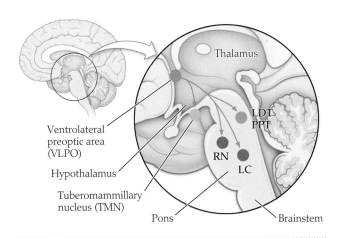

FIGURE 9.10 Sleep neural pathways. The hypothalamic projections from the ventrolateral preoptic area (VLPO) to the tuberomammillary nucleus (TMN) function to diminish wakefulness during slow wave sleep.

FIGURE 9.11 Cat naps. The sleeping posture of animals reveals information about the stage of sleep they are currently in. (a) The ability of the cat to hold its head up indicates that it is in non-REM sleep. (b) This cat has apparently lost muscle tone and entered REM sleep.

transport of cellular energy, sleep may reduce some type of cellular energy deficit established during prolonged wakefulness and its accompanying energy expenditure (Porkka-Heiskanen et al., 1997). As discussed in Chapter 4, caffeine blocks adenosine receptors, decreasing the brain's sensitivity to neurochemical markers of drowsiness (Toth & Jhaveri, 2003). Functionally, adenosine may promote the onset of sleep by inhibiting the activation of cholinergic neurons in the ARAS involved in wakefulness or facilitating activation of the sleep-promoting neurons in the VLPO (Porkka-Heiskanen et al., 1997; Schwartz & Roth, 2008).

REM Sleep. As previously described, the characteristic EEG record during REM sleep contains low-magnitude, high-frequency waves similar to those observed during wakefulness. REM is also characterized by suppressed muscle tone (**atonia**), evidenced by changes in the EMG record. For example, atonia is detected in only Figure 9.11b, suggesting that the cat is in REM sleep.

Research with cats identified a specific brain wave pattern during REM sleep, known as **pontogeniculooccipital (PGO) spikes**. PGO spikes are electrical potentials that originate in the pons and then project to the lateral geniculate nucleus of the thalamus, before making a final appearance in the occipital cortex (Morrison & Bowker, 1975). The onset of REM sleep typically occurs about 30 seconds after the appearance of these large-amplitude isolated brain potentials. Once REM is in progress, PGO spikes appear in bursts of 3–10 waves, most often correlated with rapid eye movements.

As information about the brain mechanisms involved in REM emerged, Harvard University sleep researchers Allan Hobson and Robert McCarley proposed the **activation-synthesis model of dreaming** in which brain activity was synthesized into a storyline known as a dream. Without all the appropriate brain circuits in the frontal cortex typically engaged in synthesizing material (and the requisite fact checking), the dream plots stray a bit from reality (Hobson & McCarley, 1977). For example, a fully activated frontal cortex would not accept a flying horse as realistic, but when the frontal cortex is taking a functional break during REM, that event seems just as reasonable as a running horse.

As revolutionary as the discovery of REM sleep was in humans, the identification of this sleep state in animals confirmed its evolutionary significance and provided an appropriate model for investigating it. Around the same time, in the late 1950s, William Dement and the French scientist Michel Jouvet were independently exploring REM in cats. Using the cat model, Jouvet reported that muscle atonia accompanied EEG desynchrony during REM. Although some scientists thought that REM was generated in the forebrain, careful investigations revealed that the area between the caudal medulla and the rostral midbrain (see Figure 9.12)

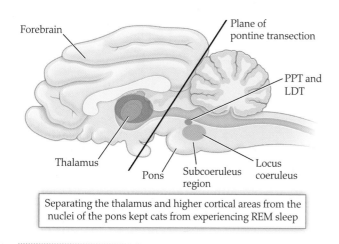

Separating the thalamus and higher cortical areas from the nuclei of the pons kept cats from experiencing REM sleep

FIGURE 9.12 Generating REM sleep. Nuclei in the pons are important for the generation of REM brain waves.

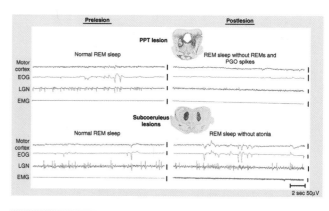

FIGURE 9.13 Pontine nuclei and REM characteristics. Lesions of pontine nuclei diminish specific aspects of REM sleep.

appeared to be sufficient for the production of REM and its accompanying effects (Adey, Bors, & Porter, 1968). Today, however, the cholinergic basal forebrain area is known to be active during REM sleep, as it is during waking hours (Vazquez & Baghdoyan, 2001).

Further research with cats and rats has also pointed to the area below the locus coeruleus, known as the **subcoeruleus region**, as an especially critical generator of REM. When this brain area was lesioned in cats, REM was decreased to a level in proportion to the percentage of cholinergic cells damaged in this area. Thus, the more cholinergic cells that were damaged in the subcoeruleus region, the lower the probability that REM sleep would be observed (Carli & Zanchetti, 1965; Webster & Jones, 1988). Researchers have observed similar effects in rats (Lu, Sherman, Devor, & Saper, 2006).

It makes intuitive sense that the loss of muscle tone during REM sleep might occur so that individuals cannot get hurt by physically acting out the bizarre storylines typical of dreams. Focusing on laboratory findings rather than courtroom testimony, however, researchers have found that when they make small lesions damaging certain portions of the subcoeruleus regions in cats, the cats retain all of the physiological signs of REM sleep (e.g., rapid eye movement, muscle twitches, respiratory changes) except for muscle atonia. This animal model allowed investigators to glimpse inside the dreams of the cats by observing their actions during REM sleep (Lai, Hsieth, Nguyen, Peever, & Siegel, 2008; Webster & Jones, 1988). These lesioned cats seemed to act out their dreams by attacking what appeared to be imaginary objects and engaging in other responses such as grooming and locomotion. Considering that these fundamental responses are related to species survival, it is possible that animals rehearse adaptive responses during REM sleep.

Subsequent experiments on specific areas throughout the midbrain, pons, and medulla have provided evidence

for specific functions of small areas located in this general brain region. As shown in Figure 9.13, lesions of the pedunculopontine tegmental nuclei in cats abolish the rapid eye movements and PGO spikes characteristic of REM sleep, whereas, as previously mentioned, lesions of the subcoeruleus area abolish the atonia typically observed in REM sleep. Generally, the cells that are maximally active during REM sleep (as opposed to during waking and non-REM sleep) are called **REM-on cells** (Siegel, 2011).

Why Sleep and Dream?

We spend up to a third of our lives engaged in sleep—it seems that a response that evolution has invested in so mightily would have obvious functions. Yet, when it comes to understanding the function of sleep, including the function of dreaming, we remain somewhat in the dark.

Evolutionary Theories of Sleep Function

Animals differ greatly in their sleep patterns, and these differences provide an opportunity for researchers to investigate how these evolved sleep specializations translate into survival advantages for various species. In addition to species differences in sleep patterns, individual differences exist. For example, you may have very different sleep habits than your roommate. As you will learn in this section, it is becoming evident that these varying sleep patterns may affect a range of other important behavioral and physiological systems.

Homeostatic Theory of Sleep Regulation. Many people believe that the function of sleep is to provide rest and recovery. This theory is sometimes referred to as the

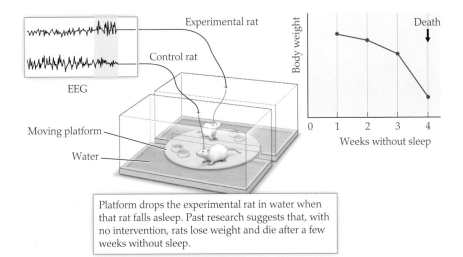

Experimental rat

Control rat

EEG

Moving platform

Water

Body weight

Death

0 1 2 3 4
Weeks without sleep

Platform drops the experimental rat in water when that rat falls asleep. Past research suggests that, with no intervention, rats lose weight and die after a few weeks without sleep.

FIGURE 9.14 Rodent model of sleep deprivation. Electroencephalograms recorded from the experimental animals activate the movement of the platform when the animal sleeps so that the disk movement and threat of falling into the water wake the animal up. The yoked animal also has its sleep patterns disrupted by the platform movement, but, unlike the experimental animal, it can engage in occasional sleep.

homeostatic theory of sleep regulation. However, only a moderate amount of evidence supports this theory. One piece of evidence for this theory is the **sleep rebound effect**, in which lost sleep is made up during the next opportunity for sleep. More specifically, such evidence would suggest that, if sleep is necessary for normal physiological functions, lost sleep would subsequently need to be made up for optimal functioning.

Although research conducted primarily on humans and rodents has revealed such supporting evidence for the homeostatic theory of sleep regulation, the sleep rebound effect is modest. Typically, such studies suggest that no more than 30% of lost sleep is recovered following sleep deprivation (Gulevich, Dement, & Johnson, 1966; Tobler, Franken, Trachsel, & Borbely, 1992). Short-term sleep deprivation such as the loss of a single sleep cycle (i.e., one cycle of slow wave and REM sleep) often leads to a non-REM sleep rebound effect, whereas longer-term deprivation, such as the lack of sleep for an entire day, leads to a REM sleep rebound effect (Siegel, 2009). Age decreases non-REM rebound effects in humans, and stress decreases REM rebound effects in both humans and rodents (Lafortune et al., 2012; Suchecki, Tiba, & Machado, 2012).

Whether or not lost sleep is typically recovered, an analysis of 19 different sleep-deprivation studies provided evidence that sleep deprivation had a significantly negative impact on cognition, motor performance, and emotional regulation (Pilcher & Huffcutt, 1996). These findings suggest that sleep does provide some "rest and renewal" function for the brain and its responses; however, we must be careful in interpreting the results of sleep-deprivation research. Sleep-deprivation studies requiring subjects to sleep fewer hours than they typically sleep are inherently stressful for the subjects. The functional impairments observed in these studies may result from that stress instead of, or in addition to, the subjects' actual reduction in sleep duration. The effects of sleep deprivation are more accurately determined by assessing individuals with established histories of sleeping a specific number of hours per night and comparing groups who report sleeping fewer hours each night with those who report sleeping more hours each night.

One source of support for the homeostatic theory has been from a research technique that prevents rats from sleeping. This technique involves placing a rat on a disk that rotates when the rat falls asleep, dropping the rat into a tray of water. A control rat also experiences the rotating disk, but the movement is not correlated with sleep; therefore, the control rat can engage in intermittent sleep (see Figure 9.14). The sleep-deprived rats in these studies indeed show signs of sickness, evidenced by decreased food consumption, inefficient temperature regulation, and, after a few weeks, death (Bergmann et al., 1989; Rechtschaffen & Bergmann, 1995).

An important aspect of these studies, however, is the fact that this technique is also very stressful for the animals (as suggested by the sleep-deprivation studies in humans), so their sickness is most accurately interpreted as an effect of both sleep deprivation and chronic stress (Peigneux, Laureys, Delbeuck, & Maquet, 2001). As previously mentioned, it is difficult for researchers to disentangle the effects of stress from those of sleep deprivation.

Perhaps the most extreme sleep deprivation study was the case of high-school student Randy Gardner, who broke the world record in 1964 by staying awake for 11 days straight. Gardner's two friends kept him awake by driving him around, taking him to a doughnut shop, and playing music (see Figure 9.15). The sleep researcher William Dement joined the high school team to monitor the effects of sleep deprivation on Gardner. After the first few days, Gardner began to exhibit significant cognitive impairment, moodiness, and even psychiatric symptoms such as hallucinations. However, he beat Dement in a pinball game on the final day of his sleep deprivation and appeared quite lucid in news interviews after breaking the world record (Ross, 1965). Perhaps the added adrenaline caused by the media

FIGURE 9.15 **Extreme sleep deprivation.** Randy Gardner stayed awake for 11 days so that the researcher William Dement could study sleep deprivation.

attention at the end of this self-experiment provided enough stimulation for him to appear competent in these tasks. This case study supports the notion that sleep supplies rest and recovery necessary for cognitive and emotional functioning. However, the fact that Gardner appeared to compensate for the extended loss of sleep with just 14 hours of sleep after the experiment suggests that there is probably more to the purpose of sleep than the maintenance of homeostatic functions.

Another piece of evidence supporting the homeostatic theory of sleep regulation is the observation that humans secrete growth hormone, important for the maintenance of physiological functions throughout life, during SWS (Born, Muth, & Fehm, 1988). Dogs and rats, in contrast, show evidence of growth hormone secretion during waking hours. Melatonin, described earlier in this chapter, is secreted maximally during sleep periods in animals that are active during the day, whereas it is secreted maximally during waking hours in animals that are active at night (Redman, 1997). These results suggest a considerable amount of flexibility built into the regulatory functions sometimes associated with sleep; that is, homeostatic functions typically associated with sleep may occur during waking hours in some cases.

Although moderate support exists for the homeostatic theory of sleep regulation, one challenge to this theory is the observation of vast differences in sleep requirements among

mammalian species. One might think that large animals would require more sleep to allow their large bodies to recover after being awake during the day. However, as shown in Figure 9.16, sleep duration varies greatly across mammalian species. When animals are closely monitored in captivity, researchers have observed that elephants sleep 3–4 hours per day, whereas the much smaller bats sleep 19 hours per day (Moorcroft, 2003).

Recent research indicates that the total sleep duration of captive animals may not accurately mirror the total sleep duration of animals in the wild. For example, although sloths were once thought to sleep 20 hours per day, scientists have recently implanted EEG "hats" in wild sloths and found that in the wild, sloths sleep only 9 hours per day (Figure 9.17; Rattenborg et al., 2008; Voirin, 2011). Perhaps, in some cases, sleep is a response to boredom more than a response to a need to replenish vanishing physiological resources.

Adaptive Theory of Sleep. When specific lifestyle characteristics and habitats are evaluated for various species, potential explanations begin to emerge for the different customary sleep durations across the animal kingdom. The **adaptive theory of sleep** suggests that animals evolved different sleep durations that help them survive. For example, Jerome Siegel, a neuroscientist at the University of California at Los Angeles, has proposed that sleep is a state of **adaptive inactivity**. Considering that some species of bats, for example, can successfully hunt for food only during a few hours around the time of dusk and early darkness, their extended periods of slumber provide protection against being consumed by predators. Elephants, in contrast, can successfully forage throughout the day. Extended durations of wakefulness allow more time to consume the large quantities of food required to maintain the large body mass of these animals. When food availability is diminished for some mammals living in harsh, cold climates, it is adaptive to conserve as much energy as possible to enable the body to continue to live in the midst of limited resources. Mammals as large as bears and as small as the Siberian hamster respond to this challenge by hibernating, as discussed earlier in the chapter (Siegel, 2009). In short, sleep can be viewed as an adaptive response linking rest–activity cycles such as sleep duration to the animal's ecological niche and physiological requirements (Toth & Jhaveri, 2003; Webb, 1974). Since humans do not have to forage all day to provide sufficient energy for a healthy body, it may have been

FIGURE 9.16 **Variations of sleep patterns.** A vast array of sleep durations is observed across the animal kingdom. These variations provide clues about the functions of sleep.

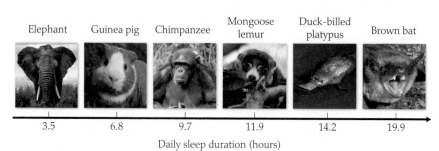

Elephant	Guinea pig	Chimpanzee	Mongoose lemur	Duck-billed platypus	Brown bat
3.5	6.8	9.7	11.9	14.2	19.9

Daily sleep duration (hours)

(a)

(b)

FIGURE 9.17 **Sloth sleep.** Observations of sleep duration patterns in sloths kept in captivity indicated that they sleep up to 20 hours per day. (a) However, when sloths' sleep is monitored in their natural habitat by placing electroencephalogram caps on them, (b) the results indicate that they sleep far less than in captivity.

adaptive for our ancestors to rest in a safe place, hidden from predators during the night.

Historical and Cultural Perspectives on Human Sleep Patterns

We are constantly reminded that we need approximately seven to eight hours of continuous sleep each night to remain healthy. Where did this advice originate, and is it valid? Examination of our ancestors' sleeping patterns reveals that humans have engaged in alternative sleep patterns longer than they have opted for eight hours of sleep per night.

The historian Roger Ekirch has extensively investigated the sleep patterns of preindustrialized societies—before the advent of electric lights—and has found repeated references

to a more segmented sleep pattern than currently practiced. As recently as the 16th century, individuals would sleep for about four hours, then wake up for a few hours to pray, meditate, write diary entries, or socialize, and then settle into about four more hours of sleep before morning. These segments were referred to as the *first sleep* and *second sleep*. As artificial lighting began to provide more opportunities to be active at night, parents started encouraging their children to sleep for a single sleep bout, saving two to three hours of "down" time between the first and second sleep (Ekirch, 2005). Ekirch's research suggests that by the 17th century, literary references to the first and second sleep started to disappear, explaining why few of us have ever heard of this common practice of our ancestors.

Contemporary research assessing human subjects' responses to days with 14 hours of darkness has also shown the segmented sleep pattern described by Ekirch. With a window into brain wave activity in these recent sleep investigations, researchers found that the first sleep was characterized by more SWS and the second sleep by more REM activity, constituting a lighter sleep that may have been easier to awaken from (Wehr, 1992).

Researchers have observed less regimented sleeping habits in the African tribe !Kung, whose members typically stay awake as long as something interesting is occurring and go to sleep when they feel like it. In this culture, no one is told to go to sleep, not even children. It is possible that cultures with more individual differences and flexibility in sleeping practices ensured that, at any given time, someone was awake, or at least in an easily disrupted second sleep, to respond to oncoming predators, environmental threats, or a sick member of the group (Worthman & Melby, 2002). This is observed in the Hazda African tribe, which has been described as a "living fossil" of humans since the contemporary members' lifestyles have remained the same over the past 10,000 years (see Figure 9.18) (Finkel, 2009). This tribe also reports variation in sleep schedules; for example, some members stay awake during the night and nap during the day (Finkel, 2009). In a recent investigation of sleep patterns in three preindustrialized societies in Bolivia, Tanzania, and Namibia, sleep durations of 5.7–7.1 hours were reported, with sleep onset occurring about 3 hours after sunset. Temperature was observed to be an important regulator of sleep patterns; for example, these individuals napped on 22% of the summer days and only 7% of the winter days (Yetish et al., 2015).

If continuous sleep is a relatively new practice, then what Western society has perceived as "sleep abnormalities," such as waking up in the middle of the night and not being able to immediately go back to sleep, may be merely a reemergence of the sleeping patterns of our ancestors. As you look at our contemporary sleep EEG throughout a bout of continuous sleep, it is easy to discern two distinct phases of sleep characterized by deep sleep (SWS) during the first half and REM sleep in the second half of the brain's sleep cycle (as described earlier in the chapter). Understanding that some

FIGURE 9.18 **Contemporary sleep fossils.** The Hazda African tribe still live as hunters and gatherers, as our ancestors did 10,000 years ago. Their sleep habits may provide clues about the origins of human sleep–wake cycles before the environmental changes associated with contemporary societies. In this culture, people often lie out in the open around a fire.

variations in sleep practices may be natural may relieve the anxiety of some individuals who think that they have a serious sleep disorder. Even so, some variations of the sleep pattern do indeed present health risks, as you will see in the discussion of sleep disorders later in this chapter.

Learning, Memory, and Survival Functions

Wouldn't it be nice if your brain could memorize dates for an upcoming history exam or master a new language you have been wanting to learn while you blissfully sleep during the night? Although several types of sleep learning programs and devices have been marketed, learning during a night's sleep does not seem to work that way. But do not lose hope; various aspects of learning and memory have indeed been observed in sleep research. Research suggests that sleep can enhance cognitive and emotional functions necessary for survival during the waking hours. Although the sleeping brain cannot interact directly with the environment, it can engage in other types of processing during this downtime. Evidence suggests that various aspects of learning and memory—from memory consolidation to the introduction of creative problem solving—occur during different stages of sleep. **Memory consolidation** refers to a process that transforms new, unstable memories into more stable memories integrated into the brain's network of existing memories (Diekelmann & Born, 2010).

Slow Wave Sleep. Generally, SWS has been shown to consistently facilitate the consolidation of information that can be consciously recalled for further processing or use

(also known as **declarative memories**). On the one hand, your memories of your high school graduation are declarative memories. **Procedural memories** (memories of how to perform certain actions), on the other hand, do not represent conscious retrieval of stored memories. Your ability to play tennis the week after receiving your first lesson may be a result of procedural memories that have consolidated outside your realm of conscious awareness. Declarative memories have been associated with hippocampal activity, whereas procedural memories have been associated with hippocampal-independent memory circuits (Diekelmann & Born, 2010). You will learn more specific information about neural processes associated with learning in Chapter 12.

Pioneering research using sleeping rodents has provided a potential explanation for how memories are consolidated during sleep episodes (M. A. Wilson & McNaughton, 1994). The Massachusetts Institute of Technology neuroscientist Matthew Wilson made a rather serendipitous discovery of sleep-reactivated hippocampal cells in rats. Wilson had implanted microelectrodes into the hippocampal cells of rats that were subsequently trained to search for food in a maze. During training, he could hear the cracking noises indicating firing patterns of neurons' action potentials as the animal was learning to navigate the maze. After concluding the training one day, however, he heard the familiar neural activity patterns in a rat that he had left hooked up to the recording equipment—but this time the rat was not running the maze; it was asleep!

Further research confirmed that the same neurons that fired during spatial tasks also fired in SWS, suggesting that learned information during waking was reexpressed, or rehearsed, in hippocampal circuits during sleep (MIT News,

2009; M. A. Wilson & McNaughton, 1994). In a subsequent study, activation of the visual cortex during sleep was also found to play a role in memory consolidation in rats learning to successfully navigate a maze. As depicted in Figure 9.19a, similar patterns of cortical and hippocampal activation were observed during the actual process of running the maze and the subsequent bout of sleeping (Ji & Wilson, 2007).

A study in humans also provided evidence that reactivation of relevant neurons during SWS facilitates the consolidation of memories acquired during the previous waking hours. As indicated in Figure 9.19b, subjects were exposed to a specific odor while learning the location of objects in a two-dimensional spatial task. Exposure to the same odor during SWS enhanced the subsequent recall of the spatial memories, an effect not observed if the odor was presented during REM sleep. Further, more pronounced hippocampal activation was observed during odor exposure in SWS than that observed in wakefulness, indicating significant activation of relevant hippocampal networks during SWS (Diekelmann & Born, 2010; Rasch, Buchel, Gais, & Born, 2007). The results provided evidence that the odor used in this study acted as

a cue to activate the relevant hippocampal circuits that enabled the subject to perform the task while awake.

The neuroscientists Chiara Cirelli and Guilio Tononi of the University of Wisconsin–Madison and their colleagues have also provided research evidence that SWS plays a role in learning and memory. These researchers are interested in the finding from past human and animal studies that suggests synaptic strengthening occurs throughout the day following exposure to both familiar and novel situations, reaching critically high levels by the day's end. To maintain the most efficient memory system, these researchers have stated that it is important to prune the neural networks, especially in the neocortex, of weak and potentially unimportant synapses to strengthen the more relevant and stronger synapses. According to their **synaptic homeostasis hypothesis**, an important function of sleep is to reduce weaker synapses to provide more energy and resources for the stronger synapses.

SWS may provide an ideal electrophysiological environment for this cortical synaptic downsizing (Hanlon, Vyazovskiy, Faraguna, Tononi, & Cirelli, 2011). Although we do not yet know whether this hypothesis is correct, it is at

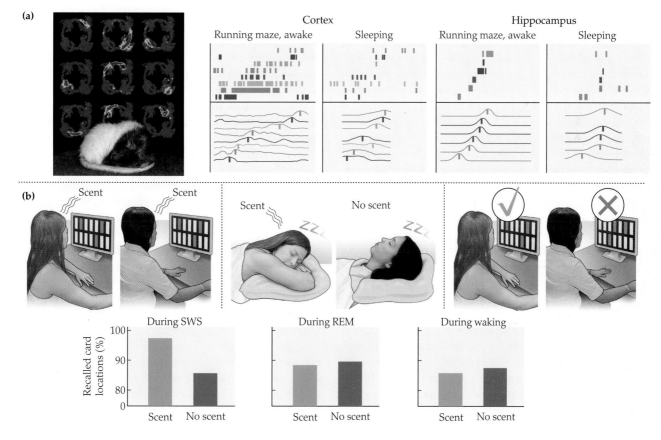

Source: Diekelmann, S. & Born, J. (2010). The memory function of sleep. *Nature Reviews Neuroscience, 11*, 114-125.

FIGURE 9.19 Sleep and learning. (a) When a rat sleeps after navigating through a maze, the same neural patterns that the rat displayed while in the maze are reactivated. (b) In humans, presentation of stimuli during a learning task and subsequently when a subject is in slow wave sleep can reactivate neural patterns similar to those active during learning, facilitating consolidation of the information.

least consistent with recent findings. In one study, for example, a specific glutamate receptor associated with synaptic strengthening was found to be at its highest level in the cortex during wakefulness and at its lowest level during sleep (Vyazovskiy, Cirelli, Pfister-Genskow, Faraguna, & Tononi, 2008). Such data suggest that the production of synapses increases during waking hours and decreases during sleeping hours.

REM Sleep. A considerable amount of research also suggests that offline processing continues in REM sleep, consolidating memories acquired during waking hours in both animals and humans (Laureys et al., 2001; Smith, 1996; Stickgold, Whidbee, Schirmer, Patel, & Hobson, 2000). REM sleep seems to be especially important for the consolidation of procedural, as opposed to declarative, memories. Human studies imposing REM sleep deprivation following acquisition of a procedural task (e.g., a logic task requiring the identification of specific codes to generate letters) found memory deficits associated with the REM sleep deprivation. Additionally, studies monitoring REM sleep following acquisition of tasks ranging from learning tricks on a trampoline to solving challenging puzzles have reported increased time spent in REM sleep as well as increased intensity of REM sleep (determined by the number of eye movements during the REM sessions) compared with REM sleep quality when learning acquisition was not taking place (Smith, 2001).

The number of rapid eye movements during sleep has also been associated with academic forms of learning. Shortly after their final exams, students exhibited a greater number of rapid eye movements than recorded earlier in the semester, when the students were engaging in less intensive studying. Specifically, the greatest number of rapid eye movements was observed during the fourth occurrence of the REM period over the night's sleep (Smith & Lapp, 1991). Isn't it interesting to think that the extent of the increased number of rapid eye movements during sleep may play a role in learning and remembering information for final exams?

The classic research conducted by Jonathan Winson of Rockefeller University (as reviewed in Winson, 2002 [1990]) provides a unique perspective on the "meaning" of dreams. Winson's research focused on the biological relevance of dreams, rather than on the unconscious motives of dreams that were hypothesized by Sigmund Freud (1900/1953). Winson postulated that **θ rhythms**, observed in the hippocampal activity of several different species of animals, were critical for the processing of survival-related behavior. In addition, Winson emphasized that θ rhythms appeared in the EEG of different species of animals during REM sleep, as shown in Figure 9.20, suggesting that REM sleep allowed

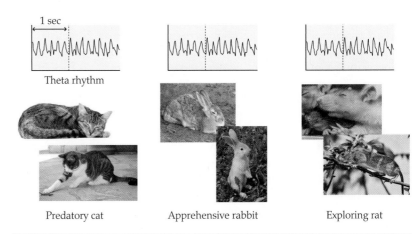

Theta rhythm

Predatory cat   Apprehensive rabbit   Exploring rat

FIGURE 9.20 θ rhythms during REM and waking behaviors. Similar θ rhythms observed during both REM and survival-related behaviors in various mammals suggest that REM brain activity may facilitate these behaviors expressed during waking hours.

animals to incorporate meaningful survival-related responses into their existing neural networks.

An unassuming mammal called the short-beaked spiny anteater, or echidna (Figure 9.21), has provided support for Winson's ideas about θ rhythms and REM processing. The echidna, one of the earliest mammals to evolve from terrestrial reptiles, lays eggs—testifying to its origins—but is warm blooded, grows hair, and suckles its young (after they emerge from the leathery eggs). The prefrontal cortex of this prehistoric mammal, however, is surprisingly large. Winson suggested that if the human prefrontal cortex were proportionately similar, we would have to carry our heads around in a wheelbarrow (Rock, 2004). Why does an echidna require such a large prefrontal cortex? Winson reported that the echidna does not have REM sleep and its accompanying θ waves, meaning that it does not have a neural format for offline processing during sleep. The result is that this animal must process survival and emotionally relevant information in "real time" as the response occurs, requiring a large amount of neocortex on hand to accomplish that task (Winson, 1990).

Additional support for the idea that REM helps encode survival-related responses comes from Michel Jouvet's previously described findings that animals appeared to be acting out species-relevant survival responses during REM sleep. Jouvet proposed that REM sleep provides a safe "dress rehearsal" for the most meaningful aspects of our waking lives (Hobson, 2004).

Subsequent research suggests that the echidna's sleep may represent more of an evolutionary precursor for both REM and non-REM sleep. However, it is distinct from sleep patterns in other mammals (Siegel, Manger, Nienhuis, Fahringer, & Pettigrew, 1996). Regardless, the sleep researcher Allan Hobson has commented that "REM sleep may constitute a protoconscious state, providing a virtual reality model of the world that is of functional use to the development and maintenance of waking consciousness" (Hobson,

(a)

(b)

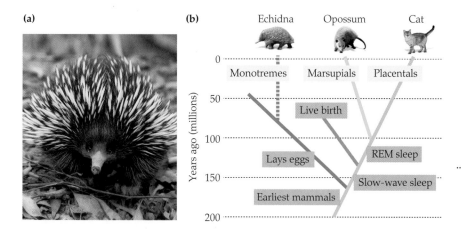

FIGURE 9.21 Evolution of REM sleep. The echidna (a), an egg-laying mammal, evolved at an earlier point than did (b) those animals that experience REM sleep.

2009, p. 803). Indeed, the consequences of making errors are much less severe in our dreams than in the real world!

At the time that Winson proposed his theory emphasizing the importance of θ rhythms and offline processing in REM, it was not clear that humans also expressed these rhythms. Since that time, however, θ rhythms have been observed in humans. Researchers have also found correlations between θ rhythms and the initiation of voluntary memories (as when you recall your movements throughout the day to remember where you left your phone). These parallel the correlations found between rodent θ waves in the hippocampus and the initiation of movement (Kaplan et al., 2012). Considering that exploration of one's environment, a function of θ rhythms, involves both muscular movement and eye movement, animals had to evolve mechanisms to suppress the physical movement to avoid harm. However, the eye movements involved in exploration may have remained because they posed no harm to the sleeper, comprising the mysterious rapid eye movements characterizing REM sleep. Thus, both laboratory and evolutionary research approaches in multiple species have confirmed the role of REM in learning and memory processes.

Before concluding this section on REM sleep, we will consider the effect of antidepressant drugs on REM sleep. Most antidepressants drastically alter sleep rhythms by greatly increasing the amount of time between falling asleep and entering REM sleep, as well as reducing the amount of time ultimately spent in REM sleep. Yet individuals taking antidepressant medication show no apparent cognitive side effects of the REM loss (S. Wilson & Argyropoulos, 2005). If REM sleep plays a critical role in consolidating information gained throughout the day, we might expect patients taking these drugs to report drug-related memory loss. However, they do not. It is possible, of course, that other non-REM compensatory mechanisms may come into play to retain memory consolidation in patients consuming antidepressant drugs. We clearly still have much to learn about the purposes and effects of REM sleep.

This section has described just a few of the many studies indicating associations among learning, memory, and various sleep phases. A different form of learning enhancement (i.e., insight learning), not linked to a specific phase of sleep, is described in "Context Matters."

CONTEXT MATTERS

Stuck on a Problem? Sleep on It!

Featured Study: Wagner, U., Gals, S., Halder, H., Verteger, R., & Born, J. (2004). Sleep inspires insight. Nature, 427, 352–355.

In Chapter 3, you learned that the Nobel Prize winner Otto Loewi was stuck on the problem of how neurons communicate with one another. Was it through an electrical spark? Physical pressure? Some type of neurochemical? The answer to the question, in the form of an experiment, came to Loewi in his dreams. We now know that neurons use chemicals to communicate with one another.

Does research support the notion that enhanced problem solving occurs following sleep? Considering that sleep changes the neural characteristics of the brain, variations in sleep can be perceived as both an internal and an experiential contextual variable. A team of German neuroscientists designed a study to determine whether insight was enhanced following sleep. Insight, in this case, was defined as a form of mental restructuring that enables an individual to arrive at a solution to a particular problem: the proverbial *A-ha* moment! For example, you struggle with a problem in calculus, go to sleep, and wake up in the morning with a new and improved strategy that helps you solve the problem. You have gained insight into the problem at hand after modifying the brain's internal (postsleep brain physiology) and experiential (different time and place) context.

(a) Task: Determine the final digit

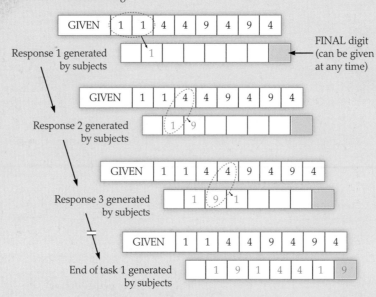

(b) Groups and procedure

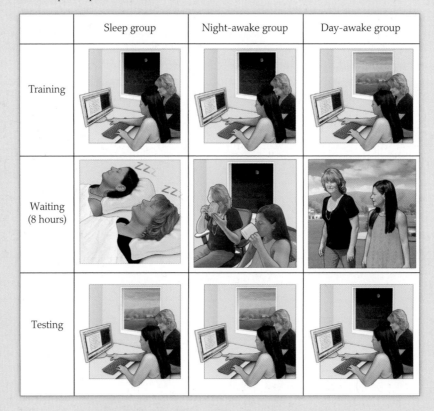

CONTEXT MATTERS FIGURE 9.1 Insight and sleep. (a) Subjects were trained on the Number Reduction Task and then (b) assigned to groups that were instructed to sleep, stay awake through the night, or simply wait until later in the day to attempt to solve the problem.

The present study investigated the idea that restructuring may go beyond that necessary for memory consolidation and, in some cases, may promote insight. To test this hypothesis, these researchers recruited 66 young adult subjects to work on a slightly frustrating cognitive task known as the number reduction task. In this task, subjects are given a series of eight digits in the first line and the first digit in the second line, as follows:

11449494
1

Each line is composed, or will be composed, solely of the digits 1, 4, and 9. The subjects' ultimate task is to determine the eighth and final digit in the second line. Initially, to generate the first missing digit in the series in the second line, subjects were instructed to compare the first two digits in the first line and apply the following two rules:

Rule 1: If the two digits match, provide that same digit.

Rule 2: If the two digits do not match, provide the third digit in the remaining three-digit system (1, 4, or 9).

After subjects determined the first missing digit in the series, they were required to make comparisons between the response they had just made and the next digit in the first line. Specifically, they were instructed to look directly above the next empty slot and one digit to the right to determine whether that digit matched the response they had just made. Then, they were required to apply Rules 1 and 2. The subjects' ultimate task was to use these rules to generate the eighth and final digit in the second line.

What was not presented to the subjects was a "hidden" rule that the last three digits generated mirrored the previous three digits. Subjects who discovered this hidden rule could solve the problems faster because they never needed to solve for the final three digits, but only provide the mirror digits for the previous three digits. In the example above, the correctly generated digits include the following:

11914419

After working through 90 of these trials, one group of subjects was allowed to sleep for 8 hours. A second group of subjects was required to stay awake all night before the second wave of trials. A final group of subjects completed the initial

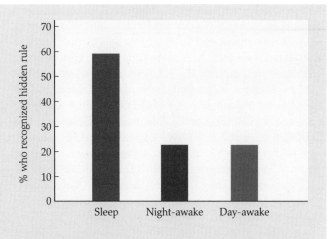

CONTEXT MATTERS FIGURE 9.2 Study results. Eight hours after the initial attempt to solve the problem, the group allowed to sleep exhibited enhanced insight.

trials in the morning, stayed awake throughout the day and then, eight hours later, tackled the second batch of trials (to control for the effects of sleep deprivation) (see Context Matters Figure 9.1).

The results indicated that the group that was allowed to sleep was more likely to discover the hidden rule and jump to the final digit after generating the third number in the sequence (Context Matters Figure 9.2). In this case, 59% of the subjects from the sleep group utilized the hidden rule during the second wave of trials. Once subjects had this "insight," the amount of time it took to solve a Number Reduction Task decreased from nine seconds to less than three seconds. The two groups that were not allowed to sleep, however, were less efficient on the task because only 23% of subjects in those groups discovered the valuable hidden rule.

Thus, for this challenging Number Reduction Task, sleep appeared to enhance insight or problem solving. This result suggests that sleep may have restructured Otto Loewi's memories and observations to enable him to arrive at his Nobel Prize–winning neurochemical solution to neural communication. These results also suggest that at least in some cases, sleep, rather than wakefulness, is the optimal brain context for insight learning. Consequently, the lesson of this study may be that after you have studied a problem extensively, sleep on it!

Potential Immune Functions

Does it seem that you are more likely to get sick when you are sleep deprived? As previously mentioned, it can be difficult to tease apart the effects of sleep deprivation from those of stress. However, the energy-consuming immune system may activate specialized operations during times of sleep, when the nervous system, also an energy guzzler, is less active.

Several studies suggest that sleep loss compromises one's health. For example, vaccines have been found to be less effective in individuals who have an interrupted night of sleep (Spiegel, Sheridan, & van Cauter, 2002). In another study, 150 adults were recruited to determine whether sleep duration and **sleep efficiency** (defined as the percentage of time in bed that one is asleep) predicted susceptibility to the common cold. After reporting their sleep information for two weeks, subjects were quarantined and given nasal drops containing a virus that can cause a cold. Subjects were subsequently monitored for objective signs of illness for five days. Results showed that a sleep duration of seven hours or less was correlated with a 3-fold increase in cold susceptibility. However, results suggested that sleep efficiency had an even greater impact on illness susceptibility assessed by the presence of symptoms of the cold. A sleep efficiency of less than 92% was associated with a 5.5-fold increase in cold susceptibility (Cohen, Doyle, Alper, Janicki-Deverts, & Turner, 2009). Although these correlations do not indicate that lack of sleep (or lack of sleep efficiency) caused the illness, the relationship between sleep and illness susceptibility deserves further investigation.

A potential mechanism for the sleep–immune system interactions may be related to the observation that neurons responsive to two immune chemicals, or cytokines **interleukin 1** and **tumor necrosis factor**, are located in sleep–wake-regulatory centers including the brainstem, hippocampus, and hypothalamus. These two immune factors also appear to increase SWS in several species. Accordingly, when these chemicals are blocked or disrupted, SWS decreases.

Another example of immune–sleep interactions is the finding in many studies that sick animals exhibit disrupted sleep, an intriguing observation that deserves further study. Imeri and Opp (2009) have proposed that disrupted sleep patterns help maintain fevers that enable the body to ward off unwelcome pathogens. The drops in body temperatures that coincide with SWS are inconsistent with maintaining high body temperatures characteristic of the fever. Frequent disruptions in SWS observed during illness may facilitate the maintenance of a fever. Shivering, also involved in heat production during a fever, is not possible during REM sleep with loss of muscle tone, which may be the reason that REM is compromised during sleep when a fever is emerging (Imeri and Opp, 2009). Increased energy conservation during non-REM sleep in times of sickness is also beneficial, considering that the body's metabolic rate dramatically increases to sustain the necessary increase in body temperature maintaining the fever. The REM and SWS modifications observed during times of sickness may explain why extended sleep durations often accompany sickness, although the **sleep architecture pattern** (the pattern of sleep stages) may be disrupted (Imeri & Opp, 2009). An opportunistic immune system may adjust the sleep architecture to maximize immune efficiency and positive health outcomes.

The varied functions and explanations of sleep proposed in this section confirm the complexity of the sleep state. Although sleep may have had a single basic function early in the evolution of mammals, research suggests that sleep may have adapted to serve several functions. Consider an office building bustling with people and activities during the working hours. It is important to conserve energy in this office building each evening, turning the lights down and adjusting the temperature setting. Even with the workers gone, many operations can be addressed during the evenings—cleaning, backup of computer files, a repair here and there—so the employees can hit the ground running the next morning. Similarly, even if we need downtime to conserve energy and avoid predators, both SWS and REM sleep benefit the processing of the brain's daily collection of relevant and irrelevant experiences. And, similar to the night watchmen protecting the office building against various threats, the immune system may take advantage of extra energy supplies each evening to produce the many immune cells and proteins necessary to ward off looming threats to the body. Likewise, sleep, perhaps more than any other behavior, may contribute in diverse ways to maintaining our health, including energy conservation, protection from harm's way, immune enhancement, memory consolidation, rehearsal of relevant behaviors, and pruning of weak neural connections.

Sleep Patterns: Typical and Atypical Variations

With so many sleep stages and the presence of predisposed individual differences in sleep–wake cycles, it is becoming increasingly evident that sleep practices are more accurately described as *flexible* rather than *fixed* in nature. Consequently, defining the boundaries representing a dysfunctional departure from the evolved sleep norm is sometimes difficult, especially with questions related to sleep deprivation and sleep disorders. Even so, research has identified distinguishing characteristics of several conditions that stray from the more typical sleep patterns. However, before we focus on disorders of sleep, we will examine the variations observed in sleep durations.

Establishing the Sleep Norm

Before it can be established that reduced sleep durations are clinically relevant, it is important to evaluate the boundaries of minimum and maximum sleep durations in humans. The UK sleep researcher Jim Horne has suggested a provocative idea, that the second half of a night's sleep, characterized by increased REM periods, can be shortened with few negative consequences. Horne's research questions whether there are any negative consequences of **sleep debt** (the difference between the amount of sleep you supposedly need and the amount of sleep you actually get).

Recent sleep surveys in the United Kingdom and the United States confirm that sleep duration in adults has a normal distribution, with an average sleep duration of about seven hours per day (see Figure 9.22; Groeger, Zijlstra, & Dijk, 2004: Krueger & Friedman, 2009). Although we tend to think that we get less sleep than our ancestors, few historic surveys indicate that our ancestors slept eight hours per day (as discussed earlier in the chapter). In fact, it appears that an influential study that was used to determine the eight-hour sleep need was a study of children and adolescents conducted in 1913 (Terman & Hocking, 1913). However, results based on children and adolescents might not generalize

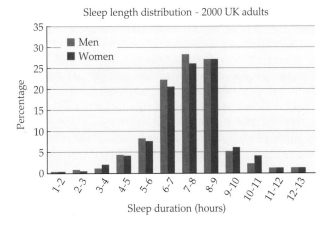

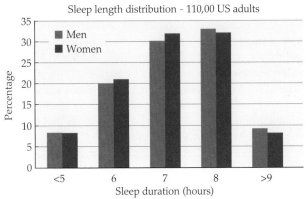

Figure 9.22a. Source: Groeger, J.A., Zijlstra, F.R.H., Dijk, D.J. (2004). Sleep quantity, sleep difficulties and their perceived consequences in a representative sample of some 2000 British adults. *Journal of Sleep Research, 13*, 359-371.

Figure 9.22b. Source: Krueger, P.M., Friedman, E.M. (2009). Sleep duration in the United States: a cross-sectional population-based study. *American Journal of Epidemiology, 169*, 1052-1063.

FIGURE 9.22 **Sleep durations in the United Kingdom and the United States.** Sleep durations are similarly distributed in (a) the United Kingdom and (b) the United States, with an average nightly sleep of approximately seven hours in both groups.

to adults. Recently, a survey of 11,000 adults asked subjects how they would spend a free hour during the day. About half the men and women reported that they would spend it sleeping. However, this response was not associated with a self-report of sleepiness and perceived sleep debt. And when given the choice, most people did not report that they would opt to sleep during that hour over other waking alternatives, such as reading or watching television. After confirming an association between a perceived sleep deficit and stressful lifestyle, these authors concluded that a desire for more sleep was more indicative of a need for "down time" than for actual sleep (Anderson and Horne, 2008).

Horne argues that, whereas abrupt reductions in sleep durations have negative consequences, an adaptation to shorter sleep durations over several weeks can be achieved without excessive daytime sleepiness. Daytime sleepiness has been traditionally viewed as an indicator of a rising sleep debt because of a failure to sleep 8 hours per night. Horne

describes individuals sleeping approximately 6 hours per night as short sleepers, arguing that they are both alert and healthy (Horne, 2011). On the other end of the spectrum, individuals whom researchers allowed to stay in bed 10 hours per night (as opposed to 8 hours) slept an extra hour compared with their baseline sleep durations, yet failed to exhibit increased daytime alertness. This finding suggests a cap on the benefits that can be gained from a night's sleep (Harrison & Horne, 1996). Based on his observations, Horne proposes that an adaptable range for sleep in human adults is 6 to 9 hours per day, a conclusion that challenges the traditional notion that adults need to sleep around 8 hours per day (Horne, 2011).

Although research on sleep patterns is far from providing definitive answers about the absolute number of hours humans need to sleep each day, contemporary researchers are questioning the traditional views of sleep patterns in an attempt to generate the most accurate views about this important behavior. Once researchers more accurately define healthy patterns of sleep, they can more accurately classify sleep disorders to develop effective therapies.

Sleep Disorders

Although no "one-size-fits-all" sleep pattern exists, some individuals suffer from atypical and dysfunctional sleep-related conditions that cause distress and disruption. The sleepwalking and violence described in the opening story of Kenneth Parks represent an example of such a variation in the normal sleep pattern. Other disorders include dreams that are extremely scary (nightmares) or sudden shifts in consciousness during SWS that result in an abrupt wakening and panic responses (**night terrors**), most often observed in children. Although children with night terrors tend not to remember the experience—unlike those who suffer from nightmares—it can be extremely frightening for their parents. We explore three other common sleep disorders in this section, beginning with the most common: insomnia.

Insomnia. Individuals diagnosed with **insomnia** experience difficulties initiating sleep, maintaining sleep, or both and suffer from sleepiness during the waking hours. Insomnia is one of the most common medical complaints reported to physicians. In a poll conducted by the National Sleep Foundation in the United States, 35% of adults reported experiencing symptoms of insomnia each night, and 58% reported experiencing these symptoms at least a few nights per week (National Sleep Foundation, 2014).

Insomnia has many potential causes, including genetic predispositions that alter neurobiological components of the sleep–wake cycle, the presence of illness or anxiety, or ill-advised sleep habits (such as taking frequent naps during the day). It is important to establish effective therapies to help individuals with insomnia obtain a satisfying night's sleep.

Pharmacotherapy is currently the treatment that is most often recommended for patients suffering from insomnia. Benzodiazepines, drugs that affect GABA receptors, have been used as hypnotic drugs to facilitate sleep. More recent variations of these drugs include Ambien (zolpidem), Sonata (zaleplon), and Lunesta (eszopiclone). Although these drugs may be effective in the short term, in the long term they produce significant side effects such as fatigue, dizziness, and nightmares. Accordingly, cognitive-behavioral therapy (CBT) has been compared with pharmacotherapy to determine the most effective and safest long-term treatment strategy for insomnia.

In one study of older adults, patients were assigned to one of the following groups: (1) a CBT group (this group included instruction in sleep mechanisms and strategies, as well as information about cognitive and relaxation strategies for enhancing sleep), (2) a sleep medication group, and (3) a placebo medication group. Following six weeks of treatment, the total duration of wake time (time awake during the sleep cycle) decreased by 52% for the CBT group compared with decreases of 4% in the drug group and 16% in the placebo group. Further, the CBT group had a better quality of sleep, with longer durations of SWS than the comparison groups. After six months of therapy, the CBT group had less wake time and better sleep efficiency (percentage of time in bed spent asleep) than the medication group did, with the medication group reporting adverse side effects such as a dry mouth, nausea, daytime sleepiness, and a bitter taste in their mouth (Siversten et al., 2006). Additional research studies have reported promising results comparing CBT with traditional sleep medications in younger adults, suggesting that more research must be conducted to determine how to use CBT as a first-line treatment approach for insomnia before medications are prescribed (G. D. Jacobs, Pace-Schott, Stickgold, & Otto, 2004; Siebern & Manber, 2011). As illustrated in Table 9.1, in CBT, multiple strategies have been found to be effective in reducing insomnia (Siebern & Manber, 2011).

Narcolepsy. Whereas people with insomnia cannot get enough sleep, those with **narcolepsy** have the opposite problem: they experience uncontrollable bouts of sleep in their waking lives. Consider the case of S.I., a 35-year-old woman diagnosed with narcolepsy. S.I.'s first symptoms appeared when she was playing basketball as a teenager—while she was shooting free throws, she felt a weakness in her knees. These periods of weakness were accompanied by droopy eyelids and progressed to the point at which she would drop things she was holding. Her symptoms progressed further when she started college. Regardless of how much she slept at night, she would fall asleep in class and at social gatherings during the day. Furthermore, she felt very sleepy during emotionally arousing times; for example, she would awkwardly fall asleep when she kissed her boyfriend. Her sleep architecture at night also seemed to be changing. As she was falling asleep, she would sometimes experience auditory and visual hallucinations—known as **hypnogogic hallucinations**—accompanied by paralysis. She also experienced muscle paralysis during the day when she was fully awake. Finally, when drifting to sleep, she entered REM almost immediately and encountered more Stage 1 and Stage 2 sleep than SWS (Moorcroft, 2003).

S.I.'s case is typical for individuals suffering from narcolepsy, a neurological disorder. In general, symptoms include excessive sleepiness, intermittent and uncontrollable episodes of sleep during waking hours, muscular weakness or paralysis known as **cataplexy**, and hypnogogic hallucinations. Because the muscular weakness typical of narcolepsy and disruptive shifts in conscious awareness/sleepiness occur during REM sleep, researchers have considered narcolepsy a REM-related disorder.

Certain breeds of dogs also exhibit narcolepsy, so researchers have used them as animal models to study the

---

TABLE 9.1.

Cognitive-Behavioral Therapy for Insomnia

ELEMENT	DESCRIPTION
Stimulus control	Set of instructions aimed at breaking conditioned arousal and strengthening the bed and bedroom as stimuli for sleep
Sleep restriction	Limiting the time allowed in bed to the patient's average reported actual sleep time and subsequently slowly increasing the time allowed in bed as sleep improves
Cognitive therapy	Targeting beliefs and thoughts that directly interfere with sleep by increasing arousal in bed or indirectly by interfering with adherence to stimulus control and sleep restriction
Relaxation techniques	Diaphragmatic breathing, progressive muscle relaxation, and visual imagery to reduce mental and physical anxiety related to sleep
Sleep hygiene education	Limiting caffeine intake, avoiding alcohol before bed, incorporating daily exercise, and keeping the bedroom quiet, dark, and at a comfortable temperature

Source: Siebern, A. T., & Manber, R. (2011). New developments in cognitive behavioral therapy as the first-line treatment of insomnia. *Psychology Research and Behavior Management, 4*, 21–28.

disorder's underlying mechanisms. This research identified a gene mutation related to altered receptors for a neuropeptide (a type of protein) that received two names, **hypocretin** and **orexin**, from two labs simultaneously identifying its importance in sleep–wake cycles. Researchers observed diminished receptor binding in the **hypocretin/orexin system** of dogs exhibiting narcoleptic symptoms (Kilduff, 2001). Postmortem examinations of humans with narcolepsy also revealed significant reductions in the number of hypocretin/orexin-producing neurons compared with that in healthy control subjects (Peyron et al., 2000). Thus, because of some sleepy dogs, the hypocretin/orexin system involved in sleep–wake cycles was identified (see Figure 9.23). Today, we appreciate the complex integrations of the hypocretin/orexin-producing neurons because they affect emotions, energy expenditure, and reward systems (Sakurai, 2007).

The exciting genetic and molecular discoveries related to narcolepsy have yet to lead to a cure for this disabling disorder. Typically, the symptoms of narcolepsy are treated individually by various pharmaceuticals. For example, antidepressants may be prescribed to dampen the emotional arousal that often precedes the onset of uncontrollable sleep episodes, stimulants to counter muscular weakness, and hypnotic drugs to enhance nighttime sleep (Moorcroft, 2003). Although these drugs can be used to successfully manage the symptoms of narcolepsy, they do not address the cause of the disorder. Until a treatment emerges that addresses the root cause, individuals with narcolepsy must continue to take these medications. Further, research with the orexin system has led to potential treatments for other sleep disorders; for example, the orexin receptor antagonist, suvorexant, was recently approved by the U.S. Food and Drug Administration for the treatment of insomnia (Lee-Iannotti & Parish, 2016).

Sleep Apnea. In contrast to narcolepsy, a disorder in which sleep invades waking hours, **sleep apnea** is a disorder characterized by waking episodes that invade the nighttime

sleep structure. Specifically, one or more pauses in breathing or the appearance of shallow breaths occur during sleeping. This disorder severely disrupted the life of R.P., a 43-year-old high school math teacher. His excessive and loud snoring had contributed to two previous divorces, and his current wife reported that her husband snored so loudly that she could hear him when she was at the opposite end of the house. R.P.'s waking hours were also troublesome. He felt that he always had to be moving around while he was teaching; if he stood still, he was overwhelmed with sleepiness. To keep himself awake while grading papers, he drank coffee and sometimes splashed his face with cold water. His excessive sleepiness prevented him from going to movies, watching television, or even playing cards—he just viewed these activities as too boring to hold his attention. Physically, R.P. was about 50 pounds overweight, and he had high blood pressure.

At the sleep lab, R.P. fell asleep within three short minutes but subsequently awakened approximately once per minute, each time making a gasping, snoring sound. Once he was in Stage 1 or Stage 2 sleep, his breathing ceased for about a minute or two, followed once again by the gasping, snoring, sound. His EEG was highly abnormal, showing virtually no SWS and greatly diminished REM sleep. He spent much of the night awake, making his sleep efficiency low; additionally, violent limb movements coincided with his arousals. Because no air entered or exited his body between snoring bouts, R.P. was diagnosed with obstructive sleep apnea, a form of sleep apnea characterized by some type of blockage of the airway (often a result of obesity). Most people with obstructive sleep apnea are unaware of their abnormal breathing during the night. Another less common form of sleep apnea, central sleep apnea, is caused by impairment of brain mechanisms that regulate breathing patterns during sleep (Li et al., 2014).

After observing R.P. sleep in the laboratory, researchers could easily understand why he was so sleepy during his waking hours. R.P. was prescribed a **continuous positive airway pressure (CPAP) machine** that consisted of a breathing mask to place over his nose each night, connected to an air pump, to deliver air pressure to hold his airway open. In this case, the results were dramatic. Within a few days, he felt more alert during the day, and his wife could enjoy a full night's sleep uninterrupted by snoring. A follow-up night in the sleep lab a few months later revealed that, when he was sleeping with his CPAP machine, his sleep EEG was typical for a male his age (Moorcroft, 2003).

Although it was not chosen as a treatment strategy in R.P.'s case, sometimes surgery is used to correct the obstructed airway. Surgery tends not to be the first treatment choice because of the risk of complications and the controversy surrounding its effectiveness (Kotecha & Hall, 2014).

Sleep apnea is recognized as a risk factor for hypertension, heart attack, and stroke (Kotecha & Hall, 2014). Additionally, prolonged, untreated sleep apnea may result in significant brain changes, as evidenced in a study that

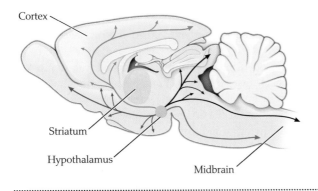

Cortex

Striatum

Hypothalamus

Midbrain

FIGURE 9.23 **The hypocretin system.** Hypocretin/orexin cells are located in the hypothalamus. They project to areas throughout the brain, influencing wakefulness and other functions related to energy expenditure and emotional processes.

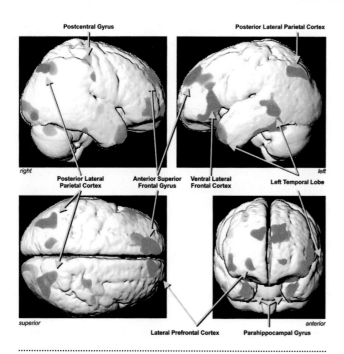

FIGURE 9.24 Sleep apnea and brain volume. Postmortem analyses of individuals with obstructive sleep apnea revealed smaller cortical areas (shown in red) compared with healthy control brains.

investigated autopsied brains from individuals diagnosed with obstructive sleep apnea. As shown in Figure 9.24, several brain areas of subjects with obstructive sleep apnea showed significant decreases in gray matter, including the frontal cortex, temporal lobe, and parietal cortex—brain areas that one needs for life-long healthy functions (Macey et al., 2002).

Altered States of Consciousness: Beyond Sleep

Throughout this chapter (and book) we have discussed varying states of consciousness, or awareness. The activation of specific neural circuits brings emotional experiences such as fear, anxiety, and happiness to the mind's forefront. These variations in conscious awareness undoubtedly modulate our responses to both our internal and our external worlds. The consumption of psychoactive drugs can also drive conscious experiences by activating specific neural circuits, although not necessarily as a real-time response to relevant environmental events. As discussed throughout this chapter, each day we ride a rollercoaster of highs and lows of conscious awareness as we cycle from heightened arousal to drowsiness to nonresponsive sleep states and back again.

Philosophers, psychologists, and neuroscientists have struggled with what is known as the "hard question" of **consciousness**, our awareness of our internal and external worlds (Hobson, 1999). That is, how do we explain the subjective experience of conscious awareness with the objective properties of the brain? A very important piece of the puzzle may come from the unfortunate cases of humans in vegetative or semiconscious states who have lost varying degrees of conscious awareness. Although we are far from having specific answers, there is no doubt that a clear understanding of consciousness will coincide with informed thoughts of the brain's role in awareness.

Neural Networks and Conscious Awareness

Consciousness includes both arousal and awareness (Goldfine & Schiff, 2011). These components are related in the sense that low arousal diminishes awareness (because you are unaware of your surroundings during sleep). Arousal can be thought of as alertness or vigilance and is related to activation of the reticular activating system, hypothalamus, and basal forebrain. But what about conscious awareness? Awareness may be targeted at environmental events (external) or directed toward one's self (internal) and has generally been associated with activation in the frontoparietal association areas. Preliminary research provides evidence that conscious awareness, associated with the neocortex, represents a relatively recently acquired function of the mind (evolutionarily speaking, that is; Bor & Seth, 2012; Mashour & Alkire, 2013).

The Belgian neurologist Steven Laureys and his colleagues have investigated more specific questions about the brain areas involved in conscious awareness (Vanhaudenhuyse et al., 2011). In one study, this research team investigated brain imaging activation patterns that differentiated external awareness from internal awareness. The researchers defined external awareness as an awareness of the environment achieved through the sensory systems (visual, auditory, and so forth). By contrast, they defined internal awareness as mental processing that did not require the presence of external sensory stimuli. Daydreaming, mind wandering, and inner speech are examples of internal awareness. While fMRI images were being acquired, subjects in this study were asked to rate their internal or external awareness for a specified time period following an auditory prompt.

The results of this study provided evidence that very different brain areas were involved in external as opposed to internal awareness (Figure 9.25). When subjects were asked

(a)

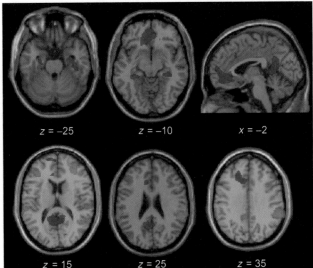

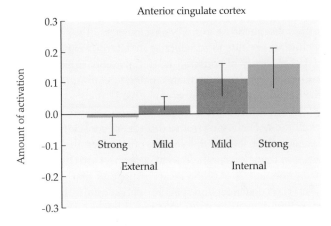

(b)

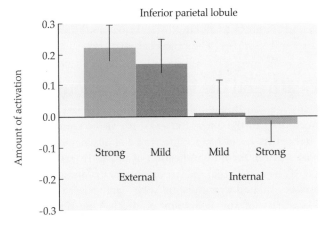

Source: Vanhaudenhuyse, A., Demertzi, A., Schabus, M., Noirhomme, Q., Bredart, S., Boly, M., . . . & Laureys, S. (2011). Two distinct neuronal networks mediate the awareness of environment and of self. *Journal of Cognitive Neuroscience, 23*, 570-578.

to focus on internal awareness, they exhibited increased activity in the cingulate cortex and parahippocampal cortex, areas active during mind wandering, daydreaming, and inner speech. External awareness, in contrast, was associated with increased activity in the dorsolateral prefrontal cortex and inferior parietal lobe, areas typically involved in goal-directed behavior and cognitive processing of external stimuli.

Additionally, this study shed some light on the mystery of consciousness by providing information about the activity of the brain when it is supposedly at rest, not directly influenced by internal or external stimuli. The resting brain is characterized by spontaneous low-frequency brain waves, reminiscent of the brain waves observed during SWS. The researchers observed that the subjects switched from internal to external awareness about every 20 seconds. Thus, it appears that the brain's default mode is to maintain vigilance as it systematically monitors both the internal and the external surroundings. Fewer switches between brain areas associated with external awareness and those associated with internal awareness are observed during SWS, under general anesthesia, and during **vegetative states** (individuals in vegetative states appear to be awake yet exhibit no awareness of external stimuli, such as a hand waving in front of their face) (Vanhaudenhuyse et al., 2011).

Disorders of Consciousness

Making accurate diagnoses of various disorders of consciousness is extremely challenging. Clinical reports indicate that a misdiagnosis is provided about 40% of the time (M. M. Monti et al., 2010). Although these patients may appear healthy and may even sit up with their eyes open, there is obviously something very wrong. When presented with verbal questions or demands, for example, they exhibit no signs of awareness. As previously described, patients in a vegetative state appear to be awake but unresponsive to the environment, whereas patients in a **minimally conscious state** may exhibit nonreflexive behaviors, such as visual tracking or responding to simple commands, but show no further evidence of awareness. Once communication is observed, however, the patient is known to have emerged from minimal consciousness to consciousness. These conditions

FIGURE 9.25 Internal and external awareness. Specific brain areas are activated during internal and external conscious awareness. These functional magnetic resonance imaging scans show more activation in the cingulate cortex and parahippocampal cortex (blue) in strong internal awareness and more activation in the dorsolateral prefrontal cortex and inferior parietal lobe (red) during strong external awareness.

differ from a more pronounced disruption of consciousness known as a **coma**, in which the person shows no signs of wakefulness or awareness (M. M. Monti et al., 2010).

How can physicians determine whether patients who cannot communicate are aware of their external or internal surroundings? In such circumstances, it is difficult to establish whether the patient is fully conscious, minimally conscious, or unconscious. Recently, recording and imaging techniques have been used to detect functional brain activity in individuals who are experiencing sensory and/or language deficits that would restrict them from responding to a verbal command. For example, in one innovative study, 54 patients diagnosed with disorders of consciousness (i.e., they were in either a minimally conscious state or an unconscious state) were asked two questions to determine whether they could willfully control their brain activity. First, the patients were asked to imagine being on a tennis court and hitting a ball back and forth to an instructor. Second, the subjects were asked to imagine themselves walking through each room in their home or navigating the streets of a familiar city. These tasks were intended to access brain circuits that were involved in motor imagery and spatial imagery, respectively. In each case, the subjects' brains were scanned so that fMRI data could be compared with the scans of healthy, fully conscious control subjects. The results provided evidence that five of the patients with disorders of consciousness could willfully control their brain activity when asked to imagine playing tennis, evidenced by a close parallel between their brain activity and the controls' activity (see Figure 9.26). Four of these five patients were considered unconscious prior to this assessment (M. M. Monti et al., 2010). By exploring the brain wave activity in these patients, researchers found evidence of awareness that was not evident by monitoring the patients' behavior.

Patients diagnosed with **locked-in syndrome** have a fully functioning brain that is essentially trapped in a body that cannot move or communicate in traditional ways (see Figure 9.27). This condition, typically caused by a brainstem lesion resulting from a stroke or tumor, afflicted a nine-year-old girl, Eve Anderson, who suffered a bleed in the region of her brainstem. In a single moment, Eve transformed from an active little girl who loved brownies and Irish dancing to someone with virtually no control over her body, whose parents had to feed her through a tube each day and tend to all of her needs. Eve is thought to be the youngest person in the world with this unfortunate diagnosis. She is now able to open her eyes and communicate by smiling, grimacing, or blinking (Bates, 2012; Bruno, Bernheim, Schnakers, & Laureys, 2008).

The disorders of consciousness described in this section are characterized by the near-total absence of movement and the absence of spoken language. Research exploring innovative ways to determine the presence of higher-order cognitive functions in these patients offers new hope in this area. Such information may also be used to make more informed decisions about aspects of consciousness that may predict future improvements, such as progression from a vegetative or minimally conscious state to a conscious state. Patients' families could also use this information to feel more prepared for the difficult decisions they face concerning the future of their loved one.

One line of research has used TMS, a method that uses magnetic fields to stimulate neurons in the brain (Chapter 3), coupled with high-density EEG, at the bedside of patients who have disorders of consciousness to determine the pervasiveness of activation across the brain. Results of one study indicated that TMS stimulated a local simple neural response in patients in a vegetative state, similar to that observed in anesthetized subjects. In minimally conscious patients, however, TMS stimulated more complex neural responses that traveled to distant cortical regions in the ipsilateral and contralateral hemispheres in similar patterns to those observed in conscious locked-in patients. This response in minimally conscious subjects was correlated with subsequent recovered consciousness. Thus, the TMS technique appears to be effective in determining the potential of recovery of consciousness in patients suffering from brain injuries that leave them unable to communicate with the outside world (Rosanova et al., 2012).

In addition to providing information about a patient's likelihood of emerging from a disorder of consciousness, the research described in this section offers clues about healthy levels of consciousness and what contributes to this complex phenomenon. The TMS research suggests that consciousness is less dependent on specific neural circuits than it is on distributed neural circuits that travel beyond local sites of stimulation. Such capacity for activation of specific areas to spread to other areas across the brain may lead to enhanced neural connections among cortical areas and from cortex to thalamus to cortex (Rosanova et al., 2012).

Death and the End of Consciousness

Have you ever thought about the defining criteria for death? According to the ancient Greeks, the heart contained the vital spirits necessary for life, and the absence of a heartbeat was the defining indication of death. It was not until the 12th century that the irreversible lack of brain function was considered synonymous with death (Bernat, 2002). Regardless of the definition of death, the 19th-century writings of Edgar Allen Poe highlighting anecdotes of being buried alive reflected fears among the general public (Laureys, 2005; Poe, 1981). Accordingly, Count Karnie-Karnicki, the chamberlain of the tsar of Russia, marketed a device added to the coffin that enabled the buried individual to ring a bell or wave a flag to indicate that he or she was still alive (Laureys, 2005) (see Figure 9.28).

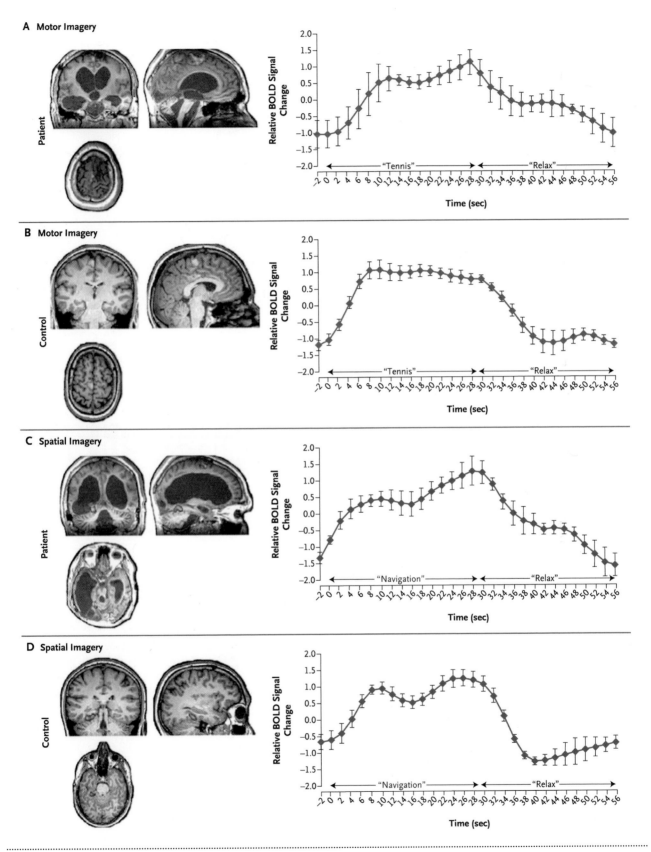

FIGURE 9.26 **Brain responsiveness of minimally conscious patient.** When asked to imagine hitting a ball on a tennis court (A/B) and navigating through a city or their home (C/D), a minimally conscious patient and a healthy individual showed similar brain response patterns.

FIGURE 9.27 **Locked-in syndrome.** Patients suffering from locked-in syndrome have a fully functioning brain that is essentially trapped in a body that cannot move or communicate in traditional ways.

It was not until the mid-20th century, however, that movement toward a clear brain-centered definition of death was achieved. The French neurologists Mollaret and Goulon were the first to introduce the term brain death, or *coma depasse* (irretrievable coma). Because the report describing this provocative information was written in French, it did not significantly impact the international community (Machado et al., 2007). This notion was made more official a decade later, when a group from Harvard Medical School published a report defining death as irreversible coma ("A Definition of Irreversible Coma," 1968). At this point, the question about the psychological and physiological criteria for death became important for other disciplines such as law, philosophy, ethics, and theology. Further research confirmed that damage to the brainstem was critical for death, leading to the notion of **brain death**, the permanent loss of brainstem function. If the brainstem is no longer functioning, the person is no longer considered alive (Laureys, 2005). As you have previously learned, the brainstem is the gateway for the majority of hemispheric input and output, as well as the center known to control both conscious awareness and respiration (Pallis & Harley, 1996). As shown in Figure 9.29, there is virtually no observable resting brain activity in PET scans of individuals diagnosed with brainstem, or brain, death (Laureys, Owen, & Schiff, 2004).

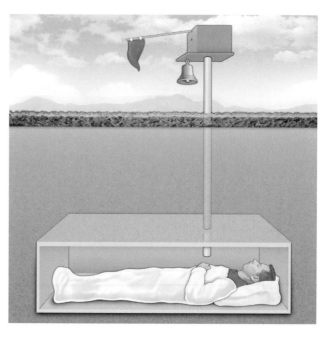

FIGURE 9.28 **Assurance against being buried alive.** Throughout history, devices were installed in coffins to enable the falsely declared deceased to communicate their recovery.

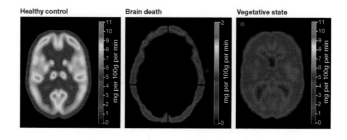

FIGURE 9.29 **Brain death.** There is virtually no observable resting brain activity in positron emission tomography scans of individuals diagnosed with brainstem, or brain, death.

When asked about the future of death research, Steven Laureys (the Belgian neurologist introduced in the section on conscious awareness) has conveyed that technological advances including brain–computer interactions, targeted stem-cell transplants, and other novel therapeutic approaches for brain repair may spur yet another dramatic change in people's understanding of death (Laureys, 2005, p. 907).

LABORATORY EXPLORATION

Optogenetics: Shining a Light on the Brain's Sleep–Wake Circuits

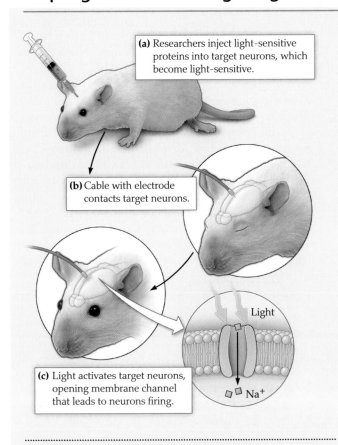

(a) Researchers inject light-sensitive proteins into target neurons, which become light-sensitive.

(b) Cable with electrode contacts target neurons.

(c) Light activates target neurons, opening membrane channel that leads to neurons firing.

Light

Na$^+$

LABORATORY EXPLORATION FIGURE 9.1 Optogenetics. (a) To use optogenetic tools, researchers inject a virus into the brain to express light-activated proteins in specific neurons. (b) An optical fiber is inserted in proximity to the targeted neurons. (c) The light activates specific neurons in the targeted area.

The Stanford neuroscientist Karl Deisseroth and his graduate student, Ed Boyden, were intrigued by the observation that certain algae could convert light into electrical energy, as photoreceptors in your eyes do. If these photoreceptive properties could be transferred to specific neurons in the brain, then those neurons could be controlled by light. By isolating the DNA coding the photoreceptive properties in the algae, these scientists were able to transfer the genes into specific rat neurons. The genes produced opsins (light-sensitive proteins, discussed in Chapter 6) in the neurons of specific targeted brain areas, enabling researchers to control the firing of specific populations of neurons by shining light on them, which alters the transport of ions (e.g., sodium, potassium) across the cell membrane (Mikulak, 2012). Consequently, researchers can use this technique to stimulate or inhibit activity in

light-sensitized brain areas, including those thought to be involved in sleep and waking.

This technique, optogenetics, is similar to electrical brain stimulation, but more specific in the cells it targets. Optogenetics can be viewed as the perfect blend of an electrode with very specific timing and a genetic probe that can target specific types of neurons (e.g., dopaminergic, serotonergic). Further, different opsins respond to different colors of light. Certain opsins such as chanelrhodopsin-2 can be used to activate neurons, whereas others such as halorhodopsin can be used to inhibit neural activity (Adamantidis, Carter, & de Lecea, 2010). If both of these opsins are infused into a specific area of the brain, the neurons can be turned either on or off depending on the color of light.

This discovery has been applied to the sleep–wake system. For example, to evaluate the role of hypocretin-producing neurons (about which you learned earlier in this chapter) in the transition from sleep to wakefulness, researchers used a virus to deliver channelrhodopsin-2 to hypocretin-producing neurons in mice. Once the DNA for the opsin was delivered to the targeted cells and incorporated into their genetic code, the neurons could be activated with light. When the hypocretin-producing neurons were activated in this manner, it increased the probability of the mice waking up from either REM or non-REM sleep (Adamantidis, Zhang, Aravanis, Deisseroth, & de Lecea, 2007). (See Laboratory Exploration Figure 9.1).

Optogenetics is one of the most exciting techniques that has been introduced to the field in the past half-century. More and more labs are using the technique for research questions beyond those related to sleep. If a certain brain area is suspected to play a role in a certain behavior or mental condition, that area can be both activated and suppressed in animal models using optogenetic technology.

What about humans? Will we be able to use optogenetics to treat neurological and psychiatric illnesses in humans in the future? Researchers are currently exploring these questions in appropriate animal models for conditions such as depression, Parkinson's disease, and blindness caused by retinitis pigmentosa (a hereditary condition that affects photoreceptors; Albert, 2014; Busskamp & Roska, 2011; Kravitz et al., 2010; Manfredsson, Bloom, & Mandel, 2012). Further, this technique has also been used to examine the role of brainstem stimuli in anxiety, a pervasive response that affects many diverse behaviors (Masseck et al., 2014). Thus, although researchers should proceed with caution since this is an invasive procedure, there may be approved clinical applications for this technique in the future.

Conclusion

In this chapter, we have explored the variations of conscious awareness that occur throughout our waking and sleeping hours. Light is a powerful stimulus that synchronizes the functions of the brain and body. However, in its absence, these regularly occurring circadian rhythms (such as sleep–wake cycles) persist. Although the daily mammalian activity of sleeping was once viewed as a passive response to a lack of stimulation, we now know that the brain is, at times, very active throughout the night.

After reading this chapter, you may appreciate that there are few absolute answers to the many questions surrounding sleep and conscious awareness. After all this time, we still are not certain about the function of sleep or dreaming, the optimal duration of sleep, or the neural basis of consciousness. Even so, scientists have made progress in many areas. It is becoming increasingly apparent that sleep and dreaming may have evolved for a single reason but now likely serve many important functions. Sleep appears to conserve energy, provide protection from predators, provide a unique environment for neural restructuring, and

enhance immune functions. REM sleep provides periodic activation to the resting brain, and this activation may be associated with the transfer or processing of recently experienced or evolutionarily significant information. Various aspects of sleep, such as timing and optimal duration, are flexible and can be influenced by culture and lifestyle. When sleep disorders lead to health problems, help may be gained through CBT, lifestyle adjustments, pharmaceutical approaches, and specific devices that improve the quality of breathing during sleep.

Variations in responsiveness throughout the sleep–wake cycle lead to broader questions related to the patterns of neural activity necessary to generate conscious awareness. Fascinating research with individuals in states of diminished consciousness has provided an opportunity to learn more about the neural correlates of both internal and external conscious awareness. Such research may one day benefit patients who have lost access to these neural circuits or may at least identify individuals with high probabilities of one day regaining conscious awareness. We will discuss altered awareness further in the next chapter, as we see how heightened arousal is typically associated with emotionally relevant events that occur in our lives.

KEY TERMS

automatism (p. 250)
electroencephalograms (EEGs) (p. 250)
parasomnias (p. 250)
rapid eye movement (REM) sleep (p. 251)

The Rhythms of Sleep and Wakefulness

circadian rhythms (p. 251)
zeitgeber (p. 251)
free-running rhythms (p. 251)
suprachiasmatic nucleus (SCN) (p. 251)
retinohypothalamic tracts (p. 251)
ultradian rhythms (p. 251)
melatonin (p. 251)
phase shift (p. 251)
jet lag (p. 251)
shift work (p. 252)
sleep (p. 253)
polysomnography (p. 253)
polysomnograph (p. 253)
electrooculogram (EOG) (p. 253)
electromyogram (EMG) (p. 253)
beta (β) waves (p. 253)
alpha (α) waves (p. 253)
theta (θ) waves (p. 253)

delta (δ) waves (p. 253)
k-complexes (p. 253)
sleep spindles (p. 253)
non-REM sleep (p. 253)
Stage 1 sleep (p. 253)
Stage 2 sleep (p. 253)
slow wave sleep (SWS) (p. 253)
hibernation (p. 254)

The Neurobiology of Sleep

ascending reticular activating system (ARAS) (p. 255)
raphe nuclei (p. 255)
basal forebrain area (p. 255)
pedunculopontine tegmental nuclei (p. 255)
laterodorsal tegmental nuclei (p. 255)
locus coeruleus (p. 255)
ventrolateral preoptic area (VLPO) (p. 256)
galanin (p. 256)
tuberomammillary nucleus (TMN) (p. 256)
adenosine triphosphate (p. 256)
atonia (p. 257)
pontogeniculooccipital (PGO) spikes (p. 257)

activation-synthesis model of dreaming (p. 257)
subcoeruleus region (p. 258)
REM-on cells (p. 258)

Why Sleep and Dream?

homeostatic theory of sleep regulation (p. 259)
sleep rebound effect (p. 259)
adaptive theory of sleep (p. 260)
adaptive inactivity (p. 260)
memory consolidation (p. 262)
declarative memories (p. 262)
procedural memories (p. 262)
synaptic homeostasis hypothesis (p. 263)
(θ) rhythms (p. 264)
sleep efficiency (p. 267)
interleukin 1 (p. 268)
tumor necrosis factor (p. 268)
sleep architecture pattern (p. 268)

Sleep Patterns: Typical and Atypical Variations

sleep debt (p. 268)
night terrors (p. 269)
insomnia (p. 269)

REVIEW QUESTIONS

1. Name and describe the stages of sleep (including differences in brain waves). Describe the mechanisms by which the sleep stages are measured in sleep studies.

2. How does brain wave activity during SWS differ from that during REM sleep? Which brain areas are involved in each of these types of sleep?

3. What have we learned from sleep-deprivation research?

4. Describe research on the role sleep plays in our ability to learn and remember. What are some of the research techniques used, and what are some findings?

5. Provide evidence that suggests a relationship between sleep and the immune system.

6. Narcolepsy and sleep apnea are both sleep disorders that cause people to fall asleep during the day. Describe the features of each and how they compare with the other sleep disorders.

7. What are some techniques used to "communicate" with patients who are in a minimally conscious or unconscious state? How do these techniques work?

CRITICAL-THINKING QUESTIONS

1. Discuss the historical and cultural differences in human sleep patterns described in this chapter. In the future, as globalization influences more cultures around the world, do you think that sleep patterns are likely to change? If so, why and how?

2. What standards or criteria should be used to distinguish individual variations in sleep patterns from sleep disorders? Should treatment be available to individuals if their symptoms do not meet the criteria for the diagnosis of a sleep disorder? Why or why not?

3. Describe how the definition of "death" has changed over the past century and how it may be expected to change in the future. Do you anticipate a time when technology will eradicate death? Explain your answer.

CHAPTER 10

Emotional Expression and Regulation

The Neurobiology of Voodoo Death

We have probably all said at some point in our lives that something nearly scared us to death. A roller coaster, a haunted house, a near-missed traffic accident, a sensitive text that was sent to the wrong person, an exam that we had somehow forgotten—our lives seem to be filled with stressful experiences. If you think about the phrase *scared to death*, however, it is interesting to consider that our emotional response could reach such an extreme level, resulting in a person's demise.

In 1942, Walter Cannon, a biopsychology pioneer who introduced the "fight-or-flight" function of the sympathetic nervous system (described in Chapter 2), explored the potential explanation of claims that people throughout history had been frightened to death. For this project, he consulted historical accounts of case studies in which a person had died for no apparent medical reason after being frightened. He read 16th-century accounts of people in South Africa who were condemned to death by "medicine men" for committing some tribal indiscretion. He also reported the case of an African tribe member who was on a journey and stopped by a friend's home for a meal. The meal was chicken, and the traveler knew that he could eat only domestic hens; the traveler was forbidden to eat wild hens. However, the host denied that the chicken being served was wild, and the traveler enjoyed the meal. Several years later, the two men met again.

This time, the previous host confessed to having served his friend, the African tribe member, the forbidden wild chicken. At that point, the African tribe member started trembling with fear and, within 24 hours, was dead (Cannon, 1942).

Cannon argued that the many cases he had presented were a result of the person believing that he or she was condemned to death because of a voodoo curse, consumption of a taboo food, or some other form of condemnation (see Figure 10A). Cannon referred to this phenomenon as **voodoo death**. More recently, the neurologist Martin Samuels has pointed out that many contemporary examples exist

FIGURE 10A Voodoo practices and emotional responses. The strong belief systems that have emerged with cultural traditions such as voodoo often translate into significant emotional and physiological effects that can have profound health consequences.

of people being frightened to death. For example, a minister in Boston was reading his Bible quietly at home when police officers mistakenly raided his dwelling. In the midst of all the excitement, this minister collapsed in shock and was found to have died of a heart attack (Das, 2006; Samuels, 2007).

Behind the Scenes

In his initial analysis, Cannon hypothesized that voodoo death stemmed from persistent and extreme activation of the sympathetic nervous system. Thus, the adrenaline release, resulting from the "cursed" victim's perceived lack of control and impending doom, overstimulated the cardiovascular system in a fashion similar to that of an overdose of cocaine. In the 1950s, another biopsychology pioneer, Curt Richter, expressed a different view. He proposed that the complementary arm of the autonomic nervous system, the parasympathetic nervous system (which is typically activated following the activation of the sympathetic nervous system; see Chapter 2), responds excessively, thereby calming the person to death. Richter arrived at this conclusion after observing that laboratory rats could survive extended swimming sessions when there was no escape route. By contrast, if the rats had to face this situation with freshly trimmed whiskers, depriving them of sensory feedback, they would drown, likely because of heart failure (Richter, 1957).

Such studies would not be approved by institutional review boards today because of strict ethical guidelines, but the findings are still informative. Perhaps the disoriented whiskerless rats saw no escape from the stressful situation, similar to a human under a curse from a respected source. After discovering that the surgical removal of the adrenal gland—a technique called an **adrenalectomy**—failed to protect the stressed swimming rats from death, Richter concluded that their death was not caused by the overexcitation of the sympathetic nervous system, but by the overstimulation of the parasympathetic nervous system. Or, more specifically, it was caused by increased **vagal tone**, inhibition of heart rate resulting from stimulation of the vagus nerve (Samuels, 2007).

Which biopsychology pioneer was correct? Samuels has suggested that both the sympathetic and the parasympathetic arms of the autonomic nervous system are likely involved, meaning that both men were partially correct. Certain systems likely predominate at different times, with the sympathetic nervous system having a greater influence earlier in the process and the parasympathetic nervous system controlling the later events. After investigating the autopsied hearts of more contemporary human case studies, Samuels also observed cardiac lesions that could lead to heart failure. Systematic studies with mice suggest that sympathetic activation, even in animals whose adrenal glands had been removed, leads to the cardiac lesions. Thus, the lesions may be a result of direct interactions between the nervous system and the heart, rather than a result of the release of stress hormones (Hawkins & Clower, 1971).

Because we will never study individuals experiencing life-threatening fear in the laboratory, much of this research depends on case studies and archived evidence (as is the case in true mysteries!). However, this nontraditional source of data has convinced Martin Samuels, also known as "Dr. Death," to continue to explore the effects of neurogenic, or voodoo, death. This research has led him to propose that we are all susceptible to being frightened to death if the fear factor is high enough and there is no perceived escape from the impending doom (Das, 2006; Samuels, 2007). ▶

Although the idea of literally being frightened to death is grim, emotions such as fear do not always lead to our demise. In fact, although we often find fear unpleasant, it is an adaptive response that mobilizes the brain and body to escape successfully from threatening situations.

In Chapter 2, you learned about the fundamental components of emotional responses, including the brain's limbic system and autonomic nervous system. This chapter will more thoroughly examine the neurobiology of emotional responses. Because emotions are intimately intertwined with the stress response, this chapter will also discuss the harmful effects of prolonged stress, as well as coping strategies that have been shown to build emotional resilience. Stress responses penetrate the body's immune functions, so any methods used to respond more effectively to emotional challenges should lead to stronger immunological defenses. Thus, an informed view of emotions, stress, and resilience prepares us to escape many of life's most stressful situations with minimal damage.

Biopsychological Perspectives of Emotional Expression

Emotional responses are difficult to define, but easy to identify when we see them. A young child bawling when left with a babysitter; football fans jumping up and down cheering on their home team; a tearful wife running to the arms of her husband and children after returning from her deployment in Afghanistan—all are experiencing strong emotional responses.

The concept of emotions is difficult to capture with an objective, clear-cut definition, but an abundance of informative research findings exists on the topic. We can define **emotions** as subjective feelings that are influenced by activation of various parts of our CNS and PNS. Activation of several neurobiological systems heightens our level of conscious awareness surrounding the internal and external circumstances of a particular event. Although elements of emotions such as aggression are observed throughout the animal kingdom, mammals display the most complex and sophisticated emotional responses. These emotional experiences can be positive or negative, fleeting or long lasting, appropriate or inappropriate. Although emotional responses appear to be a fundamental component of mammalian existence, they are virtually impossible to simulate in even the most advanced forms of artificial intelligence. Ironically, the ability of a two-year-old to throw a temper tantrum may be one of the most clearly distinctive characteristics of the mammalian nervous system.

Evolutionary and Universal Emotional Expressions

Emotions are by no means unique to humans. When my Maltese dog, Golgi, runs in circles after I ask him if he wants to go for a walk, he certainly appears to be experiencing some positive emotion. When two male lions are fighting for access to a female, they seem to be experiencing intense emotion as well. This notion that animals experience emotions is not new. In 1872, Charles Darwin published *The Expression of Emotions in Man and Animals*. Following decades of observations, he introduced the idea that animals experience emotions in a fashion similar to humans. Darwin's observations emphasized threads of continuity observed in emotional responses across species. For example, the practice of baring teeth in aggressive encounters is seen across the mammalian animal spectrum.

Darwin's 19th-century observations also emphasized that a limited set of emotions exists across species and cultures. The more aversive, or negative, emotions such as fear and aggression are clearly present in reptiles, birds, and mammals, but more positive emotions such as happiness are more difficult to observe. An increasing number of behavioral neuroscientists, however, have suggested that nonhuman mammals such as rats experience positive emotions such as joy. Positive emotional experiences are thought to involve many of the same brain mechanisms as aversive emotional experiences do, with additional activation of the brain's reward systems and neurochemicals such as opiates and GABA (Burgdorf & Panksepp, 2006). The *Laboratory Exploration* at the end of this chapter describes how researchers are considering a specific chirping response in rats as a rudimentary form of laughter related to positive emotions (Burgdorf & Panksepp, 2001). Such animal models allow scientists to explore the neurobiological mechanisms of positive emotions as they have done with the more negative emotions, such as fear and aggression.

Psychologists have conducted extensive research on universal aspects of emotion in humans, such as facial expressions. Following a visit to the oncologist to learn the latest cancer status report, a patient seldom needs words to communicate to a loved one what the doctor said. The news is unmistakably shown in a happy or sad facial expression. To test the intimate relationship between emotion and facial expressions,

the next time you tell an emotion-laden story, try to tell it with an emotion-neutral face—it is difficult to do and very dissatisfying for your audience.

The psychologist Paul Ekman conducted pioneering research a half century ago in which he identified universal facial expressions that could be understood across cultures (as described in E. Ekman, Ekman, & Marsh, 2008). As shown in Figure 10.1, facial expressions of fear, happiness, anger, contempt, surprise, disgust, and sadness are easily identified, regardless of one's home continent.

In another line of research, Ekman's team examined the facial expressions of psychiatric patients, who were known to have lied during a clinical interview by concealing their plans to attempt suicide. The researchers found certain **facial microexpressions**, defined as barely perceptible brief facial expression fragments, to be associated with deception and lying (P. Ekman, 2003). P. Ekman found another example of facial microexpressions when he analyzed the videotape of television news anchor Katie Couric's 2007 interview of the baseball star Alex Rodriguez (see Figure 10.2). In that interview, Rodriguez denied using performance-enhancing drugs, but he later admitted to using them. In Ekman's analysis of the 2007 videotape, he noted certain facial microexpressions that had been associated with lying in his past research. Rodriguez was unable to inhibit what Ekman calls the microexpressions of gestural slips, unilateral expressions of contempt, and transient expressions of fear (Marsh, 2009).

Although we tend to associate facial expressions with humans, evidence also supports strong ties between emotional responses and facial expressions in nonhuman animals. Primates display emotions with distinct facial expressions during play, aggression, and threat. Even mice may express their emotions via facial expressions, according to some research. For example, Jeffrey Mogil and his team at McGill University developed a mouse facial grimace scale to detect the intensity of pain experienced by the animals. As shown in Figure 10.3, as pain increased, the mice showed changes in the following facial characteristics: eye squinting (orbital tightening), bulging of the nose and cheek, ear position, and whisker movement. Such studies suggest that mice can communicate information about pain to other animals visually with these facial expressions. By similarly analyzing and measuring mouse facial expressions, human researchers can assess the effectiveness of pain medication in mice (Langford et al., 2010). Further, Mogil's research suggests that, far from being a uniquely human characteristic, facial expressions are more hardwired across mammalian species than previously thought—an observation that Charles Darwin would surely have recognized.

Classic Neurobiological Theories of Emotion

In the 1880s, Harvard psychology professor William James wrote a seminal paper entitled, "What Is an Emotion?" In this paper, James suggested that emotions were the body's

(a) (b) (c) (d)

(e) (f) (g)

FIGURE 10.1 Facial expressions and emotional communication. Across cultures, specific facial expressions are linked to specific emotional responses, including (a) happiness, (b) sadness, (c) contempt, (d) fear, (e) disgust, (f) anger, and (g) surprise.

FIGURE 10.2 Microexpressions and emotional communication. According to Dr. Paul Ekman, baseball player Alex Rodriguez was unable to inhibit his microexpressions during an interview in which he denied using performance-enhancing drugs.

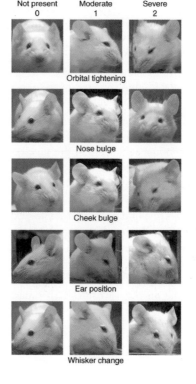

FIGURE 10.3 Mouse facial expressions. Mice experiencing various levels of pain show certain facial expressions; some resemble the human reaction to pain, especially with squinting of the eyes (orbital tightening).

adaptations and responses to stimuli of special significance, also known as *emotive stimuli* (James, 1884). Thus, if an assailant is chasing you, your nervous system tells you to run as soon as you see the assailant. Further, all the physiological responses involved in maintaining the running response contribute to your building fear. In James's view, the emotions were a by-product of the reflexive bodily responses to threatening stimuli. Around this same time, the physician Carl Lange presented a similar theory, subsequently known as the **James–Lange theory of emotion** (Dalgleish, 2004; Lange, 1885). According to this theory, the different bodily reactions that occur in response to different stimuli lead to the experience of emotions.

From our modern perspective, it is easy to see numerous theoretical and methodological holes in the James–Lange theory of emotion. Among the early researchers who challenged the theory was Walter Cannon (Figure 10.4), mentioned in the voodoo death discussion at the beginning of this chapter. As Cannon noted, some animals will still express emotions such as aggression or fear if the brain is surgically separated from the system that supplies nerves to the body. Furthermore, although there are subtle differences in bodily responses to various emotive stimuli, it seemed unlikely that the emotion to be experienced could be determined by that sole factor. Was there a certain heart rate, for example, to denote contempt as opposed to disgust? Cannon also pointed out that emotions emerge quickly—so quickly that a particular physiological response would not have time to occur before the emotion is experienced (Cannon, 1927, 1931).

Cannon based many of his criticisms on his collaborative research with Philip Bard. The two observed that cats

FIGURE 10.4 Walter Bradford Cannon. Cannon challenged the James–Lange theory of emotion and emphasized the role of the brain in emotional processing.

still expressed fear when their cortex was separated from the lower brain and spinal cord (Bard, 1928). According to the James–Lange theory of emotion, this drastic disruption of bodily feedback should have diminished emotional expression (Dalgleish, 2004). Instead, Cannon and Bard proposed that the hypothalamus was a key brain region generating the expression of emotional experiences and that higher cortical areas inhibited these evolutionarily ancient emotional responses. This hypothesis became known as the **Cannon–Bard theory of emotion**. This theory emphasized the role of the brain in emotional processing, as opposed to the James–Lange theory's emphasis on responses from other parts of the body. Supporting the Cannon–Bard theory, the removal of the cortex in cats resulted in uncontrolled displays of emotion known as **sham rage**.

The idea that the cortex served as a filter for the expression of emotions also supported earlier observations in the case of Phineas Gage, the man who survived a tamping iron blasting through his brain in a work accident (see Chapter 2). Gage's compromised emotional filters made it difficult for him to interact socially after his accident. For example, managing his team of workers as a foreman on the railroad crew was no longer possible (Rule, Shimamura, & Knight, 2002). Cannon and Bard's research was critical because it incorporated animal models into the study of emotions, or **affective neuroscience**. Further, this early research introduced the technique of using precise, experimentally induced brain lesions to investigate the fundamental mechanisms of emotions (Dalgleish, 2004).

In the 1980s, the research of Paul Ekman and colleagues provided modest support for the James–Lange theory. When they monitored heart rate during different emotional experiences in humans, they observed higher heart rates in anger and fear responses than in happiness. Thus, although it was not clear whether emotional experience depends exclusively on autonomic activity, they found evidence of emotion-specific autonomic activity (P. Ekman, Levenson, & Friesen, 1983). In another study, researchers measured emotional experience in subjects with spinal cord injury to determine whether a reduction in the intensity of autonomic responses would diminish one's ability to experience an emotion—as suggested by the James–Lange theory. When they compared these subjects with healthy subjects or with subjects who had orthopedic injuries not involving the spinal cord, they did not detect any differences in emotional awareness (Deady, North, Allan, Smith, & O'Carroll, 2010). Other researchers assessed fMRI activity in subjects with spinal cord injuries (compared with healthy control subjects) in response to a conditioned fear paradigm involving an electrical shock to the upper arm. All subjects found the shock painful. Compared with baseline values, the researchers observed diminished activation in brain areas such as the posterior cingulate and PFC in the subjects with spinal cord injuries, but no activation differences in other brain areas (Nicotra, Critchley, Mathias, & Dolan, 2006). Thus, although brain activation patterns differ from the norm in patients who have disrupted feedback from the autonomic nervous system, these patients still seem to experience emotions in a similar manner to that observed in healthy control subjects. Taken together, these studies suggest that although feedback from the autonomic nervous system likely contributes to emotional responses, the brain is predisposed to generate emotional responses with or without autonomic feedback.

In the 1960s, the **Schachter–Singer theory of emotion** (named after Stanley Schachter and Jerome Singer) acknowledged the importance of both autonomic arousal and cognitive perceptions in the expression of specific emotions. This theory emphasizes the role of context-dependent cognitive interpretation in transforming general arousal to a specific emotion such as fear or happiness. Because Schachter and Singer found evidence that the expression of a specific emotion is influenced by both cognition and physiology, the Schachter–Singer theory is sometimes known as the **two-factor theory** (see Figure 10.5).

These conclusions that emotions were influenced by both cognitive and physiological contexts were based on a study in which arousal was produced in subjects by giving them an injection of adrenaline. Following the injections, subjects were seated in a waiting room with a study confederate (i.e., an actor who pretends to be a subject but is actually working for the experimenter) who had been instructed to act either angry or happy. When subjects thought they were merely receiving a vitamin injection that should not have any emotional side effects, they were more likely to mirror the emotions of the confederate than subjects who had been told about the expected side effects. Thus, subjects who knew that the injection resulted in their feelings of arousal did not attribute their emotion to the confederate. However, subjects with no knowledge of the source of their arousal attributed it to the confederate and then refined their emotion to match the circumstances (Schachter, 1964; Schachter & Singer, 1962).

A second classic study in this area supported the role of cognition in the expression of specific emotions. An attractive female interviewer approached men on either the Capilano Suspension Bridge in Canada—a narrow, wobbly footbridge that spans a canyon 230 feet deep—or a wider, sturdier footbridge over a 10-foot ravine that typically would not arouse fear. The interviewer asked the men to fill out a questionnaire that required them to write a narrative in response to an image of a woman. The interviewer then gave the young men her telephone number in case they had any follow-up questions. The experimenters were interested in the extent to which the men ascribed sexual content to the picture, as well as whether they called the female interviewer. As you may have guessed, the men who crossed the scary bridge and likely had an accompanying sympathetic arousal response were more likely than the men who crossed the sturdy bridge to exhibit indirect evidence of sexual attraction by interpreting the picture as sexual in nature and by calling the female interviewer (Dutton & Aron, 1974). However, as important as autonomic responses and situational context are in emotional expression, the brain is the central command center. Consequently, we now turn our discussion to relevant brain areas in emotional expression.

The Brain's Role in Emotional Expression

In 1937, the neuroanatomist James Papez proposed an emotional brain circuit in a classic paper entitled *A*

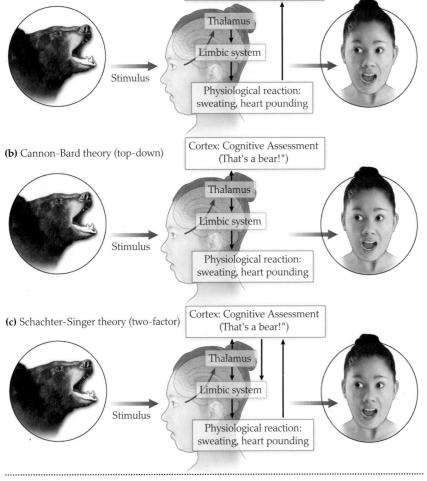

(a) James–Lange theory (bottom-up)

Cortex: Cognitive Assessment ("That's a bear!")

Thalamus

Limbic system

Physiological reaction: sweating, heart pounding

Stimulus

(b) Cannon–Bard theory (top-down)

Cortex: Cognitive Assessment ("That's a bear!")

Thalamus

Limbic system

Physiological reaction: sweating, heart pounding

Stimulus

(c) Schachter–Singer theory (two-factor)

Cortex: Cognitive Assessment ("That's a bear!")

Thalamus

Limbic system

Physiological reaction: sweating, heart pounding

Stimulus

FIGURE 10.5 Classic theories of emotion. Once threatening stimuli are received by the brain, several routes have been proposed to lead to the expression of emotions, including (a) the bottom-up James–Lange theory, (b) the top-down Cannon–Bard theory, and (c) the Schachter–Singer two-factor theory.

Proposed Mechanism of Emotion (Papez, 1937). Based on meticulous brain dissections and a thorough review of the scientific literature on neuroanatomy, Papez proposed that sensory information from the environment was processed through the thalamus and was subsequently directed toward the sensory areas of the cortex as well as the cingulate cortex. From the cingulate cortex, neural messages were projected to the hippocampus via the neural pathway known as the **cingulum**. Papez proposed that the information then traveled through the pathway known as the **fornix** to the **mammillary bodies** of the hypothalamus and on to the anterior thalamus via the pathway appropriately known as the *mammillothalamic tract*. Papez suggested that this component of the circuit allowed for cortical control of emotional processing, perhaps explaining the impact of environmental context in the emotional expression observed in the Capilano Bridge study described previously. Papez also described a second neural stream projecting directly from the thalamus to the mammillary bodies before projecting down to the body's autonomic nervous system. In this complex system, known as **Papez's circuit**, the **cingulate cortex** played a pivotal role in directing information upward and downward to ultimately result in relevant emotional thoughts and feelings (Dalgleish, 2004).

As you learned in Chapter 2, another prominent neuroanatomist, Paul MacLean, introduced the term *limbic system*, referring to a proposed circuit of specific brain areas involved in emotional processing. To form his theory, MacLean incorporated the documented Papez's circuit with relevant aspects of **Klüver–Bucy syndrome**. This condition, observed in monkeys and humans with lesioned temporal lobes, is characterized by increased exploratory behavior and a dampening of emotional responses like fear and aggression (Klüver & Bucy, 1937). MacLean concluded that the temporal lobes played a critical role in emotional expression, and he incorporated the relevant brain areas that had been identified up until that time into a proposed circuit known as the limbic system (MacLean, 1998).

A key brain area associated with emotional responses within the temporal lobes was the amygdala. Research provided evidence that bilateral lesions restricted to the amygdala resulted in the behaviors observed in Klüver–Bucy syndrome in monkeys (Weiskrantz, 1956). Further research suggested that the monkeys became so passive that they lost their social status in the important dominance hierarchies within the troop (Pribram, 1998). Both lesion studies and neuroimaging studies have supported the role of the amygdala in recognizing emotional facial expressions. Humans with amygdala damage have been observed to exhibit an impaired ability to recognize emotional facial expressions (Adolphs, Tranel, Damasio, & Damasio, 1994), and fMRI studies in healthy subjects indicate heightened amygdala activity in response to pictures of fearful faces (Breiter et al., 1996).

Essentially, MacLean's ideas expanded on the classic theories described in the preceding section. He proposed that the body's responses to environmental stimuli were interpreted by various regions of the brain, eventually leading to an emotional experience. Today, the limbic system survives as a label for a cluster of brain structures thought to be associated with emotional experience. More emphasis has been placed on the roles of the amygdala, hypothalamus, cingulate cortex, and PFC in emotional experiences compared with other brain areas (see Figure 10.6). The cingulate and PFC areas are thought to be involved in top-down processing by modulating the expression of emotions based on the integration of information processed across the brain. That is, as seen in the case of Phineas Gage, these areas are thought to influence the intensity of specific emotional responses based on the appropriateness of certain responses in specific emotional contexts (Dalgleish, 2004).

One of MacLean's most important contributions was his emphasis on integration of the relevant brain areas involved in emotional experiences. I was fortunate to have had the opportunity to interview MacLean several years ago. In speaking with me, he emphasized the importance of always respecting

(a)

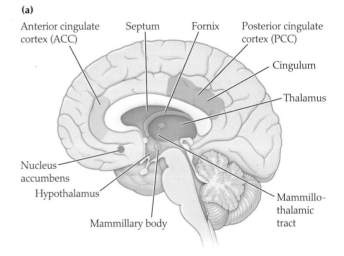

(b)

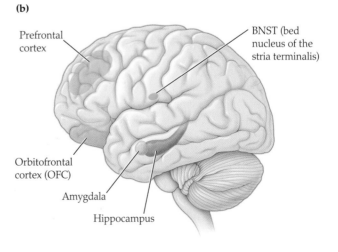

FIGURE 10.6 **The limbic system.** The network of structures radiating from the thalamus and surrounding areas to various cortical areas provides the multifaceted foundation of emotional responses.

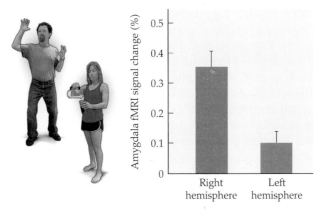

Source: De Gelder, B. (2006). Towards the neurobiology of emotional body language. *Nature Reviews Neuroscience, 7*, 242–249.

FIGURE 10.7 Amygdala sensitivity to threat posture. In this study, subjects showed more activation in the right amygdala in response to threatening body postures than in response to neutral body postures.

the positioning of brain areas and their interdependence on one another as researchers explore the functions of individual brain areas. This advice serves as a reminder that, although we spend considerable time trying to identify the functions of individual brain areas, the brain is an integrative system. In addition to examining specific brain areas, we must also consider the neuroanatomical context of brain areas.

Consider the proximity of the amygdala and hippocampus, two areas of the limbic system. According to MacLean's suggestion, this proximity likely serves an important function. Elizabeth Phelps and her colleagues at New York University have explored the question of how these two structures influence one another. In an experimental task known as the **attentional blink**, human participants are asked to focus on two target stimuli that are distinguished by a specific color and appear against a background stream of stimuli presented at a rapid pace. Typically, participants see the first target, but when the second target is presented soon after the initial target, participants typically miss it, as if their attentional system had "blinked." But there is an interesting exception: If the second target stimulus is an obscene word, participants see it with no problem. Apparently, the heightened emotional response associated with the questionable word is responsible for this effect. Thus, the attentional deficit observed in the attentional blink task (model) diminishes with an infusion of emotional processing. Individuals with amygdala damage fail to show this emotion-induced recovery of the attentional blink, suggesting that the amygdala plays an important role in this example of emotion-facilitated attention (A. K. Anderson & Phelps, 2001).

The importance of the interaction between the amygdala and hippocampus relates to the role of the hippocampus in forming memories. An event has to be noted before it can become consolidated into a memory. Phelps and her team

have suggested that the time it takes for an event to become a memory is adaptive because it allows the amygdala to first gauge the emotional relevance of the event; otherwise, all events would be processed with the same degree of relevance. In one PET study in which subjects evaluated images as either emotional or interesting, blood flow in the amygdala was significantly correlated with short-term and long-term memory recall of the image (Hamann, Ely, Grafton, & Kilts, 1999). With limited space in our brains for neural networks supporting individual memories, remembering what we had for lunch yesterday does not deserve the same priority as remembering the face of a threatening individual or some other emotionally relevant event (Phelps, 2004).

As you will recall from Chapter 2, the right hemisphere is known to be more engaged than the left hemisphere during emotional encounters. This right hemisphere dominance was observed in a study in which subjects' brains were scanned while they were shown images of either threatening body language (hands shielding the face) or neutral body language (a person pouring a liquid). As seen in Figure 10.7, fMRI scans indicated increased activation of the amygdala in the right hemisphere when the subjects viewed the threatening body posture compared with the neutral posture. This increase was not observed in the left hemisphere. Thus, this study provides evidence that, in addition to facial gestures, body posture is important in alerting us to threatening situations. Further, the right hemisphere plays an influential role in processing emotional stimuli (de Gelder, 2006).

Since the limbic system was first proposed, other relevant brain areas have been identified. For example, the nucleus accumbens, with its role in anticipation and reward, contributes to emotional expression, as does the insula. Neuroimaging studies in humans also reveal coactivation of the **anterior cingulate cortex (ACC)** and **anterior insular cortex** in subjects experiencing a wide range of emotional experiences including happiness, love, anger, disgust, indignation, empathy, and unfairness (Craig, 2009).

The Neurobiology of Aggression and Fear

Although all emotions have a functional relevance, the obvious associations among fear, aggression, and self-preservation have sparked many experiments in behavioral neuroscience. As a result, models of fear, defensive responses, and aggression have dominated the research on emotion and have resulted in a wealth of interesting findings. This section will discuss the brain areas and neurochemicals related to both aggression and fear. Additionally, although we often think of aggression and fear as negative emotional experiences, this section will explore their adaptive value. These emotions protect both human and nonhuman animals from grave danger.

Aggression

Aggressive displays represent complex social responses typically associated with defending or acquiring various types of resources. From an observer's viewpoint, aggression is characterized as behavior that appears to have the intention of harming another individual (Baron & Richardson, 1994). In humans, a fight may break out over issues as diverse as a love interest or a peanut butter and jelly sandwich. Although various forms of aggression such as maternal aggression and defensive aggression have adaptive value for humans and nonhuman animals, inappropriate displays of aggression are considered pathological by clinicians. When it comes to aggression, there is a fine line between adaptive and maladaptive consequences.

Scientists categorize aggression into two main types. **Reactive-impulsive aggression** is displayed when a person is highly emotionally aroused, as with out-of-control anger. In contrast, **controlled-instrumental aggression** is a more purposeful type of aggression. Hiring someone to murder an ex-lover is an example of controlled-instrumental aggression (Nelson & Trainor, 2007). As you might guess, reactive-impulsive aggression is more directly regulated by the limbic structures, whereas controlled-instrumental aggression is regulated by higher cortical systems.

Neuroanatomy of Aggression In rodent models of aggression, researchers create lesions of specific brain areas and observe the subsequent changes in aggressive behavior. When rodents display reduced aggression, this suggests that the lesioned area contributes to the initiation of aggression. Researchers have found evidence that lesions of the following areas result in a reduction of aggressive displays between males: the **lateral septum**, **bed nucleus of the stria terminalis (BNST)**, anterior hypothalamus, and medial amygdala. A common feature of these structures is that they receive input either directly or indirectly from the olfactory bulb (Kruk, 1991). Aggression-related information also travels to the **medial preoptic area of the hypothalamus**, the ventromedial hypothalamus, and **periaqueductal gray**, brain areas that have been investigated and found to be important in other social behaviors as well (Nelson & Trainor, 2007). In contrast, evidence indicates that lesions of the orbitofrontal cortex result in increased aggression, suggesting that this area inhibits aggressive displays (de Bruin, van Oyen, & Van de Poll, 1983). Because aggression is a social behavior, the key components of the aggression circuit are also involved in a broader social behavior circuit. As seen in Figure 10.8, these structures are interconnected.

Following fighting, male and female rodents exhibit activation of cells in the lateral septum, BNST, anterior hypothalamus, and medial amygdala (Delville, De Vries, & Ferris, 2000; Davis, & Marler, 2004; Hasen & Gammie, 2005; Kollack-Walker & Newman, 1995). In male rodents, aggression increases with electrical stimulation to the anterior hypothalamus. In contrast, aggression in

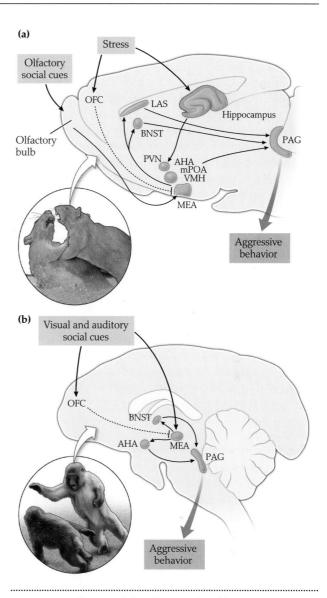

FIGURE 10.8 The amygdala and aggression. (a) In the rat, threatening olfactory stimuli are channeled to limbic structures and will specifically activate the medial amygdala-driven aggression response, whereas (b) in the primate, threatening visual and auditory stimuli are processed and directed toward the medial amygdala to trigger aggression responses.

male rodents decreases when the neuropeptide vasopressin is injected into this area. Thus, many ways exist to experimentally modulate aggressive displays in rodents. Learning that different areas and chemicals contribute to aggression informs us about how these areas may be integrated to produce aggression.

Although primate brains have not been as meticulously studied as the rodent models, the existing research suggests that the rodent findings extend to primates. In male marmoset monkeys, electrical stimulation of the VMH seemed to increase the occurrence of vocal threats such as angry chatters and loud, piercing, shrill calls; whereas lesions of the anterior hypothalamus and preoptic area appeared to reduce the occurrence of vocal threats (Dixson and Lloyd, 1988; Lipp & Hunsperger, 1978).

Explorations of the amygdala and the orbitofrontal cortex in rhesus monkeys suggest that these areas are indeed involved in aggression. However, social context determines the direction of the effect. Amygdala lesions appear to increase aggression when the monkey is introduced into groups of monkeys with more threatening males; however, these same lesions appear to decrease aggression when the monkey is placed in less threatening social situations (Emery et al., 2001; Machado & Bachevalier, 2006).

Studies of humans have emphasized the role of the frontal cortex in aggression. When the frontal cortex is damaged, aggressive behavior increases (Nelson & Trainor, 2007). For example, case studies have revealed that humans experiencing prefrontal cortex damage prior to two years of age exhibit impulsive, aggressive behavior in adulthood (S. W. Anderson, Bechara, Damasio, Tranel, & Damasio, 1999). Further, a positive correlation has been observed between the degree of amygdala activation and rates of aggression. Supporting these findings, when people diagnosed with *intermittent explosive disorder* (characterized by diminished impulse control in social situations, including aggressive encounters) were assessed in an fMRI scanner, increased activation of the amygdala was indeed observed on exposure to pictures of humans with angry facial expressions (Coccaro, McCloskey, Fitzgerald, & Phan, 2007). Additionally, individuals with tumors in the area of the amygdala (who thereby experience stimulation of the amygdala area) have been known to exhibit uncharacteristic aggression; some have even committed murder (Eagleman, 2011). Thus, experiments and case studies across humans and nonhuman animals suggest that, in general, the amygdala initiates aggressive responses, and the PFC inhibits aggression.

Neurochemistry of Aggression Several hormones and neurotransmitters influence the neural networks that are associated with aggressive behaviors. One of these is the steroid hormone testosterone, which is produced in males by specialized cells in the testes. In most mammalian species, castration results in dramatically decreased levels of aggression. However, there are exceptions. For example, when male prairie voles are castrated, their aggression levels remain unchanged. This interesting finding may be related to the observation that, in general, testosterone seems to be more influential in the developmental organization of aggression than in the activation of aggressive responses, especially in male prairie voles. Thus, particularly in this species, testosterone appears to be more important in establishing the neural foundations of the aggression brain network (organization) than in triggering the response (activation) later in the adult stages of the vole's life (Demas, Moffatt, Drazen, & Nelson, 1999). Although females also produce testosterone, a causal link to aggression is less clear

in females. Therefore, most aggression research has been conducted in males.

Studying the neurochemistry of aggression in humans is limited by ethical considerations. However, studies suggest that the relationship between testosterone and aggression is weaker in humans than in nonhuman animals (Archer, Graham-Kevan, & Davies, 2005). When human males are assessed in competitive social interactions, testosterone is positively correlated with aggression (Trainor, Kyomen, & Marler, 2006). In fact, men merely watching their favorite sports team win have increased testosterone levels, whereas men watching their teams lose have decreased testosterone levels (Bernhardt, Dabbs, & Fieden, 1998) (see Figure 10.9)!

However, researchers face numerous methodological challenges while conducting this research. One such problem is the difficulty of simulating actual aggressive responses in a laboratory setting because it would be unethical to have another person harm someone in the context of a research study. The time delay between the violent event and the current baseline testosterone levels is also a methodological problem given that testosterone is context dependent and that it is difficult to collect fluid samples from individuals while they are conducting an aggressive act. Such acts typically occur outside the laboratory in the midst of a person's day-to-day functioning (Wingfield, Hegner, Dufty, & Ball, 1990). Based on the research that has been conducted, however, the presence of testosterone receptors in key brain areas involved in aggression (e.g., orbitofrontal cortex, hypothalamus, amygdala) provides further support for the role of testosterone in aggressive responses (Batrinos, 2012).

Some researchers have assessed testosterone levels in prisoners convicted of violent crimes. Their findings suggest a strong positive relationship between criminal behavior and testosterone levels. However, as discussed above, the time delay between the violent crime and the measurement

FIGURE 10.9 Testosterone and sports. Men who watch their favorite sports teams win have shown increased levels of testosterone, a neurochemical involved in aggression.

of the criminal's testosterone levels is a methodological challenge (Wingfield et al., 1990). Without a hormone sample taken at the exact time of the aggressive encounter, it is difficult to determine the exact role of testosterone in aggression (Carre, McCormick, & Hariri, 2011; Dabbs, 1993). Currently, research suggests that fluctuations, such as the degree of increase, rather than stable levels of testosterone represent one of the most dramatic modulators of aggression (Carre et al., 2011).

Another neurochemical associated with modifications of aggressive behaviors is serotonin. Generally, high levels of serotonin are associated with reduced aggressive behavior in rodents, whereas low levels are associated with increased aggressive behavior (Chiavegatto et al., 2001). Further investigations of specific serotonin receptors suggest that the 5-HT$_{1B}$ receptor is distributed among the brain regions involved in aggression, including the periaqueductal gray, hippocampus, and lateral septum. Activation of these receptors decreases aggression; additionally, male mice that are bred to lack this receptor are hyperaggressive (Miczek, Maxson, Fish, and Faccidomo, 2001; Nelson & Chiavegatto, 2001; Olivier, 2005). PET scans in human subjects also corroborate the idea that 5-HT$_{1B}$ receptor activation is negatively correlated with aggression, providing further evidence for its inhibitory role in aggression (Nelson & Trainor, 2007). Altogether, the nonhuman and human research supports an inhibitory role of serotonin in aggression.

Other neurochemicals, including dopamine, GABA, and noradrenaline, have also been implicated in modulating aggressive responses. For example, drugs that antagonize dopamine have been associated with decreased aggression. Mice genetically engineered to lack the dopamine transporter, leading to increased extracellular dopamine, exhibit increased aggression (de Almeida, Ferrari, Parmigiana, & Miczek, 2005; Rodriguiz, Chu, Caron, & Wetsel, 2004). Furthermore, in humans, GABA receptor agonists generally decrease aggression. However, in rodents, studies provide evidence that increased GABAergic activity in the septum, an area involved with the suppression of aggression, increases aggression (Miczek & Fish, 2006; Nelson & Trainor, 2007). Although we do not yet know the cause of species-specific differences in GABA's influence on aggression, scientists are finding complex influences of both environmental and genetic variables that may even lead to occasional conflicting effects in the same species. Because aggressive encounters are stressful, high levels of noradrenaline also accompany aggression. Although the role of noradrenaline in aggression is also complex, drugs that decrease its levels (such as β blockers) have been used to treat children exhibiting excessive levels of aggression (Haller & Kruk, 2006; Nelson & Trainor, 2007).

Submission and Defeat Although aggression can be necessary for survival, it is not adaptive for animals to be excessively aggressive. Certain behaviors have evolved to prevent continuous tissue-damaging aggressive encounters. **Dominance hierarchies** that are acknowledged by animals enable them to avoid conflicts over limited resources. As a graduate student studying at the Yerkes Primate Center in Georgia, I vividly recall the behavior of the Yerkes rhesus monkeys when food was presented to them. Only certain monkeys in the group approached first. Once they had consumed the food they wanted, others approached, depending on their status in the established dominance hierarchy for that particular troop of monkeys. The process did not seem fair to the patient low-ranking monkeys as they watched the higher-ranking monkeys eat, but it reduced the fighting and injuries that would result if there were constant bickering over resources.

In other species and circumstances with less clearly defined dominance hierarchies, animals can defuse an oncoming aggressive encounter by exhibiting certain behavioral postures, sending a message of **submission** to the aggressor. As seen in Figure 10.10, Darwin noted the contrast

(a)

(b)

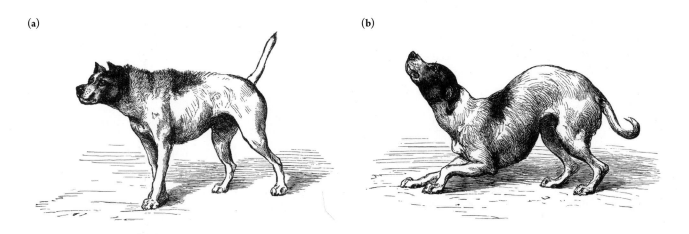

FIGURE 10.10 Emotional posturing. Darwin identified characteristic body postures in dogs that were associated with emotional responses such as (a) aggression and (b) submission.

between the aggressive and submissive postures exhibited by dogs. Submissive dogs are less likely to be involved in fights. Thus, adopting a submissive strategy on occasion may be a smart social approach that keeps an animal alive (Abrantes, 2005). Many times, despite adaptive behavioral strategies, an animal fights with another animal and loses. Defeat can have significant consequences for the animal because it often marks a pronounced loss of control over social conflicts and valuable resources (Gilbert, 2000).

Kim Huhman and her colleagues at Georgia State University have learned a lot about defeat using a hamster model of **conditioned defeat**. Although hamsters appear cute and harmless, they are a solitary species. When one hamster encounters another, both exhibit intense displays of aggression (see Figure 10.11a). Huhman has focused on a unique phenomenon that occurs in the hamsters that lose an initial aggressive encounter, that is, the defeated hamsters. Defeat is a potent stressor evidenced by increased stress neurochemicals (adrenocorticotropic hormone and glucocorticoids; see Figure 10.11b) and decreased testosterone levels in the blood (Huhman, Moore, Mougey, & Meyerhoff, 1992; Jasnow, Drazen, Huhman, Nelson, & Demas, 2001). Although the two fighting hamsters are similarly active in the initial aggressive encounter, the winner exhibits baseline levels of stress hormones during the encounter, whereas the loser exhibits heightened levels of stress hormones.

Following defeat, if the hamster is placed in the cage with a smaller, nonaggressive male hamster, the previously defeated hamster continues to exhibit submissive displays, a behavior known as *conditioned defeat*. When placed with another male, defeated males experience similar physiological effects to those observed during the initial aggressive encounter leading to defeat. Thus, because the physiological response, which may also include increased blood pressure and compromised immune function, occurs in the absence of an actual behavioral response, conditioned defeat represents a psychological stressor (Huhman et al., 1992; Jasnow et al., 2001). However, regardless of its source, stress ultimately results in a physiological response, as discussed in the next

section. Consequently, a distinction between psychological and physical stressors may not be meaningful. Conditioned defeat endures for approximately a month in male hamsters. In females, however, conditioned defeat is uncommon. If it occurs at all, it is rarely seen after the first test following the defeat (Huhman et al., 2003). Many of the same brain areas involved in emotional responses, as discussed above, are involved in conditioned defeat, including the amygdala, PFC, and BNST (in addition to being associated with aggression, this brain area has been implicated in anxiety) (Markham & Huhman, 2008; Markham, Luckett, & Huhman, 2012; Taylor, Stanek, Ressler, & Huhman, 2011).

Thus, the conditioned defeat behavioral paradigm is an interesting animal model in males for the evaluation of prolonged or chronic stress and various anxiety disorders. To the extent that it is applicable to humans, it may provide insight about the impact of persistent bullying on children—a neurochemical recipe for anxiety disorders. Interestingly, a study of South Korean middle school children indicated that victims of bullying exhibited changes in their social behavior in other contexts. Specifically, they became more dependent on adults and acted socially immature. These responses could be viewed as submissive or helpless, as observed in the defeated hamsters (Kim, Leventhal, Koh, Hubbard, & Boyce, 2006). Although few long-term studies have been conducted, existing research suggests that childhood bullying is related to both anxiety and depression in adults (Gladstone, Parker, & Malhi, 2006). A study focusing on children from both the United Kingdom and the United States found that bullying by peers during childhood produced higher rates of anxiety, depression, and self-harm in adulthood than observed in adults who experienced childhood maltreatment from adults (e.g., childhood physical, emotional, or sexual abuse; Lereya, Copeland, Costello, & Woke, 2015). Considering that approximately 10% of U.S. children and adolescents report being the victims of frequent bullying and that reported rates of bullying are much higher in other countries—for example, as high as 40% in South Korea—this topic deserves close attention (Sansone & Sansone, 2008) (Figure 10.12).

(a)

(b)

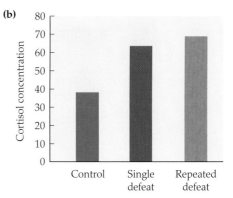

FIGURE 10.11 **The stress of defeat in hamsters.** (a) When hamsters engage in bouts of aggression, the defeated hamster adopts a submissive role. (b) Serum cortisol levels are higher in animals experiencing both single (acute) and repeated (chronic) defeat conditions.

Source: Jasnow, A.M., Drazen, D.L., Huhman, K.L., Nelson, R.J., & Demas, G.E. (2001). Acute and chronic social defeat suppresses humoral immunity of male Syrian hamsters (Mesocricetus auratus). *Hormones and Behavior, 40,* 428-433.

FIGURE 10.12 **Impact of bullying.** The mechanisms associated with defeat and submission in animal models may provide insight into the long-term biological consequences of bullying.

A final thought about the conditioned defeat response involves a concept that is central to this text: context. In these hamsters, having a history of defeat determines aggressive responses in the future. Considering that, in general, it is important to respond to real-time contextual cues to respond appropriately to threatening—and rewarding—stimuli that are critical for survival, it is difficult to understand how such prolonged periods of submission can be beneficial. Although conditioned defeat may have some adaptive value in the hamster's natural habitat, in the laboratory the response appears maladaptive, increasing the animal's susceptibility to future internal and external threats. The mismatch between response and environmental cues may be similar to the discrepancy observed between emotional responses and nonthreatening stimuli (e.g., sounds of loud, sputtering car engines or children's video games) in individuals experiencing PTSD, observed in many soldiers returning from the horrific trauma of war. The conditioned defeat research illustrates how an animal model may inform us about neurobiological mechanisms involved in human conditions such as being a victim of bullying or suffering from PTSD.

Fear

Let's face it: many things in the world can harm us. To survive, the mammalian brain evolved to steer us away from the stimuli posing the greatest threats. These evolutionary pressures have resulted in predisposed fears of threats such as heights and spiders. The nature of the most threatening stimuli has changed so drastically over the past several centuries that images that should evoke the greatest fears in contemporary society—guns, bombs, poisons—do not compare with images of the same stimuli that sent a chill down our ancestors' spines. It is ironic that a video image of a spider can cause otherwise rational adults to scream in horror, whereas a video image of a bomb rarely evokes such

a response. These observations emphasize the conserved nature of emotional responses through the years. Although our world today is drastically different from that of our prehistoric ancestors, our fears are strikingly similar.

When fear responses are observed in rats, the situational context influences the response. On detection of calls or smells from a natural predator, the rat may freeze in restricted situations, such as a laboratory cage. However, if there is an escape path, the rat may vigorously flee (Blanchard & Blanchard, 1990). Thus, effective responses to threats typically include an accurate survey of the environment. However, in cases such as conditioned fear, thorough contextual assessments are bypassed for a more immediate response.

Conditioned Fear The New York University neuroscientist Joseph LeDoux began investigating the fear response using Pavlovian classical conditioning (discussed in Chapter 12) to generate fear in rats. In his studies, a sound was paired with a brief electrical shock so that, after training, the sound elicited a fear response as the rat anticipated the delivery of the shock. The experimentally induced fear was similar to an animal's response to a natural threat such as a predator. Thus, the laboratory rats exhibited defensive behavior in the form of freezing or escape responses accompanied by altered cardiovascular and stress hormone responses (LeDoux, 2003). When LeDoux set out to map the brain circuitry of this response, he followed the brain's natural auditory processing. Specifically, the sound entered the ear and activated neural pathways continuing to the thalamus and on to the auditory cortex so that the sound could be interpreted as a threat. At that point, the appropriate subcortical emotional brain circuits could be activated, leading to a response such as RUN!

Curious about the neural connections of the auditory thalamus, LeDoux injected a chemical known as a tracer to track the neural pathways from the thalamus to other brain areas. Such chemicals, when injected into the distal processes (those located the farthest from the cell body) of a neuron, travel to the cell body, enabling scientists to confirm the origin of cell bodies in various neural networks. LeDoux observed a network directed toward the amygdala. This discovery explained previous research indicating that, although the conditioned fear paradigm required the animal to hear the stimulus, lesions of the auditory cortex did not interfere with the conditioning response. Now he knew why: some shortcut processes projected directly from the thalamus to the amygdala, and the amygdala initiated the fear response. After all, having to wait for the threatening information to travel all the way to the cortex before being interpreted might cause an animal to lose precious time in mobilizing its exit strategy (LeDoux, 1996).

As Figure 10.13 illustrates, the thalamus can use this neural shortcut for other sensory systems. In this example, when a snake is seen, the visual message travels from the eyes to the visual nucleus of the thalamus, where, in the case

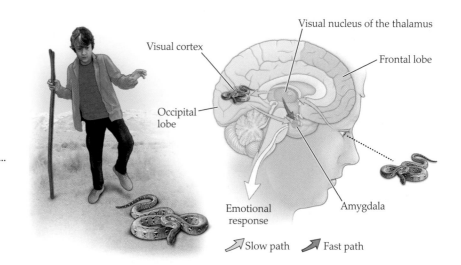

FIGURE 10.13 **Conditioned fear response.** To facilitate the fastest possible response to a threatening stimulus such as a snake, the thalamus takes on a security/protection function and directs associated neural messages right to the amygdala, bypassing the slower route including the visual cortex.

of emotional stimuli, it typically takes two roads: the high road to the visual cortex and then back to the subcortical limbic structures and the low road straight to the amygdala. The **lateral amygdala** receives the visual information and transfers the information to the **central amygdala**, which ultimately stimulates relevant brain areas that initiate the freezing response, blood pressure modifications, stress hormone release, and the startle reflex often observed in fearful situations. There is a cost, however, to this shortcut system. A police officer who shoots a person he later finds out to be holding a cell phone instead of a gun did not have the benefit of the sophisticated visual cortex weighing in on the decision. Thus, the shortcut response is a reflexive reaction that saves time; yet, the longer route activates higher circuits allowing the individual to exhibit a more informed voluntary action in response to the threat.

Building Courage in the Face of Fear Just how much control does the fear response have over our brain functions? The Roman philosopher Seneca declared that humans were slaves to their fear, suggesting that we have little control over this emotion. Yet, we have all heard of situations in which a frightened individual has stepped in to heroically save a child from an oncoming car or has run back into a burning building to save a friend.

An innovative human neuroimaging study using nonpoisonous corn snakes provided clues about how the brain overrides the fear response to muster the energy to act. In this study, participants were first divided into two groups: those with an expressed fear of snakes (fearful) and those with no fear of snakes (fearless). Participants were placed in an fMRI scanner and given the opportunity to confront their fear of snakes by moving a basket with a live corn snake within close proximity of their head in the scanner (see Figure 10.14). For a control condition, a toy bear was placed in the basket. The conveyer belt supporting the snake or toy bear was moved incrementally. For each trial, the participant had to decide to either advance the belt (to bring the object closer) or retreat the belt (to move the object away). In addition to brain activity, skin conductance was measured, and participants were asked to assess their own anxiety. Measures of skin conductance were obtained by placing recording electrodes on the skin to measure electrodermal activity. Increased activity represents heightened anxiety.

As expected, the fearful group exhibited higher levels of self-reported fear, as well as greater skin conductance reactivity. If you have ever noticed having sweaty palms during a first date or a stage performance, you have also experienced high skin conductance reactivity. When the brain scans were analyzed, the subgenual ACC was observed to be

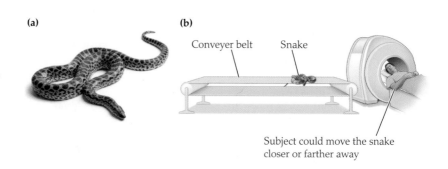

FIGURE 10.14 **Depicting courage in the brain.** This experimental setup allows experimenters to assess brain activity when subjects in the scanner are asked to activate a conveyor belt to bring a snake closer to them.

more active in the fearful group than in the fearless group when the participants were overcoming their fear and advancing the snake closer to their heads. Alternatively, when the fearful subjects succumbed to their fear by moving the snake away from their heads, increased activity was observed in the amygdala and the anterior insular cortex, a brain area that processes internal and external bodily functions including sympathetic arousal, than that observed in the condition in which the subjects advanced the snake toward them. These findings suggest that the neuroanatomical recipe for courage is an increased activation of the ACC accompanied by diminished activity in the amygdala and insula (Nili, Goldberg, Weizman, & Dudai, 2010). An improved understanding of conditioned fear responses and neural pathways to courage may lead to the establishment of additional evidence-based therapies for anxiety and fear-related disorders such as PTSD and **phobias** (a phobia is a disorder characterized by excessive fear of specific stimuli, discussed in Chapter 13).

A second study investigating the human brain's response to predisposed fears—in this case a tarantula moving toward the participant's foot—revealed additional clues about the neuroanatomical basis of fear. (Unlike participants in the snake study, these participants had not expressed a prior fear of spiders.) As the participants lay in the scanner, they saw a video feed that they believed was live, with an image of a box placed very close to their foot. The video appeared to show the tarantula approaching the participant's foot. As seen in Figure 10.15, once again, activation occurred in the ACC, as well as in the midbrain's periaqueductal gray when the tarantula was supposedly nearby and approaching. As you recall, the ACC has been implicated in courage. The periaqueductal gray is involved in the processing of pain as well as in defensive behavior. As the video feed showed the spider retreating from the participant's foot, the PFC was activated, perhaps indicating safety to the rest of the brain. Regardless of distance, if the spider was approaching the foot, the amygdala and BNST were activated; these brain areas are thought to be involved in assessing the threat value of a situation (Mobbs et al., 2010).

Courage can also be manipulated in cat-fearing rats so that they fearlessly approach their natural predators. Interestingly, this is not done with strategic neural surgeries or drugs. Rather, this "brainwashing" is accomplished by a protozoan parasite, *Toxoplasma gondii*. This parasite has a highly specialized evolutionary restriction related to its reproduction: The only place it can sexually reproduce is in the intestines of cats. Consequently, the parasite travels to the rat's brain to decrease the rat's innate fear of cat urine so that the rat's cat vigilance is relaxed, making it more likely to approach a cat. By doing so, the parasite increases its chances of arriving at its desired destination: the cat's stomach. Further, recent research suggests that not only does *T. gondii* reduce the rat's fear, likely by altering activity of the amygdala, but also it causes the rat to experience a

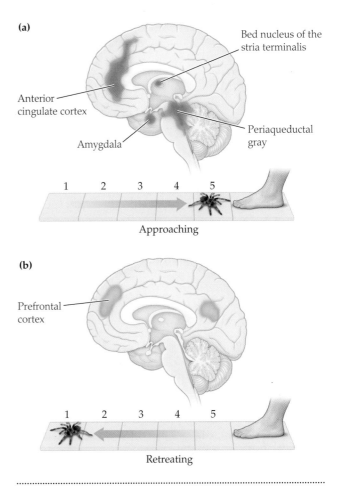

FIGURE 10.15 The brain's spider phobia. When the spider approaches the subject's foot, increased activation is observed in a fear circuit including the amygdala, bed nucleus of the stria terminalis, periaqueductal gray, and anterior cingulate cortex; alternatively, when the spider is perceived as retreating to a safe distance, the prefrontal cortex is activated.

social attraction to the cat. In this case, a single-cell parasite, without the benefit of a biopsychology course, has evolved the ability to manipulate the behavior of its mammalian host (see Figure 10.16; House, Vyas, & Sapolsky, 2011; Vyas, Kim, & Sapolsky, 2007).

The Value of Fear Although it can be fun to activate our fear responses in amusement parks and movie theaters, most of us do not enjoy these frightful feelings in our everyday lives. What would happen if our brains bypassed this fear response?

Consider the case of S.M., a 44-year-old woman who was born with a congenital disorder that eventually destroyed her amygdala during childhood (see Figure 10.17). When researchers took her to the reptile and insect section of a pet store, SM showed no sign of fear. She took a snake out of its cage, petted its scales, and touched its tongue.

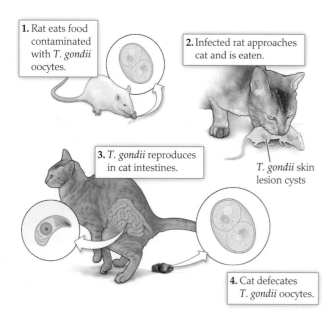

1. Rat eats food contaminated with *T. gondii* oocytes.

2. Infected rat approaches cat and is eaten.

3. *T. gondii* reproduces in cat intestines.

T. gondii skin lesion cysts

4. Cat defecates *T. gondii* oocytes.

FIGURE 10.16 Brain parasite influences emotional responses. *Toxoplasma gondii* modifies the brain and behavior of its rodent host such that *T. gondii* reaches its favored site for reproduction, inside a cat.

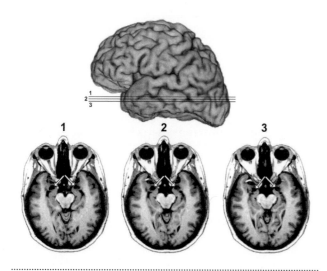

FIGURE 10.17 Living without fear. Patient S.M. lacked a functional amygdala and did not experience fear. Her case indicates fear's adaptive value in keeping us safe.

She also recalled one evening walking through an urban park when a man yelled at her to come over to the bench where he was sitting. She did not flee; she walked over to him. She remained calm when he threatened her by holding a knife to her throat. She looked around and saw a church choir that had just finished practicing and calmly told her assailant that if he was going to kill her he would have to go through God's angels (referring to the approaching choir members). The man was so confused by her response that

he let her go. In this situation, the assailant was more fearful than the victim. The next night, S.M. took a walk in the same park, providing evidence that, even after her life had been threatened in that area, the park did not evoke a fear response as it would in other people (Sohn, 2010).

Other cases of humans with compromised amygdala function are seen in the neurodevelopmental disorder **Williams syndrome**. Individuals with this genetic condition (seen in 1 in every 12,000 live births) also have specific facial features (e.g., low nasal bridge, puffiness around the eyes, a long upper lip and prominent lower lip, blue eyes with a starry pattern; see Figure 10.18), cardiovascular challenges, delayed cognitive development, and other physiological effects. Pertinent to this discussion, these individuals exhibit diminished amygdala activity in response to social situations compared with healthy control subjects. Further, they respond with less amygdala activation to images of fearful facial expressions than to images of natural disasters. Healthy controls, however, respond more intensely to fearful facial expressions. These data suggest that social threats are not considered as important in individuals diagnosed with Williams syndrome. Children born with Williams syndrome are highly social and seem to have no social stress or anxiety (Meyer-Lindenberg, Mervis, & Berman, 2006). Although enhanced tendencies to interact with others can provide many benefits, not knowing whom to approach and whom to avoid in certain contexts is dangerous (as observed in the case of S.M.). Consequently, these hypersocial children must be closely monitored.

These human cases stress the important functions of the amygdala. Although most of us would welcome a fearless day now and then, learning more about the adaptive function of the amygdala should cause us to embrace our fears or at least to appreciate their adaptive role in our safety and well-being.

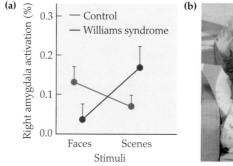

Source: Meyer-Lindenberg, A., Mervis, C.B., & Berman, K.F. (2006). Neural mechanisms in Williams syndrome: a unique window to genetic influences on cognition and behaviour. *Nature Neuroscience Reviews, 7,* 380-393.

FIGURE 10.18 Williams syndrome and amygdala response. When healthy control subjects are shown pictures of fearful faces, they respond with heightened amygdala activation; however, that is not the case for individuals with Williams syndrome.

Emotional Regulation

We will all experience emotional challenges throughout our lives. However, certain individuals, such as tortured prisoners of war, have experienced such an intense form of stress that it seems impossible that any human could have survived it. For example, consider the case of Bob Shumaker (Figure 10.19). In 1965, Bob left his pregnant wife to report for combat duty in Vietnam. Soon after his deployment, his plane was shot down north of the demilitarized zone in Vietnam. Suffering a broken back, Bob was immediately captured by the North Vietnamese. For the next eight years, he was tortured beyond imagination. He described one form of torture in which a rope was tied to both his handcuffs and his feet and tightened until his head met his feet. A metal rod was shoved down his throat to keep him from screaming.

As a prisoner-of-war in the North Vietnam prison sarcastically known as the "Hanoi Hilton," Shumaker was kept in solitary confinement for more than three years. To go even a day with no fresh air, human contact, or anything to do to pass the time seems horrible to most of us, but this was Shumaker's reality for this long period. During this time, however, Shumaker and the other prisoners kept in separate rooms devised a code in which they would tap on the wall a certain number of times for each letter of the alphabet to slowly and meticulously spell out a message. Although there was no human contact, the tap code was a form of communication that seemed to be essential for maintaining his sanity. Shumaker also passed the time by building a house in his mind . . . with all the architectural and building details including the number of bricks. He would spend 10 or 12 hours a day doing this. After spending about a year and a half on one design, he decided to implement a change, such as moving the fireplace, and started all over again.

After eight years, Shumaker was released and returned to his wife, meeting his son for the first time. By all accounts, he was healthy with no significant psychological problems. His case is significant, however, because his response to the trauma was exceptionally resilient. Consequently, researchers are interested in observing individuals such as Shumaker to gain information about such extreme cases of emotional resilience. He attained the Navy rank of rear admiral and became a college professor. He also built a new house, the one he had planned while imprisoned. Naturally, his house had many windows and expansive views.

In a recent interview, Shumaker conveyed the importance of looking inside oneself to find coping mechanisms that enable one to survive torturous circumstances and move on. This was how he built emotional resilience (Public Broadcasting System, 2009). Those words describe emotional resilience, but how do they translate into specific anatomical, neurochemical, and behavioral adaptations to maintain health and survival? This section of the chapter will address these questions.

The Stress Response, Revisited

Recall from Chapter 2 that the stress response, which is essential for survival, is composed of the sympathetic nervous system response and the related adrenaline response, as well as the hypothalamic–pituitary–adrenal (HPA) axis and corticosteroid/cortisol response. Short-term activation of the stress response is critical when one encounters a threatening stimulus. The stress hormone cortisol plays a central role in the stress response as it stimulates the sympathetic nervous system to mobilize energy resources, increases arousal, enhances vigilance, and sharpens memory. For the body to direct enough energy toward carrying out these life-saving functions, certain aspects of the PNS such as those related

(a)

(b)

FIGURE 10.19 **Prisoner of war survivor, Bob Shumaker.** (a) During the war and (b) more recently. Some individuals, such as Shumaker, exhibit extreme resilience when faced with unimaginable stressful circumstances. Researchers are interested in understanding the mechanisms of this heightened emotional resilience.

to growth, reproduction, digestion, and immune functions are temporarily compromised (Charney, 2004).

Why is energy for these important physiological functions restricted? The Stanford University biologist Robert Sapolsky explains that if your house is in the path of a hurricane, it is not the best time to decide to hang wallpaper in the guest bathroom. In such a threatening situation, all energy should be directed toward boarding up windows and securing the deck furniture to preserve the basic structure of the house (Sapolsky, 1998). Similarly, when an emotional storm is looming, energy is directed toward survival—once you are safe, more long-term investments related to romance, digestion, and immune competency once again become priorities.

When an individual is experiencing stress, it is critical for the brain to receive appropriate feedback so that baseline levels of stress hormones are reestablished once the threat has passed (Joels & Baram, 2009). Prolonged or chronic activation of the stress response will ultimately lead to allostatic overload (Chapter 2) and serious side effects, including insulin resistance and increased risk for diabetes, hypertension, immunosuppression, osteoporosis, atherosclerosis, and cardiovascular disease (Charney, 2004).

CRH is one of the brain's most important mediators of the stress response. After being released from the hypothalamus, CRH travels through the hypothalamic–pituitary portal system and triggers the eventual release of adrenocorticotropic hormone from the anterior pituitary gland and cortisol (a type of glucocorticoid found in humans) from the adrenal cortex (as discussed in Chapter 2). Additionally,

dehydroepiandrosterone (DHEA) is released from the adrenal cortex in parallel with glucocorticoids. Data indicate that natural circulating levels of DHEA provide a buffer against the effects of stress hormones in the brain and other tissue (Charney, 2004). In the brain, for example, DHEA is related to increased neurogenesis, which may protect against the onset of stress-related mental illnesses (Karishma & Herbert, 2002).

The dual efforts of the autonomic nervous system and the HPA axis in the stress response can be seen in Figure 10.20. Sympathetic activation and parasympathetic withdrawal occur almost immediately following the stressor, resulting in rapid adaptations in various physiological systems. The second tier of the stress response, the HPA axis, is a bit slower considering that the peak glucocorticoid plasma levels occur over the 20 or so minutes after the introduction of the stressor. In a sense, the autonomic nervous system sounds the body's alarm, and the HPA axis amplifies the message so that the appropriate brain areas are activated to resolve the crisis for the long term (Ulrich-Lai & Herman, 2009).

Once the brain is activated via the autonomic nervous system, HPA axis, and relevant sensory information, several brain areas play a role in managing the impending stress. Neurons in various nuclei in the amygdala respond to specific aspects of fear-related stimuli in an attempt to mobilize energy for the appropriate fear response (e.g., freeze, flee, or fight). Neurons in the locus coeruleus interact with the amygdala to further fine-tune the stress response. The PFC and hippocampus are important for interpreting the contextual aspects of the threat. The hippocampus also contains

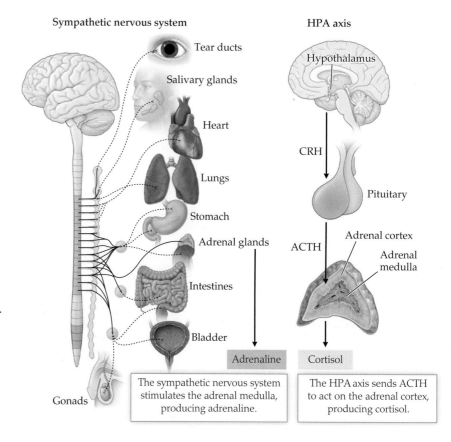

FIGURE 10.20 Dual stress systems. Because an organism's response to stress is so important, there are two systems in place to respond to threats. The sympathetic nervous system is initially triggered, with the hypothalamic–pituitary–adrenal axis activated shortly thereafter. Both systems mobilize energy to overcome the threat.

Sympathetic nervous system

Tear ducts

Salivary glands

Heart

Lungs

Stomach

Adrenal glands

Intestines

Bladder

Gonads

HPA axis

Hypothalamus

CRH

Pituitary

Adrenal cortex

ACTH

Adrenal medulla

Adrenaline

Cortisol

The sympathetic nervous system stimulates the adrenal medulla, producing adrenaline.

The HPA axis sends ACTH to act on the adrenal cortex, producing cortisol.

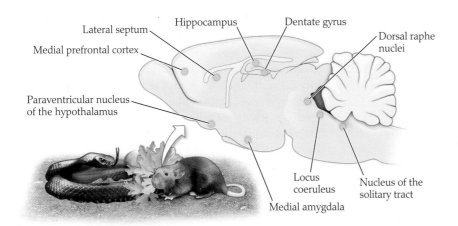

Lateral septum — Hippocampus — Dentate gyrus

Medial prefrontal cortex —

Paraventricular nucleus
of the hypothalamus —

Dorsal raphe
nuclei

Locus
coeruleus

Medial amygdala

Nucleus of the
solitary tract

FIGURE 10.21 The brain's stress detectors. Glucocorticoid receptors in areas throughout the brain monitor changes in glucocorticoid levels. The diverse distribution of these receptors indicates the importance of detecting potential threats.

neurons with receptors for glucocorticoids, neuropeptides, serotonin, and noradrenaline (Joels & Baram, 2009). In fact, as shown in Figure 10.21, glucocorticoid receptors are seen in several brain areas, suggesting that many brain areas are involved in interpreting and responding adaptively to threats. In total, these areas are involved in functions as diverse as learning, memory, decision making, and basic hormonal and neural aspects of emotional arousal.

The Neurobiology of Resilience

The term **resilience**, derived from the Latin term *re* referring to "back" and *saliere* meaning "to leap," was borrowed from the physical sciences to refer to the psychological response of springing back after a stressful situation (Stix, 2011). Just as the classic Slinky toy springs back to its original position after being stretched to the limit, resilient individuals spring back into shape after emotional trauma. Resilience also refers to an individual's ability to cope successfully with acute and chronic stressors (Feder, Nestler, & Charney, 2009).

Given the negative consequences of long-term corticosteroid exposure accompanying chronic stress (e.g., compromised hippocampus and memory, increased susceptibility for depression and anxiety disorders), anything that diminishes the stress response aids emotional resilience. DHEA, noted previously, has been shown to be related to reduced anxiety and enhanced emotional resilience. DHEA metabolites, for example, interfere with glucocorticoid receptor activation in the hippocampus, ultimately resulting in neuroprotection against damaged or dying neurons (Kimonides, Khatibi, Svendsen, Sofroniew, & Herbert, 1998; Morfin & Starka, 2001). Studies of elite special operations ("special ops") soldiers in challenging military survival tasks have found that higher levels of DHEA are associated with protection against stress-induced responses and better performance (Morgan et al., 2004). In other studies, students in a challenging college course such as organic chemistry were less likely either to fail or to drop out if they secreted higher levels of DHEA relative to cortisol levels in response to a frustrating, unsolvable task (Wemm, Koone, Blough, Mewaldt, & Bardi, 2010).

Although additional research must be conducted, there is a growing scientific interest in the role of DHEA in neuropsychiatric disorders (Maninger, Wolkowitz, Reus, Epel, & Mellon, 2008).

Neuropeptide Y (NPY), one of the most abundant peptides in the mammalian brain, is also involved in emotional resilience (Thorsell, Carlsson, Ekman, & Heilig 1999). NPY-containing neurons are densely packed in several brain areas overlapping with the areas associated with the limbic system. For example, when NPY is infused into the basolateral amygdala in rodents, a reduction in anxiety is observed (Sajdyk, Vandergriff, & Gehlert, 1999). It is not known how NPY exerts its **anxiolytic** (anxiety-reducing) effects, but evidence indicates that it may interfere with the consolidation of stressful memories (Flood, Baker et al., 1989). Additionally, NPY counteracts the **anxiogenic** (anxiety-producing) effects of CRH. Compared with healthy control subjects, lower plasma and cerebrospinal fluid levels of NPY have been observed in patients suffering from major depression (Hou, Jia, Liu, & Li., 2006) as well as in returning soldiers exhibiting symptoms of PTSD (Yehuda, Brand, & Yang, 2005). As illustrated in Figure 10.22, both DHEA and NPY counteract stress responses by interacting with the corticosteroid and CRH responses (Stix, 2011). As you will read in the next section, behavioral strategies also interact with stress and resilience brain systems.

Effective Coping Strategies Hans Selye, the Canadian scientist who introduced the term *stress* to the medical and psychobiological literature, originally thought that the stress response was extremely consistent. He thought that anyone experiencing chronic stress would exhibit effects similar to those he observed in his stressed rats (described in Chapter 2), a collection of symptoms Selye called the **generalized adaptation syndrome**. The primary stress responses Selye noted included larger adrenal glands, shrunken thymus glands (involved in immune functions), and gastric stress ulcers. To a degree, Selye was correct: the symptoms he identified are consistently associated with chronic stress. However, we now know that different

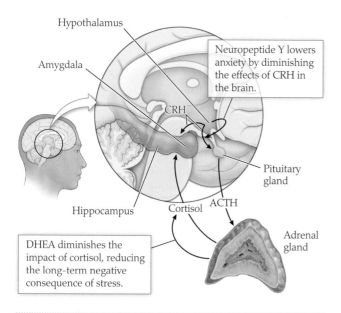

Hypothalamus

Amygdala

Neuropeptide Y lowers anxiety by diminishing the effects of CRH in the brain.

CRH

Pituitary gland

Hippocampus

Cortisol   ACTH

Adrenal gland

DHEA diminishes the impact of cortisol, reducing the long-term negative consequence of stress.

FIGURE 10.22 Neurochemical resilience. Once the stress response is engaged, chemicals such as neuropeptide Y and dehydroepiandrosterone (DHEA) have been shown to regulate the response to build resilience against the toxicity of chronic stress.

individuals possess very different strategies for coping with stress. Consequently, there is a growing scientific interest in identifying factors related to individual differences in coping strategies—and the health outcomes, if any, of these divergent **coping styles**. Have you ever wondered why you are more likely to panic when you have to take an exam, whereas your best friend appears completely calm? Answers to such questions may lead to answers about individual vulnerabilities for mental resilience and illnesses.

When given the opportunity to make varied responses to a stressor, animal models display specific coping styles. We may not be able to record animals' thoughts under various stressful conditions, but animal models provide valuable windows into their physiological functions. For example, when a predator is in the vicinity, a threatened animal may run, freeze, or attack. In one study, young pigs restrained on their backs exhibited varying responses to this stressful situation—some pigs wiggled, trying to escape, whereas others responded with no movement. Generally, the pigs that tried to escape exhibited less activation of the HPA axis and bolder responses in social competition and novel environments; hence, these animals were referred to as proactive copers. Those that did not move in the back test and had higher activation of the HPA axis appeared to be more inhibited and restrained in various environmental contexts and were referred to as reactive copers. Researchers view the more proactive responses as more adaptive since they allow the animal to change its behavior in response to changing circumstances (reviewed in Koolhaas et al., 1999).

Coping strategies have also been investigated in rats. In one study, the temperaments of young rats were categorized as either shy or bold. Once profiled, rats were exposed to a novel stimulus every six months so that both behavioral and endocrinological responses could be recorded. In addition to consistently exploring each new object, the bold rats had lower stress hormone (corticosteroid) levels than the shy rats did each time both groups were assessed. The long-term consequences of higher stress hormone levels across the life span came with a health cost because the shy rats had an average life span that was about 20% shorter than that of the bold rats (Cavigelli & McClintock, 2003).

In another coping-strategy study in which pigs were restrained on their backs, researchers noted that some of the pigs were not consistent in their response. The pigs readily switched their coping behavior from active (trying to escape) to passive (not moving) or vice versa during subsequent testing. This flexibility also seemed to be an adaptive coping response (Van Erp-Van der Kooij, Kuipers, Schrama, Eckel, & Tielen, 2000). You may imagine that if a person always responds with an intense emotional response, even when the threat does not warrant such a response, the allostatic load (Chapter 2) would build to dangerous levels, compromising other physiological systems necessary for maintaining optimal health.

To learn more about the nature of variable coping responses, researchers modified the coping test described above in the pig study for use with rats (see Figure 10.23). As observed with the piglets, when rats were gently restrained on their backs they exhibited variability in their responses. Additionally, when tested twice, some were consistently passive or active, whereas others were more variable in their responses (i.e., switched from passive to active or vice versa). The variable copers maintained variable responses in subsequent behavioral tasks. Furthermore, they had more NPY-affiliated cells in the amygdala and BNST than the more consistent copers did (Hawley et al., 2010).

Cognitive Reappraisal According to the animal models, possessing a more variable or bolder coping strategy appears to

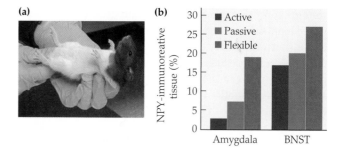

(a)

(b)

Source: Hawley, D. F., Bardi, M., Everette, A. M., Higgins, T. J., Tu, K. M., Kinsley, C. H., & Lambert, K. G. (2010). Neurobiological constituents of active, passive, and variable coping strategies in rats: Integration of regional brain neuropeptide Y levels and cardiovascular responses. *Stress, 13,* 172-183.

FIGURE 10.23 Assessing resilient coping styles. Rats profiled as flexible copers with the back test assessment have higher levels of neuropeptide Y (NPY)-cellular activity in the bed nucleus of the stria terminalis and amygdala than do rats profiled as passive or active copers.

be adaptive. But what about humans? Research suggests that first-year college students who believe that they have control over their emotional responses and can modify their emotions were more likely to exhibit healthy mental health profiles (with fewer depressive symptoms, higher social adjustment, and a heightened sense of well-being) than students who felt their emotional responses were fixed and out of their control (Tamir, John, Srivastava, & Gross, 2007). Having the perception that your emotional response is under your control is healthier than believing that you cannot control your response. Because intense emotional responses are not always appropriate, being able to modify emotional responses is often beneficial. Learning to control emotional responses, however, is not always easy. If you have ever tried to hide your nervousness when giving a speech or your jealousy when you see a former boyfriend or girlfriend on a date with someone else, you can appreciate the value of **emotional regulation**.

One way to alter the course of an emerging emotional experience is through **cognitive reappraisal**, changing one's understanding of an event in a way that also changes one's emotional response to the event. In short, cognitive reappraisal refers to the transformation of an emotional response by reinterpreting a negative experience as one that is less threatening to one's sense of well-being (Gross, 2008; Ochsner, Bunge, Gross, & Babrieli, 2002). If you pass a friend in the hall, for example, and wave and smile but note that your friend does not acknowledge your friendly gestures, it is easy to feel angry at your friend for the apparent snub. Alternatively, using cognitive reappraisal tactics, you may guide your thinking to perceiving that the friend was rushed or distracted and simply did not notice you in the hallway. Correct or not, this reappraisal results in less anger. Research also suggests that cognitive reappraisal can decrease the strength of physiological variables such as autonomic and neuroendocrine responses (Abelson, Liberzon, Young, & Khan, 2005; Stemmler, 1997). Thus, cognitive reappraisal can have a profound effect on the quality and quantity of expressed emotions.

Although the science of cognitive reappraisal is relatively new, the idea has been around for some time. Nearly 2 millennia ago, the Roman emperor Marcus Aurelius wrote, "If you are distressed by anything external, the pain is not due to the thing itself, but to your estimate of it; and this you have the power to revoke at any moment" (from Ochsner & Gross, 2005). Shakespeare's character Hamlet agreed that "there is nothing either good or bad, but thinking makes it so." In more contemporary times, clever research designs and advanced neuroimaging techniques have revealed valuable information about the effectiveness of this coping strategy.

Which brain areas are involved in emotional regulation and cognitive reappraisal? In one study, women were instructed either to react naturally to an unhappy movie or to actively suppress any emotional response to the movie. Greater activation of the prefrontal and orbitofrontal cortical areas accompanied the reappraisal task of transforming the sadness to a more neutral emotion in the subjects suppressing their emotional response (see Figure 10.24; Levesque et al., 2003). In general, brain imaging studies point to roles of the prefrontal, orbitofrontal, and cingulate cortical areas in cognitive reappraisal. As the reappraisal process successfully diminishes the emotional experience, less activation is observed in the medial orbitofrontal cortex and amygdala, suggesting that these two areas may play important roles in assessing the relevance of the emotional stimulus (Ochsner et al., 2002).

Thus, evidence from both rodent and human studies suggests that emotional responses can be modified, although some individuals seem able to do this more easily than others. The cumulative findings also suggest that emotional flexibility is adaptive. The Columbia University psychologist George Bonanno and his colleagues refer to the ability to both enhance and suppress emotions as **expressive flexibility**, emphasizing the importance of matching the emotional expression to situational demands (Westphal, Seivert, & Bonanno, 2010). In many situations, there is no need to suppress an emotional reaction. However, your outcome may be better in certain situations if your emotional expressions are less transparent. If you are playing poker, for example, being able to suppress your outward expression when you realize you have a winning (or losing) hand can be financially adaptive. Maintaining a poker face to fool other players in the game requires expressive flexibility. It is worth noting that many of our cultural heroes, including secret agents and spies (e.g., James Bond) and superhuman

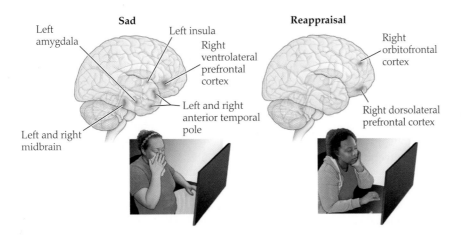

FIGURE 10.24 Brain areas involved in cognitive reappraisal. In this study, women who successfully suppressed the sadness of a film exhibited increased activation in the dorsolateral prefrontal cortex and the orbitofrontal cortex, suggesting that these brain areas play a key role in emotional regulation.

characters, are defined by their ability to remain cool under pressure. It appears that the value of expressive flexibility and emotional regulation was introduced in comic books much sooner than in biological psychology texts!

Emotions and Decision Making Being able to control emotions does not diminish one's memory of the emotional experience. Even when we suppress emotions, the experiences are still processed by the appropriate brain areas. It is critical that our brains fully process the threat value of various life events; otherwise, we will not learn from our experiences and make informed future decisions. The important role of emotions in making informed decisions is seen in the research of the University of Southern California neuroscientist Antonio Damasio and his colleagues. They have reported that individuals with frontal lobe damage experience diminished emotional responses to situations that are traditionally viewed as threatening or emotional. Subsequent investigations revealed that these individuals take more risks than others in a gambling task; further, many such individuals are currently in prison for committing crimes. Damasio's **somatic marker hypothesis** states that physiological emotional responses serve an important role in guiding the brain's decision to carry out a particular behavior, especially when making risky decisions. Without the uneasy feelings in your stomach, you are more likely to take a risk at the gambling table. In the most unfortunate cases, the lack of anxiety when thinking about harming someone may contribute to a person committing unspeakable crimes (Bechara & Damasio, 2005; Damasio, Tranel, & Damasio, 1991). The somatic marker hypothesis emphasizes the importance of physiological feedback in the expression of certain emotions (as described earlier in the chapter in the context of the James–Lange theory). In this case, diminished physiological responsiveness is associated with a weakening of an emotional response that may be necessary to inhibit certain behaviors.

Emotions and Health

Have you ever noted that you are more likely to become sick with a cold or flu after a stressful event in your life such as final exams? Or wondered why only certain members of the family catch a stomach bug although everyone lives in the same house and is exposed to it? Obviously, there are individual differences in the body's immune response. As we have seen many times in this book, the immune system engages in significant cross-talk with the nervous system. The stress response is one of the most influential mediators of psychoneuroimmunological functions. Thus, varying levels of emotional regulation and stress management will lead to different immune and health outcomes. Although the ancient Greeks acknowledged the important interactions between emotions and health, many scientists and health practitioners in more recent times (i.e., throughout most of the 20th century) dismissed the idea as a topic too subjective for empirically based health sciences. Since the times of the ancient Greeks, however, objective evidence has slowly emerged confirming that emotional experiences do indeed influence our health status (Sternberg, 2000).

Although most research findings indicate that stress results in **immunosuppression**, research conducted by the Stanford University psychoneuroimmunologist Firdaus Dhabhar suggests that, when it comes to immune functions, stress is a double-edge sword. When stress is acute or is present for short durations, much evidence suggests that stress leads to **immunoenhancement**. For example, thorough examinations suggest that some of the decreases in physiological measurement values such as the number of white blood cells (leukocytes) may represent redistribution, rather than actual degeneration, of cells to more effectively handle the immunological challenge (Cox & Ford, 1982). Dhabhar has stated that since the white blood cell numbers quickly return to baseline levels on the removal of a stressor, it is likely that the cells were not destroyed, just deployed to more active battle stations in the immunological challenge (Dhabhar & McEwen, 1996; Dhabhar, Miller, McEwen, & Spencer, 1995). Where are the white blood cells deployed in these immunological breaches of security? Dhabhar's research suggests that they are redistributed from the blood to organs such as the skin that are possible access points for pathogens, especially when an animal is exposed to an acute stressor such as an attack from a predator (Dhabhar, 2002). In other words, when an animal is about to be bitten by the pathogen-laden mouth of a lion, it is not the time for the victim to suppress immune function in its skin.

In an informative analogy, Dhabhar describes his findings as follows:

> Thus, an acute stress response may direct the body's "soldiers" (leukocytes) to exit their "barracks" (spleen and bone marrow), travel the "boulevards" (blood vessels), and take position at potential "battle stations" (skin, lining of gastro-intestinal and urinary genital tracts, lung, liver, and lymph nodes) in preparation for immune challenge. In addition to "redeploying" leukocytes to potential "battle stations," stress hormones may also better equip them for "battle" by enhancing processes like antigen presentation, phagocytosis, and antibody production. Thus, a hormonal alarm signal released by the brain upon detecting a stressor may prepare the immune system for potential challenges (wounding or infection) which may arise due to the actions of the stress-inducing agent (e.g., a predator or attacker). (Dhabhar, 2002, pp. 558–559)

How is this redistribution of immune cells accomplished? Where are the important cross-communication points between the immune and nervous systems? Research suggests that the adrenal stress hormones alert the immune system of the impending threat. Therefore, even the anticipation of an attack, because of conditioned responses, can activate the immunological response. When an animal has undergone an adrenalectomy (removal of the adrenal glands, the source of corticosteroids), the immunological response is no longer observed (Dhabhar & McEwen, 1999).

But what if the attack does not occur within a few minutes of the initial alarm? What if the stress response is prolonged for days or months, as is the case in chronic stress? In that case, the prolonged vigilance and stress response take a toll on the immune system. Ronald Glaser and Janice Kiecolt-Glaser, from the Ohio State University, have conducted extensive research on humans experiencing various forms of chronic real-life stress and have reported that immunosuppression is most often observed. For example, when assessing the immunological response in the form of antibody production to certain vaccines, medical students showed stronger virus-specific T-cell responses if they reported less emotional stress and more social support than their student counterparts with more extreme forms of stress. Additionally, individuals who were caregivers for their spouses suffering from Alzheimer's disease exhibited weaker antibody responses to vaccinations than age-matched control subjects who were not caring for a loved one suffering from Alzheimer's disease. These findings suggest that stress levels may be an important factor to consider when administering vaccinations. Further, these results highlight the increased immunological vulnerability of individuals facing chronic, unrelenting stress (Glaser & Kiecolt-Glaser, 2005).

Another index used to assess immune function in both human and animal models is the rate of wound recovery. With the increased probability of pathogens entering the body when an animal has an open wound, it appears adaptive for the wound to heal as soon as possible. In one study, when dental students received an oral wound in the hard palate of their mouths prior to either a stressful examination or vacation period, the healing rates were 40% slower in the academic stress group (Marucha, Kiecolt-Glaser, & Favagehi, 1998). Additionally, couples in hostile marital relationships (based on observed social interaction assessments conducted in the lab) exhibited a 60% reduction in the rate of wound healing compared with couples exhibiting less hostile responses (Kiecolt-Glaser et al., 2005).

Although we have only scratched the surface, ample evidence indicates that our emotions permeate immune functions. Traditional Western medicine is focused on pills, ointments, and various invasive procedures. However, an enhanced knowledge of a person's emotional state, especially stress levels, is becoming increasingly important. In addition to pharmaceutical and surgical treatment options, coping strategies such as cognitive reappraisal can be used to influence the immune system (Gianaros et al., 2014). In one study, for example, Chinese undergraduate women were shown emotionally distressing images. Afterward, they had decreased levels of an antibody, secretory **immunoglobulin A**, in their saliva. A subgroup of the women was then assigned to a cognitive reappraisal group in which they learned to imagine a positive context for the troubling image. For example, a woman weeping outside of a church could be crying tears of joy at a wedding as opposed to grieving the loss of a loved one at a funeral. Following their cognitive reappraisal training, these women had higher levels of secretory immunoglobulin A than the nontrained women (Zhang, Li, Qin, & Luo, 2012). Researchers are just beginning to try to understand both the short- and the long-term effects of emotional regulation on immune functions. More research is necessary to further clarify these relationships and inform health practitioners about how emotional regulation tactics such as cognitive reappraisal affect health outcomes.

CONTEXT MATTERS

Emotional Temperament and Longevity in Rats

Featured Study: Cavigelli, S. A., Yee, J. R., & McClintock, M. K. (2006). Infant temperament predicts life span in female rats that develop spontaneous tumors. Hormones and Behavior, 50, 454–462.

Although we typically think of external environments when considering influential contexts in our lives, this study suggests that our *internal* environment plays a critical role in health outcomes (as suggested in Chapter 1). In this case, Cavigelli, Yee, and McClintock developed an animal model to determine the role of an animal's internal environment (in the form of emotional temperament) on susceptibility to tumor development.

In this study, female rats were assessed for their tendency to explore new environments at 20 days of age and assigned to either a low-exploration, an intermediate-exploration, or a high-exploration group. Based on their prior investigations,

the researchers hypothesized that the rats that tended to avoid novelty would be more susceptible to health risks such as tumor formation and shortened life span than the rats that tended to approach novel objects. For the temperament task, an exploration arena was designed to introduce rats to an unfamiliar environment. The experimental arena was covered and the walls were opaque to reduce anxiety in the rats (who prefer dark spaces to bright habitats). Novel objects such as plastic tubes and inverted bowls were positioned throughout the unfamiliar environment. The experimenters' goal was to diminish as much of the stress response associated with the environment as possible to assess individual responses to nonthreatening novelty—that is, the novel rat-size objects. For five minutes, experimenters recorded the rats' responses.

Movement throughout the arena was assessed by counting the number of times the rats walked from one area to another area of the arena (areas were marked by nine equally sized grids). The most active rats were categorized as "neophilic" (more likely to approach novel objects) and the least active were categorized as "neophobic" (less likely to approach novel objects). The animals falling between the two extreme temperament categories were classified as "intermediate responders." This assessment was repeated when the rats were 11 months of age.

When the rats were 47 days old, they were housed in trios of sisters representing each of the three groups. Beginning at 10 months of age, the rats were routinely examined for mammary tumors (common in captive laboratory rats) to investigate the effect of these specific emotional temperaments on health outcomes. At 15 months of age, animals were placed in a restraint tube for 30 minutes. Repeated blood samples were drawn to determine corticosteroid levels at baseline and 30, 60, 90, and 150 minutes following the rat's release from the tube.

Examination of the tissue took place following each rat's death, and the rats' mammary tumors were excised and assessed. Additionally, the rats' brains were examined for the presence of pituitary tumors.

Did the results suggest that the rats' internal emotional context, that is, emotional temperament, influenced their health status? As shown in Context Matters Figure 10.1, the neophobic rats with mammary tumors died faster than their neophilic sisters (the same was true of rats with pituitary tumors). Also, neophobic rats developed mammary tumors significantly earlier than the neophilic sisters so that at all ages assessed, the neophobic rats were more likely to die of a mammary tumor. By 390 days of age, 80% of the neophobic rats had developed a detectable mammary tumor compared with only 38% of the neophilic rats. Neophobic rats lived an average of 573 days compared with 850 days for the neophilic rats. The maximum life span for the neophilic rats was 1,126 days, almost a year longer than the maximum life span of 781 days observed for neophobic rats. Further, the neophobic rats secreted lower levels of corticosterone in response to the restraint stress than the neophilic rats did, an effect hypothesized to be caused by the accelerated aging of the ovaries and HPA axis in the neophobic rats.

The results suggest that a shy, neophobic temperament in rats leads to enhanced vulnerability to tumor growth and, consequently, a shorter life span. The corticosterone results also suggest that in acute, short-term stress experiences, a greater corticosterone response was found in the rats with the healthier life outcomes (Cavigelli et al., 2006). Chronic high levels of stress hormones in humans, as discussed earlier in this chapter, are associated with negative health outcomes such as cardiovascular disease. In general, this study suggests that emotional context (e.g., personality or temperament) influences critical health markers throughout a rat's life.

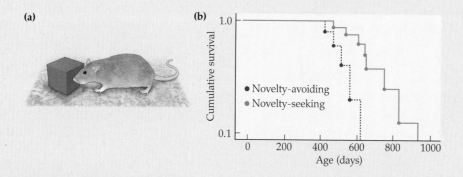

CONTEXT MATTERS FIGURE 10.1 **Temperament and health.** (a) Rats identified as having a bold, uninhibited temperament were more likely to explore unfamiliar objects in their environment. (b) These bold rats developed mammary tumors later and survived for longer than did rats with a more shy, inhibited temperament. Hence, the context of their temperament, sometimes referred to as "personality," influenced their susceptibility to disease.

LABORATORY EXPLORATION

"Laughing" Rats and Positive Emotion Research

Although most investigations of emotional responses in rodents have focused on aversive emotions such as aggression, stress, fear, and anxiety, research suggests that there is a way to systematically generate a positive emotion without the complication of the response being accompanied by food, sex, or social interactions. Jeffrey Burgdorf and Jaak Panksepp (2001) have provided convincing evidence that tickling rats on their bellies generates positive emotions. With a methodology that generates a positive emotion, various research questions can be answered about the neurobiological impact of positive emotions and may extend to human emotions (Frederickson, 1998). For example, do positive emotions strengthen the immune system in its battle against potentially toxic pathogens and diseases?

According to Burgdorf and Panksepp (2001), tickling refers to a vigorous whole-body play simulation that includes repeatedly "pinning" the animal as observed in natural rat play. Once a rat is placed in a cage or aquarium, the experimenter places one hand next to the animal and uses rapid finger and hand movements to tickle it. To avoid threatening the animal, the experimenter applies light touches to the rat's back. A nearby ultrasonic detector allows the experimenter to hear the rats' ultrasonic vocalizations and determine their quantity, duration,

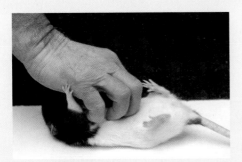

LABORATORY EXPLORATION FIGURE 10.1 Tickling and positive emotions. Rats that are tickled by the human hand emit vocalizations that are assessed by an ultrasonic detector. These chirplike vocalizations are consistent with the sounds emitted by rats engaged in other positive experiences such as rough-and-tumble play. After just five days of these tickling bouts, the rats showed increased production of new neurons (neurogenesis) in the hippocampus.

and quality. As seen in Laboratory Exploration Figure 10.1, if rats are tickled, they emit 50-kilohertz, specialized chirping vocalizations as they typically do during play with their peers. A group of rats that is lightly petted for a comparable period of time as the tickled rats (e.g., 5–10 minutes per day) serves as a control group for nontickling rat–human hand interaction.

Burgdorf and Panksepp report several lines of evidence suggesting that this specialized chirping, a response they refer to as "laughing," is a positive emotional response. For example, rats emit a similar vocalization during other positive responses such as eating and sexual behavior. Compared with social-housed animals, rats that are raised in isolation vocalize more during play sessions, perhaps because they have far less opportunity for play than social-housed animals. Further, rats have been shown to press a lever for tickle time with the experimenter's hand (Burgdorf & Panksepp, 2001). Research suggests that opioid receptors are involved in the neurochemistry of these vocalization responses. When rats were given naloxone, an opioid receptor antagonist, vocalizations were reduced in rats housed alone—an interesting finding considering that opioids are involved in both reward and pain functions. As rats were repeatedly exposed to the tickling regime, they approached the experimenter's hand more quickly, indicating a building motivation to interact with the experimenter's hand (Burgdorf & Panksepp, 2001).

The development of a technique such as the tickling protocol to assess positive emotions in rodents offers an opportunity to determine the impact of such responses on building resilience against an animal's susceptibility to negative emotions such as the expression of symptoms typically considered in rodent models of depression. German neuroscientists found that rats that emitted laughter chirps more often had more proliferation of hippocampal neurons than rats that emitted fear-related vocalizations more often. Such findings may be extremely informative for mental health investigations, considering that decreased hippocampal cell proliferation rates have been associated with susceptibility to depressive symptoms in rats (Wohr et al., 2009). Further, another study reported that tickling also enhanced hippocampal cell proliferation, providing additional support that experiencing positive emotions may be related to mental health resilience (Yamamuro et al., 2010).

Conclusion

Although the concept of emotions is difficult to capture with an objective, clear-cut definition, an abundance of informative research findings exists on the topic. The sympathetic nervous system and HPA axis work in a complementary fashion to provide the neurochemical and neurophysiological fuel for emotional responses. The brain adds the defining context, as described in the two-factor theory of emotion, to determine the final emotional expression. The resulting emotional response is often accompanied by facial expressions and other defining body gestures, conveying relevant emotional messages ranging from threat to joy.

Many of the brain areas implicated in the classically viewed limbic system are involved in aggression. Relevant information is directed to various nuclei of the hypothalamus, and areas including the medial preoptic area, lateral septum, and BNST are activated in reactive-impulsive aggression. Although testosterone is represented in these brain areas, research suggests that specific levels of testosterone do not account for individual differences in aggression. If aggression ensues and an animal is defeated, this event has significant physiological results. Defeated male hamsters exhibit a conditioned defeat response for up to a month.

As observed in the conditioned fear response, the brain has evolved a shortcut circuit to the amygdala to ensure an immediate response to various threats. Cortical areas such as the insula, anterior cingulate, and PFC are involved in less impulsive responses to threatening situations, such as exhibiting courage in the face of fear. As aversive as fear is to most individuals, this response plays a critical role in survival. Further, understanding more about conditioned fear responses and neural pathways to courage may lead to evidence-based therapies for anxiety and fear-related disorders such as PTSD and phobias.

In short durations, the acute stress response is critical for survival because it mobilizes the body and brain's resources to survive an impending challenge. Chronic stress, in contrast, diminishes one's ability to survive a threat. Various effective coping strategies, however, can enhance resilience. Both active/bold and variable coping strategies are associated with resilience markers such as NPY and DHEA, as well as longevity. In human studies, the use of strategies such as cognitive reappraisal is associated with improved emotional resilience and mental health. Thus, to maintain optimal physical and mental health, it is important to monitor both external and internal stressful contexts (McEwen, 2008).

Heightened corticosteroid levels are thought to mediate immune functions by redistributing immune cells to the body's immunological battle stations such as the bone marrow, thymus, and skin. The cross-talk between the immune system and the nervous system emphasizes the significant influence of stressors on health outcomes. Prolonged stress often leads to immunosuppression. In perhaps the most extreme example of emotion-related health outcomes, individuals have been reported to die as a result of believing that a deadly curse had been cast on them, providing at least one possible validation of the phrase *scared to death*. The voodoo death phenomenon, in which a person's beliefs and perceptions about certain life encounters may determine the difference between life and death, also provides evidence of the importance of cognitive reappraisal in emotional responses.

KEY TERMS

voodoo death (p. 281)
adrenalectomy (p. 282)
vagal tone (p. 282)

Biopsychological Perspectives of Emotional Expression

emotions (p. 282)
facial microexpressions (p. 283)
James–Lange theory of emotion (p. 285)
Cannon–Bard theory of emotion (p. 285)
sham rage (p. 285)
affective neuroscience (p. 285)
Schachter–Singer theory of emotion (p. 286)
two-factor theory (p. 286)
cingulum (p. 287)

fornix (p. 287)
mammillary bodies (p. 287)
Papez's circuit (p. 287)
cingulate cortex (p. 287)
Klüver–Bucy syndrome (p. 287)
attentional blink (p. 288)
anterior cingulate cortex (p. 288)
anterior insular cortex (p. 288)

The Neurobiology of Aggression and Fear

reactive-impulsive aggression (p. 289)
controlled-instrumental aggression (p. 289)
lateral septum (p. 289)
bed nucleus of the stria terminalis (BNST) (p. 289)

medial preoptic area of the hypothalamus (p. 289)
periaqueductal gray (p. 289)
dominance hierarchies (p. 291)
submission (p. 291)
conditioned defeat (p. 292)
lateral amygdala (p. 294)
central amygdala (p. 294)
phobias (p. 295)
Williams Syndrome (p. 296)

Emotional Regulation

dehydroepiandrosterone (DHEA) (p. 298)
resilience (p. 299)
neuropeptide Y (NPY) (p. 299)
anxiolytic (p. 299)

REVIEW QUESTIONS

1. Name three major theories of emotion and describe their key assertions. What are some key similarities and differences among the theories?

2. What are the components of the limbic system, and what is its function?

3. What are the major neurochemicals associated with aggression? Describe some limitations in the research on the role of these neurochemicals in aggression.

4. Describe the role of the amygdala in aggression and fear responses.

5. Identify the most important neurochemicals in the stress response and explain how they work.

6. How does emotional regulation differ from the classic stress response?

7. Explain the key neurobiological findings related to emotional resilience. What does research indicate about the relationship between emotional resilience and physical health?

CRITICAL-THINKING QUESTIONS

1. Discuss the pros and cons of research identifying facial-expression cues that a person is lying. How might such research be continued and expanded? What consequences might it lead to? Explain.

2. How might neurobiologists go about developing a pharmaceutical cure for fear that could be administered to soldiers, firefighters, and others who must conquer the fear response to perform their jobs? Would such a "cure" be a good idea? Why or why not?

3. To increase the level of emotional resilience in a given population, which approach do you think would be more effective: pharmacological therapy or cognitive therapy? How would you go about developing a pharmacological supplement to increase resilience? What would be the key components of cognitive therapy to increase resilience? Explain.

CHAPTER 11

Affiliative and Reproductive Strategies

The Experimental Wedding

When science writer Linda Geddes met the fellow science writer Nic Fleming, it was the beginning of a life-changing neuroendocrine experiment. Their interactions and emotional ties became more serious over time, leading to dating and, finally, a marriage proposal. To celebrate their union, they decided that the ceremony would take place in the beautiful countryside of Devon County in England.

Following a flurry of wedding plans, Linda and Nic's friends and family joined them for their big day (Figure 11A). As Linda anticipated walking down the aisle, she felt a mixture of anxiety and excitement. Wearing a beautiful strapless gown, she proceeded past her guests to join her fiancé, who wore a tux with tails. This emotional day was filled with endless traditions and rituals to mark each stage of the wedding. With their friends and family serving as witnesses, they exchanged their vows and then enjoyed a wonderful reception and dinner in a beautiful country house.

Behind the Scenes

Linda and Nic's wedding appeared to be a very traditional occasion, similar to many such emotional unions that occur each year. Yet, there was more going on at this picturesque

FIGURE 11A Linda Geddes and Nic Fleming on their wedding day. From the outside, Linda and Nic's wedding appeared to be a traditional event.

wedding than met the eye. Being science writers, Linda and Nic wanted to do a little experiment on their wedding day. Having read about the hormone oxytocin's role in love and social bonds, they wondered whether their "love hormones"

309

and those of their guests would increase during the wedding ceremony. They called neuroscientist Paul Zak at Claremont Graduate University and asked whether he would collect blood samples from the couple, family, and friends before and after the wedding ceremony. Zak enthusiastically agreed to participate and instructed Linda to locate a refrigerator and other supplies to process the blood onsite at the wedding. Linda took on the task of convincing their friends and family that it would not be so bad to donate a little blood before and after the "I do's." Linda's childhood friend who was a nurse volunteered to conduct the blood draws, after which the samples were processed and placed on dry ice for the trip back to the United States (Figure 11B).

FIGURE 11.B Drawing blood. The bride Linda, along with other members of the wedding party, had their blood drawn before and after the ceremony to measure levels of the hormone oxytocin.

In addition to oxytocin, a few additional neurochemicals were measured in the blood—vasopressin (implicated in social responses such as jealousy and possessiveness), cortisol, and testosterone. What did the results show? Oxytocin levels in the happy couple and their close relatives showed more of an increase during the ceremony than did those of the other guests. Linda, the bride, had the highest oxytocin levels, with a 28% increase during the ceremony, followed by her mother, the father of the groom, and (finally!) the groom. The groom's brother and two other members of the wedding party experienced an increase in oxytocin levels during the ceremony, but the remaining guests and one bridesmaid experienced decreases in oxytocin levels during the ceremony (Figure 11C).

Zak and the wedding couple predicted that vasopressin would increase in Nic following the ceremony because he might feel possessive of his beautiful new bride. However, Nic's vasopressin levels actually decreased. Not to anyone's surprise, the stress hormone cortisol was high in the bride before the wedding and increased even further in her post-ceremony blood sample. The groom, however, showed a decrease in cortisol immediately following the ceremony. And, whereas it was predicted that Nic's testosterone levels would decrease during this bonding ceremony, his results surprised everyone—his plasma testosterone level doubled during the ceremony. He later declared that his mind was *not* on the upcoming honeymoon, although we suspect otherwise. For now, his testosterone spike will remain a mystery.

Although the heading for this section includes the word "experimental," this is obviously far from a controlled experiment. It is a combination of a case study and field research, but one with real-world value despite the small number of subjects. Obviously, it is difficult to hold a wedding in the laboratory! Endocrinological, or hormonal, measures are traditionally highly variable with prominent individual differences, so more subjects would be required for more reliable results.

Regardless, this was an interesting case to introduce our investigation of the role of oxytocin, vasopressin, and other hormones—including the reproductive hormones testosterone and estrogen—in social relationships. Extensive research has been conducted to identify the important roles that these hormones play in building social bonds. In this chapter, you will read more about the effects of various hormones, especially those involved in affiliative behaviors (behaviors leading to social cohesiveness), such as friendship, and reproductive behaviors, such as sex and parenting. ▶

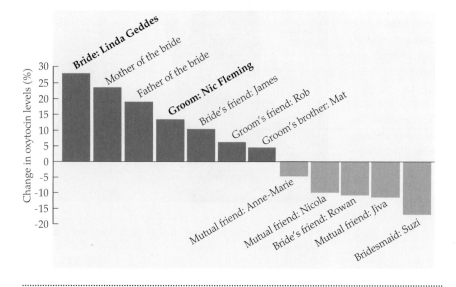

FIGURE 11.C Feeling the love. Oxytocin levels in Linda and Nic, as well as that in their close relatives, showed more of an increase during the ceremony than did those of the other guests.

Hormones and Behavior

The biological mechanisms orchestrating sexual development and behavior remained a mystery until the mid-19th century. At that point, evidence started to emerge that chemicals circulate through our bodies, playing influential roles in the development and expression of various aspects of gender-related behavior. We have learned that it is difficult to overestimate the long- and short-term effects of these chemicals on our bodies and brains.

The Endocrine System

Once the importance of hormones was identified in a general fashion, the details of how such a hormone, or endocrine, system is regulated and maintained were revealed through decades of research. Specific categories of these hormones, with specific origins and targets, regulated by specific feedback systems confirmed the complexity of the endocrine system.

Historical Background of Behavioral Endocrinology. In 1849, the German physician and researcher Arnold Berthold (Figure 11.1) conducted what is known as the first endocrinological research project. Noting that an adult male chicken looked and acted very different from an immature cockerel, Berthold wondered just how the testes contributed to the mature male characteristics (e.g., aggressive behavior and distinct plumage) observed in roosters. To answer his question, Berthold divided his group of six male chickens into three pairs, and he castrated all of them. The first castrated pair received no further "treatment." In the second pair, each chicken had one of its original testicles reimplanted into its body. In the final pair, each chicken received a transplantation of one of the other male's testicles. Berthold made sure the testes that were implanted had no vascular or neural connections. He simply implanted these sex organs into the abdomens of the second and third pairs of chickens.

The first (castration-only) pair remained small, developed no fanciful comb and tail plumage, and were never observed to exhibit sexual advances or aggressive behavior. In contrast, the two pairs receiving the implanted testicles matured into roosters with all the typical behaviors and plumage (see Figure 11.2). Berthold concluded that the testicles were transplantable organs. Because they seemed to function with no nerve supply or physiological connections with the rest of the body, he proposed that they secreted a bloodborne product that was essential for the normal development of male chickens. Because some of the observed effects were behavioral in nature, Berthold's study marked the beginning of research in behavioral endocrinology (Nelson, 1995).

If the notion of transplanting testicles in roosters seems bizarre, what about transplanting another animal's testicles into a human to enhance sexual performance? As described in Pope Brock's book *Charlatan*, "Dr." John R. Brinkley, not

FIGURE 11.1 The endocrine research pioneer, Arnold Berthold (1803–1861). Berthold conducted the first study in behavioral endocrinology.

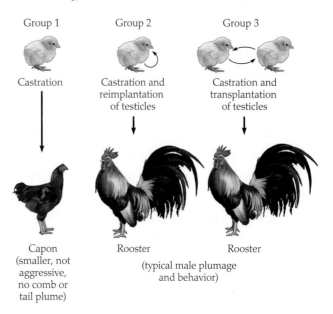

FIGURE 11.2 Castration and hormone replacement. Early endocrinological investigations revealed that the removal of gonads impacted the sexual maturation of roosters; however, replacement of hormones via gonad replacement recovered typical sexual maturation in these animals.

long after setting up a practice in Milford, Kansas, had a visit from a 46-year-old patient, the farmer Bill Stittsworth. The patient complained that he was having problems with sexual performance. Brinkley responded that he had tried various serums with patients who had similar complaints, but that none to date had been successful in improving sexual performance. The story goes that they paused and looked out the window, at which time Stittsworth commented, "Too bad I don't have billy goat nuts" (Brock, 2009, p. 29). There are two accounts of what happened next—one stating that the patient begged Brinkley to transplant the goat testicles into him and the other stating that Brinkley talked him into submitting to the experiment by offering a handsome payment.

Regardless of who initiated this testicle transplant surgery, two nights later, Stittsworth returned to the clinic. Brinkley then transplanted two goat testicles into Stittsworth's scrotum (a different insertion point than used in the roosters). Similar to the rooster transplant experiments, however, no blood or nerve connections were made. After two weeks, the patient returned with a smile on his face, conveying that the transplant was a success. Of course this was not a controlled experimental study, and the placebo effect was probably at work. But Brinkley saw this as an entrepreneurial opportunity—he started advertising this "miraculous" new procedure for improving sexual performance. In the 1920s, Brinkley reported conducting 50 surgeries a month at $750 each, earning a half a million dollars a year (equivalent to approximately $5 million in today's dollars) (see Figure 11.3). As you may surmise, subsequent information about methodological, ethical, and safety aspects (many people died from this procedure) of this testicle transplant surgery later led to the demise of Brinkley's enterprise.

Although few people today would want the reproductive organs—**gonads**—of an animal transplanted into their bodies, a vigorous market exists for treatments that enhance sexual performance. Consider the popularity of Viagra, an impotence treatment in pill form that allows for a greater blood flow into the penis when a man is sexually aroused. One year after Pfizer introduced the drug in 1998, worldwide sales topped $1 billion (Berenson, 2005). Thus, dating back to the 19th century, there has been great interest in understanding how to manipulate reproductive hormones and related physiology to enhance sexual performance. As you will see, it was time to leave the farm animals behind and head back to the laboratory.

A few decades after Brinkley's transplants, U.S. psychologist Frank Beach began delivering behavioral endocrinology lectures at New York University and wrote the definitive textbook that would launch the discipline of behavioral endocrinology, *Hormones and Behavior* (Beach, 1948). Although Berthold and Brinkley's claims about the testes being easily transplantable were a bit naive, Berthold was certainly correct about a blood-borne secretory product being essential for sexual maturation.

Primary Endocrine Glands and Hormones. Today, we know these substances to be **hormones**, chemicals released by special **endocrine glands** (see Figure 11.4) into the bloodstream, where they regulate the activity of certain cells or organs. There are variations, however, in the characteristics of neurochemicals acting as hormones. For example,

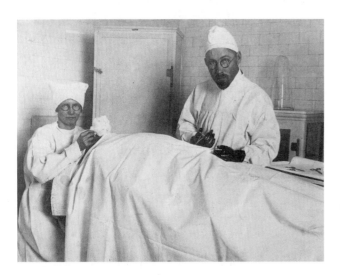

FIGURE 11.3 Gonad transplant surgery. Dr. John Brinkley and his wife prepping a patient for "testicle transplant" surgery.

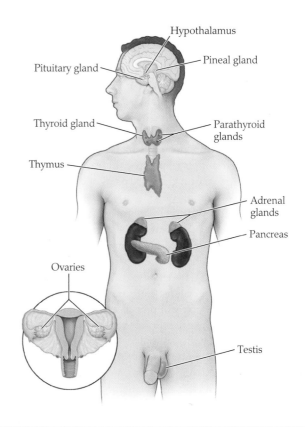

FIGURE 11.4 The endocrine system. The endocrine system consists of several endocrine glands located throughout the body.

oxytocin and **vasopressin**, the neurochemicals assessed in the wedding experiment at the beginning of this chapter, are technically neurohormones because they are released by a neuron instead of an endocrine gland. Once these neuro-hormones are released into the bloodstream, however, they travel to target organs just as other types of hormones do.

See Figure 11.4 and Table 11.1 for various hormones, release sites, and related functions. We will discuss the chemical classes of hormones in this section.

Vertebrates have several variations of hormones that use specific modes of entry into cells. Hormones may be divided into chemical classes.

TABLE 11.1.

Primary Endocrine Glands and Hormones

SITE OF RELEASE	HORMONE	CHEMICAL CLASS	PRIMARY FUNCTION(S) OF HORMONE
Hypothalamus	Corticotropin-releasing hormone	Peptide	Stimulates release of ACTH from anterior pituitary
	Thyrotropin-releasing hormone	Peptide	Regulates release of TSH from anterior pituitary
	Gonadotropin-releasing hormone	Peptide	Stimulates release of LH and FSH from anterior pituitary
	Dopamine	Amine	Inhibits release of prolactin from anterior pituitary
	Growth hormone-releasing hormone	Peptide	Stimulates release of growth hormone from anterior pituitary
	Somatostatin	Peptide	Inhibits release of growth hormone from anterior pituitary
Anterior pituitary	Adrenocorticotropic hormone (ACTH)	Peptide	Stimulates release of cortisol from adrenal cortex
	Prolactin	Protein	Stimulates breast milk production
	Luteinizing hormone (LH)	Protein	Triggers ovulation in females, stimulates progesterone following egg release in females, stimulates production of testosterone in males
	Follicle-stimulating hormone (FSH)	Protein	Promotes estrogen production in females and sperm production in males
	Thyroid-stimulating hormone (TSH)	Protein	Stimulates release of T_3 and T_4 from thyroid gland
	Growth hormone	Protein	Promotes growth
Posterior pituitary	Oxytocin	Peptide	Stimulates labor, promotes milk flow in lactating women, promotes some affiliative and parental behavior
	Vasopressin (antidiuretic hormone)	Peptide	Helps to regulate water balance in the body
Pineal gland	Melatonin	Amine	Influences circadian rhythms
Thyroid gland	Triiodothyronine (T_3)	Amine	Increases metabolic rate, regulates growth
	Thyroxine (T_4)	Amine	Increases metabolic rate, regulates growth
	Calcitonin	Peptide	Decreases blood calcium level
Parathyroid gland	Parathyroid hormone	Peptide	Increases blood calcium level
Thymus	Thymosins	Peptide	Support immune function
Adrenal cortex	Aldosterone	Steroid	Promotes long-term stress response: promotes reabsorption of sodium and excretion of potassium
	Cortisol	Steroid	Promotes long-term stress response: increases blood sugar levels, suppresses immune function
Adrenal medulla	Epinephrine	Amine	Promotes short-term stress response
	Norepinephrine	Amine	Promotes short-term stress response
Pancreas	Insulin	Protein	Decreases blood sugar levels
	Glucagon	Protein	Increases blood sugar levels
Ovaries	Estrogens	Steroid	Promotes development of female sexual characteristics
	Progesterone	Steroid	Regulates menstrual cycle
Testicles	Androgens (testosterone)	Steroid	Promotes development of male sexual characteristics

Chemical Classes of Hormones. Based on their chemical structure, hormones may be divided into four classes: steroids, amines, peptides, and proteins.

- *Steroid hormones.* **Steroid hormones**, including the reproductive hormones and stress hormones, are derived from cholesterol and are fat soluble, meaning that they can easily travel across the cell membrane (see Figure 11.5a). Examples include aldosterone, cortisol, and progesterone.
- *Amine hormones.* **Amine hormones** are derived from the amino acid tyrosine. Examples include norepinephrine, epinephrine, melatonin, and the thyroid hormones. Amine hormones cannot easily travel across the cell membrane.
- *Peptide hormones and protein hormones.* **Peptide hormones** consist of chains of amino acids. Peptide hormones that travel to the anterior pituitary from the hypothalamus (for example, CRH) are known as **hypothalamic hormones** or **releasing hormones**. Other peptide hormones include oxytocin, vasopressin, and calcitonin. Peptides with more than 50 amino acids are classified as **protein hormones**. Protein hormones include prolactin,

insulin, **glucagons**, and **luteinizing hormone** (which travels from the anterior pituitary to the gonads to influence hormone release). Like amine hormones, protein hormones cannot travel easily across the cell membrane. Consequently, they depend on activation of a specific receptor in the cell membrane that triggers the activation of additional mechanisms to carry out the protein's function (see Figure 11.5b).

Functional Relationships Between the Hypothalamus and the Pituitary Gland. Oxytocin and vasopressin, the peptide hormones that are eventually released by the posterior pituitary, are initially synthesized by neurons in the paraventricular and supraoptic nuclei of the hypothalamus. These hormones travel through the axons to the terminal endings in the posterior pituitary for storage. Action potentials from these neurons then signal the posterior pituitary to release the peptide hormones at the appropriate time. Unlike the posterior pituitary, the anterior pituitary synthesizes a different set of hormones on its own. Because no axons project from the anterior pituitary to the hypothalamus, the release of these hormones from the anterior pituitary cannot happen via an action potential from the hypothalamus. In fact, the release of the anterior pituitary hormones is triggered by releasing hormones in the hypothalamus. These releasing hormones travel through the **portal system**, a specialized blood system connecting the hypothalamus to the pituitary gland (Nelson, 1995). Figure 11.6 illustrates the hypothalamic–pituitary connections and the role of the hypothalamus in the release of the hormones from the anterior and posterior pituitary.

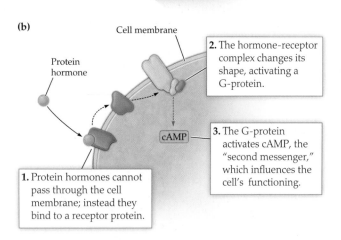

(a)

1. Steroid hormones pass through cell membrane and
2. bind to a receptor protein.
3. Hormone-receptor complex enters the nucleus and stimulates protein production

(b)

1. Protein hormones cannot pass through the cell membrane; instead they bind to a receptor protein.
2. The hormone-receptor complex changes its shape, activating a G-protein.
3. The G-protein activates cAMP, the "second messenger," which influences the cell's functioning.

FIGURE 11.5 Hormones and cellular activation. (a) Steroid hormones are able to travel across the cell membrane before attaching to a receptor protein to activate protein production by the nucleus. (b) However, nonsteroid hormones are dependent on the presence of receptors in the membrane that activate a G-protein and subsequent second messenger system to activate protein production.

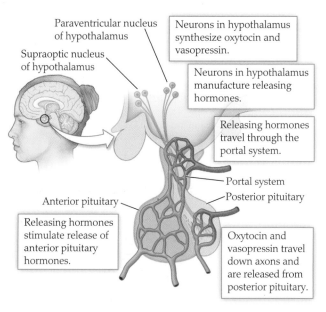

Paraventricular nucleus of hypothalamus

Neurons in hypothalamus synthesize oxytocin and vasopressin.

Supraoptic nucleus of hypothalamus

Neurons in hypothalamus manufacture releasing hormones.

Releasing hormones travel through the portal system.

Portal system
Posterior pituitary

Anterior pituitary

Releasing hormones stimulate release of anterior pituitary hormones.

Oxytocin and vasopressin travel down axons and are released from posterior pituitary.

FIGURE 11.6 The hypothalamic-pituitary system. The hypothalamus influences the release of pituitary hormones in different ways. Specifically, hypothalamic releasing hormones travel through the pituitary blood vessels to stimulate the release of anterior pituitary hormones, whereas axons from the hypothalamus extend to the posterior pituitary, where they release the posterior pituitary hormones.

Organizational and Activational Effects of Hormones During Development

In 1959, the behavioral endocrinological pioneer William C. Young published a landmark study emphasizing the importance of hormone exposure during specific critical periods of prenatal development (Phoenix, Goy, Gerall, & Young, 1959). (Some types of development rely on a certain experience occurring within a **sensitive period**—a certain period of time during which an organism is more susceptible to environmental influences or stimulation than at other times.) Thinking that feminine and masculine behavioral patterns developed in response to hormonal exposure early in development, Young's research team administered testosterone to pregnant guinea pigs during most of their 69-day gestation. Consequently, some of the female offspring were born with ambiguous external genitalia, neither clearly male nor clearly female.

Although the females possessed two ovaries, the researchers referred to these masculinized animals as **hermaphrodites** (a term technically referring to individuals who possess both male and female gonads, but, as in this case, often used for those with ambiguous external genitalia). A more contemporary version of hermaphrodite is **intersex**, a term that refers to any variation from typical XX or XY development (genetically female or male; see the discussion of sex chromosomes in Chapter 1) (Thyen, Richter-Appelt, Wiesemann, Holterhus, & Hiort, 2005). However, females exposed to lower doses of testosterone during prenatal development showed no modifications of the typical female external genitalia.

Considering that Young's research suggested that the female fetus was quite sensitive to exposure to **androgens** (male reproductive hormones) during fetal development, it is interesting to consider that **estrogens** (female reproductive hormones) start out as androgens. In the ovaries of females, the presence of a specific enzyme converts the androgens testosterone and androstenedione to estrogens. This conversion process is called **aromatization** (Nelson, 1995).

The next step for Young's team was to let the guinea pigs mature so their sexual behavior could be assessed. The mature guinea pigs had their gonads surgically removed to eliminate any natural source of reproductive hormones. They were then compared with male guinea pigs who still had their gonads intact. Later, the guinea pigs without gonads were injected with androgens and housed with intact females. The results suggested that androgen injections during prenatal development decreased the females' typical sexual responses and enhanced the likelihood that they would display male-typical sexual behavior when they received androgen injections in adulthood. The male guinea pigs exposed to the androgen injections during prenatal development did not display any modifications to their typical sexual behavior.

Young's profound observations laid the groundwork for a new conceptual framework addressing the role of hormones in development. The prenatal actions of hormones were thought to lead to the *organization*, or long-lasting structural differentiation, of the brain areas involved in sex-typical behavior. By contrast, exposure to hormones during a more mature developmental stage was thought to lead to the *activation* of those brain areas (Nelson, 1995; Phoenix et al., 1959). This revolutionary framework guided thousands of studies that provided unequivocal evidence that the presence of sex hormones early in development influences sexual differentiation of both behavior and reproductive anatomy (Berenbaum & Beltz, 2011). More recent research suggests that the organizational effects of sex hormones on the brain extend beyond the prenatal period, perhaps into adolescence (Sisk & Zehr, 2005). The extended time frame in which reproductive hormones are now known to influence the brain brings into question the more strictly defined aspects of the classic organizational effects of reproductive hormones. Indeed, the brain may never stop exhibiting organizational-like responses to steroid hormones (Arnold & Breedlove, 1985; Wright, Schwarz, Dearn, & McCarthy, 2010).

Recent research suggests that aromatization influences sexual differentiation of the brain by contributing to the production of hormonelike substances known as prostaglandins that influence sex-typical development in rats by producing more masculinized sexual behavior (e.g., mounts, ejaculations) and more dendritic spines on neurons in the medial preoptic nucleus (Amateau & McCarthy, 2002, 2004). The medial preoptic nucleus, known for its role in regulating sexual behavior, is also known as the sexually dimorphic nucleus because of its differential sizes in males and females. Typically, this structure is much larger in males than females, up to eight times larger in rats and about two times larger in human males than females (Hofman & Swaab, 1989; Zhen, Ferguson, Cui, Greenfield, & Paule, 2013). A potential mechanism for this effect is that the prostaglandins influence the glial cells known as microglia (described in Chapter 2 and known for having immune functions in the brain due to their ability to detect neural threats). As shown in Figure 11.7, newborn male rat pups have a different shape of microglial cells in the medial preoptic nucleus than females do; the shape is more compact and dense in males and more diffuse in females (Lenz, Nugent, Haliyur, & McCarthy, 2013). Thus, prostaglandins may influence microglia, thereby providing a mechanism that underlies sexual differentiation in the brain.

In humans, the presence of androgens is thought to be critical for triggering the development of either male or female external genitalia. Typically, the external genitalia will match the genetic sex (XX sex chromosomes for females and XY for males). Without the presence of a Y chromosome, the fetus will develop as a female. Further, the sex-determining region Y gene, SRY, is important for encoding a protein that initiates the male sexual differentiation process

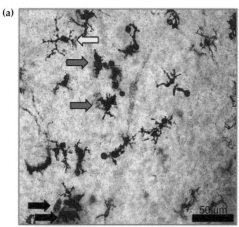

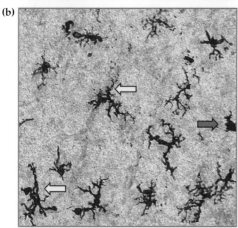

(Cortez et al., 2014). As shown in Figure 11.8, in the womb, both males and females have indistinguishable genitalia until about six weeks of development. At this time, the presence of androgens in males suppresses the **Müllerian ducts** and stimulates the transformation of the **Wolffian ducts** into the male internal genitalia, including the vas deferens, seminal vesicles, and epididymis. On further exposure to androgens, the Wolffian ducts also develop into the external genitalia, including the penis and scrotum. For females, in the absence of androgens, the Wolffian ducts are suppressed and the Müllerian ducts develop into the female internal genitalia, including the uterus, fallopian tubes, and vagina, as well as the external genitalia, including the clitoris and the labia majora and minora (Berenbaum & Beltz, 2011; Nef & Parada, 2000; Nelson, 1995).

Researchers have studied the effects of hormones on development not only by manipulating reproductive hormones in animals, but also by observing humans born with medical conditions that impact endocrine functions. One of the most extensively studied conditions is **congenital adrenal hyperplasia (CAH)**, a genetic condition resulting

in exposure to higher-than-normal levels of androgens during gestation resulting from disrupted cortisol production. This condition is observed in both males and females, but has more of an impact on the developing female fetus. The condition, marked by ambiguous-looking genitalia (as shown in Figure 11.9), is treated at birth with hormone therapy. This practice has also allowed researchers to explore the long-term effects of altered levels of adrenal steroids during the first four weeks of life. Although considerable variability existed, the research on these genetic females throughout childhood, puberty, and adulthood suggests that they engage in more masculine play than control females as children and, as adults, express more interest in male-dominated careers such as airline pilot, construction worker, or engineer (Berenbaum & Hines, 1992; Meyer-Bahlburg, Dolezal, Baker, Ehrhardt, & New, 2006). Additionally, research provides evidence that women with CAH have better spatial abilities than matched control subjects (Hampson, Rovet, & Altmann, 1998). One study that investigated sexual orientation in women with CAH at birth and in women without the condition reported that although most women in both groups were heterosexual, the CAH group showed higher rates of homosexuality and bisexuality (Meyer-Bahlburg, Dolezal, Baker, & New, 2008).

Hormone exposure during puberty also plays a role in sexual development. Some babies born with female external genitalia are actually genetic males with **5-α reductase deficiency.** This genetic condition inhibits the production of an enzyme (5-α reductase) that is necessary for the development of male external genitalia during gestation. At puberty, however, this enzyme is no longer necessary for male sexual development. Consequently, a genetic male that has been raised as a female begins developing male external genitalia and secondary sex characteristics (Ruble, Martin, & Berenbaum, 2006). In fact, in the Dominican Republic, members of a population with increased incidence of 5-α reductase deficiency have regularly adopted a new gender identity when the hormones associated with puberty are released (Berenbaum & Beltz, 2011; Nelson, 1995).

Even when there are no disruptions to hormones and related enzymes, other modifications, such as altered receptor sensitivities to the hormones, may induce variations from traditional developmental trajectories. For example, when a 22-year-old woman visited a gynecology clinic in Romania because of amenorrhea (the absence of menstruation or menstrual periods), an examination revealed that she had breasts and female genitalia, but no underarm or pubic hair. A gynecological evaluation revealed no uterus and a very short vagina. Because of this confusing revelation, the patient was sent to an endocrinologist to assess her hormone levels. A blood test indicated that she had normal levels of progesterone and estrogen; however, her testosterone level was more characteristic of a pubescent boy than of a young adult woman.

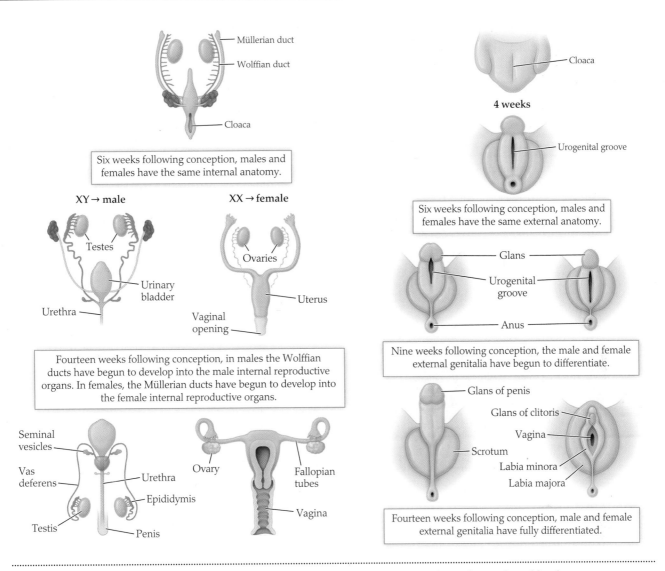

FIGURE 11.8 **Sexual differentiation.** Development and differentiation of reproductive organs and genitalia in males and females.

Genetic screening revealed that, surprisingly, the patient was genetically male, with X and Y chromosomes. In accordance with this discovery, a pelvic CT scan revealed undescended testes in the abdomen. Doctors surgically removed the testicles to prevent future health risks and also because the patient considered herself female. The patient was discharged the day after the operation and referred to the endocrinology clinic for hormone replacement therapy so that she could continue with her identity as a woman. The published case study did not indicate whether the patient was ever told that she was a genetic male: the decision of whether to tell her was left to her family. The patient was diagnosed with **androgen insensitivity syndrome (AIS)**, a disorder characterized by insensitivity to androgens during prenatal development. AIS directs the sexual organization toward the development of a female (Gingu et al., 2014).

Many women who have been diagnosed with AIS are becoming more public about their experiences and the impact of AIS on their lives. The emergence of support groups and blogs has provided an opportunity for them to share information about their personal journeys. For example, Phoebe Hart, who learned of her condition prior to having an orchidectomy (surgical removal of testicles) at age 17, produced a documentary on AIS entitled *Orchids: My Intersex Adventure* (Figure 11.10). In this film and her writings, she was brutally honest about living with AIS. Opting not to have reconstruction surgery, Hart used a special dilating device to enlarge her vagina over time. She pursued heterosexual relationships and, at the age of 28, married her (now) husband, James.

Hart reports that not being able to have children, as well as constantly needing to take hormones following the removal of her testicles, are personal challenges. On the positive side, she credits her acne-free skin, lack of inconveniences associated with monthly menstrual periods, and curvaceous shape to her compromised ability to process

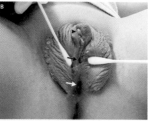

FIGURE 11.9 **Ambiguous genitalia.** Some babies with congenital adrenal hyperplasia have ambiguous genitalia at birth.

FIGURE 11.10 **Phoebe Hart and androgen insensitivity syndrome.** Phoebe Hart has spoken publically about her life as a genetic male with androgen insensitivity syndrome.

testosterone. After informally interviewing others with AIS for her documentary, Hart recommends telling children as early as possible about their condition so that they will understand why their bodies are somewhat different from those of XX females. In her opinion, being able to contact others with similar conditions as early as possible enables young girls to understand and accept the diagnosis (Graham, 2012). Of course, parents should consider recommendations from mental health professionals in making these difficult decisions.

Thus, although the genetic composition of AIS women is quite different from that of XX women, their romantic relationships are similar, in all their varied forms. For example, a recent neuroimaging study provided evidence of the similarities in brain responses between XY AIS and XX women. When these two groups of women were shown sexually arousing images, both groups responded with less amygdala activation than male subjects (Hamann et al., 2014). These results suggest that romantic relationships are influenced by more than sex chromosomes. The neurobiological underpinnings of these complex relationships are discussed in the next section.

The Neurobiology of Relationships

There are various types of affiliative (positive social) relationships, and each is accompanied by neurobiological changes that influence brains in different ways. Although we typically do not think of hormones when we are building trust with another person in an emerging friendship or forming romantic bonds with a partner, endocrine changes certainly play a role in these endeavors. Additionally, positive relationships extend to interspecies bonds, as you have likely observed if you have ever had a family pet. These relationships and their underlying neurobiology are discussed in this section.

Romantic Elixirs

Only 3–5% of mammalian species exhibit monogamy, characterized by the formation of strong pair bonds. Some monogamous species are known as **biparental species** because the males, in addition to the females, participate in raising the young (Kleiman & Malcolm, 1981). One monogamous species that has been studied extensively is the prairie vole, found in the grasslands of the central United States. These bonded couples share a nest and home range and often travel together. Unlike many humans, the prairie voles bond for life; even after one partner dies, the living partner rarely forms a new bond (Getz & Carter, 1996). Both prairie vole parents participate in building a nest, hoarding food, and tending to the pups.

Researchers have conducted considerable research with prairie voles to identify key neurobiological foundations of this bond. Generally, when given a choice between the familiar mate and a new one, the voles choose the familiar mate (Carter, DeVaries, & Getz, 1995; Williams, Catania, & Carter, 1992; see Figure 11.11). As described later, extensive research with this species has implicated the role of the posterior pituitary hormones oxytocin and vasopressin in the formation of these strong social and romantic bonds. By contrast, a closely related species, the montane vole, fails to show such intense social bonds. Consequently, the voles are viewed as a valid animal model for the exploration of neurobiological foundations of affiliative social responses. Extensive research has been conducted on the social bonds between males and females of these species.

For example, in one study, the prairie voles were allowed one hour of cohabitation with an opposite-sex prairie vole. They were then placed in an apparatus in which the prairie vole from cohabitation and a new opposite-sex prairie vole were tethered to different chambers. The test prairie vole could choose to spend time with either one (or neither). Preference is determined when the test prairie vole spends more time with one over the other. Following pretreatment

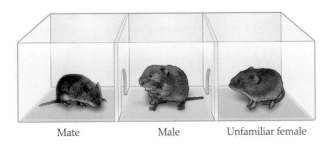

Mate   Male   Unfamiliar female

FIGURE 11.11 Pair-bonding. Following a sexual encounter, male voles were given the choice of spending time in proximity with the familiar female or an unfamiliar female. Whereas prairie vole males spent more time with the familiar female, thus exhibiting evidence of an established social bond, montane voles did not exhibit this preference.

reward. Vasopressin is distributed throughout the limbic system in brain areas including the amygdala, hypothalamus, and septum. Cells containing oxytocin are found in the medial preoptic area of the hypothalamus, in the amygdala, and in the BNST (Z. Wang, Zhou, Hulihan, & Insel, 1996). There are not drastic differences between these systems in monogamous species (such as the prairie vole) and nonmonogamous species (such as the montane vole). However, research focusing on the density of receptors indicates differences between the prairie voles and montane voles.

Prairie voles, for example, have a denser distribution of vasopressin V1a receptors than montane voles do in several brain areas, such as the olfactory bulb and BNST. Montane voles have the densest distribution of V1a receptors in the medial PFC and lateral septum. In the prairie vole, dense V1a receptor labeling was also observed in the ventral pallidum, an area in the basal ganglia implicated in reward systems (Insel, Wang, & Ferris, 1994; Lim et al., 2004; see Figure 11.12). Thus, lifelong pair-bonding is closely associated with the density of vasopressin receptors in the reward areas of the brain.

What about the distribution of oxytocin receptors in the brain? Prairie voles and other monogamous species have higher oxytocin receptor densities in the nucleus accumbens, PFC, and BNST. Nonmonogamous species have higher oxytocin receptor densities in the lateral septum, ventromedial nucleus of the hypothalamus, and amygdala (Insel & Shapiro, 1992; Young, Huot, Nilsen, Wang, & Insel, 1996). These differential receptor distributions are present shortly after birth (Wang, Liu, Young, & Insel 1997). Further, if the animals are genetically altered—for example, if a gene is inserted so that the montane vole expresses more vasopressin receptors in the ventral pallidum than it did

with either vasopressin or oxytocin, both males and females showed an increased preference for the familiar prairie vole compared with the males and females that had received no hormonal manipulation. When these neuropeptide systems were blocked with chemical antagonists, the administration of vasopressin and oxytocin failed to have an effect. Although vasopressin has been generally thought to be more influential in the male brain than in the female brain, these results provided evidence for the importance of both oxytocin and vasopressin in both males and females (Cho, DeVries, Williams, & Carter, 1999).

Recall that the bride in the opening vignette of the chapter experienced higher levels of oxytocin following her wedding ceremony than she had prior to the ceremony, perhaps the most meaningful of human social-bonding rituals. Further research on these hormones has provided additional information about their role in motivation, emotion, and

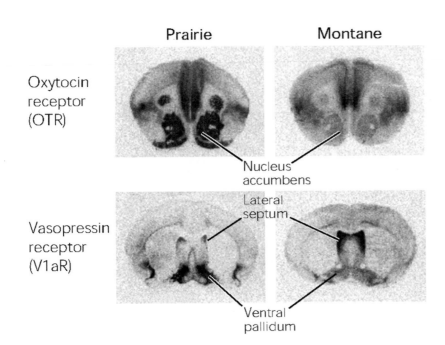

FIGURE 11.12 Social monogamy and social neuropeptides. Oxytocin and vasopressin receptors are distributed differently in the monogamous prairie vole and nonmonogamous montane vole. The darkest areas depict higher densities of receptors.

previously—the vole demonstrates increased partner preference (Young, Liu, & Wang, 2008).

Research with the prairie voles indicates that receptor densities of yet another neurochemical, dopamine, may also facilitate the tendency to form social bonds. Montane voles have more dopamine D_1 receptors than the prairie voles do in the nucleus accumbens and PFC. Prairie voles have more dopamine D_2 receptors in the medial PFC than the montane voles do (Argona, Liu, Curtis, Stephan, & Wang, 2003). As shown in Figure 11.13, when male prairie voles initially contact a female, more D_2 receptor activity is activated in the male's nucleus accumbens, whereas more D_1 receptors are activated once the bond is formed (Edwards & Self, 2006). Further, peripheral administration of a dopamine agonist that increases dopamine activity in the brain also enhances partner preference (Argona et al., 2003; Wang et al., 1999).

All this knowledge about prairie vole pair-bonding may be interesting, but what does it tell us about human social and romantic bonds? According to anthropologist Helen Fisher, the prairie vole story models social attachment more than love. However, it still demonstrates the biochemical mechanisms underlying increased motivation to be with a friend or loved one. In humans, brain-imaging studies indicate that areas of the brain such as the right PFC (which has been implicated in negative emotions) deactivate when a picture of a romantic partner is viewed; further, brain areas rich in vasopressin and oxytocin receptors are activated (Bartels & Zeki, 2004; Fisher, Aron, & Brown, 2006). Providing further evidence that nature has conserved these fundamental ingredients of romance throughout evolution, a recent study indicated a relationship between a specific vasopressin allele and the quality of pair-bonding, or romantic commitment, in humans (Walum et al., 2008).

Oxytocin: The Social Trust Molecule?

Although the hormones vasopressin and oxytocin have been found to play an important role in both rodent and human relationships, a recent trend in the commercial production of oxytocin products may be premature. A quick tour of the Internet yields several oxytocin-containing products, such as nasal spray with the name Liquid Trust, that are marketed to increase "trust" among individuals. The premise of how these products are purported to work is based on research by Paul Zak and his colleagues (who orchestrated the wedding experiment at the beginning of the chapter). This research suggests that oxytocin promotes **prosocial behaviors** such as trust, empathy, and altruism.

Zak and his colleagues have investigated the role of oxytocin in human trust by collecting blood samples in individuals playing what he calls the trust game. As shown in Figure 11.14, two subjects, Subject 1 and Subject 2, participate in this experimental game. Subject 1 is presented with $10 via her computer screen and instructed that any money she sends to Subject 2 (whom she has met, but who is

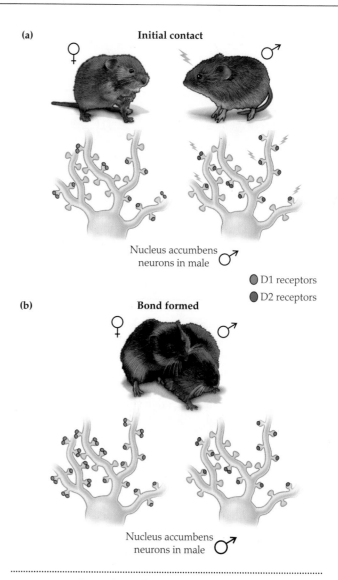

(a)   Initial contact

(b)   Bond formed

Nucleus accumbens neurons in male ♂

● D1 receptors
● D2 receptors

Nucleus accumbens neurons in male ♂

FIGURE 11.13 Dopamine and social bonding. (a) During an initial social contact, more D_2 receptors are activated in the nucleus accumbens of the male vole. Following social bonding (b), increased D_1 receptor activation is apparent.

now in a separate room) will be tripled for Subject 2 before Subject 2 is asked to send money back to Subject 1. If the two subjects cooperate, more money is available for both. According to the researchers, trust is exhibited if Subject 1 sends money to Subject 2, and trustworthiness is exhibited if Subject 2 reciprocates by returning part of the money to Subject 1.

Results indicated that 85% of the individuals in the Subject 1 role sent money to Subject 2, and 98% of individuals in the role of Subject 2 reciprocated by returning money. When individuals in the Subject 2 role received money, they exhibited a rise in oxytocin levels relative to the baseline condition, an increase that was proportional to the amount of money received. By contrast, other control subjects who were merely given money from an unknown source did not exhibit a rise in oxytocin. Finally, the Subject 2 individuals

Step 1: Subject 1 receives $10 and can decide to send some or none of it to Subject 2.

Step 2: Subject 2 gets three times what Subject 1 chose to send. Subject 2 can now send any amount of the money back to Subject 1.

$7

$21

$10

$10

Subject 1

Subject 2

Higher oxytocin levels were correlated with more generous behavior–and profit–on the part of both subjects.

FIGURE 11.14 Oxytocin and trust. Paul Zak's research indicated that the administration of oxytocin nasal spray increased trustworthiness in the trust game.

with the highest oxytocin levels sent the most money back to Subject 1 (Barraza & Zak, 2009; Zak, 2008; Zak, Kurzban, & Matzner, 2004, 2005).

Zak and his colleagues have conducted similar research to assess the effect of oxytocin in a nasal spray form. Results in the trust game suggested that a nasal dose of oxytocin enhanced the cooperative generosity of both Subjects 1 and 2 (based on the amount of money transferred; Kosfeld, Heinrichs, Zak, Fischbacher, & Fehr, 2005). The nasal spray is undergoing clinical trials, so there is no definitive word about its use for individuals who may lack social trust, such as those diagnosed with social anxiety or autism. So, for the time being, be cautious when considering those Internet ads for oxytocin-boosting nasal sprays. With these products, the goal of increasing the trust level of others is controversial. It also presents a logistical problem, considering that most people will not appreciate a stranger coming up and spraying oxytocin up their noses! Suggestions such as spraying papers so that the individuals who handle them will find themselves under the "spell" of oxytocin sound more like movie plots at this point than valid, empirically based manipulations of oxytocin. Before we get too carried away with these scenarios, we should note that Zak has written that most individuals he had sampled were producing adequate and appropriate levels of oxytocin naturally. He has even found correlations between social anxiety and higher levels of oxytocin, which may be an attempt by the brain to counteract the anxiety (Hoge, Pollack, Kaufman, Zak, & Simon, 2008; Zak, 2008). The evidence thus far suggests that we should leave trust to our brain's assessment of our actual surroundings and social interactions, just as our ancestors have always done.

The Pet Factor

If you do not have any close human relationships to boost oxytocin, vasopressin, or dopamine levels, do not worry! A trip to your local dog shelter may be just the right medicine for a little social awkwardness or anxiety (Figure 11.15). It

FIGURE 11.15 Human–pet interactions. Social bonds between pets and humans alter oxytocin levels in a manner similar to that observed between humans with established social bonds.

is estimated that humans and the ancestors of dogs began to interact socially with one another about 11,000–16,000 years ago. The relationship developed because of dogs' tameness and motivation to interact with humans (Coppinger & Schneider, 1995; Freedman et al., 2014). Research indicates that this relationship is so strong that dogs outperform wolves and apes in their understanding of human pointing or gaze cues (Hare, Brown, Williamson, & Tomasello, 2002; Miklosi et al., 2003). In fact, when dogs and wolves are raised in environments with similar exposure to humans, dogs exhibit much more attentiveness toward human gestures. These findings suggest that this predisposition toward attentiveness to humans was not a prevalent trait of wolves and has been acquired through living alongside humans for thousands of years (Udell & Wynne, 2008).

Considering the affiliative nature of these dog–human interactions, researchers wondered whether dog owners' oxytocin levels would increase when their dogs gazed at them during their interactions. To investigate this question, researchers assessed the urinary oxytocin levels of dog owners prior to and following a 30-minute interaction in which one group of owners was allowed to look at their dogs and another group of owners was not. Interestingly, the duration of gaze in the dog owners who were allowed to look at their dogs was positively correlated with the dog owners' urinary oxytocin levels. These data suggest that human–pet interactions alter oxytocin levels in a similar fashion as human–human interactions do (Nagasawa, Kikusui, Onaka, & Ohta, 2009).

Sexual Behavior and Characteristics

The dance that occurs during sexual encounters is complex. Although humans are often preoccupied with sexual behavior, it does not mean that we understand the underlying mechanisms of it. With so many variables involved, once again, it is important to begin with a simpler mammalian model. Rats have been the subject of investigation in numerous behavioral neuroscience laboratories. These studies have revealed valuable information about mammalian sexual behavior.

Rodent Model: Male and Female Sexual Behavior

Rat sexual behavior depends on the female's **estrous cycle**. As illustrated in Figure 11.16, this approximately four-day cycle is characterized by varying levels of reproductive hormones across four stages: proestrus, estrus, metestrus, and diestrus. Although the duration of the human menstrual cycle is longer, the same hormones are involved. High levels of estrogen as the rat enters the estrus phase of the estrous cycle—when the female rat is fertile—are accompanied by an increase in dendritic spine and synapse density in

the hippocampus and other limbic structures (Cooke & Woolley, 2005). Changes in cognitive strategies in learning tasks have also been observed across the estrous cycle. For example, after rats were trained to find food in a specific arm of a T-maze, their ability to switch strategies as different arms were baited with rewards (flexible learning) changed across the estrous cycle (Korol, 2004; Figure 11.17).

The female rat becomes interested in **copulation** (sexual intercourse) during proestrus as it progresses into estrus. Copulation (sexual intercourse) consists of **mounting**, intromission (penetration), and **ejaculation**. When an interested male is placed in the cage with a sexually receptive female and mounts her, the female displays a mating posture known as **lordosis**. During lordosis, she arches her back and holds her tail in a position that facilitates penetration from the male (Jenkins & Becker, 2005).

Although lordosis is considered reflexive, the female plays an active role in the solicitation of the sexual response. In the rat world, flirting, or **proceptive behavior**, consists of hopping and darting around the cage as well as wiggling the ears. Females also play an active role in pacing the timing of the penetrations from the males to maximize the chances of a resulting pregnancy (Erskine, 1989). Males prefer a more rapid pace, however, so there is a bit of conflict as each sex displays slightly different preferences to maximize reproductive fitness (the likelihood of pregnancy and viable offspring).

Regardless of the pace of the events, the sexual encounter generally consists of an initial greet in which the male sniffs the female. If the female is in the appropriate stage of estrus and is receptive, the male will eventually mount the female once she is in the lordosis position (see Figure 11.18). Following eight or more intromissions, the male's intromission is accompanied by a pronounced pelvic thrust signifying an ejaculation. After about a five-minute rest period, the process will begin again if the male is allowed to remain with the female. In this case, the male may ejaculate five or more times (Bermant 1967; Jenkins & Becker, 2005).

Research with the female rats indicates that the VNO detects pheromonal signals, which are subsequently passed through the accessory olfactory bulb to the medial

FIGURE 11.16 The estrous cycle. (a) The rodent estrous cycle occurs over a 4-day period. (b) The human menstrual cycle extends over a 28-day period. Although the durations differ, both species experience systematic fluctuations in estrogen, progesterone, luteinizing hormone, and follicle-stimulating hormone.

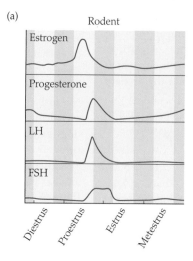
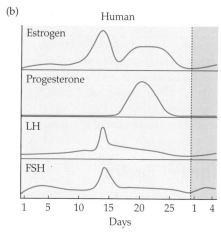
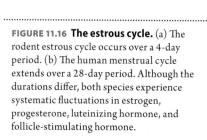

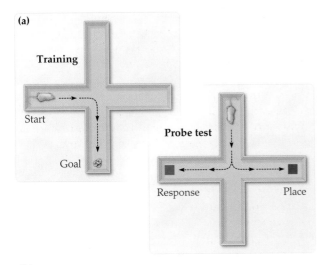

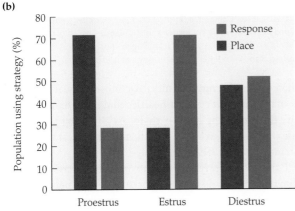

FIGURE 11.17 **Response strategies in female rats during estrous cycle stages.** (a) After being trained to find food at a particular spot, rats were placed into the mirror image of the same maze. Sometimes they went to the spot where the food had been (place preference), and at other times, they followed "directions" (e.g., turn right) that had led to the food during training (response preference). (b) The response strategy changed depending on the stage of the estrous cycle.

amygdala. From the amygdala, afferent projections target the medial preoptic area (MPOA) of the hypothalamus, sometimes incorporating the BNST. The MPOA is specifically involved in proceptive (flirting) responses such as hopping, darting, and ear wiggling to attract the male's attention (Sokolowski & Corbin, 2012). The VMH plays a role in lordosis; for example, when this area is lesioned, lordosis is diminished, whereas the behavior is triggered when the VMH is stimulated, even when no male is present (Pfaff & Sakuma, 1979). Neural control of these reproductive behaviors is also regulated by the periaqueductal gray and lower areas of the spinal cord (Lonstein & Stern, 1998; Pfaff, Schwartz-Giblin, McCarthy, & Kow, 1994). Further, considering that a female rat in estrus will cross an electric grid for a rendezvous with a male, the brain's reward circuitry, including the nucleus accumbens and related areas, is also important for this behavior. In the male, lesions of the MPOA disrupt the male's

copulatory behavior, although they leave his motivation intact. For example, these lesioned rats will still press a bar for access to females. By contrast, if the amygdala is lesioned, the male rat will not exhibit motivation to gain access to a female, but will mate with a receptive female that is present (Everitt, 1990). As observed in the female, pheromones also activate the olfactory system before activating the medial amygdala and BNST, and eventually the MPOA and VMH (Sokolowski & Corbin, 2012). The brain areas that have been implicated in rodent sexual behavior are depicted in Figure 11.18.

Following multiple ejaculations, the male appears to be exhausted and stops pursuing the female. However, if a new female is placed in the cage, he suddenly seems to regain his energy to pursue the new female. This demonstration of increased sexual behavior on the presentation of a new female is known as the Coolidge effect, named, believe it or not, after President Calvin Coolidge (Figure 11.19). Supposedly, the president and his wife were touring a farm in 1924, and for some reason they were assigned to two different tours, with his occurring after hers. When Mrs. Coolidge was on her tour, the level of sexual activity demonstrated by the rooster caught her eye, and she asked the tour guide how often the rooster exhibited such responses. Many times, the guide said. "Tell that to President Coolidge," she told the tour guide. When the tour guide mentioned this to the president during the later tour, President Coolidge asked whether this activity was with the same hen every time. The tour guide replied, "Oh no, Mr. President, a different hen each time." In response, the president recommended sharing that information with Mrs. Coolidge (Dewsbury, 2000). This effect is likely adaptive for nonmonogamous species to enable them to impregnate more females.

Although the Coolidge effect has most often been observed in the laboratory, a recent case of the Coolidge effect occurred at an animal sanctuary in Hatton Country

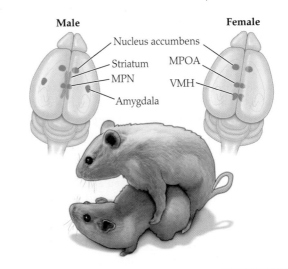

FIGURE 11.18 **Sexual behavior and brain areas.** During copulation, male and female brain activation patterns consist of both similar and different neural areas.

FIGURE 11.19 **The "source" of the Coolidge effect.** President Calvin Coolidge and his wife, Grace, are known in biopsychology texts for their famous farm tour examining fowl sexual behavior.

World in Warwickshire, England, when an unassuming male guinea pig named Randy escaped from his enclosure for one eventful night with 100 female guinea pigs (Figure 11.20; Lockley, 2014). After escaping, Randy mated with 25 of the females over the course of that memorable night before the staff discovered him exhausted and in the company of females the next day. The 100 guinea pig offspring that resulted from that single romantic evening is evidence of the Coolidge effect and its associated heightened motivation to mate with new females after previously reaching sexual satiety with another female.

Although rodent males do not appear to be selective in their potential mates, rodent females are more discriminating. The **multihistocompatibility complex (MHC)** comprises a cluster of genes that encode proteins providing information about the ongoing and potential ability of the immune system to combat a diverse array of pathogenic threats. When given a choice between a male whose MHC closely matches her own and one whose MHC is less like her own, the female rodent typically prefers the body odor of the male whose MHC is less like her own. If a female mates with a male hosting a more diverse MHC, her offspring will have more ammunition in their immunological arsenal to conquer the many pathogens animals encounter throughout their lives (Potts, Manning, & Wakeland, 1991). The immune system plays an additional role in the choice of mates of monogamous animals, such as the prairie vole.

FIGURE 11.20 **Guinea pig harem.** A guinea pig named Randy, from Warwickshire, England, exhibited the Coolidge effect when he escaped into the female enclosure and copulated with all of the females over the course of four weeks, resulting in approximately 180 offspring! Randy is shown here with some of his female partners.

When given the opportunity to choose between a potential mate with a fever or a healthy male, the female spends more time with the healthy male. As a lifelong partner, the male with the clean bill of health is the soundest investment (Klein & Nelson, 1999).

Extensive research has been conducted on rodent sexual behavior. Although many aspects of sexual behavior have been conserved through evolution, researchers must proceed with caution when generalizing to humans. Even so, similarities in the fundamental mechanisms of sexual motivation have been observed in rodents and humans. For example, although humans are not consciously aware of this process, there is also evidence that human females prefer the scents of strangers to those of family members. Of course, a stranger's MHC will be more different from that of the woman than will the MHC of one of her relatives. Scientists assessed this preference by having males wear the same t-shirt for a few days without showering. In a blind test between the smelly t-shirts, those of strangers were the most preferred (Chaix, Cao, and Donnelly, 2008).

Sex Differences and the Brain

Because of the obvious differences in sexual behaviors expressed by males and females, researchers initially proposed that the differences in the brains of males and females were found in the hypothalamus, the area most involved with sexual behavior (Levine, 1966). However, as we will discuss, more recent studies have observed differences between men and women (sex-dependent differences) in brain areas beyond the hypothalamus (Cahill, 2006).

The hippocampus contains many receptors for reproductive hormones. Rodent research reveals sex differences both in the hippocampus and in behaviors that depend on the hippocampus, including those related to spatial abilities. Although spatial abilities may seem unrelated to reproductive behavior, animals must find each other prior to sexual behavior, and parents must know the terrain to locate the appropriate resources for their offspring. Sections of the hippocampus in the male rat have a larger volume and greater density of neurons than in the female rat (Madeira & Lieberman, 1995). However, in humans, neuroimaging studies have shown that the hippocampus is larger in women than in men, in proportion to the total size of the cerebrum (Goldstein et al., 2001).

Neurochemical differences between the male and female brain have also been reported. For example, the sensitivity of glucocorticoid receptors in female rats is twice that of male rats (Turner & Weaver, 1985). Additionally, the mean rate of baseline serotonin synthesis has been observed to be 52% higher in healthy men than in healthy women (Nishizawa et al., 1997; see Figure 11.21). Considering that both glucocorticoids and serotonin have been implicated in depression, these characteristics may contribute to the higher rates of depression in women than in men.

Because the hippocampus plays an important role in learning, many researchers have assessed sex differences in various forms of learning. Shors and colleagues observed different learning effects in male and female rats exposed to stressful conditions, such as electrical shocks to the tail, prior to the learning task. After finding evidence that the stressful experiences increased the number of dendritic spines in males but decreased the number of dendritic spines in females, they found evidence that stress enhanced learning in a conditioning task in males but impaired learning in females. This finding has also been reported in human studies (Jackson, Payne, Nadel, & Jacobs, 2005; Shors, 2002).

The amygdala, another limbic structure, also shows extreme sexual differentiation. After adjusting for overall brain size, the amygdala is significantly larger in men than in women (Shors, 2002). Extensive research has confirmed the amygdala's role in emotional memories, but its specific function appears to depend on sex-related differences. In one study, the left amygdala was more involved in emotional memories in women, whereas the right amygdala was more involved in emotional memories in men (Cahill, 2000). Support for this sex-based difference comes from one rodent study in which stimulation of the right amygdala impaired memory formation in male rats, but stimulation of the left amygdala did not (Lalumiere & McGaugh, 2005).

In another study of humans, even when subjects were asked to simply rest with their eyes closed, PET scans indicated a striking difference in blood flow in the two sexes. In men, the level of activity observed in the right amygdala correlated with that in other brain areas. By contrast, in women, the level of activity in the *left* amygdala more accurately reflected the level of overall brain activity. Thus, under both baseline and emotion-based conditions, the brain seems to be more influenced by left amygdala activation in women and right amygdala activation in men (Cahill et al., 2001; Cahill, Uncapher, Kilpatrick, Alkire, & Turner, 2004; Canli, Desmond, Zhao, & Gabrieli, 2002; Lalumiere & McGaugh, 2005).

Such brain differences between males and females help us to understand the biological underpinnings of differences in male and female behavior. Although the brain areas and behaviors are diverse, each can contribute to the sex-based differences in reproductive and other sex-typical responses. Later in the chapter, we will examine parenting responses and see that although males and females have the same goal of raising healthy offspring, they accomplish this goal very differently. Brain differences between males and females likely influence the reproductive strategies related to sex and parenting.

Sexual Orientation and Transsexualism

A controversial topic in behavioral neuroscience is the notion of neurobiological mechanisms underlying sexual orientation. An interesting line of rodent research in the 1970s drew parallels between prenatal stress and sexual orientation. Male rats whose mothers were exposed to stress

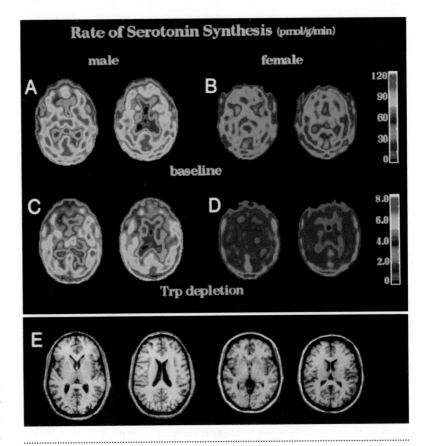

FIGURE 11.21 Sex differences and serotonin synthesis. The bright colors in these positron emission tomography scans depict higher rates of serotonin synthesis in males than in females.

during their pregnancy (i.e., by being restrained in a Plexiglas chamber for several hours each day) exhibited diminished masculine copulatory behavior. More recent research has provided evidence that, although prenatal stress demasculinizes rats (e.g., those rats perform fewer mounts and intromissions than do control rats), it does not make them more likely to approach male rats (as females do). Further, when the prenatally stressed male rats who failed to copulate with females encountered a male rat, no changes in nucleus accumbens dopamine activity were observed, suggesting that they had a lack of motivation to approach these males (C. T. Wang et al., 2006).

In 1990, Dick Swaab's research team at the Netherlands Institute for Neuroscience published the first evidence of human brain differences related to sexual orientation. The team reported that the suprachiasmatic nucleus, located in the hypothalamus, was two times larger in homosexual men than in heterosexual men (Swaab & Hofman, 1990). When this structure was pharmacologically altered in rats, the rats exhibited bisexual behavior and increased numbers of vasopressin-containing neurons in the suprachiasmatic nucleus (Swaab, Slob, Houtsmuller, Brand, & Zhou, 1995).

Also in the early 1990s, neuroscientist Simon LeVay reported that a particular nucleus in the anterior hypothalamus (INAH-3) was smaller in both homosexual men and heterosexual women compared with heterosexual men (LeVay, 1991). Additionally, researchers found that the anterior commissure was smaller in heterosexual men than in homosexual men. Further, the size of this structure in homosexual men was closer to the size of that in women. This brain structure, larger in women than in men, provides important connections between the right and left temporal cortices. It has been implicated in sex differences observed in language and other cognitive abilities, such as enhanced word fluency in females and spatial abilities in males (Mann, Sasanuma, Sakuma, & Masaki, 1990).

Despite the media attention over these earlier human studies, the methodology of these studies has been criticized for small sample sizes and its focus on autopsied brains with various diseases such as acquired immunodeficiency syndrome (AIDS). Additionally, the absence of studies replicating the initial findings, as well as the dependence on self-report for sexual practices, are considered weaknesses of these studies (Mbugua, 2003).

Brain imaging studies have provided a valuable research tool for investigating neurobiological correlates of sexual orientation in humans. These findings, although interesting, are far from conclusive. In a recent study, researchers used structural MRI to assess the volume of the cerebral and cerebellar hemispheres in living heterosexual and homosexual men and women. Additionally, they took PET measurements for a subset of the subjects so that functional connections in the form of simultaneous activation of targeted brain areas between the right and left amygdalae could be determined. The amygdala was of interest because of the previously mentioned research indicating sex differences in amygdala lateralization when emotional memories are processed; specifically, more of a left-side amygdala activation was observed in women and a right-side amygdala activation in men (Canli et al., 2002; Hamann & Canli, 2004).

Interestingly, heterosexual men and homosexual women exhibited a right-biased cerebral asymmetry (that is, the right cerebrum volume was larger than the left). However, no asymmetries were observed in the homosexual men and heterosexual women. Regarding amygdala connections to other brain areas (e.g., basal ganglia, anterior cingulate, prefrontal cortex), the projections were more widespread in the left amygdala of heterosexual women and homosexual men, whereas the connections were more widespread from the right amygdala of homosexual women and heterosexual men.

Finally, in both homosexual men and heterosexual women, prominent connections between the contralateral amygdala and the anterior cingulate were observed, whereas in heterosexual men and homosexual women, the contralateral amygdala exhibited connections with the caudate, putamen, and PFC (Savic & Lindstrom, 2008).

Although the findings varied, there were similarities between the brains of homosexual men and heterosexual women, as well as between those of homosexual women and heterosexual men. More specifically, both cerebral volume and responses to emotional stimuli were identified as two relevant factors that are similar in individuals attracted to males and individuals attracted to females. However, more research is necessary to identify the underlying causes and effects of these neuroanatomical similarities.

Research on the impact of neurochemicals on sexual orientation has suggested that in both male mice and humans, serotonin is important in various sexual behaviors such as ejaculation and orgasm (Hull & Dominguez, 2007; Hull, Muschamp & Sato, 2004). Researchers explored these findings further by assessing sexual preference in male "knockout" mice in which the researchers had inactivated the gene for tryptophan hydroxylase 2 (TPH2), an enzyme necessary for the synthesis of serotonin in the brain. When allowed to select between male and female partners, the normal ("wild-type") version of these male mice (with the gene for TPH2 intact) exhibited a clear preference for female mice over male mice. By contrast, the male knockout mice lacking serotonin did not show this preference. However, if the male knockout mice received an injection of 5-hydroxytryptophan (which was converted into serotonin), within just 35 minutes these mice preferred females at the same rate as the normal version of the mice. Although it is difficult to rule out all the potential influential factors when assessing knockout mice, this study emphasizes the potentially important role of serotonergic processing in sexual preferences (Liu et al., 2011).

Regardless of an individual's sexual orientation, do **transsexuals**, individuals who transition from the sex that was assigned at their birth to live as the other sex, have brains that differ from those of nontranssexuals? Researchers have used DTI to investigate this question.

As we saw in Chapter 1, DTI is a type of specialized magnetic resonance imaging that monitors the diffusion of molecules such as water throughout the fibers of the brain, revealing a vivid image of the white matter of the brain. DTI showed that individuals transitioning from female to male (female-to-male transsexuals) differed in several brain areas from control heterosexual females but not from control heterosexual males (who were not transitioning their gender; Rametti et al., 2011a). Specifically, the female-to-male transsexuals differed from both control males and females in the white matter in the following areas: **superior longitudinal fasciculus** (cluster of neurons connecting the anterior and posterior regions of the cerebrum in each hemisphere), right forceps minor (connects medial and lateral areas of the frontal lobes), and the right corticospinal tract.

As shown in Figure 11.22, the white matter density values for heterosexual males were higher than for heterosexual females and, in these specific areas, the female-to-male transsexual subjects fell between these two groups. Results from an additional study focusing on male-to-female transsexuals indicated that the white matter had intermediate measurements between control male and female values in the same areas as the previous study, with the addition of the right anterior cingulum (Rametti et al., 2011b). These studies provide evidence that differences in brain structure are associated with differences in gender identity. Does brain structure influence gender identity or vice versa? Alternatively, do brain structure and gender identity jointly influence each other? These challenging questions remain unanswered.

Although the results described above are intriguing, another study failed to show differences in gray or white matter volumes between heterosexual males and male-to-female transsexuals (Savic & Arver, 2011). The research literature is still mixed in this area, likely because of the vastly different experiences of subjects within each subject group. Some male-to-female transsexuals, for example, are sexually attracted to males, whereas others are attracted to females. The medical treatment for individuals seeking sex reassignment (including psychological assessment and counseling, hormone treatment, and surgery) also significantly impacts the brain baseline and response patterns.

The fact that individuals can transition from one gender to another provides evidence that gender identity may be less fixed and more flexible than once thought. A recent animal study supports this notion as well. When the naturally occurring enzyme DNA methyltransferase was suppressed in the brains of newborn female rats (that had already gone through the critical phase of fetal development for genital masculinization), their brains took on the characteristics of male brains. Specifically, their MPOA was masculinized, and they exhibited masculine sexual behavior. Although their bodies still looked female, the rats behaved like males (Nugent et al., 2015).

In one of the most public transitions from one gender to another, Chastity (now Chaz) Bono, daughter of the 1970s celebrity singing duo Sonny and Cher, decided to record her female-to-male gender transition with a film crew. Chaz also documented his story in a recent memoir, *Transition* (Bono, 2012). Chaz's body had encountered puberty as a female, solidifying the connections between female secondary sex characteristics and female genitalia established during prenatal development. However, the testosterone therapy

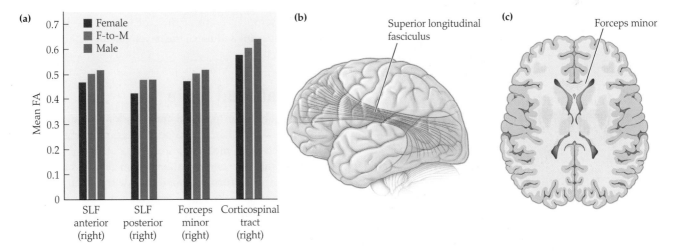

Source: Rametti, G., Carrillo, B., Gomez-Gil, E., Junque, C., Segovia, S., Gomez, A., & Guillamon, A. (2011b). White matter microstructure in female to male transsexuals before cross-sex hormonal treatment. A diffusion tensor imaging study. *Journal of Psychiatric Research, 45,* 199-204.

FIGURE 11.22 Brain involvement in transsexuals. (a) White matter structures in female-to-male transsexuals are more similar to those in heterosexual male brains than those in female brains in several brain areas, including the (b) superior longitudinal fasciculus, forceps minor, and corticospinal tract.

produced what he calls a second puberty, complete with acne, hair growth, and enhanced sex drive. Far from being fixed in the feminine mode, Chaz's body and brain changed in notable ways during the transition into a man (see Figure 11.23). "It's kind of made me sharper, and my thinking more linear, and I'm probably less talkative now and more solution-oriented," he said in a National Public Radio interview (Conan & Bono, 2011). "Before, I had a really difficult time accessing anger as an emotion at all," Bono says. "Now, that's changed, and I had to learn how to deal with that." These gender transition cases indicate the plasticity of variables influencing gender identity, even after critical developmental periods for reproductive maturation.

Although far from conclusive, the research suggests that gender-based neuroanatomical and functional differences are somewhat flexible. Even following the developmental stages of sexual maturation, the administration of hormone and surgical therapies alter gender-specific characteristics (Nugent et al., 2015). Individual human differences may account for two individuals who are genetic males identifying with different sexual orientations or sexual identities. Many gender-based variables that researchers have documented should be considered continuous rather than dichotomous.

FIGURE 11.23 Female-to-male transition. The transition of the female Chastity Bono to the male Chaz Bono was documented in the press and in his memoir.

In other words, there are many shades of gray when it comes to sexual orientation and gender identity. Regardless of one's sexual orientation or gender identity, the arrival of offspring represents a challenge to all parents invested in raising healthy progeny. Consequently, parenting, the final phase of reproduction, is discussed in the next section.

The Neurobiology of Parental Behavior

When I was expecting my first child, I was overwhelmed with anxiety about knowing how to take care of my newborn. The success of the human race confirmed that women were generally pretty good about figuring this out, but my predelivery brain did not seem ready for the impending arrival. To calm my anxiety, I consulted books like *What to Expect When You're Expecting* and took parenting classes at the local hospital. As I was wondering whether my own brain would know how to raise a healthy and happy child, I was a bit envious of my laboratory rats. They appeared to hit the ground running after delivering not 1, but 12–14 pups, providing effective maternal responses immediately after giving birth.

As you will learn in this section, the brains of all mammals undergo critical changes to enable them to care for their offspring—and in some species, behavioral modifications are observed in mammals taking care of young animals that are not their biological offspring. Research suggests that the paternal brain of some species also adapts to the arrival of offspring. It is no surprise that parents have an influence on the developing brain of their offspring. We now know that the offspring influence the development of the parental brain as well.

The Maternal Brain

In writing about the maternal brain, my long-time colleague, the University of Richmond neuroscientist Craig Kinsley, often stated that "mothers are made, not born." What he means is that the mature mammalian female brain does not automatically turn on a maternal switch when offspring arrive. Many neural adjustments take place during pregnancy, the birthing process (**parturition**), and lactation. A female mammal undergoes an extreme brain makeover as she shifts from a focus on her own survival to an investment in the survival of herself plus up to 14 offspring (that is, if you are a rat). Several of the hormones you learned about in this chapter facilitate this transformation.

The behavioral neuroendocrinologist Frank Beach, introduced earlier in the chapter, proposed that the hormones estrogen and progesterone were involved in sex-specific behaviors (behaviors that differ between males and females) such as aggression and sex. Researchers used rodent models to test this hypothesis. The Rutgers University scientists Jay Rosenblatt and Daniel Lehrman conducted research beginning around 1960 that implicated these same hormones in the expression of maternal behavior. The Tufts University neuroscientist Robert Bridges and his colleagues later demonstrated that these hormones, along with **prolactin**, showed differential levels and peaks during pregnancy to prepare the rodent mother to care for her offspring (Bridges, 1990; Bridges, DiBiase, Loundes, & Doherty, 1985; Kinsley & Lambert, 2006). (The hormone prolactin causes milk production during lactation and is also involved in other reproductive functions.) Certain levels of endorphins have been shown to prepare the mother for the pain of delivery as well as for initiating early interactions with the pups (Bridges & Ronshein, 1987).

In addition to altered levels of hormones and neurotransmitters, several specific brain regions have been implicated in a mother rat's care of her offspring. To assess the effects of these hormones, behavioral neuroscientists have identified essential behaviors that compose the maternal response. These behaviors consist of retrieving and grouping the pups into a nest so they can huddle to maintain body temperature, licking the anal–genital areas to stimulate urination and defecation, and crouching over the pups to allow them to nurse (Lambert & Kinsley, 2008). In addition to its role in sexual behavior, the MPOA of the hypothalamus plays a significant role in maternal behavior. If this area is lesioned or chemically deactivated, the mother rat will exhibit diminished or disorganized maternal responses (e.g., the pups may be scattered around the nest instead of grouped together). Further, during pregnancy, neurons in this area increase dramatically in size (Kinsley & Lambert, 2006). Paul MacLean proposed that the thalamus and its connections to the cingulate cortex were important in regulating maternal behavior. Today, we know that damage to the cingulate cortex eliminates maternal behavior in the female rodent (MacLean, 1990).

The production of new neurons (neurogenesis) may also play a role in the onset and maintenance of maternal behavior. Increased rates of neurogenesis have been observed during both pregnancy and lactation in the **subventricular zone** located in the lateral walls of the rat forebrain's lateral ventricles (Shingo et al., 2003). Increased subventricular zone neurogenesis has also been observed in the brains of foster mothers—rats that have been exposed to pups for several days and have expressed maternal behavior despite not having experienced pregnancy (Furuta & Bridges, 2009).

Once the pups are born, hormonal fluctuations, especially in oxytocin, prolactin, and endorphins, continue through lactation. After delivery of the pups, however, the brain becomes less dependent on the hormones and more dependent on the rich and diverse cues produced by the offspring. Rat pups enrich the mother's environment by making sounds when they are hungry; generating smells related to their urine, feces, and other body odors; and providing tactile stimulation when the mother touches them. The Canadian researcher Alison Fleming found that rats would press a bar in an operant chamber (or Skinner box, discussed in Chapter 12) for the reward of a pup (Lee, Clancy, & Fleming, 1999). That is, each time the rat pressed the bar, a pup was delivered to the cage (rather than food being delivered, a more traditional reward in such studies). Further, Rutgers neuroscientist Joan Morrell found that when given a choice between cocaine and pups, young rat mothers would choose their pups over cocaine. However, this maternal bliss did not last forever. Once the pups were about 16 days old, the rat mothers chose the cocaine over their pups (Wansaw, Pereira, & Morrell, 2008). Providing further evidence that pups are rewarding, fMRI data have shown that activity in the dopaminergic mesolimbic system including the nucleus accumbens, implicated in rewarding experiences, increases when the mother placed in the fMRI machine is allowed to nurse her pups (Febo & Ferris, 2008; Ferris et al., 2005).

In one study, brain scans of human mothers who were listening to their babies cry indicated that the MPOA was activated in a similar fashion to that observed in the rat mothers. Additionally, the prefrontal and orbitofrontal cortices, thought to integrate and monitor parental behaviors, were activated (Lorberbaum et al, 1999). In a different study, the nucleus accumbens was found to be activated in human mothers when they gazed at pictures of their children (Bartels & Zeki, 2004). When University of Zurich neuroscientist Erich Seifritz and his colleagues exposed men and women, both parents and nonparents, to audio recordings of infants crying and laughing, the fathers and mothers showed stronger amygdala activation when listening to infant crying, whereas the nonparents (men and women) exhibited stronger amygdala activation when listening to infant laughing (Seifritz et al., 2003). These studies, showing similarities in brain structures involved in maternal behavior in both rodents and humans, suggest that parental responses have been somewhat conserved in the evolution of mammalian species.

In our respective laboratories, Craig Kinsley and I also began to investigate brain and behavior changes that would allow the rat mothers to engage in behaviors, such as enhanced foraging and risk assessment, which, although not typically thought of as maternal behavior, would facilitate the survival of both the mother and the pups. For example, because of the increased energy demands accompanying lactation and tending to pups, a maternal rat must be very efficient with her foraging strategies. She must expend as little energy as possible and quickly return to her nest of vulnerable pups. Accordingly, we have found maternal rats to have better "foraging memory" or spatial memory than nonmothers in a task known as the dry land maze (see Figure 11.24). In this task, after learning that multiple food wells contain a food reward, rats are systematically taught to remember only one baited well throughout training. From various start positions, they are assessed to determine how quickly they return to the baited well. Mother rats perform the best on this task, followed by foster mothers and then virgin rats (rats with no sexual or reproductive experience) (Kinsley

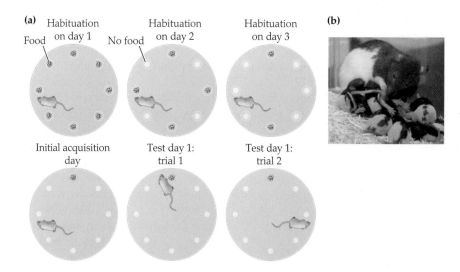

FIGURE 11.24 Maternal behavior and foraging. (a) After being trained to locate food (top row), rats began from different starting positions (bottom row). Maternal rats consistently found the food faster than nonmothers did. (b) A mother rat grooms her pups.

et al., 1999). Thus, as neurobiological changes prepare a female to engage in maternal behavior, certain "off-the-nest" behaviors appear to change to enable her to optimize care for her offspring.

Research indicating that mother rats are "smarter" than virgin rats in specific tasks contrasts with previous work with humans that revealed lower memory scores in pregnant women compared with nonpregnant women (Buckwalter et al., 1999). However, the rat experiment implemented tasks that emphasize behavior occurring in natural environments and that are essential to rat survival (finding food). By contrast, it is not clear that remembering more words in a memory recall test helps a human mother take better care of her offspring. Furthermore, my colleagues and I had tested our rats following pregnancy, after all the maternal-related neural restructuring and redirected energy toward the developing fetus had occurred. It is likely that the brain has to do some neural downsizing during pregnancy to accommodate the shifts in energy to the developing fetus (Lambert & Kinsley, 2008). Additional research with humans suggests that brains shrink during pregnancy and reach their baseline volume following birth (Oatridge et al., 2002). This effect has also been observed in rats, in which the hippocampus volume decreases during pregnancy, whereas the overall cortex volume increases after the rats give birth (Galea et al., 2000; Hamilton, Diamond, Johnson, & Ingham, 1977).

These learning benefits extend to the rat's old age as well. Over the course of two years, we tested the spatial (foraging) memory and anxiety responses of the mother rats every six months, long after they had weaned their pups. We continued to observe more efficient learning in the dry land maze, as well as diminished anxiety in an "elevated plus-maze" (as discussed in Chapter 5, a maze in which rats that venture out to uncovered alleys are considered bolder and less anxious than rats that hide in covered alleys; Love et al., 2005). Another study showed that old mother rats have fewer deposits of the amyloid precursor protein that are characteristic of Alzheimer's disease than do virgin rats of the same age (Gatewood et al., 2005).

How long does the maternal neural footprint remain in human mothers? One study used a version of MRI technology with enhanced sensitivity. Using this technique, known as voxel-based morphometry, on high-resolution MRI, the researchers collected scans of human mothers at two time points: two to four weeks and three to four months postpartum. The researchers observed increased gray matter volume in several areas, including the PFC, midbrain area, and parietal lobes at the second time point. Interestingly, the increases in gray matter volume in the midbrain area were positively correlated with the mothers' positive perceptions of their own babies at two to four weeks postpartum (Kim et al., 2010). Perhaps, as indicated in Figure 11.25, maternal love comes with the extra bonus of a bigger brain! Thus, recent research provides evidence that not only does the mother contribute to the neural health of her offspring, but also the offspring contribute to molding the mother's brain so that she is better prepared to be a successful mother (see Figure 11.26).

The Paternal Brain

I still remember the day one of my behavioral neuroscience students raised her hand after my class tutorial on the plasticity of the maternal brain and asked a simple question: Do fathers' brains change following pregnancy and the subsequent birth of their offspring?

This question presented a methodological challenge from the start. I told my student that to investigate the paternal brain, an animal model that showed paternal behavior had to be identified. The female rats we were currently using in the lab were fabulous mothers, but the fathers directed little to no nurturing attention toward the pups. Paternal animals help the mother care for and raise their offspring. As you learned in this chapter, the prairie vole fits this category—it is a monogamous, biparental species—one of the 3–5% of the mammalian species that exhibit this curious nurturing response.

My colleagues and I focused on another species, the California deer mouse (*Peromyscus californicus*), that exhibits similar paternal responses to those in the prairie voles.

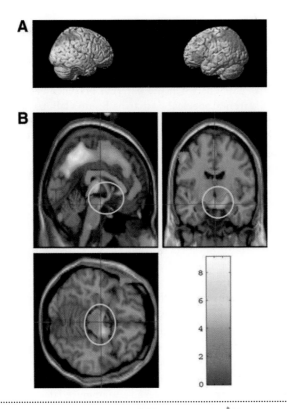

FIGURE 11.25 Changes in gray matter in the maternal human brain. (a) Gray matter volume increased from two to four weeks to three to four months following delivery. (b) The mothers who reported a more positive perception of their babies at the earliest testing period experienced enhanced volume increases in several midbrain areas, including the hypothalamus, substantia nigra, and amygdala.

When observed in the nest with a female and pups, the father California deer mouse is difficult to differentiate from the mother. It is only when the mother positions herself where the pups can be seen to be attached to her nipples that the

identification can be made with certainty. The father retrieves pups, grooms them, and crouches over them just as a nursing mother would. When one compares the California deer mouse with the common deer mouse (*Peromyscus maniculatus*), a nonpaternal species (in which biological fathers do not help raise the offspring) of the same genus, there are vast differences in fathers' responses toward pups. The common deer mouse father does not necessarily hurt his offspring when kept in the same family cage, but he does not help raise them. At times, nonpaternal species exhibit *facultative* paternal responses, meaning that, occasionally, the animals may facilitate the care of offspring. Although these rare paternal efforts provide some assistance to the maternal animals, *obligate* paternal responses such as those provided by the California mice are those that are necessary for the survival of the offspring.

Brain areas known to be involved in maternal responses, such as the MPOA, have been implicated in the paternal responses of the California deer mouse. For example, lesions to the MPOA disrupt paternal responses (Lee & Brown, 2002). Further, oxytocin and vasopressin are involved in paternal responsiveness. Specifically, increased paternal responsiveness is positively correlated with oxytocin and vasopressin levels and activity (Bielsky, Hu, Ren, Terwilliger, & Young, 2005; Gubernick, Winslow, Jensen, Jeanotte, & Bowen, 1995; Parker & Lee; 2001; Z. X. Wang, Ferris, & De Vries, 1994).

In one study, fathers from both the paternal California deer mouse and the nonpaternal common deer mouse species were removed from their offspring for 24 hours and then reunited with them so that experimenters could determine which brain areas were activated in a "family reunion." In this scenario, the nonpaternal deer mice responded to the pups with increased activation in the amygdala, involved in fear processing; the pyriform cortex, involved in olfactory processing; and the anterior cingulate, involved in emotional

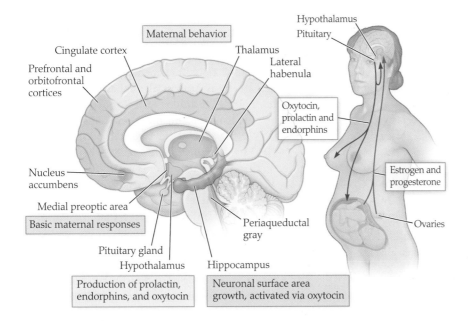

FIGURE 11.26 The maternal brain. The maternal brain requires activation of multiple brain areas to respond to and care for the offspring.

processing. The paternal California deer mice responded to pups with less fear than the nonpaternal deer mice; further, the paternal mice had more hippocampal restructuring in the form of nestin immunoreactivity (Lambert et al., 2011). As Chapter 5 notes, nestin coincides with the restructuring of existing cells in the hippocampus.

Another study of male California deer mice examined biological fathers, foster fathers (with experience around pups, but with no offspring of their own), and virgin fathers to determine whether they showed differences in hippocampal cell proliferation. The pup-exposed males (foster fathers) exhibited more cell proliferation in the hippocampus than did the biological fathers and virgin fathers (Hampton, Franssen, Bardi, & Lambert, 2010; Lambert, 2012). This result suggests that experience with the pups plays a role in preparing the male brain for paternal responses. Perhaps more for the male than for the female, parental responsiveness seems to be more of an acquired trait.

Hormonal changes have also been found to accompany fatherhood in men. In one study, researchers found higher levels of prolactin and cortisol in men just prior to the births of their babies than in control men who were not expectant fathers. Testosterone levels, however, decreased just after birth. Fathers who were more responsive to their infants had higher prolactin levels than the fathers who were less responsive to infant cues. As observed in mice, hormones may also prime the males for fatherhood (Storey, Walsh, Quinton, & Wynne-Edwards, 2000). Thus, the males' exposures to the pregnant female and to the newborn offspring are important factors that appear to mold the paternal brain.

Consequently, "face time" with infants provides opportunities for the neural mechanisms underlying nurturing and caregiving to be tapped and activated for full paternal responsiveness (Hrdy, 2009).

What happens when the paternal presence is removed in the biparental species? Katharina Braun's lab in Germany investigated this question with degus (*Octodon degus*), a South American biparental rodent species characterized by complex family structures with intense interactions among parents, older siblings, and younger pups (Reynolds & Wright, 1979). When degu offspring were deprived of a father, the mothers did not become more attentive to compensate for the father's absence. Three-week-old fatherless degus had lower densities of dendritic spines in certain regions of their orbitofrontal cortex than degus raised with fathers (Figure 11.27). Fathered peers (degus raised with fathers) reached mature spine densities by 21 days after birth. The fatherless degus did catch up with the fathered peers to some degree in spine density, but this did not happen until adulthood. Even as mature adults, the fatherless degus had shorter dendrites and suppressed synapse formation in their cortical neurons compared with fathered peers (Helmeke et al., 2009). The authors conclude that paternal deprivation during infancy results in delayed and impaired development of the orbitofrontal circuits in degus.

These results corroborated previous research with degus indicating delays in the development of neuronal circuits in the somatosensory cortex of fatherless degu pups (Pinkernelle et al., 2009). However, dendrites and spines were not altered throughout the brain; for example, no paternal deprivation effects were observed in the ACC spine density although a lower density of synapses was reported (Ovtscharoff, Helmeke, & Braiun, 2006). How might the results in fatherless degus relate to humans? Troubling statistics suggest that in human societies, children raised in the absence of a father are about four times more likely to suffer from emotional and behavioral problems such as drug or alcohol abuse, below-average academic performance, mental illness, and increased rates of criminal activity (Baskerville, 2002; Franz, Lieberz, Schmitz, & Schepank, 1999; Garfield & Isacco, 2006; O'Neill, 2002). The research conducted with these rodent models suggests that in family structures that have evolved to include two parents, the removal of the opportunity to interact with the father may have some type of long-lasting impact on the offspring.

The anthropologist Barry Hewlett has conducted extensive research on

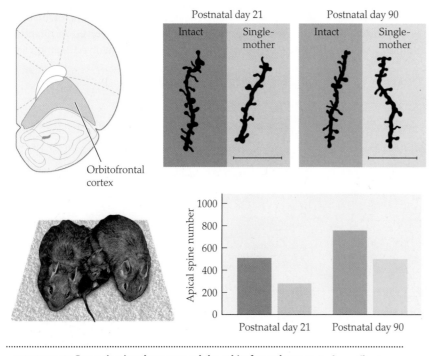

Orbitofrontal cortex

FIGURE 11.27 Parenting involvement and the orbitofrontal cortex. In degu offspring, the orbitofrontal cortex exhibits dramatic effects of not having both parents; for example, apical dendrite spines are diminished at both postnatal days 21 and 90.

the role of paternal behavior in various human cultures. Across the spectrum of cultures, vast differences exist in the contributions of human fathers to parenting. For example, !Kung fathers from the Kalahari Desert region of southern Africa spend only 2% of their time holding their children, whereas in central African nomadic communities such as the Aka (Figure 11.28), fathers spend 47% of their time holding their infants (*The Guardian*, 2005). This is a difference similar to that between common deer mice and California deer mice! The Aka fathers even let hungry children suck their nipples when their mothers are not around to nurse them. Why such diversity when it comes to this trait? How is it that some human fathers contribute a lot and some very little to the raising of offspring? This is likely a result of the persistent help of relatives and friends. As anthropologist Sarah Hrdy has expressed, when the dad is a cad (an inattentive father in this case), his offspring still survive thanks to the help of aunts and grandmothers (Hrdy, 2009).

Alloparenting

Parenting is such a demanding job that the brain goes through several transformations to be able to juggle the new demands of motherhood or fatherhood. The contributions

are worth it, considering the valuable genetic investment each offspring represents—an opportunity to perpetuate the parent's genes through the next generation. But in many species, relatives and even unrelated adults help parents care for their young, a behavior known as **alloparenting**.

Why would an individual who is not a parent invest time and energy toward caring for children? Why expend resources or, in some cases, even provide nourishment to foster the survival of another's genes? Biologists continue to investigate these puzzling questions by studying this behavior among various animal species. As anthropologist Sarah Hrdy conveys in her book *Mothers and Others* (2009), although some equate the nurturing of children other than one's own with the more sophisticated primate brains, alloparenting is observed in a diverse array of species including wolves, meerkats, scrub jays, and paper wasps (see Figure 11.29). More than a century and a half ago, Darwin pondered the question about how such seemingly selfless, or altruistic, behavior evolved.

In some cases, such as the Florida scrub jays, cooperative breeding allows animals to raise young in exposed habitats that would be unsafe if they were trying to raise their young without help. Specifically, in cooperative breeding species, a breeding pair of animals receives assistance in raising their offspring from at least one helper (alloparent). Alloparents' reproductive history and their genetic relatedness to the parents vary and has been the subject of research for biologists. If the alloparents are related to the offspring they are helping to raise, the alloparents gain some evolutionary success by facilitating the survival of an animal that carries shared genes (Bateman, 1948; Hauber & Lacey, 2005). When the parents need to forage, alloparents help guard the nest.

Thus, alloparenting results in many benefits in which the biological mothers ultimately conserve energy, obtain more nourishment, and decrease the vulnerability of their offspring to predation. The benefits also lead to accelerated

FIGURE 11.28 Paternal behavior. Aka men exhibit high rates of paternal contact.

FIGURE 11.29 Alloparenting. Meerkats use the alloparenting strategy to maximize care for offspring.

growth in the physical size of offspring, likely related to increased food availability. Among mammals that practice cooperative breeding, mothers exhibit reduced lactation and shorter intervals between pregnancies. Because the mother does not have to breastfeed the child for as long (because of accelerated growth in the child, as a result of aid in lactation and food provisioning by alloparents), she can become pregnant again more quickly, ultimately producing more offspring over her lifetime. Given the advantages offered by cooperative breeding and alloparenting, it should come as no surprise that, across many species of both birds and mammals, the number of alloparents is positively correlated with the survival of offspring. In fact, according to Hrdy, the human species, with their extremely costly and slowly maturing offspring, might have never evolved without the contributions of paternal and alloparental care.

Tim Clutton-Brock and his Cambridge University team have monitored the cooperative breeding meerkats in South Africa and noted that a single female emerges as the dominant breeder that gives birth to about 80% of the group's offspring. To facilitate this demanding role, the female undergoes a dramatic progesterone- and estrogen-induced transformation into a larger animal with a swollen head. The increase in size allows her to produce more pups and appear more intimidating to smaller subordinates who might otherwise be tempted to focus on breeding their own young (Bergmuller & Taborsky, 2005; Hrdy, 2009).

As we have seen in this section, family structures vary. Although a constant across all families is the maternal commitment, the contributions of fathers, relatives, and nonrelated acquaintances to child-rearing differ widely. Because of the immense evolutionary importance of the survival of offspring, it is likely adaptive to have several game plans, even within a single species, to respond to new and different parenting challenges, should they emerge. Indeed, the role of alloparenting in raising healthy offspring supports the African proverb, *It takes a village to raise a child.*

CONTEXT MATTERS

An Old Bird Learns a New Trick

Featured study: Velando, A., Drummond, H., & Torres, R. (2006). Senescent birds redouble reproductive effort when ill: Confirmation of the terminal investment hypothesis. Proceedings of the Royal Society B, 273, 1443–1448.

The amount of energy directed toward raising offspring is a dynamic and complex issue. Both external and internal contextual factors influence the amount of effort necessary to produce viable offspring without diminishing future reproductive capacity. According to the *terminal investment hypothesis*, however, when an animal nears the end of the reproductive stage of life, the more adaptive option is to invest all available effort to ensure the survival of its last possible offspring.

The scientists Alberto Velando, Hugh Drummond, and Roxanna Torres used an odd bird, the blue-footed booby bird, to test this interesting hypothesis. Like most birds, the booby birds are biparental, spending up to six months with each brood. In these booby birds, the contribution of the males, in the form of incubating the eggs, feeding the chicks, and defending the chicks, is essential for the survival of their offspring. The question of interest in this study was whether the age of a father would affect his parental efforts during illness. Compared with young, sick fathers, would older birds with failing health invest more energy in caring for their current brood, considering that they might not live to see another breeding season?

To test the terminal investment hypothesis, the researchers captured reproductively mature (3–9 years old) and older (more than 10 years old) booby birds on Isla Isabel in Nayarit, Mexico. The researchers randomly assigned each bird to either the experimental or the control group. To determine whether the current energy needs of the parent (e.g., if the parent is healthy or sick) would influence the males' parental investment toward raising their brood, the researchers injected the experimental group with lipopolysaccharide (LPS), molecules from bacteria that trigger an immunological response that results in the animals exhibiting signs of sickness (Context Matters Figure 11.1a). In birds, the sickness response persists for a few days, with the physiological responses ending after about two weeks (Nakamura et al., 1998; Xie, Rath, Huff, Huff, & Balog, 2000). This sickness response prompts most animals to divert resources to meet the immunological demands of sickness (such as the need for increased rest), producing the perception that health is deteriorating (Bonneaud, Mazuc, Chastel, Westerdahl, & Sorci, 2004). In addition to injecting the experimental males with LPS, experimenters gave control males an identical volume injection of the drug vehicle; that is, the inactive substance the drug was mixed in prior to injection.

To assess the success of the parenting efforts directed toward the chicks, the researchers simply monitored the nests daily to assess the survival rates of the chicks. The paternal birds' reproductive success (number of surviving chicks) increased until the tenth year of age and then progressively declined after that. The results also indicated that LPS affected neither the date that they laid their eggs nor their clutch size (Context Matters Figure 11.1b).

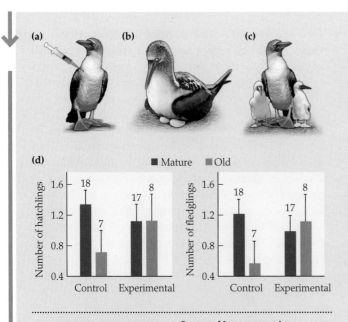

hatchlings than their healthy controls. Thus, the sickness had a negative impact on paternal birds' number of hatchlings. By contrast, the experimental older birds produced not fewer, but 59% more hatchlings (newborns). In this case, the sickness had a positive impact on the birds' number of hatchlings. Beyond hatching, did the paternal birds' parenting success differ? In other words, how successful were the fathers in producing viable fledglings (birds that are beginning to learn to fly and are more mature than the newborn hatchlings)? The younger sick males produced 18% fewer fledglings than their healthy counterparts and, once again, the older sick fathers produced 98% more fledglings than their healthy counterparts (Context Matters Figure 11.1c). In fact, the only group of fathers that successfully raised all the hatchlings to healthy fledglings was the older male group with the immune challenge. At what may be the last opportunity to reproduce, the older males managed to divert sufficient energy to combat the perceived sickness and flawlessly raise their offspring.

Thus, when these researchers merely assessed the effects of aging on paternal success in these birds, it appeared that older dads became increasingly inefficient fathers. But, in this case, the context of the fathers' health status matters when it comes to raising healthy offspring. These older booby birds transitioned into superdads when faced with the challenges of old age and compromised health.

CONTEXT MATTERS FIGURE 11.1 Parental investment in blue-footed booby birds. (a) After old and mature males received an injection that made them feel ill, (b) their paternal behavior was observed. (c and d) During the sickness, mature birds delivered less care to their offspring, whereas old birds increased their care, resulting in increased numbers of hatchlings and fledglings.

The results in the LPS study indicated that the experimental mature (younger) birds of 3–9 years produced 16% fewer

LABORATORY EXPLORATION

Manipulating Hormone Levels in Laboratory Animals with Implantable Delivery Pumps

To determine the effects of hormones on various reproductive behaviors, scientists often remove the natural source of reproductive hormones (ovaries and testicles) and subsequently replace the hormones in a systematic manner to determine the precise role of the targeted hormones. Alternatively, they leave the reproductive organs intact and deliver additional hormones to assess the effects of hormones that are present beyond natural levels.

Although injections can be used to administer hormones, implantable pumps have become increasingly popular because of their continuous infusion flow rates that are more characteristic of the natural delivery of hormones. Further, although surgery is required to implant pumps, animals with implantable pumps are able to remain undisturbed throughout experiments because the hormones are delivered through the pumps. The decreased handling and number of injections

are thought to be less stressful for the animals. Approximately 13,000 published studies confirm that implantable pumps are a popular and reliable delivery system not only for hormones, but also for drugs and other neurochemicals (Tan, Watts, & Davis, 2011).

As shown in Laboratory Exploration Figure 11.1, osmotic pumps contain a targeted amount of hormonal agent in the reservoir of the pump. As fluids are absorbed through the semipermeable membrane in the pump by natural osmotic flow to occupy the impermeable hormone reservoir, the hormonal agent is released in a constant flow through the implanted capsule into the animal's bloodstream. To enable researchers to implant these pumps, animals are anesthetized so that an incision can be made through the skin (in dorsal or ventral areas). Once the pump is implanted, the influence of targeted hormones such as estrogen or testosterone can be determined

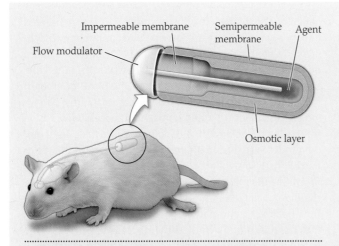

Impermeable membrane   Semipermeable membrane   Agent

Flow modulator

Osmotic layer

LABORATORY EXPLORATION FIGURE 11.1 **Osmotic pumps.** These pumps, designed to mimic physiological delivery of chemical substances over extended periods of time, are used in hormone replacement studies conducted in rodents.

by comparing the hormone group (that received the target hormone) with a control group (that received pump implants filled with inactive saline). These pumps can also be configured so that they deliver the hormone through a catheter (a thin tube) to a specific brain area such as the lateral ventricle so that the hormone can be absorbed throughout the brain.

An example of the influence of hormone delivery via osmotic pumps on rodent behavior is seen in a study that explored the effects of aromatization on sexual behaviors in male rats. When male rats were given a drug known as Fadrozole that inhibits aromatization via traditional daily injections for eight weeks, their sexual behavior (i.e., mounts, intromissions, and ejaculations) decreased. Yet, when estrogen was delivered for four weeks via osmotic pumps placed under the skin of the rats' backs, mounts and intromissions returned to baseline levels (with no effects observed on ejaculations; Roselli, Cross, Poonyagariyagorn, & Stadelman, 2003). This study is just one example of how osmotic pumps can be used to deliver a continuous flow of hormones representative of the natural release patterns of hormones into the body and brain.

Although implanting osmotic pumps in humans is more involved than simply taking a pill or injecting a drug, there are several advantages of this type of delivery system. For example, these pumps deliver the drugs in a more predictable fashion and are less affected by gastrointestinal variables than other drug delivery systems. The osmotic pumps are desirable when a precise amount of drug delivery is required for extended durations; consequently, they have been used for conditions such as hypertension, allergies, and schizophrenia (Gupta, Thakur, Jain, Banweer, & Jain, 2010).

Conclusion

Throughout this chapter we have discussed the many ways reproductive hormones, various neurotransmitters, and neuropeptides contribute to our relationships with friends, romantic partners, children, and pets. Altered patterns of these neurochemicals can also modify gender-related patterns and even secondary sex characteristics. As opportunities emerge for us to form relationships with potential lovers and friends, the brain responds by remaining flexible and exhibiting enhanced neuroplasticity. The transition from focusing solely on oneself to focusing on another likely requires brain plasticity such as increased hippocampal spine density, as well as altered levels of neurochemicals including oxytocin and vasopressin. Thus, parenting responses may have influenced fundamental social behaviors in various species as some animals evolved from solitary species to cohesive family and social units. As animals transition to parental status, the structure of the family unit varies greatly across species (including humans), ranging from stay-at-home fathers to single mothers to cooperative family structures complete with babysitters. Regardless of the species-specific form of reproductive and parenting responses, the goal of these complex behaviors is to successfully raise offspring that mature and, eventually, have their own offspring.

KEY TERMS

Hormones and Behavior

gonads (p. 312)
hormones (p. 312)
endocrine glands (p. 312)
oxytocin (p. 313)
vasopressin (p. 313)
steroid hormones (p. 314)

amine hormones (p. 314)
peptide hormones (p. 314)
hypothalamic hormones (p. 314)
releasing hormones (p. 314)
protein hormones (p. 314)
glucagons (p. 314)
luteinizing hormone (p. 314)

portal system (p. 314)
sensitive period (p. 315)
hermaphrodites (p. 315)
intersex (p. 315)
androgens (p. 315)
estrogens (p. 315)
aromatization (p. 315)

REVIEW QUESTIONS

1. Compare and contrast the role of the hypothalamus in the release of hormones from the anterior pituitary and the posterior pituitary.

2. What did William C. Young's investigations with guinea pigs reveal about the importance of hormone exposure during prenatal development? Explain.

3. What has research with prairie voles suggested about the neurobiological foundations of pair-bonding?

4. What do studies of the vasopressin receptor density in specific brain areas in the prairie vole and montane vole suggest about the role of vasopressin in pair-bonding? Explain.

5. What specific findings did Simon LeVay report in his 1991 study with regard to anatomical brain differences between homosexual men and heterosexual men? What were the limitations of LeVay's study?

6. Describe the experimental evidence that suggests that neurogenesis plays a role in the onset and maintenance of maternal behavior.

7. Which brain regions and hormones seem to play a role in the paternal behavior of the California deer mouse?

CRITICAL-THINKING QUESTIONS

1. What limitations does the model of the prairie vole and montane vole have in its ability to provide insight into the neurobiological basis of affiliative behavior in humans? Explain.

2. As you have learned, oxytocin sprays are undergoing clinical trials of their effectiveness in increasing social trust. Why should researchers and clinicians be cautious about manipulating neurochemicals such as oxytocin without considering the effect of relevant contextual factors?

3. Some human new mothers have difficulty bonding with their newborns, although they want to have a close relationship with their babies. Imagine that you are a psychologist investigating whether this difficulty in bonding has a neurobiological basis. Briefly describe possible neurobiological causes of this difficulty in bonding. What studies would you conduct to test your ideas? Explain.

Learning, Memory, and Decision Making

Clive Wearing's Fleeting Memory

As Deborah Wearing entered the room, her husband Clive ran to her, passionately calling her name and kissing her as soon as they embraced. To a casual onlooker it would have seemed obvious that the couple had been apart from one another for a long time. However, in this case, Deborah had just stepped out of the room momentarily. Each time she entered the room, she would receive Clive's passionate welcome. This bizarre scenario was not surprising to Deborah, at least not at this point. It had characterized each and every reunion with her husband for years.

Clive's unique situation resulted from an illness that had appeared in the spring of 1985, with symptoms that he originally thought nothing of. But when his symptoms persisted—chronic headache, sleepless nights, fever, and mental confusion—Clive's doting wife, Deborah, called the doctor, who suggested that Clive had the flu. Hence, Clive and Deborah did not have any warning that, when Clive woke up on Tuesday, March 26, 1985, his conscious experience would be forever altered. Although Clive retained his fundamental level of intelligence and unimpaired use of his sensory and perceptual systems, each moment of his life was almost completely erased every time he blinked (see Figure 12A).

FIGURE 12A Clive and Deborah Wearing. As the result of a brain injury, every time Clive awakens or even blinks, his memory of his life is nearly erased, except for a subset of his memories that include his love for his wife.

Nine years after the onset of Clive's illness, Deborah walked into his room, and Clive asked her how long he had been ill. When Deborah said that it was nine years, Clive returned with, "Nine years! Good heavens! Nine years. . . . I haven't heard anything, seen anything, felt anything, smelled anything, touched anything. It's been one long night lasting . . . how long?" (Wearing, 2005, p. 333). When Deborah asked him to write how he felt, Clive responded, "I am completely incapable of thinking" (Wearing, 2005, p. 155).

Clive's altered experience is passionately expressed in his daily journal entries. Each time he awoke from a night's sleep, or even blinked, seemed like his first awakening from an endless unconsciousness, and he thought the momentous occasion should be documented. Clive would document the time and then proclaim that he was finally completely awake, often beckoning for his beloved wife to come as quickly as possible. Seeing similar entries in his journal that were written just minutes before his latest profound entry, however, created frustration and angst in Clive. His response was to declare the older journal entries rubbish and to try to add superlatives to each new entry, reporting that it was indeed the first time he had been fully awake or using all capital letters and exclamation points, anything to distinguish the event from the endless similar reports that preceded it.

Behind the Scenes

Once Clive was admitted to the hospital, it was obvious to his doctors that his mental confusion was not a symptom of the flu. Eleven hours following his admission, a diagnosis was presented to Clive and Deborah. It appeared that *encephalitis*, an inflammation of the brain caused by the herpes simplex virus, was the culprit. Brain scans indicated diffuse damage throughout the cortical areas of Clive's brain—the temporal, occipital, parietal, and frontal lobes. More noteworthy to the neurologists, however, was the virus's meticulous and complete destruction of one specific area of Clive's brain, the hippocampus. As you learned in Chapter 2, the hippocampus is involved in learning and memory. Clive's case certainly corroborated past evidence that the hippocampus plays a starring role in the formation of memories.

From a psychological perspective, Clive could no longer establish memories for events such as taking a bite of his favorite food, celebrating a birthday with his family, or spending a day with his wife. Interestingly, in some cases he knew things that he could not specifically remember. For example, he could not remember his wedding, but knew Deborah was his wife; he had no memory of ever conducting a concert, but knew he was a musician. In fact, his **amnesia**, or memory loss, did not affect his ability to, after declaring no memory for a musical score, sit down and play it beautifully on the piano. The survival of a subset of Clive's memories provides evidence for the existence of various types of memory systems that will be discussed throughout this chapter.

Nearly 30 years after Clive's brain injury, his condition has not changed. Deborah regularly visits her husband in an assisted-living facility, experiencing his endless dramatic proclamations of his love for her—perhaps his most enduring memory. They both have accepted that Clive's life consists of instantaneous scenes, a literal translation of "living in the moment." ▶

Consider the picture of the rat playing basketball at the opening of this chapter. It probably comes as no surprise that rats did not evolve to play basketball. Even so, rats trained by behaviorists worldwide are amazing audiences with their athletic prowess. In my hometown, the Science Museum of Virginia declares that the Rat Basketball exhibit is among their all-time most successful exhibits.

The truth is that, although humans evolved abilities that contribute to being a successful basketball player, human athletic performance, similar to rodent athletic performance, is the product of learning, memory, and effective decision making. Apart from our reflexes, most of the behavior we engage in each day is the product of learning and memory. For example, did you drive to class today (Figure 12.1)?

Although drivers do not typically consider their actions impressive, the behavior of driving is extremely complex. It demonstrates how readily behavior can be engineered to manipulate the environment in adaptive ways. Driving enables us to accomplish goals that we perceive as necessary in our daily lives. Being able to alter our responses in changing environments is critical for the survival of our species, as well as most species on the planet. With changing resource availability, environmental threats, and social scenarios, our brains must attend to the most important aspects of the environment, adapt when necessary, commit the adaptations

FIGURE 12.1 Learning to drive. We must learn new responses before being able to drive a car; our ability to learn such complex tasks to achieve everyday goals is dependent on flexible neural networks primed to make real-time adjustments and adaptations.

to memory, and, when faced with inevitable dilemmas in the future, use both memory reserves and predictions of potential future outcomes to find the best solutions. You do all that each time you drive a car, prepare dinner, or update your social media profile. We will return briefly to the driving analogy later in the chapter as we navigate through the fields of learning, memory, and decision making.

Neurobiological Foundations of Learning and Memory Processes

Behavioral modification, or learning, has been extensively investigated on many levels using various animal models ranging from sea snails to humans. This research has identified various types of learning and associated neurobiological mechanisms.

Behavioral Approaches

Going back to the earliest written records, it is clear that mental experiences have dominated the thoughts of intellectuals throughout history. The fundamental components of these experiences, however, took investigators centuries to unravel. In his book *An Essay Concerning Human Understanding* (Locke, 1690), the 17th-century philosopher John Locke suggested that all knowledge developed through our experiences—finding no evidence that we were born with any type of knowledge. Building on the ideas of Aristotle, Locke believed that our minds at birth were a *tabula rasa*, or blank slate (Benjamin, 1993). As we have learned throughout this text, our brains are anything but a blank slate at any point of our existence. However, the notion that experience shapes our knowledge was also very true and worthy of further investigation.

It was not until the early 20th century that the truths of just how experiences shape our mental experiences started to emerge. If you have taken a general psychology course, you are familiar with Ivan Pavlov's discoveries regarding the formation of mental associations between different aspects of our environment (Pavlov, 1906). When his dogs perceived any evidence that food was about to be delivered—hearing the footsteps of workers, seeing the bowl of food, or even hearing that infamous bell—they would start salivating. The association formed between these predictors of food arrival (e.g., the food bowl) and the food itself was the product of a type of learning referred to as *classical conditioning*, or Pavlovian conditioning (Figure 12.2). Although food (the unconditioned stimulus) was previously observed to result in salivation (the unconditioned response), the dog formed associations between the bowl (conditioned stimulus) and the food (unconditioned stimulus) so that, after a while, the dog would salivate in response to just seeing the bowl (the conditioned response).

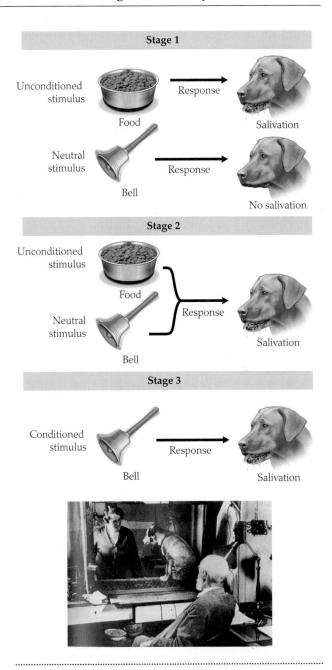

FIGURE 12.2 **Classical conditioning.** (a) Pavlov used dogs to assess saliva production in response to varying stimuli; (b) his classic work pairing conditioned and unconditioned stimuli laid the groundwork for empirical investigations.

Our lives are filled with examples of conditioned responses that occur as reflexively as breathing or blinking. If you see lightening in the sky, for example, you wince as you prepare for the clap of thunder. If you are like me, when you see the blue lights of a police car, your foot moves to the brakes automatically, regardless of your speed. Although covering our ears in the presence of lightening or tapping the brakes when we see blue lights represent acquired associations, the predictive associations among these relevant stimuli are engraved in our memories and response repertoires.

Although Pavlov was a physiologist, not a psychologist, his studies with dogs revolutionized psychological research. For example, in his now famous manifesto, *Psychology as the Behaviorist Views It* (1913), the pioneering American psychologist John B. Watson introduced insights from Pavlov's classical conditioning. Watson proclaimed that Pavlov's research opened the door for psychology, which had previously been viewed as a subjective discipline, to establish itself as an objective laboratory science. A behavioral scientist could count the number of times a conditioned stimulus and unconditioned stimulus were paired, determine the time delay between stimulus presentation and response, and evaluate the intensity of responses by counting the drops or volume of excreted saliva. Psychologists also controlled laboratory protocols, recorded data in journals, plotted graphs, and performed statistical analyses, laying the groundwork for biopsychological research. Behavioral scientists now possessed the necessary tools, although still rather crude, for investigating the neural basis of learning.

Although Pavlov's work was revolutionary, it did not explain how an individual *acquired* a behavior. How does a driver learn to turn the steering wheel, tap the brakes, and push the right buttons while keeping a two- to three-ton machine in the correct lanes of the road? Certainly, learning to drive involves more than just simple conditioned responses.

As Pavlov was exploring how two stimuli were associated in an animal's memory, an American graduate student, Edward Thorndike, was studying how animals solve problems as a means of determining their intelligence. Thorndike noted that once a chick managed to get out of a maze to receive a reward, the chick got faster with each trial. Thus, after receiving a reward for a response, the animal's behavior became more efficient. Thorndike then stepped up the complexity of the "problem" with his famous "puzzle box," in which a hungry cat was placed in a wooden crate (Figure 12.3). The cat had to determine the response that would open a door to food placed just out of reach. After trying multiple responses, the cat eventually stumbled on the response that opened the door (e.g., pressing a pedal). When given subsequent opportunities to solve the puzzle box, the cat would quickly respond by pressing the pedal.

The hungry cat learns to press the pedal to escape the box.

FIGURE 12.3 Problem solving and puzzle boxes. Thorndike observed cats' responses in puzzle boxes as they searched for ways to escape and approach the food. Once a response was observed to lead to the positive consequence of obtaining the food, that same response was repeated in future exposures to the puzzle box.

Once again, the animal's response had become more efficient (as observed with the chicks). Thorndike's investigations pointed to the important relationship between behavior and consequences, a relationship he referred to as the **law of effect** (Thorndike, 1911; see also Chance, 2003).

A few decades later, Harvard psychologist B. F. Skinner (Figure 12.4a) explored the impact of various **reinforcers**, events increasing the likelihood of a recurring response, on behavioral patterns. In the 1940s, prior to his faculty appointment at Harvard, Skinner had worked with his colleague, Keller Breland, on a wartime project. During that time, Skinner, Breland, and their colleagues began experimenting on a readily available species that they had to look no further than their windows to recruit—the pigeon. Their impromptu protocol involved snaring pigeons from the top floor of a building in Minneapolis. The researchers built an automatic feeding machine that dispensed grain for the pigeons. With their new experimental subjects and an automatic food dispenser, they began conditioning pigeon responses.

(a)

(b)

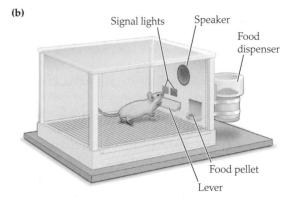

Signal lights   Speaker

Food dispenser

Food pellet

Lever

FIGURE 12.4 Operant conditioning. (a) B. F. Skinner; (b) Skinner developed operant chambers in which rats pressed levers to receive food pellets. The rats adjusted their responses to changing reinforcement schedules signaled with cues such as lights or sounds.

In the midst of serious conditioning research conducted on the pigeons, a light-hearted exploration in which researchers used the food as a reward to teach the pigeons to bowl provided insights about the acquisition of new behavioral responses. Pigeons were trained to roll a wooden ball with their beaks down a tiny alley to knock down very small pins. The conditioning was achieved using the feeding machine to reward small steps toward swiping the ball with their beaks. Amazingly, in just a few minutes, the pigeons were swiping the ball with their beaks as if they were bowling champions. Certainly, no one could claim that pigeons have an innate knowledge of bowling; this was a perfect example of a newly acquired behavior. Animals "operate" on their environment by manipulating certain aspects of it. When the response leads to a positive outcome, the actions are reinforced and repeated. Hence, this form of conditioning was known as **operant conditioning**, emphasizing the animal's active interaction with its environment.

As Skinner continued a systematic evaluation of reinforcement schedules (patterns by which reinforcements are given over time), using rodents as well as pigeons, his work continued to emphasize the importance of reinforcement contingencies. **Contingency** is the probability that a specific outcome will follow a specific response. For example, one type of contingency pattern utilized by Skinner involved time: a reward was presented one minute after a targeted response. Another contingency pattern involved response ratios in which an animal had to respond a certain number of times before the reward was presented. Although reinforcement is typically viewed as the presentation of something positive like food or money, the removal of negative or aversive stimuli such as chores or pain is considered a negative reinforcer (Skinner, 1958).

As shown in Figure 12.4b, Skinner's operant chamber, a Skinner Box, allowed researchers to manipulate reinforcement schedules. Skinner then declared that with this new knowledge came a new responsibility. For example, giving a child the candy he is screaming for in the grocery store is not the best use of reinforcement. Although it may stop the immediate screaming, this strategy reinforces the connection between screaming and getting candy, exactly the behavior a parent would want to terminate.

Learning and memory enable animals to survive in a changing real-world environment in which there are fewer absolutes than probabilities. Therefore, the notion of contingency is critical for the acquisition and memory of adaptive responses. We will continue to discuss the brain's response to various types of rewards and reinforcement schedules as we discuss the neurobiological nuances of adaptive responses throughout this chapter.

This brief introduction to the research of the behavioral pioneers will help you to understand some of the strategies that biopsychologists have used to investigate how the brain learns and remembers new information. These early studies paved the way for an understanding of the neurobiology of learning. In the next sections, we shift our focus to the brain's role in learning and memory, starting with the cells of the nervous system.

Cellular Mechanisms

Once they began to use behavioral approaches to investigate acquired behavioral responses, researchers turned their attention to the question of just how the brain accomplished this incredible feat called learning. When you sit down to study for the exam covering the material in this chapter, exactly what happens in your brain to allow you to—*let's think positively*—get the "A" that you so desperately want? With rather unsophisticated neuroscience tools available early in the 20th century, answering this question was a challenge. Even so, several dedicated scientists committed their careers to solving this problem. Although potential changes in neurons accompanying learning and memory had been previously suggested by researchers such as Santiago Ramón y Cajal (see Chapter 3), who proposed the neuronal doctrine, it was not until the mid-20th century that progress in this area started to emerge. The Canadian physiological psychologist Donald Hebb published his pioneering ideas about how neuronal circuits were established and strengthened during learning in his famous book *The Organization of Behavior* (1949). He wrote,

> *When an axon of cell A is near enough to excite a cell B and repeatedly or persistently takes part in firing it, some growth process or metabolic change takes place in one or both cells such that A's efficiency, as one of the cells firing B is increased (p. 62).... When one cell repeatedly assists in firing another, the axon of the first cell develops synaptic knobs (or enlarges them if they already exist) in context with the soma of the second cell. (p. 63)*

Hebb's ideas about modified neuronal circuits accompanying changes in behavior became known as the **Hebbian synapse theory of learning**, the precursor to the subsequent theories of neuroplasticity (Brown & Milner, 2003). Additionally, his idea of several neurons firing simultaneously during memory formation became known as the cellular assembly theory of learning and is considered a precursor to the subsequent neural network theories proposed in behavioral neuroscience (and discussed throughout this chapter; Nicolelis, Fanselow, & Ghazanfar, 1997). Further, Hebb's work is the basis for one of the most well-known sayings in behavioral neuroscience—*neurons that fire together, wire together*, articulated by the neuroscientist Carla Shatz (Shatz, 1992). Even without the benefit of actual data to inform his thoughts, Hebb's insights into how the brain changes during the learning process were remarkable. Data were the requisite next step to establish further understanding in this area.

Cellular Modifications in the Aplysia. Ironically, some of the earliest and most convincing data related to neural mechanisms underlying learning emerged in the 1960s from a most unlikely source, a large sea slug known as *Aplysia californica* (Figure 12.5b). Although the animal is not known for its intellectual capacities, its simple neuroanatomy characterized by few (approximately 20,000), but large, neurons and its ability to exhibit classical and operant conditioning made this slug an attractive model for understanding the cellular basis of learning (Zhao, Wang, & Martin, 2009). After establishing that *Aplysia* could indeed learn, the Nobel Prize–winning Columbia University neuroscientist Eric Kandel (Figure 12.5a) and his colleagues set out to understand exactly what was happening in those giant neurons during learning.

As shown in Figure 12.5c, when the *Aplysia*'s siphon is gently touched, it retracts its gill. After several touches, however, the animal will **habituate**, or adapt, and cease to respond with the gill reflex. It appeared that the gill reflex was not worth the effort for such a non-threatening stimulus. If the touch is paired with a tail shock, however, the animal will become increasingly sensitive to this threatening stimulus by responding with a much more intense gill retraction. This sensitization reflects a form of classical conditioning in the sense that the animal associated shock with the siphon touch.

In the cases of sensitization and habituation, Kandel and his colleagues discovered the importance of transmitter release between sensory and motor neurons. Specifically, a single pairing of the tail shock and siphon touch activated neurons that released serotonin. Serotonin subsequently increases levels of cyclic adenosine monophosphate (cAMP, a second messenger in cellular signaling) in the sensory neurons and leads to the production of cAMP-dependent protein kinase (PKA), an enzyme that facilitates synaptic transmission and behavioral sensitization. Without the physical stimulus, simply injecting cAMP or PKA into the sensory neuron also results in increased transmitter release. By contrast, habituation is associated

with decreased levels of serotonin. Figure 12.5 depicts how the physical stimuli interact with sensory neurons, motor neurons, and facilitating interneurons in the *Aplysia* to modulate synaptic transmission. Facilitatory interneurons influence the release of serotonin on presynaptic terminals that synapse onto the motor neurons and either enhance or diminish the response (Kandel, 2009).

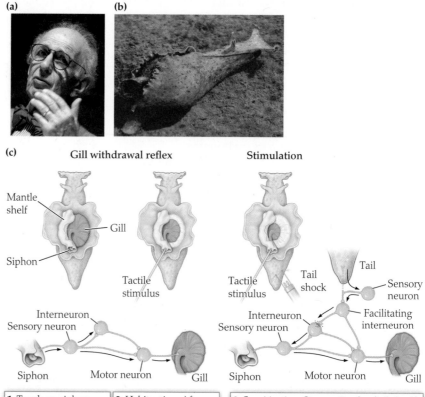

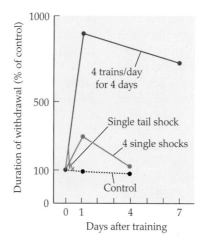

FIGURE 12.5 Cellular mechanisms of learning. (a) Eric Kandel used the (b) aplysia as a model animal to investigate cellular responses in forms of associative learning such as (c) sensitization during which stronger retention was found in animals with more training.

Understanding how serotonin increases synaptic excitability between the sensory and motor neuron requires a brief review of synaptic transmission (Chapter 3). The binding of serotonin molecules to the serotonin receptors of the sensory neuron blocks potassium (K^+) flow via the increased levels of PKA described previously. Reduced flow of K^+ extends the action potential duration, subsequently allowing greater influx of calcium (Ca^{2+}) into the synaptic terminal. Calcium, as you recall, facilitates the movement of the synaptic vesicles to the presynaptic membrane, where they expel glutamate molecules into the synaptic cleft to activate receptors on the motor neuron (Kandel, 2001).

In addition to the biochemical modifications accompanying the short-term behavioral changes or short-term memory, scientists subsequently discovered evidence of structural changes in the *Aplysia*. When the sensory neurons from the *Aplysia* demonstrated habituation to the nonthreatening touch to their siphon, fewer presynaptic terminals were observed than prior to the habituation, leading to fewer synaptic connections with motor neurons and interneurons. These observations suggested that the nervous system was restricting the neural connections in the form of synaptic connections, leading to diminished response to the nonthreatening touch. By contrast, in the sensitized animals, the number of presynaptic terminals had more than doubled. Changes were also observed in the dendrites of the postsynaptic cells in response to the added sensory input. Thus, emerging evidence suggested that structural changes in both the presynaptic and the postsynaptic cells accompanied long-term memory in the classically conditioned *Aplysia* (Bailey & Chen, 1988). We will discuss additional evidence of structural plasticity associated with learning later in this chapter. In the next section, we will explore cellular modifications in a key mammalian brain area in learning: the hippocampus.

Cellular Modifications in the Hippocampus. In 1971, two researchers working at University College London, John O'Keefe and John Dostrovsky, set out to understand why the hippocampus was so important in rats' spatial memory for laboratory mazes. When recording from individual cells in the hippocampus, it appeared that such sensory information was not activating the cells. Rather, the cells became activated when the rats were located in specific locations, or *places*, in the maze—leading to their eventually becoming known as **place cells**. Thus, the hippocampus appeared to have special sensitivities to the external environment, allowing the animal to form a cognitive, or spatial, map of its environment (O'Keefe & Dostrovsky, 1971; O'Keefe & Nadel, 1978).

Recent research has confirmed the presence of place cells in very young rats, just two days after their eyes open. As shown in Figure 12.6, additional spatial cells, known as **direction cells** and **grid cells**, have also been identified in the areas surrounding the hippocampus. Place cells in the hippocampus fire when the rat enters a specific place in the open field. Additionally, direction cells fire in the nearby **subiculum** when the animal points its head in a specific direction. Finally, grid cells, likely in the surrounding entorhinal cortex, fire as the animal crosses compartments of an imagined coordinate system grid over a spatial area to allow it to determine the cumulative distance traveled.

In 2014, three neuroscientists, John O'Keefe, May-Britt Moser, and Edvard Moser, were awarded the Nobel Prize in Physiology or Medicine for their research investigating cells that contribute to the brain's navigational systems (Burgess, 2014). Far from Locke's premise of the brain as a blank slate at birth, this research suggests that although the environment alters the brain's structures, the rat brain is hard-wired for assessing spatial information and forming neural navigational systems in new environments (Langston et al., 2010; Palmer & Lynch, 2010; Wills, Cacucci, Burgess, & O'Keefe, 2010).

About the same time that place cells were being investigated in the 1970s, the Oslo neuroscientists Timothy Bliss and Terje Lomo were looking more closely at how experience altered specific synapses in the hippocampus. They discovered that certain afferent neural pathways exhibited plasticity when stimulated with a high-frequency stimulus. Further, this modification seemed to be long-lasting, hence its name, **long-term potentiation** (LTP). As shown in Figure 12.7, the three afferent pathways shown to express plasticity are located in the hippocampus. They include the perforant pathway, the mossy fiber pathway, and the Schaffer collateral pathway. Interestingly, the perforant pathway and the Schaffer collateral pathway appear to be specialized for associative learning because LTP is contingent on the activation of the postsynaptic cell (Bliss & Lomo, 1973).

Several pieces of evidence suggested that LTP might be a biological mechanism for some forms of memory. LTP seemed to be localized in the hippocampus, an area

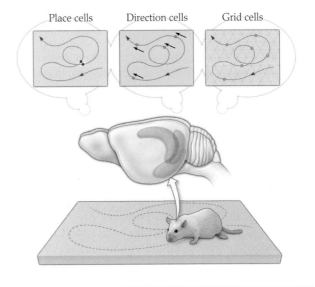

FIGURE 12.6 The brain's navigational system. Place cells and grid cells in the hippocampus and surrounding areas are important for the rat's movement of body and head around its environment.

(a)

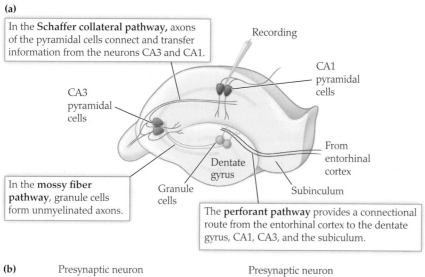

In the **Schaffer collateral pathway,** axons of the pyramidal cells connect and transfer information from the neurons CA3 and CA1.

Recording

CA1 pyramidal cells

CA3 pyramidal cells

From entorhinal cortex

Dentate gyrus

Granule cells

Subinculum

In the **mossy fiber pathway,** granule cells form unmyelinated axons.

The **perforant pathway** provides a connectional route from the entorhinal cortex to the dentate gyrus, CA1, CA3, and the subiculum.

(b)

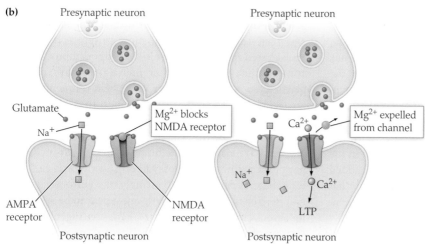

Presynaptic neuron

Presynaptic neuron

Glutamate

Na+

Mg²⁺ blocks NMDA receptor

Ca²⁺

Mg²⁺ expelled from channel

Na+

Ca²⁺

AMPA receptor

NMDA receptor

LTP

Postsynaptic neuron

Postsynaptic neuron

FIGURE 12.7 Long-term potentiation (LTP). (a) Microelectrodes are used to record postsynaptic potentials of the hippocampal neurons. (b) Postsynaptic glutamate receptors have been identified as key components of the LTP process.

previously established as important in learning and memory. The type of high-frequency stimulation used to induce LTP was similar to the θ brain wave rhythm (see Chapter 9) recorded in the hippocampus during learning. Further, when LTP was blocked in the hippocampus, learning and memory diminished. Finally, certain biochemical alterations such as the modification of the NMDA (see Chapter 4) receptor are critical in both LTP and memory formation (Lynch, 2004).

To understand the specific mechanisms involved in LTP, let's revisit the neurotransmitter glutamate, the brain's principal excitatory neurotransmitter. As described in Chapter 4, there are different types of glutamate receptors: NMDA receptors, mentioned above, and AMPA receptors. Researchers soon discovered that magnesium ions naturally block NMDA receptors, interfering with the transmission of ions into and out of the cell. The tendency for magnesium to block the NMDA receptor, however, is voltage dependent, meaning that the magnesium unblocks the receptor when the postsynaptic cell becomes depolarized.

Because postsynaptic depolarization typically occurs in response to a burst of activity from the presynaptic cell, the ultimate binding of glutamate to the NMDA receptor is contingent on simultaneous activation of the presynaptic cell and postsynaptic cell. Not unlike your need to get your friend's attention in a crowded restaurant before you can actually talk to her, the presynaptic neuron must capture the postsynaptic neuron's attention prior to actual synaptic communication that will likely establish the physical traces representing two associated events (Kandel, 2009; Neves, Cooke, & Bliss, 2008). The coactivation of the presynaptic and postsynaptic cells in LTP is reminiscent of Hebb's earlier cellular theories, described previously in this chapter (see Figure 12.7).

Researchers trying to determine whether LTP is a critical neural component of learning and memory have blocked various aspects of LTP, with subsequent evidence of impaired learning in most cases. For example, disrupting glutamate transmission or AMPA receptor availability impairs LTP and memory. Enhancing receptor binding appears to have the opposite effect, as we saw in Chapter 4 with the "Doogie mice." These transgenic mice received extra copies of the NR2B gene, a gene that enhances NMDA receptor function. With enhanced NMDA signaling, the transgenic mice performed better than their normal (non–genetically modified) counterparts in object recognition tasks. The transgenic mice explored new objects for longer than they explored familiar objects. In contrast, normal mice spent an equal amount of time with new and familiar objects, suggesting weak memories of the object they had previously explored (Shimizu, Tang, Rampon, & Tsien, 2000; Tsien, 2000). Although most of the research on the neurobiology of learning has focused on LTP, experience can also weaken connections between synapses, a process referred to as long-term depression (Collingridge, Peineau, Howland, & Wang, 2010).

Structural Neuroplasticity

How exactly does the brain rewire itself during the learning process? If Hebb's cellular assembly theory of learning is correct, how do those neuronal circuits form so that you see a picture of your grandmother and simultaneously picture her farmhouse, smell her cookies, feel her warm hugs, and recall the delicious family meals she prepared when you were a child? What part of the brain facilitates the formation of these memory cell assemblies?

The formation and rearrangement of dendrites on neurons in active regions in the brain is one likely mechanism for learning-dependent structural plasticity. Research suggests that all dendrites are not "carved in stone." Rather, dendrites can be quite transient, rearranging to form new synapses and sprouting spines in accordance with cellular demands. In fact, the memories of our lives have been likened to never-ending processes of establishing and stabilizing new synapses with newly learned associations and eliminating synapses that are no longer relevant (Caroni, Donato, & Muller, 2012).

One mechanism of synaptic restructuring includes changing the shape of dendritic spines, specifically the bulbous head at the end of the spine. Spine head shape is correlated with synaptic strength and stability. More specifically, many of the aspects of LTP such as PKA and calcium activity have been associated with spine enlargement, prompting the proposal of **activity-mediated spine enlargement** in which the shape of the spine changes with neural activity (Caroni et al., 2012). Further, structural plasticity has been observed in activated spines, prompting the emergence of new spines on dendrites located near the original activated spine set (De Roo, Klauser, & Muller, 2008). These structural changes can occur relatively quickly because new spines have been observed within a couple of hours of the original potentiation (Zito, Scheuss, Knott, Hill, & Svoboda, 2009).

Novel experiences, thus, have been associated with the formation of long-term structural modifications leading to long-term memories (Yang, Pan, & Gan, 2009). As shown in Figure 12.8, spine restructuring not only initiates rewiring of a neural circuit but also influences the intensity of the synaptic connections by increasing overall spine density (Caroni et al., 2012).

Although it is interesting to think that our learning experiences influence existing neural structures, perhaps more fascinating is the idea that entirely new neurons are created and situated within the emerging memory/learning cellular networks. Such an endeavor represents a serious investment in the learning experience, more so than the tweaking of spines on existing dendrites. As discussed in Chapter 5, neurogenesis, or the production of new neurons, continues in certain brain regions throughout adulthood. Because one area of production of these new neurons is the subgranular zone of the dentate gyrus within the hippocampus, neurogenesis is thought to be associated with the learning process.

Although this neurogenesis hypothesis of learning sounds feasible, there is a problem—timing. Compared with the rapid modifications observed in spine restructuring, it takes considerably longer for a new neuron to mature and become settled in a neural network. To understand this complex and lengthy process, let's review the developmental trajectory of a mouse hippocampal neuron. Following birth, the young cell differentiates into a neuron, rather than a glial cell. It continues to mature and then eventually migrates relatively short distances to the inner granule cell layer of the dentate gyrus so that it can begin growing modest processes in preparation for the formation of eventual synapses. Hence, during its first week of life, the neuron concentrates on its own development as it reaches its destination and continues its maturation. The neuron continues to mature during the second week following birth, as its processes have clear destinations within the hippocampus. Specifically, the dendrites migrate toward the molecular layer of the hippocampus and the axons toward the hilus and CA3 cell layer. These young neurons are distinguished from fully mature neurons by higher membrane resistance (a measure of the impediment to the flow of electric current across the membrane), leading to different action potential firing patterns.

At this early stage, the neurons start receiving GABA input from nearby interneurons. The introduction of GABA depolarizes the neurons, making them more likely to survive to maturity. By the third week of life, the neurons start

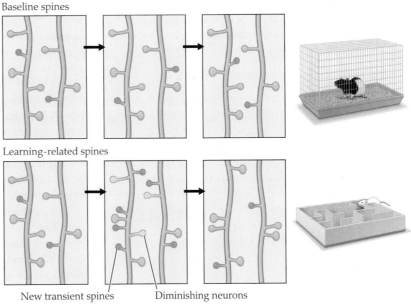

Baseline spines

Learning-related spines

New transient spines   Diminishing neurons

FIGURE 12.8 Learning-induced spine restructuring. During behavioral learning, the structures of the dendritic spines are modified in ways that are thought to facilitate neural networks supporting the newly acquired learned behavioral responses. Following learning, spine connectivity patterns are modified while spine density remains stable.

forming connections with local neural networks. The dendrites that make these connections begin to form around day 16 of a neuron's life. During this time, dendrites sprout **filopodia** that seek out existing synaptic terminals on other neurons to incorporate an existing circuit into the neuron's infrastructure. The complete process of neurogenesis takes too long for it to be the mechanism of all learning, which often must occur quickly to enhance an animal's survival or optimal resource acquisition. Still, aspects of neurogenesis have been associated with learning (Figure 12.9).

In addition to neurogenesis occurring in the hippocampus, the finding that experiences that enhance neurogenesis in the rodent (e.g., voluntary running, environmental enrichment, and spatial training) also enhance learning and memory has supported the idea that neurogenesis and learning are associated. For example, one study provided evidence that behavioral training increased the proliferation and survival of newborn neurons. As illustrated in Figure 12.10, the results of this study suggested that learning also increased the *elimination* of newborn neurons at a specific phase of development. Accordingly, inhibiting cell death also appeared to impair learning (Dupret et al., 2007).

These results suggest that learning requires a delicate balance when it comes to the brain's neurons. Neurogenesis studies suggest that the developing neurons play different roles at different stages of development. Prior to the growth of a full set of processes, the indiscriminate young neurons may modulate background neural activity and influence the firing patterns of neurons in the established neural networks. During later learning, however, the new neurons may be less necessary as the surviving developing neurons are maturing and integrating into the appropriate circuits. Finally, our brains have a limited spatial capacity. If learning requires new neurons and we have limited space in our skull for brain tissue, strategic neural downsizing must occur to maintain optimal lifelong learning.

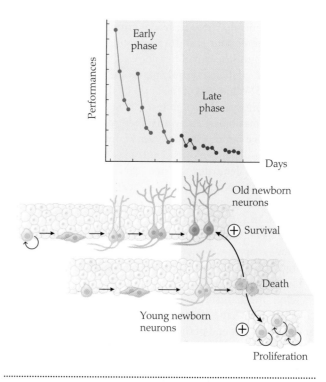

FIGURE 12.10 Learning and hippocampal cell survival. New cells have increased rates of survival early in the learning process; however, once the task is mastered, the death rate of newborn neurons increases—an event that contributes to the further development of new neurons and proliferation of new cells.

The German neuroscientist Gerd Kempermann has suggested that the mammalian brain's hallmark ability to create new neurons creates a survival advantage by allowing mammals to adapt to a changing environment. According to Kempermann (2012), "Networks that are too stable cannot acquire anything new" (p. 729). Thus, the presence of adult neurogenesis ensures that the development of the dentate gyrus never comes to an end.

As shown in Figure 12.11, the basic structure of the dentate gyrus has been conserved through vertebrate evolution. Although rudimentary origins are apparent in fish and birds, the hippocampus is much more elaborate in mammals. With the enhanced cortical development in primates, the hippocampus has dropped to the ventral areas of the brain. In the rodent, however, it has remained in the dorsal brain regions.

Also interesting from an evolutionary point of view is the observation that the hippocampus is more developed in species that are opportunistic and adapt to new environments. Rats and humans, each with respectably sized hippocampi, thrive when faced with new habitats and challenges. Although dolphins are known for their advanced cognitive abilities, their habitat is more homogenous than that of land mammals. That is, dolphins are always in the water, whereas land mammals can inhabit many different terrains, from underground burrows to trees. Accordingly, the size of dolphins' hippocampus (including the dentate gyrus) is small

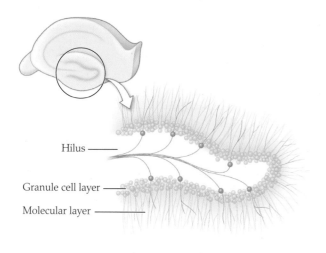

Hilus ———

Granule cell layer ———

Molecular layer ———

FIGURE 12.9 Neurogenesis and learning. As these new granule cells mature into cells with more extensive dendritic processes, they may play different roles in the neural processing that sustains learning.

Mammalian species

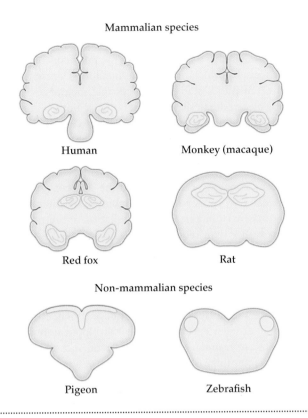

Human   Monkey (macaque)

Red fox   Rat

Non-mammalian species

Pigeon   Zebrafish

FIGURE 12.11 Varying hippocampal structures. Although the hippocampus has been conserved across vertebrates, it has taken on various forms and brain locations in mammals, especially in opportunistic mammals known for their flexible response strategies.

relative to the massive overall size of their brains (Kempermann, 2012). And, in keeping with Kempermann's proposed ideas about the function of neurogenesis and the dentate gyrus, the fox's hippocampus (including the dentate gyrus) is relatively large for its brain size. Perhaps being *sly as a fox* is based on generous neurogenesis rates!

Thus, it appears that learning experiences continuously sculpt the brain by enhancing existing neuronal connections, modulating and producing new networks, and pruning unnecessary connections when appropriate (Deng, Aimone, & Gage, 2010). The most adaptive neural strategies do not always coincide with increased numbers of neurons or connections. Later in this chapter, we will see why neural pruning and sculpting are critical for the health of the hippocampus, as they determine the events in our lives that must be committed to memory or forgotten forever.

Integrating Clinical and Laboratory Research

Prior to the development of modern neuroscience techniques such as fMRI, memory researchers often used case studies. Before Clive Wearing's unfortunate illness, the case of Henry Molaison (known in scientific publications as H.M. until his death in 2008) provided insights into the brain's ability to form new memories.

The Case of H.M. H.M., a young man in his early twenties, visited the neurosurgeon William Scoville in search of treatment for debilitating epileptic seizures. After establishing that H.M.'s seizures didn't respond to available medications, Scoville suggested removing the hippocampus. Although the function of the hippocampus was not known at this time, it had been implicated in the generation of seizures. With seemingly nothing else to lose and nowhere to turn, H.M. and his family agreed to the surgical treatment. On August 25, 1953, H.M. had his medial temporal lobes, including his hippocampus, removed.

Although the surgery decreased the frequency of his seizures, it had an unintended, significant side effect. Soon after the surgery, H.M. could no longer form long-term memories, a condition known as **anterograde amnesia**. He could recall the memories formed before the surgery. However, without the ability to form new memories, he was trapped in the perceived 1950s for the next six decades.

H.M.'s case was unique in the sense that Scoville had made a bilateral lesion of the medial temporal lobe. This lesion was much cleaner and more precise than the typical brain damage noted in patients suffering brain illness or trauma. Accordingly, the neuropsychologist Brenda Milner began systematically evaluating H.M.'s memory deficits. She and Scoville jointly published a landmark paper in 1957 describing the critical role of the hippocampus in the formation of new memories (Scoville & Milner, 1957).

Systematic evaluation of H.M. suggested that his temporal lesions caused severe deficits in the conscious retrieval of events and facts, in a type of memory known as **declarative memory** or, in some cases, **explicit memory**. Declarative memory consists of a form of autobiographical memory known as **episodic memory** as well as a memory for word meanings and concept-based knowledge known as **semantic memory**. Scoville and Milner attributed H.M.'s memory deficit to the hippocampus as opposed to the surrounding areas (Corkin, 2002). When someone asks you how your evening was, you consciously think back to all the relevant events and report the information. H.M.'s declarative memory deficit did not allow him to answer such a question. Similar to Clive Wearing, once the events were cleared from the immediate moment, they were gone, never available for recall.

The finding that a relatively small brain area played such an important cognitive function was a bombshell in the neurological literature. At that time, memory was thought to be more diffusely represented throughout the brain. The noted physiological psychologist Karl Lashley had spent his entire career searching for the **memory engram** (i.e., memory traces in the brain) in the cortex. The cortex, after all, was a logical place for the memory engram to be located because it was the most recently evolved area of the brain and learning is considered an advanced brain function. Also, in the absence of advanced surgical techniques in the laboratory, the cortex was more readily assessable than deeper brain areas. The rodents in Lashley's laboratory, however, managed to learn the mazes, regardless of the location of cortical lesions. After failing to identify a specific area of the cortex that seemed to be responsible for the transformation of experiences into memories, Lashley concluded that memory was the product of multiple regions of the cortex contributing equally to memory formation (Lashley, 1950). The theory that multiple brain areas contribute equally to a particular task or function is referred to as the **theory of equipotentiality** (Beach, 1961).

H.M.'s case suggested that a brain contender for Lashley's illusive memory engram involved the hippocampus. Milner's systematic evaluations, however, revealed that not all of H.M.'s memory systems were negatively impacted by the surgery. For example, when she asked H.M. to perform a challenging mirror-tracing motor task, she noted that his performance improved each time. Thus, although H.M. denied any memory of the task, although it was the 20th trial, his motor performance, although slower than control subjects, suggested that he did indeed remember. This motor memory that enables us to fine-tune the brain's circuitry underlying skilled performances is known as **procedural memory**. Thus, your ability to recall the number of turns you took while driving to your friend's house represents declarative, or explicit, memory. Your improved ability to stay within the lines on the road after driving for several years represents procedural, or **implicit**, memory (Eichenbaum, 2012).

Just hours following H.M.'s death in 2008, high-resolution MRI scans were made of his brain prior to its removal by the neuroanatomist Jacopo Annese. Annese accompanied H.M.'s brain to the Brain Observatory in San Diego, California, for an innovative histological project involving the digitization of more than 2,400 slices of the brain (see Figure 12.12). The final histological analysis of H.M.'s brain revealed that a portion of the posterior hippocampus remained intact. The histological examination, however, confirmed that the surgery resulted in extensive damage to the entorhinal cortex, sometimes referred to as the gateway to the hippocampus. Thus, although Scoville unintentionally left some of the hippocampus in H.M.'s brain, this area was likely isolated or at least marginalized because of the entorhinal cortex (Annese et al., 2014; see Figure 12.12).

Researchers have learned about memory consolidation (the process by which an unstable memory representation is converted into a stable and accessible memory) by implanting electrodes in the brains of humans, both volunteers and patients being monitored for epileptic seizures. This research expands on a theory originally presented in 1969 by the neuroscientist Jerry Lettvin suggesting that we may each have specific neurons that contain our memories for specific people and concepts. He introduced the concept of "grandmother cells" to convey that one's memory for one's grandmother may exist in a modest constellation of thousands of neurons rather than requiring the activation of all the billion cells in the medial temporal lobe. Another version of the grandmother cell hypothesis is that a single cell contains the memory of grandmother, but this is unlikely especially because each of our memories would be extremely vulnerable to the effects of cell loss (Quiroga, Fried, & Koch, 2013).

More recently, specific cells in the hippocampus have been found to respond to a specific person such as the *Star Wars* character Luke Skywalker or the actress Jennifer Aniston. However, instead of single cells containing the memory for a specific person or concept, it is more likely that sets of neurons make up the memory networks for specific concepts. As shown in Figure 12.13, neuroscientists debate two theories of how the brain encodes memories. One theory holds that the representation of a single memory (e.g., the image of Luke Skywalker) is distributed. That is, it is stored as bits and pieces that are distributed across millions or perhaps even billions of neurons. The alternative theory holds that thousands or ever fewer neurons constitute a "sparse" representation of an image. Each neuron will activate to different views of Luke Skywalker; a subset of these neurons will also fire to the image of the *Star Wars* character Yoda. However, a separate set of neurons will activate to the image of Jennifer Aniston. Although neuroscientists debate these two theories, there is little dispute that our rich and diverse memories consist of unique networks formed for different concepts (Quiroga, Kreiman, Koch, & Fried, 2008; Quiroga et al., 2013).

Once it was established that the medial temporal lobe, especially the hippocampus, was involved in the consolidation of memories, attention turned to this brain area in laboratory investigations. A challenge exists, however, in that most of the laboratory work is conducted on animals, who cannot simply tell us what they remember. Therefore, the researchers had to resort to innovative methods that assessed the animals' memory for details of recent events.

Animal Studies. One valuable laboratory method for assessing memory

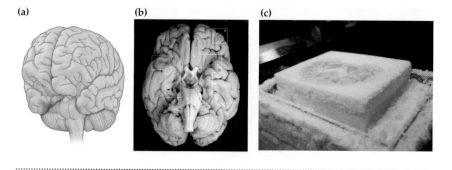

(a)   (b)   (c)

FIGURE 12.12 Lessons from H.M.'s brain. (a) Brain imaging has confirmed bilateral hippocampal damage in H.M., which impaired his declarative memory while leaving his procedural memory less impaired. (b) The ventral surface of H.M.'s brain. (c) Following H.M.'s death, neuroanatomist Jacopo Annese conducted the necessary histological analysis of the brain tissue; equipment was created to freeze and slice the whole brain into pieces that could then be studied under a microscope.

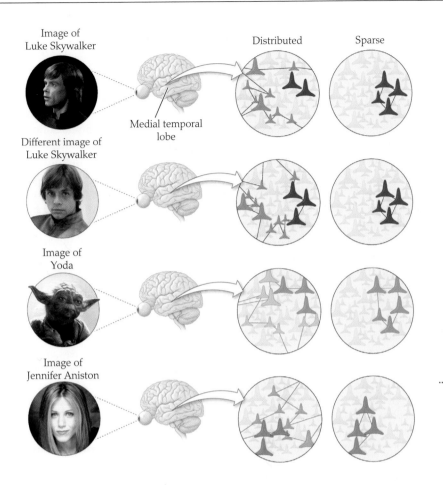

Image of
Luke Skywalker

Different image of
Luke Skywalker

Image of
Yoda

Image of
Jennifer Aniston

Distributed   Sparse

Medial temporal
lobe

FIGURE 12.13 Neural networks and memories.
Although research suggests that memories are not
represented or coded in a single cell, it is unclear
whether memories are stored in networks characterized as sparse or more distributed across the
brain.

formation is the **delayed matching-to-sample task** that
was initially designed for experiments with monkeys. In this
task, the first ("sample") phase consists of the presentation of
a single stimulus to the monkey. A delay of a designated duration follows the presentation. The real test comes with the
following "choice phase" during which two stimuli are presented, one similar to the sample stimulus and one different.
To solve the task, the monkey must be trained to reach for
the stimulus that matches the sample stimulus. In another
version of the task, the **delayed nonmatching-to-sample
task**, the successful monkey must reach for the unfamiliar object. Either way, the monkey must recall the sample
phase of the task to perform successfully. If the monkey does
not successfully perform the task, it is assumed to have a
memory deficit, or version of amnesia.

In early versions of the delayed matching-to-sample
task, research studies provided evidence that medial temporal lobe lesions impaired performance, but the magnitude of the deficit was not as severe as expected based on
observations of H.M. and other case studies. Later, the National Institutes of Health researcher Mortimer Mishkin
and his colleagues modified the task so that each presentation of stimuli included unfamiliar stimuli. For example, in
the sample phase, an unfamiliar object was presented each
time, instead of repeatedly using the same two stimuli for
the choice task. The delayed nonmatching-to-sample task is
depicted in Figure 12.14. Also depicted in Figure 12.14 are

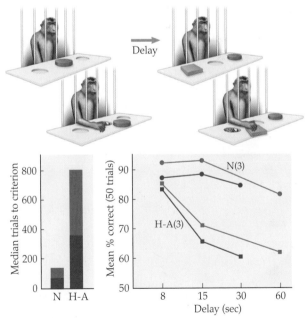

Source: Zola-Morgan, S., & Squire, L. R. (1985). Medial temporal
lesions in monkeys impair memory on a variety of tasks sensitive to
human amnesia. *Behavioral Neuroscience, 99*, 22-34.

FIGURE 12.14 Delayed nonmatching-to-sample task. (a) When
monkeys are assessed in this task that requires them to hold the
information in memory before making the correct response, (b) those
with lesions of the hippocampus and amygdala exhibit learning deficits.

graphs demonstrating that compared with monkeys with no brain damage, animals with a joint lesion of the amygdala and hippocampus exhibited a performance deficit after the eight-second delay. The lesioned animals took more trials to reach the criterion for learning the task (graph on the left) and made more errors in the 15- and 30-second delay trials (graph on the right) (Zola-Morgan & Squire, 1985).

After establishing that the temporal lobe lesion-induced amnesia generalized to nonhuman primates, researchers were also interested in establishing a rodent model of declarative memory because rodents were much easier to study than primates. After establishing that rodents with hippocampal damage were not impaired in many types of learning tasks such as classical conditioning paradigms, researchers focused on spatial learning, following up on the research indicating that "place" cells were located in the rodent hippocampus (as described earlier).

Accordingly, in 1981, Richard Morris, currently at the University of Edinburgh, introduced the **Morris water maze**, now one of the most commonly used tasks in behavioral neuroscience. This task generally involves a swimming pool filled with water that is transparent during training as the animal (typically a rat) learns where a platform is located. During testing, the water transitions to a murky color so that the animal can no longer see the platform and must rely on spatial memory to locate it. The rodent can be released from varying start positions; additionally, experimenters may include visual cues to help guide the rodent as they evaluate the extent of its memory impairment. Although rats are excellent swimmers, they do not seem to like swimming, and they try to locate the platform as quickly as possible. Researchers measure the rats' performance using tracings of the rats' spatial paths to the platform, as well as the amount of time the rats take to locate it.

In the first published investigation using this task, Morris and his colleagues showed that rats with hippocampal lesions, but not cortical lesions, were significantly impaired in the place version of the task. On the contrary, both groups of rats performed similarly in the visually cued navigation task (Morris et al., 1982). Since that time, many studies have confirmed the importance of the hippocampus in spatial learning in rodents, making the Morris water maze a "benchmark test of hippocampal function in rodents" (Eichenbaum, 2012, p. 125; see Figure 12.15).

In the late 1970s, the Johns Hopkins neuroscientist David Olton and his colleagues proposed a different task, the **radial arm maze**, which required animals to remember recent experiences to solve a problem. Although Olton referred to this as **working memory**, the current use of the term refers to keeping information readily accessible (holding it online) while working on a problem, as opposed to merely being able to remember recent events. The more contemporary view of working memory is also associated with the PFC. The incorporation of recent events required to solve the radial arm maze was considered a hippocampal-dependent ability since the skill requires a healthy hippocampus (Eichenbaum, 2012).

The radial arm maze usually consists of eight runway alleys that radiate outward from a central area, much like spokes on a wheel (Figure 12.16). In a basic version of the maze, a food reward is placed at the end of each arm, and the rat's task is to collect the rewards efficiently. Going into each arm once until all the treats are retrieved is the best strategy. Revisiting the same arm only to discover that the reward has already been retrieved is less efficient. Thus, the number of errors made in the task is a typical measure that is recorded. Similarly, when you are looking for your keys, visiting different areas until you find the lost keys is more efficient than

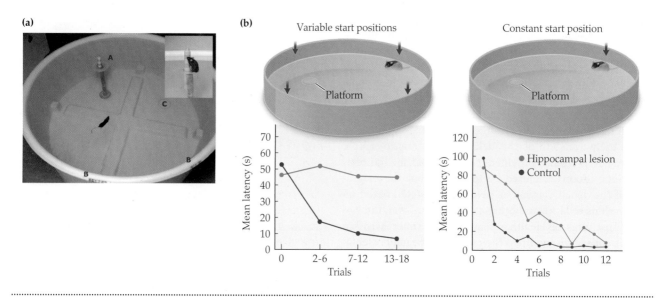

FIGURE 12.15 Morris water maze and spatial assessment. (a) When spatial ability is assessed in the Morris water maze, (b) animals with hippocampal damage perform poorly during training and testing, with longer latencies to reach the platform.

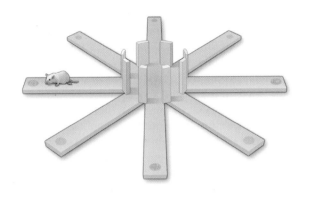

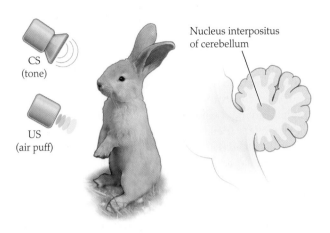

Nucleus interpositus
of cerebellum

CS
(tone)

US
(air puff)

FIGURE 12.16 The radial arm maze. Spatial memory is assessed in the radial arm maze in which animals are required to remember arms or alleys of the maze to avoid revisiting previously visited arms—a response recorded as an error.

FIGURE 12.17 Conditioned eye-blink response. The interpositus nucleus of the cerebellum is integrally involved in the rabbit conditioned eye-blink response. Following conditioning, both the conditioned stimulus (CS, tone) and the unconditioned stimulus (US, air puff) trigger the eye-blink response (either as an unconditioned response (UR) or as a conditioned response (CR)).

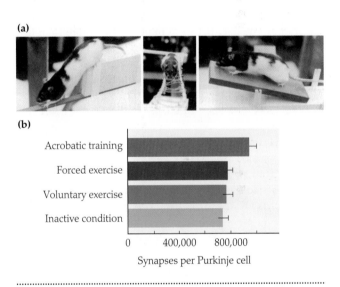

FIGURE 12.18 Obstacle course training and neuroplasticity. (a) When rats were exposed to physical training (AC) in challenging obstacle courses, (b) they exhibited more synapses in their Purkinje cells than nontrained rats.

revisiting the same areas after you have established that the keys are not there. The radial arm maze does not simply assess memory for spatial locations; it also tests the rat's memory for recent events. Damage to the hippocampus interferes severely with the ability to successfully accomplish this task (Olton, Becker, & Handelmann, 1979).

The finding that H.M.'s procedural memory was left intact has also prompted research investigating brain areas that facilitate procedural memory (although now we know that a significant portion of his hippocampus was also left intact). A classical conditioning model has been used in rabbits in which a tone is used as a conditioned stimulus and paired with a puff of air (unconditioned stimulus) delivered to the eye. In the **eye-blink reflex conditioning** task, the rabbit will learn to blink (a motor response) on presentation of the conditioned stimulus to avoid the inevitable puff of air. Research suggests that the brain area responsible for this form of motor learning is the cerebellum. Although the cerebellum lies relatively far from the hippocampus/cerebral cortex memory system for declarative memories, this revelation was not surprising because of the cerebellum's role in motor coordination (Chapter 7). Walking a balance beam or touching your finger to the tip of your nose requires the cerebellum. The cerebellum contributes to motor skills by initiating the activation of deep cerebellar nuclei that receive information from excitatory climbing mossy fibers or inhibitory processes from **Purkinje cells**, the principal inhibitory cells of the cerebellar cortex.

As shown in Figure 12.17, in the rabbit classical conditioning model, the presentation of a tone (conditioned stimulus) activates mossy fibers extending from the **pontine nuclei**, subsequently projecting to the **granule cells** in the cerebellar cortex. The **interpositus nucleus**, a deep nucleus in the cerebellum, plays a role in the conditioning necessary to form the association between the tone and the eye-blink; damage to this area impairs conditioned responses. Additionally, the length of the synapse surface area

increases in the interpositus nucleus following conditioning (see Figure 12.17; Weeks et al., 2007).

Changes in the cerebellar cortex, specifically in an area known as the **paramedian lobule** that regulates limb movement, accompany acrobatic training in rats. As shown in Figure 12.18, when compared with rats that had merely exercised (with no motor training), the rats that had been trained in a challenging obstacle course had increased numbers of synapses for each Purkinje cell (Black, Isaacs, Anderson, Alcantara, & Greenough, 1990).

Thus, procedural learning results in several forms of neuroplasticity throughout the cerebellum. The extent and duration of this plasticity remain under investigation. Have you heard the saying that *you can't teach an old dog new tricks*? Although animals can learn throughout their lifetime, procedural memories may indeed be more difficult to form in old age—even more so than declarative memories. We discussed the value of constantly updating declarative memories, but many procedural memories must remain for life. You may have also told a friend worried about forgetting a skill that *it's like riding a bike, once you learn it you never forget*. Indeed, procedural memories formed during childhood can last a lifetime. By the time a person is 70 years old it may become more difficult, but not impossible, to learn new motor skills. Although several factors may be responsible for these effects, a likely key factor comes from observations that procedural learning requires a larger neural commitment, or number of synaptic modifications, than declarative memory does. Thus, it is likely that the regulation of neuroplasticity and cellular pruning differs for different types of memory systems (Gao, van Beugen, & DeZeeuw, 2012; Woodruff-Pak et al., 2010).

Human Brain Imaging Studies. As researchers moved from case studies involving hippocampal damage to neuroimaging studies, the data began to indicate that, more than just

processing novel information, the hippocampus plays an important role in forming associations among various types of stimuli. In one study, for example, PET scans were used to assess cerebral blood flow while subjects were presented with pairs of words. The hippocampus was activated when subjects tried to associate the dissimilar words. In contrast, the hippocampus was not as activated when subjects reviewed the words to determine how familiar they were (a novelty detection task) or contemplated the meanings of the words (a semantic, or deep processing, task) (Henke, Weber, Kneifel, Wieser, & Buck, 1999).

Imaging studies have also provided evidence that the human hippocampus is involved in the sequencing of events. In one study, participants watched a movie for the first time and were subsequently asked to place four pictures of different scenes from the movie in the correct sequence. As you can imagine, this task involves evaluating the different scenes to remember their exact order in the movie. The control condition involved trying to sequence events based on how it appeared they should be sequenced (more of a logical inference task), as opposed to the participant's actual memory for the movie scenes. More activation of the hippocampus was observed in these fMRI scans during the movie sequence task compared with the baseline or logical inference conditions (see Figure 12.19; Lehn et al., 2009).

Identifying Brain-Based Memory Systems

As neuroscience research has progressed over the past several decades, have the original views of declarative and procedural memory changed at all? Although these two concepts are still regularly used in memory research, they have been modified and extended.

Eichenbaum (2000) has proposed a **cortical–hippocampal system** that underlies declarative memory. Specifically, as we form memories for everyday events and relevant factual knowledge, it has become evident that a considerable amount of communication takes place among the hippocampus, the parahippocampal region, and the more recently evolved neocortex. As shown in Figure 12.20, research from rodent models suggests that this memory network has been conserved throughout mammalian evolution. Each area contributes unique functions to the formation and use of declarative memories. As discussed previously, the hippocampus is involved in the processing and linkage of sequences of events and places. The surrounding cortical area in the parahippocampal region, however, is thought to act as a convergence pathway to the neocortical areas that add appropriate context from surrounding

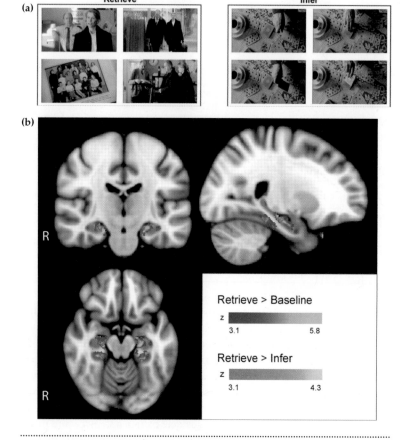

FIGURE 12.19 Retrieval, inference, and brain activation. When participants were asked to (a) retrieve and arrange movie scenes in the order in which they actually appear (as opposed to the order in which they should appear), (b) more hippocampal activation was observed.

sensory, cognitive, and motor cortical areas. Performance on the delayed nonmatching-to-sample task, for example, is not impaired with damage to the parahippocampal area (with a reasonably brief delay) but is impaired with damage to the **orbitofrontal cortex**. Thus, it appears that it is difficult to hold the information online without the support of these cortical systems.

A slightly different memory system has been proposed by Katharina Henke, a neuroscientist at the University of Bern in Switzerland. Taking into account the various brain areas involved in different aspects of learning and memory, Henke has proposed a **processing-based memory system** consisting of three processing modes that vary across three variables: fast versus slow encoding, single-item versus associative encoding, and flexible versus rigid representation (Henke, 2010; Figure 12.21).

Rapid Encoding of Flexible Associations.

As you go through your daily schedule, you are processing associations in a manner so that they can be accessed in various ways. While watching a television commercial featuring a dog one evening, you may recall a funny joke your friend told you about a dog earlier in the day and proceed to repeat the dog joke to your group of friends. Indirectly accessing the memory of the dog joke and presenting it in a novel context represents the flexible components of the episodic memory system. As shown in Figure 12.21 and as can be inferred from the research discussed thus far in the chapter, the hippocampus and neocortex are two of the most influential brain areas in this system.

Slow Encoding of Rigid Associations.

The associations acquired through classical conditioning, forms of habit, or procedural learning must be more rigid than the flexible associations previously discussed for them to be beneficial for adaptive responses. Although mammals are certainly not robots and will always have some flexibility built into their response systems, in some cases, consistency is more important than flexibility. Blinking when a threat is coming to the eye (that is, the eye-blink conditioned response) or following through

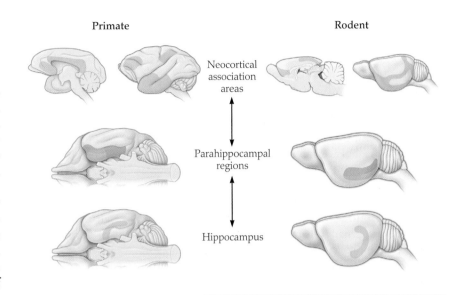

FIGURE 20.20 **Cortical–hippocampal memory system.** In both rodents and primates, the hippocampus receives and sends information to the parahippocampal and neocortical association areas. The parahippocampal region can be considered a hub or convergence area for this memory input—distributing it to the appropriate hippocampal and neocortical areas.

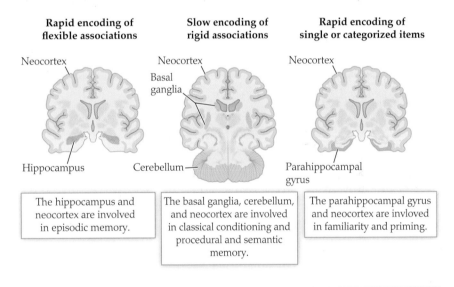

FIGURE 12.21 **Processing-based memory system.** This model distinguishes among three different types of memory systems: fast and flexible associations, slow and rigid associations, and fast processing of single-input units. Each proposed system is associated with specific brain areas.

perfectly with a dance move that has been practiced repeatedly rely more on rigid response strategies. As illustrated in Figure 12.21, these forms of memory involve the basal ganglia (involved in movement and habit formation; see Chapter 7) and the cerebellum (involved in motor coordination and learning as discussed earlier). Semantic memory, involved in the accumulation of knowledge-based concepts and memory for meaning, is also attributed to this memory system.

Your ability to memorize the definitions of terms for this course by teaching yourself the meaning and relevance of the terms and repeatedly reviewing flash cards contributes to this somewhat rigid semantic memory system. Although brain areas such as the cerebellum and basal ganglia are involved, the neocortex plays a role in this process, as it does in the acquisition of episodic memories. The degree to which you use the terms after the course ends will determine whether these semantic memories will continue to exist as long-term memories or be pruned away to make room for new memories.

Rapid Encoding of Single or Categorized Items. Once memories have been established, this memory system is involved in the recognition of how subsequent life events fit into those established memory networks. For example, a loud noise in the street outside your window will be integrated into a threat memory system if you are a military veteran who returned from a tour of duty defined by hostile combat. The noise will still get the attention of someone who recently moved to the city from the quiet countryside, but it will not be easily categorized into an existing memory system. The brain areas assessing the familiarity and relevance of stimuli encountered throughout our lives involve the area surrounding the hippocampus known as the parahippocampal gyrus, as well as the neocortex (Figure 12.21).

The neocortex is implicated in all three of the aforementioned memory processing modes. Because each of the three processing modes involves spatial, temporal, sensory, and semantic knowledge types of representations, all tapping into neocortex functions, the highly associative neocortex is considered to play a central role in most aspects of learning. Although associations can be formed by areas outside of the neocortex, lesions of the temporal neocortex inhibit the meaningfulness of the acquired associations, leading to learning and memory impairments (Adlam, Patterson, & Hodges, 2009).

A compelling argument for the importance of the neocortex in all of the memory modes is also seen in the unfortunate cases of children born with very little cerebral cortex. Although these children can categorize individuals as familiar or unfamiliar, their performance is impaired in all three memory modes (Shewmon, Holmes, & Byrne, 1999). Even with the established importance of the neocortex in each of these proposed memory modes, Henke emphasizes the role of the hippocampus, stating that "the processing-based model emphasizes the speed of relational memory formation during hippocampal processing, as no other brain structure is capable of associating the elements of our experiences on-line" (Henke, 2010, p. 529). The hippocampus, however, eventually disengages from its early essential role as learning transitions into more structured semantic categories and procedures, at which time our responses become more rigid and less flexible (Henke, 2010).

Although episodic memory appears to be an example of advanced cognitive abilities characteristic of the mammalian, or even primate, brain, a few birds remind us not to fly so quickly to conclusions about the uniqueness of human memory systems. At the University of Cambridge, the experimental psychologist Nicola Clayton has discovered impressive learning and memory abilities in scrub jays. As shown in Figure 12.22, by manipulating caching, or food storing, opportunities, she has found that the scrub jays recall where they buried certain types of food. Depending on the time elapsed from the caching to collecting, the jays will retrieve the most appropriate food source. Specifically, when only 4 hours have passed, the jays will recover the perishable worms, but after 124 hours, the jays skip the rotten worms and retrieve the peanuts (Clayton, Bussey, & Dickinson, 2003; Clayton & Dickinson, 1998). Thus, these birds appear to be recalling past events and using that information to respond adaptively in the present. Although the exact brain mechanisms have yet to be determined in this particular task, it is likely that a small hippocampus-like structure is involved (see Figure 12.22).

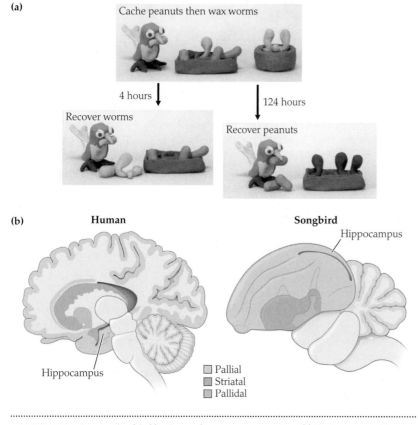

FIGURE 12.22 Impressive bird brains and memory processing. (a) Birds use memories about how much time has elapsed to influence their response targeted at recovering either perishable (worms) or nonperishable (peanuts) food items. (b) Similar to mammals, this memory processing likely involves the avian version of the hippocampus.

Modifying Memories

With so many brain areas and neuronal adaptations accompanying the formation of memories, it would seem that once the memories were formed, they would be robust and indestructible. Although the cases of Clive Wearing and H.M. show just how devastating significant memory loss can be, the truth is that healthier brains selectively forget information that is no longer relevant. And, since our lives march on with the never-ending accumulation of new episodic memories, it is always possible to modify existing memories, even without our conscious awareness.

Thus, the perfect memory system is not an infallible memory system that is carved in stone. Memory updates are necessary as we encounter new information throughout our lives. In this section, we will also consider a condition in which individuals do not have the ability to erase or forget even trivial episodic memories. Thus, the brain must balance both long-lasting and transient memories to allow us to interact optimally with our changing environment.

Rewriting Memories

When the 22-year-old college student Jennifer Thompson-Cannino heard a noise in her bedroom on July 28, 1984, she quickly realized that she was in the presence of an intruder who was going to harm her. As she was raped, however, she was determined to study the rapist's face so that, if she lived through the horrific experience, she could identify him to the police. One might expect such determined study to make Jennifer's memory for the rapist's face clearer and more reliable than her other memories of less threatening fleeting experiences. After escaping, she worked with the police to develop an accurate composite sketch. As she studied the sketch, she felt confident that she had accurately captured the face of her rapist. A photo identification was conducted a few days later; after studying the photos for about 5 minutes, she once again felt confident that she had selected the correct person. When she selected the same person, Ronald Cotton, in the physical lineup and was told that her choice matched the photo lineup choice, she was 100% confident that she had remembered the face of her rapist. Although Ronald denied any involvement in the case, with Jennifer's testimony, the jury convicted him in just 40 minutes, giving him a sentence of life plus 50 years.

During his incarceration, Ronald was a model prisoner who kept writing to his lawyer about ways to clear his name. When a fellow inmate arrived who looked like him and the composite sketch that Jennifer had developed and approved, Ronald began to think that his conviction was simply a case of mistaken identity. Although he was granted another trial, Jennifer's continuing confidence that Cotton had raped her persuaded the jury to ignore the possibility that his conviction was a result of her faulty memory. This time, he received two life sentences.

As Ronald continued to consider ways to potentially clear his name, he learned about how DNA evidence can be used in criminal cases, and he asked his lawyer to search for any remaining physical evidence associated with the case. A semen sample was located, and it showed no match to Ronald. Instead, the DNA sample showed a match to Bobby Poole, the inmate whom Ronald had suspected, confirming that Poole had committed the crime. After 11 years, Ronald was released from prison (Thompson-Cannino, Cotton, & Torneo, 2010).

As they write in their book *Picking Cotton*, Jennifer and Ronald are friends today who are adamant about informing the public about just how malleable memories are. Still today, Jennifer is shocked that her memory failed her and that she so confidently selected the wrong man (see Figure 12.23 to see how closely the two men resembled each other). Cognitive scientists who study eyewitness memory, however, are not surprised by this case. Their studies show how easy it is to nudge the human memory into becoming convinced an inaccurate photo in a lineup is the actual person of interest. If the witness's selection of a specific person in a suspect lineup is reinforced by an experimenter or officer, the original memory can be restructured in the brain. This leads to the formation of an inaccurate memory as the newly updated retrieved memory from that point forward (Wells & Loftus, 2003: Wells et al., 1998).

From a neurobiological point of view, when Jennifer's memory network for her perpetrator's face was reactivated, it was likely temporarily vulnerable to her ongoing experiences. As she studied the various faces in the photo lineup, not seeing the exact face of her perpetrator, her memory circuits may have started incorporating the face closest in appearance to Poole's, **reconsolidating**, or restructuring, her memory of her rapist's face. Although controversy still surrounds the exact nature of reconsolidation and

FIGURE 12.23 False memories. After being attacked by Bobby Poole (right), Jennifer Thompson-Cannino positively identified Robert Cotton (left) as the assailant. Thompson-Cannino's modified memory was likely a result of the individuals' similar facial features, as observed in these photos.

its function, in at least some situations, the **postretrieval lability** or instability of memories is beneficial, allowing you to upgrade your memory stores each time they are retrieved. However, this reconsolidation process makes it virtually impossible to hang on to episodic memories in the exact form they were initially consolidated. Research provides strong evidence that most long-term memories, rather than being stored in a somewhat permanent fashion, are maintained via a dynamic process. If memories are not retrieved for a long period of time, they may decay or, alternatively, change from the original version.

In the laboratory, researchers are still trying to determine the exact mechanisms of reconsolidation. To identify cellular mechanisms involved in this process, researchers use animal models to systematically track relevant neurobiological changes. One strategy is to use a simple form of training such as classical conditioning so that the animal clearly demonstrates an acquired memory. Using this form of learning, the unconditioned stimulus is presented to prompt the retrieval of the memory. When the memory is retrieved, a drug that blocks the synthesis of proteins that likely play a role in the memory-based synaptic plasticity is administered to the animals. This leads to various changes in the animals, such as blocked ion channels or restructured synaptic endings. Such studies suggest that the administration of protein synthesis inhibitors after a previously consolidated memory has been retrieved disrupts the original version of the memory (Tronson & Taylor, 2007).

Further, as we saw in our discussion of the story of Ronald Cotton, human studies have demonstrated how easily misinformation is incorporated into earlier memories and have provided strong evidence for reconsolidation in human memory. For example, college students can easily be prompted into thinking that childhood events (e.g., being lost in a mall), fabricated and introduced by experimenters in collaboration with the students' parents, actually occurred (Loftus et al., 1978). Although the notion that memory is dynamic has been accepted by cognitive psychologists for some time, researchers are still investigating the exact mechanisms of memory reconsolidation (Schiller & Phelps, 2011).

Another form of rewriting memories has been documented in patients with orbitofrontal cortex (OFC) damage. Patients with damage to this area have been observed to engage in spontaneous **confabulation**, meaning that they effortlessly make up stories to fill in gaps in their memories. Interestingly, these false memories typically include bits of true information so that, to the affected individual, fabricated segments of fuller stories seem to be fully believed as honest reflections of their currently perceived reality. For this reason, confabulation has been referred to as *honest lying.* Just as your visual system fills in the blind spot with a likely or highly probable visual picture (Chapter 6), patients with OFC damage fill in the memory gaps with somewhat realistic stories. Early accounts of confabulation were documented in chronic alcoholic patients suffering from the memory disorder known as **Korsakoff's syndrome**, in which individuals experience an atypical loss of short-term memories. Because lesions in the dorsomedial thalamic nucleus are evident in the autopsied brains of these patients, this brain area has also been cautiously implicated in spontaneous confabulations (Buckner & Wheeler, 2001; Schnider, 2003).

Memory and Emotions

The altered levels of hormones accompanying stressful events lead to both impairment and strengthening of the integrity of the memory circuits. As you recall, a destination of the stress hormone cortisol is the hippocampus. The effects of stress on memory and learning can be dramatic.

Stress and Forgetting. Perhaps the ultimate betrayal of the memory system is seen in several cases in which parents forgot that their baby was in the backseat of their car on a hot day and unknowingly left him or her to die of an extreme rise in body temperature. David Diamond, a neuroscientist at the University of South Florida, asserted that these incidents had less to do with the quality of parenting prior to the incident and more to do with the stressful circumstances the parent encountered on that unfortunate day. According to Diamond, "Memory is a machine and it is not flawless. Our conscious mind prioritizes things by importance, but on a cellular level, our memory does not. If you're capable of forgetting your cell phone, you are potentially capable of forgetting your child" (Weingarten, 2009).

If you recall the more rigid procedural memories discussed above, when a person is stressed, the brain areas such as the basal ganglia involved in procedural memories are less likely to be monitored as a parent juggles various crises and responsibilities. Returning to our driving analogy, the basal ganglia–dependent procedural memories do just fine getting you from point A to point B. However, when later asked to recall the traffic pattern, your hippocampus and prefrontal cortex may come up short, not being able to recall what was encountered along the way.

In one tragic case (described in Weingarten, 2009), a mother, after not getting much sleep the prior night as the result of babysitting for a friend and caring for her own son, who had a cold, set out to take her son to the babysitter as she drove herself to work. The baby, usually animated in the car seat, was also tired from his sleepless night and was uncharacteristically quiet. There were several factors that differed from the mother's usual routine. The car seat was in a different position than usual and was not visible in the rearview mirror, and she had to drive her husband's car. Trying to defuse a few family and work crises, she was talking on her cell phone for most of the drive to work. Consequently, she drove past the babysitter's home and parked her car in the parking lot at work. Because the babysitter had a new cell phone, she had only added the mother's cell phone number, not the office number. The babysitter's calls went unnoticed in the mother's purse all day. It was a perfect stress storm that had disastrous results. Because there is no intent to harm the children in these cases, in about 40% of the cases the authorities determine that no crime has been committed. However, in the other 60% of the cases, the parent is charged with a felony (Weingarten, 2009).

Although forgetting can be adaptive in some circumstances, in this case and in many other life situations, compromised memory can have detrimental effects. How does stress negatively affect the memory system? David Diamond and his colleagues have developed a stress model in which rats encounter unavoidable exposure to a cat, a natural predator. As shown in Figure 12.24, compared with rats simply placed in an unfamiliar cage with no cat exposure and with control rats placed in their home cage, the stressed rats that were placed in a cage with a cat positioned outside exhibited less evidence of a low-threshold version of LTP. Further, the stressed rats exhibited more errors on a water maze task, which, as you now know, is a hippocampal-dependent spatial learning task (Kim & Diamond, 2002). As you learned in Chapter 10, research with rats suggests that stress adversely affects the hippocampus by altering cell survival as well as neuronal morphological and metabolic functions. In another study in the Diamond laboratory, for example, evidence suggested that stress produced by predator exposure resulted in lower levels of neural cell adhesion molecule in the potential prey, a glycoprotein that is critical for neuronal development and synaptic plasticity in mature brains. This was accompanied by compromised spatial memory (Sandi et al., 2005).

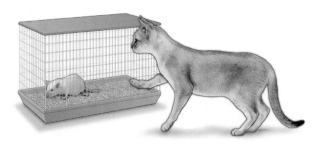

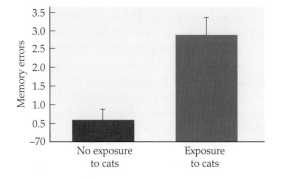

FIGURE 12.24 Stress-compromised memories. (a) In this paradigm, rats were exposed to cats prior to being tested in a memory task. (b) Rats previously exposed to cats made more errors in the radial-arm maze than nonexposed rats.

Thus, stress impairs memory systems. Learning that stress exposure compromises cognitive functioning may explain your performance on certain academic assignments and exams. However, research suggests that stress-induced memory impairment is not permanent. When rats are taken out of the stressful environment and housed in a familiar environment, memory recovers (Kim & Diamond, 2002).

Stress and Memory Enhancement. Although stress is bad for the formation of memories, in certain situations stress can facilitate the storage of a memory to the brain's hard drive. Although this is more typical with procedural memories, in these life-and-death cases, explicit memories become fixed in the threatened person's neural networks. Thus, it should not be surprising that the brain makes a special effort to remember potential threats. After a child is bitten by a neighborhood dog, it is certainly adaptive to avoid that dog at all costs in the future.

As you learned in Chapter 10's discussion of conditioned fear in rats, the amygdala has been implicated in stress-enhanced memories. This specialized cluster of nuclei in the medial temporal lobe interacts with stress hormones and other stress-related neurochemicals to facilitate the consolidation of a memory for the threatening experience. When a person has encountered severe trauma, the memory for a threatening stimulus is so strong that it leads to the development of mood and/or anxiety disorders such as **posttraumatic stress disorder (PTSD)**, a condition briefly introduced in Chapter 10. Currently, PTSD is defined as a mix of intrusive memories of a traumatic episode and accompanying avoidance of relevant triggers for the event. It typically leaves the patient with chronic hyperarousal and other emotional distortions (American Psychiatric Association, 2013). Because not everyone who experiences a traumatic experience will be diagnosed with PTSD, it is evident that biological predispositions interact with the person's encounter with an emotionally threatening event (Pitman et al., 2012).

Once PTSD has been diagnosed, a characteristic marker is a heightened autonomic response such as heart rate reactivity in response to a stimulus related to the emotional event. For example, as mentioned earlier in the chapter, war veterans may hyperrespond to loud noises in the street that sound like gunfire. Researchers have observed reduced volumes of both the hippocampus and the ventromedial PFC in PTSD patients relative to control subjects without PTSD. Further, fMRI scans implicate several brain areas in PTSD; these brain areas are shown in Figure 12.25.

The amygdala is involved in the conditioned fear response and is hyperactive in patients with a PTSD diagnosis. The insular cortex, involved in body awareness, is also hyperresponsive, as well as the ACC, an area involved in various learning tasks such as error detection and fear learning. Finally, the hippocampus, involved in the interpretation of contexts as safe or dangerous based on available cues, is typically altered—however, the direction is not always predictable because both hypo- and hyperreactivity have

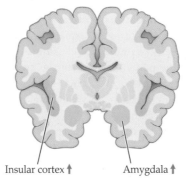
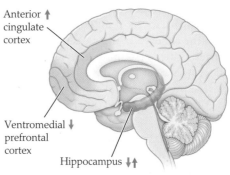

FIGURE 12.25 Posttraumatic stress disorder (PTSD) and brain activation. Imaging data reveal that PTSD is characterized by hyperactivation of the amygdala, insula, and cingulate cortex and diminished activity in the ventromedial prefrontal cortex. Both hyper- and hypoactivation have been observed in the hippocampus.

Anterior ↑ cingulate cortex

Ventromedial ↓ prefrontal cortex

Hippocampus ↓↑

Insular cortex ↑

Amygdala ↑

(a)

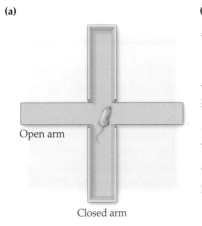

Open arm

Closed arm

(b)

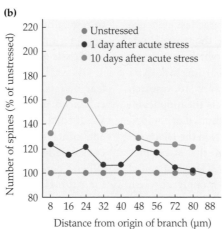

● Unstressed
● 1 day after acute stress
● 10 days after acute stress

Number of spines (% of unstressed)

Distance from origin of branch (μm)

(c)

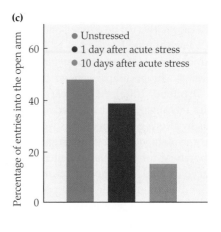

● Unstressed
● 1 day after acute stress
● 10 days after acute stress

Percentage of entries into the open arm

FIGURE 12.26 Persistent stress memories. (a) When rats were exposed to two hours of immobilization stress, (b) they exhibited more densely populated spines on neurons in the amygdala after 10 days as well as (c) persistent avoidance of the open arm in an elevated plus maze. These data reflect strong memories of the immobilization stress, with the effects building over time.

been observed. Although it would be logical to conclude that PTSD is associated with high cortisol (stress hormone) levels, this does not seem to be the case. In fact, in some cases, a cortisol deficit has been implicated in PTSD. As more animal models are created to investigate this disorder in more systematic ways, future research will likely yield evidence of complex interactions between various neurochemicals and the onset of PTSD (Pitman et al., 2012).

In one study focusing on the effects of stress on the amygdala, rats exposed to acute stress (immobilization for two hours) exhibited decreased spine density in the hippocampus, as well as increased anxiety behaviors in a task known as the elevated plus maze. In this study, both the neural and the behavioral effects seemed to build over time. No differences were observed 1 day after the stress exposure, but the effects were clearly seen 10 days after the stress exposure, suggesting that it was difficult for the rats to shift from a stress mode to a safety mode after the stress was removed (see Figure 12.26; Mitra, Jadhav, McEwen, Vyas, & Chattarji, 2005). "Context Matters" in this chapter focuses on a research study that systematically explored PTSD subjects' responses to cues related

to safety and danger. This area of research may yield fruitful results for understanding critical neurobiological events accompanying both the onset of and the recovery from PTSD.

But what about more moderate stress exposure? Does that facilitate or impair memory formation? Norepinephrine, a neurotransmitter released during stressful experiences, has been implicated as a contributing factor to the consolidation of emotionally arousing memories (Roozendaal, McEwen, & Chattarji, 2009). James McGaugh, a neuroscientist at the University of California at Irvine, has discovered that giving rats injections of epinephrine antagonists impairs memory in the Morris water maze task, whereas infusion of β-adrenergic receptor agonists enhances memory consolidation (McGaugh, 2004). Thus, according to these results, rats that are moderately emotionally aroused will perform better on a learning task than their relaxed counterparts. More research is necessary to determine whether these findings apply to human memory acquisition. As with most physiological systems, a delicate balance exists between stress and memory systems (LaBar & Cabeza, 2006).

Can Perceived Safety Diminish the Symptoms of Posttraumatic Stress Disorder?

Featured study: Jovanovic, T., Norrholm, S. D., Fennell, J. E., Keyes, M., Fiallos, A. M., Myers, K. M., ... Duncan, E. J. (2009). Posttraumatic stress disorder may be associated with impaired fear inhibition: Relation to symptom severity. Psychiatry Research, 167, 151–160.

Learning is a never-ending process that determines our lifetime collection of memories at any given point in time. As the relevance and meaning of various events in our lives change, it is extremely adaptive to alter our responses in accordance with the new contextual rules.

In this study, the researchers sought to understand how fundamental learning may contribute to PTSD. As discussed previously in this chapter, PTSD follows an emotionally traumatic event and is characterized by (1) a tendency to reexperience the troubling event via flashbacks or intrusive thoughts; (2) an avoidance of stimuli that have been associated with the event, (3) increased arousal, even when no threatening stimuli are present, and (4) negative alterations of mood and cognition (American Psychiatric Association, 2013; Bremner et al., 1999).

Accordingly, the investigators used a procedure known as *conditional discrimination* to study the impact of learning on PTSD symptoms. Under this protocol, an annoying blast of air to the larynx is used as the unconditioned stimulus. Everyone exhibits a **startle response** when that stimulus is presented! In this study, the startle response was defined by a very fast eye-blink response, not unlike the rabbits' response in the LTP research that we discussed earlier in the chapter. To establish baseline startle responses, the investigators also recorded eye-blink responses to a second type of unconditioned stimulus, a loud noise probe, which had not been

(a)

The conditioned stimuli consisted of four lights of varying colors:

● Stimulus A (green light)   ● Stimulus B (purple light)   ● Stimulus C (orange light)   ● Stimulus X (blue light)

(b)

Training Phase I:
Green light (A) → blue light (X) → airblast

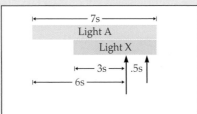

Training Phase II:
Purple light (B) → blue light (X) → no airblast

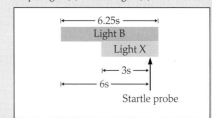

Training Phase:
All combinations of lights including new orange light with no training history are presented to subjects.

NA = Noise alone
AX = Light cues associated with air blast
BX = Light cues associated with safety or no threat
AB = Light cues with no prior threat association
AC = Light cues with no prior threat association

(c)

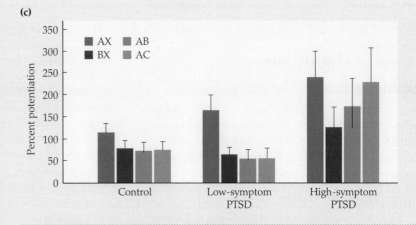

CONTEXT MATTERS FIGURE 12.1 **Posttraumatic stress disorder (PTSD) effects on conditional discrimination.** (a) After establishing light signals that predict or do not predict a threatening stimulus (air blast), (b) participants were exposed to a novel aversive noise stimulus alone and in the presence of the light cues that were associated with the air blast. (c) Participants in the high-symptom PTSD category were less likely to inhibit threat expectation in the presence of the safety signals than the control and low PTSD participants.

associated with the conditioned stimuli. The conditioned stimuli that were used to set the context for the air blast conditioned stimulus consisted of four lights of varying colors: stimulus A (green light); stimulus B (purple light); stimulus C (orange light), and stimulus X (blue light).

The participants in this study were 28 healthy adult males and 27 adult males with a PTSD diagnosis. There were three subject groups: a high-symptom PTSD group, a low-symptom PTSD group, and a healthy control group with no PTSD diagnosis.

During the training phase of the study, participants received six trials in which stimuli A and X were presented, followed by the unconditioned stimulus (air blast). These trials were followed by six trials where stimuli B and X were presented together, but were not followed by the air blast. If your attentional systems are fully engaged, you should have inferred that trials including stimulus B are never followed by the air blast and that stimulus B should therefore become accepted as a safety signal in this discrimination task.

During the testing phase, trials consisted of both A + X, B + X, and the presentation of a new stimulus light with no conditioning history (C + X). The trials were presented in an order such that the subjects could not predict the air blast using any information other than their experiences with the stimulus trials. In the actual testing phase, the air blast was no longer used, just the noise. Thus, the startle response to the noise alone with no conditioning stimuli present was compared with the startle response in the presence of the various light stimuli. Experimenters monitored subjects' eye muscles and button press responses. During conditioning, subjects had been asked to press a button reflecting their expectation of the unconditioned stimulus being presented on each trial.

Specifically, they would press "+" if they expected the air blast to follow the light, "-" if they did not expect it to follow, or "0" if they were uncertain about the outcome.

Whereas all subjects thought the air blast was aversive, indicating a perceived threat, the PTSD subjects rated the startle probe as more aversive than the control subjects rated it. All subjects startled more in response to the noise in the presence of the stimuli predicting threat (that is, A + X). As illustrated in Context Matters Figure 12.1, both the control subjects and the low-symptom PTSD subjects exhibited a suppressed startle response when the safety signal was present. However, subjects in the high-symptom PTSD group found it more difficult to discriminate between the safety (B) and threatening (A) stimuli.

In sum, the results suggest that an ability to clearly distinguish safe environments from threatening environments is important for building resilience against PTSD symptoms. After establishing conditioned responses to stimuli in one environment, as is the case for war veterans, being able to inhibit those responses to similar stimuli in a safe environment requires sophisticated learning strategies that are compromised when a person is experiencing high levels of stress. However, this ability may not be sufficient to ward off PTSD completely. The low-symptom PTSD group demonstrated an ability to inhibit the fear-potentiated startle response, yet still had developed symptoms of PTSD (although their symptoms were not as severe). More research must be conducted, but there may be some time in the future when a person's ability to inhibit previously learned conditioned responses when presented in a new environment or context may be used as a form of behavioral marker (as opposed to biomarker or physiological index) for vulnerability to PTSD.

The Case of Highly Superior Autobiographical Memory

Have you ever wished for a perfect memory or thought how wonderful it would be to have the ability to access events in your life and replay them like a movie with perfect accuracy? After reading a letter sent to Dr. James McGaugh below, you may change your mind.

Dear Dr. McGaugh,

As I sit here trying to figure out where to begin explaining why I am writing you and your colleague I just hope somehow you can help me.

I am thirty-four years old and since I was eleven I have had this unbelievable ability to recall my past, but not just recollections. My first memories are of being a toddler in the crib (circa 1967) however I can take a date, between 1974 and today, and tell you what day it falls on, what I was doing that day and

if anything of great importance (i.e., The Challenger Explosion, Tuesday, January 28, 1986) occurred on that day I can describe that to you as well. I do not look at calendars beforehand and I do not read twenty-four years of my journals either. Whenever I see a data (sic) flash on the television (or anywhere else for that matter) I automatically go back to that day and remember where I was, what I was doing, what day it fell on and on and on and on and on. It is non-stop, uncontrollable and totally exhausting.

Some people call me the human calendar while others run out of the room in complete fear but [t]he one reaction I get from everyone who eventually finds out about this "gift" is total amazement. They then start throwing dates at me to try to stump me. . . . I haven't been stumped yet. Most have called it a gift but I call it a burden. I run my entire life through my head every day and it drives me crazy!!! (Parker, Cahill, & McGaugh, 2006, p. 35)

When McGaugh and his colleague, Larry Cahill, received this letter from Jill Price, they were appropriately skeptical of this woman's claims of an infallible memory for autobiographical events and dates. However, when they brought her into the lab and subjected her to endless memory and cognitive ability tests, they were convinced that they had an authentic case of superior memory. This case, however, was different from that of the other memory champions described in the literature. Luria's famous case of "S," for example, was a professional memory expert, or mnemonist, using memory aids to facilitate his ability to recall long lists of information such as digits and words (Luria, 1987). S's autobiographical memory was not distinguishable from that of others with more normal memory systems. Interestingly, the only type of superior memory that Price exhibited was superior autobiographical memory, now known as **highly superior autobiographical memory (HSAM)**. When given long lists of words to recall, she responded with frustration and exhibited no superior abilities.

Following extensive assessment of Jill Price, McGaugh, Cahill, and their colleagues identified 10 additional patients with similar superior autobiographical memories. These subjects underwent extensive cognitive, behavioral, and brain assessments. Similar to the initial observations of Price's memories, these subjects' memories had become enhanced at around 10 years of age. Like Price, these subjects did not score above average on standard laboratory memory tests. Evidence of obsessive–compulsive disorder tendencies were observed for the subjects, expressed as the possession of meticulously organized collections of various items ranging from shoes to stamps. For example, the actress Marilu Henner (Figure 12.27) was a subject identified as HSAM, and she has a compulsive collection of shoes (CBS News, 2011). In a recent interview, as she pulled each shoe out, she conveyed when (day of week, date, and year) the shoes were purchased and last worn.

Brain-imaging assessments of these subjects revealed enhanced volumes of brain areas associated with compulsive disorders, namely the caudate and putamen in the striatum. This provides further evidence that the HSAM ability shares neurobiological connections with compulsive behavior. Certain areas of white matter serving as connections among various brain areas were also larger in the HSAM subjects than in similarly aged subjects who were not classified as having HSAM. Related more to memory enhancements, areas of the insula and parahippocampal cortex were also larger in the HSAM subjects (LePort et al., 2012). Memory researchers will follow this newly discovered memory "condition" of HSAM to learn more about types of enhanced memories.

What if you were not born with a predisposition toward enhanced memories? Most of us fall into that category. All is not lost, however, because learning about key memory mechanisms makes us more informed about behavioral and cognitive ways to enhance memory. As mentioned previously, memory-training techniques have been recognized since antiquity. For example, the well-known *Method*

FIGURE 12.27 Highly superior autobiographical memory (HSAM). The actress Marilu Henner meets the criteria for HSAM. She can tell you where she was and what she was doing on almost any day of her life.

of Loci was used by the ancient Greeks. This memory-enhancing technique requires the student to use a familiar location (e.g., his house) and mentally tack items from a memory list to various sites in the familiar location so that the list can be recalled by simply mentally walking through the familiar site. Before any information is committed to memory, however, the brain must properly attend to it. The next section will focus on the role of attention in learning and memory processes.

Focusing on Attention: Gateway to Learning and Memory

Studies of attention have been integral to learning and memory research since the birth of psychology. However, now that neuroimaging data can inform the classic attention studies conducted throughout the 20th century, the topic is of even greater interest as scientists attempt to unravel the necessary conditions for effective memory processes.

Consider a fun cognitive illusion known as **inattentional blindness**. Figure 12.28 depicts a popular example. Subjects are told to watch a video of a basketball team and count the number of times the ball is passed among members of one of the teams, ignoring the passes of the other team. During this counting task, a person in a gorilla suit walks across the basketball court, stops and beats her chest, and then exits the scene. Remarkably, at the conclusion of the counting task, half of the subjects reported that they had not seen the gorilla. Using eye tracking, researchers have shown that even when those subjects were looking at the gorilla, they did not notice it. Thus, by selectively focusing attention on the

FIGURE 12.28 Inattentional blindness. When study participants were asked to observe a video and focus on the number of times the ball was passed among the players, they failed to see the gorilla that walked across the room.

number of ball passes made by certain players, the subjects failed to attend to a visual detail that, in another situation, could be relevant for survival (Memmert, 2006; Simons & Chabris, 1999). Directing attention away from various events is a tried-and-true tactic of magicians to keep their audiences from noticing how they are manipulated in various magic tricks (Macknik et al., 2008).

Neuroimaging studies have revealed various brain areas involved in attention and are providing clues about why intelligent people may not notice a gorilla that walks in front of them. The posterior parietal cortex has been associated with attention processes in general (Cabeza, Ciaramelli, Olson, & Moscovitch, 2008). However, specific categories of attentional networks have also been identified. Building on a model proposed by the cognitive scientist Michael Posner more than three decades ago, scientists have found brain areas and neurochemicals associated with the following three forms of attention defined by Posner (Posner & Boies, 1971; Raz & Buhle, 2006; see Figure 12.29):

Alerting is characterized by heightened vigilance and sustained attention. You may be fully engaged in a conversation with your friends until you hear the ringtone on your cell phone. At this point, your involvement in the conversation is distracted as you focus on the ringtone. The frontal and parietal cortical areas, especially in the right hemisphere, are activated during alerting tasks and are modulated by the norepinephrine system arising from the locus coeruleus.

Orienting is characterized by the selection of specific stimuli in the environment from multiple sensory options. To identify the incoming call, you turn away from your friends and look down at your phone, tuning out your friends' conversation as well as the kids running in the nearby park. Brain areas involved in the visual sensory system such as specific areas of the thalamus, superior colliculus, and frontal eye fields are involved in orienting, as are portions of the temporal and parietal lobes. This aspect of attention is modulated by the cholinergic system, stemming from the basal forebrain.

Executive attention is characterized by the ability to supervise the direction of focused attention. After determining that a friend has contacted you to tell you he is stranded on the highway because of an overheated engine, you immediately respond by searching for his parents' number in your directory to contact them about arranging a tow truck and texting his roommates to tell them that he will miss dinner because of the car trouble. The ACC, a brain area involved in both cognitive conflicts (competing events attracting your attention) and error detection, and the DLPFC, also implicated in various response conflicts, are associated with the attentional executive network and are modulated by the dopaminergic system.

Further, the locus coeruleus neurons play a role in facilitating your attentional shifts through these stages of alerting, orienting, and executively attending to the incoming call. These attentional shifts are also modulated by norepinephrine. Shifting from the ringtone to problem solving is essential for encoding relevant stimuli and more accurately perceiving relevant stimuli. In one study, when rats were

(a) Alerting network

> **Brain areas activated:**
> Frontal and parietal cortical areas (lateralized to right hemisphere)
>
> **Neurochemical:**
> Norepinephrine

(b) Orienting network

> **Brain areas activated:**
> Visual sensory system (e.g., thalamus, superior colliculus, frontal eye fields), temporal and parietal cortical areas
>
> **Neurochemical:**
> Acetylcholine

(c) Executive network

> **Brain areas activated:**
> Anterior cingulate cortex, dorsolateral prefrontal cortex
>
> **Neurochemical:**
> Dopamine

FIGURE 12.29 Attentional modes in the brain. The modes of attention—alerting, orienting, and executive function—are facilitated by specific areas of the brain. Although moderate levels of widespread activation are observed in brain images, the specific areas mentioned here were designated as most important.

placed in a novel environment, behavioral activation associated with the norepinephrine system was associated with synaptic plasticity (Sara, 2009). These findings suggest that neuroplasticity circuits are primed by the locus coeruleus/norepinephrine system when entering a new environment that must be processed for relevant information.

With the importance of attentional process in learning and memory, it is no surprise that an interruption in attention is associated with the most prevalent childhood learning disorder, ADHD. Introduced in Chapter 5, this disorder is characterized by inattention, impulsivity, and hyperactivity and affects approximately 6% of children and adolescents (Willcutt, 2012). Less conservative estimates have suggested that up to 20% of boys in certain school systems have prescriptions for ADHD medication (Castellanos & Tannock, 2002). Drugs that are traditionally used to treat this disorder modulate dopamine functioning, involved in executive attention functions (as described previously).

Considering that dopamine is also involved in reward systems, pharmacological agonists for the dopamine system (e.g., methamphetamine or Ritalin) may enhance the **saliency**, or relevance, of target stimuli during the learning

process (Berridge, 2007; Schultz, 1998). For example, an enhanced sense of reward may result from arriving at the correct answer with appropriate dopaminergic activation. This focused attention could facilitate the consolidation of memories associated with various academic assignments. However, much controversy surrounds the ADHD diagnosis and the administration of methamphetamines to children. Some research documents therapeutic success, whereas other research reports no positive benefits of the drugs. Researchers also struggle to explain the rising number of diagnoses over the past several years, increasing by up to 24% in just four years (2007–2011) for certain populations of children (Getahun et al., 2012). Continuing with the controversies in this area, research also suggests that when the methodologies of ADHD studies are consistent (e.g., control for the diagnostic criteria and who is making the diagnosis), the rates of ADHD have remained constant over the past several decades (Polanczyk, Willcutt, Salum, Kieling, & Rohde, 2014). Regardless of the controversies surrounding the actual prevalence of ADHD and the best treatment, there is no denying that appropriate levels of attention are necessary for successful learning.

Decision Making

It is easy to understand why rather simplistic learning responses (e.g., classical conditioning and reinforced operant responses) are popular in laboratory investigations of learning and memory processes. However, in real life, response systems are not always that scripted. How do we make decisions between two competing options? And, when a tried-and-true learned response suddenly stops working, what do we do? How does our brain guide our behavior when there is not a straightforward and simple correct answer?

An important factor in decision making, especially for social mammals, is how the presence of other individuals, either collaborators or competitors, influences our decision to make a specific response. A scene from the movie *A Beautiful Mind*, about the Nobel Prize–winning mathematician John Nash, who suffered from schizophrenia, illustrates the intersections between social competition and response strategies. When several young women entered a bar, Nash's character told his male friends that they would be more successful meeting the women if they avoided the most attractive female and paid attention to the less attractive ones. His point was that it was important to consider the actions of others during the decision-making process. If all five friends asked the most attractive woman out, they would block each other's actions. However, if everyone initially approached individual women considered less attractive, then the success rate would increase. Although this bar scene is fictional, it describes Nash's actual

Nash equilibrium as a solution to forming strategies that incorporate the potential actions of others.

Neuroanatomy of Neuroeconomics

Questions about effective decision making have been associated with an emerging discipline known as **neuroeconomics**. This discipline investigates the neural computations that accompany value-based decisions or, in other words, the ways in which the brain makes choices among various options (Sugrue, Corrado, & Newsome, 2005). After all, the ultimate goal of behavior is to make the optimal choice that maximizes an animal's individual survival as well as the survival of its genetic code (Glimcher, 2003). For us, these decisions range from the seemingly trivial decision of selecting the best toothpaste among the many brands on the shelf to life-or-death decisions such as selecting from several treatment options for a serious illness.

Paul Glimcher, a New York University neuroscientist, has suggested that the field of neuroeconomics expands classic views of brain and behavior. Although the 17th-century philosopher René Descartes's views of simple behaviors were characterized by a specific sensory stimulus leading to a specific motor response, neuroeconomics research suggests that the input/output formula is more complicated in the complex real world. Glimcher argues that somewhere between the sensory and motor responses are brain areas devoted to computing the most optimal outcomes leading to enhanced survival.

In one series of studies focusing on perceptual choice, monkeys were trained to recognize the direction of coherent motion in a video display of random dots while the activity of their individual neurons was recorded. As seen in Figure 12.30, the dots could all be moving in a random direction, or they could be moving in a consistent direction. Thus, depending on the dot activity, the decision or choice about the direction of motion could be very difficult or very easy. This range of difficulty allowed the researchers to identify key neural areas that were associated with the animals' decision-making efforts. The researchers found that activity in the **lateral intraparietal area (LIP)** was positively correlated with the monkeys' demonstration of a final decision.

LIP activity has been suggested as a common currency for neuroeconomics because it integrates relevant information for the emergence of the final decision (Sugrue et al., 2005). A general theory of how the LIP is involved with decision making is that it contains a priority, or salience, map. Essentially, salience in this context describes any

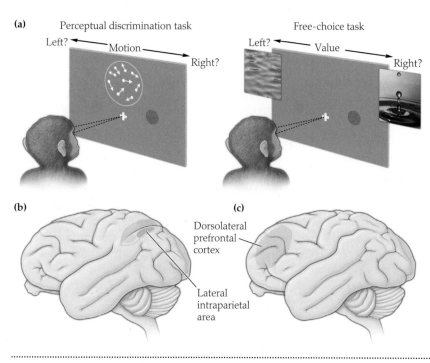

FIGURE 12.30 Decision-making task and brain activity. (a) When monkeys exposed to a random dot decision-making task decide to respond in a certain way, the (b) lateral intraparietal (LIP) area and (c) the dorsolateral prefrontal cortex (DLPFC) are activated.

stimulus that an animal deems important, either from training or via natural tendencies (Rorie, Gao, McClelland, & Newsome, 2010). The LIP is thought to encode a combination of sensory, motor, and cognitive signals that might guide the monkey's final decisions. For example, the LIP may integrate the likelihood that a visual stimulus will appear in a particular location with the magnitude of a juice reward that is associated with a motor response. Thus, although many students struggle to learn the rules of probability theory in their statistics class, the LIP has been described by Glimcher as a brain area that continuously encodes probabilities to determine the most optimal outcome of various response choices (Glimcher, 2003). Who knew that our brains were so proficient at determining probability outcomes?

The precise single-cell recording in the monkey studies described previously cannot be carried out in humans for experimental investigations because of the necessary surgical preparation and invasive placement of electrodes. A variation of the dot perceptual task, however, was used with human subjects whose brains were scanned while making decisions. Specifically, subjects were asked to decide whether ambiguous visual stimuli depicted a house or a face. Again, the difficulty level was manipulated to determine brain area activation associated with the decision-making process. In this study, another brain area, the **dorsolateral prefrontal cortex (DLPFC)**, emerged as important in the decision-making process. More research must be conducted to determine the role of the LIP, an area not easily viewed in fMRI studies, in the human brain (see Figure 12.30). Nonetheless, the DLPFC is involved in the computations associated with decision making (Heekeren, Marrett, Bandettini, & Ungerleider, 2004; Rorie & Newsome, 2005).

The probabilities computed in the brain in decision-making challenges are related to **action–outcome associations**. That is, the various rewards associated with specific actions are determined. Although more research is necessary to thoroughly understand how the brain computes action–outcome values, rat research suggests that the dorsomedial striatum and the OFC play roles in the learning and encoding of these associations. In humans, even within the same person, different valuation systems may exist that confuse action–outcome calculations and ultimate response options. For example, a person presented with the option of having a serving of ice cream is likely to reach for the spoon in the context of the goal directed toward enjoying the sweet taste of ice cream, especially if the person is hungry. However, if the person is on a diet, the action–outcome calculations could differ because the rewarding sweet taste of ice cream is offset by worries about weight gain (Rangel, Camerer, & Montague, 2008).

Another variable that influences decision making is *uncertainty*. In the real world, optimal decisions are often less than obvious because we cannot be certain of the outcomes of our actions. To systematically investigate uncertainty, a formal categorization has been proposed by the neuroscientists Dominik Bach and Raymond Dolan (2012), working at University College London and Berlin School of Mind and Brain, respectively. As shown in Figure 12.31, one can easily experience several sources of confusion when approaching an intersection. In this example, a person may experience *sensory uncertainty* when trying to determine what color the light is, *state uncertainty* when trying to determine how far the car is physically from the stop light, *rule uncertainty* when trying to determine the chances of not having an accident if the car fails to stop for the red light, and *evaluation uncertainty*, an extension of rule uncertainty, which further evaluates the outcome of the potential accident. How likely is it? Will anyone be hurt?

A detailed discussion of the many cortical areas associated with the processing of uncertainty is beyond the scope of this text; however, this variable has an important effect on adaptive decision making. As we will discuss in the next chapter, several psychiatric illnesses may be linked to the atypical processing of different aspects of uncertainty. A misinterpretation of internal or external uncertainty may lead to disorders such as depression, generalized anxiety disorder, and schizophrenia. Finally, although few of us would admit to actually enjoying experiencing uncertainty, living in a world that is always 100% predictable also has its drawbacks. According to the neuroscientists Bach and Dolan, the negative aspects of monotony may explain why "*Homo sapiens*

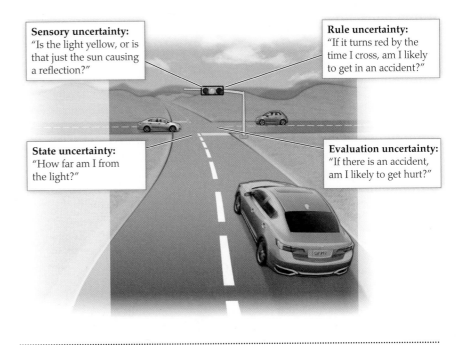

Sensory uncertainty: "Is the light yellow, or is that just the sun causing a reflection?"

Rule uncertainty: "If it turns red by the time I cross, am I likely to get in an accident?"

State uncertainty: "How far am I from the light?"

Evaluation uncertainty: "If there is an accident, am I likely to get hurt?"

FIGURE 12.31 Varying aspects of uncertainty. In everyday tasks such as driving, we encounter various categories of uncertainty including sensory, state, rule, and prediction uncertainty.

continuously strives to cross frontiers, reach higher ground, is addicted to exploration and invests so much store in scientific research—activities that abolish old uncertainties and endlessly create new ones" (Bach & Dolan, 2012, p. 584).

Unexpected Outcomes and Flexible Response Strategies

If you have lived more than about one day on this planet, you have learned that things do not always go as expected. To make the most adaptive choices in the future, the brain should take those unexpected outcomes seriously. You have already learned the importance of positive outcomes in shaping behavior—remember those operant researchers who taught pigeons to peck on a key? Each positive surprise served to reinforce the likelihood that the behavior would be repeated in the future. The brain must also give negative surprises (e.g., the lack of reward when pecking the key) equal or even higher-priority status.

The medial prefrontal cortex (mPFC) is an area that has been implicated in the recognition of unexpected outcomes. Specifically, the mPFC monitors response–outcome associations. It is inhibited if the predicted outcome occurs, and it is activated if the expected outcome fails to occur. It has been suggested that the mPFC signals the "unexpected *non-occurrence of a predicted outcome*" (Alexander & Brown, 2011, p. 1338). This is where the plasticity of our memory processes is valuable. If the contingency rules start to change, we must adapt quickly to avoid suffering the consequences of continuing with inappropriate responses. Further, the ACC is activated when an outcome occurs at an unexpected time, suggesting that the mPFC and ACC work together to signal the occurrence of negative surprises (Alexander & Brown, 2011).

When an unexpected outcome is detected, the OFC has been found to be critical for altering the established

behavior to a more adaptive default plan. The comedian who realizes that his new monologue is not getting the laughs he expected must alter the plan and revert to tried-and-true material, or at least try something different. In this case, the OFC plays a role in facilitating this switch from established behavioral strategies to new adaptive contingency strategies once unexpected outcomes are detected. Hence, the OFC is known for its role in flexible behavior, probably because it is able to rapidly encode changing relationships between specific cues and associated outcomes. For example, as shown in Figure 12.32, rats in one study were trained to associate the first odor with sugar solution and the second odor with bitter quinine solution. When the order was reversed (i.e., now the first odor predicts quinine solution), the associations needed to be rapidly recoded so that the rats would transition from avoiding odor 2 to approaching it so that they would not miss the sweet solution. Rats with OFC lesions, however, were much slower in reversing their behavior and more likely to miss their sweet rewards (Rolls, 1996; Schoenbaum, Roesch, Stainaker, & Takahashi, 2009).

The long-running television show *The Wide World of Sports* had a famous line in its introduction mentioning the "thrill of victory and the agony of defeat." Although few would argue that both victories and defeats are important to the brain, a unique fMRI study using 35 experienced physicians explored the question of whether the brain learned more from victories or defeats. In this study, brain scans were conducted while the physicians learned to discriminate between two fictional medical treatments introduced to them via virtual patient interactions. When the responses during the 64 training trials were evaluated to determine the progress of each subject, the physicians were categorized as either high- or low-performing subjects based on their performance. High performers

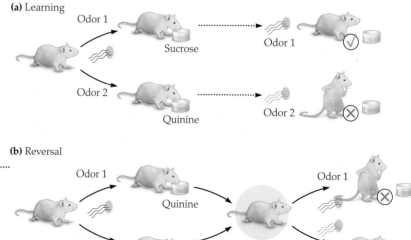

(a) Learning

Odor 1 — Sucrose ⋯⋯ Odor 1 ✓

Odor 2 — Quinine ⋯⋯ Odor 2 ✗

(b) Reversal

Odor 1 — Quinine → Rapid associative encoding → Odor 1 ✗

Odor 2 — Sucrose → Odor 2 ✓

FIGURE 12.32 Orbitofrontal cortex and flexible behavior. Rats were trained in an odor discrimination task in which one odor predicted a desired sweet fluid and another odor predicted an aversive bitter fluid. Animals with lesions were slow to inhibit the previous response–outcome association and adapt by changing their responses to avoid the bitter fluid.

appeared to learn equally from both successes and failures, whereas low performers appeared to learn significantly more from successes than from failures. Specifically, high performers exhibited higher DLPFC activity after failures, and low performers showed more activity in this area following successes. The researchers conducting this study concluded that the high performers' brains were more successful and efficient at learning because they paid attention to and learned from failures during the training sessions. The strategy used by the low performers, focusing only on the reward value of the successful trials, was less effective (Downar, Bhatt, & Montague, 2011). Thus, we may all prefer the victory of success, but we learn as much or more from the agony of defeat!

LABORATORY EXPLORATION

Using Fos Immunoreactivity to Determine Brain Activation During Learning Tasks

As discussed throughout this chapter, researchers have relied on many different types of methods to understand how the brain is involved in learning and memory. Human neuroimaging studies are valuable in that they allow researchers to track brain activity in subjects as they engage in various learning tasks. Although rodent brain scanners do exist, they are extremely rare (and expensive). Consequently, researchers using animal models have had to look to other techniques to capture the activity maps associated with an animal's real-time responses.

Immunocytochemistry (also known as immunohistochemistry) involves exposing extracted brain tissue to specific antibodies to visualize a certain substance of interest, such as brain proteins that are expressed when brain areas are active. One such protein, Fos, is produced by the immediate early gene known as c-fos. This protein is a valuable marker of recent neural events because it is produced in accordance with the activation of intracellular mechanisms. Thus, if cells are actively engaged during a learning task, increased evidence of this protein will be observed in these brain areas. More relevant for this chapter, Fos expression in the hippocampus, implicated in learning and memory, has been associated with recent firing of neurons.

After properly preparing the brain tissue, the researcher applies a primary antibody for the Fos protein to the tissue where it will bind to existing Fos in the brain. Next, to amplify the Fos protein signal, a secondary antibody is applied and will also travel to the Fos antibody and protein clusters. Subsequently, an enzyme complex is applied that will further bind and amplify the Fos protein signal. All of this will be "stained" a dark color following the addition of the enzyme substrate. This stained area is what you see in Laboratory Exploration Figure 12.1, which consists of Fos-immunoreactive cells in the rat CA1 area of the hippocampus that are activated as rats are sitting in their home cage versus exploring a new environment. Thus, these images suggest that this area of

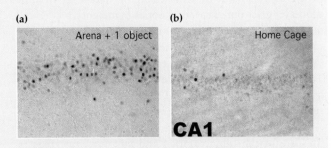

LABORATORY EXPLORATION FIGURE 12.1 Fos immunohistochemistry. In this valuable histological technique, brain tissue is exposed to the primary antibody for Fos. After several subsequent steps, stained tissue with dark cell bodies is produced indicating cells that were active during the task of interest. In this case, more hippocampal cells were active when animals were exposed to (a) novel stimuli in an arena compared with animals (b) remaining in their home cage.

the hippocampus is activated when animals are processing changing stimuli in their environment (VanElzakker, Fevurly, Breindel, & Spencer, 2008).

Although the staining patterns are not viewed as immediately as they are with fMRI scans, if the researchers wait about an hour from the rat's experience to the time of processing the tissue, they can observe an informative picture of brain activity. As discussed in Chapter 1, these imaging techniques are correlational in nature as opposed to causal, however, so further research is required to determine the specific mechanisms underlying learning and memory. Thus, when Fos data are combined with other types of brain data such as electrophysiological or lesion data, powerful inferences can be made about the causes of learning. Even with the stated limitations, the Fos technique has been extremely valuable for the identification of key brain areas enabling researchers to delve deeper in their attempts to understand how the brain learns new information.

Conclusion

This chapter introduced both historical and contemporary neurobiological approaches to the investigation of learning and memory. Prior to the introduction of sophisticated neurobiological techniques, classic behavioral paradigms were introduced by pioneers such as Ivan Pavlov, B. F. Skinner, and E. L. Thorndike. More sophisticated animal models of learning and neurobiological techniques are currently used to expand from the classic case studies to understand how the brain is altered during learning/memory. The simple nervous system of *Aplysia* revealed the important role of serotonin and calcium in synaptic transmission during learning. Research on mammals focused on the hippocampus, which was implicated in spatial memory as well as more sophisticated recognition and associative functions. The discovery of LTP in the hippocampus and the changing nature of synaptic processes grew out of earlier theories of memory-related cell networks. Case studies and human neuroimaging studies indicated the important role of the temporal lobes surrounding the hippocampus as well as the PFC and surrounding area. The brain's ability to adapt to new environments seems to require continuing alterations of the brain's memory circuits, such as neurogenesis and modifications of spine density.

The case of H.M. prompted the investigation of the role of the hippocampus and surrounding areas in declarative memory. Procedural memories have been associated with the cerebellum and are more rigid, or fixed, than declarative memories. Several animal models and human neuroimaging studies have confirmed the critical role of the hippocampus and surrounding areas in memory processes.

Memories are far from infallible: they continue to change throughout our lives. As they are recalled, they are subject to revision, creating problems for the credibility of eyewitnesses in court cases. Stress can impair memory and performance as the subcortical procedural memory systems dominate when the executive cortical areas are distracted. Alternatively, emotionally salient stimuli, mostly threatening stimuli, can lead to enhanced memory that is difficult for some individuals to suppress, even in safe environments. Autobiographical memories can be compulsively collected as evidenced by patients with HSAM.

Recently, a scientific interest in decision making has emerged, with several cortical areas implicated in the ability to solve ambiguous and complex problems. The degree of uncertainty is carefully evaluated by the brain to determine probabilities of correct responses. And when the unexpected occurs, the brain must process the information and quickly change responses to make the most informed and adaptive responses. Accordingly, our brains do not run from failures; on the contrary, these are important "teachable moments" for our neural networks.

KEY TERMS

amnesia (p. 340)

Neurobiological Foundations of Learning and Memory Processes

law of effect (p. 342)
reinforcers (p. 342)
operant conditioning (p. 343)
contingency (p. 343)
Hebbian synapse theory of learning (p. 343)
habituate (p. 344)
place cells (p. 345)
direction cells (p. 345)
grid cells (p. 345)
subiculum (p. 345)
long-term potentiation (LTP) (p. 345)
activity-mediated spine enlargement (p. 347)
filopodia (p. 348)
anterograde amnesia (p. 349)
declarative memory (p. 349)
explicit memory (p. 349)
episodic memory (p. 349)
semantic memory (p. 349)

memory engram (p. 349)
theory of equipotentiality (p. 350)
procedural memory (p. 350)
implicit memory (p. 350)
delayed matching-to-sample task (p. 351)
delayed nonmatching-to-sample task (p. 351)
Morris water maze (p. 352)
radial arm maze (p. 352)
working memory (p. 352)
eye-blink reflex conditioning (p. 353)
Purkinje cells (p. 353)
pontine nuclei (p. 353)
granule cells (p. 353)
interpositus nucleus (p. 353)
paramedian lobule (p. 353)
cortical–hippocampal system (p. 354)
orbitofrontal cortex (p. 355)
processing-based memory system (p. 355)

Modifying Memories

reconsolidating (p. 357)
postretrieval lability (p. 358)

confabulation (p. 358)
Korsakoff's syndrome (p. 358)
posttraumatic stress disorder (PTSD) (p. 359)
startle response (p. 361)
highly superior autobiographical memory (HSAM) (p. 363)

Focus on Attention: Gateway to Learning and Memory

inattentional blindness (p. 363)
saliency (p. 365)

Decision Making

Nash equilibrium (p. 366)
neuroeconomics (p. 366)
lateral intraparietal area (LIP) (p. 366)
dorsolateral prefrontal cortex (DLPFC) (p. 367)
action–outcome associations (p. 367)

REVIEW QUESTIONS

1. Although case studies have limited value in research, they often provide informed starting points for more sophisticated laboratory research. Considering the case of H.M., describe the impact this single case had on the direction of studies subsequently conducted in neurobiology of learning research.

2. What are place cells, and where in the brain are they located? How are they thought to contribute to memory?

3. What theories did Donald Hebb propose with regard to the cellular mechanisms of learning? How did these theories lay the foundation for future theories? Explain.

4. What is the difference between consolidation and re-consolidation of memories?

5. What is HSAM, and what do we know about its potential biological basis?

6. What are the differences among alerting, orienting, and executive attention? What are the differences among the brain networks that appear to modulate these forms of attention?

7. How is the LIP thought to work to determine the most optimal outcome of different response options? Explain.

CRITICAL-THINKING QUESTIONS

1. Do you think that stress more often leads to memory impairment or to memory enhancement? Explain. Give examples from your own life to support your position.

2. Based on what you have learned in this chapter, critically evaluate Henke's processing-based memory systems model. What aspects of memory does it account for and explain well? What aspects of memory does it fail to account for? Explain.

3. Do you think that the malleability of human memory is an asset, a liability, or both? Explain.

Mental Illness

Cautionary Tales in Psychiatry: The Questionable Creation of Sheri Storm's Multiple Personalities

Sitting at a local restaurant, Sheri Storm felt a wave of nausea as she opened the *Milwaukee Journal Sentinel* to read as she sipped her morning coffee. The headline that caught her eye described the case of a woman who had testified that a psychiatrist had planted false memories in her mind and then claimed that she had more than 200 personalities, including the personalities of the Bride of Satan and a duck. Sheri had eerily similar experiences with her own psychiatrist and her diagnosis of multiple personality disorder (which, as you will soon learn, is now known as "dissociative identity disorder") with an accompanying 200+ personalities. As it turned out, Sheri's psychiatrist was the same person being accused of malpractice in the newspaper article! Up until this time, Sheri had trusted that her psychiatrist had used evidence-based therapeutic practices. Now, however, she was confused about her so-called "treatment."

Sheri had sought help initially for both anxiety and insomnia following a divorce and the start of a new career. She thought that an antidepressant drug or some relaxation techniques might help build her emotional resilience. However, her psychiatrist employed other techniques, including

hypnosis and multiple medications to affect her mental state, delivered in his office and during numerous hospitalizations. According to her psychiatrist, during hypnosis Sheri had recalled being sexually abused as a child as well as being forced to participate in satanic rituals that involved the consumption of human infants.

Although these stories were bizarre to Sheri, her psychiatrist showed her video recording of sessions in which she was heavily drugged with a so-called truth serum, *sodium amytal*. Following her psychiatrist's lead, she parroted back bits and pieces of childhood abuse stories in the videos. She believed her psychiatrist's conclusion that she was a victim of satanic and sexual abuse and, to cope with this distress, had developed alter egos to deal with the pain. Further, she was terrified when told that if she did not continue with this grueling therapy, a demonic personality would emerge and likely harm her children.

As Sheri read on, she learned that the fellow patient described in the article had just received $2.4 million after accusing her psychiatrist of malpractice for using the very same techniques Sheri had encountered. Sheri's mental world collapsed as questions raced through her mind about the actual status of her memories, emotions, and mental health.

Behind the Scenes

If you think this sounds more like a movie plot than an actual case study, I would agree. But in this case, Sheri's story became personal because she contacted me after reading an article I had written about the importance of **evidence-based therapies** for mental illness. I was intrigued by her story of how, although she now understands that her particular condition is an *iatrogenic condition* (a condition that is caused by a physician or medical treatment), she still had nightmares of the horrifying satanic ritual scenes her psychiatrist had described to her.

Although Sheri suffered extended disability from her psychiatric therapy, she was somewhat comforted to learn what biological psychology could teach her about what had likely happened to her brain during these sessions. As you learned in the previous chapter, our memory systems are vulnerable because they can effortlessly reinvent our life stories. With the aid of sedative drugs and hypnosis, the mental filters we all use to discern what is "real" or not were likely severely compromised in Sheri's brain. Although many of her memories were fabricated, her brain seemed to have processed them as though they were actual events she had encountered. Consequently, it appeared that they were just as likely to emerge in her dreams and waking hours as the recollection of a shopping list or a relative's birthday.

Further, the stress associated with the mere thought of harming her children made these new memories more relevant than any information she had ever encountered. The fear associated with these memories may have sensitized her amygdala, creating heightened anxiety. These false and damaging memories remained following the hypnosis sessions, continuing to interfere with her ongoing adaptive functions and coping skills (K. G. Lambert & Lilienfeld, 2007). After two decades, Sheri remains haunted by her mental health "therapy" (Figure 13A).

Unfortunately, Sheri was just one of many who were exposed to this horrendous form of therapy. The rise in interest in multiple personality disorder, now known as **dissociative identity disorder**, coincided with the publication of a book, *Sybil*, in 1973. This book was based on the supposed true story of Shirley Mason and her multiple personalities associated with unspeakable torturous acts carried out by her mother. Within just four years of its release, *Sybil* sold more than 6 million copies in the United States. A few years later, approximately 20% of the American population watched the made-for-television movie that was based on the book.

After Shirley's Mason's death, documents revealed that her "personalities" were created in a similar way as Sheri's,

FIGURE 13A Sheri Storm. After experiencing long-term negative effects from her therapy for multiple personality disorder, Sheri (on the right) spoke to students at Randolph-Macon College about the importance of evidence-based therapies. She is shown here with her grown children.

a product of massive amounts of drugs and extended hypnosis sessions over the course of several years. Further, as was the case for Sheri, no corroborating evidence of abuse or satanic rituals was ever discovered. Accordingly, Shirley Mason's story of multiple personalities also appears to be iatrogenic, a product of her psychiatrist, Dr. Constance Wilbur (Nathan, 2011). Prior to the release of the book *Sybil*, fewer than 50 multiple personality disorder cases resulting from child abuse had been reported. However, by 1994, more than 40,000 such cases had been reported. The majority of these cases were characterized by memories of torture, satanic rituals, and cannibalism that surfaced after several years of therapy. The therapy in these cases led to estrangement from families, unemployment, and increased thoughts of suicide—pointing to the importance of using only evidence-based therapies when treating mental illness (Lambert & Lilienfeld, 2007). Fortunately, these cases are an extreme occurrence and do not represent treatment strategies in the larger field of psychiatry. ▸

Let's face it: we all have behaviors that teeter on the verge of abnormality. When I go on vacation or a business trip, I check my suitcase several times for important items, a response that could be described as compulsive in some contexts. When my daughters are later arriving home than anticipated, I reflexively generate mental scenarios in which they are injured as my fear and panic escalate until they arrive home safely. Is that a loving, concerned parent or someone with symptoms of an anxiety disorder?

My guess is that my personal brushes with variations of traditional views of mental illness are commonplace in today's society. In some cases, mental health extremes are even celebrated. Did Picasso have a fragmented perception of reality, or was he an inspired artist when he introduced cubism to the world? Did Albert Einstein exhibit symptoms of autism spectrum disorder, or was he a quiet, brilliant thinker? As you can see, determining whether someone's behavior is normal or abnormal, functional or dysfunctional, or adaptive or maladaptive is often challenging.

The Challenge of Classifying and Treating Mental Illness

The perception that the brain is involved in mental illness is somewhat recent, following a harrowing history of false perceptions and misunderstandings. The diagnostic and treatment strategies continue to evolve because, compared with other medical conditions, there are few effective treatments currently available for those suffering from various types of mental illnesses.

The Meandering Search for the Roots of Mental Illness

Before modern neurobiological techniques were available, the causes of mental illnesses were a mystery. The ancient Greeks looked to the heart as the regulator of mental and emotional functions. Hippocrates, however, insightfully pointed to the brain as the control center of the body's functions, suggesting that "from nothing else but the brain come joys, delights, laughter and sports, and sorrows, griefs, despondency, and lamentations" (Finger, 2000, p. 69).

Although Hippocrates made his insightful comments in the 5th century BCE, it would take well over a millennium for real progress to be made in understanding the brain's role in mental functions. This slow progress came at a great cost for those suffering from mental illness. This was probably never more evident than during the Middle Ages in Europe, when the Church advocated the view that abnormal behavior came from supernatural forces (e.g., demons) controlling an individual's behavior. Therapeutic approaches advocated outside of religious doctrine such as the use of laxatives, emetics (to prompt vomiting), and bleeding with leeches also fell short of effectively treating mentally ill patients (MacDonald, 1981).

The most tragic consequence of the emphasis on supernatural thinking followed the 1484 publication of *Malleus Maleficarum* (translated, *Hammer of the Witches*) that was written by the monks Heinrich Kraemer and Johann Sprenger. In stark contrast to Hippocrates' teaching, this document linked abnormal behavior to socializing with the Devil. Because most of the abnormal behavior described in *Malleus* involved women, the women were called witches. Therapies were not considered to "treat" these women; instead, the women were often tortured and then burned to death. Approximately two centuries following the initial publication of *Malleus*, the teachings of this document influenced the community of Salem, Massachusetts, resulting in 19 women being labeled witches and hanged (Finger, 2000; Shorter, 1997).

As the Middle Ages passed, various clinicians and researchers around the world explored the biological causes of mental illness. After studying medicine in Vienna in the mid-19th century, Theodor Meynert started examining brain tissue from deceased individuals who had suffered from mental illness. Using a microscope to understand a patient's odd behavior was indeed innovative at that time. Toward the end of the 19th century, he wrote, "The more that psychiatry seeks, and finds, its scientific bases in a deep and finely grained understanding of the anatomical structure [of the brain], the more it elevates itself to the status of a science that deals with causes" (quoted in Shorter, 1997, p. 77).

As Meynert was embarking on his journey to find the ultimate causes of mental illness, Emil Kraepelin was offered a professorship in the university psychiatry clinic in Heidelberg and was equally interested in mapping clinical symptoms onto the brain. Kraepelin recruited an impressive team of scientists to form one of the earliest clinical neuroscience laboratories (Figure 13.1). This team included Franz Nissl, who became known for his contribution to brain histology after using a stain to differentiate the six different layers of the cerebral cortex. Alois Alzheimer also collaborated with Kraepelin's lab and, in 1906, reported specific neuropathology that was consistent with a form of dementia, or mental deterioration. This condition now bears his name because of the progress he made in this area (Finger, 2000; Shorter, 1997).

In an attempt to understand the brain's role in mental illness, the researchers in Kraepelin's lab focused on symptoms such as memory deterioration, sadness, and false beliefs. Kraepelin suggested that separate illnesses existed that could be systematically categorized. Reviewing his records, as well as the reports of others working with clinical populations, he suggested that some patients fell into a manic–depressive category. In addition, he described a condition in which individuals exhibited mental deterioration as young adults, a category he referred to as *dementia praecox* (translated as "premature mental deterioration"). In 1908, Eugen Bleuler, a follower of Kraepelin, introduced the term **schizophrenia** for this condition, referring to the splitting of the mind's functions, leading to mismatches between cognitive and emotional responses (Finger, 2000; Shorter, 1997).

Working at the Parisian Salpêtrière Hospital during the mid-19th century, Jean-Martin Charcot was also interested in categorizing mental illnesses. He documented patients' symptoms and conducted brain autopsies following their death to identify brain pathologies that were associated with specific symptom profiles. This strategy enabled Charcot to introduce disorder categorizations such as multiple sclerosis, as well as conditions that we now call Parkinson's disease and Tourette syndrome. He was especially intrigued by patients who exhibited a behavioral problem but had no apparent brain pathology.

When a young Sigmund Freud listened to one of Charcot's lectures about mental symptoms emerging without biological causes, he embraced the idea that mental events could produce mental illness symptoms. Freud founded the field of **psychoanalysis**, emphasizing unconscious motives, not faulty neural networks, as the causes of

(a) (b) (c)

FIGURE 13.1 **Biological psychiatry pioneers.** (a) Alois Alzheimer, (b) Emil Kraepelin, and (c) Franz Nissl were part of a team of scientists who formed one of the earliest clinical neuroscience laboratories.

mental illness. Freud's theories about the origins of mental illness persisted in the United States through the mid-20th century. Despite an emphasis on evidence-based therapies and progress in understanding the role of the brain in mental functions, the perception of mental, as opposed to biologically based, mechanisms of mental health and mental illness persists even today (Finger, 2000).

Early Biological Therapies for Mental Illness

Understanding that the brain played an influential role in the symptoms characterizing mental illness was an important step toward understanding specific neurobiological mechanisms associated with some of those symptoms. Even so, the initial attempts to use this knowledge to help patients suffering from mental illness were, by today's standards, brutal and unethical.

A popular treatment for depression emerged in the 1930s in part from the Italian psychiatry professor Ugo Cerletti, who experimented with inducing seizures in dogs, so that dogs could be used as an animal model for epilepsy. This line of investigation revealed that the seizures could be produced by placing electrodes only on the head. Cerletti and his team tested the electrical current technique in 1938. After Cerletti's team systematically increased the current to prompt a seizure, his patients' psychiatric symptoms were significantly improved. This was the birth of **electroconvulsive therapy (ECT)**, which became a popular treatment for depression (Shorter, 1997).

Interest in identifying drugs that affected the brain's functions did not disappear with the emergence of ECT therapy. Sedative barbiturates, discovered at the turn of the 20th century, for example, became a popular tool for mental health professionals (Lopez-Munoz, Ucha-Udabe, & Alamo, 2005). Combinations of deep sleep therapies and barbiturate drug regimens were also used to treat mood disorders. In the mid-20th century, however, **psychopharmacologic drugs** would attract the most interest as a treatment approach, persisting as the most popular therapeutic strategy today (Kessler, Demier et al., 2005; Shorter, 1997). As described throughout this chapter, these drugs have enjoyed mixed success as treatments for mental illness.

Although biological approaches to mental illness took a long time to enter the realm of accepted practices, the idea of altering the skull and brain to provide relief from mental illness has been around since prehistoric times. The practice of **trepanning** involved drilling holes in the skull to relieve symptoms. Although trepanning was likely done initially to relieve purported evil or troubled spirits from the affected person (as some scientists believe), it also incorporated a physical, biological approach (Finger, 1994).

A new approach was introduced around 1935 by the Lisbon neurologist Egas Moniz. Moniz got his idea for this line of treatment after hearing a conference talk by the Yale neurologists Carlyle Jacobsen and John Fulton. Jacobsen and Fulton presented the results of an experiment in which they had severed the frontal lobes of two chimps, Becky and Lucy. They described learning impairments in both chimps after the operation as well as the emotional shifts in the chimps. After making an error in the learning task, Becky shifted from a presurgery agitation to a postsurgery quiescent state, whereas Lucy demonstrated the opposite effect—increased emotional agitation following the surgery. When addressing the drastic emotional change in Becky, resulting in a more relaxed demeanor, Jacobsen and Fulton conveyed that they did not know whether this type of surgery would benefit human psychiatric patients (Miller & Cummings, 2007). Collaborating with the neurosurgeon Almeida Lima, Moniz attempted on humans this experimental surgery that, to his knowledge, had been tested only in a single study of two captive chimps (with the desired effect occurring in only *one* of the chimps). In a procedure known as prefrontal leucotomy, Moniz and Lima bored two holes in the dorsal surface of the human skull, inserted a whisk-like instrument, and moved it back and forth to destroy connections to the frontal lobes.

In the United States, the neurologist Walter Freeman and the neurosurgeon James Watts followed Moniz's reports of this new surgery with great interest. They adapted the technique and introduced a procedure that they called a **lobotomy** as a treatment for psychiatric symptoms. With this method, surgeons used an instrument that resembled an icepick to enter the brain through the eye socket and jiggled the instrument around to damage neural connections. This revised version of the technique was known as a transorbital lobotomy (El-Hai, 2005). Figure 13.2 depicts the instrument used to perform a transorbital lobotomy.

This exciting new surgery was featured in a 1947 *Life Magazine* article. The lingering effect of Freud's **psychodynamic theory** was apparent in the images included with the story because it was suggested that the surgeon's knife eliminated a personality component known as the *id*, the component associated with animal-like urges, allowing the more mature and ethical ego and super-ego personality components to prevail. Also striking in this article is the statement that this procedure had *only* a 3% mortality rate.

Did the separation of the frontal lobes from the rest of the brain, namely the brain's emotional centers, end the troubling psychiatric symptoms of human patients? Although Freeman kept notes on his patients, no systematic investigation of frontal lobotomies indicated that the technique was effective. Further, the side effects were perhaps more problematic than the original symptoms.

Sadly, it turns out that the suffering associated with these surgeries could have been avoided if only Moniz had done his homework. More than a half century before his experimental surgeries with his trusting patients, physiologist David Ferrier, working at King's College in London, lesioned sections of the frontal lobes in monkeys and published the following statement:

> "For this operation I selected the most active, lively, and intelligent animals which I could obtain. . . . They seemed to me, after having studied their character carefully before and after the operation, to have

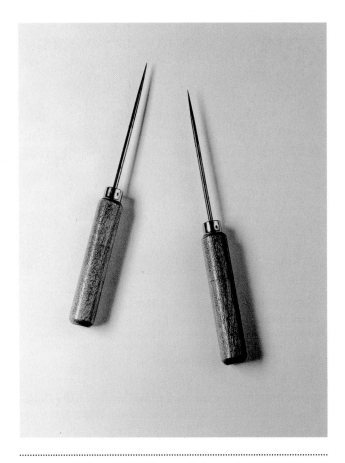

FIGURE 13.2 **Transorbital lobotomy instruments.** Although the lobotomy treatment strategy led to a Nobel Prize, it is now known that the procedure lacked empirical support and, unfortunately, resulted in severe impairment in the patients who received the "treatment." Shown here are a set of Watts–Freeman lobotomy instruments.

> undergone a great change. . . . instead of being actively interested in their home surroundings, they ceased to exhibit any interest in their environment beyond their own immediate sensations, paid no attention to, or looked vacantly and indifferently at, what formerly would have excited intense curiosity, sat stupidly quiet or went to sleep. . . . and generally appeared to have lost the faculty of intelligent and attentive observation. (Fulton, 1951, p. 21)

Further, University of Wisconsin psychologist Harry Harlow reported in 1948 that frontal lobe lesions resulted in learning deficits in monkeys (Harlow, 1989).

Despite knowledge suggesting that frontal lesions resulted in behavioral abnormalities, as well as the absence of empirical evidence of the success of the prefrontal leucotomy, Moniz was awarded the 1949 Nobel Prize for his "innovative" work in the field of mental illness. In a most unfortunate case, in 1960 Freeman (Figure 13.3) performed frontal lobotomy surgery on a 12-year-old child, Howard Dully. The boy's stepmother had reported that he had behavioral problems, such as not cleaning his room or bathing.

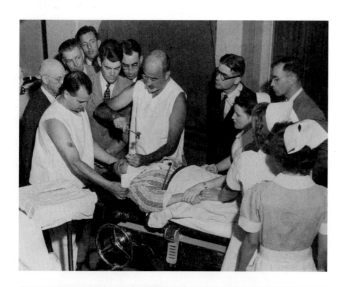

FIGURE 13.3 **Dr. Walter Freeman performs a lobotomy on an unnamed patient.** At 12 years of age, Howard Dully was lobotomized by Dr. Walter Freeman at the request of his stepmother, who was concerned about his behavioral problems, including not cleaning his room or wanting to bathe.

Howard was naively led to Dr. Walter Freeman's office, where Freeman told him that he was going to perform some tests. Ten minutes later, Howard left the office after having experienced a transorbital lobotomy. According to his book *My Lobotomy*, Howard reported that, far from being "fixed" to appease his stepmother's expectations, the surgery only damaged him, leading his parents to place him in a mental institution (Dully & Fleming, 2008).

In the rest of the chapter, you will learn that behavioral and cognitive treatment approaches are now known to alter the brain's functions without requiring invasive techniques. Additionally, as you are well aware by this point, environmental context influences the brain's functions, an observation that is also being incorporated into contemporary treatment strategies for mental illness.

Contemporary Mental Health Classifications

Currently, two diagnostic systems are used to categorize mental disorders: the *Diagnostic and Statistical Manual of Mental Disorders* (DSM) and the *International Classification of Diseases* (ICD), published by the American Psychiatric Association and the World Health Organization, respectively. The 5th version of the DSM (DSM-5) was published in 2013, and the 10th version of the ICD (ICD-10) is currently in use. The ICD encompasses all medical disorders, with a specific chapter devoted to mental disorders; by contrast, the DSM is devoted exclusively to mental disorders (Hyman, 2007).

The first DSM (DSM-I), in 1952, included diagnostic criteria for 106 disorders. The number of disorders, however, dramatically increased with subsequent revisions, and the current DSM consists of approximately 400 disorders

(American Psychiatric Association, 2013). The DSM-5 is widely used, but it is controversial. The specificity of mental illness categories can produce confusion. For example, the lack of empirical support to justify the existence of the DSM's various diagnostic categories is a topic of heated debate. In the DSM-5, several disorders were altered, introduced, or deleted in the absence of what many clinicians and researchers would view as clear evidence justifying such moves (Wakefield, 2013). For example, grieving for a lost loved one is no longer considered an exception for a depression diagnosis as it was in the DSM-IV (Wakefield, 2012). Thus, whereas a person who exhibited symptoms of depression for up to two months following the loss of a loved one would not have been diagnosed with depression and treated accordingly based on the DSM-IV, that person would now be treated as a depressed patient under the guidelines of the DSM-5. As these modifications have been evaluated, concerns have been raised about pathologizing behavioral patterns that were not viewed as consistent with mental illness prior to the release of the DSM-5 (Wakefield, 2013).

The truth is that no blood tests or brain activity patterns exist to objectively identify a specific mental disorder, making diagnosis far more subjective than with other diseases. Because of the varying nature of the diagnostic categories and lack of specificity related to associated causes, the term *mental disorder* is thought to be more appropriate than *mental disease* (Stein et al., 2010). The lack of specific tangible diagnostic criteria allows value judgments to play a role in the determination of disordered behavior. For example, homosexuality was characterized as a disorder in the first DSM but was removed in the 1973 version, the DSM-II. No key biological discovery or pivotal research study accompanied the removal of homosexuality as a mental disorder, just as no objective research finding accompanied its inclusion as a disorder in DSM-I. In this case, it appeared that the change simply represented a shift in values and social tolerance (Caplan, 1996).

Evidence suggests that common neurobiological mechanisms may be expressed as different mental illnesses. Recent research focusing on genetic markers associated with five disorders including bipolar disorder, major depressive disorder, schizophrenia, autism spectrum disorder, and ADHD suggests that, at the causal level, various mental illnesses may be more similar than different. As researchers searched for **single-nucleotide polymorphisms (SNPs)**, or variations in adenosine, guanine, thymine, or cytosine nucleotide bases (see Chapter 1) that were specific to each disorder, to their surprise, they found that specific SNPs were more generally associated with all of the targeted disorders. Further, of the four SNPs that were identified as relevant, two were associated with voltage-activated calcium channels in neuronal membranes. This provides evidence that specific genes may influence multiple manifestations of mental illness, suggesting that a single gene may have multiple neurobiological effects (Cross-disorder Group of the Psychiatric Genomics Consortium et al., 2013).

Although the classifications and defining diagnostic criteria for mental illnesses are still evolving, much research has been conducted on the neurobiological factors associated with these disorders. Accordingly, several representative disorders, along with their proposed causes and treatments, are discussed in the rest of this chapter. Specifically, you will encounter historical and contemporary research on schizophrenia, mood disorders, anxiety disorders, and anxiety-related disorders. Although they are far from complete, these synopses will give you an idea of the progress and continued challenges facing researchers and clinicians as they attempt to treat these debilitating disorders.

Schizophrenia

Schizophrenia, affecting about 1% of the population is, for most individuals, a disabling and persistent psychiatric illness (Dobbs, 2010). This disorder is typically diagnosed in late adolescence (Gogtay, Vyas, Testa, Wood, & Pantelis, 2011). Although symptom expression may vary in males and females, schizophrenia is equally likely to occur in males and females (Ochoa, Usall, Cobo, Labad, & Kulkarni, 2012; Canuso & Pandina, 2007). As previously mentioned, schizophrenia is characterized by mental fragmentation and associated mental conflicts experienced by patients (Freedman, 2010). Because of its emphasis on the splitting of mental functions, schizophrenia is often confused with dissociative identity disorder, previously known as multiple personality disorder. However, schizophrenia and dissociative identity disorder are very different. For diagnostic purposes, schizophrenia is characterized by delusions (false beliefs), hallucinations (perceptions that are not accompanied by a physical stimulus), diminished or confused speech, agitated behavior (e.g., repetitive behaviors), and other symptoms that cause social or occupational dysfunction.

Traditionally, schizophrenia symptoms have been categorized as positive or negative. Generally, **positive symptoms** such as delusions and hallucinations are viewed as abnormal behaviors that are present in people with schizophrenia but not in healthy individuals. **Negative symptoms** are associated with the diminishment or absence of the normal emotional responses or thought processes that are seen in healthy individuals.

This positive–negative categorization of symptoms for psychiatric illnesses was initially proposed by the 19th-century neurologist John Hughlings Jackson, known for his contributions to the understanding of epilepsy (Chapter 3). Jackson hypothesized that positive symptoms were associated with decreased inhibitory control and that negative symptoms resulted from malfunctioning "neural arrangements" (Foussias & Remington, 2010). These views were reinforced when the first effective drug treatments decreased the positive symptoms, but had little effect on the negative symptoms. More recently, it has been suggested that the positive and negative symptoms should be considered part of a triad of symptom categories, along with cognitive dysfunctions such as disorganized or interrupted thoughts. Thus, cognitive impairments associated with schizophrenia could contribute to both the positive and the negative symptoms (Bencherif, Stachowiak, Kucinski, & Lippiello, 2012).

To some extent, negative symptoms are to be expected in individuals considered mentally healthy. For example, it is not unusual to briefly experience bouts of social withdrawal or emotional or cognitive confusion. Although the positive symptoms are viewed as extremely rare and indicative of psychiatric illness, these symptoms also occur in healthy individuals. Research suggests that auditory hallucinations, for example, are somewhat common during the transition from a waking to a sleeping state. Grieving individuals have also reported hearing the voice of a recently deceased person. Unlike a person diagnosed with schizophrenia, healthy individuals experience such hallucinations only briefly and recognize them as false, likely because of functional neuronal filters that determine whether an event is real or imagined.

Causes

Extensive research has been conducted to identify the single most likely cause of the debilitating symptoms of schizophrenia. Neurochemical, neuroanatomical, and genetic causes have been the focus of research; however, no single cause has been identified.

Neurochemical Candidates. Although more than a century has passed since Eugen Bleuler introduced the term *schizophrenia*, a single direct cause remains elusive. For a while, however, researchers thought they had solved the mystery. The key to the puzzle was a purple dye known as **chlorpromazine** that was initially synthesized from coal tar in the 19th century. Approximately 70 years later, a drug company purchased the rights to the dye after discovering that it had properties of an antihistamine. Clinical trials for human safety and effectiveness consisted of giving drugs to individuals suffering from incurable illnesses. Out of pure coincidence, the population that received the experimental drug happened to be patients diagnosed with schizophrenia who resided in a French mental hospital.

Unexpectedly, medical staff reported that patients were somewhat calmer, not as responsive to external stimuli, and less anxious, although they also showed diminished initiative. In a sense, this chemical seemed to have produced effects similar to that of the prefrontal lobotomy, but without the risk, cost, and side effects. The other chemicals that had previously been used on the patients were barbiturates that resulted in very heavy sedation, making chlorpromazine an attractive alternative because it induced less sedation. Essentially, it calmed the patients without putting them to sleep. Consequently, two French psychiatrists, Pierre Deniker and Jean Delay, suggested that chlorpromazine was a **neuroleptic drug**. The term *leptic* is associated with seizures, suggesting that the drug's effects may have been considered similar to those of the seizure-producing drugs and electroconvulsive therapy that were used at that time to treat mental illness (Freedman, 2010). The observation that the drug diminished symptoms of schizophrenia also suggested that it was most effective in treating the positive symptoms. In addition to being referred to as neuroleptics, drugs that reduced these schizophrenia symptoms were also known as **antipsychotics**.

With the neuroleptic drug chlorpromazine touted as an effective treatment, the next step was to determine exactly how the drug worked in the brain. The Swedish physiologist Arvid Carlsson, who won the Nobel Prize for his work establishing that dopamine was a neurotransmitter in the brain, proposed the **dopamine theory of schizophrenia** by demonstrating that the dopaminergic system was the primary target of the neuroleptic drugs (see Figure 13.4). Further, when dopamine agonists were given to patients (typically for movement disorders such as Parkinson's disease), schizophrenia symptoms often emerged. Thus, the dopamine theory suggested that schizophrenia was caused by excessive activity of the brain's dopamine system (Yeragani, Tancer, Chokka, & Baker, 2010). Providing further support for the role of dopamine in schizophrenia, subsequent research reported that the D_1 and D_2 dopamine receptors were located in brain areas involved with emotion, memory, and cognition. The clinical efficacy of the neuroleptic drugs correlated with how effectively they blocked dopamine receptors (Byne, Kemether, Jones, Haroutanian, & Davis, 1999; Freedman, 2003).

However, several findings have provided evidence against the theory that excessive dopamine activity is a principal cause of schizophrenia. The observation that the neuroleptic drugs merely calmed patients without curing them suggested that the dopamine theory of schizophrenia fell short. Robert Freedman, a psychiatrist at the University of

Colorado, has identified inconsistencies with the dopamine theory of schizophrenia. The observation that the symptoms are not entirely alleviated with neuroleptics, as well as the fact that alternative treatments with marginal success influenced other neurotransmitter systems, suggested that dopamine was not a principal cause of schizophrenia. Additionally, when neuroleptics were observed to reduce positive symptoms, tests failed to demonstrate reduced levels of dopamine metabolites or receptors. This suggested a disconnect between the dopaminergic system and symptom expression (Byne et al., 1999; Freedman, 2003). Scientists continue to debate the role of dopamine in schizophrenia. Although researchers are hesitant to completely abandon the dopamine theory, it has been suggested that a reconceptualized theory of schizophrenia should incorporate other neurochemicals.

Schizophrenic patients themselves proposed another neurochemical candidate for contributing to schizophrenia symptoms—acetylcholine. Interestingly, schizophrenia patients are among the heaviest consumers of tobacco, with about 80% smoking cigarettes (compared with approximately 20% of the general population, as noted in Chapter 4). Knowing that nicotine consumption influences the acetylcholine system, researchers began to wonder whether chain-smoking cigarettes was a form of self-medication (Winterer et al., 2013).

The way these patients smoke has provided further clues about their neurochemistry. Researchers have found that schizophrenia patients inhale more deeply than other smokers and hold their breath longer (Winterer, 2010). This exaggerated inhalation may be necessary to activate the less sensitive nicotinic receptors. The α 7-nicotinic receptor has been scrutinized for its potential involvement in schizophrenia since it is more than 10 times less sensitive than other nicotinic receptors and would require the deeper breaths to activate these less responsive receptors. Additional support for the involvement of nicotinic acetylcholine receptors is provided by the finding that 50% more nicotine per smoked cigarette is found in the urine of schizophrenia patients compared with healthy (yet smoking) controls. Finally, schizophrenia patients are more likely than smokers without schizophrenia to prefer the cigarette butts—the section of the cigarette with the highest concentration of nicotine (Freedman, 2010).

The ubiquitous neurotransmitter glutamate has also been implicated in contributing to the cognitive dysfunction and negative symptoms of schizophrenia. High doses of the glutamate receptor antagonist phenylcyclohexylpiperidine, originally developed as an anesthetic, produce symptoms of schizophrenia, suggesting that the glutamate system may be involved in schizophrenia. More specifically, drugs modulating the **NMDA receptor** improve negative and cognitive symptoms associated with schizophrenia (Coyle, 2006).

An interesting case study also emphasizes the critical role of NMDA receptors in the production of schizophrenia symptoms. When 24-year-old Susannah Cahalan quickly

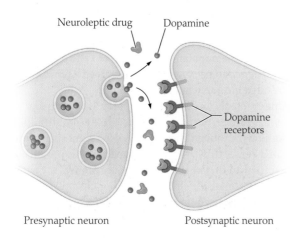

FIGURE 13.4 Neuroleptic drugs and dopamine transmission. Neuroleptic drugs such as chlorpromazine block dopamine D_2 receptors.

Neuroleptic drug   Dopamine

Dopamine receptors

Presynaptic neuron   Postsynaptic neuron

transitioned from a highly functioning reporter for the *New York Post* to a patient strapped to a bed after exhibiting hallucinations, delusions, and emotional outbursts, a diagnosis of schizophrenia seemed imminent. Because of the sudden onset of symptoms and the emergence of seizures, she found herself in the care of neurologists rather than psychiatrists or psychologists. As Susannah chronicles in her book *Brain on Fire: My Month of Madness*, the mysterious psychiatric and neurological symptoms eventually led to a rare diagnosis, anti-NMDA receptor autoimmune encephalitis. This disorder is characterized by excessive numbers of antibodies known to attack NMDA receptors, which are prevalent throughout the cortex and limbic structures. Susannah's brain was inflamed as a result of an immunological attack against a staple neurotransmitter system that is necessary for normal brain functioning (Cahalan, 2012). After Susannah was placed on an aggressive immunological regimen, her symptoms disappeared.

When researchers exposed neurons to CSF from a patient suffering from anti-NMDA receptor autoimmune enchphalitis, they observed intense immunoreactivity, indicating a dense population of NMDA receptors interacting with the antibodies. Further, as seen in Figure 13.5b, rat brain tissue exposed to the affected CSF illustrates that the

(a)

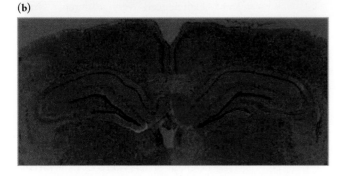

(b)

FIGURE 13.5 Autoimmune encephalitis and schizophrenia-like symptoms. (a) Susannah Cahalan exhibited characteristic symptoms of schizophrenia after developing anti-NMDA receptor autoimmune encephalitis. (b) When cerebrospinal fluid from patients with this disorder is applied to rat brains, antibodies for NMDA receptors occupy the hippocampus (shown in blue).

dense population of NMDA receptors is attacked by antibodies in the hippocampus. Considering the role of the hippocampus in memory (Chapter 12), this may explain why a characteristic feature of patients who recover from this condition is amnesia for the time in which they were most severely affected (Dalmau et al., 2008). Cases such as this one remind us that there may be multiple causes for the symptoms typically associated with schizophrenia.

Dopamine, acetylcholine, and glutamate represent just three of the many neurochemicals that are involved in the symptoms of schizophrenia. As you know, neurochemicals influence the structures of the brain. In the next section, we will examine changes in brain anatomy that accompany the symptoms of schizophrenia.

Neuroanatomical Candidates. The brains of patients diagnosed with schizophrenia have been extensively compared with normal brains in an attempt to learn which brain areas influence symptoms. Compared with healthy controls, the following neuroanatomical differences have been observed (Rund, 2009):

- Larger lateral ventricles (see Figure 13.6)
- Smaller temporal lobes
- Smaller frontal lobes
- Slightly smaller volume of thalamus
- Significant loss of gray matter (up to 10%) during adolescence

Thus, brain tissue loss is generally thought to progress through the initial phase of onset of the disorder. However, several lines of reasoning suggest that this decline does not persist after this time. An improvement in cognitive functioning, for example, is often observed after the first remission, when the symptoms subside (Rund, Landro, & Orbeck, 1997). Such functional improvement would probably not accompany continued neuroanatomical decline. Additionally, few biomarkers of neural degeneration (e.g., cellular degeneration at autopsy) exist in the autopsied brains of patients with schizophrenia (Weinberger & Marenco, 2003).

The vulnerability of the brain during adolescence has prompted many researchers to focus on this developmental

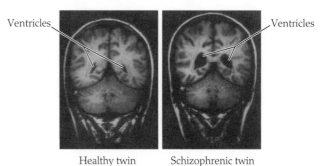

Ventricles   Ventricles

Healthy twin   Schizophrenic twin

FIGURE 13.6 Ventricle size and schizophrenia. In identical twins disconcordant for schizophrenia, the twin with schizophrenia has larger ventricles.

stage to reveal critical variables associated with the onset of schizophrenia. The University of Pittsburgh psychiatrist David Lewis and his colleagues have focused on changes occurring in the DLPFC. As previous chapters note, this area is important for the integration of cognitive and emotional information. Additionally, the DLPFC is known to continue to develop during childhood and adolescence and is influenced by both genetic and environmental factors. Lewis's work has revealed that the pyramidal neurons in the third layer of the DLPFC cortex have smaller cell bodies and fewer dendritic spines in patients with schizophrenia than that in healthy controls (Lewis & Gonzalez-Burgos, 2008).

Typically, the pruning away of unnecessary neurons during adolescence strengthens cognitive functions. In the case of schizophrenia, however, as cells are pruned from a patch of neurons with weak synaptic connections, the brain is left with pyramidal cells with weaker connections than that in normal developing brains. Whereas the weak synapses may have been masked with an abundance of neurons present prior to the onset of adolescence, cognitive impairment emerges in the individual in the initial **prodromal phase of schizophrenia**. As Lewis stated, "our suspicion is that early on, when someone destined for schizophrenia has an excess of synapses, the quality of the synapse doesn't matter so much, and the person does okay. Then later, when the pruning starts, the problems slowly become apparent, because they've lost their reserves" (Dobbs, 2010, p. 155).

As shown in Figure 13.7, a smaller cell known as the **chandelier cell** is positioned adjacent to the pyramidal cells in layer 3 of the DLPFC cortex. In individuals with schizophrenia, the proteins in the synapses of chandelier cells are greatly reduced in number compared with that in healthy controls, leading to dysfunctional synapses. It is thought that these compromised chandelier cells further compromise the

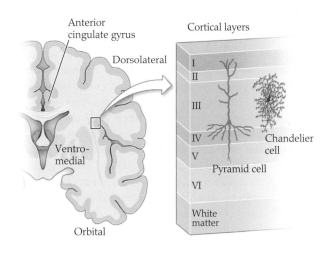

FIGURE 13.7 **Schizophrenia and chandelier cells.** When compared with healthy controls, individuals diagnosed with schizophrenia have altered receptors in the chandelier cells of the cortex. These chandelier cells are thought to communicate with the cortical pyramidal cells.

already weak synaptic connections associated with the pyramidal cells (Dobbs, 2010; Lewis & Gonzalez-Burgos, 2008).

Finally, misaligned neurons in the hippocampus have been observed in individuals with schizophrenia. As seen in Figure 13.8, the traditional north–south orientation of the neurons is replaced by a more sporadic orientation (Bunney & Bunney, 1999; Kovelman & Scheibel, 1984).

Genetic and Environmental Factors. The case of the identical Genain quadruplets born in 1930 illustrates genetic and environmental factors in the origins of schizophrenia. By their early twenties, each young woman had been hospitalized with symptoms of schizophrenia. If schizophrenia were solely influenced by genetic factors, the course of schizophrenia in each of the quadruplets should have been similar. This was not the case. The Genain sisters experienced very different symptoms despite their presumably identical genotypes (Mirsky et al., 2000). One sister was never able to graduate from high school or live on her own, whereas another married, parented two sons, and maintained a career as a secretary. The functionality of the other two sisters fell between that of these two sisters. Thus, although the Genain sisters were born with the same genotype, environmental differences such as varying birth complications and different social interactions throughout their childhood may have led to the different levels of severity of their schizophrenia symptoms.

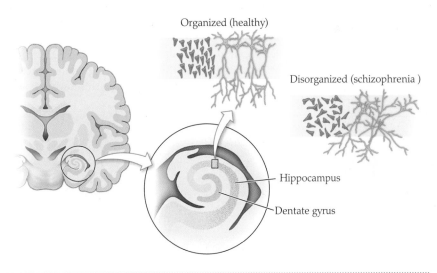

FIGURE 13.8 **Neuronal misalignment in schizophrenia.** In the hippocampus of a person with schizophrenia, pyramidal cells are characterized as being disorganized in comparison to the more organized alignment observed in healthy controls, a structural effect that likely affects neuronal processing in this brain structure.

As suggested by the Genain case, genetic factors play a significant role in the expression of schizophrenia, with a **concordance rate** of about 50% between monozygotic (identical) twins. To evaluate genetic contributions of various illnesses, the concordance rate is very important in that it compares the likelihood of two individuals developing the same disorder. For example, if the concordance rate for two identical (monozygotic) twins developing schizophrenia is higher than the concordance rate from two nonidentical (dizygotic) twins, then the genetic contribution appears to be a prevalent contributing causal factor. The fact that there is only a 50% chance that a twin will develop schizophrenia when his or her twin has been diagnosed with the disorder suggests that other (nongenetic) variables contribute to schizophrenia. With the exception of the cases of monozygotic twins, the risk of developing schizophrenia if a first-degree family member (parent, sibling) has schizophrenia is approximately 10%, whereas it drops to approximately 3% if a second-degree relative (aunt, uncle, or grandparent) has schizophrenia (Freedman, 2010). The heritability of schizophrenia, or the degree in which genetic variability contributes to phenotype variability such as varying degrees of symptoms of schizophrenia, in different degrees of relatives is depicted in Figure 13.9. Further studies have established that the risk of developing schizophrenia persists when a baby from a mother with the disorder is adopted by a healthy mother (Freedman, 2010).

As you have probably guessed based on the variant nature of the symptoms of schizophrenia and the lack of a 100% concordance rate, no single gene has been identified as a causal agent. Several gene candidates have been identified thus far on about nine chromosomes that, not surprisingly, have been implicated in neurochemical systems that have been linked to schizophrenia, such as glutamate and acetylcholine (Heinrichs, 2001; McDonald & Murphy, 2003; Riley & Kendler, 2006). Additionally, as described earlier in this chapter in the discussion of SNPs, a few polymorphisms, common genetic markers leading to a diverse expression of symptoms, have been identified with multiple psychiatric disorders. Thus, although the genetic contributions to schizophrenia are clearly important, researchers are far from having definitive answers in this area.

Focusing on the environment, an interesting series of studies have identified that schizophrenia occurs more commonly in individuals who live in cities than in those who live in other settings. That's right, growing up in a hustling-and-bustling city may nudge a genetically predisposed individual toward the expression of the schizophrenia phenotype. Chapter 1 considered the impact of urban environments on the brain.

The most common psychiatric disorder associated with city living is schizophrenia. Although this does not mean that city living causes schizophrenia, researchers have explored potential factors related to city living that may predispose individuals toward schizophrenia. Although the findings are far from conclusive, some potential factors include toxic exposure, crowded households, and decreased social contacts outside of the home. One Danish study ranked areas from more to less urban. Generally, the risk of developing schizophrenia increased with the degree of urbanicity, and the risk was positively associated with the amount of time an individual had lived in the city (Figure 13.10). For example, the risk of schizophrenia in individuals living in the most urban conditions the first 15 years of their life was greater than that observed in residents of rural areas (Pedersen & Mortenson, 2001). This effect, also observed in Ireland, may be more potent in male urban residents (Kelly et al., 2010).

But isn't it just as likely that individuals predisposed to schizophrenia may be more likely to live in cities? That is a very good question, but the relationship between the more intense urban environment and higher incidence rates suggests that something about the urban environment makes an individual more vulnerable to developing schizophrenia. The variable of *social capital* may be an important factor in this nature/nurture puzzle. In neighborhoods in which individuals know each other for extended periods of time, there may be more mutual trust, social bonding, and perceived safety. These cognitive and emotional perceptions may help to build emotional resilience against the onset of the disorder (Krabbendam & van Os, 2005). A study focusing on the city of London found that individuals characterized as living in low social cohesion areas (i.e., with minimal social support) were twice as likely to be diagnosed with schizophrenia, even after all relevant factors, such as socioeconomic status, were appropriately controlled. However, individuals in areas characterized as having the highest levels of social cohesion

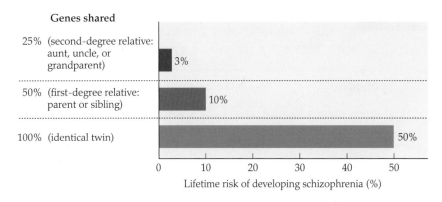

Source: Freedman, R. (2010). *The madness within us*. New York, NY: Oxford University Press.

FIGURE 13.9 Heritability of schizophrenia. Because the highest concordance rate of schizophrenia is observed in identical twins and the lowest concordance rate in individuals who are not related, a genetic component is acknowledged and is being investigated by researchers.

(a)

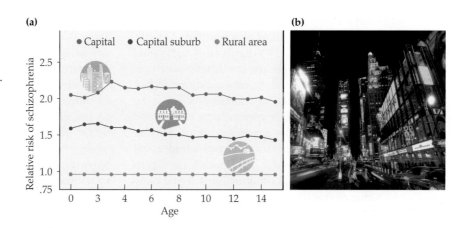

(b)

FIGURE 13.10 **Urbanization and schizophrenia risk.** When individuals lived in the more urban settings (capital or capital suburb) at any time during the first 15 years of their lives, this variable was associated with a higher risk of schizophrenia. Additional analyses indicated that individuals living in urban settings for the entire first 15 years had the highest rates of schizophrenia.

were also vulnerable (Kirkbride et al., 2008). This study suggests that both extremely low and extremely high levels of social cohesion increase vulnerability to schizophrenia.

Treatment Strategies

The most popular treatment strategy for schizophrenia is the pharmacological approach. As previously described, the serendipitous discovery that chlorpromazine reduced positive symptoms heavily influenced the treatment of this disorder. Although this antipsychotic medication was viewed as a breakthrough, clinicians soon realized that it had a rather troubling side effect that impaired the patient's motor coordination. Specifically, the patient's gait became slow and was characterized by awkward, brief shuffles.

When scientists learned that chlorpromazine's effectiveness was related to its status as a dopamine antagonist, more potent dopamine antagonists were developed, including haloperidol, which was 100 times more potent than chlorpromazine. This increased potency, however, came with an additional worrisome side effect of uncontrollable

facial and tongue movements, a condition known as **tardive dyskinesia**.

The early pharmaceutical treatments, or **first-generation antipsychotics**, have had mixed success. Approximately 20% of patients responded well to the drugs, exhibiting a complete remission. In other patients, some experienced symptom reduction, but others did not. And the success of the drugs was threatened by the debilitating side effects. To address the unwanted side effects, a wave of **second-generation antipsychotics** was developed. Clozapine, a second-generation drug that was introduced in the United States in 1989, had fewer motor side effects but reduced the number of white blood cells in a small percentage of individuals. This drug, in addition to affecting the dopamine D_2 receptors, also affected dopamine D_1 and D_4 receptors. Additionally, it antagonized serotonin and norepinephrine receptors while increasing acetylcholine release. Because clozapine has such diverse physiological effects, it is known as an **atypical antipsychotic** (Barondes, 1993; Freedman, 2010). The physiological effects of representative first- and second-generation antipsychotics are included in Table 13.1.

TABLE 13.1.

Antipsychotic Drugs, Targets, and Physiological Effects

DRUG	PHARMACOLOGICAL TARGET	PHYSIOLOGICAL EFFECT
Haloperidol	Dopamine D_2 antagonist	Blocks dopaminergic pyramidal neuron activation
Olanzapine, risperidone	Dopamine D_2 and serotonin 2_A antagonism	Blocks dopaminergic pyramidal neuron activation as well as the impact of serotonin on glutamate secretion
Clozapine	Diverse action (affects neurotransmitters such as serotonin in addition to dopaminergic effects)	Antagonizes dopamine and serotonergic processing resulting in decreased pyramidal neuronal activation; increases acetylcholine release; antagonizes norepinephrine leading to increased interneuron communication with pyramidal neurons
Amisulpride	Dopamine D_2 and D_3 antagonism	Blocks cortical dopamine receptors with minimal effect on basal ganglia

Adapted from Freedman, 2003, and K. Lambert & Kinsley, 2010.

Although some of the second-generation drugs such as clozapine have been shown to be more effective than the earlier drugs at treating the positive and negative symptoms of schizophrenia, these drugs also had side effects (e.g., weight loss, increased risk for diabetes mellitus; see Freedman 2003; Leucht et al., 2009; Tamminga, 1999). Still, extreme variability in the effectiveness of these drugs persisted for patients. Thirty percent of patients who did not respond to the first-generation drugs, for example, responded successfully to clozapine.

Because of the remaining problems with the existing antipsychotics, research continues to seek more effective pharmacological treatments. Whereas the early treatments were discovered accidentally, current research is based on evidence directing the researchers toward logical therapeutic approaches. As described previously, several candidate variables have been identified. Glutamate and the NMDA receptor is certainly an attractive therapeutic target. Research suggests that NMDA agonists decrease negative schizophrenia symptoms (Tuominen, Tiihonen, & Wahlbeck, 2005). Extending from the initial observation of excessive smoking rates in schizophrenia patients, the cholinergic system has become a therapeutic target, especially the α-7 nicotinic agonists, which have been shown to successfully treat cognitive dysfunction (Bencherif et al., 2012). Further research has implicated calcium channel inhibitors as a novel therapeutic approach for schizophrenia (Bigos et al., 2010). As described earlier in this chapter, two of the single-nucleotide polymorphisms associated with several psychiatric disorders were associated with calcium channels in neuronal membranes. The investigation of these novel pharmacological approaches is still in its infancy. Time will tell whether they will lead to more effective treatment strategies that will successfully minimize the troubling symptoms of schizophrenia.

Although the pharmaceutical approach is much more humane than some of the earlier treatments, such as lobotomies and insulin-induced comas, it is estimated that about 30% of schizophrenia patients fail to respond to any variation of antipsychotic medications (Kurita et al., 2012). This has led to an interest in identifying nonpharmacological treatment approaches, especially for the cognitive symptoms, which, if improved, may also have beneficial effects on the more classic symptoms such as hallucinations and social withdrawal. For example, using cognitive strategies to differentiate reality-based from non-reality-based perceptions and beliefs could provide a buffer against the positive symptoms of schizophrenia. Additionally, using more effective cognitive strategies could diminish fragmented thoughts and confused speech.

Two categories of nonpharmacological approaches are cognitive remediation treatment and compensatory therapy. **Cognitive remediation treatment** is aimed at restoring cognitive and brain functioning through various types of cognitive exercises. The goal of this therapy is to stimulate neuroplasticity to enhance the structure of neural networks and accompanying neural communication necessary for maintaining healthy cognitive functions. Alternatively, **compensatory therapy** instructs patients on effective tools and strategies to help them compensate for the cognitive impairment accompanying schizophrenia (Wexler, 2007).

Several studies have assessed the effectiveness of cognitive remediation treatments. Figure 13.11 shows increases in brain activity in the frontal lobe in one schizophrenia patient following 10 weeks of memory exercises. This study suggested that cognitive training could enhance verbal memory in accordance with frontal lobe activation (Wexler, Anderson, Fulbright, & Gore, 2000). In another study, fMRI scans of medicated schizophrenia patients following memory-focused training showed increased activation of the PFC when compared with that of nontrained patients (Haut, Lim, & MacDonald, 2010).

Another study used a gaming format for cognitive and social recognition training for 50 hours across 10 weeks. When compared with a group of schizophrenia patients who merely interacted with video games, the schizophrenia patients who received training demonstrated improvement in facial emotion recognition, an effect accompanied

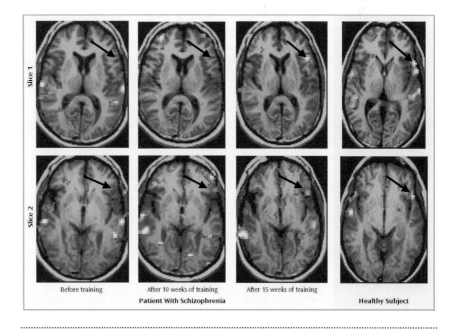

FIGURE 13.11 Cognitive training enhances frontal lobe activation. Following 10 and 15 weeks of cognitive training, this patient experienced increased activation in the left inferior frontal gyrus (slice 1) and left lateral orbital gyrus (slice 2). Activation at these levels was closer to that of the healthy subject than observed prior to training.

by increased activation of the right postcentral gyrus (known to be involved in facial recognition; Hooker et al., 2012). Other studies on cognitive remediation treatment have demonstrated improved cognitive functions in patients with schizophrenia. For example, after 10 weeks of practice, nearly 75% of the outpatients with schizophrenia performed as well as the best of the healthy controls assessed in the study (Wexler et al., 1997). These results demonstrated the potential for this type of training to move patients toward more normal cognitive responses. This is especially relevant considering that the degree of cognitive impairment is the strongest predictor of improved functional outcome in schizophrenia patients, perhaps leading to more relevant social interactions and an increased likelihood of securing employment (Wexler, 2007).

The results from cognitive training appear to be just as encouraging as the early pharmacological studies with one important missing element: negative side effects. Michael Merzenich, whose research investigating the effects of experience on neural recovery in owl monkeys was discussed in Chapter 5, has worked with other scientists to assess the effectiveness of specifically designed cognitively, socially, and emotionally stimulating software developed in a gaming format for schizophrenia patients (Fisher, Holland, Merzenich, & Vinogradov, 2009). This approach is currently undergoing trials by the U.S. Food and Drug Administration to establish safety and efficacy (Hayden, 2012). Figure 13.12 shows some sample images from this software program.

Focusing on more specific brain involvement and systematic assessment, researchers have assessed the value of cognitive training using an animal model of schizophrenia in which the ventromedial hippocampus is lesioned in newborn rats, producing cognitive impairment. In one study, compared with lesioned rodents receiving no cognitive training (e.g., an avoidance task in which animals learn that a specific arm of a T-maze is associated with shock exposure), adult rodents with this early brain damage showed diminished cognitive impairment with cognitive training during the adolescent phase of development, comparable to the prodromal phase of schizophrenia in humans. After just a few days of training in an avoidance task, the trained lesioned animals were protected against the expected cognitive impairment in adulthood. As shown in Figure 13.13, cognitive training failed to reduce the cell loss evident in both trained and untrained lesioned groups. However, the training appeared to significantly improve performance such that the performance of the lesioned trained group was indistinguishable from that of a healthy control group. Although brain damage was not repaired, EEG recordings provided evidence that cognitive training enhanced the effective firing patterns of hippocampal neurons. These researchers suggested that cognitive training could help prevent the symptoms of mental illness if administered when the earliest signs of the disorder became apparent (Lee et al., 2012).

FIGURE 13.12 Computer training as potential schizophrenia treatment. Although it is still being investigated and evaluated, (a) engaging computer training has been shown to reduce specific cognitive, verbal, and sensory impairments representative of the symptoms of schizophrenia. (b) This treatment strategy was developed by the neuroscientist Michael Merzenich.

Fewer brain imaging studies have been conducted to assess the effectiveness of compensatory therapy. However, patients with schizophrenia who have undergone compensatory therapy have shown significant improvements in day-to-day functioning. Strategies such as instructing patients to use labels, signs, and calendars facilitate day-to-day functioning in patients. The social skills of patients with schizophrenia also appear to be enhanced by coaching on strategies to improve interview skills and interpersonal interactions (Wexler, 2007).

Next, we turn to depression, a more prevalent disorder than schizophrenia. You will note several similarities in the

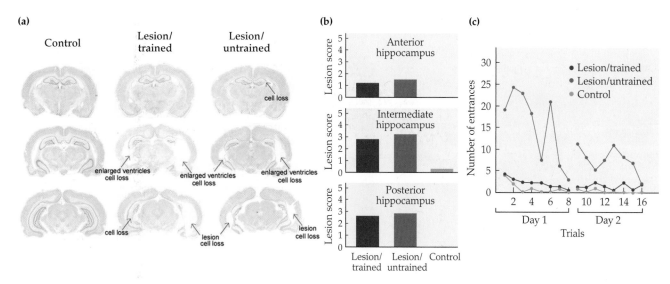

Source: Lee, H., Dvorak, D., Kao, H.Y., Duffy, A.M., Scharfman, H.E., Fenton, A.A. (2012). Early cognitive experience prevents adult deficits in a neurodevelopmental schizophrenia model. *Neuron, 75(4)*, 714-724.

FIGURE 13.13 **Brain damage in lesioned rats with and without cognitive training.** (a) Although the lesioned areas were similar in both trained and untrained groups, confirmed by (b) similar lesion size scores, (c) the trained animals performed similar to the nonlesioned controls in the cognitive task, with fewer entrances into a shock zone than the nontrained animals over the course of two days of trials.

treatment strategies used in depression and schizophrenia, such as an emphasis on pharmacological therapies with increasing interest in cognitive-behavioral therapies with high efficacy rates.

Depression

Major depression (also called major depressive disorder) is characterized by profound sadness, diminished pleasure, decreased motivation, cognitive slowing, lethargy, and, at its worst, thoughts of suicide. Whereas about 1% of the population will suffer from schizophrenia, approximately 17% of the U.S. population will suffer from depression at some point during their lives, with approximately 6% of the population suffering from depression at any given time (Fava & Kendler, 2000; Kessler et al., 2012). Close to 21% of women will experience depression compared with 13% of men (Yonkers, Kando, Hamilton, & Halbreich, 2000). Depression has a strong genetic component, with concordance rates in identical twins reaching about 50–70% and rates of 20–30% observed in fraternal twins (Edvardsen et al., 2009; Sanders, Detera-Wadleigh, & Gershon, 1999). This section will address the most prevalent form of depression, major depression; however, a brief discussion of **bipolar disorder** appears at the end.

Causes

Although altered neurochemicals have been viewed as the most likely cause of depression, neural complexity and associated neural networks have also been implicated. Effective

treatment strategies ultimately depend on the identification of the specific factors related to the onset of this debilitating disease.

Neurochemical Candidates. Like the antipsychotics, the earliest antidepressants were discovered accidentally, around the mid-20th century. Clinicians noted that drugs developed for other purposes improved the mood of depressed patients. Iproniazid, for example, was originally developed for tuberculosis before clinicians noted that it also elevated depressed patients' moods. Imipramine was originally given to patients as an antihistamine, but it was also observed to have antidepressant effects.

When the most effective antidepressant drugs were further inspected, researchers reported increased extracellular concentrations of two monoamine neurotransmitters, serotonin and norepinephrine, leading to the **monoamine hypothesis of depression**. This hypothesis stated that depression symptoms were caused by low levels of serotonin and norepinephrine at critical synaptic sites in the brain (Castren, 2005). As shown in Figure 13.14, one way these drugs (imipramine, in this example) act is by blocking the reuptake of the monoamines, thereby keeping them in the synapse longer. Alternatively, they may increase serotonin levels by blocking the deactivating enzyme, monoamine oxidase (iproniazid). These discoveries were the first to suggest that depression resulted from a chemical imbalance in the brain rather than from a dysfunctional childhood, as previously suggested.

Researchers have further investigated the roles of each of these neurochemicals in depression. In addition to the effectiveness of the monoamine drugs, lower levels of

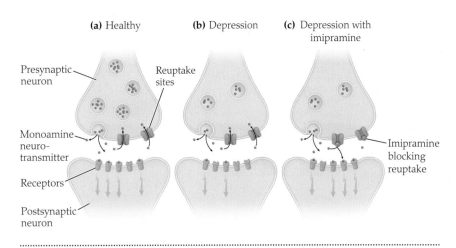

(a) Healthy   **(b)** Depression   **(c)** Depression with imipramine

Presynaptic neuron

Reuptake sites

Monoamine neurotransmitter

Receptors

Postsynaptic neuron

Imipramine blocking reuptake

FIGURE 13.14   Imipramine influence on the synapse. Imipramine blocks the reuptake of the monoamines, thereby keeping them in the synapse longer.

5-hydroxyindoleacetic acid, a breakdown product of serotonin, were found in the CSF of patients diagnosed with depression (Cheetham, Katona, & Horton, 1991). But there were holes in the theory that serotonin was *directly* responsible for depression. For example, little evidence of diminished serotonergic activity has been found in depressed patients. A diet low in tryptophan, a dietary precursor to serotonin, has not been found to transform healthy patients into depressed patients (Delgado, 2000). However, dietary tryptophan depletion can exacerbate depression symptoms in subjects with histories of depression and antidepressant medication use (Van Steenbergen, Booij, Band, Hommel, & van der Does, 2012). Further, although antidepressant drugs have an immediate impact on the brain's synapses, relief from depression symptoms is not typically experienced until several weeks after the initial dose (Lam, 2010; Nestler, 1998). Finally, further challenging the monoamine hypothesis of depression, a selective serotonin reuptake *enhancer*, which has effects opposite to those of **selective serotonin reuptake inhibitors (SSRIs)**, has been shown to be as effective as SSRIs in treating the symptoms of depression (Baune & Renger, 2014; Nickel et al., 2003). SSRIs such as Prozac, Paxil, and Zoloft block the reuptake of serotonin in the synapse. Although past research has challenged the direct relationship between serotonin and depression, the discovery of SSRIs in the 1980s catapulted serotonin as the most popular candidate neurochemical in depression, leading to the **serotonin hypothesis of depression**.

Given these uncertainties associated with the monoamine hypothesis of depression, attention has been directed toward the **molecular hypothesis of depression**, which suggests that depression is the product of long-term molecular changes in the brain and that antidepressants work by counteracting these molecular changes. Recently, modified theories have emphasized the importance of tryptophan breakdown products known as **catabolites** on various neuroplasticity measures, stress reactivity, and immune functions that have been implicated in the onset of depression

symptoms (Lopresti, Maker, Hood, & Drummond, 2014; Maes, Leonard, Myint, Kubera, & Verkerk, 2011). These newly revised theories are more complex than the original serotonin hypothesis of depression (Castren, 2005).

Norepinephrine, another target monoamine, has also been investigated as a candidate neurochemical in depression. The norepinephrine hypothesis was initially proposed in 1965 by Joseph Schildkraut at Harvard University. However, this hypothesis has paled in comparison to the wildly popular serotonin hypothesis. The spotlight may have faded inappropriately, suggests one study in which blood samples were collected from subjects suffering from depression as well as from healthy controls. The samples revealed lower norepinephrine plasma concentration levels in depressed subjects compared with healthy subjects; however, no difference in serotonin levels was found (G. Lambert, Hohansson, Agren, & Friberg, 2000).

The neurochemical corticosteroids have also been implicated in depression. As you have already learned, stress significantly impacts both physical and mental health. In fact, levels of corticosteroids appear more clearly associated with depression symptoms than do levels of monoamines. Compared with healthy control subjects, higher levels of adrenocorticotropic hormone, cortisol, and CRH are found in depressed patients (Nemeroff et al., 1984; Rubin, Poland, Lesser, Winston, & Blodgett, 1987). The HPA axis seems to be altered as well. For example, when depressed patients are administered a synthetic form of cortisol known as dexamethosone, they respond with less sensitivity and negative feedback, exhibiting consistently higher levels of cortisol compared with nondepressed individuals (Carroll, 1982). Further, compared with the brains of nondepressed individuals who died of causes other than suicide, the brains of depressed patients who ultimately committed suicide revealed fewer binding sites for CRH (recall the discussion of CRH in Chapter 10). This effect may be a compensatory response to high circulating CRH levels (Nemeroff, Owens, Bissette, Andorn, & Stanley, 1988). Further involvement of stress hormones in major depression is suggested by the observation that antidepressants increase glucocorticoid receptors as well as reduce the heightened activation of the hypothalamic–adrenal axis (de Kloet, Joels, & Holsboer, 2005). Thus, techniques used to diminish stress and enhance emotional resilience (as observed in Chapter 10) also hold promise as antidepressant techniques.

BDNF has also been implicated as a key neurochemical in the onset of depression (Krishnan & Nestler, 2008). As described in Chapter 5, BDNF is involved in neuronal development but is also critical in adulthood for neuronal survival and adaptive functions, including synaptic plasticity. Stress decreases BDNF, so the contribution of stress to depression could be a result of diminished levels of BDNF. This observation is supported by reports of diminished BDNF in autopsied brains of suicide victims compared with the brains of nondepressed individuals (Duman & Aghajanian, 2012; Karage, Vaudan, Schwald, Perroud, & LaHarpe, 2005). In addition to the finding that antidepressants seem to result in increased BDNF activity, behaviors such as exercising that are known to work as antidepressants are also associated with increases in BDNF (Hill, Storandt, & Malley, 1993; Nibuya, Morinobu, & Duman, 1995).

Further supporting the role of BDNF in depression, mice genetically altered with a BDNF gene variant associated with BDNF dysfunction exhibited decreased length of dendrite branches and less complex synaptic functioning in the hippocampus and prefrontal cortex (two areas implicated in depression) when compared with mice with normal BDNF function. As shown in Figure 13.15, results suggested that this genetic manipulation resulted in decreased dendritic branching, with a more dramatic effect in the group with the most severe genetically altered reduction

Natural, "wild type" mouse

Moderately decreased BDNF

Intensely decreased BDNF

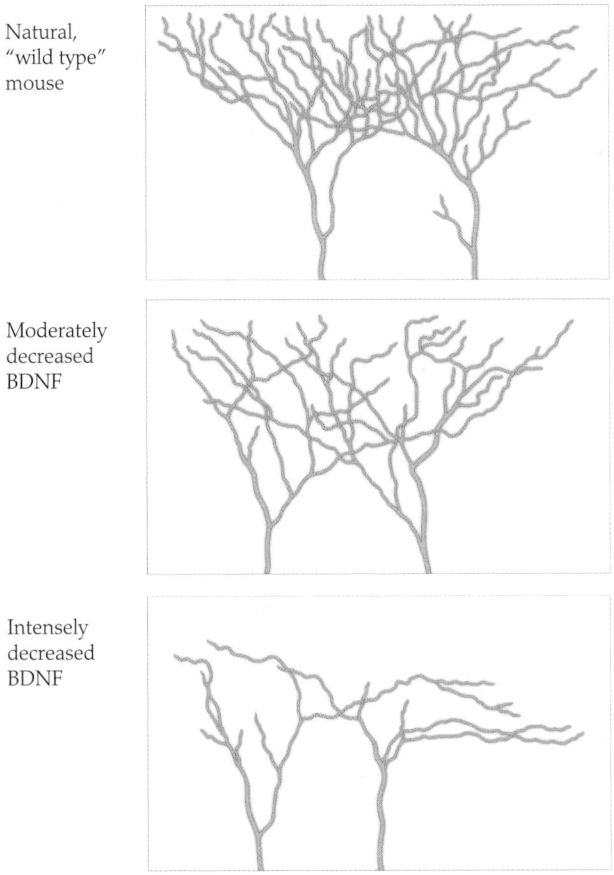

FIGURE 13.15 Brain-derived neurotrophic factor (BDNF) and depression susceptibility. In an investigation of the role of varying levels of BDNF on brain areas implicated in depression, mice with significantly reduced BDNF levels exhibited increased atrophy of the dendritic branches in the medial prefrontal cortex.

in BDNF transport. These data help explain why humans with a similar genetic variation have smaller hippocampal volumes accompanied by cognitive impairments (Duman & Aghajanian, 2012; Liu et al., 2011)

It is beyond the scope of this text to cover all the neurochemicals that have been implicated in major depression: those described in this section represent a mere sample. Our discussion of the brain areas involved in and treatment strategies for major depression will also include additional neurochemicals such as dopamine and glutamate.

Neuroanatomical Candidates. One helpful strategy for identifying brain areas involved in depression is to use the symptoms as a guide. Research investigating both living and autopsied brains of patients with depression provides additional neuroanatomical clues.

Let's begin with the lack of pleasure, or anhedonia effect, experienced by depressed patients. When this symptom emerges, typical pleasures such as spending time with cherished friends, eating a delicious dessert, or listening to one's favorite music lack their usual positive emotional response. With a diminished sense of reward, depressed patients also experience a lack of motivation to engage in previously enjoyable and meaningful activities. For this prominent symptom, the nucleus accumbens, with its role in reward and motivation, is a likely candidate brain area.

In one study investigating the role of the nucleus accumbens in depression, subjects diagnosed with depression were given an injection of *d*-amphetamine, a dopamine agonist drug that should stimulate the accumbens area. The researchers were interested in how the activation of this area influenced depression symptoms as assessed with the standard self-report scale known as the Hamilton Depression Scale. Compared with healthy controls, the depressed subjects reported more positive feelings after receiving the drug. Does this mean that the pleasure center is working more effectively in depressed patients? Revisiting your knowledge of adaptive modifications in synaptic transmission (Chapter 3), if dopamine levels were naturally lower in depressed subjects, it is very likely that dopamine receptors would become more sensitive as a compensatory effect. Consequently, if the receptors had increased sensitivity, then a more dramatic response would occur with *d*-amphetamine (Naranjo, Tremblay, & Busto, 2001).

On close inspection of the anatomical connections of the nucleus accumbens, one theory has emphasized connections to the brain's central motor system, the striatum. As introduced in Chapter 8, the nucleus accumbens is divided into a central area, the *core*, that extends to the striatum and an outer area, the *shell*, which extends to the brain's emotional circuits. The observation that the neuroanatomical structure most closely associated with reward and pleasure has connections with movement introduces a novel perspective to depression symptoms. The **effort-based reward theory** emphasizes the importance of established contingencies (predictions of probabilities of future rewards) between effort and expected rewards in the maintenance of mental health and adaptive functioning. This theory further suggests that increased rates of depression in contemporary Western societies may be related to decreased physical activity (K. G. Lambert, 2006). Research indicates that individuals in their twenties and thirties today are up to 200% more likely to have reported suffering from depression than adults born prior to 1950 (Kessler, Berglund, et al., 2005; Kessler, Petukhova, et al., 2012).

Recall the learned persistence task (see Chapter 8) in which rats trained to dig up coveted sweet cereal rewards persisted longer than nontrained rats in trying to solve an unsolvable task. Thus, perhaps the five weeks of contingency training digging up cereal strengthened connections between the striatal and accumbens circuits, enhancing the anticipation of the reward. Connections extending from the accumbens to the PFC, influencing cognitive abilities that are also affected in depression, may have also been affected in the trained animals. Additionally, rats with flexible coping styles (as described in Chapter 10) exhibit lower levels of stress hormones following training, another factor implicated in depression resilience (Bardi, Rhone et al., 2012; Bardi, True et al., 2012).

The PFC also behaves abnormally in patients with major depression. In depression, this area is associated with the lack of concentration or other cognitive difficulties that patients often report. Postmortem examination of brains of depressed patients has revealed cellular loss and atrophy in the prefrontal cortex (Rajkowaska, 2000). In living subjects, decreased blood flow has been observed in depressed brains compared with healthy control brains (Gotlib & Hamilton, 2009). Because the PFC plays an important role in sustaining an animal's attention toward both the external and the internal environments, this brain area has been labeled the *crucial convergence zone*. It facilitates the negotiation of our emotional worlds with our external reality (Liotti & Mayberg, 2001). Further, when healthy subjects were instructed to generate sad autobiographical memories, decreased activity in the PFC was observed when compared with more neutral memories, implicating this cortical area in the sadness symptoms of depression (Liotti et al., 2000).

Another brain area that has been implicated in depression, the hippocampus, has reciprocal neural connections with both the PFC and the emotion-related limbic structures such as the amygdala. Considering that chronic stress results in hippocampal atrophy and depressed patients have higher levels of stress hormones than those observed in nondepressed individuals, it is not surprising that depressed patients have smaller hippocampal volumes than nondepressed individuals (Bremner et al., 2000; Castren, 2005; Sheline, Wang, Gado, Csernansky, & Vannier, 1996).

The Network Hypothesis. The brain's neurochemicals influence our moods, thoughts, and behavior by modifying the existing neural circuitry. In his Nobel Prize acceptance speech addressing chemical neurotransmission, Arvid Carlsson stated, "However, it must be recognized that the brain is not a chemical factory but an extremely complicated survival machine" (Carlsson, 2001). We now know that the complex interactions of neurons positioned in larger neural networks are essential for the information transfer that is required for recovery from depression and other mental illnesses. As healthy individuals go through their daily lives, interactions with the environment and with other people activate neural networks in ways that appropriately modify synaptic plasticity to maintain mental health. This *activity-dependent neuroplasticity* enables the optimal processing and storage of relevant information for future adaptive responses.

The role of BDNF in depression, as described previously, provides further evidence that depression may be the result of some disturbance in activity-dependent neuroplasticity. The delay between when patients start taking antidepressants and when they report relief from symptoms also suggests that the impact of these drugs on neuroplasticity (such as increasing neurogenesis), rather than restoring a proposed chemical imbalance, may be the most accurate reflection of how the drugs eventually improve symptoms in some patients.

Eero Castren (2005), working at the University of Helsinki Neuroscience Center, has proposed that antidepressants may, in addition to increasing neurogenesis, facilitate more subtle neuroplasticity functions such as promoting the sprouting of axons and dendrites in depressed patients. The antidepressant fluoxetine (Prozac), for example, has been found to reinstate plasticity in the adult rat visual cortex (Maya et al., 2008). As shown in Figure 13.16, depression symptoms may be associated with diminished connections in certain neural networks that are restored beyond the original state during pharmacological treatment. Subsequently, the unnecessary connections forming synapses are pruned back to resemble the network configuration prior to the onset of depression. Thus, according to the **network hypothesis of depression**, the condition of neural networks (rather than a specific chemical imbalance) has the most direct impact on moods (Castren, 2005; Castren & Rantamaki, 2010). This hypothesis is preliminary at this point because of the difficulty of assessing changing neural networks in humans. The identification of suitable animal models will provide further information confirming or disconfirming this hypothesis.

Treatment Strategies

In addition to the consideration of effectiveness of various treatment strategies for depression, side effects must also be considered. Additionally, it is important to disentangle placebo effects from actual treatment effects before prescribing specific therapies. As described throughout this section, several different types of therapies offer much-needed relief for individuals suffering from depression.

Electroconvulsive Therapy. Electroconvulsive (shock) therapy (ECT) was first used as a treatment for depression in

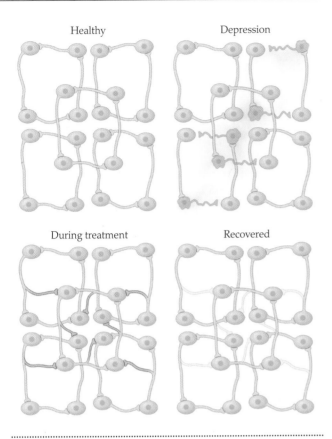

Healthy   Depression

During treatment   Recovered

FIGURE 13.16 **Network hypothesis of depression.** This theoretical model proposes that depression results from compromised neural networks, and that the symptoms subside when the networks are recovered through effective treatments.

the 1930s. As discussed earlier in this chapter, ECT involves delivering electrical stimulation to anesthetized patients to induce seizures that, in ways that are not entirely clear to researchers, alleviate or diminish depressive symptoms. Although it seems crude, ECT remains an important therapy approach today for **treatment-resistant** patients (patients who have failed to respond to any treatment) or severely depressed patients (Krystal et al., 2000; Shorter, 2009).

In its contemporary form, although patients are closely monitored in a hospital setting, the parameters associated with the delivery of this treatment are varied. Overall, research has provided evidence that, in general, ECT improves the patient's depressed mood, at least in the short term. However, memory impairment often accompanies ECT, especially for the time leading up to and following the treatment. The studies are far from controlled in most cases, but evidence indicates that ECT is more effective than simulated ECT (in which patients are anesthetized but do not receive stimulation) and pharmacotherapy, at least as an acute treatment strategy. Even so, this therapy should be reserved as a last resort after patients have failed to respond to other forms of therapy (Pagnin, de Queiroz, Pini, & Cassano, 2004; UK ECT Review Group, 2003).

Less intense treatment strategies that also alter the electrical activity of the brain's neurons—TMS and **repetitive**

transcranial magnetic stimulation (rTMS), a variant of TMS that uses repetitive stimulation of varying frequencies— were introduced in the mid-1980s and 1990s, respectively (Barker, Jalinous, & Freeston, 1985; Bolognini & Ro, 2010; George et al., 1999). Treatment with rTMS involves positioning a very powerful electromagnet on the scalp that ultimately depolarizes underlying neurons (Figure 13.17). For depression, the PFC has been a traditional rTMS target area (Bakkar et al., 2015). Unlike ECT, rTMS therapies do not require hospitalization and anesthesia because they are administered in outpatient settings. Because rTMS does not induce actual seizures, fewer side effects are observed, although some patients have reported headaches.

In one study, patients with depression who received two weeks of daily rTMS delivered to the left PFC experienced significant relief in their symptoms of depression compared with patients with depression who received sham treatment (George et al., 2000). Additional research suggests varied efficacy rates with rTMS. Specifically, this treatment does not seem to be as effective for treatment-resistant depression patients as ECT. Better outcomes have been observed with longer treatment schedules and with varied targeted sites such as the cerebellum (Couturier, 2005; Daskalakis, 2005; Schutter & van Honk, 2005). More recently, the dorsal ACC and anterior insula, together known as the salience network, have been shown to be effective rTMS targets for treating depression (Downar, Blumberger, & Daskalakis, 2016). Further research is necessary to generate treatment strategies that maximize the effectiveness of rTMS.

Although the actual mechanisms of ECT and rTMS remain a mystery, there seems to be something unique about the seizure or abrupt change in electrical fields associated with key neuronal groups that serves as a kick-start for symptom alleviation.

Pharmacotherapy. You have already been introduced to the initial drugs discovered in the 1950s that were eventually

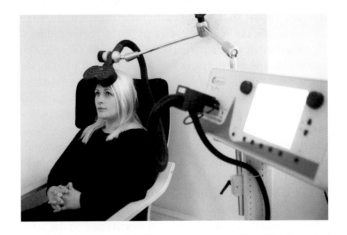

FIGURE 13.17 **Repetitive transcranial magnetic stimulation (rTMS).** Treatment with rTMS involves positioning a very powerful electromagnet on the scalp that ultimately depolarizes underlying neurons.

marketed as antidepressants. As research on the mechanisms of the early drugs was conducted, it became apparent that drugs such as iproniazid inhibited the deactivating enzyme, monoamine oxidase, which deactivates monoamine transmitter substances after being released into the synapse (as described in Chapter 3). Accordingly, iproniazid was assigned to a class of drugs known as **monoamine oxidase inhibitors (MAOIs)**. Patients taking MAOIs are instructed to avoid foods such as cheese that contain high levels of the amino acid tyramine because of the possibility of dangerously high blood pressure. In contrast to MAOIs, the other popular antidepressant drug, imipramine, was found to alter synaptic functioning by blocking the reuptake of the monoamine transmitters. This class of drugs became known as the **tricyclic antidepressants**. The earliest antidepressants affected three neurotransmitters: norepinephrine, serotonin, and dopamine. In the early 1970s, however, David Wong and his colleagues at the Eli Lilly pharmaceutical company developed the first SSRI (Barondes, 1993; Shorter, 2009). Fluoxetine (Prozac) was the first drug in this category; it was licensed in the United States for use with depression in 1987 (Richelson, 2001). In addition to SSRIs, other versions of drugs have been developed focusing on variations of the three monoamines. For example, serotonin–norepinephrine reuptake inhibitors have been shown in some cases to be as effective as SSRIs (Baune & Renger, 2014; Herrara-Guzman et al., 2010). However, no such drug has surpassed the popularity of the SSRIs.

How effective are these drugs at treating the symptoms of depression? Despite nearly a 400% increase in antidepressant use from 1988–1994 to 2005–2008 in the United States, no reductions in the rates of depression have been observed (Pratt, Brody, & Gu, 2011). In fact, depression rates have been observed to rise within this time frame (Kessler et al., 2012; Nemeroff & Owens, 2002; Olfson & Marcus, 2010). Currently, 350 million people worldwide suffer from depression (Ledford, 2014).

The clinical psychologist and researcher Irving Kirsch has raised a potential problem with the methodology used to assess the efficacy of antidepressants (2010). After conducting a meta-analysis comparing the effects of SSRIs to placebo control groups, he was surprised to see that the placebo response was an important factor in the success of antidepressants. First, SSRIs outperformed placebos (i.e., sugar pills) by only a small amount in some studies, with no difference observed in others. Kirsch suggested that, although these pharmacological studies were conducted under the assumption that a double-blind protocol was being used in which neither the doctor nor the patient knew whether the patient was receiving the drug or placebo, the studies may not have actually been double-blind control studies. Because serotonin affects so many of the brain's functions, SSRIs have a plethora of side effects, including gastrointestinal disturbances, sexual dysfunction, and insomnia (Ferguson, 2001).

Imagine participating in such a study. If you experienced any of these side effects, you would likely conclude that you were taking the drug as opposed to the sugar pill. Further, because you told the physician in the study that you were experiencing these symptoms, the physician would also conclude that you were on the drug. Once you determine that you are taking the drug, you may decide that your chances of recovery are optimal, providing enough hope to boost a recovery or at least an improvement in symptoms. According to Kirsch (2010), unless an *active placebo drug* is used—in the case of SSRIs, a drug that does not affect serotonergic functions but does promote a few of the side effects—these studies can be considered experimentally confounded, unable to distinguish between the drug effect and the placebo effect.

The association between the placebo effect and improved depression symptoms emphasizes the cognitive aspects of depression, especially the role of expectancy. It is difficult to disentangle cognitive expectancy and drug-induced symptoms related to either improvement (placebo) or worsening of symptoms (nocebo). The **nocebo effect** refers to the presence of side effects, even in placebo control groups, that may emerge if subjects are told to expect them (Enck & Hauser, 2012; Hauser, Hansen, & Enck, 2012). For example, in one study, 25% of the subjects identified as lactose intolerant who were given what they thought was a lactose pill but was in actuality a placebo reported gastrointestinal symptoms (Vernia, di Camillo, Foglietta, Avallone, & De Carolis, 2010). The identification of the pivotal role of cognition and expectancy leads us to the topic of the next treatment strategy, cognitive and behavioral therapies.

Cognitive and Behavioral Therapies. The University of Pennsylvania psychiatrist Aaron Beck is known for establishing the cognitive therapeutic approach to treat depression. Clinical efficacy for this approach, established in the 1970s, suggested its effectiveness for both individual and group therapy structures as well as in inpatient and outpatient settings. This therapy required patients to play a more active role in their treatment by learning how cognition influences emotional responses and, accordingly, how their therapist could work with them to change both cognition and behaviors, thereby diminishing the symptoms of depression (Deckersbach, Gershuny, & Otto, 2000).

The traditional form of cognitive therapy, focusing on the role of inaccurate beliefs and faulty information processing, has been the subject of more research than the forms incorporating more extensive behavioral strategies. When cognitive therapy is compared with antidepressant medications, the efficacy rates have been found to be similar, but with fewer side effects (see Figure 13.18; DeRubeis, Siegle, & Hollon, 2008; Jacobsen & Hollon, 1996) although in some cases medications have been deemed more effective for severely depressed patients.

Beyond the alleviation of acute depressive symptoms, however, cognitive therapy has been shown to have longer-lasting effects than antidepressant drug therapy. For example, after eight weeks of antidepressant drug therapy, subjects in the aforementioned study were assigned to either

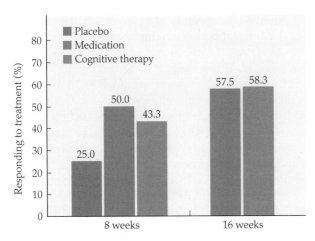

Source: Jacobson, N.S., & Hollon S.D. (1996). Prospects for future comparisons between drugs and psychotherapy: lessons from the CBT-versus pharmacotherapy exchange. *Journal of Consulting Clinical Psychology, 64*, 104-108.

FIGURE 13.18 Efficacy rates of various depression therapies. At two time points, 8 weeks and 16 weeks, there is little difference between antidepressant and cognitive therapies.

a placebo control condition or a condition in which they continued with their therapy. For the cognitive therapy group, the therapy was also discontinued for the subjects after eight weeks, although three booster sessions were distributed across the next year. After treatment ended, more than twice the number of subjects taking antidepressants relapsed compared with the cognitive therapy subjects. Continuing with the medication therapy was more effective than the placebo group but was not more effective than the discontinued cognitive therapy group. Once these patients were taken off the drug, their relapse rates were much higher than the relapse rates of subjects who had previously received cognitive therapy (Jacobsen & Hollon, 1996).

Because of the enduring effects of cognitive therapy, as well as the lack of side effects, this approach is extremely valuable for treating the symptoms of depression. Researchers have proposed that this form of therapy resets the level of prefrontal activity, facilitating more adaptive top-down processing so that emotional regulation (and likely accompanying amygdala activation) can be maintained. Antidepressants, in contrast, have been proposed to reset the limbic structures initially, providing more of a bottom-up therapeutic approach (DeRubeis, Siegle, & Hollon, 2008). The recruitment of more adaptive prefrontal-associated regulatory mechanisms represents an important lifelong skill that, even after therapy ends, protects against relapse.

Therapies that focus more on behavioral interventions are also effective. **Behavioral Activation Therapy** focuses on how the patient interacts with the environment with the objective of identifying behaviors that keep the patient from achieving his or her goals (Martell, Addis, & Jacobsen, 2001). For example, a student feeling socially withdrawn and isolated would learn to identify avoidance behaviors such as

eating in the dorm room alone or hesitating to join clubs or other social groups. Recognizing these avoidance behaviors can lead to more productive behaviors that will help to achieve treatment goals and alleviate depressive symptoms.

The psychologist Sona Dimidjian and her colleagues at the University of Washington found that behavioral therapies have higher efficacy rates than SSRI and cognitive therapies. An important factor in outcome success, however, was the observation that subjects receiving either cognitive or behavioral therapy were more likely to continue with the therapy than subjects in the SSRI group (Dimidjian et al., 2006). Research also suggests that, similar to cognitive therapy, the effects of behavioral activation are long-lasting (Dobson et al., 2008). The previously discussed effort-based reward rodent model may suggest how enhanced behavioral effort and strengthened associations between actions and positive outcomes may lead to diminished depressive symptoms and enhanced emotional and cognitive functions.

Emerging Therapeutic Approaches. Although several treatment strategies exist for depression, disappointing efficacy rates motivate researchers to continue to search for effective treatment strategies (Figure 13.19). One such novel approach is DBS, for patients who fail to respond to other therapy approaches. As noted in Chapter 7 ("Movement"), DBS is an existing therapy for patients suffering from Parkinson's disease. This approach was initially considered for depression when Parkinson's patients revealed elevations in their mood while neurosurgeons tested electrode placement.

Although a closer examination of key areas associated with the self-reported boosts in mood has implicated several areas, the **subcallosal cingulate gyrus** has emerged as a key area contributing to profound sadness in depressed patients (Holtzeimer et al., 2012; Lozano et al., 2012). The subcallosal cingulate gyrus is an area of the anterior cingulate gyrus and has projections to and from the area of the ventral

FIGURE 13.19 Helen Mayberg, a neuroscience clinical researcher at Emory University School of Medicine, has conducted pioneering research on the effectiveness of DBS for treatment-resistant depression.

striatum and nucleus accumbens shell as well as the limbic structures—areas involved with symptoms related to sadness, anhedonia, and anxiety. Further connections have been observed with the BNST (also involved in anxiety), the hypothalamus, and the dorsal raphe nuclei containing serotonergic neurons (Hamani et al., 2011). Imaging studies indicate that the subcallosal cingulate gyrus is hyperactive in depressed patients (Lozano et al., 2012). Another area that exhibits hyperresponsiveness in depressed patients and has been a target of DBS for depression is the *lateral habenula*, an area thought to be involved with freezing responses in animal models (Sartorius, 2010; Sartorius & Henn, 2007; Yang et al., 2008). When some mammals detect danger, especially the threat of a predator, they will remain motionless, which increases the probability of remaining hidden from the threatening predator. Thus, depression symptoms related to avoiding threats may be viewed as an extension of such a freeze response in which individuals are reluctant to leave the safety of their homes for fear of encountering some type of threat or aversive situation.

In a recent study, electrodes were implanted in the subcallosal cingulate area of each hemisphere in 21 patients diagnosed with treatment-resistant depression. Assessments using the Hamilton Rating Scale for Depression indicated that 57% had met criteria for symptom improvement, with the numbers falling slightly at 6 months (48%) and 12 months (29%) (Lozano et al., 2012). Compared with the frontal lobotomy technique, DBS is reversible and leads to minimal tissue damage. However, it is an invasive treatment that is not without adverse side effects (ranging from chest pain to gastrointestinal problems). Further, it is considered unethical to subject patients to this invasive brain surgery without the promise of the actual treatment, meaning that these investigations lack proper controls although the stimulation can be turned off without the patient's knowledge (meaning that, in some cases, patients can serve as their own controls). Consequently, researchers and clinicians will proceed cautiously to establish the cost/benefit analysis for this type of surgical therapeutic strategy.

Another therapeutic strategy that scientists are exploring is a different type of pharmacological treatment that enhances synaptic functions. A promising new line of research has come from the recent finding that the hallucinogenic drug ketamine (see Chapter 4), an NMDA receptor antagonist, has fast-acting antidepressant effects (in this case, within hours, compared with weeks for traditional antidepressant medications). In animal models, ketamine leads to a rapid production of synaptic proteins as well as increased activity of spines in layer V of the PFC. Additionally, ketamine seems to reverse many of the negative brain effects observed in chronically stressed animals. The fast-acting effects on synaptogenesis have been found to be associated with BDNF functions, important in facilitating brain plasticity. Because ketamine (also known as the street drug Special K) has limited therapeutic value as a result of its abuse potential, researchers continue to explore new therapeutic agents that optimize symptom relief with few side effects (Duman & Aghajanian, 2012).

As illustrated in Figure 13.20, effective treatment strategies for depression can induce activity-dependent plasticity; that is, when the presynaptic neuron is activated sufficiently to release neurotrophic chemicals (e.g., BDNF) necessary for neural plasticity. Most of the therapies that have been shown to be effective, including antidepressant medication, ECT, cognitive therapy, and even exercise, appear to lead to enhanced neuroplasticity. The exact method of achieving this increased neuroplasticity is probably less important than the end result of relieving the symptoms of depression (Castren, 2005).

Bipolar Disorder

Bipolar disorder is characterized by the depressed emotions observed in major depression along with elevated moods (referred to as manic episodes) and changes in activity and energy. Much less prevalent than major depression, bipolar disorder will occur in 1 to 1.5% of the population during their lifetimes (Strakowski, DelBello, Adler, Cecil, & Sax, 2000). Patients with bipolar disorder often ride an emotional rollercoaster as they cycle from the heights of mania to the depths of depression. As the disorder progresses, emotional cycling becomes increasingly dangerous, especially during manic episodes when patients typically engage in risky behaviors that can cause harm, such as gambling away one's life savings or consuming dangerous doses of alcohol and/or drugs. Brain imaging studies have detected various abnormalities throughout the brains of subjects with bipolar disorder (compared with healthy control subjects), including the limbic structures

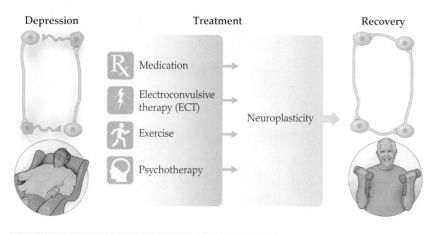

FIGURE 13.20 The many paths to neuroplasticity recovery. Several treatment strategies have the common result of increased neural plasticity that restores the neural networks for competent, as opposed to impaired, functions.

and PFC, as well as distinct changes in density of the brain's white matter, known as *white matter hyperintensities* (Chen et al., 2012; Stoll, Renshaw, Yurgelun-Todd, & Cohen, 2000). It has also been suggested that reduced densities of astrocytes, known as a homeostatic cell of the CNS, may contribute to bipolar disorder. This hypothesis is supported by the observation that drugs shown to be effective treatments (e.g., valproic acid, lithium salts) influence astrocyte genes and signaling (Peng, Li, & Verkhratsky, 2016).

One prominent difference between major depression and bipolar disorder is the type of pharmacological approach used to treat the two disorders. **Lithium** is the drug of choice for bipolar disorder. In the 1940s, the Australian psychiatrist John Cade became convinced that some toxic substance was the cause of the mood swings observed in bipolar disorder. In his studies, he eventually found that injecting lithium solution into guinea pigs resulted in a calm, tranquil response, even when the guinea pigs were placed in an uncomfortable position on their backs.

Excited that he might have been onto something, Cade translated his animal findings to clinical research in humans by developing a lithium pill and, after testing it on himself for a safety check, gave it to patients who were manic. After taking lithium, patients who had been so debilitated by their illness that they had to be institutionalized were released from the hospital. Cade's study was published in 1949 in the *Medical Journal of Australia* but received little fanfare from other researchers in the area. Although it took several decades, the U.S. Food and Drug Administration eventually approved lithium as a therapy for bipolar disorder in the early 1970s.

Although lithium's exact mechanism of action is unknown, research suggests that it increases presynaptic activity within the serotonergic system. Further, the similarity of this drug to other ions that are critical for neuronal functioning may lead to a recalibration type of effect within the nervous system (Manji, McNamara, & Lenox, 2000). Despite unwanted side effects including weight gain, tremors, gastrointestinal problems, and risk of toxicity resulting from intentional or accidental overdoses, lithium is still heralded as a pharmacological success (Oruch, Elderbi, Khattab, Pryme, & Lund, 2014; Strakowski et al., 2000). Although drugs with fewer side effects have been used to treat bipolar disorder (e.g., anticonvulsant drugs such as valproate; Monti, Polazzi, & Contestabile, 2009), lithium is still considered the most effective treatment for acute mania, with some studies reporting diminished symptoms in up to 70–80% of patients (Shorter, 2009).

Anxiety Disorders and Other Related Disorders

When 28-year-old Charlie Beljan was carried off the golf course in an ambulance during the Professional Golfers' Association (PGA) tour in November 2012, he feared that he was suffering a heart attack (Figure 13.21). Although his game remained strong, his anxiety, fear, chest pains, and dizziness all pointed to some type of impending cardiovascular event. Talk about horrible timing. If he could have just kept going, his goal was to win the tournament and maintain his eligibility for the coveted PGA championship. After spending the night in the hospital and learning that the many tests conducted indicated no cardiovascular risk, Beljan returned to the golf course the next day, persisted through his remaining symptoms, and won the tournament (Crouse and Pennington, 2012).

It turns out that the timing of Beljan's symptoms was important in the determination that he had suffered a panic attack rather than a heart attack. The stress generated by the tournament, in addition to many life changes such as a recent marriage and birth of his first child, all seemed to culminate in this intense emotional response on national television while he was playing the most important game of his life. On further investigation, it was revealed that anxiety was no stranger to Beljan prior to this particularly stressful year. In the popular media, he reported a lifelong history of being anxious about food. For example, if certain foods touched each other, it caused him anxiety, prompting his mother to send him to college with divided plates typically used by small children. The mere presence of certain foods that he did not like also caused anxiety. Because of these fears, social dining prompted intense anxiety as well.

Although Beljan has admitted to several forms of anxiety-induced responses that are considered odd by many, he remains a highly functioning, successful person. Because several different anxiety disorders are described in this section, it is important to remember that anxiety is a staple of all of our emotional lives, serving adaptive functions as it steers us from harm's way. In some cases, however, anxiety becomes out of control and disrupts functions that are

FIGURE 13.21 **Public panic attacks.** During a professional golf tournament, the golfer Charlie Beljan experienced a panic attack. After spending a night in the hospital, he returned to the course and won the tournament.

normally adaptive. Although the disorders described below are clearly distinguished from one another in the DSM-5, an unchecked stress and anxiety response is the most prevalent cause for all of these disorders.

Diagnoses of Anxiety Disorders and Other Related Disorders

Anxiety is a necessary response for survival and exists in two varieties in its nonpathological form. **State anxiety** reflects the immediate situation, and **trait anxiety** represents a person's more permanent tendencies to experience and express anxiety. Charlie Beljan's high levels of trait anxiety, coupled with equally high levels of state anxiety associated with the pressure of a professional golf tournament, culminated in a form of anxiety that is considered pathological and categorized as **panic disorder**. Heightened anxiety can express itself in the form of other disorders including **generalized anxiety disorder**, **social phobia**, **specific phobia**, **obsessive–compulsive disorder**

(OCD), and PTSD (discussed in Chapter 12). The distinctive characteristics of these disorders appear in Table 13.2. Altogether, these disorders have an approximate 20% lifetime incidence rate and are accompanied by an annual cost approaching $44 billion in the United States (Gross & Hen, 2004; Michael, Zetsche, & Margraf, 2007).

Common Causes

It should come as no surprise that anxiety disorders appear to be triggered by excessive levels of anxiety. Compared with healthy control subjects, when the brains of subjects with anxiety disorders have been subjected to fMRI scans, baseline activity is increased in the parahippocampal gyrus and cingulate cortex, both involved in emotional processing (Osuch et al., 2000). When an anxiety-provoking stimulus is present, increased activation in the amygdala has been consistently observed in subjects with anxiety disorders compared with healthy controls (Davidson, Abercrombie, Nitschke, & Putnam, 1999). In general, the forebrain has

TABLE 13.2. °

Anxiety and Other Related Disorders: Symptoms, Prevalence, and Treatment

DISORDER	SYMPTOMS	LIFETIME PREVALENCE (%)	TREATMENTS
Generalized anxiety disorder	Unrealistic, excessive, and long-lasting worry, motor tension, restlessness, irritability, difficulty sleeping, hypervigilance	5	Benzodiazepines, SSRIs, cognitive-behavioral therapy
Panic disorder	Brief, recurrent, unexpected episodes of terror (peak within 10 minutes), sympathetic activation, shortness of breath, fear of dying and losing control, derealization (perception that external world is no longer real)	3	SSRIs, cognitive/behavioral therapy
Social phobia (social anxiety disorder)	Aversion, fear, autonomic arousal in unfamiliar social settings	13	SSRIs, benzodiazepines, cognitive/behavioral therapy
Specific phobia	Aversion, fear, autonomic arousal in specific situations (for example, exposure to certain animals, the sight of blood, and so on)	11	Behavioral therapy (exposure)
Obsessive–compulsive disorder	Recurrent obsessions and compulsions: obsessions are persistent, intrusive or inappropriate thoughts that cause anxiety; compulsions are repetitive acts that the sufferer feels driven to perform to alleviate anxiety	2	SSRIs, behavioral therapy
Posttraumatic stress disorder	Following an extremely stressful event (involving actual or threatened injury), recurrent episodes of fear often triggered by reminders of initial trauma (reexperiencing and avoidance), autonomic arousal, persistent negative alterations in cognitions and mood	3	SSRIs, cognitive-behavioral therapy

SSRI, selective serotonin reuptake inhibitor.
From Gross & Hen, 2004, p. 546, and Andrews, Papakosta, & Barnes, 2013.

been implicated in maintaining high rates of excitatory neurotransmission. Accordingly, suppression of the brain's principal inhibitory system, the GABAergic system, may contribute to the emergence of anxiety symptoms. Supporting this hypothesis, genetically engineered mice lacking certain GABA receptors involved in calming the brain's functions fail to respond to anxiolytic drugs (i.e., drugs that reduce anxiety) such as benzodiazepines that bind to GABA receptors (Low et al., 2000).

Closely associated with the perception of anxiety is the physiological stress response. As discussed in Chapter 10, whereas the acute stress response keeps us from harm's way, the chronic stress response often results in some form of biomedical dysfunction that can evoke negative symptoms in the brain and/or body. Revisiting the core of the brain's stress circuit, the HPA axis, you will recall that the stress hormone released by the adrenal cortex, cortisol in humans, is circulated through the blood–brain barrier, where it interacts with specific receptors throughout the limbic structures.

The multifaceted stress response is mediated by two different glucocorticoid receptor systems, the **glucocorticoid receptor (GR)** and **mineralocorticoid receptor (MR)**. The primary difference between the receptors is their affinity for glucocorticoids. Specifically, MR are 10 times more sensitive than GR. The less-sensitive GR are activated during more prevalent increases in glucocorticoid secretion accompanying both stress and circadian changes that occur predictably each day. The MR system remains active following the initial stress activation because of the receptors' high affinity for lower circulating levels of stress hormones.

It has been hypothesized that the MR system regulates the neural circuits associated with stress, including playing a role in the brain's appraisal of incoming sensory information necessary to activate the stress response if required. The GR system, in contrast, plays an important role in maintaining homeostasis by terminating the stress response once it has been activated and mobilizing energy if sustained activation is necessary. Although the MR and GR are located throughout the limbic structures, they are both located in the hippocampus, emphasizing the role of this structure in the stress response. A delicate balance of these two systems is likely important for keeping anxiety responses at a relatively safe level for optimal and adaptive functioning (de Kloet et al., 2005).

As shown in Figure 13.22, genetic predispositions and stressful life events interact to produce responses

that are vulnerable to the emergence of an anxiety disorder. If a person has a genetic vulnerability that is subsequently accompanied by life events such as childhood trauma, exposure to a chronic stressor later in life alters gene expression that, weeks later, results in increased susceptibility to anxiety disorders. Gene-expression modifications that may ultimately lead to an anxiety disorder include modifications of MR and GR, atrophy of hippocampal CA3 dendrites, slowed cell turnover in the dentate gyrus, reduced expression of various serotonin receptors, reduced long-term potentiation, and cognitive impairment (de Kloet et al., 2005). In essence, highly functioning anxiety responses are similar to a highly sensitive security system in that they must be able to accurately detect the presence of a threat. However, if the responses are unnecessarily activated, the effectiveness diminishes as they deplete the brain's valuable resources and compromise the ability to distinguish between threats and opportunities. Following this logic, a security system that is too easily activated and is very difficult to turn off is not particularly useful.

The distribution of MR and GR systems has been suggested to be a causal factor for another anxiety-related disorder, PTSD, in which a decreased sensitivity of the brain's negative feedback system has been observed. In an animal model in which mice were exposed to a single prolonged stressor, a decrease in the expression of both MR and GR in the hippocampus was observed. These results suggest that the intensity of the stress experienced in patients with PTSD has likely changed the brain's distribution of these

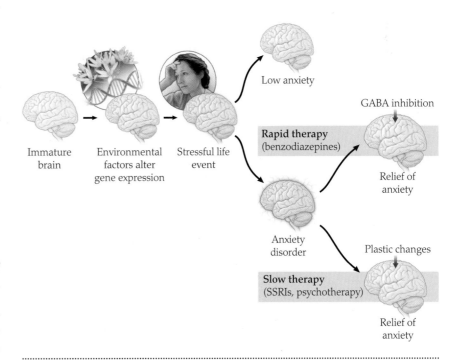

FIGURE 13.22 Genetic predispositions, environmental factors, and anxiety disorders. Exposure to the same life stressors can result in different anxiety response outcomes in individuals with varying genetic predispositions and environmental histories. For those developing an anxiety disorder, both rapid and slow therapeutic options are available.

differentially sensitive receptors, leading to a less efficient feedback system (Zhe, Fang, & Yuxiu, 2008).

The interaction of various brain areas proposed to contribute to the final anxiety-related disorder discussed in this chapter, OCD, can be seen in Figure 13.23. OCD, characterized by recurring upsetting thoughts known as *obsessions* and compensatory ritualistic acts known as *compulsions*, affects up to 3% of the population. Concordance rates between identical twins range from about 45% to 65%, suggesting that the environment also plays a significant causal role (Pauls, Mundo, & Kennedy, 2002).

In Figure 13.23, the patient experiences anxiety after leaving his parked car in the shopping mall parking lot. The anxiety prompts obsessive worrying, likely mediated by increased activity in the OFC, about whether he remembered to lock the car. The worried response expands to relevant limbic structures, including the cingulate cortex and amygdala, which result in full-blown terror about someone likely stealing his car. The fear prompts a compensatory response

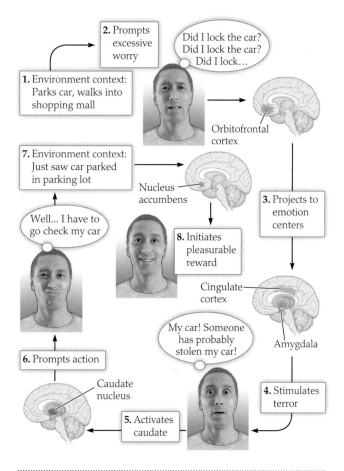

FIGURE 13.23 Context and obsessive–compulsive disorder (OCD). Environmental contexts, such as leaving a car in the parking lot, can prompt sufficient uncertainty and anxiety to trigger obsessions characteristic of OCD. For example, as fear and worry are experienced, this may ultimately lead to a response resulting in reduced anxiety (e.g., going back to the parking lot to make sure the car is locked).

mediated by the striatum's caudate nucleus to walk out to the parking lot to make sure the car is safely locked and unharmed. Once the checking behavior is initiated, satisfaction mediated through the nucleus accumbens circuitry diminishes the fear, even if is only a temporary relief (K. Lambert & Kinsley, 2010).

Treatment Strategies

Although the barbiturates and benzodiazepines were among the original drugs prescribed for anxiety disorders, their addictive properties present a drawback (Lader, 1976). Recall from Table 13.2 that SSRIs have become a common treatment for anxiety disorders. One functional difference between these drugs, however, is that the benzodiazepines have a more rapid effect than the SSRIs. Research discussed previously in this chapter has shown that SSRIs result in long-term changes in plasticity (as depicted in Figure 13.20). This property provides a potential explanation of why relief from anxiety symptoms is relatively slow with SSRIs, as is the case with the alleviation of depression symptoms. Before SSRIs gained favor in the treatment for anxiety disorders, **clomipramine (Anafranil)**, a tricyclic antidepressant, was frequently used to treat OCD. The more specific SSRIs, however, have fewer side effects (Kobak, Greist, Jefferson, Katzelnick, & Henk, 1998).

Psychosurgery has also been used to combat the symptoms of OCD. The surgeries are much more precise than the original lobotomies, although various pathways traveling through the limbic structures are damaged with the goal of dampening some of the intense emotions traveling to the PFC via the rich limbic circuitry traversing through the cingulate cortex. Various types of psychosurgery exist, with various success rates. An example is the limbic leucotomy introduced in the 1970s that involves making bilateral lesions to the lower medial OFC and the anterior cingulate bundle area. Although there are no appropriate control groups, systematic evaluations of patient symptoms following surgery reveal success rates as high as 84%. Obviously, this extremely invasive treatment strategy should be attempted only after less invasive and dangerous strategies have failed (Perse, 1988).

A noninvasive treatment approach for many of the anxiety disorders is the use of behavioral strategies (review Table 13.2). Behavioral treatment strategies are particularly effective in the case of specific phobias. In this disorder, intense fear of an object such as a spider or a bridge can be so disabling that individuals structure their daily routines to avoid encountering the feared objects. Such phobias can lead to maladaptive and restrictive lifestyles. **Exposure therapy** is a type of behavioral therapy in which patients are progressively confronted with a fear-inducing object. The efficacy rate of this type of therapy exceeds that of any other treatment for mental illness. Specifically, it has been reported that 95% of the patients undergoing exposure therapy for specific phobias improve after just one session lasting several

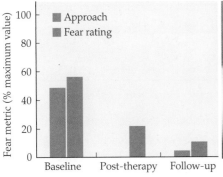

Source: Hauner, K.K., Mineka, S., Voss, J.L., & Paller, K.A. (2012). Exposure therapy triggers lasting reorganization of neural fear processing. *PNAS, 109*, 9203-9208.

FIGURE 13.24 Effectiveness of exposure therapy. A two-hour exposure therapy session resulted in persistent decreases in self-reported phobia symptoms and, as indicated in the graph, the ability to approach a live tarantula, and the fear associated with that fear.

hours—with the improvement maintained at the one-year follow up visit (Ost, Alm, Brandberg, & Breitholtz, 2001; Ost, Hellstrom, & Kaver, 1992). It is difficult to overstate the impressive efficacy rate of this treatment strategy. The lack of side effects is equally impressive.

How does exposure therapy affect the brain? An examination of brain changes accompanying the decreased fear provides important clues. In one study, subjects with a spider phobia completed a single two-hour session of exposure therapy. The therapy ended with the subject holding a live tarantula in his or her hand. Few would argue that this result does not represent a clear recovery. To understand how the brain is involved in exposure therapy, subjects were shown an image of a spider and a neutral image of a moth both before and after a one-time exposure therapy treatment while fMRI scans were acquired. Prior to treatment, the spider image activated a network including the cingulate cortex, insula, and amygdala when compared with the brain response to the moth images.

Other researchers have reported abnormal activation in the thalamus during exposure to feared stimuli (Del Casale et al., 2012). Following therapy, less activation was observed in this network and the PFC was activated. The study provided evidence that the fear network was still suppressed six months later on exposure to the spider image, with the absence of the prefrontal activation suggesting that the PFC was no longer necessary to prevent the phobic response. Without drugs or surgery, these results provide evidence that behavioral therapy used for phobias reorganizes neural responses to fear-generating stimuli. Researchers in this study found no evidence of recurring phobias at the six-month follow-up visit in any patients, an impressive 0% relapse rate (see Figure 13.24; Hauner, Mineka, Voss, & Paller, 2012).

If therapists do not welcome the idea of keeping snakes and spiders in their office, the phobic stimuli can also be introduced with virtual reality technology (Figure 13.25). Although virtual reality is not the same as encountering the actual stimuli, it introduces feared objects or scenarios in a

FIGURE 13.25 Using virtual reality to fight phobias. Although virtual reality is not the same as encountering the actual stimuli, it introduces feared objects or scenarios in a naturalistic and engaging context. Shown here, a patient wearing a virtual reality headset undertakes a therapy session in the psychiatric unit of Conception Hospital in Marseille, France.

naturalistic and engaging context that allows for precise manipulation of stimulus exposure. Virtual reality has clear advantages when treating people with a fear of flying because it is much more economical than scheduling multiple flights! This suggests that the visual experience is quite engaging and, although there are differences, is perceived by the brain as an actual representation of the targeted scenario (Bohil, Alicea, & Biocca, 2011). Preliminary studies suggest that the efficacy rates of virtual reality therapy are comparable to the actual therapy (Botella et al, 2007). Further, when the drug *d*-cycloserine, a partial glutamatergic NMDA agonist, is used in combination with virtual therapy and other exposure therapies, some studies have reported increased rates of recovery (Hofman, Wu, & Boettcher, 2013; Smits et al., 2013). The importance of using slightly varied contexts to present feared stimuli during virtual reality therapy is emphasized in this chapter's "Context Matters."

Virtual Reality Therapy for Spider Phobias

Featured study: Shiban, Y., Pauli, P. & Muhlberger, A. (2013). Effect of multiple context exposure on renewal in spider phobia. Behaviour Research and Therapy, 51, 68–74.

Although relapse rates are low for exposure therapy, various forms of exposure therapy have variable long-term effects for different phobias. This study explored the value of using virtual reality therapy with variable contexts to determine whether multiple context exposure (MCE), being exposed to relevant stimuli in multiple contexts, enhanced the robustness of the therapy by decreasing relapse rates.

Sixty subjects diagnosed with a spider phobia were recruited by advertisements in local newspapers. Following extensive testing, 15 subjects were assigned to the MCE group and 15 to the single context exposure (SCE). All subjects were female, had normal vision, and ranged in age from 18 to 58. The MCE group was exposed to spiders presented in five distinctive virtual rooms, each with a light of a different color. Besides the color of the light, the other variables were consistent across the rooms. In each trial, the virtual spider was positioned in the center of the virtual room and was animated so that it wiggled slowly.

Four measures were collected both prior to and subsequent to the virtual therapy. First, a structured clinical interview was used to determine subjects' degree of the phobia from a clinical perspective. Second, a behavioral approach test was used to assess responses. Specifically, a female spider *Grammostola rosea* measuring 8 centimeters from the front legs to the body was placed in a transparent box on a slide 3 meters from each subject. Each subject was asked to pull the spider as close as she felt possible so that the distance could be assessed. Third, subjects reported fear ratings at several points during exposure to the spider. Finally, two surface electrodes were placed on the subjects' nondominant hands to assess electrodermal activity (also referred to as skin conductance level), a physiological measure of anxiety.

Following habituation to the relevant aspects of the virtual reality equipment, the training sessions commenced. Training consisted of four 5-minute spider exposure sessions

with the MCE group exposed to four different virtual room colors and the SCE group exposed to four sessions with the same virtual room (Context Matters Figure 13.1a). Following the four sessions, the test session was another 5-minute exposure with a novel environment for both groups to assess whether MCE suppressed fear of the virtual spider in the final test. Subjects reported fear ratings throughout the virtual exposure session.

Results showed that the fear ratings decreased within each session and between sessions for both MCE and SCE groups. A similar effect was observed with the skin conductance data. In the novel environment test, fear was higher in the SCE group. Finally, in the final behavior avoidance test using the actual spider, the MCE group pulled the spider closer than the SCE group (Context Matters Figure 13.1b).

The results support the hypothesis that MCE suppresses renewal of phobia fear following virtual reality exposure treatment sessions. The researchers reported that this study was the first published account of the clinical benefits of MCE over more traditional exposure strategies in subjects with a phobia.

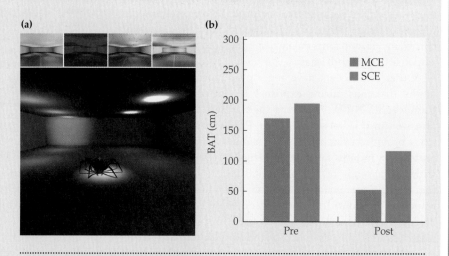

CONTEXT MATTERS FIGURE 13.1 Multiple context exposure and spider phobias. (a) After multiple context exposure (MCE) therapy in which participants are exposed to spiders in various colored room contexts or the single context exposure (SCE) therapy, (b) the participants in the MCE group were able to move a live spider in a box closer to them in the behavioral approach test (BAT).

Evolutionary Roots

Although it has generally been a challenge for researchers to identify appropriate animal models for schizophrenia and depression, compulsive behavior is often seen in various mammals. For example, the excessive grooming observed in some rodents, described in Chapter 8, confirms that compulsive responses are not unique to humans. Like grooming in rodents or handwashing in humans, many of the forms of behavior that are taken to excess are adaptive responses when considered on a smaller scale.

The fact that similar types of obsession occur across various cultures also provides support for the adaptive nature of these responses. Contaminating germs, for example, represent the most prevalent obsession in the United States, India, the United Kingdom, Japan, Denmark, and Israel (Sasson et al., 1997), suggesting that humans are biologically predisposed to keep our bodies clean to avoid sickness. The importance of an evolved biological predisposition to avoid certain stimuli, such as very small spiders, but not very dangerous objects such as guns, suggests that our evolutionary roots affect how readily we associate fear with an object. Although a gun is much more likely to harm us, it is rare to read about a person undergoing therapy for a gun phobia. It takes many generations for such a genetic predisposition to emerge.

The case of the comedian Howie Mandel provides further evidence of the evolutionary roots of obsessions and compulsions based on their relevance for the survival of our human ancestors. Mandel has severe germ phobia that leads him, for example, to use fist bumps instead of handshakes (Figure 13.26). In his memoir *Here's the Deal: Don't Touch Me*, he described the origin of his abnormal behavior. The fear began during a childhood vacation to Miami. During this trip, he was bitten by sand flies, which was unpleasant enough, but the flies also laid eggs under his skin. The affected skin was irritated and, when he scratched these

areas, the larvae would crawl under his skin. According to Mandel's account, his encounter with these insects literally made his skin crawl, an experience that would be traumatic for most people, especially a six-year-old child. Thus, this experience, combined with his persistent trait anxiety, resulted in a lifelong fear of germs and compensatory responses to avoid them. In addition to avoiding shaking hands in public, he wears a surgical mask each time he flies (Mandel, 2009). Based on the research described in this chapter, exposure therapy may provide the necessary top-down processing to allow Mandel to shake hands in public and remove his mask during his next flight.

FIGURE 13.26 Howie Mandel's fist bump. To avoid germ transmission and calm his anxiety, the comedian Howie Mandel greets others by tapping fists rather than shaking hands.

LABORATORY EXPLORATION

Schizophrenia and Prepulse Inhibition

Researchers have faced many challenges in identifying appropriate animal models for schizophrenia. For example, how do you know when a rat is experiencing hallucinations? However, one characteristic of schizophrenia that has been modeled in rodents is the sensory-gating deficit known as reduced **prepulse inhibition**. Prepulse inhibition is a decrease in the response to a startling stimulus when another weaker stimulus precedes it closely in time. In other words, the startle response does not habituate in safe environments as it does in healthy subjects. For example, when you tour a haunted house and your friend approaches you from the back and grabs your shoulders and shouts *boo!*, your state of anxiety is influenced

by being in a dark scary house, prompting you to respond with a dramatic startle response (and depending on the intensity of anxiety, a scream as well). In the context of a haunted house, this is a normal response. But, imagine that your so-called friend repeats the shoulder grab just two minutes later. This time you are on to your friend and you do not respond with the same exaggerated response exhibited by the first scare. In contrast, individuals with schizophrenia do not habituate or filter the shoulder tap and respond with equal intensity following each tap. Whereas the healthy person inhibits the response because of the familiar stimuli (prepulse inhibition), this effect is not observed in schizophrenia (Geyer & Moghaddam, 2002).

Prepulse inhibition can be assessed in animals by placing rats in a small box, typically known as an **acoustic** or **startle response box** that has a restrainer positioned on a weight-sensitive platform that assesses the latency to jump, or startle, as well as the intensity of the response by monitoring weight fluctuations on the platform (see Laboratory Exploration Figure 13.1). In one study, the prepulse stimulus was a single 85-decibel noise that was followed by a louder 115-decibel sound. When the 115-decibel stimulus was presented with no 85-decibel warning,

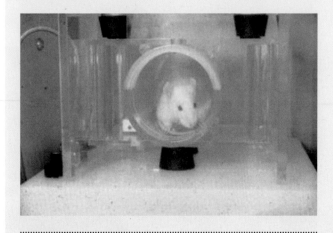

LABORATORY EXPLORATION FIGURE 13.1 Measuring the startle response. Rats are positioned in restraint tubes to assess startle responses when preceded by warning signals as an index of prepulse inhibition—a response similar to prepulse inhibition responses in patients diagnosed with schizophrenia.

the startle response is stronger than when it is preceded with the 85-decibel warning. After receiving dopamine agonists, a diminished prepulse inhibition is observed in rodents.

As described earlier in this chapter, dopamine has been implicated in schizophrenia because of the effectiveness of neuroleptic drugs that act as dopamine antagonists. Further, research implicating the role of dopamine in anticipation (discussed in Chapter 8) explains the function of dopamine in this sensory-gating task. If the upcoming loud noise is anticipated, the rodent prepares for the aversive stimulus by suppressing the full-blown startle response following the 115-decibel stimulus. When a person tries to prepare you for upsetting news by saying "brace yourself," this is a form of verbal filter for an upcoming upsetting stimulus.

Using this model, various neuroanatomical and neurochemical variables have been manipulated. In one study using the 85- and 115-decibel stimuli, lesions of the entorhinal cortex (involved in routing information to the hippocampus) compromised the rat's prepulse inhibition response (Goto, Ueki, Iso, & Morita, 2002). Other studies have also implicated the temporal and prefrontal cortical areas, as well as the ventral tegmental area, brain areas known for dopamine involvement. This model is also useful for identifying certain genetic models that are susceptible to compromised prepulse inhibition (Swerdlow, Geyer, & Braff, 2001). With animal models such as the prepulse inhibition model, neurobiological factors can be identified as risk factors. Further, such models can guide informed research, potentially leading to effective treatment strategies for schizophrenia symptoms.

Conclusion

One goal of this chapter is to emphasize that most forms of mental illnesses stem from the brain's attempt to assess accurately both our internal and our external environments to enhance our survival. When the brain's neurons fire out of step with reality in patients with schizophrenia, mental experiences are constructed to explain the confusion. The result is a blurred perception of reality that represents the brain's attempt to justify the malfunctioning neurophysiological responses. When fears heighten because of threatening circumstances, individuals may become more passive in their responses to life's challenges and, as a result, are more susceptible to a diagnosis of depression. Finally, anxiety typically corresponds with situations that are, to some extent, considered threatening. The responses consistent with various anxiety disorders, although they may be disruptive, are often effective in keeping us from encountering those dreaded stimuli. Thus, the symptoms associated with most mental illnesses are mere variants of normal responses—with the lines between normal and abnormal, as conveyed in the beginning of this chapter, being very fuzzy in some cases.

The extreme variations of the responses that comprise the symptoms of mental illnesses, however, often require professional intervention to recalibrate the brain's adaptive functions. Pharmacological treatment is standard, and it is attractive because of its ease of delivery. However, patients' response rates to pharmacological treatment are often disappointing, especially considering the side effects and relapse rates. Even so, the SSRIs have been associated with activation of various neuroplasticity systems that have been associated with recovery from mental illness. Other types of therapies have also been associated with enhanced neuroplasticity, including exercise therapy and ECT. Neuroplasticity may also be enhanced by various methods that diminish chronic stress and promote a sense of control, as observed in various behavioral and cognitive therapies.

It is encouraging that the nature of therapeutic approaches has changed over the past century. Although the treatments are far from perfect, the welfare of the patients is a concern as cost/benefit analyses are conducted when new therapeutic approaches are evaluated. Perhaps more so than with any other topic discussed in this text, we must learn from the past failed attempts to treat mental illness. As new treatment strategies emerge, including computer training tasks and virtual reality exposure, the importance of using evidence-based therapies will help us avoid unfortunate cases such as those of Sheri Storm and Howard Dully in the future.

KEY TERMS

evidence-based therapies (p. 373)
dissociative identity disorder (p. 374)

The Challenge of Classifying and Treating Mental Illness

schizophrenia (p. 375)
psychoanalysis (p. 375)
electroconvulsive therapy (ECT) (p. 376)
psychopharmacologic drugs (p. 376)
trepanning (p. 376)
lobotomy (p. 377)
psychodynamic theory (p. 377)
single-nucleotide polymorphisms
  (SNPs) (p. 378)

Schizophrenia

positive symptoms (p. 379)
negative symptoms (p. 379)
chlorpromazine (p. 379)
neuroleptic drug (p. 380)
antipsychotics (p. 380)
dopamine theory of schizophrenia
  (p. 380)
NMDA receptor (p. 380)
prodromal phase of schizophrenia
  (p. 382)
chandelier cell (p. 382)

concordance rate (p. 383)
tardive dyskinesia (p. 384)
first-generation antipsychotics (p. 384)
second-generation antipsychotics
  (p. 384)
atypical antipsychotic (p. 384)
cognitive remediation treatment (p. 385)
compensatory therapy (p. 385)

Depression

major depression (p. 387)
bipolar disorder (p. 387)
monoamine hypothesis of depression
  (p. 387)
selective serotonin reuptake inhibitors
  (SSRIs) (p. 388)
serotonin hypothesis of depression
  (p. 388)
molecular hypothesis of depression
  (p. 388)
catabolites (p. 388)
effort-based reward theory (p. 389)
network hypothesis of depression
  (p. 390)
treatment resistant (p. 391)
repetitive transcranial magnetic
  stimulation (rTMS) (p. 391)

monoamine oxidase inhibitors
  (MAOIs) (p. 392)
tricyclic antidepressants (p. 392)
nocebo effect (p. 392)
Behavioral Activation Therapy (p. 393)
subcallosal cingulate gyrus (p. 393)
lithium (p. 395)

Anxiety Disorders and Other Related Disorders

state anxiety (p. 396)
trait anxiety (p. 396)
panic disorder (p. 396)
generalized anxiety disorder (p. 396)
social phobia (p. 396)
specific phobia (p. 396)
obsessive–compulsive disorder
  (OCD) (p. 396)
glucocorticoid receptor (GR) (p. 397)
mineralocorticoid receptor (MR)
  (p. 397)
clomipramine (Anafranil) (p. 398)
exposure therapy (p. 398)
prepulse inhibition (p. 401)
acoustic response box (p. 402)
startle response box (p. 402)

REVIEW QUESTIONS

1. How did Jean Martin Charcot's ideas on mental illness influence the thinking of Sigmund Freud? How did the ideas of Charcot and Freud collectively advance the study of mental illness?

2. What is a prefrontal lobotomy and for what purpose was it used in humans? What side effects did the people who underwent this procedure suffer?

3. What is the difference between the "positive symptoms" and "negative symptoms" of schizophrenia? Explain, and provide examples of positive symptoms and negative symptoms.

4. Describe the evidence that genetic and environmental factors contribute to the onset of schizophrenia. Are genetic and environmental factors thought to interact to cause schizophrenia? Explain.

5. Describe the methods of and rationale for ECT and rTMS for treating depression.

6. Overall, which is more effective for treating depression, antidepressants or cognitive therapy? Explain.

7. What is exposure therapy? How has it been used to treat phobias? What are some potential ways this therapeutic approach is thought to influence neural functions?

CRITICAL-THINKING QUESTIONS

1. If you had a suitable animal model, how would you test the network hypothesis of depression?

2. For which types of phobias do you think virtual reality exposure therapy would be most helpful and for

which types of phobias do you think it would be least helpful? Explain.

3. What sociocultural factors do you think inform how we define abnormal behavior?

Epilogue:

Expanding the Contextual Boundaries of Biopsychology

Throughout this text, I have emphasized the important influence of relevant biological psychology contexts on the brain's complex responses. We have learned that the same brain with the same neural networks responds differently in varying situations. For example, you may be very studious and reflective while sitting in your biological psychology class, but come across as funny and outgoing when interacting with your friends. Alternatively, you may be a whiz at solving problems in chemistry lab, but freeze when trying to figure out how to escape from a growling Rottweiler running your way. In short, you have learned that when it comes to understanding the brain and its responses, context matters.

In this Epilogue, we will explore various innovative research questions and ideas that test the contextual limits of the brain's functions. Consideration of these contextual challenges will give your neural networks much to ponder as you consider the future of biological psychology. One of my personal measures of success as a professor is observing students continuing a class discussion on their own *after* the class has been dismissed. I would be equally thrilled to know that you walked away from this text and this course with a continued interest in the many unsolved mysteries of biological psychology—perhaps even starting discussions related to these topics with unsuspecting friends!

Here, you will encounter three variations of the topic of context that I have focused on throughout this text. First, we will discuss one of the most fundamental elements of our environmental context, gravity, as we consider research on rats developing in microgravity (very low-gravity) environments in space. Second, we will look at the physical context of the brain as we examine the recent success of brain–machine interfaces in facilitating responses in cases such as humans who are paralyzed. Finally, we will consider the value of stepping outside of the traditional context of the biopsychology laboratory in exploring creativity and innovative responses in shelter-seeking octopuses, nest-decorating bowerbirds, problem-solving raccoons and chimps, and freestyle-rapping humans. These topics should stretch the limits of the more traditional contexts that we have become so familiar with in each of this book's chapters.

Extreme Environmental Context Modification: Rats Undergoing Prenatal Development in Space

Although we have considered the influences of varying contexts throughout this text, laboratory versions of altered environments generally include rather mundane contextual changes such as the introduction of new objects or a slight change in the light–dark schedule. For example, in one line of studies that you read about in Chapter 1, experimenters provided new toys, or other objects, in rats' cages to create what is known as an "enriched" environment. We have learned that, for the most part, rats and other mammals are adept at adjusting to modifications in their environments.

But how well would rats adjust to *extreme* contextual changes? For example, what if they developed in an environment with almost no gravity? Human astronauts have demonstrated their ability to adapt to microgravity environments since the first space missions in the 1960s. Although the gravitational force is not completely absent in these environments, it is very different from the gravitational fields of our familiar environment on Earth. If you have ever experienced a feeling of "free fall" on a roller coaster, you have some perception of what a microgravity environment is like (Figure 14.1). After sufficient training in specialized microgravity enclosures on Earth, highly specialized astronauts learn to adapt their floating to direct themselves to targets. They make key adaptations to enable themselves to carry out behaviors, such as eating and washing their hair, that are so simple when performed with the gravitational force on Earth.

The neuroscientist Jeffrey Alberts began studying the impact of low-gravity environmental contexts on mammalian development after being approached by both the former Soviet Union and the *National Aeronautics and Space Administration* (NASA) in the 1980s to investigate the effects of space flight on pregnant rats. Subsequently, Alberts started his own company, known as STAR Enterprises (STAR is RATS spelled backward), to develop habitats to investigate rodents in space. Considering that all living animals on Earth have evolved to exist in Earth's gravitational forces, how would a mammal respond to developing in its mother's womb in an environmental context with very little gravity?

FIGURE 14.1 Microgravity perception. The perception of "free fall" in amusement park rides simulates a microgravity environment and triggers a dramatic response in the willing participants of this experiment in changing environmental contexts.

In the first study, the scientists were interested in the effects of microgravity on developing rat pups born on Earth after having spent days 13–18 of their 21-day gestational period aboard the unmanned Soviet biosatellite *Cosmos 1514*. Would developing in a mother's womb in a microgravity environment compromise their movement and balance later in life (similar to how being deprived of light early in development compromises visual acuity later in life)? Based on his knowledge of developmental systems, Alberts hypothesized that the developing rats' vestibular system, a sensory system of the inner ear that controls balance, would not develop normally if the rats were deprived of gravity during fetal development. He further predicted that it would be difficult for such "space rats" to differentiate *up* from *down* and to balance themselves when they were later born on gravity-bound Earth.

Was Albert's hypothesis correct? The space rats adapted better than expected. Researchers did not observe any drastic deficits in their postnatal behaviors. The only behavioral effect in the Soviet space study was related to movement. On Earth, mammals typically move forward or backward, rarely proceeding in an angular direction to move across an area. For example, if we are standing in a courtyard and notice a friend in a northwest direction, we turn toward our friend and proceed to walk in a forward direction until we reach our social destination. It would be odd to stay facing our original direction and simply move our bodies in a northwest direction until we reach our friend. These gravity-deprived rats, however, were more likely to engage in this angular movement compared with rats whose pregnant mothers had remained Earth-bound. This result provided evidence that the microgravity environment contributed to the rats being more sensitive to this type of movement (Alberts, Serova, Keefe, & Apanasenko, 1985).

After that initial space flight, Alberts and his colleagues sent pregnant rats on NASA's small space shuttle around the time of mid-pregnancy (9th–11th gestational days). On the pregnant rats' return to Earth just prior to the time they were due to give birth, the fetuses were removed. This removal occurred before the fetuses had time to adjust to Earth's gravity. Unlike the flight in the Soviet space study, the NASA flight in this study had a crew who videotaped the pregnant rats during their spaceflight. Pregnant rats in space rolled around much more than their pregnant Earth-bound counterparts. This finding was not unexpected because walls and ceilings are all perceived as floors in a weightless environment, where *up* and *down* are less clearly defined. These rolling movements exposed the developing fetuses to more angular accelerations, explaining the findings related to sensitivity to angular movement (described previously) in the first Soviet rat mission.

To assess the developing vestibular systems in these rat pups, the experimenters gently restrained the rat pups on their backs against a contact surface in one test (contact test) and, in a second balance assessment, held the rat pups on their backs submerged in a warm bath (water test).

The researchers videotaped the rat pups' responses to determine how effectively they could "right" themselves from the position on their backs.

In the contact test, the rat pups showed no deficits in righting themselves. In this test, the rat pups could rely on several types of stimuli, including tactile and vestibular cues (e.g., the floor surface and the perception of being upright). Therefore, they could compensate for any vestibular impairment using other senses in the contact test. However, the water test was a purer test of the rat pups' vestibular sensory cues. When they were submerged in water during this test, the group of space rat pups took longer to right themselves than a control group of Earth-bound rat pups did for almost the first week of life. According to Alberts, after spending a week in a microgravity environment in the womb, the space rat pups had difficulty discerning *up* from *down* and reestablishing their balance (Shere, 2004). However, they caught up after the first week outside the womb, showing similar righting responses as the Earth-bound rat pups (Ronca, Fritsch, Bruce, & Alberts, 2008; see Figure 14.2).

Now that the space data are in, it is clear that developing rats can adapt to Earth's gravitational pull following gestational development in a microgravity environment. The adaptation of fully developed astronauts to a weightless environment suggests that humans would be equally as flexible adapting to changes in gravity. Given the degree of adaptability that rats and humans demonstrate here on Earth, this is yet another example of the great functionality the brain provides via its ability to consistently change and evolve even in an environment as foreign as space.

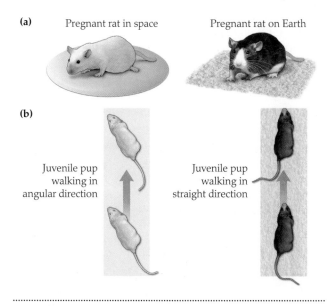

(a)   Pregnant rat in space   Pregnant rat on Earth

(b)

Juvenile pup walking in angular direction

Juvenile pup walking in straight direction

FIGURE 14.2 Rats in space. (a) After being exposed to a uterine environment either in space or on Earth, (b) the movement patterns of the pups were assessed following birth, with the space offspring exhibiting more movement in an angular direction than the pups experiencing gestational growth on Earth.

Changing the Context of the Brain's Infrastructure: Building Brain–Machine Interfaces

In Mary Shelley's novel *Frankenstein*, a dead brain was brought to life by being stimulated with electricity. In the *Matrix* films, computers connected to human brains projected virtual images that appeared realistic. As research life has imitated art, the *brain–machine interface* has transitioned from a component of fictitious storylines to a component of reality. In the 1960s, Manfred Clynes and Nathan Kline introduced the term *cyborg* (for "cybernetic organism") to refer to the merging of biological and artificial systems, such as the integration of electronic systems with human bodies. Although the initial plan for cyborgs was to enable humans to change their physiology to adapt to space exploration (as in the rat studies discussed previously), the current focus is on more earthly challenges, such as providing lost function to many populations with disabilities (Clynes & Kline, 1960; Mussa-Ivaldi & Miller, 2003).

The initial brain–machine interface was the cochlear implant, an electronic device designed to provide a sense of hearing to deaf or severely hard-of-hearing patients (Loeb, 1990). Today, more than 324,000 patients worldwide have cochlear implants (U.S. Department of Health and Human Services, 2013). The cochlear implant is an example of a *neuroprosthesis*: a device that restores lost sensory, motor, or cognitive function.

In another application of brain–machine interfaces, more recent research has focused on enabling paralyzed patients to perform motor tasks. In general, this has been accomplished by training subjects to maintain certain cortical rhythms in brain areas such as the sensorimotor cortex. During training, these EEG waves are recorded over the sensorimotor cortex as subjects engage in tasks such as actually reaching for a cup or imagining reaching for a cup. With such training techniques, both healthy subjects and subjects with disabilities have been taught to control their brain waves to control a cursor on a monitor. This activity provided a method of communication as well as a form of movement control for patients with motor impairments (Wolpaw, Birbaumer, McFarland, Pfurtscheller, & Vaughan, 2002; Wolpaw, Flotzinger, Pfurtscheller, & McFarland, 1997; Wolpaw & McFarland, 1994).

As microelectrodes and computer technologies became more sophisticated, researchers began to merge machines and brains in more direct ways. For example, in one study with rats, a small group of neurons in the part of the motor cortex that controls the forelimb was stimulated with

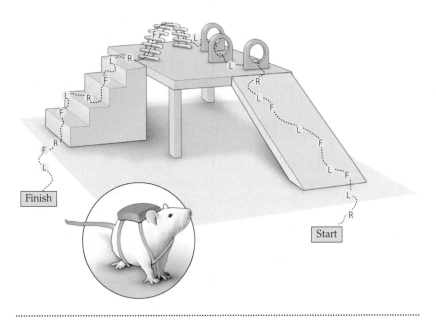

FIGURE 14.3 Remote-control rats. Rats received stimulation to the medial forebrain bundle, coupled with specific somatosensory input associated with the right or left whisker representations to guide their movement within a challenging obstacle course.

microwires. The activation of this group of neurons was transferred as input to a computer program designed to move a robotic arm. The rats eventually learned to use their neural signals to operate the robotic arm to press a lever for water—without moving their own arms (Chapin, Moxon, Markowitz, & Nicolelis, 1999). Monkeys have also been trained to manipulate brain–machine interfaces using visual cues to control a cursor on a computer screen as well as robotic arms (Blake, 2012). In another study, rats were trained to associate electrical stimulation of the somatosensory cortex with stimulation to the medial forebrain bundle (part of the brain's reward system). Consequently, researchers could control the movement of the rat, like a remote-control car, via a remote device that stimulated the brain's reward center when the rat approached a specific location (see Figure 14.3; Talwar et al., 2002).

Although individuals with paralysis have not successfully used their brains to move their own muscles in some time, they can learn to use the same brain areas to enable tools to respond as those muscles would. The brain appears to retain the ability to generate motor commands even when it can no longer control movement because of the conditions contributing to paralysis. This suggests that although the brains of these patients have been functionally disconnected from their bodies, if the damaged motor circuits were repaired, the brain would be ready to reestablish neural control of the lost movement (Lebedev et al., 2011).

Remarkably, patients have demonstrated an ability to maintain the function of these motor planning neuronal networks, even after years of lost function. For example, scientists at Brown University implanted a tiny grid with

96 microelectrodes (about the size of a baby aspirin) into the motor cortex of a 58-year-old patient, 15 years after she had suffered a brainstem stroke that had left her with quadriplegia (paralysis of all four limbs). The scientists positioned the microelectrodes to record the activity of the neurons that are associated with planned movement. The Brain–Computer Interface system known as *BrainGate2* reads this patient's neural inputs, recorded by the microelectrode grid implanted in the motor cortex, and translates them into commands to operate devices such as a robotic arm with a bottle of coffee. Thus, instead of making the precise movements with her own arm to pick up a cup of coffee and drink it, the patient generates actions in the motor cortex to move the robotic arm in the same way.

As Figure 14.4 illustrates, this patient was able to guide the robotic arm with her motor neurons to serve herself a sip of coffee for the first time in 15 years. Although paralyzed human patients had previously been trained to move cursors in a two-dimensional pattern over a visual screen to indicate responses or letters for communicating, this was the first demonstration of a patient manipulation of a device in a three-dimensional space to perform a task as her own arm had once done (Hochberg et al., 2012).

Now that brain–machine interfaces have been developed to enable individuals to use brain activity to operate robotic devices, new hope exists for patients who are suffering from paralysis. Of course, a neuroprosthesis that functions as a person's actual limb is an even better option for such patients and has recently been attempted in two paralyzed individuals. These patients' neuroprostheses have allowed them to

FIGURE 14.4 Brain–machine interface provides autonomy to patient. Using *BrainGate2*, this paralyzed patient is able to move the robotic arm by sending neural signals to activate her motor cortex. The result is a much-anticipated sip of coffee and a smile.

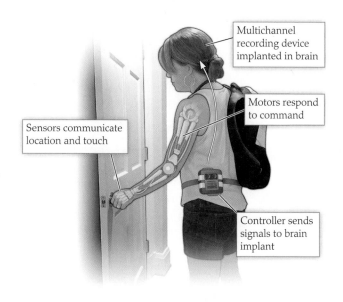

Multichannel recording device implanted in brain

Motors respond to command

Sensors communicate location and touch

Controller sends signals to brain implant

FIGURE 14.5 Real-world applications of brain–machine interface research. Current research on fully implantable brain–machine interface technology is aimed at allowing humans with limb paralysis or amputations to gain control of their natural or prosthetic limbs, so they may carry out everyday activities.

gain limited shoulder, elbow, forearm, wrist, and hand movement (Memberg et al., 2014). As shown in an artist's rendering of a theoretical neuroprosthesis in Figure 14.5, multiple sensory and motor input channels are necessary for such a device to be used successfully in one's arm. Thus, the nervous system appears to readily adapt to the contextual changes of interacting with various types of hardware to accommodate for loss of function. Scientists hope that these promising research discoveries will translate into mainstream treatments to restore function in individuals facing the rest of their lives with brains that can no longer directly control their body movements (Lebedev & Nicolelis, 2006).

Stepping Outside the Context of the Laboratory: Creativity and the Brain

Although you probably have a good sense of what the term *creativity* means, it is a difficult term for scientists to define operationally. Creativity is generally thought to be related to the production of an idea or product that is both novel and useful in a particular setting. Further, the novel end product of the creative process is often described as *innovative* (Kaufman, Butt, Kaufman, & Colbert-White, 2011). An important question for biopsychological researchers interested in creative responses is whether creativity can be systematically investigated. And, if creativity can indeed be systematically investigated, can it be observed in the controlled and often less-than-engaging laboratory environment?

Creativity is often viewed as one of the defining features of intelligence (Jauk et al., 2013). But is creativity uniquely human? Probably not. In fact, creativity may not even be unique to vertebrates! Octopuses have been shown to find a creative use for coconut shells they find on the ocean floor by turning the shells into functional homes (Figure 14.6b). As shown in Figure 14.6c, these animals have developed an innovative method of transporting their new shelters to their home territory, a manner of walking described as "stilt walking." The concave surface of the coconut is positioned upright while the octopus positions its arms around the coconut and uses the remaining parts of its limbs as a form of rigid walking sticks (Finn, Tregenza, & Norman, 2009).

In the world of vertebrates, male bowerbirds, introduced in Chapter 8, also appear to exhibit creative responses when they build elaborate nests out of various plant materials and then "decorate" the nests with colored ornaments such as shells, flower petals, or other items they collect from local trash bins (see Figure 14.7). Research suggests that the male bower birds prefer colored objects that contrast with the color of their own plumage as well as the nest material, perhaps to give their nest ornaments more of a visual impact. Why such a fuss about a nest? These decorative elements, in combination with the males' plumage, attract female suitors to the nest (Endler & Day, 2006). Interestingly, the male bower bird's brain volume has been positively correlated with the complexity of its nest, reinforcing the relationship between brain complexity and this complex nest-building behavior (Day, Westcott, & Olster, 2005).

Of course, if creativity is indeed a sophisticated cognitive response, more evidence of creative responses should be apparent in mammals, especially primates, which possess elaborate and extensive cortical tissue. A classic study that Wolfgang Köhler (1925) conducted with chimps demonstrates their novel and creative solution to a problem. When chimps were placed in a room with a banana dangling from the ceiling—out of reach—they had to determine a way to obtain the banana. As Figure 14.8 indicates, when boxes were also present in the room, the chimps stacked the boxes on top of one another, pushed the stack under the bananas, and climbed up to pick their banana from the ceiling. Köhler used the term *insight* to refer to this apparently novel use of items in the environment to solve a problem. Researchers have replicated this finding with pigeons (Epstein, Kirshnit, Lanza, & Rubin, 1984).

Other than primates, the animal that has been most closely associated with creativity and innovation is the raccoon. Further, the raccoon has been associated with another characteristic related to human cognition known as *curiosity*. According to the pioneering psychologists G. Stanley Hall and Theodate Smith, curiosity is the highest form of learning. These psychologists viewed curiosity as a form of attention

(a)

(b)

(c)

(a)

(b)

(c)

FIGURE 14.6 Creativity in invertebrates? (a) An octopus exhibits a creative use for a coconut shell, (b) using it as a habitat and (c) moving it using an innovative mode of transportation known as stilt walking.

FIGURE 14.7 Bower bird interior design. (a) The male bower birds (b) build complex nests with colors that coordinate in various ways with plumage color. (c) The complexity and color scheme of the nest attracts female bower birds. Thus, this nest-building behavior, perhaps a model of creativity, is selected for in male bower birds when the females mate with the builders of the most elaborate nests.

FIGURE 14.8 **Chimpanzee problem solving.** This chimp demonstrated a novel approach to solving the problem of having to reach a banana hanging from the ceiling.

that was stripped of all functional thoughts, such as the facilitation of eating or avoidance of a threat (Pettit, 2010). It is one thing for an animal to persist on a problem to obtain a food treat, especially if it is hungry, but something very different if the animal persists on a problem when no food or other visible tangible reward is associated with the task.

Before scientists selected the rat as the typical animal of study in psychology labs in the United States, the raccoon was a contender, at least for a short time. One early advocate of the raccoon model was Lawrence Cole at the University of Oklahoma. His research early in the 20th century suggested that the raccoon provided a unique and valuable model of human cognition (see Figure 14.9). Using the puzzle boxes introduced by Thorndike (described in Chapter 12), Cole found that raccoons could successfully open several types of latches to reach a goal. After he had spent considerable time training these raccoons, Cole stated that, based on his observations, curiosity, rather than food, seemed to drive their behavior.

Another researcher at the time noted the raccoons' unique spontaneous attention directed toward problem solving in the absence of training and their persistent tendency to investigate their surroundings (Davis, 1907). Although researchers were intrigued by raccoons' sophisticated cognitive abilities, these very abilities ultimately became a problem. It became virtually impossible to keep raccoons inside a laboratory—they were constantly manipulating and

destroying their cages and were even reported to escape through a lab's ventilation system! Because of the difficulty in maintaining raccoons in the laboratory, the more manageable and agreeable rat emerged as a more desirable laboratory animal for the investigation of cognitive functions (Pettit, 2009).

Although rats have provided a wealth of information about the brain's control of behavior, perhaps it is time to revisit the sophisticated antics of the raccoons. If raccoons cannot be assessed in laboratories, can they be investigated in their natural habitat? If scientists observe raccoons in their natural habitats, can we learn more about creativity and curiosity? Recently my students and I observed free-ranging, wild raccoons in a park setting where they were given food daily. Outside of the constraints of the laboratory, the raccoons seemed to exhibit curiosity, as well as highly social behavior, similar to primates we were observing at the same time.

Behaviors such as maternal-offspring interactions of long durations, social grooming, exploration of novel nonfood objects, and adult play suggest that these animals engage in complex social and cognitive behaviors (Pitt, Lariviere, & Messier, 2008; see Figure 14.9). We wondered whether the specialized neurons implicated in the heightened social, cognitive, and emotional functions of humans, the von Economo neurons (discussed in Chapter 3), were present in the raccoon brain.

FIGURE 14.9 Exploring raccoon intelligence and innovation. Raccoons were considered a model animal for psychological experiments early in the history of the discipline by researchers such as Lawrence Cole (a). In their natural habitat, raccoons exhibit complex behaviors such as (b) social play, (c) problem-solving behavior, and (d) robust exploration of novel objects.

As seen in Figure 14.10, we observed cells in the raccoon's frontoinsular cortex that have been confirmed to be von Economo neurons; although speculative at this point, these neurons may facilitate advanced social and cognitive functions that share characteristics with some primates (Landis, Bardi, Hyer, Rzucidlo, & Lambert, 2014). Further, the raccoon has more neurons in its cerebral cortex than other carnivores do; for example, although a golden retriever has a larger cortex volume than the raccoon, the raccoon has 60% more neurons (Messeder, Lambert, Noctor, Manger, & Herculano-Houzel, 2015).

As useful as animal models of creativity are, however, valuable information can be gathered about human creativity by conducting research on . . . you guessed it . . . humans. One innovative study investigated which brain areas are active during the creative process of generating freestyle rap music. Freestyle rap music is a form of hip-hop music in which the artist improvises lyrics (that rhyme!) in novel patterns, with the improvised lyrics guided by an instrumental

beat. With some researchers emphasizing the real-time nature, or rather effortless flow, of creativity, the spontaneous generation of rhythmic lyrics seems to be an optimal model for creativity (Abraham et al., 2013). In one study, adult male subjects who were freestyle rap artists performed two separate tasks. In the experimental condition, subjects underwent fMRI scans as they generated (improvised) their own freestyle lyrics. By contrast, in the control condition, subjects underwent fMRI scans as they recited lyrics they had memorized prior to the fMRI scans. Hence, the key difference between the conditions was whether subjects were required to creatively generate the lyrics.

As Figure 14.11 illustrates, subjects in the experimental (freestyle improvisation) condition showed less activity in the DLPFC and more activity in the mPFC compared with the control condition. We saw in Chapter 12 that the mPFC has been implicated in the regulation of motivation, incentives, intentions, and, in general, one's drive to achieve a goal. The mPFC sends signals to the DLPFC, which is involved in

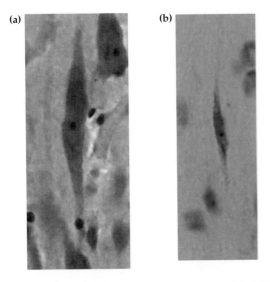

FIGURE 14.10 **von Economo neurons.** Similarly structured von Economo neurons exist in both (a) humans and (b) raccoons, especially in the frontoinsular cortex. Although more research is needed, these neurons have been implicated in advanced social and cognitive functions.

controlling the activity of the mPFC. The inhibitory regulation by the DLPFC is typically very adaptive in that it keeps us out of harm's way. However, in the case of freestyle rap, the investigators believe, there is no time to monitor the generation of rhythms and rhyming lyrics. As a result, to produce this innovative outcome, the mPFC literally must "go with the brain flow" without the advice of the DLPFC (Liu et al., 2012). These results suggest that creative behavior may, at times, involve working without a DLPFC brain net!

You may have noted that, to assess creativity and innovation, researchers have had to engage their own creative neural circuits. Not only do neuroscientists and biological psychologists need to think creatively, but also they need to think out of the lab—or at least outside of the traditional views of the typical biopsychology laboratory. Thus, when it comes to future research, the focus on animals housed individually in less-than-engaging laboratory environments may not provide an adequate *context* to investigate complex cognitive and intellectual functions. In many cases, in an attempt to provide the tightest of laboratory controls for studies, we have systematically removed any form of a natural lifestyle from the animals. This is not a new concern.

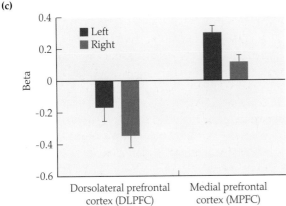

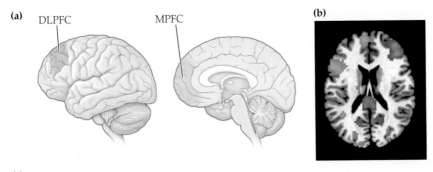

Source: Liu, S., Chow, H. M., Xu, Y., Erkkinen, M. G., Swett, K. E., Eagle, M. W., Rizik-Baer, D. A., & Braun, A.R. (2012). Neural correlates of lyrical improvisation: An fMRI study of freestyle rap. *Scientific Reports*, 2, 834.

FIGURE 14.11 **Freestyle rap–induced brain activity.** Compared with conventional rap, improvised rap was characterized by (a) decreased activity in the right and left dorsolateral prefrontal cortex and increased activity in the medial prefrontal cortex in each hemisphere indicated in (b) functional magnetic resonance imaging scans, with orange representing increased activity and blue representing decreased activity, (c) as well as in average signal changes (improvisational to conventional) across subjects.

The McGill University comparative psychologist Wesley Mills addressed this issue more than a century ago, when he likened the restrictive cages of laboratory animals to placing a "living man in a coffin, lowering him against his will into the earth, and attempting to deduce normal psychology from his conduct" (Mills, 1899, p. 266).

As I close this Epilogue, my hope is that the information you have learned throughout this text will inform your decisions about selecting enriching, engaging, and healthy contexts for your own brain throughout the rest of your life journey. Put another way, *may the healthiest contextual forces be with you!*

Appendix:

Major Research Methods in This Text

This listing includes major research methods and where the text discusses each one.

METHOD	USED IN	CHAPTER	PAGES
Physical damage			
Case studies	Humans	1	21
Gene knockout	Animals	1	26
Lesion studies	Animals	1	25–26
Lobotomy	Humans and animals	13	377
Stereotaxic surgery	Animals	1	25–26
Physical recording			
Electroencephalography (EEG)	Humans	1	21–23
Event-related potentials (ERPs)	Humans	1	21–22
Magnetoencephalography	Humans	1	23
Polysomnography	Humans	9	253
Single-cell recording	Humans and animals	1	22
Physical stimulation			
Brain stimulation from electrode	Animals	1	26
Deep brain stimulation (DBS)	Humans	7	206

(continued)

METHOD	USED IN	CHAPTER	PAGES
Optogenetics	Animals	9	277
Repetitive transcranial magnetic stimulation (rTMS)	Humans	13	391
Transcranial magnetic stimulation (TMS)	Humans	3	82, 84–85
Imaging living brain			
Brainbow	Animals	2	59–60
Computed tomography (CT)	Humans	1	23
Diffusion tensor imaging (DTI)	Humans	1	23
Functional magnetic resonance imaging (fMRI)	Humans	1	23–24
Positron emission tomography (PET)	Humans	1	23
Structural magnetic resonance imaging (MRI)	Humans	1	23
Imaging nonliving brain			
Fos immunoreactivity	Animals	12	369
Histological staining	Animals	2,3	33
Behavioral tests			
Classical conditioning	Animals	12	341–342
Iowa Gambling Task	Humans	3	63–64
Morris water maze	Animals	12	352
Operant conditioning	Animals	12	342–343
Polysomnography	Humans	9	253
Radial arm maze	Animals	12	352–353
Skin conductance response (SCR)	Humans	3	63
Social preference test	Animals	1	26–27
Two-bottle test	Animals	1	26
Other lab techniques			
Behavioral phenotyping	Animals	5	147–148
Cortical mapping	Animals	6	182
Field research	Animals	1	27
Genetic engineering	Animals	1, 5	26, 147–148
Laughing rats and positive emotion research	Animals	10	305
Microdialysis	Animals	8	244–245
Osmotic delivery pump	Humans and animals	11	335–336
Prepulse inhibition	Animals	13	401–402
Vaccination	Humans	4	115–116

Glossary

absolute threshold   The lowest intensity of a stimulus that a person can detect 50% of the time. [6]

accessory olfactory system   A sensory system that detects pheromones consisting of the vomeronasal organ—located in the nasal cavity—and its neuronal projections to the accessory olfactory bulbs, which then project to the hypothalamus and amygdala. [6]

acetylcholine   A natural chemical substance secreted by neurons that is transported across the synapse during synaptic transmission. [3]

acoustic response box   A small box for assessing prepulse inhibition in animals, equipped with a restrainer positioned on a weight-sensitive platform that assesses the latency to jump, or startle, as well as the intensity of the response by monitoring weight fluctuations on the platform. (Also called "startle response box.") [13]

acquired immune system (adaptive immune system)   As distinct from the innate immune system, a component of the immune system that allows immune cells to adapt to unfamiliar threats—viruses, bacteria, and other dangerous substances. [2]

action potential   The nerve impulse, the critical element of neural functioning, triggered in response to information from the environment or another neuron. [3]

action–outcome associations   The probable relationships between specific actions and outcomes and various rewards that are computed by the brain during decision-making challenges. [12]

activation-synthesis model of dreaming   Proposed idea that activity in the dreaming brain is synthesized by key brain areas involved in the maintenance of sleep without the engagement of all the appropriate brain circuits in the frontal cortex, whereby dream plots stray a bit from reality. [9]

activity-mediated spine enlargement   A possible mechanism of synaptic restructuring in which aspects of long-term potentiation change the shape of dendritic spines, specifically the bulbous head at the end of the spine, prompting the emergence of new dendritic spines nearby. [12]

activity-stress   Refers to heightened activity observed in laboratory rats restricted to one-hour feedings per day, yet given unlimited access to activity wheels, resulting in maladaptive health effects. [8]

adaptations   Biological modifications that enhance the chances of survival in different environments. [1]

adaptive inactivity   A theoretical characterization of sleep as an adaptive response to an animal's ecological niche and physiological requirements. [9]

adaptive theory of sleep   The idea that sleep is an adaptive response linking rest–activity cycles to an animal's ecological niche and physiological requirements and that animals have evolved different sleep durations to help them survive. [9]

additive response   An integrated neural response that is proportionately smaller than a superadditive neural response. [6]

adenosine   An inhibitory neurotransmitter; caffeine modulates this system. [4]

adenosine triphosphate (ATP)   Coenzyme essential for the production and transport of cellular energy. [9]

adequate stimulus   The type of physical energy that is required to cause a sensory nerve to respond effectively. [6]

adipsia   An apparent absence of thirst. [8]

adrenalectomy   The surgical removal of the adrenal gland. [10]

adrenocorticotropic hormone   A chemical produced by pituitary gland that travels through the blood to the adrenal gland, where it triggers the release of stress hormones called glucocorticoids. [2]

affective neuroscience   The study of the neurobiology of emotions. [10]

afferent nerves   The sensory nerves that transmit information from the environment or other body areas toward the central nervous system. [2]

affinity   When speaking of neurotransmitters, a tendency for close binding. [4]

aggregation   In the aggregation phase of neuronal development, cells differentiate and form neural *communities* consisting of similar types of neurons. [5]

agonist   A drug that mimics or enhances the effects of specific neurotransmitters. [4]

agouti-related peptide (AgRP)   A neurochemical produced by hypothalamic neurons that works in conjunction with neuropeptide Y neurons to maintain energy regulation by increasing appetite and decreasing energy expenditure. [8]

akinesia   A diminished capacity for voluntary movement. [7]

aldosterone   A hormone, triggered by angiotensin II and released by the adrenal cortex, that stimulates reabsorption of sodium and water to restore appropriate fluid and solute levels to the blood. [8]

alleles   Alternative forms of a given gene. Humans have two alleles at each gene location on the chromosome, one from each parent. [1]

alloparenting   A behavior found in many species in which relatives and even unrelated adults help parents care for their young. [11]

all-or-none law   The principle that as long as the membrane potential reaches the threshold value, an action potential occurs; but if the membrane potential does not reach the threshold value, no action potential is triggered. [3]

allostasis   The body's change in physiological response to varying situational demands. [2]

alpha (α) waves   The fairly regular, consistently shaped, and slightly slow (8–12 Hertz) brain waves that are predominant in awake, but drowsy, brains. [9]

Alzheimer's disease (AD)   A disease characterized by severe memory loss and eventual loss of essential functions such as swallowing; increases dramatically with age. [5]

amacrine cells   Along with horizontal cells, a type of specialized cells that process information in a lateral direction in the retina to facilitate the integration of information processed in the retina. [6]

amine hormones   Hormones derived from the amino acid tyrosine; cannot easily travel across the cell membrane. [11]

amino acid neurotransmitters   A major category of neurotransmitter; among the most abundant in the central nervous system. [4]

amino acids The organic compounds that combine to make proteins. [1]

amnesia Memory loss. [12]

AMPA receptor One type of receptor activated by the neurotransmitter glutamate, called AMPA receptor because of its affinity for α-amino-3-hydroxy-5-methyl-4-isoxazole *propionic acid*. [4]

amphetamine A stimulant drug. [4]

amygdala A limbic structure closely associated with fear. [2]

amyloid plaque protein Deposits of the protein known as β-amyloid found in spaces between neurons. [5]

amyotrophic lateral sclerosis A neuromuscular disease resulting from the degeneration of motor neurons. [7]

analgesics Drugs that relieve pain. [4]

anandamide The first endocannabinoid to be identified. Involved in hippocampal plasticity in close association with the glutamatergic neurotransmitter system. [4]

androgen insensitivity syndrome (AIS) A disorder characterized by insensitivity to androgens during prenatal development, resulting in sexual organization toward the development of a female in individuals genetically male (XY). [11]

androgens Traditionally viewed as male reproductive hormones. [11]

angiogenesis The production of new blood vessels. [7]

angiotensin II A protein that works to increase blood pressure by constricting blood vessels, triggering the release of aldosterone and vasopressin and stimulating drinking, thus restoring appropriate fluid and solute levels. [8]

angular gyrus A formation in the parietal lobe involved in the visual and auditory processing of words. [7]

anhedonia The inability to experience pleasure in activities that were previously rewarding or enjoyable. [4, 8]

animal model The substitution of a specific animal species as an experimental subject in a scientific investigation when the use of a human subject is not appropriate. [1]

anorexia nervosa An eating disorder characterized by a significantly low body weight for one's developmental stage, an exaggerated fear of gaining weight, an unrealistic perception of weight, and persistent behavior that interferes with weight gain. [8]

anorexigenic Appetite suppressing. [8]

antagonistic muscles Muscles that produce actions that are opposite of one another. [7]

antagonists Neurochemicals that block or decrease the effects of specific neurotransmitters. [4]

anterior A specific term of anatomical direction meaning "toward the front or mouth." Also known as *rostral*. [2]

anterior cingulate cortex (ACC) The front portion of the cingulate cortex, activated during a wide range of emotional experiences, including happiness, love, anger, disgust, indignation, empathy, and unfairness. [10]

anterior commissure A thick band of myelinated axons, providing more ventral communication between the left and right cerebral hemispheres. [2]

anterior corticospinal tract The smaller proportion of corticospinal fibers (20%) that do not cross over in the medulla, but decussate at the level of the lower motor neuron and control the muscles of the core or midline of the body, sometimes called the ventral corticospinal tract. [7]

anterior insular cortex The front portion of the insular cortex, activated during a wide range of emotional experiences, including happiness, love, anger, disgust, indignation, empathy, and unfairness. [10]

anterograde amnesia The inability to form long-term memories. [12]

antibodies Chemical tags secreted by B cells to identify pathogens to be destroyed by T cells. [2]

antidiuretic hormone Another name for vasopressin, a neuropeptide that reduces the production of urine. [8]

antigens Any substances leading to the production of antibodies. [2]

antipsychotics Drugs that reduce schizophrenia symptoms, such as delusions, hallucinations, paranoia, and cognitive dysfunction. [13]

anxiogenic Anxiety producing. [10]

anxiolytic Anxiety reducing. [10]

aphasias Specific language disorders. [7]

apoptosis A form of programmed cell death. [5]

aqueous humor The watery substance that occupies the space between the cornea and lens of the eye. [6]

arcuate fasciculus A bundle of fibers connecting Broca's area and Wernicke's area, involved in the processing of language production and speech perception. [7]

arcuate nucleus An area of the hypothalamus with receptors that are activated by insulin. [8]

area postrema An area of the brain with a weak blood–brain barrier, located in the medulla, known as the vomiting center. [3]

Area V2 The visual cortex area that responds to outlines or defining shapes, including illusory contours that do not actually exist. [6]

Area V3 The visual cortex area involved in form analysis and motion, facilitating, for example, the interpretation of a fast-moving visual stimulus. [6]

Area V4 The visual cortex area that facilitates the ability to identify objects, as well as color perception. [6]

Area V5 The visual cortex area, also known as the medial temporal area, which contributes to the perception of motion. [6]

aromatization The process that converts the androgens testosterone and androstenedione to estrogens in the presence of a specific enzyme in the ovaries of females. [11]

ascending reticular activating system (ARAS) A neural network system, involved in sleep–wake cycles, which sends projections from the brainstem and hypothalamus throughout the forebrain. [9]

astrocytes The most abundant type of glial cell. Star-shape cells that fill the spaces between neurons and transport nutrients from blood vessels to the neurons; also regulate the blood flow and chemical environs of the brain. [2]

atonia Suppressed muscle tone. [9]

attentional blink An experimental task in which human participants are asked to focus on two target stimuli that are distinguished by a specific color and appear against a background stream of stimuli presented at a rapid pace. [10]

atypical antipsychotic An antipsychotic drug, such as clozapine, that has diverse physiological effects. [13]

auditory nerve The nerve that carries auditory signals from the cochlea of the ear to the brainstem; a component of the eighth cranial nerve, which controls both hearing and balance. [6]

autism spectrum disorder (ASD) A disorder characterized by disruptions in social interactions and communication, as well as the presence of repetitive behaviors. [3]

automaticity The ability to perform skills using less of the brain, usually as a result of practice. [7]

automatism An involuntary complex response that occurs outside of conscious awareness. [9]

autonomic nervous system The part of the peripheral nervous system that controls involuntary functions, such as heart rate or digestion. [2]

axoaxonic A type of synaptic arrangement such that axon synapses onto axon. [3]

axodendritic A type of synaptic arrangement such that axon synapses onto dendrite. [3]

axon hillock The gate of the axon through which nerve signals enter the neuron. [2]

axon shearing A process of damage that occurs as axons twist and tear. [5]

axons Specialized extensions of the neuron that receive neural messages and propagate them away from the soma to another nerve cell. [2]

axosomatic A type of synaptic arrangement such that axon synapses onto soma. [3]

B cells Cells that originate in bone marrow and, on recognizing a pathogen in the bloodstream, secrete antibodies to tag infected cells for T cells to destroy. [2]

barbering, The plucking of whiskers and fur of cagemates in laboratory rodents. [8]

baroreceptors Specific pressure receptors located in the blood vessels. [8]

basal forebrain area A part of the ascending reticular activating system. A brain area involved in wakefulness. [9]

basal ganglia A subcortical brain structure located in the telencephalon and composed of the caudate, globus pallidus, and putamen that modulates complex information processing critical for the regulation of movement. [2]

basilar membrane The receptive area of the cochlea in the ear containing hair cells and contacting the tectorial membrane. [6]

Bayesian decision theory The idea that applies probabilistic reasoning about uncertain circumstances using past experiences and current likelihoods to make inferences. [7]

bed nucleus of the stria terminalis (BNST) Forebrain structure thought to serve as a key relay for social behavior, anxiety, and aggression-related information from limbic forebrain structures to hypothalamic and brainstem regions associated with autonomic and neuroendocrine functions; receives input from the olfactory bulb. [10]

Behavioral Activation Therapy The treatment for depression that focuses on how the patient interacts with the environment with the objective of identifying behaviors that prevent a patient from achieving his or her goals. [13]

behavioral phenotyping A form of behavioral profiling given to genetically engineered mouse strains to determine whether the new mouse strain is a "match" for the human disorder of interest. [5]

benzodiazepines Sedative drugs similar to barbiturates. [4]

beta (β) waves The most active waves: fast (13–30 Hertz), irregular, low-intensity waves that typically occur in brains that are awake and active. [9]

Betz cells Giant pyramidal cells located in layer V of the primary cortex. [7]

binocular vision Vision dependent on two eyes. [6]

biofeedback techniques Practices that use one's thoughts to control functions that are usually considered involuntary, such as heart rate or blood flow. [2]

biofeedback Training techniques to control physiological responses that are typically viewed as involuntary, such as heart rate or blood pressure. [7]

biological psychology Discipline that combines knowledge from the fields of biology, neuroscience, and psychology to reveal how the brain produces behavior. Also known as *biopsychology*. [1]

biopsychology Discipline that combines knowledge from the fields of biology, neuroscience, and psychology to reveal how the brain produces behavior. Also known as *biological psychology*. [1]

biparental species Monogamous species in which males, in addition to the females, participate in raising the young. [11]

bipolar cells Cells at the back of the eye, which receive signals from the rods and cones and form synapses with ganglion cells. [6]

bipolar disorder A mental disorder characterized by the depressed emotions observed in major depression alternating with elevated moods (manic episodes) and changes in activity and energy. [13]

bipolar neuron A nerve cell with two processes extending from the soma (a dendrite and an axon), generally found in sensory areas of the brain. [2]

blind spot A small section of the retina that possesses no photoreceptors. [6]

blind studies Clinical studies in which patients do not know whether they are being administered the actual medication under trial or an inactive placebo. [4]

blood–brain barrier The brain's primary security system. Acts as a filter and protects the brain from potentially harmful substances. [2]

bottom-up visual processing The processing of specific visual information in increasing levels of complexity (e.g., the firing of ganglion cells). [6]

brain circuits Neural networks linking multiple brain areas in critical ways so that they are concurrently involved in certain functions. [1]

brain death Irreversible loss of basic functions such as respiration that are necessary for survival; considered as a criterion for death

brain stimulation techniques A method of research whereby a permanent electrode is surgically implanted to stimulate a specific brain area and observe the effects of increased activation on behavior. [1]

brain-derived neurotrophic factor (BDNF) Neurochemicals that alter the programmed genetic development of neurons and promote the maturation of neurons and synapse formation throughout the brain; implicated in complex behaviors such as learning and in disorders such as depression. [5]

brainstem The base of the brain connecting with the spinal cord. Formed by the medulla oblongata (or myelencephalon), the pons, and the midbrain. [2]

bregma The connection point between parts of the skull at the top of the head. [1]

brightness The perceived intensity of a light stimulus. [6]

Bruce effect A classic example of pheromonal processing, in which pregnancy is blocked when a female mouse is exposed to the scent of an unfamiliar male's urine. [6]

Buerger's disease A condition characterized by inflammation and blockage of blood vessels in the hands and feet that is triggered by smoking cigarettes. [4]

bulimia nervosa An eating disorder characterized by the behaviors of binging (excessive overeating) and purging (removing food from one's system via strategies such as self-induced vomiting or use of laxatives). [8]

caffeine A stimulant found naturally in the leaves, seeds, and fruit of several plants, such as tea and coffee; the earth's most widely used psychoactive drug. [4]

cannabinoid receptors   Receptors activated by δ-9-tetra-hydrocannabinol; concentrated in the basal ganglia, substantia nigra, cerebellum, hippocampus, and cerebral cortex. [4]

cannabis   Marijuana. [4]

Cannon–Bard theory of emotion   The idea proposing that the hypothalamus was a key brain region generating the expression of emotional experiences and that higher cortical areas inhibited these evolutionarily ancient emotional responses. [10]

cardiac muscle   Heart muscle. [7]

case studies   Investigations of individual examples, such as of a patient with a brain injury. [1]

catabolites   Substances produced by the metabolic breakdown of more complex molecules. [13]

cataplexy   Muscular weakness or paralysis. [9]

catecholamines   A class of monoamine neurotransmitter that includes the neurotransmitters dopamine, norepinephrine, and epinephrine. [4]

caudal   A specific term of anatomical direction meaning "toward the tail." Also known as *posterior*. [2]

caudate   A component of the basal ganglia (along with the globus pallidus and the putamen) located in the telencephalon and critical for the regulation of movement. [2]

caudate nucleus   A primary component of the basal ganglia; communicates regularly with the cerebral cortex to contribute to the efficient execution of appropriate movements. [7]

cell-adhesion molecules (CAMs)   Membrane proteins located on the cell's surface that react differentially to other cell surfaces and, by being attracted to certain proteins located on specific types of cells, provide one manner of neuron migration. [5]

central amygdala   The portion of the amygdala that stimulates relevant brain areas to initiate the freezing response, blood pressure modifications, stress hormone release, and startle reflex in a fearful situation after receiving emotionally stimulating visual information from the lateral amygdala. [10]

central nervous system (CNS)   The part of the nervous system that consists of the brain and spinal cord. [2]

central pattern generators   Networks of neurons that spontaneously generate patterns of activity such as walking. [7]

cerebellar cognitive affective syndrome   A clinical disorder characterized by the emergence of cognitive deficits following cerebellar damage. [7]

cerebellar peduncles   Neural communication transit system at the foot of the cerebellum; connects to other brain areas such as the cerebral cortex. [7]

cerebellum   Literally, "little brain." A large neural structure that dangles off the dorsal section of the brainstem. It regulates balance and motor coordination and contains up to 80% of all the brain's neurons. [2]

cerebral cortex   The brain's outer layer of neurons. [2]

cerebral hemispheres   The two sides of the brain, left and right, above the brainstem. [2]

cerebrospinal fluid (CSF)   A clear fluid that fills the ventricles of the central nervous system, providing an appropriate environment for the brain's cells. [2]

chandelier cell   A smaller cell positioned adjacent to the pyramidal cells in layer 3 of the dorsolateral prefrontal cortex. In individuals with schizophrenia, the proteins in the synapses of chandelier cells are greatly reduced in number, leading to dysfunctional synapses. [13]

chlorpromazine   A purple dye initially synthesized from coal tar in the 19th century that was accidentally found to be effective in treating symptoms of psychotic patients in the 1950s. [13]

choroid plexus   The dense collection of small blood vessels located in the ventricles that produces cerebrospinal fluid. [2]

chromosomes   Threadlike structures in the nucleus of every living cell containing the DNA instructions passed from parents to offspring. [1]

chronic traumatic encephalopathy (CTE)   A condition due to head injuries from boxing, originally referred to as *dementia pugilistica* or *punch-drunk syndrome*, that appears to result in progressive neurological deterioration. [5]

cilia   The tiny hair growths, contained in the hair cells of the basilar membrane of the ear, which move against the tectorial membrane, translating sound wave characteristics to neural energy. [6]

cingulate cortex   Cortex surrounding the cingulate gyrus immediately above the corpus callosum. Plays a pivotal role in directing information upward and downward to ultimately result in relevant emotional thoughts and feelings. [10]

cingulum   Neural pathway projecting from the cingulate cortex to the hippocampus. [10]

circadian rhythms   Responses, such as the timing of sleep and wake cycles, with distinct daily rhythms. [9]

clinical efficacy   Medical effectiveness. [5]

clomipramine (Anafranil)   A tricyclic antidepressant pharmaceutical drug, used to treat obsessive–compulsive disorder before selective serotonin reuptake inhibitors gained favor in the treatment for anxiety disorders. [13]

cocaine   A stimulant that combats the effects of hunger and fatigue; the active ingredient of the coca plant. [4]

cochlea   Greek for *land snail*. The fluid-filled portion of the ear that receives vibrations from the ossicles of the middle ear. [6]

cochlear implant   A small electronic device that can restore some aspects of sound perception. [6]

cognitive neuroscience   The exploration of brain functions that accompany various cognitive functions such as perception, memory, and language. [1]

cognitive reappraisal   Changing one's understanding of an event in a way that also changes one's emotional response to the event. [10]

cognitive remediation treatment   A nonpharmacological approach to treating schizophrenia, aimed at restoring cognitive and brain functioning through various types of cognitive exercises. [13]

color constancy   The ability to continue to perceive that an object is a specific color even under varying perceptual conditions. [6]

coma   A pronounced disruption of consciousness such that a person shows neither signs of wakefulness nor awareness. [9]

compensatory therapy   A nonpharmacological approach to treating schizophrenia that instructs patients on effective tools and strategies to help them compensate for their cognitive impairments. [13]

complex cells   V1 cortical cells that respond to bar-shape stimuli but are less selective about the location of the bar in the visual field than V1 simple cells. [6]

computed tomography (CT)   A scanning technique using X-rays and computer technology to generate cross-sectional views of neuroanatomy. [1]

concentration gradient   The varying distribution of ions inside and outside of the axon. [3]

concentric receptive field   Characteristic of cells in the retina and lateral geniculate nucleus that respond to detailed visual information only in very specific areas of their representative visual fields. [6]

concordance rate   Compares the likelihood of two individuals developing the same disorder; important in evaluating the genetic contributions of various illnesses. [13]

concussions Brain injuries with symptoms ranging from loss of consciousness to a sustained headache to memory loss. [5]

conditioned cues Exposure to environmental circumstances that are strongly associated with drug use. [4]

conditioned defeat A behavior in which a previously defeated animal continues to exhibit submissive displays. [10]

conditioned place-preference test A laboratory task to assess the motivation to consume a drug and its relationship to positive and stimulating environmental conditions. [4]

cones Visual photoreceptors clustering in the center of the retina that enable the detection of color and visual detail. The human retina contains approximately 5 million cones. [6]

confabulation The rewriting of memories by inventing stories to fill in gaps, typically including bits of true information with fabricated segments, to seem fully believable as honest recollection. [12]

confounding variables Variables other than the independent variable of interest that may affect dependent variables under study. [1]

congenital adrenal hyperplasia (CAH) A genetic condition, especially affecting females, resulting in exposure to higher-than-normal levels of androgens during gestation because of disrupted cortisol production; marked by ambiguous-looking genitalia. [11]

connexons In electrical synapses, the specific channels that align to form a gap junction between two neurons. [3]

consciousness Our awareness of our internal and external worlds. [9]

conservative process In evolutionary theory, the idea suggested by the prevalence of similarities between species, that certain principles are *conserved* during evolution. [5]

conspecific Of the same species. [6]

constraint-induced movement therapy A behavioral therapy that restricts the use of a functional limb to encourage the use of an impaired limb, forcing new neural circuits to be formed that regulate the performance of the impaired limb. [5]

context frames Prepackaged visual perceptual templates that we are likely to encounter based on past experience. [6]

context The specific setting in which an event occurs, including the circumstances surrounding an event and the unique interactions that exist among behavior, the brain, and one's external and internal environment. It includes both *environmental context*, in the form of external or internal conditions, and *experiential context*, representing past or future personal events. [1]

contingency The probability that a specific outcome will follow a specific response. [12]

continuous positive airway pressure (CPAP) machine A medical device consisting of a breathing mask over the nose, connected to an air pump, that delivers air pressure; it holds a sufferer of sleep apnea's airway open during slumber. [9]

contrast enhancement The perceived contrast emphasized by lateral inhibition in retinal cells. [6]

controlled-instrumental aggression Purposeful aggression, regulated by higher cortical systems; one of the two main types of aggression. [10]

coping styles The varying and divergent individual strategies for coping with stress. [10]

copulation Sexual intercourse. [11]

cornea The transparent surface that covers the pupil and iris of the eye. Along with the lens, it helps focus images projected to the back of the eye. [6]

corona radiata A projection of nerve fibers that connect the cerebral cortex to the brainstem and spinal cord. [7]

corpus callosum The thick band of myelinated axons that connects the dorsal sections of the left and right cerebral hemispheres. [2]

cortical association areas Portions of the cortex that process or integrate more than one sense, allowing more complex cognition and adaptive response. [6]

cortical–hippocampal system A memory network underlying declarative memory, composed of the hippocampus, the parahippocampal region, and the more recently evolved neocortex. [12]

corticospinal tracts The bundles of axons that descend from the cerebral motor cortex and connect to the spinal cord, including two separate tracts—the lateral corticospinal tract and the anterior corticospinal tract—and essential for voluntary control over the skeletal muscles. [7]

corticotropin-releasing hormone A chemical produced by the hypothalamus and sent to the pituitary gland, prompting the release of adrenocorticotropic hormone as part of the sympathetic nervous response to a stressor in the environment. [2]

crack A street drug created by mixing cocaine hydrochloride with baking soda to make a more efficient form for smoking. [4]

cranial nerves The 12 nerves that exit various areas of the brain and extend to target destinations in the head, face, and shoulder region. They have primarily motor, sensory, or mixed (motor and sensory) functions. [2]

cross-fostering A technique whereby offspring are removed from their biological parents and raised by nonbiological "foster" parents. [8]

cross-modal stimuli Stimuli from two senses. [6]

cross-modality Integration between senses. [6]

cross-sensitization A sensitivity to one substance inducing a sensitivity to a different substance. [8]

cytoskeleton The cellular infrastructure made up of the fibers contained within the cell's cytoplasm. [5]

Dalila effect Another name for hair and whisker plucking seen in laboratory rodents, derived from the biblical story of Samson and Dalila. [8]

declarative memories Information that can be consciously recalled for further processing or use. [9]

declarative memory The conscious retrieval of events and facts; sometimes called "explicit memory." [12]

decussation Crossing over. [7]

deep brain stimulation A type of surgery involving the placement of electrodes into various areas of the brain to reduce Parkinson's symptoms. [7]

dehydroepiandrosterone (DHEA) A hormone released from the adrenal cortex in parallel with glucocorticoids, providing a buffer against the effects of stress hormones; related to increased neurogenesis, which may protect against the onset of stress-related mental illnesses and to reduced anxiety and enhanced emotional resilience. [10]

delayed matching-to-sample task A laboratory method for assessing memory formation, initially designed for monkeys, in which a single stimulus is presented ("sample phase") followed by a timed delay, after which two stimuli—one similar to the sample stimulus and one different—are presented ("choice phase"). The monkey must choose the stimulus that matches the sample stimulus to be rewarded. [12]

delayed nonmatching-to-sample task A laboratory method for assessing memory formation, initially designed for monkeys, in which a single stimulus is presented ("sample phase") followed by a timed delay, after which two stimuli—one similar to the sample stimulus and one different—are presented ("choice phase"). The monkey must choose the unfamiliar stimulus to be rewarded. [12]

delta (δ) waves   Low-frequency sleep waves (0.5–3 Hertz), characteristic of slow wave sleep. [9]

denaturing   Weakening the internal bonds of food proteins (e.g., by cooking or pickling) to increase digestibility. [8]

dendrites   The branching portions of the neuron that typically extend from multiple points on the soma. Named after the Greek word for "tree" because of their similarity to a tree's branches. [2]

dendritic spines   Small protrusions located throughout the dendritic processes, or branches, that greatly increase the surface area of a nerve cell. [2]

dentate nucleus   Structure within the lateral cerebellar hemispheres of the cerebellum that communicates in a structured, maplike fashion with the various motor and nonmotor areas of the cerebral cortex. [7]

deoxyribonucleic acid (DNA)   The unit of inheritance. The double-strand molecular component of chromosomes that carries an organism's genetic information. [1]

dependent variable   The variable that is affected and measured in an experiment in response to manipulations of the *independent variable*, on which it is said to "depend." [1]

depolarization   An alteration of a neuron's membrane potential by making its inside less negative. [3]

depressants   Drugs that suppress arousal. [4]

dermatome   A distinct area of skin served by a single spinal nerve. [2]

difference threshold   The minimum amount that a stimulus must change for a subject to detect a difference. Also known as *just noticeable difference*. [6]

diffusion tensor imaging (DTI)   Technique that uses the movement of water in the brain to detect characteristics in the fibers composing the white matter, or the communication pathways, in the brain. [1]

direction cells   Cells (similar to place cells) that fire in the subiculum, near the hippocampus, when a rat points its head in a specific direction. [12]

dissociative identity disorder   A mental disorder thought to be caused by early childhood trauma and characterized by confused and disconnected thoughts about one's identity (formerly called "multiple personality disorder"). [13]

distal   A specific term of anatomical direction meaning "farther" from the central nervous system. [2]

DNA methylation   A technique in which genes can be modified by the addition of a methyl chemical compound to the cytosine nucleotide base in DNA. The presence of a methyl group at a gene promoter usually prevents the expression of the gene in question. [5]

docosahexaenoic acid (DHA)   The ω-3 fatty acid that most commonly appears in the cell membranes of neurons. [8]

dominance hierarchies   Adaptive social ranking systems acknowledged by animals that enable them to avoid aggressive encounters over limited resources. [10]

dominant   In genetics, when a dominant gene is paired with a recessive gene, the characteristics of the dominant gene are expressed. [1]

dopamine   A monoamine neurotransmitter produced in the substantia nigra and ventral tegmental area that is involved in movement, reward systems, and increased vigilance. [4]

dopamine theory of schizophrenia   The idea that schizophrenia is caused by excessive activity of the brain's dopamine system, as suggested by the demonstration that the dopaminergic system is the primary target of the neuroleptic drugs. [13]

dopaminergic nigrostriatal bundle   The collective name of fibers connecting the substantia nigra and the striatum, involved in motor and sensory systems. [8]

dorsal   A specific term of anatomical direction meaning "toward the top or back." [2]

dorsal column–medial lemniscus pathway   The route of axons carrying information about tactile discrimination to the relay nucleus of the thalamus specialized for somatosensation. [6]

dorsal stream   Visual pathway extending from V1 that contributes information about the location of particular objects. [6]

dorsolateral prefrontal cortex (DLPFC)   A brain area involved in the computations associated with the decision-making process. [12]

dose–response curves   Measurements of outcome to determine the lowest amount of drug necessary to produce optimal responses. [4]

double-blind studies   Clinical studies in which neither the patients nor the researchers know whether the patients are being administered the actual medication under study or an inactive placebo. [4]

drug addiction cycle   Clinically characterized as including a compulsion to seek and consume a drug, an inability to control the intake of a drug, and the onset of a negative emotional state when access to the drug is prevented. [4]

drug dependence   An individual's need for a drug to maintain physiological functions. [4]

dura mater   Just below the skull, the tough outer layer of the meninges, which encase and protect the brain and spinal cord. [2]

dyslexia   A disorder characterized by difficulty reading. [7]

echolocation   An auditory adaptation whereby the generation of sounds and analysis of echoes is used to navigate instantaneously. [6]

efferent nerves   Motor nerves; the nerves that are activated to cause movement. [2]

efficacy   Ability to produce desired effects for a targeted condition. [4]

effort-based reward theory   The idea emphasizing the importance of a relationship between effort and expected rewards in maintaining mental health. The theory further suggests that increased rates of depression may be related to decreased physical activity. [13]

ejaculation   The final stage of copulation; the discharge of semen by the male. [11]

electrical gradient   The distribution of oppositely charged particles, which tend to attract in nature. [3]

electroconvulsive therapy (ECT)   A treatment for depression popular in the 1930s, using electrodes placed only on the head to induce seizures that, in ways not entirely understood, alleviate or diminish depressive symptoms. Still used today for treatment-resistant and severely depressed patients. [13]

electroencephalograms (EEGs)   Tests that track and record the electrical activity of the brain using electrodes attached to the scalp. A primary tool for investigating the biological basis of sleep. [9]

electroencephalography (EEG)   A technique using electrodes at regularly spaced intervals on the scalp to measure brain activity by detecting the electrical activity of large populations of a brain's cells. [1]

electromagnetic spectrum   All possible wavelengths of electromagnetic radiation (of which light is only a narrow band). [6]

electromyogram (EMG)   A physiological record that assesses muscle tension. [9]

electrooculogram (EOG)   A physiological record that assesses eye movements. [9]

emotional regulation   The intentional modification and control of emotional behavior, especially when intense emotional response is inappropriate. [10]

emotions   Subjective feelings that are influenced by activation of various parts of our central and peripheral nervous systems. [10]

empirical evidence   Information gathered through observation or experimentation that provides support for a scientific claim. [1]

Encephalization Quotient (EQ) An index determined by comparing the actual brain mass of an animal with the expected brain mass for an animal of that particular body mass based on measurements of representative mammals. [5]

endocannabinoids Substances produced by the body itself that mimic the physiological effects of the cannabis (marijuana) plant. [4]

endocrine glands Organs found in the brain and elsewhere in the body that release hormones. [11]

endogenous Produced within the organism itself. [4]

endorphins A type of opioid peptide that interacts with the dopamine system by diminishing GABA's inhibitory effects, leading to increased secretion of dopamine. [4]

enkephalin Literally, "in the brain"; a natural peptide that inhibits pain. [4]

enriched environment A setting containing stimulating objects, the interaction with which appears to increase physical and social interaction and physiological growth. [1]

entorhinal cortex A section of the medial temporal lobe involved with memory and navigation. [6]

environmental context The internal or external conditions of a subject of observation or an experimental subject. [1]

enzymatic deactivation A process whereby a neurotransmitter terminates its activation of a postsynaptic receptor, in this case by being broken down by enzymes. (Also see *reuptake*.) [4]

enzyme A protein that facilitates a chemical reaction but is not changed by it. [1]

epigenetics Changes in phenotypic expression caused, not by changes in DNA sequence, but by variations in the life experience or the environment of an organism. [1]

epinephrine A member of the catecholamine class of monoamine neurotransmitters, released from the adrenal gland atop the kidney, and involved in increased vigilance, focused attention, and enhanced energy. [4]

episodic memory A form of autobiographical memory.

estrogens Traditionally viewed as female reproductive hormones. [11]

estrous cycle Reproductive cycle during which female animals are sexually receptive and solicit a sexual response. Characterized by varying levels of reproductive hormones across four stages: proestrus, estrus, metestrus, and diestrus. [11]

eudaimonia The Greek word meaning *a life well lived*. According to Aristotle, one of the two fundamental aspects of happiness. [8]

event-related potentials (ERPs) The small voltages resulting while recording the brain's electroencephalography response to a specific task, stimulus, or event. [1]

evidence-based therapies Methods of diagnosing and treating mental disorders based on research findings that are of objectively proven effectiveness. [13]

excitatory postsynaptic potential (EPSP) The change produced in a postsynaptic membrane when a neurotransmitter–receptor binding depolarizes membrane potential (with an influx of sodium ions into the membrane). [3]

exocytosis The release of neurotransmitters out of the synaptic vesicles and into the synaptic cleft. [3]

experiential context The past experiences, assumptions, motives, and feelings of a subject of observation. [1]

explicit memory The conscious retrieval of events and facts; usually called "declarative memory." [12]

exposure therapy A type of behavioral therapy for the treatment of specific phobia in which patients are progressively confronted with a fear-inducing object. [13]

expressive flexibility The ability to both enhance and suppress emotions, matching emotional expression to situational demands. [10]

extracellular Outside of cells. [8]

extracellular space The space outside the cell. [3]

extrafusal fibers Muscle cells that contract to shorten a muscle. [7]

extraocular muscles The muscles around the eye that hold the eye in the optic socket. [6]

extrastriate cortex The visual cortex located outside of the primary visual cortex. [6]

eye-blink reflex conditioning A classical conditioning model, used in rabbits, in which a tone is used as a conditioned stimulus and paired with a puff of air (an unconditioned stimulus) delivered to the eye to investigate procedural memory. [12]

facial microexpressions Barely perceptible brief facial expression fragments. [10]

field research Observations conducted in a subject's natural habitat, whereby limitations of a laboratory environment can be avoided. [1]

fight-or-flight response A term that refers to the function of the sympathetic nervous system in preparing the body for strenuous physical responses to threats. [2]

filopodia Dendritic sprouts, appearing around day 16 of a neuron's life, that seek out existing synaptic terminals on other neurons to incorporate an existing circuit into the neuron's infrastructure. [12]

first-generation antipsychotics Early pharmaceutical treatments, characterized by mixed success, including complete remission, some reduction of symptoms, and debilitating side effects. [13]

5-α reductase deficiency A genetic condition inhibiting the production of an enzyme (5-α reductase) necessary for the development of male external genitalia during gestation, resulting in genetic males with female external genitalia. [11]

flavor A perception based on the convergence of cues from several senses including vision, smell, taste, and touch. [6]

flocculonodular lobe The oldest part of the cerebellum, thought to support fundamental motor functions such as the maintenance of balance and posture. [7]

FM-FM neurons Specialized nerve cells that allow bats to echolocate by processing the time delay between the emitted sonar signal and the perception of the returning signal. [6]

fornix Neural pathway from the hippocampus to the mammillary bodies of the hypothalamus and on to the anterior thalamus (the latter more properly known as the *mammillothalamic tract*). [10]

Fos A protein used to identify recent neuronal activation in a particular brain area. [8]

fovea The center of the retina; the most densely populated area of cones, and the part of the retina where our vision is sharpest. [6]

free nerve endings Touch receptors in the skin that respond to tissue damage and temperature changes, experienced as pain. [6]

free-running rhythms Internal mechanisms that regulate daily rest and activity cycles. [9]

frequency modulation (FM) Frequency of a sound wave. [6]

frontal lobe One of the four large areas of the cerebral cortex, involved in interpreting sensory information. [2]

frontostriatal A brain area implicated in the self-regulation necessary to perform a spatial task; connects the frontal cortex to the striatum. [8]

functional MRI (fMRI) The scanning technique that measures brain activity by detecting changes in blood flow and oxygenation in different areas. [1]

fusiform face area An area of the cortex associated with the perception of individual faces. [6]

galanin An inhibitory neurotransmitter that is widely expressed throughout the brain, playing a role in sleep–wake cycles, eating, learning, mood regulation, and protection of neurons from damage. [9]

gamma (γ)-aminobutyric acid (GABA) The principal inhibitory neurotransmitter in the brain; derived from glutamate. [4]

ganglia Clusters of neurons; singular *ganglion*. [2]

ganglion cells Cells that receive signals from the bipolar cells of the eye and bundle to comprise the optic nerve that exits at the back of the eyeball. [6]

gap junction In electrical synapses, the place where connexons between two neurons align, across which electrical currents can be exchanged bidirectionally. [3]

gated ion channels Ion channels that open and close based on the environmental conditions around the membrane. [3]

gene knockout A genetic engineering research approach in which a specific targeted gene is rendered inoperative to determine the impact on the test animal's function. [1]

gene–environment interactions The response of genotypes to environmental variation. [1]

generalized adaptation syndrome A collection of symptoms, including larger adrenal glands, shrunken thymus glands (involved in immune functions), and gastric stress ulcers, consistently associated with chronic stress. [10]

generalized anxiety disorder A pathological form of anxiety characterized by unrealistic, excessive, and long-lasting worry, motor tension, restlessness, irritability, difficulty sleeping, and hypervigilance. [13]

genes The basic biological units of heredity. Genes contain the inherited information for the particular parts of a cell that control or influence the growth, appearance, and other physical characteristics of living things. [1]

genetics The study of heredity, or how the characteristics of living things are transmitted from one generation to the next. [1]

genome The complete set of genes for a given species. [1]

genotype An individual's collection of genes; also, the two alleles inherited for a particular gene. The genotype is expressed when the gene's DNA is used to make protein and RNA molecules. [1]

ghrelin A chemical secreted by endocrine cells in the stomach. Ghrelin is a satiety signal secreted outside of the central nervous system that is subsequently detected in the brain to regulate hunger and food consumption. [8]

glia A class of nerve cell distinct from neurons, once thought to merely support neurons, but more recently believed to also have other critical ongoing functions. [2]

globus pallidus A primary component of the basal ganglia located in the telencephalon and critical for the regulation of movement; output typically inhibits unwanted movements. [2, 7]

glomeruli After the Latin *glomus*, meaning "ball." Axonal and dendritic processes contained in the olfactory bulbs. [6]

glucagons Protein hormones released by the pancreas; increase blood sugar levels. [11]

glucocorticoid receptor (GR) The less sensitive of the two glucocorticoid receptor systems that mediate stress response, activated during more prevalent increases in glucocorticoid secretion accompanying both stress and circadian changes that occur predictably each day. (Also see *mineralocorticoid receptor*.) [13]

glucocorticoids Stress hormones released from the adrenal cortex of the adrenal gland. [2]

glucose A simple sugar, considered a fuel for the brain. [1]

glutamate A type of amino acid neurotransmitter for excitatory signaling pathways in the brain, especially notable for its role in synaptogenesis facilitating learning and memory. [4]

glycine A prevalent major inhibitory neurotransmitter in the brainstem and spinal cord that plays an important role in the control of many sensory and motor pathways. [4]

Golgi tendon organ A sensory organ located in the tendon that sends a message back to the nervous system to initiate compensatory action if a muscle contracts excessively. [7]

gonads The reproductive organs. [11]

G-protein A protein, coupled with the energy-storing molecule guanosine triphosphate, that is activated when a ligand binds to a metabotropic receptor, in turn activating second messengers within the postsynaptic neuron. [3]

granule cells Cells in the cerebellar cortex that receive signals from the pontine nuclei within the cerebellum. [12]

gray matter Neuronal cell bodies in the brain. [2]

grid cells Cells, likely in the entorhinal cortex surrounding the hippocampus, that fire as a rat crosses compartments of an imagined coordinate system grid over a spatial area, allowing the rat to determine cumulative distance traveled. [12]

grooming Biologically programmed movement sequences serving to maintain the skin and fur by removing parasites, transmitting important odors, facilitating wound healing, and maintaining thermoregulation; also help to reduce anxiety. [8]

gyri The bulges of the cerebral cortex; singular, *gyrus*. [2]

habituate Adapt, or get used to. [12]

hair cells The cells in the basilar membrane of the ear containing tiny hair growths that form synapses with the auditory nerve stretching into the cochlea. [6]

hallucinogenic drugs Psychoactive chemical substances that alter perception, such as lysergic acid diethylamide, psilocybin mushrooms, and peyote.

Hebbian synapse theory of learning The basic idea, proposed by Donald Hebb, that nerve cell circuits are established, strengthened, and modified by the learning and memory formation that accompany changes in behavior. [12]

hedonia The Greek word for *pleasure*. According to Aristotle, one of the two fundamental aspects of happiness. [8]

heredity The biological transmission of physical and mental characteristics from parents to offspring. [1]

hermaphrodites Technically, individuals who possess both male and female gonads, but often also used to refer to those with ambiguous external genitalia. [11]

heroin A manufactured form of morphine, highly potent when injected. [4]

heterozygous Having one of each of two different alleles. [1]

hibernation A form of prolonged sleep on a seasonal rhythm found in some animals. It enhances survival by allowing withdrawal from harsh environmental conditions. [9]

highly superior autobiographical memory (HSAM) A type of memory characterized by an infallible recall for autobiographical events and dates; usually associated with obsessive–compulsive tendencies and otherwise normal memory. [12]

hippocampus A limbic structure activated by stress hormones involved in learning and memory. [2]

histological technique Method to study the microscopic structure and cellular organization of body tissues. [2]

histones Proteins located in cellular nuclei that act as spools around which DNA coils. [5]

homeostasis The body's tendency to preserve a constant internal environment. [2]

homeostatic theory of sleep regulation The widely held theory that the function of sleep is to provide rest and recovery. [9]

homologous Having the same relative position. [7]

homozygous When an individual has two of the same allele, whether dominant or recessive. [1]

horizontal cells Along with amacrine cells, specialized cells that process information in a lateral direction in the retina to facilitate the integration of information processed in the retina. [6]

hormones Chemicals released by special endocrine glands into the bloodstream, where they regulate the activity of certain cells or organs, affecting body function and growth. [2, 11]

hue The perceived color, or wavelength, of a light stimulus. [6]

Human Genome Project A large-scale research project completed in 2000 to decode and sequence the nearly 3 billion nucleotide base pairs of human DNA. [1]

hypercomplex cells V1 cortical cells that respond to bars of a particular length by detecting endpoints as well as aspects of position and orientation. [6]

hyperphagia Overeating. [8]

hyperpolarization An alteration of a neuron's membrane potential by making its inside more negative. [3]

hypertonic solution A solution that has a higher concentration of solutes outside the cell than exists inside the cell. [8]

hypnogogic hallucinations Auditory and visual hallucinations, sometimes accompanied by paralysis, while falling asleep. [9]

hypocretin A neuropeptide (also called *orexin*) affecting sleep–wake cycles, as well as emotions, energy expenditure, and reward systems. [9]

hypocretin/orexin system A neuropeptide involved in sleep–wake cycles. Complex integrations of the hypocretin/orexin-producing neurons also affect emotions, energy expenditure, and reward systems. [9]

hypothalamic hormones Peptide hormones that travel to the anterior pituitary from the hypothalamus (for example, corticotropin-releasing hormone). Also called releasing hormones. [11]

hypothalamic–pituitary–adrenal axis The body's system of stress-induced response that modulates cardiovascular function, brain activity, and other physiological systems. [2]

hypothalamus A brain structure below the thalamus, prominent in motivational systems. [2]

hypotheses Testable scientific predictions; singular *hypothesis*. [1]

hypotonic solution A solution that has a lower concentration of solutes outside the cell than exists inside the cell. [8]

hypovolemia Low blood volume. [8]

immune system A means of bodily protection that surveys the body and brain for evidence of invasions of pathogens (disease-causing agents). [2]

immunoenhancement Increase in immune response or effectiveness. [10]

immunoglobulin A Important antibody found in mucous secretions from the tear glands, salivary glands, mammary glands, the respiratory system, the genitourinary tract, and the gastrointestinal tract. [10]

immunosuppression Reduction in immune response or effectiveness. [10]

implicit memory The motor memory that consists in fine-tuning the brain's circuitry to enable skilled performances; also called "procedural memory." [12]

inattentional blindness A cognitive illusion whereby a selectively focused attention to one detail results in the failure to notice other details. [12]

independent variable The variable that stands on its own and can be chosen, changed, controlled, and manipulated during an experiment. Usually the variable that is thought to affect the *dependent variable*. [1]

indolamines A class of monoamine neurotransmitter; includes the neurotransmitter serotonin. [4]

inferior colliculi A set of nuclei in the tectum of the midbrain important for processing and localizing auditory information. [2]

inferior colliculus A midbrain structure that receives auditory signals from the cochlear nucleus and superior olivary nucleus, and sends them to the medial geniculate nucleus. [6]

inhibitory postsynaptic potential (IPSP) The change produced in a postsynaptic membrane when a neurotransmitter–receptor binding makes the membrane channels more permeable to negative ions, which makes the membrane potential hyperpolarized. [3]

innate immune system The barrier system of the body that dispatches cells to engulf and digest pathogens that have breached the skin or digestive tract. [2]

insomnia One of the most common medical complaints, a disorder characterized by difficulties initiating sleep, maintaining sleep, or both, and sleepiness during the waking hours. [9]

insula A portion of the cerebral cortex that reports on the state of the body to other brain regions by integrating input both from within the body and from the external environment. Also known as *insular cortex*. [2]

insular cortex A portion of the cerebral cortex that reports on the state of the body to other brain regions by integrating input both from within the body and from the external environment. Also known as *insula*. [2]

insulin resistance A condition whereby a diet high in fat and sugar decreases insulin's effectiveness at lowering blood glucose levels, resulting in increased food consumption and fat storage. [8]

insulin A hormone produced by the pancreas that regulates blood sugar levels; important for metabolism and energy utilization throughout the body. [8]

interleukin 1 An immune chemical found in sleep–wake regulatory centers, including the brainstem, hippocampus, and hypothalamus. Also called *cytokines IL-1*. [9]

interneuron Neurons that transmit impulses between other neurons. [2]

interpositus nucleus A deep nucleus in the cerebellum that experiences lengthening of the synapse surface following conditioning. [12]

intersex Any variation from typical XX or XY development (genetically female or male). [11]

intracellular space The space inside the cell. [3]

intracellular Inside of cells. [8]

intrafusal fibers Muscle cells that detect changes in muscle length. [7]

ion channels Pores composed of proteins in the neuronal cell membrane. [3]

ion pumps Elements of the cell membrane that play an essential role in the distribution of ions inside and outside the neuron. [3]

ionic flux A condition in nerve cells caused by a decrease in cerebral blood flow that interrupts the delivery of glucose and oxygen, and that is characterized by altered concentrations of ions (such as decreased levels of magnesium and potassium and increased levels of calcium). [5]

ionotropic receptors   Postsynaptic receptors that alter the membrane potential immediately on binding to neurotransmitters. [3]

ions   Charged molecules. [3]

iris   The diaphragm that controls the size of the pupil of the eye. [6]

ischemia   The disruption of blood flow, often following an accident or a stroke. [5]

isotonic solution   A solution that has equal concentrations of solutes (dissolved substances) inside and outside a cell. [8]

James–Lange theory of emotion   The idea that different bodily reactions that occur in response to different stimuli lead to the experience of emotions. [10]

jet lag   Sleep problems resulting from a desynchronization of biological rhythms. [9]

just noticeable difference (JND)   The minimum amount that a stimulus must change for a subject to detect a difference. Also known as *difference threshold*. [6]

k-complexes   Large waves with a slow rise to a peak followed by a faster decline, characteristic of Stage 2 sleep electroencephalograms. [9]

Klüver–Bucy syndrome   A condition, observed in monkeys and humans with lesioned temporal lobes, characterized by increased exploratory behavior and a dampening of emotional responses like fear and aggression. [10]

koniocellular layer   One of three types of cellular layers in the lateral geniculate nucleus of the thalamus, the koniocellular layer is associated with color perception. [6]

Korsakoff's syndrome   Memory disorder suffered by chronic alcoholics, characterized by an atypical loss of short-term memories and damage to the dorsomedial thalamic nucleus. [12]

lateral   A specific term of anatomical direction meaning "toward the side." [2]

lateral amygdala   In a fearful situation, this portion of the amygdalatransfers emotionally stimulating information from the thalamus to the central amygdala, which ultimately stimulates relevant brain areas that initiate the freezing response, blood pressure modifications, stress hormone release, and startle reflex. [10]

lateral cerebellar hemispheres   The largest portions of the cerebellum, containing the deep nuclei that communicate with the various motor and non-motor areas of the cerebral cortex. [7]

lateral corticospinal tract   The majority of corticospinal fibers (approximately 80%) in the pyramidal area that cross over to the other (contralateral) side of the body, playing an integral role in the conscious motor control of the distal limbs and digits. [7]

lateral geniculate nucleus (LGN)   The portion of the thalamus that receives visual information from the optic tract and transmits to the primary visual cortex via fibers called optic radiations. [6]

lateral hypothalamus (LH)   A part of the hypothalamus that plays a role in initiating food intake and responding to the taste and sight of food. [8]

lateral inhibition   The process whereby visual information about edges and contrasts is perceived, in which a cell's neighboring neurons inhibit the activation of that particular cell. [6]

lateral intraparietal area (LIP)   A cortical area involved in decision making that integrates relevant sensory, motor, and cognitive information to determine the most optimal outcome of various response choices. [12]

lateral septum   Nuclei below the corpus callosum with strong projections to hypothalamic and midbrain regions, having a role in processing emotion, mood, and social behavior in stress responses, such as fear, anxiety, worry, and anger. [10]

lateralization   Difference in function or specialization between the right and left hemispheres of the brain. [2]

laterodorsal tegmental nuclei   Cholinergic pons/midbrain area that contributes to producing and sustaining wakefulness. [9]

law of effect   The important relationship between behavior and consequences, first cited by Edward Thorndike. [12]

L-DOPA (L-3 4-dihydroxyphenylalanine)   A drug used to treat Parkinson's disease by increasing levels of dopamine in patients experiencing deficits in this essential neurotransmitter. [7]

learned helplessness   An acquired shift in motivation in which animal test subjects not previously able to escape a shock no longer attempt to escape; thought to be a model for depression in humans. [8]

learned persistence   The idea that experience with work that consistently produces rewards leads to increased persistence when the problem becomes more difficult and unfamiliar, such that animal test subjects continue attempting to improve their situation regardless of the effectiveness of their latest attempt; the opposite of learned helplessness. [8]

lens   A transparent membrane located behind the pupil that, along with the cornea, helps focus images projected to the back of the eye. [6]

leptin   A hormone that plays a key role in hunger regulation by decreasing appetite. [8]

Lewy bodies   Abnormal protein deposits present in the cell body of brain areas affected by Parkinson's disease. [7]

Lewy neurites   Abnormal protein deposits present in the neuronal processes of brain areas affected by Parkinson's disease. [7]

ligand-gated channels   Channels in synaptic membranes involved in the neurotransmitter binding process. (Chemicals that bind to other chemicals are known as ligands.) Also called neurotransmitter-gated channels. [3]

limbic system   A subcortical system of the telencephalon consisting of a collection of structures (the fornix, septum, amygdala, cingulum, and hippocampus) that surround the thalamus and are involved in the regulation of emotional expression as seen in mammals. [2]

lithium   Pharmacological drug used to treat acute mania during bipolar disorder, possibly by increasing presynaptic activity within the serotonergic system. [13]

lobotomy   A 20th-century surgical treatment for psychiatric symptoms, in which surgeons use an instrument resembling an icepick to enter the brain through the eye socket and damage neural connections of the frontal lobes. [13]

localization of brain function   The process of mapping specific mental functions onto specific areas of the brain. [1]

locked-in syndrome   A diagnosis wherein patients have a fully functioning brain that is essentially trapped in a body that cannot move or communicate in traditional ways; typically caused by a brainstem lesion resulting from a stroke or tumor. [9]

locus coeruleus   A brainstem area involved in arousal; one of the locations where norepinephrine is produced; activates thalamocortical neurons (neurons projecting from the thalamus to the cortex). [4, 9]

long-term potentiation (LTP)   Long-lasting alteration to specific afferent synapses in the hippocampus when stimulated with a high-frequency stimulus; possible biological mechanism for some forms of memory. [12]

lordosis   Mating posture during which female animal reflexively arches her back and holds her tail in a position that facilitates penetration from the male. [11]

loudness   The perceived intensity of sound waves measured as intensity. [6]

lower motor neurons   Essential motor neurons in the gray matter of the spinal cord that specifically arise from the ventral horn of the spinal cord. [7]

luteinizing hormone   Protein hormone that travels from the anterior pituitary to the gonads to influence hormone release. [11]

macrophages   Cells dispatched by the innate immune system that engulf and digest pathogens via a process called phagocytosis. [2]

magnetic resonance imaging (MRI)   A high-resolution scanning technique utilizing a powerful magnetic field to detect brain structure. [1]

magnocellular layers   One of three types of cellular layers in the lateral geniculate nucleus of the thalamus, the magnocellular layer is characterized by larger cells and provides information about the position of a visual stimulus. [6]

major depression   A mental disorder characterized by profound sadness, diminished pleasure, decreased motivation, cognitive slowing, lethargy, and thoughts of suicide (also called "major depressive disorder"). [13]

mammillary bodies   Two small, round bodies beneath the hypothalamus that relay information from the hypothalamus to the anterior thalamus and, as a part of Papez's circuit, have an integral role in spatial memory and emotional processing. [10]

McGurk effect   The perceptual experience whereby slightly mismatched pairs of auditory and visual cues cause listeners to report hearing something more consistent with their visual input. [6]

MDMA   A "designer" drug commonly known as ecstasy, a form of amphetamine (3,4-methylenedioxymethamphetamine). [4]

mechanoreceptor   A receptor in the skin that responds to touch or pressure. [6]

medial   A specific term of anatomical direction meaning "toward the center." [2]

medial frontal cortex   The cortex of the rat brain comparable to the human medial prefrontal cortex; contributes to a rat's decision to exert effort to obtain a high-value reward. [8]

medial geniculate nucleus   Part of the auditory pathway, a region in the thalamus that receives signals from the inferior colliculus and projects them to the primary auditory cortex. [6]

medial preoptic area of the hypothalamus   A part of the hypothalamus that processes aggression-related information. Found to be important in other social behaviors as well. [10]

medulla oblongata (myelencephalon)   The most ventral (lower) area of the brain through which neural information enters from the spinal cord, regulating fundamental life-supporting systems such as respiration, blood pressure, arousal, and muscle tone. [2]

medullary pyramids   The areas in the brainstem medulla containing the corticospinal tracts, where the lateral corticospinal tracts cross over, or decussate. [7]

Meissner's corpuscles   Skin receptors that are sensitive to light touch and are concentrated in sensitive areas such as fingers and lips. [6]

melatonin   Hormone produced by the pineal gland that is involved in sleep/wake cycles

membrane potential   The difference in charge between the inside and outside of a cell. [3]

membrane   In neurons, a double layer of phospholipids that isolates the cell's inner components from the extracellular fluid, yet is also porous. [3]

memory consolidation   A process that transforms new, unstable memories into more stable memories integrated into the brain's network of existing memories. [9]

memory engram   Memory traces in the brain. [12]

meninges   A three-layer structure (dura mater, arachnoid mater, and pia mater) covering the outside of the brain and the spinal cord. [2]

mental faculties   The specific functions of the brain. [1]

mesolimbic pathway   The dopamine pathway from the ventral tegmental area to the brain reward area (including the nucleus accumbens). [4]

messenger RNA (mRNA)   The type of RNA that transmits the DNA's prescriptions to a ribosome for protein manufacture within the cell. [1]

metabotropic receptors   Postsynaptic receptors that respond more slowly than ionotropic receptors to neurotransmitter release using intracellular molecules as intermediaries. [3]

metencephalon   The brain area just above the medulla oblongata, containing the pons and the cerebellum. [2]

methamphetamine   A highly addictive drug that stimulates the central nervous system and alters the secretion of the neurotransmitter dopamine. [4]

methylphenidate   A psychostimulant drug, also called Ritalin. [4]

microdialysis,   A method, using the principle of the separation movement of solutes, to determine the levels of targeted neurotransmitters or drug concentrations in brain tissue. [8]

microglia   Smaller glial cells that monitor the microenvironment of the nervous system and serve to protect the brain by cleaning up dead cells and cellular debris. [2]

mineralocorticoid receptor (MR)   The more sensitive of the two glucocorticoid receptor systems that mediate stress response. Remains active following the initial stress activation because of the receptors' high affinity for lower circulating levels of stress hormones. (Also see *glucocorticoid receptor*.) [13]

minimally conscious state   An absence of consciousness such that patients may exhibit nonreflexive behaviors such as visual tracking or responding to simple commands, but show no further evidence of awareness. [9]

mirror neurons   Specialized neurons theorized to be involved in imitative (mirroring) behavior and proposed to play a role in empathy, speech perception, and other social behaviors. [3]

mirror system hypothesis of language   The idea that the primate mirror system involved in grasping responses eventually evolved into critical components that prepared the human brain for language. [7]

molecular hypothesis of depression   The idea suggesting that depression is the product of long-term molecular changes in the brain and that antidepressants work by counteracting these molecular changes. [13]

monoamine hypothesis of depression   The idea that depression symptoms are caused by low levels of serotonin and norepinephrine at critical synaptic sites in the brain. [13]

monoamine oxidase inhibitors (MAOIs)   A class of antidepressant drugs that inhibit the enzyme, monoamine oxidase, which deactivates monoamine transmitter substances after being released into the synapse. [13]

monoamines   A major category of neurotransmitter, widely distributed throughout the brain and characterized by containing a single amine group; composed of two classes: catecholamines and indolamines. [4]

monosynaptic spinal reflex   A reflex arc containing a single synapse of one sensory neuron and one motor neuron. [7]

morphine   The principal psychoactive substance in opium. [4]

Morris water maze   One of the most commonly used tasks in behavioral neuroscience. Measures spatial memory in rats using tracings of spatial paths to a goal, plus the amount of time required to locate it. [12]

motor end plate   A section of the extrafusal muscle fiber that is highly excitable and appropriate for the initiation of action potentials; forms a synapse with the axon terminal of a motor neuron. [7]

motor homunculus   Literally, "little man." A map depicting the proportion of motor cortex areas devoted to certain body parts. [7]

motor neurons   Neurons involved in initiating movement. [2]

motor theory of speech perception   The notion that speech is perceived as an extension of gestures generated by individuals articulating communicative sounds. [7]

motor unit   The α motor neuron in the ventral horn of the gray matter of the spinal cord, its axon, and the extrafusal muscle fibers it innervates. [7]

mounting   The first stage of copulation; cooperative behavior whereby an interested male approaches a sexually receptive female preliminary to penetration and ejaculation. [11]

Müllerian ducts   Embryonic features that, in females, in the absence of androgen, develop into the female internal genitalia (the uterus, fallopian tubes, and vagina) and the external genitalia (the clitoris and the labia majora and minora). In males, these ducts are suppressed by the presence of androgen. [11]

multihistocompatibility complex (MHC)   A cluster of genes that encode proteins with information about the ongoing and potential ability of the immune system to combat a diverse array of pathogenic threats. [11]

multiple sclerosis   A neuromuscular disease caused by the degeneration of the myelin sheath and associated with sensory and motor impairments. [2, 7]

multipolar neurons   The most common shape of neuron in the nervous system, with multiple dendrites extending from a single soma. [2]

multisensory integration   Adaptive processing of the various sensory stimuli decoded by our brains as we interpret information from multiple sensory systems. [6]

multisensory neuron   A nerve cell that responds to multiple senses, containing several receptive fields for different sensory modalities. [6]

muscle spindle   An intrafusal muscle sensory organ for detecting stretch in the muscle, with receptor endings that extend from γ motor neurons in the spinal cord to wrap around the intrafusal muscle fibers. [7]

mutation   A random but permanent alteration that suddenly occurs in the DNA sequence of a gene. [1]

myelin sheath   Found in many vertebrate axons, the special insulating covering that ensures the strength and speed of a nerve signal. [2]

narcolepsy   A neurological disorder characterized by excessive sleepiness, intermittent and uncontrollable episodes of sleep during waking hours, muscular weakness or paralysis, and hypnogogic hallucinations. [9]

Nash equilibrium   In a noncooperative game, the point at which each player finds the best response by considering the strategies of the other players during the decision-making process. [12]

NDMA receptor   One type of receptor activated by the neurotransmitter glutamate, called NMDA receptor because of its affinity for *N-methyl-d-a*spartate. [4]

negative plastic changes   Changes associated with cognitive decline that occur during aging as the signal-to-noise ratio discerned by the brain's neurons becomes less and less distinct. [5]

negative symptoms   A traditional category of schizophrenia symptoms, abnormal behaviors reflecting the diminishment or absence of the normal emotional responses or thought processes seen in healthy individuals. (Also see *positive symptoms*.) [13]

nerve-growth factor (NGF)   A protein neurochemical that facilitates the growth of axons and dendrites and enhances the probability of neuronal survival. [5]

nerves   The cabled axons extending beyond the central nervous system that travel to various sites in the peripheral nervous system. Also called *peripheral nerves*. [2]

network hypothesis of depression   The idea suggesting that the condition of neural networks (rather than a specific chemical imbalance) has the most direct impact on mood. [13]

neural circuits   The communicative collaborations of brain cells to produce behavioral and physiological responses. [3]

neuroeconomics   The discipline that investigates the neural computations accompanying value-based decisions, or the ways in which the brain makes choices among various options. [12]

neuroethology   The study of the neural basis of animals' natural behavior. [5]

neurogenesis   The process whereby the adult mammalian brain can create new neurons in certain brain areas. [2]

neuroleptic drug   A name for a drug whose effects on schizophrenia patients were similar to those of the seizure-producing drugs and electroconvulsive therapy that were used to treat mental illness in the 1950s. [13]

neuromuscular junction   The synapse formed when the axon terminal of a motor neuron positions itself in the motor end plate, an area that is highly excitable and appropriate for the initiation of action potentials. [7]

neuron   A nerve cell, the fundamental unit of the nervous system. [2]

neuropeptide Y (NPY)   A neuropeptide neurotransmitter that causes increased food intake; one of the most abundant peptides in the mammalian brain, found in neurons densely packed in several brain areas overlapping with limbic system areas. [8, 10]

neuroplasticity   The brain's ability to restructure itself. [5]

neuropsychopharmacology   The scientific study that seeks to identify specific drugs that interact with the nervous system to alter behavior that has been disrupted by disease, injury, or environmental factors. [4]

neurotransmitters   Neurochemicals exchanged between neurons. [3]

neurotrophic factors   Nerve growth factors. [3]

nicotine   An addictive substance, the active ingredient in tobacco. [4]

night terrors   Abrupt wakening and panic responses, most often observed in children. [9]

nigrostriatal pathway   The dopamine pathway from the substantia nigra to the striatum (caudate and putamen). [4]

nitric oxide   When released by postsynaptic neurons to affect the axons of presynaptic neurons, a gas that can act as a retrograde neurotransmitter, readily passing through the cell membrane to modulate neurotransmission. [4]

NMDA receptor   Receptor in nerve cells that is activated by the ubiquitous neurotransmitter glutamate; implicated in contributing to the cognitive dysfunction and negative symptoms of schizophrenia. [13]

nocebo effect   The presence of side effects, even in placebo control groups, that may emerge if subjects are told to expect them. [13]

nodes of Ranvier   Tiny gaps between segments of myelin sheath in a neuronal axon. [2]

non-REM sleep A stage of night sleep, composed of three distinct stages: Stage 1 sleep, Stage 2 sleep, and slow wave sleep. [9]

norepinephrine A member of the catecholamine class of monoamine neurotransmitters, produced in the locus coeruleus, and involved in increased vigilance, focused attention, and enhanced energy. [4]

nuclei In neuroanatomy, the clusters of neurons in the midbrain where fine-tuned sensory and motor messages interact, enhancing responsiveness to complex environments. Singular, *nucleus*. [2]

nucleotide bases The chemical building blocks of DNA, appearing as the base pairs adenine–thymine and cytosine–guanine. [1]

nucleus The command center of the cell that contains the genetic code, which directs the cell's functioning. [1]

nucleus accumbens A brain area known for its role in reward and motivational responses. [4]

nucleus tractus solitari A group of cells in the medulla involved in the sensory component of the autonomous nervous system. [8]

ob/ob mice Mice expressing the recessive gene that makes them leptin deficient; hence, they become obese. [8]

obesity An overabundance of body fat to the detriment of health. [8]

obsessive–compulsive disorder (OCD) A pathological form of anxiety characterized by recurrent, persistent, intrusive, or inappropriate thoughts that cause anxiety (obsessions) and repetitive acts that the sufferer feels driven to perform to alleviate anxiety (compulsions). [8, 13]

occipital lobe One of the four large areas of the cerebral cortex, involved in visual processing. [2]

odorant molecules Molecules that we can smell. [6]

off-center cells Retinal cells inhibited when a light is focused on the center of the cell. [6]

olfactory bulbs Organs that lie at the ventral surface of the brain just above the olfactory epithelium containing clusters of axonal and dendritic processes known as olfactory glomeruli. [6]

olfactory epithelium The mucous membrane located at the top of the nasal cavity containing olfactory sensory neurons. [6]

oligodendrocytes The type of glial cells that make up the myelin sheath that encapsulates axons of myelinated neurons located *within* the brain and spinal cord. They have multiple projections, each serving as one segment of the neuron's myelin sheath. Also known as *oligogendroglia*. [2]

omega (ω)-3 Essential fatty acids that must be ingested (since the body cannot make them). Has a role in supporting cognitive function by activating genes involved in neuroplasticity. [8]

on-center cells Retinal cells stimulated when a light is focused on the center of the cell. [6]

operant conditioning The form of learning resulting from an animal's active interaction with its environment, wherein active responses that lead to a positive outcome are reinforced and repeated. [12]

opioid receptors Receptors found throughout the brain for which opioids have a strong affinity. [4]

opioids Substances derived from opium, such as morphine and heroin. [4]

opium A pain reliever derived from the liquid extracts of certain poppy plants. [4]

opponent-process theory of color vision The idea that the visual system was designed to detect opposed pairs of colors, specifically, green versus red, blue versus yellow, and black versus white. [6]

opsin A specific type of protein found in photopigments of photoreceptors in the retina of the eye. [6]

optic chiasm A midline structure where portions of the optic nerves of each eye cross over so that signals from the right and left visual field proceed to the contralateral hemisphere. [6]

optic nerve The bundle of axons emerging from the ganglion cells that exits the back of the eyeball. [6]

optic tract The pathway of visual information after exiting the optic chiasm that proceeds to the lateral geniculate nucleus of the thalamus. [6]

optimal actions Actions that minimize costs and maximize benefits. [7]

orbitofrontal cortex Prefrontal cortex region of the brain; associative area required for effective memory processing and learning. [12]

orexigenic Appetite stimulating. [8]

orexin A neuropeptide (also called *hypocretin*) affecting sleep–wake cycles, as well as emotions, energy expenditure, and reward systems. [9]

organ of Corti The area of the cochlea that contains the receptive cells (hair cells) for audition. [6]

organum vasculosum of the lamina terminalis (OVLT) Brain structure of the anterior third ventricle, lacking a blood–brain barrier, and containing very sensitive osmoreceptors that sample and respond to changes in solutes and fluid levels in the brain. [8]

orientation columns The organization of V1 cortical cells as determined by the tendency of cells that respond to lines of a particular orientation to group together. [6]

osmoreceptors Cells that are sensitive to cellular dehydration. [8]

osmosis The net movement of fluid (e.g., water) through a semipermeable membrane into a region of higher solute concentration. [8]

ossicles The three tiny bones located behind the eardrum in the middle ear—the hammer, anvil, and stirrup—that transmit air vibrations from the eardrum to the cochlea. [6]

oval window The portion of the cochlea on which the pitch of the sound waves project activating various sections of the basilar membrane. [6]

oxygen free radicals Highly reactive molecules containing oxygen that can harm vulnerable neurons. [5]

oxytocin A peptide hormone released by the posterior pituitary; produces prosocial behaviors such as trust, empathy, and altruism. [11]

Pacinian corpuscles Touch receptors in the skin that respond to deep pressure. [6]

panic disorder A pathological form of anxiety produced by heightened levels of both trait anxiety and state anxiety and characterized by brief, recurrent, unexpected episodes of terror, sympathetic activation, shortness of breath, fear of dying and losing control, and derealization (the perception that the external world is no longer real). [13]

Papez's circuit Neural circuit originally thought to process emotional expression, relaying from the cingulate cortex to the hippocampus via the cingulum, then through the fornix to the mammillary bodies of the hypothalamus and on to the anterior thalamus, together with a second circuit directly from the thalamus to the mammillary bodies and then to the autonomic nervous system. [10]

parabiosis A technique in which portions of two animals are surgically bound so that the blood supply is shared between them. [5]

parahippocampal cortex (PHC) Cortical area sensitive to contextual relations based on the presence of other objects to facilitate accurate object recognition. [6]

paramedian lobule   An area in the cerebellar cortex that specifically regulates limb movement. [12]

paraplegic   Paralyzed in the lower half of the body.

parasomnias   Talking, walking, and eating during sleep. [9]

parasympathetic nervous system   The part of the autonomic nervous system that reestablishes normal baseline functions after a threat has passed. It extends from the cranial and sacral areas of the spinal cord and has long preganglionic fibers and short postganglionic fibers that extend to the final organ destination. [2]

paraventricular nucleus   An area of the hypothalamus thought to be involved with both the inhibition of appetite and—by stimulating the agouti-related peptide neurons in the arcuate nucleus—the enhancement of hunger. [8]

parietal lobe   One of the four large areas of the cerebral cortex, involved in interpreting sensory information. [2]

Parkinson's disease   A degenerative neuromuscular disease that results from suboptimal activation of the basal ganglia after these structures fail to receive adequate supplies of the neurotransmitter dopamine, causing problems with movement such as slowness, involuntary tremor, or rigidity. [2, 7]

parturition   The birthing process. [11]

parvocellular layers   One of three types of cellular layers in the lateral geniculate nucleus of the thalamus, the parvocellular layer provides identifying details about a visual stimulus. [6]

pedunculopontine tegmental nuclei   Cholinergic pons/midbrain area that contributes to producing and sustaining wakefulness. [9]

peptide hormones   Hormones consisting of chains of amino acids. [11]

peptide neurotransmitter   A major category of neurotransmitter; includes neurotransmitters such as endorphins, oxytocin, and vasopressin. [4]

peptides   Molecules consisting of approximately 3–40 amino acids. [4]

perception   The interpretation of information about our environmental context. [6]

periaqueductal gray   The central region of the tegmentum of the midbrain, involved in the sensation of pain; an interface between the forebrain and the lower brainstem that processes aggression-related information. [2, 10]

peripheral nervous system (PNS)   The part of the nervous system that lies outside of the brain and spinal cord. [2]

phagocytes   Cells dispatched by the innate immune system that engulf and digest pathogens via a process called phagocytosis. [2]

phagocytosis   The process of engulfing and digesting pathogens as part of the innate immune system. [2]

pharmacodynamics   The effects of a drug and the mechanisms of how the drug works; what a drug does to the body. [4]

pharmacokinetics   The process by which a drug is absorbed, distributed, metabolized, and eliminated by the body; what the body does to a drug. [4]

phase shift   Realignment. [9]

phenotypes   The observable physical characteristics of an organism, such as shape and color. [1]

pheromones   Chemicals released from one animal and detected by another. [6]

phobias   Disorders characterized by excessive fear of specific stimuli. [10]

phosphodiesterase   An enzyme in the rods of the retina that reduces cyclic guanosine monophosphate concentrations that maintain the open channels, resulting in the closure of the sodium channels and hyperpolarization of the receptor. [6]

photopigments   Molecules present in photoreceptors, consisting of opsin and retinal, that are required to convert physical energy to neural energy. [6]

photoreceptors   Specialized neurons that are sensitive to light. [6]

phrenology   From the Latin *phren* (mind) and *logos* (discourse), refers to the now-debunked theory that bumps on the skull correlate to different mental characteristics. [1]

pia mater   The fine layer of the meninges immediately covering the brain's surface. [2]

piriform cortex   An evolutionarily ancient structure in the telencephalon that receives olfactory axons from the olfactory bulbs; involved with the process of smelling. [6]

pitch   The perceived frequency of sound waves. [6]

pituitary gland   The size of a pea, a component of the endocrine system (the body's hormonal system), located beneath the hypothalamus, that triggers the release of various hormones related to fertility, growth, and anxiety, among others. [2]

place cells   Cells that become activated when rats are located in specific locations, or *places*, in a maze. [12]

placebo   An inactive substance, administered in experiments to compare with the effects of administering the substance under study. [1]

placebo effect   A patient's subjective perception that treatment with an inactive substance presented as an actual medicine is having a therapeutic effect. [4]

planum temporale   An area of the temporal cortex that is thought to be involved in language. [2]

pluripotent   Cells that are able to become many different types of cells. [5]

polysomnograph   The record of brain wave activity, eye movements, and muscle tension produced by the physiological recording technique called polysomnography. [9]

polysomnography   A physiological recording technique that simultaneously records brain wave activity, eye movements, and muscle tension. [9]

pons   From the Latin term for *bridge*. A structure in the metencephalon, the bulge on the ventral side of the brain rich in nerve-fiber pathways that transfer information to more dorsal (upper) areas and from one side of the brain to the other. [2]

pontine nuclei   Deep cerebellar nuclei that contain excitatory climbing mossy fibers and project to the granule cells in the cerebellar cortex. [12]

pontogeniculooccipital (PGO) spikes   A specific brain wave pattern during REM sleep that originates in the pons and projects to the lateral geniculate nucleus of the thalamus before making a final appearance in the occipital cortex. [9]

portal system   A specialized blood system that facilitates the travel of releasing hormones from the hypothalamus to the pituitary gland. [11]

positive symptoms   A traditional category of schizophrenia symptoms, abnormal behaviors that are present in people with schizophrenia, such as delusions and hallucinations, but not in healthy individuals. (Also see *negative symptoms*.) [13]

positron emission tomography (PET)   A scanning technique that provides real-time images of functioning in areas of the brain by observing the metabolism of radioactive glucose by the brain. [1]

posterior   A specific term of anatomical direction meaning "toward the tail." Also known as *caudal*. [2]

posterior parietal cortex   Cortical area activated when subjects are asked to localize certain sounds. [6]

postretrieval lability   Instability of memories. [12]

postsynaptic membrane   The neuron surface containing receptors for the specific neurotransmitter released by the synaptic vesicles of an adjoining neuron's presynaptic membrane. [3]

posttraumatic stress disorder (PTSD)   A mood and anxiety disorder mixing intrusive memories of a traumatic episode and accompanying avoidance of relevant triggers for the event, typically accompanied by chronic hyperarousal and negative emotional distortions. [12]

potency   The strength or ability to produce an effect. [4]

premotor cortex   Located ventral to the supplementary motor complex and directly in front of the primary motor cortex, cortex activated for motor skills less dependent on self-initiation and more dependent on the external guidance of movement. [7]

prepulse inhibition   A decrease in the response to a startling stimulus when another weaker stimulus precedes it closely in time. [13]

presupplementary motor area (pre-SMA)   A part of the motor cortex that is activated during tasks involving executive control, such as deciding to suppress a response or switch tasks, perhaps while conducting a difficult procedure with constantly changing conditions. [7]

presynaptic facilitation   The effect of synaptic interactions resulting in increased excitation and neurotransmitter release. [3]

presynaptic inhibition   The effect of synaptic interactions resulting in decreased neurotransmitter release. [3]

presynaptic membrane   The surface membranes of axon terminals on which synaptic vesicles cluster. [3]

presynaptic terminal   The axon terminal. [3]

primary auditory cortex   The cortical area that receives projections from the medial geniculate nucleus in the thalamus. [6]

primary motor cortex   A region in the frontal lobe controlling motor function. [2]

primary somatosensory cortex   A region in the parietal lobe that processes sensory signals from the body; the main cortical area for processing tactile information. [2, 6]

primary visual cortex (V1)   The large region of the cortex that receives visual input from the richly detailed foveal region of the retina. Also called striate cortex. [6]

priming effect   An exposure to a drug whereby an individual is reminded of an earlier memory of effects of the drug. [4]

procedural memories   Memories of how to perform certain actions. [9]

procedural memory   The motor memory that consists in fine-tuning the brain's circuitry to enable skilled performances; also called "implicit memory." [12]

proceptive behavior   Behavior that attracts attention from a potential sexual partner; flirting. [11]

processing-based memory system   A proposed memory system consisting of three processing modes that vary across three variables: fast versus slow encoding, single-item versus associative encoding, and flexible versus rigid representation. [12]

prodromal phase of schizophrenia   The initial time period, usually in adolescence, when cognitive impairment emerges in the individuals destined for schizophrenia. [13]

progenitor cells   A category of rapidly dividing cells that retain their ability to eventually produce a specific type of cell, but do not have the ability to produce pluripotent cells. [5]

progesterone   A reproductive hormone that may help facilitate the remyelination of axons affected by demyelinating diseases such as multiple sclerosis. [3]

prolactin   A protein hormone released by the anterior pituitary; stimulates breast milk production. [11]

proliferative areas   Cell-producing areas. [5]

proprioception   The ability to sense the position, orientation, and movement of one's own body. [7]

prosocial behaviors   Cooperative behaviors such as trust, empathy, and altruism. [11]

prosopagnosia   The inability to recognize faces. [6]

protein hormones   Peptides with more than 50 amino acids; cannot travel easily across the cell membrane and consequently depend on activation of a specific receptor in the cell membrane to trigger the activation of additional mechanisms to carry out their function. [11]

protolanguage   Early vocal-based language. [7]

protosigns   Manual movements, theorized to provide a neural groundwork for vocal language. [7]

proximal   A specific term of anatomical direction meaning "closer" to the central nervous system. [2]

proximal causes   The short-term causes of behavior, such as an unexpected loud noise or a hormonal change. [1]

psychoactive drug   A natural or artificial chemical substance that acts on the central nervous system to affect moods, feelings, thoughts, and behavior. [4]

psychoanalysis   Mental health field founded by Sigmund Freud, emphasizing unconscious motives, not faulty neural networks, as the causes of mental illness. [13]

psychodynamic theory   The idea, emphasizing unconscious motives, that a personality is composed of the interrelationship of three elements: an instinctual id, a moralizing super-ego, and a realistic ego that mediates between the other two. [13]

psychoneuroimmunology   The study of the integration of the nervous system and immune function that seeks to establish the connections among psychology, neuroscience, and the immune system. [2]

psychopharmacologic drugs   Therapeutic drugs that affect the brain's functions. [13]

Psychophysics   The measurable relationship between the physical qualities of a sensory stimulus and the perception of that stimulus. [6]

pupil   The portal through which light enters the eye. [6]

Purkinje cells   The principal inhibitory cells of the cerebellar cortex. [12]

putamen   A primary component of the basal ganglia located in the telencephalon; communicates regularly with the cerebral cortex to contribute to the efficient execution of appropriate movements. [2, 7]

quadriplegia   Paralysis of arms, legs, and torso. [7]

radial arm maze   A task used in behavioral neuroscience that tests an animal's memory of recent experiences to solve a problem. [12]

radial cells   Certain glial cells that play an extremely important role in the developing cortex by providing a pathway for developing neurons to follow to their destinations. Radial cells may turn into astrocytes or may continue to exist as radial cells. [5]

raphe nuclei   The area of the brain where serotonin is synthesized from the dietary amino acid tryptophan; also a heterogeneous group of serotonergic neurons in the brain stem that activate neurons projecting from the thalamus to the cortex, some contributing to sleep and some contributing to wakefulness.. [4, 9]

rapid eye movement (REM) sleep   A stage of sleep during which the eyes move back and forth. [9]

ratio strain   The upper boundary of the amount of work an animal will do to receive a desired outcome. [8]

reactive-impulsive aggression   One of the two main types of aggression, displayed when a person is highly emotionally aroused, as with out-of-control anger; more directly regulated by the limbic structures. [10]

receptive fields   Sections in sensory neurons that receive information from a specific sensory area. [6]

recessive   In genetics, heritable characteristics that are expressed in offspring only when inherited from both parents. [1]

reconsolidating   Restructuring (said of long-term memories that may change during formation, augmentation, storage, or retrieval). [12]

red nucleus   A pinkish area, prominent within the *substantia nigra* region of the tegmentum in the midbrain, that seems to have evolved as limbs (such as arms) evolved because it plays a role in limb movement. [2]

red–green colorblindness   The most common form of color blindness in which a person has difficulty differentiating red and green

reflex arc   Very fast neural network that processes a motor reaction to a sensory stimulus outside the domain of the cortex. [7]

reflexes   Very fast involuntary movement responses to stimuli. [7]

refractory period   The time period after an action potential sequence of a nerve cell that sets a maximum limit on a neuron's firing frequency. [3]

reinforcers   Events that increase the likelihood of a recurring response. [12]

relapse   The recurrence of drug use following a period of abstinence. [4]

releasing hormones   Peptide hormones that travel to the anterior pituitary from the hypothalamus (for example, corticotropin-releasing hormone). Also called hypothalamic hormones. [11]

REM-on cells   Generally, the cells that are maximally active during REM sleep (as opposed to during waking and non-REM sleep). [9]

renin   The hormone that is released into the circulatory system when hypovolemia is detected by the kidneys. [8]

repetitive transcranial magnetic stimulation (rTMS)   A therapy for treating depression, less intense than electroconvulsive therapy, that provides repetitive stimulation of varying frequencies using a powerful electromagnet on the scalp to depolarize underlying neurons; introduced in the 1990s. [13]

resilience   The psychological response of springing back after a stressful situation, providing the ability to cope successfully with acute and chronic stressors. [10]

response inhibition   The ability to inhibit irrelevant responses that interfere with the completion of the task. [5]

resting membrane potential   The unequal distribution of ions contributing to the negative polarity of a resting neuronal membrane. [3]

restraint stress   An experimental condition in which test animals are confined to small spaces for a period of time. [3]

reticular formation   The cluster of nuclei and fibers located throughout the central area of the brainstem. [2]

retina   The layer of specialized photoreceptors that line the back of the eye. [6]

retinal   Fatty substances that, along with opsin, comprise photopigments of photoreceptors in the retina of the eye. [6]

retinohypothalamic tracts   Tracts extending from the retina that stimulate a nucleus of the hypothalamus known as the suprachiasmatic nucleus. [9]

retrosplenial cortex   Cortical area implicated in context perception. [6]

reuptake   A process whereby a neurotransmitter terminates its activation of a postsynaptic receptor, in this case by being transported back to the presynaptic neuron and repackaged for reuse. (Also see *enzymatic deactivation*.) [4]

rhodopsin   The photopigment in the rods of the retina of the eye. [6]

ribonucleic acid (RNA)   A single-strand molecule, similar to DNA but with the base uracil instead of thymine. [1]

rods   Visual photoreceptors most densely packed around the periphery of the retina at the back of the eye and most sensitive to light. The human retina contains approximately 100 million rods. [6]

rostral   A specific term of anatomical direction meaning "toward the front or mouth." Also known as *anterior*. [2]

round window   The structure that allows fluids to move back and forth within the cochlea, making it more responsive to vibrations. [6]

saliency   Relevance. [12]

saltatory conduction   The jumping movement of an action potential from one short unmyelinated section of axon to another. It greatly enhances the speed of neural processing. [3]

saturation   The perceived purity of a light stimulus, represented by the precision of the wavelength bandwidth of the visual output. [6]

Schachter–Singer theory of emotion   The theory of emotion that emphasizes the role of context-dependent cognitive interpretation in transforming general arousal to a specific emotion; acknowledges the importance of both autonomic arousal and cognitive perceptions in the expression of specific emotions. [10]

schizophrenia   A complex category of mental disorder in which individuals exhibit mental deterioration as young adults and begin experiencing delusions, hallucinations, paranoia, and cognitive dysfunction. [13]

Schwann cells   Pancake-shape glial cells that wrap their entire cell body around the axon of myelinated neurons located *outside* of the brain and spinal cord. [2]

second messengers   Intracellular molecules that act as intermediaries to cause changes in the postsynaptic neuron, including the opening of ion channels. [3]

second-generation antipsychotics   Pharmaceutical treatments of patients diagnosed with schizophrenia that address the unwanted side effects of earlier treatments. [13]

selective serotonin reuptake inhibitors (SSRIs)   Pharmaceutical drugs that treat depression by blocking the reuptake of serotonin in the synapse, such as Prozac, Paxil, and Zoloft. [13]

semantic memory   A memory for word meanings and concept-based knowledge. [12]

sensation   The detection of information about our environmental context. [6]

sensitive period   A certain period of time during which an organism is more susceptible to environmental influences or stimulation than at other times. [11]

sensitization   An increase in drug efficiency upon repeated use. [4]

sensory adaptation   The natural adjustment of sensory receptors to reduce signals that are no longer meaningful. [6]

sensory neurons   The neurons that detect incoming information from the environment and body areas. [2]

sensory receptors   Specialized neurons that receive external stimuli (e.g., receptors in the eye's retina and olfactory cells in the nasal cavity). [6]

sensory-specific satiety   A phenomenon linking the sensory perception of food and appetite regulation, such that although an appetite may be sated by the consumption of one food, it may be immediately increased by the sensory perception of a new food. [8]

septal nuclei   A limbic structure that, in rats, has been implicated in pleasure and reward as well as the modulation of fear and anxiety. [8]

serotonin   A member of the indolmine class of monoamine neurotransmitters, produced in the raphe nuclei, and affecting mood regulation, sleep/wake cycles, temperature regulation, sexual activity, and aggression. [4]

serotonin hypothesis of depression   The idea suggesting that low levels of the neurochemical serotonin are the cause of depression. [13]

sex chromosomes   The chromosome pair, differently shaped from other chromosomes, decisive for determining the sex of an offspring, XX for female and XY for male. [1]

sham lesion   A surgical operation analogous to a placebo that includes the anesthesia, incision, and postoperative care, but omits the lesion that is under study, used as an experimental control. [1]

sham rage   Uncontrolled displays of emotion following the removal of the cortex in cats. [10]

shift work   Employment that requires employees to periodically change their work hours around the clock on a rotating basis. [9]

simple cells   V1 cortical cells that respond to bar-shape stimuli located in specific areas in specific orientations (e.g., vertical, horizontal). [6]

single-nucleotide polymorphisms (SNPs)   Variations in adenosine, guanine, thymine, or cytosine nucleotide bases that are generally associated with all of the targeted disorders. Further, of the four SNPs that were identified as relevant, two were associated with voltage-activated calcium channels in neuronal membranes. [13]

single-unit recording   A research technique using a microelectrode positioned to record the activity of a single neuron. [1]

skeletal (striatal) muscles   The muscles found throughout the body, considered to depend on volition to be activated. [7]

skin conductance response (SCR)   A measure in human experiments indicating a heightened emotional response characterized by increased electrodermal activity in the palms of the subjects (e.g., sweaty palms). [3]

skin theory of color vision   The idea that the colors emphasized in our visual repertoire allow us to see changes in skin color that provide information about a person's health or emotional status. [6]

sleep   A reversible state characterized by minimal movement, a relaxed posture, and diminished attention directed to the environment. [9]

sleep apnea   A disorder characterized by excessive snoring and abnormal pauses or shallowness in breathing during sleep. [9]

sleep architecture pattern   The pattern of sleep stages.

sleep debt   The difference between the amount of sleep you supposedly need and the amount of sleep you actually get. [9]

sleep efficiency   The more time spent asleep during the entire time spent dedicated to sleep, the higher the sleep efficiency index.

sleep rebound effect   The evidence that lost sleep is made up during the next opportunity for sleep, suggesting that, if sleep is necessary for normal physiological functions, lost sleep must be made up for optimal functioning. [9]

sleep spindles   Characteristic of Stage 2 sleep electroencephalograms, moderately fast and intense oscillations (12–14 Hertz) that last up to 1.5 seconds. [9]

slow wave sleep (SWS)   Sleep dominated by low-frequency δ waves and extreme grogginess. [9]

smooth muscles   Muscles located in organs such as the stomach, considered under involuntary control. [7]

social facilitation of eating   The effect whereby people eat more when they are with others. [8]

social phobia   A pathological form of anxiety characterized by aversion, fear, and autonomic arousal in unfamiliar social settings (also called "social anxiety disorder"). [13]

sodium–potassium pump   A type of ion pump that plays an important role in maintaining the unequal distribution of sodium ions and potassium ions across the neuronal membrane. [3]

soma   A prominent cell body that encloses a collection of microstructures found in all cells throughout the body. [2]

somatic marker hypothesis   The idea that physiological emotional responses serve an important role in guiding the brain's decision to carry out a particular behavior, especially when making risky decisions. [10]

somatic nervous system   The part of the peripheral nervous system that generally controls voluntary movement. [2]

somatosensation   Tactile sensation reported from the mechanoreceptors in the skin. [6]

somatosensory system   The skin-related sensory system that relays information about the body's interaction, through touch, position, and movement, with the external world. [6]

spatial summation   The process in which multiple synaptic inputs originating from different locations have a cumulative effect on depolarizing or hyperpolarizing a neuron, whereby the action potential threshold is reached. [3]

specific phobia   A pathological form of anxiety characterized by aversion, fear, and autonomic arousal in specific situations (such as the sight of blood). [13]

spike-initiation zone   The area in a neuron in which the action potential is initiated. [3]

spinal nerves   The left–right pairs of nerves that shuttle information to and from all areas of the body. There are 31 pairs in humans, including 8 cervical spinal nerve pairs, 12 thoracic spinal nerve pairs, 5 lumbar spinal nerve pairs, 5 sacral spinal nerve pairs, and 1 coccygeal spinal nerve pair. [2]

spinothalamic (anterolateral) pathway   The route of axons mediating pain and temperature sensation in the skin. [6]

split-brain patients   Patients who have had their corpus callosum (the bundle of nerve cells that connects the cerebral cortex of the left and right hemispheres of the brain) surgically severed to diminish the severity of their epileptic seizures. [2]

Stage 1 sleep   The initial phase of non-REM sleep characterized by a transition from β waves to α waves, relaxing muscles, and slow eye movements. [9]

Stage 2 sleep   A phase of non-REM sleep characterized by the appearance of k-complexes and sleep spindles and a lack of eye movements. [9]

startle response box   A small box for assessing prepulse inhibition in animals, equipped with a restrainer positioned on a weight-sensitive platform that assesses the latency to jump, or startle, as well as the intensity of the response by monitoring weight fluctuations on the platform. (Also called "acoustic response box.") [13]

startle response   An instantaneous defensive motor response to an intrusive stimulus, such as a very fast eye-blink response to a sudden blast of air. [12]

state anxiety   A nonpathological form of anxiety, concern relating to an immediate, temporary stressful situation. [13]

stem cells   The category of cells that are able to become many different types of cells. [5]

stereotaxic apparatus   A precise surgical instrument composed of an orthogonal frame of reference using a set of three coordinates in the *x*-, *y*-, and *z*-axes. [1]

stereotaxic atlas   A guidebook or brain atlas used to ascertain the location of a brain area of interest based on the locations of specific anatomical landmarks. [1]

stereotaxic surgery   Precision surgery using a spatial coordinate apparatus to pinpoint locations within the body during operations with minimal collateral damage. [1]

steroid hormones   Hormones derived from cholesterol that easily travel across the cell membrane; includes reproductive hormones and stress hormones. [11]

stimulants   Drugs that facilitate arousal. [4]

stress response   A means of bodily protection produced by the sympathetic branch of the peripheral nervous system that helps guide both behavioral and physiological responses to danger. [2]

striate cortex   Another name for the primary visual cortex (V1), called striate because of a notable stripe in the tissue. [6]

striatum   An area of the brain; part of the nigrostriatal pathway; a term that refers to the caudate and putamen of the basal ganglia collectively. [4, 7]

stroke   Brain trauma caused by the interruption of oxygen and nutrients to the brain when a blood vessel carrying blood to the brain is blocked or bursts. [1]

subadditive neural response   The integrated neural response that is even less exaggerated than an additive response. [6]

subcallosal cingulate gyrus   An area of the anterior cingulate gyrus with projections to and from the area of the ventral striatum and nucleus accumbens shell as well as the limbic structures; hyperactive in depressed patients, it is a key area contributing to profound sadness in depressed patients. [13]

subcoeruleus region   The area below the locus coeruleus, an especially critical generator of REM. [9]

subdural hematoma   A localized blood clot on the brain. [5]

subfornical organ (SFO)   Circumventricular organ, lacking a blood–brain barrier, containing very sensitive osmoreceptors that sample and respond to changes in solutes and fluid levels in the brain. [8]

subgranular zone   A discrete area of the mature mouse brain in which neurogenesis occurs; cells in the subgranular zone of the dentate gyrus in the hippocampus eventually mature and migrate to the existing neurocircuitry of the dentate gyrus, where they likely play a role in learning and memory. [5]

subiculum   Area near the hippocampus where direction cells fire when a rat points its head in a specific direction. [12]

submission   Strategy, in the absence of clearly defined dominance hierarchies, of avoiding potentially injurious aggressive encounters by exhibiting unthreatening messages and postures. [10]

substantia nigra   Literally, "black substance." A left–right pair of regions of the tegmentum in the midbrain known for the production of a neurochemical important for smooth physical movement; communicates with the basal ganglia. [2, 7]

subventricular zone   A discrete area of the mature mouse brain in which neurogenesis occurs; cells generated in the subventricular zone of the lateral ventricle give rise to cells that migrate to the olfactory bulb and differentiate into interneurons that have olfactory function. [5, 11]

sulci   The grooves of the cerebral cortex; singular, *sulcus*. [2]

superadditive neural response   An exaggerated integrated response, much stronger than any of its components. [6]

superior colliculi   A left–right pair of nuclei in the tectum of the midbrain important for processing visual information. [2]

superior colliculus   A midbrain region that receives inputs from the optic tract, involved in eye movements, visual orientation, and visual vigilance. [6]

superior longitudinal fasciculus   Cluster of neurons connecting the anterior and posterior regions of the cerebrum in each hemisphere. [11]

superior olivary nucleus   A portion of the auditory pathway that receives projections from the auditory nerve and synapse in the cochlear nuclei in the brainstem and projects to the inferior colliculus. [6]

superior orbital sulcus   Cortical area activated in tasks that require higher-order integration to continuously update the interpretation of a visual stimulus. [6]

supplementary motor area (SMA)   A part of the motor cortex that activates when a person imagines performing a complex motor task, such as the finger movement sequences of a musician. [7]

supplementary motor complex   A cluster of cortical areas located in the dorsomedial frontal cortex that helps to guide the execution of complex voluntary movements. [7]

suprachiasmatic nucleus (SCN)   A nucleus of the hypothalamus that receives stimulation from light via tracts extending from the retina. [9]

sympathetic nervous system   The part of the autonomic nervous system that switches to high alert and prepares the body for strenuous physical responses to life threats and challenges. It extends from the thoracic and lumbar areas of the spinal cord and has short preganglionic fibers and long postganglionic fibers that extend to the final organ destination. [2]

synapse   Literally, "to clasp." The structure consisting of the presynaptic and postsynaptic membranes as well as the minuscule gap between neurons that allows one neuron to communicate with another neuron. [3]

synaptic cleft   The narrow gap (approximately 20 nanometers) between two neuron membranes. [3]

synaptic homeostasis hypothesis   The idea that an important function of sleep is to reduce weaker synapses to provide more energy and resources for stronger synapses. [9]

synaptic transmission   The process by which a neuron communicates with another neuron or neurons across a synapse. [3]

synaptic vesicles   Small neurochemical-containing spheres clustering around the active zones of the terminals of axons. [3]

synaptogenesis   The formation of new synapses among neurons. [3, 5]

synesthesia   A rare condition in which stimulation of one sense triggers additional, seemingly unrelated perceptual experiences, e.g., "seeing" music. [4, 6]

T cells   Cells that form in the bone marrow and then mature in the thymus, with specialized detection abilities to migrate to infected areas to kill pathogens. [2]

tardive dyskinesia Uncontrollable facial and tongue movements. [13]

taste buds Small structures of soft tissue located on the tongue, soft palate, and areas of the throat that contain receptors that detect salty, sweet, sour, bitter, and umami (a rich, meaty taste). [6]

Tau (τ) protein Knotted threads of protein, important in supporting the microtubules that form the infrastructure of the neuron. [5]

tectorial membrane The part of the cochlea positioned above the hair cells of the basilar membrane. [6]

tectum Literally, "roof." The region of the midbrain that contains two sets of nuclei related to sensory processing, the *superior colliculi* and the *inferior colliculi*. [2]

tegmentum Literally, "floor." A region of the midbrain composed of several nuclei, including the most dorsal region of the reticular formation, the *periaqueductal gray* central region, and the *substantia nigra*. [2]

telomeres Repetitive DNA sequences located at the end of chromosomes that are critical for keeping genes intact during chromosome replication, but get worn down and lose their ability to function during aging. [5]

temporal lobe One of the four large areas of the cerebral cortex, involved in hearing, language, visual processing, and emotional processing. [2]

temporal summation The process in which a single neuron synapsing onto the postsynaptic membrane is stimulated quickly in succession before the first transmitter release decays. [3]

terminal ending The end of an axon where a nerve impulse or message is transmitted to another neuron or to nonneuronal tissue, such as a muscle or gland. [2]

thalamus An evolutionarily old brain structure; part of the diencephalon, consisting of two large egg-shape structures, one in each hemisphere, and composed of several nuclei that filter and direct all sensory stimuli (except smell) to higher areas in the cerebral cortex. [2]

THC The primary active ingredient in marijuana: δ-9-tetrahydrocannabinol. [4]

theory of equipotentiality The theory that multiple brain areas contribute equally to a particular task or function. [12]

theory of natural selection The idea that species that are biologically adapted to the physical conditions of their habitats are more likely to survive than species that are not. These survivors then pass on these adaptive traits to their offspring, thereby increasing, in each succeeding generation, the proportion of organisms with adaptive traits. [1]

therapeutic effects The targeted and beneficial consequences of a medical procedure. [4]

theta (θ) rhythms Hippocampal activity rhythms appearing in the electroencephalogram of different species of animals during REM sleep; it has been suggested that REM sleep allows animals to incorporate meaningful survival-related responses into their existing neural networks. [9]

theta (θ) waves Low-intensity, slow (3–7 Hertz) brain waves of the sleeping brain. [9]

threshold A neural membrane potential that must be reached to trigger an action potential, or nerve impulse. [3]

tolerance When an individual's reaction to a drug decreases with repeated exposure to that drug, such that increasingly larger doses of the drug are required to achieve the same desired effect. [4]

top-down processing Cognitive control that requires executive cognitive function to override the impulse to focus on the stimulus. [5]

top-down visual processing The processing of more integrated visual information based on context and expectations (e.g., cortical processing of a visual scene). [6]

tracts The cabled axons found within the central nervous system (the brain and spinal cord). [2]

trait anxiety A nonpathological form of anxiety, representing a person's ordinary tendencies to experience, attend to, and report fears and worries across many situations. [13]

transcranial magnetic stimulation An experimental laboratory technique to temporarily disrupt neural processing by placing a magnet over the cortex and then administering brief electrical currents in a specific region of the cerebral cortex. [3]

transduction The conversion of physical energy to neural energy. [6]

transgenerational In genetics, characteristics influenced by life events of a single generation that extend across multiple subsequent generations. [5]

transgenic Genetically engineered, such as mice whose genes have been inserted with fluorescent protein genes. [2]

transporters The proteins that act to provide neurotransmitter reuptake back into the presynaptic membrane. [4]

transsexuals Individuals who transition from the sex that was assigned at their birth to live as the other sex. [11]

trapezoid body A region near the cochlear nucleus that receives projections from the auditory nerve and synapse in the cochlear nuclei in the brainstem. [6]

traumatic brain injury (TBI) Injuries caused by strokes, seizures, and other debilitating diseases, as well as wounds from accidents and firearms. [5]

treatment resistant Said of patients who have failed to respond to any treatment. [13]

trepanning The practice of drilling holes in the skull to relieve symptoms and provide relief from mental illness. First used in prehistoric times. [13]

trichotillomania, A disorder characterized by compulsive hair plucking; one of the earliest documented psychiatric disorders. [8]

tricyclic antidepressants Class of antidepressant drugs found to alter synaptic functioning by blocking the reuptake of the monoamine transmitters. [13]

tuberomammillary nucleus (TMN) Brain area involved in sleep-wake cycles and circadian rhythms that also contains histamine neurons that are active during immune functions such as allergic responses. [9]

tumor necrosis factor An immune chemical located in sleep–wake-regulatory centers including the brainstem, hippocampus, and hypothalamus. [9]

two-factor theory Another name for the Schachter–Singer theory of emotion, called "two-factor" theory because the expression of a specific emotion is influenced by both cognition and physiology. [10]

tympanic membrane The eardrum, which vibrates when stimulated by sound waves. [6]

ultimate causes The long-term evolutionary causes of physical and behavioral characteristics. [1]

ultradian rhythms Biological rhythms with a period shorter than 24 hours. [9]

unipolar neuron A nerve cell with one process extending from the cell body that divides into an axonal and dendritic segment, generally found in sensory areas of the brain. [2]

upper motor neurons The bundles of axons extending from the cell bodies in the motor cortex that comprise the corticospinal tracts and project to the lower motor neurons of the anterior gray horns of the spinal cord. [7]

vagal tone Inhibition of heart rate resulting from stimulation of the vagus nerve. [10]

validity The degree to which a chosen test actually measures what the researcher seeks to measure. [1]

vasopressin Neuropeptide released from the posterior pituitary gland in response to hypovolemia that constricts the blood vessels to increase blood pressure and triggers a response in the kidneys to reduce fluid release to the bladder; plays roles in motivation, emotion, and reward. [8, 11]

vegetative states An absence of consciousness such that individuals appear to be awake yet exhibit no awareness of external stimuli and are unresponsive to the environment. [9]

ventral A specific term of anatomical direction meaning "toward the bottom or chest." [2]

ventral pallidum A site for considerable output from the nucleus accumbens and a crucial component of the reward circuit. [4]

ventral posterior nucleus of the thalamus The relay nucleus of the thalamus specialized for somatosensation. [6]

ventral stream Visual pathway extending from V1 that provides information about the identification of various objects. [6]

ventral tegmental area An area of the brain; one of the places where the neurotransmitter dopamine is produced. [4]

ventricles The chambers of the central nervous system that are filled with cerebrospinal fluid. [2]

ventrolateral preoptic area (VLPO) The one brain area in which the neurons increase their activation levels during slow wave sleep. Neurons in this area characterized as GABAergic and galaninergic neurons (because they produce GABA and galanin) project to the tuberomammillary nucleus. [9]

ventromedial hypothalamus (VMH) Area in the hypothalamus related to hunger regulation. [8]

vermis A functional section of the cerebellum in the midline, thought to regulate muscle tone. [7]

visual acuity Clearness of vision. [6]

vitreous humor The jellylike substance that fills the internal cavity of the eye and helps maintain its healthy condition. [6]

voltage-gated ion channel Passages in the neural membrane that open and close in response to changes in the membrane potential. [3]

vomeronasal organ (VNO) A structure located in the nasal cavity that can detect pheromones as part of an accessory olfactory system. [6]

von Economo neuron A large type of bipolar neuron that may enhance the speed of communication among neural areas and has been implicated in our ability to make quick, intuitive assessments of complex situations. [3]

voodoo death Mortality resulting from a person believing that he or she was condemned to death because of a voodoo curse, consumption of a taboo food, or some other form of condemnation (sometimes called *neurogenic death*). [10]

Weber's law The empirical principle that the just noticeable difference is a constant proportion of the initial stimulus. [6]

Wernicke's area A cortical area known for its involvement in speech perception, typically localized in the left hemisphere. [7]

white matter Myelinated axons of the brain. [2]

Williams syndrome Genetic neurodevelopmental disorder characterized by specific facial features (e.g., low nasal bridge, puffiness around the eyes, a long upper lip and prominent lower lip, blue eyes with a starry pattern), cardiovascular challenges, delayed cognitive development, and other physiological effects. Individuals exhibit diminished amygdala activity in response to social situations. [10]

withdrawal symptoms Drug cravings and troubling feelings of fatigue, irritability, agitation, and anxiety experienced by addicts when first abstaining from drug use. [4]

Wolffian ducts Embryonic features that are suppressed, in females, by the absence of androgen but that in males, in the presence of androgen, transform into the male internal genitalia (including the vas deferens, seminal vesicles, and epididymis and the external genitalia—the penis and scrotum). [11]

working memory Keeping information readily accessible while working on a problem (as opposed to merely being able to remember recent events); associated with the prefrontal cortex. [12]

Young–Helmholtz trichromatic theory of color vision The idea that specialized receptor cells respond specifically to medium, short, and long wavelengths of light, thus enabling the perception of all recognized colors. [6]

zeitgeber German for *time-giver*. Events such as daylight, alarm clocks, city sounds, and the voices of family members that regulate or synchronize rest and activity cycles. [9]

α motor neurons Lower motor neurons, the axons of which exit the spinal cord via the ventral roots, directly responsible for contractions of skeletal muscles. [7]

γ motor neurons Efferent nerve cells in the spinal cord that innervate muscle spindles. [7]

References

CHAPTER 1

Alexander, B. K., Beyerstein, P. F., Hadaway, P. F., & Coambs, R. B. (1981). Effect of early and later colony housing on oral ingestion of morphine in rats. *Pharmacology, Biochemistry and Behavior, 15,* 571–576.

Anand, B. K., & Brobeck, J. R. (1951). Hypothalamic control of food intake in rats and cats. *Yale Journal of Biology and Medicine, 24,* 123–140.

Baker, M. (2011). Inside the minds of mice and men. *Nature, 475,* 123–128.

Bateson, P., & Laland, K. N. (2013). Tinbergen's four questions: An appreciation and an update. *Trends in Ecology & Evolution, 28,* 712–718.

Becker, M. W., Alzahabi, R., & Hopwood, C. J. (2013). Media multitasking is associated with symptoms of depression and social anxiety. *Cyberpsychology, Behavior and Social Networking, 16,* 132–135.

Bennett, E. L., Diamond, M. C., Krech, D., & Rosenzweig, M. R. (1964). Chemical and anatomical plasticity of the brain, *Science, 164,* 610–619.

Berdoy, M. (2002). *The laboratory rat: A natural history.* Film, Oxford University. Retrieved from http://www.RATLIFE.org.

Boulter, M. (2010). *Darwin's garden: Down house and the origin of species.* Berkeley, CA: Counterpoint.

Bowden, R., MacFie, T. S., Myers, S., Hellenthal, G., Nerrienet, E., Bontrop, R. E., . . . Mundy, N. I. (2012). Genomic tools for evolution and conservation in the chimpanzee: *Pan troglodytes ellioti* is a genetically distinct population. *PLoS Genetics, 8,* e1002504. doi:10.1371/journal.pgen.1002504

Bravo, J. A., Forsythe, P., Chew, M. V., Escaravage, E., Savignac, H. M., Dinan, T. G., . . . Cryan, J. F. (2011). Ingestion of Lactobacillus strain regulates emotional behavior and central GABA receptor expression in a mouse via the vagus nerve. *Proceedings of the National Academy of Sciences of the USA, 108,* 16050–16055.

Brune, M. (2007). On human self-domestication, psychiatry, and eugenics. *Philosophy, Ethics & Humanities in Medicine, 2,* 21. doi:10.1186/1747–5341–2-21

Bulmer, M. (1999). The development of Francis Galton's ideas on the mechanism of heredity. *Journal of the History of Biology, 32,* 263–292.

Castelhano-Carlos, M. J., & Baumans, V. (2009). The impact of light, noise, cage cleaning and in-house transport on welfare and stress on laboratory rats. *Laboratory Animals, 43,* 311–322.

Choi, C. Q. (2009). Humans still evolving as our brains shrink. *LiveScience.* Retrieved from http://www.livescience.com/7971-humans-evolving-brains-shrink.html

Cohen, J. (2010). The human genome, a decade later. *MIT Technology Review.* Retrieved from http://www.technologyreview.com/featuredstory/422140/the-human-genome-a-decade-later/

Dethlefsen, L., Huse, S., Sogin, M. L., & Relman, D. A. (2008). The pervasive effects of an antibiotic on the human gut microbiota, as revealed by deep 16S rRNA sequencing. *PLOS Biology, 6,* e280. doi:10.1371/jounal.pbio.0060280

Diamond, M. C. (1988). *Enriching heredity: Impact of the environment on brain development.* New York, NY: Free Press.

Diamond, M. C., Krech, D., & Rosenzweig, M. R. (1964). The effects of an enriched environment on the rat cerebral cortex. *Journal of Comparative Neurology, 123,* 111–119.

Dick, D. M., & Rose, R. J. (2002). Behavior genetics: What's new? What's next? *Current Directions in Psychological Science, 11,* 70–74.

Dobrossy, M. D., & Dunnett, S. B. (2001). The influence of environment and experience on neural grafts. *Nature Reviews Neuroscience, 2,* 871–879.

Dolan, R. J. (2008). Neuroimaging of cognition: Past, present, and future. *Cell, 60,* 496–502.

Donnay, A. (1999). On the recognition of multiple chemical sensitivity in medical literature and government policy. *International Journal of Toxicology, 18,* 383–392.

Draganski, B., Gaser, C., Busch, V., Schulerer, G., Bogdahn, U., & May, A. (2004). Changes in grey matter induced by training. *Nature, 427,* 311–312.

Draganski, B., Gaser, C., Kempermann, G., Kuhn, H. G., Winkler, J., Buchel, C., & May, A. (2006). Temporal and spatial dynamics of brain structure changes during extensive learning. *The Journal of Neuroscience, 26,* 6314–6317.

Dye, C. (2008). Health and urban living. *Science, 319,* 766–769.

Finger, S. (1994). *Origins of neuroscience.* New York, NY: Oxford University Press.

Finger, S. (2000). *Minds behind the brain.* New York, NY: Oxford University Press.

Hartig, T. (2007). Three steps to understanding restorative environments as health resources. In C. Ward-Thompson & P. Travlou (Eds.), *Open space, people space* (p. 165). New York, NY: Taylor & Francis.

Hawrylycz, M. J., Lein, E. S., Guillozet-Bongaarts, A. L., Shen, E. H., Ng, L., Miller, J. A, . . . Jones, A. R. (2012). An anatomically comprehensive atlas for the adult human brain transcriptome. *Nature, 489,* 391–399.

Hemmer, H. (1990). *Domestication: The decline of environmental appreciation.* Cambridge, UK: Cambridge University Press.

Henig, R. M. (2000). *The monk in the garden.* New York, NY: Mariner Books.

Kaufman, C., Brown, M., Tschirhart, M., Rzucidlo, A., Hyer, M., Bardi, M., & Lambert, K. (2012). *Natural elements in enriched environments enhance emotional resilience in male Long Evans rats.* Poster presented at the International Behavioral Neuroscience Society, Kona, HI.

Keynes, R. D. (2001). *Charles Darwin's beagle diary.* Cambridge, UK: Cambridge University Press.

Kulathinal, R. J. (2010). Commemorating the 20th century Darwin: Ernst Mayr's words and thoughts, five years later. *Genome, 53,* 157–159.

Kuo, F. E., & Sullivan, W. C. (2001). Aggression and violence in the inner city: Effects of environment via mental fatigue. *Environment and Behavior, 33,* 543–571.

Lalano, K. N., Sterelny, K., Odling-Smee, J., Hoppitt, W., & Uller, T. (2011). Cause and effect in biology revisited: Is Mayr's proximate–ultimate dichotomy still useful? *Science, 334*, 1512–1516.

Lambert, K. (2011). *The lab rat chronicles*. New York, NY: Perigee.

Lambert, K. G., Nelson, R. J., Jovanovic, T., & Cerda, M. (2015). Brains in the city: Neurobiological effects of urbanization. *Neuroscience and Biobehavioral Reviews, 58*, 107–122.

Lander, E. (2011). Initial impact of the sequencing of the human genome. *Nature, 470*, 197–192.

Lander, E.S., Linton, L. M., Birren, B., Nusbaum, C., Zody, M. C., Baldwin, J., . . . Szustakowki, J. (2001). Initial sequencing and analysis of the human genome. *Nature, 409*, 860–921.

Lathe, W., Williams, J., Mangan, M., & Karolchik, D. (2008). Genomic data resources: Challenges and promises. *Nature Education, 1*, 2.

Lederbogen, F., Kirsch, P., Haddad, L., Streit, F., Tost, H., Schuch, P., . . . Meyer-Lindenberg, A. (2011). City living and urban upbringing affect neural social stress processing in humans. *Nature, 474*, 498–501.

Loh, K. K., & Kanai, R. (2014). Higher media multi-tasking activity is associated with smaller gray-matter density in the anterior cingulate cortex. *PLoS One, 9*, e106698.

Luby, J. L., Barch, D. M., Belden, A., Gaffrey, M. A., Tillman, R., Babb, C., . . . Botteron, K. N. (2012). Maternal support in early childhood predicts larger hippocampal volumes at school age. *Proceedings of the National Academy of Sciences of the USA, 109*, 2854–2859.

Maddox, B. (2002). *Rosalind Franklin*. New York, NY: Perennial.

Majerus, M. E., & Mundy, N. I. (2003). Mammalian melanism: Natural selection in black and white. *Trends in Genetics, 19*, 585–588.

Mardis, E. R. (2011). A decade's perspective on DNA sequencing technology. *Nature, 470*, 198–203.

Maurin, T., Zongaro, S., & Bardoni, B. (2014). Fragile X syndrome: From molecular pathology to therapy. *Neuroscience & Biobehavioral Reviews, 46*(2), 242–255. doi:10.1016/j.neubiorev.2014.01.006

McAuliffe, K. (2011, September). If modern humans are so smart, why are our brains shrinking? *Discover Magazine*. Retrieved from http://discovermagazine.com/2010/sep/25-modern-humans-smart-why-brain-shrinking#.UYFxjsrf2dk

Mensen, A., Poryazova, R., Schwartz, S., & Khatami, R. (2014). Humor as a reward mechanism: Event-related potentials in the healthy and diseased brain. *PLoS One, 9*(1), e85978. doi:10.1371/journal.pone.0085978

Nachman, M. W, Hoekstra, H. E., & D'Agostino, S. L. (2003). The genetic basis of adaptive melanism in pocket mice. *Proceedings of the National Academy of Sciences, 100*, 5268–5273.

Narayanan, N. S., Cavanagh, J. F., Frank, M. J., & Laubach, M. (2013). Common medial frontal mechanisms of adaptive control in humans and rodents. *Nature Neuroscience, 16*, 1888–1895.

National Institutes of Health. (2012). Tay–Sachs disease. In *Genetics home reference*. Retrieved from http://ghr.nlm.nih.gov/condition/tay-sachs-disease

O'Conner, C. (2008). Developing the chromosome theory. *Chromosomes and Cytogenetics*. Retrieved from http://www.nature.com/scitable/topicpage/developing-the-chromosome-theory-164

Oishi, K., Mielke, M. M., Albert, M., Lyketsos, C. G., & Mori, S. (2011). DTI analyses and clinical applications in Alzheimer's disease. *Journal of Alzheimer's Disease, 26*, 287–296.

Ophir, E., Nass, C., & Wagner, A. D. (2009). Cognitive control in medial multitaskers. *Proceedings of the National Academy of Sciences of the USA, 106*, 15583–15587.

Ploghaus, A., Narain, C., Beckmann, C. F., Clare, S., Batick, S., Wise, R., . . . Tracey, I. (2001). Exacerbation of pain by anxiety is associated with activity in a hippocampal network. *The Journal of Neuroscience, 21*, 9896–9903.

Pollack, A. (2011). DNA sequencing caught in deluge of data. *New York Times*. Retrieved from http://www.nytimes.com.2011/12/01/business/dna-sequencing-caught-in-deluge-of-data.html

Pontzer, H., Raichlen, D. A., Wood, B. M., Mabulla, A. Z. P., Racette, S. B., & Marlowe, F. W. (2012). Hunter-gatherer energetics and human obesity. *PLoS ONE, 7*, e40503. doi:10.1371/journal.pone.0040503

Public Broadcasting Service. (2001). *Cracking the code of life*. Retrieved from http://www.pbs.org/wgbh/nova/body/cracking-the-code-of-life.html

Reardon, S. (2011). The secrets of bear hibernation. *Science NOW*. Retrieved from http://news.sciencemag.org/sciencenow/2011/02/the-secrets-of-bear-hibernation.html

Rosenbloom, M., Sullivan, E. V., & Pfefferbaum, A. (2003).Using magnetic resonance imaging and diffusion tensor imaging to assess brain damage in alcoholics. *Alcohol Research and Health, 27*, 146–152.

Ruoso, C. (2011, February). The monkey who went into the cold. *National Geographic*, 126–137.

Schnell, M. J., McGettigan, J. P., Wirblich, C., & Papaneri, A. (2010). The cell biology of rabies: Using stealth to reach the brain. *Nature Reviews Microbiology, 8*, 51–61.

Sillaber, I., Rammes, G., Zimmermann, S., Mahal, B., Zieglgansberger, W., Wurst, W., . . . Spanagel, R. (2002). Enhanced and delayed stress-induced alcohol drinking in mice lacking functional CRH1 Receptors. *Science, 296*, 931–933.

Silverman, J. L., Yang, M., Lord, C., & Crawley, J. N. (2010). Behavioral phenotyping assays for mouse models of autism. *Nature Reviews Neuroscience, 11*, 490–502.

Stam, C. J. (2010). Use of magnetoencephalography (MEG) to study functional brain networks in neurodegenerative disorders. *Journal of the Neurological Sciences, 289*, 128–134.

Suls, J., & Wan, K. C. (1989). Effects of sensory and procedural information on coping with stressful medical procedures and pain: A meta-analysis. *Journal of Consulting and Clinical Psychology, 57*, 372–379.

Sur, S., & Sinha, V. K. (2009). Event-related potential: An overview. *Industrial Psychiatry Journal, 18*, 70–73.

Taylor, A. F., Kuo, F. E., & Sullivan, W. C. (2002). Views of nature and self-discipline: Evidence from inner city children. *Journal of Environmental Psychology, 22*, 49–63.

Venter, J. C., Adams, M. D., Myers, E. W., Li, P. W., Mural, R. J., Sutton, G. G., . . . Zhu, X. (2001). The sequence of the human genome. *Science, 291*, 1304–1351.

Volkow, N. D., Wang, G. J., Franceschi, D., Fowler, J. S., Thanos, P. K., Maynard, L., . . . Li, T. K. (2006). Low doses of alcohol substantially decrease glucose metabolism in the human brain. *Neuroimage, 29*, 295–301.

Wilmer, W. H. (1921). Effects of carbon monoxide upon the eye. *American Journal of Ophthalmology, 73*–90.

Zeveloff, S. I. (2002). *Raccoons: A natural history*. Washington, DC: Smithsonian Institution Press.

CHAPTER 2

Ader, R., & Cohen, N. (1975). Behaviorally conditioned immunosuppression. *Psychosomatic Medicine, 37*, 333–340.

Ader, R., Cohen, N., & Felten, D. (1995). Psychoneuroimmunology: Interactions between the nervous system and the immune system. *The Lancet, 345*, 99–103.

Adolphs, R., Tranel, D., Damasio, H., & Damasio, A. R. (1995). Fear and the human amygdala. *The Journal of Neuroscience, 15,* 5879–5891.

Atwell, D., Buchan, A. M., Charpak, S., Lauritzen, M., MacVicar, B. A., & Newmen, E. A. (2010). Glial and neuronal control of blood flow. *Nature, 468,* 232–243.

Blaine, D. (2009, October). *David Blaine: How I held my breath for 17 minutes* [Video file]. Retrieved from http://www.ted.com/speakers/david_blaine.html

Bullock, T. H., Bennett, M. V. L., Johnston, D., Josephson, R., Marder, E., & Fields, R. D. (2005). The neuron doctrine, redux. *Science, 310,* 791–793.

Cannon, W. B. (1915). *Body changes in pain, hunger, fear and rage.* New York, NY: Appleton.

Churchland, P. (2011). *Braintrust.* Princeton, NJ: Princeton University Press.

Craig, A. D. (2010a). The sentient self. *Brain Structure and Function, 214,* 563–577.

Craig, A. D. (2010b). Once an island, now the focus of attention. *Brain Structure and Function, 214,* 395–396.

Critchley, H. G., Wiens, S., Rotshtein, P., Ohman, A., & Dolan, R. J. (2004). Neural systems supporting interoceptive awareness. *Nature Neuroscience, 7,* 189–195.

Davalos, D., Grutzendler, J., Yang, G., Kim, J. V., Zuo, Y., Jung, S., . . . Gan, Wen-Biao. (2005). ATP mediates rapid microglial response to local brain injury in vivo. *Nature Neuroscience, 8,* 752–758.

deCharms, R., C., Maeda, F., Glover, G. H., Ludlow, D., Pauly, J. M., Soneji, D., . . . Mackey, S. C. (2005). Control over brain activation and pain learned by using real-time functional MRI. *Proceedings of the National Academy of Sciences of the USA, 102,* 18626–18631.

Dworkin, B. R., & Miller, N. E. (1986). Failure to replicate visceral learning in the acute curarized rat preparation. *Behavioral Neuroscience, 100,* 299–314.

Fiala, J. C., and Harris, K. M. (1999). Dendrite structure. In G. Stuart, N. Spruston, & M. Hausser (Eds.), *Dendrites* (Chap. 1, pp. 1–28). New York, NY: Oxford University Press.

Fields, R. D. (2004, April). The other half of the brain. *Scientific American,* 54–61.

Fields, R. D. (2009). *The other brain.* New York, NY: Simon & Schuster.

Fink, G. (2009). *Stress science: Neuroendocrinology.* New York, NY: Academic Press.

Fischl, B., & Dale, A. M. (2000). Measuring the thickness of the human cerebral cortex from magnetic resonance images. *Proceedings of the National Academy of Sciences of the USA, 97,* 11050–11055.

Foundas, A. L., Leonard, C. M., Gilmore, R., Fennell, E., & Heilman, K. M. (1994). Planum temporale asymmetry and language dominance. *Neuropsychologia, 32,* 1225–1231.

Fox, P. T., Ingham, R. J., Ingham, J. C., Zamarripa, F., Xiong, J. H., & Lancaster, J. L. (2000). Brain correlates of stuttering and syllable production: A PET performance-correlation analysis. *Brain, 123,* 1985–2004.

Gage, F. H., & van Praag, H. (2002) Neurogenesis in adult brain. In K. L. Davis, J. T. Charney, J. T. Coyle, & C. Nemeroff (Eds.), *Neuropsychopharmacology: The fifth generation of progress.* Brentwood, TN: American College of Neuropsychopharmacology.

Gazzaniga, M. S., Bogen, J. E., & Sperry, R. W. (1962). Dyspraxia following division of the cerebral hemispheres. *Proceedings of the National Academy of Sciences of the USA, 48,* 1765–1769.

Gazzaniga, M. S., Ivry, R. B., & Mangun, G. R. (1998). *Cognitive neuroscience.* New York, NY: Norton.

Gazzaniga, M. S., & Sperry, R. W. (1967). Language after section of the cerebral commissures. *Brain, 90,* 131–148.

Gould, E., Cameron, H. A., Daniels, D. C., Woolley, C. S., & McEwen, B. S. (1992). Adrenal hormones suppress cell division in the adult rat dentate gyrus. *Journal of Neuroscience, 12,* 3642–3650.

Greve, D. N., Van der Haegen, L., Cai, Q., Stufflebeam, S., Sabuncu, M. R., Fischl, B., & Brysbaert, M. (2013). A surface-based analysis of language lateralization and cortical asymmetry. *Journal of Cognitive Neuroscience, 25,* 1477–1492.

Gruber, P., & Gould, D. J. (2010). The red nucleus: Past, present, and future. *Neuroanatomy, 9,* 1–3.

Haanpaa, M., Laippala, P., & Nurmikko, T. (1999). Pain and somatosensory dysfunction in acute herpes zoster. *Clinical Journal of Pain, 15,* 78–84.

Halpern, M. E., Gunturkun, O., Hopkins, W. D., & Rogers, L. J. (2005). Lateralization of the vertebrate brain: Taking the side of model systems. *The Journal of Neuroscience, 25,* 10351–10357.

Hamilton, N. B., & Attwell, D. (2010). Do astrocytes really exocytose neurotransmitters? *Nature Reviews Neuroscience, 11,* 227–238.

Herculano-Houzel, S. (2009). The human brain in numbers: A linearly scaled-up primate brain. *Frontiers in Human Neuroscience, 3.* doi:10.3389/neuro.09.031.2009

Herculano-Houzel, S. (2010). Coordinated scaling of cortical and cerebellar numbers of neurons. *Frontiers in Neuroanatomy, 4.* doi:10.3389/nana.2010.00012

Herculano-Houzel, S., Collins, C. E., Wong, P., Kaas, J. H., & Lent, R. (2008). The basic nonuniformity of the cerebral cortex. *Proceedings of the National Academy of Sciences of the USA, 26,* 12593–8.

Herculano-Houzel, S., Collins, C. E., Wong, P., & Kaas, J. H. (2007). Cellular scaling rules for primate brains. *Proceedings of the National Academy of Sciences of the USA, 104,* 3562–3567.

Herculano-Houzel, S., & Lent, R. (2005). Isotropic fractionator: A simple, rapid method for the quantification of total cell and neuron numbers in the brain. *Journal of Neuroscience, 25,* 2518–2521.

Hilgetag, C. C., & Barbas, H. (2009). Are there ten times more glia than neurons in the brain? *Brain Structure and Function, 213,* 365–366.

Jacobs, G. D. (2001). The physiology of mind–body interactions: The stress response and the relaxation response. *The Journal of Alternative and Complementary Medicine, 7,* 83–92.

Joels, M., & Baram, T. Z. (2009). The neuro-symphony of stress. *Nature Reviews, 10,* 459–466.

Kim, S. U., & de Vellis, J. (2005). Microglia in health and disease. *Journal of Neuroscience Research, 81,* 302–313.

Kocsis, J. D., & Waxman, S. G. (2007). Schwann cells and their precursors for repair of central nervous system myelin. *Brain, 130,* 1978–1980.

Lehrer, J. (2009). Neuroscience: Making connections. *Nature, 457,* 524–527. doi:10.1038/457524a

Li, L., Lu, J., Tay, S. S. W., Moochhala, S. M., & He, B. P. (2007). The function of microglia, either neuroprotection or neurotoxicity, is determined by the equilibrium among factors released from activated microglia *in vitro. Brain Research, 1159,* 8–17.

Lichtman, J. W., Livet, J., & Sanes, J. R. (2008). A technicolor approach to the connectome. *Nature Reviews, 9,* 417–422.

Lichtman, J. W., & Smith, S. J. (2008). Seeing circuits assemble. *Neuron, 60,* 441–445;

MacLean, P. (1990). *The triune brain in evolution.* New York, NY: Plenum Press.

MacMillan, M. (2002). *An odd kind of fame.* Cambridge, MA: Bradford Books/MIT Press.

Macmillan, M., & Lena, M. L. (2010). Rehabilitating Phineas Gage. *Neuropsychological Rehabilitation, 20,* 641–658.

Mazzarello, P. (2010). *Golgi*. New York, NY: Oxford University Press.

McEwen, B. S. (2009). Stress: Homeostasis, rheostasis, allostasis and allostatic load. In G. Fink (Ed.), *Stress science: Neuroendocrinology* (pp. 10–14). New York, NY: Academic Press.

Miller, M. B., Sinnott-Armstrong, W., Young, L., King, D., Paggi, A., Fabri, M., . . . Gazzaniga, M. S. (2010). Abnormal moral reasoning in complete and partial callosotomy patients. *Neuropsychologia, 48*, 2215–2220.

Miller, N. E. (1969). Learning of visceral and glandular responses. *Science, 163*, 434–445.

Miller, N. E. (1978). Biofeedback and visceral learning. *Annual Review of Psychology, 29*, 373–404.

Nedergaard, M. (1994). Direct signaling from astrocytes to neurons in cultures of mammalian brain cells. *Science, 263*, 1768–1771.

Neumann, S., Braz, J. M., Skinner, K., Llewellyn-Smith, I. J., & Basbaum, A. I. (2008). Innocuous, not noxious, input activity PKC gamma interneurons of the spinal dorsal horn via myelinated afferent fibers. *Journal of Neuroscience, 28*, 7936–44.

Nolte, J. (2002). *The human brain*. St. Louis, MO: Mosby.

Olave, M. J., Puri, N., Kerr, R., & Maxwell, D. J. (2002). Myelinated and unmyelinated primary afferent axons form contacts with cholinergic interneurons in the spinal dorsal horn. *Experimental Brain Research, 145*, 448–456.

Ousman, S. S., & Kubes, P. (2012). Immune surveillance in the central nervous system. *Nature Neuroscience, 8*, 1096–1101.

Popovich, P. G., & Longbrake, E. E. (2008). Can the immune system be harnessed to repair the CNS? *Nature Reviews Neuroscience, 9*, 481–493.

Qian, L., & Flood, P. M. (2008). Microglial cells and Parkinson's disease. *Immunological Research, 41*, 155–164.

Reese, R. M., Bhatnagar, S., & Young, B. A. (2009). Evolutionary origins and functions of the stress response. In G. Fink (Ed.), *Stress science: Neuroendocrinology*. New York, NY: Academic Press.

Sapolsky, R. M. (2001). Depression, antidepressants, and the shrinking hippocampus. *Proceedings of the National Academy of Sciences of the USA, 98*, 12320–12322.

Sapolsky, R. M. (2010). *Why zebras don't get ulcers* (3rd ed.). New York, NY: Holt.

Siegel, G. J., Agranoff, B. W., Albers, R. W., Fischer, S. K., & Uhler, M. D. (Eds.). (1999). *Basic neurochemistry: Molecular, cellular and medical aspects* (6th ed.). Philadelphia, PA: Lippincott–Raven.

Sterling, P. (2004). "Chapter 1. Principles of Allostasis." In J. Schulkin (Ed.), *Allostasis, homeostasis, and the costs of physiological adaptation*. New York, NY: Cambridge University Press.

Stranahan, A. M., Khalil, D., & Gould, E. (2006). Social isolation delays the positive effects of running on adult neurogenesis. *Nature Neuroscience, 9*, 526–533.

Strick, P. L., Dum, R. P., & Fiez, J. A. (2009). Cerebellum and nonmotor function. *Annual Review of Neuroscience, 32*, 413–434.

Strebhardt, K., & Ullrich, A. (2008). Paul Ehrlich's magic bullet concept: 100 years of progress. *Nature Reviews Cancer, 8*, 473–480.

Strittmatter, S. (2010). Spinal cord regeneration: Ready, set, nogo. *Eukaryon, 6*, 55–60.

Tien, R. D., Felsberg, G. J., Krishnan, R., & Heinz, E. R. (1994). MR imaging of diseases of the limbic system. *American Journal of Roentgenology, 163*, 657–665.

Tierney, J. (2008). This time, he'll be left breathless. *The New York Times*. Retrieved from http://www.nytimes.com/2008/04/22/science/22tier.html

Toy, D., & Namgung, U. (2013). Role of glial cells in axonal regeneration. *Experimental Neurobiology, 22*, 68–76.

Twomey, S. (2010). Phineas Gage: Neuroscience's most famous patient. *Smithsonian Magazine*. Retrieved from http://www.smithsonianmag.com/history-archaeology/Phineas-Gage-Neurosciences-Most-Famous-Patient.html.

Van Horn, J. D., Irimia, A., Torgerson, C. M., Chambers, M. C., Kikinis, R., & Toga, A. W. (2012). Mapping connectivity damage in the case of Phineas Gage. *PLoS ONE, 7*, e37454.

Van Praag, H., Christie, B. R., Sejnowski, T. J., & Gage, F. H. (1999). Running enhances neurogenesis, learning and long-germ potentiation in mice. *Proceedings of the National Academy of Sciences of the USA, 96*, 13427–13431.

Wehrlin, J. P., Zuest, P., Hallon, J., & Marti, B. (2006). Live hightrain low for 24 days increases hemoglobin mass and red cell volume in elite endurance athletes. *Journal of Applied Physiology, 100*, 1938–1945.

Wolman, D. (2012). A tale of two halves. *Nature, 483*, 260–263.

CHAPTER 3

Abela, A. R., & Chudasama, Y. (2013). Dissociable contributors of the ventral hippocampus and orbitofrontal context to decision-making with a delayed or uncertain outcome. *European Journal of Neuroscience, 37*, 640–647.

Adrian, R. H. (1975). Conduction velocity and gating current in the squid giant axon. *Proceedings of the Royal Society of London, Biological Sciences, 189*, 81–86.

Alexander, W. H., & Brown, J. W. (2011). Medial prefrontal cortex as an action-outcome predictor. *Nature Neuroscience Reviews, 14*, 1338–1344.

Allman, J. M., Tetreault, N. A., Hakeem, A. Y., Manaye, K. F., Semendeferi, K., Erwin, J. M., . . . Hof, P. (2010). The von Economo neurons in frontoinsular and anterior cingulated cortex in great apes and humans. *Brain Structure and Function, 214*, 495–517.

Allman, J. M., Tetreault, N. A., Hakeem, A. Y., Manaye, K. F., Semendeferi, K., Erwin, J. M., . . . Hof, P. R. (2011). The von Economo neurons in fronto-insular and anterior-cingulate cortex. *Annals of the New York Academy of Sciences, 1225*, 59–71.

Allman, J. M., Watson, K. K., Tetreault, N. A., & Hakeem, A. Y. (2005). Intuition and autism: A possible role for Von Economo neurons. *Trends in Cognitive Sciences, 9*, 367–373.

Araque, A., Parpura, V., Sanzgiri, R. P., & Haydon, P. G. (1999). Triparitite synapses: Glia, the unacknowledged partner. *Trends in Neuroscience, 22*, 208–215.

Assaf, Y., Blumenfeld-Katzir, J., Yovel, Y., & Basser, P. J. (2008). AxCaliber: A method for measuring axon diameter distribution from diffusion MRI. *Magnetic Resonance in Medicine, 59*, 1347–1354.

Aston, C., Jiang, L., & Sokolov, B. P. (2005). Transcriptional profiling reveals evidence for signaling and oligodendroglial abnormalities in the temporal cortex from patients with major depressive disorder. *Molecular Psychiatry, 10*, 309–322.

Aziz-Zadeh, L., Wilson, S. M., Rizzolatti, G., & Iacoboni, M. (2006). Congruent embodied representations for visually presented actions and linguistic phrases describing actions. *Current Biology, 16*, 1818–1823.

Barker, A. T., Jalinous, R., & Freeston, I. L. (1985). Non-invasive magnetic stimulation of human motor cortex. *Lancet, 1*, 1106–1107.

Barres, B. A. (2008). The mystery and magic of glia: A perspective on their roles in health and disease. *Neuron, 60*, 430–440.

Bechara, A., Damasio, H., Tranel, D., & Damasio, A. R. (1997). Deciding advantageously before knowing the advantageous strategy. *Science, 275*, 1293–1295.

Bush, T. G., Puvanchandra, N., Homer, C. H., Plito, A., Ostenfield, T., Svendsen, C. N . . . Sofroniew, M. V. (1999). Leukocyte infiltration, neuronal degeneration, and neurite outgrowth after ablation of scar-forming, reactive astrocytes in adult transgenic mice. *Neuron, 23,* 297–308.

Butti, C., Sherwood, C. C., Hakeem, A. Y., Allman, J. M., & Hof, P. R. (2009). Total number and volume of von Economo neurons in the cerebral cortex of cetaceans. *Journal of Comparative Neurology, 515,* 243–259.

Cahoy, J. D., Emery, B., Kaushal, A., Foo, L. C., Zamanian, J. L., Christopherson, K. S., . . . Barres, B. A. (2008). A transcriptome database for astrocytes, neurons, and oligodendrocytes: A new resource for understanding brain development and function. *Journal of Neuroscience, 28,* 264–278.

Castren, E. (2005). Is mood chemistry? *Nature Reviews Neuroscience, 6,* 241–246.

Chouinard, P. A., & Paus, T. (2010). What have we learned from "perturbing" the human cortical motor system with transcranial magnetic stimulation? *Frontiers in Human Neuroscience, 4.* doi:10.3389/fnhum.2010.00173.

Christopherson, K. S., Ullian, E. M., Stokes, C. C., Mullowney, C. E., Hell, J. W., Agah, A., Lawler, J., . . . Barres, B. A. (2005). Thrombospondins are astrocyte-secreted proteins that promote CNS synaptogenesis. *Cell, 120,* 421–433.

Colbert, C. M., & Johnston, D. (1996). Axonal action-potential initiation and Na+ channel densities in the soma and axon initial segment of subicular pyramidal neurons. *The Journal of Neuroscience, 16,* 6676–6686.

Craig, M. T., & McBain, C. J. (2014). The emerging role of GABAB receptors as regulators of network dynamics: Fast actions from a "slow" receptor? *Current Opinion in Neurobiology, 26,* 15–21.

Critchley, H. D., Mathias, C., & Dolan, R. (2001). Neural activity in the human brain relating to uncertainty and arousal during anticipation. *Neuron, 29,* 537–545.

Dapretto, M., Davies, M. S., Pfeifer, J. H., Scott, A. A., Sigman, M., Bookheimer, S. Y., & Iacoboni, M. (2006). Understanding emotions in others: Mirror neuron dysfunction in children with autism spectrum disorders. *Nature Neuroscience, 9,* 28–30.

D'Ausilio, A., Pulvermuller, F., Salmas, P., Buflari, I., Begliomini, C., & Fadiga, L. (2009). The motor somatotopy of speech perception. *Current Biology, 19,* 381–385.

Dinstein, I., Thomas, C., Behrmann, M., & Heeger, D. J. (2008). A mirror up to nature. *Current Biology, 18,* 13–18.

Di Pellagrino, G., Fadiga, L., Fogassi, L., Gallese, V. & Rizzolatti, G. (1992). Understanding motor events: A neurophysiological study. *Experimental Brain Research, 91,* 176–180.

Dzhala, V. I., Talos, D. M., Sdrulla, D. A., Brumback, A. C., Mathews, G. C., Benke, T. A., Delpire, E., Jensen, F. E., Staley, K. J. (2005). NKCC1 transporter facilitates seizures in the developing brain. *Nature Medicine, 11,* 1205–13.

Edgar, N., & Sibille, E. (2012). A putative functional role for oligodendrocytes in mood regulation. *Translational Psychiatry,* e109. doi:10.1038/tp.2012.34

Erecinska, M., & Dagani, F. (1990). Relationships between the neuronal socium/potassium pump and energy metabolism. *Journal of General Physiology, 95,* 591–616.

Evrard, H. C., Forro, T., & Logothetis, N. K. (2012). Von Economo neurons in the anterior insula of the macaque monkey. *Neuron, 74,* 482–489.

Falck-Ytter, T., Gredeback, G., & von Hofsten, C. (2006). Infants predict other people's action goals, *Nature Neuroscience, 9,* 878–79.

Ferrari, P. F., Paukner, A., Ionica, C., & Suomi, S. J. (2009). Reciprocal face-to-face communication between rhesus macaque mothers and their newborn infants. *Current Biology, 19,* 1768–1772.

Ferrari, P. F., Visalberghi, E., Paukner, A., Fogassi, L., Ruggireo, A., & Suomi, S. J. (2006). Neonatal imitation in rhesus macaques. *PLoS Biology, 4,* 1501–1508.

Finger, S. (2000). *Minds behind the brain.* New York, NY: Oxford.

Fogassi, L., Gallese, V., & Rizzolatti, G. (1992), Understanding motor events: A neurophysiological study. *Experimental Brain Research, 9,* 176–180.

Foxx, R. M. (2008). Applied behavior analysis treatment of autism: The state of the art. *Child and Adolescent Psychopath Clinics of North America, 17,* 821–836.

Funatsuka, M., Fujita, M., Shirakawa, S., Oguni, H., & Osawa, M. (2001). Study on photo-pattern sensitivity in patients with electronic screen game-induced seizures (ESGS): Effects of spatial resolution, brightness, and pattern movement. *Epilepsia, 42,* 1185–1197.

Gadsby, D. C. (2009). Ion channels vs. ion pumps: The principal difference, in principle. *Nature Reviews Molecular Cell Biology, 10,* 344–352.

Gallese, V., Gernsbacher, M. A., Hayes, C., Hickock, G., & Iacoboni, M. (2011). Mirror neuron forum. *Perspectives on Psychological Science, 6,* 369–407.

Gazzola, V., Aziz-Zadeh, L., & Keysers, C. (2006). Empathy and the somatotopic auditory mirror system in humans. *Current Biology, 16,* 1824–1829.

Hakeem, A. Y., Sherwood, C. C., Bonar, C. J., Butti, C., Hof, P. R., & Allman, J. M. (2009). Von Economo neurons in the elephant brain. *The Anatomical Record, 292,* 242–248.

Heiser, M., Iacoboni, M., Maeda, F., Marcus, J., & Mazziotta, J. C. (2003). The essential role of Broca's area in imitation. *European Journal of Neuroscience, 17,* 1123–1128.

Heyes, C. M. (2010). Where do mirror neurons come from? *Neuroscience and Biobehavioral Reviews, 34,* 575–583.

Holtmaat, A., & Svoboda, K. (2009). Experience-dependent structural synaptic plasticity in the mammalian brain. *Nature Reviews Neuroscience, 10,* 647–658.

Hursh, J. B. (1939). The properties of growing nerve fibers. *American Journal of Physiology, 127,* 140–153.

Hussain, R., El-Etr, M., Gaci, O., Jennifer, R., Macklin, W. B., Kumar, N., . . . Goumari, A. M. (2011). Progesterone and nestorone facilitate axon remyelination: A role for progesterone receptors. *Endocrinology, 152,* 3820–3831.

Hyman, R. (1977). Cold reading: How to convince strangers that you know all about them. In J. Mickell, B. Karr, & T. Genoni (Eds.), *The outer edge: Classic investigations of the paranormal.* New York, NY: CSICOP.

Iacoboni, M. (2005). Understanding others: Imitation, language, empathy. In S. Hurley & N. Chater (Eds.), *Perspectives on imitation: From cognitive neuroscience to social science* (pp. 77–100). Cambridge, MA: MIT Press.

Iacoboni, M. (2009a). Imitation, empathy, and mirror neurons. *Annual Review of Psychology, 60,* 653–670.

Iacoboni, M. (2009b). *Mirroring people.* New York, NY: Picador.

Iacoboni, M., & Dapretto, M. (2006). The mirror neuron system and the consequences of its dysfunction. *Nature Neuroscience Reviews, 7,* 942–951.

Ibegbu, A. O., Umana, U. E., Hamman, W. O., & Adamu, A. S. (2014). Von Economo neurons: A review of the anatomy and functions. *Austin Journal of Anatomy, 1,* 1026–1030.

Insel, T. R., & Young, L. J. (2001). The neurobiology of attachment. *Nature Reviews Neuroscience, 2,* 129–136.

Kinsley, C. H., Trainer, R., Stafisso-Sandoz, G., Quadros, P., Marcus, L. K., Hearon, C., Meyer, E. A., . . . Lambert, K. G. (2006). Motherhood and the hormones of pregnancy modify concentrations of hippocampal neuronal dendritic spines. *Hormones and Behavior, 49*(2), 131–142.

Kirsch, I. (2010). *The emperor's new drugs: Exploding the antidepressant myth*. New York, NY: Basic Books.

Klin, A., Jones, W., Schultz, R., Volkmar, F., & Cohen, D. (2002). Visual fixation patterns during viewing of naturalistic social situations as predictors of social competence in individuals with autism. *Archives of General Psychiatry, 59*, 809–816.

Kocsis, R. N., Hayes, A. F., & Irwin, H. J. (2002). Investigative experience and accuracy in psychological profiling of a violent crime. *Journal of Interpersonal Violence, 17*, 811–823.

Lo, W. K., & Reese, T. S. (1993). Multiple structural types of gap junctions in mouse lens. *Journal of Cell Science, 106*, 227–235.

Loewi, O. (1960). An autobiographical sketch. In: *Perspectives in Biology and Medicine, 3*–25.

MacDermott, A. B., Role, L. W., & Siegelbaum, S. A. (1999). Presynaptic ionotropic receptors and the control of transmitter release. *Annual Review of Neuroscience, 22*, 443–485.

Marin-Burgin, A., Eisenhart, F. J., Baca, S. M., Kristan, W. B., & French, K. A. (2005). Sequential development of electrical and chemical synaptic connections generates a specific behavioral circuit in the leech. *The Journal of Neuroscience, 25*, 2478–2489.

Mauch, D. H., Nagler, K., Schumacher, S., Goritz, C., Muller, E. C., Otto, A., & Pfrieger, F. W. (2001). CNS synaptogenesis promoted by glia-derived cholesterol. *Science, 294*, 1354–1357.

McCormick, C. M., Smythe, J. W., Sharma, S., & Meaney, M. (1995). Sex-specific effects of prenatal stress on hypothalamic–pituitary–adrenal responses to stress and brain glucocorticoid receptor density in adult rats. *Developmental Brain Research, 84*, 55–61.

McCormick, D. A. (1999). Membrane potential and action potential. In M. J. Zigmond, F. E. Bloom, S. C. Landis, J. L. Roberts, & L. R. Squire (Eds.), *Fundamental Neuroscience* (pp. 129–154). New York, NY: Academic Press.

McKittrick, C., Magarinos, A., Blanchard, D. C., Blanchard, R. J., McEwen, B., & Sakai, R. (2000). Chronic social stress reduces dendritic arbors in CA3 of hippocampus and decreases binding to serotonin transporter sites. *Synapse, 36*, 85–94.

Mukamel, R., Ekstrom, A. D., Kaplan, J., Iacoboni, M., & Fried, I. (2010). Single neuron responses in humans during execution and observation of actions. *Current Biology, 20*, 750–756.

Mychasiuk, R., Gibb, R., & Kolb, B. (2011). Prenatal bystander stress induces neuroanatomical changes in the prefrontal cortex and hippocampus of developing rat offspring. *Brain Research, 1412*, 55–62. doi:10.1016/j.brainres.2011.07.023

Oberman, L. M., McCleery, J. P., Hubbard, E. M., Bernier, R., Wiersema, J. R., Raymakers, R., & Pineda, J. A. (2013). Developmental changes in mu suppression to observed and executed actions in autism spectrum disorders. *Social Cognitive and Affective Neuroscience, 8*, 300–304.

Oberman, L. M., & Ramachandran, V. S. (2007). The stimulating social mind: The role of the mirror neuron system and simulation in the social and communicative deficits of autism spectrum disorders. *Psychological Bulletin, 133*, 310–327.

Pascual-Leone, A., Bartres-Faz, D., & Keenan, J. P. (1999). Transcranial magnetic stimulation: Studying the brain–behavior relationship by induction of "virtual lesions." *Philosophical Transactions of the Royal Society of London B: Biological Sciences, 354*, 1229–1238.

Paukner, A., Ferrari, P. F., & Suomi, S. J. (2011). Delayed imitation of lipsmacking gestures by infant rhesus macaques (*Maccaca mulatta*). *PLoS ONE*, e28848. doi:10.1371/journal.pone.0028848

Penfield, W., & Erikson, T. C. (1941). *Epilepsy and cerebral localization*. Baltimore, MD: Thomas.

Pereda, A. E. (2014). Electrical synapses and their functional interactions with chemical synapses. *Nature Reviews Neuroscience, 15*, 250–263.

Pereda, A., E., Curtis, S., Hoge, G., Cachope, R., Flores, C. E., & Rash, J. E. (2013). Gap junction mediated electrical transmission: Regulatory mechanisms and plasticity. *Biochimica et Biophysica Acta, 1828*, 134–146.

Perkins, T., Stokes, M., McGillivray, J., & Bittar, R. (2010). Mirror neuron dysfunction in autism spectrum disorders. *Journal of Clinical Neuroscience, 17*, 1239–1243.

Pfrieger, F.W., & Barres, B. A. (1997). Synaptic efficacy enhanced by glial cells in vitro. *Science, 277*, 1684–1687.

Radley, J. J., & Sawchenko, P. E. (2011). A common substrate for prefrontal and hippocampal inhibition of the neuroendocrine stress responses. *Journal of Neuroscience, 31*, 9683–9695.

Ragsdale, D. S., McPhee, J. C., Scheuer, T., & Catterall, W. A. (1994). Molecular determinants of state-dependent block of Na+ channels by local anesthetics. *Science, 265*, 1724–1728.

Ramachandran, V. S., & Seckel, E. L. (2011). Synchronized dance therapy to stimulate mirror neurons in autism. *Medical Hypotheses/Correspondence, 76*, 144–151.

Rapport, R. (2005). *Nerve endings: The discovery of the synapse*. New York, NY: Norton.

Rizzolatti, G., & Craighero, L. (2004). The mirror-neuron system. *Annual Review of Neuroscience, 27*, 169–192.

Rosenthal, J. J. C., & Bezanilla, F. (2002). A comparison of propagated action potentials from tropical and temperate squid axons: Different durations and conduction velocities correlate with ionic conductance levels. *The Journal of Experimental Biology, 205*, 1819–1830.

Santos, M., Uppal, N., Butti, C., Wicinski, B., Schmeidler, J., Giannakopoulos, P., . . . Hof, P. R. (2011). Von Economo neurons in autism: A stereologic study of the frontoinsular cortex in children. *Brain Research, 1380*, 206–217.

Scharfman, H. E. (2007). The neurobiology of epilepsy. *Current Neurological Neuroscience Reports, 7*, 348–354.

Shepherd, M. S. (1991). *Foundations of the neuron doctrine*. New York, NY: Oxford University Press.

Snook, B., Cullen, R. M., Bennell, C., Taylor, P. J., & Gendreau, P. (2008). Profiling illusion: What's behind the smoke and mirrors? *Criminal Justice and Behavior, 35*, 1257–1276.

Southgate, V., Johnson, M. H., Osborne, T., & Csibra, G. (2009). Predictive motor activation during activation observation in human infants. *Biology Letters, 5*, 769–772.

Suomi, S. (2011). *Risk, resilience, and gene environment interplay in primates*. Keynote address delivered at annual meeting of International Behavioral Neuroscience Society meeting, May 29, 2011, Steamboat Springs, Colorado.

Tucker, G. J. (2005). Seizures. In J. M. Silver, T. W. McAllister, & S. C. Yudofsky (Eds.), *Textbook of traumatic brain injury*. Washington, DC: American Psychiatric Press.

Turella, L., Pierno, A. C., Tubaldi, F., & Castiello, U. (2008). Mirror neurons in humans: Consisting or confounding evidence? *Brain & Language 108*, 10–21.

Turnbull, O. H., Bowan, C. H., Shanker, S., & Davies, J. L. (2014). Emotion-based learning: Insights from the Iowa Gambling Task. *Frontiers in Psychology, 5*, 162. doi:10.3389/fpsyq.2014.00162

Valenstein, E. S. (2005). *The war of the soups and the sparks.* New York, NY: Columbia University Press.

Von Economo, C., & Koskinas, G. (1925). *Die Cytoarchitectonik der Hirnrinde des erwachsenen Menschen.* Berlin, Germany: Springer.

Waxman, S. G., Kocsis, J. D., & Stys, P. K. (1995). *The axon: Structure, function and pathophysiology.* New York, NY: Oxford University Press.

Weinstein, D. E. (1999). Review: The role of Schwann cells in neural regeneration. *Neuroscientist, 5,* 208–216.

Williams, J. H., Whiten, A., Suddendorf, T., & Perrett, D. I. (2001). Imitation, mirror neurons and autism. *Neuroscience and Biobehavioral Reviews, 25,* 287–295.

CHAPTER 4

Amitai, N., & Markou, A. (2009). Chronic nicotine improves cognitive performance in a test of attention but does not attenuate cognitive disruption induced by repeated phencyclidine administration. *Psychopharmacology, 202,* 275–286.

Anderson, B.M., Rizzo, M., Block, R.I., Pearlson, G.D., & O'Leary, D.S. (2010). Sex differences in the effects of marijuana on simulated driving performance. *Journal of Psychoactive Drugs, 42,* 19–30.

Anton, R. E. (1999). What is craving? Models and implications for treatment. *Alcohol Research & Health, 23*(3), 165–173.

Arkkila, P. E. (2006). Thromboangiitis obliterans (Beurger's disease). *Orphanet Journal of Rare Diseases, 1,* 14; doi:10.1186/1750-1172-1-14

Artinian, L., Tornieri, K., Zhong, L., Baro, D., & Rehder, V. (2010). Nitric oxide acts as a volume transmitter to modulate electrical properties of spontaneously firing neurons via apamin-sensitive potassium channels. *The Journal of Neuroscience, 30,* 1699–1711.

Atkins, K., Burks, T., Swann, A. C., & Dafny, N. (2009). MDMA (ecstasy) modulates locomotor and prefrontal cortex sensory evoked activity. *Brain Research, 1302,* 175–182.

Bachhuber, M. A., Saloner, B., Cunningham, C. O., & Barry, C. L. (2014). Medical cannabis laws and opioid analgesic overdose mortality in the United States, 1999–2010. *JAMA, 174,* 1668–1637.

Barr, A. M., & Phillips, A. G. (1999). Withdrawal following repeated exposure to d-amphetamine decreases responding for a sucrose solution as measured by a progressive ratio schedule of reinforcement. *Psychopharmacology, 141,* 99–106,

Basavarajappa, B. S. (2007). Neuropharmacology of the endocannabinoid signaling system-molecular mechanisms, biological actions and synaptic plasticity. *Current Neuropharmacology, 5,* 81–97.

Berman, S., O'Neill, J., Fears, S., Bartzokis, G., & London, E. D. (2008). Abuse of amphetamines and structural abnormalities in the brain. *Annals of the New York Academy of Sciences, 1141,* 195–220.

Berman, S. M., Kuczenski, R., McCracken, J. T., & London, E. D. (2009). Potential adverse effects of amphetamine treatment on brain and behavior: A review. *Molecular Psychiatry, 14,* 123–142.

Blakemore, S. J., & Robbins, T. W. (2012). Decision-making in the adolescent brain. *Nature Neuroscience, 15,* 1184–1191.

Bon, C. I. M., & Garthwaite, J. (2003). On the role of nitric oxide in hippocampal long-term potentiation. *Journal of Neuroscience, 23,* 1941–1948.

Boyette, C., & Wilson, J. (2015, January 7). Is weed legal in your state? Retrieved from http://www.cnn.com/2015/01/07/us/recreational-marijuana-laws/

Budney, A. J., Moore, B. A., Rocha, H. L., & Higgins, S. T. (2006). Clinical trial of abstinence-based vouchers and cognitive-behavioral therapy for cannabis dependence. *Journal of Consulting and Clinical Psychology, 74*(2), 307–316.

Bullen, C., Willimen, J., Howe, C., Laugean, M., McRobbie, H., Paraq, V., & Walker, N. (2013). Study protocol for a randomized controlled trial of electronic cigarettes vs. nicotine patch for smoking cessation. *BMC Public Health, 13,* 210.

Burgess, C., O'Donohoe, A., & Gill, M. (2000). Agony and ecstasy: A review of MDMA effects and toxicity. *European Psychiatry, 15,* 287–294.

Caine, S. B., Heinrichs, S. C., Coffin, V. L., & Koob, G. F. (1995). Effects of the dopamine R-1 antagonist sCH 23390 microinjected into the accumbens, amygdala or striatum on cocaine self-administration in the rat. *Brain Research, 692,* 47–45.

Caine, S. B., Humby, T., Robbins, T. W., & Everitt, B. J. (2001). Behavioral effects of psychomotor stimulants in rats with dorsal or ventral subiculum lesions: Locomotion, cocaine self-administration, and prepulse inhibition of startle. *Behavioral Neuroscience, 115,* 880–894.

Caine, S. B, Thomsen, M., Gabriel, K. I., Berkowitz, J. S., Gold, L. H., Koob, G. F., . . . Xu, M. (2007). Lack of self-administration of cocaine in dopamine D1 receptor knock-out mice. *Journal of Neuroscience, 115,* 880–894.

Campbell, G. A., & Rosner, M. H. (2008). The agony of ecstasy: MDMA (3,4-methylenedioxmethamphetamine) and the kidney. *Clinical Journal of the American Society of Nephrology, 3,* 1852–1860.

Capela, J. P., Carmo, H., Remiao, F., Bastos, M. L., Meisel, A., & Carvalho, F. (2009). Molecular and cellular mechanisms of ecstasy-induced neurotoxicity: An overview. *Molecular Neurobiology, 39,* 210–271.

Cardinal, R. N., & Everitt, B. J. (2004). Neural and psychological mechanisms underlying appetitive learning: Links to drug addiction. *Current Opinion in Neurobiology, 14,* 156–162.

Carroll, K. M., & Onken, L. S. (2005). Behavioral therapies for drug abuse. *American Journal of Psychiatry, 162,* 1452–1460.

Corrigall, W. A., Franklin, K. B., Coen, K. M., & Clarke, P. B. (1992). The mesolimbic dopaminergic system is implicated in the reinforcing effects of nicotine. *Psychopharmacology, 107,* 285–289.

Courtney, K. E., & Polich, J. (2009). Binge drinking in young adults: Data, definitions, and determinants. *Psychological Bulletin, 135,* 142–156.

Courtwright, D. T. (2001). *Forces of habit: Drugs and the making of the modern world.* Cambridge, MA: Harvard University Press.

Dawson, T. M., & Snyder, S. H. (1994). Gases as biological messengers: Nitric oxide and carbon monoxide in the brain. *The Journal of Neuroscience, 14,* 5147–5159.

Devane, W. A., Dysarz, F. A., III, Johnson, M. R., Melvin, L. S., & Howlett, A. C. (1988). Determination and characterization of a cannabinoid receptor in rat brain. *Molecular Pharmacology, 34,* 605–613.

Diana, M., Pistis, M., Carboni, S., Gessa, G. I., & Rosetti, Z. L. (1993). Profound decrement of mesolimbic dopaminergic neuronal activity during ethanol withdrawal syndrome in rats: Electrophysiological and biochemical evidence. *Proceedings of the National Academy of Sciences of the USA, 90,* 7966–7969.

Erb, S., Hitchcott, P. K., Rajabi, H., Mueller, D., Shaham, Y., & Stewart, J. (2000). Alpha-2 adrenergic receptor agonists block stress-induced reinstatement of cocaine seeking, *Neuropsychopharmacology, 23,* 138–150.

Erb, S., & Stewart, J. (1999). A role for the bed nucleus of the stria terminalis, but not the amygdala, in the effects of corticotrophin-releasing factor on stress-induced reinstatement of cocaine seeking. *Journal of Neuroscience, 19,* 1–6.

Everitt, B. J., Belin, D., Economidou, D., Pelloux, Y., Dalley, J. W., & Robbins, T. W. (2008). Neural mechanisms underlying the vulnerability to develop compulsive drug-seeking habits and addiction. *Philosophical Transactions of the Royal Society of London, 363*, 3125–3135.

Everitt, B. J., & Robbins, J. V. (2005). Neural systems of reinforcement for drug addiction: From actions to habits to compulsion. *Nature Neuroscience, 8*, 1481–1489.

Exley, R., & Cragg, S. J. (2008). Presynaptic nicotinic receptors: A dynamic and diverse cholinergic filter of striatal dopamine neurotransmission. *British Journal of Pharmacology, 153*, S283–S297.

Fadda, F., & Rossetti, Z. (1998). Chronic ethanol consumption: From neuroadaptation to neurodegeneration. *Progress in Neurobiology, 56*, 385–431.

Farley, T., & Cohen, D. (2005). *Prescription for a healthy nation.* Boston, MA: Beacon Press.

Fastbom, J., Pazos, A., & Palacios, J. M. (1987). The distribution of adenosine A1 receptors and 5-nucleotidase in the brains of some commonly used experimental animals. *Neuroscience, 22*, 813–826.

Felder, C. C., and Glass, M. (1998). Cannabinoid receptors and their endogenous agonists. *Annual Review of Pharmacology, 38*, 179–200.

Foderaro, L. W. (1988, December 11). Psychedelic drug called ecstasy gains popularity in Manhattan nightclubs. *The New York Times.* http://www.nytimes.com/1988/12/11/nyregion/psychedelic-drug-called-ecstasy-gains-popularity-in-manhattan-nightclubs.html?pagewanted=all&src=pm

Fredholm, B. B., & Dunwiddie, T. V. (1988). How does adenosine inhibit transmitter release? *Trends in Pharmacological Science, 9*, 130–134.

Gardner, E. L. (2011). Addiction and brain reward and antireward pathways? *Advances in Psychosomatic Medicine, 30*, 22–60.

Goode E. 1993. *Drugs in American Society.* (4th ed.) New York, NY: McGraw-Hill.

Grant, I., Atkinson, J. H., Gouaux, B., & Wilsey, B. (2012). Medical marijuana: Clearing away the smoke. *The Open Neurology Journal, 6*, 18–25.

Green, A. R., King, M. V., Shortall, S. E., & Fone, K. C. F. (2012). Lost in translation: Preclinical studies on 3, 4-methylenedioxymethamphetamine provide information on mechanisms of action, but do not allow accurate prediction of adverse events in humans. *British Journal of Pharmacology, 166*, 1523–1536.

Griffiths, R. R., & Mumford, G. K. (1995). Caffeine—A drug of abuse? In F. E. Bloom & J. Kopler (Eds.), *Psychopharmacology: The Fourth Generation of Progress* (pp. 1699–1713). New York, NY: Raven Press.

Hanks, J. B., & Gonzalez-Maeso, J. (2012). Animal models of serotonergic psychedelics. *ACS Chemical Neuroscience, 4*, 33–42.

Heilig, M., Goldman, D., Berrettini, W., & O'Brien, C.P. (2011). Pharmacogenetic approaches to the treatment of alcohol addiction. *Nature Reviews Neuroscience, 12*, 670–684.

Herkenham, M., Lynn, A. B., Johnson, M. R., Melvin, C. S., de Costa, B. R., & Rice, K. C. (1991). Characterization and localization of cannabinoid receptors in rat brain: A quantitative in vitro autoradiographic study. *The Journal of Neuroscience, 11*, 563–583.

Heyser, C. J., Roberts, A. V., Schulteis, G., & Koob, G. F. (1999). Central administration of an opiate antagonist decreases oral ethanol self-administration in rats. *Alcohol, Clinical and Experimental Research, 23*, 1468–76.

Hofmann, A. (1979). How LSD originated. *Journal of Psychedelic Drugs, 11*, 53–60.

Holst, B. D., Vanderklish, P. W., Krushel, L. A., Zhou, W., Langdon, R. B., McWhirter, J. R., . . . Crossin, K. L. (1998). Allosteric modulation of AMPA-type glutamate receptors increases activity of the promoter for the neural cell adhesion molecule, N-CAM. *Proceedings of the National Academy of Sciences of the USA, 95*, 2597–2602.

Hubner, C. B., & Koob, G. F. (1990). The ventral pallidum plays a role in mediating cocaine and heroin self-administration in the rat. *Brain Research, 508*, 20–29.

Hughes, I. (1975). Search for the endogenous ligand of the opiate receptor. *Neuroscience Research Program Bulletin, 13*, 55–58.

Hyytia, P., & Koob, G. F. (1995). GABAA receptor antagonism in the extended amygdala decreases ethanol self-administration in rats. *European Journal of Pharmacology, 283*, 151–159.

Ingole, S. R., Rajput, S., & Sharma, S. S. (2008). Cognition enhancers: Current strategies and future perspectives. *CRIPS (Current Research and Information on Pharmaceutical Sciences), 3*, 42–48.

Iverson, L., (2003). Cannabis and the brain. *Brain, 126*, 1252–1270.

Jaffe, J. H. (1975). Drug addiction and drug abuse. In L. S. Goodman & A. Gilman (Eds.), *The Pharmacological Basis of Therapeutics* (5th ed., pp. 284–324). New York, NY: Macmillan.

Jaffe, J. H., Cascell, N. G., Kumor, K. M., & Sherer, M. A. (1989). Cocaine-induced cocaine craving. *Psychopharmacology, 97*, 59–64.

Jo, Y. H., Chen, Y. J., Chua, S. C., Talmage, D. A., & Role, L. R. (2005). Integration of endocannabinoid and leptin signaling in an appetite-related neural circuit. *Neuron, 48*, 1055–1066.

Johnson, R. A., & Johnson, F. K. (2000). The effects of carbon monoxide as a neurotransmitter. *Current Opinion in Neurology, 13*, 709–713.

Johnston, L. D., O'Malley, P. M., Bachman, J. G., & Schulenberg, J. E. (2009). *Monitoring the future national results on adolescent drug use: Overview of key findings, 2008* (NIH Publication No. 09-7401).

Jones, S., Sudweeks, S., & Yakes, J. L. (1999). Nicotinic receptors in the brain: Correlating physiology with function. *Trends in Neuroscience, 22*, 555–561.

Killen, J. D., & Fortmann, S. P. (1997). Craving is associated with smoking relapse: Findings from three prospective studies. *Experimental and Clinical Psychopharmacology, 5*, 137–142.

Kolodny, A., Courtwright, D. T., Hwang, C. S., Kreiner, P., Eadie, J. L., Clark, T. W., & Alexander, G. C. (2015). The prescription opioid and heroin crisis: A public health approach to an epidemic of addiction. *Annual Review of Public Health, 36*, 559–74.

Koneru, A., Satyanarayana, S., & Rizwan, S. (2009). Endogenous opioids: Their physiological role and receptors. *Global Journal of Pharmacology, 3*, 149–153.

Koob, G. F. (2008). A role for brain stress systems in addiction. *Neuron, 59*, 11–34.

Koob, G. F. (2009). Dynamics of neuronal circuits in addiction: Reward, antireward and emotional memory. *Pharmacopsychiatry, 42*, 32–41.

Koob, G. F., Kandel, D., & Volkow, N. D. (2008). Pathophysiology of addiction. In A. Tasman, K. Kay, J. A. Leberman, M. First, & M. Maj (Eds.), *Psychiatry* (3rd ed., vol. 1, pp. 354–378). Chichester, United Kingdom: Wiley.

Koob, G. F., & Le Moal, M. (1997). Drug abuse: Hedonic homeostatic dysregulation. *Science, 278*, 52–58.

Koob, G. F., & Volkow, N. D. (2010). Neurocircuitry of addiction. *Neuropsychopharmacology, 35*, 217–238.

Kozlowski, L. T., Whetzel, C. A., Stellman, S. D., & O'Connor, R. J. (2008). Ignoring puff counts: Another shortcoming of the Federal Trade Commission cigarette testing programme. *Tobacco Control, 17*, 6–9.

Kreitzer, A. C. (2005). Neurotransmission: Emerging roles of endo-cannabinoids. *Current Biology, 15*, R549–R551.

Krentzman, A. R., Robinson, E. A. R., Moore, B. C., Kelly, J. F., Laudet, A. B., White, W. L., . . . Strobbe, S. (2011). How alcoholics anonymous (AA) and narcotics anonymous (NA) work: Cross-disciplinary perspectives. *Alcohol Treatment Quarterly, 29*, 75–84.

Kuriyama, K., & Ohkuma, S. (1995). Role of nitric oxide in central synaptic transmission: Effects on neurotransmitter release. *Japanese Journal of Pharmacology, 69*, 1–8.

Lambert, K. G., & Kinsley, C. H. (2010). *Clinical neuroscience: Psychopathology and the brain* (2nd ed.). New York, NY: Oxford University Press.

Landolt, H. P., Dijk, D. J., Gaus, S. E., & Borbely, A. A. (1995). Caffeine reduces low frequency delta activity in the human sleep EEG. *Neuropsychopharmacology, 12*, 229–238.

Le Doux, J. E. (2000). Emotion circuits in the brain. *Annual Review of Neuroscience, 23*, 155–184.

Lee, B., London, E. D., Poldrack, R. A., Farahi, J., Nacca, A., Monterosso, J. R., . . . Mandelkern, M. A. (2009). Striatal dopamine D2/D3 receptor availability is reduced in methamphetamine dependence and is linked to impulsivity. *The Journal of Neuroscience, 29*, 14734–14740.

Lockner, J. W., Lively, J. M., Collins, K. C., Vendruscolo, J. C. M., Azar, M. R., & Janda, K. D. (2015). A conjugate vaccine using enantiopure hapten imparts superior nicotine-binding capacity. *Journal of Medicinal Chemistry, 58*, 1005–1011.

Long, M. (2011, May 3). Quest for vaccines to treat addiction. *The Wall Street Journal.* Retrieved from http://online.wsj.com/article/SB10001424052748704436004576298980739463392.html

Mansour, A., & Watson, S. J. (1993). Anatomical distribution of opioid receptors in mammalians: An overview. In A. Herz (Ed.), *Opioids I. Handbook of Experimental Pharmacology* (Vol. 104, pp. 79–106). New York, NY: Springer-Verlag.

Martinez, D., Broft, A., Foltin, R. W., Slifstein, M., Hwang, D. R., Huang, Y., Perez, A., . . . Laruelle, M. (2004). Cocaine dependence and D2 receptor availability in the functional subdivisions of the striatum: Relationship with cocaine-seeking behavior. *Neuropsychopharmacology, 29*, 1190–1202.

Martinez, D., Gil, R., Slifstein, M., Hwang, D. R., Huany, Y., Perez, A., . . . Abi-Dargham, A. (2005). Alcohol dependence is associated with blunted dopamine transmission in the ventral striatum. *Biological Psychiatry, 58*, 779–786.

McGregor, A., & Roberts, D. C. S. (1993). Dopaminergic antagonism within the nucleus accumbens or the amygdala produces differential effects on intravenous cocaine self-administration under fixed and progressive ration schedules of reinforcement. *Brain Research, 624*, 245–252.

McGregor, C., Srisurapanont, M., Jittiwutikarn, J., Laobhripatr, S., Wongtan, T., & White, J. M. (2005). The nature, time course and severity of methamphetamine withdrawal. *Addiction, 100*, 1320–1329.

Mechoulam, R. (1970). Marihuana chemistry. *Science 168*, 1159–1166. Retrieved from http://www.garfield.library.upenn.edu/classics1983/A1983QV00900002.pdf

Meier, M. H., Caspi, A., Ambler, A., Harrington, H., Houts, R., Keefe, R. S. E., . . . Moffitt, T. E. (2012). Persistent cannabis users show neuropsychological decline from childhood to midlife. *Proceedings of the New York Academy of Science, 109*, E2657–E2664.

Moore, B. A., Augustson, E. M., Moser, R. P., & Budney, A. J. (2004). Respiratory effect of marijuana and tobacco use on a U.S. sample, *Journal of General Internal Medicine, 20*, 33–37.

Moreno, A. Y., Azar, M. R., Warren, N. A., Dickerson, T. J., Koob, G. F., & Janda, K. D. (2010). A critical evaluation of a nicotine vaccine with a self-administration behavioral model. *Molecular Pharmaceuticals, 7*, 431–441.

Moszczynska, A., Fitzmaurice, P., Ang, L., Kalasinsky, K. S., Schmunk, G. A., Peretti, F. J., . . . Kish, S. J. (2004). Why is parkinsonism not a feature of human methamphetamine users? *Brain*, 363–370.

Naqvi, N. H., Rudrauf, D., Damasio, H., & Bechara, A. (2007). Damage to the insula disrupts addiction to cigarette smoking. *Science, 315*, 531–534.

National Institute on Drug Abuse. 2011. Drug facts: Nationwide trends. Retrieved from http://www.drugabuse.gov/publications/drugfacts/nationwide-trends

National Institute on Drug Abuse. (2012). Principles of drug addiction treatment: A research-based guide (3rd ed.). Retrieved from http://www.drugabuse.gov/sites/default/files/podat_1.pdf

National Survey on Drug and Health (2014). http://www.samhsa.gov/data/sites/default/files/NSDUH-FRR1-2014/NSDUH-FRR1-2014.pdf

Nestler, E.J. (2005). The neurobiology of cocaine addiction. *Science and Practice Perspectives, 3*, 4–10.

Neugebauer, V., Li, W., Bird, G. C., & Han, J. S. (2004). The amygdala and persistent pain. *Neuroscientist, 10*, 221–234.

New York Times (2012, November 30). Marijuana and medical marijuana. Retrieved from http://topics.nytimes.com/top/reference/timestopics/subjects/m/marijuana/index.html .

Nichols, D. E. (2004). Hallucinogens. *Pharmacology & Therapeutics, 101*, 131–181.

Nyilas, R., Dudok, B., Urban, G. M., Mackie, K., Watanabe, M., Cravatt, B. F., . . . Katona, I. (2008). Enzymatic machinery for endocannabinoid biosynthesis associated with calcium stores in glutamatergic axon terminals. *The Journal of Neuroscience, 28*, 1058–1063.

O'Brien, C. P., & McLellan, A. T. (1996). Myths about the treatment of addiction. *The Lancet, 347*, 237–240.

Orsini, C., Koob, G. F., & Pulvirenti, L. (2001). Dopamine partial agonist reverses amphetamine withdrawal in rats. *Neuropsychopharmacology, 25*, 789–792.

Pandey, G. N., Dwivedi, Y., Rizavi, H. S., Ren, X., Pandey, S. C., Pesold, C., . . . Tamminga, C. A. (2002). Higher expression of serotonin 5-HT2A receptors in the postmortem brains of teenage suicide victims. *The American Journal of Psychiatry, 159*, 419–429.

Parrott, A. C. (2002). Recreational ecstasy/MDMA, the serotonin syndrome, and serotonergic neurotoxicity. *Pharmacology, Biochemistry and Behavior, 71*, 837–844.

Parrott, A. C., & Kaye, F. J. (1999). Daily uplifts, hassles, stresses and cognitive failures: In cigarette smokers, abstaining smokers and non-smokers. *Behavioral Pharmacology, 10*, 639–646.

Passie, T., Halpern, J. H., Stichtenoth, D. O., Emrich, H. M., & Hintzen, A. (2008). The pharmacology of lysergic acid diethylamide: A review. *CNS Neuroscience & Therapeutics, 14*, 295–314.

Paul, L. A., Grubaugh, A. L., Frueh, B. C., Ellis, C., & Egede, L. E. (2011). Associations between binge and heavy drinking and health behaviors in a nationally representative sample. *Addictive Behaviors, 36*, 1240–1245.

Paul, S. M. (2006). Alcohol-sensitive GABA receptors and alcohol antagonists. *Proceedings of the National Academy of Sciences of the USA, 103*, 8307–8308.

Paulus, M. P., Hozack, N. E., Zauscher, B. E., Frank, L., Brown, G. G., Braff, D. L., & Scheckit, M. A. (2002). Behavioral and functional neuroimaging evidence for prefrontal dysfunction in methamphetamine-dependent subjects. *Neuropsychopharmacology*, 26, 53–63.

Pendergrast, M. (1999). *Uncommon grounds*. New York, NY: Basic Books.

Peng, X. Q., Xi, Z. X., Li, X., Spiller, K., Li, J., Chun, L., . . . Gardner, E. L. (2010). Is slow-onset long-acting monoamine transport blockade to cocaine as methadone is to heroin? Implication for anti-addiction medications. *Neuropsychopharmacology*, 35, 2564–2578.

Pert, C. B., & Snyder, S. H. (1973). Properties of opiate receptor binding in rat brain. *Proceedings of the National Academy of Sciences of the USA*, 79, 2243–2247.

Peto, R., Lopez, A. D., Boreham, J., Thun, M., & Health, C., Jr. (1992). Mortality from tobacco in developed countries: Indirect estimation from national vital statistics. *Lancet*, 339, 1268–1278.

Phillis, J. W., & Edstrom, J. P. (1976). Effects of adenosine analogs on rat cerebral cortical neurons. *Life Science*, 19, 1041–1053.

Pierce, R. C., & Kumaresan, V. (2006). The mesolimbic dopamine system: The final common pathway for the reinforcing effect of drugs of abuse? *Neuroscience and Biobehavioral Reviews*, 30, 215–238.

Pubill, D., Canudas, A. M., Pallàs, M., Camins, A., Camarasa, J., & Escubedo, E. (2003). Different glial response to methamphetamine- and methylenedioxy-methamphetamine-induced neurotoxicity. *Naunyn Schmiedeberg's Archives of Pharmacology*, 367, 490–499.

Quenqua, D. (2011, October 3). An addiction vaccine, tantalizingly close. *The New York Times*. Retrieved from http://www.nytimes.com/2011/10/04/health/04vaccine.html?pagewanted=all

Rahman, S., Lopez-Hernandez, G. Y., Corrigall, W. A., & Papke, R. L. (2008). Neuronal nicotinic receptors as brain targets for pharmacotherapy of drug addiction. *CNS & Neurological Disorders-Drug Targets*, 7, 422–441.

Ritz, M. C., Lamb, R. J., Goldberg, S. R., & Kuhar, M. J. (1988). Cocaine self-administration appears to be mediated by dopamine uptake inhibition. *Progress in Neuropsychopharmacological and Biological Psychiatry*, 12, 233–239.

Roberto, M., Madamba, S. G., Moore, S. D., Tallent, M. K., & Siggins, G. R. (2003). Ethanol increases GABAergic transmission at both pre-and postsynaptic sites in rat central amygdala neurons. *Proceedings of the National Academy of Sciences of the USA*, 100, 2053–2058.

Robison, A. J., & Nestler, E. J. (2012). Transcriptional and epigenetic mechanisms of addiction. *Nature Reviews Neuroscience*, 12, 623–637.

Robledo, P., & Koob, G. F. (1993). Two discrete nucleus accumbens projection areas differentially mediate cocaine self-administration in the rat. *Behavioral Brain Research*, 55, 159–166.

Roiko, S. A., Harris, A. C., Keyler, D. E., Lasage, M. G., Zhang, Y., & Pentel, P. R. (2008). Combined active and passive immunization enhances the efficacy of immunotherapy against nicotine in rats. *The Journal of Pharmacology and Experimental Therapeutics*, 325, 985–993.

Ross, V., & DeJong, W. (2008). Alcohol and other drug abuse among first-year college students. The Higher Education Center for Alcohol and Other Drug Abuse and Violence Prevention. Retrieved from http://www.higheredcenter.org

Salo, R., Nordahl, T. E., Possin, K., Leamon, M., Givson, D. R., Galloway, G. P., . . . Sullivan, E. V. (2002). Preliminary evidence of reduced cognitive inhibition in methamphetamine-dependent individuals. *Psychiatry Research*, 111, 65–74.

Schoenborn, C. A., & Adams, P. F. (2010). *Vital and health statistics* (Vol. 10). Washington, DC: US Department of Health and Human Services; Health behaviors of adults: United States, 2005–2007.

Sciolino, E. (2008, January 3). Even France, haven of smokers, is clearing the air. *The New York Times*. Retrieved from http://www.nytimes.com/2008/01/03/world/europe/03smoking.html?pagewanted=print

Shaham, Y., Highfield, D., Delfs, J., Leung, S., & Stewart, J. (2000). Clonidine blocks stress-induced reinstatement of heroin seeking in rats: An effect independent of the locus coeruleus noradrenergic neurons. *European Journal of Neuroscience*, 12, 1–11.

Sheff, D. (2005, February 6). My addicted son. *The New York Times*. Retrieved from http://www.nytimes.com/2005/02/06/magazine/06ADDICT.html?pagewanted=print&position&_r=0

Sheff, D. (2008). *Beautiful boy*. New York, NY: Houghton Mifflin.

Sherwood, N. (1993). Effects of nicotine on human psychomotor performance. *Human Psychopharmacology*, 8, 155–184.

Silins, E., Horwood, J. L., Patton, G. C., Fergusson, D. M., Olsson, C. A., Hutchinson, D. M., . . . Mattick, R. P. (2014). Young adult sequelae of adolescent cannabis use: an integrative analysis. *The Lancet Psychiatry*, 1(4), 286–293.

Snyder, S. H. (1977). Opiate receptors and internal opiates. *Scientific American*, 236, 44–56.

Snyder, S. H., & Pasternak, G. W. (2003). Historical review: Opioid receptors. *Trends in Pharmacological Science*, 24, 198–205.

Solinas, M., Chauvet, C., Thiriet, N., El Rawas, R., & Jaber, M. (2008). Reversal of cocaine addiction by environmental enrichment. *Proceedings of the National Academy of Sciences of the USA*, 105, 17145–17150.

Stewart, J. (2000). Pathways to relapse: The neurobiology of drug- and stress-induced relapse to drug-taking. *Journal of Psychiatry & Neuroscience*, 24, 125–136.

Stewart, J., & Badiani, A. (1993). Tolerance and sensitization to the behavioral effects of drugs. *Behavioral Pharmacology*, 4, 289–312.

Stewart, J., & Vezina, P. (1988). A comparison of the effects of intra-accumbens injections of amphetamine and morphine on reinstatement of heroin intravenous self-administration behavior. *Brain Research*, 457, 287–294.

Substance Abuse and Mental Health Services Administration, Center for Behavioral Health Statistics and Quality. (2014). *Results from the 2013 national survey on drug use and health: Summary of national findings* (NSDUH Series H-48, HHS Publication No. (SMA) 14–4863). Retrieved from http://www.samhsa.gov/data/sites/default/files/NSDUHresultsPDFWHTML2013/Web/NSDUHresults2013.pdf

Takahashi, H., Yamada, M., & Suhara, T. (2012). Functional significance of central D1 receptors in cognition: Beyond working memory, *Journal of Cerebral Blood Flow and Metabolism*, 32, 1248–1258.

Terenius, L., & Wahlstrom, A. (1974). Inhibitor(s) of narcotic receptor binding in brain extracts and cerebrospinal fluid. *Acta Pharmacologica et Toxicologica*, 35(Suppl. 1), 87. (Abst) In Meyer & Quenzer (2005).

Thompson, P. M., Hayashi, K., Simon, S. I., Geaga, J. A., Hong, M. S., Sui, Y., . . . London, E. D. (2004). Structural abnormalities in the brains of human subjects who use methamphetamine. *Journal of Neuroscience*, 24, 6028–6036.

Tomkins, D. M., & Sellers, E. M. (2001). Addiction and the brain: The role of neurotransmitters in the cause and treatment of drug dependence. *Canadian Medical Association Journal*, 164, 817–821.

Tsien, J. Z. (2000). Building a brainier mouse. *Scientific American*, 282, 62–68.

Ufnal, M., & Sikora, M. (2011). The role of brain gaseous transmitters in the regulation of the circulatory system. *Current Pharmaceutical Biotechnology*, 12, 1322–1333.

Vickers, S. P., & Kennett, G. A. (2005). Cannabinoids and the regulation of ingestive behavior. *Current Drug Targets, 6*, 215–223.

Vogel-Sprott, M. (1997). Is behavioral tolerance learned? *Alcohol Health and Research World, 21*, 161–176.

Volkow, N. D., Chang, L., Wang, G. J., Fowler, J. S., King, Y. S., Sedler, M., . . . Pappas, N. (2001). Low level of brain dopamine D2 receptors in methamphetamine abusers: Association with metabolism in the orbitofrontal cortex. *American Journal of Psychiatry, 158*, 2015–2021.

Volkow, N. D., & Swanson, J. M. (2003). Variables that affect the clinical use and abuse of methylphenidate in the treatment of ADHD. *American Journal of Psychiatry, 160*, 1909–1918.

Vollenweider, F. X., & Kometer, M. (2010). The neurobiology of psychedelic drugs: Implications for the treatment of mood disorders. *Nature Reviews Neuroscience, 11*, 642–651.

Volpp, K. G., Troxel, A. B., Pauly, M. V., Glick, H. A., Puig, A., Asch, D. A., . . . Audrain-McGovern, J. (2009). A randomized, controlled trial of financial incentives for smoking cessation. *The New England Journal of Medicine, 360*, 699–709.

Walcher, S., Koc, J., Reichel, V., Schlote, F., Verthein, U., & Reimer, J. (2016). The opiate dosage adequacy scale for identification of the right methadone dose—A prospective cohort study. *BMC Pharmacology and Toxicology, 17*, doi:10.1186/s40360-016-0058-9

Wallner, M., Hanchar, H. J., & Olsen, R. W. (2006). Low dose acute alcohol effects on GABA A receptor subtypes. *Pharmacology & Therapeutics, 112*, 513–528.

Wechsler, H., Moeykens, B., Davenport, A., Castillo, S., & Hansen, J. (1995). The adverse impact of heavy episodic drinkers on other college students. *Journal on Studies of Alcohol and Other Drugs, 56*(6), 628–634.

Willis, T. A., & Winder, D. G. (2013). Ethanol effects on N-methyl-d-aspartate receptors in the bed nucleus of the stria terminalis. *Cold Spring Harbor Perspectives on Medicine, 3*(4), a012161. doi:10.1101/schperspect.a012161

World Health Organization. (2011). *Global status report on alcohol and health.* Retrieved from http://www.who.int/substance_abuse/publications/global_alcohol_report/en/index.html

World Health Organization. (2012). *Management of substance abuse: The global burden.* Retrieved from http://www.who.int/substance_abuse/facts/global_burden/en/

World Health Organization. (2013). *Report on the global tobacco epidemic.* Retrieved from http://www.who.int/tobacco/global_report/2013/en/

World Health Organization (2014). http://www.who.int/gho/publications/world_health_statistics/2014/en/

Xue, L., Farrugia, G., Miller, S. M., Ferris, C. D., Snyder, S. H., & Szurszewski, J. H. (2000). Carbon monoxide and nicotinic oxide as coneurotransmitters in the enteric nervous system: Evidence from genomic deletion of biosynthetic enzymes. *Proceedings of the National Academy of Sciences of the USA, 97*, 1851–1855.

Zorick, T., Nestor, L., Miotto, K., Sugar, C., Hellemann, G., Scanlon, G., . . . London, E.D. (2010). Withdrawal symptoms in abstinent methamphetamine-dependent subjects. *Addiction, 105*, 1809–1818.

SECONDARY SOURCES USED FOR CHAPTER 4

Doweiko, H. (2009). *Concepts of chemical dependency* (8th ed.). Belmont, CA: Brooks/Cole Learning.

Feldman, R. S., & Quenzer, L. F. (1984). *Fundamentals of neuropsychopharmacology,* Sunderland, MA: Sinauer.

Meyer, J. S., & Quenzer, L. F. (2005). *Psychopharmacology: Drugs, the brain and behavior.* Sunderland, MA: Sinauer.

Purves, D., Augustine, G. J., Fitzpatrick, D., Katz, L. C., LaMantia, A. S., O McNamara, J., & Williams, S. M. (Eds.). (2001). *Neuroscience* (2nd ed.). Sunderland, MA: Sinauer.

CHAPTER 5

Abbott, A. (2009). One hundred years of Rita. *Nature, 458*, 564–567.

Abrous, D. N., Koehl, M., & Le Moal, M. (2005). Adult neurogenesis: From precursors to network and physiology, *Physiological Review, 85*, 523–569.

Akinbami, L. J., Liu, X., Pastor, P. N., & Reuben, C. A. (2011). *Attention deficit hyperactivity disorder among children aged 5–17 years in the United States, 1998–2009 (NCHS Data Brief, 70).* Retrieved from http://www.cdc.gov/nchs/data/databriefs/db70.pdf

Alzheimer's Association. (2011). Alzheimer's disease facts and figures. *Alzheimer's and Dementia, 7* (2).

American Psychiatric Association. (2013). *Diagnostic and statistical manual of mental disorders* (5th ed.). Arlington, VA: American Psychiatric Publishing.

Amiri-Kordestani, L., & Fojo, T. (2012). Why do phase III clinical trials in oncology fail so often? *Journal of the National Cancer Institute, 104*, 568–569.

Asato, M. R., Terwilliger, R., Woo, J., & Luna, B. (2010). White matter development in adolescence: A DTI study. *Cerebral Cortex, 20*, 2122–2131.

Azevedo, F. A., Carvalho, L. R., Grinberg, L. T., Farfel, J. M., Ferretti, R. E., Leite, R. E., . . . Herculano-Houzel, S. (2009). Equal numbers of neuronal and nonneuronal cells make the human brain an isometrically scaled-up primate brain. *Journal of Comparative Neurology 513*, 532–541.

Ball, K., Berch, D. B., Helmers, K. F., Jobe, J. B., Leveck, M. D., Marsiske, M., . . . the Advanced Cognitive Training for Independent and Vital Elderly Study Group. (2002). Effects of cognitive training interventions with older adults: A randomized controlled trial. *Journal of the American Medical Association, 288*, 2271–2281.

Bao, S., Chen, L., Qiao, X., & Thompson, R. F. (2011). Transgenic brain-derived neurotrophic factor modulates a developing cerebellar inhibitory synapse. *Learning and Memory, 6*, 276–283.

Barker, D. J. P. (1995). Fetal origins of coronary heart disease. *British Journal of Medicine, 311*, 171.

Beatty, W. W., Dodge, A. M., Dodge, L. J., White, K., & Panksepp, J. (1982). Psychomotor stimulants, social deprivation and play in juvenile rats. *Pharmacology Biochemistry and Behavior, 16*, 417–422.

Bishop, N. A., Lu, T., & Yankner, B. A. (2010). Neural mechanisms of ageing and cognitive decline. *Nature, 464*, 529–535.

Bohacek, J., & Mansuy, I. M. (2015). Molecular insights into transgenerational non-genetic inheritance of acquired behaviours. *Nature Reviews Genetics, 16*, 641–652.

Braun, C., Schweizer, R., Elbert, T., Birbaumer, N., & Taub, E. (2000). Differential activation in somatosensory cortex for different discrimination tasks. *The Journal of Neuroscience, 20*, 446–450.

Buchen, L. (2010). In their nurture. *Nature, 467*, 146–148.

Buffo, A., Inmaculada, R., Pratibha, T., Lepiert, A., Colak, D., Horn, P., Mori, T., & Gotz, M. (2008). *Proceedings of the National Academy of Sciences (PNAS), 105*, 3581–86.

Burgdorf, J., Kroes, R. A., Beinfeld, M. C., Panksepp, J., & Moskal, J. R. (2010). Uncovering the molecular basis of positive affect using rough-and-tumble play in rats: A role for insulin-like growth factor I. *Neuroscience, 168*, 769–777.

Bygren, L. O., Kaati, G., & Edvinsson, S. (2001). Longevity determined by ancestors' overnutrition during their slow growth period. *Acta Biotheoretica, 49*, 53–59.

Cairo, O. (2011). External measures of cognition. *Frontiers in Human Neuroscience, 5,* doi:10.3389/fnhum.2011.00108

Cameron, H. A., & McKay, R. D. (2001). Adult neurogenesis produces a large pool of new granule cells in the dentate gyrus. *Journal of Comparative Neurology, 435,* 406–417.

Carlen, M., Cassidy, R. M., Brismar, H., Smith, G. A., Enquist, L. W., & Frisen, J. (2002). Functional integration of adult-born neurons. *Current Biology, 12,* 606–608.

Casey, B. J., Jones, R. M., & Hare, T. A. (2008). The adolescent brain. *Annals of the New York Academy of Sciences, 1124,* 111–126.

Centers for Disease Control and Prevention. (2010). *The association between school based physical activity, including physical education, and academic performance.* Atlanta, GA: U.S. Department of Health and Human Services.

Chambers, R. A., Taylor, J. R., & Potenza, M. N. (2003). Developmental neurocircuitry of motivation in adolescence: A critical period of addiction vulnerability. *American Journal of Psychiatry, 160,* 1041–1052.

Champagne, F. A., & Curley, J. P. (2009). Epigenetic mechanisms mediating the long-term effects of maternal care on development. *Neuroscience & Biobehavioral Reviews, 33,* 593–600.

Charles, J. R., Wolf, S. L., Schneider, J. A., & Gordon, A. M. (2007). Efficacy of a child-friendly form of constraint-induced movement therapy in hemiplegic cerebral palsy: A randomized control trial. *Developmental Medicine & Child Neurology, 48,* 635–642.

Chen, Y., & Swanson, R.A. (2003). Astrocytes and brain injury. *Journal of Cerebral Blood Flow and Metabolism, 23,* 137–149.

Clee, S. M., Nadler, S. T., & Attie, A. D. (2005). Genetic and genomic studies of the BTBR ob/ob mouse model of Type 2 diabetes. *American Journal of Therapeutics, 12,* 491–498.

Clements, R. (2004). An investigation of the status of outdoor play. *Contemporary Issues in Early Childhood, 5,* 68–80.

Cloud, J. (2010). Why your DNA isn't destiny. *Time Magazine.* Retrieved from http://content.time.com/time/magazine/article/0,9171,1952313,00.html

Cohen, B. A., Inglese, M., Rusinek, H., Babb, J. S., Grossman, R. I., & Gonen, O. (2007). Proton MR spectroscopy and MRI-volumetry in mild traumatic injury. *American Journal of Neuroradiology, 28,* 907–913.

Cohen, S., Levi-Montalcini, R., & Hamburger, V. (1954). A nerve growth-stimulating factor isolated from sarcomas 37 and 180. *Proceedings of the National Academy of Sciences of the USA, 40,* 1014–1018.

Curley, J. P., Jensen, C. L., Mashoodh, R., & Champagne, F. A. (2010). Social influences on neurobiology and behavior: Epigenetic effects during development. *Psychoneuroendocrinology, 36*(3), 352–371.

Dobbs, D. (2011, October). Beautiful brains. *National Geographic,* pp. 37–59.

Elbert, T., Pantev, C., Wienbruch, C., Rockstroh, B., & Taub, E. (1995). Increased cortical representation of the fingers of the left hand in string players. *Science, 270,* 305–307.

Eriksson, P. S., Perfilieva, E., Björk-Eriksson, T., Alborn, A-M., Nordborg, C., Peterson, D. A., & Gage, F. H. (1998). Neurogenesis in the adult human hippocampus. *Nature Medicine, 4,* 1313–1317.

ESPN. (2010, September 13). Penn's Owen Thomas had CTE. Retrieved from http://sports.espn.go.com/ncf/news/story?id=5569329

Faul, M., Xu, L., Wald, M. M., & Coronado, V. G. (2010). *Traumatic brain injury in the United States: Emergency department visits, hospitalizations, and deaths.* Atlanta, GA: Centers for Disease Control and Prevention, National Center for Injury Prevention and Control.

Gazzaniga, M. (2008). *Human: The science behind what makes us unique.* New York, NY: Harper

Girgis, J., Merrett, D., Kirkland, S., Metz, G. A. S., Verge, V., & Fouad, K. (2007). Reaching training in rats with spinal cord injury promotes plasticity and task specific recovery. *Brain, 130,* 2992–3003.

Giza, C. C., & Hovda, J. J. (2001). The neurometabolic cascade of concussion. *Journal of Athletic Training, 36,* 228–235.

Gordon, N. S., Kollack-Walker, S., Akil, H., & Panksepp, J. (2002). Expression of c-fos gene activation during rough and tumble play in juvenile rats. *Brain Research Bulletin, 57,* 651–659.

Gould, E. (2007). How widespread is adult neurogenesis in mammals? *Nature Reviews Neuroscience, 8,* 481–488.

Gratzner, H. G. (1982). Monoclonal antibody to 5-bromo- and 5-iododeoxyuridine: A new reagent for detection of DNA replication, *Science, 218,* 474–475.

Green, E. J., Greenough, W. T., & Schlumpf, B. E. (1983). Effects of complex or isolated environments on cortical dendrites of middle-aged rats. *Brain Research, 264,* 233–240.

Greenough, W. T., McDonald, J. W., Parnisari, R. M., & Camel, J. E. (1986). Environmental conditions modulate degeneration and new dendrite growth in cerebellum of senescent rats. *Brain Research, 380,* 136–143.

Grier, C. F., Terwilliger, R., Teslovich, T., Velanova, K., & Luna, B. (2010). Immaturities in reward processing and its influence on inhibitory control in adolescence, *Cerebral Cortex, 20,* 1613–1629.

Harcourt, R. (1991). Survivorship costs of play in the South American fur seal. *Animal Behaviour, 42,* 129–162.

Harvey, W. J., Reid, G., Bloom, G. A., Staples, K., Grizendo, N., Mbekou,V., . . . Joober, R. (2009). Physical activity experiences of boys with and without ADHD. *Adapted Physical Activity Quarterly, 26,* 131–150.

He, M., Xiang, F., Zeng, Y., Mai, J., Chen, Q., Zhang, J., . . . Morgan, I. G. 2015. Effect of time spent outdoors at school on the development of myopia among children in China: A randomized clinical trial. *Journal of the American Medical Association, 314,* 1142–1143. doi:10.1001/jama.2015.10803

Hendrickson, M. L., Rao, A. J., Demerdash, O. N. A., & Kalil, R. E. (2011). Expression of nestin by neural cells in the adult rat and human brain. *Plos One.* doi:10.10371/journal.pone.0018535

Herculano-Houzel, S. (2009). The human brain in numbers: A linearly scaled-up primate brain. *Frontiers in Human Neuroscience.* doi:10.3389/neuro.09.031.2009

Herculano-Houzel, S. (2010). Coordinated scaling of cortical and cerebellar numbers of neurons. *Frontiers in Neuroanatomy, 4.* doi:10.3389/fnana.2010.00012

Herculano-Houzel, S. (2011a). Brains matter, bodies maybe not: The case for examining neuron numbers irrespective of body size. *Annals of the New York Academy of Sciences, 1225,* 191–199. doi:10.1111/j.1749–6632.2011.05976.x

Herculano-Houzel, S. (2011b). Not all brains are made the same: New views on brain scaling in evolution. *Brain, Behavior, and Evolution, 78,* 22–36. doi:10.1159/000327318

Herculano-Houzel, S. (2012). The remarkable, yet not extraordinary, human brain as a scaled up private brain and its associated cost. *Proceedings of the National Academy of Sciences, 109,* 10661–10668.

Herculano-Houzel, S., Collins, C. E., Wong, P., & Kaas, J. H. (2007). Cellular scaling rules for primate brains. *Proceedings of the National Academy of Sciences of the USA, 104,* 3562–3567.

Herculano-Houzel, S., de Souza, K. A., Neves, K., Porfirio, J., Messeder, D., Ferjo, L. M., Maldonado, J., & Manger, P. R. (2014).

The elephant brain in numbers. *Frontiers in Neuroanatomy, 8,* 46. doi: 10.3389/fnana.2014.00046

Hofman, M. A. (2014). Evolution of the human brain: When bigger is better. *Frontiers in Neuroanatomy, 8,* 15. doi:10.3389/fnana.2014.00015

Holtmaat, A., & Svoboda, K. (2009). Experience-dependent structural synaptic plasticity in the mammalian brain. *Nature Reviews Neuroscience, 10,* 647–658.

Hopwood, N. (2006). Pictures of evolution and charges of Fraud: Ernest Haeckel's embryological illustrations. *Isis, 97,* 260–301.

Jaskelioff, M., Muller, F. L., Paik, J. H., Thomas, E., Jiang, S., Adams, A. C., . . . DePinho, R. A. (2011). Telomerase reactivation reverses tissue degeneration in aged telomerase-deficient mice. *Nature, 469,* 102–107.

Jenkins, L. W., Lyeth, B. G., Lewelt, W., Moszynksi, K., DeWitt, D. S., Balster, R. L., . . . Hayes, R. L. (1988). Combined pre-trauma scopolamine and phencyclidine attenuate posttraumatic increased sensitivity to delayed secondary ischemia. *Journal of Neuotrauma, 5,* 275–287.

Jenkins, W. M., Merzenich, M. M., Ochs, M. T., Allard, T., & Gulc-Robles, E. (1990). Functional reorganization of primary somatosensory cortex in adult owl monkeys after behaviorally controlled tactile stimulation. *Journal of Neurophysiology, 63,* 82–104.

Kaas, J. H. (1991). Plasticity of sensory and motor maps in adult mammals. *Annual Review of Neuroscience, 14,* 137–161.

Kaati, G., Bygren, L. O., & Edvinsson, S. (2002). Cardiovascular and diabetes mortality determined by nutrition during parents' and grandparents' slow growth period. *European Journal of Human Genetics, 10,* 682–688.

Kessler, R. C., Berglund, P., Demler, O., Jin, R., Merikangas, K. R., & Walters, E. E. (2005). Lifetime prevalence and age-of-onset distributions of DSM-IV disorders in the National Comorbidity Survey Replication. *Archives of General Psychiatry, 62,* 593–602.

Knutson, B., & Panksepp, J. (1997). Effects of serotonin depletion on the play of juvenile rats. *Annals of the New York Academy of Sciences, 807,* 475–7.

Kraus, J. F., & Chu, L. D. (2005). Epidemiology. In J. M. Silver, T. W. McAllister, & S. C. Yudofsky (Eds.), *Textbook of traumatic brain injury.* Washington, DC: American Psychiatric Publishing.

Kriegstein, A., & Alvarez-Buylla, A. (2009). The glial nature of embryonic and adult neural stem cells. *Annual Review of Neuroscience, 32,* 149–184.

Lambert, C. (2010, January–February). Hits, helmets, heads. *Harvard Magazine.* Retrieved from http://harvardmagazine.com

Langlois, J. A., Rutland-Brown, W., & Wald, M. M. (2006). The epidemiology and impact of traumatic brain injury: A brief overview. *Journal of Head Trauma Rehabilitation, 21,* 375–378.

Larsen, D. D., & Krubitzer, L. (2008). Genetic and epigenetic contributions to the cortical phenotype in mammals. *Brain Research Bulletin, 75,* 391–397.

Lashley, K. S. (1923). Temporal variation in the function of the gyrus precentralis in primates. *American Journal of Physiology, 65,* 585–602.

Lent, R., Azevedo, F. A. C., Andrade-Moraes, C. H., & Pinto, A. V. O. (2011). How many neurons do you have? Some dogmas of quantitative neuroscience under revision. *European Journal of Neuroscience, 35,* 1–9.

Levi-Montalcini, R., & Hamburger, V. (1951). Selective growth stimulating effects of mouse sarcoma on the sensory and synaptic nervous system of the chick embryo. *Journal of Experimental Zoology, 116,* 321–361.

Luna, B., Garver, K. E., Urban, T. A., Lazar, N. A., & Sweeney, J. A. (2004). Maturation of cognitive processes from late childhood to adulthood. *Child Development, 75,* 1357–1372.

Luna, B., Padmanabhan, A., & O'Hearn, K. (2010). What has fMRI told us about the development of cognitive control through adolescence? *Brain and Cognition, 72,* 101–113.

Luna, B., & Sweeney, J. A. (2001). Studies of brain and cognitive maturation through childhood and adolescence: A strategy for testing neurodevelopmental hypotheses, *Schizophrenia Bulletin, 27,* 443–455.

Ma, D. K., Marchetto, M. C., Guo, J. U., Ming, B., Gage, F. H., & Song, H. (2010). Epigenetic choreographers of neurogenesis in the adult mammalian brain. *Nature Neuroscience, 13,* 1338–1341.

MacLean, P. D. (1990). *The Triune brain in evolution: Role in paleocerebral functions.* New York, NY: Plenum Press.

Mahncke, H. W., Bronstone, A., & Merzenich, M. (2006). Brain plasticity and functional losses in the aged: Scientific bases for a novel intervention. *Progress in Brain Research, 157,* 81–109.

Masis-Calvo, M., Sequeira-Cordero, A., Mora-Gallegos, A., & Fornaguers-Trias, J. (2013). Behavioral and neurochemical characterization of maternal care effects on juvenile Sprague-Dawley rats. *Physiology & Behavior, 118,* 212–217.

McCartt, A. T., Shabanova, V. I., & Leaf, W. A. (2003). Driving experience, crashes and traffic citations of teenage beginning drivers. Accident analysis and prevention. *Archives of General Psychiatry, 35,* 311–320.

McClain, D. A., & Edelman, G. M. (1982). A neural cell adhesion molecule from human brain. *Proceedings of the National Academy of Sciences of the USA, 79,* 6380–6384.

Meaney, M. J. (2001). Maternal care, gene expression, and the transmission of individual differences in stress reactivity across generations. *Annual Review Neuroscience, 24,* 1161–1192.

Meaney, M. J. (2009). Epigenetic regulation of the glucocorticoid receptor in human brain associates with childhood abuse. *Nature Neuroscience, 12,* 342–348.

McKee, A. C., Cantu, R. C., Nowinski, C. H., Hedley-Whyte, T., Gavett, B. E., Budson, A. E., . . . Stern, R. A. (2009). Chronic traumatic encephalopathy in athletes: Progressive taupathy after repetitive head injury. *Journal of Neuropathology and Experimental Neurology, 68,* 709–735.

Merzenich, M. M., & Kaas, J. H. (1982). Reorganization of somatosensory cortex in animals following peripheral nerve injury. *Trends in Neuroscience, 5,* 435–436.

Merzenich, M. M., Nelson, R. J., Stryker, M. P., Cynader, M. S., Schoppmann, A., & Zook, J. M. (1984). Somatosensory cortical map changes following digit amputation in adult monkeys. *The Journal of Comparative Neurology, 224,* 591–605.

Monteggia, L. M., Barrot, M., Powell, C. M., Berton, O., Galanis, V., Gemelli, T., . . . Nestler, E. J. (2004). Essential role of brain-derived neurotrophic factor in adult hippocampal function. *Proceedings of the National Academy of Sciences of the USA, 101,* 10827–10832.

Morrison, J. H., & Hof, P. R. (1997). Life and death of neurons in the aging brain. *Science, 278,* 412–419.

Murphy, M. R., MacLean, P. D., & Hamilton, S. C. (1981). Species-typical behavior of hamsters deprived from birth of the neocortex. *Science, 213,* 459–461.

Nicholls, J. G., Martin, A. R., Wallace, B. G., & Fuchs, P. A. (2001). *From neuron to brain* (4th ed.). Sunderland, MA: Sinauer.

Nolte, J. (1988). *The human brain* (2nd ed.). St. Louis, MO: Mosby.

Normansell, L., & Panksepp, J. (1990). Effects of morphine and naloxone on play-rewarded spatial discrimination in juvenile rats. *Developmental Psychobiology, 23,* 75–83.

Pakkenberg, B., & Gundersen, H. J. (1997). Neocortical neuron number in humans: Effect of sex and age. *Journal of Comparative Neurology, 384*, 312–320.

Panksepp, J. (2007). Can play diminish ADHD and facilitate the construction of the social brain? *Journal of the Canadian Academy of Child and Adolescent Psychiatry, 16*, 57–66.

Panksepp, J. (2010). Play behavior. In G. Koob, M. Le Moal, & R. Thompson (Eds.), *Encyclopedia of behavioral neuroscience* (pp. 87–93). New York, NY: Elsevier.

Panksepp, J., & Beatty, W. W. (1980). Social deprivation and play in rats. *Behavioral and Neural Biology, 30*, 197–206.

Park, D. C., & Gutchess, A. H. (2003). Long-term memory and aging: A cognitive neuroscience perspective. In R. Cabeza, L. Nyberg, & D. Park (Eds.), *Cognitive neuroscience of aging: Linking cognitive and cerebral aging* (pp. 218–245). New York, NY: Oxford University Press.

Park, D. C., Smith, A. D., Lautenschlager, G., Earles, J. D., Frieske, D., Zwahr, M., & Gaines, C. L. (1996). Mediators of long-term memory performance across the life span. *Psychological Aging, 11*, 621–637.

Paus, T., Keshavan, M., & Giedd, J. N. (2008). Why do many psychiatric disorders emerge during adolescence? *Nature Reviews Neuroscience, 9*, 947–956.

Pellegreni, A. D., Horvat, M., & Huberty, P. (1998). The relative cost of children's physical play. *Animal Behavior, 55*, 1053–1061.

Pellis, S., & Pellis, V. (2009). *The playful brain.* New York, NY: Oneworld.

Pellis, S. M., Pellis, V. C., & Whishaw, I. Q. (1992). The role of the cortex in play fighting by rats: Developmental and evolutionary implications. *Brain, Behavior and Evolution, 39*, 270–84.

Polli, F. E., Barton, J. J., Cain, M. S., Thakkar, K. N., Rauch, S. L., & Manoach, D. S. (2005). Rostral and dorsal anterior cingulate cortex make dissociable contributions during antisaccade error commission. *Proceedings of the National Academy of Sciences of the USA, 102*, 15700–15705.

Rakic, P. (2009). Evolution of the neocortex: A perspective from developmental biology. *Nature Reviews Neuroscience, 10*, 724–735.

Raymond, G. V., Bauman, M. L., & Kemper, T. L. (1996). Hippocampus in autism: A Golgi analysis. *Acta Neuropathologica, 91*, 117–119.

Raz, N., & Rodrigue, K. M. (2006). Differential aging of the brain: Patterns, cognitive correlates and modifiers. *Neuroscience and Biobehavioral Reviews, 30*, 730–748.

Ridgway, S. H., & Hanson, A. C. (2014). Sperm whales and killer whales with the largest brains of all toothed whales show extreme differences in cerebellum. *Brain, Behavior, and Evolution, 83*, 266–274.

Roberts, G. W., Allsop, D., & Bruton, C. (1990). The occult aftermath of boxing. *Journal of Neurology, Neurosurgery and Psychiatry, 53*, 577–592.

Romer, D. (2010). Adolescent risk taking, impulsivity, and brain development: Implications for prevention. *Developmental Psychobiology, 52*, 263–276.

Rozenbeek, B., Maas, A. I., & Menon, D. K. (2013). Changing patterns in the epidemiology of traumatic brain injury. *Nature Reviews Neurology, 9*, 231–236.

Sahler, C. S., & Greenwald, B. D. (2012). Traumatic brain injury in sports: A review. *Rehabilitation Research and Practice, 2012.* doi:10.1155/2012/659652

Salthouse, T. A. (1996). The processing speed theory of adult age differences in cognition. *Psychological Review, 103*, 403–428.

Scattoni, M. L., Gandhy, S. U., Ricceri, L., & Crawley, J. N. (2008). Unusual repertoire of vocalizations in the BTBR T+tf/J mouse model of autism. *Plos One, 8*, e3067.

Shaw, P., Greenstein, D., Lerch, J., Clasen, L., Lenroot, R., Gogtay, N., . . . Giedd, J. (2006). Intellectual ability and cortical development in children and adolescents. *Nature, 440*, 676–679.

Silverman, J. L., Yang, M., Lord, C., & Crawley, J. N. (2010). Behavioural phenotyping assays for mouse models of autism. *Nature Reviews Neuroscience, 11*, 490–502.

Simon, M. (June 7, 2012). 2,000 players unite in suing NFL over head injuries. CNN. http://edition.cnn.com/2012/06/07/sport/football/nfl-concussion-lawsuit/index.html

Siviy, S. M., & Panksepp, J. (2011). In search of the neurobiological substrates for social playfulness in mammalian brains. *Neuroscience and Biobehavioral Reviews, 35*, 1821–1830.

Song, H., Stevens, C. F., & Gage, F. H. (2002). Neural stem cells from adult hippocampus develop essential properties of functional CNS neurons. *Nature Neuroscience, 5*, 438–445.

Spear, L. (2007). The developing brain and adolescent-typical behavior patterns: An evolutionary approach. In D. Romer & E. F. Walker (Eds.), *Adolescent psychopathology and the developing brain: Integrating brain and prevention sciences* (pp. 9–30). New York, NY: Oxford University Press.

Stahnisch, F. W., & Nitsch, R. (2002). Santiago Ramon y Cajal's concept of neuronal plasticity: The ambiguity lives on. *Trends in Neurosciences, 25*, 589–591.

Stein, D. G. (2011). Is progesterone a worthy candidate as a novel therapy for traumatic brain injury? *Dialogues in Clinical Neuroscience, 13*, 352–359.

Stein, D. G. (2015). Embracing failure: What the Phase III progesterone studies can teach about TBI clinical trials. *Brain Injury, 29*, 1259–1272. doi:10.3109/02699052.2015.1065344

Steinberg, L. (2007). Risk taking in adolescence. *Current Directions in Psychological Science, 16*, 55–59.

Stephenson, D. T., O'Neill, S. M., Narayan, S., Tiwari, A., Arnold, E., Samaroo, H. D., . . . Morton, D. (2011). Histopathologic characterization of the BTBR mouse model of autistic-like behavior reveals selective changes in neurodevelopmental proteins and adult hippocampal neurogenesis. *Molecular Autism, 2*, 7. Retrieved from http://www.molecularautism.com/content/2/1/7

Tau, G. Z., & Peterson, B. S. (2010). Normal development of brain circuits. *Neuropsychopharmacology, 35*, 147–168.

Taub, E., Ramey, S. L., DeLuca, S., & Echols, K. (2004). Efficacy of constraint-induced movement therapy for children with cerebral palsy with asymmetric motor impairment. *Pediatrics, 113*, 305–12.

Thompson, T., & Red, C. (2013, August 29). NFL reaches agreement on $765 million settlement with more than 4,500 former players to end concussion-related lawsuits. *New York Daily News.* Retrieved from http://www.nydailynews.com

Thurman, D. J., Branche, C. M., & Sniezek, J. E. (1998). The epidemiology of sports-related traumatic brain injuries in the United States: Recent developments. *Journal of Head Trauma Rehabilitation, 13*, 1–8.

Tricoles, R. (2007). The promise of progesterone. *Emory Medicine, Winter*, 19–21.

Uhl, G. R., & Drgonova, J. (2014). Cell adhesion molecules: Druggable targets for modulating the connectome and brain disorders. *Neuropsychopharmacology, 39*, 235.

Vanderschuren, L. J. M. J., Niesink, R. J. M., Spruijt, B. M., & Van Ree, J. M. (1995a). μ- and κ-opioid receptor-mediated opioid effects on social play in juvenile rats. *European Journal of Pharmacology, 276*, 257–266.

Vanderschuren, L. J. M. J., Niesink, R. J. M., Spruijt, B. M., & Van Ree, J. M. (1995b). Effects of morphine on different aspects of social play in juvenile rats. *Psychopharmacology, 117*, 225–231.

Velanova, K., Wheeler, M. E., & Luna, B. (2008). Maturational changes in anterior cingulate and frontoparietal recruitment support the development of error processing and inhibitory control. *Cerebral Cortex, 18*, 2505–2522.

Vidal, C. N., Nicolson, R., DeVito, T. J., Hayashi, K. M., Geaga, J. A., Drost, D. J., . . . Thompson, P. M. (2006). Mapping corpus callosum deficits in autism: An index of aberrant cortical connectivity. *Biological Psychiatry, 60*, 218–225.

Villeda, S. A., Luo, J., Mosher, K. I., Zou, B., Britschgi, M., Bieri, G., . . . Wyss-Coray, T. (2011). The ageing systemic milieu negatively regulates neurogenesis and cognitive function. *Nature, 477*, 90–94.

Weaver, I. C. G., Cervoni, N., Champagen, F. A., D'Alessio, A. C., Sharma, S., Seckl, J. R., . . . Meaney, M. J. (2004). Epigenetic programming by maternal behavior. *Nature Neuroscience, 7*, 847–854.

Weir, K. (2013). Progesterone's promise. *Monitor on Psychology, 44*, 33.

Willis, S. L., Tennstedt, S. L., Marsiske, M., Ball, K., Elias, J., Koepke, K. M., Morris, J. N., Rebok, G. W., Unverzagt, F. W., Stoddard, A. M., Wright, E., & ACTIVE Study Group (2006). Long-term effects of cognitive training on everyday functional outcomes in older adults. *Journal of the American Medical Association (JAMA), 298*, 2805–14.

Winocur, G. (1998). Environmental influences on cognitive decline in aged rats. *Neurobiology of aging, 19*, 589–97.

Wojtowicz, J. M., & Kee, N. (2006). BrdU assay for neurogenesis in rodents. *Nature Protocols, 1*, 1399–1405.

Wright, D. W., Kellermann, A. L., Hertzberg, V. S., Clark, P. L., Frankel, M., Goldstein, F. C., . . . Stein, D. G. (2007). ProTECT: A randomized clinical trial of progesterone for acute traumatic brain injury. *Annals of Emergency Medicine, 49*, 391–402.

Zikopoulis, B., & Barbas, H. (2010). Changes in prefrontal axons may disrupt the network in autism. *Journal of Neuroscience, 30*, 14595–14609.

CHAPTER 6

Appler, J. M., & Goodrich, L. V. (2011). Connecting the ear to the brain: Molecular mechanisms of auditory circuit assembly. *Progress in Neurobiology, 93*, 488–508.

Bar, M. (2004). Visual objects in context. *Nature Reviews Neuroscience, 5*, 617–629.

Bar, M., & Aminoff, E. (2003). Cortical analysis of visual context. *Neuron, 38*, 347–358.

Barraclough, N. E., Xiao, D., Baker, C. I., Oram, M. W., & Perrett, D. I. (2005). Integration in visual and auditory information by superior temporal sulcus neurons responsive to the sight of actions. *Journal of Cognitive Neuroscience, 17*, 377–391.

Berson, D. M. (2007). Phototransduction in ganglion-cell photoreceptors. *European Journal of Physiology, 454*, 849–855.

Birnbaum, M. (2011). *Season to taste: How I lost my sense of smell and found my way.* New York, NY: Harper Collins.

Boehnke, S. E., Berg, D. J., Marino, R. A., Baldi, P. F., Itti, L., & Monoz, D. P. (2011). Visual adaptation and novelty responses in the superior colliculus. *European Journal of Neuroscience, 34*, 766–779.

Burn, C. (2008). What is it like to be a rat? Rat sensory perception and its implications for experimental design and rat welfare. *Applied Animal Behaviour Science, 112*, 1–32.

Buzas, S. P., Kobor, Pl., Petyko, A., Telkes, I., Martin, P. R., & Lenard, L. (2013). Receptive field properties of color opponent neurons in the cat lateral geniculate nucleus. *The Journal of Neuroscience, 33*, 1451–1461.

Cattaneo, Z., Vecchi, T., Cornoldi, C., Mammarella, I., Bonino, D., Ricciardi, E., & Pietrini, P. (2008). Imagery and spatial processes in blindness and visual impairment. *Neuroscience and Biobehavioral Reviews, 32*, 1346–1360.

Cauna, N., & Ross, L. L. (1960). The fine structure of Meissner's touch corpuscles of human fingers. *The Journal of Cell Biology, 8*, 467–482.

Changizi, M. (2009). *The vision revolution.* Dallas, TX: Benbella.

Chaudhari, N., & Roper, S. D. (2010). The cell biology of taste. *The Journal of Cell Biology, 190*, 285–296.

Chou, I. C., Trakht, T., Signori, C., Smith, J., Felt, B. T., Vazquez, D. M., & Barks, J. D. E. (2001). Behavioral/environmental intervention improves learning after cerebral hypoxia–ischemia in rats. *Stroke, 32*, 2192–2197.

Codina, C., Pascalis, O., Mody, C., Toomey, P., Rose, J., Gummer, L., & Buckley, D. (2011). Visual advantage in deaf adults linked to retinal changes. *PLoS One, 6*, e20417. doi:10.1371/journal.pone.0020417

Correll, J., Park, B., Judd, C. M., & Wittenbrink, B. (2002). The police officer's dilemma: Using ethnicity to disambiguate potentially threatening individuals. *Journal of Personality and Social Psychology, 85*, 1314–1329.

DeValois, R. L., Albrecht, D. G., & Thorell, L. G. (1982). Spatial frequency selectivity of cells in macaque visual cortex. *Vision Research, 22*, 545–559.

Downing, P. E. (2007). Face perception: Broken into parts. *Current Biology, 17*(20), R888–R889. doi:10.1016/j.cub.2007.08.008

Eagleman, D. (2010). Synaesthesia. *British Medical Journal, 340*, 221–223.

Felleman, D. J., & Van Essen, D. C. (1987). Receptive field properties of 147 neurons histologically verified to be located in area V3 of macaque monkey extrastriate cortex. *Journal of Neurophysiology, 57*, 889–920.

Field, T., Schanberg, S., Scafidi, F., Bauer, C. R., Vega-Lahr, N., Garcia, R., . . . Kuhn, C. M. (1986). Tactile/kinesthetic stimulation effects on preterm neonates. *Pediatrics, 77*, 654–658.

Finkel, M. (2011, March 1). The blind man who taught himself to see. *Men's Journal.* Retrieved from http://www.mensjournal.com/magazine/the-blind-man-who-taught-himself-to-see-20120504

Frank, M. E., & Hettinger, T. P. (2005). What the tongue tells the brain about taste. *Chemical Senses, 30*, 168–169.

Gainotti, G. (2013). Is the right anterior temporal variant of prosopagnosia a form of "associative prosopagnosia" or a form of "multimodal person recognition disorder"? *Neuropsychology Review, 23*, 99–110.

Ghazanfar, A. A., & Schroeder, C. E. (2006). Is neocortex essentially multisensory? *TRENDS in Cognitive Science, 10*, 278–285.

Gibb, R. L., Gonzalez, C. L. R., Wegenast, W., & Kolb, B. E. (2010). Tactile stimulation promotes motor recovery following cortical injury in adult rats. *Behavioral Brain Research, 214*, 102–107.

Grosof, D. H., Shapley, R. M., & Hawken, M. J. (1993). Macaque V1 neurons can signal "illusory" contours. *Nature, 365*, 550–552.

Halpern, M., & Martinez-Marcos, A. (2003). Structure and function of the vomeronasal system: An update. *Progress in Neurobiology, 70*, 245–318.

Hartline, H. K. (1949). Inhibition of activity of visual receptors by illuminating nearby retinal areas in the *Limulus* eye. *Federation Proceedings, 8*(1), 69–69.

Hendry, S. H. C., & Reid, R. C. (2000). The koniocellular pathway in primate vision. *Annual Review of Neuroscience, 23*, 127–153.

Hubel, D. H., & Wiesel, T. N. (1962). Receptive fields, binocular interaction and functional architecture in the cat's visual cortex. *Journal of Physiology, 160*, 106–154.

Hunt, M. (1993). *The story of psychology*. New York, NY: Doubleday.

Hurvich, L. M., & Jameson, D. (1949). Helmholtz and the three-color theory: An historical note. *The American Journal of Psychology, 62*, 111–114.

Jacobs, G. H. (2009). Evolution of colour vision in mammals. *Philosophical Transactions of the Royal Society: B/Biological Sciences, 364*, 2957–2967.

Johnson, D. M. G., Illig, K. R., Behan, M., & Haberly, L. B. (2000). New features of connectivity in piriform cortex visualized by intracellular injection of pyramidal cells suggest that "primary" olfactory cortex functions like "association" cortex in other sensory systems. *The Journal of Neuroscience, 20*, 6974–6982.

Jones, M. P., Pierce, K. E., & Ward, D. (2007). Avian vision: A review of form and function with special consideration to birds of prey. *Journal of Exotic Pet Medicine, 16*, 69–87.

Kaufman, P. L., Alm, A., & Adler, F. (2003). *Adler's physiology of the eye: Clinical applications* (10th ed.). New York, NY: Mosby.

Keller, H. (1914). *The story of my life*. New York, NY: Doubleday, Page.

Keller, M., Baum, M., Brock, O., Brennan, P. A., & Bakker, J. (2009). The main and the accessory olfactory systems interact in the control of mate recognition and sexual behavior. *Behavioural Brain Research, 200*, 268–276.

Klinge, C., Eippert, F., Roder, B., & Buchel, C. (2010). Cortico-cortical connections mediate primary visual cortex responses to auditory stimulation in the blind. *Journal of Neuroscience, 30*, 12798–12805.

Kubota, C., Nagano, T., Baba, H., & Sato, M. (2004). Netrin-1 is crucial for the establishment of the dorsal column-medial lemniscal system. *Journal of Neurochemistry, 89*(6), 1547–1554.

Kupers, R., Pietrini, P, Ricciardi, E., & Ptito, M. (2011). The nature of consciousness in the visually deprived brain. *Frontiers in Psychology, 2*, 19. doi:10.3389/fpsyg.2011.00019

Lamb, T. D., Collin, S. P., & Pugh, E. N. (2007). Evolution of the vertebrate eye: Opsins, photoreceptors, retina and eye cup. *Nature Reviews Neuroscience, 8*, 960–975.

Lambert, K. (2011). *The lab rat chronicles*. New York, NY: Perigee.

Laurant, G. (2005). Olfaction: A window into the brain. *Engineering and Science, 68*, 42–51.

Lotto, B. (2009, October). Optical illusions show how we see [Video file]. Retrieved from http://www.ted.com/talks/beau_lotto_optical_illusions_show_how_we_see

MacKinnon, D. A., Gross, C. G., & Bender, D. B. (1976). A visual deficit after superior colliculus lesions in monkeys. *Acta Neurobiologiae Experimentalis, 36*, 169–180.

Mancuso, K., Hauswirth, W. W., Li, Q., Connor, T. B., Kuchenbecker, J. A., Mauck, M. C., . . . Neitz, M. (2009). Gene therapy for red–green colour blindness in adult primates. *Nature, 461*, 784–787.

Martin, P. R., White, A. J., Goodchild, A. K., Wilder, H. D., & Sefton, A. E. (1997). Evidence that blue-on cells are part of the third geniculocortical pathway in primates. *European Journal of Neuroscience, 9*, 1536–1541.

Martin, R. D. (1979). Phylogenetic aspects of prosimian behavior. In G. A. Doyle, & R. D. Martin (Eds.), *The study of prosimian behavior* (pp. 45–78). New York, NY: Academic Press.

Martin, R. D. (1990). *Primate origins and evolution*. Princeton, NJ: Princeton University Press.

McLaughlin, E. C. (2010, September 8). Giant rats put noses to work on Africa's land mine epidemic. *CNN.com*. Retrieved from http://www.cnn.com/2010/WORLD/africa/09/07/herorats.detect.landmines/

Menini, A., Lagostena, L., & Boccaccio, A. (2004). Olfaction: From odorant molecules to the olfactory cortex. *News in Physiological Science, 19*, 101–104.

Mennella, J. A., & Forestell, C. A. (2008). Children's hedonic responses to the odors of alcoholic beverages: A window to emotions. *Alcohol, 42*, 249–260.

Mollon, J. D., Estevez, O., & Cavonius, C. R. (1990). The two subsystems of colour vision and their roles in wavelength discrimination. In C. Blakemore (Ed.), *Vision: Coding and efficiency* (pp. 119–131). Cambridge, UK: Cambridge University Press.

Montell, C. (1999). Visual transduction in Drosophila. *Annual Review of Cell and Developmental Biology, 15*, 231–268.

Murray, D. J. (1983). *A history of western psychology*. Englewood Cliffs, NJ: Prentice Hall.

Nassi, J. J., & Callaway, E. M. (2009). Parallel processing strategies of the primate visual system. *Nature Reviews Neuroscience, 10*, 360–372.

National Institutes of Health. (2012). Cochlear implants. Retrieved from http://www.nidcd.nih.gov/health/hearing/pages/coch.aspx

Ohshiro, T., Angelaki, D. E., & DeAngelis, G. C. (2011). A normalization model of multisensory integration. *Nature Neuroscience, 14*, 775–782.

Platanov, A., & Goosens, J. (2013). The role of lateral inhibition binocular motion rivalry. *Journal of Vision, 13*, 1–16.

Pointer, M. R., & Attridge, G. G. (1998). The number of discernible colours. *Color Research Applications, 23*, 52–54.

Preston, C. (2000). *Wild bird guides: Red-tailed hawk*. Mechanicsburg, PA: Stackpole.

Purves D., & Lotto R. B. (2003) *Why we see what we do: An empirical theory of vision*. Sunderland, MA: Sinauer.

Rauschecker, J. P., & Tian, B. (2000). Mechanisms and streams for processing of "what" and "where" in auditory cortex. *Proceedings of the National Academy of Sciences of the USA, 97*, 11800–11806.

Regan, B. C., Julliot, C., Simmens, B., Vienot, F., Charles-Cominique, P., & Mollon, J. D. (2001). Fruits, foliage and the evolution of primate colour vision. *Philosophical Transactions of the Royal Society: B/Biological Sciences, 356*, 229–283.

Ricciardi, E., Bonino, D., Sani, L., Vecchi, T., Guazzelli, M., Haxby, J. V., . . . Pietrini, P. (2009). Do we really need vision? How blind people "see" the actions of others. *Journal of Neuroscience, 29*, 9719–9124.

Roe, A. W., Chelazz, L., Conner, C. E., Conway, B. R., Fujita, I., Gallant, J. L., . . . Vanduffel W. (2012). Toward a unified theory of visual area V4. *Neuron, 74*, 12–29.

Rowe, T., Macrini, T. E., & Luo, Z. X. (2011, May 20). Fossil evidence on origin of the mammalian brain. *Science, 332*(6032). doi:10.1126/science. 1203117

Saygin, Z. M., Osher, D. E., Koldewyn, K., Reynolds, G., Gabrieli, J. D., & Saxe, R. R. (2011). Anatomical connectivity patterns predict face selectivity in the fusiform gyrus. *Nature Neuroscience, 15*, 321–327.

Schoenfeld, M. A., Neuer, G., Tempelmann, C., Schubler, K., Noesselt, T., Hopf, J. M., & Heinze, H. J. (2004). Functional magnetic resonance tomography correlates of taste perception in the human primary taste cortex. *Neuroscience, 127*, 347–353.

Seaburg, M. (2012, May 1). He's got a way about him. *Psychology Today*. Retrieved from http://www.psychologytoday.com/blog/tasting-the-universe/201205/hes-got-way-about-him

Seelke, A. M. H., Dooley, J. C., & Krubitzer, L. A. (2012). The emergence of somatotopic maps of the body in S1 in rats: The correspondence between functional and anatomical organization. *PLoS ONE, 7*(2). doi:10.1371/journal.pone.0032322

Shapley, R., & Hawkins, M. J. (2011). Color in the cortex: Single- and double-opponent cells. *Vision Research, 51*, 701–717.

Sinclair, S. (1985). *How animals see: Other visions of our world.* Bechenham, Kent, UK: Croom Helm.

Slotnick, B., Schellinck, H., & Brown, R. (2005). Olfaction. In I. Q. Whishaw & B. Kolb (Eds.). *The behavior of the laboratory rat* (pp. 90–104). New York, NY: Oxford University Press.

Solomon, S. G., & Lennie, P. (2007). The machinery of colour vision. *Nature Reviews Neuroscience, 8*, 276–286.

Spence, C., Levitan, C. A., Shankar, M. U., & Zampini, M. (2010). Does food color influence taste and flavor perception in humans? *Chemical Perception, 3*, 68–84.

Stahlbaum, C. C., & Houpt, K. A. (1989). The role of the Flehmen response in the behavioral repertoire of the stallion. *Physiology and Behavior, 45*, 1207–1214.

Stein, B. E., & Stanford, T. R. (2008). Multisensory integration: Current issues from the perspective of the single neuron. *Nature Reviews Neuroscience, 9*, 255–266.

Stephen, I. D., Coetzee, V., Smith, M. L., & Perrett, D. I. (2009). Skin blood perfusion and oxygenation colour affect perceived human health. *PLoS ONE, 4*(4). doi:10.137/journal.pone.0005083

Sternberg, E. (Actor), Cohen, M., & Cohen, R. (Producers). 2010. *The science of healing with Dr. Esther Sternberg* [DVD]. Arlington, VA: Public Broadcasting Service.

Tirindelli, R., Dibattista, M., Pifferi, S., & Menini, A. (2009). From pheromones to behavior. *Physiological Reviews, 89*, 921–956.

Tootell, R. B., Tsao, D., & Vanduffel, W. (2003). Neuroimaging weighs in: Humans meet macaques in "primate" visual cortex. *Journal of Neuroscience, 23*, 3981–3989.

Trotier, D. (2011). Vomeronasal organ and human pheromones. *European Annals of Otorhinolaryngology, Head and Neck Diseases, 128*(4), 184–190.

Wang, X., Vaingankar, V., Sanchez, C. S., Sommer, F. T., & Hirsch, J. A. (2011). Thalamic interneurons and relay cells use complementary synaptic mechanisms for visual processing. *Nature Neuroscience, 14*, 224–231.

Wasner, G., Lee, B. B., Engel, S., & McLachlan, E. (2008). Residual spinothalamic tract pathways predict development of central pain after spinal cord injury. *Brain 131*(9), 2387–2400.

Wassle, H. (2004). Parallel processing in the mammalian retina. *Nature Reviews Neuroscience, 5*, 1–11.

Wenstrup, J. J., & Portfors, C. V. (2011). Neural processing of target distance by echolocating bats: Functional roles of the auditory midbrain. *Neuroscience and Biobehavioral Reviews, 35*, 2073–2083.

Whitman, A. (1968). Helen Keller, 87, dies. *New York Times.* Retrieved from http://www.nytimes.com/learning/general/onthisday/bday/0627.html

Zeki, S. (2004). Thirty years of a very special visual area, area V5. *The Journal of Physiology, 557*, 1–2.

Zeki, S., Watson, J. D., Lueck, C. J., Friston, K. J., Kenard, C., & Frackowiak, R. S. (1991). A direct demonstration of functional specialization in human visual cortex. *Journal of Neuroscience, 11*, 641–649.

Zeveloff, S. I. (2002). *Raccoons: A natural history.* Washington, DC: Smithsonian Institution Press.

CHAPTER 7

Ackermann, H., & Riecker, A. (2004). The contribution of the insula to motor aspects of speech production: A review and a hypothesis. *Brain and Language, 89*, 320–328.

Ai Masri, O. (2011). An essay on the human corticospinal tract: History, development, anatomy and connections. *Neuroanatomy, 10*, 1–4.

Arbib, M. A. (2005). From monkey-like action recognition to human language: An evolutionary framework for neurolinguistics. *Behavioral and Brain Sciences, 28*, 105–167.

Barker, R. A., Barrett, J., Mason, S. L., & Bjorklund, A. (2013). Fetal dopaminergic transplantation trials and the future of neural grafting in Parkinson's disease. *The Lancet Neurology, 12*, 84–91.

Bash, D. (April 10, 2013). "Stronger, better, tougher": Giffords improves but she'll never be the same. *CNN Politics*. Retrieved from http://www.cnn.com/2013/04/09/politics/giffords-health/index.html/

Beilock, S. (2010). *Choke: What the secrets of the brain reveal about getting it right when you have to.* New York, NY: Atria.

Bjorklund, A., Dunnett, S. B., Brundin, P., Stoessl, A. J., Freed, C. R., Breeze, R. E., . . . Barker, R. (2003). Neural transplantation for the treatment of Parkinson's disease. *The Lancet Neurology, 2*, 437–445.

Blakemore, S. J., Wolpert, D. M., & Frith, C. D. (1998). Central cancellation of self-produced tickle sensation. *Nature Neuroscience, 1*, 635–640.

Boatman, D., Freeman, J., Vining, E., Pulsifer, M., Miglioretti, D., Minahan, R., Carson, B., . . . McKhann, G. (1999). Language recovery after left hemispherectomy in children with late-onset seizures. *Annals of Neurology, 46*, 579–586.

Bregman, B. S., Kunkel-Bagden, E., Rier, P. J., Dai, H. N., McAtee, M., & Gao, D. (1993). Recovery of function after spinal cord injury: Mechanisms underlying transplant-mediated recovery of function differ after spinal cord injury in newborn and adult rats. *Experimental Neurology, 123*, 3–16.

Bregman, B. S., McAtee, M., Dai, H. N., & Kuhn, D. L. (1997). Neurotrophic factors increase axonal growth after spinal cord injury and transplantation in the adult rat. *Experimental Neurology, 148*, 475–94.

Brundin, P., Li, J. Y., Holton, J. L., Lindvall, O., & Revesz, T. (2008). Research in motion: The enigma of Parkinson's disease pathology spread. *Nature Reviews Neuroscience, 9*, 741–745.

Changizi, M. (2011). Harnessed: How language and music mimicked nature and transformed ape to man. Dallas, TX: BenBelle Books.

Chiueh, C. C., Markey, S. D., Burns, R. S., Johannessen, J. N., Jacobowitz, D. M., & Kopin, K. J. (1984). Neurochemical and behavioral effects of MPTP in rat, guinea pig and monkey. *Psychopharmacology Bulletin, 20*, 548–553.

Choi, C. (2007, May 24). Strange but true: When half a brain is better than a whole one. *Scientific American*. Retrieved from http://www.scientificamerican.com/article/strange-but-true-when-half-brain-better-than-whole/

Chouinard, P. A., & Paus, T. (2010). What have we learned from "perturbing" the human cortical motor system with transcranial magnetic stimulation? *Frontiers in Human Neuroscience, 4*, 173. doi:10.3389/fnhum.2010.00173

Colcombe, S. J., Erickson, K. L., Raz, N., Webb, A. G., Cohen, N. J., McAuley, E., & Kramer, A. F. (2003). Aerobic fitness reduces brain tissue loss in aging humans. *Journal of Gerontology Series A (Biological Science and Medical Sciences), 58*, 176–180.

Dayan, E., & Cohen, L. G. (2011). Neuroplasticity subserving motor skill learning. *Neuron, 72,* 443–454.

DeCaro, M. S., Thomas, R. D., Albert, N. B., & Beilock, S. L. (2011). Choking under pressure: Multiple routes to skill failure. *Journal of Experimental Psychology. General. 140,* 390–406.

Deuschl. G., Schade-Brittinger, C., Krack, P., Volkmann, J., Schäfer, H., Bötzel, K., . . . Voges, J. (2006). A randomized trial of deep-brain stimulation for Parkinson's disease. *The New England Journal of Medicine, 355,* 896–908.

DeWitt, I., & Rauschecker, J. P. (2012). Phenome and word recognition in the auditory ventral system. *Proceedings of the National Academy of Sciences of the USA, 109,* E505–E514.

Doyon, J., Bellec, P., Amsel, R., Penhune, V., Monchi, O., Carrier, J., . . . Benali, H. (2009). Contributions of the basal ganglia and functionally related brain structures to motor learning. *Behavioral Brain Research, 199,* 61–75.

Duman, R. S. (2005). Neurotrophic factors and regulation of mood: Role of exercise, diet and metabolism. *Neurobiology of Aging, 26,* 88–93.

Earhart, G. M. (2009). Dance as therapy for individuals with Parkinson Disease. *European Journal of Physical Rehabilitation Medicine, 45,* 231–238.

Enard, W. (2011). FOXP2 and the role of cortico-basal ganglia circuits. *Current Opinions in Neurobiology, 21,* 415–424.

Engel, B. T. (2003). Clinical feedback: A behavioral analysis. *Neuroscience and Biobehavioral Reviews, 5,* 397–400.

Ericsson, K. A., Krampe, R. T. & Tesch-Romer, C. (1993). *Psychological Review, 100,* 363–406.

Ferguson, T. A., & Son, Y. J. (2011). Extrinsic and intrinsic determinents of nerve regeneration. *Journal of Tissue Engineering.* doi:10.1177/2041731411418392

Foster, K. R., & Kokko, H. (2009). The evolution of superstitious and superstition-like behavior. *Proceedings of the Royal Society, 276,* 31–37.

Franklin, D. W., & Wolpert, D. M. (2011). Computational mechanisms of sensorimotor control. *Neuron, 72,* 425–442.

Franklin, R. J. M., & Blakemore, W. F. (1990). The peripheral nervous system–central nervous system regeneration dichotomy: A role for glia cell transplantation. *Journal of Cell Science, 95,* 185–190.

Gernsbacher, M. A., & Kaschak, M. P. (2003). Neuroimaging studies of language production and comprehension. *Annual Review of Psychology, 54,* 91–114.

Gharbawie, O. A., Gonzalez, C. L. R., Williams, P. T., Kleim, J. A., & Whishaw, I. Q. (2005). Middle cerebral artery (MCA) stroke produces dysfunction in adjacent motor cortex as detected by intracortical microstimulation in rats. *Neuroscience, 130,* 601–610.

Ghez, C. (1991). The cerebellum. In E. R. Kandel, J. H. Schwartz, & J. M. Jessell (Eds.), *Principles of neural science* (3rd ed.). New York, NY: Elsevier.

Goulding, M. (2009). Circuits controlling vertebrate locomotion: Moving in a new direction. *Nature Reviews Neuroscience, 10,* 507–518.

Goymer, P. (2009, November 19). Bird behavior, Darwin and dance. *Nature, 462,* 288.

Graybiel, A. M. (2008). Habits, rituals, and the evaluative brain. *Annual Review of Neuroscience, 31,* 359–387.

Gulie, S. (2007, March). A shock to the system. *Wired.* Retrieved from http://www.wired.com/wired/archive/15.03/brainsurgery_pr.html/

Halsband, U., Matsuzaka, Y., & Tanji, J. (1994). Neuronal activity in the primate supplementary, pre-supplementary and premotor cortex during externally and internally instructed sequential movements. *Neuroscience Research, 20,* 149–155.

Halsey, A. (2010, January 13). Cellphone use, texting in 28 percent of crashes. *The Washington Post.* Retrieved from http://articles.washingtonpost.com/2010-01-13/news/36800274_1_focusdriven-cellphone-hands-free-devices/

Herculano-Houzel, S. (2010, March 10). Coordinated scaling of cortical and cerebellar numbers of neurons. *Frontiers in Neuroanatomy.* doi:10.3389/fnana.2010.00012

Hoppenbrouwers, S. S., Schutter, D. J. L. G., Fitzgerald, P. B., Chen, R., & Daskalakis, Z. J. (2008). The role of the cerebellum in the pathophysiology and treatment of neuropsychiatric disorders: A review. *Brain Research Reviews, 59,* 185–200.

Horwitz, B., Amunts, K., Bhattacharyya, R., Patkin, D., Jeffries, K., Zilles, K., & Braun, A. R. (2003) Activation of Broca's area during the production of spoken and signed language: A combined cytoarchitectonic mapping and PET analysis. *Neuropsychologia, 41*(14), 1868–1876.

Hoshi, E., Tremblay, L., Feger, J., Carras, P. L., & Strick, P. L. (2005). The cerebellum communicates with the basal ganglia. *Nature Neuroscience, 11,* 1491–1493.

Jakeman, L. B., & Reier, P. J. (1991). Axonal projections between fetal spinal cord transplants and the adult spinal cord: A neuroanatomical tracing study of local interactions. *Journal of Comparative Neurology, 307,* 311–34.

Kang, C., & Drayna, D. (2011). Genetics of speech and language disorders. *Annual Review of Genomics and Human Genetics, 12,* 145–164.

Kleim, J. A., Barbay, S., Cooper, N. R., Hogg, J. M., Reidel, C. N., Remple, M. S., & Nudo, R. N. (2002). Motor learning-dependent synaptogenesis is localized to functionally reorganized motor cortex. *Neurobiology of Learning and Memory, 77,* 63–77.

Klein, A., Sacrey, L. A. R., Whishaw, I. Q., & Dunnett, S. B. (2012). The use of rodent skilled reaching as a translational model for investigating brain damage and disease. *Neuroscience and Biobehavioral Reviews, 36,* 1030–1042.

Kramer, A. F., Colcombe, S. J., McAuley, E., Scalf, P. E., & Erickson, K. I. (2005). Fitness, aging and neurocognitive function. *Neurobiology of Aging, 26,* S124–S127.

Langston, J. W., & Palfreman, J. (1995). *The case of the frozen addicts.* New York, NY: Pantheon.

Leblois, A., Boraud, T., Meissner, W., Bergman, H., & Hansel, D. (2006). Competition between feedback loops underlies normal and pathological dynamics in the basal ganglia. *Journal of Neuroscience, 26,* 3587–2583.

Liegeois, F., Morgan, A. T., Stewart, L. H., Cross, J. H., Vogel, A. P., & Vargha-Khadem, F. (2010). Speech and oral motor profile after childhood hemispherectomy. *Brain and Language, 114,* 126–134.

Loddenkemper, T., Dinner, D. S., Kuba, C., Prayson, R., Bingaman, W., Bagirmanjian, A., & Wyllie, E. (2004). Aphasia after hemispherectomy in an adult with early onset epilepsy and hemiplegia. *Journal of Neurology, Neurosurgery, and Psychiatry, 75,* 149–151.

Meister, I. G., Wilson, S. M., Deblieck, C., Wu, A. D., & Iacoboni, M. (2007). The essential role of premotor cortex in speech perception. *Current Biology, 17,* 1692–1696.

Milton, J., Solodkin, A., Hlustik, P., & Small, S. L. (2007). The mind of expert motor performance is cool and focused. *Neuroimage, 35,* 804–813.

Murray, D. J. (1983). *A history of western psychology.* Englewood Cliffs, NJ: Prentice Hall.

Nachev, P., Kennard, C., & Husain, M. (2008). Functional role of the supplementary and pre-supplementary motor areas. *Nature Reviews Neuroscience, 9*, 855–869.

National Institute of Neurological Disorders and Stroke. (last updated July 1, 2013). Retrieved from http://www.ninds.nih.gov/disorders/sci/detail_sci.htm/

Neave, N., McCarty, K., Freynik, J., Caplan, N., Honekopp, H., & Fink, B. (2010). Male dance moves that catch a woman's eye. *Biology Letters.* doi:10.1098/rsbl.2010.0619

Obeso, J. A., Concepcio, M., Rodriguez-Oroz, C., Blesa, J., Benitez-Temino, B., Mena-Segovia, J., . . . Olanow, C. W. (2008). The basal ganglia in Parkinson's disease: Current concepts and unexplained observations. *Annals of Neurology, 64*, 30–46.

Okun, M. S., & Zeilman, P. R. (2014). *Parkinson's disease: Deep brain stimulation: A guide for patients and their families.* Retrieved from http://www.parkinson.org/

Pollick, A. S., & de Waal, F. B. M. (2007). Ape gestures and language evolution. *Proceedings of the National Academy of Science of the USA, 104*, 8184–8139.

Porras, G., Li, Q., & Bezard, E. (2012). Modeling Parkinson's disease in primates: The MPTP model. *Cold Spring Harbor Perspectives in Medicine, 2*(3). doi:10.1101/cshperspect.a009308

Portugal, E. M. M., Cevada, T., Monteiro-Junior, R. S., Guimaraes, T. T., Rubini, E. D. C., Lattari, E., . . . Deslandes, A. C. (2013). Neuroscience of exercise: From neurobiology mechanisms to mental health. *Neuropsychology, 68*, 1–14.

Redgrave, P., Rodriguez, M., Smith, Y., Rodriguez-Oraz, M. C., Lehericy, S., Bergman, H., Agid, Y., . . . Obeso, J.A. (2010). Goal-directed and habitual control in the basal ganglia: Implications for Parkinson's disease. *Nature Neuroscience Reviews, 11*, 760–772.

Reier, P. J., Stokes, B. J., Thompson, F. J., & Anderson, D. K. (1992). Fetal cell grafts into resectin and contusion/compression injuries of the rat and cat spinal cord. *Experimental Neurology, 115*, 177–88.

Roland, P. E., Larsen, B., Lassen, N. A., and Skinhoj, E. (1980). Supplementary motor area and other cortical areas in organization of voluntary movements in man. *Journal of Neurophysiology, 43*, 118–136.

Rubchinsky, L. L., Kopell, N., & Sigvardt, K. A. (2003). Modeling facilitation and inhibition of competing motor programs in basal ganglia subthalamic nucleus–pallidal circuits. *Proceedings of the National Academy of Sciences of the USA, 100*, 14427–14432.

Russo-Neustadt, A., Ha, T., Ramirez, R., & Kesslak, J. P. (2001). Physical activity–antidepressant treatment combination: Impact on brain-derived neurotrophic factor and behavior in an animal model. *Behavior Brain Research, 120*, 87–95.

Rymer, R. (July, 2012). Vanishing languages, *National Geographic.* Retrieved from http://ngm.nationalgeographic.com/2012/07/vanishing-languages/rymer-text/

Schaar, K. L., Brenneman, M. M., & Savitz, S. I. (2010). Functional assessment in the rodent stroke model. *Experimental and Translational Stroke Medicine, 2*, 13. doi:10.1186/2040-7378-2-13

Schmahmann, J. D., Weilburg, J. G., & Sherman, J. C. (2007). The neuropsychiatry of the cerebellum—Insights from the clinic. *Cerebellum, 6*, 254–267.

Science Daily. (2012). Walking and running after spinal cord injury. Retrieved from http://www.sciencedaily.com/releases/2012/05/120531145714.htm/

Scott, S. H. (2003). The role of primary motor cortex in goal-directed movements: Insights from neurophysiological studies on non-human primates. *Current Opinion in Neurobiology, 13*, 671–677.

Scott, S. K., McGettigan, C., & Eisner, F. (2009). A little more conversation, a little less action—Candidate roles for the motor cortex in speech perception. *Nature Reviews Neuroscience, 10*, 295–302.

Shima, K., & Tanji, J. (2006). Binary-coded monitoring of a behavioral sequence by cells in the pre-supplementary motor area. *The Journal of Neuroscience, 26*, 2579–2582.

Stoodley, C. J., Valera, E. M., & Schmahmann, J. D. (2012). Functional topography of the cerebellum for motor and cognitive tasks: An fMRI study. *Neuroimage, 16*, 1560–70

Swain, R. A., Harris, A. G., Wiener, E. C., Dutka, M. V, Morris, H. D., Theien, B. T., . . . Greenough, W. T. (2003). Prolonged exercise induces angiogenesis and increases cerebral blood volume in primary motor cortex of the rat. *The Journal of Neuroscience, 117*, 1037–1046.

Tedesco, A. M., Chiricozzi, F. R., Clausi, S., Lupo, M., Molinari, M., & Leggio, M. G. (2011). The cerebellar cognitive profile. *Brain.* doi:10.1093/brain/awr266

Thuret, S., Moon, L. D. F., & Gage, F. H. (2006). Therapeutic interventions after spinal cord injury. *Nature Reviews Neuroscience, 7*, 628–643.

Van den Brand, R., Heutschi, J., Barraud, Q., DiGiovanna, J., Bartholdi, K., Huerlimann, M., Friedl, L., Vollenweider, I., Moraud, E.M., Duis, S., Dominici, N., Micera, S., Musienko, D., & Courtine, G. (2012). Restoring voluntary control of locomotion after paralyzing spinal cord injury. *Science, 336*, 1182–5.

Van Praag, H. (2009). Exercise and the brain: Something to chew on. *Trends in Neurosciences, 32*, 283–290.

Van Praag, H., Kempermann, G., & Gage, F. H. (1999). Running increases cell proliferation and neurogenesis in the adult mouse dentate gyrus. *Nature Neuroscience, 2*, 266–270.

Vargha-Khadem, F., Gadian, D. G., Copp, A., & Mishkin, M. (2005). FOXP2 and the neuroanatomy of speech and language. *Nature Reviews Neuroscience, 6*, 131–138.

Vicario, C. M., (2013). FOXP2 gene and language development: The molecular substrate of the gestural-origin theory of speech? *Frontiers in Behavioral Neuroscience.* doi:10.3389/fnbeh.2013.00099

Westbrook, B. K., & McKibben, H. (1989). Dance/movement therapy with older adults who have sustained neurological insult: A demonstration project. *American Journal of Dance Therapy, 19*, 135–160.

Whishaw, I. Q. (2005). Prehension. In I. Q. Whishaw & B. Kolb (Eds.), *The behavior of the laboratory rat.* New York, NY: Oxford University Press.

Wilkinson, A. (2007, April 16). No obstacles: Navigating the world by leaps and bounds. *The New Yorker.*

Wojtecki, L., Colosimo, C., & Fuentes, R. (2012). Deep brain stimulation for movement disorders—A history of success and challenges to conquer. *Frontiers in Integrative Neuroscience, 6*, 1–2.

Wolpert, D. (2009). Moving in an uncertain world: Computational principles of human motor control. Fred Kavli distinguished international scientist lecture. *Annual Meeting for the Society for Neuroscience*, Chicago, Illinois.

Yarrow, K., Browin, P., & Krakauer, J. W. (2009). Inside the brain of an elite athlete: The neural processes that support high achievement in sports. *Nature Reviews Neuroscience, 10*, 585–596.

Zimmer, C. (2012). The common hand. *National Geographic*, 98–105.

CHAPTER 8

Aiello, L., & Wheeler, P. (1995). The expensive-tissue hypothesis: The brain and the digestive system in human and primate evolution. *Current Anthropology, 36*, 199–221.

Aldridge, J. W. (2005). Grooming. In I. Q. Whishaw & B. Kolb (Eds.), *The behavior of the laboratory rat: A handbook with tests* (pp. 141–149). New York, NY: Oxford University Press.

Amianto, R., Caroppo, P., D'Aqata, F., Spalatro, A., Lavagnino, L., Caglio, M., . . . Fassino, S. (2013). Brain volumetric abnormalities in patients with anorexia and bulimia nervosa: A voxel-based morphometry study. *Psychiatry Research: Neuroimaging, 213,* 210–216.

Amsel, Al., & Roussel, J. (1952). Motivational properties of frustration. III. Relation of the frustration effect to antedating goal processes. *Journal of Experimental Psychology, 53,* 126–131.

Anand, B. K., & Brobeck, J. R. (1951). Localization of a feeding center in the hypothalamus of the rat. *Proceedings of the Society for Experimental Biology and Medicine, 77,* 323–324.

Andersson, B. (1953). The effect of injections of hypertonic NaCl solutions into different parts of the hypothalamus of goats. *Acta Physiologica Scandinavica, 28,* 188–201.

Andersson, B. (1978). Regulation of water intake. *Physiological Review, 58,* 582–603.

Andersson, B., & Eriksson, L. (1971). Conjoint action of sodium and angiotensin in brain mechanisms controlling water and salt balances. *Acta Physiologica Scandinavica, 81,* 18–29.

Audenaert, K., Van Laere, K., Dumont, F., Vervaet, M., Goethals, I., Slegers, G., . . . Dierckx, R. A. (2003). Decreased 5-HT2A receptor binding in patients with anorexia nervosa. *Journal of Nuclear Medicine, 44,* 163–169.

Avena, N. M., & Hoebel, B. G. (2003). A diet promoting sugar dependency causes behavioral cross-sensitization to a low dose of amphetamine. *Neuroscience, 122,* 17–20.

Avena, N. M., Rada, P., & Hoebel, B. G. (2008). Evidence for sugar addiction: Behavioral and neurochemical effects of intermittent, excessive sugar intake. *Neuroscience and Biobehavioral Reviews, 32,* 20–39.

Bailer, U. F., Frank, G. K., Henry, S. E., Price, J. C., Meltzer, C. C., Weissfeld, L., . . . Kaye, W. H. (2005). Altered brain serotonin 5-HT1A receptor binding after recovery from anorexia nervosa measured by positron emission tomography and (Carbonyl11C)WAY-100635. *Archives of General Psychiatry, 62,* 1032–1041.

Berridge, K. C. (1989). Substantia nigra 6-OHDA lesions mimic striatopallidal disruption of syntactic grooming chains—A neural systems analysis of sequence control. *Psychobiology, 17,* 377–385.

Berridge, K. C. (2007). The debate over dopamine's role in reward: The case for incentive salience. *Psychopharmacology, 191,* 391–431.

Berridge, K. C., & Aldridge, J. W. (2000). Super-stereotype I: Enhancement of a complex movement sequence by systemic dopamine D1 agonists. *Synapse, 37,* 194–204.

Berridge, K. C., & Fentress, J. C. (1987). Deafferentation does not disrupt natural rules of action syntax. *Behavioural Brain Research, 23,* 69–76.

Berridge, K. C., Ho, C., Richard, J. M., & DiFeliceantonio, A. G. (2010). The tempted brain eats: Pleasure and desire circuits in obesity and eating disorders. *Brain Research, 1350,* 43–64.

Berridge, K. C., & Kringelbach, M. L. (2008). Affective neuroscience of pleasure: Reward in humans and animals. *Psychopharmacology, 199,* 457–480.

Blüher, S., & Mantzoros, C. S. (2009). Leptin in humans: Lessons from translational research. *American Journal of Clinical Nutrition, 89,* 991S–997S.

Brace, C. L. (1995). *The stages of human development* (5th ed.). Englewood Cliffs, NJ: Prentice Hall.

Carelli, R. M. (2004). Nucleus accumbens cell firing and rapid dopamine signaling during goal-directed behaviors in rats. *Neuropharmacology, 47* (Suppl. 1), 180–189.

Chang, G. Q., Gaysinskaya, V., Karatayev, O., & Leibowitz, S. F. (2008). Maternal high-fat diet and fetal programming: Increased proliferation of hypothalamic peptide-producing neurons that increase risk for overeating and obesity. *Journal of Neuroscience, 28,* 12107–12119.

Chou, S. H., & Mantzoros, C. (2014). 20 years of leptin: Role of leptin in human reproductive disorders. *The Journal of Endocrinology, 223,* T49–T62.

Christenson, G. A., & Mansueto, C. S. (1999). Trichotillomania: Descriptive characteristics and phenomenology. In D. Stein, G. Christenson, & E. Hollander (Eds.), *Trichotillomania: Current concepts* (pp. 1–411). Washington, DC: American Psychiatric Press.

Clark, J. M., Clark, A. J. M., Bartle, A., & Winn, P. (1991). The regulation of feeding and drinking in rats with lesions of the lateral hypothalamus made by N-methyl-d-aspartate. *Neuroscience, 45,* 631–640.

Clark, J. T., Kalra, P. S., Crowley, W. R., & Kalra, S. P. (1984). Neuropeptidy Y and human pancreatic polypeptide stimulate feeding behavior in rats. *Endocrinology, 115,* 427–429.

Colantuoni, C., Rada, P., McCarthy, J., Patten, C., Avena, N. M., Chadeayne, A., & Hoebel, B. G. (2002). Evidence that intermittent, excessive sugar intake causes endogenous opioid dependence. *Obesity Research, 10,* 478–488.

Craig, A. D. (2003). Interoception: The sense of the physiological condition of the body. *Current Opinion in Neurobiology, 13,* 500–505.

Cromwell, H. C., & Berridge, K. C. (1996). Implementation of action sequences by a neostriatal site: A lesion mapping study of grooming syntax. *Journal of Neuroscience, 16,* 3444–3458.

Darwin, C. (1874). *The descent of man, and selection in relation of sex.* New York: Merrill and Baker Publishers, p. 54.

Davidoff, A. J., Mason, M. M., Davidson, M. B., Carmody, M. W., Hintz, K. K., Wold L. E., . . . Ren, J. (2004). Sucrose-induced cardiomyocyte dysfunction is both preventable and reversible with clinically relevant treatments. *American Journal of Physiology, Endocrinology, &. Metabolism, 286,* E718–E724.

De Castro, J. M. (2000). Eating behavior: Lessons from the real world of humans. *Ingestive Behavior and Obesity, 16,* 800–813.

Deci, E. L., & Ryan, R. M. (2008). Hedonia, Eudaimonia and well-being: An introduction. *Journal of Happiness Studies, 9,* 1–11.

Denton, D. A., Shade, R., Zammarippa, F., Egan, G., Blair-West, J. R., McKinley, M. J., & Fox, P. (1999). Neuroimaging of genesis of thirst, and satiation of thirst. *Proceedings of the National Academy of Sciences of the USA, 96,* 5304–5309.

Dorey, N. R., Rosales-Ruiz, J., Smith, R., & Lovelace, B. (2009). Functional analysis and treatment of self-injury in a captive olive baboon. *Journal of Applied Behavior Analysis, 42,* 785–794.

DuFour, B. D., & Garner, J. P. (2010). An ethological analysis of barbering behavior. In A. V. Kalueff, J. L. LaPorte, & C. L. Bergner (Eds.), *Neurobiology of Grooming Behavior* (pp. 184–225). Cambridge, UK: Cambridge University Press.

Erikson, J. C., Holloopeter, G., & Palmiter, R. D. (1996). Attenuation of the obesity syndrome of ob/ob mice by the loss of neuropeptide Y. *Science, 274,* 1704–1707.

Erlanson-Albertsson, C. (2005). How palatable food disrupts appetite regulation. *Basic & Clinical Pharmacology & Toxicology, 97,* 61–73.

Farooqi, I. S., Matarese, G., Lord, G. M., Keogh, J. M., Lawrence, E., Agwu, C., . . . O'Rahilly, S. (2002). Beneficial effects of leptin on obesity, T cell hyporesponsiveness, and neuroendocrine/metabolic dysfunction of human congenital leptin deficiency. *The Journal of Clinical Investigation, 110,* 1093–1103.

Farr, O. M., Gavrieli, A., & Mantzoros, C. S. (2015). Leptin applications in 2015: What have we learned about leptin and obesity? *Current Opinion in Endocrinology, Diabetes, and Obesity, 22,* 353–359.

Farrell, M. J., Egan, G. F., Zamarripa, F., Shade, R., Blair-West, J., Fox, P., & Denton, D. A. (2006). Unique, common, and interacting cortical correlates of thirst and pain. *Proceedings of the National Academy of Sciences of the USA, 103,* 2416–2421.

Fentress, J. C., & Stilwell, F. P. (1973). Letter: Grammar of a movement sequence in inbred mice. *Nature, 244,* 52–53.

Ferrari, P. F., van Erp, A. M., Tornatzky, W., & Miczek, K. A. (2003). Accumbal dopamine and serotonin in anticipation of the next aggressive episode in rats. *European Journal of Neuroscience, 17,* 371–378.

Finkel, M. (2009, December). The Hazda. *National Geographic,* 94–119.

Frank, C., Bailer, U. F., Henry, S. E., Drevets, W., Meltzer, C. C., Price, J. C., . . . Kaye, W. H. (2005). Increased dopamine D2/D3 receptor binding after recovery from anorexia nervosa measured by positron emission tomography and [11C]raclopride. *Biological Psychiatry, 58,* 908–912.

Friedman, J. M., & Halaas, J. L. (1998). Leptin and the regulation of body weight in mammals, *Nature, 395,* 763–770.

Fullerton-Smith, J. (2007). *The truth about food: What you eat can change your life.* London, UK: Bloomsbury.

Galic, M. A., & Persinger, M. A. (2002). Voluminous sucrose consumption in female rats: Increased "nippiness" during periods of sucrose removal and possible oestrus periodicity. *Psychological Reports, 90,* 58–60.

Garner, J. P., Dufour, B., Gregg, L. E., Weisker, S. M., & Mench, J. A. (2004). Social and husbandry factors affecting the prevalence and severity of barbering ("whisker trimming") by laboratory mice. *Applied Animal Behaviour Science, 89,* 263–282.

Gomez-Pinilla, F. (2008). Brain foods: The effects of nutrients on brain function. *Nature Reviews Neuroscience, 9,* 568–578.

Grossman, S. P. (1967). *A textbook of physiological psychology,* New York, NY: Wiley.

Grossman, S. P. (1973). *Essentials of physiological psychology,* New York, NY: Wiley.

Hahn, T. M., Breininger, J. F., Baskin, D. G., & Schwartz, M. W. (1998). Coexpression of AgRP and NPY in fasting-activated hypothalamic neurons. *Nature Neuroscience, 1,* 271–272.

Harris, J. L., Bargh, J. A., & Brownell, K. D. (2009). Priming effects of television food advertising on eating behavior. *Health Psychology, 28,* 404–413.

Hauber, W., & Sommer, S. (2009). Prefrontostriatal circuitry regulates effort-related decision making. *Cerebral Cortex, 10,* 2240–2247.

Heath, R. G. (1972). Pleasure and brain activity in man. Deep and surface electroencephalograms during orgasm. *Journal of Nervous and Mental Disease, 154,* 3–18.

Hewson, A. K., Tung, L. C., Connell, D. W., Tookman, L., & Dickson, S. L. (2002). The rat arcuate nucleus integrates peripheral signals provided by leptin, insulin, and a ghrelin mimetic, *Diabetes, 51,* 3412–3419.

Hibbeln, J. R. (1998). Fish consumption and major depression. *Lancet, 35,* 12–13.

Hoek, H. W. (2006). Incidence, prevalence and mortality of anorexia nervosa and other eating disorders. *Current Opinions in Psychiatry, 19,* 389–394.

Horvath, T. L., & Diano, S. (2004). The floating blueprint of hypothalamic feeding circuits. *Nature Reviews Neuroscience, 5,* 662–667.

Howard, E. C., Schier, C. J., Wetzel, J. S., & Gonzales, R. A. (2009). The dopamine response in the nucleus accumbens core-shell border differs from that in the core and shell during operant ethanol self-administration. *Alcohol Clinical Expression Research, 33,* 1355–1356.

Huta, V., & Ryan, R. M. (2010). Pursuing pleasure or virtue: The differential and overlapping well-being benefits of hedonic and eudaimonic motives. *Journal of Happiness Studies, 11,* 735–762.

Johnson, P. M., & Kenney, P. J. (2010). Dopamine D2 receptors in addiction-like reward dysfunction and compulsive eating in obese rats. *Nature Neuroscience, 13,* 635–641.

Kalueff, A. V., Aldridge, J. W., LaPorte, J. L., Murphy, D. L., & Touhimaa, P. (2007). Analylzing grooming microstructure in neurobehavioral experiments. *Nature Protocols, 2,* 2538–2544.

Kalueff, A. V., & Touhimaa, P. (2005). The grooming analysis algorithm discriminates between different levels of anxiety in rats: Potential utility for neurobehavioral stress research. *Journal of Neuroscience Methods, 143,* 169–177.

Kaye, W. H., Frank, G. K., & McConaha, C. (1999). Altered dopamine activity after recovery from restricting-type anorexia nervosa. *Neuropsychopharmacology, 21,* 503–506.

Kaye, W. H., Fudge, J. L., & Paulus, M. (2009). New insights into symptoms and neurocircuit function of anorexia nervosa. *Nature Reviews Neuroscience, 10,* 573–584.

Kaye, W. H., Wierenga, C. E., Bailer, U. F., Simmons, A. N., & Bischoff-Grethe, A. (2013). Nothing tastes as good as skinny feels: The neurobiology of anorexia nervosa. *Trends in Neurosciences, 36*(2), 110–120. doi:10.1016/j.tins.2013.01.003

Kehr, J. (1999). Monitoring chemistry of brain microenvironment: Biosensors, microdialysis and related techniques. Chapter 41. In U. Windhorst & H. Johansson (Eds.), *Modern techniques in neuroscience research* (pp. 1149–1198). Heidelberg, Germany: Springer-Verlag GmbH.

Kim, J. K., Gimeno, R. E., Higashimori, T., Kim, H. J., Choi, H., Punreddy, S., . . . Shulman, G. I. (2004). Inactivation of fatty acid transport protein 1 prevents fat-induced insulin resistance in skeletal muscle. *Journal of Clinical Investigation, 113,* 756–763.

Kontis, D., & Theochari, E. (2012). Dopamine in anorexia nervosa: a systematic review. *Behavioral Pharmacology, 23,* 496–515.

Krashes, M. J., Shah, B. P., Madara, J. C., Olson, D. P., Strochlic, D. E., Vong, L., . . . Lowell, B. B. (2014). An excitatory paraventricular nucleus to AgRP neuron circuit that drives hunger. *Nature, 507,* 238–242.

Lai, S., Lai, H., Page, J. B., & McCoy, C. B. (2000). The association between cigarette smoking and drug abuse in the United States. *Journal of Addictive Diseases, 19,* 11–24.

Lambert, K. G. (1993). The activity-stress paradigm: Possible mechanisms and applications. *Journal of General Psychology, 120,* 21–32.

Lambert, K. G., & Hanrahan, L. (1990). The effect of ambient temperature on the activity-stress ulcer paradigm. Paper presented at the Southern Society for Philosophy and Psychology, Louisville, KY.

Lambert, K. G., & Porter, J. H. (1992). Pimozide mitigates excessive running in the activity-stress paradigm. *Physiology & Behavior, 52,* 299–304.

Lambert, K. G., Tu, K., Everette, A., Love, G., McNamara, I., Bardi, M., & Kinsley, C. H. (2007). Explorations of coping strategies, learned persistence, and resilience, in Long–Evans rats: Innate vs. acquired characteristics. In: *Resilience in children* (pp. 319–324). New York, NY: New York Academy of Sciences.

Leyton, M. (2009). The neurobiology of desire: Dopamine and the regulation of mood and motivational states in humans. In M. L. Kringelback & K. C. Berridge (Eds.), *Pleasures of the brain* (pp. 222–243). Oxford, UK: Oxford University Press.

Maier, S. F., Grahn, R. E., Kalman, B. A., Sutton, L. C., Wiertelak, E. P., & Watkins, L. R. (1993). The role of the amygdala and dorsal raphe nucleus in mediating the behavioral consequences of inescapable shock. *Behavioral Neuroscience, 107*, 377–389.

Maier, S. F., & Watkins, L. R. (2005). Stressor controllability and learned helplessness: The roles of the dorsal raphe nucleus, serotonin, and corticotropin-releasing factor. *Neuroscience and Biobehavioral Reviews, 29*, 829–841.

Markou, A., & Koob, G. F. (1991). Postcocaine anhedonia; An animal model of cocaine withdrawal. *Neuropsychopharmacology, 4*, 17–26.

Marsh, R., Horga, G., Wang, Z., Wang, P., Klahr, K. W., Berner, L. A., . . . Peterson, B. S. (2011). An fMRI study of self-regulatory control and conflict resolution in adolescents with bulimia nervosa. *American Journal of Psychiatry, 168*, 1210–1220.

Mather, J. G. (1981). Wheel-running activity: A new interpretation. *Mammal Review, 11*, 41–51.

McCann, J. C., & Ames, B. N. (2005). Is docosahexaenoic acid, an n-3 long chain polyunsaturated fatty acid, required for development of normal brain function? An overview of evidence from cognitive and behavioral tests in humans and animals. *American Journal of Clinical Nutrition, 82*, 281–295.

McKinley, M. J., & Johnson, A. K. (2004). The physiological regulation of thirst and fluid intake. *News in Physiological Sciences, 19*, 1–6.

Mills, E. (1909). The beaver and his works. Retrieved from http://abob.libs.uga.edu/bobk/beavwork.html/

Morell, V. (2010). Bowerbirds. National Geographic, http://ngm.nationalgeographic.com/2010/07/bowerbirds/morell-text

Mutlu, O., Gumuslu, E., Ulak, G., Celikyurt, I. K., Kokturk, S., Kir, H. M., . . . Erden, F. (2012). Effects of fluoxetine, tianeptine and olanzapine on unpredictable chronic mild stress-induced depression-like behavior in mice. *Life Sciences, 91*, 1252–1262.

Ogden, C. L., Carroll, M. D., Kit, B. K., & Flegal, K. M. (2012). Prevalence of obesity and trends in body mass index among US children and adolescents, 1999–2010. *Journal of the American Medical Association, 307*, 483–490.

Olds, J., & Milner, P. (1954). Positive reinforcement produced by electrical stimulation of septal area and other regions of a rat brain. *Journal of Comparative and Physiological Psychology, 47*, 419–427.

Pare, W. P. (1975). The influence of food consumption and running activity on the activity-stress ulcer in the rat. *Digestive Diseases, 20*, 262–273.

Pare, W. P. (1976). Activity-stress ulcer in the rat: Frequency and chronicity. *Physiology and Behavior, 16*, 699–704.

Pare, W. P. (1977). Body temperature and the activity-stress ulcer in the rat. *Physiology and Behavior, 16*, 699–704.

Powell, L. M., Szczypka, G., Chaloupka, F. J., & Braunschweig, C. L. (2007). Nutritional content of television food advertisements seen by children and adolescents. *Pediatrics, 120*, 576–583.

Preuss, T. M. (1995). Do rats have prefrontal cortex? The Rose–Woolsey–Akert program reconsidered. *Journal of Cognitive Neuroscience, 7*, 1–24.

Reynolds, S. M., & Berridge, K. C. (2008). Emotional environments retune the valence of appetitive versus fearful functions in nucleus accumbens. *Nature Neuroscience, 11*, 423–425.

Rohner-Jeanrenaud, F., & Jeanrenaud, B. (1980). Consequences of ventromedial hypothalamic lesions upon insulin and glucagon secretin by subsequently isolated perfused pancreases in the rat. *Journal of Clinical Investigations, 65*, 902–910.

Rolls, E. T. (1981a). Central nervous mechanisms related to feeding and appetite. *British Medical Bulletin, 37*, 131–134.

Rolls, E. T. (1981b). Processing beyond the inferior temporal visual cortex related to feeding, learning, and striatal function. In Y. Katsuki, R. Norgren, & M. Sato (Eds.), *Brain mechanisms of sensation* (chap. 16, pp. 383–393). New York, NY: Wiley.

Rolls, E. T. (1986). Neuronal activity related to the control of feeding. In R. Ritter, S. Ritter, & C. Barnes (Eds.), *Feeding behavior: Neural and humoral controls* (chap. 6, pp. 163–190). New York, NY: Academic Press.

Rolls, E. T., Sanghera, M. K., & Roper-Hall, A. (1979). The latency of activation of neurons in the lateral hypothalamus and substantia innominata during feeding in the monkey, *Brain Research, 164*, 121–135.

Salamone, J. D., & Correa, M. (2002). Motivational views of reinforcement: Implications for understanding the behavioral functions of nucleus accumbens dopamine. *Behavioral Brain Research, 137*, 3–25.

Salamone, J. D., Correa, M., Farrar, A., & Mingote, S. M. (2007). Effort-related functions of nucleus accumbens dopamine and associated forebrain circuits. *Psychopharmacology, 191*, 461–482.

Salamone, J. D., Correa, M., Nunes, E. J., Randall, P. A., & Pardo, M. (2012). The behavioral pharmacology of effort-related choice behavior: Dopamine, adenosine, and beyond. *Journal of the Experimental Analysis of Behavior, 97*, 125–146.

Salamone, J. D., Steinpreis, R. E., McCullough, L. D., Smith, P., Grebel, D., Mahan, K. (1991). Haloperidol and nucleus accumbens dopamine depletion suppress lever pressing for food but increase free food consumption in a novel food choice procedure. *Psychopharmacology, 104*, 515–521.

Sarna, J. R., Dyck, R. H., & Whishaw, I. Q. (2000). The Dalila effects: C57BL6 mice barber whiskers by plucking. *Behavioral Brain Research, 108*, 39–45.

Schwartz, M. W., Marks, J. L., Sipols, A. J., Baskin, D. G., Woods, S. C., Kahn, S. E., & Porte, D. (1991). Central insulin administration reduces neuropeptide Y mRNA expression in the arcuate nucleus of food-deprived lean (Fa/fa) but not obese (fa/fa) Zucker rats. *Endocrinology, 128*, 2645–2647.

Scott, D. J., Heitzeg, M. M., Koeppe, R. A., Stohler, C. S., & Zubieta, J. K. (2007). Individual differences in reward responding explain placebo-induced expectations and effects. *Neuron, 55*, 325–336.

Seeley, R. J., & Woods, S. C. (2003). Monitoring of stored and available fuel by the CNS: Implications for obesity. *Nature Reviews Neuroscience, 4*, 901–909.

Shippenberg, T. S., & Thompson, A. C. (2001). Overview of microdialysis. *Current Protocols in Neuroscience.* doi:10.1002/0471142301.ns07.1s00

Smith, G. P., & Geary, N. (2002). The behavioral neuroscience of eating. In K. L. Davis, D. Charney, J. T. Coyle, & C. Nemeroff (Eds.), *Neuropsychopharmacology: The fifth generation of progress* (chap. 15, pp. 1666–1673). Brentwood, TN: American College of Neuropsychopharmacology.

Smolinsky, A. N., Bergner, C. L., LaPorte, J. L., & Kalueff, A. V. (2009). Analysis of grooming behavior and its utility in studying animal stress, anxiety, and depression. In T. D. Gould (Ed.). Mood and anxiety related phenotypes in mice. *Neuromethods, 42.* doi:10.1007/978-1-60761-303-9-2

Spruijt, B. M., van Hooff, J. A., & Gispen W. H. (1992). Ethology and neurobiology of grooming behavior. *Physiological Review, 72*, 825–852.

Stilwell, M. F., & Fentress, J. C. (2010). Grooming , sequencing, and beyond: How it all began. In A. V. Kalueff, J. L. LaPorte, & C. L. Bergner (Eds.). *Neurobiology of Grooming B. Behavior.* Cambridge: Cambridge University Press.

Stocker, S. D., Stricker, E. M., & Sved, A. F. (2001). Arterial baroreceptors mediate the inhibitory effect of acute arterial blood pressure on thirst. *American Journal of Physiology, 282,* 1718–1729.

Story, M., & French, S. (2004). Food advertising and marketing directed at children and adolescents in the U.S. *International Journal of Experimental Social Psychology, 38,* 556–568.

Stout, S. C., Boughner, R. L., & Papini, M. R. (2003). Reexamining the frustration effect in rats: Aftereffects of surprising reinforcement and nonreinforcement. *Learning and Motivation, 34,* 437–456.

Tindell, A. J., Smith, K. S., Berridge, K. C., & Aldridge, J. W. (2009). Dynamic computation of incentive salience: "Wanting" what was never "liked." *The Journal of Neuroscience, 29,* 12220–12228.

Trivedi, B. P. (2014). Dissecting appetite. *Nature, 508,* 564–565.

U.S. Department of Health and Human Services, National Institutes of Health, National Institute of Diabetes and Digestive and Kidney Diseases. (2012). *Overweight and obesity statistics.* Retrieved from http://www.niddk.nih.gov/health-information/health-statistics/Pages/overweight-obesity-statistics.aspx/

U.S. Department of Labor, Bureau of Labor Statistics. (2013). American time use survey. Retrieved from http://www.bls.gov/tus/charts/students.htm/

Van den Broek, F. A. R., Omtzigt, C. M., & Beynen, A. C. (1993). Whisker trimming behavior in A2g mice is not prevented by offering means of withdrawal from it. *Lab Animal, 27,* 270–272.

Walters, E. E., & Kendler, K. S. (1995). Anorexia nervosa and anorexic-like syndromes in a population-based female twin sample. *American Journal of Psychiatry, 152,* 64–71.

Walton, M. E., Bannerman, D. M., & Rushworth, M. F. (2002). The role of rat medial frontal cortex in effort-based decision making. *Journal of Neuroscience, 24,* 10996–11003.

Waterman, A. S. (1993). Two conceptions of happiness: Contrasts of personal expressiveness (eudaimonia) and hedonic enjoyment. *Journal of Personality and Social Psychology, 64,* 678–691.

White, M. P., & Dolan, P. (2009) Accounting for the richness of daily activities. *Psychological Science, 20,* 1000–1008.

Wideman, C. H., Nadzam, G. R., & Murphy, H. M. (2005). Implication of an animal model of sugar addiction, withdrawal and relapse for human health. *Nutritional Neuroscience, 8,* 269–276.

Winn, P., Tarbuck, A., & Dunnett, S. B. (1984). Ibotenic acid lesions of the lateral hypothalamus: Comparison with electrolytic lesion syndrome. *Neuroscience, 12,* 225–240.

Wise, R. A., & Schwartz, H. V. (1981). Pimozide attenuates acquisition of lever pressing for food in rats. *Pharmacology, Biochemistry, and Behavior, 15,* 655–656.

Woods, S. C., Schwartz, W., Baskin, D. G., & Seeley, R. J. (2000). Food intake and the regulation of body weight. *Annual Review of Psychology, 51,* 255–277.

World Health Organization. (2014). Obesity and overweight. Factsheet No. 311. Retrieved from http://www.who.int/mediacentre/factsheets/fs311/en/

Wrangham. R. (2009). *Catching fire.* New York, NY: Basic Books.

Wren, A. M., Small, C. J., Fribbens, C. V., Neary, N. M., Ward, H. L., Seal, L. J., . . . & Bloom, S. R. (2002). The hypothalamic mechanisms of the hyophysiotropic action of ghrelin. *Neuroendocrinology, 76,* 316–324.

Wu, A., Ying, Z., & Gomez-Pinilla, F. (2007). Omega-3 fatty acids supplementation restores mechanisms that maintain brain homeostasis in traumatic brain injury. *Journal of Neurotrauma, 10,* 1587–1595.

Zink, C. F., Pagnon, G., Martin-Skurski, M. E., Chappelow, J. C., & Berns, G. S. (2004). Human striatal responses to monetary reward depend on saliency. *Neuron, 42,* 509–517.

CHAPTER 9

Adamantidis, A. R, Carter, M. C., & de Lecea, L. (2010). Optogenetic deconstruction of sleep–wake circuitry in the brain. *Frontiers in Molecular Neuroscience, 2.* doi:10.3389/neuro.02.031.2009

Adamantidis, A. R., Zhang, F., Aravanis, A. M., Deisseroth, K., & de Lecea L. (2007). Neural substrates of awakening probed with optogenetic control of hypocretin neurons. *Nature, 450,* 420–424.

A definition of irreversible coma. (1968). Report of the Ad Hoc Committee of the Harvard Medical School to Examine the Definition of Brain Death. *Journal of the Medical Association, 205,* 337–340.

Adey, W. R., Bors, E., & Porter, R. W. (1968). EEG sleep patterns after high cervical lesions in man. *Archive of Neurology, 19,* 377–383.

Albert, P. R. (2014). Light up your life: Optogenetics for depression? *Journal of Psychiatry and Neuroscience, 39,* 3–5.

Anderson, C., & Horne, J. A. (2008). Do we really want more sleep? A population-based study evaluating the strength of desire for more sleep. *Sleep Medicine, 9,* 184–187.

Arendt, J. (2010). Shift work: Coping with the biological clock. *Occupational Medicine, 60,* 10–20.

Aserinsky, E., & Kleitman, N. (1953). Regularly occurring periods of eye motility and concomitant phenomena during sleep. *Science, 118,* 273–274.

Bates, C. (2012). Parents of world's youngest locked-in syndrome sufferer, nine, reveal heartache over daughter who blinks to communicate. Retrieved from http://www.dailymail.co.uk/health/article-2194189/Parents-worlds-youngest-locked-syndrome-sufferer-reveal-heartache-daughter-blinks-communicate.html#ixzz26I8oOr9Q/

Batini, C., Beaumanoir, A., & Tyc-Dumont, S. (2011). Guiseppe Moruzi, experimental epilepsy and reticular homeostasis: The French connection. *Archives Italiennes de Biologie, 149,* 115–123.

Batini, C., Moruzzi, G., Palestini, M., Rossi, G. F., & Zanchetti, A. (1958). Persistent patterns of wakefulness in the pretrigeminal midpontine preparation. *Science, 128,* 30–32.

Bergmann, B. M., Kushida, C. A., Everson, C. A., Gilliland, M. A., Obermeyer, W., & Rechtschaffen, A. (1989). Sleep deprivation in the rat: II. Methodology. *Sleep, 12,* 5–12.

Bernat, J. L. (2002). The biophilosophical basis of whole-brain death. *Social Philosophy and Policy, 19,* 324–342.

Bjorness, T. E., Kelly, C. L., Gao, T., Poffenberger, V., & Greene, R. W. (2009). Control and function of the homeostatic sleep response by adenosine A1 receptors. *Journal of Neuroscience, 29,* 1267–1276.

Bor, D., & Seth, A. K. (2012). Consciousness and the prefrontal parietal network: Insights from attention, working memory, and chunking. *Frontiers in Psychology, 3.* doi:10.3389/fpsyg.2012.00063

Born, J., Muth, S., & Fehm, H. L. (1988). The significance of sleep onset and slow wave sleep for nocturnal release of growth hormone (GH) and cortisol. *Psychoneuroendocrinology, 13,* 233–243.

Brown, C. (2003). The stubborn scientist who unraveled a mystery of the night. *Smithsonian Magazine,* http://www.smithsonianmag.com/science-nature/the-stubborn-scientist-who-unraveled-a-mystery-of-the-night-91514538/?no-ist

Bruno, M., Bernheim, J. L., Schnakers, C., & Laureys, S. (2008). Locked-in: Don't judge a book by its cover. *Journal of Neurosurgery and Psychiatry, 79,* 2.

Busskamp, V., & Roska, B. (2011). Optogenetic approaches to resting visual function in retinitis pigmentosa. *Current Opinion in Neurobiology, 21,* 942–946.

Cajochen, C., Krauchi, K., & Wirz-Justice, A. (2003). Role of melatonin in the regulation of human circadian rhythms and sleep. *Journal of Neuroendocrinology, 15,* 432–437.

Carli, G., & Zanchetti, A. (1965). A study of pontine lesions suppressing deep sleep in the cat. *Archives of Italian Biology, 103,* 725–750.

Cohen, S., Doyle, W. J., Alper, C. M., Janicki-Deverts, D., & Turner, R. B. (2009). Sleep habits and susceptibility to the common cold. *Archives of Internal Medicine, 169,* 62–67.

Dement, W., & Kleitman, N. (1957). The relation of eye movements during sleep to dream activity: An objective method for the study of dreaming. *Journal of Experimental Psychology, 53,* 339–346.

Diekelmann, S., & Born, J. (2010). The memory function of sleep. *Nature Reviews Neuroscience, 11,* 114–125.

Ekirch A. R. (2005). *At day's close: Night in times past.* New York, NY: Norton.

Everson, C. A., Smith, C. B., & Sokoloff, L. (1994). Effects of prolonged sleep deprivation on local rates of cerebral energy metabolism in freely moving rats. *Journal of Neuroscience, 14,* 6769–6778.

Finkel, M. (2009, December). The Hazda. *National Geographic.* Retrieved from http://ngm.nationalgeographic.com/2009/12/hazda/finkel-text/2/

Freud, S. (1900/1953). The Interpretation of Dreams. In J. Strachey (Ed. and Trans.), *The Standard edition of the complete psychological works of Sigmund Freud* (Vols. 4, 5). London: Hogarth Press.

Gallup, A. C. (2011). Why do we yawn? Primitive versus derived features. *Neuroscience and Biobehavioral Reviews, 35,* 765–769.

Gallup, A. C., & Gallup, G. G. (2007). Yawning as a brain cooling mechanism: Nasal breathing and forehead cooling diminish the incidence of contagious yawning. *Evolutionary Psychology, 5,* 92–101.

George, D. B., Webb, C. T., Farnsworth, M. L., O'Shea, T. J., Bowen, R. A., Smith, D. L., . . . Rupprecht, C. E. (2011). Host and viral ecology determine bat rabies seasonality and maintenance. *Proceedings of the National Academy of Sciences of the USA.* doi:10.1073/pnas.1010875108

Goldfine, A. M., & Schiff, N. D. (2011). Consciousness: Its neurobiology and the major classes of impairment. *Neurologic Clinics, 29,* 723–737.

Groeger, J. A., Zijlstra, F. R. H., & Dijk, D. J. (2004). Sleep quantity, sleep difficulties and their perceived consequences in a representative sample of some 2000 British adults. *Journal of Sleep Research, 13,* 359–371.

Gulevich, G., Dement, W., & Johnson, L. (1996). Psychiatric and EEG observations on a case of prolonged (264 hours) wakefulness. *Archives of General Psychiatry, 15,* 29–35.

Hanlon, E. C., Vyazovskiy, V. V., Faraguna, U., Tononi, G., & Cirelli, C. (2011). Synaptic potentiation and sleep need: Clues from molecular and electrophysiological studies. *Current Topics in Medical Chemistry, 11,* 2472–2482.

Harrison, Y., & Horne, J. A. (1996). Long-term extension to sleep—Are we chronically sleep deprived? *Psychophysiology, 33,* 22–30.

Hobson, J. A. (1999). *Consciousness.* New York, NY: Scientific American Library.

Hobson, J. A. (2009). REM sleep and dreaming: Towards a theory of protoconsciousness. *Nature Reviews Neuroscience, 10,* 803–813.

Hobson, J. A. (2004). Michel Jouvet: A personal tribute. *Archives of Italiennes de Biologie, 142,* 347–352.

Hobson, J. A., & McCarley, R. (1977). The brain as a dream state generator: An activation-synthesis hypothesis of the dream process. *American Journal of Psychiatry, 134,* 1335–1348.

Holmstrand, E. C., & Sesack, S. R. (2011). Projections from the rat pedunculopontine and laterodorsal tegmental nuclei to the anterior thalamus and ventral tegmental area arise from largely separate populations of neurons. *Brain Structure and Function, 216,* 331–345.

Honma, K., von Goetz, C., & Aschoff, J. (1983). Effects of restricted daily feeding on freerunning circadian rhythms in rats. *Physiology and Behavior, 30,* 905–913.

Horne, J. (2011). The end of sleep: "Sleep debt" versus biological adaptation of human sleep to waking needs. *Biological Psychology, 87,* 1–14.

Imeri, L., & Opp, M. R. (2009). How (and why) the immune system makes us sleep. *Nature Reviews Neuroscience, 10,* 199–210.

Jacobs, B. L., & Fornal, C. A. (1991). Activity of brain serotonergic neurons in the behaving animal. *Pharmacological Review, 43,* 563–578.

Jacobs, G. D., Pace-Schott, E. F., Stickgold, R., & Otto, M. W. (2004). Cognitive behavior therapy and pharmacotherapy for insomnia. *Archives of Internal Medicine, 164,* 1888–1896.

Ji, D., & Wilson, M. A. (2007). Coordinated memory replay in the visual cortex and hippocampus during sleep. *Nature Neuroscience, 10,* 100–107.

Jones, B. E., & Muhlethaler, M. (1999). Cholinergic and GABAergic neurons of the basal forebrain: role in cortical activation. In R. Lydic & H. Baghdoyan (Ed.), *Handbook of behavioral state control: Cellular and molecular mechanisms* (pp. 213–234). Boca Raton, FL: CRC Press.

Kaplan, R., Doeller, C. F., Barnes, G. R., Litvak, V., Duzel, E., Bandettini, P. A., & Burgess, N. (2012). Movement-related theta rhythm in humans: Coordinating self-directed hippocampal learning. *PLoS Biology, 2,* e1001267.

Kilduff, T. S. (2001). Sleepy dogs don't lie: A genetic disorder informative about sleep. *Genome Research, 11,* 509–511.

Kotecha, B. T., & Hall, A. C. (2014). Role of surgery in adult obstructive sleep apnoea. *Sleep Medicine Reviews.* doi:10.1016/j.smrv.2014.02.003

Kravitz, A. V., Freeze, B. S., Parker, P. R. L., Kay, K., Thwin, M. T., Deisseroth, K., & Kreitzer, A. C. (2010). Regulation of Parkinsonian motor behaviors by optogenetic control of basal ganglia circuitry. *Nature, 466,* 622–626.

Krueger, P. M., & Friedman, E. M. (2009). Sleep duration in the United States: A cross-sectional population-based study. *American Journal of Epidemiology, 169,* 1052–1063.

Lafortune, M., Gagnon, J. F., Latreille, V., Vandewalle, G., Martin, N., Filipini, D., Doyon, J., & Carrier, J. (2012). Reduced slow-wave rebound during daytime recovery sleep in middle-aged subjects. *PLOS ONE, 7,* e43224.

Lai, Y. Y., Hsieth, K. C., Nguyen, D., Peever, J., & Siegel, J. M. (2008). Neurotoxic lesions at the ventral mesopontine junction change sleep time and muscle activity during sleep: An animal model of motor disorders in sleep. *Neuroscience, 154,* 431–443.

Laureys, S. (2005). Death, unconsciousness and the brain. *Nature Reviews Neuroscience, 6,* 899–909.

Laureys, S., Owen, A. M., & Schiff, N. D. (2004). Brain function in coma, vegetative state, and related disorders. *Lancet Neurology, 3,* 537–546.

Laureys, S., Peigneux, P., Phillips, C., Fuchs, S., Dequelche, C., Aerts, J., Del Fiore, G., et al. (2001). Experience-dependent changes in cerebral functional connectivity during rapid eye movement sleep. *Neuroscience, 105,* 521–525.

Lee-Iannotti, J. K., & Parish, J. M. (2016). Suvorexant: A promising, novel treatment for insomnia. *Neuropsychiatric Disease and Treatment, 12,* 491–495.

Leone, A., Ferrari, P. F., & Palagi, E. (2014). Different yawns, different functions? Testing social hypotheses on spontaneous yawning in *Theropithecus gelada. Scientific Reports, 4.* doi:10.1038/srep04010

Li, J., Li, M. X., Liu, S. N., Wang, J. H., Huang, M., Wang, M., & Wang, S. (2014). Is brain damage really involved in the pathogenesis of obstructive sleep apnea? *Neuroreport, 25,* 593–595.

Lu, J., Sherman, D., Devor, M., & Saper, C. B. (2006). A putative flip-flop switch for control of REM sleep. *Nature, 441,* 589–594.

Macey, P. M., Henderson, L. A., Macey, K. E., Alger, J. R., Frysinger, R. C., Woo, M. A., . . . Harper, R. M. (2002). Brain morphology associated with obstructive sleep apnea. *American Journal of Critical Care Medicine, 166,* 1382–1387.

Machado, C., Korein, J., Ferrer, Y., Portela, L., de la C. Barcia, M., Manero, J. M. (2007). The concept of brain death did not evolve to benefit organ transplants. *Journal of Medical Ethics, 33,* 197–200.

Manfredsson, F. P., Bloom, D. C., & Mandel, R. J. (2012). Regulated protein expression for invivo gene therapy for neurological disorders: Progress, strategies and issues. *Neurobiology of Disease, 48,* 212–221.

Mashour, G. A., & Alkire, M. T. (2013). Evolution of consciousness: Phylogeny, ontogeny, and emergence from general anesthesia. *Proceedings of the National Academy of Science of the USA, 110,* 10357–10364.

Masseck, O. A., Spoida, K., Dalkara, D., Maejima, T., Rubelowski, J. M., Wallhorn, L., . . . Herlitze, S. (2014). Vertebrate cone opsins enable sustained and highly sensitive rapid control of Gi/0 signaling in anxiety circuitry. *Neuron, 81,* 1263–1273.

Mershon, J. L., Sehlhorst, C. S., Rebar, R. W., & Liu, J. H. (1992). Evidence of a corticotropin-releasing hormone pulse generator in the macaque hypothalamus. *Endocrinology, 130,* 2991–2996.

Mikulak, A. (2012). Behavioral science at the speed of light. *Observer, 25*(3). Retrieved from http://www.psychologicalscience.org/index.php/publications/observer/2012/march-12/behavioral-science-at-the-speed-of-light.html/

MIT News. (2009). In profile: Matt Wilson. Retrieved from http://web.mit.edu/newsoffice/2009/profile-wilson.html/

Monti, J. M. (2010). The structure of the dorsal raphe nucleus and its relevance to the regulation of sleep and wakefulness. *Sleep Medicine Reviews, 14,* 307–317.

Monti, M. M., Vanhaudenhuyse, A., Coleman, M. R., Boly, M., Pickard, J. D., Tshibanda, L., Owen, A. M., & Laureys, S. (2010). Willful modulation of brain activity in disorders of consciousness. *The New England Journal of Medicine, 362,* 579–589.

Moorcroft, W. H. (2003). *Understanding sleep and dreaming.* New York, NY: Kluwer Academic/Plenum.

Morrison, A. R., & Bowker, R. M. (1975). The biological significance of PGO spikes in the sleeping cat. *Acta Neurobiologiae Experimentalis, 35,* 821–840.

Moruzzi, G., & Magoun, H. W. (1949). Brain stem reticular formation and activation of the EEG. *Electroencephalography and Clinical Neurophysiology, 1,* 455–473.

Mukhametov, L. M., Supin, A. Y., & Polyakova, I. G. (1977). Interhemispheric asymmetry of the electroencephalographic sleep pattern in dolphins. *Brain Research, 134*(3), 581–584.

National Sleep Foundation. (2014). *Insomnia.* Retrieved from http://sleepfoundation.org/sleep-disorders-problems/insomnia/

Nir, Y., Staba, R. J., Andrillon, T., Vyazovskiy, V. V., Cirelli, C., Fried, I., & Tononi, G. (2011). Regional slow waves and spindles in human sleep. *Neuron, 70,* 153–169.

Pallis, C., & Harley, D. H. (1996). *ABC of brainstem death* (2nd ed.) London, UK: BMJ.

Peigneux, P., Laureys, S., Delbeuck, X., & Maquet, P. (2001). Sleeping brain, learning brain. The role of sleep for memory systems. *NeuroReport, 12,* A11–A24.

Peter-Derex, L., Magnin, M., & Bastuji, H. (2015). Heterogeneity of arousals in human sleep: A stereo-electroencephalographic study. *Neuroimage, 123,* 229–244. doi:10.1016/j.neuroimage.2015.07.057

Peyron, C., Faraco, J., Rogers, W., Ripley, B., Overeem, S., Charney, Y., . . . Mignot, E. (2000). A mutation in a case of early onset narcolepsy and a generalized absence of hypocretin peptides in human narcolepsy brains. *Nature Medicine, 6,* 991–997.

Pilcher, J. P., & Huffcutt, A. I. (1996). Effects of sleep deprivation on performance: A meta-analysis. *Sleep, 19,* 318–326.

Poe, E. A. (1981). In *The Complete Edgar Allan Poe Tales* (pp. 432–441). New York, NY: Avenel.

Porkka-Heiskanen, T. R., Strecker, E., Thakkar, M., Bjorkum, A. A., Greene, R. W., & McCarley, R. W. (1997). Adenosine: A mediator of the sleep-inducing effects of prolonged wakefulness. *Science, 276,* 1265–1268.

Provine, R. R., Hamernik, H. B., & Curchack, B. B. (1987). Yawning: Relation to sleeping and stretching in humans. *Ethology, 76,* 152–160.

Purves, D., Augustine, G. J., Fitzpatrick, D., Katz, L. C., LaMantia, A.-S., McNamara, J. O., & Williams, S. M. (2001). *Neuroscience* (2nd ed.). Sunderland, MA: Sinauer.

Rajaratnam, S. M., & Arendt, J. (2001). Health in a 24-h society. *The Lancet, 358,* 999–1005.

Ralph, M. R., Foster, R. G., Davis, F. C., & Menaker, M. (1990). Transplanted suprachiasmatic nucleus determines circadian period. *Science, 247,* 975–978.

Rasch, B., Buchel, C., Gais, S., & Born, J. (2007). Odor cues during slow-wave sleep prompt declarative memory consolidation. *Science, 315,* 1426–1429.

Rattenborg, N. C., Voirin, B., Vyssotski, A., Kays, R. W., Spoelstra, K., Kuemmeth, F., . . . Wikelski, M. (2008). Sleeping outside the box: Electroencephalographic measures of sleep in sloths inhabiting a rainforest. *Biology Letters, 4,* 402–405.

Rechtschaffen, A., & Bergmann, B. M. (1995). Sleep deprivation in the rat by the disk-over-water method. *Behavioral Brain Research, 69,* 55–63.

Redman, J. R. (1997). Circadian entrainment and phase shifting in mammals with melatonin. *Journal of Biological Rhythms, 12,* 581–587.

Rock, A. (2004). *The mind at night.* New York, NY: Basic Books.

Rosanova, M., Gosseries, O., Casarotto, S., Boly, M., Casali, A. G., Bruno, M. A., . . . Massimini, M. (2012). Recovery of cortical effective connectivity and recovery of consciousness in vegetative patients. *Brain, 135,* 1308–1320.

Ross J. (1965). Neurological findings after prolonged sleep deprivation. *Archives of Neurology, 12*(4), 399–403.

Sacks, R. L., Brandes, R. W., Kendall, A. R., & Lewy, A., (2000). Entrainment of free-running circadian rhythms by melatonin in blind people. *The New England Journal of Medicine, 343,* 1070–1077.

Sakai, K. (2011). Sleep–waking discharge profiles of dorsal raphe nucleus neurons in mice. *Neuroscience, 197,* 200–224.

Sakurai, T. (2007). The neural circuit of orexin (hyporetin): Maintaining sleep and wakefulness. *Nature Reviews Neuroscience, 8,* 171–181.

Saper, C. G., Chou, T. C., & Scammell, T. E. (2001). The sleep switch: Hypothalamic control of sleep and wakefulness. *Trends in Neuroscience, 24,* 726–731.

Schenck, C. (2011, October 25). The curious case of Kenneth Parks [Video file]. Retrieved from http://www.worldsciencefestival.com/2011/10/the_curious_case_of_kenneth_parks/

Schwartz, J. R. L., & Roth, T. (2008). Neurophysiology of sleep and wakefulness: Basic science and clinical implications. *Current Neuropharmacology, 6,* 367–378.

Sherin, J. E., Shiromani, P. J., McCarley, R. W., & Saper, C. B. (1996). Activation of ventrolateral preoptic neurons during sleep. *Science, 271,* 216–218.

Siclari, F., Khatami, R., Urbaniok, F., Nobili, L., Mahowald, M. W., Schenck, C. H., . . . Bassetti, C. (2010). Violence in sleep. *Brain, 133,* 3494–3509.

Siclari, F., Tononi, G., & Bassetti, C. (2012, July/August). Death by sleepwalker. *Scientific American Mind,* 38–41.

Siebern, A. T., & Manber, R. (2011). New developments in cognitive behavioral therapy as the first-line treatment of insomnia. *Psychology Research and Behavior Management, 4,* 21–28.

Siegel, J. M. (2009). Sleep viewed as a state of adaptive inactivity. *Nature Reviews Neuroscience, 10,* 747–753.

Siegel, J. M. (2011). REM sleep. In M. H. Kryger, T. Roth, & W. C. Dement, *Principles and practice of sleep medicine.* St. Louis, MO: Elsevier Saunders.

Siegel., J. M., Manger, P. R., Nienhuis, R., Fahringer, H. M., & Pettigrew, J. D. (1996). The echidna *Tachglossus aculeatus* combines REM and non-REM aspects in a single sleep state: Implications for the evolution of sleep. *The Journal of Neuroscience, 16,* 3500–3506.

Siversten, B., Omvik, S., Passesen, S., Bjorvatn, B., Odd, E. H., Kvale, G., . . . Nordhus, I. (2006). Cognitive behavioral therapy vs. Zopiclone for treatment of chronic primary insomnia in older adults. *JAMA, 295,* 2851–2858.

Smith, C. T. (1996). Sleep states, memory processes and synaptic plasticity. *Behavioral Neuroscience Research, 78,* 49–56.

Smith, C. T. (2001). Sleep states and memory processes in humans: Procedural vs. declarative memory systems. *Sleep Medicine Reviews, 5,* 491–506.

Smith, C., & Lapp, L. (1991). Increases in number of REMs and REM density in humans following an intensive learning period. *Sleep, 14,* 325–330.

Spiegel, K., Sheridan, J. F., & Van Cauter, E. (2002). Effect of sleep deprivation on response to immunization. *JAMA, 288,* 1471–1472.

Spiga, F., Walker, J. J., Terry, J. R., & Lightman, S. L. (2014). HPA axis rhythms. *Comprehensive Physiology, 4,* 1273–1298.

Steriade, M., & Contreras, D. (1995). Relations between cortical and thalamic cellular events during transition from sleep patterns to paroxysmal activity. *Journal of Neuroscience, 15,* 623–642.

Stickgold, R., Whidbee, D., Schirmer, B., Patel, V., & Hobson, J. A. (2000). Visual discrimination task improvement: A multistep process occurring during sleep. *Journal of Cognitive Neuroscience, 12,* 246–254.

Suchecki, D., Tiba, P. A., & Machado, R. B. (2012). REM sleep rebound as an adaptive response to stressful situations. *Frontiers in Neurology.* doi:10.3389/neur.2012.00041

Terman, L. M., & Hocking, A. (1913). The sleep of schoolchildren: Its distribution according to age and its relation to physical and mental efficiency. *Journal of Educational Psychology, 4,* 138–147.

Tobler, I. I., Franken, P., Trachsel, L., & Borbely, A. A. (1992). Models of sleep regulation in mammals. *Journal of Sleep Research, 1,* 125–127.

Toth, L. A., & Jhaveri, K. (2003). Sleep mechanisms in health and disease. *Comparative Medicine, 53,* 473–486.

Vanhaudenhuyse, A., Demertzi, A., Schabus, M., Noirhomme, Q., Bredart, S., Boly, M., . . . Laureys, S. (2011). Two distinct neuronal networks mediate the awareness of environment and of self. *Journal of Cognitive Neuroscience, 23,* 570–578.

Vazquez, J., & Baghdoyan, H. A. (2001). Basal forebrain acetylcholine release during REM sleep is significantly greater than during waking. *American Journal of Psychological Regulatory Integrative Comp Physiology, 280,* R598–R601.

Voirin, B. (2011). Why do animals sleep? New York Times.com. Retrieved from http://scientistatwork.blogs.nytimes.com/2011/03/18/why-do-animals-sleep/

Vyazovskiy, V. V., Cirelli, C., Pfister-Genskow, M., Faraguna, U., & Tononi, G. (2008). Molecular and electrophysiological evidence for net synaptic potentiation in wake and depression in sleep. *Nature Neuroscience, 11,* 200–208.

Wagner, U., Gals, S., Halder, H., Verteger, R., & Born, J. (2004). Sleep inspires insight. *Nature, 427,* 352–355.

Waite, E. J., McKenna, M., Kershaw, Y., Walker, J. J., Cho, K., Piggins, H. D., & Lightman, S. L. (2012). Ultradian corticosterone secretion is maintained in the absence of circadian cues. *European Journal of Neuroscience, 36,* 3142–3150.

Webb, W. B. (1974). Sleep as an adaptive response. *Perceptual and Motor Skills, 38,* 1023–1027.

Webster, H. H., & Jones, B. E. (1988). Neurotoxic lesions of the dorsolateral pontomesencephalic tegmentum–cholinergic cell area in the cat II. Effects upon sleep–waking states *Brain Research, 458,* 285–302.

Wehr, T. A. (1992). In short photoperiods, human sleep is biphasic. *Journal of Sleep Research, 1,* 103–107.

Wilson, M. A., & McNaughton, B. L. (1994). Reactivation of hippocampal ensemble memories during sleep. *Science, 265,* 676–679.

Wilson, S., & Argyropoulos, S. (2005). Antidepressants and sleep: A qualitative review of the literature. *Drugs, 65,* 927–947.

Winson, J. (2002, updated from original 1990 (Nov) version). The meaning of dreams. *Scientific American,* 54–61.

Worthman, C. M., & Melby, M. (2002). Toward a comparative developmental ecology of human sleep. In M. A. Carskadon (Ed.), *Adolescent sleep patterns: Biological, social, and psychological influences* (pp. 69–117). New York, NY: Cambridge University Press.

Yetish, G., Kaplan, H., Gurven, M., Wood, B., Pontzer, H., Manger, P. R., . . . Siegel, J. M. (2015). Natural sleep and its seasonal variations in three pre-industrial societies. *Current Biology, 25,* 2862–2868.

CHAPTER 10

Abelson, J. L., Liberzon, I., Young, E. A., & Khan, S. (2005). Cognitive modulation of the endocrine stress response to a pharmacological challenge in normal and panic disorder subjects. *Archives of General Psychiatry, 62,* 668–675.

Abrantes, R. (2005). *The Evolution of Canine Social Behavior* (2nd ed.), Naperville, IL: Wakan Tanka.

Adolphs, R., Tranel, D., Damasio, H., & Damasio, A. (1994). Impaired recognition of emotion in facial expressions following bilateral damage to the human amygdala. *Nature, 372,* 669–672.

Anderson, A. K., & Phelps, E. A. (2001). Lesions of the human amygdala impair enhanced perception of emotionally salient events. *Nature, 411,* 305–309.

Anderson, S. W., Bechara, A., Damasio, H., Tranel, D., & Damasio, A. R. (1999). Impairment of social and moral behavior related to early damage in human prefrontal cortex. *Nature Neuroscience, 2,* 1032–1037.

Archer, J., Graham-Kevan, N., & Davies, M (2005). Testosterone and aggression: A reanalysis of Book, Starzyk, and Quinsey's (2001) study. *Aggression, Violence and Behavior, 10,* 241–261.

Bard, P. A. (1928). A diencephalic mechanism for the expression of rage with special reference to the central nervous system. *American Journal of Physiology, 84,* 490–513.

Baron, R. A., & Richardson, D. (1994). *Human aggression.* New York, NY: Plenum.

Batrinos, M. L. (2012). Testosterone and aggressive behavior in man. *International Journal of Endocrinological Metabolism, 10,* 563–568.

Bechara, A., & Damasio, A. R., (2005). The somatic marker hypothesis: A neural theory of economic decision. *Games and Economic Behavior, 52,* 336–372.

Bernhardt, P. C., Dabbs, J. M., Fieden, J. A., & Lutter, C. D. (1998). Testosterone changes during vicarious experiences of winning and losing among fans at sporting events. *Physiology & Behavior, 65,* 59–62.

Blanchard, R. J., & Blanchard, D. C. (1990). In N. McNaughton & G. Andrews (Eds.), *Anxiety* (pp. 24–33). Dunedin, New Zealand: Otago University Press.

Breiter, H. D., Etcoff, N. L., Whalen, P. J., Kennedy, W. A., Rauch, S. L., Buckner, R. L., . . . Rosen, B. R. (1996). Response and habituation of the human amygdala during visual processing of facial emotion. *Neuron, 17,* 875–887.

Burgdorf, J., & Panksepp, J. (2001). Tickling induces reward in adolescent rats. *Physiology & Behavior, 72,* 167–173.

Burgdorf, J., & Panksepp, J. (2006). The neurobiology of positive emotions. *Neuroscience and Biobehavioral Reviews, 30,* 173–187.

Cannon, W. B. (1927). The James–Lange theory of emotions, a critical examination and an alternative theory. *American Journal of Psychology, 39,* 106–24.

Cannon, W. B. (1931). Against the James–Lange and the thalamic theories of emotion. *Psychological Review, 38,* 281–295.

Cannon, W. B. (1942). "Voodoo" death. *American Anthropologist, 44,* 169–181.

Carre, J. M., McCormick, C. M., & Hariri, A. (2011). The social neuroendocrinology of human aggression. *Psychoneuroendocrinology, 36,* 935–944.

Cavigelli, S. A., & McClintock, M. K. (2003). Fear of novelty in infant rats predicts adult corticosterone dynamics and an early death. *Proceedings of the National Academy of Sciences of the USA, 100,* 16131–16136.

Cavigelli, S. A., Yee, J. R., & McClintock, M. K. (2006). Infant temperament predicts life span in female rats that develop spontaneous tumors. *Hormones and Behavior, 50,* 454–462.

Charney, D. S. (2004). Psychobiological mechanisms of resilience and vulnerability: Implications for successful adaptation to extreme stress. *American Journal of Psychiatry, 161,* 195–214.

Chiavegatto, S., Dawson, V. L., Mamounas, L. A., Koliatsos, V. E., Dawson, T. M., & Nelson, R. J. (2001). Brain serotonin dysfunction accounts for aggression in male mice lacking neuronal nitric oxide synthase. *Proceedings of the National Academy of Sciences of the USA, 98,* 1277–1281.

Coccaro, E. F., McCloskey, M. S., Fitzgerald, D. A., & Phan, K. L. (2007). Amygdala and orbitofrontal reactivity to social threat in individuals with impulsive aggression. *Biological Psychiatry.* doi:10.1016/j.biopsych.2006.08.024

Cox, J. H., & Ford, W. L. (1982). The migration of lymphocytes across specialized vascular endothelium. IV. Prednisolone acts at several points on the recirculation pathway of lymphocytes. *Cellular Immunology, 66,* 407–422.

Craig, A. D. (2009). How do you feel—Now? The anterior insula and human awareness. *Nature Reviews Neuroscience, 10,* 59–70.

Dabbs, J. M. (1993). Salivary testosterone measurements in behavioral studies. *Annals of the New York Academy of Sciences, 694,* 177–183.

Dalgleish T. (2004). The emotional brain. *Nature Reviews Neuroscience, 582,* 582–589.

Damasio, A. R., Tranel, D., & Damasio, H. (1991). Somatic markers and the guidance of behavior: Theory and preliminary testing. In H. S. Levin, H. M. Eisenberg, & A. L. Benton (Eds.), *Frontal lobe function and dysfunction.* New York, NY: Oxford University Press.

Darwin, C. (1872/1965). *The expression of the emotions in man and animals.* Chicago, IL: Chicago University Press.

Das, A. (2006). Scared to death. *Boston Globe.* Retrieved from http://www.boston.com/news/globe/magazine/articles/2006/08/06/scared_to_death/

Davis, E. S., & Marler, C. A. (2004). C-fos changes following an aggressive encounter in female California mice: A synthesis of behavior, hormone change and neural activity. *Neuroscience, 127,* 611–624.

Deady, D. K., North, N. T., Allan, D., Smith, M. J., & O'Carroll, R. E. (2010). Examining the effect of spinal cord injury on emotional awareness, expressivity and memory for emotional awareness, expressivity and memory for emotional material. *Psychology, Health and Medicine, 15,* 406–419.

De Almeida, R. M., Ferrari, P. M., Parmigiani, S., & Miczek, K. A. (2005). Escalated aggressive behavior: dopamine, serotonin and GABA. *European Journal of Pharmacology, 526,* 51–64.

De Bruin, J. P., van Oyen, H. C., & Van de Poll, N. (1983). Behavioural changes following lesions of the orbital prefrontal cortex in male rats. *Behavioral and Brain Research, 10,* 209–232.

De Gelder, B. (2006). Towards the neurobiology of emotional body language. *Nature Reviews Neuroscience, 7,* 242–249.

Delville, Y., De Vries, C. J., & Ferris, G. F. (2000). Neural connections of the anterior hypothalamus and agonistic behavior in golden hamsters. *Brain Behavior and Evolution, 55,* 53–76.

Demas, G. E., Moffatt, C. A., Drazen, D. L., & Nelson, R. J. (1999). Castration does not inhibit aggressive behavior in adult male prairie voles (*Microtus ochrogaster*). *Physiology and Behavior, 66,* 59–62.

Dhabhar, F. S. (2002). A hassle a day may keep the doctor away: Stress and the augmentation of immune function. *Integrative and Comparative Biology, 42,* 556–564.

Dhabhar, F. S., & McEwen, B. S. (1996). Stress-induced enhancement of antigen-specific cell-mediated immunity. *Journal of Immunology, 156,* 2608–2615.

Dhabhar, F. S., & McEwen, B. S. (1999). Enhancement of the immunization/sensitization phase of cell-mediated immunity: The role of acute stress and adrenal stress hormones. *Neuroimmunomodulation, 6,* 213.

Dhabhar, F. S., Miller, A. H., McEwen, B. S., & Spencer, R. L. (1995). Effects of stress on immune cell distribution—Dynamics and hormonal mechanisms. *Journal of Immunology, 154,* 5511–5527.

Dixson, A. F., & Lloyd, S. A. C. (1988). Effects of hypothalamic lesions upon sexual and social behaviour of the male common marmoset (*Callithrix jacchus*). *Brain Research, 463,* 317–329.

Dutton, D. G., & Aron, A. P. (1974). Some evidence for heightened sexual attraction under conditions of high anxiety. *Journal of Personality and Social Psychology, 30,* 310–317.

Eagleman, D. (2011). The Brain on Trial. *The Atlantic* (June/July), http://www.theatlantic.com/magazine/archive/2011/07/the-brain-on-trial/308520/

Ekman, E., Ekman, P., & Marsh, J. (2008, Fall). Can I trust you? *Greater Good,* 20–24.

Ekman, P. (2003). Darwin, deception, and facial expression. *Annals of the New York Academy of Science, 1000,* 205–221.

Ekman, P., Levenson, R. W., & Friesen, W. V. (1983). Autonomic nervous system activity distinguishes among emotions. *Science, 221,* 1208–1210.

Emery, N. J., Capitanio, J. P., Mason, W. A., Machado, C. J., Mendoza, S. P., & Amaral, D. G. (2001). The effects of bilateral lesions of the amygdala on dyadic social interactions in rhesus monkeys (*Macaca mulatta*). *Behavioral Neuroscience, 115,* 515–544.

Feder, A., Nestler, E. J., & Charney, D. S. (2009). Psychobiology and molecular genetics of resilience. *Nature Neuroscience Reviews, 10,* 446–457.

Flood, J. F., Baker, M. L., Hernandez, E. N., & Morley, J. E. (1989). Modulation of memory processing by neuropeptide Y varies with brain injection site. *Brain Research, 503,* 73–82.

Fredrickson, B. L. (1998). What good are positive emotions? *Review of General Psychology, 2,* 300–319.

Gianaros, P. J., Marsland, A. L., Kuan, D. C-H., Schirda, B. L., Jennings, J. R., Sheu, L. K., Hariri, A. R., Gross, J. J., & Manuck, S. B. (2014). An inflammatory pathway links atherosclerotic and cardiovascular disease risk to neural activity evoked by the cognitive regulation of emotions. *Biological Psychiatry, 75,* 738–745.

Gilbert, P. (2000). Varieties of submissive behavior as forms of social defense: Their evolution and role in depression (pp. 3–45). In P. Gilbert & L. Sloman (Eds.), *Subordination and defeat: An evolutionary approach to mood disorders and their therapy.* Mahwah, NJ: Erlbaum.

Gladstone, G. L., Parker, G. B., & Malhi, G. S. (2006). Do bullied children become anxious and depressed adults: A cross-sectional investigation of the correlates of bullying and anxious depression. *The Journal of Nervous and Mental Disease, 194,* 201–208.

Glaser, R., & Kiecolt-Glaser, J. K. (2005). Stress-induced immune dysfunction: Implications for health. *Nature Reviews Immunology, 5,* 10–18.

Gross, J. J. (2008). Emotion regulation. In M. Lewis, J. M. Haviland-Jones, & L. F. Barrett (Eds.), *Handbook of emotions.* New York, NY: Guilford Press.

Haller, J., & Kruk, M. R. (2006). Normal and abnormal aggression: Human disorders and novel laboratory models. *Neuroscience and Biobehavioral Reviews, 30,* 292–303.

Hamann, S. B., Ely, T. D., Grafton, S. T., & Kilts, C. D. (1999). Amygdala activity related to enhanced memory for pleasant and aversive stimuli. *Nature Neuroscience, 2,* 289–293.

Hasen, N. S., & Gammie, S. C. (2005). Differential FOS activation in virgin and lactating mice in resonse to an intruder. *Physiology & Behavior, 84,* 681–695.

Hawkins, W. E., & Clower, B. R. (1971). Myocardial damage after head trauma and simulated intracranial haemmorrhage in mice: The role of the autonomic nervous system. *Cardiovascular Research, 5,* 524–529.

Hawley, D. F., Bardi, M., Everette, A. M., Higgins, T. J., Tu, K. M., Kinsley, C. H., & Lambert, K. G. (2010). Neurobiological constituents of active, passive, and variable coping strategies in rats: Integration of regional brain neuropeptide Y levels and cardiovascular responses. *Stress, 13,* 172–183.

Hou, C., Jia, F., Liu, Y., & Li, L. (2006). CSF serotonin, 5-hydroxyindolacetic acid and neuropeptide Y levels in severe major depressive disorder. *Brain Research, 1095,* 154–158.

House, P. K., Vyas, A., and Sapolsky, R. (2011). Predator cat odors activate sexual arousal pathways in brains of Toxoplasma gondii infected rats. *PLoS ONE.* http://dx.doi.org/10.1371/Journal.pone.0023277.

Huhman, K. L., Moore, T. O., Mougey, E. H., & Meyerhoff, J. L. (1992). Hormonal responses to fighting in hamsters: Separation of physical and psychological causes. *Physiology & Behavior, 51,* 1083–1086.

Huhman, K. L., Solomon, M. B., Janicki, M., Harmon, A. C., Lin, S. M., Israel, J. E., Jasnow, A. M. (2003). Conditioned defeat in male and female Syrian hamsters. Hormones & *Behavior, 44,* 293–299.

James, W. (1884). What is an emotion? *Mind, 9,* 188–205.

Jasnow, A. M., Drazen, D. L., Huhman, K. L., Nelson, R. J., & Demas, G. E. (2001). Acute and chronic social defeat suppresses humoral immunity of male Syrian hamsters (*Mesocricetus auratus*). *Hormones and Behavior, 40,* 428–433.

Joels, M., & Baram, T. Z. (2009). The neuro-symphony of stress. *Nature Reviews Neuroscience, 10,* 459–466.

Karishma, K. K., & Herbert, J. (2002). Dehydorepiandrosterone (DHEA) stimulates neurogenesis in the hippocampus of the rat, promotes survival of newly formed neurons and prevents corticosterone-induced suppression. *European Journal of Neuroscience, 16,* 445–453.

Kiecolt-Glaser, J. K., Loving, T. J., Stowell, J. R., Malarkey, W. B., Lemeshow, S., Dickinson, S. L., & Glaser, R. (2005). Hostile marital interactions, proinflammatory cytokine productions, and wound healing, *Archives of General Psychiatry, 62,* 1377–1384.

Kim, Y. S., Leventhal, B. L., Koh, Y. J., Hubbard, A., & Boyce, W. T. (2006). School bullying and youth violence: Causes or consequences of psychopathologic behavior? *Archives of General Psychiatry, 63,* 1035–1041.

Kimonides, V. G., Khatibi, N. H., Svendsen, C. N., Sofroniew, M. V., & Herbert, J. (1998). Dehydroepiandrosterone (DHEA) and DHEA-sulfate (DHEAS) protect hippocampal neurons against excitatory amino acid in neurotoxicity. *Proceedings of the National Academy of Sciences of the USA, 95,* 1852–1857.

Klüver, H., & Bucy, P. C. (1937). Psychotic blindness and other symptoms following bilateral temporal lobectomy. *American Journal of Physiology, 221,* 1208–1210.

Kollack-Walker, S., & Newman, S. W. (1995). Mating and agonistic behavior produce different patterns of FOS immunolabeling in the male Syrian hamster brain, *Neuroscience, 66,* 721–736.

Koolhaas, J. M., Korte, S. M., De Boer, S. F., Van Der Begt, B. J., Van Reenen, C. G., Hopsger, H., . . . Blokhuis, H. J. (1999). Coping styles in animals: Current status in behavior and stress-physiology. *Neuroscience and Biobehavioral Reviews, 23,* 925–935.

Kruk, M. R. (1991). Ethology and pharmacology of hypothalamic aggression in the rat. *Neuroscience and Biobehavioral Reviews, 15,* 527–538.

Lange, C. (1885). In E. Dunlap (Ed.), *The emotions.* Baltimore, MD: Williams & Wilkins.

Langford, D. J., Bailey, A. L., Chanda, M. L., Clarke, S. E., Drummond, T. E., Echols, S., . . . Mogil, J. S. (2010). Coding of facial expressions of pain in the laboratory mouse. *Nature Methods, 7,* 447–449. doi:10.1038/nmeth.1455

LeDoux, J. (1996). *The emotional brain.* New York, NY: Simon & Schuster.

LeDoux, J. (2003). The emotional brain, fear, and the amygdala. *Cellular and Molecular Neurobiology, 23,* 727–738.

Lereya, S. T., Copeland, W. E., Costello, E. J., & Woke, D. (2015). Adult mental health consequences of peer bullying and maltreatment in childhood: Two cohorts in two countries. *The Lancet Psychiatry, 2,* 524–531.

Levesque, J., Eugene, F., Joanette, Y., Paquette, V., Mensour, B., Beaudoin, G., . . . Beauregard, M. (2003). Neural circuitry underlying voluntary suppression of sadness. *Biological Psychiatry, 53,* 502–510.

Lipp, H. P., & Hunsperger, R. W. (1978). Threat, attack, and fight elicited by electrical stimulation of the ventromedial hypothalamus of the marmoset monkey *Callithrix jacchus. Brain Behavior and Evolution, 15,* 260–293.

Machado, C. J., & Bachevalier, J. (2006). The impact of selective amygdala, orbital frontal cortex, or hippocampal formation lesions on established social relationships in rhesus monkeys (*Macaca mulatta*). *Behavioral Neuroscience, 120,* 761–786.

MacLean, P. (1998). Paul D. MacLean. In L. S. Squire (Ed.), *The history of neuroscience in autobiography* (pp. 244–275). New York, NY: Academic Press.

Maninger, N., Wolkowitz, O. M., Reus, V. I., Epel, E. S., & Mellon S. H. (2008). Neurobiological and neuropsychiatric effects of dehydroepiandrosterone (DHEA) and DHEA sulfate (DHEAS). *Frontiers in Neuroendocrinology, 30,* 65–91.

Markham, C. M., & Huhman, K. L. (2008). Is the medial amygdala part of the neural circuit modulating conditioned defeat in Syrian hamsters? *Learning and Memory, 15,* 6–12.

Markham, C. M., Luckett, C. A., & Huhman, K. L. (2012). The medial prefrontal cortex is both necessary and sufficient for the acquisition of conditioned defeat. *Neuropharmacology, 62,* 933–939.

Marsh, B. (2009, February 14). The voice was lying. The face may have told the truth. *The New York Times.* Retrieved from http://www.nytimes.com/2009/02/15/weekinreview/15marsh.html?_r=0

Marucha, P. T., Kieclot-Glaser, J. K., & Favagehi, M. (1998). Mucosal wound healing is impaired by examination stress. *Psychosomatic Medicine, 60,* 362–365.

McEwen, B. (2008). Central effects of stress hormones in health and disease: Understanding the protective and damaging effects of stress and stress mediators. *European Journal of Pharmacology, 583,* 174–185.

Meyer-Lindenberg, A., Mervis, C. B., & Berman, K. F. (2006). Neural mechanisms in Williams syndrome: A unique window to genetic influences on cognition and behaviour. *Nature Neuroscience Reviews, 7,* 380–393.

Miczek, K. A., & Fish, E. W. (2006). Monoamines, GABA, glutamate, and aggression. In R. J. Nelson (Ed.), *Biology of aggression* (pp. 114–149). New York, NY: Oxford University Press.

Miczek, K. A., Maxson, S. C., Fish, E. W., & Faccidomo, S. (2001). Aggressive behavioral phenotypes in mice. *Behavioral Brain and Research, 125,* 167–181.

Mobbs, D., Yu, R., Rowe, J. B., Elch, H., FeldmanHall, O., & Dalgleish, T. (2010). Neural activity associated with monitoring the oscillating threat value of a tarantula. *Proceedings of the National Academy of Sciences of the USA, 47,* 20582–20585.

Morfin, R., & Starka, L. (2001). Neurosteroid 7-hydroxylation products in the brain. *International Review of Neurobiology, 46,* 79–95.

Morgan, C. A., Southwick, S., Hazlett, G., Rasmusson, A., Hoyt, G., Zimolo, A.,& Charney, D. . (2004). Relationships among plasma dehydroepiandrosterone sulfate and cortisol levels, symptoms of dissociation, and objective performance in humans exposed to acute stress. *Archives of General Psychiatry, 61,* 819–825.

Nelson, R. J., & Chiavegatto, S. (2001). Molecular basis of aggression. *Trends in Neuroscience, 24,* 713–719.

Nelson, R. J., & Trainor, B. C. (2007). Neural mechanisms of aggression. *Nature Reviews Neuroscience, 8,* 536–546.

Nicotra, A., Critchley, H. D., Mathias, C. J., & Dolan, R. J. (2006). Emotional and autonomic consequences of spinal cord injury explored using functional brain imaging. *Brain, 129,* 718–728.

Nili, U., Goldberg, H., Weizman, A., & Dudai, Y. (2010). Fear thou not: Activity of frontal and temporal circuit in moments of real-life courage. *Neuron, 66,* 949–962.

Ochsner, K. N., Bunge, S. A., Gross, J. J., & Babrieli, J. D. E. (2002). Rethinking feelings: An fMRI study of the cognitive regulation of emotion. *Journal of Cognitive Neuroscience, 14,* 1215–1229.

Ochsner, K. N., & Gross, J. J. (2005). The cognitive control of emotion. *Trends in Cognitive Sciences, 9,* 242–249.

Olivier, B. (2005). Serotonergic mechanisms in aggression. *Novartis Foundations Symposium, 268,* 171–183.

Panksepp, J., & Burgdorf, J. (2003). "Laughing" rats and the evolutionary antecedents of human joy? *Physiology & Behavior, 79,* 533–547.

Papez, J. W. (1937). A proposed mechanism of emotion. *Archives of Neurology and Psychiatry, 38,* 725–743.

Phelps, E. A. (2004). Human emotion and memory: Interactions of the amygdala and hippocampal complex. *Current Opinion in Neurobiology, 14,* 198–202.

Pribram, K. H. (1998). Karl H. Pribram. In L. S. Squire (Ed.), *The history of neuroscience in autobiography* (pp. 306–349). New York, NY: Academic Press.

Public Broadcasting System. (2009). *This emotional life.* Retrieved from http://www.pbs.org/thisemotionallife

Richter, C. P. (1957). On the phenomenon of sudden death in animals and man. *Psychosomatic Medicine, 19,* 191–198.

Rodriguiz, R. M., Chu, R., Caron, M. G., & Wetsel, W. C. (2004). Aberrant responses in social interaction of dopamine transporter knockout mice. *Behavior Brain Research, 148,* 185–198.

Rule, R. R., Shimamura, A. P., & Knight, R. T. (2002). Orbitofrontal cortex and dynamic filtering of emotional stimuli. *Cognitive, Affective & Behavioural Neuroscience, 2,* 264–270.

Sajdyk, T. J., Vandergriff, M. G., & Gehlert, D. R. (1999). Amygdalar neuropeptide Y Y1 receptors mediate the anxiolytic-like actions of neuropeptide Y in the social interaction test. *European Journal of Pharmacology, 368,* 143–147.

Samuels, M. A. (2007). "Voodoo" death revisited: The modern lessons of neurocardiology. *Cleveland Clinic Journal of Medicine, 74,* S8–S16.

Sansone, R. A., & Sansone, L. A. (2008). Bully victims: Psychological and somatic aftermaths. *Psychiatry, June,* 62–64.

Sapolsky, R. (1998). *Why zebras don't get ulcers.* New York, NY: Holt.

Schachter, S. (1964). The interaction of cognitive and physiological determinants of emotional state. In L. Berkowitz (Ed.), *Advances in experimental social psychology.* New York, NY: Academic Press.

Schachter, S., & Singer, J. E. (1962). Cognitive, social and physiological components of the emotional state. *Psychological Review, 69,* 379–399.

Sohn, E. (2010). The no-fear woman (and what her brain reveals). *Discovery News,* December 16, 2010. Retrieved from http://www.seeker.com/the-no-fear-woman-and-what-her-brain-reveals-1765153069.html

Stemmler, G. (1997). Selective activation of traits: Boundary conditions for the activation of anger. *Personality and Individual Differences, 22,* 213–233.

Sternberg, E. M. (2000). *The balance within: The science connecting health and emotions.* New York, NY: Freeman.

Stix, G. (2011). The neuroscience of grit. *Scientific American, 304,* 28–33.

Tamir, M., John, O. P., Srivastava, S., & Gross, J. J. (2007). Implicit theories of emotion: Affective and social outcomes across a major life transition. *Journal of Personality and Social Psychology, 92,* 731–744.

Taylor, S. L., Stanek, L. M., Ressler, K. J., & Huhman, K. L. (2011). Differential brain-derived neurotrophic factor expression in limbic brain regions following social defeat or territorial aggression. *Behavioral Neuroscience, 125,* 911–920.

Thorsell, A., Carlsson, K., Ekman, R., & Heilig, M. (1999). Behavioral and endocrine adaptation, and up-regulation of NPY expression in rat amygdala following repeated restraint stress. *Neuroreport, 10,* 3003–3007.

Trainor, B. C., Kyomen, H. H., & Marler, C. A. (2006). Estrogenic encounters: How interactions between aromatase and the environment modulate aggression. *Frontiers in Neuroendocrinology, 27,* 170–179.

Ulrich-Lai, Y. M., & Herman, J. P. (2009) Neural regulation of endocrine and autonomic stress responses. *Nature Reviews Neuroscience, 10,* 397–409.

Van Erp-Van der Kooji, E., Kuipers, H. H., Schrama, J. W., Eckel, E. D., & Tielen, M. J. M. (2000). Individual behavioral characteristics in pigs and their impact on production. *Applied Animal Behavior Science, 66,* 171–185.

Vyas, A., Kim, S. K., Sapolsky, R. M. (2007). The effects of toxoplasma infection on rodent behavior are dependent on dose of the stimulus. *Neuroscience, 148*(2), 342–348

Weiskrantz. L. (1956). Behavioral changes associated with ablation of the amygdaloid complex in monkeys. *Journal of Comparative and Physiological Psychology, 49,* 381–391.

Wemm, S., Koone, T., Blough, E. R., Mewaldt, S., & Bardi, M. (2010). The role of DHEA in relation to problem solving and academic performance. *Biological Psychology, 85,* 53–61.

Westphal, M., Seivert, N. H, & Bonanno, G. A. (2010). Expressive flexibility. *Emotion, 10,* 92–100.

Wingfield, J. C., Hegner, R. E., Dufty, A. M., & Ball, G. F. (1990). The "challenge hypothesis": Theoretical implications for patterns of testosterone secretion, mating systems, and breeding strategies. *American Naturalist, 136,* 829–846.

Wohr, M., Kehl, M., Borta, A., Schanzer, A., Schwarting, R., & Hoglinger, G. U. (2009). New insights into the relationship of neurogenesis and affect: Tickling induces hippocampal cell proliferation in rats emitting appetitive 50-kHz ultrasonic vocalization. *Neuroscience, 163,* 1024–1030.

Yamamuro, T., Senzaki, K., Iwamoto, S., Nakagawa, Y., Hayashi, T., Hori, M., Sakamoto, S., & Urayama, O. (2010). Neurogenesis in the dentate gyrus of the rat hippocampus enhanced by tickling stimulation with positive emotion. *Neuroscience Research, 68,* 285–289.

Yehuda, R., Brand, S., & Yang, R. K. (2005). Plasma neuropeptide Y concentrations in combat exposed veterans: Relationship to trauma exposure, recovery from PTSD, and coping. *Biological Psychiatry, 59,* 660–663.

Yehuda, R., Brand, S. R., & Golier, J. A., & Yang, R. K. (2006). Clinical correlates of DHEA associated with post-traumatic stress disorder. *Acta Psychiatrica Scandinavica, 114,* 187–193.

Zhang, W., Li, F., Qin, S., & Luo, J. (2012). The integrative effects of cognitive reappraisal on negative affect: Associated changes in secretory immunoglobulin A., unpleasantness and ERP activity. *Public Library of Science ONE, 7,* e30761.

CHAPTER 11

Amateau, S. K., & McCarthy, M. M. (2002). A novel mechanism of dendritic spine density plasticity involving estradiol induction of prostaglandin-E2. *Journal of Neuroscience, 22,* 8586–8596.

Amateau, S. K., & McCarthy, M. M. (2004). Induction of PGE2 by estradiol mediates developmental masculinization of sex behavior. *Nature Neuroscience, 7,* 643–650.

Argona, B. J., Liu, Y., Curtis, J. T., Stephan, F. K., & Wang, Z. (2003). A critical role for nucleus accumbens dopamine in partner-preference formation in male prairie voles. *Journal of Neuroscience, 23,* 3483–3490.

Arnold, A. P., & Breedlove, S. M. (1985). Organizational and activational effects of sex steroids on brain and behavior: A reanalysis. *Hormones and Behavior, 19,* 469–498.

Barraza, J. A., & Zak, P. J. (2009). Empathy toward strangers triggers oxytocin release and subsequent generosity. Values, empathy, and fairness across social barriers. *Annals of the New York Academy of Sciences, 1167,* 182–189.

Bartels, A., & Zeki, S. (2004). The neural correlates of maternal and romantic love. *Neuroimage, 21,* 1155–1166.

Baskerville, S. (2002). The politics of fatherhood. *Political Science & Politics, 35,* 695–699.

Bateman, A. J. (1948). Intra-sexual selection in Drosophila. *Heredity, 2,* 349–368.

Beach, F. A. (1948). *Hormones and behavior.* New York, NY: Hoeber.

Berenbaum, S. A., & Beltz, A. M. (2011). Sexual differentiation of human behavior: Effects of prenatal and pubertal organizational hormones. *Frontiers in Neuroendocrinology, 32,* 183–200.

Berenbaum, S. A., & Hines, M. (1992). Early androgens are related to childhood sex-typed toy preferences. *Psychological Science, 3,* 203–206.

Berenson, A. (2005, December 5). Sales of impotence drugs fall, defying expectations. *The New York Times.* Retrieved from http://www.nytimes.com/2005/12/04/business/yourmoney/04impotence.html/

Bergmuller, R., & Taborsky, M. (2005). Experimental manipulation of helping in a cooperative breeder: Helpers "pay to stay" by preemptive appeasement. *Animal Behaviour, 69,* 19–28.

Bermant, G. (1967). Copulation in rats. *Psychology Today, 1,* 52–60.

Bielsky, I. F., Hu, S. B., Ren, X., Terwilliger, E. F., & Young, L. J. (2005): The V1z vasopressin receptor is necessary and sufficient for normal social recognition: a gene replacement study. *Neuron, 47,* 503–513.

Bonneaud, C., Mazuc, J., Chastel, O., Westerdahl, H., & Sorci, G. (2004). Terminal investment induced by immune challenge and fitness traits associated with major histocompatibility complex in the house sparrow. *Evolution, 58,* 2823–2830.

Bono, C. (with P. Fitzpatrick). (2012). *Transition: Becoming who I was always meant to be.* New York, NY: Plume.

Bridges, R. S. (1990). Endocrine regulation of parental behavior in rodents. In N. A. Krasnegor & R. S. Bridges (Eds.), *Mammalian parenting: Biochemical, neurobiological, and behavioral determinants* (pp. 93–117). New York, NY: Oxford University Press.

Bridges, R. S., Dibiase, R., Loundes, D. D., & Doherty, P. C. (1985). Prolactin stimulation of maternal behavior in female rats. *Science, 227*, 782–784.

Bridges, R. S., & Ronsheim, P. M. (1987). Immunoreactive beta-endorphin concentrations in brain and plasma during pregnancy in rats: Possible modulation by progesterone and estradiol. *Neuroendocrinology, 45*, 381–388.

Brock, P. (2009). *Charlatan: America's most dangerous huckster, the man who pursued him and the age of the flimflam.* New York, NY: Broadway Books.

Buckwalter, J. G., Stanzyk, F. Z., McCleary, C. A., Bluestein, B. W., Buclwalter, D. K., Rankin, K. P., . . . Goodwin, T. M. (1999). Pregnancy, the postpartum, and steroid hormones: Effects on cognition and mood. *Psychoneuroendocrinology, 24*, 69–84.

Cahill, L. (2000). Modulation of long-term memory in humans by emotional arousal: Adrenergic activation and the amygdala. In J. Aggleton (Ed.). *The amygdala: A functional analysis* (pp. 425–444). London, UK: Oxford University Press.

Cahill, L. (2006). Why sex matters for neuroscience. *Nature Reviews Neuroscience, 7*, 477–484.

Cahill, L., Haier, R. J., White, N. S., Fallon, J., Kilpatrick, L., Lawrence, C., . . . Alkire, M. T. (2001). Sex-related difference in amygdala activity during emotionally influenced memory storage. *Neurobiology, Learning and Memory, 75*, 1–9.

Cahill, L., Uncapher, M., Kilpatrick, L., Alkire, M. T., & Turner, J. (2004). Sex-related hemispheric lateralization of amygdala function in emotionally influenced memory: An fMRI investigation. *Learning and Memory, 11*, 261–266.

Canli, T., Desmond, J., Zhao, Z., & Gabrieli, J. D. E. (2002). Sex differences in the neural basis of emotional memories. *Proceedings of the National Academy of Science of the USA, 99*, 10789–10794.

Carter, C. S., DeVaries, A. C., & Getz, L. L. (1995). Physiological substrates of monogamy: The prairie vole model. *Neuroscience and Biobehavioral Reviews, 19*, 303–314.

Chaix, R., Cao, C., & Donnelly, P (2008). Is mate choice in humans MHC-dependent? *PLoS Genetics, 4*, e1000184.

Cho, M. M., DeVries, A. C., Williams, J. R., & Carter, C. S. (1999). The effects of oxytocin and vasopressin on partner preference in male and female prairie voles (*Microtus ochrogaster*). *Behavioral Neuroscience, 113*, 1071–1079.

Conan, N. (Interviewer), & Bono, C. (Interviewee). (2011, May 15). "Through 'transition,' Chastity Bono becomes Chaz." *Talk of the Nation* [interview transcript]. Retrieved from http://www.npr.org/2011/05/10/136177386/through-transition-chastity-becomes-chaz

Cooke, B. M., & Woolley, C. S. (2005). Gonadal hormone modulation of dendrites in the mammalian CNS. *Journal of Neurobiology, 64*, 34–46.

Coppinger, R., & Schneider, R. (1995). Evolution of working dogs. In J. Serpell (Ed.), *The domestic dog: Its evolution, behaviour and interactions with people* (pp. 21–47). Cambridge, UK: Cambridge University Press.

Cortez, D., Marin, R., Toledo-Flores, D., Froidevaux, L., Lichti, A., Waters, P. D., . . . Kaessmann, H. (2014). Origins and functional evolution of Y chromosomes across mammals. *Nature, 508*, 488–493.

Dewsbury, Donald A. (2000) Frank A. Beach, master teacher. *Portraits of Pioneers in Psychology, 4*, 269–281.

Edwards, S., & Self, D. W. (2006). Monogamy: Dopamine ties the knot. *Nature Neuroscience, 9*, 7–8. doi:10.1038/nn0106-7

Erskine, M. S. (1989). Solicitation behavior in the estrous female rat: A review. *Hormones and Behavior, 23*, 473–502.

Everitt, B. J. (1990). Sexual motivation: A neural and behavioural analysis of the mechanisms underlying appetitive and copulatory responses of male rats. *Neuroscience and Biobehavioral Reviews, 16*, 217–232.

Febo, M., & Ferris, C. F. (2008). Imaging the maternal rat brain. In R. S. Bridges (Ed.), *Neurobiology of the Parental Brain*. New York, NY: Academic Press.

Ferris. C. F., Kulkarni, P., Sullivan, J. M., Jr, Harder, J. A., Messenger, T. L, & Febo, M. (2005). Pup suckling is more rewarding than cocaine: Evidence from functional magnetic resonance imaging and three dimensional computational analysis. *Journal of Neuroscience, 25*, 149–156.

Fisher, H., Aron, A., & Brown, L. L. (2006). Romantic love: A mammalian brain system for mate choice. *Philosophical Transactions of the Royal Society, 361*, 2173–2186.

Franz, M., Lieberz, K., Schmitz, N., & Schepank, H. (1999). The missing father. Epidemiological findings on the significance of early absence of the father for mental health in later life. *Z Psychosomatic Medicine and Psychotherapy, 45*, 260–278.

Freedman, A. H., Gronau, I., Schweizer, R. M., Vecchyo, D., Han, E., Silva, P. M., . . . Novembre, J. (2014). Genome sequencing highlights the dynamic early history of dogs. *PLOS Genetics, 10*, e1004016. doi:10.1371/journal.pgen.1004631

Furuta, M., & Bridges, R. S. (2009). Effects of maternal behavior induction and pup exposure on neurogenesis in adult, virgin female rats. *Brain Research Bulletin, 80*, 408–413.

Galea, L. A., Ormerod, B., Sampath, S., Kostaras, X., Wilkie, D., & Phelps, M. (2000). Spatial working memory and hippocampal size across pregnancy in rats. *Hormones and Behavior, 37*, 86–95.

Garfield, C. F., & Isacco, A. (2006). Fathers and the well-child visit. *Pediatrics, 117*, e637–e645.

Gatewood, J. D., Morgan, M. D., Eaton, M., McNamara, I. M., Stevens, I. F., Macbeth, . . . Kinsley, C. H. (2005). Motherhood mitigates aging-related decrements in learning and memory and positively affects brain aging in the rat. *Brain Research Bulletin, 66*, 91–98.

Getz, L. L., & Carter, S. C. (1996). Prairie vole partnerships. *American Scientist, 84*, 56–62.

Gingu, C., Dick, A., Patrascoiu, S., Domnisor, L., Mihai, M., Harza, M., & Sinescu, I. (2014). Testicular feminization: Complete androgen insensitivity syndrome. Discussions based on a case report. *Roman Journal of Morphological Embryology, 55*, 177–181.

Goldstein, J. M., Seidman, L. J., Horton, N. J., Makris, N., Kennedy, D. N., Caviness, V. S., Jr., . . . Tsuang, M. T. (2001). Normal sexual dimorphism of the adult human brain assessed by in vivo magnetic resonance imaging. *Cerebral Cortex, 11*, 490–497.

Graham, L. (2012). I'm proud to be a hermaphrodite. Body+Soul, Retrieved from http://www.bodyandsoul.com.au/sex+relationships/wellbeing/im+proud+to+be+a+hermaphrodite,16555/

Gubernick, D. J., Winslow, J. T., Jensen, P., Jeanotte, L., & Bowen, J. (1995): Oxytocin changes in males over the reproductive cycle in the monogamous, biparental California mouse, *Peromyscuscalifornicus*. *Hormones and Behavior, 29*, 59–73.

Gupta, B. P., Thakur, N., Jain, N. P., Banweer, J., & Jain, S. (2010). Osmotically controlled drug delivery system with associated drugs. *Journal of Pharmacy and Pharmacological Science, 13*, 571–588.

Hamann, S., & Canli, T. (2004). Individual differences in emotion processing. *Current Opinions in Neurobiology, 14*, 233–238.

Hamann, S., Stevens, J., Vick, J. H., Bryk, K., Quigley, C. A., Berenbaum, S. A., & Wallen, K. (2014). Brain responses to sexual images in 46 XY women with compete androgen insensitivity syndrome are female-typical. *Hormones and Behavior, 66,* 724–730.

Hamilton, W. L., Diamond, M. C., Johnson, R. E., & Ingham, C. A. (1977). Effects of pregnancy and differential environments on rat cerebral cortical depth. *Behavioral Biology, 19,* 333–340.

Hampson, E., Rovet, J. F., & Altmann, D. (1998). Spatial reasoning in children with congenital adrenal hyperplasia due to 21-hydroxylase deficiency. *Developmental Neuropsychology, 14,* 299–238.

Hampton, J. E., Franssen, C. L., Bardi, M., & Lambert, K. G. (2010). Paternal experience alters neuroplasticity and cell proliferation in California deer mice (*Peromyscus californicus*). Poster presented at the *International Behavioral Neuroscience Society* meeting in Sardinia, Italy.

Hare, B., Brown, M., Williamson, C., & Tomasello, M. (2002). The domestication of social cognition in dogs. *Science, 298,* 1634–1636.

Hauber, M. E., & Lacey, E. A. (2005). Bateman's principle in cooperatively breeding vertebrates: The effects of non-breeding alloparents on variability in female and male reproductive success. *Integrative Comparative Biology, 45,* 903–914.

Helmeke, C., Seidel, K., Poeggel, G., Bredy, T. W., Abraham, A., & Braun, K. (2009). Paternal deprivation during infancy results in dendrite- and time-specific changes of dendritic development and spine formation in the orbitofrontal cortex of the biparental rodent *Octodon degus. Neuroscience, 163,* 790–798.

Hofman, M. A., & Swaab, D. F. (1989). The sexually dimorphic nucleus of the preoptic area in the human brain: a comparative morphometric study. *Journal of Anatomy, 164,* 55–72.

Hoge, E. A., Pollack, M. H., Kaufman, R. E., Zak, P. J., & Simon, N. M. (2008). Oxytocin levels in social anxiety disorder. *CNS Neuroscience and Therapeutics, 14,* 165–170.

Hrdy, S. B. (2009). *Mothers and others.* Boston, MA: Harvard University Press.

Hull, E. M., & Dominguez, J. M. (2007). Sexual behavior in male rodents. *Hormones and Behavior, 52,* 45–55.

Hull, E. M., Muschamp, J. W., & Sato, S. (2004). Dopamine and serotonin: Influences on male sexual behavior. *Physiology and Behavior, 83,* 291–307.

Insel, T. R., & Shapiro, L. E. (1992). Oxytocin receptor distribution reflects social organization and monogamous and polygamous voles. *Proceedings of the National Academy of Sciences of the USA, 89,* 5981–5985.

Insel, T. R., Wang, Z. X., & Ferris, C. F. (1994). Patterns of brain vasopressin receptor distribution associated with social organization in microtine rodents. *Journal of Neuroscience, 14,* 381–392.

Jackson, E. D., Payne, J. D., Nadel, L., & Jacobs, W. J. (2005). Stress differentially modulates fear conditioning in healthy men and women. *Biological Psychiatry, 59,* 516–522.

Jenkins, W. J., & Becker, J. B. (2005). Sex. In I. Whishaw & B. Kolb (Eds.), *The behavior of the laboratory rat* (pp. 307–320). New York, NY: Oxford University Press.

Kim, P., Leckman, J. F., Mayes, L. C., Feldman, R., Wang, X., & Swain, J. E. (2010). The plasticity of human maternal brain: Longitudinal changes in brain anatomy during the early postpartum period. *Behavioral Neuroscience, 123,* 695–700.

Kinsley, C. H., & Lambert, K. G. (2006, January). The maternal brain. *Scientific American,* 72–79.

Kinsley, C. H., Madonia, L., Gifford, G. W., Tureski, K., Griffin, G. R., Lowry, C., . . . Lambert, K. G. (1999). Motherhood improves learning and memory, *Nature, 402,* 137–138.

Kleiman, D. G., & Malcolm, J. R. (1981). The evolution of male parental investment in mammals. In D. J. Gubernick & P. H. Klopfer (Eds.), *Parental care in mammals* (pp. 347–387). New York, NY: Plenum.

Klein, S. L., & Nelson, R. J. (1999). Activation of the immune-endocrine system with lipopolysaccharide reduces affiliative behaviors in voles. *Behavioral Neuroscience, 113,* 1042–1048.

Korol, D. (2004) Role of estrogen in balancing contributions from multiple memory systems. *Neurobiology, Learning and Memory, 82,* 309–323.

Kosfeld, M., Heinrichs, M. Zak, P. J., Fischbacher, U., & Fehr, E. (2005). Oxytocin increases trust in humans. *Nature, 435,* 673–676.

Lalumiere, R. T., & McGaugh, J. L. (2005). Memory enhancement induced by post-training intrabasolateral amygdala infusions of B-adrenergic or muscarinic agonists requires activation of dopamine receptors involvement of right, but not left, basolateral amygdala. *Learning and Memory, 12,* 527–532.

Lambert, K. G. (2012). The parental brain: Transformations and adaptations. *Physiology and Behavior, 107,* 792–800.

Lambert, K. G., Franssen, C. L., Bardi, M., Hampton, J. E., Hainley, L., Karsner, S., . . . Kinsley, C. H. (2011). Characteristic and distinct neurobiological patterns differentiate paternal responsiveness in two Peromyscus species. *Brain, Behavior, and Evolution, 77,* 159–175.

Lambert, K. G., & Kinsley, C. H. (2008). The neuroeconomics of motherhood: Costs and benefits of maternal investment. In R. Bridges (Ed.), *The parental brain.* New York, NY: Elsevier.

Lee, A., Clancy, S., & Fleming, A. S. (1999). Mother rats bar-press for pups: Effects of lesions of the MPOA and limbic sites on maternal behavior and operant responding for pup reinforcement. *Behavioural Brain Research, 100,* 15–31.

Lee, A. W., & Brown, R. E. (2002). Medial preoptic lesions disrupt parental behavior in both male and female California mice (*Peromysus californicus*). *Behavioral Neuroscience,* 968–975.

Lenz, K. M., Nugent, B. M., Haliyur, R., & McCarthy, M. M. (2013). Microglia are essential to masculinization of brain and behavior. *Journal of Neuroscience, 33,* 2761–2772.

LeVay, S. (1991). A difference in hypothalamic structure between heterosexual and homosexual men. *Science, 253,* 1034–1037.

Levine, S. (1966). Sex differences in the brain. *Scientific American, 214,* 84–90.

Lim, M. M., Wang, Z., Olazabal, D. E., Ren, X., Terwilliger, E. F., & Young, L. J. (2004). Enhanced partner preference in a promiscuous species by manipulating the expression of a single gene. *Nature, 429,* 754–757.

Liu, Y., Jiang, Y., Si, Y., Kim, J., Chen, Z., & Rao, Y. (2011). Molecular regulation of sexual preference revealed by genetic studies of 5-HT in the brains of male mice. *Nature, 472,* 95–99.

Lockley, M. (2014). Randy the guinea pig becomes dad to 100—And there's 80 more on the way. Birmingham Mail, UK. Retrieved from http://www.birminghammail.co.uk/news/midlands-news/randy-guinea-pig-becomes-dad-7633280/

Lonstein, J. S., & Stern, J. M. (1998). Site and behavioral specificity of periaqueductal gray lesions on postpartum sexual, maternal, and aggressive behaviors in rats. *Brain Research, 804,* 21–35.

Lorberbaum, J. P., Newman, J. D., Dubno, J. R., Horwitz, A. R., Nahas, Z., Teneback, C., . . . George, M. S. (1999). Feasibility of using fMRI to study mothers responding to infant cries. *Depression and Anxiety, 10,* 99–104.

Love, G., Torrey, N., McNamara, I., Morgan, M., Banks, M., Hester, N. W., . . . Lambert, K. G. (2005). Maternal experience produces long-lasting behavioral modifications in the rat. *Behavioral Neuroscience, 119,* 1084–1096.

Madeira, M. D., & Lieberman, A. R. (1995). Sexual dimorphism in the mammalian limbic system. *Progress in Neurobiology, 45,* 275–333.

Mann, V. A., Sasanuma, S., Sakuma, N., & Masaki, S. (1990). Sex differences in cognitive abilities in cross-cultural perspective. *Neuropsychologia, 28,* 1063–1077.

MacLean, P. D. (1990). *The triune brain in evolution (role in paleocerebral functions).* New York, NY: Plenum Press.

Mbugua, K. (2003). Sexual orientation and brain structures: A critical review of recent research. *Current Science, 84,* 173–178.

Meyer-Bahlburg, H. F. L., Dolezal, C., Baker, S. W., Ehrhardt, A. A., & New, M. I. (2006). Gender development in women with congenital adrenal hyperplasia as a function of disorder severity. *Archives of Sexual Behavior, 35,* 667–684.

Meyer-Bahlburg, H. F., Dolezal, C., Baker, S. W., & New, M. I. (2008). Sexual orientation in women with classical or nonclassical congenital adrenal hyperplasia as a function of degree of prenatal androgen excess. *Archives of Sexual Behavior, 37,* 85–99.

Miklosi, A., Kubinyi, E., Topal, J., Gacsi, M., Viranyi, Z., & Csanyi, V. (2003). A simple reason for a big difference: Wolves do not look back at humans, but dogs do. *Current Biology, 13,* 763–766.

Moorhead, J. (2005, June 15). Are the men of the African Aka tribe the best fathers in the world? *The Guardian.* Retrieved from http://www.guardian.co.uk/

Nagasawa, M., Kikusui, T., Onaka, T., & Ohta, M. (2009). Dog's gaze at its owner increases owner's urinary oxytocin during social interaction. *Hormones and Behavior, 55,* 434–444.

Nakamura., K., Mitarai, Y., Yoshioka, M., Koizumi, N., Shibahara, T., & Nakajima, Y. S. (1998). Serum levels of interleukin-6 alpha 1-acid glycoprotein, and corticosterone in two-week-old chickens inoculated with *Escherichia coli* lipopolysaccharide. *Poultry Science, 77,* 908–911.

Nef, S., & Parada, L. F. (2000). Hormones in male sexual development. *Genes and Development, 14,* 3075–3086.

Nelson, R. J. (1995). *An introduction to behavioral endocrinology,* Sunderland, MA: Sinauer.

Nishizawa, S., Benkelfat, C., Young, S. N., Leyton, M., Mzengeza, S., de Montigny, C., Blier, P., & Diksic, M. (1997). Differences between males and females in rates of serotonin synthesis in human brain. *Proceedings of the National Academy of Sciences of the USA, 94,* 5308–5313.

Nugent, B. M., Wright, C. L., Shetty, A. C., Hodes, G. E, Lenz, K. M. Mahurkar, A., Russo, . . . McCarthy, M. M. (2015). Brain feminization requires active repression of masculinization via DNA methylation. *Nature Neuroscience,* 2015. doi:10.1038/nn.3988

Oatridge, A., Holdcroft, A., Saeed, N., Hajnal, J. V., Puri, B. K., Fusi, I., & Bydder, G. M. (2002). Change in brain size during and after pregnancy: Study in healthy women and women with preeclampsia. *American Journal of Neuroradiology, 23,* 19–26.

O'Neill R. (2002). Experiments in living: The fatherless family. *Civitas, September,* 1–20.

Ovtscharoff, W., Helmeke, C., & Braiun, K. (2006). Lack of paternal care affects synaptic development in the anterior cingulate cortex. *Brain Research,* 663–673.

Parker, K. J., & Lee, T. M. (2001). Central vasopressin administration regulates the onset of facultative paternal behavior in *Microtus pennsylvanicus* (meadow voles). *Hormones and Behavior, 39,* 285–294.

Pfaff, D. W., & Sakuma, Y. (1979). Deficit in the lordosis reflex of female rats caused by lesions in the ventromedial nucleus of the hypothalamus. *Journal of Physiology, 288,* 203–210.

Pfaff, D. W., Schwartz-Giblin, S., McCarthy, M. M., & Kow, L. M. (1994). Cellular mechanisms of female reproductive behaviors. In E. Knobil & J. D. Neill (Eds.), *The physiology of reproduction* (2nd ed., pp 107–220). New York, NY: Raven.

Phoenix, C. H., Goy, R. W., Gerall, A. A., & Young, W. C. (1959). Organizing action of prenatally administered testosterone propionate on the tissues mediating mating behavior in the female guinea pig. *Endocrinology, 65,* 369–382.

Pinkernelle, J., Abraham, A., Seidel, K., & Braun, K. (2009). Paternal deprivation induces dendritic and synaptic changes and hemispheric asymmetry of pyramidal neurons in the somatosensory cortex. *Developmental Neurobiology, 69,* 663–673.

Potts, W. K., Manning, C. J., & Wakeland, E. K. (1991). Mating patterns in seminatural populations of mice influenced by MHC genotype. *Nature, 352,* 619–621.

Rametti, G., Carrillo, B., Gomez-Gil, E., Junque, C., Segovia, S., Gomez, A., & Guillamon, A. (2011a). White matter microstructure in female to male transsexuals before cross-sex hormonal treatment. A diffusion tensor imaging study. *Journal of Psychiatric Research, 45,* 199–204.

Rametti, G., Carrillo, B., Gomez-Bil, E., Junque, C., Zubiarre-Elorza, L., Segovia, S., . . . Guillamon, A. (2011b). The microstructure of white matter in male to female transsexuals before cross-sex hormonal treatment. A DTI study. *Journal of Psychiatric Research, 45,* 949–954.

Reynolds, T. J., & Wright, J. W. (1979). Early postnatal physical and behavioural development of degus (*Octodon degus*). *Laboratory Animals, 13,* 93–100.

Roselli, C. E., Cross, E., Poonyagariyagorn, H. K., & Stadelman, H. L. (2003). Role of aromatization in anticipatory and consummatory aspects of sexual behavior in male rats. *Hormones and Behavior, 44,* 146–151.

Ruble, D. N., Martin, C. L., & Berenbaum, S. A. (2006). Gender development. In W. Damon & R. M. Lerner (Series Eds.), *Handbook of child psychology.* In N. Eisenberg (Vol. Ed.). *Social, emotional, and personality development* (Vol. 3, pp. 858–932). New York, NY: Wiley.

Savic, I., & Arver, S. (2011). Sex dimorphism of the brain in male-to-female transsexuals. *Cerebral Cortex, 21,* 2525–2533.

Savic, I., & Lindstrom, P. (2008). PET and MRI show differences in cerebral asymmetry and functional connectivity between homo- and heterosexual subjects. *Proceedings of the National Academy of Sciences of the USA, 105,* 9403–9408.

Seifritz, E., Esposito, F., Neuhoff, J. G., Luthi, A., Mustovic, H., Drammann, G., . . . Di Salle, A. (2003). Differential sex-independent amygdala response to infant crying and laughing in parents versus nonparents. *Biological Psychiatry, 54,* 1367–1375.

Shingo, T., Gregg, C., Enwere, E., Fukikawa, H., Hassam, R., Greary, C., . . . Weiss, S. (2003). Pregnancy-stimulated neurogenesis in the adult female forebrain mediated by prolactin. *Science, 299,* 117–120.

Shors, T. (2002). Opposite effects of stressful experience on memory formation in males and females. *Dialogues in Clinical Neuroscience, 4,* 139–147.

Sisk, C. L., & Zehr, J. L. (2005). Pubertal hormones organize the adolescent brain and behavior. *Frontiers in Neuroendocrinology, 26,* 163–174.

Sokolowski, K., & Corbin, J. G. (2012). Wired for behaviors: From development to function of innate limbic system circuitry. *Frontiers in Molecular Neuroscience, 5.* doi:10.3389/fnmol.2012.00055

Storey, A. E., Walsh, C. J., Quinton, R. L., & Wynne-Edwards, K. E. (2000). Hormonal correlates of paternal responsiveness in new and expectant fathers. *Evolution and Human Evolution, 21,* 79–95.

Swaab, D. F., & Hofman, M. A. (1990). An enlarged suprachiasmatic nucleus in homosexual men. *Brain Research, 537,* 141–148.

Swaab, D. F., Slob, A. K., Houtsmuller, E. J., Brand, T., & Zhou, J. N. (1995). Increased number of vasopressin neurons in the suprachiasmatic nucleus (SCN) of "bisexual" adult male rats following perinatal treatment with the aromatase blocker kATD. *Developmental Brain Research, 85,* 273–279.

Tan, T., Watts, S. W., & Davis, R. P. (2011). Drug delivery: Enabling technology for drug discovery and development. iPRECIO Micro IN fusion pump: Programmable, refillable, and implantable. *Technology Report, 44.* doi:10.3389/fphar.2011.00044

Thyen, U., Richter-Appelt, H., Wiesemann, C., Holterhus, P. M., & Hiort, O. (2005). Deciding on gender in children with intersex conditions: Considerations and controversies. *Treatments in Endocrinology, 4,* 1–8.

Turner, B. B., & Weaver, D. A. (1985). Sexual dimorphism of glucocorticoid binding in rat brain. *Brain Research, 343,* 16–23.

Udell, M. A. R., & Wynne, C. D. L. (2008). A review of domestic dogs' (*Canis familiaris*) human-like behaviors: Or why behavior analysts should stop worrying and love their dogs. *Journal of the Experimental Analysis of Behavior, 89,* 247–261.

Velando, A., Drummond, H., & Torres, R. (2006). Senescent birds redouble reproductive effort when ill: Confirmation of the terminal investment hypothesis. *Proceedings of the Royal Society B, 273,* 1443–1448.

Walum, H., Westberg, L., Henningsson, S., Neiderhiser, J. M., Reiss, D., Igl, W., . . . Lichtenstein, P. (2008). Genetic variation in the vasopressin receptor 1a gene (AVPR1A) associates with pair-bonding behavior in humans. *Proceedings of the National Academy of Sciences of the USA, 16, 37,* 14153–14156.

Wang, C. T., Shui, H. A., Huang, R. L., Tai, M. Y., Peng, M. T., & Tsai, Y. F. (2006). Sexual motivation is demasculinized, but not feminized, in prenatally stressed male rats. *Neuroscience, 138,* 357–364.

Wang, Z. X., Ferris, C. F., & De Vries, G. J. (1994). Role of septal vasopressin innervation in paternal behavior in prairie voles (*Microtus ochrogaster*). *Proceedings of the National Academy of Sciences of the USA, 91,* 400–404.

Wang, Z., Zhou, L., Hulihan, J. J., & Insel, T. R. (1996). Immunoreactivity of central vasopressin and oxytocin pathways in microtine rodents: A quantitative comparative study. *Journal of Comparative Neurology, 306,* 726–727.

Wang, Z., Liu, Y., Young, L. J., & Insel, T. R. (1997). Developmental changes in forebrain vasopressin receptor binding in prairie voles (*Microtus ochrogaster*) and montane voles (*Microtus montanus*). *Annals of the New York Academy of Sciences, 807,* 510–513.

Wang, Z., Yu, G., Cascio, C., Liu, Y., Ginrich, B., & Insel, T. D. (1999). Dopamine D2 receptor-mediated regulator of partner preferences in feral prairie voles (*Microtus ochrogaster*): A mechanism for pair-bonding? *Behavioral Neuroscience, 113,* 602–611.

Wansaw, M. P., Pereira, M., & Morrell, J. P. (2008). Characterization of maternal motivation in the lactating rat: Contrasts between early and late postpartum responses. *Hormones and Behavior, 54,* 294–301.

Williams, J. R., Catania, K. C., & Carter, C. S. (1992). Development of partner preferences in female prairie voles *Microtus ochrogaster*: The role of social and sexual experience. *Hormones and Behavior, 26,* 339–349.

Wright, C. L., Schwarz, J. S., Dearn, S. L., & McCarthy, M. M. (2010). Cellular mechanisms of estradiol-mediated sexual differentiation of the brain. *Trends in Endocrinology and Metabolism, 21,* 553–561.

Xie, H., Rath, N. C., Huff, G. R., Huff, W. E., & Balog, J. M. (2000). Effects of *Salmonella typhimurium* lipopolysaccharide on broiler chickens. *Poultry Science, 79,* 3–40.

Young, L. J., Huot, B., Nilsen, R., Wang, Z., & Insel, T. R. (1996). Species differences in central oxytocin receptor gene expression: Comparative analogy of promoter sequences. *Journal of Neuroendocrinology, 8,* 777–783.

Young, K. A., Liu, Y., & Wang, Z. X. (2008). Neurobiology of social attachment: A comparative approach to behavioral, neuroanatomical and neurochemical studies. *Comparative Biochemistry and Physiology, 148,* 401–410.

Zak, P. J. (2008, November 10). The oxytocin cure [Blog post]. Retrieved from http://www.psychologytoday.com/blog/the-moral-molecule/200811/the-oxytocin-cure/

Zak, P. J., Kurzban, R., & Matzner, W. T. (2004). The neurobiology of trust. *Annals of the New York Academy of Science, 1032,* 224–227.

Zak, P. J., Kurzban, R., & Matzner, W. T. (2005). Oxytocin is associated with human trustworthiness. *Hormones and Behavior, 48,* 522–527.

Zak, P. J. (2008, June). The neurobiology of trust. *Scientific American.* Retrieved from http://www.scientificamerican.com/

Zhen, H., Ferguson, S. A., Cui, L., Greenfield, L. J., & Paule, M. G. (2013). Development of the sexually dimorphic nucleus of the preoptic area and the influence of estrogen-like compounds. *Neural Regeneration Research, 8,* 2763–2774.

CHAPTER 12

Adlam, A. L. R., Patterson, K., & Hodges, J. R. (2009). I remember it as if it were yesterday: Memory for recent events in patients with semantic dementia. *Neuropsychologia, 47,* 1344–1351.

Alexander, W. H., & Brown, J. W. (2011). Medial prefrontal cortex as an action–outcome predictor. *Nature Neuroscience Reviews, 14,* 1338–1344.

American Psychiatric Association. (2013). *Diagnostic and statistical manual of mental disorders* (5th ed.). Arlington, VA: American Psychiatric Publishing.

Annese, J., Schenker-Ahmed, N. M., Bartsch, H., Maechler, P., Sheh, C., Thomas, N., . . . Corkin S. (2014). Postmortem examination of patient H.M.'s brain based on histological sectioning and digital 3D reconstruction. *Nature Communications, 5,* 3122. doi:10.1038/ncomms4122

Bach, D. R., & Dolan, R. J. (2012). Knowing how much you don't know: A neural organization of uncertainty estimates. *Nature Neuroscience Reviews, 13,* 572–586.

Bailey, C. H., & Chen, M. (1988). Long-term memory in *Aplysia* modulates the total number of varicosities of single identified sensory neurons. *Proceedings of the National Academy of Sciences of the USA, 85,* 2373–2377.

Beach, F. (1961). A biographical memoir [of Karl Lashley]. *Biographical Memoirs of the National Academy of Sciences, 3,* 162–204.

Benjamin, L. T. (1993). *A history of psychology in letters.* Dubuque, IA: Brown Communications.

Berridge, K. C. (2007). The debate over dopamine's role in reward: The case for incentive salience, *Psychopharmacology, 191,* 391–431.

Black, J. E., Isaacs, K. R., Anderson, B. J., Alcantara, A. A., & Greenough, W. T. (1990). Learning causes synaptogenesis, whereas motor activity causes angiogenesis, in cerebellar cortex of adult rats. *Proceedings of the National Academy of Sciences of the USA, 87,* 5568–5572.

Bliss, T. V., & Lomo, T. (1973). Long-lasting potentiation of synaptic transmission in the dentate area of the anaesthetized rabbit following stimulation of the perforant path. *Journal of Physiology, 232*, 331–356.

Bremner, J. D., Staib, L. H., Kaloupek, D., Southwick, S. M., Soufer, R., & Charney, D. S. (1999). Neural correlates of exposure to traumatic pictures and sound in Vietnam combat veterans with and without posttraumatic stress disorder: A positron emission tomography study. *Biological Psychiatry, 45*, 806–816.

Brown, R. E., & Milner, P. M. (2003). The legacy of Donald O. Hebb: More than the Hebb synapse. *Nature Reviews Neuroscience, 4*, 1013–1019.

Buckner, R. L., & Wheeler, M. E. (2001). The cognitive neuroscience of remembering, *Nature Reviews Neuroscience, 2*, 624–634.

Burgess, N. (2014). The 2014 Nobel Prize in Physiology or Medicine: A spatial model for cognitive neuroscience. *Neuron, 84*, 1120–1125.

Cabeza, R., Ciaramelli, E., Olson, I. R., & Moscovitch, M. (2008). The parietal cortex and episodic memory: An attentional account. *Nature Neuroscience Reviews, 9*, 613–625.

Caroni, P., Donato, F., & Muller, D. (2012). Structural plasticity upon learning: Regulation and functions. *Nature Neuroscience Reviews, 13*, 478–490.

Castellanos, F. X., & Tannock, R. (2002). Neuroscience of attention-deficit/hyperactivity disorder: The search for endophenotypes, *Nature Neuroscience Reviews, 3*, 617–628.

CBS News. (June, 2011). Marilu Henner's Super Memory Summit featured on news show *60 Minutes*. Retrieved from http://www.cbsnews.com/8301-504803_162-20072052-10391709.html/

Chance, P. (2003). *Learning and behavior*. Belmont, CA: Wadsworth.

Clayton, N. S., Bussey, T. J., & Dickinson, A. (2003). Can animals recall the past and plan for the future? *Nature Reviews Neuroscience, 4*, 685–691.

Clayton, N. S., & Dickinson, A. (1998). Episodic-like memory during cache recovery by scrub jays. *Nature, 395*, 272–274.

Collingridge, G. L., Peineau, S., Howland, J. G., & Wang, Y. T. (2010). Long-term depression in the CNS. *Nature Reviews Neuroscience, 11*, 459–473.

Corkin, S. (2002). What's new with the amnesic patient H.M.? *Nature Reviews Neuroscience, 3*, 153–160.

Deng, W., Aimone, J. G., & Gage, F. H. (2010). New neurons and new memories: How does adult hippocampal neurogenesis affect learning and memory? *Nature Reviews Neuroscience, 342*, 339–350.

De Roo, M., Klauser, P., & Muller, G. (2008). LTP promotes a selective long-term stabilization and clustering of dendritic spines. *PLoS Biology, 6*, e219.

Dittrich, L. (2010). The brain that changed everything. *Esquire*. Retrieved from http://www.esquire.com/features/henry-molaison-brain-1110-6/

Downar, J., Bhatt, M., & Montague, P. R. (2011). Neural correlates of effective learning in experienced medical decision-makers. *PLoS ONE, 6*, e27768.

Dupret, D., Fabre, A., Dobrossy, M. D., Panatier, A., Rodriguez, J. J., Lamarque, S., . . . Abrous, D. N. (2007). Spatial learning depends on both the addition and removal of new hippocampal neurons. *PLoS Biology, 5*, e214. doi:10.1371/journal.pbio.0050214

Egner, T. (2011). Surprise! A unifying model of dorsal anterior cingulate function? *Nature Neuroscience, 14*, 1219–1220.

Eichenbaum, H. (2000). A cortical–hippocampal system for declarative memory. *Nature Reviews Neuroscience, 1*, 41–50.

Eichenbaum, H. (2012). *The cognitive neuroscience of memory* (2nd ed.). New York, NY: Oxford University Press.

Gao, Z., van Beugen, B. J., & De Zeeuw, C. I. (2012). Distributed synergistic plasticity and cerebellar learning. *Nature Reviews Neuroscience, 13*, 619–635.

Getahun, D., Jacobsen, S. J., Fassett, M. J., Chen, W., Demissie, K., & Rhoads, G. G. (2012). Recent trends in childhood attention-deficit/hyperactivity disorder, *JAMA Pediatrics*. doi:10.1001/2013.jamapediatrics.401

Glimcher, P. W. (2003). *Decisions, uncertainty, and the brain*. Cambridge, MA: MIT Press.

Hebb, D. O. (1949). *The organization of behavior*. New York, NY: Wiley.

Heekeren, H. R., Marrett, S., Bandettini, P. A., & Ungerleider, L. G. (2004). A general mechanism for perceptual decision-making in the human brain. *Nature, 431*, 859–862.

Henke, K. (2010). A model for memory systems based on processing modes rather than consciousness. *Nature Reviews Neuroscience, 11*, 523–532.

Henke, K., Weber, B, Kneifel, S., Wieser, H. G., & Buck, A. (1999). Human hippocampus associates in formation in memory. *Proceedings of the National Academy of Science USA, 96*, 5884–5889.

Jovanovic, T., Norrholm, S. D., Rennell, J. E., Keyes, M., Fiallos, A. M., Myers, K. M., . . . Duncan, E. J. (2009). Posttraumatic stress disorder may be associated with impaired fear inhibition: Relation to symptom severity. *Psychiatry Research, 167*, 151–160.

Kandel, E. R. (2001). The molecular biology of memory storage: A dialogue between genes and synapses. *Science, 294*, 1030–1038.

Kandel, E. R. (2009). The biology of memory: A forty-year perspective. *The Journal of Neuroscience, 29*, 12748–12756.

Kempermann, G. (2012). New neurons for "survival of the fittest." *Nature Reviews Neuroscience, 13*, 727–735.

Kim, J. J., & Diamond, D. M. (2002). The stressed hippocampus, synaptic plasticity and lost memories. *Nature Reviews Neuroscience, 3*, 453–462.

LaBar, K., & Cabeza, R. (2006). Cognitive neuroscience of emotional memory. *Nature Reviews Neuroscience, 7*, 54–64.

Langston, R. F., Aine, J. A., Couey, J. J., Canto, C. B., Bjerknes, T. L., Witter, M. P., . . . Mosey, M.B. (2010). Development of the spatial representation system in the rat. *Science*, 1576–1580.

Lashley, K. (1950). In search of the engram. In *Physiological mechanisms in animal behaviour*, Symposium of the Society for Experimental Biology, No. IV, pp. 454–482.

Lehn, H., Steffenach, H-A, van Strien, N. M., Veltman, D. J., Witter, M. P., & Haberg, A. (2009). A specific role of the human hippocampus in recall of temporal sequences. *The Journal of Neuroscience, 29*, 3475–3485.

LePort, A. K. R., Mattfeld, A. T., Dickinson-Anson, H., Fallon, J. H., Stark, C. E. L., Kruggel, F., . . . McGaugh, J. L. (2012). Behavioral and neuroanatomical investigation of highly superior autobiographical memory (HSAM). *Neurobiology of Learning and Memory, 98*, 78–92.

Locke, J. (1690). An essay concerning human understanding (1975 edition). Oxford, UK: Clarendon Press (as referenced in Benjamin, 1993).

Loftus, E. F. (1979). The malleability of human memory. *American Scientist, 67*, 312–320.

Loftus, E. F., Miller, D. G., & Burns, H. J. (1978). Semantic integration of verbal information into a visual memory. *Journal of Experimental Psychology, Human Learning and Memory, 4*, 19–31.

Luria, A. R. (1987). *The mind of a mnemonist*. Cambridge, MA: Harvard University Press.

Lynch, M.A. (2004). Long-term potentiation and memory. *Physiological Review, 84*, 87–136.

Macknik, S. L., King, M., Randi, J., Robbins, A., Teller, Thompson, J., & Martinez-Conde, S. (2008). Attention and awareness in stage magic: Turning tricks into research. *Nature Reviews Neuroscience, 9,* 871–879.

McGaugh, J. L. (2004). The amygdala modulates the consolidation of memories of emotionally arousing experiences. *Annual Review of Neuroscience, 27,* 1–28.

Memmert, D. (2006). The effects of eye movements, age, and expertise on inattentional blindness. *Conscious Cognition, 15,* 620–627.

Mitra, R., Jadhav, S., McEwen, B. S., Vyas, A., & Chattarji, S. (2005). Stress duration modulates the spatiotemporal patterns of spine formation in the basolateral amygdala. *Proceedings of the National Academy of Sciences of the USA, 102,* 9371–9376.

Morris, R. G. M., Garrud, P., Rawlins, J. N. P., & O'Keefe, J. (1982). Place navigation impaired in rats with hippocampal lesions. *Nature, 297,* 681–683.

Neves, G., Cooke, S. F., & Bliss, T. V. P. (2008). Synaptic plasticity, memory and the hippocampus: A neural network approach to causality. *Nature Reviews Neuroscience, 9,* 65–75.

Nicolelis, M. A., Fanselow, E. E., & Ghazanfar, A. A. (1997). Hebb's dream: Minireview; The resurgence of cell assemblies. *Neuron, 19,* 219–221.

Olton, D. S., Becker, J. T., & Handelmann, G. E. (1979). Hippocampus, space and memory. *Behavioral and Brain Sciences, 2,* 313–322.

O'Keefe, J., & Dostrovsky, J. (1971). The hippocampus as a spatial map. Preliminary evidence from unit activity in the freely-moving rat. *Brain Research, 34,* 171–175.

O'Keefe, J., & Nadel. L. (1978). *The hippocampus as a cognitive map.* Oxford, UK: Clarendon.

Palmer, L., & Lynch, G. (2010). A Kantian view of space. *Science, 328,* 1487–1488.

Pavlov, I. P. (1906). The scientific investigation of the psychical faculties or processes in the higher animals. *Science, 24,* 613–619.

Parker, E. S., Cahill, L., & McGaugh, J. L. (2006). A case of unusual autobiographical remembering. *Neurocase, 12,* 35–49.

Pitman, R. K., Rasmusson, A. M., Koenen, K. C., Shin, L. M., Orr, S. P., Gilbertson, M. W., . . . Liberzon, I. (2012). Biological studies of post-traumatic stress disorder. *Nature Reviews Neuroscience, 13,* 769–786.

Polanczyk, G. V., Willcutt, E. G., Salum, G. A., Kieling, C., & Rohde, L. A. (2014). ADHD prevalence estimates across three decades: An updated systematic review and meta-regression analysis. *International Journal of Epidemiology.* doi:10.1093/ije/dyt261

Posner, M. I., & Boies, S. J. (1971). Components of attention. *Psychological Review, 78,* 391–408.

Quiroga, R. Q., Fried, I., & Koch, C. (2013). Brain cells for grandmother. *Scientific American, February,* 31–35.

Quiroga, R. Q., Kreiman, G., Koch, C., & Fried, I. (2008). Sparse but not "grandmother-cell" coding in the medial temporal lobe. *Trends in Cognitive Sciences, 12,* 87–91.

Rangel, A., Camerer, C., & Montague, P. R. (2008). A framework for studying the neurobiology of value-based decision making. *Nature Reviews Neuroscience, 9,* 545–556.

Raz, A., & Buhle, J. (2006). Typologies of attentional networks, *Nature Reviews Neuroscience, 7,* 367–379.

Rolls, E. T. (1996). The orbitofrontal cortex. *Philosophical Transactions of the Royal Society of London, Series B, Biological Sciences, 351,* 1433–1443.

Roozendaal, B., McEwen, B. S., & Chattarji, S. (2009). Stress, memory, and the amygdala. *Nature Reviews Neuroscience, 10,* 423–433.

Rorie, A. E., Gao, J., McClelland, J. L., & Newsome, W. T. (2010). Integration of sensory and reward information during perceptual decision-making in lateral intraparietal cortex (LIP) of the macaque monkey. *PLoS ONE, 5,* e9308.

Rorie, A. E., & Newsome, W. T. (2005). A general mechanism for decision-making in the human brain? *Trends in Cognitive Sciences, 9,* 41–43.

Sandi, C., Woodson, J. C., Haynes, V. F., Park, C. R., Touyarot, K., Lopez-Fernandez, M. A., . . . Diamond, D. M. (2005). Acute stress-induced impairment of spatial memory is associated with decreased expression of neural cell adhesion molecule in the hippocampus and prefrontal cortex. *Biological Psychiatry, 57,* 856–864.

Sara, S. J. (2009). The locus coeruleus and noradrenergic modulation of cognition. *Nature Reviews Neuroscience, 10,* 211–223.

Schiller, D., & Phelps, E. A. (2011). Does reconsolidation occur in humans? *Frontiers in Behavioral Neuroscience, 5.* doi:10.3389/fnbeh.2011.00024

Schoenbaum, G., Roesch, M. R., Stainaker, T. A., & Takahashi, Y. K. (2009). A new perspective on the role of the orbitofrontal cortex in adaptive behavior. *Nature Reviews Neuroscience, 10,* 885–892.

Schnider, A. (2003). Spontaneous confabulation and the adaptation of thought to ongoing reality. *Nature Reviews Neuroscience, 4,* 662–671.

Schultz. W. (1998). Predictive reward signal of dopamine neurons. *Journal of Physiology, 80,* 1–27.

Scoville, W. B., & Milner, B. (1957). Loss of recent memory after bilateral hippocampal lesions. *Journal of Neurology, Neurosurgery, and Psychiatry, 20,* 11–21.

Shatz, C. J. (1992) The developing brain. *Scientific American, 267,* 60–67.

Shewmon, D. A., Holmes, G. L., & Byrne, P. A. (1999). Consciousness in congenitally decorticate children: Developmental vegetative state as self-fulfilling prophecy. *Developmental Medicine & Child Neurology, 41,* 364–374.

Shimizu, E., Tang, V. P., Rampon, C., & Tsien, J. Z. (2000). NMDA receptor-dependent synaptic reinforcement as a crucial process for memory consolidation. *Science, 290,* 1170–1174.

Simons, D. J., & Chabris, C. F. (1999). Gorillas in our midst: Sustained inattentional blindness for dynamic events. *Perception, 28,* 1059–1074.

Skinner, B. F. (1958). Reinforcement today. *The American Psychologist, 13,* 94–99.

Sugrue, L. P., Corrado, G. S., & Newsome, W. T. (2005). Choosing the greater of two goods: Neural currencies for valuation and decision making. *Nature Reviews Neuroscience, 6,* 363–375.

Thompson-Cannino, J., Cotton, R., & Torneo, E. (2010). *I picked Cotton.* New York, NY: St. Martin's Griffin.

Thorndike, E. L. (1911). *Animal intelligence: Experimental studies.* New York, NY: Hafner.

Tronson, N. C., & Taylor, J. R. (2007). Molecular mechanisms of memory reconsolidation. *Nature Reviews Neuroscience, 8,* 262–275.

Tsien, J. Z. (2000). Building a brainier mouse. *Scientific American,* 62–68.

VanElzakker, M., Fevurly, R. D., Breindel, T., & Spencer, R. L. (2008). Environmental novelty is associaated with a selective increase in Fos expression in the output elements of the hippocampal formation and the perirhinal cortex. *Learning and Memory, 15,* 899–908.

Watson, J. B. (1913). Psychology as a behaviorist views it. *Psychological Review, 20,* 158–177.

Wearing, D. (2005). *Forever today: A true story of lost memory and never-ending love.* London, UK: Corgi.

Weeks, A. C. W., Connor, S., Hinchcliff, R., LeBoutillier, J. C., Thompson, R. F., & Petit, T. L. (2007). Eye-blink conditioning is associated with changes in synaptic ultrastructure in the rabbit interpositus nuclei. *Learning & Memory, 14,* 385–389.

Weingarten, G. (2009, March 8). Fatal distraction: Forgetting a child in the backseat of a car is a horrifying mistake. Is it a crime? *The Washington Post.* Retrieved from http://www.washingtonpost.com/wp-dyn/content/article/2009/02/27/AR2009022701549.html?sid=ST2009030602446/

Wells, G. L., & Loftus, E. F. (2003). Eyewitness memory for people and events. *Handbook of Psychology, 3,* 149–160.

Wells, G. L., Small, M., Penrod, S., Malpass, R. S., Fulero, S. M., & Brimacombe, C. A. E. (1998). Eyewitness identification procedures: Recommendations for lineups and photospreads. *Law and Human Behavior, 22,* 1–39.

Willcutt, E. G. (2012). The prevalence of DSM-IV attention-deficit/hyperactivity disorder: A meta-analytic review. *Neurotherapeutics, 9,* 490–499.

Wills, J., Cacucci, F., Burgess, N., & O'Keefe, J. (2010). Development of the hippocampal CS map in preweaning rats. *Science, 328,* 1573–1576.

Woodruff-Pak, D. S., Foy, M. R., Akopian, G. G., Lee, K. H., Zach, J., Nguyen, K. P. T., . . . Thompson, R. F. (2010). Differential effects and rates of normal aging in cerebellum and hippocampus. *Proceedings of the National Academy of Sciences of the USA, 107,* 1624–1629.

Yang, G., Pan, F., & Gan, W. B. (2009). Stably maintained dendritic spines are associated with lifelong memories. *Nature, 462,* 920–924.

Zhao, Y., Wang, D.O., & Martin, K.C. (2009). Preparation of Aplysia sensory-motor neuronal cell cultures. *Journal of Visual Experimentation.* doi: 10.3791/1355.

Zito, K., Scheuss, V., Knott, C., Hill, T., & Svoboda, K. (2009). Rapid functional maturation of nascent dendritic spines. *Neuron, 61,* 247–258.

Zola-Morgan, S., & Squire, L. R. (1985). Medial temporal lesions in monkeys impair memory on a variety of tasks sensitive to human amnesia. *Behavioral Neuroscience, 99,* 22–34.

CHAPTER 13

American Psychiatric Association. (2013). *Diagnostic and statistical manual of mental disorders* (5th ed.). Arlington, VA: American Psychiatric Publishing.

Andrews, N. A., Papakosta, M., & Barnes, N. M. (2013). Discovery of novel anxiolytic agents—The trials and tribulations of preclinical models of anxiety. *Neurobiology of Disease.* doi:10.1016/j.nbd.2013.10.116

Bakkar, N., Shahab, S., Giacobbe, P., Blumberger, D. M., Daskalakis, Z. J., Kennedy, S. H., & Downar, J. (2015). rTMS of the dorsomedial prefrontal cortex for major depression: Safety, tolerability, effectiveness, and outcome predictors for 10 Hz versus intermittent theta-burst stimulation. *Brain Stimulation, 8,* 208–215.

Bardi, M., Rhone, A. P., Franssen, C. L., Hampton, J. E., Shea, E., Hyer, M. M., . . . Lambert, K. G. (2012). Behavioral training and predisposed coping strategies interact to influence resilience in male Long–Evans rats: Implications for depression. *Stress, 15,* 306–317.

Bardi, M., True, M., Franssen, C. L., Kaufman, C., Rzucidlo, A., & Lambert, K. G. (2012). Effort-based reward (EBR) training enhances neurobiological efficiency in a problem-solving task: Insights for depression therapies. *Brain Research, 490,* 101–110.

Barker, A. T., Jalinous, R., & Freeston, I. L. (1985). Noninvasive magnetic stimulation of the human motor cortex. *Lancet, 1,* 1106–1107.

Barondes, S. H. (1993). *Molecules and mental illness.* New York, NY: Freeman.

Baune, B. T., & Renger, L. (2014). Pharmacological and non-pharmacological interventions to improve cognitive dysfunction and functional ability in clinical depression—A systematic review. *Psychiatry Research, 219,* 25–50.

Bencherif, M., Stachowiak, M. K, Kucinski, A. J., & Lippiello, P. M. (2012). Alpha7 nicotinic cholinergic neuromodulation may reconcile multiple neurotransmitter hypotheses of schizophrenia. *Medical Hypotheses, 78,* 594–600.

Bigos, K. L., Mattay, V. S., Callicott, J. H., Straub, R. E., Vakkalanka, R., Lolachana, B., . . . Weinberger, D. R. (2010). Genetic variation in CACNA1C affects brain circuitries related to mental illness. *Archives of General Psychiatry, 67,* 939–945.

Bohil, C. J., Alicea, B., & Biocca, F. A. (2011). Virtual reality in neuroscience research and therapy. *Nature Reviews Neuroscience, 12,* 752–762.

Bolognini, N., & Ro, T. (2010). Transcranial magnetic stimulation: Disrupting neural activity to alter and assess brain function. *The Journal of Neuroscience, 30,* 9647–9650.

Botella, C., Garcia-Palacios, A., Villa, H., Banos, R.M., Queros, S., Alcaniz, J., & Riva, G. (2007). Virtual reality exposure in the treatment of panic disorder and agoraphobia: A controlled study. *Clinical Psychology and Psychotherapy, 14,* 164–175.

Bremner, J. D., Narayan, M., Anderson, E. R., Staib, L. H., Miller, H. L., & Charney, D. S. (2000). Hippocampal volume reduction in major depression. *American Journal of Psychiatry, 157,* 115–118.

Bunney, W. F., & Bunney, B. S. (1999). Neurodevelopmental hypothesis of schizophrenia. In D. S. Charney, E. J. Nestler, & B. S Bunney (Eds.), *Neurobiology of mental illness* (pp. 225–235). New York, NY: Oxford University Press.

Byne, W., Kemether, E., Jones, L., Haroutunian, V., & Davis, K. (1999). The neurochemistry of schizophrenia. In D. S. Charney, E. J. Nestler, & B. S. Bunney (Eds.), *Neurobiology of Mental Illness* (pp. 236–257). New York, NY: Oxford University Press.

Cahalan, S. (2012). *Brain on fire: My month of madness.* New York, NY: Free Press.

Canuso, C. M. & Pandina, G. (2007). Gender and schizophrenia. *Psycholpharmacology Bulletin, 40,* 178–190.

Caplan, P. J. (1996). *They say you're crazy: How the world's most powerful psychiatrists decide who's normal.* Reading, MA: Addison–Wesley.

Carlsson, A. A. (2001). A half-century of neurotransmitter research: Impact on neurology and psychiatry. *ChemBioChem, 2,* 484–493.

Carroll, J. (1982). Clinical applications of the dexamethasone suppression test for endogenous depression. *Pharmacopsychiatry, 15,* 19–24.

Castren, E. (2005). Is mood chemistry? *Nature Reviews Neuroscience, 6,* 241–246.

Castren, E., & Rantamaki, T. (2010). The role of BDNF and its receptors in depression and antidepressant drug action: Reactivation of developmental plasticity. *Developmental Neurobiology, 70,* 289–2010.

Cheetham, S. C., Katona, C. L. E., & Horton, R. W. (1991). Postmortem studies of neurotransmitter biochemistry in depression and suicide. In R. W. Horton & C. L. E. Katona (Eds.), *Biological aspects of affective disorders* (pp. 192–331). London, UK: Academic Press.

Chen, Z., Cui, L., Li, M., Jiang, L., Deng, W., Ma, X., . . . Li, T. (2012). Voxel based morphometric and diffusion tensor imaging analysis in male bipolar patients with first episode mania. *Progress in Neuro-Psychopharmacology and Biological Psychotherapies, 36,* 231–238.

Couturier, J. L. (2005). Efficacy of rapid-rate repetitive transcranial magnetic stimulation in the treatment of depression: A systematic review and meta-analysis. *Journal of Psychiatry and Neuroscience, 30,* 83–90.

Coyle, J. T. (2006). Glutamate and schizophrenia: Beyond the dopamine hypothesis. *Cellular and Molecular Neurobiology, 26,* 365–384.

Cross-Disorder Group of the Psychiatric Genomics Consortium, Lee, S. H., Ripke, S., Neale, B. M., Faraone, S. V., Purcell, S. M., . . . Wray, N. R. (2013). Genetic relationship between five psychiatric disorders estimated from genome-wide SNPs. *Nature Genetics, 45*(9), 984–994. doi: 10.1038/ng.2711

Crouse, K., & Pennington, B. (Nov 13, 2012). Panic attack leads to hospital on way to golfer's first victory. *The New York Times,* p. A1.

Dalmau, J., Gleichman, A. J., Hughes, E. G., Rossi, J. E., Peng, X., Lai, M., . . . Lynch, D. R. (2008). Anti-NMDA-receptor encephalitis: Case series and analysis of the effects of antibodies. *Lancet Neurology, 7,* 1091–1098.

Daskalakis, Z. J. (2005). Repetitive transcranial magnetic stimulation for the treatment of depression: To stimulate or not to stimulate? *Journal of Psychiatry and Neuroscience, 30,* 81–82.

Davidson, R. J., Abercrombie, H., Nitschke, J. G., & Putnam, K. (1999). Regional brain function, emotion and disorders of emotion. *Current Opinion in Neurobiology, 9,* 228–234.

Deckersbach, T., Gershuny, B. S., & Otto, M. W. (2000). Cognitive-Behavioral therapy for depression: Applications and outcomes. *The Psychiatry Clinics of North America, 23,* 795–809.

Del Casale, A., Ferracuti, S., Rapinesi, C., Serata, D., Piccirilli, M., Savoja, V., . . . Girardi, P. (2012). Functional neuroimaging in specific phobia. *Psychiatry Research: Neuroimaging, 202,* 181–197.

De Kloet, E. R., Joels, M., & Holsboer, F. (2005). Stress and the brain: From adaptation to disease. *Nature Reviews Neuroscience, 6,* 463–475.

Delgado, P. L. (2000). Depression: The case for a monoamine deficiency. *Journal of Clinical Psychiatry, 61,* 5–12.

DeRubeis, R. J., Siegle, G. J., & Hollon, S. D. (2008). Cognitive therapy versus medication for depression: Treatment outcomes and neural mechanisms. *Nature Reviews, 9,* 788–796.

Dimidjian, S., Hollon, S. D., Dobson, K. S., Schmaling, K. G., Kohlenberg, R., Addis, M., . . . Jacobson, N. S. (2006). Randomized trial of behavioral activation, cognitive therapy, and antidepressant medication in the acute treatment of adults with major depression. *Journal of Consulting and Clinical Psychology, 74,* 658–670.

Dobbs, D. (2010). The making of a troubled mind. *Nature, 468,* 154–156.

Dobson, K. S., Hollon, S. D., Dimidjian, S., Schmaling, K. B., Kohlenberg, R. J., & Gallup, R. J. (2008). Randomized trial of behavioral activation, cognitive therapy and antidepressant medication in the prevention of relapse in MDD. *Journal of Consulting and Clincial Psychology, 76,* 468–477.

Downar, J., Blumberger, D. M., & Daskalakis, Z. J. (2016). The neural crossroads of psychiatric illness: An emerging target for brain stimulation. *Trends in Cognitive Sciences, 20,* 107–120.

Dully, H., & Fleming, C. (2008). *My lobotomy.* New York, NY: Broadway.

Duman, R. S., & Aghajanian, G. K. (2012). Synaptic dysfunction in depression: Potential therapeutic targets. *Science, 338,* 68–72.

Edvardsen, J., Torgersen, S., Roysamb, E., Lygren, S., Skre, I., Onstad, S., & Oien, P. A. (2009). Unipolar depressive disorders have a common genotype. *Journal of Affective Disorders, 117,* 30–41.

El-Hai, J. (2005). *The lobotomist.* Hoboken, NJ: Wiley.

Enck, P., & Hauser, W. (2012, August 10). Beware the nocebo effect. *New York Times.* Retrieved from http://www.nytimes.com/2012/08/12/opinion/sunday/beware-the-nocebo-effect.html?/

Fava, M., & Kendler, K. S. (2000). Major depressive disorder. *Neuron, 28,* 335–341.

Ferguson, J. M. (2001). SSRI antidepressant medications: Adverse effects and tolerability, *Primary Care Companion Journal of Clinical Psychiatry, 3,* 22–27.

Finger, S. (1994). *Origins of neuroscience.* New York, NY: Oxford University Press.

Finger, S. (2000). *Minds behind the brain.* New York, NY: Oxford University Press.

Fisher, M., Holland, C., Merzenich, M. M., & Vinogradov, S. (2009). Using neuroplasticity-based cognitive training to impact verbal memory in schizophrenia. *American Journal of Psychiatry, 166,* 805–811.

Foussias, G., & Remington, G. (2010). Negative symptoms in schizophrenia: Avolition and Occam's razor. *Schizophrenia Bulletin, 36,* 359–369.

Freedman, R. (2003). Schizophrenia. *New England Journal of Medicine, 349,* 1738–1749.

Freedman, R. (2010). *The madness within us.* New York, NY: Oxford University Press.

Fulton, J. F. (1951). *Frontal lobotomy and affective behavior: A neurophysiological analysis.* New York: Norton.

George, M. S., Nahas, Z., Kozel, R. A., Goldman, J., Molloy, M., & Oliver, N. (1999). Improvement of depression following transcranial magnetic stimulation. *Current Psychiatry Reports, 1,* 114–124.

George, M. S., Nahas, Z., Molloy, M., Speer, A. M., Oliver, N. C., Li, X., . . . Ballenger, J. C. (2000). A controlled trial of daily left prefrontal cortex TMS for treating depression. *Biological Psychiatry, 48,* 962–970.

Geyer M. A., & Moghaddam, B. (2002). Animal models relevant to schizophrenia disorders. In K. L. Davis, D. Charney, J. T. Coyle, C. Nemeroff (Eds.), *Neuropsychopharmacology: The fifth generation of progress* (pp. 689–701). Philadelphia, PA: Lippincott Williams and Wilkins.

Gogtay, N., Vyas, N. S., Testa, R., Wood, S. J., & Pantelis, C. (2011). Age on onset of schizophrenia perspectives from structural neuroimaging studies. *Schizophrenia Bulletin, 37,* 504–513.

Gotlib, I. H., & Hamilton, J. P. (2009). Neural functioning in major depression disorder. *Frontiers in Neuroscience, 3,* 244–256.

Goto, K., Ueki, A., Iso, H., & Morita, Y. (2002). Reduced prepulse inhibition in rats with entorhinal cortex lesions. *Behavioral Brain Research, 134,* 201–207.

Gross, C., & Hen, R. (2004). The developmental origins of anxiety. *Nature Reviews Neuroscience, 5,* 545–552.

Hamani, C., Mayberg, H., Stone, S., Laxton, A., Haber, S., & Lozano, A. M. (2011). The subcallosal cingulate gyrus in the context of major depression. *Biological Psychiatry, 69,* 301–308.

Harlow, H. (1989). *Biographical memoirs* (Vol. 58). Washington, DC: National Academies Press.

Hauner, K. K., Mineka, S., Voss, J. L., & Paller, K. A. (2012). Exposure therapy triggers lasting reorganization of neural fear processing. *Proceedings of the National Academy of Sciences of the USA, 109,* 9203–9208.

Hauser, W., Hansen, E., & Enck, P. (2012). Nocebo phenomena in medicine. *Deutsches Arzteblatt International, 109,* 459–465.

Haut, K. M., Lim, K. O., & MacDonald, A. (2010). Prefrontal cortical changes following cognitive training in patients with chronic schizophrenia: Effects of practice, generalization, and specificity. *Neuropsychopharmacology, 35,* 1850–1859.

Hayden, E. C. (2012). Treating schizophrenia: Game on. *Nature, 483,* 24–26.

Heinrichs, R. W. (2001). *In search of madness: Schizophrenia and neuroscience.* New York, NY: Oxford University Press.

Herrara-Guzman, I., Herrera-Abarca, J. E., Gudayol-Ferre, E., Herrera-Guzman, D., Gomez-Carbajal., L., Pena-Olvira, M., . . . Joan, G. O. (2010). Effects of selective serotonin reuptake and dual serotonergic–noradrenergic reuptake treatments on attention and executive functions in patients with major depressive disorder. *Journal of Psychiatric Research, 43,* 855–863.

Hill, R. D., Storandt, M., & Malley, M. (1993). The impact of long-term exercise on training on psychological function in older animals. *Journal of Gerontology, 48,* 12–17.

Hofman, S. G., Wu, J. Q., & Boettcher, H. (2013). *d*-Cycloserine as an augmentation strategy for cognitive behavioral therapy of anxiety disorders. *Biology of Mood and Anxiety Disorders, 3,* 11. Retrieved from http://www.biolmoodanxietydisord.com/content/3/1/11/

Holtzeimer, P. E., Kelley, M. E., Gross, R. E., Filkowski, M. M., Garlow, S. J., Barrocas, A., . . . Mayberg, H. S. (2012). Subcallosal cingulate deep brain stimulation for treatment-resistant unipolar and bipolar depression. *Archives of General Psychiatry, 69,* 150–158.

Hooker, C. I., Bruce, L., Fisher, M., Verosky, Sc., Miyakawa, A., & Vinogradov, S. (2012). Neural activity during emotion recognition after combined cognitive plus social cognitive training in schizophrenia. *Schizophrenia Research, 139,* 53–59.

Hyman, S. E. (2007). Can neuroscience be integrated into the DSM-V? *Nature Reviews Neuroscience, 8,* 725–732.

Jacobson, N. S., & Hollon, S. D. (1996). Prospects for future comparisons between drugs and psychotherapy: Lessons from the CBT-versus pharmacotherapy exchange. *Journal of Consulting Clinical Psychology, 64,* 104–108.

Karage, F., Vaudan, G., Schwald, M., Perroud, N., & La Harpe, R. (2005). Neurotrophin levels in postmortem brains of suicide victims and the effects of antemortem diagnosis and psychotropic drugs. *Brain Research and Molecular Brain Research, 136,* 29–37.

Kelly, B. D., O'Callaghan, E., Waddington, J. L., Feeney, L., Browne, S., Sully, P. J., Clarke, M., Quinn, J. F., McTique, O., Morgan, M. G., Kinsella, A., & Larkin, C. (2010). Schizophrenia and the City: A review of literature and prospective study of psychosis and urbanicity in Ireland. *Schizophrenia Research, 116,* 75–89.

Kessler, R. C., Berglund, P. A., Demler, O., Jin, R., & Walters, E. E. (2005). Lifetime prevalence and age-of-onset distributions of DSM-IV disorders in the National Comorbidity Survey Replication (RCS-R). *Archives of General Psychiatry, 62,* 593–602.

Kessler, R. C., Demier, O., Frank, R. G., Olfson, M., Pincus, H. A., Walters, E. E., Wang, P., . . . Zaslavsky, A. M. (2005). Prevalence and treatment of mental illnesses. *New England Journal of Medicine, 354,* 2515–2523.

Kessler, R. C., Petukhova, M., Sampson, N. A., Zaslavsky, A. M., & Wittchen, H. U. (2012). Twelve-month and lifetime prevalence and lifetime morbid risk of anxiety and mood disorders in the United States. *International Journal of Methods in Psychiatric Research, 21,* 169–184.

Kirkbride, J. B., Barker, P., Cowden, R., Stamps, M., Yang, M., Jones, P. B., Coid, J. W. (2008). Psychoses, ethnicity, and socioeconomic status, *British Journal of Psychiatry, 193,* 18–24.

Kirsch, I. (2010). *The emperor's new drugs: Exploding the antidepressant myth.* New York, NY: Basic Books.

Kobak, K. A., Greist, J. H., Jefferson, J. W., Katzelnick, D. J., & Henk, H. J. (1998). Behavioral versus pharmacological treatments of obsessive disorder: A meta-analysis. *Psychopharmacology, 136,* 205–216.

Kovelman, J. A., & Scheibel, A. B. (1984). A neurohistological correlate of schizophrenia. *Biological Psychiatry, 19,* 1601–1621.

Krabbendam, L., & van Os, J. (2005). Schizophrenia and urbanicity: A major environmental influence—Conditional or genetic risk. *Schizophrenia Bulletin, 31,* 795–799.

Krishnan, V., & Nestler, E. J. (2008). The molecular neurobiology of depression. *Nature, 455,* 894–902.

Krystal, A. D., West, M., Prado, R., Greenside, H., Zoldi, S., & Weiner, R. D. (2000). EEG effects of ECT: Implications for rTMS. *Depression and Anxiety, 12,* 157–165.

Kurita, M., Holloway, T., Garcia-Bea, A., Kozlenkov, A., Friedman, A. K., Moreno, J. L., . . . Gonzalez-Maeso, J. (2012). HDAC2 regulates atypical antipsychotic responses through the modulation of mGlu2 promoter activity. *Nature Neuroscience, 15,* 1245–1255.

Lader, M. (1976). Antianxiety drugs: Clinical pharmacology and therapeutic use. *Drugs, 12,* 362–373.

Lam, R. W. (2010). The importance of early symptom relief in antidepressant treatment: Focus on agomelatine. *Journal of Psychopharmacology, 24,* 27–30.

Lambert, G., Hohansson, M., Agren, H., & Friberg, P. (2000). Reduced brain norepinephrine and dopamine release in treatment-refractory depressive illness. *Archives of General Psychiatry, 57,* 787–703.

Lambert, K. G. (2006). Rising rates of depression in today's society: Consideration of the roles of effort-based rewards and enhanced resilience in day-to-day functioning. *Neuroscience and Biobehavioral Reviews, 30,* 497–510.

Lambert, K., & Kinsley, C. H. (2010). *Clinical neuroscience: Psychopathology and the brain.* New York, NY: Oxford University Press.

Lambert, K. G., & Lilienfeld, S. O. (2007, October/November). Brainstains: Traumatic therapies can have long-lasting effects on mental health. *Scientific American Mind,* 46–53.

Ledford, H. (2014). If depression were cancer. *Nature, 515,* 182–187.

Lee, H., Dvorak, D., Kao, H. Y., Duffy, A. M., Scharfman, H. E., & Fenton, A. A. (2012). Early cognitive experience prevents adult deficits in a neurodevelopmental schizophrenia model. *Neuron, 75*(4), 714–724.

Leucht, S., Komossa, K., Rummel-Kluge, C., Corves, C., Hunger, H., Schmid, F., Aseno Lobos, C., Schwarz, S., Davis, J.M. (2009). A meta-analysis of head to head comparisons of second-generation antipsychotics in the treatment of schizophrenia. *American Journal of Psychiatry, 166,* 152–163.

Lewis, D. A., & Gonzalez-Burgos, G. (2008). Neuroplasticity of neocortical circuits in schizophrenia. *Neuropsychopharmacology, 33,* 141–165.

Liotti, M., & Mayberg, H. S. (2001). The role of functional neuroimaging in the neuropsychology of depression. *Journal of Clinical and Experimental Neuropsychology, 23,* 121–136.

Liotti, M., Mayberg, H. S., Brannan, S. K., McGinnis, S., Jerabek, P., & Fox, P. T. (2000). Differential cortico-limbic correlates of sadness and anxiety in healthy subjects: Implication for affective disorders. *Biological Psychiatry, 29,* 887–899.

Liu, R. J., Lee, F. S., Li, X. Y., Bambico, F., Duman, R. S., & Aghaja-nian, G. K. (2011). Brain-derived neurotrophic factor Val66Met allele impairs basal and ketamine-stimulated synaptogenesis in prefrontal cortex. *Biological Psychiatry, 71,* 996–1005.

Lopez-Munoz, F., Ucha-Udabe, R., & Alamo, C. (2005). The history of barbiturates a century after their clinical introduction. *Neuropsychiatric Disease and Treatment, 1,* 329–343.

Lopresti, A. L., Maker, G. L., Hood, S. D., & Drummond, P. D. (2014). A review of peripheral biomarkers in major depression: The potential of inflammatory and oxidative stress biomarkers. *Progress in Neuro-Psychopharmacology & Biological Psychiatry, 48,* 102–111.

Low, K., Crestani, F., Keist, R., Benke, D., Brunig, I., Benson, J. A., . . . Rudolph, U. (2000). Molecular and neuronal substrate for the selective attenuation of anxiety. *Science, 290,* 131–134.

Lozano, A. M., Giacobbe, P., Hamani, C., Rizvi, S. J., Kennedy, S. H., Kolivakis, T. T., . . . Mayberg, H. S. (2012). A multicenter pilot study of subcallosal cingulate area deep brain stimulation for treatment-resistant depression. *Journal of Neurosurgery, 116,* 315–322.

MacDonald, M. (1981). *Mystical bedlam: Madness, anxiety, and healing in seventeenth-century England.* New York, NY: Cambridge University Press.

Maes, M., Leonard, B. E., Myint, A. M., Kubera, M., & Verkerk, R. (2011). The new "5-HT" hypothesis of depression: Cell-mediated immune activation induces indoleamine 2,3-dioxygenase, which leads to lower plasma tryptophan and an increased synthesis of detrimental tryptophan catabolites (TRYCATS), both of which contribute to the onset of depression. *Progress in Neuro-Psychopharmacology & Biological Psychiatry, 35,* 702–721.

Mandel, H. (2009). *Don't touch me.* New York, NY: Bantam.

Manji, H. K., McNamara, R. K., & Lenox, R. H. (2000). Mechanisms of action of lithium in bipolar disorder. In U. Halbreich & S.A. Montgomery (Eds.), *Pharmacotherapy for mood anxiety, and cognitive disorders* (pp. 111–142). Washington, DC: American Psychiatric Press.

Martell., C. R., Addis, M. E., & Jacobson, N. S. (2001). *Depression in context.* New York, NY: Norton.

Maya Vetencourt, J. F., Sale, A., Viegi, A., Baroncelli, L., De Pasquale, R. O'Leary, O. F., Castren, E., Maffei, L. (2008). The antidepressant fluoxetine restores plasticity in the adult visual cortex. *Science, 18,* 385–388.

McDonald, C., & Murphy, K. C. (2003). The new genetics of schizophrenia. *Psychiatric Clinics of North America, 26,* 41–63.

Michael, T., Zetsche, U., & Margraf, J. (2007). Epidemiology of anxiety disorders. *Psychiatry, 6,* 136–142.

Miller, B. L., & Cummings, J. L. (Eds.). (2007). *The human frontal lobes: Functions and disorders.* New York, NY: Guilford Press.

Mirsky, A. F., Bieliauskas, L. A., French, L. M., van Kammen, D. D., Jonsson, E., & Sedvall, G. (2000). A 39-year followup of the Genain quadruplets. *Schizophrenia Bulletin, 26,* 699–708.

Monti, B., Polazzi, E., & Contestabile, A (2009). Biochemical, molecular and epigenetic mechanisms of valproic acid neuroprotection. *Current Molecular Pharmacology, 2,* 95–109.

Naranjo, C. A., Tremblay, L. K., & Busto, U. E. (2001). The role of the brain reward system in depression. *Progress in Neuropsychopharmacology and Biological Psychiatry, 25,* 781–823.

Nathan, D. (2011). *Sybil exposed.* New York, NY: Free Press.

Nemeroff, C. B., & Owens, M. J. (2002). Treatment of mood disorders. *Nature Neuroscience* supplement, *5,* 1068–1070.

Nemeroff, C. B., Owens, M. J., Bissette, G., Andorn, A. C., & Stanley, M. (1988). Reduced corticotropin-releasing factor binding sites in the frontal cortex of suicide victims. *Archives of General Psychiatry, 45,* 377–379.

Nemeroff, C. B., Widerlov, E., Bissette, B., Walleus, H., Karlsson, I., Eklund, K., . . . Vale, W. (1984). Elevated concentrations of CSF corticotropin-releasing factor-like immunoreactivity in depressed patients. *Science, 226,* 1342–1344.

Nestler, E. J. (1998). Antidepressant treatments in the 21st century. *Biological Psychiatry, 44,* 526–533.

Nibuya, M., Morinobu, S., Duman, R.S. (1995). Regulation of BDNF and trkB mRNA in rat brain by chronic electroconvulsive seizure and antidepressant drug treatments. *Journal of Neuroscience, 15,* 7539–7547.

Nickel, T., Sonnatg, A., Schill, J., Zobel, A. W., Ackl, N., Brunnauer, A., . . . Holsboer, F. (2003). Clinical and neurobiological effects of tianeptine and paroxetine on major depression. *Journal of Clinical Psychopharmacology, 23,* 155–168.

Ochoa, S., Usall, J., Cobo, J., Labad, X., & Kulkami, J. (2012). Gender differences in schizophrenia and first episode psychosis: A comprehensive literature review. *Schizophrenia Research and Treatment.* doi: 10.1155/2012/916198.

Olfson, M., & Marcus, S. C. (2010). National patterns in antidepressant medication treatment. *Archives of General Psychiatry, 67,* 1265–1273.

Oruch, R., Elderbi, M. A., Khattab, H. A. Pryme, I. F., & Lund, A. (2014). Lithium: A review of pharmacology, clinical uses, and toxicity. *European Journal of Pharmacology, 740,* 464–473.

Ost, L. G., Alm, T., Brandberg, M., & Breitholtz E. (2001). One vs five sessions of exposure and five sessions of cognitive therapy in the treatment of claustrophobia. *Behavioral Research Therapy, 39,* 167–183.

Ost, L. G., Hellstrom, K., & Kaver, A. (1992). One versus five sessions of exposure in the treatment of injection phobia. *Behavioral Therapy, 23,* 263–281.

Osuch, E. A., Ketter, T. A. , Kimbrell, T. A., George, M. S., Benson, B. E., Willis, M. W., . . . Post, R. M. (2000). Regional cerebral metabolism associated with anxiety symptoms in affective disorder patients. *Biological Psychiatry, 48,* 1020–1023.

Pagnin, D., de Queiroz, V., Pini, S., & Cassano, G. B. (2004). Efficacy of ECT in depression: A meta-analytic review. *Journal of ECT, 20,* 13–20.

Pauls, D. L., Mundo, E., & Kennedy, J. L. (2002). The pathophysiology and genetics of obsessive-compulsive disorder. In K. I. Davis, D. Charney, J. T. Coyle, & C. Nemeroff (Eds.), *Neuropsychopharmacology: The fifth generation of progress* (pp. 1610–1619). Philadelphia, PA: American College of Neuropsychopharmacology.

Pedersen, C. B., & Mortensen, P. B. (2001). Evidence of a dose-response relationship between urbanicity during upbringing and schizophrenia risk. *Archives of General Psychiatry, 58,* 1039–1046.

Peng, L., Li, B., & Verkhratsky, A. (2016). Targeting astrocytes in bipolar disorder. *Expert Review of Neurotherapeutics, 16,* 649–657.

Perse, T. (1988). Obsessive–compulsive disorder: A treatment review. *Journal of Clinical Psychiatry, 49,* 48.

Pratt, L. A., Brody, D. J., & Gu, Q. (2011). Antidepressant use in persons aged 12 and over: United States, 2005–2008. NCHS data brief, No. 76. Hyattsville, MD: National Center for Health Statistics.

Rajkowska, G. (2000). Postmortem studies in mood disorders indicate altered numbers of neurons and glial cells. *Biological Psychiatry, 48,* 766–777.

Richelson, E. (2001). Pharmacology of Antidepressants. *Mayo Clinic Proceedings, 76,* 511–527.

Riley, B., & Kendler, K. S. (2006). Molecular genetics of schizophrenia. *European Journal of Human Genetics, 14,* 669–680.

Rubin, R. T., Poland, R. E., Lesser, I. M., Winston, R. A., & Blodgett, A. L. N. (1987). Neuroendocrine aspects of primary endogenous depression. *Archives of General Psychiatry, 44,* 328–336.

Rund, B. R. (2009). Is there a degenerative process going on in the brain of people with schizophrenia? *Frontiers in Human Neuroscience, 3.* doi:10.3389/neuro.09.036.2009

Rund, B. R., Landro, N. I., & Orbeck, A. L. (1997). Stability in cognitive dysfunctions in schizophrenia patients. *Psychiatry Research, 69,* 131–141.

Sanders, A. R., Detera-Wadleigh, S. D., & Gershon, E. S. (1999). Molecular genetics of mood disorders. In D. S. Charney, E. J. Nestler, & B. S. Bunney (Eds.), *Neurobiology of mental illness* (pp. 299–316). New York, NY: Oxford University Press.

Sartorius, A., & Henn, F. A. (2007). Deep brain stimulation of the lateral habenula in treatment resistant major depression. *Medical Hypotheses, 69,* 1305–1308.

Sartorius, A., Kiening, K. L., Kirsch, P., von Gull, C. C., Haberkorn, U., Unterberg, A. W., Henn, F. A., & Meyer-Lindenberg, A. (2010). Remission of major depression under deep brain stimulation of the lateral habenula in a therapy-refractory patient. *Biological Psychiatry, 67,* 9–11.

Sasson, Y., Zohar, J., Chopra, M., Llustig, M., Iancu, I., & Hendler, T. (1997). Epidemiology of obsessive-compulsive disorder: A worldview. *Journal of Clinical Psychiatry, 58,* 7–10.

Schutter, D. J., & van Honk, J. (2005). A framework for targeting alternative brain regions with repetitive transcranial magnetic stimulation in the treatment of depression. *Journal of Psychiatry and Neuroscience, 30,* 91–97.

Sheline, Y. I., Wang, P., Gado, M., Csernansky, J., & Vannier, M. (1996). Hippocampal atrophy in recurrent major depression. *Proceedings of the National Academy of Sciences of the USA, 93,* 3908–3913.

Shiban, Y., Pauli, P., & Muhlberger, A. (2013). Effect of multiple context exposure on renewal in spider phobia. *Behaviour Research and Therapy, 51,* 68–74.

Shorter, E. (1997). *A history of psychiatry.* New York, NY: Wiley.

Shorter, E. (2009). *Before Prozac: The troubled history of mood disorders in psychiatry.* New York, NY: Oxford University Press.

Smits, J. A., Rosenfield, D., Otto, M. W., Powers, M. B., Hofmann, S. G., . . . Tart, C. D. (2013). *d*-Cycloserine enhancement of fear extinction is specific to successful exposure sessions: Evidence from the treatment of height phobia. *Biological Psychiatry, 73,* 1054–1058.

Stein, D. J., Phillips, K. A., Bolton, P, Fulford, K. W. M., Sadler, J. Z., & Kendler, K. S. (2010). What is a mental/psychiatric disorder? From DSM-IV to DSM-V. *Psychological Medicine, 40,* 1759–1765.

Stoll, A. L., Renshaw, P. F., Yurgelun-Todd, D. A., & Cohen, B. M. (2000). Neuroimaging in bipolar disorder: What have we learned? *Biological Psychiatry, 48,* 505–517.

Strakowski, S. M., DelBello, M. P., Adler, C., Cecil, K. M., & Sax, K. W. (2000). Neuroimaging in bipolar disorder. *Bipolar Disorder, 2,* 148–164.

Swerdlow, N. R., Geyer, M. A., & Braff, D. L. (2001). Neural circuit regulation of prepulse inhibiton of startle in the rat: Current knowledge and future challenges. *Psychopharmacology, 156,* 194–215.

Tamminga, C. A. (1999). Principles of the pharmacotherapy of schizophrenia. In D. S. Charney, E. J. Nestler, & B. S. Bunney (Eds.), *Neurobiology of mental illness* (pp. 272–285). Oxford, UK: Oxford University Press.

Tuominen, H. J., Tiihonen, J., & Wahlbeck, K. (2005). Glutamatergic drugs for schizophrenia: A systematic review and meta-analysis. *Schizophrenia Research, 72,* 225–334.

UK ECT Review Group. (2003). Efficacy and safety of electroconvulsive therapy in depressive disorders: A systematic review and meta-analysis. *The Lancet, 361,* 799–808.

Van Steenbergen, H., Booij, L., Band, G. P. H., Hommel, B., van der Does, A. J. (2012). Affective regulation of cognitive-control adjustments in remitted depressive patients after acute tryptophan depletion. *Cognitive and Affective Behavioral Neuroscience, 12,* 280–286.

Vernia, P., Di Camillo, M., Foglietta, T., Avallone, V. E., & De Carolis, A. (2010). Diagnosis of lactose intolerance and the "nocebo" effect: The role of negative expectations. *Digestive and Liver Disease, 42,* 616–619.

Wakefield, J. C. (2012). DSM-5: Proposed changes to depressive disorders. *Current Medical Research and Opinion, 28,* 335–343.

Wakefield, J. C. (2013). DSM-5: An overview of changes and controversies. *Clinical Social Work Journal, 41,* 139–154.

Weinberger, R. D., & Marenco, S. (2003). Schizophrenia as a neurodevelopmental disorder. In S. R. Hirsch & D. R. Weingerger (Eds.), *Schizophrenia* (2nd ed.). London, UK: Blackwell.

Wexler, B. E. (2007). Nonpharmacological interventions for the management of cognitive symptoms. *Johns Hopkins Advanced Studies in Medicine, 7,* 79–84.

Wexler, B. E., Anderson, M., Fulbright, R. K., & Gore, J. C. (2000). Preliminary evidence of improved verbal working memory performance and normalization of talk-related frontal lobe activation in schizophrenia following cognitive exercises. *American Journal of Psychiatry, 57,* 1694–697.

Wexler, B. E., Hawkins, K. A., Rounsaville, B., Anderson, M., Serriyak, J. J., & Green, M. F. (1997). Normal neurocognitive performance of extended practice in patients with schizophrenia. *Schizophrenia Research, 62,* 173–180.

Winterer, G. (2010). Why do patients with schizophrenia smoke? *Current Opinion in Psychiatry, 23,* 112–119.

Winterer, G., Gallinat, J., Brinkmeyer, J., Musso, F., Kornhuber, J., Thuerauf, N., . . . Streffer, J. R. (2013). Allosteric alpha-7 nicotinic receptor modulation and P50 sensory gating in schizophrenia: A proof-of-mechanism study. *Neuropharmacology, 64,* 197–204.

Yang, L.-M., Hu, B., Zia, Y-H., Zhang, B-L., & Zhao, H. (2008). Lateral habenula lesions improve the behavioral response in depressed rats via increasing the serotonin level in dorsal raphe nucleus. *Behavioral Brain Research,* 84–90.

Yeragani, V. K., Tancer, M., Chokka, P., & Baker, B. B. (2010). Arvid Carlsson and the story of dopamine. *Indian Journal of Psychiatry, 52,* 87–88.

Yonkers, K. A., Kando, J. C., Hamilton, J. A., & Halbreich, U. (2000). Gender differences in treatment of depression and anxiety. In U. Halbreich & S. A. Montgomery (Eds.), *Pharmacotherapy* (pp. 59–72). Washington, DC: American Psychiatric Press.

Zhe, D., Fang, H., & Yuxiu, S. (2008). Expression of hippocampal mineralocorticoid receptor (MR) and glucocorticoid receptor (GR) in the single-prolonged stress rats. *Acta Histochem Cytochem, 41,* 89–95.

EPILOGUE

Abraham, A. (2013). The promises and perils of the neuroscience of creativity. *Frontiers in Human Neuroscience.* doi: 10.3389/fnhum.2013.00246.

Alberts, J. R., Serova, L. V., Keefe, J. R., & Apanasenko, Z. (1985). Early postnatal development of rats gestated during flight of *Cosmos 1514. The Physiologist, 28,* S81–S82.

Blake, D. T. (2012). How brains learn to control machines. *Nature, 483*, 284–285.

Chapin, J. K., Moxon, K. A., Markowitz, R. S., & Nicolelis, M. A. L. (1999). Real-time control of a robot arm using simultaneously recorded neurons in the motor cortex. *Nature Neuroscience, 2*, 664–670.

Clynes, M. E., & Kline, N. S. (1960). Cyborgs and space. In *Astronautics* (pp. 26–27, 74–75). American Rocket Society.

Day, L. B., Westcott, D. A., & Olster, D. H. (2005). Evolution of bower complexity and cerebellum in bowerbirds. *Brain, Behavior and Evolution, 66*, 67–72.

Davis, H. G. (1907). The raccoon: A study in animal intelligence. *American Journal of Psychology, 18*, 447–489.

Endler, J. A., & Day, L. B. (2006). Ornament colour selection, visual contrast and the shape of colour preference functions in great bowerbirds, *Chlamydera nuchalis. Animal Behavior, 72*, 1405–1416.

Epstein, R., Kirshnit, C. E., Lanza, R. P., & Rubin, L. C. (1984). Insight in the pigeon: Antecedents and determinants of an intelligent performance. *Nature, 308*, 61–62.

Finn, J. K., Tregenza, T., & Norman, M. D. (2009). Defensive tool use in a coconut carrying octopus. *Current Biology, 19*, R1069–R1070.

Hochberg L. R., Bacher, D., Jarosiewicz, B., Masse, N. Y., Simeral, J. D., Vogel J., . . . Donoghue, J. P. (2012). Reach and grasp by people with tetraplegia using a neutrally controlled robotic arm. *Nature, 485*, 372–375.

Jauk, E., Benedek, M., Dunst, B., & Neubauer, A. C. (2013). The relationship between intelligence and creativity: New support for the threshold hypothesis by means of empirical breakpoint detection. *Intelligence, 41*, 212–221.

Kaufman, A. B., Butt, A. E., Kaufman, J. C., & Colbert-White, E. N. (2011). Towards a neurobiology of creativity in nonhuman animals. *Journal of Comparative Psychology, 125*, 255–272.

Köhler, W. (1925). *The mentality of apes.* London, UK: Routledge & Kegan Paul.

Landis, T., Bardi, M., Hyer, M., Rzucidlo, A., & Lambert, K. (2014). Explorations of creative problem-solving and social responses in free-ranging raccoons: A potential role of von Economo neurons? Poster presented at the International Behavioral Neuroscience Society held in Las Vegas, NV.

Lebedev, M. A., & Nicolelis, M. A. L. (2006). Brain–machine interfaces: Past, present and future. *Trends in Neuroscience, 29*, 536–546.

Lebedev, M. A., Tate, A. J., Hanson, T. L., Li, Z., O'Doherty, T. E., Winans, J. A., . . . Nicolelis, M. A. L. (2011). Future developments in brain–machine interface research. *Clinics, 66*, 25–32.

Liu, S., Chow, H. M., Xu, Y., Erkkinen, M. G., Swett, K. E., Eagle, M. W., . . . Braun, A. R. (2012). Neural correlates of lyrical improvisation: An fMRI study of freestyle rap. *Scientific Reports, 2*, 834. doi:10.1038/srep00834

Loeb, G. E. (1990). Cochlear prosthetics. *Annual Review of Neuroscience, 13*, 357–337.

Memberg, W. D., Polasek, K. H., Hart, R. L., Bryden, A. M., Kilgore, K. L., Nemunaitis, G. A., . . . Kirsch, R. F. (2014). Implanted neuroprosthesis for restoring arm and hand function in people with high level tetraplegia. *Archives of Physical Medicine and Rehabilitation, 95*(6), 1201–1211.e1.

Messeder, D. J., Lambert, K., Noctor, S., Manger, P. R., & Herculano-Houzel, S. (2015). Neuronal scaling rules for the brain of carnivores. Presentation at the Annual Society for Neuroscience meeting, Chicago, IL.

Mills, W. (1899). The nature of animal intelligence and the methods of investigating it. *Psychological Review, 3*, 262–274.

Mussa-Ivaldi, F. A., & Miller, L. E. (2003). Brain–machine interfaces: Computational demands and clinical needs meet basic neuroscience. *TRENDS in Neuroscience, 26*, 329–334.

Pettit, M. (2010). The problem of raccoon intelligence in behaviourist America. *British Journal for the History of Science, 43*, 391–421.

Pitt, J. A., Lariviere, S., & Messier, F. (2008). Survival and body condition of raccoons at the edge of the range. *Wildlife Management.* doi: 10.2093/2005-761.

Ronca, A. E., Fritsch, B., Bruce, L. L., & Alberts, J. R. (2008). Orbital spaceflight during pregnancy shapes function of mammalian vestibular system. *Behavioral Neuroscience, 122*, 224–232.

Shere, J. (2004). Rats in space. *Indiana University Research and Creative Activity, 27.* Retrieved from http://www.indiana.edu/~rcapub/v27n1/rats.shtml/

Talwar, S. K., Xu, S., Hawley, E. S., Weiss, S. A., Moxon, K. A., & Chapin, J. K. (2002). Behavioral neuroscience: Rat navigation guided by remote control. *Nature, 417*, 37–38.

U.S. Department of Health and Human Services, National Institutes of Health, National Institute on Deafness and Other Communication Disorders. (2013). *NIDCD Fact Sheet: Cochlear implants* (NIH Publication No. 11-4798). Retrieved from https://www.nidcd.nih.gov/health/hearing/pages/coch.aspx/

Wolpaw, J. R., Birbaumer, N., McFarland, D. J., Pfurtscheller, G., & Vaughan, T. M. (2002). Brain–computer interfaces for communication and control. *Clinical Neurophysiology, 113*, 767–791.

Wolpaw, J. R., Flotzinger, D., Pfurtscheller, G., & McFarland, D. J. (1997). Timing of EEG-based cursor control. *Journal of Clinical Neurophysiology, 14*, 529–538.

Wolpaw, J. R., & McFarland, D. J. (1994). Multichannel EEG-based brain–computer communication. *Electroencephalography and Clinical Neurophysiology, 90*, 444–449.

Credits

Chapter 1

Figure 1.2: Shutterstock/Sergey Uryadnikov; **Figure 1.4:** © tbkmedia.de/Alamy Stock Photo; **Figure 1.7 a:** © National Geographic Creative/Alamy Stock Photo; **Figure 1.7 b:** Shutterstock/Sokolova23; **Figure 1.8 b:** Shutterstock/Razvan Ionut Dragomirescu; **Figure 1. 8 c:** © imageBROKER/Alamy Stock Photo; **Figure 1.8 d:** Shutterstock/decade3d - anatomy online; **Figure 1.8 e:** Shutterstock/Horoscope; **Figure 1.8 f:** Shutterstock/Victoria Antonova; **Figure 1.8 g:** Shutterstock/ buttet; **Figure 1.8 h:** Shutterstock/Pop Paul-Catalin; **Figure 1.8 i:** Shutterstock/ChameleonsEye; **Figure** 1.8 j Shutterstock/Lindsay Franklin; **Figure** 1.10 © Gina Kelly/ Alamy Stock Photo; **Figure 1.11:** Fig. 3. N. F. Dronkers et al. Paul Broca's Historic Cases: High Resolution MR Imaging of the Brains of Leborgne and Lelong. Brain (2007) 130 (5): 1432–1441. Copyright © 2007 the Authors. By permission of Oxford University Press; **Figure 1.16 a:** Shutterstock/ vitstudio; **Figure 1.16 b:** vitstudio/Shutterstock.com; **Figure 1.16 c:** Robert S. McNeil/Baylor College of Medicine/Science Source; **Figure 1.16 d:** Alfred Pasieka/Science Source; **Figure 1.16 e:** Shutterstock/Jesada Sabai; **Figure 1.16 f:** Shutterstock/pathdoc; **Figure 1.17:** Dr. Fred Hossler/Getty Creative; **Figure 1.18 b:** M. Spencer Green/The Associated Press; **Figure 1.19:** © wunkley/Alamy Stock Photo; **Figure 1.20 a:** Mensen A, Poryazova R, Schwartz S, Khatami R (2014) Humor as a Reward Mechanism: Event-Related Potentials in the Healthy and Diseased Brain. PLoS ONE 9(1): e85978; **Figure 1.20 b:** Mensen A, Poryazova R, Schwartz S, Khatami R (2014) Humor as a Reward Mechanism: Event-Related Potentials in the Healthy and Diseased Brain. PLoS ONE 9(1): e85978; **Figure 1.22 a:** Nora D. Volkow et al. "Low doses of alcohol substantially decrease glucose metabolism in the human brain." NeuroImage January 2006;29(1): 295–301. Used by permission of Elsevier via Copyright Clearance Centre; **Figure 1.22 b:** Margaret Rosenbloom, Edith V. Sullivan, and Adolf Pfefferbaum, "Using Magnetic Resonance Imaging and Diffusion Tensor Imaging to Assess Brain Damage in Alcoholics." Alco Res Health 2003;27(2): 146–52; **Figure 1.22 c:** Hugh Myrick et al. "Differential Brain Activity in Alcoholics and Social Drinkers to Alcohol Cues: Relationship to Craving." Neuropsychopharmacology (2004) 29, 393–402. © 2004 Nature Publishing Group; **Figure 1.23:** © Juice Images/Alamy Stock Photo; **Figure 1.26:** World Biomedical Frontiers; **Figure 1.27:** © 2014 ter Horst, van der Mark, Kentrop, Arp, van der Veen, de Kloet and Oitzl. This is an open-access article distributed under the terms of the Creative Commons Attribution Licens; **Figure 1.28:** Getty Images/Cyril Ruoso/ Minden Pictures

Chapter 2

Chapter Opener: info@mbfbioscience.com; **Figure 2.A:** epa european pressphoto agency b.v./Alamy Stock Photo; **Figure 2.2:** © INTERFOTO/Alamy Stock Photo; **Figure 2.14 b:** ScienceSource; **Context Matters Figure 2.1 c:** Reprinted by permission from Macmillan Publishers Ltd: Nature Neuroscience (doi: 10.1038/nn1668), copyright (2006); **Figure 2.19 a:** Creative Commons Attribution 3.0 License - UC Regents Davis campus, 2005–2015; **Figure 2.19 b:** The Brain Biodiversity Bank and the National Science Foundation; **Figure 2.27 a:** johnij@aol.com; **Figure 2.27 b:** johnij@ aol.com; **Figure 2.27 c:** johnij@aol.com; **Figure 2.29:** © Van Horn et al. 2012. Van Horn JD, Irimia A, Torgerson CM, Chambers MC, Kikinis R, Toga AW (2012) Mapping Connectivity Damage in the Case of Phineas Gage. PLoS ONE 7(5): e37454. doi:10.1371/journal.pone.0037454; **Figure 2.34:** Getty Images/Bettmann; **Figure 2.35 a–c:** Science Source; Science Source/Science Photo Library; Biology Pics/ Science Source; **Laboratory Exploration Figure 2.1:** Image by Tamily Weissman, Harvard University, Cambridge, MA.

Chapter 3

Chapter Opener: Daniel Schroen/ Science Source; **Figure 3.1 a:** © INTERFOTO/Alamy Stock Photo; **Figure 3.1 b:** Science Photo/ Science Source; **Context Matters Box Figure 3.2:** RonMervis@neurostructural.org RONALD F. MERVIS, PH.D. - NEUROSTRUCTURAL RESEARCH LABORATORIES, INC; **Figure 3.6 a:** © Keystone Pictures USA/Alamy Stock Photo; **Figure 3.6 b:** © Keystone Pictures USA/Alamy Stock Photo; **Figure 3.9:** Science Source; **Figure 3.10 b:** © Keystone Pictures USA/Alamy Stock Photo; **Figure 3.18:** Reprinted by permission from Macmillan Publishers Ltd: Nature Reviews Neuroscience (doi:10.1038/nrn2024), copyright (2006); **Figure 3.20:** Reprinted by permission from Macmillan Publishers Ltd: Current Biology, November 2009 (http://dx.doi.org/10.1016/j.cub.2009.08.055); **Figure 3.22:** Reprinted by permission from Macmillan Publishers Ltd: Nature Reviews Neuroscience (doi:10.1038/nrn2024), copyright (20016)

Chapter 4

Chapter Opener: Shutterstock/Roman Samborskyi; **Figure 4.A:** Getty/WireImage/Shawn Ehlers/Stringer; **Figure 4.10:** CC-BY-AA Monitoring the Future, Institute for Social Research, The University of Michigan; **Figure 4.14:** Universal History Archive/Contributor via Getty Images; **Figure 4.17:** Shutterstock/Ijansempoi; **Figure 4.18:** Getty/Universal Images Group; **Figure 4.19:** http://dx.doi.org/10.1016/j.

pmn.2007.02.004; **Figure 4.20:** Getty/Bettmann; **Figure 4.21:** ray.thibodeau@contentednet.com; **Figure 4.24:** Brandon Carmichael; **Figure 4.25:** Shutterstock/Monkey Business Images; **Figure 4.26:** George F Koob, and Nora D Volkow, "Neurocircuitry of Addiction," Neuropsychopharmacology Reviews (2010) 35, 217–238. Copyright © 2009, Rights Managed by Nature Publishing Group.

Chapter 5

Chapter Opener: Shutterstock/Vitalinka; **Figure 5.2 a–b:** Kölliker, 1893; **Figure 5.3 b:** Getty/ullstein bild; **Figure 5.3 c:** Shutterstock/Lisa Hagan; **Figure 5.3:** Shutterstock/Rudmer Zwerver; **Figure 5.4 b:** © Juice Images/Alamy Stock Photo; **Figure 5.6:** Herculano-Houzel S (2009). The human brain in numbers: a linearly scaled-up primate brain. Front. Hum. Neurosci. 3:31. doi: 10.3389/neuro.09.031.2009 © 2009 Herculano-Houzel; **Figure 5.7 b:** Reprinted from Physiology & Behavior, 118, Masís-Calvo, M., Sequeira-Cordero, A., Mora-Gallegos, A., & Fornaguera-Trías, J., Behavioral and neurochemical characterization of maternal care effects on juvenile Sprague–Dawley rats, 212–21, Copyright 2013, with permission from Elsevier; **Figure 5.7 c:** Reprinted from Physiology & Behavior, 118, Masís-Calvo, M., Sequeira-Cordero, A., Mora-Gallegos, A., & Fornaguera-Trías, J., Behavioral and neurochemical characterization of maternal care effects on juvenile Sprague–Dawley rats, 212–21, Copyright 2013, with permission from Elsevier; **Figure 5.12:** Getty/Mondadori Portfolio; **Figure 5.14 a–c:** http://onlinelibrary.wiley.com/doi/10.1002/hipo.20550/abstract; **Figure 5.15:** Copyright © 2009 Elsevier Inc. All rights reserved. Reprinted from Brain and Cognition, Vol 72/Issue 1, Beatriz Luna, Aarthi Padmanabhan, and Kirsten O'Hearn, What has fMRI told us about the Development of Cognitive Control through Adolescence?, 101–113 Copyright (2011), with permission from Elsevier; **Figure 5.16:** Copyright © 2008, Oxford University Press; **Figure 5.17:** Reprinted from Ann N Y Acad Sci. 1124 March, "The Adolescent Brain," B.J. Casey, Rebecca M. Jones, and Todd A. Hare. 111–126;Copyright © 2008, with permission from Elsevier. Context Matters Box; **Figure 5.1 a–b:** Reprinted by permission from Macmillan Publishers Ltd: Nature 477, 90–94 (01 September 2011), copyright 2011; **Figure 5.22:** Bob Sheperd, University of Alabama at Birmingham; **Figure 5.23:** Shutterstock/Helga Esteb; **Figure 5.2:** http://www.bu.edu/experts/profiles/ann-mckee/; **Figure 5.25:** Melanie Lei, The Daily Pennsylvanian; **Figure 5.26:** Xenith, LLC; **Laboratory Exploration Figure 5.1:** Reprinted by permission from Macmillan Publishers Ltd: Nature Reviews Neuroscience (doi:10.1038/nrn2851), copyright 2010.

Chapter 6

Chapter Opener: Shutterstock/szefei/; **Figure 6.A:** CC BY-SA 2.0 PopTech; **Figure 6.1:** Photo Researchers, Inc/Alamy; **Figure 6.2:** Universal Images Group North America LLC/DeAgostini/Alamy; **Figure 6.3 b:** Photo by Dina Rudick/The Boston Globe via Getty Images; **Figure 6.3 b:** Dina Rudick/The Boston Globe via Getty Image; **Figure 6.8:** Editorial Images/Science Source; **Figure 6.1:** Monica Schroeder/Science Source; **Figure 6.17:** Reprinted from Current Biology, 17(20), Paul E. Downing, Face Perception: Broken into Parts, R888–R889., Copyright (2007), with permission from

Elsevier; **Figure 6.20:** Reprinted by permission from Macmillan Publishers Ltd: Nature Reviews Neuroscience, Moshe Bar, "Visual objects in context," 5(8), 617–629, copyright 2004; **Figure 6.21:** Reprinted by permission from Macmillan Publishers Ltd: Nature Reviews Neuroscience, Moshe Bar, "Visual objects in context," 5(8), 617–629, copyright 2004; **Figure 6.24 a–b:** http://www.lottolab.org/; **Figure 6.25:** Shutterstock/Beata Becla; **Figure 6.26:** Ian D. Stephen, Vinet Coetzee, Miriam Law Smith, and David I. Perrett, "Skin Blood Perfusion and Oxygenation Colour Affect Perceived Human Health." PLoS ONE. 2009;4(4): e5083; **Figure 6.27:** Neitz Laboratory; **Figure 6.28:** Shutterstock/Michal Ninger; **Figure 6.33:** Photo by ullstein bild/ullstein bild via Getty Images; **Figure 6.36 b:** CC BY-SA 2.0 Gaby Müller; **Figure 6.36 c:** Dave Watts/Alamy; **Context Matters Figure 6.1 c:** Reprinted from Behavioral Brain Research, 214, Gibb, R. L., Gonzalez, C. L. R., Wegenast, W., & Kolb, B. E., Tactile stimulation promotes motor recovery following cortical injury in adult rats, 102–107, Copyright 2010, with permission from Elsevier; **Figure 6.40:** Shutterstock/eastern light photography; **Figure 6.41:** Getty/Science Picture Co; **Figure 6.42:** APOPO; **Figure 6.43 a:** Shutterstock/chris froome; **Figure 6.43 b:** Shutterstock/gillmar; **Figure 6.43 c:** Shutterstock/Bernhard Richter; **Figure 6.43 d:** Reprinted from Neuron, 56(2). Leah Krubitzer, The Magnificent Compromse: Cortical Field Evolution in Mammals, 201–208, Copyright 2007, with permission of Elsevier.

Chapter 7

Chapter Opener: Getty/MENAHEM KAHANA/Stringer; **Figure 7A:** WGBH Educational Foundation; **Figure 7.1:** Shutterstock/littlesam; **Figure 7.2 a:** Getty/DON EMMERT; **Figure 7.2 b:** Nicolas Armer/picture-alliance/dpa/AP Images; **Figure 7.3 a:** Getty/Boris Spremo; **Figure 7.3 c:** NATURAL HISTORY MUSEUM, LONDON/SCIENCE PHOTO LIBRARY; **Figure 7.16:** © Action Plus Sports Images/Alamy Live News; **Figure 7.17:** Getty/Jamie Squire; **Context Matters Figure 7.1:** Getty/Boston Globe; **Figure 7.19:** Shutterstock/Syda Productions; **Figure 7.20:** Michael Leidel; **Figure 7.22:** Reprinted from NeuroImage, 35(2), John Milton, Ana Solodkin, Petr Hluštík, Steven L. Small, The mind of expert motor performance is cool and focused, 804–813, Copyright 2007, with permission from Elsevier; **Figure 7.23:** ASSOCIATED PRESS; **Figure 7.24:** Stanley J. Colcombe, Kirk I. Erickson, Naftali Raz, Andrew G. Webb, Neal J. Cohen, Edward McAuley, Arthur F. Kramer. "Aerobic Fitness Reduces Brain Tissue Loss in Aging Humans." Journals of Gerontology - Series A: Biological Sciences and Medical Sciences. 2003, 58(2): M176-M180, by permission of Oxford University Press; **Figure 7.27 a:** Courtesy of Kelly Snydor; **Figure 7.27 b:** Courtesy of Kelly Snydor; **Figure 7.28:** Center for Neuroprosthetics and Brain Mind Institute, Swiss Federal Institute of Technology in Lausanne, Switzerland, May 31, 2012. Photo ©Lionel Maillot; **Figure 7.29 a:** Amy S. Pollick and Frans B. M. de Waal. "Ape gestures and language evolution," PNAS 2007 104(19), 8184–8189. Photograph by Frans de Waal; **Figure 7.29 b:** Shutterstock/Monkey Business Images; **Figure 7.30:** Shutterstock/g-stockstudio; **Figure 7.33:** Ida Mae Astute/ABC via Getty Images; **Figure 7.34 a–b:** Reprinted from Brain and Language, 114(2), Frédérique

Andrea Soddu, Andre Luxen, Gustave Moonen, and Steven Laureys, wo Distinct Neuronal Networks Mediate the Awareness of Environment and of Self, J Cog Neurosci, 2011, 23(3), 570–578. Reprinted by permission of MIT Press Journals; **Figure 9.26:** From The New England Journal of Medicine, Marton M. Monti, Audrey Vanhaudenhuyse, Martin R. Coleman, et al. Willful Modulation of Brain Activity in Disorders of Consciousness, 362(7) Copyright © 2010 Massachusetts Medical Society. Reprinted with permission from Massachusetts Medical Society; **Figure 9.27:** AP Photo/Republican-American, Tracey O'Shaughnessy; **Figure 9.29:** Reprinted by permission from MacMillan Publishers Ltd: Nature Reviews Neuroscience, Steven Laureys, "Death, unconsciousness, and the brain," 6(11), 899–909, copyright 2005.

Chapter 10

Chapter Opener: Shutterstock/Happy Together; **Figure 10.a:** Shutterstock/Vera Petruk; **Figure 10.1 a:** Shutterstock/Daniel M Ernst; **Figure 10.1 b:** Shutterstock/Ollyy; **Figure 10.1 c:** Shutterstock/blvdone; **Figure 10.1 d:** Shutterstock/ArtFamily; **Figure 10.1 e:** Shutterstock/Gorich; **Figure 10.1 f:** Shutterstock/Dan Kosmayer; **Figure 10.1 g:** Shutterstock/Nejron Photo; **Figure 10.2:** Photo by Mark Makela/Corbis via Getty Images; **Figure 10.3:** Reprinted by permission from Macmillan Publishers Ltd: Nature Publishing Group 7(6), copyright 2010; **Figure 10.4:** Granger Historical Picture Archive/Alamy; **Figure 10.7 c:** Adapted by permission from Macmillan Publishers Ltd: Nature Reviews Neuroscience 7(3), 242–249, copyright 2006; **Figure 10.9:** Richard Wareham Fotografie/Alamy Stock Photo; **Figure 10.11 a:** Juniors Bildarchiv GmbH/Alamy Stock Photo; **Figure 10.12:** Shutterstock/Monkey Business Images; **Figure 10.14 a:** Shutterstock/cellistka; **Figure 10.16 a:** Shutterstock/Pakhnyushchy; **Figure 10.17:** Reprinted from Current Biology, 21 (1), Justin S. Feinstein, Ralph Adolphs, Antonio Damasio, Daniel Tranel, The Human Amygdala and the Induction and Experience of Fear, 34–38, Copyright 2011, with permission of Elsevier; **Figure 10.18 b:** ASSOCIATED PRESS; **Figure 10.19 a:** Van Bao; **Figure 10.19 b:** Naval Historical Foundation; **Figure 10.23 b:** Neurobiological constituents of active, passive, and variable coping strategies in rats: Integration of regional brain neuropeptide Y levels and cardiovascular responses, Hawley, D. F., Bardi, M., Everette, A. M., Higgins, T. J., Tu, K. M., Kinsley, C. H., & Lambert, K. G., Stress, 2010, reprinted by permission of the publisher (Taylor & Francis Ltd,http://www.tandfonline.com). **Context Matters Figure 10.1 a–b:** Reprinted from Hormones and Behavior, 50(3), Sonia A/ Cavigelli, Jason r. Yee, Martha K. McClintock, Infant temperament predicts life span in female rates that develop spontaneous tumors, 454–464, Copyright (2006), with permission from Elsevier; **Laboratory Exploration Figure 10.1:** Jaak Panksepp, Ph.D.

Chapter 11

Chapter Opener: CC-by-2.0 Robert Whitehead; **Figure 11.a:** Linda Geddes; **Figure 11.b:** New Scientist/Jon Hurst; **Figure 11.c:** New Scientist; **Figure 11.3:** Kansas Historical Society; **Figure 11.7:** Republished with permission of the Society for Neuroscience from "Microglia are essential to masculinization of brain and behavior." Kathryn M. Lenz, Bridget M. Nugent, Rachana Haliyur, and Margaret M. McCarthy.

Society for Neuroscience 33(7) 2013;permission conveyed through Copyright Clearance Center; **Figure 11.9:** From The New England Journal of Medicine, Po-Jui Ko, Ming-Lun Yeh, "Congenital Adrenal Hyperplasia," 372(24), e32. Copyright © 2015 Massachusetts Medical Society. Reprinted with permission from Massachusetts Medical Society."; **Figure 11.10:** Phoebe Hart; **Figure 11.12:** Hemanth P. Nair, Larry J. Young. "Vasopressin and Pair-Bond Formation: Genes to Brain to Behavior." Physiology. 2006 Vol. 21 no. 2, 146–152 © 2006 Int. Union Physiol. Sci./Am. Physiol. Soc; **Figure 11.14:** Redrawn from an illustration by Logan Parsons. From Paul J. Zak. "The Neurobiology of Trust." Scientific American 298, 88–95 (2008); **Figure 11.15:** Radharani/Shutterstock.com; **Figure 11.19:** Glasshouse Images/Alamy; **Figure 11.20:** Peter Corns; **Figure 11.21:** Nishizawa, S., Benkelfat, C., Young, S.N., Leyton, M., Mzengeza, S., de Montigny, C., Blier, P., & Diksic, M. (1997). Differences between males and females in rates of serotonin synthesis in human brain. Proceedings of the National Academy of Sciences, 94, 5308–5313; **Figure 11.23 a:** Everett Collection Historical/Alamy Stock Photo; **Figure 11.23 b:** Allstar Picture Library/Alamy; **Figure 11.23 c:** ZUMA Press, Inc./Alamy; **Figure 11.23 d:** Photo by Rich Polk/CB/Getty Images; **Figure 11.25:** Copyright © 2010 by the American Psychological Association. Reproduced with permission. Kim, P., Leckman, J.F., Mayes, L.C., Feldman, R., Wang, X., & Swain, J.E. (2010). "The plasticity of human maternal brain: Longitudinal changes in brain anatomy during the early postpartum period." Behavioral Neuroscience, 123, 695–700. The use of APA information does not imply endorsement by APA; **Figure 11.27 a:** "Paternal deprivation during infancy results in dendrite- and time-specific changes of dendritic development and spine formation in the orbitofrontal cortex of the biparental rodent Octodon degus C. Helmeke, K. Seidel, G. Poeggel, T.W. Bredy, A. Abraham, K. Braun Neuroscience Elsevier"; **Figure 11.27 b:** "Paternal deprivation during infancy results in dendrite- and time-specific changes of dendritic development and spine formation in the orbitofrontal cortex of the biparental rodent Octodon degus C. Helmeke, K. Seidel, G. Poeggel, T.W. Bredy, A. Abraham, K. Braun Neuroscience Elsevier"; **Figure 11.28:** robertharding/Alamy; **Figure 11.29:** EcoPic/iStock Photo; **Context Matters Figure 11.1 d:** "Alberto Velando,Hugh Drummond,Roxana Torres, ""Senescent birds redouble reproductive effort when ill: confirmation of the terminal investment hypothesis,"" Proceedings B, 273, 2006, 1593, 1443–1448, by permission of the Royal Society."

Chapter 12

Chapter Opener: © Michael Waine Photography; **Figure 12.A:** © Jiri Rezac 2006; **Figure 12.1:** aastock/Shutterstock.com; **Figure 12.2 b:** Sovfoto/UIG via Getty Images; **Figure 12.5 a:** epa european pressphoto agency b.v./Alamy; **Figure 12.5 b:** Elliotte Rusty Harold/ Shutterstock.com; **Figure 12.12 b:** Reprinted by permission from Macmillan Publishers Ltd: Nature Communications, 5, Article number: 3122, copyright 2014; **Figure 12.12 c:** Diego Mariscal; **Figure 12.13 a:** Moviestore collection Ltd./Alamy; **Figure 12.13 b:** Photos 12/Alamy; **Figure 12.13 c:** Philippa Griffith-Jones/Alamy; **Figure 12.13 d:** Lifestyle pictures/Alamy; **Figure 12.15 a:** Peter van Meer, Jacob Raber. "Mouse behavioural analysis in systems biology." Biochemical Journal Aug 01, 2005, 389 (3) 593–610. By

Chapter 13

Chapter 14

Name Index

484

Subject Index